International Directory of
COMPANY
HISTORIES

International Directory of
COMPANY HISTORIES

VOLUME 34

Editor

Jay P. Pederson

ST. JAMES PRESS

AN IMPRINT OF THE GALE GROUP

DETROIT • NEW YORK • SAN FRANCISCO
LONDON • BOSTON • WOODBRIDGE, CT

STAFF

Jay P. Pederson, *Editor*

Miranda H. Ferrara, *Project Manager*

Michelle Banks, Laura Standley Berger, Joann Cerrito, Jim Craddock, Steve Cusack, Kristin Hart,
Laura S. Kryhoski, Margaret Mazurkiewicz, Carol Schwartz, Christine Thomassini,
Michael J. Tyrkus, *St. James Press Editorial Staff*

Peter M. Gareffa, *Managing Editor, St. James Press*

Library of Congress Catalog Number: 89-190943

British Library Cataloguing in Publication Data

International directory of company histories. Vol. 34
I. Jay P. Pederson
338.7409

ISBN 1-55862-393-0

Printed in the United States of America
Published simultaneously in the United Kingdom

St. James Press is an imprint of The Gale Group

Cover photograph: Pacific Stock Exchange Trading Floor
(courtesy of The Pacific Stock Exchange)

10 9 8 7 6 5 4 3 2 1

CONTENTS _____

Company Histories

PREFACE _____

The St. James Press series *The International Directory of Company Histories (IDCH)* is intended for reference use by students, business people, librarians, historians, economists, investors, job candidates, and others who seek to learn more about the historical development of the world's most important companies. To date, *IDCH* has covered over 4,650 companies in 34 volumes.

Inclusion Criteria

Most companies chosen for inclusion in *IDCH* have achieved a minimum of US$50 million in annual sales and are leading influences in their industries or geographical locations. Companies may be publicly held, private, or nonprofit. State-owned companies that are important in their industries and that may operate much like public or private companies also are included. Wholly owned subsidiaries and divisions are profiled if they meet the requirements for inclusion. Entries on companies that have had major changes since they were last profiled may be selected for updating.

The *IDCH* series highlights 10% private and nonprofit companies, and features updated entries on approximately 45 companies per volume.

Entry Format

Each entry begins with the company's legal name, the address of its headquarters, its telephone, toll-free, and fax numbers, and its web site. A statement of public, private, state, or parent ownership follows. A company with a legal name in both English and the language of its headquarters country is listed by the English name, with the native-language name in parentheses.

The company's founding or earliest incorporation date, the number of employees, and the most recent available sales figures follow. Sales figures are given in local currencies with equivalents in U.S. dollars. For some private companies, sales figures are estimates and indicated by the abbreviation *est.* The entry lists the exchanges on which a company's stock is traded and its ticker symbol, as well as the company's NAIC codes.

Entries generally contain a *Company Perspectives* box which provides a short summary of the company's mission, goals, and ideals, a *Key Dates* box highlighting milestones in the company's history, lists of *Principal Subsidiaries, Principal Divisions, Principal Operating Units, Principal Competitors,* and articles for *Further Reading.*

American spelling is used throughout *IDCH*, and the word "billion" is used in its U.S. sense of one thousand million.

Sources

Entries have been compiled from publicly accessible sources both in print and on the Internet such as general and academic periodicals, books, annual reports, and material supplied by the companies themselves.

Cumulative Indexes

IDCH contains two indexes: the **Index to Companies**, which provides an alphabetical index to companies discussed in the text as well as to companies profiled, and the **Index to Industries**, which allows researchers to locate companies by their principal industry. Both indexes are cumulative and specific instructions for using them are found immediately preceding each index.

Suggestions Welcome

Comments and suggestions from users of *IDCH* on any aspect of the product as well as suggestions for companies to be included or updated are cordially invited. Please write:

The Editor
International Directory of Company Histories
St. James Press
27500 Drake Rd.
Farmington Hills, Michigan 48331-3535

ABBREVIATIONS FOR FORMS OF COMPANY INCORPORATION

A.B.	Aktiebolaget (Sweden)
A.G.	Aktiengesellschaft (Germany, Switzerland)
A.S.	Atieselskab (Denmark)
A.S.	Aksjeselskap (Denmark, Norway)
A.Ş.	Anomin Şirket (Turkey)
B.V.	Besloten Vennootschap met beperkte, Aansprakelijkheid (The Netherlands)
Co.	Company (United Kingdom, United States)
Corp.	Corporation (United States)
G.I.E.	Groupement d'Intérêt Economique (France)
GmbH	Gesellschaft mit beschränkter Haftung (Germany)
H.B.	Handelsbolaget (Sweden)
Inc.	Incorporated (United States)
KGaA	Kommanditgesellschaft auf Aktien (Germany)
K.K.	Kabushiki Kaisha (Japan)
LLC	Limited Liability Company (Middle East)
Ltd.	Limited (Canada, Japan, United Kingdom, United States)
N.V.	Naamloze Vennootschap (The Netherlands)
OY	Osakeyhtiöt (Finland)
PLC	Public Limited Company (United Kingdom)
PTY.	Proprietary (Australia, Hong Kong, South Africa)
S.A.	Société Anonyme (Belgium, France, Switzerland)
SpA	Società per Azioni (Italy)

ABBREVIATIONS FOR CURRENCY

DA	Algerian dinar	Dfl	Netherlands florin
A$	Australian dollar	Nfl	Netherlands florin
Sch	Austrian schilling	NZ$	New Zealand dollar
BFr	Belgian franc	N	Nigerian naira
Cr	Brazilian cruzado	NKr	Norwegian krone
C$	Canadian dollar	RO	Omani rial
RMB	Chinese renminbi	P	Philippine peso
DKr	Danish krone	PLN	Polish Zloty
E£	Egyptian pound	Esc	Portuguese escudo
EUR	Euro Dollars	Ru	Russian ruble
Fmk	Finnish markka	SRls	Saudi Arabian riyal
FFr	French franc	S$	Singapore dollar
DM	German mark	R	South African rand
HK$	Hong Kong dollar	W	South Korean won
HUF	Hungarian forint	Pta	Spanish peseta
Rs	Indian rupee	SKr	Swedish krona
Rp	Indonesian rupiah	SFr	Swiss franc
IR£	Irish pound	NT$	Taiwanese dollar
L	Italian lira	B	Thai baht
¥	Japanese yen	£	United Kingdom pound
W	Korean won	$	United States dollar
KD	Kuwaiti dinar	B	Venezuelan bolivar
LuxFr	Luxembourgian franc	K	Zambian kwacha
M$	Malaysian ringgit		

International Directory of

COMPANY
HISTORIES

Advanced Marketing Services, Inc.

5880 Oberlin Drive, Suite 400
San Diego, California 92121
U.S.A.
Telephone: (858) 457-2500
Fax: (858) 452-2237
Web site: http://www.admsweb.com

Public Company
Incorporated: 1982
Employees: 491
Sales: $501.1 million (1999)
Stock Exchanges: NASDAQ
Ticker Symbol: ADMS
NAIC: 422920 Books Wholesaling; 511130 Book
   Publishing

Advanced Marketing Services, Inc. (AMS) is the primary supplier of general interest books, hardcover bestsellers, mass market paperback books, and related merchandise to more than 3,000 membership warehouses, including Sam's Club and Costco. AMS serves warehouse clubs and a variety of specialty retail stores in the United States, Canada, Mexico, and the United Kingdom through distribution centers located in Baltimore, Dallas, Indianapolis, Sacramento, Mexico City, and London. Book distribution services include advertising and promotional programs, in-store book department management, and customized book recommendations in accordance with region, customer base, and marketing strategy. AMS publishes books under three imprints. Thunder Bay Press publishes promotional and gift books, including coffee-table books; Silver Dolphin publishes children's books; and Laurel Glen publishes general interest books on gardening, natural history, interior decoration, art, cooking, and other topics.

Beginnings in 1982: Anticipating the Supply Chain Needs of Warehouse Clubs

AMS originated in 1982 when its three founders saw an opportunity to provide wholesale book distribution services to the new membership warehouse stores. Warehouse clubs charged annual membership fees, but sold brand name goods at low cost, compensating for low profit margins with high volume sales. Charles C. Tillinghast III, Loren C. Paulsen, and Craig Shafer intended to grow their book jobber business along with the warehouse clubs by shaping AMS to the needs of warehouse club operators. To this endeavor Tillinghast brought experience in publishing; Paulsen, mass-marketing; and Shafer, book distribution.

The three started with $6,000, a 5,000-square-foot distribution center, and branch offices at their homes. They also had the promise of book business from Price Club through an associate of Tillinghast. Tillinghast and Paulsen delivered AMS's first order of books, 25 copies of *Baseball Becky,* to a San Diego Price Club from the trunk of Tillinghast's Volvo in August 1982. Within the first nine months of operation AMS served nine locations, including four Price Clubs and a Sam's Club, a subsidiary of Wal-Mart, which received its first delivery in March 1983. For the fiscal year ended March 31, 1983, sales reached $2.7 million, with net income of $70,000.

AMS served the warehouse clubs by offering books at a low, 15 percent markup over AMS's already low cost. AMS obtained volume discounts from publishers, paying less than the bookstore chains for inventory. This allowed the warehouse clubs to sell books at 30 to 45 percent below the publishers' suggested retail price. In addition to addressing the club stores' need for bargain-priced books, AMS merchandisers sifted through thousands of books published every year, as well as the million books in print, and advised customers on potential bestsellers and value-priced titles for fast turnover and high sales volume. AMS grew through the use of trade credit as book inventory sold before publisher billing.

As new warehouse clubs opened in the next three years AMS obtained purchase orders to serve those companies, including Pace Membership Warehouse, B.J.'s Wholesale Club, and Costco Wholesale. When the first Office Depot store opened in 1986, AMS provided the office supply superstore with low-cost computer and business books. After five years in business, revenues at AMS reached $70 million with 12 customers at 200 locations. A proprietary computer software linked the company's distribution centers to the main office in San Diego, allowing for shipment of most orders within 48 hours.

> ## Company Perspectives:
>
> *AMS uses its unique book industry expertise to source, distribute and promote general interest books and related media. AMS has owned the largest market share of book distribution to membership warehouse clubs since beginning operations in 1982. The Company's insightful ability to provide exceptional service to this segment has driven its revenue growth and financial results. AMS intends to continue to nurture and grow its core business and solid financial position while leveraging its competitive advantages to accelerate further growth.*

Just-in-time delivery gave retailers a high profit margin relative to the space used for display and inventory.

With a 90 percent share of the warehouse club book market, AMS's success has been attributed to its ability to choose book titles that appealed to an upscale yet dollar-conscious consumer. For example, coffee-table books proved to be a popular impulse item for their perceived value in a discount shopping environment. AMS ordered special reprints of previously published titles, offered boxed sets of classics, and designed special packages, such as children's coloring books with crayons and gardening books with pruning shears. From 170 publishers AMS provided a continually changing inventory of approximately 200 titles with flexibility for seasonal demand, such as gift books for the Christmas holiday and gardening books in the spring.

AMS became a public company in July 1987 with an offering of 1.6 million shares of common stock at $13 per share. At the end of fiscal 1988, AMS reported revenues of $110 million and net income of $3.6 million. That year AMS distributed 15 million books, with 42 percent of revenues garnered from 38 Price Club stores and 22 percent of revenues from Sam's Club stores. Audio cassettes packages with children's books and video cassettes accounted for nine percent of sales and calendars contributed three percent of revenues. A second offering of stock in August 1998 provided capital for large, seasonal printings and an in-house publishing company, Thunder Bay Press, established in 1990.

The 1990s: Challenges of Growth

Along with widespread growth in distribution and sales, AMS experienced the challenges of growing quickly. Despite revenues of $207.2 million, AMS reported a 50 percent decline in income for fiscal 1990. The number of office supply stores AMS served increased from 60 to 261 locations and the number of warehouse clubs rose from 283 to 357 locations; however, AMS lowered the price of its merchandise to compete in new markets while expenses increased. In anticipation of growth in market share AMS augmented warehouse support, as the company relocated two distribution centers to larger facilities, and hired additional merchandise service representatives. The company experienced a high volume of store level overstock and returns of unsold books. Because AMS purchased 85 percent of its inventory on a nonreturnable basis, the company decided to cut the volume of books purchased while it sought to gain a better sense of its clients' customer base. AMS marketed excess inventory through eight new retail stores in factory outlet malls nationwide. The Publishers Outlet Service stores carried gift books, such as art and coffee-table books, basic reference books, and some children's books.

By the end of fiscal 1993 AMS rebounded with a $2.9 million profit on $258.4 million in revenues. Participation in publishers' promotions and strong sales of calendars, gift books, juvenile, and computer books improved the company's profit margins. AMS operated ten outlet stores, which sold $4 million to $5 million in inventory annually, and planned to open another two stores in 1994. Improved distribution methods allowed AMS to reduce the number of distribution centers to four. In addition to consolidating the Atlanta facility into its Baltimore center in June 1993, AMS closed the San Diego facility a year later.

In alignment with the company's intention to grow with the warehouse clubs, AMS supplied books to some portion of all 25 membership warehouse companies in the early 1990s. Growth followed international expansion as AMS supplied Costco stores in Europe and Price Club and Sam's Club stores in Mexico. The company established subsidiary operations in London and Mexico City in 1993 and 1994, respectively, and AMS began to carry Spanish-language books. AMS reached an agreement with Kmart to supply both English- and Spanish-language books to six to eight stores that opened in Mexico in early 1994.

Although AMS maintained a 90 percent market share in book distribution for the warehouse clubs in the mid-1990s, the company again miscalculated its growth potential. In 1993 the company served 600 warehouse clubs and 650 office supply stores. AMS added 83 Sam's Club outlets to its distribution roster in 1994 but reported an operating loss due to increased expenses related to international expansion, larger warehouse facilities, and an increase in staff. A weak economy resulted in slower store-level sales at warehouse clubs, producing a high volume of book returns and the expense of processing returns. In addition, the merger of Costco and Price Club led to some store closures and a reduction in sales. AMS cut costs by reducing the staff at its main headquarters by ten percent. The company rebounded in 1995 with strong sales in the computer, children's, cookbook, and audio categories. AMS also added 65 Sam's Club stores to its customer roster, becoming that company's major vendor, serving 356 of 428 stores.

AMS continued to have a problem of high book returns, which the company addressed through implementation of the Vendor Management Inventory system (VMI) in late 1996. The return rate on unsold books increased from 22 percent in 1995 to 28 percent in 1997. VMI provided more efficient tracking of point-of-sale inventory at each store and stock replenishment forecasting based on historical sales data and comparable titles. In conjunction with Independent Service Representatives, who provided custom book recommendations, VMI improved the book supply mix and fostered store level turnover for increased sales. Through implementation at 600 Costco and Sam's Club locations the return rate decreased to 21 percent in 1998.

Diversification and Expansion on the Agenda: Late 1990s

With 80 percent of AMS's total revenues originating from Costco and Sam's Club, AMS decided to diversify its customer base. In the fall of 1995 AMS created a new division to provide book inventory to online retailers, including the Home Shopping Network's Prodigy outlet and America Online's Global Plaza. AMS began to supply specialty retailers, including computer superstores, Petco pet supply stores, sporting goods stores, and catalog retailers. In April 1996 AMS gained Phar-Mor, Inc. as a customer, providing children's books, bestsellers, and promotional and gift books to the chain of 96 retail pharmacies in the Midwest. To improve methods of supplying specialty retailers, which tended to order less than a full carton of one title, the company instituted the Acupak customer fulfillment system at the Indianapolis facility in 1996 and in Sacramento in 1998.

Diversification at AMS involved intensifying in-house publishing activities under the newly formed Advantage Publishers Group. To Thunder Bay Press AMS added two new imprints. Laurel Glen published general interest nonfiction for bookstore chains, including Borders and Barnes & Noble, as well as for the warehouse clubs. Under the Silver Dolphin imprint AMS published reprints of *Curious George* and other popular children's titles. Silver Dolphin developed a series of children's activity books, called *Let's Start,* which included project materials, and a series of interactive nature books illustrated by award-winning, wildlife artist Maurice Pledger. The company's largest effort involved publication of 100,000 copies of *D.A.R.E. to Keep Your Kids Off Drugs.*

Expansion involved new products as well as new clients. Through an August 1997 agreement with International Periodical Distributors (IPD), which provided magazines from 1,500 publishers to 6,500 retailers, AMS diversified its customer base as well as its product line. The agreement made IPD services available to AMS customers, while AMS offered book programs to IPD customers. New clients involved the distribution of books to ten Fedco superstores in southern California and paperback books to 228 Kmart stores in California, Oregon, and Washington.

In the United Kingdom AMS diversified into supplying books to specialty retailers through acquisitions and new clients. AMS made its first acquisition of another company in March 1998 with the $6.8 million purchase of Aura Books plc, a supplier of books to department stores and specialty retailers, such as garden centers, gift shops, and the Mothercare chain of superstores for baby and toddler goods. Under AMS Aura Books expanded distribution to Mothercare from 73 to 340 stores. In March 1999 AMS acquired Metrastock Ltd., a book supplier to specialty retailers in the garden, craft, and gift markets. New distribution agreements for AMS involved Center Parcs, a prestigious vacation resort company, and Focus Retail Groups, a chain of home improvement stores, with increased distribution from 67 to 180 stores. AMS consolidated operations of Metrastock, Aura Books, and AMS at a new 74,000-square-foot distribution center that opened in Bicester, Oxfordshire, in December 1999.

To facilitate international expansion AMS created a new position, vice-president—international, for which the company hired Bruce Derkash in November 1998 for his marketing experience in Latin America, Asia, and Europe. Under Derkash international distribution spread to Korea, Indonesia, Argentina, and Australia. Despite earlier efforts to improve operations in Mexico, when AMS had added staff with expertise in Mexican products and Spanish-language books, the subsidiary continued to operate at a loss. AMS developed relationships with Mexican publishers to provide Spanish-language books to Spanish-speaking markets in the United States as well as for distribution in Mexico. In 1999 AMS's distribution in Mexico grew to include VIP's, an eatery that combined book and music sales into its concept. In addition, distribution to Office Depot grew from 16 to 32 stores.

AMS involvement in North American distribution grew with the September 1999 acquisition of a 25 percent interest in Raincoast Book Distribution, a traditional book wholesaler based in Vancouver. Raincoast's operations included the exclusive distribution for 40 publishers and in-house publishing of books on travel, health, popular science, personal finance, and other topics. Raincoast also acquired the rights to publish books for Canadian markets, such as J.K. Rowling's bestselling series of Harry Potter children's books.

Expectations for Continued Success into the Future

At the end of the 1990s the volume of AMS's purchases from book publishers ranked fifth nationally in the late 1990s, giving the company the advantage of the highest discount available from publishing companies. AMS purchased books from 295 publishers in 1998, with 15 percent of purchases from Penguin Putnam, 12 percent each from Random House and Bantam Doubleday, 11 percent from Simon & Schuster, and ten percent from Little, Brown. AMS was the number one customer for many publishers and often purchased 30 percent to 100 percent of a first printing. In 1999 AMS purchased 700,000 of the first 2.5 million copies printed of John Grisham's book *The Testament.* AMS estimated that 25 percent of recent bestselling books sold in the United States had been distributed through the company.

Although growth in sales and income was steady at AMS, reliance on a few customers made potential investors reluctant to buy. Costco and Sam's Club still accounted for more than 75 percent of AMS's revenues as comparable store sales rose more than six percent in 1998 and 1999. Trading of AMS stock on the NASDAQ increased as growth in earnings continued and the company paid its first ever stock dividend on fiscal 1998 income of $9.1 million, a 42 percent increase over 1997. In 1999 AMS's stock value rose some 120 percent. Much of that increase occurred after the July/August 1999 issue of *Equities* placed AMS among the "Fastest Growing NASDAQ Companies Rankings" in America. Of the 5,000 companies on NASDAQ, AMS ranked 77th based on earnings over the previous five years with a 39 percent compound annual earnings growth rate. The company's stock split twice, in January 1999 and January 2000, and AMS planned to pay quarterly dividends adjusted for the increase in shares.

AMS continued to improve operations and to seek growth in new domestic and international markets. As the Vendor-Managed Inventory system continued to improve the rate of return on unsold books, the company began to close its outlet stores in 1998 and 1999. AMS formed a team of sales associates to sell returned product, thus providing for a low overhead method of sales. A distribution agreement with Borders bookstores helped to improve sales for the 1999 holiday season and AMS expanded distribution with Borders in the spring of 2000. In March 2000 AMS acquired Bookwise International of Australia, which generated $4.1 million in sales to 2,500 customers in New Zealand and Australia. For more than 50 years Bookwise distributed specialty books on fine art, architecture, photography, music, wine, and other topics to traditional bookstores, chain bookstores, and department stores.

Principal Subsidiaries

Advanced Marketing Europe, Ltd.; Advanced Marketing S. de R.L. de C.V. (Mexico); Aura Books plc (U.K.); Metastock Ltd. (U.K.).

Principal Competitors

Baker & Taylor Corporation; Chas Levy Company LLC; Ingram Industries, Inc.

Further Reading

"Advanced Marketing Services, Inc.," *San Diego Business Journal,* April 15, 1991, p. A8.

Allen, Mike, "AMS Reads the Needs of Giant Big Box Stores," *San Diego Business Journal,* August 16, 1999, p. 1.

"AMS Acquires U.K. Distributor," *Publishers Weekly,* March 16, 1998, p. 15.

"AMS Adds Kmart to Client List," *Publishers Weekly,* August 24, 1998, p. 34.

"AMS and the Clubs: Onward and Upward," *California Business,* March 1993, p. 19.

"AMS Has Record Period, Borders Deal," *Publishers Weekly,* January 31, 2000, p. 14.

"AMS Inks Deal with Phar-Mor," *Publishers Weekly,* April 29, 1996, p. 16.

"AMS Invests in Canada's Raincoast," *Publishers Weekly,* September 27, 1999, p. 17.

"AMS Looking for More Double-Digit Growth in Fiscal 1994," *Publishers Weekly,* July 19, 1993, p. 8.

"AMS Names International V-P," *Publishers Weekly,* November 30, 1998, p. 14.

"AMS' Record Year," *Publishers Weekly,* May 20, 1996, p. 27.

"AMS to Supply Mexican Kmarts," *Publishers Weekly,* August 2, 1993, p. 13.

Bary, Andrew, "The Trader," *Barron's,* March 29, 1999.

"Business Brief: Advanced Marketing Services: Firm Says Profits Declined in Fiscal Fourth Quarter," *Wall Street Journal,* April 6, 1989, p. 1.

"Earnings, Margin Both Up at AMS in Fiscal '93," *Publishers Weekly,* May 24, 1993, p. 27.

"Financing Business: Advanced Marketing Services, Inc.," *Wall Street Journal,* August 12, 1988, p. 1.

"Fiscal '95 Sales Up Over 14% at AMS," *Publishers Weekly,* June 5, 1995, p. 16.

Flaherty, Robert J., "America's Fastest-Growing Companies," *Equities,* July/August 1999.

Green, Frank, "AMS Is Writing Book on Sales," *San Diego Union-Tribune,* February 8, 2000, p. C1.

Kinsman, Michael, "AMS Capital Hits $20 Million," *San Diego Union-Tribune,* August 12, 1988, p. AA1.

Kraul, Chris, "AMS Finds Its Niche in Books and Expands It," *Los Angeles Times,* March 15, 1988, p. 2A.

——, "Distributor of Books Plans Stock Offering," *Los Angeles Times,* August 3, 1988, p. 2A.

Kupfer, Andrew, "The Final Word in No-Frills Shopping?," *Fortune,* March 13, 1989, p. 30.

McWilliams, Brian, "A . . . Unique Wholesaling Proposition," *Computerworld,* August 22, 1994, p. 77.

Milliot, Jim, "A Disappointing Fiscal '94 Prompts Changes at AMS: Warehouse Club Consolidation Means Higher Returns, Lower Profits," *Publishers Weekly,* May 23, 1994, p. 28.

——, "Advanced Marketing Services Has Another Record Quarter," *Publishers Weekly,* August 2, 1999, p. 12.

——, "AMS Looking to Diversify Customer Base in '97," *Publishers Weekly,* August 5, 1996, p. 273.

——, "AMS Looks to Expand Customer Base, Cut Returns," *Publishers Weekly,* August 11, 1997, p. 235.

——, "BDD Closes Promotional Book Co.; Sells Inventory," *Publishers Weekly,* May 10, 1993, p. 9.

——, "Gains for Industry Stocks in 1999," *Publishers Weekly,* January 10, 2000, p. 10.

——, "Overseas Profits Elusive for AMS," *Publishers Weekly,* July 13, 1998, p. 12.

Moore, Brenda, "Branching Out Could Help Make Advanced Marketing a Bestseller," *Wall Street Journal,* July 14, 1999.

"More Sam's for AMS," *Publishers Weekly,* September 18, 1995, p. 20.

"New AMS Deal Will Expand Book Reach," *Publishers Weekly,* November 10, 1997, p. 14.

"New AMS Stress on Electronic Publishing," *Publishers Weekly,* May 10, 1995, p. 12.

"Nicita Joining AMS from Golden-Lee," *Publishers Weekly,* November 7, 1994, p. 16.

Order, Norman, "How the Other Book Buyers Use the ABA Show; Price Clubs, Remainder Dealers Are Prowling the Aisles for Special Bargains, New Contracts," *Publishers Weekly,* June 10, 1996, p. 34.

"Returns Dampen Record Year at AMS," *Publishers Weekly,* May 26, 1997, p. 12.

Riggs, Rod, "San Diego's AMS Stock Goes on Market," *San Diego Union-Tribune,* July 2, 1987, p. E1.

Schifrin, Matthew, "Streetwalker," *Forbes,* December 27, 1999, p. 256.

See, Lisa, and John F. Baker, "AMS Sales Improve, to Publishers' Relief," *Publishers Weekly,* March 9, 1992, p. 6.

Smith, Sarah, "Advanced Marketing Services, Inc.," *Fortune,* June 20, 1988, p. 96.

Zeitchik, Steven M., "AMS Has Record Year, Will Pay Dividend," *Publishers Weekly,* May 25, 1998, p. 16.

—Mary Tradii

Aer Lingus 🍀

Aer Lingus Group plc

Dublin Airport, Dublin
Ireland
Telephone: 353 (1) 886-2222
Toll Free: (800) IRISH AIR
Fax: 353 (1) 886-3832
Web site: http://www.aerlingus.ie

State-Owned Company
Incorporated: 1936 as Aer Lingus Teoranta
Employees: 7,300
Sales: IR£901.4 million (EUR 1.15 billion; US$1.34
   billion) (1998)
NAIC: 481111 Scheduled Passenger Air Transportation;
   481212 Nonscheduled Chartered Freight Air
   Transportation; 481211 Nonscheduled Chartered
   Passenger Air Transportation; 56152 Tour Operators;
   561599 All Other Travel Arrangement and
   Reservation Services

A relatively late starter among European flag carriers, Aer Lingus Group plc has grown quickly in its first few decades to a stature belying the size of its tiny home base. Although Ireland has less than four million inhabitants, about six million passengers a year fly Aer Lingus, which also handles a significant amount of cargo.

Origins

On April 11, 1928, Major James Fitzmaurice, Officer Commanding the Air Corps, had made the first aerial east-west crossing of the Atlantic with Hermann Koehl and Günther Freiherr von Hünefeld, leaving Baldonnel, county Dublin in a Junkers W33. In spite of the celebrity he achieved, Fitzmaurice was unable to persuade the Irish government to start a national airline, probably because the venture would have likely lost money at first.

Nevertheless, in the next few years a number of air companies sprang up, at least on paper, eager to supply transatlantic air service to the Emerald Isle. Richard F. O'Connor, County Cork Surveyor, originally proposed the name "Aer Lingus Éireann." His prospectus noted that Bulgaria was the only other European country that had not yet started its own airline. Interestingly, Ireland was also the only country which allowed civil aircraft to fly into all its military airfields.

When the illustrious British aviator Sir Alan Cobham pulled out of a prospective cross-channel venture with the Irish government, Captain Gordon Olley was left as the government's partner. The new company, then referred to as Irish Sea Airways, was based at 39 Upper O'Connell Street in Dublin. It had just a handful of staff. The airfield, in somewhat remote Baldonnel, doubled as a sheep pasture.

The airline was formally incorporated on May 22, 1936, as Aer Lingus Teoranta, a corruption of the Gaelic for "Air Fleet (*Loingeas*) Limited." At the same time, Aer Rianta was established as a holding company for diverse national aviation interests including Aer Lingus itself.

The company's first plane, a twin-engined de Havilland DH-84 Dragon, was dubbed *Iolar*, Irish for "eagle." Transferred from Olley Air Services, it had cost £2,900 new. Its first Aer Lingus flight, carrying five passengers, was from Baldonnel near Dublin to Bristol on May 27. However, the maiden voyage of the luxury liner *Queen Mary* stole any hope of press coverage that day.

In fact, the board would come to avoid publicity of the airline's regularly unreliable service at the hands of uncertified crew. Nevertheless, the company's route system grew within the first year, adding the Isle of Man and Liverpool. Sightseeing flights around Dublin were even made part of the program.

Aer Lingus purchased a second aircraft in September, a DH-86A. A DH-89 followed and two years later the company ordered a couple of Lockheed 14 aircraft, which were soon sold and replaced by the ubiquitous Douglas DC-3. In spite of the large number of types flown, at any one time the company fielded but a handful of aircraft. Aer Lingus flew 4,987 passengers in 1938, a more than fourfold increase from 1936's 1,130.

North American aviator Robert Logan was hired as manager in 1938. He effected improvements in all areas of operations. A new airport at Collinstown, near Dublin, opened in January 1940. J.F. Demsey became manager of Aer Lingus and Aer Rianta in January 1943.

Although Ireland was neutral during World War II, the conflict scuttled plans for a continental route, either to Paris or Amsterdam. Aerial warfare complicated service to England, closing access to cities under bombardment and necessitating complex approach procedures and camouflage. Even these flights were suspended with Allied preparations for the Normandy invasion.

Postwar Growth

Demand took off after the war. Several other aircraft types went through Aer Lingus's hands in quick succession as the company struggled to find enough suitable planes. It acquired five more DC-3s (converted from C-47s) in 1945. The Irish Air Corps briefly transferred to the airline a Supermarine Walrus amphibian for training. The company bought seven Vickers Vikings in 1947 due to a spare parts crisis for one of its crash-damaged DC-3s. Five new Lockheed Constellations were bought the same year (at US$892,000 apiece) in anticipation of reaching a market of 40 million ethnic Irish in the United States with transatlantic service. Although yet another Aer Rianta subsidiary, Aerlínte Éireann, was created for these operations, an unfavorable political climate grounded these efforts. Both the Vikings and the Constellations were sold off in 1948.

In 1946, Aer Lingus was reorganized as a joint venture between the state-owned holding company Aer Rianta (60 percent) and two British carriers, BEA (30 percent) and BOAC (ten percent). The purpose was to develop international air traffic to, from, and through Ireland.

After World War II, the airline began naming its planes after Irish saints such as St. Malachy and St. Ronon. They were even blessed in an annual ceremony. Still, one of the DC-3s crashed in Wales in 1952, killing all 20 persons aboard. The new pride of the fleet, sleek turboprop-driven Vickers Viscounts, first arrived in 1954. (Unfortunately, three of the Viscounts were destroyed in crashes in 1967 and 1968.) Another new aircraft was the Fokker F27, five of which were ordered.

The seasonal nature of Anglo-Irish air traffic helped create IR£50,000 of losses for 1954. However, expansion to more

points on the continent helped bring a turnaround by 1956 (the company attaining an operating surplus of IR£159,000). That same year, the British shareholding in Aer Lingus was reduced to just ten percent, and BEA began to fly competing routes.

Aer Lingus finally inaugurated transatlantic service to New York in April 1958 on a single leased Super Constellation aircraft, billed as "the great emerald fleet." This and two other "Connies" were soon replaced by the company's first jets—three Boeing 720s brought on-line beginning in December 1960. Aer Lingus showed a record profit of IR£277,000 in 1961, whereas its sister company Aerlínte lost IR£94,000 over the North Atlantic. Aer Lingus added several new routes to Europe, particularly France.

The Boeing 720s lacked sufficient range with the full payloads they were carrying, and they began to be replaced with Boeing 707s in 1964. Aer Lingus also used Carvairs—converted from DC-4s—for car ferries to Great Britain, and acquired a couple of Airspeed Consuls for training and charters. However, a request to buy French Caravelle jets was denied by the finance ministry on the grounds the buy would result in excess capacity.

Aer Lingus bought a 25 percent stake in Irish Intercontinental Hotels in 1960 in cooperation with Aer Rianta, International Hotels Corporation (owned by Pan Am), the Gresham Hotel of Dublin, and others. It later briefly invested in Ryan's Tourist Holdings, and opened its own hotel, the London Tara, in 1973. In the 1970s it invested in leisure resorts and bought control of the Dunfey family's New England hotel empire.

Aer Lingus and Aerlínte were cut off from the national treasury in 1963, and required to borrow whatever funds they needed at commercial rates. A restructuring in 1965 relegated Aer Rianta to airport management after BEA withdrew entirely from Aer Lingus. Aerlínte continued to operate. Airline staffed numbered about 5,400 in the mid-1960s, most of them based in Ireland.

Charters became an important source of business. Aer Lingus carried British football teams to the continent, bingo players from Liverpool to New York, and on one occasion installed a dance floor in a Boeing 747 to allow the Arthur Murray School of Dancing to foxtrot to Ireland. The carrier also leased out aircraft in the off season. In the case of tiny Air Siam, this was accompanied by a significant commitment of Aer Lingus support personnel as well.

Aer Lingus began flying new British Aerospace BAC 1-11 jets in 1965. It also ordered some larger Boeing 737s, making it an early operator of one of the most successful short-haul jets ever. The flight simulator installed for this type allowed Aer Lingus to begin training pilots for third parties. Booming transatlantic service seemed to justify ordering two of the enormous Boeing 747s for IR£20 million in 1967. (Aer Lingus began flying them in 1971.) Aer Lingus also bought out Shannon Repair Services, a privately owned competitor to its maintenance unit, in 1967. Michael Dargan became general manager in that year.

Aer Lingus contracted with IBM Ireland to install its computer reservation system, Advanced System of Telecommunica-

Key Dates:

1936: Aer Lingus is incorporated in Dublin.
1958: Transatlantic service is launched.
1972: U.S.-Ireland landing rights dispute nearly costs Aer Lingus access to New York.
1983: Aer Lingus Commuter is launched.
1999: Aer Lingus joins the OneWorld alliance.

tions and Reservations for Aer Lingus (ASTRAL), making it an early player in this most important area of technology. The company was soon selling access to the system to other airlines. In 1971 these operations were spun off as Cara Computing.

The Trying 1970s

During the 1970s, violence in Northern Ireland kept many Americans at home, decimating transatlantic traffic, and increasing insurance rates. Talks of developing a joint venture, Northern Ireland Air Services, fell through due to political disturbances. Aer Lingus and Aerlínte posted their first combined loss in 12 years—IR£2,390,000—in 1971. Around this time, plans were being made to merge the two companies; however, they were to wait for more than a dozen years.

The 1970s opened with tense negotiations between the United States and Ireland over landing rights. Soon after receiving its first Boeing 747 jumbo, dubbed *St. Colmcille*, Aer Lingus learned that the United States would be suspending its landing rights in New York in August 1972. The closure of the New York route was deferred and the issue was finally resolved in June 1973; Pan Am and TWA received the right to fly directly to Dublin rather than Shannon. However, TWA operated the route only briefly and Pan Am not at all; the oil crisis of 1973 removed any hope of profits there. During the next year, fuel costs would increase five times and inflation would rise to 20 percent.

Charters remained the fastest-growing area of traffic to the continent even after Ireland joined the Common Market in 1973. Pursuing the budget traveler, Aer Lingus invested in a couple of wholesale travel agencies specializing in southern Europe. Aer Lingus also acquired a ten percent share in the Guinness Peat Group at the end of 1973, ensuring access to favorable terms and clearing the way for the Guinness Peat Aviation aircraft brokerage venture in 1975. Aviation Traders (Engineering), based at London's Stansted Airport, was acquired in 1976. Other engineering, catering, and personnel management enterprises were bought or started throughout the decade.

David Kennedy was designated Michael Dargan's replacement as CEO when Dargan retired in March 1974. The company streamlined its shamrock logo and introduced new uniforms for flight attendants, part of a campaign to establish a "Friendliaer Lingus." The Tara Circle frequent fliers program was also launched.

British authorities removed the carrier's fifth freedom rights in Manchester (the ability to pick up passengers in a foreign country to transport beyond that country). As a result, Aer Lingus phased out destinations in Germany, Belgium, the Netherlands, and Scandinavia. The carrier also closed money-losing routes to Montreal and Chicago in 1979 and 1980. Fuel prices had made the routes uneconomical for the Boeing 707s, which were then phased out.

In addition to political violence at home and in the Middle East, Aer Lingus endured significant labor unrest, culminating in a bitter strike in March and April 1978. However, a papal visit to Ireland the next year gave Aer Lingus staff a chance to demonstrate the fullest extent of their hospitality. Another oil crisis later in the year, though, precipitated staff reductions and other austerity measures.

Aer Lingus helped many developing countries (Lesotho, Netherlands Antilles, Kenya, Zambia) establish their own airlines in the 1970s. Ireland's own status as a former colony made it appear a sympathetic partner. By decade's end, 40 airlines worldwide were contracting with Aer Lingus for some ancillary service or another.

Post-Deregulation Complications

Deregulation of U.S. air carriers and open skies agreements around the world complicated the competitive scenario for Aer Lingus, which posted a IR£11.2 million loss in 1981. Within a few years the company closed high-profile offices in Paris and New York City and other sales offices in North America and the United Kingdom.

Still, the company continued to grow internally and by acquisition. After nearly a decade of discussions, Aer Lingus acquired a 54 percent interest in tiny, all-cargo Aer Turas in 1980. Four years later, one of its DC-8s became the first Irish plane to circle the globe (it made a dozen stops en route). Irish Helicopters was also acquired. Airmotive Ireland, an engine overhaul specialist, opened in 1981. The unit took some years to develop profitability. At the same time, the Aviation Traders subsidiary suffered a downturn in work due to a worldwide phasing out of Boeing 707s.

The U.S. government also pressured the company to turn away lucrative business from United Arab Airlines. Aer Lingus had a direct brush with terrorism when flight EI 164 from Dublin to London was hijacked on May 2, 1981. Fortunately, no one was injured and the hijacker, who had wanted to go to Iran, was arrested after a few hours of negotiations on the tarmac at Le Tourquet, France.

A new commuter service subsidiary was launched in May 1983 to keep routes between Dublin and provincial cities open in the face of dwindling economic justification. Interestingly, the commuter line used Shorts 330 and 360 aircraft built in Belfast—the first time Aer Lingus flew Irish-made planes.

There were more reasons for the Irish to take pride in their aviation industry. In 1984, the CEO of Aer Lingus, David Kennedy, held the presidency of the International Air Transport Association (IATA), while Ireland also supplied presidents to the European Civil Aviation Conference (ECAC) and the European Community. On the occasion of its Golden Jubilee in 1986, Aer Lingus restored a de Havilland DH-84 aircraft for exhibitions at air shows.

A four-day pilots' strike in July 1985, though, demonstrated some internal disharmony. Aer Lingus faced renewed transatlantic competition from Pan Am and Delta. Fortunately, Aeroflot was feeding the company transatlantic passengers from Moscow. Cargo operations also helped this route. Aer Lingus carried 20,000 tons of cargo on it, a third of its total. After falling sharply the year before, traffic on the North Atlantic grew more than 20 percent in 1985, reaching 292,000 passengers. The airline carried 1.9 million on European routes. Aer Lingus attained a IR£14.3 million profit, but had to brace itself for the replacement of its aging fleet.

A small independent competitor, Avair, went out of business in 1985, unable to compete after Aer Lingus denied it access to the Astral computer reservation system. The launch of independent Irish carrier Ryanair in 1987 brought Aer Lingus intense low-fare competition in the European market.

In 1989, Aer Lingus canceled a ticket-exchange deal with British Midland after it announced a competing London-Dublin service. In 1992, the European Community Commission fined Aer Lingus EUR 750,000 (US$933,000) for market abuse and ordered Aer Lingus to resume the cooperation.

Regrouping in the 1990s

In 1990, maintenance operations were made a separate company known as TEAM Aer Lingus ("The Experts in Aircraft Maintenance"). It boasted 2,100 employees and a new US$60 million hangar. However, the unit would lose money for the next few years due to the global recession.

Unemployment in Ireland, at 20 percent, was the highest in Europe in the early 1990s. Preparing for privatization in this type of political climate was a long process. Further, scandals rocked other flotations at Telecom Eireann and Irish Sugar. Still, after it lost IR£1.12 billion in 1994, Aer Lingus underwent a profound restructuring. It was able to cut costs 20 percent in the next two years as traffic rose by 30 percent. The company added Newark to its three other U.S. destinations—New York, Boston, and Chicago. Aer Lingus retired its Boeing 747s in 1995. Leased Airbus A330s took over the transatlantic routes while Air Lingus Commuter added three BAe 146 jets to its fleet of Fokker 50s.

The company unveiled a new corporate identity on February 14, 1996. By this time, Ireland's economy had become one of the hottest in Europe and Aer Lingus was one of the 25 most profitable airlines in the world (operating profits of IR£41 million or US$67 million). Still, the carrier searched for a strong U.S. partner to help it remain viable in the era of global alliances.

Sales continued to rise, and Aer Lingus boasted pre-tax profits of IR£55 million in 1998. The company sold TEAM Aer Lingus to Denmark-based FLS Aerospace, and reportedly spent US$85 million to buy the staff out of their contracts.

Service to Los Angeles was added in May 1999, giving Aer Lingus a much-desired West Coast stop. The company pitched Dublin as a more convenient portal to the United States for U.K. travelers than crowded Heathrow Airport in London. Later in the year, Aer Lingus joined the OneWorld alliance made up of American Airlines, British Airways, Canadian Airlines, Qantas, and others. The Irish government remained ostensibly committed to its eventual privatization.

Principal Subsidiaries

Aer Lingus Limited; Aer Lingus Shannon Limited; Aer Lingus Commuter Limited; Aer Lingus Beachey Limited; Compania Hispania Irlandesa de Aviacion SA (Futura) (Spain; 85%); Timas Limited (75%).

Principal Divisions

Transatlantic; London; Continental Europe; Aer Lingus Commuter; Cargo; London Heathrow—Ground Handling; Futura.

Principal Competitors

Ryanair Holdings plc; British Airways plc; Delta Air Lines Inc.

Further Reading

Craig, Carole, "Shannon Airport Mandatory Stopover Becomes Difficult Irish Business Issue," *Wall Street Journal*, June 19, 1992.
"Curtains for Aer Lingus Props," *Airfinance Journal*, May 1995, p. 8.
Donoghue, J.A., "Focused on Future Profits," *Air Transport World*, August 1997, pp. 94–95.
——, "Timely Turnaround," *Air Transport World*, September 1997, pp. 55–59.
Duffy, Paul, "Aer Lingus's 'School to Ops' Bridge," *Air Transport World*, December 1993, pp. 96f.
Marks, Debra L., "Ireland Puts State Asset Sales on Hold—Scandals and Job Fears Ground Privatization Effort," *Wall Street Journal*, September 8, 1992, pp. A9Bff.
Reed, Arthur, "TEAMates," *Air Transport World*, November 1999, pp. 97–98.
Share, Bernard, *The Flight of the Iolar: The Aer Lingus Experience 1936–1986*, Dublin: Gill and Macmillan, 1986.

—Frederick C. Ingram

Agence France-Presse

3, place de la Bourse
75002 Paris
France
Telephone: +33 1-40-41-46-46
Fax: +33 1-40-46-32
Web site: http://www.afp.com

Private Company
Incorporated: 1835 as Agence Havas
Employees: 1,400
Sales: FFr 1.4 billion (US$233 million)(1999)
NAIC: 51411 News Syndicates

Agence France-Presse (AFP) is the world's oldest news agency and one of the world's top three, behind the United Kingdom's Reuters and The Associated Press of the United States. Unlike its publicly traded rivals, AFP remains largely controlled by the French government, along with a number of its top media clients. In this capacity, AFP's operations are restricted by a series of requirements first legislated in 1957, such as precluding opening the company's shares to private investors and a requirement that AFP present a balanced budget for each year. These two restrictions, in particular, have limited AFP's ability to raise the capital needed to invest in new products and outlets, including the Internet, and to compete head-to-head with its wealthier rivals. Nonetheless, AFP maintains an unsurpassed reputation for the integrity and independence of its reporting. The company's 200 photographers, 1,200 reporters, and more than 2,000 stringers, located in over 160 countries, allow AFP to offer more extensive coverage than its competitors. Each day the company distributes more than two million words in French, English, German, Spanish, Portuguese, and Arabic. Moreover, AFP is the leading supplier of news and images to the Asian, African, and Middle Eastern regions. Through subsidiary AFX News, AFP also offers specialized coverage of the world's financial markets. Its archives of seven million photographs, dating back to the 1930s, is one of the world's largest. AFP operates editing facilities in Paris, Hong Kong, Cyprus, Montevideo, and Washington, D.C. Under the new leadership of Eric Giuily, named CEO in 1999, AFP has focused on pressing for changes in the rules surrounding its corporate status, pertaining particularly to allowing the company to take on private investment capital. In 1999 AFP broke a long tradition when it hired a non-French editor-in-chief, Eric Wishart, a Scotsman.

Founding a News Service in the 19th Century

In France, the liberty of the press was first guaranteed under Article XI of the *Declaration des Droits d'homme*, published in 1789. With this guarantee, the country saw a sudden jump in the number of newspapers and periodicals available, with some 1,500 appearing in just six months of that year. While the press suffered a series of setback in the rocky political climate of the early 19th century, a number of technical developments had made printing easier, cheaper, and faster; the printed press was more widely available than ever before. As the technology for distributing newspapers developed, a need arose for new sources of news and information, not only on a local basis, but on a national and even international scale.

Charles-Louis Havas founded his Agence Havas in 1835 in order to provide this information for France's newspapers, periodicals, and magazines. The creation of an agency devoted to news gathering and dissemination marked a first worldwide and was soon emulated in other countries, leading to the development of Associated Press, formed in the United States in 1848, and the Reuters news service, founded in the United Kingdom in 1852.

At first, Agence Havas used traditional news distribution methods, such as carrier pigeons, horse-drawn carriages and coaches, and mounted couriers to transmit news during a period of widespread social and political strife. Then the creation of France's railroad system in 1842 offered new alternatives for distributing news. The invention of the telegraph in 1845 gave Agence Havas its first taste of modern news transmission and quickly became a primary means of distribution throughout France and across Europe as well. By the end of its first decade, Agence Havas was already an international news distribution service.

Until the middle of the 19th century, advertising had remained a rarity. The development of new distribution systems, however, gave rise to new markets for publicity and advertising initiatives. Agence Havas quickly recognized the potential of adding advertising services to its distribution activities, forming a specialized ad division in 1852. This activity was boosted in 1857 when Havas merged its publicity business with that of the Société Générale des Annonces. The newly enlarged Havas division took Havas firmly into the advertising industry, where the company became one of the foremost advertising agencies in France and throughout Europe.

Offering both news distribution and advertising services gave Agence Havas a great deal of prominence among political circles as well, as the company was able to use its powerful position to influence public opinion on the day's crucial issues. Holding more or less a monopoly on news distribution in France also made Agence Havas a much sought after partner for foreign companies and businesses eager to achieve the recognition and approval of the French government and people. At the same time, Agence Havas was able to serve the country's interests overseas, especially during wartime. The use of propaganda had become increasingly sophisticated in the early years of the 20th century, and took on a higher degree of importance as Europe geared up for a new war. For France, Agence Havas played a key role in helping to disseminate the company's propaganda across the continent.

Yet this same powerful position in the French news and media markets came to be Agence Havas's downfall. With the outbreak of World War II, Agence Havas was stripped of its news distribution service, which was placed under French government control and renamed the Office Français d'Information (French Information Office, or FIO). This new agency was quickly seized by the Nazis after the French capitulation in 1940. During the war, the former Agence Havas's international distribution network was used to serve Nazi and Vichy government interests.

Postwar Rebirth

The taint of collaboration doomed the FIO by war's end. Legislation was passed prohibiting the collaborationist press— that is, all newspapers and journals that continued to publish after 1942—from continuing their activities, putting an end to the FIO. The same legislation, however, seeking to stimulate the creation of new, untainted newspaper and news organizations, also promised government financial assistance, of up to one million francs, toward the formation of new journals.

In 1944, the FIO news agency's operations were taken over by a group of former members of the French Resistance. Renamed Agence France-Presse (AFP), they resumed operations that same year and quickly recaptured much of the former Agence Havas's worldwide reputation and structure. Yet, heavily subsidized by the French government, which also became the company's chief client, AFP was soon placed under the government's control.

AFP remained a government arm until the mid-1950s. By then, the company faced new competition on the domestic front, in the form of the Agence Centrale Presse, operating since 1951, as well as internationally, particularly with the growing strength of the Associated Press, as well as the Reuters news service, both of which had benefited from the Allied victory after World War II. While these agencies operated as independent, commercial businesses, AFP found itself limited by its status as a government-led agency. Under the direction of Jean Marin, who had been named CEO of the company in 1954 and remained in this capacity until 1975, AFP began to agitate for a change in status.

In 1957, AFP was granted its liberty, firmly establishing its independence for not only its commercial development, but, more importantly, for its editorial policy as well. Nonetheless, the French government retained a strong control over the company. Along with legislation establishing AFP as a commercial entity, the news agency found itself placed within a series of restrictions. While the new legislation, passed in October 1957, qualified AFP as an "autonomous organization with a civil character," it also prohibited the company from raising capital through sales of shares to private investors, while at the same time demanded that the company present a balanced budget for each year. A further burden for the company was the provision for the presence of its major clients—including eight representatives from the country's major daily newspapers and some five government representatives—on the AFP board of directors.

If AFP had gained its independence in name, these restrictions effectively placed the company in a position of continued reliance on the French government, which, through its various agencies, remained AFP's principal source of revenues. The situation well suited the French government, which, especially during the De Gaulle administration and later during the period of political dominance by the Socialist Party, enjoyed a tight control on much of French industry and commercial life.

AFP soon found itself at a vast disadvantage vis-à-vis its competitors. Where Reuters and the Associated Press were quick to adopt new technologies for information distribution— Reuters, for example, had begun investing in using computer-based data networks as early as 1964—AFP, lacking the capital for such investments, would be forced to rely on the slower, traditional transmission methods until as late as the 1990s. AFP's influence diminished especially among the world's financial markets, which turned to Reuters in particular. If the French news agency remained influential in certain regions traditionally favorable to the French, such as the Middle East and North Africa, its position was eroding among the more economically powerful Western world.

Jean Marin's continued efforts to guarantee the company's editorial independence—which, although required by the 1957 legislation, faced constant pressure from the French government—eventually cost Marin his job in 1975, when the government, led by Valery Giscard d'Estaing, forced Marin to resign. AFP now entered into a period of revolving-door CEOs; the 1957 legislation had, in effect, made this possible by calling for the election of a CEO every three years. With the departure of Marin,

Key Dates:

1835: The agency's precursor, Agence Havas, is founded by Charles-Louis Havas.

1852: Agence Havas launches an advertising division.

1857: The agency's advertising activities are merged with Société Générale des Annonces.

1941: The agency's news division is spun off as Office Français d'Informations (French Information Office, or FIO).

1944: The FIO is disbanded and reforms as Agence France-Presse (AFP).

1957: Independent status is granted AFP in a 1957 legislative decree.

1985: Decentralization of operations begins.

1991: AFP enters a joint venture, called AFX News, with the *Financial Times.*

1997: AFP launches Internet financial new service called ''Mine and Yours Trésorie.''

1999: Companynews Internet news service is initiated.

2000: AFP purchases 100 percent controlling interest of AFX.

the CEO position became something of a political football, as the newspaper representatives on the board of directors, seeking pricing benefits, negotiated with the board's government representatives, who, in turn, sought to place in position CEOs favorable to the government's policies and political objectives.

By the mid-1980s, AFP found its financial position in disarray, with a steady string of losses—culminating in some FFr 200 million in the red in 1986—and annual revenues, at around FFr 700 million, representing only a small percentage of those of its major competitors. In 1985, the company took steps to modernize its operations, taking into account the developing global realities of the era. After some 150 years operating from its Paris headquarters, Agence France-Presse restructured, decentralizing its operations into a new worldwide network, with headquarters and distribution facilities not only in Paris, but also in Washington, D.C., Hong Kong, and Nicosia, Cyprus. These new offices strengthened the company's ability to respond to the particular nature of the European, North and South American, Far Eastern, and Middle Eastern and African regions, respectively.

These moves helped improve the company's financial position, boosting revenues to FFr 850 million by 1989, and putting it—temporarily—in the black. Nevertheless, more than 50 percent of the company's sales were generated by the French government.

Diversification for the 1990s

At the start of the 1990s, AFP began to take steps to regain its technological edge and to improve its position among the financial and business communities. In 1991, the company launched a new subsidiary, AFX News, a financial news wire service, in a joint venture with the *Financial Times* of England. The success of the AFX service, which extended its operations

to more than 30 offices across Europe, North America, and Asia during the 1990s, led AFP to take full control of the subsidiary in March 2000.

Despite the success of the AFX venture, AFP, continually hampered by budget restraints, lagged behind its competitors, who were rapidly adopting new technologies, perhaps most importantly the Internet and World Wide Web, for their distribution activities. The early adoption of these technologies led to a wider gap between AFP and its competitors. By the mid-1990s, for example, AFP's annual sales had reached FFr 1.13 billion—while Reuters was posting annual revenues some 16 times greater.

Toward the end of the decade, however, AFP began diversifying its activities, adding new technology and targeting new markets, such as the satellite broadcasting market with subsidiary PolyCom, a joint venture with France Telecom and the Bourse of Paris. By the year 2000, PolyCom had extended its network to more than 5,000 stations in over 100 countries. Another initiative, launched in 1999 in cooperation with Agefi, the France-based financial news provider, was Companynews, dedicated to providing press releases and financial commentary on corporations worldwide, yet with an emphasis on French companies, which made up some 50 percent of Companynews' company list. The new subsidiary was technology savvy from the start, offering its services not only through satellite and internet, as well as through fax and France's Minitel network, but also through the booming GSM mobile telephone market.

In 1997, AFP made its delayed debut on the Internet, with the launch of a financial information service directed toward the world's stock markets, ''Mine and Yours Trésorie,'' in conjunction with leading French broker Groupe Roussin. That same year, the company began placing its photo archives, one of the world's largest with images dating to the 1930s, online as well.

By the late 1990s, analysts were forecasting that the mobile telephone market would become the world's dominant means of both data and voice transmission in the early years of the 21st century, a forecast that appeared increasingly more likely with the introduction of the WAP (wireless application protocol) standard in 1999. AFP made a strong move toward establishing a position in this new market when it signed a global cooperation agreement with mobile telephone giant Nokia, of Finland, in December 1999. Under terms of the agreement, AFP began providing sports, financial, and general news transmissions in English, French, German, Portuguese, and Spanish to a market expected shortly to undergo a huge expansion; by 2005, industry analysts expected mobile telephones to replace personal computers as the chief means of accessing the Internet.

As AFP entered the new century, however, it remained hampered by its quasi-governmental status. New CEO Eric Giuily, elected in 1999, began his tenure proposing changes to the legislation governing AFP's operations. He was particularly interested in opening the company to private investors; he also promised to orient the company more toward English-language news. Vehement protests to the latter by the company's journalists, who shut down the company during a strike, forced Giuily to back off from this proposal. Nonetheless, it seemed evident that in order to maintain its position as one of the world's top three news agencies, AFP needed a new and more financially independent status.

Principal Subsidiaries

AFX News; AFP GmbH (Germany); Sports-Informations-Dienst (Germany); PolyCom (joint venture); Companynews (joint venture); Nolis; Inédit.

Principal Competitors

The Associated Press; Reuters Holdings PLC; Bloomberg L.P.; Corbis Corporation; Crain Communications, Inc.; Dow Jones & Company, Inc.; Knight Ridder, Inc.; United Press International, Inc.

Further Reading

Berls, Jodi, ''Without Fraternity, No Liberty or Equality,'' *Passport*, March 16, 2000.

Feraud, Jean-Christophe, ''L'avenir de l'AFP à nouveau en question,'' *Les Echos*, November 30, 1999, p. 20.

Gasquet, Pierre de, ''AFP: Quitte ou double,'' *Les Echos*, February 6, 1996, p. 46.

Sanai, Darius, ''Scotching Rumors,'' *Independent*, August 24, 1999, p. 16.

—M. L. Cohen

Airborne Freight Corporation

3101 Western Avenue
Seattle, Washington 98121
U.S.A.
Telephone: (206) 285-4600
Fax: (206) 281-1444
Web site: http://www.airborne.com

Public Company
Incorporated: 1946 as Airborne Flower Traffic
    Association of California
Employees: 23,500
Sales: $3.14 billion (1999)
Stock Exchanges: New York Pacific
Ticker Symbol: ABF
NAIC: 481112 Scheduled Freight Air Transportation;
    49211 Couriers; 481212 Nonscheduled Chartered
    Freight Air Transportation; 488111 Air Traffic
    Control; 488119 Other Airport Operations; 48819
    Other Support Activities for Air Transportation

Airborne Freight Corporation is the third largest express delivery company in the United States. Better known as "Airborne Express," the company keeps a lower profile than rivals FedEx and United Parcel Service of America Inc. (UPS). Airborne boasts the lowest cost structure and targets high-volume corporate customers. A deal with the U.S. Postal Service in 1999 has brought Airborne into the low-margin market of residential deliveries.

1940s Pacific Origins

Airborne Express originated in two companies based on the West Coast—Pacific Air Freight, Inc. and Airborne Freight Corporation. Pacific Air Freight, an air freight forwarder, was founded in Seattle in 1947 by former Army Air Corps officer Holt W. Webster. Airborne Freight began in San Francisco in 1946 as the Airborne Flower Traffic Association of California, concerned with shipping fresh tropical flowers from Hawaii to the Mainland. It also provided freight forwarding services to

Seattle and Alaska. In 1968, the two companies merged, keeping the California company's name and the Washington-based company's management. John D. McPherson, the chairperson of Airborne Freight, kept his position; Holt W. Webster, the president of Pacific Air Freight, became president and chief executive of the new company. Stock in this company was divided equally between shareholders in the former companies.

During the 1970s Airborne Express maintained the role of air freight forwarder. In the last half of the decade, however, the company became interested in the air express business and began expanding operations in that direction. Deregulation of the airline industry occurred in 1977–78, giving air carriers the liberty to fly anywhere in the United States using any size aircraft. A carrier could purchase a fleet of larger aircraft and operate cost effectively in the air express field. For this purpose, in 1980 Airborne purchased both Midwest Air Charter, a fleet of propeller and propeller-jet airplanes, and Wilmington Airport in Wilmington, Ohio, a former Strategic Air Force Command base.

The first air carrier to buy its own airport, the company developed its property into Airborne Air Park, which became the central sorting facility for Airborne's air express services. A nationwide distribution system in which packages and letters were flown into the Wilmington center, sorted, and flown out for next-day delivery, operated from this location. The operation was supported by nearby Airborne Commerce Park which housed such services as a customs and brokerage operation; a Central Printing Center; the Airborne Stock Exchange, a parts warehouse with overnight shipping capacity; warehouse facilities available to companies wishing to ship their goods quickly from a centralized location; and an animal quarantine and exotic plant isolation and inspection center.

Airborne's shipping capacity was also enhanced by the convenient flight schedules of airports in Dayton, Columbus, and Cincinnati, Ohio. While upgrading the airport into a modern sorting and delivery center, the company developed its fleet of aircraft to include more than 60 DC-8s, DC-9s, and YS-lls. A regional stock exchange system with centers in 40 U.S. cities to service customers with same-day shipping needs was initiated. Sky Courier, a subsidiary of Airborne Express, provided 29 Stock Exchange locations for their customer St. Jude Medical,

---

Inc., which manufactured artificial heart valves needing rapid delivery.

Consolidation in the 1980s

Airborne faced tough competition in launching air courier services during the 1980s. The industry leader, Federal Express, dictated market conditions, and such companies as Emery Air Freight, the U.S. Postal Service's Express Mail, and Purolator Courier Corporation, battled with Airborne for second place in the market and a share of the profits. Survival depended on providing consumers with the fastest possible service.

As a newcomer to the air courier business Airborne was initially unable to compete. In 1984, Tom Rooney, a vice-president of marketing at Airborne, remarked in *Advertising Age* that the company had originally, in 1980, presented a product not up to industry standards and had "considered the market, the product, the category, to be simply next-day. Not until we got into focus groups did we find out it was really before noon. We just had to understand, and the market told us very clearly that if you're not a before-noon service, forget it, get out." Airborne aggressively pursued this goal, and in 1982, began to exhibit growth exceeding Emery Air Freight's shipment volume.

In 1983 and 1984 Airborne laid siege to Federal Express's undisputed position as number one by employing advertising campaigns—including national television spots—designed to emphasize the impersonal nature of Federal Express's handling of shipment tracing and Airborne's speedy delivery time. As Kent W. Freudenberger, an executive vice-president in marketing at Airborne, stated in *Advertising Age,* "There's no room in this industry for the meek. Competition is probably stronger now than at any time in our history. We cannot wait for the marketplace to come to us. We have to go out aggressively and communicate to the marketplace how good we are." The pitch worked. During one three-month period in 1983, the company averaged 29,800 shipments per day, compared to 22,000 during the same period in 1982. While revenues fluctuated from a high of $295.2 million in 1982 to $243.4 million in the first half of 1983, earnings grew steadily between 1982 and 1984, showing a particularly dramatic 104 percent increase between 1982 and 1983.

Although in 1983 Wall Street skeptics predicted that Airborne could not survive the cutthroat competition of the air freight industry, the company demonstrated consistent growth over the next eight-year period. By 1987, with revenues of approximately $630 million, Airborne was ranked third; UPS, with revenues of $8.6 billion, captured second place behind Federal Express, whose revenues reached $3.2 billion that year. Airborne shipped approximately 35 million packages in 1987 compared to 5.7 million in 1982, constituting 12 percent of the U.S. market and earning approximately $12 million in profits.

Robert S. Cline, named chair and chief executive officer of Airborne in 1984, described Airborne's successful business strategy in *Forbes* magazine: "Federal Express is the Cadillac of this business. High profile, lots of bells and whistles. UPS is the Chevrolet. Less dramatic, less service-oriented, less expensive for the infrequent user. We've tried to position ourselves in between." To accomplish this, Airborne targeted the corporate client, tailoring discounts and special services to each customer as incentives for using the company. Airborne also provided inexpensive pickup on demand and next-day delivery before noon. These tactics paid off early in 1987, when Airborne received a three-year contract to ship all of IBM's air express mail weighing less than 150 pounds. The prominent account became instrumental in attracting other corporate customers such as Xerox.

Meanwhile, impressed by Airborne's growth rate and assets, an Australian transport company, TNT Limited, attempted to buy out the company in 1986. Though TNT amassed 15 percent of Airborne's stock, no further negotiations between the companies followed after Airborne rejected the bid.

Competition among air express companies remained strong during the latter part of the 1980s due to several consolidation moves. In 1986 Emery Air Freight bought Purolator Courier Corporation; in 1989 Federal Express purchased Tiger International for $880 million. Both acquisitions caused concern that Airborne's position in the industry might be under threat. Airborne did, however, maintain a high growth pattern, with shipments up approximately 40 percent in 1989.

During the same year, the company began negotiations to consolidate Airborne's Japanese interests with those of Japanese transport giant Mitsui & Company. Under the terms of the agreement, Airborne's operations in Japan would merge with Panther Express International, which was owned by Mitsui and Tonami Transportation Co.—also based in Japan. Airborne would receive $100 million for aircraft financing and Mitsui and Tonami would invest $40 million in Airborne stock, allowing one member from each company to sit on Airborne's board. Negotiations were successful and Airborne Express Japan became a reality in 1990, with Airborne owning 40 percent, Mitsui possessing 40 percent, and Tonami holding 20 percent of the new company. The company shipped freight, packages, and letters worldwide, providing Airborne, now the fourth largest air courier in Japan, with a solid Asian base of operations in a market growing 25 percent yearly and anticipating doubled growth by 1996.

Early 1990s Price Wars

Joint ventures became typical of Airborne's international expansion strategy during the 1990s, allowing the company to maximize its U.S. distribution system and capitalize on its strong base of international companies already in place. Chairman Cline elaborated in *Forbes* magazine: "The Japanese market is very nationalistic, and having a local partner is key to having better penetration. That, in a nutshell, is our philosophy for overseas expansion." Joint operating agreements were also negotiated with Purolator Courier Ltd. of Canada and with Thailand. In addition to Japanese and Canadian interests, Airborne had offices in the Far East, Australia, New Zealand, and the United Kingdom. In 1991 Airborne reached 90 percent of the world's markets, yet international sales accounted for only 20 percent of the overall profits and the corporation's market share was only 1 percent. The air carrier hoped that foreign expansion would increase these profits in the 1990s.

Between the mid-1980s and mid-1990s, Airborne created several innovative customer services. The PACE program, geared toward small to medium-sized businesses, offered the mid-range customer the same discounts usually offered only to larger companies with a higher volume of shipments. Such services as next-morning delivery, pickup on demand, computer tracking, free shipping supplies and preprinted airbills, and a flat worldwide delivery rate made Airborne a viable choice for consumers. The communications network, able to track shipment status anywhere in the world at any time, was designed to facilitate customer access to the progress of parcels. In 1986 Airborne introduced Electronic Data Interchange (EDI), a computer system that allowed customers to view Airborne shipping data on their own mainframe computers.

Increasingly during the 1990s, Airborne was recognized for contributions to the air carrier industry by businesses and professional organizations. In 1990 the International Cargo Forum, an organization that awards excellence in the transportation industry, presented Airborne with an award for performance and service. The following year Glaxo, a pharmaceutical manufacturer, honored Airborne with an Air Express Carrier Award, and *Computerworld Magazine* cited the company as one of the top 100 information systems users in the United States. A consulting firm for EDI users presented Airborne with an award for excellent usage of the data system in implementing service to customers in 1992.

Airborne's foreign expansion program and uniquely innovative services positioned the air carrier strongly in the fiercely competitive business atmosphere of the 1990s. Sales for 1991 hit the $1 billion mark and Airborne's 108,996 shipments reflected a 20 percent increase from the 88,220 parcel figure of

1990. Federal Express's estimated growth during the same period was only 5 percent, while UPS's growth was estimated at 10 percent. Industry analysts cautioned, however, that Airborne's fleet of aircraft was mostly second hand, jet fuel was expensive, and the company relied heavily upon major corporate customers prone to recession difficulties—all factors that might slow growth in future markets. Although revenues rose nine percent to $1.48 billion in 1992, net earnings fell from $27.2 million to $2.4 million.

Cutthroat competition in the early 1990s reduced industry prices 20 percent in the early 1990s. Unable to reduce costs any more, Airborne focused on finding new business. International markets were particularly strong, although, along with other U.S. shippers, the company complained of biased treatment in Mexico in spite of the NAFTA trade accord. In 1996, Airborne posted net earnings of $27.2 million on revenues of $2.5 billion, up 11 percent.

New Markets in the Late 1990s

A strike at UPS in August 1997 may have seemed like a boon for Airborne. However, the low-margin ground shipments involved were not an attractive business to express shippers, and Airborne itself suffered some labor discord. Specifically, in 1998, the Teamsters protested the firing of a pilot who refused to fly a test flight. They had complained three years earlier of Airborne's use of more part-time and nonunionized labor.

When the United States Postal Service announced a discount program for private shippers in 1999, Airborne was one of the first to sign up. This effectively meant mail carriers would deliver Airborne's packages from local post offices to residential addresses; the company had entered a segment traditionally dominated by UPS, just as e-commerce shipments were heating up.

After UPS banned handguns on its ground delivery system, seeking to reduce liability due to loss and theft, Airborne banned all firearms and ammunition deliveries. While UPS had been the gun industry's preferred shipper, Airborne had traditionally carried few firearms anyway.

Third-party logistics were an important source of new revenues. Airborne Logistics Services doubled in size between 1996 and 1999, when it accounted for $150 million in revenues. Online retailing fueled much of the growth. Overall revenues increased two percent in 1999 to $3.1 billion; earnings fell to $17 million from $38 million in 1998.

Principal Subsidiaries

ABX Air, Inc.; Airborne Forwarding Corporation d.b.a. Sky Courier; Inc.; Airborne Freight Limited (New Zealand).

Principal Divisions

Airborne Logistics Services.

Principal Competitors

Federal Express Corporation; United Parcel Service of America Inc.; DHL Worldwide Express Inc.; United States Postal Service.

Further Reading

"Airborne Delivers Challenge," *Advertising Age,* August 29, 1983.

"Airborne Delivers on Underdog Status," *Advertising Age,* January 9, 1984.

"Airborne Express Background," Seattle, Airborne Freight Corporation, 1991.

"Airborne Freight Outlines Venture, Investment Plans," *Wall Street Journal,* December 7, 1989.

Barron, Kelly, "Low-Flier," *Forbes,* September 6, 1999, p. 274.

"Beating the Big Guys," *Forbes,* September 30, 1991.

Beauchamp, Marc, "Flying Harder," *Forbes,* September 7, 1987.

Blackmon, Douglas A., "Delivery Firms Prepare to Curb Gun Shipments," *Wall Street Journal,* October 13, 1999, p. A6.

——, "FedEx Delivers Sunday Punch for Expanding Workweek—Stakes Are Large in Battle with UPS, But Market Is Small for Weekend Couriers," *Wall Street Journal,* April 13, 1998, p. B4.

——, "US Post Office Plans to Deliver for Airborne," *Wall Street Journal,* June 3, 1999, p. A28.

Bleakley, Fred R., "Going for Growth," *Wall Street Journal,* July 5, 1996, p. A1.

Brannigan, Martha, "Air-Freight Firms Gain Unexpectedly from an Expired Federal Excise Tax," *Wall Street Journal,* January 3, 1996, p. A4.

Deogun, Nikhil, Martha Brannigan, and Anna Wilde Mathews, "UPS Walkout Delivers Opportunities for Some," *Wall Street Journal,* August 8, 1997, p. A2.

Frank, Robert, and Helene Cooper, "US Claims NAFTA Violations by Mexico in Treatment of Express-Delivery Firms," *Wall Street Journal,* April 27, 1995, p. A2.

"Hitching a Ride," *Forbes,* January 7, 1991.

Lazere, Cathy, "Resisting Temptation," *CFO: The Magazine for Senior Financial Executives,* December 1997, pp. 64–70.

Scheraga, Dan, "Taking Stock," *Chain Store Age,* October 1999, pp. 172–74.

—Grace Jeromski
—updated by Frederick C. Ingram

American Locker Group Incorporated

608 Allen Street
Jamestown, New York 14701-3966
U.S.A.
Telephone: (716) 664-9600
Toll Free: (800) 828-9118
Fax: (716) 664-2949
Web site: http://www.americanlocker.com

Public Company
Incorporated: 1958
Employees: 135
Sales: $35 million (1999)
Stock Exchanges: NASDAQ
Ticker Symbol: ALGI
NAIC: 337215 Lockers (Except Refrigerated)
    Manufacturing; 337127 Institutional Furniture
    Manufacturing; 42144 Other Commercial Equipment
    Wholesalers; 333311 Automatic Vending Machine
    Manufacturing; 334419 Other Electronic Component
    Manufacturing

Through its wholly owned subsidiary American Locker Security Systems, Inc., American Locker Group Incorporated ranks as one of the world's leading supplier of secure locker storage. Fully 70 percent of its business, however, is conducted with the United States Postal Service, for which it supplies mailbox clusters for use in multi-family dwellings. The estate of former CEO Harold Ruttenberg, who died in 1998 at the age of 84, controls 21 percent of American Locker.

Origins of American Locker Group

American Locker Group traces its origins, at least in part, to the U.S. Voting Machine Company, which was founded in 1958 to exploit Thomas Edison's pioneering invention to ensure honest election results. The company was bought by Pittsburgh-based Rockwell Manufacturing Company and then spun off to shareholders in 1964 and renamed the Automatic Voting Ma-

chine Corporation (AVM). Rockwell continued to supply the management team, including executives Lloyd A. Dixon, Sr., and Lloyd A. Dixon, Jr. AVM's subsidiary company American Locker Group, Inc., was originally incorporated on December 15, 1958. In April 1964 shares of American Locker were distributed to AVM stockholders and American Locker became a publicly held corporation. In its heyday, AVM had 15 divisions, making everything from auto parts and furniture to air-conditioning components.

Management Problems: 1972–73

In August 1972, Lloyd Dixon, Sr., died, just after signing a $19 million contract with the Republic of Venezuela to deliver 10,000 voting machines in time for the 1973 presidential elections. This huge contract was canceled shortly after AVM had borrowed money to fill the order. In an unrelated problem, Lloyd Dixon, Jr., was indicted by a federal grand jury in Buffalo, being charged with bribing Buffalo officials in order to sell them voting machines. He resigned in disgrace on January 10, 1973. He eventually was found not guilty of the bribery charge, but was nonetheless found to have violated Securities and Exchange Commission rules.

The Ruttenberg Era: 1973

Ex-labor union economist Harold J. Ruttenberg, who as Philip Murray's right-hand man had helped organize the United Steelworkers of America, stepped in to save the day. Ruttenberg had proposed that steelworkers' wages be tied to increased mill productivity, becoming chief economist and director of research for the union. He later became president of Stardill-Keystone, merging four companies into one, and then helped manage Portsmouth Steel. He was appointed president and chief executive officer of AVM on April 17, 1973, replacing Alvin Dawson.

Reorganization: 1973–89

Ruttenberg began raising needed cash by suspending AVM's dividends, and by selling off seven divisions over the

---

Company Perspectives:

With the motto "Security is our Business," American Locker Security Systems, Inc., headquartered in Jamestown, NY, is the world's premier supplier of secure locker storage. An international company with product lines ranging from classic coin-operated lockers to computer-controlled distribution systems, American Locker currently dominates a sizeable portion of the locker specialty field and is viewed as the industry standard for secure storage around the world.

---

next two decades, including the voting machines unit, the airport checking locker businesses, the domestic locker concessions, and the steel office furniture division, Signore Inc., which was sold to its employees in 1989 at a $1.7 million loss.

After reorganization, American Locker Group, Inc. was the sole surviving division of the original firm and the nation's leading maker of storage lockers for business and recreation. Part of the reorganization involved the development of new markets. A key element in the company's new direction was the successful development of high-quality molded plastic cluster box units that could be built by outside manufacturers for its lucrative U.S. Postal Service contract.

American Locker's sales offices were centrally located throughout the United States, with general access provided via e-mail through corporate headquarters; international representatives around the world provided expert consultation on product selection, operation, and specific security needs. American Locker's National Service Center, located in Ellicottville, New York, supplied parts to customers throughout the world. In addition to stocking and supplying parts for virtually all American Locker products, the Service Center also cut keys, repaired locks, assisted customers with problems over the telephone, and, in some areas, provided customers with on-site service.

Lockers were outfitted with rugged self-closing rubber cushioned doors, corner returns, and stainless steel double loop hinges. All modules come factory-assembled in single- to triple-wide tiers containing up to 18 compartments per module. Ease of installation meant that a great number of modules could be installed in minimum time.

Cash Flow Positive in the 1990s

Unlike many publicly traded companies, American Locker operated as a cash flow positive enterprise with shareholder value firmly in the forefront of management's concerns. With the help of its lucrative Postal Service contract, American Locker's net income from operations expanded from $472,535 in 1996 to $1.46 million in 1997. At around this time the company adopted a policy of repurchasing shares in order to enhance shareholder value. By the end of 1997, American Locker had repurchased nearly 25 percent of the common shares it had outstanding at the end of 1996, resulting in increased per-share earnings for the year. A four-for-one stock split took place on June 25, 1998, triggering a 50 percent advance in the company's stock price within five days.

Sales Increase: 1997–98

At the end of the third quarter of 1998, net sales for the preceding nine months were $36.8 million, up over 120 percent from the same period in 1997, with a net income of $3.4 million. Plastic locker sales were up by nearly 200 percent, although sales of metal products were somewhat lower.

End of the Ruttenberg Era: 1998

On August 15, 1998, American Locker announced the death by heart failure of 84-year-old Harold J. Ruttenberg, chairman, CEO, and treasurer. At the time of his death, he owned about 30 percent of the company. On September 3, 1998, the board of directors appointed Ruttenberg's eldest son, 52-year-old Edward F. Ruttenberg, to replace his father. With the Ruttenberg family still owning approximately 33 percent of the business, Edward Ruttenberg had much incentive to continue where his father left off.

Preparing for the Future

Since 1996 American Locker had been actively pursuing corrective Y2K actions. After assessing its information technology systems in 1997, the company decided to scrap all existing hardware and software. Implementation of the new IT system, which connected to a Novell PC network, was scheduled for early 1999, with the existing IT system running parallel to the new network until it had been fully tested. American Locker also surveyed the company's entire vendor base during the third quarter of 1998, to verify that its major suppliers were working towards year 2000 compliance, and that reasonable contingency plans were in place to allow uninterrupted production of products to continue.

American Locker Group had maintained sufficient resources and enough capital liquidity to continue the expansion of its operations indefinitely. Indeed, its working capital steadily increased in the late 1990s, with a line of credit also available for contingencies. A "Safe Harbor" statement filed by American Locker, in accordance with the Private Securities Litigation Reform Act, included the company's plans, strategies, objectives, expectations, intentions, and adequacy of resources, projecting that future capital needs could be met primarily through cash proceeds from its own operations.

In February 1999, American Locker was named number three by *Business Wire* in its list of the top ten 1998 technology stock performance winners. Thanks to the far-seeing efforts of founder Harold Ruttenberg, the company remained well run, both financially and operationally, and was consistently recommended as a "good risk" for savvy investors.

While ALGI's prospects for the future seemed bright, the rosy scenario was based almost entirely on maintenance of its lucrative United States Postal Service contracts. Should those agreements change suddenly, or should eager competitors underbid American Locker (which did not have patent protection on its cluster units), or should necessary components and materials suddenly become scarce or unavailable, the outlook would become considerably more clouded. Having laid its financial "eggs" solely in the post office's "basket," the company's future was tied inexorably to USPS concerns. Fortunately for

Key Dates:

1895: U.S. Voting Machine Company is founded.
1958: American Locker Group is incorporated.
1964: Business is spun off from Rockwell Manufacturing and renamed Automatic Voting Machine Corporation (AVM).
1973: Harold J. Ruttenberg becomes new president and CEO and American Locker Group becomes sole surviving corporate entity of AVM.
1998: Ruttenberg dies and is replaced by his eldest son, Edward F. Ruttenberg; company issues a four-for-one stock split.

investors, these concerns seemed minimal in 1999, and the company's current financial basis remained rock solid.

Principal Subsidiaries

American Locker Security Systems, Inc.; Canadian Locker Company, Ltd.

Principal Competitors

Cutler Manufacturing.

Further Reading

"Alvin Dawson, 90, Founded Plastics Company," *Boston Globe*, December 11, 1988, p. 83.

"American Locker Chairman, CEO Named," *Dow Jones News Service*, September 3, 1998.

"American Locker Chairman Ruttenberg Dies at 84," *Dow Jones Online News*, August 18, 1998.

"American Locker Group, Inc.," *Wall Street Journal*, June 7, 1996, p. B2.

"American Locker Group Posts $1.2 Million Profit," *Buffalo News*, July 25, 1998, p. B12.

"American Locker Group Sells Unit to Employees...," *Dow Jones News Service*, January 5, 1990.

"American Locker Group Shares Climb Following 4-for-1 Stock Split," *Dow Jones Online News*, June 30, 1998.

"American Locker Rescinds Pension Plan Termination," *Dow Jones News Service*, September 18, 1987.

Barrett, William P., "Indestructible," *Forbes*, February 8, 1999, p. 76.

"The Best 200 Small Companies," *Forbes*, November 2, 1998, p. 250.

"Harold J. Ruttenberg (obituary)," *New York Times*, August 18, 1998, p. B9.

"Harold J. Ruttenberg Labor Leader Turned Entrepreneur," *Pittsburgh Post-Gazette*, August 16, 1998, p. B5.

Robinson, David, "American Locker Sees Profits Triple in Third Quarter," *Buffalo News*, November 4, 1998, p. B4.

—Robert Reginald and Mary A. Burgess

America West Holdings Corporation

4000 East Sky Harbor Boulevard
Phoenix, Arizona 85034
U.S.A.
Telephone: (480) 693-0800
Fax: (480) 693-5546
Web site: http://www.americawest.com

Public Company
Incorporated: 1981
Employees: 12,200
Sales: $2.2 billion (1999)
Stock Exchanges: New York
Ticker Symbol: AWA
NAIC: 481111 Scheduled Passenger Air Transportation;
    56152 Tour Operators; 561599 All Other Travel
    Arrangement and Reservation Services

Of the more than 150 U.S. airlines launched during the post-deregulation start-up boom, only one survived to become a major carrier: America West Airlines (AWA), owned by America West Holdings Corporation. Propelled by strong economies in Phoenix and Las Vegas, AWA has added another hub in Ohio. America West Holdings Corporation also owns The Leisure Company (TLC), built out of the airline's travel businesses.

Origins

America West was incorporated in 1981 by ten investors, including Edward R. Beauvais, an accountant and airline consultant; the investors took out second mortgages on their homes and borrowed against their credit cards to raise funds for the endeavor. With the company still short millions of dollars, Beauvais made dozens of trips to New York over a two-year period before he was able to convince an investment banking firm to underwrite a stock issue for the new airline, raising $18.7 million from the sale of 3.5 million shares at $7.50 a piece. With this capital, America West took to the skies on August 1, 1983. Operating three leased Boeing 737 aircraft, the fledgling airline offered flights from its hub in Phoenix to four cities: Colorado Springs, Colorado; Los Angeles, California; Kansas City, Missouri; and Wichita, Kansas.

The company's strategy was to make Phoenix an east-west transfer point by routing travelers from its network of Midwestern cities through Sky Harbor Airport to California. With business travelers as its targeted market, America West aimed to increase passenger traffic on the routes it served through a combination of full-quality service, frequent flights, and low fares. To set itself apart from competitors, the company adopted perks such as onboard ticketing and free 12-ounce drinks.

In entering a crowded and highly competitive industry, Beauvais, who became America West's chairman and CEO, and President Michael J. Conway, brought a different approach to the traditional problems of running an airline. To avoid head-to-head competition with the better established major airlines, the company decided to restrict its activities to the area west of the Mississippi. To circumvent high labor costs, Conway and Beauvais devised a mandatory employee stock ownership program, in which its employees, none of whom belonged to a union, were required to purchase shares in the company equal to one-fifth of their starting salary. The airline touted this angle in its advertising, which featured a picture of a company employee under the slogan, "There's something unusual about Laurie: she owns an airline."

In an effort to build team spirit and keep workers interested in their jobs, America West structured its workforce in a deliberately non-hierarchical fashion. All employees earned a low base salary, supplemented by earnings from a profit-sharing program that allotted 15 percent of all pre-tax earnings to be distributed among employees. Pilots were expected to fill in as dispatchers or in other ground jobs when they were not in the cockpit. Customer service personnel rotated between various tasks, acting as baggage handlers, flight attendants, gate and ticket counter agents, and reservations agents. A *Wall Street Journal* reporter who flew the airline in its second month wrote that customer service representatives servicing a newly landed plane on the tarmac looked like "college students preparing a homecoming float" and described one worker backing a catering truck into a conveyor belt.

America West expanded rapidly in its first months of operation, adding two more planes and service to Omaha, Nebraska, and Ontario, California, outside of Los Angeles, on October 1, 1983. At the end of that month, an additional plane to Las Vegas was brought on line. On December 1 of that year, the airline inaugurated service to four more cities east of Phoenix—Des Moines, Iowa; Tulsa, Oklahoma; Oklahoma City, Oklahoma; and Albuquerque, New Mexico—and also began flying to San Diego, California, to bring its total of destinations served to 12 and its number of planes leased to ten. Although the airline lost money in its first two months as a result of start-up costs, its passenger traffic was picking up, and the company had nearly tripled its 280-person workforce by the end of the year.

By the end of 1984 America West had 21 aircraft serving 22 cities. Although the carrier had attained a dominant position in its home market, Phoenix, it had done so by racking up $19 million in losses in its first 15 months in operation. In November 1984 the airline announced its first profitable month of operations, and the following month it rejected an offer by rival Southwest Airlines to purchase the company.

First Profit in 1985

In 1985 America West shed its initial difficulties and came into its own, doubling its revenues to $241 million to post its first profit, $11.4 million. The company had earned a one-third market share in its hub in Phoenix, offering 66 flights to California every day and 122 flights total. Overall, it flew 32 planes to 26 different cities. As a complement to its passenger service, the company inaugurated an air cargo service as well as a small package service. Offering passengers free sandwiches and copies of the *Wall Street Journal* on its flights, America West wooed business travelers and maintained a higher percentage of seats filled on its flights than the industry average. "We gave Midwesterners California at half the price and twice the frequency," said Conway, explaining the company's startling growth to the *New York Times*.

By 1986 the airline was set to undergo a period of transition, building on the success of its early years of limited operations to expand the scope of its activities. Now serving 30 cities, including its first international destinations, Calgary and Edmonton in

western Canada, America West announced its intention to include an additional 10 to 20 points on its route map within the next two years.

The company also planned to inaugurate service using smaller planes to ferry customers from the start-up cities of Yuma and Flagstaff, Arizona, to connecting flights at its hub in Phoenix. In addition, America West broke ground on a new maintenance complex in Phoenix. The cost of this expansion, coupled with an expensive fare war the airline was waging with Southwest Airlines, cut back profits in 1986 to $3 million, less than a third of the previous year's total.

By 1987 America West had opened a second hub of operations in Las Vegas, with 102 daily departures, as the airline looked to double its size by the end of the year. In part, this rapid pace of expansion was designed to ward off unwanted consolidation with a larger airline, the fate of many other small carriers during the late 1980s. America West ventured outside the safe harbor of its Western base for the first time in May 1987, inaugurating service to Chicago's O'Hare International Airport. Six weeks later it extended its reach even further east, scheduling flights from Phoenix and Las Vegas to Baltimore and New York. In order to do this, the company added seven Boeing 757s to its fleet. These moves resulted in an unprofitable first half of 1987, as the airline racked up losses of nearly $15 million, and left America West vulnerable to competition from the powerful major airlines who dominated service from these areas. The company's leaders insisted, however, that their targeted markets were underserved or overcharged, leaving a window of opportunity open for their airline with its low operating costs.

Despite the fact that the U.S. airline industry was undergoing a frenzy of mergers and takeovers during this time, America West was able to remain largely removed from this activity. The company's stock option plan for employees had put 18 percent of the airline's outstanding shares in workers' hands, and members of the company's management controlled an additional 12 percent. Nevertheless, a one-fifth stake in America West was purchased by Ansett Airlines, an Australian company half-owned by media mogul Rupert Murdoch. America West had previously leased planes from the company in August of 1987, providing the airline with a much needed infusion of additional cash. Regardless of this measure of financial health, the company's stock price remained static, as Wall Street analysts expressed doubts about the company's ambitious plans for expansion.

By the end of 1987 America West had added 3,200 employees, 23 aircraft, and ten new destinations in just one year, becoming the nation's tenth largest airline. However, passenger traffic failed to grow as fast as the airline's capacity, and persistent fare wars in some markets cut margins of profitability. These factors led to a $45.7 million loss on revenues of $575 million for the year.

Faced with this bad news, America West announced plans for a cutback in operations in early 1988 in an attempt to regain profitability. The airline set out to trim flight operations by 10 percent, removing 15 planes from service, shutting down service to Chicago's Midway airport and to Springfield, Missouri, and shrinking its staff by 500 employees. America West was teetering on the brink of disaster. "They're flying into oblivion. It's only a matter of time," opined one pessimistic airline analyst in *Business Week*. The company's planes were flying half-full, below the break-even point, and the airline's success in Phoenix had attracted the interest of powerful competitors, who were increasing their service to this market.

Nevertheless, the cost-cutting measures proved effective, and, benefiting from a strong economy, America West ended 1988 in the black, showing a profit of $9.4 million after a debt refinancing. Despite a disastrous first quarter, the company's operating profits had grown steadily throughout the last nine months of the year, as the percentage of seats filled on each plane improved and some ticket prices were raised. Rivals pronounced the turnaround "extraordinary."

Rebounding in 1989

Buoyed by the company's resurrection, America West's president announced plans to add flights to major markets on the East Coast, including New York-LaGuardia and Washington-National Airport, using boarding gates abandoned by ailing Eastern Airlines. Despite its heavy burden of debt, which had reached 85 percent of operating capital, the airline looked even farther afield to Hawaii and Australia, where it planned to hook up with part-owner Ansett Airlines and other points on the Pacific Rim. Undeterred by the company's recent brush with disaster, CEO Beauvais explained the need for continued expansion to a *Business Week* reporter, asserting: "You cannot just sit still and survive."

In keeping with this philosophy, America West made a bid in the spring of 1989 to acquire Eastern Airlines' shuttle service between Washington, D.C., New York City, and Boston. Although this attempt was ultimately unsuccessful, the airline did inaugurate service from the west to New York City and Washington, D.C., in July 1989 as well as service to Hawaii in November 1989. Although the flights to Hawaii lost money due to stiff competition on the route, they helped to fill connecting flights to Phoenix and lent cachet to the airline's frequent flier program, which could now reward customers with a vacation in the islands. In addition, the airline envisioned Hawaii as a potential hub for a network of flights radiating out to points across the Pacific.

In May 1989 America West lost a hard-fought bid to provide service to Tokyo, the first of its planned Pacific Rim destina-

tions. It pressed on, however, with efforts to win permission to fly to Nagoya, a large Japanese industrial center, and also to Hong Kong and Taipei. The airline also took steps to increase the size of its fleet, ordering an additional 25 jets from Boeing as well as six more small commuter planes from another manufacturer. America West ended 1989 in the black, posting a profit of $20 million.

In the first half of 1990, America West was reclassified as a major airline by the United States Department of Transportation, and the company's sales rose as the airline carried 40 percent more revenue passenger miles than it had in the previous year. Curtailed by high fuel costs and heavy interest payments on its large debt, however, earnings remained small. To counteract its higher costs, America West raised fares by 10 percent in August 1990.

As other airlines in poor financial shape, such as TWA, underwent radical reorganization, America West explored the possibility of taking over some of their operations. In the fall of 1990 the company made its second serious inquiry into an East Coast shuttle, entering into talks with Pan Am about taking over its Washington-New York-Boston route. Although those talks, too, fell through, the company did receive a much-coveted approval from the federal government to start service between Honolulu and Nagoya. This boon shortly followed a September 1990 announcement that America West intended to lease more than 100 planes from Airbus Industrie, the European aircraft consortium, for use on possible new routes. (AWA chose the Airbus jets over Boeings largely for the cockpit and maintenance commonality across various types in the Airbus family.) Despite these signs of aggressive expansion, the airline ended 1990 in poor financial shape, racking up losses of $74.7 million.

1991 Bankruptcy

Performance in 1991 continued to be weak. Although America West added coast-to-coast flights between New York City and Orange County, California, began service to Atlanta, and stepped up flights to Honolulu, it prepared to scale back its growth. The war in the Persian Gulf in early 1991 cut air traffic dramatically, as travelers wary of possible terrorist attacks stayed home. By the middle of the year it was clear that America West's expansion had left it with too small a financial cushion to fall back on in lean times. Although the airline had grown to the point of serving 54 cities with a fleet of 109 planes, 87 of those aircraft were leased from their owners; the lack of cash to make payments on these planes forced the airline to file Chapter 11 bankruptcy on June 27, 1991. The airline petitioned for protection from its creditors while it attempted to reorganize its finances without being forced to suspend operations.

Since the generally poor state of the American airline industry made the likelihood of a bail-out by a foreign airline or a domestic competitor small, AWA looked to pare its unprofitable operations and emphasize its strengths. To do this, it moved away from head-to-head competition with more efficient Southwest Airlines on short-haul flights and restructured its route map to stress longer flights to eastern destinations. As part of this process, the company announced plans to shed its commuter airline operation. Desperate to lure passengers back to the air, America West was forced to sell tickets at half-price, weakening its earnings. The company laid off 15 percent of its employees and slapped the others with a 10 percent pay cut. In addition, 15 planes were taken out of service. In August 1991 the airline received some essential financial help from Northwest Airlines and a British group, and a creditor pledged additional loans in December of that year. Even with these measures, America West ended 1991 $213.8 million in the red.

Still alive and kicking in 1992, despite the predictions of doomsayers, America West transferred the focus of its attention from Phoenix, its historical base of operations, to Columbus, Ohio. By building a hub in Ohio, the airline's leaders predicted, the company could avoid damaging competition with Southwest Airlines and garner profitable business fliers from the area's high concentration of corporate headquarters. By March 1, 1992, 26 flights left Columbus daily, and the company had made its entry into the Florida market.

As part of its new eastern focus, America West also sold off its recently acquired route to Nagoya, Japan, adding $15 million of cash to the airline's coffers. Passenger bookings were up, as the airline aggressively courted travel agents to regain their lost confidence. In addition, the company's costs had sunk to the lowest levels in the industry as America West prepared to submit a plan for reorganization to its bankruptcy court in 1992. While Conway told *Business Week* that "this airline is too tough to die," industry observers predicted that America West's fate hung with the rest of the economy: a robust economic upswing could save it, while continued recession would almost certainly doom it.

Beauvais left America West in 1992 as William A. Franke, leader of a group of Arizona angels who invested in the company, became chairman. A. Maurice Myers, president and CEO of Aloha Airlines, replaced Conway in January 1994 after the airline had become profitable again (earning $37 million in 1993) and pressure mounted to pick a reorganization plan.

The America West board chose that of AmWest Partners, which included Continental Airlines chairman David Bonderman, James Coulter, Continental Airlines itself, Mesa Airlines, and Fidelity Investments. It invested $215 million in America West, which continued to cut costs and post profits. The Bonderman group declared an alliance with Continental would produce enough value to repay creditors. The two airlines began conducting joint flights in October 1994.

Record profits in 1995 fueled further expansion around the Phoenix hub. The airline added six routes from Acapulco to Anchorage. Company officials stated there was enough room for America West and Southwest Airlines to coexist in Arizona, which had one of the fastest-growing economies in the United States. America West specialized in longer trips than Southwest, which typically operated point-to-point routes.

The company began to outsource its heavy maintenance to BF Goodrich's Tramco unit in December 1995. However, the transition was awkward and costly in terms of canceled flights and lost revenues. Personnel shortages contributed to a loss of $50 million in the third quarter of 1996; the carrier posted an undersized $8.5 million profit on sales of $1.7 billion for the year.

Richard Goodmanson was named president in February 1996. By this time, America West was boasting the lowest operating costs among major U.S. airlines—lower even than Southwest's. However, in spite of efforts to win big-spending business flyers, AWA remained dependent on low-rent leisure traffic. Its Nite Flight service to Las Vegas, the company's nocturnal hub, accounted for 15 percent of revenues and helped keep its moonlighting planes profitable.

AWA's travel package offerings grew handsomely, warranting the creation of a separate subsidiary, The Leisure Company (TLC), in January 1998. This unit specialized in bundling air travel with accommodations under the America West Vacations and Destination Leisure brands. TLC launched FareBusters, a ticket consolidator, in April 1998 and acquired The Vacation Store (TVS), a $30 million-a-year business, in October.

America West sought to distance itself from any budget carrier connotations with a $10 million advertising effort in 1999. It reassured business travelers in particular that "Every flight counts," a message also aimed at its own fractious employees (flight attendants nearly walked off the job in March).

Principal Subsidiaries

America West Airlines; The Leisure Company.

Principal Competitors

AMR Corporation; Delta Air Lines Inc.; Southwest Airlines Co.; UAL Corporation.

Further Reading

Alsop, Stewart, "My Trip on America West, Or Why Customer Service Still Matters," *Fortune,* November 22, 1999.

Bayer, Tom, "America West Flies with Personal Touch," *Advertising Age,* August 1, 1983.

Cuneo, Alice Z., and David Goetzl, "America West Aspires to Reach Airlines' Top Tier," *Advertising Age,* April 12, 1999, p. 6.

DiDio, Laura, "www.window-seat.com," *Computerworld,* December 22, 1997, p. 37.

Dornheim, Michael A., "Creditors May File Alternate America West Recovery Plan," *Aviation Week & Space Technology,* March 7, 1994, p. 31.

——, "Profitable America West Turns to Expansion," *Aviation Week & Space Technology,* November 13, 1995, pp. 28, 30.

Harris, Roy J., Jr., "New Airline Surmounting Labor Dilemma," *Wall Street Journal,* September 12, 1983.

Henderson, Danna K., "America West: Back in the Saddle," *Air Transport World,* June 1997, pp. 84–90.

Kane, Sid, "The Cloudless Skies of America West," *New York Times,* June 8, 1986.

——, "Surprise Attack," *Financial World,* November 17, 1987.

Loeffelholz, Suzanne, "Staying Power," *Financial World,* September 5, 1989.

McKenna, James T., "Continental, America West Increase Ties, Cut Jobs," *Aviation Week & Space Technology,* January 23, 1995, pp. 48–49.

Salpukas, Agis, "A Young Airline's Battle to Survive Lean Times," *New York Times,* June 29, 1991.

Schine, Eric, "Can These Upstart Airlines Handle the Heavy Weather?," *Business Week,* October 1, 1990.

——, ''Someone up There Loves America West,'' *Business Week,* March 16, 1992.

Schine, Eric, and Wendy Zellner, ''This Bird Is No Longer an Ugly Duckling,'' *Business Week,* February 28, 1994, p. 40.

Smith, Bruce A., ''America West Expands Routes Served,'' *Aviation Week & Space Technology,* December 19, 1983.

——, ''America West Tackles Operational Problems,'' *Aviation Week & Space Technology,* September 23, 1996, pp. 44–45.

——, ''America West to Upgrade Fleet, Facilities, Employee Salaries,'' *Aviation Week & Space Technology,* August 25, 1986.

Toy, Stewart, ''America West Is Flying High Again—But for How Long?,'' *Business Week,* February 6, 1989.

——, ''The Last of the Upstarts May Be Falling,'' *Business Week,* March 14, 1988.

——, ''This Upstart Could Be Flying a Bit Too High,'' *Business Week,* June 15, 1987.

—Elizabeth Rourke
—updated by Frederick C. Ingram

Ameritrade Holding Corporation

4211 South 102nd Street
Omaha, Nebraska 68127
U.S.A.
Telephone: (402) 331-7856
Toll Free: (800) 237-8692
Fax: (402) 597-7789
Web sites: http://www.ameritradeholding.com
          http://www.ameritrade.com

Public Company
Incorporated: 1975 as First Omaha Securities, Inc.
Employees: 2,379
Sales: $315.3 million (1999)
Stock Exchanges: NASDAQ
Ticker Symbol: AMTD
NAIC: 52312 Securities Brokerage; 334611 Reproduction
    of Software; 551112 Offices of Other Holding
    Companies

Ameritrade Holding Corporation is a discount broker-dealer that operates through four subsidiaries: Ameritrade, Accutrade, Advance Clearing, and AmeriVest. Through its subsidiaries, Ameritrade Holding provides trading services to individual investors and institutions, with a particular emphasis on providing trading services via the Internet. Known for its low commissions, the company ranks as the fifth largest online broker, having maintained a presence on the Internet since 1995. Ameritrade and Accutrade, the company's two discount retail brands, provide online, telephone, and fax trading. Advanced Clearing provides clearing services and AmeriVest provides discount brokerage services to financial institutions.

Founder's Background

As a teenager growing up in Nebraska, J. Joe Ricketts dreamed of some day becoming a doctor or a lawyer. The future chairman and chief executive officer of Ameritrade Holding made his first step toward gaining his professional degree by enrolling at Creighton University in 1959. Within weeks, Rick-

etts lost his boyhood passion, quickly finding the classwork not to his liking. Growing restless at Creighton, Ricketts followed the advice of a friend and signed up for a course in economics, which introduced him to the writings and theories of Adam Smith. Ricketts's academic malaise immediately gave way to a life-changing zeal for matters of the business world. He later reminisced in a January 28, 2000 interview with the *Standard:* "I knew that this was what turned me on."

Ricketts discovered the general direction of his professional life while at Creighton, but he did not land on the specific path of his calling until more than a decade after he left school. Ricketts was employed as a Dean Witter salesman when he reached his second life-defining epiphany. In May 1975, the federal government deregulated the securities industry, touching off sweeping changes in the business where Ricketts made his living. One of the pertinent effects of deregulation for Ricketts was the advent of negotiated commissions for individual investors, a facet of the securities industry that would become best known as discount brokerage. Facing a potential flood of new competitors who would be willing to undercut any transaction fee charged by Dean Witter salespeople, Ricketts grew anxious. The new rules meant he would have to substantially increase his efforts to beat back a wave of aggressive rivals. Ricketts was not opposed to more work, but he was opposed to investing more of his time on behalf of Dean Witter. "If I was going to have to work longer and harder," Ricketts informed the *Standard* in his January 28, 2000 interview, "[I knew] I'd rather be working for myself."

Ricketts Establishes Ameritrade Holding's Predecessor in 1975

The 1975 deregulation of the brokerage industry led Ricketts down the path of entrepreneurialism. Determining that his days working under the aegis of Dean Witter were at an end, Ricketts left for Chicago in pursuit of membership into the Chicago Board of Options Exchange. While in Chicago, Ricketts ran into a Creighton alumnus who was a principal in a discount brokerage firm, one of the new breed of securities companies that found fertile ground in the post-deregulation era. Ricketts's former classmate invited him to have a look at his brokerage operation and Ricketts agreed, leading to his fortuitous intro-

Company Perspectives:

Our mission is to be the largest broker in the world for individual consumer investors as measured by agency trades (not revenues, not investment banking, not market making, and not principal trades—only agency trades).

duction into the nascent world of retail discount brokerage. "There were three people in a small room answering phones and writing tickets as fast as they could," Ricketts told the *Standard,* recalling his first impression of the business that would become his life's work. "To me, that was heaven."

Inspired and filled with purpose, Ricketts returned to Omaha, determined to establish himself as an operator of a discount brokerage firm. He found four investors who each were willing to contribute $12,500 to his cause. Ricketts added another $12,500, obtaining the money from family and friends. With the $62,500 (which eventually grew into a $2 billion personal fortune), Ricketts took over First Omaha Securities, Inc. in 1975, a company that had been established four years earlier as a local investment bank. Ricketts immediately gave the company a new business direction, creating a discount brokerage firm that offered the lowest transaction fees in the industry. By charging $25 to trade 100 shares on the New York Stock Exchange or over-the-counter, Ricketts, not for the last time, touched off a revolution in the securities industry. The company made $700 during its first month. Ricketts later confessed he had little idea about what he was doing, but First Omaha thrived nevertheless. Before the end of his first year of business, Ricketts was ready to take on a bigger challenge and court a national clientele. To apprise industry observers of his intentions, Ricketts changed the name of the company to the more geographically expansive First National Brokerage Services, Inc.

First National developed a sound foundation during its formative years, broadening its operations as its business volume grew. In 1983, Ameritrade Clearing, Inc. was established as a clearing broker, adding another facet to the brokerage business governed by Ricketts. By all measures, the company was a success during its first decade of business, but the extent of its success was limited. First National attracted little national attention, occupying what was regarded as the second tier of the securities industry, competing against a smaller breed of competitors than the country's elite brokerage firms. The company's stature would change during its second decade of business, altered substantially by Ricketts's pioneering advancements in the securities industry. He had gained his business footing through aggressive pricing, but Ricketts national fame and the prolific growth of his company were ignited by his intrepid incorporation of new technology. From the late 1980s forward, Ricketts's company consistently embraced new ways of doing business in the securities industry, resulting in the company's promotion from a market underling to one of the leaders of the industry.

Touchtone Telephone Trading Debuts in 1988

Before taking his first big risk in the field of technology, Ricketts changed the name of First National to TransTerra Co.

in 1987. TransTerra served as the holding company for Ameritrade Clearing and the company's discount brokerages, led by the flagship operation, Accutrade. Shortly after the name change, Ricketts began seriously considering allowing customers to place orders via touchtone telephone, a service that would greatly reduce his costs once the investment in the technology had been made. The idea was a gamble. No other company had tested the technology, but Ricketts was willing to take the risk. He canvassed his customers and formed focus groups, trying to determine whether there would be a demand for touchtone telephone trading. The market studies showed unequivocally that customers had no desire to use their telephones to buy and sell securities, but, remarkably, Ricketts pressed ahead with his plans. He was convinced automated trading would reduce costs significantly, resulting in savings that he could pass on to customers. Ricketts invested in the technology and announced the new service in 1988, becoming the first in the industry to offer touchtone telephone trading. Customers who had flatly stated they would not use the service quickly changed their minds when they learned that they could trade for three cents a share, an exceedingly low commission. Although the technology required a heavier investment than Ricketts had anticipated, the decision to offer automated trading proved to be a resounding success, substantiating Ricketts's belief in the potential of technology.

Beginning of Online Trading: 1994

During the 1990s, Ricketts's company recorded explosive growth primarily because of his willingness to incorporate emerging technologies into the securities business. After his experience with touchtone telephone trading, Ricketts needed little encouragement to dive headlong into online trading. "The Internet wasn't a puzzle," he informed the *Standard* in his January 28, 2000 interview. "We were crystal clear from the beginning that customers would migrate to this," he added. The era of online trading officially began in August 1994, when K. Aufhauser & Company became the first brokerage outfit to offer Internet trading. Ricketts acquired K. Aufhauser the following year, as well as All American Brokers, Inc., quickly forging a sizable presence in the new market niche. Accutrade for Windows, the first online investing system that used preprogrammed investment parameters, debuted in January 1996, giving individual investors a trading system that previously was only available to institutions. In May 1996, another online trading brand was added to TransTerra's portfolio called eBroker, which functioned as an Internet-only broker organized as a subsidiary of All American Brokers.

Ricketts's faith in online trading paid substantial dividends, fueling his company's prolific growth during the latter half of the 1990s. After the company's expansion in online trading in 1996, the effect on business volume was swift and decisive. "We've seen a near doubling of our core discount brokerage accounts in the past year and a 300 percent increase in online business in one year," Ricketts told *Knight-Ridder/Tribune Business News* on September 4, 1997. "We have a unique opportunity before us, and we are intensifying our focus on account growth, particularly online accounts with the Ameritrade brand," he added. The Ameritrade brand was a product of the several important organizational changes implemented in

Key Dates:

1975: J. Joe Ricketts establishes First Omaha Securities, Inc. as a discount broker.
1987: First Omaha is renamed TransTerra Co.
1988: Accutrade, a TransTerra subsidiary, is the first company to introduce touchtone telephone trading.
1995: TransTerra acquires K. Aufhauser & Co., the first company with an Internet trading site.
1997: Ricketts completes initial public offering of newly named Ameritrade Holding Corporation.
1998: Ameritrade Holding enables customers to invest overseas for the first time through an agreement with German concern Deutsche Bank AG.

1997 that followed a change in the company's corporate title from TransTerra to Ameritrade Holding Corporation in November 1996. The newly named company filed for an initial public offering (IPO) in February 1997 and completed its IPO the following month. In October 1997, the company established its new brand Ameritrade, Inc., which represented an amalgamation of K. Aufhauser, eBroker, and Ceres Securities, Inc., a deep discount brokerage Ricketts formed in 1994.

The impetus for the structural changes of 1997 stemmed in part from Ricketts's miscalculation of the online trading market. His prediction that consumers would migrate to online trading—evinced by his acquisition of K. Aufhauser in 1995—had come true, but he had underestimated how fast individual investors would embrace the Internet age. What Ricketts believed would take years to develop was happening in a matter of months, which put Ameritrade Holding in the uncomfortable position of lagging behind other brokerage firms who had carved a deeper presence in online trading services. By mid-1997, Ameritrade Holding was trailing a handful of brokerage firms that included Charles Schwab, E-Trade, and TD Waterhouse, a market position that Ricketts sought to improve by consolidating his discount brands into Ameritrade and announcing a new industry low for online trading fees. Concurrent with the debut of Ameritrade, Ricketts lowered his commission to $8 per equity market order and invested an unprecedented $14 million into the company's "Eight Bucks a Trade" marketing program.

Although Ameritrade Holding continued to trail the industry leaders in the wake of Ameritrade's formation, the company's rate of growth increased substantially. A month-and-a-half after launching its marketing campaign, the company's online accounts increased 50 percent, prompting Ricketts to assume a more aggressive marketing posture. He set aside an additional $44 million for another marketing campaign, which underpinned a remarkable rise in the company's business volume during the late 1990s. Between 1997 and 1999, as the prospect of trading online gripped millions of individual investors, Ameritrade's accounts soared from 98,000 to 560,000. Significantly, Ameritrade averaged more than six trades per quarter, per account, by far eclipsing the average activity of accounts held by E-Trade and TD Waterhouse and more than three times the average recorded by Charles Schwab.

By the end of the 1990s, Ameritrade Holding ranked as the fifth largest online investment broker in the United States, a position the company was poised to improve upon during the first decade of the 21st century. Important agreements had been reached during the late 1990s to ensure the company's visibility on the Internet, particularly marketing agreements with America Online and MSN, The Microsoft Network online service, both reached in 1997. Additionally, Ricketts had begun to expand beyond U.S. borders by the end of the decade, opening new growth channels for his company to explore in the 21st century. In November 1998, Ameritrade Holding and Deutsche Bank AG formed a joint marketing agreement to allow their customers to trade online in both the U.S. and German securities markets. In March 1999, Ameritrade and a European discount broker named Cortal announced a similar agreement that opened access to French securities markets. A foray into Japan was expected to be made in the early years of the 2000s.

Ricketts was expected to pass operational control over Ameritrade Holding to co-CEO Thomas Lewis in the first half of 2000, leaving behind a company with a market capitalization of more than $3 billion. During Ricketts's last few months at the helm, Ameritrade Holding took steps to prepare itself for rapid growth in the near future. Two new facilities were expected to be completed during the first half of 2000, an enormous data center in Kansas City, Missouri, and a four-story building in Annapolis Junction, Maryland, to house the company's Advanced Technology Development Center. Once its processing capabilities were improved, Ameritrade Holding claimed it would be able to handle 400,000 trades per day, or approximately six times the company's capacity in 1999. With its focus centered on capturing the business to take advantage of its potential, Ameritrade Holding moved resolutely forward, intent on becoming the market leader in the decade ahead.

Principal Subsidiaries

Ameritrade, Inc.; Accutrade, Inc.; Advanced Clearing, Inc.; AmeriVest, Inc.

Principal Competitors

E*Trade Group, Inc.; TD Waterhouse Group, Inc.; The Charles Schwab Corporation.

Further Reading

Booth, Tamzin, "Day Traders Beware," *Institutional Investor International Edition,* March 1999, p. 23.
"Discount Brokerage Ameritrade Reorganizes," *Knight-Ridder/Tribune Business News,* September 4, 1997, p. 904B1072.
Frederick, Jim, "Why Online Brokers Can Win the Web War," *Money,* July 1, 1999, p. 103.
Garrity, Brain, "Ameritrade Stock Woes Cost Chairman and Underwriters," *Investment Dealers' Digest,* August 2, 1999, p. ITEM9921100A.
Loizos, Constance, "Online Brokers Turn to—Gasp!—Service," *Investment News,* October 11, 1999, p. 14.
Rasmussen, Jim, "Earnings, AOL Propel Stock of Omaha, Neb., Brokerage Ameritrade," *Knight-Ridder/Tribune Business News,* July 24, 1998, p. OKRB982051EB.

——, "Earnings Top Expectations at Omaha, Neb.-Based Ameritrade," *Knight-Ridder/Tribune Business News,* October 30, 1997, p. 1030B0927.

——, "High Volume Overwhelms Ameritrade Online Brokerage Service," *Knight-Ridder/Tribune Business News,* September 15, 1998, p. OKRB982570EC.

Rodriguez, Karen, "Casting a Wider Net," *Business Journal,* January 7, 2000, p. 17.

Snael, Ross, "Snubbed by Banks, Ameritrade Unit Turns to 'Screen Scraping,'" *American Banker,* January 10, 2000, p. 1.

Taylor, John, "Few Midlands Stocks Escape Dow's Big Drop," *Knight-Ridder/Tribune Business News,* August 4, 1998, p. OKRB982160E9.

—Jeffrey L. Covell

Amtran, Inc.

7337 West Washington Street
Indianapolis, Indiana 02861
U.S.A.
Telephone: (317) 247-4000
Toll Free: (800) I-FLY-ATA; (800) 435-9282
Fax: (317) 243-4162
Web site: http://www.ata.com

Public Company
Incorporated: 1973 as Ambassadair
Employees: 7,000
Sales: $1.12 billion (1999)
Stock Exchanges: NASDAQ
Ticker Symbol: AMTR
NAIC: 481211 Nonscheduled Chartered Passenger Air
    Transportation; 481212 Nonscheduled Chartered
    Freight Air Transportation; 481111 Scheduled
    Passenger Air Transportation; 481112 Scheduled
    Freight Air Transportation; 56152 Tour Operators

Amtran, Inc. has outlasted most of its pre-deregulation peers to become America's largest charter carrier and the biggest airline, according to *Forbes*, that no one's ever heard of. The holding company's American Trans Air (ATA) subsidiary flies seven million passengers a year, mostly tourists.

1970s–80s: Early Growth

Airline founder J. George Mikelsons was born in Riga, Latvia, and moved with his family first to Australia, then to Germany, and finally to Indianapolis, Indiana, in 1960. There he trained as a pilot, and in 1965 he took a position as a DC-7 copilot for a local travel club known as Voyager 1000.

In 1973, Mikelsons started his own travel club, Ambassadair, taking out a second mortgage on his home to fund the venture. For Ambassadair, Mikelsons not only flew the plane, a leased Boeing 720 dubbed "Miss Indy," but he also drove the passengers to the airport in a second-hand school bus, loaded their baggage, and took them sightseeing once they reached their destination. As a travel club, Mikelsons' start-up could not publish rate or schedule information; it could only serve its members. A second plane, acquired by Ambassadair in 1978, the year of deregulation in the American airline industry, was named "Spirit of Indiana."

During this time, another entity, known as American Trans Air (ATA), was set up by Mikelsons to manage Ambassadair's flight and travel operations. In 1981, however, ATA received its certification as a charter carrier and added eight Boeing 707s to the fleet. It began flying charters for the U.S. Department of Defense. Employees numbered 320 in 1982, when revenues were $30.5 million.

Mikelsons next formed Amtran, Inc., a holding company for Ambassadair and ATA, in 1984. ATA ditched the 707s in favor of 727s during this time and began operating wide-body aircraft as well, in the form of McDonnell Douglas DC-10s and Lockheed L-1011s. By the mid-1980s, Amtran had become the largest charter operator in North America and, according to *Inc.* magazine, the seventh fastest-growing private company in the United States.

In 1986, ATA launched its first scheduled service, between Indianapolis, Indiana, and four destinations in Florida. As a scheduled passenger carrier, ATA sought to distinguish itself by keeping its fares low and imposing few restrictions on travel times. Mikelsons remained involved in tour packages, and in 1987 created the ATA Vacations, Inc. subsidiary to oversee these operations.

The broader scope of Amtran's operations necessitated a move to new corporate headquarters in Indianapolis, as well as construction of ATA's own maintenance center at Indianapolis Airport. Amtran's annual revenues had multiplied eight times in six years, reaching $254 million in 1988 and involving a workforce of 1,800. In 1989, ATA began operating four Boeing 757s, formerly owned by Singapore Airlines, and soon thereafter created ATA ExecuJet, a corporate jet and helicopter charter service. A freight handling subsidiary was created in 1991.

Company Perspectives:

At American Trans Air, safety has always been our number one objective. With over twenty-five years in the airline business, we have come a long way from our origins as a travel club back in 1973, but have never compromised our commitment to your safety. Our Safety Division, headed by a company Vice President reporting directly to the CEO, is continuously engaged in audits of the other divisions of the company to ensure appropriate standards are met or exceeded. Furthermore, the division is constantly reviewing its own programs with the objective of maintaining our proactive safety leadership.

During the Persian Gulf War, ATA carried more troops (108,000) for the U.S. military than any other civil airline. These flights contributed some $50 million in revenues. However, as Operation Desert Storm ended, ATA was forced to lay off some of its workforce. The company posted its first loss, $2 million, in 1990. Between 85 and 90 percent of the company's business at the time came from civil and military charters.

In the early 1990s, consolidation was expected to thin the ranks of independent carriers willing to deal with tour operators, much to ATA's benefit. The company sought to raise the public perception of charter flights during this time by offering top-notch wine, food, and cabin service. In 1993, in addition to its considerable military transport duties, Amtran offered an around-the-world flight on an L-1011 priced at $45,000 a ticket. The trip reportedly took in $1 million for the company.

When it began flying out of Midway Airport in 1992, ATA carried 500,000 passengers out of Chicago alone. Operating revenues at this time reached $422 million and the workforce had increased to 2,400. ATA operated 12 L-1011s and seven 727s. The Ambassadair Travel Club had 27,000 members in 1992. Another club, Ports of Call, had also been established, and both clubs offered installment payment plans to their members.

Going Public in 1993

Amtran completed an initial public offering (IPO) on the NASDAQ in May 1993. Until that point, founder George Mikelsons had been the company's sole shareholder; after the IPO he still retained a 73 percent stake in Amtran. The $40 million Amtran raised through the IPO helped strengthen its debt-heavy balance sheet after a couple of unprofitable years, while about half the money was earmarked for buying new planes. ATA also opened a new reservations center in Chicago and began flying out of Milwaukee. John Tague, a former Midway Airlines executive who joined ATA in 1991, was promoted to president and chief operating officer in 1993.

Scheduled flights accounted for between 25 and 30 percent of ATA's revenues of $468 million in 1993. Vacation traffic accounted for 80 percent of ATA's revenues, and the carrier soon began renewing its focus on vacation travelers. In alliance with tour operator Pleasant Hawaiian Holidays, ATA began flying to Hawaii from Los Angeles, San Francisco, and Chicago. (In 1992 ATA had become the first airline certified for

extended—180 minute—flights over water in the Boeing 757.) The company soon acquired another Lockheed L-1011 and Boeing 757 aircraft to keep up with demand for seats.

By the mid-1990s, Amtran was retaining a workforce of 3,200. Membership at its Ambassadair travel club had reached some 90,000, and ATA was the largest charter carrier and the tenth largest airline in the United States. ATA carried more than five million passengers on its 25 jets in 1995. After the city of St. Petersburg, Florida, courted ATA to relocate its headquarters there, Indianapolis assembled a $40 million incentive package to keep the carrier at home. Much of the tax credits in this plan, which ATA accepted, hinged on the airline's planned expansion in Indianapolis.

Also during this time, ATA became a global concern. A weak dollar and lower labor costs helped make ATA attractive in Europe, where charter airlines already enjoyed a better public perception. ATA opened a sales office in Frankfurt and began operating seasonal routes to Ireland (Shannon and Dublin) from New York's JFK International Airport. The company also opened another maintenance hangar at Midway to service its fleet there and launched the ATA Connection in conjunction with Chicago Express, a shuttle service that linked Chicago, Grand Rapids, Des Moines, and Dayton. Lansing, Michigan, and Madison, Wisconsin, were soon added to the ATA Connection route. Amidst this expansion, Tague, the company's president and COO, left the Amtran executive team to start his own consulting practice.

Troubled Times: 1996

The year 1996 marked the beginning of increased competition from a major player in the industry. In January 1996, Southwest Airlines, the king of budget carriers, entered ATA's Florida markets. This was just the beginning of the bad news. Like most budget carriers, ATA saw a dip in bookings after the ValuJet crash in the Everglades on May 11, 1996. Although ATA should have clearly been differentiated from the flock of start-up airlines at the time, being a well-established company with a good safety record, one of the company's jets suffered a decompression incident on May 12, 1996, that was widely reported in the immediate aftermath of the ValuJet disaster. With its reputation suddenly under media scrutiny, the company also experienced financial stress in the form of rising fuel costs.

A change in leadership was imminent. Mikelsons stepped down as CEO of Amtran in August 1996, remaining active as chairman. Stanley L. Pace, leader of a consulting team dispatched by Boston-based Bain & Co., was named CEO and president, filling the vacancy left by Tague. Pace brought considerable experience to Amtran, having helped develop a turnaround strategy for Continental Airlines.

Competitive pressure from Southwest Airlines and Delta Express forced ATA to retrench from the scheduled market. Increased sales on this side had not led to increased profits. Amtran trimmed its route structure, cutting scheduled service to Boston entirely. It also canceled leases on five Boeing 757s. In the fall, the company announced plans to lay off 1,000 of its 5,300 workers. Amtran lost $27 million in 1996, its worst year ever. Positive developments for the year were few and included

Key Dates:

1973: Pilot J. George Mikelsons starts his own tour company, Ambassadair.
1981: American Trans Air (ATA), another Mikelsons entity, begins flying military charters.
1984: Amtran, Inc. holding company is formed.
1993: Amtran goes public.
1996: High fuel costs, competition, and the ValuJet crisis produce ATA's worst year ever.
1998: An invigorated ATA takes on United and America at their own hubs, and thrives.

the launch of ATA's new web site, which began offering special bargain fares on the web, and was able to take and record reservations online.

Stanley Pace left the company in May 1997, returning to his home state of Texas. Ironically, the $2 million it cost to pay off his contract wiped out the company's second quarter earnings. Before he left, he had recommended that Amtran merge with the beleaguered ValuJet, a proposal Mikelsons promptly vetoed. ValuJet eventually merged with AirWays Corporation to form AirTran Holdings, Inc., and Tague returned to Amtran in the roles of president and CEO.

A Sterling 25th Anniversary in 1998

Nevertheless, at the company's 25th anniversary in 1998, there were plenty of reasons to celebrate. From origins as a simple travel club, the company had nearly achieved major carrier status; it was the 11th largest in the country in that capacity, as well as the country's largest charter operator. The airline began to post record results in a booming economy with lowered fuel costs. ATA carried more than six million passengers in 1998, and revenues reached $919 million.

In this optimistic environment, ATA ordered more planes and reserved a dozen gates at a new terminal at Midway Airport. Only Southwest Airlines had a larger presence there. ATA boosted flight frequencies at Midway 50 percent in the summer of 1998 and announced plans to hire 500 workers in the area. ATA also began competing with United Airlines on the route between that major airline's two largest hubs, Chicago and Denver. It also took on American Airlines, offering connections from that airline's biggest hubs, Dallas and Chicago. The two majors soon cut fares in response to ATA's threat. Still, the risky bet seemed to pay off in record earnings for Amtran. Mikelsons had once told *Air Transport World,* "If there is a cornerstone to our philosophy it is cowardice."

Amtran postponed a planned stock offering in August 1998 due to a general softening among airline stocks. Amtran's stock originally sold for $16 a share, slipped to $9 in 1996, and rose to $28 in July 1998 before falling to $23. The offering would have brought in $37 million and reduced Mikelsons' holding to a minority.

Acquisitions characterized the late 1990s at Amtran. In March 1999, Amtran bought out T.G. Shown Associates Inc., which owned the other half of its $13 million a year Amber Air Freight venture. A few weeks later, it announced plans to sell at least part of its stake in Chicago Express Airlines. The unit operated nine turboprop planes and brought in $9 million a year in sales. Amtran also bought Chicago Express, Key Tours, and Travel Charter.

Principal Subsidiaries

ATA; Ambassadair; ATA Vacations, Inc.; ExecuJet; Amber Air Freight; American Trans Air Training Corporation.

Principal Competitors

Southwest Airlines Co.; Delta Express; US Airways Group, Inc.

Further Reading

Dinnen, S.P., "Future Location of Indiana Charter Flight Company Headquarters Uncertain," *Indianapolis Star,* September 13, 1996.
——, "Seven-Year Search for New Amtran CEO Ends; Pace to Head Indianapolis Airline," *Indianapolis Star,* August 13, 1996.
Eckert, Toby, "ATA Faces Incentive Deadline," *Indianapolis Business Journal,* September 23, 1996, p. 1.
——, "Mikelsons: Pace Left for Personal Reasons; Ex-CEO Gives No Explanation for Leaving," *Indianapolis Business Journal,* June 2, 1997, p. 4A.
Edelhart, Courtenay, "Airways-ValuJet Merger Announcement Came After Amtran Talks Failed," *Indianapolis Star,* July 22, 1997.
Flint, Perry, "Back in Chartered Waters," *Air Transport World,* January 1997, pp. 39–40.
——, "Jack of All Trades," *Air Transport World,* June 1992, pp. 54ff.
——, "Schedule Change," *Air Transport World,* January 1994, pp. 71ff.
Gross, Daniel, "The Great State Giveaway," *CFO: The Magazine for Senior Financial Executives,* January 1996, pp. 24–29.
Hayes, John R., "Penny-Pincher," *Forbes,* September 12, 1994, pp. 96f.
Horgan, Sean, "Parent Firm May Sell Chicago-Based Commuter Carrier," *Indianapolis Star,* May 12, 1999.
Kjelgaard, Chris, "IPO Heralds New Era for American Trans Air," *Airfinance Journal,* August 1993, pp. 8ff.
Lacey, Peter, "J. George Mikelsons," *Chief Executive,* June 1994, p. 20.
Leonhardt, David, "Small Airline, Tricky Flight Plan," *Business Week,* June 22, 1998, pp. 96–98.
O'Malley, Chris, "American Trans Air Has Grown But Kept Low Fares," *Indianapolis News,* February 1, 1998.
——, "Amtran Stock Rises on Good Season, Changes in Service," *Indianapolis News,* April 6, 1998.
——, "Indianapolis Airline Amtran Inc. Delays Stock Sale," *Indianapolis News,* August 4, 1998.
Ott, James, "Recovering ATA Plans on Midway Expansion," *Aviation Week & Space Technology,* February 23, 1998, p. 53.

—Frederick C. Ingram

Anheuser-Busch Companies, Inc.

One Busch Plaza
St. Louis, Missouri 63118
U.S.A.
Telephone: (314) 577-2000
Toll Free: (800) 342-5283
Fax: (314) 577-2900
Web site: http://www.anheuser-busch.com

Public Company
Incorporated: 1979
Employees: 23,645
Sales: $11.70 billion (1999)
Stock Exchanges: New York London Frankfurt Tokyo
    Paris Zurich Geneva Basel Boston Midwest
    Cincinnati Pacific Philadelphia
Ticker Symbol: BUD
NAIC: 31212 Breweries; 332431 Metal Can
    Manufacturing; 71311 Amusement and Theme Parks;
    23311 Land Subdivision and Land Development

Anheuser-Busch Companies, Inc. is the largest brewer in the world, producing more than 100 million barrels of beer each year. The company's primary brands, Budweiser, Bud Light, Michelob, and Busch, are market leaders, enabling the massive St. Louis enterprise to claim nearly 50 percent of the U.S. beer market. Anheuser-Busch also operates nine theme parks, including Busch Gardens and Sea World properties at several locations.

19th-Century Origins

Anheuser-Busch has been overseen by a member of its founding family since 1852, when Eberhard Anheuser, a prosperous soap manufacturer in St. Louis, bought a failing brewery from Bavarian immigrant George Schneider. The brewery's cool underground caverns near the Mississippi River were conducive to good brewing, and Anheuser was determined to turn the business around, but he lacked experience in the industry. Therefore, he hired his son-in-law, Adolphus Busch, a recent German immigrant schooled in the art of brewing, as his general manager. Together, Anheuser and Busch approached the enterprise with an aggressive business strategy and knowledge in quality brewing, two factors that have informed Anheuser-Busch's history ever since.

According to a popular company legend, Adolphus Busch obtained the recipe for his beer during a visit to a German monastery. There, monks provided him with a recipe and some of their brewer's yeast, the secret of their excellent beer. That recipe became the basis of Anheuser-Busch beers, and the original strain of yeast, allegedly preserved for years in Adolphus's ice cream freezer, remained in use in the 1990s. Although fictitious, the story highlighted two important philosophies at Anheuser-Busch: only the finest "European" ingredients were to be used and the basic recipe would remain essentially unchanged.

In 1853, Anheuser and Busch increased the rejuvenated brewery's capacity from 3,000 to 8,000 barrels per year and began to expand their sales effort into Texas and Louisiana, as well as their home state of Missouri. The beverage became increasingly popular, as cowboys reportedly deserted their beloved red-eye whiskey for the light Bohemian beer, which became known as Budweiser in 1891, when the company purchased the rights to the name from the Bohemian brewer of "Budweis."

Budweiser's formula was enhanced by innovations in the brewing industry, particularly as pasteurization allowed for longer preservation periods. Moreover, newly invented refrigerated railroad cars permitted the transport of beer across state borders, and the bottling of beer allowed for easier distribution throughout the country. Regional brewers lost their advantage to large breweries such as Anheuser-Busch, which had found the means to supply beer to every state in the union. Despite the growth of its market, however, Anheuser-Busch still referred to itself as a "regional brewery"—an institution that understood the distinct needs and tastes of local people.

Anheuser gave over the day-to-day operations to Busch in the 1870s. The company continued to prosper, and its workforce increased. During his tenure, Busch initiated the concept of considering employees members of a family: cared for and

<table>
</table>

Company Perspectives:

Innovation, a long-standing strategy at Anheuser-Busch, represents the path to greatness. Adolphus Busch employed this strategy 120 years ago to make Budweiser the first national beer—using new ideas like pasteurizing beer, refrigerating railcars to transport it across the country and mobilizing grassroots salespeople to market the product. Today, Anheuser-Busch has some of the most innovative brewing, packaging and adventure-park facilities in the world. Leaders keep their eye on the future and continually find new ways to think about their business. Anheuser-Busch is no exception.

nurtured by the company and expected to remain loyal to the company for a lifetime. Anheuser-Busch considered this unique relationship between employer and employee, intimate and co-operative, vital in producing an outstanding product.

In the 1890s, Pabst, a competitor, was the best-selling beer in the United States. Busch and his "family" thwarted the competition, however, with the introduction of Michelob in 1896. Forceful and frequent advertising promoted Budweiser and Michelob as the most popular beers in the country, and this goal was realized in 1901, when Anheuser-Busch became the leading national brewery.

Busch died in 1913, and his son, August A. Busch, Sr., took over; the younger Busch soon focused on diversifying the company's interests. Toward this end, Busch patented the first diesel engine, which was installed in the brewery to increase production. With the onset of World War I, Busch founded a subsidiary to produce the engines for Navy submarines. In addition, the Anheuser-Busch family purchased sufficient war bonds to finance two bombers—each named "Miss Budweiser."

After the war, in November 1918, President Woodrow Wilson signed the bill that instituted Prohibition. During this hiatus, Anheuser-Busch diversified into related fields. Malt syrup was canned and sold to people who required malt for their homemade brews. A refrigeration car company was established to transport perishables. Bevo, a soft drink made from ingredients similar to those in beer, was a great success for three years; it later failed when Prohibition laws concerning the use of yeast forced the company to change ingredients. Nevertheless, Anheuser-Busch began a trend toward diversification that would thereafter characterize the history of the company.

When Prohibition ended, the company experienced an unforeseen problem: people had become used to the sweet taste of the soft drinks and homemade brews that were available during Prohibition and were not willing to return to the more bitter commercial beer. In response, many brewers changed their formulas to achieve a sweeter taste. However, Anheuser-Busch refused to alter the formula for best-selling Budweiser, a decision endorsed by Dr. Robert Gall, the company's post-Prohibition brewmaster. Instead, the company initiated a major advertising campaign, challenging consumers to a "five-day test." Busch predicted that after five days of drinking Budweiser the consumer would not drink a sweet beer again. The advertising

campaign was successful and established a trend for future consumer appeals.

During World War II, the company, led by Adolphus Busch III, again made substantial contributions to the war effort. Anheuser-Busch supplied the military with ammunition hoists, which were in production at a new company subsidiary. Moreover, the distribution of Budweiser beer was withdrawn from the Pacific Coast in order to supply the government with additional freight cars for war essentials, and spent grain was sold to financially troubled wartime farmers for poultry and livestock food. These patriotic actions elevated sales and advanced Anheuser-Busch's image as a patriotic company.

Between 1935 and 1950, the demand for Anheuser-Busch beer consistently exceeded the supply. In 1941, three million barrels of beer were produced, a figure that doubled by 1950. After the death of Adolphus Busch III in 1946, the company temporarily relinquished its lead in the industry. But with the succession of his brother, August "Gussie" Busch, Jr., the company became the nation's top brewer once again.

Post-World War II Expansion and Diversification

August Busch, Jr., continued the practice of aggressive advertising established by his brother and father, which had involved the distribution of pocket knives and gold pieces; advertisements featuring reproductions of patriotic art such as "Custer's Last Stand"; and the 1933 introduction of the famous Clydesdale horses, which remained popular in the 1990s. Under August Busch, Anheuser-Busch became the first brewery to sponsor a radio network. Positive consumer response prompted William Bien, the vice-president of marketing, to design a legendary advertising campaign: "pick-a-pair-of-six-packs." The campaign cost $2.5 million for two months, but was the most successful promotion in the history of the beer industry.

Despite its successful promotions, Anheuser-Busch entered a close competition at the beginning of the 1950s with Carling beer. During this time, a holiday was declared in Newark, New Jersey, in honor of the opening of a new Anheuser-Busch factory in that city. The new facility and new equipment necessitated a price hike, however, and Carling profited when its economical beer attracted customers put off by Anheuser-Busch's higher prices. In response, Busch introduced a new, low-priced lager beer and also pursued aggressive advertising promotions. In 1953, Anheuser-Busch bought the St. Louis Cardinals baseball team, targeting sports fans as a new category of consumers. Ultimately, the company was successful in rebuffing Carling's challenge.

Another brewery soon attempted to displace Anheuser-Busch from its number one market ranking. Decreasing the price of its beer in the 1960s, the Schlitz brewery hoped to force Anheuser-Busch into a price war. August Busch, Jr., remained confident that consumers would recognize Anheuser-Busch beer as superior in quality. Public opinion, however, was never tested, as Schlitz committed several marketing and advertising mistakes, and Anheuser-Busch retained its ranking.

During this time, August Busch III began his career at his father's company. After attending college for two years in Arizona and undergoing instruction in the art of brewing at a school

Key Dates:

1852: St. Louis soap merchant Eberhard Anheuser acquires the Bavarian Brewery.
1853: Anheuser, together with son-in-law Adolphus Busch, expand sales into Texas and Louisiana.
1876: Budweiser is introduced.
1896: Michelob is introduced.
1936: Budweiser is packaged in cans for the first time.
1955: The Busch brand is launched.
1959: Company's first amusement park, Busch Gardens, opens in Tampa, Florida.
1964: Annual production reaches ten million barrels.
1982: Bud Light is introduced.
1984: Through licensed brewers, Budweiser is introduced in England and Japan.
1989: Anheuser-Busch Companies purchases Sea World.
1997: Worldwide annual production eclipses 100 million barrels.

in Chicago, Busch III started in an entry-level position at the company. In 1979, he took over as CEO, vowing to uphold Adolphus Busch's philosophy that natural ingredients be used to distinguish the company's fine brewing from the lower quality brewing of other beers.

The Miller Brewing Company challenged this philosophy during the 1970s and 1980s. Miller introduced a light, low-calorie beer in 1974, which became the best-selling beer for a few months. Although Anheuser-Busch soon edged back into the top ranking, it remained closely followed by the Miller brewery. In response to Miller's challenge, Anheuser-Busch introduced two light beers in 1977, Natural Light and Michelob Light, and the popular Budweiser Light was introduced soon thereafter.

Under Busch III, the company developed a unique strategy for dealing with competition that included introducing new brands, increasing the advertising budget, and expanding its breweries. Moreover, Busch III refocused the company's marketing practices to target more specific groups of consumers. He hired a team of 100 college graduates to promote the sale of Anheuser-Busch beers on college campuses. He also oversaw the development of new advertisements designed to appeal to the working class. In the process, the company's marketing budget quadrupled, and sales increased.

Busch III also adopted a "management control system" that increased the efficiency of the company, redefining it as a modern corporation rather than a small family business. The new management system emphasized planning, teamwork, and communications, controls that, ironically, were intended to promote Anheuser-Busch's image as a regional brewery producing different beers to satisfy individual tastes. Anheuser-Busch continued to rank first in the brewing industry into the 1980s. By 1980, sales had reached 50 million barrels, increasing to 86.8 million barrels by 1992. Although competition with Miller remained intense, the Budweiser brand outsold its next four competitors combined.

Anheuser-Busch initially espoused an acquisition policy of purchasing companies that would enhance its brewing operations, including malt plants in Wisconsin and Minnesota, beer can factories in Florida and Ohio, and yeast plants in Missouri, New Jersey, California, and Florida. The St. Louis Refrigerator Car Company inspected and maintained the 880 refrigerated railroad cars used to transport the company's beer across the country. Manufacturers Railway shipped Anheuser-Busch beer after it was manufactured at the brewery with help from the malt and yeast subsidiaries.

Other subsidiaries, however, were soon established that were not directly related to the beer industry. Campbell-Taggart, Inc., the second largest bakery in the United States, was acquired in 1982, associating Anheuser-Busch's name with the food industry. In the 1980s, 6.7 percent of Anheuser-Busch's operating income was spent on food products. Another acquisition, Eagle Snacks, Inc., nationally distributed food products to bars, taverns, and convenience stores. Despite intense competition from Frito-Lay and Planters Peanuts, Eagle Snacks enhanced Anheuser-Busch's beer business by targeting consumers likely to purchase beer to complement their food products.

Anheuser-Busch also developed and acquired theme parks, forming the Busch Entertainment Corporation in 1979. The first "Busch Gardens" opened 20 years earlier in Tampa, Florida, and featured a 300-acre park boasting one of the world's largest collections of wildlife under private ownership. Another tourist attraction, "The Old Country," in Williamsburg, Virginia, was modeled after villages in 17th-century Europe. Anheuser-Busch also acquired the eight-park Sea World chain of mostly aquatic theme parks in 1989 for $1.3 billion. Although these entertainment parks were not particularly profitable, they helped expose Anheuser-Busch's name to a new target group—a younger generation and their parents—and enhanced the company's reputation for contributing to the public welfare. Anheuser-Busch's ownership of the St. Louis Cardinals served a similar function.

Anheuser-Busch also devoted considerable energy to nurturing its foreign market. The corporation formed Anheuser-Busch International, Inc. in 1981 to expand its presence in the global beer market through joint ventures, licensing agreements, and equity investments in foreign brewers. The corporation's timing in this venture proved fortuitous: the fall of trade barriers and conversion of formerly communist and socialist governments to free enterprise systems opened a wealth of opportunity for Anheuser-Busch. By 1993, the company's beers were offered in 21 European countries and ranked as the second most popular lager beer in the Republic of Ireland and the United Kingdom. Budweiser was introduced to Japan in 1981 and stood as that country's leading import by the early 1990s because of successful promotion to the young adult market. With a nine percent market share worldwide, Anheuser-Busch had the largest export volume of any American brewer in 1993, accounting for more than 45 percent of U.S. beer exports.

Adjusting to a New Marketplace: 1990s

During the early 1990s, Anheuser-Busch was compelled to face the declining—and more discerning—use of alcoholic beverages among Americans. The company had introduced LA, the first low alcohol beer, in 1984, but this product did not prove widely successful. LA was replaced by O'Doul's in 1990, however, which soon became the nation's most popular nonalcohol brew. Moreover, as Americans' tastes grew more refined and microbreweries made unprecedented inroads into the modern beer industry, Anheuser-Busch sought to enhance the appeal of its brew. The company introduced eight new beers between 1984 and 1991, and, by 1993, Anheuser-Busch offered 19 beer brands, three of which were imports. Anheuser-Busch's Bud Dry and Ice Draft from Budweiser appealed to such premium beer drinkers. New brand introductions did not seem to detract from Budweiser's brand power; the new variations captured 17 percent of the market, while Bud only lost half a share point.

As the decade progressed, so too did the growth of the craft-brewing industry, forcing the nation's three largest brewers to take heed of the beer industry's upstarts. Anheuser-Busch's closest rivals, Adolph Coors Company and Miller Brewing Company, introduced a host of new brands during the mid-1990s as a riposte. Anheuser-Busch followed suit, but to a much lesser extent, pursuing a more conservative strategy that proved to be a prudent approach later in the decade when many of the specialty brands introduced by the big breweries were confirmed failures. Bill Weintraub, the senior vice-president of Adolph Coors, noted as much. "I think they've (Anheuser-Busch) understood that supporting their core brands is a smarter way to build brands over the long term," he conceded in the May 5, 1997 issue of *Brandweek.* Although Anheuser-Busch invested substantially in the craft-brewing phenomenon—including signing a distribution and equity partnership agreement in 1994 with Red Hook Brewery, a leading craft brewer—the company's primary focus was on its core brands.

Amid a flurry of new beer brands introduced during the mid-1990s, Anheuser-Busch scaled back its operations, divesting properties while other large brewers expanded their portfolios. In 1995, the company announced it was severing its ties with Eagle Snacks after 17 years of losses. Concurrently, Anheuser-Busch announced it was divesting itself of the St. Louis Cardinals and Busch Memorial Stadium properties. In 1994, the baseball franchise posted a loss of $12 million, and Eagle Snacks racked up $25 million in losses. The divestitures were made so that the company could direct more of its attention and resources to beer and theme parks, the two principal areas of Anheuser-Busch's focus for the future.

Of particular importance was injecting new life in the company's all-important Budweiser brand, which was suffering from stagnant sales growth as the company entered the mid-1990s. Internationally, the company was realizing encouraging growth, thanks in large part to investments such as the 50 percent of Grupo Modelo (brewer of Corona beer) acquired in 1993 and the majority stake purchased in the Chinese brewer Budweiser Wuhan International Brewing Company, in 1995, but domestically the brand's sales had flattened. The task of spurring Budweiser sales fell to August Busch IV, whom many regarded as the next in line to lead the family business. (In 1997, August Busch III announced his intention to retire in 2003.) Under the 30-year-old's direction, a revamped marketing plan was developed that aimed at winning over younger consumers, who had gravitated to imports and microbrews. "There was a culture weaved into the Budweiser brand," the younger Busch explained to *Fortune* on January 13, 1997. "No one wanted to change it." August Busch IV spearheaded the widely popular "talking frogs" advertising campaign for Budweiser and the successful "I Love You Man" advertising campaign for Bud Lite, both of which were credited with lifting sales. In 1997, two years after the irreverent, youth-oriented advertising campaigns were launched, annual worldwide beer volume (including the interests Anheuser-Busch held in other breweries) eclipsed 100 million barrels for the first time, as Budweiser sales moved measurably upward.

At the end of the 1990s, Anheuser-Busch's dominance of the U.S. beer industry testified to the prolific growth of the company during the 20th century. By 1999, the company's share of the U.S. beer market had risen to 47.5 percent, fueling confidence that August Busch III's goal of capturing 60 percent of the market by 2005 could be achieved.

Principal Subsidiaries

Anheuser-Busch, Inc.; Busch Entertainment Corporation; Manufacturers Railway Company; St. Louis Refrigerator Car Company; Busch Properties, Inc.; Metal Container Corporation; Anheuser-Busch Recycling Corporation; Anheuser-Busch International, Inc.; Busch Media Group, Inc.; Busch Creative Services Corporation; Busch Agricultural Resources, Inc.; Precision Printing & Packaging, Inc.

Principal Competitors

Miller Brewing Company; Adolph Coors Company; Heineken N.V.

Further Reading

Baron, Stanley Wade, *Brewed in America: A History of Beer and Ale in the U.S.,* New York: Arno Press, 1972.

Delaney, Lawrence, Jr., "Beer Brawl," *World Trade,* March 1993, pp. 34–40.

The History of Anheuser-Busch Companies—A Fact Sheet, St. Louis: The Anheuser-Busch Companies, Inc., 1992.

Khermouch, Gerry, "Tapped Out Brewers," *Brandweek,* May 5, 1997, p. 42.

Krebs, Roland, *Making Friends Is Our Business: 100 Years of Anheuser-Busch,* St. Louis: Cuneo Press, 1953.

Lubove, Seth, "Unfinished Business," *Forbes,* December 10, 1990, pp. 170, 172.

Melcher, Richard A., "How Eagle Became Extinct," *Business Week,* March 4, 1996, p. 68.

Sellers, Patricia, "Bud-Weis-Heir," *Fortune,* January 13, 1997, p. 90.

Wells, Melanie, "Are Dynasties Dying?," *Forbes,* March 6, 2000, p. 126.

—updated by Jeffrey L. Covell

Arjo Wiggins Appleton p.l.c.

Gateway House, Basing View
Basingstoke, Hampshire RG21 4EE
United Kingdom
Telephone: +44-1-25-672-3000
Fax: +44-1-25-672-3723
Web site: http://www.fine-papers.com

Public Company
Incorporated: 1991
Employees: 19,043
Sales: £3.36 billion (US$2.1 billion) (1999)
Stock Exchanges: London
Ticker Symbol: WTPL
NAIC: 322121 Paper (Except Newsprint) Mills; 322222
    Coated and Laminated Paper Manufacturing; 32223
    Stationery Product Manufacturing

Arjo Wiggins Appleton p.l.c. is one of the world's leading producers of premium paper products, ranging from carbonless papers used for facsimile paper, forms, and credit card receipts, to thermal papers, and premium fine papers and specialty papers, such as art and tracing papers. Until 2000, Arjo Wiggins Appleton was also a world-leading paper distributor. In February of that year, the company spun off its merchanting division, renamed Antalis, as a separate company, distributing all shares in Antalis to its shareholders. A product of a series of mergers in the early 1990s, Arjo Wiggins spent most of that decade struggling to achieve integrated operations. A thorough restructuring starting in 1999, led by Chairman Ken Minton, reorganized the company into separate operating companies grouped along product lines, each with its own chief executive officer. After beginning the Antalis demerger process, expected to be completed by the third quarter of 2000, the company regrouped around its two remaining divisions—Carbonless and Thermal papers, and Premium Fine, Specialty & Coated papers. These two divisions together accounted for a little more than half of Arjo Wiggins Appleton's 1999 sales of £3.36 billion. Despite the impending demerger of the Antalis division, which remains Europe's leading paper distributor and among the top paper distributors worldwide, Arjo

Wiggins Appleton has continued to invest in its growth, including the acquisition of two European wholesale promotional products distributors, Röder & Co. of Germany and Mostra Importaciones S.A. of Spain. At the same time, the company, which remains the leading manufacturer of carbonless papers worldwide, has taken steps to reduce its exposure to what is seen as a mature—and possibly doomed—market by boosting its activities in other value-added papers categories. Arjo Wiggins Appleton also holds a 40 percent share of publicly traded SOPORCEL, Portugal's leading pulp producer. Some 40 percent of Arjo Wiggins Appleton itself is held by the SOMEAL (Agnelli family) investment vehicle, taking over the stake formerly held by French conglomerate St. Louis.

Cross-Continental Mergers in the 1990s

Arjo Wiggins Appleton was formed by the mergers of three companies: Wiggins Teape of the United Kingdom, Appleton Papers of the United States, and Arjomari-Prioux of France. These three companies represented operations dating back to the early 18th century and beyond. The oldest of the three was Wiggins Teape, which was known as Jones, Wiggins and Teape in 1850, when Henry Teape and Edward Wiggins purchased partnerships in a paper mill already in existence for more than 100 years. Teape and Wiggins later took over full ownership of the paper company, renaming it Wiggins Teape Ltd. During the 20th century, Wiggins Teape shifted its production to the growing market for specialty papers—a segment that included papers for artistic drawing and painting, tracing papers used in the engineering and architectural markets, and other paper types.

Wiggins Teape built up a strong share of the specialty paper market in the United Kingdom, becoming one of the region's largest by the end of the 1950s. Wiggins Teape also extended its range into the so-called "carbonless" paper market, a new technology that enabled customers to dispense with carbon paper for making copies, such as for credit card receipts or business invoices and other uses, especially requiring signatures. Carbonless paper represented a high-growth sector until the mid-1990s, when, with the emergence of new printing and electronic invoicing and other technologies, the carbonless papers had reached maturity.

	Key Dates:
1850:	Jones, Wiggins and Teape (later Wiggins Teape) is formed.
1950:	Arjomari is formed.
1962:	British American Tobacco (BAT) begins acquiring stake in Wiggins Teape.
1968:	Arjomari and Prioux-Dufournier merge.
1970:	BAT acquires 100 percent ownership of Wiggins Teape.
1978:	BAT acquires Appleton Papers.
1989:	Wiggins Teape and Appleton Papers are spun off from BAT.
1990:	Wiggins Teape and Appleton Papers merge.
1991:	Merger with Arjomari-Prioux forms Arjo Wiggins Appleton.
Late 1990s:	Company undergoes major reorganization while the Agnelli family assumes a 40 percent ownership position.
2000:	Merchanting division spun off as independent company.

The 1950s saw the emergence of one of Wiggins Teape's later partners. During that decade, four French paper mills—those of Arches, Johannot, Marais, and Rives—merged their businesses, using the beginning of each mill's name to create the Arjomari paper company. Arjomari, with operations located primarily in the Lorraine region, soon became one of France's leading paper producers. By the end of the 1960s, Arjomari had begun to grow into one of the principal paper producers, especially of specialty and decorative papers, in Europe. In 1968, the company merged with fellow French paper producer Prioux-Dufournier, changing its name to Arjomari-Prioux. By the end of the 1980s, Arjomari-Prioux was one of Europe's top five paper producers. It also had powerful financial backing, with French conglomerate St. Louis holding 40 percent of the company's shares.

Meanwhile, Wiggins Teape Ltd. had acquired new ownership. In the early 1960s, as the first antismoking laws were being introduced, tobacco giant British American Tobacco (BAT) had begun diversifying its operations in order to reduce its reliance on tobacco. As part of its diversification, BAT began buying up shares in Wiggins Teape. By the end of the 1960s, BAT had acquired full ownership of Wiggins Teape. BAT continued to build up its paper holdings through the 1970s, culminating by the end of the decade in the acquisition of Appleton Papers of the United States, giving the conglomerate not only paper operations on two continents, but also the world's leading share of the carbonless paper market. Appleton, long one of Wiggins Teape's main competitors, remained a separate—and often competing—company under BAT's ownership.

Reorganizing for the 21st Century

By the late 1980s, BAT itself had come under attack. Weakened by steadily tightening antismoking legislation and by the troubled stock market, BAT found itself the subject of famed corporate raider Jimmy Goldsmith's attention. Goldsmith's hostile takeover attempt targeted the whole of BAT for breakup, a popular means of generating shareholder profits in the late 1980s. To fight off the attack, BAT instead spun off its paper division in 1989. The following year, Wiggins Teape and Appleton Papers formally joined forces, becoming Wiggins Teape Appleton. The new independent company ranked in the world's top five paper producers, with annual revenues worth approximately US$1.5 billion.

By 1991, Wiggins Teape Appleton, which maintained BAT's former global leading position in the carbonless paper market, sought to extend its market dominance into other paper product sectors. The company joined with France's Arjomari-Prioux, which by then, with annual revenues of more than FFr 8.2 billion, had taken the French lead in paper production, ahead of rival Aussedat Rey, a subsidiary of International Paper. The merged entity, renamed Arjo Wiggins Appleton, headed into the troubled decade.

As the *Independent* wrote in 1999: Arjo Wiggins Appleton was "a text-book example of how mergers—especially cross-border ones—go wrong." With more than 45 paper mills in Europe and the United States, as well as a 43 percent share of SOPORCEL, a pulp producer based in Portugal and jointly held with the Portuguese government, Arjo Wiggins Appleton represented one of the worldwide paper industry's heavyweights. Yet the company made little effort to merge its far-flung operations. Instead, the three units continued to be operated as more or less independent companies and focused on geographic divisions rather than product lines. As a result, Arjo Wiggins Appleton came to find itself saddled with an inefficient, often redundant operation.

This situation was exacerbated by the collapsing economic climate of the late 1980s and early 1990s. The recession of the period, which in Europe extended well into the middle of the decade, created a price war among paper producers. The paper industry in turn responded by ramping up production, quickly leading to a market glut. At the same time, pulp prices dropped sharply. Arjo Wiggins Appleton's inability to integrate its multinational operations left it top-heavy and unable to respond quickly enough to the changed economic climate.

By 1993, the company had lost the CEO behind the merger, Stephen Walls, who was replaced by Alain Soulas. Arjo Wiggins Appleton's CEO office seemed to have a revolving door during the decade: less than three years after his arrival, Soulas was dismissed. This trend was to continue through the decade. In the meantime, the company attempted something of a restructuring, closing some of its plants, including a paper mill in Germany, while cutting back its workforce. Between 1990 and 1993, the company had shed 12 percent of its payroll.

Nonetheless, Arjo Wiggins Appleton's problems continued into mid-decade. The company appeared rife for a breakup, especially after the departure of Alain Soulas and the arrival of St. Louis chairman Daniel Melin as Arjo Wiggins Appleton's deputy chairman and chief executive. Melin led the company on a strategic review—with analysts suggesting the industry brace itself for a breakup of the company's components, particularly its European manufacturing operations. Yet the company's slumping share prices made a breakup less than attractive.

Instead, Arjo Wiggins Appleton continued shedding jobs and engaging in what was suggested was a halfhearted attempt to restructure operations. In 1996, the company announced a new series of job cuts across its European operations, amounting to some seven percent of its European workforce. Slumping sales across the industry, as customers held back on orders while waiting for falling pulp prices to be reflected in paper prices, only added to Arjo Wiggins Appleton's woes. In March 1997, Melin stepped down, replaced by Philippe Beylier, who had been one of the chief architects in building Arjomari in the late 1980s.

The collapse of pulp prices opened the way for a wave of consolidation moves across the paper industry, highlighted by the merger between Kimberly-Clark and Scott Paper in 1996. In 1997, Arjo Wiggins Appleton, too, began looking for partners—turning to South Africa's Sappi International for a merger of the two companies' coated wood-free papers operations. The proposed merger fell through, however. Meanwhile, Arjo Wiggins Appleton continued the restructuring begun in 1995, including cutting more jobs.

While struggling to raise its position in the late 1990s, Arjo Wiggins Appleton was confronted with its exposure to the carbonless paper market. Said to have long reached its maturity, carbonless paper had started to see declines in its sales, as new technologies, such as the use of laser printers, electronic invoicing methods, and the introduction of fax machines capable of using plain papers, began to offer cheaper and more attractive alternatives. By the end of the 1990s, Arjo Wiggins Appleton had made little progress in reducing its pressures. Despite maintaining profitability through the second half of the decade, the company's revenues were slipping, back from a high of £3.56 billion in 1995.

The arrival of a new majority shareholder, as the Agnelli family of Italy—through their investment vehicle SOMEAL—took over St. Louis's 40 percent shareholding, seemed to offer the company new perspectives. The company's new chairman, Ken Minton, began taking long overdue steps to integrate the company's operations along product lines, rather than according to geographic location. During 1999, the company's new organization was put into place. Arjo Wiggins Appleton now was separated into three divisions—Carbonless and Thermal; Premium Fine, Specialty & Coated; and Merchanting—which were to operate more or less as independent companies. Instead of a single CEO for the entire group, each division was appointed its own chief executive, resulting in the departure of Beylier in 1999.

As part of the new restructuring drive, the company began streamlining its operations, closing plants, and eliminating redundancies in production. The company also made a series of strategic acquisitions, including the purchases of Papel del Solto, of Brazil, in January 2000, and Van Houton Palm, a Netherlands manufacturer of banknote paper, in February. At the same time, the company strengthened its paper distribution division with the acquisition of Röder & Co. of Germany and Mostra Importaciones S.A. of Spain, both of which boosted the merchanting arm's position in the wholesale promotional products sector.

The year 2000 marked more significant changes, as Minton announced that the company intended to merge all of its distribution subsidiaries into a single, internationally operating concern, Antalis. The new company was to be spun off from Arjo Wiggins Appleton by year's end, with shares of Antalis being distributed to the company's shareholders. The spinoff was greeted as a strong move toward concentrating Arjo Wiggins Appleton's operations around a manufacturing core, as the company moved to retain its position as one of the world's primary paper producers for the 21st century.

Principal Subsidiaries

Appleton Papers Inc. (U.S.A.); Arjo Wiggins Ltd.; Arjo Wiggins Belgium SA (Belgium); Arjo Wiggins Deutschland GmbH (Germany); Arjo Wiggins Italia Srl (Italy); Arjo Wiggins Limited; Arjo Wiggins SA (France); Bernard Dumas S.A. (France); Industria de Papel de Solto Ltda (Brazil); Newton Falls Inc. (U.S.A.); Papeteries du Bourray S.A. (France); SOPORCEL (Portugal; 40%); Usiplast S.A. (France).

Principal Competitors

Amcor Limited; Boise Cascade Corporation; Buhrmann; Champion International Corporation; FiberMark; Georgia-Pacific Group; International Paper Company; Mead Corporation; Nashua Corporation; Oji Paper Co., Ltd.; PWA Group; Rexam PLC; Svenska Cellulosa Aktiebolaget SCA; UPM-Kymmene Corporation.

Further Reading

Anderson, Simon, "Arjo Shakes Up Paper Operations in Europe," *Daily Telegraph,* April 10, 1999.

Larsen, Peter Thal, "Arjo Chief Quits in Radical Revamp," *Independent,* January 13, 1999, p. 14.

Lea, Robert, "Arjo Absorbs Restructure Costs to Prompt Share Lift," *Times,* March 2, 2000.

——, "Arjo Wiggins Lifts Production to Grow Business," *South American Business Information,* January 12, 2000.

——, "Going Down: Arjo Wiggins," *Independent on Sunday,* August 29, 1999, p. 4.

—M. L. Cohen

Ashtead Group plc

Ashtead House
Business Park 8, Barnett Wood Lane
Leatherhead, Surrey KT22 7DG
United Kingdom
Telephone: (+44) 1-372 362-300
Fax: (+44) 1-372 376-610
Web site: http://www.ashtead-group.com

Public Company
Incorporated: 1947 as Ashtead Plant Hire Company
Employees: 3,735
Sales: £256 million (US$412.6 million)(1999)
Stock Exchanges: London
Ticker Symbol: AHT
NAIC: 532412 Construction, Mining, and Forestry
    Machinery and Equipment Rental and Leasing; 53249
    Other Commercial and Industrial Machinery and
    Equipment Rental and Leasing

England's Ashtead Group plc is a leading provider of non-manned equipment rental services with operations primarily in the United States and the United Kingdom. Ashtead is comprised of three core businesses: A-Plant, in the United Kingdom; Sunbelt, with principal operations in the eastern region of the United States; and Ashtead Technologies, providing specialized equipment to offshore oil and gas platforms in the Aberdeen, Scotland area and elsewhere in the United Kingdom. Together these subsidiaries provide equipment ranging from woodworking tools and other handheld equipment to forklifts, cranes, dump trucks, industrial pump and power generation systems, to highly sophisticated underwater testing and inspection equipment and other submersible equipment. In total, Ashtead's inventory contains more than half a million rental items. The company itself is comprised of more than 350 branch locations—which Ashtead calls "Profit Centres"—situated in the United Kingdom, the United States, and the Far East. In the 1990s, Ashtead achieved impressive growth, rising from a small construction hire business to an international leader producing revenues of more than £250 million per year. The company expects to continue its expansion,

particularly in the United States, where the equipment rental market remains highly fragmented and more or less undeveloped. Toward that end, in April 2000, Ashtead announced that it would double in size through the acquisition of BET USA, an American equipment hire business and subsidiary of Rentokil Initial plc. Ashtead is led by Peter Lewis, chairman, and George Burnett, managing director, who led a buyout of Ashtead's original owners in the early 1980s.

Reinventing Renting in the 1980s

Founded as Ashtead Plant Hire Company in 1947, Ashtead largely concentrated on providing equipment rental (called "plant hire" in the United Kingdom) services to the construction industry through the 1980s. While profitable, the company remained a small, regional business. By 1984, Ashtead Plant Hire was posting annual sales of £1.5 million, with 60 employees working out of five branch offices, including Ashtead's headquarters in Leatherhead, in Surrey, England. The company was typical of the equipment rental industry in the United Kingdom, which remained fragmented among a large number of relatively small companies.

In 1984, however, Ashtead was bought up by a group of investors, headed by the team of Peter Lewis and George Burnett, who took on the roles of chairman and managing director, respectively. Lewis and Burnett recognized the potential to build Ashtead into a national force, partly through internal growth, but also through acquisitions of other rental companies as the United Kingdom's plant hire industry moved toward consolidation.

In order to fund Ashtead's growth, Lewis and Burnett took the company public in 1986. The public listing enabled the company to begin its expansion. Through the rest of the decade, however, Ashtead remained linked to the construction industry, which continued to produce nearly 100 percent of Ashtead's rental revenues. The United Kingdom's construction market collapsed in the late 1980s—the result of the stock market crash of 1987, which revealed an over-saturated office building and hotel market, additionally crippled by the outbreak of the Persian Gulf War, helping to lead the United Kingdom into the worldwide recession of the early 1990s.

Company Perspectives:

We will develop Ashtead into an internationally based industrial rentals Group, meeting customer needs at a worthwhile profit to our enterprise in markets where we have scope to build a significant presence.

Ashtead was quick to seize on the new opportunities offered by a construction market reluctant to invest in new equipment purchases. The United Kingdom's construction industry turned toward the country's plant hire specialists for its non-manned equipment needs. By the late 1990s, more than 30 percent of the country's construction industry were renting equipment, ranging from power hammers to fleets of dump trucks. As its U.K. business expanded, Ashtead looked overseas at the huge and highly fragmented rental market in the United States. In 1990, Ashtead acquired Sunbelt Rentals, an equipment rental provider with operations along the southeastern coast. Ashtead began extending Sunbelt's reach farther up north, with locations growing from eight to ten coastal states. With the addition of Sunbelt, Ashtead became Ashtead Group; the company's United Kingdom operations were renamed A-Plant.

At the same time, Ashtead began to reinvent itself. Recognizing that the construction slump was likely to continue toward the middle of the 1990s, Ashtead began looking to diversify its business in order to protect itself from the downturns and overall cyclical nature of its core market. In its diversification moves, Ashtead, breaking from the rental industry's focus on the construction market, began to woo potential clients in other sectors, including industries such as the automotive and offshore oil industries, but also markets that were less vulnerable to business cycles, such as water utility operations and the equipment needs of local governments. As part of its new sales strategy, Ashtead began a series of major equipment investments, eventually boosting its catalog to more than 500,000 items. The company also invested in its sales department, doubling the size of its staff.

Building a Rental Powerhouse in the 1990s

By 1991, Ashtead was reporting annual sales of more than £31 million, posting a net profit for that year of £4 million. If the company's growth since the buyout in 1984 had been impressive, Ashtead's growth in the next decade was still more so. By the end of the 1990s, the company's sales had leaped to £256 million, with a payroll of more than 3,700 employees.

In 1993, Ashtead launched a new subsidiary, Ashtead Technology, based in Aberdeen, Scotland. Ashtead Technology continued the parent company's equipment rental business, with a specialized focus on the market for testing, inspection, analysis, and other equipment needed for the offshore oil and gas platforms near the Scottish coast. The Aberdeen location soon began providing equipment for the oil exploration industries in West Africa and South America as well. In the mid-1990s, Ashtead Technology opened a second branch office in Singapore, serving the oil and gas industry in Southeast Asia. Later in the decade, Ashtead Technology launched a third profit centre,

this time in the heart of the oil industry in the United States, in Houston, Texas. By the late 1990s, Ashtead Technology had captured the world-leading position in its market. Despite its growth, Ashtead Technology remained the smallest part of the Ashtead Group, posting revenues of £9.3 million in 1999.

Ashtead Group's largest growth came through its core equipment rentals businesses. The company's growth was particularly strong in the United Kingdom, which saw more and more industries turning to equipment rentals for their machine tools and equipment needs. By the mid-1990s, Ashtead, through its A-Plant subsidiary, had succeeded in capturing some 13 percent of the total U.K. equipment rental market. By 1994, the company posted sales of £43.8 million, from more than 70 branch locations. Just two years later, the number of Ashtead locations had swelled to 164, providing nearly £96 million in revenues.

The company, which had grown in part through acquisition, in part through the establishment of greenfield sites, switched its acquisition drive into higher gear. Raising more than £67 million in fresh capital through a two-for-one rights issue, Ashtead went on a buying spree. In 1996, the company acquired Leada Acrow, adding that company's 19 locations across the United Kingdom and Ireland. Purchasing an additional five branches in Ireland in October 1996, A-Plant took the leading position for the Irish plant hire market. That same year, Ashtead purchased McLean Rentals, doubling its Sunbelt subsidiary's size and extending its reach from Maryland to Florida. With more than 24 profit centres, Sunbelt had built its share of the highly fragmented and largely undeveloped U.S. rentals market to one percent.

Further growth in the United States, however, was to come primarily through the establishment of greenfield locations, as Lewis and Burnett judged the prices of potential acquisitions to be too high. Nonetheless, with rental prices tending to be higher overseas, Ashtead looked to the United States as a primary growth market. By the mid-1990s, the company's U.S. business had grown to more than one-third of its total sales.

Back home, Ashtead continued to consolidate its leadership position. As many of its competitors faltered, Ashtead's early diversification moves gave it the flexibility to absorb the difficulties of the U.K. construction industry, just starting to come out of its long slump by mid-decade. By then, however, Ashtead had successfully reduced its construction industry contracts to just 40 percent of sales.

Ashtead's good health enabled it to snatch up some of its competitors. In August 1997, Ashtead paid £39 million to acquire one of its chief rivals, Sheriff Holdings, adding 48 branches to boost its total number of profit centers in the United Kingdom to 204. By the following year, the company's location list had grown to 275 locations worldwide.

While continuing to enjoy leadership status in the U.K. market, Ashtead's operations were developing more slowly. The U.S. equipment rentals market had remained fragmented through the first half of the decade. Yet, in the second half of the 1990s, a wave of consolidation began to affect the market, as a small number of Ashtead's competitors began buying up other businesses, in turn driving up the cost of acquisitions among the industry. Ashtead, which lacked the funds for acquisitions in the

United States, remained largely on the sidelines, concentrating instead on building organic growth through the opening of new branch offices.

By mid-1999, however, Ashtead's position in the U.S. market had fallen to 12th among that country's market leaders. Lewis and Burnett, fearing that Ashtead would be transformed into a marginal player, but lacking the funds to participate in the wave of consolidation sweeping the equipment rentals industry, began exploring more radical options for maintaining Sunbelt—and Ashtead's—future growth. In August 1999, the company announced that it had hired management consultants Salomon Smith Barney to field purchase offers for Ashtead Group.

While shares in Ashtead soared after the announcement, employee morale suffered, and the company saw increased turnover in its workforce. Ashtead's position on the sales block did not last long. In September 1999, share prices among Ashtead's competitors, and especially those leading the industry consolidation, crashed. The sagging share prices also lowered Ashtead's value—and the value of the merger offers it had received. Meanwhile, Sunbelt's policy of greenfield growth had left it in good health relative to its more acquisitive competitors.

By early 2000, Lewis, who was preparing his retirement at the same time, announced that Ashtead Group was no longer up for sale and would instead maintain its independent course. The company continued, however, to target the United States for its strongest growth, announcing plans to more than double its business within three years and to capture a leading share of the rentals market in its southeast coast—stretching from New Jersey to Florida, and including Tennessee—core operations. These goals seemed near realization when in April 2000, Ashtead announced that it would purchase BET USA, an American subsidiary of Rentokil Initial plc, for £186 million cash plus £134 million in convertible notes. When finalized, the deal would double the size of Ashtead, making it the fifth largest equipment renter in the United States as well as the top such company in Britain. Moreover, Ashtead's U.S. presence would expand to include 26 states. CEO Lewis noted at the time, that Ashtead would next look to make more acquisitions in the United Kingdom. Leadership of these expansion plans would likely be turned over to George Burnett in the 21st century, as Lewis was slated to retire in December 2000.

Principal Subsidiaries

Ashtead Plant Hire Co. Ltd.; Ashtead Plant Hire Co. (Ireland) Ltd.; Ashtead Technology Ltd.; Ashtead Technology (South East Asia) Pte Ltd. (Singapore); Ashtead Technology, Inc. (U.S.A.); Sunbelt Rentals, Inc. (U.S.A.).

Principal Competitors

Aggreko plc; Chancellor Corporation; Hewden Stuart plc; Mitcham Industries, Inc.; NationsRent; United Rentals Inc.

Further Reading

"Ashtead," *Investors Chronicle*, July 16, 1999.
Hyland, Anne, "Ashtead Goes in Search of Potential Suitors," *Daily Telegraph*, September 1, 1999.
"Investors Vent Their Anger at Undisclosed Bids for Ashtead," *Independent*, February 4, 2000, p. 19.
Lamsden, Quentin, "Taking Plant Hire to a Higher Plane," *Independent on Sunday*, October 13, 1996. p. 6.
Larsen, Peter Thal, "US Hire Sales Look Good for Ashtead," *Independent*, July 14, 1998, p. 21.
Pratley, Nils, "Ashtead Worthy of Its Hire," *Daily Telegraph*, January 20, 1998, p. 27.
"US Constraints Force Ashtead to Plan for Sale," *Financial Times*, September 1, 1999.
Wood, Martin, "Expanding Ashtead Has a Great American Dream," *Birmingham (England) Post*, January 20, 1998, p. 19.

—M. L. Cohen

ASV, Inc.

840 Lily Lane
P.O. Box 5160
Grand Rapids, Minnesota 55744
U.S.A.
Telephone: (218) 327-3434
Fax: (218) 327-9122
Web site: http://www.asvi.com

Public Company
Incorporated: 1983 as All Seasons Vehicles, Inc.
Employees: 110
Sales: $36.2 million (1999)
Stock Exchanges: NASDAQ
Ticker Symbol: ASVI
NAIC: 33312 Construction Machinery Manufacturing

ASV, Inc. designs, builds, and markets the Posi-Track, an all-season, rubber-tracked, work vehicle notable for its versatility. The crawler, which exerts a low level of ground pressure, is marketed primarily to the construction, agriculture, and landscaping industries and performs the functions of skid-steer loaders, small dozers, and small tractors. Rapidly growing demand led to a 1998 agreement with Caterpillar, Inc., which gave ASV access to vast financial resources and a worldwide distribution network.

Off the Beaten Trail: 1950s–80s

Sparsely populated northern Minnesota provided the perfect proving ground for off-road vehicle industries beginning in the 1950s. Edgar Hetteen founded two of the snowmobile industry's largest companies, first Polaris Industries Inc. and later Arctic Enterprises. Gary D. Lemke, in turn, built one of the country's largest Arctic Cat dealerships, in Grand Rapids, Minnesota. But a shortage of snow, high interest rates, and foreign competition sideswiped the seasonal industry in the early 1980s. Arctic Cat filed for chapter 11 reorganization, and Lemke's dealership went under.

Hetteen and Lemke, who were friends as well as fellow veterans of the highs and lows of the snowmobile industry, decided to use their combined expertise to build a year-round work vehicle using snowmobile-like track technology. Lemke had begun selling a winter-only, Swedish-built vehicle sporting a full-length metal track, but found customers wanted something that would give them a wider range of use, something that did less damage to ground and paved surfaces.

Since neither of the men could fund the endeavor, Lemke asked his friends and neighbors on North Star Lake in Marcell, Minnesota, to back the concept, which was still in design form. Lemke and Hetteen's salesmanship raised $70,000 from seven local investors. Included among them was Twin Cities real estate magnate Philip Smaby, who owned a cabin in the area and had purchased one of Lemke's first snowmobiles. Many of the other investors had retired to the area, which was blessed with hundreds of lakes.

In 1983, Lemke and Hetteen established All Seasons Vehicles, Inc. (ASV) in Marcell. The village was located about 200 miles north of the Twin Cities or around 30 miles from Grand Rapids, on the edge of Minnesota's iron mining region. ''The only evidence ASV even existed was its one tin building stuck in the sand by the only road through Marcell. When it rained, the parking lot was a muddy stew; when it froze, a jagged, rutted mess. To make it all work under those conditions, Hetteen told *Corporate Report Minnesota* in 1999, 'You have to be a little naive.' ''

The local investors stopped by regularly to check on the progress. When the first unit rolled out for a test drive, one of them went along for the ride. Seventeen additional investors signed on once the prototype was completed. All Season Vehicles sold the second unit off the line to the State of Minnesota's Department of Natural Resources (DNR) for cross-country ski trail grooming.

The Track Truck, more versatile than full-length metal track vehicles, could maneuver through snow, sand, brush, swamps, and bogs. The patented steering system allowed the driver to separately control the dual rubber tracks located under the rear three-quarters of the small truck. The front end could be equipped with either wheels or skis. By October 1985, the company employed 15 people and was selling Track Trucks to companies, government agencies, and individuals for search and rescue missions and worker transport, as well as for farm and recreation purposes. Nine U.S. distributors carried the $16,000 vehicle.

A couple years later, Lemke and Hetteen discovered customers had been adapting the Track Truck for unintended purposes, like bolting on attachments to create a snowblower or plow. Picking up the cue, the men began working on a second vehicle, one with more flexibility than the Track Truck.

On Track with a New Product: Late 1980s to Early 1990s

In 1988, ASV presented a prototype to trade shows. The vehicle's undercarriage support system stood out from tractors, dozers, and skid-steers and quickly garnered interest. ASV's new product weighed in at 5,800 pounds but exerted ground pressure of just 1.5 pounds per square foot, about the same as a child.

A lengthy research and development stage was out of the question—just meeting weekly payroll had been known to cause some tense moments. Lemke and Hetteen decided to sell the fully tracked machine to a hand-picked group of customers who would be willing to test the product on the job. (The field testing would ultimately lead to the development of ASV's patent-pending Maximum Traction and Support System undercarriage.)

ASV's new offering, the Posi-Track, produced sales of $223,000 in 1991. The company's first product, the Track Truck, brought in $750,000 that year and served primarily as a utility vehicle and trail groomer. The Posi-Track, on the other hand, was built to carry a wide range of attachments and targeted the landscaping, construction, and agricultural industries. Looking much like a small front-end loader on rubber tracks, the Posi-Track could traverse wet, steep, fragile, or rough terrain.

By 1993, the Posi-Track had nearly overtaken the Track Truck in sales, and its strong showing encouraged Lemke and Hetteen to take the 30-employee company public. ASV netted $3.4 million in the August 1994 initial public offering (IPO) of 1.2 million shares at $3.25 per share. ASV planned to use part of the money raised for debt retirement and part for working capital. Two Iron Range economic development organizations funded the construction of a 42,000-square-foot manufacturing facility in Grand Rapids. The new facility, opened in 1995, tripled the company's available production space and allowed ASV to bring some processes, previously outsourced, in-house.

The $34,000 Posi-Track's closest competitor, the well-known Bobcat skid-steer, held 50 percent of its market. JI Case followed behind with a 20 percent market share. The multipurpose Posi-Track, however, was unique. "They're kind of out there with a totally new product and normally those things don't sell in large numbers overnight. But I think [ASV] has the potential to do that," said Tom Niemiec in a 1995 *Corporate Report Minnesota* article. Niemiec was vice-president of corporate finance for Minneapolis-based Summit Investment Company, the underwriter for ASV's IPO.

Negotiating New Terrain: Mid-to-Late 1990s

ASV's overall sales had grown by 50 percent annually since Posi-Track's introduction in 1991, reaching $8.2 million in 1995. The Minnesota company exceeded Wall Street estimates in the first half of 1996. Sales jumped 44 percent, and earnings more than doubled.

For the first decade of business, early investors such as Hazel Harris saw no returns from ASV but kept faith in the company's future. Harris served on the board from 1983 to 1996 and knew each employee by name up until the time the operation moved to Grand Rapids. Another early board member, ad executive Leland T. Lynch of Minneapolis-based Carmichael Lynch, had come on as a director in 1987, serving without a fee for many years. Lynch's agency had worked with both Polaris and Arctic Cat.

The board makeup began to shift as the company's fortunes headed upward. James H. Dahl, Florida investment firm head and junk bond pioneer, saw a Posi-Track at a Florida Caterpillar dealership in the mid-1990s. Impressed, he went to Minnesota to find out more and became an investor and board member in 1996. Dahl would bring in R.E. (Teddy) Turner IV, son of Turner Communication's Ted Turner. From January to September 1996 ASV stock climbed from $6.25 to $18.50.

Demand also continued to climb, but ASV's limited manufacturing capacity forced the company to turn away potential Posi-Track dealers. To alleviate the problem, ASV made a $5 million private placement of convertible debentures, during fourth quarter 1996, to enlarge the Grand Rapids manufacturing plant, purchase equipment, and infuse working capital. An additional $1.8 million from the Iron Range Resource and Rehabilitation Board helped fund the 60,000-square-foot expansion.

Net sales for 1996 were $12.3 million with earnings nearing the $1 million mark. In February 1997, the company moved from a NASDAQ small cap listing to the NASDAQ national market.

ASV ramped up product development as well as production during 1997 as customers continued to find new ways to use the vehicle. A range of attachments allowed the Posi-Track to work, for example, as a loader, backhoe, planer, auger, mover, or snowplow, but because the vehicle exerted such low ground pressure the Posi-Track had been seen leveling grain inside cargo ships, laying out large rolls of sod, and moving between rows of grapevines. The military had used a remote-controlled unit to clear surface munitions from a Nevada test and training range, and ASV was developing an attachment for antiterrorist operations.

Mark Rupe, a John Kinnard analyst, predicted continued rapid growth for the company during 1998 but also saw some potential pitfalls, according to a December 1997 *St. Paul Pioneer Press* article by Dave Beal. "Rupe ticks off a list of adversities that could rise to smite the company: less acceptance of its products; a relatively illiquid stock; trouble in expanding its dealer network; and inability to manage fast growth; too much dependence on key suppliers; competition from big-hitter companies such as John Deere, Caterpillar, Case, Ingersoll-Rand."

According to *Investor's Business Daily,* Melroe Co., the Ingersoll-Rand Co. subsidiary that built Bobcat skid-steer loaders and excavators, sold 40,000 units through 900 dealers in 75 countries during 1997. ASV expected to sell about 850 vehicles through its 116 dealers in 37 states in 1998.

"It's the versatility that sells the machine," said Kevin Robbins, vice-president of the Posi-Track's largest U.S. dealer, in a June 1998 *Duluth News-Tribune* article. Since the concept was unfamiliar, June Brissett reported, potential customers needed to see the Posi-Track in action. ASV vastly improved its visibility quotient in October 1998, when it struck a deal with Caterpillar, Inc.

Big Deal for Small Company: For 1999 and Beyond

The world's largest manufacturer of construction and mining equipment agreed to buy one million shares of ASV stock at $18 per share, 8.8 percent of the company, and received warrants to buy up to 51 percent of ASV at $21 per share. ASV eventually would gain access to Caterpillar's worldwide distribution network—1,400 dealers in more than 200 countries. Conversely, Caterpillar, which had sales of $18.93 billion in 1997, gained a foothold in the small equipment market and access to ASV's low pressure technology.

Caterpillar Vice-President Dick Benson, quoted in a *Duluth News-Tribune* article, said, "By combining ASV's suspension system technology with Caterpillar's legendary track know-how, ASV will be ideally positioned to develop new business and new products around the world."

ASV President Lemke said in a company news release, "We've known for 10 years that we're building, pound-for-pound, the best work vehicle in the world. With Caterpillar behind us, we expect to push our company's momentum years ahead of schedule."

Via the agreement, ASV would receive management, financial, and engineering support, and two Caterpillar members would join the board of directors. For the meantime, ASV would retain its independent status, and yet be in a stronger position to compete with big companies such as John Deere should they enter the low-pressure niche.

On the heels of the announcement, ASV debuted at number 14 on the *Forbes* list of the 200 Best Small Companies based on factors such as profitability, growth, sales, net income, and market value. Earlier in the year, ASV found a spot on *Individual Investor* magazine's 100 fastest-growing companies list. On *Investor Business Daily's* top issues list, ASV ranked 11th, outperforming high-profile issues such as Starbucks Corporation and Yahoo! Inc. ASV stock price climbed by more than 1,000 percent from August 1994 to 1998, and the company racked up a string of 15 quarters of record sales as of October 1998.

ASV shareholders ratified the Caterpillar deal by an overwhelming margin in January 1999. The $18 million raised was earmarked for capital equipment, research and development, and working capital.

ASV's transition to the Caterpillar distribution network hurt performance from fourth quarter 1998 into third quarter 1999. Some existing dealers dropped the line following the announcement of ASV's deal with Caterpillar, resulting in canceled orders and product returns. New Caterpillar dealers, in line for product training, held off on placing substantial orders.

Another glitch occurred when a Florida Caterpillar dealer, one that served seven southern states and produced 21 percent of ASV's 1998 sales, pulled out of Georgia, Mississippi, Alabama, Louisiana, and North and South Carolina, leaving Caterpillar dealers in those states to pick up Posi-Track distribution. (About 40 percent of ASV's total sales had already been coming by way of Caterpillar dealers prior to the stock agreement.) Analysts generally agreed that the downturn was temporary and, by year end, revenue, earnings, and stock price would again turn upward.

Caterpillar, meanwhile, reassigned one of its project managers to assist ASV with the dealership system changes. Furthermore, during the period, ASV had its first chance to show off its products for dealers and customers at Caterpillar's Arizona testing ground. The two companies also began planning their first joint project, a rubber-tracked tractor for agricultural use. Finally, the Posi-Track MD2800 Series had been receiving recognition from construction trade journals as one of the top products of 1998.

The Posi-Track produced virtually all of ASV's sales, and the company worked to deliver new models for ever broadening applications. The Posi-Track 4810, the first ASV vehicle to carry a Caterpillar engine, had start-up delays during 1999, which contributed to lower third quarter earnings but helped boost sales in the fourth quarter.

For the year overall numbers dropped. The slower-than-expected dealership overhaul, R&D costs, and sales commissions to Caterpillar resulted in lower net income: $1.4 million in 1999 versus $3.4 million in 1998. Net sales for 1999 were $36.2 million, down from $39 million in 1998.

Despite the ups and downs of the transition period following ASV and Caterpillar's agreement, the Posi-Track line appeared poised for a bright future, based on its solid technology and access to an international market.

Principal Competitors

Ingersoll-Rand Co. (Bobcat).

Further Reading

"ASV Does Placement," *St. Paul Pioneer Press,* October 8, 1996, p. 2D.

"ASV, Inc.," *Corporate Report Fact Book 2000,* p. 136.

"A.S.V. in New Facility," *St. Paul Pioneer Press,* June 22, 1995, p. 2E.

Beal, Dave, "A.S.V. and Tower Automotive Are Going Public," *St. Paul Pioneer Press,* August 12, 1994, p. 2E.

——, "ASV Inc. Founders on the Right Track," *St. Paul Pioneer Press,* December 15, 1997, p. 1F.

Benjamin, Matthew, "Deal with Equipment Giant to Power ASV's Tractor Sales," *Investor's Business Daily,* October 29, 1998, p. 4A.

"Briefly . . . ," *St. Paul Pioneer Press,* August 2, 1996, p. 2E.

Brissett, Jane E., "Analysts See Better Days Ahead for ASV," *Duluth News-Tribune,* June 4, 1999, p. 1F.

——, "Caterpillar Buying Part of ASV," *Duluth News-Tribune,* October 15, 1998, pp. 1F, 3F.

——, "Tiny Company Going Gangbusters," *Duluth News-Tribune,* June 19, 1998, p. 1F.

Brissett, Jane E., and Jill P. Burcum, "Developing a Growth Vehicle," *Corporate Report Minnesota,* February 1995, p. 16.

"Earnings in 1999 Down for ASV Inc. of Grand Rapids," *Duluth News-Tribune,* March 2, 2000, p. 1E.

"Expansion Money Ok'd," *St. Paul Pioneer Press,* October 10, 1996, p. 2C.

Forster, Julie, "Marcell's Millionaires," *Corporate Report Minnesota,* September 1999, pp. 22–28.

Fredrickson, Tom, "ASV Expansion Rumored," *Minneapolis/St. Paul CityBusiness,* July 19, 1996, p. 5.

——, ASV's Sales Are Riding a Strong Growth Track," *Minneapolis/St. Paul CityBusiness,* October 6, 1995, p. 7.

——, "ASV Stays on Track," *Minneapolis/St. Paul CityBusiness,* March 7, 1997, p. 7.

Kratz, Vikki, "Red Flag," *Corporate Report Minnesota,* January 1997, p. 9.

"Largest IPOs," *Corporate Report Minnesota,* March 1995, pp. 58, 60.

Meyer, Harvey, "On the Right Tracks," *Minnesota Business Journal,* October 1985, p. 83.

St. Anthony, Neal, "ASV Rose from Ashes of Lean Period for Snowmobiles," *Star Tribune* (Minneapolis), November 10, 1998, pp. 1D, 2D.

——, "Caterpillar to Acquire Stake in ASV," *Star Tribune* (Minneapolis), October 15, 1998, pp. 1D, 2D.

Steinfeldt, Laurie, "Done Deals: ASV, Inc.," *Minnesota Ventures,* November/December 1994, pp. 40–41.

"200 Best Small Companies," *Forbes,* November 2, 1998, p. 250.

Weintraub, Adam, "ASV Hits Bumpy Stretch," *Minneapolis/St. Paul CityBusiness,* August 27, 1999, p. 1.

Youngblood, Dick, "Hetteen's Back in the Driver's Seat," *Star Tribune* (Minneapolis), October 7, 1996, p. 2D.

—Kathleen Peippo

Audiovox Corporation

150 Marcus Boulevard
Hauppauge, New York 11788
U.S.A.
Telephone: (631) 231-7750
Toll Free: (800) 645-4994
Fax: (631) 231-2968
Web site: http://www.audiovox.com

Public Company
Incorporated: 1960
Employees: 950
Sales: $1.16 billion (fiscal 1999)
Stock Exchanges: NASDAQ Chicago
Ticker Symbol: VOXX
NAIC: 42169 Other Electronic Parts & Equipment
    Wholesalers; 443112 Radio, Television & Other
    Electronics Stores; 513322 Cellular & Other Wireless
    Telecommunications

Audiovox Corporation is an international leader in the marketing of cellular telephones, consumer electronics, auto sound, vehicle security, and mobile video systems. The company markets its products under its own brands and private labels through a distribution network that includes Bell operating companies. International sales are also handled through several joint ventures. Audiovox purchases most of its products from sources in Asia, Europe, and the United States. One supplier, Japanese-based TALK Corporation, is 31 percent-owned by Audiovox.

From Car Radios to Cell Phones: 1965–95

John J. Shalam, the son of an Egyptian textile merchant, immigrated to New York City with his family in 1948. He founded Audiovox as an import trading company in 1960. In 1965 Shalam found that the 2,000 car radios he was forced to dispose of when a deal to sell them fell through were so popular that he began doing business exclusively in auto sound. By 1982 Audiovox was one of the top three companies in the custom auto sound industry, according to Shalam, selling radios

and sound systems both to car dealers and retail customers. The company also had a Protector division providing aftermarket products ranging from paint sealants to car burglar alarms. Cellular mobile telephones were added in 1984. Company sales grew from $157.88 million in fiscal 1985 (the year ended November 30, 1985) to $203.83 million in fiscal 1986. Net income increased from $2.73 million to $3.45 million during this period.

Audiovox became a public corporation in 1987, raising $37.62 million by selling about one-sixth of its Class B common stock at $16 a share in its initial offering. Shalam retained control over a majority of the shares. Although the company had been carrying mobile cell phones for only three years, they accounted for almost half of its income in 1987. Audiovox held the largest market share of this product, with approximately 20 percent of the total cellular market, and was selling them to seven regional Bell operating companies, as well as other telephone companies, distributors, and mass merchandisers in the United States and Canada, including two joint ventures. Audiovox was also selling, installing, and servicing cell phones through its 16 Quintex retail locations.

Automotive sound equipment was still the largest sector of Audiovox's business in 1987. These products included radios (including stereo cassette radios), compact disc players, speakers, amplifiers, and antennas, marketed through five product divisions to car dealers, mass merchandisers, catalogue showrooms, and audio specialists. A wide variety of automotive accessories included security systems, radar detectors, cruise controls, video cassette players, and chemical protection treatments. Audiovox was also selling cordless telephones. Shintom Co., Ltd., an Asian company in which Audiovox held an interest, was supplying Audiovox with about one-third of its products, but the majority of its cell phones were coming from Toshiba Corporation. Toshiba subsequently replaced Shintom as Audiovox's leading supplier. Sales were being made under such registered trademarks as Audiovox, Hi-Comp, SPS, and Protector as well as private labels.

In 1989 Audiovox introduced a $399 wireless home security system with remote dialing. The following year it added facsimile machines, and in 1991 it marketed what supplier Toshiba called the world's smallest portable telephone. But this was a recessionary period in the national economy, and Audiovox lost money in fiscal years 1989–91, including $14.7 million in the last year alone. In 1993 Audiovox sold part of its 50 percent share in CellStar Corp., operator of the retail chain National Auto Cellular, for $27.5 million. Audiovox was also seeking to improve its balance sheet by adding to its export sales volume, which came to about $10 million in 1993. The following year Audiovox took a 30 percent interest in a new Japanese company, TALK Corporation, established to market and distribute cellular phones, electronic pagers, videocassette recorders, and other products for Audiovox, Shintom, and Rainbowstar Co. Also in 1994, Audiovox formed a Malaysian joint venture and opened a subsidiary in Singapore.

Exploiting the Cell Phone Boom in the Late 1990s

Although now far behind Motorola Inc., Audiovox was still the second largest distributor of cellular phones in the United States, with 14 percent of a domestic market that continued to climb. By 1997, it had also fallen behind Ericsson Inc. and Nokia Inc., though retaining 11 percent of the handset market. By this time cellular phones accounted for 70 percent of the company's sales. To stay abreast of the competition Audiovox cut prices, which contributed to a net loss in fiscal 1995 and 1996, following record net income of $26.2 million in 1994. The company shut down 90 of 120 unprofitable retail outlets in 1995.

In 1998 Audiovox introduced Pursuit Vehicle Trak, a system designed to allow motorists without even a mobile phone to communicate with an emergency help center. It automatically monitored a car whenever it moved more than 1,000 feet from where it had been parked and could slow down and shut off the car if it had been stolen. Other systems features would start the car, warm the engine, and unlock the doors. Also that year, Audiovox introduced a cellular phone using a built-in global positioning satellite (GPS) service to pinpoint a caller's location.

The cellular industry was moving from analog to digital phones during 1998–99. The digital ones offered clearer reception and added features such as caller ID. Audiovox came out with a digital phone using a CDMA chip in 1998 and TDMA and GSM models in 1999. The company offered wireless carriers special marketing packages, including providing warranty repairs. "They're relatively quick to respond to the changing dynamics of the industry and to us as a customer," a United States Cellular executive told Pradnya Joshi of *Newsday* in 1998. Digital sales outstripped analog sales worldwide for the first time in 1999.

Audiovox's sales nearly doubled in 1999 as its new line of digital phones became available in the United States, and its net income rose from $2.97 million to a record $27.25 million.

The company was expecting even better results in 2000 because of the recent introduction of TDMA and GSM sets, which served, respectively, as the standard in Latin America and Europe and Asia. Audiovox's international cellular phone sales as a percentage of its overall sales had dropped from 20 percent in 1996 to 13 percent in 1998 partly because it did not have a GSM model to compete in Europe.

With a full digital line in place, Audiovox was projecting sales of 5.3 million handsets in 1999 and 7.1 million in 2000. During 1999 it moved from fifth to third place among handset suppliers in North America, according to a survey. For 2000, the company was planning to add such features as Internet access and other interactive technologies. It was also planning tri-mode products combining digital and analog technologies. It moved from the American to the NASDAQ exchange in early 2000 and completed a secondary offering of stock, raising $97.5 million after deducting expenses.

Audiovox in 1999

Audiovox was divided in 1999 into a Wireless Group and an Electronics Group. The Wireless Group, acting through Audiovox Communications Corp., a 95 percent-owned subsidiary, was selling handsets and accessories. It raised its sales 110 percent in 1999 and accounted for 80 percent of company revenue. Digital products grew to 56 percent of the unit's sales, compared to 19 percent in 1998. The group also was selling a complete line of accessories, including batteries, hands-free kits, battery eliminators, cases, and hands-free earphones.

The Wireless Group was operating about 20 subscriber facilities under the names Quintex or American Radio and was licensing the trade names Audiovox, Quintex, and American Radio to five retail outlets in the United States. Its five largest wireless customers were Bell Atlantic Mobile, AirTouch Communications Inc., PrimeCo Personal Communications LP, MCI Worldcom, and United States Cellular Corporation. Acting through Audiovox Communications, it was also operating several retail locations under the Quintex name. Although not engaged in manufacturing, the company was working closely with both customers and suppliers in the design, development, and testing of its products.

The Electronics Group consisted of two major categories: mobile electronics and consumer electronics. The former included auto sound products, such as radios, speakers, amplifiers, and DC changers, and mobile video products, including console mobile entertainment systems, videocassette players, game options, automotive security and remote start systems, and automotive power accessories. The latter included home and portable stereos, two-way radios, LCD televisions, and MP-3 Internet music player/recorders. These products were being marketed under the Audiovox brand name and several other company-owned trade names, including Prestige, Pursuit, and Rampage.

The Electronics Group's customers included a variety of mass merchants, chain stores, specialty retailers, distributors,

---

Key Dates:

1960: Audiovox is founded as an import trading company.
1965: Audiovox begins dealing exclusively in auto sound systems.
1984: Audiovox begins selling cellular telephones.
1989: The company introduces a wireless home security system.
1997: Cellular phones account for 70 percent of revenue.
1999: Audiovox markets a full line of cell phones.

---

new car dealers, and subsidiaries of auto manufacturers. Its five biggest customers in 1999 were Gulf States Toyota, Kmart Corporation, Southeast Toyota, Alkon International, and Costco. Sales of Audiovox's Malaysian and Venezuelan subsidiaries fell under the Electronics Group. TALK Corporation continued to be the joint venture that held distribution rights for products manufactured by Shintom Ltd., with Audiovox holding exclusive distribution rights on all its wireless personal communications products for most of the world. Audiovox Specialized Applications, a joint venture formed in 1997, was responsible for distributing products for van, RV, and other specialized vehicles. Also formed in 1997, Bliss-Tel Company, Ltd. distributed wireless products and accessories in Thailand.

Audiovox was leasing 33 facilities in 11 states and a Canadian province in 1999. It also owned and leased facilities in Malaysia and Venezuela. Company headquarters remained in an industrial park in Hauppauge, Long Island. Shalam was still president and chief executive officer of Audiovox. The company's long-term debt was $122.8 million at the end of fiscal 1999. Shalom owned 20.7 percent of the company's Class A shares in February 2000.

Principal Subsidiaries

Audiovox Canada Limited (Canada); Audiovox Communications Corp. (95%); Audiovox Communications (Malaysia) Sdn. Bhd.; Audiovox Holding Corp.; Audiovox Holdings (M) Sdn. Bhd.; Audiovox Venezuela C.A. (Venezuela); Quintex Mobile Communications Corp.

Principal Operating Units

Electronics Group; Wireless Group.

Principal Competitors

Nokia Inc.; CellStar Corp.; Ericsson Inc.; Motorola Inc.; Motor Sound Corp.

Further Reading

"Audiovox Expanding Lineup of Aftermarket Products," *Automotive News,* June 7, 1982, p. 16.
"Audiovox to Enter Home Security, Unveil Cellular Phone, Car Stereo," *HFD,* December 26, 1988, p. 79.
Bernstein, James, "Audiovox Broadens Its Marketing in Asia," *Newsday,* August 30, 1994, p. A41.
Demery, Paul, "Audiovox Is Playing Big Overseas," *LI Business News,* April 15, 1991, p. 3.
Einstein, David, "911 Cell-Phone Location Just a Jingle Away," *San Francisco Chronicle,* September 1, 1998, p. C3.
Joshi, Pradnya, "Audiovox Finds Its Calling," *Newsday,* November 6, 1998, pp. C8–C9.
——, "Calling All Cars! New Options on Tap," *Newsday,* December 18, 1997, p. A68.
Siemplenski, Janel, "Cellular Dealer Dials IPO," *Dallas Business Journal,* October 29, 1993, p. 1.
Sutton, Judy, "1996 Hall of Fame: John Shalam, Audiovox—On Top of Technology," *Dealerscope Consumer Electronics Marketplace,* January 1996, p. 10.
"Toshiba Develops Small Telephone," *New York Times,* March 26, 1991, p. D5.
Walzer, Robert, "Audiovox Sets Internat'l Push," *LI Business News,* September 17, 1999, p. 1A.

—Robert Halasz

Ault Incorporated

7105 Northland Terrace
Minneapolis, Minnesota 55428
U.S.A.
Telephone: (763) 592-1900
Fax: (763) 592-1911
Web site: http://www.aultinc.com

Public Company
Incorporated: 1960
Employees: 438
Sales: $50.9 million (fiscal 1999)
Stock Exchanges: NASDAQ
Ticker Symbol: AULT
NAIC: 335311 Power, Distribution, and Specialty
  Transformer Manufacturing; 335999 All Other
  Miscellaneous Electrical Equipment and Component
  Manufacturing

Ault Incorporated, the leading independent external power conversion manufacturer in North America, develops and sells standard, semi-custom, and custom products to original equipment manufacturers (OEMs) producing data communications, small computers and peripherals, telecommunications, and medical equipment. Beginning in late 1970, Ault created a market for its goods by tapping into the trend toward smaller and smaller equipment. Ault's power supplies, transformers, and battery chargers change the voltages supplied by power companies to lower voltages needed to operate its customers products. Ault entered the year 2000 holding 12 percent of the $400 million external power conversion niche.

Slow Start-up: 1960s to Late 1970s

Joseph Ault, a contract engineer with Honeywell, created his own business in 1960. Luther T. Prince, Jr., an engineering supervisor interested in expanding his own horizons, signed on to serve as an advisor and board member for the custom power supply operation in 1961. Prince came on board full time as general manager the next year.

The start-up company began by building power supply units for a single customer, Control Data Corporation (CDC). The computer maker dropped the Ault-produced parts in 1966, but by that time the small manufacturer had lined up additional customers. Meanwhile, Prince and Ault found themselves at odds over the direction of the company: Prince believed Ault was allocating too much money for a ''pet project,'' according to an April 1982 article by Marc Hequet.

In 1967, with sales at $1.6 million and losses at $114,000, Ault's board of directors ousted the company's founder and put Prince in charge. A stipulation tied to the Small Business Administration (SBA) loan restricted Joseph Ault's voting rights and therefore prevented him from stopping the move.

Prince, on the other hand, was in control but also in a bind. If he saved the company and paid back the loan, Ault, who held 70 percent of the stock, would be in a position to fire him. Prince sought buyers for the company, ones who would support his leadership in the future, but they failed to materialize. Consequently, Prince moved to buy controlling interest of the company himself.

No one other than Ault held more than five percent of the company—shares were spread among employees, former employees, and friends of Ault. Prince's game plan was to buy enough of the founder's stock to gain control; turn the business around; take the company public; and finally, sell off enough equity to pay off his debt. Given the company's track record, the plan was a hard sell. Furthermore, Prince was an African-American, a fact which further complicated matters in the United States of the late 1960s.

Prince called on his community contacts to get the $100,000 he needed to gain 55 percent ownership. ''He went to Philip M. Harder, Sr., then top lending officer with First National Bank of Minneapolis. Prince and Harder were active together in the Twin Cities Urban Coalition, a group trying to defuse racial tension,'' wrote Hequet for *Corporate Report Minnesota.*

Harder got Prince in the door. Although other First National bankers, doubting Prince's ability to turn the company around, opposed the loan, Harder pushed the deal through. ''I enjoyed

---

Company Perspectives:

The Ault Objective is the unifying vision for the company: Our objective is to be a world class corporation using a customer driven, team approach that focuses on the prevention of waste through continuous process improvement.

---

his courage," he said in *Black Enterprise* magazine in 1982. "He really kept hammering away. I always found him absolutely straight to deal with. If there was trouble, he said so."

Ault agreed to part with his business but negotiated to retain a product line he'd been developing. He went on to begin a new enterprise. As for Prince, he was headed down a path he had not anticipated while growing up in Fort Worth, Texas.

Prince's early aspirations revolved around aviation, not business. When dreams of flying were sidetracked, he enrolled in Ohio State University. In 1946, the draft interrupted his college studies. After three years in the army, Prince entered the Massachusetts Institute of Technology (MIT), where he earned bachelor's and master's degrees in electric engineering. Minneapolis-based Honeywell recruited him in 1953; there, he designed missile and aircraft-flight control systems.

As head of Ault, Prince had to find a way to control a stream of red ink. The company's downhill spiral continued over the next two years. Sales of $2.2 million produced losses of $48,000 in 1968. The losses skyrocketed to $382,000 the following fiscal year, as sales fell to $1.7 million. During the period, an $850,000 infusion from lenders and investors kept Ault Inc. aloft, but just barely.

Late in 1969, Prince asked his former employer and current customer, Honeywell, for a $350,000 advance on an outstanding order. The Honeywell cash paid the bills, and Prince appealed to plant workers for help. "He wanted production volume of $250,000 in November 1969, even though Ault had never done better than $200,000 in any month. But in November 1969, Ault production hit $290,000," wrote Hequet.

Prince's persuasive ability helped him survive another crisis, but the roller-coaster ride continued: in 1970, sales climbed to $3.1 million but were followed by decreased sales in 1971 and 1972. Sales peaked again at $3.3 million in 1974 before taking another skid as manufacturers began moving power supply production in-house. The 1974–75 recession further depressed sales, which bottomed out at $2.1 million in fiscal 1976.

Ault had been operating primarily as a custom producer of electrical power converters for data communications and telecommunications original equipment manufacturers (OEMs), a position which made the company particularly vulnerable. On the one hand, if a customer canceled an order, Ault could not just sell the special order parts to another buyer. On the other hand, the internally situated power supply units Ault produced required safeguards, ones which drove up the size, weight, and cost of the OEM's final product. During tough economic times, manufacturers sought ways to cut costs.

A Move Outward: Early 1980s

Prince determined the company's best bet was to begin making a standardized external power supply. Hequet wrote in *Black Enterprise*, "It all sounds logical in retrospect, but it was a desperation move at the time. 'That market didn't exist,' Prince says. 'We created it.'"

The introduction of the Aulternatives line in 1977 propelled company growth, and Luther Prince was inducted into the Minnesota Business Hall of Fame in November 1982, becoming the first African-American Minnesota businessman to receive the award. Ault's sales had grown from $2 million to $7 million over a five-year period, and the number of employees jumped from 100 to 300. The company ranked among the top 100 black-controlled U.S. businesses.

Ault's product line multiplied as well over the period, expanding to more than 100 products including: step-down transformers, uninterruptible power sources, line regulators, DC-regulated power supplies, and battery chargers. Ault counted among its customers electronics giants such as Western Electric, Texas Instruments, and IBM.

Ault made its initial public offering (IPO) in August 1983. According to an early 1984 *Minnesota Business Journal* article, the newly public company was experiencing rapid sales growth and strong net income, and also anticipated increased market share. William R. Hegeman saw Ault's dependency on one company, Texas Instruments (TI), for one-third of its fiscal 1983 sales as a less promising sign for investors.

Significantly, the Ault IPO was driven in large part by a single contract, one to manufacture external power supplies for IBM's new PC Jr. IBM diverted from the norm by designing a personal computer with an external power source. The move was calculated to make the machine lighter and smaller, and to run more coolly and safely. Additionally, the external power supply afforded IBM an easier way to adapt its machine to foreign voltage requirements. The Ault IPO funded part of the production.

Ault had expected the IBM PC Jr. contract to boost the bottom line over the next several years, instead IBM scrapped the poorly performing project after a year. The machine lacked the versatility and power required for business purposes and was unable to compete with the Macintosh. A TI home computer also failed in the market. Ault's stock price took a beating.

Just as Ault was trying to regroup from the home computer fiasco, AT&T received a court order to divest its Bell Systems. The transition period resulted in lost contracts for Ault; Bell had been one its most consistent customers for several years. To add insult to injury, Taiwanese competitors were undercutting Ault's U.S. market by selling similar products for 50 percent less.

Changes Inside: Late 1980s to Early 1990s

Ault's revenue went into a freefall: dropping from $17.5 million in fiscal 1984 to $10 million in 1986. Ault racked up nearly $2 million in losses for fiscal 1986 due primarily to costs related to the closing of the plant opened to build PC Jr. power supplies. Frederick M. Green succeeded Prince as president and

<table>
<tr><td colspan="2">Key Dates:</td></tr>
<tr><td>1960:</td><td>Joseph Ault forms company to build custom power supplies for computers and computer peripherals.</td></tr>
<tr><td>1968:</td><td>Luther T. Prince, Jr., acquires controlling interest of company.</td></tr>
<tr><td>1977:</td><td>Introduces standard line of external power supply products.</td></tr>
<tr><td>1983:</td><td>Initial public stock offering.</td></tr>
<tr><td>1987:</td><td>Opens subsidiary in Korea.</td></tr>
<tr><td>1993:</td><td>Introduces line of low-cost transformers manufactured in China.</td></tr>
<tr><td>1997:</td><td>Appears on Business Week's 100 "Hot Growth Companies" list.</td></tr>
<tr><td>1999:</td><td>Ault reaches $50 million in revenues.</td></tr>
</table>

CEO in 1985. (Prince, who had originally recruited Green from CDC, remained on the board of directors until 1993.)

The string of negative events, caused in part by Ault's dependency on a few customers, led Green to strengthen the sales and marketing systems especially in key East and West Coast territories. The company also accelerated efforts to gain customers in Canada and Europe.

Concerned with the influx of cheaper foreign power supply products, Ault opened a plant in South Korea, in 1987, becoming the only U.S. external power supply maker with a wholly owned subsidiary in the Far East. Unfortunately, the newly renovated plant's roof collapsed, resulting in delayed production and greatly increased expenses.

Ault revenues resumed an upward trend, reaching $15.7 million in fiscal 1988. About 20 percent of Ault's revenue was generated by the Korean subsidiary, which concentrated on high-volume, low-margin production runs; the majority of engineering and design work remained in Minnesota. Enthusiasm over the revenue recovery was tempered by Korean production start-up problems which contributed to a loss for the year.

By 1989, Ault was producing 300 different products for more than 300 customers, mainly telecommunications, data communications, computers and peripherals, and medical equipment makers. The company had succeeded in broadening its customer base: Northern Telecom, its largest customer, generated just 7 percent of sales.

Even though the prospects for profitability looked brighter and order backlogs were growing during the first half of fiscal 1989, investors still shied away from Ault. Clint Morrison, analyst with investment firm Dain Bosworth, surmised they were put off by the memory of the PC Jr. debacle. Nora Leven, in an April 1989 *Corporate Report Minnesota* article, said Morrison was "unenthusiastic about the power supply industry in general" due to high labor needs and lack of proprietary products. Another analyst, Michael Sabbann of Piper, Jaffray & Hopwood, viewed the industry and Ault more positively, pointing to the size-conscious laptop computer, modem, and telecommunications equipment makers and their growing demand for external power supplies.

Green was determined to stay competitive. In 1991, Ault Inc. became one of the first U.S. power supply companies to achieve ISO 9002 status; they upgraded their quality certification to ISO 9001 two years later. In spite of Green's efforts, the company continued to be buffeted by market volatility.

Ault produced a record $23.3 million in sales during fiscal 1992, but weakness in the electronics industry forced Ault to downsize its Korean subsidiary in 1993–94. When the market rebounded in fiscal 1995, Ault's earnings—the first in two years—were somewhat diluted by costs related to rebuilding the Korean manufacturing infrastructure.

The successful introduction of new products during the year was a hopeful sign. They helped boost the year's sales 51 percent to $27.1 million. Moreover, the Aultra line of low-cost transformers, manufactured under subcontracting arrangements in the People's Republic of China since 1993, garnered 25 percent of total sales. North American electronics manufacturers had been going to Far East producers for similar products.

New Products Driving Sales: Late 1990s and Beyond

Ault recorded sales of $33.78 million in fiscal 1996, an increase of 25 percent over 1995, and produced another year of net earnings. Fifteen new products were introduced in 1996. When combined with the 13 from the previous year, Ault's new product output was the greatest in the company's 35-year history.

The effort expanded Ault's range of products at both the upper and lower ends of the external power supply market. Basic transformers and linear power supplies complemented battery chargers/power supply combinations and positioned Ault as a single source supplier for a number of its customers. Ault claimed to be the largest U.S.-based independent maker of external power conversion products.

A secondary public offering, in December 1996, raised net proceeds of $10.6 million, used primarily to pay down debt and acquire equipment and a factory in the People's Republic of China. Ault appeared on *Business Week's* 100 "Hot Growth Companies" list, in May 1997, based on three-year sales, profits, and return on capital. In addition to increased sales and net income, Ault improved gross margins significantly in fiscal 1997 thanks in part to a shift in the sales mix toward Ault's highest-margin products, switching power supplies and battery chargers.

Ault introduced its first switching power supply using its patented high-density technology during 1997, thus moving the company into the 50-watt range versus the 25-to-35 range of earlier technology and opening the way for new product applications, such as for printers, high-powered personal computers, and video conferencing. In all, Ault introduced 18 new product families in fiscal 1997.

The external power supply market had been growing at a rate of 12 percent annually. The segment produced 10 percent of the $16 billion generated by the power supply market as a whole. Merchant suppliers, such as Ault, were growing at a rate of 18 percent annually and produced $1 billion in revenues for the niche, according to a July 1997 *Twin Cities Business Monthly* article by Mark Hoonsbeen.

A slower than anticipated ramp-up time in the cable modem industry, resulting in lower than expected orders, hindered Ault's performance in fiscal 1998. Yet, the company reported increased sales and solid operating income and earnings: "a reflection of our improved infrastructure and sales concentration in other market segments and other geographic areas," Ault reported to shareholders.

The following year, sales rose 24 percent to a record $50.94 million. Operating income and net income also made strong gains, 38 percent and 51 percent, respectively. A significant portion of the sales growth was generated by cable modems and the growing ADSL modem market—ADSLs facilitate the convergence of voice, high-speed data, and video communications on a single broadband "pipeline." Ault's sales of external power supplies to major OEMs making digital cameras, new wireless phone systems, analog PC modems, industrial instrumentation, and business phone systems also grew in fiscal 1999.

Ault completed its first acquisition during the fiscal year: the operating assets of Maryland-based LZR Electronics' power supply division. The unit produced a series of flexible platforms or subassemblies which could quickly be modified according to customers' specifications. The acquisition, restructured as Ault Express, gave the company entry into the low-volume market niche.

During fiscal 2000, the company continued to benefit from the strong growth in the broadband modem market. Outside factors, such as the sharp rise in oil prices and the high volatility among technology stocks, had somewhat of a negative impact on the company's numbers. But Ault Incorporated now had 40 years of experience under its belt and appeared to have eliminated the extreme ups and downs of its earlier years.

Principal Subsidiaries

Ault Korea Corporation.

Principal Competitors

Exide Electronics Group, Inc.; ZEXEL U.S.A. Corp.; Tripplite; Advanced Energy Industries; Maxwell Technologies; Spectrolab; Acme Electric Corp.; International Components Corp.

Further Reading

"Ault Inc.," *Corporate Report Fact Book 2000,* p. 152.

"Ault Inc. Official Resigns," *St. Paul Pioneer Press,* January 5, 1993, p. 9C.

"Ault Starts Power Supply Express Service," *Electronic News,* August 3, 1998, p. 42.

Carideo, Tony, "Shareholder, Top Officer Disagree on Whether Ault Is Good Buyout Candidate," *Star Tribune* (Minneapolis), October 2, 1993, p. 2D.

DeSilver, Drew, "Ault to Enter Japan with New Partner," *Minneapolis/ St. Paul CityBusiness,* November 15, 1996, p. 1+.

"The Fastest Growing High-Tech Companies (and the Fast Receding)," *Corporate Report Minnesota,* October 1987, pp. 62–63.

Fiedler, Terry, "An Abundant Resource," *Minnesota Business Journal,* January 1983, pp. 24–31.

Hegeman, William R., "Three Prospects," *Minnesota Business Journal,* January 1984, p. 46.

Hequet, Marc, "A Princely Solution at Ault," *Black Enterprise,* April 1982, pp. 45–46.

——, "Profile: Luther Prince," *Corporate Report Minnesota,* December 1981, pp. 52–53.

Hoonsbeen, Mark, "More Power to Ya," *Twin Cities Business Monthly,* July 1997, pp. 16–17.

Leven, Nora, "Recharging Ault," *Corporate Report Minnesota,* April 1989, pp. 33–36, 104.

Mack, Gracian, "Keeping Stride with Telecommunications," *Black Enterprise,* October 1996, p. 57.

Monahan, Michael J., "Periscope: Ault Inc.," *Corporate Report Minnesota,* September 1984, pp. 166–67.

Schafer, Lee, "Obsessed with Change," *Corporate Report Minnesota,* December 1992, p. 71

Weintraub, Adam, "Ault Builds with Workers," *Minneapolis/St. Paul CityBusiness,* June 25, 1999, p. 11.

Wieffering, Eric, "State Tech Stocks Take a Shellacking: NASDAQ Rout Hits Locally," *Star Tribune* (Minneapolis), April 5, 2000, p. 1D.

—Kathleen Peippo

Automobili Lamborghini Holding S.p.A.

via Modena 12
40019 Sant'Agata Bolognese
Bologna
Italy
Telephone: (051) 68-17-611
Fax: (051) 68-17-644
Web site: http://www.lamborghini.it

*Wholly Owned Subsidiary of AUDI AG, a 99-Percent
    Owned Subsidiary of Volkswagen Aktiengesellschaft*
Incorporated: 1963 as Automobili Lamborghini S.p.A.
Employees: 327
Sales: L 73 billion (1998 est.)
NAIC: 336111 Automobile Manufacturing; 333618 Other
    Engine Equipment Manufacturing; 551112 Offices of
    Other Holding Companies

Automobili Lamborghini Holding S.p.A. is one of the world's most renowned manufacturers of high-performance sports cars. The company sells fewer than 300 cars in a given year (more than 100 of them in the United States, its largest market), but the hefty price tags—upwards of US$300,000, for example, for the limited edition Diablo GT—make up for small volume. Lamborghini has had a troubled history featuring a revolving door of owners, including Chrysler Corporation, an Indonesian consortium of investors, and, starting in 1998, AUDI AG, which is itself owned by Volkswagen Aktiengesellschaft. Under its German owners, the company was restructured into a holding company with three separately operated companies: Automobili Lamborghini S.p.A., manufacturer of cars; Motori Marini Lamborghini S.p.A., maker of marine engines; and Automobili Lamborghini Artimarca S.p.A., a licensing and merchandising arm.

Ferruccio Lamborghini's Road to Car Making

The founder of Automobili Lamborghini, Ferruccio Lamborghini, was born in 1916 in the village of Renazzo, near Bologna. As a boy he was fascinated by the mechanics of revolutionary machines such as the automobile and airplane. As soon as he could, he went to Bologna, and he completed studies in mechanics just before the start of World War II. During the war he worked as a supervisor of the Italian Army's vehicle maintenance unit in Rodi, Greece.

Lamborghini's experience in the motor pool prepared him to assume the role of entrepreneur when he returned to Italy after the war. He immediately purchased old military vehicles and collected abandoned German tanks in order to reconfigure them and produce tractors, equipment that was essential for Italy to rebuild itself after the destruction caused by the war. The young businessman was so successful with this enterprise that he purchased a large factory and workshop in Centro during the early part of 1948.

During the 1950s, Lamborghini focused on his tractor business. Sales expanded rapidly, not only in Italy, but soon in other war-ravaged European countries. As revenues increased, he traveled to the United States to acquire technology for the manufacture of heating systems, air conditioners, and automobile parts. During the late 1950s, one of the company's most innovative products was an air-cooled automobile engine. The company's financial stability provided Lamborghini with the opportunity to pursue one of his lifelong ambitions: the manufacture of helicopters. Unfortunately, the Italian government refused to grant him a license.

A well-circulated tale describes the genesis of Lamborghini's sports car company during the early 1960s: As he grew more interested in automobiles, Lamborghini purchased a Ferrari, one of the most prestigious, high-performance sports cars in the world. One day, while taking a pleasure drive, he noticed a sound in the front of his car and discovered a faulty part. He drove the car to Modena, the headquarters of Ferrari, and asked them to repair or replace the faulty part. He was kept waiting for such a long time that he finally demanded to see Enzo Ferrari, the founder. Ferrari, already a great man in the international race car circuit, also kept Lamborghini waiting. Angry and frustrated with the way he had been treated, Lamborghini decided to establish his own high-performance sports car company.

1963–72: Successful Early Years

Situated in Sant'Agata, near Bologna, the Automobili Lamborghini S.p.A. car factory began operations in 1963. Lambor-

Key Dates:

1963: The Automobili Lamborghini S.p.A. car factory begins operations.

1964: The first Lamborghini sports car, the 350 GT, is delivered.

1966: The 400 GT and the Miura P400 are introduced.

1968: The Islero 400 GT and the Espada make their debut.

1972: The Urraco P250 and the Jarama 400GTS (the last front-engined Lamborghini) are introduced.

1974: The Countach LP400 goes into production; Ferruccio Lamborghini sells his remaining 49 percent stake in the company and retires to his estate; the company he founded soon falls into bankruptcy.

1976: The Silhouette is introduced.

1980: The Bologna Court sells the firm to the Mimram brothers.

1982: The Countach LP500S and the Jalpa make their debuts.

1987: Chrysler Corporation purchases Automobili Lamborghini.

1988: The Countach is taken out of production, after 25 years of manufacturing.

1990: The Diablo, the world's fastest production car, is first produced.

1994: Chrysler sells Lamborghini to MegaTech, which is controlled by Indonesian conglomerate SEDTCO.

1995: Ownership of Lamborghini is restructured: Indonesia company V'Power Corp. holds 60 percent interest, MyCom Bhd., a Malaysian company, owns 40 percent.

1996: Vittorio Di Capua becomes president and CEO and initiates a major cost-cutting and restructuring program.

1998: Volkswagen, through its AUDI AG subsidiary, acquires Lamborghini.

1999: Company is restructured into a holding company, Automobili Lamborghini Holding S.p.A., with Automobili Lamborghini S.p.A. an auto making subsidiary; Di Capua resigns as head of the company and is replaced by Giuseppe Greco.

ghini hired a brilliant automotive engineer by the name of Paolo Stanzani and asked him to establish one of the most technologically advanced car-making facilities in the world. The first Lamborghini sports car was delivered in 1964 and created a sensation in automotive circles. The 350 GT, an aerodynamic sports car with a four-cam V12, five-speed transmission, four-wheel disk brakes, and four-wheel independent suspension, was soon competing for customers that had previously purchased such high-performance cars as Porsche and Jaguar. Especially gratifying to Lamborghini was the fact that his cars were as well received by automobile critics as Enzo Ferrari's.

In 1966 the company produced the 400 GT, while at the same time building its own transmissions. During the same year, Automobili Lamborghini produced the Miura P400, which created a buzz in the crowd during the Geneva Motorshow due to its compact 3929 cc transverse V12 powertrain and bare chassis. In

1968 the Islero 400 GT was introduced, featuring a luxury interior, four-wheel independent suspension, disc brakes, and an all-aluminum quad cam V12 engine. Also in 1968, Lamborghini produced the Espada, a four-seater engineered with a one-piece, solid steel body. Within a short time, the Espada became one of the most popular of all the Lamborghini models, and sales of the model remained brisk for years. The company was now known around the world for its sleek, low-slung sports cars, and sold models to celebrities including Grace Kelly and Frank Sinatra, who ordered a custom-made Lamborghini and requested that the interior decoration include genuine leopard skin.

From 1970 to 1972 the company was at the height of its success. A new version of the Miura P400, the Miura P400 SV, was introduced in 1971 and featured a completely redesigned suspension system and leather interior. Another new prototype, the Countach LP500, had its debut at that year's Geneva Motor Show. The design included a handmade aluminum body, aerodynamic contours for high-speed performance, and a dramatic new "wedge" look. In 1972 the company introduced the Urraco P250 at the Turin Motor Show, and later introduced the Jarama 400GTS. With a unique hood scoop, five bolt wheels, and significantly increased horse power, the Jarama was the last Lamborghini sports car to exhibit a front engine. With such new and exciting models, the company seemed destined for even greater financial rewards and international recognition.

1973–87: Fall into and Recovery from Bankruptcy

Unfortunately, the year 1973 was a turning point for the company. Automobili Lamborghini was hit hard by the oil embargo and by the crisis created by the worldwide recession. The market for high-speed, gas-guzzling sports cars suddenly dried up, and the firm was confronted with rapidly decreasing sales. Disappointed, Ferruccio Lamborghini decided to sell his shares of the company and retire to a 740-acre estate on Lake Trasimeno; in 1974 he sold his remaining 49 percent stake to René Leimer, a friend of the man who earlier in the decade had purchased a 51 percent stake, Swiss businessman Georges-Henri Rossetti. Lamborghini Automobili was controlled by the government for a short time, then suffered the indignity of compulsory liquidation.

Yet, due to the determination of the remaining employees, the company continued to manufacture sport cars. In 1974 the Countach LP400 went into production with a 3.9 liter V12 engine and a tubular chassis. In 1975 the Urraco 300 was manufactured and, one year later, the Silhouette was introduced at the Geneva Motor Show. In 1977, in an attempt to revive the company's profitability, production of off-road vehicles for the military was initiated. However, the design of the prototype vehicle was altered when management discovered that the general public was more interested in purchasing the models than was the military.

Despite the seemingly fast-paced production schedule, the company's fate remained uncertain throughout the decade. In 1980 the Bologna Court sold the firm to the Mimram brothers, young and famous entrepreneurs in the food industry who had a passion for sleek sports cars. They immediately started a comprehensive restructuring program, including the infusion of large amounts of capital to rehabilitate the dilapidated manufacturing facilities in Sant'Agata, and then initiated a worldwide search for highly qualified automotive engineers and designers.

Results from the investment made by the Mimram brothers began to pay off immediately. In 1982 the Countach LP500S was introduced with a new 5-liter, 375-horsepower engine. A brand new model, the Jalpa, was also introduced during the same year. The Jalpa, a two seater, included a 5-speed transmission and a new transverse-mounted V8 engine. In 1985 the Countach underwent its third major redesign and was renamed the LP500S QV. Unfortunately, the rapid production pace did not generate increased income, and the Mimram brothers soon realized that the amount required for capital expenditure was beyond the financial means of individual investors such as themselves. Looking for an experienced and financially stable partner, they met with representatives of Chrysler Corporation.

1987–93: The Chrysler Era

Chrysler Corporation was attractive to Lamborghini due to the company's committed management, its ability to introduce new models in a relatively short time and, of course, the mystique of the Lamborghini sports car. Chrysler paid approximately US$25 million for Automobili Lamborghini and took control of the company in April 1987. Chrysler management immediately poured US$50 million worth of capital into the Italian automobile manufacturer, primarily to increase production and to expand into the United States.

Under Chrysler management, the most popular and successful of all Lamborghini models, the Countach, went out of production in 1988 after 25 years and a total output of 1,997. The Countach was replaced by the Diablo, the fastest car in the world made on a production line (202 m.p.h.), at a base price of US$239,000. In 1990, sales of the car were so brisk that Lamborghini showed a profit of US$15,000. During this same time, Chrysler established a United States branch to sell Lamborghini's new models. Chrysler developed Lamborghini's U.S. network from a disorganized and loosely connected jumble of private distributors into a highly efficient franchise with support services such as maintenance and service agreements and spare parts distribution. Under Chrysler's direction, Lamborghini also began to manufacture marine engines for the offshore racing circuit. In addition, a new factory was opened in Modena, Italy, called Lamborghini Engineering, to design and produce Formula One racing cars. For its diligence, Chrysler saw Lamborghini production rise to 673 cars in 1991, and profits increase to US$1.32 million.

For all Chrysler's efforts, however, its success with Lamborghini was brief. By 1992 production had dropped to 166 cars, and the company lost nearly US$19.3 million. Sales had dropped precipitously, in spite of an expanding franchise network in the United States. Americans just were not buying the US$239,000 Diablo, so plans were initiated to develop an exotic car with a price of US$100,000, a range more accessible to American sports car enthusiasts. Yet development of the car lagged, and Chrysler became more and more frustrated with the difficulties involving Lamborghini production methods. Total production for the company amounted to just 215 cars in 1993, a figure that did not satisfy the executives at Chrysler who were used to high-volume car production. As a result, Chrysler began to look for an investor to take Automobili Lamborghini off its hands.

1994–98: Indonesian/Malaysian Ownership Period

In late 1993, Chrysler reached an agreement with Mega-Tech, Ltd. to sell Lamborghini for approximately US$40 million. MegaTech was a holding company registered in Bermuda and wholly owned by SEDTCO Pty., a large Indonesian conglomerate. SEDTCO, headed by Setiawan Djody and Tommy Suharto, the son of the premier of Indonesia, had extensive worldwide holdings in mining, manufacturing, and shipping. The agreement, which was consummated in February 1994, included the sale of Automobili Lamborghini in Sant'Agata, Lamborghini Engineering, the manufacturer of Formula 1 race cars, and Lamborghini USA. Djody owned a 35 percent stake in Vector Automotive Corporation, a manufacturer of sports cars with an average sticker price of US$450,000, and he thought Vector and Lamborghini might collaborate on the design and marketing of new models for the high-performance sports car market.

With Djody acting as chairman, the new owners hired Michael J. Kimberly as president and managing director of the company. Kimberly had worked with Jaguar and Lotus and finally as executive vice-president of General Motors in Malaysia before he was hired for the position at Lamborghini. Kimberly began a comprehensive analysis of the entire Lamborghini operation. He concluded that the company needed more than just one or two models to sell, and he began to make plans for the development of Lamborghini cars at a price accessible to the American car enthusiast. At the same time, he implemented a marketing strategy to raise awareness of the attractiveness and mystique of the Lamborghini sports car. By the beginning of 1995, sales of Lamborghini models had jumped 14 percent in the United States and 34 percent worldwide. During 1995 the ownership of Lamborghini was restructured. Suharto, through his company V'Power Corp., held a 60 percent interest, with the remaining 40 percent owned by My-Com Bhd., a Malaysian company controlled by Jeff Yap.

Despite the improved sales, the company continued to operate deeply in the red. Vittorio Di Capua was hired in November 1996 as president and CEO to attempt to turn Lamborghini around. Di Capua was a veteran of the car industry, having spent more than 40 years at Fiat S.p.A. The new CEO immediately launched a major cost-cutting and restructuring program. A number of executives and consultants were let go, and the production process was overhauled to achieve a 50 percent productivity gain. In 1996 Lamborghini would have had to have sold 450 Diablos just to break even (it sold only 211); the following year the break-even point had been cut to 196 units—209 Diablos were actually sold, resulting in a net US$120,000 profit, the first in years. Di Capua also worked to leverage the well-known Lamborghini brand and image by taking a more aggressive approach to merchandising and licensing deals. In addition, he moved forward with a US$100 million development budget for both a high-performance version of the Diablo, nicknamed the Super Diablo, and a smaller version dubbed the Baby Diablo.

1998 and Beyond: Germans in Charge

Di Capua's turnaround program set the stage—with the help of the Asian economic crisis that erupted in 1997—for another ownership change. The chairman of Volkswagen AG, Ferdinand Piëch, grandson of Volkswagen's founder, Ferdinand

Porsche, decided to take his company upmarket through acquisitions. During a 1998 buying spree, Volkswagen acquired Lamborghini for about US$110 million. Lamborghini thereby became a subsidiary of Volkswagen's luxury car subsidiary, AUDI AG. Audi spokesman Juergen de Graeve told the *Wall Street Journal* that Lamborghini "could strengthen Audi's sporty profile, and on the other hand Lamborghini could benefit from our technical expertise." Lamborghini also needed a deeper pocketed owner if it was to successfully expand its line of products.

In the immediate aftermath of the acquisition, management changes and an organizational reorganization were the first orders of business. By early 1999 Lamborghini had been restructured into a holding company called Automobili Lamborghini Holding S.p.A., with Franz-Josef Paefgen, president of AUDI, as chairman. The holding company controlled three subsidiaries: Automobili Lamborghini S.p.A., handling the manufacture of cars; Motori Marini Lamborghini S.p.A., taking over marine engine production; and Automobili Lamborghini Artimarca S.p.A., which was responsible for licensing and merchandising. These separately run companies could now focus more completely on their specific duties. Di Capua initially headed Automobili Lamborghini S.p.A. but resigned in June 1999. Hired to take over was Giuseppe Greco, another automotive veteran with previous experience at Fiat, Alfa Romeo, and Ferrari. During 1999 Lamborghini increased its sales to 265 units, a 24 percent jump from the previous year. Helping to boost sales was the introduction of the US$308,000 Diablo GT, a high-performance version of the Diablo featuring a six-liter, 575-horsepower engine that translated into a top speed of 210 m.p.h.—said to make the car the fastest production model on the market. The GT was limited to a production of 80; as a limited edition, the GT was not exported to the United States because the low volume made it uneconomical to go through the process of gaining official emissions and crashworthiness approval.

In place at the turn of the millennium, with AUDI's support, was a five-year plan to relaunch Lamborghini. Through the year 2003 the company planned to spend US$161 million to overhaul its engineering and production facilities at Sant'Agata Bolognese. During that period two new models were to be developed: a successor to the Diablo, scheduled for introduction in late 2001,

and the former Baby Diablo, now simply code-named L140. The latter was still expected to be positioned as a more affordable Lamborghini. By 2003 Lamborghini was aiming to produce 1,500 vehicles—two-thirds of them L140s and one-third the Diablo successor—which would represent an astounding leap forward and cap the German rescue of an Italian legend.

Principal Subsidiaries

Automobili Lamborghini S.p.A.; Motori Marini Lamborghini S.p.A.; Automobili Lamborghini Artimarca S.p.A.

Principal Competitors

Bayerische Motoren Werke AG; DaimlerChrysler AG; Ferrari S.p.A.; Fiat S.p.A.; Ford Motor Company; General Motors Corporation; Dr. Ing. h. c. F. Porsche AG.

Further Reading

Automobili Lamborghini News, Number 17, 1994.

Cowell, Alan, "Ferruccio Lamborghini," *New York Times,* February 22, 1993.

Kurylko, Diana T., "Chrysler Sells Lamborghini to Indonesian Group," *Automotive News,* November 22, 1993, p. 18.

Lamborghini: The Man and the Company, Lamborghini USA company document, 1995.

Lamborghini, Tonino, *Onora il padre e la madre: storia di Ferruccio Lamborghini,* Venice: Editoria Universitaria, 1997, 140 p.

Massaro, Sergio, *Lamborghini: le granturismo,* [Milan]: Ediauto, [1991], 126 p.

Pasini, Stefano, *Automobili Lamborghini: catalogue raisonné, 1963–1998,* Milan: Automobilia, 1998, 271 p.

Rechtin, Mark, "$100,000 Lamborghini Due in '96," *Automotive News,* June 20, 1994, p. 36.

Rive Box, Rob de la, and Richard Crump, *History of Lamborghini,* Isleworth, England: Transport Bookman Publications, 1980, 173 p.

Shari, Michael, "Has Lamborghini Landed on Its Wheels?," *Business Week,* October 24, 1994, pp. 92D+.

"The World's Fastest Car Is Now—A Chrysler?," *Business Week,* February 12, 1990, p. 44.

—Thomas Derdak
—updated by David E. Salamie

Baltek Corporation

10 Fairway Court
Northvale, New Jersey 07647-0195
U.S.A.
Telephone: (201) 767-1400
Fax: (201) 387-6631
Web site: http://www.baltek.com

Public Company
Incorporated: 1969
Employees: 1,315
Sales: $86.02 million (1999)
Stock Exchanges: NASDAQ
Ticker Symbol: BTEK
NAIC: 321999 All Other Miscellaneous Wood
   Manufacturing; 321918 Other Millwork (Including
   Flooring) (pt); 114112 Shellfish Fishing

A multinational manufacturing and marketing company, Baltek Corporation operates in two lines of business. The first is supplying core materials, primarily balsa wood and balsa wood products, linear and cross-linked PVC foam products, and non-woven polyester mat. Indeed, the name Baltek derives from the words ''Balsa technology,'' a niche industry in which the company has long been a leader. The second is aquaculture, specifically the farming and processing of shrimp, a business the company entered in 1983 and remains equally committed to. The founders sons, brothers Jacques and Jean Kohn, own 32 percent of the company.

From Balsa to Wooden Airplanes and Boats: 1927–69

During the 1920s in France, the father of Baltek President and CEO Jacques Kohn was operating a successful lumber company near Paris and had begun to experiment with balsa. The Frenchman had inherited the business from his own father, who since the mid-1880s had been importing tropical hardwoods to be processed for the furniture industry. By the early 1930s, however, just as balsa had found a niche with the model airplane market, he saw dark changes on the horizon and decided to set up operations in the United States. The rest of the Kohn family remained in France until the father's return in 1941, at which time all the Kohns, who were Jewish, fled the Nazi onslaught.

By this time, Baltek Corporation was underway as a primary supplier of balsa wood. Established in 1940, Baltek was the point guard of sandwich composite technology. The company supplied the balsa core used to build the nearly 8,000 legendary World War II plywood-skinned British Mosquito attack bombers, versatile aircraft used extensively from 1940 until after the war, and very effective against the heavier German planes, such as the He219. The ''wooden wonders'' could exceed 400 miles per hour in flight, an incredible feat for 1941 combat planes. Later in the 1940s, balsa core metal-faced laminates were developed for the aircraft and transportation industries. Baltek branched out as well, introducing balsa core to the marine industry in 1951 for use in building the Crosby Hydrodyne fiberglass runabouts.

During the war years, Jean, after attending school in Cuba, lied about his age in order to join the Allied effort. He spent much of the war participating in covert operations in French Indochina before parachuting into France and joining the resistance fighters there. Jacques, the older of the two, stayed at the family's main balsa plant in Guayaquil, Ecuador, serving as assistant manger in charge of production.

Following the war, demand for balsa came to a standstill. It fell to Jacques to find new markets for the family's core product. Ultimately he hit upon the use of Balsa composites by the boating industry, which Jacques felt was about to take off. Despite his father's refusal to finance the necessary expenditures for research and testing, the younger Kohn went ahead. He and his wife, Margot, emptied their savings account of $14,000 and pursued the dream. With a patent in hand and their first order from Hatteras Yachts in North Carolina, the business that would save the family firm was launched.

Eventually the company embraced an even wider field of activities, supplying non-woven reinforcements and PVC foam cores to the composites industry. By the early 1980s, the company's products were being sold throughout the United States,

Canada, Europe, Japan, Australia, and Latin America to some 1,600 ultimate users. The company made approximately 30 percent of its domestic core material product sales directly, through the use of a huge sales force in position; the remainder of the sales were handled through regional distributors in the United States, Europe, Canada, and the Pacific Rim. Sales of the company's Contourkore product to customers outside the United States by this time were being handled through a wholly owned foreign sales corporation.

Jumping on the Aquaculture Bandwagon: 1983

In 1983, the company branched out still further and entered the growing world of aquaculture, specifically shrimp farming in Ecuador. Since the company was already doing business in Ecuador with its balsa wood operations and, since the Latin American country, which began shrimp farming in 1968 had quickly grown to become the fourth largest exporter of shrimp in the world, it seemed like a logical connection to the Kohns.

In a 1986 article by Jill Barnes in *Nation's Business*, Henri-Armand Kohn explained: ''I had a friend who wanted us to get into the business [of shrimp farming]. I looked it over but forgot about it. Then, [in 1983], we were looking for a chance to invest in something new, so we began to study the shrimp farming idea again.'' Knowing nothing more about shrimp than ''that it was good to eat,'' Barnes reported, ''Kohn called the Commerce Department, which referred him to Cornelius Mock, of the National Marine Fisheries Service, in Galveston, Texas.'' Mock, who had created a technique for growing shrimp in a hatchery, called The Galveston Method, was helpful to Kohn, who later adopted Mock's technique in the Baltek shrimp yards.

Baltek Corporation bought a small island off of Ecuador's coast, about an hour's trip by boat from the city of Guayaquil. ''The island was mostly salt flats and marshes with brackish water, and covered with mangrove trees, which are important to the survival of young shrimp,'' said Barnes. Baltek spent some $4 million to create the shrimp farm. ''[We] had to build everything on the island, from the hatchery, to ponds to grow the shrimp, to houses for the workers,'' said Henri-Armand, complete with biologists who monitored the shrimp, as well as the filtering, saline, algae, and pH systems for the ponds. Barnes reported, ''Baltek's first harvest in April 1984 produced some 200,000 pounds of shrimp. As a result, Baltek's net earnings went from $1.5 million in 1984 to $1.8 million in 1985.''

In February 1986, the company opened its own $300,000 hatchery, ''so we can produce our own larvae . . . breed our own shrimp and look to producing the best possible. It's done with chickens and cattle, so why not shrimp?'' Kohn said in the *Nation's Business* article. Following that, Baltek's acquisitions in the aquaculture industry began, as the company expanded wholeheartedly into its new venture. The company acquired a shrimp packing plant in 1987; all of the outstanding capital stock of an existing shrimp farming operation adjacent to the company's already existing shrimp farm in Ecuador, for approximately $1.415 million, in July 1990; a 444-acre Ecuadorian shrimp farm in October 1997 for $965,000; and certain assets and inventory of the seafood importing U.S. subsidiary, located in Fort Lee, New Jersey, of Japanese conglomerate Nissho Iwai Corporation for an undisclosed sum, in April 1999. In 1998, approximately 42 percent of all the company's shrimp production was sold to the U.S. market through food brokers; the balance was sold to the European market. Baltek raised both *penaeus vannamei* (white shrimp) and *penaeus stylirostris* (blue shrimp) species at its farms.

Operations in the 1990s

Meanwhile, a joint venture with Sins, Switzerland-based Alusuisse Airex S.A., a $52.8 million company founded in 1956, brought together two of the oldest core material producers for structural sandwich composites in the world, and made Baltek the sole North American source for Airex and AirLite structural PVC foams. The alliance gave Baltek access to PVC foams with densities of 2.5 lbs. per cubic foot and up, in addition to its already-extensive line of engineered and end-grain balsa structural materials. Additionally, the two companies pooled their technical expertise to create a product called AirLite, making it the most advanced structural foam sandwich core in the world, expanding Baltek's capability to serve marine, industrial, transportation, aerospace, and other related markets.

Foam and mat products, together with the company's balsa products, positioned the company as a complete supplier to the composite structural core market. The core materials were typically used by the company's customers to manufacture a variety of products by laminating metal or fiberglass reinforced plastic skins to both sides of the core material, thereby creating a sandwich structure. The products manufactured by the company's customers included fiberglass boats of all types manufactured by some 1,000 builders throughout the world.

In the transportation industry, the company provided materials to manufacture aircraft flooring, aircraft cargo pallets, overhead compartments, galleys, storage units, and cabin partitions; highway container bodies; intermodal container and bulk cargo; hopper rail cars; buses; rapid transit car flooring and bulkheads; recreational vehicles; cryogenic insulation; and NASA lunar vehicles. In the industrial industry, the company's products were used to manufacture wind turbine blades; stacks; scrubbers; ducting; chemical process and storage tanks; fiberglass storage and processing tanks; and fiberglass tub and shower bottoms. For architectural uses, the company helped provide material for fascias, concrete forms, decorative panels, portable shelters, columns, partitions; and, in the military, air cargo and air drop pallets, air transportable containers, U.S. Navy and

Key Dates:

1940: Baltek is founded.
1941: Kohn family makes their escape from the south of France in advance of the Nazi invasion.
1945: World War II concludes and the demand for balsa abruptly halts.
1955: Balsa industry takes off.
1980s: Company's products are being sold around the globe.
1983: Baltek enters the shrimp farming business.
2000: Members of the Kohn family control approximately one-third of the company.

Coast Guard vessels, landing craft, and in the hull bottoms of the famed World War II PBY Catalina patrol bombers.

Baltek's balsa lumber was used mostly by the hobby industry to manufacture model airplanes. The company milled and sold graded and finished balsa lumber in standard sizes and balsa wood strips and blocks.

The company also manufactured and sold custom-made bonded panels, bonded blocks of balsa wood, and flexible balsa wood block mats called ''Contourkore,'' ''Coremat,'' and ''Baltekmat.'' The company's mat products were imported from Holland and Japan and resold without further manufacturing. One of the principal outlets for mat products was the pleasure boat industry. The company, additionally, was the sole North American source and non-exclusive distributor in Central and South America of Airex and AirLite, structural PVC foam products. The foam was purchased from Airex for further processing in the United States and was sold to customers as rigid or flexible panels in various thicknesses.

New products and products made from Baltek materials abounded in 1999. In April, at the JEC Trade Show in Paris, the company released SuperLite, its new and most advanced core product to be used in high-end, high-tech applications. In the fall of 1999, Alden Yachts released the Alden 72 performance cruiser, the largest fiberglass Alden sailboat, designed by J.G. Alden Naval Architects, with three densities of Baltek core. The company by this time also had more than 16,000 acres of balsa farmlands under cultivation in Ecuador.

Thus, with the unlikely combination of balsa wood, composite construction materials, and shrimp, the company continued to grow in the late 1990s. Total revenue for 1997 reached $56.1 million and, the following year, jumped 20.7 percent, to $67.7 million, and net income climbed 83 percent, to reach $3.3 million. At the end of 1999, several generations and branches of the Kohn family still worked for the company, with Jacques as president, Jean as executive vice-president, Margot as secretary, and Henri-Armand as a vice-president. Baltek looked forward to the future with great hope and anticipation. As Jacques Kohn remarked to Andrew Rusnak in 1997, ''The potential is enormous. The composites industry fascinates like nothing else.''

Principal Subsidiaries

Balmanta S.A.; Balsa Development Corporation; Balsa Ecuador Lumber Corporation; Baltek Foreign Sales Corporation; Baltek GmbH; Baltek, Ltd.; Baltek, S.A.; Baltek Scandinavia Aps; Compania Ecuatoriana de Balsa, S.A.; Crustacea Corporation; Cryogenic Structures Corporation; Ecuatoriana de Crustaceos, S.A.; Maderas Secas C.A. (Maseca); Marines C.A.; Pacific Timber Ltd.; Plantaciones de Balsa, S.A.; Productos del Pacifico, S.A.; Recorcholis, S.A.; Sanlam Corporation; Servicios Contables, S.A.; Vanalarva, S.A.

Principal Competitors

British Vita PLC; Glassmaster Company; Seaboard Corporation.

Further Reading

''Baltek Buys Nissho Iwai Assets,'' *Wall Street Journal*, April 26, 1999, p. A11(W)/C14(E).

''Baltek Corporation Announces Higher Second Quarter and Six Months Sales,'' *Business Wire*, August 16, 1999, p. NA.

Barnes, Jill, ''Big on Shrimp Farming,'' *Nation's Business*, July 1986, p. 62.

Birtles, Philip, *Mosquito: A Pictorial History of the DH98*. London, New York: Jane's, 1980.

Miller, Clark, ''Baltek's New Coated Balsa Core Keeps Weight Down, Strength Up,'' *National Fisherman*, September 1986, p. 34.

''Net Income Increase 45% with a 22% Revenue Gain,'' *Wall Street Journal*, March 9, 1999, p. C11.

''Net Income Jumps by 84% on a 16% Increase in Sales,'' *Wall Street Journal*, November 12, 1998, p. A15.

Rusnak, Andrew, ''The Application of Jacques Kohn,'' *Composites Fabrication*, November/December 1997, pp. 2–7.

—Daryl F. Mallett

BARRICK

Barrick Gold Corporation

Royal Bank Plaza, South Tower
200 Bay Street, Suite #2700
Toronto
Canada M5J 2J3
Telephone: (416) 307-7442
Fax: (416) 861-0727
Web site: http://www.barrick.com

Public Company
Founded: 1980 as Barrick Petroleum Corporation
Employees: 5,000
Sales: US$1.42 billion (1999)
Stock Exchanges: Toronto New York London Swiss
    Paris
Ticker Symbol: ABX
NAIC: 21221 Gold Ore Mining

Barrick Gold Corporation is an anomaly in the gold exploration and mining industry; it has little debt and low-cost production, yet high yield and even higher sales. Though Barrick began as a less than spectacular petroleum and oil company in Canada founded by Peter Munk and David Gilmour, they turned to prospecting in 1983 and became the quintessential success story. While gold mining operations may spend decades searching for the motherlode, Barrick began by acquiring established mines and bringing them to new levels of productivity and profit. On its Goldstrike Property on the Carlin Trend in Nevada, Barrick has established the Betze-Post and Meikle Mines: the former is the richest and most productive mine in the United States while the latter is the largest underground mine in North America. Ongoing exploration and drilling continue in the region, as well as on properties in Canada, South America, and Africa, with projections to reach more than five million ounces of gold production by 2003. Since Barrick's mining and processing facilities are among the most technologically advanced in the world, this is all but a fait accompli.

From Inauspicious Beginnings
Come Great Things: 1980–85

The story of gold is as old as time itself. Ancient civilizations appreciated the beauty and malleability of the precious metal and many rulers had their likenesses fashioned onto coins. Gold's value was always an absolute; the possessor wielded both wealth and power. Barrick Gold Corporation's mission was never unique; yet how the company forged a name for itself and became the world's most profitable gold producer has been fodder for Canada's history books and led to studies at prestigious business schools. Few tales rival Barrick's meandering path to become a gold industry giant.

Although the gold standard was established in 1821, the story of Barrick Gold Corporation did not begin until more than 160 years later. Hungarian-born Peter Munk, whose family fled from the Nazis to Switzerland, came to Canada in 1948 with big dreams and even bigger ambition. After several ventures—some hits, others misses—Munk, his longtime partner David Gilmour, and several Arab investors founded Barrick Petroleum Corporation in 1980. The new company drew little notice until Munk and Gilmour bought Viking Petroleum and began working with the legendary D.O. ''Swede'' Nelson to find oil. Much to their dismay, the partners never found any gushers and the industry bottomed out.

Munk then decided to go into precious metals, selecting gold as his venue, a field drastically in need of a boost. Targeting European pension funds with gold investments in South Africa, the new Barrick Resources Corporation (later renamed American Barrick Resources Corporation) hoped to get fund managers to invest their capital in North American gold stocks. With growing discord in South Africa's political and financial arenas, Munk and his partners believed Barrick could offer a more prudent investment. The new Barrick went public on the Toronto Stock Exchange in May 1983 with 1.3 million shares. The sale garnered only C$2.5 million, just enough to get the fledgling company on its way.

The company's mission was simple yet of grand scale: dominate the gold industry by becoming North America's larg-

Company Perspectives:

Barrick is a compelling investment choice, for reasons that stand out in any diversified basket of stocks: for aggressive growth and financial strength that would make it a leader in any industry; and beyond that, for excellent leverage to rising gold prices.

est producer; acquire established properties with sound futures; be fiscally conservative; and protect the bottom line through an aggressive hedging program. Hedging, used by precious metals producers, was the use of complicated financial contracts to arrange forward sales at fixed prices, regardless—or rather in spite of—market fluctuations. The seemingly win-win formula—if prices went down, producers were protected by their contracted prices; if prices rose, they could sell additional reserves on the open market—was a boon for Barrick and such rivals as Vancouver's Placer Dome.

Barrick's second business tenet, to acquire working mines with potential, came into play just months after the company went public. The company bought a 23 percent stake in gold deposits in Alaska's Valdez Creek region, then joined up with Alaska Power & Light and the city of Juneau to explore over two dozen sites. Barrick's next move was to buy a half-interest in Ontario's Renabie mine. Though both the Valdez and Renabie mines produced gold, the former was eventually sold and the latter was closed.

In 1984 the tide turned with the acquisition of the debt-laden Camflo Mines Ltd. of Quebec. Camflo had a solid reputation for low cost gold production and top notch people, including Robert Smith, Alan Hill, and Brian Meikle, who stayed on board to work with Barrick. In addition to the Camflo mine came stakes in two other mines, one near Reno, Nevada, and another by Ontario's Kirkland Lake. The Ontario interest later became the Holt-McDermott Mine, Barrick's first major find from initial exploration to full production. The Nevada property led Munk and his team to staggering success and the coveted title of the world's most profitable gold producer. But first there were trials and tribulations to wade through.

Barrick went public on the New York Stock Exchange in 1985, issuing shares at C$1.40 each. Though more successful than its IPO on the Toronto exchange, the company was still relatively unknown to Wall Street and its investors. With minor triumphs from mining operations at the Valdez and Camflo, and ongoing development of the Holt-McDermott mine, Barrick was not only making money but hedging to stave off any market downswings. Bob Smith, who had come on board with the Camflo deal, was now Munk's leading developer and righthand man. Smith helped spearhead Barrick's next acquisition, Utah's oft-closed Mercur Mine, a neglected property Texaco Inc. was looking to unload.

After arduously pulling together the $40 million asking price, Barrick excitedly took possession of Mercur Mine and its surrounding property in Utah. During the long negotiations, Smith and his other former Camflo colleagues, Hill and Meikle,

discovered Mercur had much more to offer than expected. The acquisition turned out to be a major coup—not only because of additional gold deposits—but because Texaco had poured over $100 million into updating the mine before deciding to sell. Barrick paid less than half what Texaco had put into the mine, while gaining a property with considerably more assets than anticipated. Mercur Mine brought Barrick into the big leagues of gold production; Barrick, in turn, brought increased production and state-of-the-art processing to Mercur. In the course of two years, Barrick's fortunes had multiplied: revenues jumped from $13 million with gold production of 34,000 ounces in 1984 to $42 million and 116,000 ounces in 1985.

All That Glitters Is Gold: 1986–92

In 1986 Barrick had another year of hidden advantages after the company's prospectors traveled to the gold country of the Carlin Trend in north central Nevada. On the surface, buying the Goldstrike Property, along the United States' richest gold vein, was a good purchase; beneath the layers of rock, Goldstrike more than lived up to its name. The legendary Carlin Trend was home to several mines and mining companies, including one of Barrick's chief rivals, Newmont Mining Corporation. Newmont's Genesis Mine was a huge operation and located adjacent to the Goldstrike Property. After negotiating two separate deals, each worth 50 percent, Barrick had complete control of Goldstrike. Despite some initial setbacks, Goldstrike was confirmed as the richest gold deposit in North America and a wholly owned part of Barrick's growing empire.

By the late 1980s the Goldstrike Property was home to the exceptionally prolific Betze mine (named for the two geologists who discovered it, Bettles and Kornze), with several developments underway. Barrick had increased productivity, sold some gold, and stored the rest for a rainy day. By now hedging was no longer a trend but the industry norm, with Barrick one of its leading proponents. Yet some analysts felt hedging was not in the best interests of shareholders if prices rose significantly, to which Munk said, "Isn't it more important to have no downside?" Then he needed only point to the numbers—stock valuation had gone up nearly 190 percent on the NYSE for 1987 alone.

In 1989 Munk was the conquering hero to shareholders and the industry when gold prices took a dive to their lowest point in three years. Amazingly, Barrick's earnings were robust, up over 20 percent, while stock prices rose an incredible 94 percent. Hedging, at least the Barrick way, had paid off tremendously. The same was true again in 1991 when lackluster prices brought devastating losses for many of Canada's producers. Yet Barrick surprised its shareholders and competitors with a 59 percent leap in earnings and a 68 percent jump in production. The next year Barrick reaped even greater rewards, with net income climbing 89 percent to $175 million on total revenues of $554 million, with production costs *falling* instead of rising, and gold production reaching a new high of 1.3 million ounces.

Yet 1992 was most significant for two other reasons: the first, to continue its exploration of the Carlin Trend's Deep Post region, Barrick and rival Newmont agreed to a joint venture for the land adjacent to both their properties. This amicable agreement, the Newmont/Barrick HD Venture, came not long after

Barrick considered a takeover of Newmont, which fell apart. In exchange for a 40 percent stake, Barrick performed the onsite drilling, while Newmont was responsible for the processing. Given the region's spectacular gold deposits, both companies had high hopes for the venture. Second, Barrick announced its intention to develop a massive underground reserve in what was called the Purple Vein. The new Meikle Mine, named after Brian Meikle, had over 6.5 million ounces of particularly high-grade gold.

"Do a Barrick": 1993–96

The next year, 1993, Munk received Canada's highest honor, when he was named an Officer of the Order of Canada for his contributions to the country and beyond. The honor was both a personal and professional triumph for Munk, who had come to Canada with high hopes—though no one had envisioned just how far he would take those aspirations. Barrick, meanwhile, was full speed ahead. In 1994 came another banner year when the company won a bidding war for Lac Minerals Ltd., which turned out to be the biggest gold company acquisition in North and South America at the time. Lac Minerals owned several properties, but the most exciting were in the El Indio gold belt in the Andes Mountains, and Barrick's development team hoped El Indio's deposits might rival those found at Goldstrike.

By 1995 Barrick had ten working mines and four in development. At the close of the year the company had produced 3.1 million ounces of gold and reported reserves of 37.6 million ounces, an all-time high; sales surpassed the billion-dollar mark at $1.28 billion. In 1996 Barrick was in fantastic form with gold reserves of over 51 million ounces, a 40 percent upswing from the previous year's reserves. The company had become the planet's most profitable gold company and its second largest producer (behind Newmont). Not only had Barrick mined three million ounces of gold during the year at an average cost of $193 per ounce (as opposed to the industry's standard of $269 per ounce), but the company had identified an additional 25 million ounces of new resources in the form of gold mineralization. In addition, the company had two years' worth of gold production in its hedging program, and in nearly a decade of hedging had created $500 million in extra revenues.

The company's name had even entered the vernacular, with investors and analysts searching for outfits that could "do a Barrick," or become as successful as Barrick had over the 13-plus years since it segued into gold mining. With the August takeover of Arequipa Resources, Ltd. of Vancouver, came the Pierina mine and an additional 47 properties in Peru with promising futures. Barrick put the Pierina deposits into development and continued its exploration of Chile's Pascua, which was now up to ten million ounces in production. The two properties were expected to generate up to one million additional ounces of gold to Barrick's annual output within a few years, while the company's joint venture with Newmont had brought in 1.2 million ounces in reserves since its creation the year before. The new Meikle Mine on the Goldstrike property in Nevada also began production in 1996, on time and on budget. Sales for the year were $1.3 billion for 3.12 million ounces.

Just before the end of the year, Barrick seemingly had its industry by the tail—excellent cash flow, high gold reserves, and some of the richest gold properties in the world. Yet a new gold find in Indonesia was about to rock the gold industry, and Barrick would be right in the middle of the resulting maelstrom.

The Bubble Bursts: 1997–99

By the beginning of 1997, Barrick announced its pact with the Indonesian government to acquire a 75 percent stake in the Bulsang gold deposit, believed to be the biggest gold find since South Africa's Witwatersrand. Completion of the deal meant Barrick would shed its rank as second largest gold producer in the world, and rise to number one. Gold prices, however, bottomed out and no one was left unscathed. As Munk wrote in the company's 1997 annual report, "The past year brought a new and sobering reality to the gold business." This was putting it mildly as Barrick was assaulted on all fronts—financially, in the press, and by a lawsuit filed by Bre-X Minerals Ltd. Although Barrick's size and reserves protected it from much financial fallout, the company announced the closure of its less efficient mines (numbering four) and took a major hit in the third quarter. According to *Maclean's*, the company had been valued on the stock market at $15.4 billion, and by the end of 1997 had fallen to $8.6 billion with gold at a 12-year low of $295 per ounce.

Barrick also took heat for its hedging practices, with detractors accusing the company and the other major producers of manipulating the gold market, which Munk vehemently denied. In addition, the Bulsang gold project in Borneo had become a vicious mess. Initially, Barrick believed it had secured a 75 percent share of the mine, much to the dismay of the Calgary-based Bre-X, who had staked the claim and wound up with only a 25 percent interest. It was a classic David and Goliath struggle; Bre-X accused Barrick of influence peddling, in the form of former Canadian Prime Minister Brian Mulroney (a Barrick board member since 1993) and former President George Bush (who had joined the board in 1995) to gain access to Indonesia's Suharto government. Before the dust settled accusations of graft and greed touched everyone involved, including Bre-X, who then leveled a lawsuit at Barrick for attempting to steal the golden egg. Barrick eventually withdrew from negotiations; Munk maintained the company pulled out because the Indonesian government wanted too much control of the operation as well as ten percent of the action.

For Barrick, 1997 had been a rude awakening; the company was not above major market fluctuations regardless of its hedging program, which Munk still firmly believed in. Yet despite an earnings loss for the year, revenues were still a robust $1.28 billion, and gold production was three million ounces. The troubled year also brought a few executive changes: Bob Smith, president of Barrick since 1985, left his post to become vice-chairman and John K. Carrington was named the new president and COO. Barrick, however, bounced back the following year: in 1998 operating cash flow was an amazing $539 million, after costs had declined 12 percent due to the program implemented the previous year. Having slashed its operating mines to five, gold sales remained almost the same at $1.28 billion (up by $3 million) for the year, income topped $300 million for the first time, and gold production increased by 200,000 ounces. Barrick was still the most profitable gold company in the world, and for every ounce of gold sold, the company earned six times more profit than its competitors.

In October 1998, Barrick suffered a heavy blow when Vice-Chairman Bob Smith passed away. Generally referred to as ''the soul of Barrick,'' Smith had helped steer the company to its preeminence in the 1990s. Smith's successor as vice-chairman was Carrington, and Randall Oliphant, formerly executive vice-president and CFO, took over as president and CEO.

The company again came under fire in the late 1990s for its hedging practices, during another industry slump causing substantial losses. With prices reaching their lowest point in 20 years, and Barrick's sales soaring in 1999, the finger-pointing was inevitable. Barrick was accused of dumping too much gold on the market, triggering lower prices, when some of the blame lay with banks and the International Monetary Fund's plans to unload substantial amounts of their gold reserves. Ironically, Munk lobbied hard to get the banks and the IMF to reconsider, since the gold market was in such disarray. They complied; gold prices soared; everybody was content—until the next downswing. Several of the industry's top producers, however, including Barrick, Placer Dome, and Cambior, Inc., vowed to decrease their hedging programs.

While the Indonesian debacle was over but not forgotten, Barrick still went after promising properties. In 1999, following Placer Dome's lead, Barrick went to Africa and soon acquired Sutton Resources. Sutton had been exploring the Bulyanhulu property, situated in northwestern Tanzania, extolled as East Africa's largest gold deposit with reserves of 8.8 million ounces of exceptionally high-grade gold. For every Bulsang, there was a Bulyanhulu—and Barrick had far more of the latter than the former. The company finished the year with gold sales of $1.42 billion, net income of $331 million (up 10 percent from the previous year), and production up another 500,000 ounces for a total of 3.7 million ounces of gold.

2000 and Beyond

Barrick on the brink of a new century was much the same as Barrick historically—acquisitions, steady production, and exceptional profit. In March, the company reached an agreement with TNR Resources to buy many of its Argentinian properties, an area in which Barrick was already established through its El Indio gold belt explorations and mining. Yet Peter Munk was determined *not* to take his company's fortunes for granted. Quoted in the corporate history by Peter C. Newman, which Barrick commissioned and published in 1995, Munk said: ''. . . We tell each other not to get too euphoric. I remind them [his executive management team] not to be caught in the deadly sin of hubris. We must never start believing we're invincible; that would be fatal. I keep repeating to my people—and I make them repeat it back to me so I'm sure they get it—that we are still the same human beings we were 10 years ago when we were struggling. Balance sheets change but people don't. We'll never get too big for our britches.''

Principal Operating Units

Bulyanhulu Property (Tanzania); Goldstrike Property; Pascua-Lama Property (Chile); Pierina Property (Peru).

Principal Competitors

Anglo American Corporation; Cambior Inc.; Goldfields of South Africa; Homestake Mining Company; Newmont Mining Corporation; Placer Dome Inc.

Further Reading

Chadwick, John, ''Barrick Goldstrike,'' *Mining Magazine*, November 1995, pp. 250+.

''El Indio Rejuvenated Under Barrick Gold,'' *Mining Magazine*, January 1996, p. 6.

''Good for Barrick, Bad for Gold?,'' *Business Week*, October 25, 1999, p. 134.

Newman, Peter C., *Dreams & Rewards: The Barrick Story,* Toronto: Barrick Gold Corporation, 1995.

——, ''Mining the Riches of Urban Real Estate,'' *Maclean's*, September 22, 1997, p. 60.

——, ''Peter Munk: A Dreamer Who Became a King,'' *Maclean's*, December 9, 1996, p. 42.

''Newsroom Notes: The Making of a Mega-Deal,'' *Maclean's*, December 9, 1996, p. 4.

Rohmer, Richard, *Golden Phoenix: The Biography of Peter Munk*, Toronto: Key Porter Books, 1999.

Ross, Priscilla, ''Barrick Buys into Top E African Mine,'' *African Business*, April 1999, p. 31.

''The Shine Is Off Barrick's Gold,'' *Maclean's*, December 8, 1997, p. 60.

Wells, Jennifer, ''Greed, Graft, Gold: Canadians Find Treasure in One of the World's Most Corrupt Countries,'' *Maclean's,* March 3, 1997, p. 38.

——, ''Gunning for Gold,'' *Maclean's*, February 17, 1997, p. 52.

——, ''King of Gold: The Inside Story of Peter Munk's Indonesian Gold Coup,'' *Maclean's*, December 9, 1996, p. 32.

—Nelson Rhodes

Boy Scouts of America

The Boy Scouts of America

1325 W. Walnut Hill Lane
Irving, Texas 75015-2079
U.S.A.
Telephone: (972) 580-2000
Fax: (972) 580-2502
Web site: http://www.bsa.scouting.org

Nonprofit Company
Incorporated: 1910
Employees: 500
Sales: $251.5 million (1998)
NAIC: 81341 Civic and Social Organizations; 51112
    Periodical Publishers; 51113 Book Publishers

Rooted in Victorian values, The Boy Scouts of America (BSA) is a 20th-century phenomenon and a powerful civic force. More than a million Boy Scouts and half a million adult volunteers contribute 50 million service hours a year. BSA is unique among the country's largest nonprofit groups in that volunteers at the local level are responsible for much of its planning.

Famous Eagle Scouts include Steven Spielberg, H. Ross Perot, Gerald Ford, and Neil Armstrong.

Edwardian Origins

Although many ideas were incorporated into the Boy Scouts of America, a chance encounter on a foggy London night in 1909 connected all the threads. Chicago publisher William D. Boyce was on his way to a safari in Africa. On a layover in London, he became lost and was rescued by a helpful Boy Scout who refused to take a tip for his good deed. This inspired Boyce to set up a meeting with the man who had started the movement in 1907, Major General Robert S.S. Baden-Powell.

Baden-Powell, a plucky Boer War hero, penned *Scouting for Boys* in 1908 after learning the popularity of his survival manual among schoolboys. Feeling modern males lacked the kinds of initiation rites found in primitive society, and disdaining the urban decadence and declining influence of the British military

in Edwardian Britain, Baden-Powell developed his own program for building character among youths in a setting of outdoor recreation. Besides African tribes, he looked to the early British and Irish, the Japanese, the Spartans, and to contemporary American youth movements for inspiration. Although scouting was in its infancy when Boyce discovered it, the movement had already recruited more than 100,000 Boy Scouts across the British Empire. Baden-Powell was knighted for his work in 1910.

Initially unable to obtain a federal charter, Boyce incorporated the Boys Scouts of America on February 8, 1910, in the District of Columbia. He then delegated some of the start-up work to Edgar M. Robinson, who was heading a scouting program for the YMCA (Young Men's Christian Association). On June 21, 1910 dozens of representatives from various boys' agencies met at BSA's temporary headquarters at a New York YMCA to elect a steering committee. By this time, newspaper magnate William Randolph Hearst had organized his own "American Boy Scouts."

From the start, the Boy Scouts of America (BSA) was surrounded by men of influence and means. President William Howard Taft and Theodore Roosevelt were named honorary president and vice-president. The group's president was Colin Livingstone, president of the American National Bank of Washington. Scottish émigré Ernest Thompson Seton, who had founded the Woodcraft Indians and would write the BSA handbook, was chosen first Chief Scout in 1910. Another buckskin-wearing naturalist, Daniel Carter Beard, was first national scout commissioner. He designed the original uniform and merged his own boys' group, the Sons of Daniel Boone, with BSA. James E. West, the first Chief Scout Executive, was an inspirational figure. Handicapped and an orphan, he had furthered himself along the lines of a Teddy Roosevelt. However, he antagonized the more athletic types, like Seton, who was forced out of the organization.

BSA established its National Council office at 200 Fifth Avenue, New York on January 2, 1911. It had just seven staff members but membership reached 61,495 that year. President Taft spoke at the group's first annual meeting, held at the White House.

Boys' Life magazine was launched that same year and scouting spread to all states by the next year. In 1913, BSA com-

Company Perspectives:

The mission of the Boy Scouts of America is to prepare young people to make ethical choices over their lifetimes by instilling in them the values of the Scout Oath and Law.

Scouting helps develop strong values that stay with youth throughout their lives. This is particularly true for boys who stay in Scouting for five or more years.

The Boy Scouts asked Louis Harris & Associates to accept the challenge of scientifically uncovering the foundational elements to the success of Scouting programs. The research determined that Scouting is effective because it meets six critical elements of healthy youth development: 1) Strong personal values and character; 2) a sense of self-worth; 3) caring and nurturing relationships with parents, other adults, and peers; 4) a desire to learn; 5) productive and creative use of time; 6) social adeptness.

menced publication of *Scouting* magazine for Scout volunteers. BSA finally received a federal charter in June 1916 which limited membership to U.S. citizens. Membership stood at 245,183 at year-end. Boy Scouts soon became known for their patriotic service, selling millions of dollars worth of war bonds during World War I.

First World Jamboree in 1920

In 1920, BSA sent 301 members to the first World Jamboree in England, attended by Boy Scouts from 32 of 52 scouting countries. The Boy Scouts adopted the left-handed handshake in 1923. By this time, more than two million people had participated in the program and active membership—boys and volunteers—was nearly 600,000.

Boyce's Lone Scouts merged with BSA in 1924. The next year, BSA sent a promotional delegation to South America. In 1927, the headquarters relocated to roomier accommodations at 2 Park Avenue, New York.

The Cub Scouts program for younger boys was officially launched in 1930. Total membership exceeded one million by BSA's 25th anniversary in 1935. Unfortunately, an epidemic of infantile paralysis that year caused the national jamboree to be canceled.

In 1938, BSA received an enormous gift from Waite Phillips, who gave the agency 36,000 acres of land in the Rocky Mountains near Cimarron, New Mexico. Three years later, Phillips added another 91,000 acres to the gift, which became the Philmont Scout Ranch, the world's largest. The Philtower Building in Tulsa, Oklahoma, accompanied the donation and provided income to run the camp.

Being Prepared: During and After World War II

Boy Scouts again assisted their country during World War II. The range of tasks undertaken included distributing war bonds and propaganda, salvaging critical materials such as rubber, and helping medical and fire brigades.

After the war, BSA's World Friendship Fund gave money to help restore scouting in war-torn areas including the Philippines, which received $10,000. Conservation education featured highly in the scouts' program at home. Membership passed two million in 1946.

The U.S. Post Office issued the first stamp honoring the Boy Scouts in 1950. The next year, the scouts collected two million pounds of clothing for various relief efforts. Another "Good Turn" was hanging millions of "Get-Out-the-Vote" reminders on doorknobs. Civil defense education was also on the agenda.

The National Council relocated to New Brunswick, New Jersey, in October 1954. BSA started a foreign exchange program with the gift of transportation on U.S. military planes. The International Geophysical Year, 1958, saw an Explorer (adult volunteer) scout accompany an arctic expedition sponsored by the National Academy of Sciences. Total membership reached five million the next year.

BOYPOWER '76

As part of its golden jubilee, BSA opened the Johnston Historical Museum in New Brunswick in June 1960. By 1965, 40 million boys had been part of the BSA program, 500,000 of them becoming Eagle Scouts. The National Council launched the BOYPOWER '76 eight-year plan in 1968, aiming to boost membership and to raise $65 million.

In the 1970s, the Scouts tried to Save Our American Resources (SOAR). An anti-drug campaign, Operation Reach, was also launched. In conjunction with the Bicentennial, Boy Scouts displayed a massive exhibition of scouting skills on the Mall in Washington, D.C. Twelve scouts gave the Report to the Nation to President Gerald Ford, himself a former Eagle Scout.

Under pressure to keep membership numbers up in order to maintain donations from the United Way, some troop leaders were found to have exaggerated their enrollment statistics in 1974. At any rate, the BOYPOWER campaign ultimately proved unsuccessful. BSA had but 4.6 million members in 1976, down 1.1 million from 1969. Membership continued to wane. BSA had even introduced an action figure, Steve Scout, which also failed.

In 1978, updating its image, BSA unofficially dubbed itself "Scouting USA." It launched a new "Campaign for Character" to raise $49 million. National Council headquarters relocated again in 1979, to Irving, Texas, while the 15th World Jamboree was postponed due to events in the host country of Iran.

Membership figures started to rise again in 1980. Perhaps the new uniforms designed by Oscar de la Renta helped. Scouts nationwide urged participation in the census. They formed new relationships with other government agencies, such as the Department of the Interior and the Department of Energy. Cub Scouting turned 50 and signed up its 30 millionth Cub Scout.

BSA counted its one millionth Eagle Scout in 1982. At the same time, the organization had launched its "Shaping Tomorrow" program. New categories of scouting—Tiger Cubs for 7-year-old boys and athletics-oriented Varsity Scouting for 14- to 17-year-olds—emerged.

Key Dates:

1907: Scouting begins in England as the brainchild of Robert Baden-Powell.

1908: Baden-Powell publishes *Scouting for Boys.*

1909: American William D. Boyce is introduced to scouting through a chance occurrence.

1911: National Council offices are launched in the United States; first issue of *Boys' Life* is published.

1912: Scouting spreads to all 50 states.

1920: The first Boy Scout World Jamboree is held in England.

1930: Cub Scouts, a program for younger boys, is launched.

1982: The millionth Eagle Scout is registered; the Tiger Cubs program for first graders is launched.

2000: The Boy Scouts of America celebrates its 90th birthday.

In 1985, the year of BSA's 75th anniversary, scouts lit campfires outside each state capitol and carried the ashes in a three-month procession across the country. Membership continued to climb, exceeding five million by the end of 1986.

That year, Boy Scouts promoted the cause of organ donation. Societal issues (''unacceptables'') tackled by BSA in the late 1980s included drug abuse, child abuse, illiteracy, youth unemployment, and hunger. Backed by corporate supporters such as Quaker Oats and the United Way, scouts collected 60 million containers of food in 1988 alone. BSA recognized the potential for child abuse in its own organization and structured activities to eliminate one-on-one encounters between scouts and adult volunteers.

New Frontiers in the 1990s

The collapse of the Soviet empire opened new frontiers for the Boy Scouts. Czechoslovakia and Hungary soon began their own programs. In 1990, a BSA delegation sought opportunities in Moscow, then continued to the Vatican City to present Pope John Paul II with a commendation. At home, the Hispanic Emphasis and Urban Emphasis targeted underrepresented segments of the population.

A sophisticated TV ad campaign aimed to swell the ranks of the Boy Scouts in the United States, who numbered only one million in 1990. Cub Scouting, aimed at younger boys, was much more popular as teenagers found traditional Boy Scout activities such as knot-tying decidedly unhip. In-school Scouting brought many new members in urban areas, although purists protested the perceived dilution of the curriculum.

BSA's policy barring homosexuals prompted Levi Strauss, Bank of America, and Wells Fargo to cancel their support for the organization (which together amounted to about $100,000 a year) in 1992. Conservative groups boycotted the three San Francisco-based firms in response, and Bank of America soon resumed its contributions. BSA also banned atheists, as one of its three founding principles was a belief in God. An appellate court ruled that the Boy Scouts were a private group not subject to civil rights laws. Although it won a 1987 lawsuit from a woman scorned, BSA subsequently allowed women into scoutmaster positions.

A restructuring in 1992 reduced the number of councils from 408 to 340 and the number of regions from six to four. BSA also sold off underutilized real estate, switched from mainframe computers to PCs, and began benchmarking practices from the world of business. It also began to reduce its staffing levels.

Jere Ratcliffe was picked to lead the National Council in 1993, taking over from Norm Augustine, CEO of Lockheed Martin. BSA started systematically searching for more endowment money. Operating revenues were $411 million in 1995, a fifth of it provided by the United Way, which was cutting back its contribution. While it had 3,300 professional employees, more than a million volunteers did most of the work. Operation First Class sought adults from diverse backgrounds to fill the ranks.

Although a much beloved organization among Americans of all ages and ethnic backgrounds, The Boy Scouts of America was not without its share of ongoing problems and controversies. For example, in 1999 the New Jersey Supreme Court ruled in favor of James Dale, a scoutmaster whom BSA had expelled for being gay. BSA appealed the case to the U.S. Supreme Court. Apparently, whether gays would be tolerated within its ranks remained an as yet unanswered question. Nonetheless, the organization looked to the future with optimism, celebrating its 90th anniversary in 2000 and rededicating itself to the traditions that had served it so well throughout its history.

Principal Divisions

Tiger Cubs BSA; Cub Scouting; Boy Scouting; Varsity Scouting; Venturing; National Eagle Scout Association.

Principal Competitors

Boy's Clubs of America; Young Men's Christian Association (YMCA).

Further Reading

Byrne, John A., ''Prepared at Last,'' *Forbes,* October 10, 1983, pp. 32f.

Cochran, William F., ''Confessions of a Jamboree Scoutmaster,'' *Harper's,* February 1951, pp. 59–67.

Dean, John I., ''Scouting in America: 1910–1990,'' D.Ed. diss., University of South Carolina, 1992.

Ferguson, Tim W., ''Departures from Tradition: Airlines, Yes; Scouts, No,'' *The Wall Street Journal,* August 25, 1992, p. A15.

Lambert, Wade, ''Boy Scouts Can Prevent Atheists from Joining Group, Court Rules,'' *Wall Street Journal,* May 19, 1993, p. B8.

MacLeod, David Irving, ''Good Boys Made Better: The Boy Scouts of America, Boys' Brigades, and YMCA Boys' Work, 1880–1920,'' Ph.D. diss., University of Wisconsin, 1973.

Miller, Cyndee, ''Quayle's Comments Fuel Boycott Against Three Firms,'' *Marketing News,* July 20, 1992, p. 1.

Mullin, Rick, ''Reorienting the Boy Scouts,'' *Journal of Business Strategy,* July/August 1996, pp. 21ff.

Pechter, Kerry, ''Round the Campfire They'll Sing: 'Hail, Hail, the Gang's All Here','' *Wall Street Journal,* March 22, 1990, p. B1.

Peterson, Robert W., *The Boy Scouts,* New York: American Heritage, 1985.

——, ''Happy Birthday, Boys,'' *Boys' Life,* February 2000, pp. 14–17.

Rivera, Elaine, "All for a Scout's Honor," *Time,* August 16, 1999, p. 33.

Stein, Benjamin J., "The Magic of Scouting," *Wall Street Journal,* April 17, 1997.

Wagner, Carolyn Ditte, "The Boy Scouts of America: A Model and a Mirror of American Society," Ph.D. diss., Johns Hopkins University, 1978.

Young, David, "Boy Scout Numbers Down Since Exposé," *Chicago Tribune,* September 19, 1975.

——, "Phantoms Fill Boy Scout Roles; Scout Records Falsified— Scout Pledge Lost in Sign Up Drive," *Chicago Tribune,* June 10, 1974, pp. 1, 23.

—Frederick C. Ingram

Brass Eagle Inc.

1201 S.E. 30th Street
Bentonville, Arkansas
U.S.A.
Telephone: (501) 464-8700
Fax: (501) 464-8701
Web site: http://www.brasseagle.com

Public Company
Incorporated: 1882 as Plymouth Iron Windmill Company
Employees: 230
Sales: $68.23 million (1999)
Stock Exchanges: NASDAQ
Ticker Symbol: XTRM
NAIC: 33992 Sporting and Athletic Goods Manufacturing

Brass Eagle Inc. is recognized as the worldwide leader in the paintball industry, manufacturing paintball markers, paintballs, and accessories. Brass Eagle is the only company of its kind to manufacture a comprehensive list of paintball merchandise, including a variety of markers—ranging from inexpensive to expensive models—and protective equipment. The company is also the only paintball manufacturer to distribute its products to mass merchandisers. Wal-Mart and Kmart each accounted for more than ten percent of the company's sales in 1999.

Origins

The Brass Eagle of the late 1990s began its corporate life in the 19th century as Plymouth Iron Windmill Company, a manufacturer of windmills based in Plymouth, Michigan. Although the connection between Brass Eagle and windmill operations in Michigan was a distant one, the evolution of Plymouth Iron in the 1880s and 1890s set a precedent that was followed a century later, leading to the modern manifestation of Brass Eagle.

Plymouth Iron started business in 1882, but before long company officials struggled to exist in the new era of industrialization. Their salvation came through the intervention of a local inventor named Clarence Hamilton, who approached the company in 1886 with a metal and wire contraption that used compressed air to fire a small lead ball. The president of Plymouth Iron fired Hamilton's creation and, according to company lore, exclaimed, "Boy, that's a daisy!" His enthusiastic reaction not only gave the company a new business to pursue but also provided the inspiration for the company's new name.

Initially, before Plymouth Iron found it difficult to attract customers, the company gave Hamilton's compressed-air gun to farmers as a gift when they purchased a windmill. The farmers' positive response soon prompted Plymouth Iron management to begin manufacturing the guns exclusively. The name given to Hamilton's invention was adopted as the company's new name, ratified by the board of directors in 1895, when Daisy Manufacturing Company, Inc. officially was born. Daisy Manufacturing introduced generations of Americans to the BB gun, an air-powered rifle that carved a new industry niche populated by a host of competitors. In the decades to follow, Daisy Manufacturing threw itself into feeding the BB gun craze it had started, becoming in the process a fixture in 20th-century American industry.

The Invention of the Paintball Gun in 1970

Daisy Manufacturing existed in its original incarnation for a century before the same events that triggered its birth also triggered its transformation into another company. Like Hamilton's metal and wire apparatus, the currents of change were sparked by invention, but unlike the forces that caused Daisy Manufacturing's creation, the source of innovation came from within the company's organization. In 1970, a Daisy Manufacturing engineer named James Hale invented and patented a device called the "Splotchmarker," which propelled a projectile of encapsulated, oil-based paint. Hale's Splotchmarker was marketed as a device to mark cattle and trees for later identification, an innovation that created a sidelight business for Daisy Manufacturing, at the time enjoying considerable success manufacturing various models of air-powered rifles. Daisy Manufacturing signed a contract to manufacture the paint markers for a company named Nelson Paint Company, which sold them commercially. The business relationship endured for years, as Hale's invention took considerably longer than the nine years it took Hamilton's invention to fundamentally alter the strategic focus of Daisy Manufacturing.

In the two decades following the invention of the Splotchmarker, a less utilitarian but more commercially viable use for Hale's creation developed. People began to use the air-powered gun to mark each other with paint, conducting mock battles fought in open fields, forests, or wherever the new breed of paintball enthusiasts collected on the weekends. At first, and for quite some time, the new recreational activity was taken up by a group commonly referred to as survivalists: adult males, generally, who adopted many of the characteristics of a military lifestyle. For years, paintball existed as such, as a little-known activity practiced by those living on the fringe of society, but gradually the use of markers, as the paint guns were called, began to attract a much broader fan base. During the 1990s, a number of sports and recreational activities previously characterized as peripheral pursuits moved into the mainstream, gaining legitimacy and recognition amid widespread exposure. Paintball was one of those niche activities whose participation rate mushroomed in the 1990s, becoming a business worth hundreds of millions of dollars in revenue each year.

Paintball's rapid rise in popularity was not entirely an organic phenomenon. The marketing and promotional efforts of corporations contributed mightily to the sport's growth, perhaps none more than those undertaken by a Canadian company named Brass Eagle. Based in Mississauga, Ontario, Brass Eagle crossed paths with Daisy in 1993, when Daisy terminated its agreement with Nelson Paint Company and signed a royalty agreement with Brass Eagle to manufacture, market, and distribute paintball products for the Canadian company. The relationship forged with Brass Eagle in 1993 marked the beginning of a concerted and serious effort to take the business of paintball to a new level, an objective management planned to achieve by developing a plan with several important initiatives.

The primary concern was to shed the perception of paintball as the exclusive domain of eccentric survivalists and replace it with an image that would appeal to a much larger audience. To accomplish such a task, management comprehensively changed the way paintball products were distributed, marketed, and merchandised, implementing a multi-pronged strategic plan that distinguished the Daisy-Brass Eagle partnership from all competitors. The rapid growth of paintball as a new sport for the 1990s was the result.

Before the intervention of Daisy-Brass Eagle management, the characteristics of the paintball market were consistent with the sport's existence on the periphery of society. The few products that were available—generally limited to markers and paintballs—were sold either by catalogue distributors or in a small number of hard-to-find specialty stores, where they were retailed as high-precision instruments with hefty price tags attached. Daisy-Brass Eagle executives realized substantial revenues could not be gained from marketing a small number of high-priced markers. Instead, they knew they had to market to the masses, which, if done right, would also promote the growth of the sport. Consequently, they developed a full line of markers distinguished by price and performance, giving nearly every potential paintball customer a model he or she could afford. Further, the products marketed under the Brass Eagle name represented a host of accessories, including face masks, protective eyewear, and other items. Equally as important as fleshing out their product line, the officials in charge radically altered their distribution methods by concentrating on mass merchandisers, such as Kmart and Wal-Mart, and major sporting goods retailers.

1990s Transformation of Daisy Manufacturing into Brass Eagle

Implementing the changes that created a foundation capable of supporting broadly based growth did not occur overnight. The Daisy-Brass Eagle partnership gradually made the necessary changes, and as their efforts matured, so did the market for paintball equipment. By the mid-1990s, great strides had been achieved, prompting Daisy management to up its ante in what for years had been a sidelight business. In October 1995, Daisy purchased the Brass Eagle name, trademarks, patents, and other assets, including tools, dies, jigs, and molds, from Brass Eagle.

The Brass Eagle purchase occurred exactly a century after the board of directors of Plymouth Iron ratified the transformation into Daisy Manufacturing. The precedence took on fuller meaning less than two years later when Daisy Manufacturing management demonstrated its willingness to completely alter its business direction. In September 1997, Daisy Manufacturing changed its corporate title to Brass Eagle Inc., a profound decision for a company whose legacy as a firearms manufacturer was deeply woven into the fabric of American society. More fundamental changes followed a month later when the company initiated a sweeping corporate reorganization. In November 1997, the company transferred all its non-paintball related assets, operations, and liabilities to a newly created subsidiary, Daisy Manufacturing Company, which was spun off as a separate, private company. Concurrently, Brass Eagle converted to public ownership.

By the time Brass Eagle completed its IPO, the company's commitment to paintball had realized encouraging results. In 1993, when the company began a serious effort to promote and capitalize on paintball, annual revenues from the sport amounted to less than $5 million. By the end of 1996—the first year Brass Eagle introduced a full line of paintball accessories—revenues had climbed to $13.8 million and then soared to $36.1 million shortly after the completion of the IPO. Company officials were after far more, however, targeting a lion's share of what was estimated to be a $250 million market annually.

To achieve substantial revenue growth, Brass Eagle further developed its self-assumed role as the ambassador of paintball,

---

Key Dates:

1882: Plymouth Iron Windmill Company is launched in Plymouth, Michigan.
1895: The windmill manufacturer transforms itself into Daisy Manufacturing Company, Inc. in honor of Daisy line of compressed-air guns.
1970: An engineer for Daisy Manufacturing invents the Splotchmarker, the first paintball gun.
1993: Daisy Manufacturing signs a royalty agreement with Brass Eagle.
1995: Daisy Manufacturing acquires Brass Eagle.
1997: Daisy Manufacturing sells all non-paintball assets and changes its name to Brass Eagle.
1999: Brass Eagle acquires CM Support, Inc.

---

championing its growth by escorting it into the mainstream market and increasing the number of playing facilities. Historically, paintball had been played in secluded, rural areas, yet another characteristic of the sport that Brass Eagle officials realized they needed to alter to promote widespread growth. Accordingly, in the months following the IPO, the company began promoting a modular paintball field concept suitable for play in relatively small, self-contained areas. Before the end of the decade, the company began marketing a version of the concept called Pursuit Park, which was designed to be incorporated into existing family amusement centers, including miniature golf courses, baseball batting cages, and go-cart tracks. Along this same vein, Brass Eagle joined forces with other partners and began developing Challenge Park Xtreme, located on 154 acres on the Des Plaines River in Joliet, Illinois. The facility, which was expected to open in September 2000, was designed as a combination sports and entertainment complex, featuring several paintball fields, skateboarding ramps, climbing walls, mountain biking trails, a BMX track, and an inline skating rink.

As Brass Eagle's influence over the development of paintball widened, its leadership role translated into ever increasing financial figures and national recognition. In 1998, when sales leaped to $75.1 million, the company was coming off a three-year period of prolific growth, registering a 137 percent rate in annual revenue growth and a more than 300 percent rate in annual earnings growth. The financial gains did not go unnoticed, as the business press paid tribute to a company regarded as the worldwide leader in the manufacturing and distribution of makers, paintballs, and numerous accessories. In

1998, *Business Week* magazine heralded Brass Eagle as one of its "Hot Growth" companies, selecting the company as 39th in a list of 100 fast-growth companies. *Industry Week* also praised Brass Eagle, naming it as one of the top 25 small manufacturers in the country for its ability to effectively coordinate growth, innovation, and profits.

By the end of the 1990s, Brass Eagle management had forged a powerful manufacturing, distributing, and marketing force. In October 1998, the company launched its first national television advertising campaign, debuting on networks such as MTV, ESPN, and ESPN2. The commercials, featuring a recurring character named Francis, were expected to reach a target audience of 30 million viewers during their first month on the air. Another series of commercials was slated for broadcast in 1999. In January 1999, Brass Eagle acquired CM Support, Inc., a leading manufacturer of paintball accessories that previously had been a major supplier of products to Brass Eagle. Concurrent with the $5 million CM Support acquisition, the company announced an agreement with The Outdoor Research Group Inc. for the Los Angeles-based company to manufacture 13 paintball products for Brass Eagle, including knee pads, gear bags, and ball haulers.

As Brass Eagle entered the 21st century, the paintball market it helped to create was growing at an estimated 25 percent annual rate. As the only company to offer a full line of merchandise and the only company to distribute its products to mass merchandisers, Brass Eagle occupied a singular and dominant position in its industry, enabling it to assume an aggressive posture toward future growth. Looking ahead, the company anticipated further acquisitions to bolster its capabilities. In March 2000, Brass Eagle signed an agreement to acquire JT USA, LP, a leading manufacturer of protective accessories and apparel for the paintball industry. Expansion into Europe and South America also factored into the company's plans.

Principal Competitors

R.P. Scherer Corporation; eCom eCom.com, Inc.

Further Reading

Lovel, Jim, "Brass Eagle Acquires Company, Receives National Recognition," *Arkansas Business,* January 11, 1999, p. 10.
McLean, Bethany, "Companies: Who Said Paintball Is for the Lunatic Fringe?," *Fortune,* March 2, 1998, p. 46.
Wood, Jeffrey, "Paintball 'Brass' Targets Market, Gaming Safety," *Arkansas Business,* August 1999, p. 14.

—Jeffrey L. Covell

BRITISH-BORNEO

British-Borneo Oil & Gas PLC

9th Floor, East Wing, Bowater House
68 Knightsbridge
London SW1X 7BN
United Kingdom
Telephone: +44 (0) 20 7590 6400
Fax: +44 (0) 20 7590 6499
Web site: http://www.british-borneo.co.uk

Public Company
Founded: 1912 as The British-Borneo Petroleum Syndicate
Employees: 131
Sales: £133 million (1999)
Stock Exchanges: London
Ticker Symbol: BBOR.L
NAIC: 211111 Crude Petroleum and Natural Gas
   Extraction; 211112 Natural Gas Liquid Extraction

Formerly known as The British-Borneo Petroleum Syndicate, British-Borneo Oil & Gas PLC is one of the United Kingdom's oldest oil companies. It is also the U.K.'s third largest independent oil company (following Enterprise Oil PLC and LASMO PLC), the U.K.'s sixth largest overall oil company (adding Shell Transport and Trading Co. PLC, Premier Oil PLC, and Cairn Energy PLC), and one of the leading oil and gas exploration and production companies in the world. The company is active on six continents, with a core focus in the United States, the United Kingdom, and Australia, particularly in deepwater drilling in the Gulf of Mexico and on low-risk exploration on the U.K. Continental Shelf in the North Sea.

Gas Progenitors: 1792–1948

As far back as 1792 in England, William Murdoch (1754–1839) piped gas into his home at Redruth to light it. Employed as an engineer at Cornwall-based Boulton & Watt, Murdoch moved shortly thereafter to Birmingham to develop gas lighting commercially. Together with another former Boulton & Watt employee, Samuel Clegg (1781–1861), who became his assistant in 1801, Murdoch began installing commercial plants in 1805. Fredrick Albert Winsor (1763–1830) meanwhile, who

had seen gas lighting experiments by Philippe Lebon (d. 1804), began giving lectures on the subject at the Lyceum Theatre in 1804, as well as demonstrations at Pall Mall and Carlton House Terrace in 1807. This led to Winsor's attempt to create a national company to produce gas at central stations and pipe the gas to users all over England, which Murdoch opposed. In 1810, Winsor secured an Act to create The Gas Light and Coke Company, which was financed and commenced operations in 1812, and Preston became the first city to be so lit, in 1816.

Thus began over 150 years of stiff regulation of the gas industry by the British government, including The Gas Works Clauses Acts (1847, 1871), The Sale of Gas Act (1859), the founding of The Gas Workers' Union (1889), The Gas Regulation Act (1920), and The Gas Act (1948), which nationalized the gas industry in England, Scotland, and Wales.

British-Borneo Petroleum Syndicate: 1912–88

Founded in 1912, British-Borneo Petroleum Syndicate was created to oversee oil and gas licenses in British North Borneo and Brunei, where it also carried out exploration operations until 1925. Exploration continued in other areas of the world until World War II. By this time, there were over 1,000 local gas interests in the United Kingdom. With the institution of The Gas Act in 1948, they were divided into 12 Area Boards, all of which reported to the newly created Gas Council (1949), which was to act as a liaison to The Ministry of Fuel and Power. With the stringent regulations and nationalization of the industry, British-Borneo left the active exploration of the industry and entered into a period of relative dormancy—running for more than half a century—in which it operated as an investment company with a bias towards the oil sector, investing in other firms such as British Petroleum, Royal Dutch/Shell, and Ultramar.

The Gas Council was abolished in 1973 and replaced by The British Gas Corporation (BGC). With the passing of The Oil and Gas (Enterprise) Act in 1982, the British government allowed BGC to carry third-party gas to users. In turn, this led to the privatization of the industry on August 24, 1986, when the government transferred the assets of BGC to British Gas PLC, then owned entirely by the government. Shares were offered for the first time in December 1986.

+---+
| **Company Perspectives:** |
| |
| *We are an independent oil and gas explora- |
| tion and production company with booked |
| reserves of 254 million barrels oil equivalent|
| (boe). We aim to combine the best practices |
| of a major with the innovation and rapid |
| response of an independent.* |
+---+

Acquisitions and Changing Core Competencies: 1989–99

With the privatization of the gas and oil industries, British-Borneo began to come out of the cocoon of safe investments it had wrapped itself in. In 1989, the company, which until that time had no full-time employees, hired Alan J. Gaynor, formerly of Whitehall Petroleum, a North Sea exploration company which was later acquired by Amerada Hess, and also a former executive of British Petroleum (now BP Amoco PLC). Gaynor, who had just sold his own company, GB Petroleum, was charged with helping the company liquidate its £20 million in investments in other companies and put the proceeds into safe oil exploration assets, thus avoiding large capital gains taxes. Gaynor turned British-Borneo's focus back to direct participation in the oil and gas industry, as the company, during the next three years, began extensive efforts to expand its business in the United Kingdom, most notably through the £55 million purchase of Norsk Hydro's U.K. assets, as well as acquiring a ten percent stake in the Victor gas field and Unocal's remaining U.K. business. Gaynor also brought in more talent, securing Steve Holliday, formerly of Exxon, as international director in charge of managing international expansion, and Peter Hill, Hardy's former exploration director, as technical director, to oversee the company's exploration efforts.

In 1995, the company acquired the deep water Morpeth field from Shell Oil, making British-Borneo the only independent in the industry with a deep water presence in the Gulf of Mexico. In conjunction with Houston, Texas-based firm Atlantia, the company created a new mono-hull tension leg platform called SeaStar.

In 1997, the company purchased an eight percent interest in Australia-based Petroz, giving British-Borneo assets in the cooperative zone between Timor, Indonesia, and Australia. Also that year, the company received a 17.5 percent stake in two highly prospective areas in the Shetlands region of the United Kingdom.

More growth occurred in September 1998, when British-Borneo acquired 62.8 percent of rival U.K. independent Hardy Oil & Gas. The merger strengthened British-Borneo's position in the United Kingdom, as well as gave it entrance to the Australian market and the emerging Pakistani market; Hardy, meanwhile, received funding for exploration and appraisal efforts, easier financing for development projects, and access to the Gulf of Mexico deep water fields. The combined company, now known as British-Borneo Oil & Gas PLC, placed itself in the top ranks of independent British oil and gas firms.

Later that year, a major field was discovered in Pakistan, and a joint-venture between British-Borneo's Hardy division, Pakistan Petroleum Limited, and Exploration GmbH began to develop it. Also during 1998, the company began utilizing its SeaStar platforms off the coast of Brazil in joint ventures with Amerada Hess, PETROBRAS, and Odebrecht.

The Bayu-Undan liquids and gas development project (of which British-Borneo owned 6.72 percent), located in the Zone of Cooperation between East Timor and Australia, made significant progress in 1999. In November of that year, the partners (which included Phillips Petroleum Company) sanctioned development of the first (liquids) phase of the project (comprising the offshore facilities) to produce and process 1.1 billion standard cubic feet per day of raw gas, extraction of 110,000 barrels per day of condensate and liquid petroleum gas, and the re-injection of the resulting dry gas. Total cost for this first phase was estimated to be US$1.4 billion, with British-Borneo footing US$92.9 million of that, and production was scheduled to begin in late 2003 or early 2004. In the second phase of the project, Bayu's significant gas resource would be exported to shore near Darwin, Australia, where the company continued to make progress developing options for both domestic gas sales within Australia and possible export.

Another example of British-Borneo's drilling success in 1999 was the company-operated Woollybutt, Australia oil field—of which British-Borneo owned 30 percent—where a successful appraisal well was drilled in 1999. The "rationalization" of the company's Australian portfolio was completed in early 1999, with the sale of its producing interests in Harriet and East Spar for US$80 million, together with interests in a number of exploration leases in the Gulf of Mexico. Finally, the company was awarded a 50 percent interest in a deep-water block in the Canning Basin, offshore Western Australia, during that year; the other 50 percent went to U.S.-based Kerr-McGee Corporation.

During 1999, British-Borneo's oil and gas production more than doubled from 1998, to 43,233 barrels of oil equivalent (boe) per day, and the company had proven and probable reserves of 262 million boe. Total revenue for 1999 climbed to £133 million, up from £62 million in 1998, and net profit on the year climbed back into the black, reaching £16.9 million, following 1998's net loss of £81 million.

However, things were not coming up all roses. A number of setbacks plagued the company. Delivery of Morpeth development wells was slow, resulting in what CEO Gaynor called in the fiscal 1998 annual report "a substantial cost overrun and delayed peak production." A sustained fall in world oil prices during 1997–98, which brought them to their lowest levels for 12 years, combined with what CEO Gaynor called in the fiscal 1998 annual report "a slower than anticipated build-up in production at [the] Morpeth field in the deep water Gulf of Mexico" significantly "reduced cashflow and increased [the company's] borrowing requirement." Early abandonment of the Durward and Dauntless fields in the North Sea cost the company some £14 million and operational problems led to lower productions than forecast at both the Allegheny and Morpeth fields. In the latter half of 1999, difficult sea conditions known as "loop currents" shut down operations on both the Morpeth and Allegheny platforms for nearly three months, increasing costs and delaying planned drilling and completion work. Around October, Allegheny went back on stream, but only had three producing wells,

<table>
<tr><td colspan="2">Key Dates:</td></tr>
<tr><td>1912:</td><td>British-North Borneo Petroleum Syndicate is founded.</td></tr>
<tr><td>1925:</td><td>The oil and gas management and exploration firm begins a lengthy period of shelved operations, choosing instead to function as an investment company.</td></tr>
<tr><td>1989:</td><td>British-Borneo resurfaces, liquidating its £20 million investment cache and ultimately pursuing oil and gas exploration once again.</td></tr>
<tr><td>1998:</td><td>Name changes to British-Borneo Oil & Gas PLC after merger with U.K. rival Hardy Oil & Gas.</td></tr>
<tr><td>2000:</td><td>British-Borneo agrees to be purchased by Italian energy group ENI (Ente Nazionale Idrocarburi) S.p.A.</td></tr>
</table>

two of which did not perform as expected, and one of which was shut pending rededication in 2000.

By the end of 1999, the company was facing a total debt of £525 million and, according to the company's fiscal 1999 annual report, "cash flow and debt level [were] adversely affected, greatly reducing the company's financial resilience. Consequently the Board has been seeking purchasers for its Gulf of Mexico business and certain other assets to reduce borrowings and restore financial flexibility."

To that end, in September 1999 British-Borneo entered into an agreement with Jehan Energy Limited to sell the entire share capital of Hardy Exploration & Production India Inc. to Jehan. Under the terms of the agreement, Jehan took over the entire business of Hardy in India with the exception of the interest in the contact area known as CB-OS/1. All national staff continued in their positions and expatriate management was supplemented by Jehan personnel.

Changing Hands: 2000

As the company moved into its new headquarters at Bowater House, Knightsbridge, London in March 2000, British-Borneo agreed to an offer to be purchased by Agip (U.K.) Ventures PLC, a division of Italian energy group ENI S.p.A., for approximately £788 million in cash and debt acquisition, ending nearly a century as an independent British oil and gas company.

One of the world's largest oil and gas operators, ENI was also one of Italy's largest companies. Based in Rome, ENI operated natural gas networks, electric power plants, refineries, service stations, and engineering firms. The acquisition of British-Borneo allowed ENI's hydrocarbon production group to double its production in the Gulf of Mexico, as well as strengthen its position in Australia and Brazil, and provide the Italian concern new entry into the emerging Asian markets.

Principal Competitors

Enterprise Oil PLC; LASMO PLC; Shell Transport and Trading Co. PLC; Premier Oil PLC; Cairn Energy PLC.

Further Reading

Blitz, James, "British-Borneo Stake in Gulf of Mexico Field," *Financial Times*, August 28, 1997, p. 21.

"British-Borneo Buys into U.K. Wave Energy," *Oil and Gas Journal*, October 19, 1998, p. 42.

"British-Borneo Hikes Morpeth Reserves," *Oil and Gas Journal*, February 24, 1997, p. 36.

Chan, Karen, and Angela Macdonald-Smith, "British-Borneo to Acquire Hardy Oil: Stock Transaction Is Valued at $573 Million," *Wall Street Journal, Europe*, September 15, 1998, p. 3.

Collin, Jane, "Sun Appears Ready to Set on British-Borneo as Independent," *Oil Daily*, February 8, 2000.

Corzine, Robert, "British-Borneo Shares Fall on 'Disappointing' Report," *Financial Times*, April 5, 1997, p. 20.

——, "Production Rise Helps Brit-Borneo," *Financial Times*, September 2, 1994, p. 19.

Crowden, Michael, "Atlantia, British-Borneo Develop SeaStar," *Offshore*, February 1996, p. 16.

Delmar, Robert J., "Progress in Australia-Timor's Bayu-Undan," *Offshore*, September 1999, p. 20.

DeLuca, Marshall, "Bayu-Undan Beginning to Roll, but ZOCA Agreement Needed Soon," *Offshore*, November 1999, p. 122.

——, "Production Has Commenced from the SeaStar Mono-Hull TLP," *Offshore*, November 1998, p. 11.

Forster, Christine, "Equity in Phillips' Timor Gap Bayu-Undan Project May Shift," *Platt's Oilgram News*, October 28, 1999, p. 2.

Forster, Christine, and Jim Washer, "London Wonders: What Is Borneo's Aim for Petroz?," *Platt's Oilgram News*, February 18, 1998, p. 1.

Furlow, William, "British-Borneo Solution Clarified," *Offshore*, April 1998, p. 28.

Harverson, Patrick, "British Borneo Jumps to 8.1m Pounds Sterling," *Financial Times*, September 12, 1996, p. 34.

Holberton, Simon, "Hanson Gas Arm Signs 100m Pounds Sterling Deal," *Financial Times*, August 15, 1996, p. 17.

Hollinger, Peggy, "British Borneo Makes Cash Call for 54 Million Pounds Sterling," *Financial Times*, January 27, 1996, p. 9.

——, "Gas Move Benefits British Borneo," *Financial Times*, March 18, 1994, p. 24.

——, "Reid to Head British-Borneo," *Financial Times*, March 24, 1995, p. 26.

Knott, David, "U.K. Independents Try New Approaches in Expanded Worldwide Exploration Push," *Oil and Gas Journal*, September 30, 1996, p. 36.

Levi, Jim, "Drilling Deep in the Gulf of Mexico," *Petroleum Economist*, June 1999, p. 50.

Marsh, Virginia, "British-Borneo Steps Up Global Diversification," *Financial Times*, September 19, 1997, p. 23.

——, "British-Borneo Warns on 'Silly' Lease Bids," *Financial Times*, March 20, 1998, p. 28.

Martinson, Jane, "British Borneo Announces Rights Issue to Raise 167 Million Pounds Sterling," *Financial Times*, July 17, 1997, p. 25.

——, "British-Borneo to Double Exploration Spending," *Financial Times*, March 21, 1997, p. 21.

Mortis, Guntis, "Shell Advancing Gulf Deepwater Developments," *Oil and Gas Journal*, April 28, 1997, p. 26.

Peel, Michael, "British-Borneo Bids for Hardy," *Financial Times*, September 15, 1998, p. 29.

Smith, Jennifer E., "Loop Currents, Lack of Specialists Cited for Rise in Costs," *Offshore*, November 1999, p. 24.

Washer, Jim, "Focus on Enterprise As British Borneo Stock Jumps," *Platt's Oilgram News*, May 24, 1999, p. 1.

Wold, Melanie, "United We Stand: British-Borneo Won't Let Hardy Rest on Its Laurels," *Euroil*, October 1998, p. 12.

—Daryl F. Mallett

Broadcom Corporation

16215 Alton Parkway
P.O. Box 57013
Irvine, California 92619-7013
U.S.A.
Telephone: (949) 450-8700
Fax: (949) 450-8710
Web site: http://www.broadcom.com

Public Company
Incorporated: 1991
Employees: 500
Sales: $518.2 million (1999)
Stock Exchanges: NASDAQ
Ticker Symbol: BRCM
NAIC: 334413 Semiconductor and Related Device
Manufacturing; 334419 Other Electronic Component
Manufacturing

Broadcom Corporation is one of several companies contributing to the infrastructure that will bring high-speed Internet and other services directly to homes and offices. The company specializes in designing high-speed integrated circuits (ICs), or chips, that are used in applications such as cable TV set-top boxes, cable modems, and local area network (LAN) cards. The company also provides key technology and products in emerging broadband markets such as digital subscriber loop (DSL), fixed wireless, direct broadcast satellite, and terrestrial digital broadcast. Extremely popular with investors since going public in 1998, the company has used its stock to acquire smaller high-tech companies and integrate their technology.

Communications Markets: 1991–95

Broadcom was founded as a private company in 1991 by Henry T. Nicholas III, Ph.D., and Henry Samueli, Ph.D. The two men had 35 years combined experience in communications integrated circuits (IC). Nicholas was Broadcom's president and CEO, while Samueli was the company's vice-president of research and development. While working at TRW Inc., the pair gained experience in the Defense Department's Very High-Speed IC (VHSIC) program that later enabled them to create powerful silicon compilers for the quick design of commercial integrated circuits (ICs). Samueli was a tenured electrical engineering professor at UCLA and Nicholas's doctoral program adviser.

The company's basic strategy was to focus on emerging markets in communications that used cable or wire. Using its design cell library and silicon compiler technology, it was able to quickly develop chip products, or integrated circuits (ICs), for applications such as Fast Ethernet or advanced cable TV systems. Leveraging its military-based technology, Broadcom was able to accelerate the development of its commercial ICs.

Broadcom got its first big break in 1993 with a contract from Scientific-Atlanta, Inc. of Norcross, Georgia, which was supplying TV set-top boxes for Time Warner Corp.'s experimental cable system in Orlando, Florida. Broadcom initially supplied Scientific-Atlanta with a three-chip set for digital demodulation in the set-top boxes, and within ten months had integrated the solution into one IC using a technology called quadrature-amplitude modulation (QAM).

For the first few years Broadcom relied on full-custom designs and licensing agreements for revenue as well as funding from its two founders. Its early custom-chip customers included Rockwell International, Analog Devices, and U.S. Air Force contractors producing global positioning systems. The small and relatively unknown company was able to gain such customers because of what its engineers accomplished and the quality of its engineering team, including the two founders.

In 1994 the company's revenues exceeded $5 million. It also received about $5 million in corporate financing from Intel Corporation, which was interested in Broadcom's Fast Ethernet chips for networking. In the fall of 1994 it began shipping volume production quantities of chips using the production capacities of American Microsystems Inc. of Pocatello, Idaho, and Taiwan Semiconductor Manufacturing Co. Revenues were expected to increase fourfold in 1995. Fast Ethernet, with 100-megabit/second ICs, was seen as a new market for potential growth. The company had about 50 employees.

<table><tr><td>**Company Perspectives:**

Broadcom believes that one of its key competitive advantages is its broad base of core technologies encompassing the complete design space from systems to silicon. The company has developed and continues to build on four primary technology foundations: proprietary communications systems algorithms and protocols; advanced digital signal processing hardware architectures; silicon compiler design methodologies and advanced cell library development for both standard cell and full-custom IC design; high-performance analog and mixed-signal circuit design using industry-standard CMOS processes.</td></tr></table>

Supporting High-Speed Internet Access: 1996

As Internet usage quickly expanded in 1996, regional Bell operating companies were competing with cable operators to become the dominant providers of Internet access. It was not yet clear whether cable modems hooked to coaxial cables or telephone modems with asymmetrical digital subscriber lines (ADSL) would become the dominant provider of Internet access. Broadcom was positioned to support both technologies. It was developing an ASDL transceiver for Northern Telecom (Nortel) and also rolling out a cable modem chipset for coaxial cable applications.

Using the same QAM technology that it used for its QAMLink line of devices for cable TV set-top boxes, Broadcom implemented QAM in cable modems and ADSL transceivers. Broadcom's QAMLink cable modem chipset provided 1,000 times the bandwidth then available over phone lines at 28.8 kilobits-per-second. Supporting the chipsets through strategic alliances with Broadcom were such original equipment manufacturers (OEMs) as General Instrument, Motorola, Hewlett-Packard, and Scientific-Atlanta.

By 1997 Broadcom's vision was to provide the technology to make the Internet accessible without a personal computer. The company was making the silicon chips inside nearly every cable modem and digital set-top box. *Red Herring,* a technology monthly, named Broadcom the best private company in the United States, and Nicholas and Samueli were named to the "Top 50 Cyber Elite" by *Time Digital.* It was estimated that cable companies deployed about 20,000 cable modems in 1996 and 100,000 in 1997. The demand for cable modems was expected to explode to one million in 1998. Each cable modem contained about $35 worth of Broadcom chips. For 1997 Broadcom reported a net loss of $1.2 million on revenues of $37 million.

For 1998 Broadcom forecast it would provide $30–$45 worth of chips for two million digital cable set-top boxes. Demand, however, was dependent on the ability of cable systems to upgrade their infrastructures. Most systems were not designed for 500 channels or two-way communication with the Internet.

Going Public, Rising in Valuation: 1998–2000

Broadcom went public in April 1998. It had grown to about 320 employees and boasted 36 Ph.D.s on its payroll. The company was popular with investors, because it was making or preparing to make devices that supported high-speed voice and data transmission for computer networks, cable modems and digital TV set-top boxes, high-speed telephone modems, and direct broadcast satellite systems. In other words, Broadcom appeared to be positioned to play a big role in the convergence of computers, telephones, and television. Its two biggest customers were 3Com Corporation and General Instrument Corporation.

In the first six months following the IPO, Broadcom's stock doubled in price and occasionally traded above $72, three times its original price. In September 1998 the company issued another three million shares to the public. By January 1999 Broadcom's two founders were billionaires. At least 300 employees became millionaires, from engineers to receptionists. The firm's stock hit $100 in December 1998 and was approaching $200 a share in early January. The company's revenues for 1998 were $203.1 million and net income was $36.4 million.

Series of Acquisitions: 1999

In 1999 Broadcom began making a series of acquisitions that would expand its technological capabilities. In January 1999 Broadcom acquired startup Maverick Networks, a developer of multi-layer switching technology for enterprise networks, for about $104 million in stock. The acquisition of the two-year-old company gave Broadcom the means to enter the market for corporate enterprise switches.

In February Broadcom announced it would provide products for in-home networking that would transmit voice, video, and data at high speeds over existing telephone wires. The company dubbed its home networking technology MediaShare. Nortel Networks, anxious to maintain a competitive edge in the broadband arena, adopted very high speed digital subscriber line (DSL) technology that was jointly developed with Broadcom. Nortel said its new scalable DSL transceiver would support digital television, high-speed Internet access, videoconferencing, and multiple Internet protocol data streams.

In an effort to reach small and medium sized companies, Broadcom selected Insight Electronics as its first authorized distributor. Through Insight, which was selected because of its technical expertise, Broadcom products would be made available throughout North and South America. Until now Broadband's customer focus had been on large companies, such as Cisco Systems, Nortel Networks, 3Com, Motorola, and Scientific-Atlanta.

Broadcom acquired Epigram Inc., a leader in home networking silicon technology, in April 1999 for $316 million in stock. Home networking was still in its infancy, but analysts estimated the home networking market could reach $1.4 billion in four years. The acquisition helped boost Broadcom's market capitalization by more than $850 million as investors drove up the stock price. Purchasing Epigram all but assured Broadcom it would be first to market with its own home networking technology. Epigram's technology was widely expected to be the basis for the Home Phoneline Networking Alliance's 2.0 standard, an expectation that was confirmed by the Alliance's announcement in July 1999 that it had chosen technologies from Broadcom and

Lucent Technologies as the basis for the next generation in home networks.

Broadcom introduced a new, faster chip (IC) that could transmit data, voice, and video signals on a copper line at one gigabit per second, ten times faster than existing technology and a speed then attained only on fiber optic cables. Cisco Systems, 3Com, Nortel, Hewlett-Packard, and Dell were all developing products based on the new chip. Again, the company's stock soared on rumors of the announcements.

Amedia Inc., a design engineering firm and developer of advanced silicon technology that was based in India, was acquired. Then Broadcom purchased HotHaus Technologies of Vancouver, British Columbia, for $280 million in stock. HotHaus made software for embedded digital signal processors. The acquisition added to Broadcom's portfolio of ICs for broadband applications in DSL, cable modem, and wireless environments. The company hoped to bring Voice Over IP to home through an outside provider's broadband network, such as a cable operator, a DSL service provider, or via satellite provider. The Voice Over IP market was forecast to exceed $1.8 billion by 2003, up from $290 million in 1999.

In August 1999 Broadcom acquired AltoCom Inc., a maker of software-based modems, or ''soft modems,'' for $180 million in stock. The acquisition gave Broadcom access to another area of Internet technology, enabling Broadcom to build chips that would work with both cable and phone lines.

Rumors began circulating in the summer of 1999 that Broadband cofounder Henry Nicholas would purchase the California Angels and the Anaheim Mighty Ducks from the Walt Disney Company. In August 1999 he gave the University of California-Irvine's rowing team a $1.28 million stock donation, the largest athletic donation in UCI's history. By mid-1999 70 percent of the 300 employees when the company went public were millionaires or better.

In October 1999 Nicholas and Samueli formed a partnership with Marvin Winkler, chairman of Gotcha International, to launch the Broadband Interactive Group (BIG). The privately held group planned to use Broadcom's high-speed communications chips to deliver interactive programming about sports and surfing. While Broadband was manufacturing interactive TV chips for cable set-top boxes, hardly anyone was using that technology, because hardly anyone was offering interactive TV services. BIG's goal was to create a demand for such services. It purchased all of Gotcha's media operations, including Gotcha TV, Gotcha.com, and three magazines. The three partners also discussed the possibility of forming a group to run the day-to-day operations of the Angels and the Ducks with the Walt Disney Co. Finally, though, Nicholas had to put an end to the rumors that the group was planning to buy the two sports teams.

Perhaps relieved that Nicholas and Samueli were not interested in owning a professional sports team, Wall Street sent Broadcom's stock surging in November 1999. With its stock price rising over $200 a share, the company's market capitalization was approaching $22 billion. The rise came in anticipation of a stock split, which often precedes a run-up in a company's stock price. By January 2000, the stock was trading at more than $300 a share. A two-for-one split was subsequently announced for February 11.

At the end of 1999 Henry Samueli, together with his wife Susan, donated $20 million to the University of California-Irvine's engineering program and $30 million to the engineering program at University of California-Los Angeles (UCLA).

Broadcom continued acquiring companies in 2000. In January it acquired BlueSteel Networks Inc., a maker of chips that scramble and unscramble data sent over the Internet, for $123 million in stock at the stock's closing price of $328.50. BlueSteel's high-performance security processors protected Internet transmissions from hackers. Broadcom noted a growing trend to include security in every application across networks, especially for consumers who wanted to participate in areas such as electronic commerce and home banking.

In March Broadcom acquired Digital Furnace Corp., an Atlanta, Georgia-based developer of software that increased the flow of information over cable lines, for about $136 million in stock. Digital Furnace's software compressed data sent over cable lines, thus tripling the capacity of cable networks equipped with Broadcom's high–speed communication chips. That same month Broadcom acquired Stellar Semiconductor for about $162 million. Stellar was a Silicon Valley designer of 3D video chips. Its cable modem chips could accelerate 3D graphics by reducing the amount of data and time it took cable TV set-top boxes to display three-dimensional pictures on TV screens.

Following the February stock split, Broadcom's stock continued to soar, reaching nearly $250 a share. The company's market capitalization was more than $50 billion. As a result of its acquisitions in 1999, Broadcom reported revenues of $518.2 million that year, nearly two-and-a-half times 1998 revenue; net income reached $83.3 million, more than three times 1998's net income. Broadcom continued to be popular with investors and was positioned as a supplier of high-speed chips to the growing communications industry.

Principal Competitors

LSI Logic Corporation; VLSI Technology Inc.; Advanced Micro Devices, Inc.; AT&T; Motorola Inc.; National Semiconductor Corporation; Hughes Electronics Corporation; Raytheon Company; Texas Instruments Inc.; Intel Corporation; Conexant Systems Inc.

Further Reading

Ascierto, Jerry, and Arik Hesseldahl, "Broadcom Acquires AltoCom; Releases First Product from Maverick Acquisition," *Electronic News (1991)*, August 23, 1999, p. 18.

Bartimo, Jim, "Broadcom: Pumping Network Iron," *PC Magazine*, October 19, 1999, p. 95.

Biagi, Susan, "A.M. Report; Nortel Adopts Broadcom VDSL Chipset," *Telephony*, March 15, 1999.

"Broadcom Enters Home Networking with MediaShare," *Electronic News (1991)*, February 15, 1999, p. 23.

Campbell, Ronald, "Broadcom of Irvine, Calif., Celebrates Fame by Returning to Work," *Knight-Ridder/Tribune Business News*, May 14, 1998.

——, "Broadcom of Irvine, Calif., Makes the Computer Chips in Most Cable Modems," *Knight-Ridder/Tribune Business News*, October 31, 1997.

——, "California-Based Broadcom to Sell More Stock to Public," *Knight-Ridder/Tribune Business News*, September 30, 1998.

——, "Group Chooses Technology of Broadcom, Lucent for Future Home Networks," *Knight-Ridder/Tribune Business News*, July 27, 1999.

——, "Irvine, Calif.-Based Broadcom Demonstrates New, Super-Fast Chip," *Knight-Ridder/Tribune Business News*, May 13, 1999.

——, "Irvine, Calif.-Based Broadcom Reaches New Financial Heights," *Knight-Ridder/Tribune Business News*, January 8, 1999.

——, "Irvine, Calif.-Based Firm Prepares for Future of Home Networking," *Knight-Ridder/Tribune Business News*, May 2, 1999.

Cohen, Sarah, "Broadcom in Middle of Internet Access Fray," *Electronic News (1991)*, September 2, 1996, p. 14.

Elliott, Heidi, "Broadcom Gains Insight," *Electronic News (1991)*, April 19, 1999, p. 40.

Farnsworth, Chris, "Broadcom Co-Founder Donates $20 Million to California College," *Knight-Ridder/Tribune Business News*, December 21, 1999.

——, "Broadcom Co-Founders, Media-Company Executive Launch Interactive-TV Firm," *Knight-Ridder/Tribune Business News*, October 3, 1999.

——, "California Billionaire Denies Reports of Offers on Hockey, Baseball Teams," *Knight-Ridder/Tribune Business News*, October 6, 1999.

——, "Chip Maker Broadcom to Buy Mountain View, Calif.-Based Software Firm," *Knight-Ridder/Tribune Business News*, August 11, 1999.

——, "Irvine, Calif.-Based Communications-Chipmaker Buys Designer," *Knight-Ridder/Tribune Business News*, March 1, 2000.

——, "Irvine, Calif.-Based Communications-Chip Maker Sees Stock Price Soar," *Knight-Ridder/Tribune Business News*, November 22, 1999.

——, "Irvine, Calif., Communications-Chip Maker Buys Internet-Security Firm," *Knight-Ridder/Tribune Business News*, January 19, 2000.

——, "Irvine, Calif. Firm Acquires Atlanta-Based Software Developer," *Knight-Ridder/Tribune Business News*, March 1, 2000.

——, "Orange County, Calif., Tech Firm Broadcom Announces Purchase, Stock Split," *Knight-Ridder/Tribune Business News*, January 20, 2000.

——, "Orange County, Calif., Technology Stocks Do Well Amid Downturn," *Knight-Ridder/Tribune Business News*, March 9, 2000.

Farnsworth, Chris, and Barbara Kingsley, "Internet Firm Gives Irvine, Calif., Crew Team $1.28 Million in Stock," *Knight-Ridder/Tribune Business News*, August 22, 1999.

Hesseldahl, Arik, "Another Broad Deal," *Electronic News (1991)*, January 24, 2000, p. 18.

——, "Broadcom Acquires Epigram," *Electronic News (1991)*, May 3, 1999, p. 36.

——, "Broadcom Acquires HotHaus," *Electronic News (1991)*, July 26, 1999, p. 30.

——, "Broadcom Makes Stellar Acquisition," *Electronic News (1991)*, March 6, 2000, p. 14.

Lashinsky, Adam, "San Jose Mercury News, Calif., Silicon Street Column," *Knight-Ridder/Tribune Business News*, June 21, 1998.

Ristelhueber, Robert, "Broadcom Buys Startup for $104M," *Electronic News (1991)*, February 1, 1999, p. 16.

Rosen, Carol, "Broadcom Turns Defense Technology Knowhow into Communication ICs," *Electronic Business Buyer*, March 1995, p. 57.

Sanders, Edmund, "Modem Chip Maker Broadcom Becomes Top Public Firm in Orange County, Calif.," *Knight-Ridder/Tribune Business News*, January 11, 1999.

—David P. Bianco

Bufete Industrial, S.A. de C.V.

Moras 850, Colonia del Valle
Mexico, D.F. 03100
Mexico
Telephone: (525) 723-4721
Fax: (525) 420-8903
Web site: http://www.bufete.com

Public Company
Incorporated: 1977
Employees: 12,986
Sales: 5.56 billion pesos (US$561.1 million) (1998)
Stock Exchanges: Mexico City New York (ADRs)
Ticker Symbol: BUFETE (Mexico City); GBI (New York)
NAIC: 23491 Water, Sewer and Pipeline Construction; 23331 Manufacturing and Industrial Building Construction; 23493 Nonbuilding Structure Construction; 54133 Engineering Services; 551112 Offices of Other Holding Companies

Bufete (or Grupo Bufete) Industrial, S.A. de C.V. is a Mexican holding company that, through its subsidiaries, provides integrated engineering, procurement, and construction services in ten countries. These services are divided into three areas: industrial process and power generation plants; urban projects; and infrastructure projects and manufacturing plants. Bufete also provides planning, consulting, and appraisal services to its clients. The company has completed more than 1,000 large-scale projects in a variety of industries. It has the largest engineering work force in Mexico.

Successful Start-Up: 1949–77

Bufete Industrial was founded in 1949 by José Mendoza Fernandez and two other recent chemical engineering graduates of the National Autonomous University in Mexico City, one of whom was Rafael Pardo Grandison (who was president of operations as late as 1977). Mendoza had already distinguished himself while working part-time for Sosa Texcoco S.A., a producer of caustic soda and soda ash, by acting promptly in manually closing a recalcitrant safety valve whose malfunction threatened to cause an explosion. Mendoza won a scholarship to the Massachusetts Institute of Technology but turned it down to go into business.

Bufete was Mexico's only process engineering firm for about ten years, a period in which Mendoza never took a vacation. Its first contract came from a friend of Mendoza's father, who hired the fledgling firm for technical consulting and then entrusted it with the construction and start-up of a US$3 million sodium sulfate plant in Viesca, located in the state of Coahuila. Another important early client was the Mexican subsidiary of E.I. du Pont de Nemours & Co., for which it built a plant for titanium bioxide in Altimira, Tamaulipas. By the end of the 1950s Bufete's roster of clients also included Union Carbide Corporation and Celanese Mexicana. Soon after, General Motors Corporation, Kimberly Clark de Mexico, S.A. de C.V., Petroleos Mexicanos (Pemex), and Mexico's federal electricity commission were also clients for engineering, procurement, or construction contracts.

Pemex, Mexico's biggest industrial company, was an especially important client in the 1960s. Bufete's first major project for the government-owned firm, a cyclohexane plant, was the first Pemex facility for which all the project engineering work was done in Mexico. By the end of 1977 Bufete had performed about 20 projects for Pemex, including a refinery in Cadereyta, Nuevo Leon, on which the company spent more than one million man-hours for the engineering. Some 35 percent of its engineering personnel were devoted to the petroleum and petrochemical industries at this time.

Other Bufete projects completed by that date included a newsprint plant, various sugar refineries, a General Motors factory in Toluca, a thermoelectric power plant in central Mexico, and a Kimberly Clark plant in Orizaba using sugarcane bagasse for paper production. The company had been offering its services abroad for more than ten years, with completed projects including a paper plant in Argentina, sugar and textile plants in Venezuela, and food and pulp and paper projects in the Dominican Republic.

Good Times and Bad: 1977–94

By 1977, when Bufete was reorganized as a holding company, it was the 53rd ranking Mexican company, with sales that year of 2.01 billion pesos (US$88.2 million) and some 8,000 to 10,000 employees. In an interview for the Mexican business magazine *Expansion,* Mendoza described the firm's principal objective as "to offer all services necessary to start up a factory, from its conception to the beginning of production."

In the following years Bufete became a major builder of refineries and plants for government-owned petroleum, fertilizer, steel, and power generation companies. Business boomed so much in this period that the company had to import steel, cement, and skilled personnel. By 1982 Bufete had developed more than 600 projects, including ones for the petroleum, petrochemical, steel, paper, and sugar industries, and it had exported its technology to Europe, Latin America, the United States, and Japan. Among its nine subsidiaries was Houston-based Process Projects International.

The collapse of the peso in 1982, following the end of the oil-price boom that had fueled economic expansion in Mexico, was costly to Bufete. Sales dropped 65 percent in 1982. Mendoza later told Christopher Palmeri of *Forbes,* "It took six years to recover from the 1982 crisis." In return for its loans, Banamex, Mexico's largest private bank, held a 40 percent share of the company in 1984. As late as 1985 Bufete was still slashing employment, from 6,000 to 4,050.

By 1988 Bufete was conducting 750 projects in many areas of industry, including chemicals, petrochemicals, petroleum, sugar refining, pulp and paper, textiles, food, electrical energy, hydraulics, public transportation, and urban development. The company was employing more than 14,000 workers and had six subsidiaries in Mexico City, two in Guadalajara, two in Monterrey, and an international group that began work on a project to modernize some 20 hotels in Havana. The following year Bufete sold a 25 percent interest in the firm to Houston-based M.W. Kellogg Co., a U.S. corporation also engaged in engineering and construction services. Bufete's association with Kellogg enabled it to win contracts in the next few years for engineering work on an ethylene plant in Westlake, Louisiana, and a smaller one in Bulgaria, and two petrochemical plants in Kuantlan, Malaysia.

Bufete was trying to wean itself from dependence on government contracts and on Mexico's boom-and-bust economy generally. "It was the recession of the 1980s that made Bufete decide it was time to no longer depend so much on Mexican economic cycles and to go abroad," a company executive later told Michael Tangleman of *Infrastructure Finance.* But, he added, "Going abroad is no easy feat. It takes years of bidding in different countries to develop the necessary image and profile that allows you to win contracts."

In addition to Kellogg's 25 percent share, Bufete was 60 percent owned by Mendoza and 15 percent by the company's employees when it went public in 1993, selling about 25 percent of its shares on the Mexican stock exchange. Mendoza still owned 52 percent of the stock at the end of 1993. That year Bufete was doing business in ten countries—for the most part in Latin America, but also in the United States, Bulgaria, Malaysia, and Spain. Nearly 90 percent of company revenues were coming, however, from projects for Pemex and Mexico's federal electricity commission. Services related to infrastructure work, manufacturing plants, and urban projects accounted for the remainder. Revenues came to 1.33 billion pesos (about US$420 million) and consolidated net income amounted to 113 million pesos (about US$36 million) that year. Subsidiaries now included an environmental engineering firm and a computer services company.

In the past the Mexican government and its state-run enterprises, such as Pemex, would parcel out projects among subcontractors: for example, one for engineering, another for design, a third for procuring materials, and a fourth for actual construction. But by the 1990s, to avoid duplication and other inefficiencies, it increasingly turned to "turnkey" contractors—that is, companies who would do the entire job. (Bufete's first such project had consisted of two thermoelectric plants in Chihuahua for a Japanese firm, contracted in 1982 for US$100 million.) In 1994 Bufete's big projects included the construction and management of a system of water distribution for Mexico City, in collaboration with the French firm Lyonnaise des Eaux Dumet.

Struggling to Survive in the Late 1990s

The flight of capital in late 1994, followed by the devaluation of the peso and subsequent economic crisis was a major blow to Bufete, as to other Mexican companies. Bufete lost 808.2 million pesos (US$123.8 million) in 1995 and 79.5 million pesos (US$10.4 million) in 1996. Its debt reached as high as US$384 million in 1995, and the majority of that was short-term bank debt. There were some bright spots, however. The 1994 purchase of Chilean general contractor Empresa de Obras y Montajes Ovalle Moore, S.A. won it many lucrative contracts in Chile's booming mining, engineering, and construction markets. In the United States, Bufete was participating with Kellogg in petrochemical and oil refinery projects, along with urban and infrastructure projects of its own. Foreign-earned income grew from less than 3 percent of total revenues in 1993 to 29 percent in 1995.

Bufete was a very different company by the time the worst of this economic crisis had passed. With the Mexican government forced to cut back on its spending, more than 82 percent of the company's US$570 million backlog in orders in mid-1996 was from private companies. Among the projects in which Bufete was engaged in 1996 was the construction of a steel plant in Lazaro Cardenas for an Indian company, Ispat, which had purchased a company previously owned by the Mexican government. Another was a resin plant in Altamira for a subsidiary of Shell Oil Co. In 1997 Bufete formed a unit focused on the disposal of medical waste.

The company earned 50.6 million pesos (US$6.4 million) in 1997, but its revenues fell from 6.03 billion pesos (US$786.24 million) the previous year to 4.1 billion pesos (US$627.9 million), and its short-term bank debt began to rise again. The Mexican government, wary of spending money for big projects, was awarding concessions to companies that would finance, build, and operate such facilities itself. To raise the money and assemble the necessary expertise, Mexican contractors needed to form joint ventures with foreign partners. Of the nation's big three—the other two being Empresas ICA and Grupo Tribasa—Bufete was having the most difficulty creating such alliances. "It's the first time that for these large projects the name of the game is not engineering and construction so much as operating and financing," a Bufete executive conceded to Henry Tricks of *Financial Times.*

At the end of 1998 Bufete was executing projects in the Bahamas, Chile, Columbia, El Salvador, Peru, Trinidad, Tobago, and the United States, as well as Mexico. About 38 percent of its 1998 revenues and 14 percent of its backlog at the end of the year were related to projects outside Mexico. Bufete's backlog of work in early 1999, according to the company, included mineral-metallurgical, chemical, petrochemical, and pharmaceutical projects, electrical cogeneration plants, a variety of manufacturing plants, and the construction of a new building for General Motors Mexico.

Although Bufete raised its revenues to 5.56 billion pesos (US$561.1 million) in 1998, it suffered a loss of 495.8 million pesos (US$50.1 million). The short-term bank debt swelled to 1.43 billion pesos (US$144 million). Bufete was able to meet payments on its debts in 1998 only because it received 846 million pesos (US$90.5 million) from the federal electricity commission for work on two earlier projects and five loans from a government bank. By 1999 Bufete was scrambling to find enough money to pay more than US$100 million due in debt over the next six months. The company defaulted on a US$100 million Eurobond in July. Its total debt was about US$280 million.

In February 2000, Citibank of Mexico, the Bank of New York, and Banco Serfin, the principal representatives of Bufete's creditors, decided to assume control of the enterprise, proposing to exchange about half its debt—US$92 million—in return for 90 percent of its capital. Mendoza, who had held 41 percent of the company, retained the remaining ten percent but

retired from active management. Enron Corporation signed a preliminary agreement to provide a management team for Bufete and financing for ongoing projects. The largest of these was a US$170 million oil drilling platform for Pemex and a US$76 million gasoline plant at a Colombian oil refinery.

Principal Subsidiaries

Bufete Industrial Inc. (U.S.A.); Bufete Industrial Construcciones, S.A. de C.V.; Bufete Industrial Disenos y Proyectos, S.A. de C.V.; Bufete Industrial Infrastructura, S.A. de C.V.; Bufete Industrial Ingenieria, S.A. de C.V.; Bufete Industrial Ingenieria Ambiental, S.A. de C.V.; Constructora Urbec, S.A. de C.V.; Empresa de Obras y Montajes Ovalle Moore y Cia. Ltda. (Chile); Tecnologia y Servicios de Agua, S.A. de C.V. (51%); Urbec Construction Inc. (U.S.A.).

Principal Competitors

Empresas ICA Sociedad Controladroa, S.A. de C.V.; Grupo Tribasa, S.A. de C.V.

Further Reading

"Bufete Industrial: Los fabricantes de fabricas," *Expansion,* November 23, 1977, pp. 52–53, 55–56, 59.

"Enron Reportedly to Manage Bufete Industrial," *Los Angeles Times,* March 3, 2000, Bus. Sec., p. 2.

Gatsiopoulos, Georgina, "Acreedores de Bufete se unen para tomar a la compania," *El financiero,* February 2, 2000, p. 23.

——, "Bufete Industrial, tras un nuevo milagro," *El financiero,* January 14, 1999, p. 22.

Mandel-Campbell, Andrea, "Bufete in Talks to Sell Crucial Stake to Iconsa," *Financial Times,* December 9, 1999, p. 20.

Martinez Staines, Javier, "Bufete Industrial: negocios llave en mano," *Expansion,* July 21, 1993, pp. 39–41, 43–44.

Mejia Prieto, Jorge, *Mexicanos que escalaron el exito,* Mexico City: Editorial Diana, 1988, pp. 67–73.

Palmeri, Christopher, "Cool in the Face of Adversity," *Forbes,* July 29, 1996, p. 69.

Parkinson, Gerald, "What If He'd Gone to MIT?," *Chemical Engineering,* December 1993, pp. 67–68, 70.

"Pocos materiales para la reconstruccion de la industria," *Expansion,* June 26, 1985, p. 43.

Tangeman, Michael, "Mexican Multinationals," *Infrastructure Finance,* November 1996, pp. 41–44.

Torres, Craig, "Mexican Construction Firm Bufete Industrial Is Seen by Some Analysts As Poised for Rebound," *Wall Street Journal,* June 19, 1995, p. C2.

Tricks, Henry, "Bufete Is Forced to Take Hard Knocks," *Financial Times,* March 26, 1998, p. 41.

"Una actividad que ya tiene cimientos," *Expansion,* August 18, 1982, pp. 47–49.

—Robert Halasz

Canal Plus

85-89, quai André Citroën
75015 Paris Cedex 15
France
Telephone: (+33) 1 44 25 10 00
Fax: (+33) 1 44 25 12 34
Web site: http://www.cplus.fr

Public Company
Incorporated: 1984
Employees: 3,900
Sales: EUR 3.29 billion (1999)
Stock Exchanges: Paris
Ticker Symbol: CNPLY
NAIC: 51321 Cable Networks; 51211 Motion Picture and
    Video Production

With nearly 14 million subscribers across Europe and Africa, Canal Plus ranks as one of the world's premiere subscription-based television providers. In addition to its Canal+ pay-TV service, with operations in France, Sweden, the Netherlands, and Spain, until early 2000 the company held a nearly 70 percent stake in CanalSatellite, the French satellite television provider, as well as a more than 70 percent stake in Multithematiques, providing theme channels to the cable and satellite television markets. Aggressive investments in Hollywood and the creation of its own production companies have made Canal Plus an important player in both the American and European film industries, and especially in France, where the company has a hand in nearly 90 percent of all French film production activities, allowing the company to profit from its powerful involvement on both continents. Turning toward the future, Canal Plus has joined with former major shareholder Vivendi in the 50–50 partnership Vivendi-Net (V-Net), created to combine the two companies' Internet interests. Canal Plus has also stepped up development of its own Internet-access set-top boxes, planning to invest some 220 million euros in this project in the year 2000. In January 2000, Canal Plus announced that French arms and media conglomerate Lagardère Group SCA had purchased a major stake in the company's digital television wing, taking 34 percent of Ca-

nalSatellite and nearly 27.5 percent of Multithematiques, for a price of more than FFr 7 billion.

Pioneering Pay-TV in France in the 1980s

Canal Plus was the creation of André Rousselet, president of the French media and advertising giant Havas. While some observers were surprised that the top publicity group in France would become involved in a medium that needed no outside publicity, Havas hoped that the innovative move would open up a potentially profitable market. Rousselet decided to launch a subscription television channel in November 1984 to offer the French public an alternative to the comedies and variety shows typically featured on the three government-owned channels then in existence. Contending that no one would pay for television programming, critics dubbed the company "Canal Minus."

In fact, subscriptions were extremely low at the onset, and the company announced first year losses of FFr 330 million. Moreover, some politicians, including Laurent Fabius, France's prime minister, were not in favor of commercial television and petitioned for a retraction of the Canal Plus broadcasting license. Rousselet, however, was a personal friend, golf partner, and former chief of staff of President François Mitterand; he was able to acquire a government concession that gave Canal Plus an all but official monopoly on subscription television. In addition, Rousselet and Pierre Lescure, the company's director-general, put forth an aggressive spring schedule of blockbuster films, depleting all its programming for the next season, in an effort to attract viewers. Suddenly, subscriptions picked up. This initial success convinced Canal Plus that giving viewers what they were not able to get on government television— American hit comedies and French drama—was central to its future success.

In addition to Rousselet's effective political networking and the channel's innovative programming, Canal Plus benefited from lack of competition, high taxes on home video recorders, and a sluggish video market. The use of an existing broadcast channel and decoders allowed the station to avoid paying cable companies to broadcast shows and gave the station almost immediate national coverage. These advantages proved to be worth the expense the company incurred to improve early decoders, which were known for having technical problems.

Moreover, Canal Plus was exempt from regulations that required free channels to air films only three nights of the week and to wait three years to show a movie after its box-office release. Thus, Canal Plus was able to broadcast feature films only a year after their cinema releases. The channel also managed to use some restrictions to its own advantage. For example, the Socialist government's regulations required Canal Plus to broadcast a few hours a day with an unscrambled signal so that all television viewers could gain from the new service, and these unscrambled broadcasts were turned into ideal free promotion for the channel's regular programming. Two of every three subscribers first watched the channel during these free hours, according to Pierre Lescure. The government also required the channel to devote no more than 45 percent of its air time to films. This restriction encouraged Canal Plus to develop other interesting programming; as a result, sports programs became one of the channels specialties, with the network gaining exclusive rights to national soccer matches and top-quality coverage of boxing and American football. When the government succumbed to pressure from the film industry to ban the company's movie broadcasting during peak cinema-going hours, the station expanded its programming beyond films to interview shows, documentaries, and soft pornography.

In 1985, Mitterand announced the opening of private commercial television stations. While these new stations offered serious competition to Canal Plus, the company managed to break even the following year. Growth since then remained around 25 percent annually, as each new subscriber added about FFr 2,000 in annual turnover, but required far less additional cost. Aggressive advertising and competent management of the viewer base kept subscriptions high. A policy of debiting fees from subscribers' bank accounts contributed to the extremely high viewer subscription renewal rate of around 95 percent. Canal Plus's financial stability was thus greatly increased, as subscriber fees accounted for almost 90 percent of all turnover. By the time the company's stock went on the market in 1987, and soared from FFr 275 to FFr 575 per share in just one year, the station was thriving, with profits at $100 million in 1988. The channel had penetrated 15 percent of the 18 million French households. By 1989, Canal Plus had almost three million subscribers, representing a comparable penetration rate in France as Home Box Office Inc. (HBO) had accomplished in the United States, without HBO's 12-year head start.

With a secure base in France, Canal Plus was looking to expand internationally. Its attempts to link up with Lausanne-based Telecine Romandie were thwarted by the Swiss government in 1988. However, the next year, Canal Plus launched a channel in Belgium, of which it controlled 33 percent, and entered into a consortium with Prisa, a media group, which gained a license to begin a private television station in Spain. In partnership with Bertelsmann and the Kirch Group, Canal Plus launched Germany's first national pay TV service, the Premiere channel.

While Canal Plus faced increased competition and had fewer political connections abroad, its local partners helped tailor its programming of films and sports to match local tastes. In France, as well, Canal Plus created new theme channels featuring specialized programming, including children's shows and classic movies. While these new foreign and domestic channels initially lost money, they proved sound investments by edging out local competitors. By the time Canal Plus had expanded to Africa in 1990 with Canal Horizons, the channel had become the most successful subscription channel in Europe and was second only to HBO worldwide.

In the mid-1980s, Canal Plus began trying to acquire television rights to popular American television shows. Initially dismissed as a newcomer, the French channel soon won over Hollywood with its success and its international expansion, but remained very dependent on American film studios for the blockbusters, which were essential to its programming. In fact, by 1991, Canal Plus was paying $100 million a year just to acquire American movie rights. Hoping to avoid paying Hollywood's high prices, Canal Plus moved directly into film production itself, acquiring a five percent stake in Carolco Pictures, an independent U.S. studio, for $30 million in 1991. That year, the company also launched Studio Canal Plus, its own Hollywood production company, which had a working capital of $200 million and which later joined with Universal Pictures to co-produce films. Canal Plus also entered into a deal with Warner Brothers and the German media outfit Scriha & Deyhle to help finance Arnon Milchan's independent production company, Regency International. Through these various investments, Canal Plus contributed to the production of such hit movies as *Terminator 2, JFK,* and *Basic Instinct.*

The company's attempts to secure its position in the cinema industry did not all go smoothly, however, as it had to write off the $20 million it had invested in Carolco to help that company out of bankruptcy. This loss was not received well by investors, and Canal Plus stock prices fell. During this time, Canal Plus also gradually withdrew its equity partnership with Milchan, producer of the hit film *Pretty Woman.* Still, Canal Plus continued its investment in Carolco and did not stop buying the European rights to most Milchan films. The company, in fact, undertook another production venture in the form of Hexicon Films, a wholly owned production company, which released a film called *Money Men.*

The important role of Canal Plus in both the American and French film industries became especially evident in the early 1990s. In 1992, Canal Plus was Europe's biggest purchaser of American movie rights and remained important to U.S. studios wishing to have access to the European Community market, in light of the increasingly protectionist attitude of the European film industry. At the same time, Canal Plus's management expressed the desire to play a leading role in modernizing and strengthening European film production. The company's obligations to spend ten percent of its revenue on French-made films increased its clout in the ailing French cinema industry, which had at first regarded the subscription channel as a competitor. With the increasing number of Hollywood movies entering the European market, Canal Plus came to be regarded as a savior for the French film industry, with its significant investments in French movies.

Canal Plus began to broadcast by satellite in 1992 to reach parts of France not hooked up to the cable network, developing subsidiaries to build satellite antennas and decoders. However, this venture produced conflicts with the government over the use of the D2-Mac standard for satellite broadcasting. The government's support of this standard broke the monopoly that Canal Plus had enjoyed in the decoder market. Nonetheless, Canal Plus was still reaching more and more viewers, passing the four million mark in France, which was long thought to be the saturation level.

The company continued its policy of European expansion, investing in such cable channels as European Sports Network and entering the market in Britain with a ten percent stake in TVS. In 1992, the channel joined with BSkyB, another powerful European subscription television service, to offer digital, multichannel pay-TV to Europe. Canal Plus also teamed up with Rupert Murdoch's News Corporation to develop new television services throughout Europe in 1992.

Between 1988 and 1993, Canal Plus stock increased 378 percent, and sales rose to $1.5 billion. While the channel's earnings growth and return on capital were expected to decline slightly throughout the 1990s, due to its investment in cable television and foreign channels, continued growth patterns were expected to bolster profits once the company passed the break-even point in its new investments. Indeed, by the late 1990s, most of the company's operations proved profitable. However, continued international expansion—particularly into the under-developed Italian market—kept the company's net earnings in the red.

In February 1994, Rousselet quit the board, citing disagreement with equity moves, but also reportedly because of a disagreement over government intrusion into the company's operations. Rousselet was replaced by Pierre Lescure, who kept Canal Plus on its course to build one of Europe's dominant media networks. Meanwhile, Canal Plus had begun to face new competition, at home in the form of satellite broadcaster AB Sat and a pay-per-view initiative from Lyonnaise Communications, and abroad as well from the six-channel satellite service, Taurus Programming, in Spain, and the expansion onto the continent of the United Kingdom's BSkyB satellite service.

In the late 1990s, Canal Plus nevertheless held its lead and continued to set the pace for television broadcasters. In 1996, the company was the first to launch digital satellite transmissions. At the same time, the company boosted its programming stock by buying up the library from Carolco Pictures, as well as that of UGC DA, one of Europe's largest. The following year,

Canal Plus bought up Nethold, based in Holland, making the French group Europe's largest digital television provider. Canal Plus also took majority control of France's NC Numericable (formerly CGV), giving it one of the country's largest cable television networks. The following year, the company added digital television services to Scandinavia and Poland.

Canal Plus, which had launched its own web site in 1995, joined the rush to the Internet for the new millennium. After reaching a content-provision agreement with AOL (America Online in Europe) and Bertelsmann AG, the company formed, with then-major shareholder Vivendi, a 50–50 partnership called V-Net (Vivendi-Net) with the intent of providing content to the array of new information transmission markets, and especially the mobile telephone market, which, with the development of WAP (wireless application protocol) was expected to become the chief means of accessing the Internet within the first decade of the new century.

Canal Plus continued to explore new partnerships. After aborting merger talks with BSkyB in 1999, the company announced an agreement with mobile telephony giant Vodaphone to join V-Net in the launch of Vodaphone's MAP, a Europe-wide interactive content portal service. Then in January 2000, Canal Plus announced that French arms and media conglomerate Lagardère had acquired a major shareholding position in two of Canal Plus's subsidiaries—CanalSatellite and Multithematiques–a move that would serve to boost Canal Plus's content offering. At the same time, Canal Plus strengthened its upstream arm, announcing the merger of its Ellipse Programme television production subsidiary into major French programming provider Expand, a move announced in February 2000.

Despite posting a loss of EUR 136 million in 1999, due almost entirely to the company's efforts to establish its Italian operations, Canal Plus continued to mark strong growth, boosting its sales to EUR 3.3 billion. In that year, the company's total subscription base topped 13.7 million, marking an increase of 17 percent over the previous year. Its early investment in digital television, however, looked to become its strongest growth market; with four million subscribers in 1999, the company posted a subscriber growth rate of 58 percent in a single year. With a relatively undeveloped subscriber-based television market across Europe, and the company's strong moves into the Internet and multiaccess content markets, Canal Plus looked likely to maintain its leadership position.

Principal Subsidiaries

Antennes Tonna (51%); CANAL + Finance; CANAL + Image (97%); CANAL + Nederland; CANAL + Television (Sweden); CanalSatellite (70%); Expand (35%); Le Studio CANAL +; Mutlithematiques (27.42%); NC Numericable (85%); Sogecable (25%; Spain); TELE + (Italy; 90%); Tobis-Studio CANAL + (Germany; 60%).

Principal Competitors

Audiofina; Bertelsmann AG; DirectTV; France Telecom Group; Groupe AB; Liberty Media Corporation; Mediaset; News Corporation Limited; Pathé SA; Télévision Française 1; Time Warner Inc.; United PanEurope.

Further Reading

"Canal Plus Confirms BSKYB Discussions," *Cable Europe,* March 3, 1999.

"Canal Satellite Tops 800,000," *Interspace,* January 13, 2000.

Checketts, Peter, "News Corp., Canal Plus Are Partners," *Broadcasting,* October 12, 1992, p. 14.

Echikson, William, "The Big Payoff in French Pay-TV," *Fortune,* May 3, 1993, pp. 48–49.

Grantham, Bill, "Euromoguls," *Forbes,* December 9, 1991, pp. 140–46.

Jaques, Bob, "Swiss Govt Nixes Canal Plus Link with Troubled Telecine," *Variety,* March 16, 1988, p. 68.

Landau, Sue, and Nathalie Meistermann, "Canal, Lagardere TV Deal Leaves Future Open," *Reuters Business Report,* January 13, 2000.

Marcom, John, Jr., "TV de Triomphe," *Forbes,* October 16, 1989, p. 124.

Matlack, Carol, "Why Two TV Titans Might Finally Get Hitched," *Business Week International Editions,* June 21, 1999, p. 23.

Moore, Lisa, "Will Taurus' Pay-TV Plans Fly in Spain?," *Variety,* June 14, 1993, pp. 37, 39.

"Putting Europe on the Box," *Economist,* July 11, 1992.

Riemer, Blanca, "Canal Plus: The Latest French Sensation," *Business Week,* May 13, 1991, p. 55.

Sasseen, Jane, "Return on Capital," *International Management,* January/February 1993, pp. 61–62.

——, "Star of the Small Screen," *International Management,* June 1991, pp. 42, 45.

"Stock Leap Leaves Top 12 Execs Sitting Pretty on a Pile of Coins," *Variety,* November 30, 1988, pp. 50, 60.

Williams, Michael, "New Broadcast Standard Threatens Canal Plus," *Variety,* March 9, 1992, pp. 40, 45.

——, "Paris Test Bodes Well for PPV," *Variety,* August 2, 1993, pp. 27, 48.

—Jennifer Kerns
—updated by M.L. Cohen

Canandaigua Brands, Inc.

300 Willowbrook Office Park
Fairport, New York 14450
U.S.A.
Telephone: (716) 218-2169
Fax: (716) 218-2155
Web site: http://www.cbrands.com

Public Company
Incorporated: 1972 as Canandaigua Wine Company, Inc.
Employees: 4,230
Sales: $1.98 billion (1999)
Stock Exchanges: New York
Ticker Symbol: CDB
NAIC: 312120 Breweries; 312130 Wineries; 312140
Distilleries; 422810 Beer and Ale Wholesaling;
422820 Wine and Distilled Alcoholic Beverage
Wholesalers; 312112 Bottled Water Manufacturing

Canandaigua Brands, Inc.—which changed its name from Canandaigua Wine Company, Inc. in 1997—is one of the largest and most successful producers and marketers of wines, beers, and distilled spirits in the United States and the United Kingdom. The company produces and markets more than 180 brands of alcohol through 1,000 wholesale distributors in the United States, and distributes products to more than 16,000 U.K. customers. Canandaigua is the second largest domestic producer of wines, the second largest importer of foreign beers, and the fourth largest distributor of distilled spirits within the United States. The company's manufacturing operations include 20 production facilities in the United States, Canada, and the United Kingdom. Canandaigua's brands of table wine, sparkling wines, dessert wines, foreign and domestic beers, hard liquor, and hard cider are famous, including such well-known names as Almaden, Arbor Mist, Cook's, Dunnewood, Inglenook, J. Roget, Manischewitz, Paul Masson, Marcus James, and Richard's Wild Irish Rose in the wine sector; Corona, Double Diamond, Modelo Especial, Negra Modelo, Pacifico, Peroni, Point, St. Pauli Girl, Tetley's English Ale, and Tsingtao in the beer sector; Barton, Black Velvet, Canadian LTD, Chi-

Chi's, Fleischmann's, Inver House, Montezuma, Mr. Boston, Paul Masson Grande Amber, and Ten High in the hard liquor category; and Blackthorn, Diamond White, and Olde English in the U.K. cider sector.

Early History: From North Carolina to Wild Irish Rose

In 1935, some years after the repeal of the Volstead Act and the end of prohibition, Mack Sands opened the Car-Cal Winery. Located in North Carolina, Car-Cal Winery produced varietal table wines for limited distribution. Mack's son, Marvin, learned about the wine industry from his father, and was soon determined to open a winery of his own. In 1945, Marvin's dream materialized when his family purchased a sauerkraut factory-turned-winery located in Canandaigua, New York (in the Finger Lakes region), and he established Canandaigua Industries.

Sands hired eight workers to produce and sell bulk wine in wooden barrels to companies that would bottle them on the East Coast. In just two years, business was so good that Sands decided to significantly change the direction of his company. With a steady flow of cash to deal with unforeseen emergencies, the head of Canandaigua Industries was determined to produce and sell wine using his own name brands. In 1948, the Car-Cal operation run by Mack Sands was closed, and all wine production was transferred to the facility in Canandaigua. In the same year, Marvin Sands purchased the Mother Vineyard Wine Company, located in Manteo, North Carolina, the first in a long line of strategic acquisitions designed to expand Canandaigua's market position.

Primarily concentrating on regional markets, Canandaigua's new brand of wines were moderately successful. In 1951, the younger Sands opened Richards Wine Cellars in Petersburg, Virginia, and asked his father to assume control of the operation. Not long afterwards, the Onslow Wine Company was added to the growing list of regional wine producers owned and operated by Canandaigua. Both Richards Wine Cellars and Onslow Wine Company produced a wine called Scuppernong, made from varietal grapes grown primarily in the southern United States which serve as a popular source of wines throughout the region. In spite of this expansion, sales remained relatively slow and the company's business did not grow rapidly.

In 1954, however, Sands was lucky enough to come across something most entrepreneurs only dream about—a widely successful product that catapults a company into a future of rapid growth and high profits. This product became known as the Richard's Wild Irish Rose brand of dessert wines (named after his son Richard), and spearheaded Canandaigua's development for years and years. Quickly realizing the potential of his new product, Sands implemented an extremely innovative franchising system, the very first in the wine industry. The franchising network included an agreement between Canandaigua and five independent bottling companies located in various parts of the United States. These bottlers were given the franchise rights to bottle and distribute Wild Irish Rose brands in their areas. With a minimum capital investment, Sands reaped the rewards of seeing his hot-selling Wild Irish Rose gain a larger and larger part of the dessert wine market.

During the late 1950s, revenues generated from the widespread sale of Wild Irish Rose allowed Canandaigua to concentrate on increasing its own production facilities. As sales of the dessert wine brand continued to grow, the company expanded to meet the explosive demands of the marketplace. People were hired to help extend the company's sales network, and a wholesale distributor operation was also established. During the early and mid-1960s, both the sales staff and the wholesale distributor network was strengthened to meet the ever-growing demand for Wild Irish Rose brands. As sales increased, Sands continued his policy of strategic acquisition by purchasing the Tenner Brothers Winery, located in South Carolina, in 1965, and adding Hammondsport Wine Company in 1969. The acquisition of Hammondsport gave Canandaigua an entry into the sparkling wine market, a direction that Sands had wanted his company to take for years.

1970s and 1980s: Going Public, Adding New Brands, and Riding the Wine Cooler Boom

In 1972 the company was incorporated as Canandaigua Wine Company, Inc. One year later, it became a public corporation and issued an initial sale of company stock on the NASDAQ. Several important brands of wine were produced at Richards Wine Cellars, but it was the acquisitions strategy that continued to shape the company. The most significant acquisition was made in 1974 when Canandaigua purchased the Bisceglia Brothers Winery in Madera, California. This gave the

company access to a large varietal wine market in the western United States. Another milestone in the firm's history was the production of its own brand of champagne, J. Roget, in 1979. This champagne was an immediate triumph, and contributed to Canandaigua's seemingly endless string of successful product introductions.

The 1980s were boom years for the company. In 1984, Canandaigua introduced Sun Country Wine Cooler, a concoction of wine, spritzer, and fruit flavorings. The cooler caught like wildfire across the United States and revenues for the product skyrocketed. During the early 1980s, the firm purchased Robin et Cie, a French producer of high-quality table wine, and renamed it the Batavia Wine Company. Batavia soon began to create different brands of sparkling wines, including champagne. In 1986 Richard Sands, son of founder Marvin, took over as president of the company. The following year, Canandaigua purchased a plant in McFarland, California, in order to produce grape juice concentrate and grape spirits.

The two most important acquisitions in 1987, however, included Widmer's Wine Cellars, and the Manischewitz brands from Monarch Wine Company. Widmer's Wine Cellars, located in Naples, New York, was one of the most successful and popular producers of table wine on the East Coast. Producing a wide range of table wines, from Dry Riesling to California varietals, Widmer had won a host of awards in wine competitions. In the late 1980s, Manischewitz was the best-selling brand name in kosher wines. When Canandaigua purchased the Manischewitz assets, all the production facilities were relocated to the Widmer plant in Naples, New York. Canandaigua's commitment to the production of the Manischewitz brands involved a separate facility which maintained strict supervision for the making of kosher wine under the auspices of the Union of Orthodox Jewish Congregations of America.

1990s: Diversification Through Acquisition

In 1988, the company added Cal-Products in order to produce grape spirits. During the same year, the company purchased the Cisco brand name products from Guild Wineries, a maker of table wines, dessert wines, and champagnes. Canandaigua was so pleased with the revenue generated by these products that it acquired Guild Wineries in 1991 for $60 million. This purchase brought with it the popular brands of Dunnewood wines, Cribari vermouth, and Cook's champagne. Italian Swiss Colony brand dessert wines were also bought at this time. During the late 1980s and early 1990s, in addition to the acquisition of domestic firms that produced wines, champagnes, and juices, the company began to import the Marcus James brand of table wines from Brazil, the popular Mateus brand from Portugal, the Keller Geister brand of table wines from Germany, and Mondoro Asti Spumante from Italy.

During the decade of the 1990s, with Sands heading the company as chairman of the board of directors, and with son Richard serving first as president then as CEO as well starting in 1993, Canandaigua continued to expand. One of the most significant acquisitions included Barton Incorporated, which was purchased in June 1993 for approximately $123 million in cash, one million shares of Canandaigua stock, and the assumption of $47.9 million in debt. Barton, located in Chicago, Illinois, was

Key Dates:

1945: The Sands family purchases a winery located in Canandaigua, New York; Marvin Sands establishes Canandaigua Industries to run the winery.

1948: Sands purchases the Mother Vineyard Wine Company, located in Manteo, North Carolina.

1951: Sands opens Richards Wine Cellars in Petersburg, Virginia.

1954: Company introduces the Richard's Wild Irish Rose brand of dessert wines, which becomes the firm's top brand.

1969: Canandaigua acquires Hammondsport Wine Company, gaining entry into the sparkling wine sector.

1972: Company is incorporated as Canandaigua Wine Company, Inc.

1973: Company goes public and is listed on the NASDAQ.

1974: Bisceglia Brothers Winery, a West Coast varietal wine maker, is acquired.

1979: Company begins production of its own champagne brand, J. Roget.

1984: Canandaigua enters the wine cooler market with the Sun Country brand, leading to skyrocketing revenues.

1986: Richard Sands, son of Marvin, is named president of the company.

1987: Widmer's Wine Cellars, an East Coast table wine producer, and Manischewitz, the bestselling kosher wine brand, are acquired.

1991: Company acquires Guild Wineries, including the Dunnewood and Cook's brands.

1993: Company acquires Barton Incorporated, a leading producer of distilled spirits and a leading importer of foreign beers; and Vintners International, owner of the Paul Masson and Taylor California Cellars brands.

1994: Canandaigua acquires Almaden Vineyards and Inglenook Vineyards from Heublein, Inc.

1995: Company purchases from United Distillers Glenmore, Inc. 12 distilled spirits brands, including Canadian LTD, Chi-Chi's, Fleischmann's, Inver House, and Mr. Boston.

1997: Company changes its name to Canandaigua Brands, Inc.

1998: Company moves its headquarters to Fairport, New York; acquires Matthew Clark plc, a leading U.K. producer and distributor of hard cider, wine, and bottled water.

1999: Canandaigua acquires eight Canadian whiskey brands from Diageo plc, including Black Velvet; company enters premium wine category through purchases of Franciscan Vineyards, Inc. and Simi Winery, Inc.; Richard Sands takes over as chairman following his father's death.

---

one of the largest producers of distilled spirits and also one of the largest importers of foreign beers. A firm with additional facilities in Carson, California, and Atlanta, Georgia, Barton was in the midst of its own expansion program when acquired by Canandaigua. This purchase provided Canandaigua with an entry into the lucrative distilled spirits market. Barton's brands were already selling well, including Scotch whiskeys such as House of Stuart and Speyburn single malt, Canadian whiskeys such as Canadian Host and Northern Light, and American whiskeys named Corby's Reserve and Kentucky Gentleman. At the time of the acquisition, Barton Vodka was one of the largest selling domestically made vodkas in the United States. The Barton Beer division was just beginning to reap the rewards of importing such popular items as Corona Light from Mexico and Tsingtao from the People's Republic of China.

In October 1993, Canandaigua purchased Vintners International Company, Inc., including Paul Masson and Taylor California Cellars, for $148.9 million in cash. The Paul Masson brand, one of the most popular and respected in the wine industry, was given a new label with a heavy television advertising campaign that included the familiar phrase, "We will sell no wine before its time." Taylor California Cellars brand of table wines, one of the best-selling brands in the country, was given a new price structure. Less than one year after the purchase of the Vintners brands, wholesale orders began to exceed company estimates, and sales steadily increased. In July 1994, Canandaigua became the sole American importer and distributor of Cordorniu sparkling wines. Established in 1972 by the Cordorniu family in Barcelona, Spain, the winery was the first

to produce Methode Champernoise sparking wines on the Iberian peninsula. In 1992, Cordorniu built a facility in Napa Valley where it began to produce the popular Cordorniu Napa Valley Brut Cuvee.

A very significant acquisition for Canandaigua occurred in August 1994 when the company purchased both Almaden Vineyards and Inglenook Vineyards from Heublein, Inc. for $130.6 million. Inglenook Vineyards, founded in 1879 by a sea captain from Finland—Gustave Niebaum—and Almaden Vineyards, established by Etienne Thee and Charles LeFranc in 1852, were two of the oldest and most well-respected wineries in the United States. Together the two companies sold approximately 15 million cases of wines in 1993, and Almaden ranked fifth while Inglenook ranked sixth in table wine sales within the United States. Almaden alone, before its acquisition by Canandaigua, had captured over six percent of the American table wine market. Inglenook had cornered over five percent of the domestic table wine market.

With these acquisitions, Canandaigua owned and operated four of the five GAMIT brands (GAMIT is the acronym for the five major wine brands in the United States: Gallo, Almaden, Paul Masson, Inglenook, and Taylor California Cellars). These wineries produced significant amounts of varietal wines, and Canandaigua positioned itself to take advantage of the growing varietal wine market through its acquisition strategy. At the same time, the company also improved upon its ranking as the second leading wine producer in the United States. Under new marketing techniques implemented by management at Canandaigua, Almaden wines such as Mountain Burgundy and Golden Chardonnay grew in popularity, increasing company revenues. A new pricing structure for Inglenook varietal wines, such as Premium Select, Estate Cellars, and Napa Valley, also led to increasing sales.

Double-digit sales growth during the early 1990s catapulted Canandaigua into one of the largest and most popular of the alcoholic beverage producers and importers in the United States. From 1990 to 1994, the company's gross sales shot up from $201 million to $861 million, nearly a fourfold increase. In 1994, net income was recorded at $26 million, a 71 percent increase over the previous year. The acquisition of Barton resulted in a sales increase of $211 million for 1994, while the purchase of Vintners generated $119 million for the same fiscal year. In just one month of sales, the Almaden and Inglenook acquisition added an impressive $17 million to the 1994 year in sales.

That same year, the company announced a comprehensive restructuring program that was estimated to save approximately $1.7 million in 1995 and over $13.3 million by 1996. The acquisition of Barton and Vintners gave rise to an integration of sales staff, improvement of customer services, a more focused marketing campaign, more efficient production techniques, an implementation of up-to-date information systems, and more effective finance and administrative operations. During the mid-1990s, Canandaigua consolidated all its facilities already located in California, enabling the company to group three separate bottling operations in one location. The new facility, the Mission Bell plant in Madera, California, began bottling more than 22 million cases annually.

Under the continued leadership of Marvin Sands, Canandaigua in the mid-1990s appeared to be headed for even greater profitability in the future. The company had captured 32 percent of the domestic champagne market, the largest in the industry. By the mid-1990s, the company's Barton Beer Division held ten percent of the total market share for imported beers in the United States. In 1994, the division's domestic brand, Point Special, increased sales by an astounding 25 percent. The company's Dunnewood brand, a California varietal wine, also increased its sales by 25 percent in 1994. With such popular brands, and astute management that foresaw opportunities and took advantage of trends in the marketplace, it was no surprise that the company's stock price increased by a record 37 percent for fiscal 1994.

Acquisitions continued in the second half of the 1990s, highlighted early on by the September 1995 purchase of 12 distilled liquor brands from United Distillers Glenmore, Inc. for $141.8 million. Among the key brands added to the Canandaigua portfolio were Canadian LTD whiskey; Chi-Chi's cocktails; Fleischmann's gin, vodka, and whiskey; Inver House scotch; and Mr. Boston liqueurs, brandies, and schnapps. This acquisition propelled Canandaigua from the eighth largest distributor of distilled spirits in the United States to the fourth largest.

The company suffered a brief setback during the 1996 fiscal year after running into operational difficulties stemming from the aggressive string of acquisitions of the previous half-decade. Canandaigua subsequently restructured its production, market-

ing, and distribution operations to cut costs, increase production, and improve profitability. Another key to the turnaround was the beefing up of the company's upper management ranks, including the addition of Daniel Barnett as president of the wine division and Thomas Summer as CFO. Marvin Sands remained chairman of the company, while son Richard continued serving as president and CEO.

The company's 1990s diversification led to the September 1997 company name change to Canandaigua Brands, Inc. The wine division thereupon adopted the Canandaigua Wine Company name, while the spirits and beer operations were organized within Barton Incorporated. In early 1998 the company moved its headquarters from Canandaigua to Fairport, New York (located east of Rochester). For the fiscal year ending in February 1998, Canandaigua Brands reported record net sales of $1.21 billion; the net income of $50.1 million was nearly double the $27.7 million figure for the preceding year.

In the spring of 1998 Canandaigua succeeded with the launch of a new wine brand, Arbor Mist. The new line consisted of fruit-flavored varietal wines, with a low alcohol content of six percent, aimed at first-time and younger wine consumers, particularly women. By the fall Arbor Mist had already captured 1.2 percent of the U.S. wine market. With acquisition prospects in the United States dwindling, Canandaigua began seeking international opportunities in 1998. In December of that year, the company acquired Matthew Clark plc for $475 million. Founded in 1810, the U.K.-based company was a leading producer and distributor of hard cider, wine, and bottled water in its home country. Among the company's brands were Blackthorn and Diamond White cider, Stowells of Chelsea and QC wines, and Strathmore sparkling water. In April 1999 Canandaigua spent $185.5 million to acquire eight Canadian whiskey brands and production facilities in the provinces of Alberta and Quebec from Diageo plc. The top brand gained thereby was Black Velvet, the number three Canadian whiskey brand in the United States.

A rapidly growing sector of the wine industry in the late 1990s was the premium category, an area in which Canandaigua Brands lacked any presence. That changed in June 1999 when the company completed two separate acquisitions of Franciscan Vineyards, Inc. and Simi Winery, Inc., and began operating them as a separate division called Franciscan Estates. The purchases instantly vaulted Canandaigua into the ranks of the major makers of fine wines, with a portfolio that featured several well-respected brands: Quintessa, Veramonte, Mount Veeder, Franciscan Oakville Estate, Estancia, and Simi.

From the start of its acquisition spree in 1991 through the fiscal 1999 year, Canandaigua Brands achieved a remarkable level of growth, with both net sales and net income increasing at a rate of 33 percent per year. Net sales for 1999 were a shade under $1.5 billion. In August 1999, soon after the company's entry into the premium wine category, Marvin Sands died at the age of 75, after more than 50 years of leading the company. Richard Sands took over as chairman, gaining full responsibility for taking the rapidly growing company through the initial years of the 21st century.

Principal Subsidiaries

Batavia Wine Cellars, Inc.; Canandaigua Wine Company, Inc.; Canandaigua Europe Limited; Canandaigua B.V. (Netherlands); Canandaigua Limited (U.K.); Polyphenolics, Inc.; Roberts Trading Corp.; Barton Incorporated; Barton Brands, Ltd.; Barton Beers, Ltd.; Barton Brands of California, Inc.; Barton Brands of Georgia, Inc.; Barton Canada, Ltd.; Barton Distillers Import Corp.; Barton Financial Corporation; Schenley Distilleries Inc./Les Distilleries Schenley Inc. (Canada); Stevens Point Beverage Co.; Monarch Import Company; The Viking Distillery, Inc.; Matthew Clark plc (U.K.); Freetraders Group Limited (U.K.); Matthew Clark Wholesale Limited (U.K.); Matthew Clark Brands Limited (U.K.); Strathmore Mineral Water Company Limited (U.K.); Taunton Cider plc (U.K.); The Gaymer Group Europe Limited (U.K.); The Gaymer Group Limited (U.K.).

Principal Competitors

Brown-Forman Corporation; Diageo plc; E. & J. Gallo Winery; H.P. Bulmer Holdings PLC; Halewood Vintners; Heaven Hill Distilleries, Inc.; Heineken N.V.; Interbrew S.A.; Jim Beam Brands; Molson Inc.; Perrier; Tavern; Waverley Vintners; The Wine Group.

Further Reading

Astor, Will, "Canandaigua Sets Move of Headquarters," *Rochester Business Journal,* December 12, 1997, p. 1.

Chao, Mary, "Canandaigua Brands Aims to Boost 'Undervalued' Stock," *Rochester Business Journal,* January 1, 1999, p. 3.

——, "Canandaigua Capitalizing on New Taste for Wines," *Rochester Business Journal,* November 14, 1997, p. 13.

——, "Canandaigua Eyes Acquisitions," *Rochester Business Journal,* October 10, 1997, p. 4.

——, "Canandaigua Uncorks New Line of Dessert Wines," *Rochester Business Journal,* September 18, 1998, p. 14.

——, "More Canandaigua Brands Growth Projected," *Rochester Business Journal,* July 24, 1998, p. 8.

Cowan, Alison Leigh, "For Smaller Maker, a Rough Fight Just to Survive," *New York Times,* October 19, 1987, p. D10.

Fisher, Lawrence M., "Marvin Sands, Winery's Chairman, Dies at 75," *New York Times,* August 31, 1999, p. A18.

"A 47-Year History of Canandaigua Wine Company," *Cellar Echo* (Canandaigua Wine Co., Inc. Employee Newsletter), November 1992.

Johnston, David Cay, "The Wine Maker Canandaigua Is Riding High. But Can It Continue?," *New York Times,* March 3, 1995, p. D6.

Khermouch, Gerry, "Made in the Mist," *Brandweek,* July 12, 1999, pp. 18–19.

Kimelman, John, "Canandaigua Wine: Grape Expectations," *Financial World,* February 2, 1993, p. 16.

Lane, Randall, "Who's Afraid of Big, Bad Gallo?," *Forbes,* February 13, 1995, p. 180.

O'Connell, Vanessa, "A Wine Label with a Bouquet of Controversy," *Wall Street Journal,* December 8, 1998, p. B1.

Prial, Frank J., "Growing a Giant in the Vineyard," *New York Times,* August 22, 1999, sec. 3, p. 2.

Reflecting on Success, Canandaigua, N.Y.: Canandaigua Wine Co., Inc., 1995.

Roberts, Catherine, "Analysts Laud Changes at Canandaigua Wine," *Rochester Business Journal,* July 18, 1997, p. 6.

——, "Canandaigua Wine Unit Undergoes Restructuring," *Rochester Business Journal,* October 18, 1996, p. 6.

Siwolop, Sana, "Canandaigua Wine Tries to Get Its Bottles in a Row," *New York Times,* February 9, 1997, sec. 3, p. 4.

Stern, Willy, "Bottom Fishing in an Empty Pond," *Financial World,* March 14, 1995, p. 40.

Whiskeyman, Dolores, "Canandaigua Wine Sets New Course," *Rochester Business Journal,* January 16, 1989, p. 2.

—Thomas Derdak
—updated by David E. Salamie

Carl-Zeiss-Stiftung

Carl-Zeiss-Strasse 2-60
73446 Oberkochen
Germany
Telephone: (7364) 200
Fax: (7364) 6808
Web site: http://www.zeiss.de

Private Foundation
Incorporated: 1889
Employees: 31,806
Sales: DM 5.98 billion (US$3.3 billion) (1998)
NAIC: 327211 Flat Glass Manufacturing; 327212 Other
Pressed and Blown Glass and Glassware Manufacturing; 327213 Glass Container Manufacturing; 331524
Aluminum Foundries (Except Die-Casting); 331528
Other Nonferrous Foundries (Except Die-Casting);
333314 Optical Instrument and Lens Manufacturing;
333315 Photographic and Photocopying Equipment
Manufacturing; 334413 Semiconductor and Related
Device Manufacturing; 334519 Other Measuring and
Controlling Device Manufacturing; 339112 Surgical
and Medical Instrument Manufacturing; 339115
Ophthalmic Goods Manufacturing; 421460
Ophthalmic Goods Wholesalers; 421490 Other
Professional Equipment and Supplies Wholesalers

The Carl-Zeiss-Stiftung, a "juridical person" under German civil law, is the sole owner of two industrial enterprises, Carl Zeiss of Oberkochen and Schott Glas of Mainz. These enterprises develop, produce, and sell high-quality precision-engineered optical glass and electronic products, including ophthalmic products, binoculars, camera lenses, medical and surgical instruments and systems, microscopes, semiconductor technologies, measuring machines, surveying instruments, glass for household appliances, consumer glassware, laboratory glassware, glass tubing, and glass pharmaceutical packaging. The Carl-Zeiss-Stiftung enterprises have—as a percentage of sales—one of Germany's highest research and development budgets. The company has no private or state associates, and no shareholders. *Stiftung* is sometimes inaccurately translated as a special type of "foundation," a term suggesting an institution with purely charitable or scientific aims. The Carl-Zeiss-Stiftung, however, is a business organization with specific technological, scientific, economic, and social aims and functions. Usually companies are owned by individuals, banks, or states. The above-mentioned enterprises, however, are owned by the Stiftung and owe much of their character to its 1896 statute provisions.

Microscopic Origins

The origins of the Carl-Zeiss-Stiftung date from 1846, when Carl Zeiss, later awarded the title of university mechanic by the Grand Duke of Sachsen-Weimar, opened an instrument maker's shop in Jena. He soon specialized in the manufacture of microscopes. At the request of Carl Zeiss, the physicist Ernst Abbe developed the wave theory of microscopic imaging and, based on this theory, designed instruments with better resolution power and better color rendition than was hitherto possible. These improved microscopes sold from 1872, and—in particular microscopes with homogenous immersion objectives, introduced in 1877, and those with apochromatic objectives, available in 1886—greatly assisted bacteriologists' identification of infectious bacteria.

At that time the availability of only a small number of glass types with different optical properties limited progress in microscope image quality. In 1884 the chemist Otto Schott, together with Ernst Abbe, Carl Zeiss, and the latter's son Roderich, established a glass research laboratory, which developed into the Jenaer Glaswerk Schott & Genossen. By 1886, 44 different types of optical glass were in production. In cooperation with Ernst Abbe, Otto Schott carried out systematic research work into the dependence of optical and other glass on chemical composition. Schott's inventions included thermometer glass and chemical- and heat-resistant borosilicate glass. His optical glass contributed to the development of modern optical instruments. For microscopes and later also for telescopes, optical systems with apochromatic correction, that is, considerably reduced color aberrations, were designed.

Abbe's achievements as a social reformer of employment conditions were as significant as his scientific innovations. In 1889, the year following the death of Carl Zeiss, Abbe founded the Carl-Zeiss-Stiftung, which in 1891 he made the sole owner of the Zeiss works and a partner in the Schott works. In 1919 Schott made his own share of the glass works available to the Carl-Zeiss-Stiftung, which thus became the sole owner of both enterprises. In the 1896 statute of the Carl-Zeiss-Stiftung, Ernst Abbe formulated its aims and principles. The guiding principle of the Zeiss and Schott works and their associated enterprises throughout the world was to secure their economic, scientific, and technological future and in this way to improve the job security of their employees. The Stiftung's enterprises were obliged to produce high-quality, precision-engineered instruments, optical glass, and similar products, to fulfill long-term social welfare obligations to their employees, to support science and technology outside as well as within the enterprises, and to participate in projects that served the general good. The employment and career of an employee would depend only on his capabilities and performance, not on his origin, religion, or political views. The employees were to elect their own representation on the works council, and they received the right to a fixed minimum income, paid holidays, sickness benefit, profit sharing, disablement and pension benefits, and a nine-hour day, all of which was realized as early as 1896. In 1900 the eight-hour day was introduced.

Early Diversification and Growth

This scientific and social basis was reinforced economically by product diversification and by a growing export organization. In addition to microscopes Zeiss marketed photo lenses from 1890, measuring instruments from 1893, and terrestrial telescopes from 1894. Astronomical optics followed in 1897, medical instruments in 1898, photogrammetrical instruments in 1901, surveying instruments in 1908, and eyeglasses in 1912. Schott solved the cooling problem for large optical components with a diameter of up to 1.4 meters, as early as 1894. In 1913

Schott offered 97 types of optical glass, and by 1923 the number had increased to 114.

International relations were cultivated at an early stage. Zeiss visited the Paris World Fair in 1867, and Schott was repeatedly active as a manager in Spain, establishing a chemical factory in Oviedo and a production facility for window glass in Reinosa. These were not, however, owned by Schott. Abbe exchanged ideas with British microscopists, and from 1878 he published papers in English.

In 1899 about two-thirds of Zeiss instruments were sold abroad. A network of branches and agencies was built up, beginning with Zeiss sales offices in London, in 1901, and Vienna, in 1902. Branch factories were established in Vienna; in Györ, Hungary; Riga; and London in the first years of the 20th century.

In this period the Carl-Zeiss-Stiftung financed a number of projects for the benefit of Jena University and of the community, including a university building in 1908 and the Volkshaus, literally the "People's House," but in reality a palace with a library, museums, lecture halls, and a concert hall. Other projects in which the Stiftung was involved included a school of opticians, a children's hospital, and a public baths.

The Carl-Zeiss-Stiftung's constituent businesses, according to its statute, do not have a president but have several board members instead. This arrangement provides a degree of continuity even if a manager retires or dies. When Abbe retired in 1903 and died in 1905, Otto Schott, Siegfried Czapski, and Rudolf Straubel took over the burden of responsibility. Long-standing leaders of the organization included Erich Schott, who created a glass electric division in the glass works and was a board member from 1927 to 1968, and Walther Bauersfeld, who was a Zeiss board member from 1908 to 1959. Bauersfeld received worldwide esteem for his invention of a planetarium, which strikingly demonstrated the real and apparent movements of the sun, moon, fixed stars, and planets by projection on the inside of a dome.

The reputation of the Carl-Zeiss-Stiftung, the excellence of its products, and the commercial success of its enterprises had a far-reaching impact on the industries in which it was involved. Bausch & Lomb of Rochester, New York, acquired licenses from Zeiss, who bought shares in this U.S. company in 1908. World War I put an end to this successful collaboration in 1915. Another well-known microscope manufacturer, Rudolf Winkel of Göttingen, was reorganized in 1911 after some financial problems with the help of Carl Zeiss, which became the principal shareholder.

From 1910 to 1926 various German camera factories were amalgamated step-by-step into the Zeiss Ikon AG, famous for its Contax brand. In 1910 Zeiss acquired shares and in 1931 the majority of the Prontor-Werk Alfred Gauthier GmbH, later a producer of items for Carl Zeiss instruments. In 1927 the Schott works acquired a majority share in a company later called Schott-Zwiesel-Glaswerke AG that produced consumer glassware. Three years later a majority share was acquired in the company later known as Deutsche Spezialglas AG, a manufacturer of ophthalmic glass and various types of special technical glass. In 1928 Carl Zeiss acquired shares of the M. Hensoldt &

Key Dates:

1846: Carl Zeiss opens an instrument maker's shop in Jena.

1872: Working for Zeiss, Ernst Abbe develops the wave theory of microscopic imaging and designs the first microscopes based on this theory.

1884: With Abbe and Zeiss, chemist Otto Schott establishes a glass research laboratory.

1889: Abbe founds the Carl-Zeiss-Stiftung.

1890: Company diversifies into photo lenses.

1891: The Carl-Zeiss-Stiftung is made the sole owner of the Zeiss works and a partner in the Schott glass works.

1893: Company diversifies into measuring instruments.

1894: Company diversifies into terrestrial telescopes.

1896: Abbe formulates the aims and principles of the Carl-Zeiss-Stiftung in the foundation's statute.

1919: Schott turns over his share of the glass works to the Carl-Zeiss-Stiftung.

1927: Entry into consumer glassware through the acquisition of a majority stake in a company later called Schott-Zwiesel-Glaswerke AG.

1930: Majority stake is acquired in a company later known as Deutsche Spezialglas AG, maker of ophthalmic glass and special technical glass.

1933: A National Socialist is appointed foundation deputy.

1934: Following board and workforce resistance, the Nazi foundation deputy is ousted from his post and replaced by Abraham Esau, a professor loyal to the Stiftung.

1945: Following World War II, the Allies bring the entire management and the leading scientists of the Stiftung enterprises to Heidenheim.

1948: The two Jena-based enterprises are expropriated by the East Germans and turned into state-owned entities, including VEB Carl Zeiss Jena.

1949: Heidenheim becomes the new, West German, legal base for the Carl-Zeiss-Stiftung.

1954: Carl-Zeiss-Stiftung reinstates the employment rights of its workers.

1967: Schott Glass Technologies Inc. is founded in Duryea, Pennsylvania, for the production of optical glass.

1969: Schott-Ruhrglas GmbH is established to make special glass tubing.

1971: An agreement is reached between the east and west branches of the Carl-Zeiss-Stiftung regarding the worldwide use of the Zeiss name.

1990: Reunification of Germany sets the stage for the reuniting of eastern and western Carl Zeiss enterprises; Carl Zeiss Jena is converted into a limited company, Jenoptik Carl Zeiss Jena GmbH.

1991: Jenoptik Carl Zeiss sheds its nonoptical activities and changes its name to Carl Zeiss Jena GmbH; Carl Zeiss, Oberkochen, gains 51 percent stake in Carl Zeiss Jena and Jenaer Glaswerk, marking the beginning of the reuniting of the Carl-Zeiss-Stiftung.

1994: The Carl-Zeiss-Stiftung is domiciled in both Jena and Heidenheim.

1995: Carl Zeiss, Oberkochen, gains full control of Carl Zeiss Jena and Jeaner Glaswerk.

1997: Schott Glaswerke shortens its name to Schott Glas.

Söhne Wetzlar Optische Werke AG, which later produced Carl Zeiss telescopes and riflescopes. Hermann Anschütz-Kaempfe, the inventor of the gyrocompass, was impressed by the ideas of the Carl-Zeiss-Stiftung, to which he offered majority share of his company Anschütz & Co. GmbH, producers of navigation instruments, shortly before his death in 1931.

Thanks to its solid foundations the Carl-Zeiss-Stiftung survived through times of hardship. During World War I, the workforce was considerably enlarged due to the demands of riflescope, distancemeter, and aerial camera production. After the war and the subsequent period of hyperinflation it became necessary to reduce personnel. In accordance with the statute of the Carl-Zeiss-Stiftung, compensation for dismissal was paid.

In 1933 a National Socialist was appointed to the post of *Stiftungskommissar* (foundation deputy), as the one-man supervising authority of the Carl-Zeiss-Stiftung. The board members and workforces of both enterprises, Carl Zeiss and Schott Glaswerke, offered concerted resistance. The foundation deputy was ousted from his post in 1934, and Abraham Esau, a professor loyal to the Stiftung, took his place.

After 1933 production of a wide range of glass materials, glass products, and optical instruments continued. New developments included the phase contrast microscope, the prototype of which was first seen in 1936, and a new instrument for rapid surveying, in 1942. During World War II demand for military optics—range finders, rifle scopes, and periscopes for example—increased again. The additional workforce consisted of both Germans and laborers from occupied countries.

Postwar Reconstruction in a Divided Germany

In 1945, after World War II, the Allied government brought the entire management and the leading scientists of the enterprises of the Carl-Zeiss-Stiftung to Heidenheim. Four years later, Heidenheim became its new legal base after the two Jena enterprises were expropriated in 1948 by the East German authorities without compensation. Only in West Germany could it continue its existence on the basis of Abbe's statute. The Schott Glaswerke and Carl Zeiss were thereby able to regain international renown for their numerous technical innovations.

Nevertheless, the 126 managers and scientists in West Germany had to overcome enormous difficulties. Having arrived without technical documents, they had to rely on memory. In 1946, in Oberkochen near Heidenheim—in what is today Baden-Württemberg—a new optical plant was established, initially in rented premises. The glass experts continued production in Zwiesel and Landshut, Bavaria, until 1952, when a new factory was opened in Mainz. The manufacture of microscopes was transferred to Göttingen and the facilities of Rudolf Winkel, which was fully taken over by Carl-Zeiss-Stiftung in 1957.

Schott also established a number of production and sales subsidiaries at home and abroad; for example, ampule factories in Brazil and France between 1954 and 1974. In 1967 Schott Glass Technologies Inc. of Duryea, Pennsylvania, in the United States was founded for the production of optical glass. In Germany the Schott-Ruhrglas GmbH, manufacturing special glass tubing, was established in 1969. Carl Zeiss acquired two spectacles factories—Marwitz & Hauser, in which it had acquired a majority shareholding in 1958, and Titmus Optical Inc., of the United States—in 1974. The contact lens maker Wöhlk became a Zeiss subsidiary in 1980, when Carl Zeiss acquired a major stake.

After the postwar reconstruction of the company, the employment rights of the workers became effective once more; they had not been practicable during the state of emergency after World War II. On the occasion of this event Federal President Theodor Heuss visited Oberkochen on May 1, 1954, and stated: "German destiny is branded on few establishments of world significance as it is on this Zeiss establishment."

The original plants in Jena were dismantled by the Russian authorities in 1946, and more than 300 specialists were forced to work in Russia for some years. The Zeiss and Schott enterprises in Jena were temporarily struck off the trade register. Expropriation and nationalization of its former factories had removed the basis of the existence of the Carl-Zeiss-Stiftung in Jena. Nevertheless, the factories in Jena were restored to working order as part of a state-owned enterprise called VEB Carl Zeiss Jena, which was created in 1948. By the 1960s, this entity was transformed into an East German "combine," eventually becoming the largest and most prestigious such conglomerate in the country. While continuing to produce microscopes, telescopes, medical instruments, and other optical products—and thereby competing directly with the West German Carl Zeiss—Carl Zeiss Jena also diversified into military technology, microchips, cameras, and a host of other areas. (Cameras provided an interesting contrast between Carl Zeiss east and west; the latter exited from camera making in 1971 under pressure from Japanese competitors, while the former started making cameras in 1986 at the prodding of the East German government.) Carl Zeiss Jena was so important to the East German economy that its head was also a member of the Communist Party Central Committee.

From 1954 there were legal disputes in many countries regarding the matter of identity of the Carl-Zeiss-Stiftung and the use of the name Zeiss and its trademarks. In 1971 a compromise contract was finally drawn up in London. Under the contract, the Carl-Zeiss-Stiftung, Heidenheim, could exclusively use its name and trademarks with the component Zeiss in West Germany and some other Western countries, including the United States. The Jena party received corresponding exclusive rights within the Comecon (Council for Mutual Economic Assistance, representing communist countries) and some other countries. In certain countries, such as the United Kingdom and Spain, both parties could use the name Zeiss. As far as the identity of the Carl-Zeiss-Stiftung was concerned, the parties adhered to their differing opinions, each claiming to be the true representative of the foundation set up by Ernst Abbe. For the

glass works, a settlement valid worldwide was reached in 1981; the enterprise in Mainz was renamed Schott Glaswerke and the Jena enterprise took the name Jenaer Glaswerk.

1990s Reunification

The July 1990 reunification of Germany provided the opportunity for the reuniting of the eastern and western sides of the Carl-Zeiss-Stiftung. In February of that year the first exploratory talks were held between the two sides. In June 1990 Carl Zeiss Jena was converted into a limited company under the name Jenoptik Carl Zeiss Jena GmbH, the shares of which were acquired by the Treuhandanstalt, the Berlin-based agency in charge of privatizing the enterprises of what was soon to be the former East Germany. In November the two sides reached a general agreement to reunite, an agreement that also provided a framework for the restructuring of both Jenoptik Carl Zeiss and Jenaer Glaswerk.

By early 1991, then, Jenoptik Carl Zeiss had slashed its workforce by nearly 60 percent, from 69,000 to 25,800, and had jettisoned a number of noncore operations. In 1991, in anticipation of reunification, the Jena-based firm spun off its remaining nonoptical activities into a new entity called Jenoptik GmbH, which became owned by the state of Thuringia, where Jena is located. The optical activities were organized in the newly founded Carl Zeiss Jena GmbH. In June 1991 a final agreement was reached whereby the Oberkochen Carl Zeiss took a 51 percent controlling stake in both Carl Zeiss Jena and Jenaer Glaswerk, with the state of Thuringia, through its ownership of Jenoptik, holding the remaining 49 percent stakes in each. In May 1995 the interests held by Jenoptik were acquired by the Oberkochen Carl Zeiss. The four Carl Zeiss enterprises—the Oberkochen Carl Zeiss, Schott Glaswerke, Carl Zeiss Jena, and Jenaer Glaswerk—were thereby fused within the umbrella of the Carl-Zeiss-Stiftung. In a victory for the western side, the foundation was reconstituted based on the Heidenheim version of the charter, although in 1994 it adopted dual headquarters in Heidenheim and Jena. Rounding out the legal changes, Schott Glaswerke shortened its name to Schott Glas in 1997, while the Jena-based glass works were renamed Schott Jenaer Glas GmbH.

Despite nearly US$400 million in assistance from the German government, the reunification proved extremely difficult. The eastern German companies continued to lose money into the late 1990s, in spite of further workforce reductions, which left only about 3,000 Zeiss workers in Jena (about 10,000 jobs went over to Jenoptik GmbH). The operations of Carl Zeiss Jena suffered from the loss of most of its reliable customers in eastern Europe and Russia in the wake of the economic difficulties that accompanied the transition from state planning to capitalism. A deep recession in Germany did not help matters. Further layoffs followed, and in 1995 the entire Carl Zeiss group reorganized its product areas into smaller customer-oriented business groups.

For the 1996–97 fiscal year, the Carl Zeiss group broke even, following several years in the red. The Carl-Zeiss-Stiftung reported improving results in the late 1990s with net sales increasing from DM 5.1 billion in 1996 to DM 5.98 billion in 1998. Net income was on the rise as well, improving from DM 166 million in 1996 to DM 318 million in 1998. For the

1999 fiscal year, however, the Carl-Zeiss-Stiftung reported weaker results, in part because of the Asian financial crisis. This downturn led the foundation's management to consider a more radical reorganization, whereby the foundation would be transformed into a holding company, with Carl Zeiss and Schott Glas turned into separate incorporated firms. Such a makeover would follow similar transformations at other large German foundation companies, such as Bertelsmann AG.

Principal Subsidiaries

CARL ZEISS: Carl Zeiss Beteiligungs-GmbH; Carl Zeiss Industrielle Meátechnik GmbH; Carl Zeiss Jena GmbH; Carl Zeiss Lithos GmbH; Carl Zeiss Vision GmbH; Hensoldt AG; Hensoldt Systemtechnik GmbH; Marwitz & Hauser GmbH; MICROM Laborgeräte GmbH (74.9%); Prontor-Werk Alfred Gauthier GmbH; Schott-Zeiss Assekuranzkontor GmbH (50%); Wöhlk Contact-Linsen GmbH; Zeiss Optronic GmbH; Carl Zeiss N.V.-S.A. (Belgium); Carl Zeiss S.A. (France); Schott-Zeiss France Holding S.à.r.l. (France; 25.5%); Carl Zeiss Ltd. (U.K.); Carl Zeiss S.p.A. (Italy); Carl Zeiss B.V. (Netherlands); Carl Zeiss AS (Norway); Carl Zeiss GmbH (Austria); Carl Zeiss AB (Sweden); Carl Zeiss AG (Switzerland); Optiswiss Thaler AG (Switzerland); Carl Zeiss S.A. (Spain); Carl Zeiss Hungaria Optikai Kft. (Hungary); CAZE Szemüvegkeret Gyártó Kft. (Hungary); Carl Zeiss Holding Co. Inc. (U.S.A.); Carl Zeiss IMT Corporation (U.S.A.); Carl Zeiss Inc. (U.S.A.); Carl Zeiss Optical Inc. (U.S.A.); Carl Zeiss Canada Ltd.; Carl Zeiss (Pty.) Ltd. (South Africa); Carl Zeiss Far East Co. Ltd. (Hong Kong); Carl Zeiss Co. Ltd. (Japan); Humphrey Co. Ltd. (Japan); Carl Zeiss SDN. BHD. (Malaysia); Carl Zeiss Pte. Ltd. (Singapore); Carl Zeiss Co. Ltd. (Thailand; 49%); Carl Zeiss Pty. Ltd. Canberra Company (Australia); Carl Zeiss (N.Z.) Ltd. (New Zealand). SCHOTT GLAS: Schott Auer GmbH; Schott Desag AG (92.2%); Schott Jenaer Glas GmbH; LIB Industrie Beteiligung GmbH; Schott Medica GmbH; Schott-Geräte GmbH; Schott Glas Export GmbH; Schott Glaswerke Beteiligungs-GmbH; Schott-Rohrglas GmbH; Schott Spezialglas GmbH; Schott Glaskontor; Schott ML GmbH; Schott-Zeiss Assekuranzkontor GmbH (50%); Schott-Zwiesel AG (71.9%); Schott Amphabel S.A. (Belgium); Schott Verrerie Médicale S.à.r.l. (France); Schott France S.à.r.l.; Schott-Zeiss France Holding S.à.r.l. (74.5%); Schott SFAM Société Française d'Ampoules Mécaniques S.à.r.l.; VTF Industries S.à.r.i.; Schott Fibre Optics (UK) Ltd.; Schott Glass Ltd. (U.K.); Schott Industrial Glass Ltd. (U.K.); T.G.S. S.p.A. (Italy; 80%); V.I.T. Italvetro S.p.A. (Italy; 80%); Pieterman Glas B.V. (Netherlands); Schott Glaverbel B.V. (Netherlands; 75%); Schott Glaverbel Holding B.V. (Netherlands; 66.7%); Schott Benelux B.V. (Netherlands); Schott Svenska AB (Sweden); Schott Atevi S.A. (Spain); Schott Ibérica S.A. (Spain); Travisa Transformadora del Vidrio S.A. (Spain); Schott Electronic Packaging Lanskroun s.r.o. (Czech Republic); STV Glass a.s. (Czech Republic; 51%); Gemtron Corporation (U.S.A.; 51%); Schott Corporation (U.S.A.); Schott Fiber Optics Inc. (U.S.A.); Schott Glass Technologies Inc. (U.S.A.); Schott Scientific Glass Inc. (U.S.A.); Schott Pharmaceutical Packaging Inc. (U.S.A.); SGBM Inc. (U.S.A.); Day Specialties Corporation (Canada; 51%); Schott Canada Inc.; Schott Vitronac Ltda. (Brazil); Schott Glaverbel do Brasil Ltda. (Brazil; 70%); Schottbras Indústria de Vidros Ltda. (Brazil); Schott Vitrofarma Ltda. (Brazil); Schott Vitrosul Ltda. (Brazil); Gemtron de México S.A. de C.V.; Schott Igar Glass (Indonesia); Schott Nippon KK (Japan); Schott Glass (Malaysia) SDN. BHD. (93%); Schott Electronic Packaging Asia Pte. Ltd. (Singapore).

Principal Operating Units

CARL ZEISS GROUP: Consumer Optics Business Group; Medical Systems Business Group; Microscopy Business Group; Opto-Electronic Systems Business Group; Semiconductor Technology Business Group; Industrial Metrology Business Group. SCHOTT GROUP: Home Appliances Business Group; Television Business Group; Consumer Glassware Business Group; Industry Business Group; Optics Business Group; Opto-Electronics Business Group; Tubing Business Group; Pharmaceutical Packaging Business Group.

Principal Competitors

Avimo Group Limited; BMC Industries, Inc.; Brown & Sharpe Manufacturing Company; Corning Incorporated; Fisher Scientific International Inc.; JDS Uniphase Corporation; LG Electronics; LightPath Technologies, Inc.; Nikon Corporation; Nippon Sheet Glass Company, Limited; Pilkington plc; PPG Industries, Inc.; Southwall Technologies Inc.; ThermoSpectra Corporation; US Precision Glass Company.

Further Reading

Abbe, Ernst, *Gesammelte Abhandlungen,* Volumes I-IV, Jena, Germany: G. Fischer, 1904–1928.

Aeppel, Timothy, "German Firm Finds Reuniting Hard to Do," *Wall Street Journal,* December 14, 1990, p. B3C.

Auerbach, Felix, *The Zeiss Works and the Carl Zeiss Foundation in Jena,* London: W. & G. Foyle, [1927], 273 p.

"Cold War," *Economist,* May 18, 1991, p. 81.

Colitt, Leslie, "East Germany's High-Flying Company Comes Down to Earth," *Financial Times,* December 14, 1990, p. 2.

Dempsey, Judy, "Zeiss 'Marriage' a Unification Story Ending in Tears," *Financial Times,* November 1, 1994, p. 2.

Düllberg, H., et al., *Meilensteine der Zeiss Fernglasgeschichte und ihre Dokumentation,* Stuttgart: Dongowski & Simon, [1993], 99 p.

Fisher, Andrew, "New Focus at Zeiss," *Financial Times,* December 13, 1991, p. 14.

——, "Two Parts of Zeiss Rejoin After 45 Years," *Financial Times,* November 12, 1991, p. 28.

Goodhart, David, "Reuniting a Corporate Symbol of German Division: The Future of Carl Zeiss Jena," *Financial Times,* July 2, 1990, p. 10.

Hermann, Armin, *Nur der Name war geblieben—Die abenteuerliche Geschichte der Firma Carl Zeiss,* Stuttgart: DVA, 1989, 367 p.

Kiaulehn, Walther, *Der Zug der 41 Glasmacher,* Mainz, Germany: Schott Glaswerke, 1959.

Kühnert, Herbert, *Der Briefwechsel zwischen Otto Schott und Ernst Abbe über das optische Glas 1879–1881,* Jena, Germany: G. Fischer, 1946.

Nash, Nathaniel C., "Zeiss Bears Brunt of German Unity," *New York Times,* November 8, 1994, p. D1.

O'Boyle, Thomas F., "Zeiss Claimed by Communists, Capitalists: German Optical Twins Thrive on Both Sides of Iron Curtain," *Wall Street Journal,* January 13, 1989.

100 Jahre Carl-Zeiss-Stiftung, Heidenheim, Germany: Carl-Zeiss-Stiftung, 1988.

Rohr, Moritz von, *Zur Geschichte der Zeissischen Werkstätte bis zum Tode Ernst Abbes,* Jena, Germany: G. Fischer, 1936.

Roth, Terence, "Zeiss of East Germany Set to Re-enter Free Market via Merger with Namesake," *Wall Street Journal,* June 22, 1990.

Schares, Gail E., "Is There a Silicon Valley in the East German Rubble?," *Business Week,* December 21, 1992, p. 86D.

Schomerus, Friedrich, *Geschichte des Jenaer Zeisswerkes, 1846–1946,* Stuttgart: Piscator, 1952, 348 p.

——, *Werden und Wesen der Carl-Zeiss-Stiftung,* Stuttgart: G. Fischer, 1955, 253 p.

Schott, Erich, *Von Jena nach Mainz,* Mainz, Germany: [n.p.], 1984.

Volkmann, Harald, "Ernst Abbe and His Work," *Applied Optics,* November 1966.

Willam, Horst Alexander, "Otto Schott und das Zeiss Werk," *Klinische Monatsblätter für Augenheilkunde,* 1966.

—Wolfgang Pfeiffer
—updated by David E. Salamie

Cathay Pacific Airways Limited

35th Floor, Two Pacific Place
88 Queensway
Hong Kong
Telephone: +852-2747-5210
Toll Free: (800) 233-2742
Fax: +852-2810-6563
Web site: http://www.cathaypacific.com

Public Company
Incorporated: 1946 as Cathay Pacific Airways
Employees: 14,000
Sales: HK$28.70 billion (1999)
Stock Exchanges: Hong Kong Singapore
NAIC: 481111 Scheduled Passenger Air Transportation;
    481112 Scheduled Freight Air Transportation

After World War II, Cathay Pacific Airways Limited grew from a small regional airline to a prosperous international carrier fueled by trade and tourism. After the 1997 transition to Chinese rule in Hong Kong, the carrier has had to redefine its role at the gateway of southern China. In spite of a traditional determination to go it alone, Cathay Pacific joined the one-world alliance, spearheaded by American Airlines and British Airways, to economically maintain a global presence.

Origins

Cathay Pacific's roots date back to 1946 when 34-year-old American businessman and pilot Roy Farrell teamed up with an adventurous 32-year-old Australian pilot, Sydney de Kantzow, who had been flying the ''Hump'' (the route from Calcutta over Burma to Chungking) during World War II. Originally operating out of Shanghai with a lone DC-3, the two entrepreneurs soon moved their operations to Hong Kong, where they were required to officially register their company with the British colonial government. Together they registered Cathay Pacific Airways' corporate papers on September 24 of that year, also forming the Roy Farrell Import-Export Company which, for tax purposes, would lease aircraft from Cathay Pacific. By the end

of 1946 the airline had acquired a second DC-3 and had carried 3,000 passengers and 15,000 kilos of cargo between Australia and Asia.

In 1947 Cathay Pacific added five more DC-3s and two smaller aircraft known as Catalina ''flying boats,'' which allowed the airline to begin service to Macao, a nearby Portuguese colony on the coast of China. In these years immediately following World War II, Farrell and de Kantzow had to contend with Asia's shifting political boundaries, and their passengers enjoyed few of the comforts that today's transcontinental passengers have come to expect. The Roy Farrell Import-Export Company proved to be a profitable enterprise, operating out of an office on Ice House Street in Hong Kong; at this time it was advertising Australian oysters (considered a delicacy in the British Crown Colony) available by air within 32 hours of their harvesting.

By 1948 Cathay Pacific had a passenger ticket office in the lobby of the Peninsula Hotel, among the colony's most prestigious establishments. While flight crews were recruited mostly from Australia and the United States, de Kantzow began staffing passenger flights with Portuguese stewardesses from Macao and Hong Kong.

Swire Invests in 1948

Early in 1948, Farrell and de Kantzow were informed by the British governor of Hong Kong that, as foreigners, they were barred from owning more than 20 percent of the airline; a British partner would have to be recruited. After negotiations with the British air transport company Skyways ended unsuccessfully, Cathay Pacific's founders turned to John Kidston ''Jock'' Swire, head of Butterfield & Swire, a leading trading company in Hong Kong.

Farrell and de Kantzow believed that a British partner would be willing to pay a great deal to join their profitable business. The airline industry was at a crossroads, as ''tramp'' airlines running charter flights were giving way to increasingly competitive scheduled airline operations. Since 1946, the Bermuda agreement between the United States and the United Kingdom had regulated the routes airlines could service and the fares they could charge, marking a new era of government restrictions. Swire's influence with the British government made him an advantageous partner. From Swire's point of view, Cathay Pacific had a convenient competitor: Hong Kong Airways, run by Swire's longtime business rival, Jardine Matheson. Negotiations with Swire were fruitful, and in July 1948 the new Cathay Pacific Airways was officially registered.

The first known incident of air piracy occurred that same month when a Cathay Pacific flight, ten miles from Macao and carrying 23 passengers, was hijacked by a Chinese gunman who apparently believed the plane was carrying a cargo of gold bullion. The flight's captain, Dale Cramer, was shot in the head, and the plane crashed into the Pearl River estuary; there was only one survivor. De Kantzow and Farrell decided to use metal detectors on all passengers and baggage on subsequent flights.

The same year, Farrell's wife became ill and he decided to sell his stake in the airline and return to Texas, leaving Cathay Pacific a 90 percent British-owned company. The airline faced increasing competition from Hong Kong Airways, which had been purchased by the British Overseas Airways Corporation (BOAC—now British Airways). While the British government in London tended to give favorable treatment to BOAC, Hong Kong's local government had grown more independent as the colony gained economic power, and gave its support to Cathay Pacific.

Cathay Pacific had an additional advantage. Hong Kong Airways was obliged to offer its European passengers all the luxury and personal service they had come to expect from BOAC. Cathay Pacific, on the other hand, as a regional airline increasingly catering to the small Chinese traders accustomed to traveling on Swire's ships, did not have to offer expensive frills and consequently saved on overhead costs.

Under Swire's tutelage, de Kantzow instituted a number of changes. Swire's right-hand man Ian Grabowsky revamped Cathay Pacific's lax accounting procedures. More pilots were hired and each flew fewer hours, to stave off fatigue and possible mishaps. Eventually de Kantzow tired of Swire's control and announced his resignation from Cathay Pacific in April 1951. The parting appeared to be an amicable one.

Cathay Pacific suffered losses in 1951 approaching HK$1.5 million, a figure which increased over the next few years. Swire recognized the need to replace the airline's aging fleet with new aircraft, and began to look for a new partner for the company. In 1953 the London-based P&O shipping company paid HK$2.5 million for a 31.2 percent stake in the airline.

At this time, two important executives joined Cathay Pacific's management team: Captain Kenneth Steele became flight superintendent in charge of training flight crews, and senior engineer Jack Gething took over the Hong Kong Aviation Engineering Company, a division of Cathay Pacific responsible for airplane maintenance.

In September 1958, a new 8,350-foot runway was opened at Hong Kong's Kai Tak airport, in time for the arrival of Cathay Pacific's new DC-6 aircraft. That same year, Captain Bob Howell took the first DC-6 from Hong Kong to London. The larger, more modern airplane also pioneered the Hong Kong-Taipei-Tokyo route.

Merging into the 1960s

In 1959 BOAC, having endured heavy losses throughout the decade, agreed to merge Hong Kong Airways with Cathay Pacific. Swire's organization gained control of the airline, while BOAC received a seat on its board of directors. By the following year, Cathay Pacific's fleet of new aircraft included a DC-3, a DC-4, a DC-6, a DC-6B, and, notably, two Electra jets. At this time, Bill Knowles became the airline's chairman and Duncan Bluck its commercial manager.

Hong Kong's growing importance as an economic power resulted in an increasing number of routes serviced by Cathay Pacific. Late in 1959 the airline began flights to Sydney, prompting Qantas, Australia's national airline, to retaliate by announcing its own Sydney-Hong Kong jet service. The British government urged Swire to aggressively compete with Qantas to prevent an Australian concern from gaining an economic foothold in Hong Kong. This scenario proved typical in years to come: Swire saw his company simply as a regional airline flying to regional destinations such as Manila and Singapore, but to the British government Cathay Pacific was a British-owned company playing a major role in advancing Hong Kong to a position of economic prosperity and leadership in the region. In this instance, the matter was settled in August 1961 when Qantas, with the help of government subsidies, began flying newer, more expensive Boeing 707s to Hong Kong, forcing Cathay Pacific out of that particular market.

The loss of the Sydney-Hong Kong route to Qantas convinced Swire not to attempt to compete with government-backed intercontinental carriers; to his thinking, the objective was to offer the best service in the Asian market, not necessarily the best in the world. But Swire's regional view was opposed by commercial manager Bluck. Throughout the early 1960s, Bluck argued for more flights to Japan, which had experienced tremendous economic growth in the postwar years, and for flights to Canada and the United States, which were doing an increasing amount of business with Asian nations. Bluck also urged the purchase of better, more expensive planes for Cathay Pacific's fleet.

Key Dates:

1946: American and Australian pilots establish Cathay Pacific in Shanghai.
1948: Swire trading house buys into Cathay Pacific.
1959: Cathay Pacific merges with BOAC's Hong Kong Airways.
1987: China invests in Cathay Pacific through CITIC.
1996: Swire reduces its holdings to 44 percent.
1997: Great Britain returns Hong Kong to China.
1998: Cathay Pacific posts its first loss in 36 years.

Bluck's boardroom arguments succeeded. In January 1962, Cathay Pacific announced that it would purchase new Convair 880 jets manufactured by General Dynamics in the United States. The first Convair 880 arrived in Hong Kong in November 1964. By 1968, Cathay Pacific had five of the jets in its fleet, having retired or sold its other aircraft.

During this time there had been changes in management as well: in 1963 Gething and Steele retired and were succeeded by Don Delaney as engineering director and Dave Smith as flight superintendent. A year later, Bill Knowles retired from his position as chairman and was replaced by H.J.C. (John) Browne.

Early in 1965 Browne informed Cathay Pacific's board that the expansion into the Japanese market was a success, with passenger traffic for the airline up 26 percent over the previous year and well over half a million passengers carried into and out of Kai Tak airport in 1964. Three ticket offices had opened in Japan, which, along with Taiwan, now accounted for 90 percent of the airline's passenger capacity. In 1965, Jock Swire retired, leaving Cathay Pacific in the hands of his two sons, John and Adrian.

On June 15, 1972, one of Cathay Pacific's Convair jets was involved in what seemed at first to have been a midair collision over Vietnam. After initial speculation regarding the identity of the other aircraft, investigators turned to the possibility of a bomb having been placed on board. British and Hong Kong police identified their prime suspect: a Thai policeman whose recently insured wife and child had been on board the flight. Charged with sabotage and murder, in May 1974 the policeman was found not guilty; no further suspects were ever brought to trial.

Global Expansion in the 1970s and 1980s

The tragedy did not dissuade Cathay's directors from expansion. By 1974, eleven 707s had been added to the airline's fleet. That same year, Cathay renewed its Hong Kong-Sydney service with 707s, putting its earlier defeat by Qantas behind it. The success of the Australian run was followed in 1976 by thrice-weekly flights to the Arabian Gulf, first to Bahrain, and later to Dubai in the United Arab Emirates. Asian laborers were increasingly in demand throughout the Gulf following the 1973 oil crisis and newly wealthy Arab sheiks were eager to purchase the high-tech electronic products then available in Hong Kong.

But getting acceptance from London for Cathay Pacific, sporting a union jack on its tail, to fly the "Golden Route" from Hong Kong to London proved a surprisingly drawn-out process. In December 1979, the Hong Kong airline applied to the United Kingdom's Civil Aviation Authority for a license to land in London. But British Airways, enjoying a monopoly on the Hong Kong-London route, fought Cathay Pacific's application at Civil Aviation Authority hearings. To complicate matters still further, British Airways' rival British Caledonian joined with Laker Airways to compete with Cathay Pacific for the run to Hong Kong. Finally, in March 1980, London authorities ruled against Cathay's application, choosing British Caledonian instead. The news was difficult to accept in the Cathay boardroom. The Hong Kong airline appealed, and was finally granted a license in June of that year to land in London. Cathay Pacific joined other deluxe international carriers by taking two jumbo 747s into its fleet.

In 1981, Cathay Pacific carried over three million passengers and 97 million kilos of cargo to 23 destinations. A year later, six 747s were employed on its routes, some flying to London nonstop in 14 hours. Another international destination added in 1983 was Vancouver, which had one of the largest Chinese communities abroad.

In 1984 Bluck, who had become chairman of Cathay Pacific, answered charges that Asian airlines were prospering because of the low wages paid to their workers and lower overheads than faced by Western airline carriers. Bluck, quoted in Gavin Young's *Beyond Lion Rock,* responded, "Japanese cars, VTRs and TV sets have been able to penetrate western markets because of quality, reliability, the application of modern technology and price. So too will Asia-Pacific airlines continue to win customer support, not by low prices but by quality of service."

In 1986 Cathay Pacific carried nearly 4.2 million passengers and 182 million kilos of cargo on its way to becoming a beneficiary of the economic boom then developing in the Asian Pacific region. Hong Kong's proximity to burgeoning centers of growth in southern China were expected to further benefit Cathay Pacific. The impending takeover of the colony in 1997 by the Chinese government, however, was seen as a potential liability. The political change was expected to hinder the airline's attempts to win crucial air service rights through bilateral agreements with other countries.

In anticipation of the change in government, the Swire Group announced in January 1987 that it was reducing its share of ownership in Cathay Pacific. This was followed by an announcement that the China International Trade and Investment Corporation (CITIC), China's principal commercial arm in Hong Kong, was taking a 12.5 percent shareholding in the airline. The Chinese government stake, coupled with the airline's welcoming a new director onto its board—Larry Yung, son of the CITIC's chairman—was seen by observers as proof that China was sincerely interested in the future prosperity of Cathay Pacific and Hong Kong in general.

New Rules in the 1990s

In 1991, the airline posted profits of HK$2.95 billion, just slightly below 1990 profits of HK$2.99 billion. Maintaining its profitability was an impressive achievement at a time when many U.S. and European airlines were floundering amid recessionary and Gulf War woes. Also at that time, drawn-out negotiations between London and Peking appeared close to ending, suggesting agreement on a new international airport to be built on Hong Kong's Chek Lap Kok Island at an estimated cost of HK$13 billion. Scheduled to open in 1997, the new airport was expected to face increasing competition from low-cost airports in neighboring Macao and Shenzen, China.

Cathay's forecasts predicted its cargo business growing by eight percent per year throughout the 1990s. Transporting freight had contributed approximately 20 percent of overall airline revenue in the first six months of 1991. Richard Cater, Cathay Pacific's cargo marketing manager, stated in the February 24, 1992 issue of *Aviation Week & Space Technology,* "We see ourselves as a passenger airline with a very important cargo element." The growing cargo business was welcome at a time of recessionary gloom in much of the Western world, and falling airline passenger traffic due to the Persian Gulf War.

Although Cathay Pacific remained profitable under the Swire Group's control, lingering uncertainties over the outlook for Hong Kong under Chinese rule clouded the company's business strategy. Despite the instability of the world economy, Cathay Pacific counted on its reputation as a premier Asian carrier and on a continuation of the Asian-Pacific economic boom to maintain its place in the global airline trade.

Peter Sutch led Cathay Pacific as managing director beginning in 1992. He subsequently became chairman of the company as well as its parent, John Swire & Sons (HK) Ltd. David M. Turnbull took over as managing director in December 1996, replacing Rod Eddington, who returned to Australia to lead Ansett Airlines.

In 1996, Swire Pacific sold a major portion of its airline holdings to Chinese interests. It reduced its stake in Cathay Pacific from 53 to 44 percent and its stake in Hong Kong Dragon Airlines (Dragonair) from 43 to 26 percent. CITIC upped its holdings in CX (Cathay's IATA designation) from ten to 25 percent while selling some of its shares in Dragonair to the China National Aviation Corporation (CNAC), which also held about five percent of Cathay Pacific. The Chinese reportedly had threatened to set up their own airline in Hong Kong, pressuring Swire into diluting its holdings (it issued new shares rather than selling the ones it owned). Cathay Pacific eventually acquired three-quarters of another small competitor, Air Hong Kong.

Because of its strong position in Asia, Cathay Pacific was being courted by many global airline alliances, but the carrier felt inclined to go it alone, remaining true to its regional focus. The company did set up a new direct route to New York. It also teamed up on the ground, setting up a maintenance company in Xiamen, China, with Singapore Airlines and Japan Airlines.

Before the change of government in Hong Kong, CX had begun to build its first proper headquarters (the HK$448 million Cathay Pacific City) and had reworked its corporate image (it had until then painted Union Jacks on its planes). Thanks in part to the sale of Dragonair shares, the company posted a profit of HK$3.8 billion (US$488 million) for 1996, up 28 percent.

However, tourism after the handover of Hong Kong on July 1, 1997 was less than expected. The number of Japanese visitors fell 62 percent in the second half of 1997 compared to the same period in 1996—from 1.4 million to just over 500,000. CZ upped its flight frequencies to Europe, Australia, and the United States, following tourist dollars.

The Asian financial crisis cut business traffic. Further, since Hong Kong tied its currency to the U.S. dollar, Cathay's costs rose in comparison to those of its neighbors. Significant gains in cargo operations were temporarily threatened by computer problems at the new airport's shipping center.

Steep landing fees at the new Hong Kong International Airport at Chek Lap Kok added to Cathay's burden. Billed as "the world's largest construction project," the new airport did give CZ the impressive setting it lacked to showcase its sterling service. However, it was expensive. Cathay Pacific provided half the total commercial investment–HK$1 billion, including the cost of its new headquarters.

The company laid off 760 employees in January 1997. The cost-cutting was not sufficient to avoid a loss of HK$542 million (US$70 million) for 1998, its first in 36 years. (Most of this came from write-offs of older aircraft.) A falling share price prompted Hong Kong to invest in both Cathay and Swire. For its part, Cathay attempted to take over struggling Philippine Airlines Inc. in late 1998.

As cockpit crew accounted for 40 percent of labor costs, company executives asked this well-paid bunch for concessions in 1999. The pilots reluctantly agreed, after two weeks of "too stressed to fly" sick-outs that cost the company an estimated HK$500 million. (Flight attendants had held a three-week strike in 1993 that cost Cathay Pacific HK$200 million.) The *Wall Street Journal* reported that most of Cathay's pilots were British, and not one of them was an ethnic Chinese from Hong Kong.

Cathay Pacific adopted a new corporate identity in 1999. During the year, passenger levels rose on nearly all routes, particularly U.S. ones, and e-commerce helped push up cargo revenues 20 percent to HK$8.4 billion. The company posted a profit of HK$2.2 billion in 1999 on sales of HK$28.7 billion. The optimistic figures prompted the conservative management to begin to expand its fleet again with Airbus planes and two Boeing 747 freighters.

After years of courtship, Cathay Pacific finally succumbed to the economic appeal of code sharing and joined the oneworld alliance led by American Airlines and British Airways. The airline saw Hong Kong as more of a hub than a destination by then. The opening of China's airways raised the prospect of CX flying passengers directly to the mainland again, rights the carrier had lost after it acquired a portion of Dragonair in 1990.

Principal Subsidiaries

Cathay Pacific Catering Services; Hong Kong Aircraft Engineering Co. (HAECO); Hong Kong Dragon Airlines (18%).

Principal Competitors

British Airways plc; China Airlines; Singapore Airlines Ltd.

Further Reading

Arnold, Wayne, "Cathay Pacific Executives Seek to Trim One of Aviation's Fattest Paychecks," *Wall Street Journal,* March 24, 1999.

Bangsberg, P.T., "Cargo Gains Fail to Offset Decline at Cathay Pacific," *Journal of Commerce,* August 8, 1997, p. 13A.

Cathay Pacific Airways: An Illustrated History, Cathay Pacific Public Relations, 1990.

"Cathay's Mix of 7775 Confirms Interest in Stretched Version," *Aviation Week & Space Technology,* April 20, 1992.

"Critical Time As Cathay Reviews Its Future," *Duty-Free News International,* May 15, 1999.

Donoghue, J.A., "Through the Changes," *Air Transport World,* January 1997, pp. 52–53.

——, "The Wing Takes Flight," *Air Transport World,* March 1999, pp. 85–86.

Field, Catherine, "The Selling of a Grand Old Airline," *Worldbusiness,* July/August 1996, p. 12.

Feldman, Joan, "Cathay's Conservative Challenge," *Air Transport World,* April 1999, pp. 53–54.

Ionedes, Nicholas, "Cathay Buys Remainder of Catering Service," *South China Morning Post,* March 20, 1996, p. 2.

——, "Haeco Riding Out Turbulence," *South China Morning Post,* December 27, 1995. p. 2.

Lo, Joseph, "Cathay Plots New Course; Hubbing Holds the Key As Airline Re-Invents Itself," *South China Morning Post,* November 23, 1999, p. 22.

Mungan, Christina, and Erik Guyot, "Cathay Pacific Senior Pilots Accept Cuts in Pay, Averting a Threatened Strike," *Wall Street Journal,* June 11, 1999, p. A14.

Quak Hiang Whai, "Cathay's Crisis Far from Over Despite Pilot Salary Accord," *Business Times* (Singapore), June 15, 1999, p. 17.

Saunier, Veronique, "Cathay's Sale of Dragonair Shares Pushes '96 Profits to $488 Million," *Aviation Week & Space Technology,* March 17, 1997, p. 41.

"Second Half Turnaround at Cathay Pacific," *Financial Times,* March 25, 1992.

"Serving Dinner for 80,000 Requires a Lot of Refrigeration," *Air Conditioning, Heating & Refrigeration News,* December 7, 1998, pp. 34–35.

Tabakoff, Nick, "Cathay Emphasises Go-It-Alone Strategy," *South China Morning Post,* March 3, 1997, p. 2.

Thomas, Geoffrey, "Normally Profitable, Cathay Posts First Loss," *Aviation Week & Space Technology,* March 15, 1999, p. 40.

"Thriving Regional Economies, Automation Spark Growth of Asian Cargo Carriers," *Aviation Week & Space Technology,* February 24, 1992.

Tong, Amy, "Cathay Pacific to Trim Staff, Add Planes; Carrier Won't Cut Flights, Despite Asian Turmoil, Fewer Japanese Tourists," *The Nikkei Weekly,* February 23, 1998, p. 22.

"Towards Open Skies," *Flight International,* February 19–25, 1992.

Westlake, Michael, "A Tale of Two Airlines," *Far Eastern Economic Review,* July 1, 1999, pp. 46–48.

Young, Gavin, *Beyond Lion Rock: The Story of Cathay Pacific Airways,* London: Hutchinson, 1988.

—Etan Vlessing
—updated by Frederick C. Ingram

Childtime Learning Centers, Inc.

38345 West 10 Mile Road
Suite 100
Farmington Hills, Michigan 48335
U.S.A.
Telephone: (248) 476-3200
Fax: (248) 476-1168
Web site: http://www.child-time.com

Public Company
Incorporated: 1995
Employees: 6,000
Sales: $112.96 million (1999)
Stock Exchanges: NASDAQ
Ticker Symbol: CTIM
NAIC: 62441 Child Day Care Services (pt)

Childtime Learning Centers, Inc. offers child-care and preschool services through its network of more than 290 centers in 22 states and the District of Columbia. The company serves more than 30,000 families and provides care for children aged 6 weeks to 12 years through its Childtime Centers and employer-sponsored, at-work facilities. Childtime experienced considerable growth in the 1990s and has plans to continue expanding at the rate of about 30 new centers a year to boost revenues.

Building Business in the Early Years: 1967–90

What eventually evolved into Childtime Learning Centers was founded in Illinois in 1967. The child-care firm was acquired by Michigan-based baby food manufacturer Gerber Products Company in 1973, and the name was changed to Gerber Children's Centers, Inc. The company grew swiftly and expanded into New York, Illinois, California, Florida, Oklahoma, Ohio, Michigan, Maryland, Virginia, Georgia, Texas, and Arizona by the late 1980s.

Gerber was a pioneer in the development of employer-sponsored child-care services, opening its first corporate child-care center in 1981 at the Hurley Medical Center in Flint, Michigan. The center provided daycare and child-care services

to employees of the hospital as well as members of the community. Gerber followed up the success of the Hurley center with centers at the Fresno Hospital in Fresno, California, in 1983, on the campus of Prince Georges Community College in 1984, at Mercy Hospital in Oklahoma City, Oklahoma, in 1986, and at Henry Ford Hospital in Detroit, Michigan, in 1987. In early 1990 Gerber opened a center at Edward W. Sparrow Hospital in Lansing, Michigan, and one at William Beaumont Hospital, located in Royal Oak, Michigan. The Beaumont facility turned a profit after only six months in operation.

Gerber Children's Centers built a reputation for focusing on education, but its rapid expansion and what some in the industry viewed as poor management led to financial struggles in the late 1980s. The business suffered losses of about $3 million, and enrollment sagged—the centers, which numbered 115 in 1990, operated at about 60 percent of capacity at best, and 19 of the total were only half full. Attention from parent company Gerber Products was lacking as well; Gerber Products had diversified to the detriment of its primary business of baby food, and in the late 1980s the company began to shed its unprofitable, noncore operations, which included a trucking firm and businesses that manufactured toys, infant car seats, sleepwear, and children's furniture, in order to return its attention to baby food. The Gerber Children's Centers business was considered extraneous as well, and in 1990 Gerber Products announced the sale of its child-care subsidiary to KD Acquisition Corporation, a private investment firm based in New York. The sale was completed in July, and new ownership began the task of turning around the ailing business.

New Ownership and Restructuring in the Early 1990s

The U.S. child-care industry was highly fragmented, filled with many independent and local providers. In the early 1990s the largest child-care companies controlled only about four percent of the entire $15 billion market, leaving ample room for growth. The child-care industry was forecast to grow considerably as the number of working mothers increased, and the new owners of Gerber Children's Centers hoped to tap into this growth. As Deborah Ludwig, executive vice-president and general manager of Gerber Children's Centers, explained in a company press

Company Perspectives:

The Children entrusted to our care will receive the best in learning environments in an atmosphere of acceptance, understanding, respect, and love.

The Parents of our children shall receive support in meeting the developmental and educational needs for their children and, as customers of our service, be treated with courtesy and respect.

The Shareholders will view shares of Childtime as an opportunity for meaningful return.

The Community will be served by a responsible corporate citizen supporting those activities which improve the quality of life for all children.

The Women and Men who, as members of our company, are directly responsible for its success, will enjoy a professionally fulfilling, participative, work life.

We commit ourselves to the quest of meeting our objectives in a manner that will allow us to truthfully say: "We Make a Difference."

release, "Nearly 75 percent of all pre-school children will have employed mothers by 1995. . . . And more women with infants are choosing to stay employed than ever before in the history of this country. This, along with an overall rise in births—4.5 percent from July 1989 to July 1990—all point to growth opportunities for reputable providers of child care."

The new owners of Gerber Children's Centers wasted no time getting to work on reviving the company. Expansion, primarily in the growing field of employer-sponsored facilities, was a goal, and in December 1990 the company acquired Supertots, a provider of at-work child-care services, from Ogden Services Corporation. The purchase of the ten Supertots locations cemented the position of Gerber Children's Centers as one of the five largest child-care providers in the nation. Among the centers acquired by Gerber Children's Centers were those at Prudential Insurance Company of America in Iselin, New Jersey, and at Schering-Plough Corporation in Union, New Jersey.

Another major change for the company came in 1991. Under terms of the sale, KD Acquisition agreed to give up the Gerber name. To select a new company name, Gerber Children's Centers staged a contest that resulted in more than 3,000 entries. Two people came up with the winning name, Childtime Children's Centers, and for their efforts they were each given a $25,000 college scholarship bond.

The company moved its headquarters from Fremont, Michigan, to Brighton to be nearer to a major airport and assembled a new management team. Harold Lewis was recruited from Thomas Cook Travel Inc. to serve as president and CEO. Lewis, who had no previous work experience in the child-care industry, implemented a new management strategy that focused more heavily on the business aspect of running a child-care center. Lewis told *Crain's Detroit Business,* "We make it clear to our center directors that there's no inconsistency at all in being profitable and in caring for and teaching young children. . . . Without profitability, we can't invest back into the business in

terms of new equipment for the children." Incentive programs that rewarded center directors for increasing enrollment and running more efficient operations were launched, and the company began offering management courses for directors that included classes on planning budgets, recruiting and firing staff members, marketing, and finance. Childtime also implemented a marketing program that targeted dual-income families with young children. The program used direct mail to entice prospective customers and marketed its services to businesses located close to Childtime facilities to attract working parents.

The emphasis on business and management did not mean Childtime ignored the care of children. The company installed computer systems in the majority of Childtime centers and hired an educational consultant to develop a curriculum for each age group served by the facilities. Childtime educational programs emphasized the process of learning and discovery, and children were placed into groups depending on their social, intellectual, emotional, and physical maturity. To retain business, Childtime made it a policy to keep parents informed regarding the activities and progress of their children, and thus the centers distributed the curriculum and periodic report cards to parents.

Childtime moved its headquarters again in 1992, to Farmington Hills, Michigan, and by the end of that year business was on the upswing—of the 19 centers that had been running at half capacity at the beginning of the decade, 16 had recovered and become profitable. By 1993 Childtime posted revenues of $44 million and a profit of $1 million. In 1993 the company opened two new at-work facilities, one at St. Francis Hospital in Evanston, Illinois, and one at the Northern Illinois Medical Center in McHenry. The following year Childtime began operating a facility for Blue Cross and Blue Shield of Mississippi and opened the Child Development Center at the Tulsa State Office Building in Oklahoma. To realize its goal of adding about 20 new centers a year, Childtime continued to expand through strategic acquisitions as well, and in 1994 the company bought Little Learners, a child-care provider in Syracuse, New York. The acquisition boosted Childtime's numbers to 135 centers covering 14 states and Washington, D.C.

By the mid-1990s Childtime's recovery seemed complete. For the fiscal year ended March 31, 1995, Childtime enjoyed record growth. The company reported revenues of $55 million, an increase of $7 million from the previous year, and net income of about $2.7 million. Harold Lewis commented on the company's accomplishments in a prepared statement and said, "Our growth over the past three years, in a very competitive market, is primarily the result of target marketing and focused management." Lewis also noted that the company's achievements were all the more remarkable when considering the slim profit margins in the child-care industry.

Steady Growth and Increasing Revenues in the Late 1990s

Childtime welcomed new challenges as it entered the second half of the decade. The company reincorporated as Childtime Learning Centers, Inc. in November 1995 and completed its initial public offering in February 1996. Childtime shares were offered on the NASDAQ exchange at $10 a share. In addition, although the child-care industry was growing rapidly,

```
┌─────────────────────────────────────────────────┐
│                  Key Dates:                     │
│                                                 │
│  1967:  Company begins operations in Illinois.  │
│  1973:  Original company is acquired by Gerber  │
│         Products Company and renamed Gerber     │
│         Children's Centers, Inc.                │
│  1990:  KD Acquisition Corporation buys Gerber  │
│         Children's Centers.                     │
│  1991:  Gerber Children's Centers is renamed    │
│         Childtime Children's Centers.           │
│  1995:  Childtime Learning Centers, Inc. is     │
│         incorporated.                           │
│  1996:  Company goes public and begins trading  │
│         on the NASDAQ.                          │
└─────────────────────────────────────────────────┘
```

Childtime planned to expand steadily but conservatively, aiming to open about 25 to 30 new facilities a year until the end of the decade. Lewis told the *Detroit News,* "The problem with expanding any faster is coming up with the capital and human resources. We don't want any handicaps. Our goal is to maintain steady growth with high-quality facilities." Each newly built center cost about $1 million to build. The spacious centers ranged from 6,400 to 8,000 square feet. To ensure the success of the centers it opened, Childtime sought locations in residential areas with a high density of dual-income families and in regions with numerous office buildings. The company also looked for opportunities managing employer-sponsored, at-work facilities.

Differing state regulations, high employee turnover, and low profit margins all posed problems to those in the child-care industry, but the potential for growth in the U.S. market outweighed the cons. Thomas Johnson of Kindercare Learning Centers, Inc., one of the largest child-care providers in the United States, explained in *Crain's Detroit Business* in 1996, "There are 51 million children under the age of 12. . . . Even if you total 50 of the largest for-profit child-care centers in the country, they'd be able to take care of only 1 percent of the nation's children." By the late 1990s the industry had grown to a $30 billion market, and consolidation had begun, indicating acknowledgment by investors of the growth potential of the business. In 1997 Kindercare was purchased by Kohlberg Kravis Roberts & Co., and La Petite Academy was acquired by Chase Manhattan. In 1998 Children's Discovery Center was bought by Knowledge Universe, an investment company led by infamous junk bond dealer Michael Milken, Milken's brother Lowell, and Oracle Systems Corporation Chairman Lawrence Ellison.

Childtime's growth strategy proved successful, and the company's revenues grew steadily. Childtime's revenues for fiscal 1997 reflected a 20 percent increase over 1996 revenues and reached $78.63 million. The company opened 37 centers that year, including the takeover of Bureautots, an at-work facility serving employees of the U.S. Census Bureau in Suitland, Maryland. Childtime also won contracts to operate centers on the campus of the New Jersey Institute of Technology and the Veterans Affairs Medical Center in Pennsylvania. In 1997 the company made its entry into the state of Washington when it acquired nine centers from Abundant Life Childcare Centers in Seattle. Childtime also secured a contract to assume operation of an at-work center sponsored by the General Services Administration in downtown Seattle.

By the end of fiscal 1999, which ended April 2, the number of Childtime facilities had grown to 270 spanning 19 states and Washington, D.C. Childtime's revenues reached $112.96 million, up from $97.83 million in 1998. Net income also increased, from $4.35 million in 1998 to $5.1 million. Enrollment in the centers had grown from 26,000 to 30,000 children, and the company added 30 new facilities. Childtime gained seven centers in Nevada through an acquisition, and two contracts involved the management of child-care facilities located at mass transit stops. The centers, in Baltimore, Maryland, and Des Moines, Iowa, were designed to promote mass transit commuting by working parents.

In August 1999 Childtime announced that its first quarter results would fall below estimates. The company blamed high electricity bills, caused by an unseasonably warm summer, and expenses from unsuccessful acquisition negotiations for the fall in earnings. Childtime also stated plans to close seven of its centers, which resulted in a severe one-day drop in the company's share price of 13.2 percent. The company indicated that it could possibly close six to ten additional underperforming centers during the year, but that plans to open 35 to 40 new facilities were in place.

Childtime may have hit a few snags as it neared the turn of the century, but the company was not discouraged. The company was included on "The 200 Best Small Companies in America," an annual list compiled by *Forbes,* in 1999. Childtime continued to grow and expand, adding 11 new centers in North Carolina, Georgia, and Texas at the end of 1999 and winning a management contract for the Lovelace Child Development Center, which provided services for the employees and members of Lovelace Health Systems, a health maintenance organization. In September Childtime partnered with ParentWatch, an Internet company that provided parents with live video access via the World Wide Web to their children at participating child-care facilities. To enhance its educational programs, Childtime formed a joint venture with Oxford Learning Centres of Canada. Known as Oxford Learning Centers of America, the venture was designed to offer after-school tutoring and enrichment programs to children from kindergarten through the eighth grade.

In the course of one decade, Childtime not only had defied its demise but it also had grown from 115 centers to more than 280 facilities in 22 states and the District of Columbia. For the first nine months of fiscal 2000, Childtime reported revenues of $96.37 million, up from $84.88 million for the comparable period of 1999. Net income fell from $3.5 million to $3.2 million, but Childtime remained confident in its future. The company planned to continue growing and expanding to meet the demands of working families in the 21st century.

Principal Subsidiaries

Childtime Childcare, Inc.; Childtime Childcare—Michigan, Inc.; Childtime Childcare—PMC, Inc.

Principal Competitors

KinderCare Learning Centers, Inc.; La Petite Academy, Inc.; ARAMARK Corporation.

Further Reading

Adelson, Andrea, "Child-Care Industry Is Showing Signs of a Growth Spurt," *Austin American-Statesman,* August 1, 1998, p. 4.

Burge, Katrina, " 'What Did You Do in School Today, Darling?' Harold Lewis Is in the Business of Taking Care of Other People's Kids, But He's Smart Enough to Realize That His Real Customers Are the Parents," *Forbes,* December 1, 1997, p. 106.

Child, Charles, "Day-Care HQ in Brighton," *Crain's Detroit Business,* February 18, 1991, p. 1.

Grugal, Robin M., "The New America—Childtime Learning Centers Inc.," *Investor's Business Daily,* October 31, 1996, p. A4.

Hoffman, Gary, "Childtime Learning Readies $18-Million Initial Stock Offering," *Detroit News,* January 10, 1996, p. E1.

Kosseff, Jeffrey, "Childtime Skins Knees: But Some Analysts See Upside to Closings," *Crain's Detroit Business,* August 23, 1999, p. 2.

Raphael, Steve, "Minding Business: Chain Mixes Caring, Profits," *Crain's Detroit Business,* August 8, 1994, p. 3.

Seymour, Liz, "This Isn't Child's Play: Childtime Seeing Shamrock Green—Possibly $65M of It," *Crain's Detroit Business,* March 18, 1996, p. 3.

Smith, Joel J., "Day-Care Centers Running Out of Room," *Detroit News,* June 18, 1996, p. B1.

Snavely, Brent, "Childtime Sprouts Up: But Child Care Company's Stock Hasn't Followed," *Automotive News,* December 20, 1999, p. 2.

Waldsmith, Lynn, "Child Care Provider Gains in Earnings, Not on Market: Childtime Centers Sales Climb 20% Since Going Public in '96," *Detroit News,* September 9, 1997, p. B1.

—Mariko Fujinaka

China Airlines

131 Nanking East Rd., Section 3
Taipei
Taiwan
Telephone: 886 (2) 2715-2233
Fax: 886 (2) 2514-6005
Web sites: http://www.china-airlines.com
http://usa.china-airlines.com

Public Company
Incorporated: 1959
Employees: 9,200
Sales: NT$51.9 billion (US$1.61 billion) (1998)
Stock Exchanges: Taipei
Ticker Symbol: CAIR-TP
NAIC: 481111 Scheduled Passenger Air Transportation;
481112 Scheduled Freight Air Transportation; 481211
Nonscheduled Chartered Passenger Air
Transportation; 48819 Other Support Activities for
Air Transportation

Although China Airlines (CAL) became something of a pariah when the United Nations recognized the People's Republic of China as that country's true government, the sheer power of the Taiwanese economy propelled it to become one of the world's most profitable airlines, thriving even in global recessions. CAL also benefited from strong government support; however, critics charge that the "Retired Generals' Club" that has controlled CAL for so long is responsible for its dismal safety record. CAL controls about a third of Taiwan's international air traffic; more than seven million passengers a year fly the accident-prone carrier, which assures them, "We treasure each encounter."

Nationalist Origins

As aviation historian R.E.G. Davies recounts it, CAL was founded on December 10, 1959, by a group of retired Chinese Air Force officers in Taipei, the Republic of China (Taiwan). Initial capitalization was NT$400,000. Operations began with two PBY-5A Catalina flying boats and 26 employees. Military charter work formed the bulk of its business. Within a couple of years, however, CAL had obtained a few war surplus C-47 (DC-3) and C-46 transports which it used to link several points around the island.

CAL was not Taiwan's first carrier. Civil Air Transport (CAT) had been founded before the mass exodus of Chinese Nationalists from the mainland. In time CAT became Taiwan's flag carrier, although the U.S. Central Intelligence Agency (CIA) owned 60 percent of it through the Pacific Corporation. It had been steadily losing influence when China Airlines was created. CAL, other regional carriers, and even Air America, also sponsored by the CIA, succeeded in parceling out CAT's routes. After a few disastrous crashes, the Taiwanese government closed down CAT in May 1968. CAL subsequently became the official state airline.

CAL had meanwhile started its first international service to Saigon on a used Lockheed Super Constellation in December 1966. It also bought a couple of Boeing 727 jets to ferry Japanese tourists to Taipei and Hong Kong. Its fleet then numbered 32 and employment exceeded 2,000. Ben Chow was the company's president.

The International Air Transport Association (IATA) admitted CAL in January 1969. However, the carrier automatically lost its International Civil Aviation Organization (ICAO) membership in October 1971 when the United Nations (UN) officially recognized the communist People's Republic of China (PRC) as that country's true government.

Growth in the 1970s and 1980s

CAL grew furiously—by a factor of 80 percent—in 1972 and 1973. However, a number of factors caused this growth to fall off sharply in the next two years. Japan and Malaysia canceled air agreements with CAL following the UN declaration. Losing access to Tokyo left CAL unable to fly to Korea as well. Within a short time, CAL lost access to Saigon due to the fall of South Vietnam. The 1973 oil crisis dealt another severe blow.

In the early 1970s, CAL began serving San Francisco first via Tokyo and Anchorage, then via Honolulu. In 1974, it dedicated a Boeing 707 freighter to a Los Angeles route as cheap exports poured out of Taiwan. The carrier had the confidence to lease a giant Boeing 747 for transpacific service in 1975, while it added three Boeing 737s for important regional routes. It left many marginally profitable short-haul routes to the likes of Far Eastern Air Transport and Yung Shing ("Forever Prosperous") Airlines (later Formosa Airlines).

CAL was able to resume service to Tokyo (Haneda Airport) in October 1975. It also entered into tentative cooperation with Jordan for a westerly route network meeting in Bangkok. However, CAL was ditched in favor of Air Siam for this service. CAL did sign a similar, more lasting agreement with Saudi Arabian Airlines in February 1976. Chang Lin-tech assumed the company presidency around this time.

This western expansion extended into Europe by decade's end. In 1978, CAL agreed to buy four Airbus A300 widebody jets, a deal rumored to help the carrier pry open the market there. Taiwan also allowed a couple of Luxembourg air freight companies to serve Taipei.

CAL posted its first ever loss in 1980 as rail and road transportation improved considerably on the island of Taiwan. The airline's global expansion continued nonetheless. Cargo flights stretched all the way to New York City beginning in 1981, and the next year CAL added its first European cargo service, to Luxembourg. In 1984, CAL added a new around-the-world route via New York and Amsterdam for passengers and cargo. It also added the super-luxurious Dynasty Class. Tragedy marred these accomplishments, though, when CAL lost a Boeing 737 into the Taiwan Strait in February 1986, killing 13. Later that year, one China Airlines pilot—who formerly flew U-2 spy planes for the United States—hijacked his own Boeing 747 freighter, landing in his ancestral homeland at Canton.

As Taiwanese were allowed to visit mainland China in the late 1980s, CAL was able to fly them partway, to Hong Kong or Tokyo, where they continued on airlines of the PRC (Air China, China Eastern, China Southern, etc.) The pilgrimage attracted 750,000 in 1990. That year, another 257,000 flew to the United States.

Another of CAL's Boeing 737s was lost in October 1989 when it flew into a mountain, killing 54 people. Five crew members were lost when a Boeing 747 crashed, again into a mountain, in December 1991. These incidents would not be the last.

1990s: Decade of Disaster

China Airlines had 7,200 employees as it began the 1990s. CAL was reorganized as a registered corporation in 1991, though it remained 84 percent government-owned through the China Aviation Development Foundation (CADF), created in 1988 as a kind of quasi-governmental holding company.

A new crop of local operators opened up the prospect of competition. The Evergreen shipping empire founded Eva Air in 1991, filling in points not easily reached by CAL. Eva Air was somehow able to connect to Great Britain, one of the first countries to accept Beijing's sovereignty in 1957. Foshing Airlines, a small charter operator, changed its name to TransAsia Airways and began flying shuttles around Taiwan with Airbus A320 jets in 1992. CAL reduced its domestic network to just the Taipei-Kaohsiung route, focusing on international expansion.

In 1992, CAL bought Mandarin Airlines, a two-year-old carrier formed to service countries which objected to CAL's use of the word "China" in its name. Meanwhile, some European airlines (British Airways, Lufthansa, Air France), unable to fly to both mainland China and Taiwan, began to serve the latter through subsidiaries. Cathay Pacific competed with service to Hong Kong, from which it could fly to both China and Taiwan.

In spite of the crowded market and poor safety record, CAL had become one of the five most profitable carriers in the world. It earned profits of $125 million on revenues of $1.7 billion in 1993. Cargo contributed 20 percent of revenues. CAL had developed extensive maintenance facilities at Chiang Kai Shek Airport. It owned 19 percent of Far Eastern Air Transport. It also had hotel interests and continued to diversify. The company had 8,000 employees in 1993, when it was listed on the Taiwan Stock Exchange.

According to some observers, a huge trade imbalance in Taiwan's favor pressured CAL into buying American, ordering ten U.S.-made jets. CAL lost a $145 million Boeing 747 in November 1993 when it overshot the runway in Hong Kong. Fortunately no one was killed in this accident. However, the next April, 264 died in Nagoya, Japan, after a copilot in training reportedly pushed the controversial "go around" button while landing, then fought the controls until the Airbus 300 stalled and fell to the ground.

Chairman Liu Ming-the and President Yuan Hsing-yuan resigned after the Nagoya crash, one of the ten worst air disasters in history. The two were replaced by Chiang Hung-i and Fu Chun-fan, respectively. The carrier's close links with the military were placed under scrutiny, and Chiang was also a retired air force general. Critics believed the carrier skimped on flight simulators and training time. CAL's profits fell to US$24 million (NT$642 million) in 1994.

CAL unveiled a new corporate identity in October 1995. While touting its devotion to safety, the carrier replaced the Taiwanese flags on its planes with less controversial pink plum blossoms ("We blossom every day"). Change purportedly ran deeper than the aircraft skin. CAL had shaken up its management and brought in Lufthansa Technik as a safety consultant. CAL remained focused on expansion. It ordered 15 advanced Boeing 737 medium-haul jets worth $750 million in December 1995, and acquired one-third of Formosa Airlines in 1996.

Hong Kong, for decades a colony leased by Great Britain, reverted to Chinese ownership in 1997. CAL was able to continue flying to it, a fact which its softened image probably helped.

That year, CAL earned about US$90 million (NT$2.77 billion) on revenues of US$1.7 billion. It entered a code-sharing arrangement with American Airlines on transpacific routes. CAL was ranked one of the top ten cargo airlines in the world in 1997 and placed first in Taiwan, controlling one quarter of the market.

In spite of such impressive statistics, management struggled to cut costs as the number of new airline seats threatened to outpace traffic growth projections. However, the carrier still boasted impressive load factors (the percentage of seats filled). Meanwhile, the Taiwanese government, which then owned 71 percent of CAL, looked for a foreign investor to acquire 16 percent of the company.

Just as a recovery seemed in hand, a CAL jet crashed in Taipei in February 1998, killing 203. A few weeks later, a Formosa Airlines Saab 340 crashed with 13 on board. The accidents decimated traffic at the country's 17 airlines, and at CAL in particular. Further, 130 flight attendants left the carrier after the crash.

Interestingly, the next president, Sandy K.Y. Liu, was the son of Liu Ming-the, the CAL chairman who resigned after the Nagoya crash—just one indication of the "revolving door syndrome" in Taiwan's aviation industry. However, by this time, a third of CAL's pilots were brought in from outside the country, thinning the ranks of former military aviators.

CAL still had a long way to go; critics charged that old military styles of thinking continued to dominate. In April 1998, a new $120 million maintenance facility opened. However, regulators found problems there as well, although CAL was aiming to increase third party work at this unit. The carrier obtained two senior pilots from Singapore Airlines (SIA) in August 1998 to direct flight safety operations. However, they both left a few months later, citing profound differences in flight training philosophies. SIA had also agreed to take an equity stake in the carrier, but soon canceled over a disagreement on the size of the stake. The government, through the CADF, began to shop around a 35 percent stake in the company, hiring Salomon Smith Barney to help find a buyer. Taiwan-based China Development Bank stepped up as a likely candidate, but insisted on having control of the management.

The Asian financial crisis ended a ten-year string of growth in departure traffic and CAL lost US$92.6 million (NT$2.96 billion) in 1998 on sales of US$1.61 billion (NT$51.9 billion). However, it restored profitability in the first half of 1999. CAL merged its Formosa and Mandarin airlines subsidiaries and on August 11, 1999, announced its largest order ever—$5.6 billion for 24 Boeing and 12 Airbus jets. It was Boeing's largest order ever for dedicated freighters (17). Another CAL jet crashed on August 23. The MD-11 flipped over while landing in strong crosswinds at Hong Kong. Three people were killed and 200 injured.

Although some safety factors remained out of CAL's control, such as Taipei's suboptimal air traffic control system, the long string of accidents had observers asking how many crashes could a single airline bear. Still, CAL planned to spend $5 billion on new Airbus and Boeing jets. It was recognized for excellent customer service and attained ISO 9001 certification. In early 2000, Northwest Airlines and CAL discussed areas of cooperation short of an equity investment.

Principal Subsidiaries

Mandarin Airlines Ltd.; CAL-Dynasty International, Inc. (U.S.A.); CAL-Asia Investment, Inc. (BVI); Hwa Hsia Company, Ltd.; Hwa Sheng Investment Co., Ltd.; Abacus Distribution System Taiwan, Ltd. (95%); Taiwan Airport Services Company, Ltd. (58.35%); Taoyuan International Airport Services Co., Ltd. (55%); China Pacific Laundry Services, Ltd. (55%); Dynasty Holidays, Inc. (51%); China Pacific Catering Services, Ltd. (51%); Formosa Airlines Corporation (40.77%); Global Sky Express, Ltd. (25%); Asian Compressor Technology Services Co., Ltd. (24.5%); Spacehab Taiwan, Inc. (21.62%).

Principal Competitors

Cathay Pacific Airways Limited; Eva Air.

Further Reading

Baum, Julian, "Losing Height," *Far Eastern Economic Review,* September 2, 1999, pp. 44–45.
——, "Safety First," *Far Eastern Economic Review,* June 16, 1994, pp. 74+.
Brady, Diane, "Taiwan's China Air Drops Flag Logo, Stresses Safety in Recasting Its Image," *Wall Street Journal,* October 9, 1995.
Carey, Susan, "China Airlines Plans Stock Offerings, Joining Other Asian Lines Going Public," *Wall Street Journal,* October 14, 1991.
Chang, Leslie, and Diane Brady, "China Air Is on Course to Repeat Mistakes: Taiwan Carrier's Safety Record Scares Off Passengers," *Wall Street Journal,* April 29, 1998, pp. A19ff.
"China Airlines, SIA Part Ways," *Aviation Week & Space Technology,* May 31, 1999, p. 38.
Davies, R.E.G., "Airline Transfer to an Offshore Island," *Airlines of Asia Since 1920,* London: Putnam, 1997, pp. 362–82.
Drury, Rick, "Black Rain," *Airways,* November 1999, pp. 79–80.
Flannery, Russell, "Taiwan Retains Airline Executives, Facilitating Sale," *Wall Street Journal,* August 30, 1999, p. A23.
——, "Taiwan Still Urges Sell-Off at China Air—Government Raises Pressure on Carrier's 71 Percent Owner Despite Latest Crash," *Wall Street Journal,* August 25, 1999, p. A14.
——, "Taiwan Vows Curbs on China Airlines If It Was at Fault in Sunday's Crash," *Wall Street Journal,* August 24, 1999, p. A14.

Hill, Leonard, ''Louder Than Words,'' *Air Transport World,* August 1999, pp. 27–30.

Jones, Dominic, ''Competition Intensifies in Taiwan's Air Transport Market,'' *Airfinance Journal,* April 1997, pp. 34–35.

Moore, Jonathan, ''Can China Air Climb Again?,'' *Business Week,* March 2, 1998, p. 55.

Sterba, James P., ''Negotiations for Return of Hijacked Jet Just a New Twist to an Old Chinese Game,'' *Wall Street Journal,* May 21, 1986.

''Taiwan and China Progress Slowly in Plane Talks,'' *Wall Street Journal,* May 19, 1986.

''Taiwan Regionals Forced to Merge,'' *Aviation Week & Space Technology,* April 20, 1998, p. 36.

Vandyk, Anthony, ''Rising Above Its Identity,'' *Air Transport World,* August 1993, p. 87.

—Frederick C. Ingram

CISCO SYSTEMS

Cisco Systems, Inc.

170 West Tasman Drive
San Jose, California 95134-1706
U.S.A.
Telephone: (408) 526-4000
Toll Free: (800) 553-6387
Fax: (408) 526-4100
Web site: http://www.cisco.com

Public Company
Incorporated: 1984
Employees: 26,140
Sales: $12.15 billion (1999)
Stock Exchanges: NASDAQ
Ticker Symbol: CSCO
NAIC: 334210 Telephone Apparatus Manufacturing;
334418 Printed Circuit Assembly (Electronic Assembly)
Manufacturing; 334419 Other Electronic Component
Manufacturing; 511210 Software Publishers; 541512
Computer Systems Design Services

Cisco Systems, Inc. is the world's leading supplier of computer networking products, systems, and services. The company's product line includes routers, switches, remote access devices, protocol translators, Internet services devices, and networking and network management software, all of which link together geographically dispersed local area networks (LANs), wide area networks (WANs), and the Internet itself. Cisco serves three main market segments: large organizations—including corporations, government entities, utilities, and educational institutions—needing complex networking solutions that typically bridge multiple locations; service providers, including Internet access providers, telephone and cable companies, and providers of wireless communications; and small and medium-sized businesses whose needs include operating networks, connecting to the Internet, and/or connecting with business partners. The company is increasingly developing expertise in the area of fiber-optic networking as well as the concomitant expertise in multiservice networks, which offer video and voice capabilities in addition to the traditional data capability.

Beginnings in Multiprotocol Routers

Cisco Systems was founded in December 1984 in Menlo Park, California, by a husband and wife team from Stanford University, Leonard Bosack and Sandra Lerner. Bosack was the manager of the computer science department's laboratory, and Lerner oversaw the computers at the graduate school of business. At Stanford, Bosack devised a way to connect the two local area networks in the respective departments where he and his wife worked, 500 yards across campus.

Lerner and Bosack initially tried to sell the internetworking technology that Bosack had developed to existing computer companies, but none were interested. They then decided to start their own business, Cisco Systems, based on this technology (they came up with the name, a shortened form of San Francisco, while driving across the Golden Gate Bridge). Bosack and Lerner were joined by colleagues Greg Setz, Bill Westfield, and Kirk Lougheed, as cofounders. Stanford University later tried to obtain $11 million in licensing fees from the new company, because Bosack had developed the technology while an employee at the university, but eventually the university settled for $150,000 and free routers and support services.

The company was established on a very tight budget. In fact, Bosack and Lerner had to mortgage their house, run up credit card debts, and defer salaries to their friends who worked for them in order to get the venture off the ground, and, even after two years of business, Lerner maintained an outside salaried job to supplement the couple's income.

Cisco's primary product from the beginning was the internetworking router, a hardware device incorporating software that automatically selects the most effective route for data to flow between networks. Cisco's routers pioneered support for multiple protocols or data transmission standards, and could therefore link together different kinds of networks, those having different architectures and those built on different hardware, such as IBM-compatible personal computers, Apple Macintosh computers, UNIX workstations, and IBM mainframes. Cisco thus became the first company to commercially provide a multiprotocol router when it shipped its first product in 1986, a router for the TCP/IP (Transmission Control Protocol/Internet Proto-

111

Company Perspectives:

Cisco is better positioned than ever before to lead the Internet economy and help change the way we work, live, play, and learn.

---

col) protocol suite. A year later, Cisco was selling $250,000 worth of routers per month. Sales for the fiscal year ending July 1987 were $1.5 million, and the company had only eight employees at the time.

Cisco initially marketed its routers to universities, research centers, the aerospace industry, and government facilities by contacting computer scientists and engineers via ARPANET, the precursor to what was later known as the Internet. These customers tended to use the TCP/IP protocols and UNIX-based computers. In 1988, the company began to target its internetworking routers at mainstream corporations with geographically dispersed branches that used different networks. To that end, Cisco developed routers serving an even greater array of communications protocols and subsequently distinguished its routers by enabling them to support more protocols than those of any other router manufacturer. By the late 1980s, when the commercial market for internetworking began to develop, Cisco's reasonably priced, high-performance routers gave it a head start over the emerging competition.

Although Cisco had a high rate of sales growth, the young company was still short of cash; in 1988 Bosack and Lerner were forced to turn to a venture capitalist, Donald T. Valentine of Sequoia Capital, for support. Valentine, however, required that the owners surrender to him a controlling stake in the company. Valentine thus became chairperson and then hired an outsider, John Morgridge, as the company's new president and chief executive officer. Morgridge, who had an M.B.A. from Stanford University, was chief operating officer at laptop computer manufacturer GRiD Systems Corp. and prior to that had spent six years as vice-president of sales and marketing at Stratus Computer. Morgridge replaced several Cisco managers, who were friends of Bosack and Lerner, with more qualified and experienced executives. In February 1990, Cisco went public, after which Bosack and Lerner began selling their shares. Sales for the fiscal year ending July 1990 were $69.8 million, net income was $13.9 million, and the company had 254 employees.

Under Morgridge, Bosack had been given the title of chief scientist and Lerner was made head of customer service. However, Lerner reportedly did not get along well with Morgridge and, in August 1990, she was fired, whereupon Bosack also quit. When they left the company, Bosack and Lerner sold the remainder of their stock for $100 million, for a total divestiture of about $200 million. The couple subsequently gave away the majority of their profits to their favorite charities.

Early 1990s: Rapid Growth As Networks Proliferate

Meanwhile, Morgridge built up a direct sales force to market the products to corporate clients. At first, Cisco's corporate clients were the scientific departments of companies which already maintained large internal networks. Later, Cisco was able to market its products to all kinds of major corporations to help them link the computer systems of their headquarters, regional, and branch offices. As Cisco's client base grew, the company's greatest challenge became meeting customer support service needs. The large size of the network systems for which Cisco supplied products made the user support task especially complex.

The company grew at a tremendous rate as its market rapidly expanded. In the early 1990s, companies of all sizes were installing local area networks (LANs) of personal computers. As such, the potential market for linking these networks, either with each other or with existing minicomputers and mainframe computers, also grew. Cisco's sales jumped from $183.2 million in fiscal 1991 to $339.6 million in 1992, and net income grew from $43.2 million to $84.4 million during the same period. In 1992, *Fortune* magazine rated Cisco as the second fastest growing company in the United States. In its role as the leading internetworking router provider, Cisco could redefine and expand the market as it grew.

While new communications technologies became widespread, Cisco adapted and added the capabilities of handling new protocols to its products. In the fall of 1992, Cisco introduced Fiber Distributed Data Interface (FDDI) and Token-Ring enhancements to its high-end router. Around the same time, the company also introduced the first Integrated Services Digital Network (ISDN) router for the Japanese market.

Until 1992, Cisco's products had not addressed IBM's System Network Architecture (SNA), a proprietary network structure used by IBM computers. In September 1992, however, after IBM announced plans to license its Advanced Peer-to-Peer Networking (APPN) protocol used for SNA, Cisco responded by announcing plans for a rival Advanced Peer-to-Peer Internetworking (APPI) protocol for supporting SNA. By August 1993, Cisco had decided not to develop a rival protocol, because IBM made it clear that APPN would be a more open, multivendor protocol than originally intended. Cisco then proceeded to work with IBM on further defining the APPN standard and bought a license to use APPN technology.

The emergence of asynchronous transfer mode (ATM) technology as a new standard method for multiprotocol data communications posed a challenge to Cisco and the router industry. ATM is a cell-switching technique that can provide high-speed communications of data, voice, video, and images without the use of routers. In early 1993, Cisco entered into a joint development project with AT&T and StrataCom to develop standards that would ensure that ATM operated within existing Frame Relay networks. Cisco also became one of the four founding members of the ATM Forum to help define the emerging standard. In February 1993, Cisco announced a strategy to include ATM among the protocols supported by its products. In fiscal 1994, Cisco introduced its first ATM switch.

In January 1993, Cisco introduced a new flagship product, the Cisco 7000 router, which featured a 50 percent improvement in performance over the AGS+, Cisco's existing high-end router. In June of that year, Cisco introduced a new low-end, lower-priced product line, the Cisco 2000 router family.

Key Dates:

1984: Cisco Systems, Inc. is founded by Leonard Bosack and Sandra Lerner.

1986: Company ships its first product, a router for the TCP/IP protocol suite.

1988: Donald T. Valentine, a venture capitalist, gains control of the company; John Morgridge is named president and CEO.

1990: Company goes public; Lerner is fired and Bosack quits.

1993: Cisco completes its first acquisition, that of Crescendo Communications.

1994: Revenues exceed $1 billion for the first time.

1995: John T. Chambers is named CEO.

1996: Company acquires StrataCom, Inc., maker of switching equipment, for $4.67 billion.

1998: Cisco's market capitalization passes the $100 billion mark.

1999: Company acquires 17 businesses, including: GeoTel Communications Corp., a maker of software for routing telephone calls, for $1.9 billion; Cerent Corporation, maker of fiber-optic networking equipment, for $7.2 billion; Aironet Wireless Communications Inc., maker of wireless LAN equipment, for $800 million; and the fiber-optic telecommunications equipment business of Italy's Pirelli S.p.A. for about $2.2 billion.

2000: Company's market capitalization reaches $450 billion.

The Cisco 2000 was aimed at companies desiring to link their smaller, remote branches or even remote individual employees, but unwilling to pay a premium price. Also during this time, the first network with over 1,000 Cisco routers was created.

International sales became an important part of Cisco's business. Subsidiaries were established in Japan and Australia, and a European Technical Assistance Center was established in Brussels, Belgium. In March 1993, Cisco Systems (HK) Ltd. became a new subsidiary in Hong Kong. International sales steadily increased, accounting for 35.6 percent of sales in fiscal 1991, 36 percent in fiscal 1992, 39 percent in fiscal 1993, and 41.9 percent in fiscal 1994. Most of Cisco's international sales were through distributors, whereas in the United States the majority of sales (65 percent in early 1994) were made directly to the end users.

Cisco also began to market its technology, especially its software, more aggressively to long-distance telephone companies, as the deregulation of U.S. telephone carriers enabled these companies to provide more kinds of data communications products and services. For example, Cisco entered into a joint marketing agreement with MCI International to integrate Cisco's routers into end-to-end data networks over telephone lines. In 1992, Cisco entered new distribution agreements with Bell Atlantic Corp. and U.S. West Information Systems Inc. Cisco also signed marketing agreements in fiscal 1993 with Pacific Bell, whereby Cisco became a preferred router supplier for the company's network systems.

Cisco similarly began contracting with major European telecommunications companies at about the same time. British Telecom became an original equipment manufacturer (OEM) client of all of Cisco's products. Other European telecommunications companies that entered into OEM relationships with Cisco included Alcatel of France and Siemens A.G. of Germany. Olivetti of Italy agreed to market Cisco's products under a value-added reseller agreement late in 1992.

Cisco made other strategic alliances to position itself better in the maturing internetworking market. To reach out to less technical clients, Cisco entered into joint agreements with Microsoft Corporation to market Cisco's first PC-based router card with Microsoft's Windows NT Advanced Server networking software through Microsoft's marketing channels. Similarly, Cisco established a partnership with Novell to integrate Cisco's routers with Novell's Netware network software so as to provide links between Netware and UNIX-based networks. Additionally, Cisco began working with LanOptics Ltd. to develop remote-access products.

1993–94: First Wave of Acquisitions

In September 1993, Cisco made its first acquisition. For $95 million, it acquired Crescendo Communications, which had pioneered products for a new technology called Copper Distributed Data Interface (CDDI). Crescendo's development of ATM technology was also a leading reason for the acquisition. Crescendo Communications was renamed the Workgroup Business Unit, and its switching technologies under development were later incorporated into Cisco's routers. Cisco made its second acquisition, that of Newport Systems Solutions for $93 million in stock, in August 1994. Newport Solutions sold the LAN2LAN product line, software used in linking local area networks.

Early in 1994, Cisco announced a new networking architecture, CiscoFusion, to provide clients with a gradual transition from routers to the new switched networking technologies of ATM and LAN switching. CiscoFusion allowed users to take advantage of both routing and switching techniques. As part of this architecture, several new switching products were introduced in March 1994, including the ATM Interface Processor and the Catalyst FDDI-to-Ethernet LAN switch. The latter was the first new product of the Workgroup Businesses Unit since the acquisition of Crescendo.

During this time, Cisco moved its headquarters from one end of Silicon Valley to the other, from Menlo Park to a newly constructed office building complex in San Jose, California. The growing size of the company had necessitated larger office space. The company's workforce had grown from 1,451 in July 1993 to 2,262 in July 1994, as Cisco hired talent from smaller, struggling networking companies which were laying off personnel. In fiscal 1994, Cisco topped $1 billion in sales, ending the year on July 31, 1994, with $1.24 billion in net sales, a 92 percent increase over the previous year, and $314.9 million in net income, 83 percent more than fiscal 1993. Later in 1994, in October, Cisco completed two more acquisitions of firms involved in the switching sector. It spent $240 million for Kalpana, Inc., a maker of Ethernet switching products; and

$120 million for LightStream Corp., which was involved in ATM switching and Ethernet switching and routing.

Astounding Growth Under John Chambers Starting in 1995

In January 1995 John T. Chambers was named CEO of Cisco, with Morgridge becoming chairman and Valentine vice-chairman. Chambers, who had previous stints at IBM and Wang Laboratories before joining Cisco in 1991, stepped up the company's acquisition pace to keep ahead of its rivals and to fill in gaps in its product line, aiming to provide one-stop networking shopping to its customers. The company completed 11 acquisitions in 1995 and 1996, including Grand Junction, Inc., maker of Fast Ethernet and Ethernet switching products, purchased for $400 million in September 1995; and Granite Systems Inc., a maker of high-speed Gigabit Ethernet switches, bought for $220 million in September 1996. The largest deal during this period, however, was that of StrataCom, Inc., a $4.67 billion acquisition completed in April 1996. StrataCom was a leading supplier of ATM and Frame Relay WAN switching equipment capable of handling voice, data, and video. The addition of Frame Relay switching products to the Cisco portfolio was particularly important as that technology was being rapidly adopted by telecommunications companies needing to increase the capacity of their networks. The deal was also a key step in Cisco's attempt to move beyond its core customer area of "enterprise" customers—i.e., large corporations, government agencies, utilities, and educational institutions—into the area of telecommunications access providers, an area in which it faced entrenched and formidable competition in the form of such giants as Alcatel, Lucent Technologies Inc., and Nortel Networks Corporation.

Cisco continued its blistering acquisitions pace in 1997 and 1998, completing 15 more deals. The largest of these was the April 1998 purchase of NetSpeed, Inc., a specialist in digital subscriber line (DSL) equipment, an emerging technology providing homes and small offices with high-speed access to the Internet via existing telephone lines. Another emerging networking technology was that of voice-over-IP (Internet Protocol), which essentially enables the routing of telephone calls over the Internet. The acquisitions of LightSpeed International, Inc. in April 1998 and Selsius Systems, Inc. in November 1998 helped Cisco gain a significant presence in the Internet telephony sector. The areas of DSL and voice-over-IP provided additional examples of Cisco's strategy of acquiring its way into emerging networking sectors.

By the late 1990s Cisco Systems was the undisputed king of the networking world. In July 1998 the company's market capitalization surpassed the $100 billion mark, just 12 years after its initial public offering—a time frame believed to be a record for achieving that level. Revenues reached $12.15 billion by fiscal 1999, a more than sixfold increase over the fiscal 1995 result of $1.98 billion. During 1999 Cisco became even more acquisitive, snatching up an additional 17 companies, in the process gaining presences in two more emerging areas: fiber-optic networking and wireless networking. Several fiber-optic companies were acquired, including start-up Cerent Corporation, which was purchased for about $7.2 billion in the company's largest acquisition yet. Fiber-optic networks were particularly being built by telecommunications firms aiming to take advantage of their capacity for handling massive quantities of voice, video, and data, making Cisco's entry into this segment of vital importance. In late 1999 Cisco announced that it would acquire the fiber-optic telecommunications equipment business of Italy's Pirelli S.p.A. for about $2.2 billion, gaining Pirelli gear that takes a beam of light and breaks it into as many as 128 "colors," each of which can carry a separate stream of voice, data, or video. Cisco's key wireless acquisition also came in late 1999 with the announcement of the $800 million purchase of Aironet Wireless Communications, Inc., maker of equipment that creates LANs without wires in small and medium-sized businesses. The technology was also expected to be transferred to the home environment, where Cisco aimed to capture what was predicted to be an area of rapid early 21st century growth: the networked home. During 1999 Cisco also acquired GeoTel Communications Corp., a maker of software for routing telephone calls, for about $1.9 billion.

By early 2000—following 1999's frenzied bull market in high-tech stocks—Cisco's market value surpassed $450 billion, making it the third most valuable company in the world, behind Microsoft and General Electric Company (for a brief period in late March, Cisco actually ranked as the most valuable company in the world, with a total market capitalization of $555 billion). Revenues were soaring, as were earnings, which reached $906 million for the second quarter of the 2000 fiscal year alone. Rather than slowing it down, Chambers planned to increase the company's acquisition pace, with the addition of as many as 25 companies during 2000. Through acquisitions and through strategic alliances with such industry giants as Microsoft, Hewlett-Packard Company, and Intel Corporation, Chambers aimed to increase Cisco Systems' revenues to $50 billion by 2005. Cisco's presence in nearly every networking sector, the speed with which it typically entered emerging areas, and its proven ability to absorb and expand acquired companies provided evidence that the company was likely to reach this lofty goal and to continue in its role as the undisputed leader of the networking equipment industry.

Principal Subsidiaries

Cisco Systems Canada Limited; Cisco Systems Europe, S.A.R.L. (France); Cisco Systems Import/Export Corporation (U.S. Virgin Islands); Cisco Systems Belgium, S.A.; Cisco Systems Limited (U.K.); Cisco Systems Australia PTY. Limited; Nihon Cisco Systems, K.K. (Japan); Cisco Systems de Mexico, S.A. de C.V.; Cisco Systems New Zealand Limited; Cisco Systems (HK) Limited (Hong Kong); Cisco Systems GmbH (Germany); Cisco Systems (Italy) Srl; Cisco Systems GmbH (Austria); Cisco do Brasil Ltda. (Brazil); Cisco Systems (Korea) Ltd.; VZ, Cisco Systems, C.A. (Venezuela); Cisco Systems South Africa (Pty) Ltd.; Cisco Systems Sweden Aktiebolag; Cisco Systems (Switzerland) AG; Cisco Systems Capital, B.V.; Cisco Systems International Netherlands, B.V.; Cisco Systems Czech Republic, s.r.o.; Cisco Systems Spain, S.L.; Cisco Systems Argentina S.A.; Cisco Systems Chile, S.A.; Cisco Sistemas de Redes S.A. (Costa Rica); Cisco Systems Malaysia, Sdn. Bhd.; Cisco Systems (USA) Pte. Ltd., Singapore; Cisco Systems Thailand, Ltd.; Cisco Systems Peru, S.A.; Cisco Systems Greece, S.A.; Cisco Systems Poland, Sp.zo.o; Cisco Systems Israel, Ltd.; Cisco Systems Internetworking

Iletsim Hizmetlieri Ltd. Sirketi (Turkey); Cisco Systems (India), Ltd.; Cisco Systems Capital Corp.; Cisco Systems (Taiwan), Ltd.; Cisco Systems (Colombia), Ltda; Cisco Technology, Inc.; Cisco Systems Sales & Service, Inc.; Cisco Systems Co. (Canada); Telebit Corporation; Cisco Systems Danmark AS; Cisco Systems Norway AS; Cisco Systems Hungary, Ltd.; Cisco Systems Management B.V.; Cisco Systems (Puerto Rico) Corp.; Cisco Systems Finland Oy; Cisco Systems (China) Networking Technologies Ltd.; Cisco Systems Romania SRL; Cisco Systems Croatia Ltd. for Trade; Cisco Systems Slovakia, spol. sr.o.

Principal Competitors

ADC Telecommunications, Inc.; Alcatel; Cabletron Systems, Inc.; Compaq Computer Corporation; D-Link Corporation; ECI Telecom Ltd.; Fujitsu Limited; Hewlett-Packard Company; Intel Corporation; International Business Machines Corporation; Juniper Networks, Inc.; Kingston Technology Company; Lucent Technologies Inc.; Madge Networks N.V.; Microsoft Corporation; Motorola, Inc.; MRV Communications, Inc.; NEC Corporation; Network Associates, Inc.; Newbridge Networks Corporation; Nokia Corporation; Nortel Networks Corporation; Novell, Inc.; Sterling Software, Inc.; Telefonaktiebolaget LM Ericsson; 3Com Corporation.

Further Reading

Baker, Stephen, "Cisco's Telecom Two-Step in Europe," *Business Week* (international edition), October 11, 1999.

Baum, Geoff, "John Chambers," *Forbes ASAP*, February 23, 1998, pp. 52–53+.

Byrne, John A., "The Corporation of the Future," *Business Week*, August 31, 1998, pp. 102+.

Carlsen, Clifford, "Rolling on the Info Superhighway," *San Francisco Business Times*, August 20, 1993, p. 6A.

Carroll, Paul B., "Cisco Systems Will Acquire StrataCom, Computer Switch Maker, for $4 Billion," *Wall Street Journal*, April 23, 1996, p. A3.

Clark, Don, "Cisco Is Buying GeoTel for $1.92 Billion in Stock," *Wall Street Journal*, April 14, 1999, p. A3.

Daly, James, "John Chambers: The Art of the Deal," *Business 2.0*, October 1999.

Donnelly, George, "Acquiring Minds: Cisco and Lucent Buy into the Telecom Revolution with Strategies That Clash and Converge," *CFO Magazine*, September 1999.

Emigh, Jacqueline, "Cisco Unveils ATM Interfacing Router," *Telephony*, February 1, 1993, pp. 24+.

Goldblatt, Henry, "Cisco's Secrets," *Fortune*, November 8, 1999, pp. 177–78+.

Gomes, Lee, "Cisco Tops $100 Billion in Market Capital," *Wall Street Journal*, July 20, 1998, p. B5.

Hutheesing, Nikhil, and Jeffrey Young, "Curse of the Market Leader," *Forbes*, July 29, 1996, pp. 78+.

Kupfer, Andrew, "The Real King of the Internet," *Fortune*, September 7, 1998, pp. 84–86+.

Mardesich, Jodi, "Cisco's Plan to Pop Up in Your Home," *Fortune*, February 1, 1999, pp. 119–20.

Musich, Paula, "Cisco Chief Plots Router Course: Outlines Plans for ATM Technology," *PC Week*, September 13, 1993, pp. 49+.

——, "Cisco Revamps Router Strategy: Shifts Product, Distribution Tactics for Maturing Market," *PC Week*, November 22, 1993, p. 123.

——, "Cisco, Wellfleet Ride Router Market to Success," *PC Week*, December 14, 1992, pp. 163+.

Osterland, Andrew, "No Kidding. Cisco Isn't Done Yet," *Financial World*, January 21, 1997, pp. 62–64, 66.

Pitta, Julie, "Long Distance Relationship," *Forbes*, March 16, 1992, pp. 136+.

Reinhardt, Andy, "Meet Mr. Internet," *Business Week*, September 13, 1999, pp. 128–31+.

Reinhardt, Andy, Peter Burrows, and Amy Barrett, "Cisco Crunch Time for a High-Tech Wiz," *Business Week*, April 28, 1997, pp. 80+.

Schlender, Brent, "Computing's Next Superpower," *Fortune*, May 12, 1997, pp. 88–90+.

Schonfeld, Erick, "Cisco and the Kids: Are They As Scary As They Look?," *Fortune*, April 14, 1997, pp. 200–202.

Thurm, Scott, "Cisco to Acquire Networking Firm Cerent," *Wall Street Journal*, August 26, 1999, p. A3.

——, "For Cisco, Focus on Small Companies Pays Off," *Wall Street Journal*, May 27, 1999, p. B8.

——, "Joining the Fold: Under Cisco's System, Mergers Usually Work; That Defies the Odds," *Wall Street Journal*, March 1, 2000, pp. A1, A12.

Thurm, Scott, and Deborah Ball, "Cisco to Buy a Pirelli Unit for $2 Billion," *Wall Street Journal*, December 20, 1999, p. A3.

Tully, Shawn, "How Cisco Mastered the Net," *Fortune*, August 17, 1998, pp. 207–8, 210.

—Heather Behn Hedden
—updated by David E. Salamie

Comair Holdings, Inc.

P.O. Box 75021
Cincinnati, Ohio 45275
U.S.A.
Telephone: (859) 767-2550
Fax: (859) 767-2278
Web site: http://www.comair.com

Wholly Owned Subsidiary of Delta Air Lines, Inc.
Incorporated: 1977 as Comair, Inc.
Employees: 4,382
Sales: $763.3 million (1999)
NAIC: 481111 Scheduled Passenger Air Transportation;
551112 Offices of Other Holding Companies

Wholly owned by Delta Air Lines, Inc. since January 2000, Comair Holdings, Inc. is the parent firm of subsidiary Comair, Inc., a regional airline catering to business travelers from its hubs in Cincinnati and Orlando. These are also Delta hubs, so Comair is able to connect Delta passengers to its destinations: 89 cities in 32 states, Toronto and Montreal, Canada, and Nassau in the Bahamas. Comair also participates in the Delta frequent flyer program. Comair has about 100 aircraft in its fleet, 75 percent of which are regional jets; Comair is in the process of converting to an all-jet fleet. Comair Holdings also operates a flight training service, a charter service, and a small package delivery service.

Early Years

Comair was established in Cincinnati in April 1977 by the father and son team of Raymond and David Mueller. A couple of years earlier, David Mueller had been working as a corporate pilot for a Cincinnati bank, when he first observed the inadequacy of flight service in the area. He and his father decided to found a company that would provide higher frequency flights between cities lacking efficient, reliable air service. Raymond Mueller was the company's first president and David Mueller, aged 25, was the executive vice-president.

From their base at the Greater Cincinnati International Airport, David Mueller also served as pilot, reservationist, and baggage clerk at the fledgling company. With a fleet of three Piper-Navajo aircraft, the company's first scheduled flights offered transportation between Cincinnati, Cleveland, Detroit, and Akron-Canton, all within a 500-mile radius. As the company grew, larger nine-passenger Piper-Chieftain aircraft were added to the fleet.

The company had been in business for only two years when tragedy struck. In 1979 a Comair plane crashed at the Greater Cincinnati International Airport, killing eight people. The settlements and fines cost Comair approximately $500,000. Moreover, the company garnered considerable negative national publicity, as increasing numbers of Americans began to question the safety of the smaller planes used by regional airlines. In 1980 the company reported an earnings loss and faced what the younger Mueller would later refer to as "the company's darkest moment."

Describing the company's plans to overcome the setback, in a March 1984 interview in the *Cincinnati Post*, Mueller asserted that he and his father "decided to bet the family jewels" on their ability to turn Comair around, noting that they eventually were just "plain lucky." Specifically, Comair focused on keeping costs low, increasing the frequency of flights to selected cities, and providing comfortable seating in planes carrying 50 or fewer travelers. The strategy paid off. Comair not only overcame the crash, but also secured a solid place among regional air carriers in the Midwest. The company also benefited from the deregulation of the airline industry in the early 1980s. As the major airlines dropped unprofitable routes in the face of intensified competition, Comair and other regional fliers were quick to fill the gap in service.

In 1981 Comair began a major enhancement program, adding more modern turboprop aircraft and doubling the size of its fleet with the addition of ten Brazilian-made Embraer Bandeirante twin-engine airplanes. The following year, Comair added SB3-30s to its fleet; with a capacity of 30 passengers, these were the first Comair aircraft to feature flight attendants, lavatories, and in-flight food and beverage service. With plans for a $1 million expansion of its home base, Comair was taken public in 1981, trading on the NASDAQ National Market System for the first time in July of that year. The IPO raised $5.5 million.

With continued investments in new aircraft, Comair was able to increase the frequency of its flights. While most regional airlines were focusing on hooking up passengers with major airline flights, 70 percent of Comair's passengers (the vast majority of which were businesspeople) were reaching their final destination on Comair. Although this meant that the smaller Comair was competing directly with industry giants, Comair had the advantage of offering more frequent flights.

Middle to Late 1980s: Broadening Customer Base Through Delta Connection

Nevertheless, Comair recognized the value of linking its service to that of the major airlines and in December 1981 began its relationship with Delta Air Lines, becoming part of the Deltamatic computerized reservation system. Within three years, Delta and Comair had entered into a marketing agreement under which Comair became an official Delta Connection carrier. Comair's Cincinnati departures were thereafter coordinated to help customers catch Delta flights at other airports in 15 cities located in seven states. With the expansion of Delta Air Lines' Cincinnati operations and the growth of the Greater Cincinnati area, the two companies oversaw more than 100 daily departures from the Cincinnati Airport in 1984.

Comair's fleet at this time consisted of approximately 21 jet-prop aircraft, having been augmented by the September 1984 addition of a Saab-Fairchild 340 airliner, the first airplane designed specifically for regional service. Designed through a joint venture between manufacturers Fairchild Industries and Saab-Scania AB, this craft could travel at faster speeds and offered increased passenger comfort, and Comair soon ordered 12 more of the same model. Such growth prompted the company to expand its facilities at the Cincinnati Airport with the construction of a $1.8 million corporate office building as well as a new hangar.

Remarking on the success of Comair's relationship with Delta in a December 1984 *Cincinnati Enquirer* article, Charles Curran, Comair's senior vice-president for marketing, noted that since becoming the Delta Connection, Comair had tripled its business. The following year found Comair reporting considerable increases in all areas used by the industry to measure an airline's vitality.

Indeed, in a 12-month period beginning in August 1984, the company increased the number of passengers it flew from the Cincinnati Airport by 200 percent, making Comair the airport's

busiest airline, with more daily departures (93) than any other airline. Moreover, the company ranked second only to Delta at the airport for the number of passengers carried. During this time, the company served 23 markets from Cincinnati and flew as far north as Toronto, as far east as Richmond, Virginia, and as far south as Chattanooga, Tennessee. Comair ranked seventh in size among national regional carriers.

Because the airline now carried a wider variety of passengers seeking connections with Delta flights, rather than Cincinnati-based business travelers only, it began to broaden its scope in the mid-1980s. Tapping Delta's diverse customer base, Comair eventually expanded its services to include limited weekend flights, as well as flights to tourist destinations and smaller cities of as few as 150,000 people.

A series of unfortunate events, however, contributed to Comair's first quarterly loss as a public company in March 1986. One factor in this loss was a tornado that hit two Comair hangars on March 10, severely damaging four planes and the airline's offices. Although the loss was insured, business for March was disrupted while repairs were made; March was usually the company's busiest month of the quarter. In addition, in December 1985, the Federal Aviation Administration (FAA) grounded all ten of Comair's Saab-Fairchild 340s, citing problems with their twin turboprop engines that could cause the planes to catch fire in icy weather. In order for the 340s to resume flying, they had to be fitted with a system for continuous engine ignition, and this was not completed at Comair until January 5. A final factor in the company's depressed earnings, one that industry analysts regarded as perhaps the most crucial, was that Comair had operated with excess seating capacity over the year. Preparing for a proposed expansion of Delta's flight service from Cincinnati, Comair had purchased several new planes and was having a hard time filling seats as it waited for Delta to complete the expansion project.

Delta's expanded hub did materialize the following year, and the two companies soon were overseeing more than 125 Cincinnati departures daily. Moreover, the company's fortunes brightened in the second period of 1986, when the company was able to battle fierce fare competitions by reducing unit costs per available seat-mile to less than 17 cents for the first time in history. Despite the early quarterly loss, Comair showed a profit for the 1986 fiscal year. Charles Curran reminded the public, in a September 1986 *Cincinnati Post* article, that Comair had "never had an unprofitable year since its inception on April 1, 1977."

In May 1986, Comair issued 1.85 million new shares of common stock to Delta, generating $16.9 million for Comair. Delta thus emerged with a 20 percent interest in the regional airline and a new seat on Comair's board of directors. Commenting on the transaction in the *Cincinnati Post,* a Delta official stated that the company had made the investment "to solidify and enhance the Delta Connection program in which the two companies have successfully engaged the past two years." Comair used the increase in capital to replace its lost hangars and office and to continue upgrading its fleet of 37 aircraft. By July 1987, Comair was flying to 29 cities and had plans to add other locations at a rate of four or five per year.

Key Dates:

1977: The father and son team of Raymond and David Mueller founds Comair, Inc.

1979: A Comair plane crashes at the Cincinnati airport, killing eight people.

1981: Company goes public; begins relationship with Delta Air Lines by becoming part of the Deltamatic computerized reservation system.

1984: Comair enters into a marketing agreement with Delta and becomes an official Delta Connection carrier.

1986: A March tornado severely damages four Comair planes, two hangars, and the airline's offices; Delta acquires a 20 percent stake in Comair for $16.9 million.

1987: Comair opens its Orlando hub.

1988: Comair, Inc. is reorganized into a subsidiary of a new parent firm, Comair Holdings, Inc.

1991: Comair places an order with Bombardier for its first Canadair jets.

1993: Company acquires its first 50-passenger Canadair jet.

1994: Comair begins operating from a 53-gate, 170,000-square-foot terminal at the Cincinnati airport, doubling its passenger capacity.

1995: Comair reaches an agreement with Bombardier to expand its fleet of Canadair jets to more than 75 by the end of the decade.

1997: A Comair turboprop, Flight 3272, crashes near Detroit in icy conditions, killing all 29 people on board.

1998: An order is placed for 50 more Canadair regional jets, including the first 70-seaters.

2000: Comair is acquired by Delta, becoming a wholly owned subsidiary.

Also in 1987, Comair began flying to Florida at the request of Delta, which had recently become the official airline for Walt Disney World in Orlando and needed the regional carrier to feed its airliners bound for larger cities. Comair joined with Delta to open hubs in Orlando and Ft. Lauderdale, and its success was immediate; the Florida market was profitable by the fifth month of operation. The number of daily Florida flights steadily increased until the figure rivaled that reported at the home base of Cincinnati.

Not surprisingly, David Mueller, who had replaced his father as president, announced at the company's September 1988 annual shareholder meeting that Comair would be looking for "any and all aviation related business in which we can be successful." Preparing for acquisitions, Comair, Inc. was soon reorganized into a subsidiary of a new Kentucky parent firm, Comair Holdings, Inc. The regional airline, along with CVG Aviation, a jet charter service concern that provided services for noncommercial planes at the Cincinnati Airport, were both now subsidiaries of the new Comair Holdings. Eventual acquisitions included a flight training company, an investment company, and an aircraft leasing company.

1990s: Transitioning to an All-Jet Fleet

Comair's flight service was expanded to include routes between Cincinnati and Chicago's Midway Airport as well as routes between Florida and the Bahamas. In addition, as Delta announced plans in 1990 for a $319 million expansion, Comair officials expected to almost double the company's operations over the next few years. Comair placed orders for more than 100 planes, 60 of which were Brazilian planes that would enable Comair to more than double its flying radius from its current hubs. Comair also set its sights on moving from its one-gate operation to a separate facility with a minimum of 25 to 30 gates.

In October 1990, David A. Siebenburgen succeeded David Mueller as president of Comair Holdings Inc. Siebenburgen remained in his previous capacity as chief operating officer as well, while Mueller retained his roles as chairman and chief executive officer. Over the next two years, Comair focused on adding flights both in frequency and to new locations. By 1991, Comair's aircraft fleet had grown to 75, including five new 340s for the Cincinnati market and 20 Embraer Brasilias for the Florida market. Naturally, the company's workforce grew in accordance, surpassing 2,000 by the spring of 1990. In 1991 Comair made the important decision of transitioning its fleet from turboprops to jets. That year, it placed an order for 50 regional jets from Canada's Bombardier Inc. In the spring of 1992, Comair began seasonal flights to vacation sites such as Myrtle Beach.

In April 1992, American Airlines announced rate changes that would affect the entire airline industry. While American simplified and lowered their fares, other major airlines moved to match these rates, hoping that increased passenger volume would offset losses from lower fares. Some industry analysts warned that the regional airlines affiliated with major airlines would suffer from the fare war, but Comair was nevertheless able to utilize cost containment strategies to come out ahead. In addition, one company official stated in a May 1992 *Cincinnati Business Courier* that "a major financial blow to Delta would not necessarily have an equal impact on Comair. Unlike other regional carriers that are totally dependent on a major airline, Comair connects only 45 to 50 percent of its business with Delta. And the break-even load factor—the percentage of seats that must be sold for a flight to break even—is 39 percent for Comair vs. about 70 percent for major carriers." Indeed, in the early 1990s, while the major airlines reported a collective loss of $10 billion, Comair was one of the few airlines to remain profitable. Comair's combination of good planning for future growth and a tight rein on costs had once again seen it through a rough time.

In the spring of 1993, Comair announced the acquisition of its first 50-passenger Canadair jet from Bombardier. Known as the world's quietest jet airplane, the Canadair had a top cruising speed of 530 miles per hour, and its range was 1,500 miles—three times the range of Comair's then-current fleet and well beyond the typical two-hour flight limit of most regional airlines with turboprops. The jets also provided Comair with a competitive advantage in that most consumers preferred them to noisy, bumpy turboprops. With these more powerful airplanes, Comair planned to enter markets in 36 new cities through 1995.

On September 3, 1994, Comair began leasing and operating from a new $50 million terminal built by the Greater Cincinnati International Airport. With 53 gates, the 170,000-square-foot facility enabled Comair to double its passenger capacity. Amenities in the terminal included automated teller machines, a combination newsstand and gift shop, and a food court, with McDonald's, PizzaHut Express, and other fast-food restaurants commonly found in larger airline terminals, but not as prevalent in a regional airline terminal. Another unique item was the ''Kid's Corner,'' a space filled with large, bright plastic toys and a play yard for children.

Commuter airlines began a shaky few months in October 1994, when an American Eagle plane crashed in Indiana. As Federal regulators investigated the matter, suggesting that commuter airline restrictions and safety regulations were perhaps inadequate, the public lost some confidence in their commuter flights. In addition, Comair felt specific pressure from new cost-cutting measures implemented by the major airlines and new low-fare competition. As a result, Comair's stock fell to $17 a share in December of that year, down from a high of $34.50 in late 1993.

Referring to the volatility of Comair's stock price, in an August 1994 article in the *Cincinnati Enquirer,* CEO Mueller suggested to shareholders that Comair was being unfairly associated with other commuter air linkups. ''While the carrier continues to make money, investors lump Comair together with other regional airlines—even those that haven't performed as well,'' he noted.

Comair sustained the bad publicity generated by the American Eagle crash; in 1994 the company reported record revenues of $297 million, posted record profits of $28.5 million, and carried a record 2.7 million passengers over the course of the year. Moreover, Comair's expansion continued. In January 1995, the company reached an agreement with Canada's Bombardier Inc. to acquire five more Canadair Jet aircraft, with conditional orders and available options to purchase 35 more. Once a formal purchase agreement was completed, delivery was expected to continue through fiscal 1999. Fulfillment of the order would give Comair 70 Canadair jets, which would help the company continue to enhance its Cincinnati and Orlando hubs.

Comair suffered a couple more setbacks as it moved into the late 1990s. In 1996 the company announced plans to acquire Spirit Airlines Inc., a discount carrier based in Detroit, but the deal fell through. The following January Comair suffered the second fatal crash in its history when Flight 3272 crashed near Detroit in icy conditions, killing all 29 people on board. The National Transportation Safety Board's investigation concluded that a thin layer of ice had built up on the turboprop's wings, causing the pilot to lose control. The board also faulted the crew for flying in bad weather conditions and criticized Comair for its guidelines for flying in icy conditions and the FAA for failing to set minimum speeds for flying safely in such circumstances.

For the fiscal year ending in March 1997, Comair Holdings continued to post record results. Revenues reached $563.8 million, more than double the level of 1993, when the airline was just beginning to switch its fleet to jets. Net income for 1997 was $75.4 million, translating into a net profit margin of 13.4 percent and making Comair one of the most profitable airlines in the industry. It was generally acknowledged that the impetus for this growth and continued stellar financial performance was the company's gamble on jets. Comair was outperforming its regional airline rivals because its jets, which numbered more than 50 by 1997, enabled the airline to start new routes, cater to business travelers, and command higher prices. While other regional carriers were scrambling to catch up by purchasing their own regional jets, Comair had by 1997 vaulted into the number two spot among the regionals, trailing only AMR Corporation's Simmons Airlines (later merged into AMR's American Eagle). In October 1998 Comair placed a follow-up order with Bombardier for 50 more Canadair regional jets, a deal worth more than $1 billion. With this order, which included 20 70-seat jets in addition to 30 50-seaters, Comair hoped to create an all-jet fleet by the early 21st century. The 70-seat jets, which were not slated to be ready until late 2001, were to be used on the airline's most heavily traveled routes.

2000 and Beyond: Operating As a Delta Subsidiary

By the end of the 1999 fiscal year, Comair was carrying more than 600,000 passengers each month and operated more than 750 daily flights. More than 6.4 million passengers flew on a Comair flight that fiscal year. Revenues reached $763.3 million, a 17 percent increase over the previous year, and net income stood at $132.9 million, a 30 percent jump. Only a few months after the announcement of this good news, Comair faced a critical deadline. In October 1999 the long-term marketing agreement between Delta and Comair was due to expire. According to Amy Higgins of the *Cincinnati Enquirer,* the regional carrier had three choices. It could sign a new marketing agreement, but Delta was unlikely to agree to a deal as favorable to Comair as the previous one had been in terms of the revenue split. It could choose not to renew with Delta, and either enter into an alliance with another major carrier or attempt to go it alone. But with this option, Comair faced the prospect of heightened competition and the concomitant loss of revenues, profits, and stock value.

Comair was then left with the third choice: agreeing to be acquired by Delta. With Comair's stock deflated to less than $18 a share, in part because of increasing oil prices, Comair announced on October 18 that it had agreed to be purchased by Delta for about $1.8 billion, or $23.50 a share, a 31 percent premium. The acquisition was completed in January 2000 and Comair Holdings thereby became a wholly owned subsidiary of Delta and part of a new unit called Delta Connection Inc., which was charged with overseeing all of the airline's regional carriers, including Comair and Atlantic Southeast Airlines; the latter served the Southeast and East Coast through hubs in Atlanta and Dallas/Fort Worth. Siebenburgen was appointed president and CEO of Delta Connection, and Randy D. Rademacher, who had been CFO of Comair Holdings, was named president of Comair Holdings. David Mueller agreed to serve as an advisor for a three-year period. Soon after the acquisition was completed, *Air Transport World* named Comair ''Regional Airline of the Year'' for 1999, a fitting climax to the airline's era of quasi-independence.

Principal Subsidiaries

Comair, Inc.; Comair Services, Inc.; Comair Investment Company.

Principal Competitors

AirTran Holdings, Inc.; AMR Corporation; ASA Holdings, Inc.; Continental Airlines, Inc.; Mesa Air Group, Inc.; Mesaba Holdings, Inc.; Southwest Airlines Co.; TransWorld Airlines, Inc.; UAL Corporation; US Airways Group, Inc.

Further Reading

Agnew, Ronnie, "Comair Wants to Be Top Gun in Fla.," *Cincinnati Enquirer,* October 24, 1988, p. F5.

Beaupre, Becky, Joel J. Smith, and James Tobin, "29 Killed As Plane Dives into Field Near Monroe," *Detroit News,* January 10, 1997, p. A1.

Boulton, Guy, "Comair Outlook: Blue Skies," *Cincinnati Enquirer,* June 22, 1997.

Boyer, Mike, "Following a Year of Turbulence, Comair May See Brighter Skies," *Cincinnati Enquirer,* January 5, 1987, p. E4.

——, "Profitable Comair Takes Off on Major Expansion," *Cincinnati Enquirer,* March 14, 1993, pp. H1, H10.

Brannigan, Martha, "Delta to Buy Remainder of Comair," *Wall Street Journal,* October 18, 1999, p. A3.

Bryant, Adam, "Commuter Airlines Like Comair Expect Growth Despite Problems," *New York Times,* December 7, 1994, p. C6.

Carey, Susan, "Comair, Once the Little Kid on the Block, Stands Tall," *Wall Street Journal,* September 10, 1997, p. B4.

Chipello, Christopher J., and Susan Carey, "Comair Orders 50 Regional Jets from Bombardier," *Wall Street Journal,* October 2, 1998, p. B6.

Deveny, Kathleen, "A Commuter Airline That's Stretching Its Wings," *Business Week,* July 29, 1985, pp. 72+.

Frazier, Mya, "Delta Left Comair Little Choice," *Cincinnati Business Courier,* October 22, 1999, p. 1.

Gleason, Mark, "Cost-Cutting Helps Comair Fly High Again," *Cincinnati Business Courier,* November 9, 1992, pp. 3, 39.

Harrington, Jeff, "Analysts Rate Comair As High Flier Even with Flat Earnings," *Cincinnati Enquirer,* July 1, 1991, p. C6.

Heidenreich, Rob, "Comair Successful by Many Measures," *Cincinnati Enquirer,* September 12, 1985, p. D9.

Kennedy, Rick, "Piloting Comair Higher," *Cincinnati Post,* March 6, 1984, p. B1.

Lewis, Arnold, "The New Standard for Regional Terminals," *Business & Commercial Aviation,* January 1995, pp. C2–C6.

Marino, Jacqueline, "Comair's Business Soars," *Cincinnati Enquirer,* June 26, 1994, pp. E1, E3.

Merwin, John, "Riding in the Slipstream," *Forbes,* December 31, 1984, pp. 40+.

Moorman, Robert W., "The 'National' Regional," *Air Transport World,* December 1998, pp. 46–47, 50, 52.

"NTSB Report Faults Airspeed, Flaps in Crash That Killed 29," *Detroit News,* May 8, 1997, p. A1.

Olson, Thomas, "Comair Takes Off into New Markets," *Cincinnati Business Courier,* June 18–24, 1990, pp. 1, 18.

Ott, James, "Buying Comair, Delta Carves a Huge Regional Network," *Aviation Week & Space Technology,* October 25, 1999, p. 30.

——, "Cincinnati Expansion Project Key to Delta, Comair Future," *Aviation Week & Space Technology,* October 18, 1993, p. 51.

——, "RJ Fuels Growth in Comair's Traffic," *Aviation Week & Space Technology,* December 12, 1994, pp. 40, 42.

Prendergast, Jane, "Comair Gets New Home at Airport," *Cincinnati Enquirer,* August 31, 1994, pp. B1, B4.

Rawe, Dick, "Comair Enjoys the Sun," *Cincinnati Post,* February 11, 1988, p. C7.

——, "Comair Growing in New Ways," *Cincinnati Post,* March 12, 1993, p. A5.

——, "Stock Deal, Links with Delta Air to Thrust Comair to New Heights," *Cincinnati Post,* May 30, 1986, p. A7.

Rhodes, Gary, "Comair Unveils New Jet," *Cincinnati Post,* May 14, 1993, p. C10.

Schaber, Greg, "For Comair, Rate Game Means Wait Game," *Cincinnati Business Courier,* May 11–17, 1992, pp. 1, 8.

Troxell, Thomas N., Jr., "Winging Ahead: Comair, a Regional Airline, Carves Out a Market," *Barron's,* October 10, 1983, p. 54.

Turner, Patrick, "The Public File: Comair Holdings, Inc.," *Business Record,* August 15, 1994, p. 10.

Weathers, William A., "Comair to Build $1.8 Million Office at Airport," *Cincinnati Enquirer,* December 22, 1984, p. B5.

—Jennifer Voskuhl Canipe
—updated by David E. Salamie

Compass Group PLC

Cowley House
Guildford Street, Chertsey
Surrey KT16 9BA
United Kingdom
Telephone: (44) 1932-573-000
Fax: (44) 1932-569-956
Web site: http://www.compass-group.com

Public Company
Incorporated: 1987
Employees: 191,400
Sales: £4.81 billion (US$7.92 billion) (1999)
Stock Exchanges: London
Ticker Symbol: CMSGY
NAIC: 72331 Food Service Contractors; 72332 Caterers

As the world's largest foodservice company, Compass Group PLC is aptly named. Catering to more than 70 countries, Compass Group's operations provide food and beverages in myriad form from vending machines and corporate catering to bringing popular franchises such as Burger King, Kentucky Fried Chicken, Taco Bell, Pizza Hut, T.G.I.-Fridays, and Harry Ramsden's to alternative outlets, including schools, airports, military bases, and correctional and healthcare facilities. Compass Group also has its own profitable brands, including Caffé Ritazz, Café Select, Upper Crust, Not Just Donuts, Franks, and Sushi Q restaurants. With annual turnover exceeding £4.8 billion (US$7.9 billion), Compass Group sits well within the FTSE 100 as one of the U.K.'s most successful conglomerates.

From Something Established, Something New: 1987–94

Compass Group PLC started with a bang. The year in which the company became a reality—1987—was fraught with ups and downs. In the political arena, Margaret Thatcher was reelected to her third term as prime minister yet failed to stop the publication of Peter Wright's MI5 memoir, *Spycatcher,* in Australia. Politics paled, however, when compared to Black Monday, which sent the

stock markets and financial world stumbling. What became the world's most extensive foodservice empire had begun as the contract services division of Grand Metropolitan, a London-based food and spirits company. When Grand Metropolitan agreed to sell its catering unit to members of the parent company's management for £164 million (US$260 million), it was hailed as Europe's most expensive spinoff in history. Hence the auspicious formation of Compass Group PLC was underway.

Compass Group was headed by Gerry Robinson, who took the helm as CEO, albeit on an abbreviated basis. Robinson soon departed for British television giant Granada Group, and subsequently steered it into the foodservice industry. Robinson's segue provided added incentive for Compass Group, as the two companies became competitors. By the time Compass Group went public in 1988 on the London Stock Exchange, Robinson had made a crucial acquisition by purchasing Sutcliffe's to head up Granada's catering division. Yet Granada was more heavily into television programming and hotels than the foodservice industry and did not pose a more serious threat to Compass Group until later in the decade. In the meantime, Compass Group began its climb to the top with meticulous attention to the evolving foodservice industry and its key players.

In 1991 came a changing of the guard and a major turning point at Compass with the appointment of Francis Mackay as chief executive. Soon after Mackay took control came the ambitious plan to become the world's largest foodservice company, to be attained through both organic growth and by buying up rivals and companies leading various sectors within the industry. Among the early acquisitions were railway caterer Traveller's Fare (later renamed Upper Crust), bought from British Rail in 1992, Scandinavian Airlines Systems' catering business in 1993 (which marked Compass Group's jump into airlines and airports), and the 1994 acquisition of Canteen Corp., the third largest vending and foodservice company in the United States. With the Canteen purchase came the formation of the North American Division, headed by Michael Bailey, a former chef with Gardner Merchant who joined Compass a year earlier to oversee the company's branded foods division.

As Compass grew, so did the competition. Chief among its rivals were Gardner Merchant in the United Kingdom, France's

Company Perspectives:

Our mission is to achieve leadership in our chosen foodservice markets through the constant pursuit, in partnership with our clients and partners, of superior levels of quality, efficiency, and service. The total dedication of our staff to achieving excellence is the major factor in our success.

Sodexho Alliance, and the U.S.-based Aramark. Gardner Merchant had bought the U.S.-based Morrison Hospitality Group in 1994 and was then gobbled up by Sodexho. The combined clout of Merchant and Sodexho were a force to be reckoned with; their merger made them the world's largest contract foodservice company, with combined assets of over US$4 billion. Not to be outdone, Compass engineered a coup of its own: the purchase of Accor's Eurest International for US$931 million. In return for selling Eurest, Accor received a 22.5 percent share of the newly energized company, and Compass Group bested its rivals to claim the top spot as the largest foodservice company in the world.

Being Number One: 1996–98

Compass Group's domination of the global foodservice industry was in full swing by 1996. The company's management, however, was not content to sit upon their laurels; they were keenly aware their three rivals—Sodexho, Aramark, and Marriott Managed Services—had aggressive expansion plans. Though Compass had ended up spending over £3.9 billion (US$2.5 billion) in its buying frenzy to reach the top, the downside was a hefty debt load, which translated into lower profit margins than expected, but not significantly so. Since its debut as a publicly held company, the Compass Group had yet to have a loss or any serious downturns—in fact, turnover and profits continued to climb, though perhaps more modestly than some had hoped. Revenues for 1994 and 1995, despite major expenditures for acquisitions, were a healthy £917.9 million and £1.51 billion, respectively, with corresponding operating profits of £62.8 million and £91.2 million.

Since Compass Group seemed to be engaged in constant one-upmanship, its next win or "trophy" contract was a big step in preserving its status as number one. Touted at the time as the largest contract of its kind in the United States, Compass's coup was a five-year, US$250 million agreement with IBM to serve 100,000 employees at locations in 29 states. In 1996 and 1997 came several strategic acquisitions, Professional Food-Service Management and Service America for the North American division, and France's SHRM to bolster home operations. Then controversy arose when Compass beat out Sodexho for a US$40 million EuroDisney contract; Sodexho cried foul, stating Compass had "undercut" them and was willing to lose money on the contract to win it. Mackay countered that such claims were ludicrous, that Compass Group's purpose was to make money, not lose it. The Disney agreement, one of the U.K.'s three largest catering contracts, was a feather in Compass Group's increasingly well-plumed hat.

Turnover soared from 1996's £2.65 billion (itself a 29 percent from 1995) to 1997's £3.7 billion. Broken down by geo-

graphic region, nearly half of Compass's turnover was represented by its European/World division, at £1.8 billion; followed by the North American division, at £1.2 billion; and U.K. operations at just over £668 million. Tallied by operating division, the business and industrial segment represented more than half of the company's overall revenue.

With its increased presence in the foodservice industry and the clout its number-one status carried, Compass Group had not only earned a solid reputation but was able to bolster its bottom line by negotiating more favorable terms with suppliers. Better pricing on its own supplies meant the company could seek larger contracts more aggressively. In 1998 the North American division sought and won a contract for the Smithsonian Institution, including sites in the National Museum of American History, the American Art & Portrait Gallery, and the National Museum of Natural History. This same division also acquired the U.S.-based Restaurant Associates, for US$90 million. By the end of the year Compass Group's stock value had quadrupled since its introduction a decade earlier, and profits had increased by 14 percent to £54.3 million from 1997. Compounded growth figures from 1994 to 1998 showed a tremendous growth rate of 46.4 percent in turnover, a 36.5 percent increase in operating profits, and shareholder return for the same period up by 32.2 percent.

In 1998 the playing field became stacked in favor of Sodexho, when the company's U.S. arm, Sodexho USA, merged with Marriott Managed Services, a part of Marriott International. The result, Sodexho Marriott Services, of which Sodexho Alliance owned over 48 percent, was a powerhouse in the U.S. foodservice arena and tough competition for Compass Group's North American division.

Preparing for a New Century

Compass Group's continued success was due in part to its clear delineation of business segments, covering the broadest spectrum of food and beverage services. Unlike Aramark, both Compass and Sodexho Alliance were not as diversified into related businesses and remained firmly entrenched in the foodservice industry (though Compass had owned a hospital management company which it sold in 1996). Aramark, on the other hand, was a major player in the hospitality field, providing maintenance, housekeeping, and food services around the world, in addition to its massive uniform rental agency (ranked second in the United States).

By the end of the 1990s, Compass Group had seven major operating groups: Eurest, in the business and industrial marketplace, including multinational companies with many locations as well as offshore and remote sites. Medirest and Bateman, catering to the healthcare community in hospitals, rehabilitation centers, and nursing homes; Chartwells and Scolarest, which covered the educational market from preschool to university in both the United States and the United Kingdom; Flik and Roux Fine Dining, providing elite dining services, often working with well known international chefs such as Albert Roux; Canteen Vending Services, along with Selecta (Europe's top vending operator, partly owned by Compass Group), supplying outlets primarily in the United States as well as other international contracts; Select Service Partner (SSP) food and beverage units in airports, rail stations, shopping malls, and other quick-stop concessions; and lastly, Letheby & Christopher and Restaurant Associates, both of which catered high-end sports, social, or leisure outings in the United Kingdom and the United States, such as the English Open, the U.S. Open, PGA European Golf Tour, Rugby World Cup, and Ryder Cup.

Within its seven market segments were Compass Group's increasingly popular proprietary brands, including Ritazza and Caffé Ritazza outlets (coffee), Stopgap (convenience marts), Upper Crust (breads and sandwiches), Not Just Donuts (breakfast foods), and Profiles (workplace dining with a twist—chefs preparing dishes while interacting with clients). Compass had also been putting its mark on franchising as well, with such high visibility food chains as Burger King, Pizza Hut, Sbarro, T.G.I. Friday's, and a more recent venue, Harrods Tea Room in association with the famous department store.

Compass Group's management was full speed ahead with further expansion, in particular with its German subsidiaries in railway stations, airports, conference centers, and sports facilities, in an effort to capture a larger slice of that country's ever growing £10 billion catering marketplace. Beyond Germany, Compass Group's extensive empire represented less than a third of the £170 billion foodservice marketplace and the company was intent on controlling more through both acquisitions and bigger contracts. New contracts included its role as the official caterer for the 2002 Winter Olympics in Salt Lake City (worth an estimated US$25–$40 million); contracts for rail stations with Spain's Renfe as well as a similar contract with Spanair in Madrid; an agreement to provide food, coffee, and vending services at 11 MCI Worldcom sites in the United States; a new contract with Crown Cork & Seal for up to 40 sites in Africa, Europe, and the Middle East; and a ten-year, US$300 million contract for 27 United Technologies sites.

Investments and acquisitions included buying a 50 percent stake in Brazil's largest catering company, Générale Restauration S.A., and purchasing P&O Australia, making Compass Group the leading remote-site caterer in Australia. Internally, Compass picked up Brake Brothers as a new catering supplier, after the company was dropped by rival Granada Group. The company's SSP division, meanwhile, operating in 56 airports in 18 countries worldwide, had received high approval ratings for its Copenhagen Airport operations, and was awarded a new contract with the Toronto Airport. SSP hoped the Toronto deal would open further doors in North American airports and railway stations. Eurest Dining Services' North American arm was similarly praised, receiving a Supplier Excellence Award from the Prudential Insurance Company, while Chartwells USA was named the fastest growing contract foodservice company by *Nation's Restaurant News*.

In July 1999 Mackay assumed the role of chairman, while the North American division's Michael Bailey was named group chief executive. Compass Group finished the year with turnover of £4.81 billion (US$7.92 billion), a 14.3 percent increase over 1998 and with operating profits of £261.4 million, another substantial increase over the previous year's £218 million. Accor, the French hotel giant who once owned nearly 23 percent of Compass, had sold most of its shares and possessed only 4.5 percent of the world's largest foodservice company.

The Future: 2000 and Beyond

In 2000 the clash of the foodservice titans continued with each contributing to the industry's record expansion (with almost a decade of uninterrupted growth). Compass Group was still the leader, yet Sodexho Alliance was close on its heels and gaining as the United Kingdom's second largest foodservice provider. The privately operated, third-ranked Aramark, with rumors of its impending IPO still swirling after several years, pursued further domestic expansion and had steadily gained an increased international presence. All three conglomerates were adding further focus to in-house proprietary brands, offering unusual foods and beverages to suit wide-ranging tastes and tailoring outlets to particular clients' needs. Additionally, Compass Group and its major rivals had not only one another to worry about but how to continue to out-muscle smaller competitors through clout, reputation, and incentives.

While the business and industrial segments carried the big name corporate contracts or the "trophies" in the industry, the correctional facility and child care segments had much potential. In this respect, Aramark was already ahead in the game, servicing correctional facilities in nearly three dozen U.S. states, light years ahead of both Compass Group and Sodexho Alliance. Yet all three companies were headed in the same direction, to exploit new markets and gain more control of existing markets through organic growth and acquisitions. Two disparate quotes sum up the industry, its potential, and its dangers for the new millennium: first, from the December 1, 1999 issue of *Restaurants & Institutions,* Compass Group's North American division head Gary Green stated, "Being big, bigger, biggest means nothing. Being the best is what it's all about." Second, Dennis Reynolds, covering the foodservice industry for *Cornell Hotel & Restaurant Administration Quarterly,* reminded, ". . . You're only as good as your last meal." Both men, intimates of the industry, spoke the truth.

Principal Subsidiaries

Compass Group UK Ltd.; Compass Services France S.A.; SHRM S.A. (France); Compass Group Deutschland GmbH (Germany); Compass Group Holdings Spain S.L.; Compass Group Nederland B.V. (Netherlands); Compass Group Norge A/S (Norway); Compass Holdings, Inc. (U.S.A.).

Principal Operating Units

Bateman and Medirest; Chartwells and Scolarest; Eurest; Flik and Roux Fine Dining; Canteen Vending Services; Select Service Partner (SSP); Letheby & Christopher and Restaurant Associates.

Principal Competitors

Aramark Corporation; Fine Host; Granada Group PLC; Sodexho Alliance SA; HDS Services.

Further Reading

"Company Report—Compass Group," *Investext,* May 21, 1997.
"Expanding Fast in All Directions," *Financial Times,* August 15, 1997.

Matsumoto, Janice, "Contractors," *Restaurants & Institutions,* September 15, 1999, p. 72.
Reynolds, Dennis, "Managed-Services Companies," *Cornell Hotel & Restaurant Administration Quarterly,* June 1997, p. 88.
——, "Managed-Services Companies: The New Scorecard for On-Site Food Service," *Cornell Hotel & Restaurant Administration Quarterly,* June 1999, p. 64.
——, "Productivity Analysis in the On-Site Food-Service Segment," *Cornell Hotel & Restaurant Administration Quarterly,* June 1998, p. 22.
Rousseau, Rita, "Compass Points to Global Future," *Restaurants & Institutions,* December 1, 1996, p. 23.
——, "Contractors," *Restaurants & Institutions,* August 1, 1996, p. 40.

—Nelson Rhodes

Cramer, Berkowitz & Co.

100 Wall Street
New York, New York 10005
U.S.A.
Telephone: (212) 742-4480
Fax: (212) 587-2905

Private Partnership
Founded: 1987 as Cramer & Co.
Employees: 11
Total Assets: $265 million (1999 est.)
NAIC: 52599 Other Financial Vehicles

Cramer, Berkowitz & Co. is a private limited partnership that runs a Wall Street hedge fund named Cramer Partners. The general partners are its managers, James J. Cramer and Jeff Berkowitz, while the limited partners are a small number of wealthy people who have each invested millions of dollars. Cramer, Berkowitz has a record of outperforming the returns of a broad stock market gauge, the Standard & Poor index of 500 stocks. Its high profile on Wall Street is due to Cramer, who frequently appears on television, writes columns that appear in print and online publications, and is the founder of TheStreet.com, an online financial news company. He is considered an inspiration for the growing number of Americans who spend their days buying and selling stock on the Internet.

Cramer's interest in the stock market began in the second grade, when he started keeping meticulous records of the trades he would have made if he had the money. A graduate of Harvard College in 1977, he was president of the *Harvard Crimson,* generally considered the most prestigious post in college journalism. After four years as a reporter, he enrolled in Harvard Law School, but following graduation went to work instead for the elite Wall Street investment banking house of Goldman Sachs & Co. While in law school Cramer had begun to play the stock market for real, reportedly tripling a $500,000 investment made by Martin Peretz, publisher of the liberal weekly the *New Republic* and the husband of an heiress to the Singer sewing-machine fortune. Peretz was the best man at Cramer's wedding, and when Cramer formed his own firm in

1987, Peretz was one of the first two clients. The other was Michael Steinhardt, a legendary hedge-fund operator who also donated office space to the new venture.

Cramer & Co.: 1987–96

Cramer & Co., the firm he founded, was a hedge fund rather than a mutual fund. Unlike a mutual fund, a hedge fund only takes as a client someone willing to make a large initial investment—generally at least $1 million—and only allows redemption of funds during a limited period rather than at any time. Asked by Kathleen Doler of *Upside* in 1998 why he had made this choice, Cramer replied, ''The compensation's better. And there are fewer clients. It's easier, and it lets me focus more on doing what I like to do, which is pick stocks.'' Cramer said that his future wife, a Steinhardt trader, advised him a week before the 1987 Wall Street crash to sell everything. He did so and broke even for the year, while the Standard & Poor index lost 18 percent. Cramer & Co. gave its clients a higher yield on their money than the S&P or the Dow Jones Industrials average every year between 1988 and 1996—according to the firm—and all but two years in that period, according to another account.

Cramer was also writing for the *New Republic* and contributing a financial column for *Manhattan Lawyer.* In 1993 he also became a columnist for *SmartMoney,* a new personal finance magazine. This became an issue in 1995, when a front page *Washington Post* story charged that the Cramer & Co. hedge fund had made $2.5 million as a major stockholder in three thinly traded small companies whose stock soared in value after favorable mention in a *SmartMoney* column by Cramer. Moreover, Cramer had bought large amounts of shares in these companies after submitting the column to the editors but before the magazine reached readers. As a result of this incident, *SmartMoney* added disclosures about the stock holdings of its contributors and barred them from writing about stocks in which they held large positions or that were thinly traded.

Cramer denied any conflict of interest and pointed out that he had not cashed in during the rally. ''I have the most strict disclosure rules of anyone in the business,'' he was later quoted by Suzanna Andrews in *Vanity Fair.* ''I am a commentator, not

---

Key Dates:

1987: Former Goldman Sachs trader James (''Jim'') Cramer founds hedge fund Cramer & Co.
1996: Cramer assumes 35 percent ownership of Internet information service provider TheStreet.com.
1999: Firm is managing some $265 million in assets.

---

a journalist, who is trying to explain what he sees. I don't recommend stocks. I try to teach people the hows and whys of investing.'' The Securities and Exchange Commission implicitly supported this position by taking no action after investigating the matter. Joseph Nocera—a friend of Cramer's—in a *Time* column, also backed the money manager, writing, ''The value of Cramer's column lies precisely in the fact that its author is a professional trader, not a professional journalist. The fact that he has his own firm's money at risk gives his work a credibility that is largely absent from the bland and scattershot advice so often parceled out by the personal-finance fraternity.''

Cramer's impact on Wall Street trading became even stronger in 1996, when he and Peretz each took 35 percent ownership of TheStreet.com, a publication for investors appearing on the World Wide Web. In order to quell any further conflict-of-interest controversy, Cramer made an arrangement with the SEC by which he was removed from the publication's editorial management and agreed not to tell its reporters about individual stocks unless he refrained from buying and selling these stocks for 30 days. Staffers of TheStreet.com also agreed not to discuss stocks with any of Cramer's employees at his investment firm, which was now Cramer, Berkowitz & Co., with the addition of co-partner Jeff Berkowitz, a former Goldman, Sachs colleague who was put in charge of research.

Cramer's Frenetic Schedule in 1997

By the spring of 1997 Cramer's profile was higher than ever. In addition to his daily contribution for TheStreet.com he was writing for *Worth* and for *Slate,* Microsoft Corporation's online magazine. He was also appearing on ''Bull Session,'' a television show on CNBC, a cable network, and other programs. Cramer, Berkowitz was now managing about $250 million for 70 clients, with about half the money—according to Melanie Warner of *Fortune*—in small companies that he considered undervalued. The other half was employed in making about 200 trades a day through five staffers. Evaluated another way by Alan Deutschman for *GQ/Gentleman's Quarterly,* Cramer, Berkowitz was keeping about half its portfolio in what Cramer considered long-term investments—stocks and bonds held for at least one year.

In his 1997 profile on Cramer, Deutschman wrote, ''There's no quick and easy key to Cramer's style of investing, no simple set of commandments or rules that encapsulate and explain his stock market philosophy. . . . Cramer characterizes his style as 'eclectic and chameleonlike,' with a willingness to adapt his strategy to changing circumstances in the market.'' Deutschman continued, ''He also thrives on understanding and outwitting the psychology of the market and has a strong con-

trarian bent for knowing when the market has overreacted to news about a stock. Perhaps most important, he benefits from his experience and frame of reference—his ability to compare market situations to similar ones he encountered weeks or years ago, taking advantage of his *Rain Man*/Mr. Memory acuity.''

A typical working day for the hyperactive Cramer—who claimed to sleep three hours a night—started with an hour or two of work at home, beginning at 3:30 in the morning, followed by a chauffeur-driven trip from his Long Island home to his Wall Street office. He read 26 newspapers—including more than one edition of the *Wall Street Journal* and *New York Times*—noting changes in emphasis—and hundreds of research reports and news releases every day. He also called chief executive officers and responded to the dozens of daily e-mail messages he received from the public. During a typical trading day, viewing six computers on his desk and barking orders to seven staffers, he would make 100 stock and 50 option trades—according to Deutschman—buying and selling constantly to earn a profit of 50 cents a share.

''The vast majority of what I do,'' Cramer told Jill Dutt of the *Washington Post* in 1997, ''is try to assess whether the market itself is wrong [that is, too optimistic or pessimistic] on a short-term basis.'' But his frenetic trading also had another purpose—earning large commissions for brokerage houses that in turn afforded him access to their best analysts. After the markets closed, Cramer would depart for home, where he would write as many as six columns each evening for TheStreet.com under the contrarian heading *Wrong!*

In one example of profiting from the market's pessimism, Cramer bought 300,000 shares of Philip Morris stock after investors, in just one day, had taken its value down $10 billion following an adverse court ruling. When the stock quickly rose again, he earned $1.05 million. ''Morris is a hugely emotional stock,'' he explained to Deutschman. ''People trade it with emotions, not brains.'' Cramer described as his best trade the purchase, in 1989, of Intel Corporation shares. Following the 1994 news of a flaw in Intel's Pentium chip, Cramer chose to double his investment in the company. As the price of Intel's shares continued to fall, Cramer tripled, then quadrupled, his holdings. ''At one point I had 60 percent of my assets in Intel,'' he told Dutt. ''I just didn't believe this flaw could matter that much. At one point I thought, 'Oh, my God, I have to sell everything because all I have is Intel.' '' By the spring of 1997 Intel's stock had risen more than fivefold from its nadir.

On the other hand, Cramer lost $8 million as the largest stockholder in Rexon, a producer of backup computer tapes that filed for bankruptcy protection in 1995. In addition, five months after buying 1.1 million shares of Dow Jones & Co. in early 1997, he sold almost all of it because, he said, he was tired of waiting for the company to sell its unprofitable electronic financial information unit, formerly named Telerate. At one point Dow Jones stock comprised about 15 percent of Cramer, Berkowitz's portfolio. Cramer took a $4 million profit on the investment, but Dow Jones sold the unit in early 1998 and Cramer was said to have conceded that he had made a mistake.

Falling Out with Peretz: 1998–99

Besides managing his investors' money for Cramer, Berkowitz and writing columns for TheStreet.com, Cramer was, in June 1998, appearing as a guest cohost on CNBC and a commentator on ABC's ''Good Morning America,'' plus also writing columns regularly for *GQ* and the *New York Observer.* By this time all his writings and television appearances were accompanied by some kind of disclaimer to the effect that he did not intend to, and would not be allowed to, profit as a money manager in his capacity as a journalist. During the summer he said he had cut down on his activities, rejecting most requests to go before the TV cameras and even taking a two-week vacation with his family.

A new conflict-of-interest controversy developed after Cramer, appearing on the CNBC program ''Squawk Box'' in December 1998, said that he had called his broker to say that he wanted to short-sell the stock of WavePhore Inc., a developer of online broadcasting technology, ''because I think this is a big speculative bubble.'' When WavePhore's stock immediately sank in value, the company demanded an investigation, and CNBC temporarily suspended Cramer from its show. He returned after the network confirmed that Cramer had not actually shorted the stock, either before or after the program. A CNBC spokesperson said Cramer always submitted his financial holdings before he appeared on the air.

More serious to Cramer's credibility was a February 1999 *New York Times* article that reported Cramer, Berkowitz had earned only two percent in 1998, after fees, for its investors, compared to about 29 percent for the S&P index. The *Times* said it had obtained a letter to the fund's investors claiming that Cramer, Berkowitz's performance had been damaged by redemptions that forced it to sell stocks at the bottom of the 1998 market—during concerns over a possible Asian financial collapse—when it intended to buy. (During this period Long-Term Capital Management, a larger hedge fund, suffered heavy losses and had to be rescued by a consortium of banks and brokerage houses.)

According to a *Vanity Fair* article by Suzanna Andrews, Cramer was enraged by the *Times* story and was convinced that only Peretz could have leaked the fund's letter to its investors. Her article reported that Peretz—who denied leaking the letter—had withdrawn all his money from Cramer, Berkowitz and that his differences with Cramer stemmed from disputes concerning TheStreet.com. Peretz told her that he had closed his account because Cramer had abruptly resigned as a trustee from several Peretz family trusts without telling him. Cramer, in turn, called Peretz's account a ''canard'' but conceded he had resigned because, he said, he was not being consulted. Bitter over Peretz's defection and his alleged leak to the press, he told

Andrews, ''They all pulled out, and I had to sell into the worst market possible,'' in order to raise the money needed to pay off these investors.

Peretz also closed his Crimson Investments account with Cramer, Berkowitz. This account consisted of a pool of small sums invested by Harvard graduate journalist friends of his and Cramer's, among them Jonathan Alter, Fred Barnes, Eric Breindel, Michael Kinsley, Charles Krauthammer, and Leon Wieseltier. Journalists not in this pool but later brought into the fund by Cramer included Kurt Andersen, Steve Brill, and James Stewart. The minimum initial investment in Cramer, Berkowitz for the firm's 70 or so limited partners was $2.5 million. A staff of nine principals was assisting Cramer and Berkowitz in late 1998. The fund reportedly had $265 million in assets in March 1999. The firm was taking as its profit the standard 20 percent charged by hedge funds on what they earned for their clients, plus a one percent asset management fee, also standard.

Principal Competitors

Long-Term Capital Management.

Further Reading

Andrews, Suzanna, ''Wild on TheStreet.Com,'' *Vanity Fair,* June 1999, pp. 86, 88, 90, 92, 94, 96, 98, 100.
Bryant, Adam, ''Money's Loud Voice,'' *Newsweek,* March 19, 1999, pp. 44–46.
Deutschman, Alan, ''It's 3:45 A.M. Do You Know Where Jim Cramer Is?,'' *GQ/Gentleman's Quarterly,* August 1997, pp. 146–48, 150–55, 202–03.
Doler, Kathleen, ''James Cramer, Columnist, Trader, and Wild Man,'' *Upside,* November 1998, pp. 70–72, 74–75, 120, 122, 124.
Dutt, Jill, ''In the 'Foxhole,' A Trader Awaits Fed's Zero Hour,'' *Washington Post,* May 21, 1997, pp. A1, A8.
Jones, Tim, ''CNBC Welcomes Back Analyst, Explains Its Disclosure Policies,'' *Chicago Tribune,* December 24, 1998, Sec. 3, p. 3.
Kahn, Joseph, ''For a Triple Threat, a Less-Than-Stellar Season,'' *New York Times,* February 25, 1999, pp. C1, C7.
Lux, Hal, ''Cramer Vs. Cramer,'' *Institutional Investor,* July 1997, pp. 55–58.
Napoli, Lisa, ''Investment Site Co-Founder Is at Home on the Internet,'' *New York Times,* June 29, 1998, p. D8.
Nocera, Joseph, ''A Fatuous Furor,'' *Time,* March 6, 1995, p. 73.
Sanger, Elizabeth, ''Dow Jones Critic Sells His Shares,'' *Newsday,* June 5, 1997, p. A56.
Warner, Melanie, ''Are His 15 Minutes Up Yet?,'' *Fortune,* August 17, 1998, p. 226.
——, ''The Trader Who Won't Shut Up,'' *Fortune,* May 12, 1997, pp. 19–20, 22.
Zuckerman, Laurence, ''Smart Money Rethinks Conflict Rule,'' *New York Times,* February 20, 1995, p. D2.

—Robert Halasz

DAIMLERCHRYSLER

DaimlerChrysler AG

Epplestrasse 225
70546 Stuttgart
Germany
Telephone: (711) 17 1
Fax: (711) 17 94022
Web site: http://www.daimlerchrysler.com

Public Company
Incorporated: 1998
Employees: 466,938
Sales: EUR 149.99 billion (US$151.04 billion) (1999)
Stock Exchanges: Frankfurt Berlin Bremen Düsseldorf Hamburg Hanover Stuttgart Munich New York Chicago Pacific Philadelphia Wien Montreal Toronto Paris London Tokyo Basel Geneva Zurich
Ticker Symbol: DCX
NAIC: 336111 Automobile Manufacturing; 336112 Light Truck and Utility Vehicle Manufacturing; 336120 Heavy Duty Truck Manufacturing; 336211 Motor Vehicle Body Manufacturing; 336322 Other Motor Vehicle Electrical and Electronic Equipment Manufacturing; 336411 Aircraft Manufacturing; 336412 Aircraft Engine and Engine Parts Manufacturing; 336414 Guided Missile and Space Vehicle Manufacturing; 336415 Guided Missile and Space Vehicle Propulsion Unit Parts Manufacturing; 336510 Railroad Rolling Stock Manufacturing; 421110 Automobile and Other Motor Vehicle Wholesalers; 522220 Sales Financing; 522291 Consumer Lending; 532112 Passenger Cars Leasing; 541512 Computer Systems Design Services; 514210 Data Processing Services

DaimlerChrysler AG—one of the five largest automakers in the world with a global market share of nine percent—is the product of the November 1998 merger of Daimler-Benz Aktiengesellschaft of Germany and Chrysler Corporation of the United States. Vehicles built by the resultant powerhouse include Mercedes-Benz luxury passenger cars; a microcompact car sold under the name ''Smart''; Chrysler, Jeep, and Dodge cars, pickup trucks, and sport utility vehicles (the Plymouth brand was in the process of being phased out at the turn of the millennium); and commercial vehicles, including vans, trucks, and buses, under the brand names Mercedes-Benz, Freightliner, Sterling, Setra, and Thomas Built Buses. The company's revenue stream is heavily weighted toward the United States and Europe. More than 52 percent is generated in the U.S. market, while Germany accounts for about 19 percent and the rest of Europe a little more than 14 percent. About eight percent derives from the rest of the Americas, with only just more than three percent originating in Asia. This last figure was likely to change with the early 2000 announcement that DaimlerChrysler was buying a 34 percent stake in Mitsubishi Motors Corporation, the fourth largest Japanese automaker.

In addition to its vehicle manufacturing operations, DaimlerChrysler is active in a number of other areas—with many of these activities stemming from a 1980s Daimler-Benz diversification drive. DaimlerChrysler Services is a leading provider of information technology services in Germany and offers a variety of financial services—including vehicle sales and leasing financing, dealer financing, and insurance services—primarily in North America and Europe. DaimlerChrysler Aerospace is involved in commercial aircraft, helicopters, military aircraft, satellites, defense technology, and space technology. At the turn of the millennium, these aerospace operations were slated to be merged into a new firm called European Aeronautic Defence and Space Company (EADS), which would be 30 percent-owned by DaimlerChrysler. EADS would be the largest aerospace firm in Europe and hold an 80 percent stake in Airbus Industrie, the number two commercial aircraft maker in the world. Three other DaimlerChrysler units are also worth noting: ADtranz, a maker of railroad vehicles and equipment; MTU Motoren- und Turbinen-Union, which produces diesel engines and gas turbines for large boats and ships, aircraft, rail vehicles, and heavy trucks; and TEMIC TELEFUNKEN microelectronic, which specializes in automotive electronic systems.

The Predecessors of Daimler-Benz AG

The roots of Daimler-Benz go back to the mid-1880s and two engineers, Carl Benz and Gottlieb Daimler, who are cited by most authorities as the most important contributors to the development of the internal combustion engine. Despite the fact that they were both concerned with the same idea at virtually the same time, and they lived within 60 miles of each other, the two apparently never even met. They certainly never envisioned the 1926 merger of their two companies.

Although Benz drove his first car in 1885 and Daimler ran his in 1886, neither was actually the first to create gasoline-powered vehicles. They were, however, the first to persist long enough to make them viable as transportation. At this time the obstacles to motorized vehicles were enormous: gasoline was considered dangerously explosive, roads were poor, and few people could afford an automobile in any case. Nevertheless, Benz dedicated himself to revolutionizing the world's transportation with the internal combustion engine.

Early in 1885 Benz—who had formed Benz & Companies in Mannheim in 1883—sat in a car and circled a track next to his small factory, while his workers and his wife stood nearby. The car had three wheels and a top speed of ten mph. This engineering triumph was only slightly marred by Benz's first public demonstration, which took place shortly afterward, in which he forgot to steer the car and smashed into the brick wall around his own home. Despite this inauspicious debut, Benz's cars quickly became known for their quality of materials and construction. By 1888 Benz had 50 employees building his three-wheeled car. Two years later, he began making a four-wheeled vehicle.

Daimler's convictions about the internal combustion engine were as intense as Benz's. Originally a gunsmith, Daimler later trained as an engineer, studying in Germany, England, Belgium, and France. After working for a number of German and British firms, he became technical director for the Gasmotorenfabrik Deutz. Disillusioned by the company's limited vision, he and researcher Wilhelm Maybach resigned in 1882 to set up their own experimental engine workshop near Stuttgart. They tested their first engine on a wooden bicycle. Later, they put engines into a four-wheeled vehicle and a boat. Daimler sold the French rights to his engines to Panhard-Levassor (which later fought him for the use of his name). In 1896 he granted a patent license to the British Daimler company, which eventually became independent of the German Daimler-Motoren-Gesellschaft, which was incorporated in 1890.

The story of how Daimler found a new brand name for its cars has become legendary. In 1900 Austro-Hungarian Consul-General and businessman Emil Jellinek approached the company with a suggestion. He offered to underwrite the production of a new high-performance car. In return, he asked that the vehicle be named after his daughter—Mercedes. Daimler's Mercedes continued to make automotive history. In 1906 the young engineer Ferdinand Porsche took the place of Daimler's oldest son, Paul, as chief engineer at the company's Austrian factory. (Paul Daimler returned to the main plant in Stuttgart.) In the five years Porsche was with Daimler, he produced 65 designs, which made him one of the most influential and prolific automotive designers ever. Approximately the same time, in 1909, the Mercedes star emblem was registered; it has embellished the radiators of all the company's cars since 1921.

In 1924 the Daimler and Benz companies began coordinating designs and production, but maintained their own brand names. They merged completely in 1926 as Daimler-Benz Aktiengesellschaft and began producing cars under the name Mercedes-Benz. The merger undoubtedly saved the two companies from bankruptcy in the poverty and inflation of post-World War I Germany.

World War II and the Postwar Recovery

The company continued to grow throughout the 1930s. The most consistently successful participant in automobile racing history, Mercedes-Benz scored international victories that added to its reputation. The company's racing success was also used as propaganda by the Third Reich in the years before World War II. The Mercedes-Benz became Adolph Hitler's parade transportation. Whenever he was photographed in a vehicle, it was a Mercedes. In 1939 the state took over the German auto industry, and during the war Daimler-Benz developed and produced trucks, tanks, and aircraft engines for the Luftwaffe—using, in large part, the slave labor of prisoners. The company's importance to the German war machine made Daimler-Benz a primary target for Allied bombing raids. Two weeks of air strikes in September 1944 destroyed 70 percent or more of the company's plants. Although little was left of the company, workers returned to resume their old jobs after the war. To the surprise of many people, the factories recovered and the company again became one of the most successful auto manufacturers in the world.

Much of Daimler-Benz's growth in the 1950s occurred under the direction of stockholder Friedrich Flick. A convicted war criminal, Flick lost 80 percent of his steel fortune at the end of World War II. Yet he still had enough money to purchase a little more than 37 percent interest in Daimler-Benz between 1954 and 1957. By 1959 his US$20 million investment was worth US$200 million, and he had become Germany's second ranking industrialist. Flick's holdings allowed him to push the company in 1958 to buy 80 percent of competitor Auto Union GmbH and its Audi make, to gain a smaller car for the Daimler product line. The acquisition made Daimler-Benz the fifth largest automobile manufacturer in the world and the largest outside the United States.

The acquisition probably lessened the competitive impact of the new U.S. compact cars introduced in the 1950s; moreover, Daimler-Benz faced a lesser threat than other European automakers because the Mercedes appealed to the market segment made up of wealthy, status-conscious customers, and its appeal grew steadily. By 1960 Daimler-Benz already had 83,000 employees

---

Key Dates:

1882: Gottlieb Daimler and Wilhelm Maybach set up an engine workshop near Stuttgart.

1883: Carl Benz forms Benz & Companies in Mannheim.

1885: Benz drives the first car of his own design.

1890: Daimler-Motoren-Gesellschaft is incorporated.

1900: The Mercedes brand is used for the first time.

1924: Maxwell Motor Corporation, headed by Walter P. Chrysler, introduces the Chrysler Six model.

1925: Maxwell changes its name to Chrysler Corporation.

1926: Daimler and Benz are merged to form Daimler-Benz Aktiengesellschaft, which begins producing cars under the name Mercedes-Benz.

1928: Chrysler acquires Dodge Corporation.

1939: The German auto industry is taken over by the Third Reich.

1944: Most of Daimler-Benz's plants are destroyed in Allied bombing raids.

1958: Daimler-Benz gains control of Auto Union GmbH and its Audi make.

1966: Daimler-Benz sells Auto Union to Volkswagenwerk AG.

1978: Lee Iacocca is named CEO of Chrysler.

1979: Through passage of the Chrysler Loan Guarantee Bill, the U.S. government guarantees US$1.2 billion in loans to Chrysler.

1980: Chrysler posts a loss of nearly US$1.8 billion, the largest ever for a U.S. company.

1981: Daimler-Benz acquires Freightliner Corporation, a U.S.-based maker of heavy trucks.

1983: Chrysler pays off its loan guarantees seven years early.

1984: Chrysler introduces the first minivan.

1985: Daimler-Benz gains full control of Motoren- und Turbinen-Union and purchases a 65.6 percent interest in Dornier.

1986: Daimler-Benz acquires AEG.

1987: Chrysler acquires American Motors Corporation.

1989: Daimler-Benz InterServices (Debis) is created as an internal services arm.

1992: Robert Eaton takes over as CEO of Chrysler.

1993: Daimler-Benz reports its first loss since the end of World War II and becomes the first German firm listed on the New York Stock Exchange.

1995: Jürgen Schrempp takes over as Daimler-Benz's chairman and chief executive; Daimler-Benz and ABB Asea Brown Boveri form railcar-making joint venture, ADtranz; Daimler-Benz posts a loss for the year of nearly US$4 billion, the largest in German history.

1997: Schrempp initiates a sweeping reorganization, creating a new structure with several divisions: passenger cars, commercial vehicles, aerospace, and services.

1998: Daimler-Benz and Chrysler merge to form DaimlerChrysler AG.

1999: DaimlerChrysler agrees to merge the company's aerospace arm, Deutsche Aerospace AG (DASA), into European Aeronautic Defence and Space Company (EADS); DaimlerChrysler gains full control of ADtranz.

2000: DaimlerChrysler agrees to buy a 34 percent stake in Mitsubishi Motors Corporation.

---

in seven West German plants. Additional plants were located in Argentina, Brazil, and India, and the company had established assembly lines in Mexico, South Africa, Belgium, and Ireland. In 1966 Auto Union was sold to Volkswagenwerk AG.

Surviving the Difficulties of the 1970s and Early 1980s

Daimler-Benz's conservative outlook was evident in its strategy of gradual growth, concentration on areas of expertise, foresight, and willingness to sacrifice short-term sales and earnings for long-term benefits. This conservatism helped soften the effect of the recession and gasoline shortages that had severely affected other automakers in the 1970s. While many manufacturers were closing facilities and cutting workers' hours, Daimler-Benz registered record sales gains. Chairman Joachim Zahn, a lawyer, said the company had foreseen "the difficult phase" the auto industry was about to confront. Between 1973 and 1975, Zahn had set aside some US$250 million as "preparation" for bad times. While other automakers spent time and money on model changes, Daimler-Benz had invested in engines powered by inexpensive diesel fuel. These vehicles comprised 45 percent of its output by the mid-1970s. The company was not without problems during these years, as high labor costs and the increasing value of the deutsche mark were making

Mercedes-Benz automobiles more expensive than ever. Rather than reducing costs or cutting corners, however, the company began to speak of its cars as "investments."

Although primarily known for its passenger cars, Daimler-Benz's commercial truck line was its largest source of profits for many years. The company profited from the oil price increase of the late 1970s, when demand for its commercial vehicles rose dramatically in the Middle East. Most of the company's trucks were made outside of Germany, unlike its cars. Later, the commercial line led the company into one risk that was stalled by unfortunate timing. In 1981 Daimler-Benz purchased the U.S.-based Freightliner Corporation, a manufacturer of heavy trucks, just as sales ground to a halt in the face of a U.S. recession.

Some risk-taking was inevitable, of course; usually it paid off. Daimler-Benz increased its car production from 350,000 to 540,000 units a year between 1975 and 1983. Most of the increase was due to the introduction in 1983 of its "190" model, a smaller version of its sedan. Despite some concern that the 190 would cannibalize sales of its larger cars, the 190 expanded Daimler-Benz's customer base, and the updated image of the new model attracted younger customers, lowering the average age of a Mercedes owner from 45 to 40.

As a manufacturer of luxury automobiles, Daimler-Benz was less vulnerable than most automakers to shifts in demand during the early 1980s. Most Mercedes-Benz customers were wealthy enough to rise above concerns about finance rates, inflation, recession, gasoline prices, or tax breaks. In early 1985, for example, German lawmakers vacillated over tax breaks for buyers of cars with lower exhaust emissions, and many Germans delayed purchasing a car until they could see which way the balance would swing. While other auto manufacturers suffered through the falling sales that resulted, Daimler-Benz was unaffected. Not only were its diesel-powered cars producing fewer fumes, but most Mercedes drivers were unconcerned about tax perks.

Another traditional safeguard for Daimler-Benz was its longstanding policy of making only as many cars as it could expect to sell, especially during a recession. The result was usually a backlog of demand when a recession ended. In addition, since the company's sales were good even when the market was poor, Daimler-Benz never had to cater to demands from dealers. Although the United States comprised Daimler-Benz's largest export market, its 500 American dealers unsuccessfully requested more cars in 1985. Why wouldn't Daimler-Benz increase shipments? One reason was that sharp upswings in supply tended to lower the value of used Mercedes, which meant that owners were less likely to sell and buy a new one. Resales were vital to the company's success: 90 percent of West German owners bought another Mercedes when they changed cars. In foreign markets, the repurchase rate was often as high as 80 percent.

Due to limitations that the company placed on production and exports, a "grey market" in Mercedes-Benz cars operated in the United States. Dealers imported recent models from other countries without Daimler-Benz's authority, often illegally, and modified them to meet U.S. safety and emission standards; they then sold the cars at a lower price than regular dealer franchises. Daimler-Benz often tried to protect its carefully controlled market against these "grey market" dealers, but with little success. During the mid-1980s Daimler-Benz was confronted with a dramatic increase in competition for the luxury car market, the fastest-growing segment of the automobile business. Along with this market competition was the increasing speed and sophistication of competitors' automotive research. For example, pioneering Daimler-Benz engineers spent 18 years developing anti-skid brakes to enable drivers to keep control of their vehicles during sudden stops. A few months after the company introduced the breakthrough in the United States, Lincoln brought out a similar system as standard equipment.

Middle to Late 1980s Diversification at Daimler-Benz

Competition and the high price of research and development were two of the factors precipitating the sudden moves Daimler-Benz made between February 1985 and February 1986. Industry analysts were surprised when the company acquired, in quick succession, three large conglomerates. This was a departure from Daimler-Benz's tradition of gradual growth. In February 1985 Daimler-Benz acquired Motoren- und Turbinen-Union, which made aircraft engines and diesel motors for tanks and ships. Daimler already had a 50 percent interest in the company, and when MAN (a Daimler-Benz partner and manufacturer of heavy trucks and buses) wanted to acquire some cash, the company bought MAN's share for US$160 million (Motoren- und Turbinen-Union sales were US$768 million in 1984).

The second acquisition followed in May 1985. Daimler-Benz spent US$130 million for 65.6 percent of Dornier, a privately held manufacturer of spacecraft systems, commuter planes, and medical equipment with 1984 sales of US$530 million. In early 1986 Daimler-Benz made its third acquisition, paying US$820 million for control of AEG, a high-technology manufacturer of electronic equipment such as turbines, robotics, and data processing, as well as household appliances. Although the company's annual sales in 1984 were an impressive US$3.7 billion, the company had just emerged from bankruptcy after losing US$904 million in nine years building nuclear power plants. Many industry watchers were dubious about the diversification of a company that was already doing so well. Profits had increased every year but one between 1970 and 1985, and increased more than 50 percent in 1985 alone. Some analysts also questioned the speed of Daimler-Benz's purchases, as well as management's ability to hold such a large and diverse enterprise together.

Yet Werner Breitschwerdt, chairman of Daimler-Benz's management board, maintained full confidence in the moves. Breitschwerdt, an electrical engineer, joined the passenger car division of the company in 1953 and served as head of styling and product development. He became a member of the managing board in 1977 and chairman in 1983 after the death of his predecessor, Dr. Gerhard Prinz. Breitschwerdt was the first engineer to head the company in decades and the only research and development expert to hold that position. By bringing the technical and research expertise of the new subsidiaries to Daimler-Benz, Breitschwerdt hoped to significantly expand the company's research base. The prospects were highly promising for the automotive division, whose engineers were already interested in developing "intelligent" cars. In this area, the radar technology of AEG and the materials expertise of Dornier would be extremely useful.

The Deutsche Bank (which owned 28 percent of Daimler-Benz) became increasingly troubled, however, by Breitschwerdt's apparent lack of a clear program for integrating the company's US$5.5 billion in recent acquisitions, and in July 1987 Breitschwerdt announced his resignation. Despite the major reservations of several board members, but with Deutsche Bank's full approval, Edzard Reuter, the company's chief strategic planner, was appointed to succeed Breitschwerdt. These upheavals seemed to have little impact on Daimler-Benz's performance; it still emerged as the largest industrial concern in Germany. Notwithstanding its recent diversification, the company remained closely identified with its line of expensive automobiles.

In 1989 Daimler-Benz InterServices AG (Debis) was created to handle data processing, financial and insurance services, and real estate management for the Daimler group. Modeling Debis after similar internal service divisions at Eastman Kodak, General Motors, and IBM, Debis's primary function was to trim much of the company's corporate fat. The following year the dismantling of the Berlin Wall had both positive and negative repercussions for Daimler-Benz: although the recently acquired aeronautical and defense businesses were hurt, the resulting unification provided a welcome jump in demand for Daimler-Benz's automotive division.

Serious Downturn in the Early 1990s

By the early 1990s the German economy took a turn for the worse, and the consequences of Daimler-Benz's mid-1980s spending spree began to take their toll. For the first time in its history, Daimler-Benz was forced to eliminate jobs (14,000 of them, through early retirement and attrition) in its automotive division as Mercedes sales plunged and Daimler's overall profit dropped 25 percent in 1992. Hoping to bolster sales by expansion, Mercedes-Benz bought a five percent stake in Korea's Ssangyong Motor Company in December to build four-wheel-drive vehicles, vans, and, later, passenger cars using Mercedes engines and technology.

First quarter figures for 1993 reflected Germany's widening recession, with Daimler-Benz's net income plummeting by 96 percent to US$12.4 million on sales of US$13.1 billion, while Mercedes' sales (65 percent of the group's) fell 24 percent for the period. Yet with long-term goals in mind, Daimler-Benz announced hidden reserves of US$2.45 billion in an effort to become the first German firm listed on the New York Stock Exchange. The disclosure by Daimler-Benz, which had been prevented from admittance in the past by discrepancies between German and U.S. accounting procedures, was the first of several compliances offered to satisfy U.S. regulators. By midyear, using stringent U.S. accounting procedures, Daimler-Benz reported sales of US$69.6 billion and its first loss since the end of World War II. Yet the company's financial maneuvering earlier in the year had paid off: in October 1993, Daimler-Benz triumphantly listed its stock on the Big Board of the NYSE.

Mercedes-Benz, meanwhile, was busy with both internal and external expansion. A new lower-priced C-Class Mercedes (known as the ''Baby-Benz'') was introduced in 1993 to appeal to younger buyers in the United States and Europe, while plans were announced to build a US$300 million manufacturing facility in Tuscaloosa, Alabama, in return for massive tax breaks, investments from Jefferson County and the city of Birmingham, and a host of other incentives many labeled extravagant. Other big moves in 1993 included Debis's construction of new headquarters in Berlin, rewarded by US$5.1 billion in sales, nearly double those of 1990. Also in 1993, the company's aerospace arm, Deutsche Aerospace AG (DASA), acquired a controlling 51 percent stake in Fokker, a Dutch airplane manufacturer. Daimler-Benz finished 1993 with overall revenue of US$70 billion, with sales constrained by higher interest rates, an increase in value-added taxes, and a sluggish European market. The year's losses amounted to US$1.3 billion, including an US$88.3 million deficit from DASA, which continued to hemorrhage for the next several years.

In 1994 Mercedes-Benz initiated a sweeping reorganization that included manufacturing more car parts outside Germany, appealing to younger buyers through radically different U.S. advertising, and developing more of the smaller, C-Class Mercedes or Baby-Benz models, as well as sport utility vehicles and minivans built at the new Alabama plant. Near the end of the year Mercedes announced plans for a micro-Mercedes, a four-seat, four-door version of its luxurious A-Class car to be marketed to Americans as a ''city'' car for under US$20,000, while an even tinier compact called the ''Swatchmobile'' would be built in France and sold through a partnership with Swiss businessman Nicolas Hayek (the driving force behind Swatch wristwatches). Also on the drawing board was a new model in Mercedes' E-Class full-size cars.

While Mercedes streamlined operations, Daimler-Benz's workforce reductions from 1992 to 1994 now totaled 20 percent of its 350,000 worldwide employees (bringing with it a US$2.5 billion restructuring charge). Believing it had weathered the worst of its recessionary storms, Daimler-Benz climbed back to profitability in 1994 with earnings of US$750 million, due in part to a sharp increase in both buying and selling outside Germany. Yet 1995 brought a series of highs and lows beginning with a changing of the guard: Edzard Reuter was forced out as CEO and was succeeded by former protege Jürgen E. Schrempp, former chairman of DASA.

Schrempp-Engineered Daimler-Benz Turnaround in the Mid-1990s

Among Schrempp's first moves was to stem the flow of red ink at Daimler-Benz Industrie. Arranging a 50/50 merger with the Swedish-Swiss ABB Asea Brown Boveri Ltd. in exchange for US$900 million in cash from Daimler-Benz, the new venture, ABB Daimler-Benz Transportation (ADtranz), would become the world's largest international rail systems provider, generating sales in the neighborhood of US$4.5 billion annually. With the climb of the mark in 1995, Daimler-Benz was saddled with higher labor costs and serious setbacks as the dollar remained weak. Anointed as the Daimler-Benz group's savior, Mercedes-Benz, which earned US$1.3 billion in 1994, was held up as a model to its ailing parent. Always Daimler-Benz's cash cow, Mercedes had just agreed to a US$1.2 billion joint venture with Nanfang South China Motor Corp. to build minivans and engines in China, as well as a second US$50 million venture with Yangzhou Motor Coach Manufacturing Co. to build touring buses and commercial undercarriages. Nevertheless, the still-troubled DASA and Daimler-Benz Industrie posted huge losses in 1995, in part because of writeoffs, leading the company deeply into the red: a nearly US$4 billion loss, the largest in German industrial history.

Fokker was a major burden for Daimler-Benz, causing Schrempp to cut off funding in January 1996, leading to the aircraft maker's bankruptcy. That same month, Schrempp tackled another headache when he distributed the remnants of the troubled AEG electronics subsidiary into other divisions. The revitalization of the Mercedes-Benz unit continued in 1996 with the introduction of the SLK, a convertible roadster sold for about US$40,000 and aimed at younger buyers. That same year, three others models were launched: C-Class and E-Class station wagons and a V-Class minivan. In early 1997 the A-Class made its debut with the launch of the A140, a 141-inch-long compact sporting a small 82-horsepower engine located underneath the floor, and selling for as little as US$17,000—expensive for a compact but cheap for a Mercedes. The A-Class got off to a rough start when an early version showed a tendency to flip over during sharp turns at full speed. The car was quickly pulled from the market and reengineered with an electronic stabilizing system.

Spearheading the risky effort to transform Mercedes-Benz into a full-range carmaker aiming to sell 1.2 million cars a year was the unit's chief executive, Helmut Werner. The key to his strategy was to find market niches in which buyers were willing to pay more for a Mercedes-Benz because of its reputation for luxury and quality. His plan appeared to be working as Mercedes' worldwide passenger car sales increased from about 500,000 in 1993 to nearly 650,000 in 1996. In January 1997, however, Werner resigned in a power struggle with Schrempp. Werner's departure was in anticipation of a sweeping reorganization, which Schrempp launched in April 1997. As part of a dismantling of the holding company structure adopted by Daimler-Benz during its 1980s diversification, Mercedes-Benz AG, which had operated since the 1980s as a subsidiary with its own board of directors, was merged into its parent. Daimler-Benz was then organized into several divisions: passenger cars, commercial vehicles, aerospace (DASA), and services (Debis). The new structure also included three units directly managed by Daimler-Benz: rail systems (the ADtranz joint venture), Motoren- und Turbinen-Union (the diesel engine and gas turbine maker), and TEMIC TELEFUNKEN microelectronic (a specialist in automotive electronic systems). The reorganization significantly flattened the management structure, eliminated hundreds of management positions, and yielded annual cost savings of US$125 million.

Other developments in 1997 included the debut of the first Mercedes sport utility vehicle, the M-Class, which was built at the plant in Alabama. In February 1997 Daimler-Benz acquired the U.S. heavy truck business of the Ford Motor Company, which later in the year began operating under the Sterling brand name.

By early 1998 Schrempp's restructuring efforts had reduced the company's workforce by 63,000 and had seen the divestment of a dozen unprofitable businesses. During 1998, while the merger with Chrysler was in the negotiating and then the pending stages, Daimler-Benz was busy on a number of other fronts. In the commercial vehicle area, the company acquired Thomas Built Buses, a leading North American maker of school buses, and formed a partnership with Nissan Motor Co., Ltd. to make light commercial trucks. Daimler-Benz also sold its semiconductor business to Vishay Intertechnology, Inc. of the United States. Daimler-Benz saw its partnership with the maker of Swatch watches disintegrate in 1998, but moved ahead with development of the microcompact car on its own. Later that year the car made its debut in Europe under the brand name ''smart.'' In November 1998 Daimler-Benz merged with Chrysler, which like Daimler went through tough times in the 1970s and 1980s and emerged in the mid-1990s as one of the most successful car companies in the world.

Early History of Chrysler

The story of the Chrysler Corporation begins in 1920, when the company's founder, Walter Percy Chrysler, resigned his position as president of Buick and vice-president of General Motors (GM) over policy differences with GM's founder, William C. Durant. Chrysler was soon asked by a group of New York bankers to restore the Maxwell Motor Corporation to solvency; in the process, he designed a new Maxwell model, the Chrysler Six. First exhibited in 1924, the car was an immediate success, and before year's end the company sold 32,000 cars at a profit of more than US$4 million. In 1925 Chrysler renamed the company Chrysler Corporation.

The enthusiasm with which the Chrysler Six was met encouraged Walter Chrysler to design four additional models for the coming year: the 50, 60, 70, and Imperial 80. These model numbers referred to the maximum velocity that the cars could reach on a level stretch of road. Until that time, Ford's Model T had enjoyed the reputation of the fastest car, achieving a modest 35 mph. Alarmed by Chrysler's technological breakthrough, the Ford Motor Company closed its doors for nine months and emerged with a replacement for the Model T. By 1927, however, the Chrysler Corporation had firmly established itself with a sale of 192,000 cars, becoming the fifth largest company in the industry.

Walter Chrysler realized that to exploit his firm's manufacturing capacities to their fullest, he would have to build his own plants. Since he could not afford the estimated US$75 million to achieve this, he approached the New York banking firm of Dillon Read and Company. Dillon Read had bought the Dodge Corporation of Detroit from the widows of the Dodge brothers and was happy to reach an agreement with the now highly regarded Walter Chrysler. In July 1928, Dodge became a division of the Chrysler Corporation; overnight, the size of the company increased fivefold. Soon thereafter, the company introduced the low-priced Plymouth and the DeSoto.

Walter Chrysler, carefully avoiding the dangers associated with rapid growth, discontinued his policy of manufacturing as many parts as possible for his cars. Although he paid more for components than other car makers, he was able to maintain greater flexibility in models and designs. This proved to be extremely important in an age of rapid technological advance. Indeed, Walter Chrysler's farsightedness helped the company to survive the Great Depression far better than most in the industry, and his strategy of spending money on research, ''no matter how gloomy the outlook,'' may have been responsible for his firm's sound financial standing until well into the 1940s.

Along with the rest of Detroit's motor industry, Chrysler converted to war production during World War II. The manufacture of its Chrysler, Dodge, and Plymouth cars was put on hold while the corporation specialized in defense hardware such as small arms ammunition and submarine nets. But chief among its war products were B-29 bomber engines and anti-aircraft guns and tanks. Chrysler's wartime service earned it a special Army-Navy award for reliability and prompt delivery.

Postwar Doldrums

The corporation's problems started in the immediate postwar period. The ambition and spirit that drove the company to constant innovation and experimentation in the early days had been lost. The auto market had exhausted fundamental engineering breakthroughs, and American tastes had changed. It seemed that the public was more excited by the sleeker, less traditional, and sometimes less reliable models being produced by Chrysler's rivals. In short, the car industry was becoming a ''marketer's game,'' and Chrysler's management was not playing.

In 1950, L.L. Colbert, a lawyer hired by Walter Chrysler in 1929, became the corporation's president. By this time, some major overhauling was necessary, and Colbert hired the management consulting firm of McKinsey and Company. Three reforms were instituted: Chrysler developed international markets for its cars, its management was centralized, and the role of the engineering department was redefined.

Colbert's reforms did little to revive the company's flagging fortunes, and two years later there was another change of management. Lynn Townsend, the new corporate head, proved to be more effective. He consolidated the Chrysler and Plymouth car divisions, closed some unproductive plants, and generally tightened operations; he also reduced the workforce and installed an IBM computer system to replace 700 members of the clerical staff. Most important, he enhanced sales by improving the quality of the Chrysler automobile, introducing the best warranty the industry had yet seen and instituting a more aggressive marketing policy. In less than five years, Townsend had revitalized the corporation.

Success led to expansion: a space division was formed, and Chrysler became the prime contractor for the Saturn booster rocket. By the end of the 1960s, Townsend's international strategy yielded plants in 18 foreign countries. But before the decade was over, the domestic market was undergoing major changes. Inflation was taking its toll on U.S. auto manufacturers, imports of foreign vehicles had substantially increased, and the price of crude oil had risen drastically. Chrysler's troubles were compounded by internal factors: it was more concerned with competing against Ford and General Motors than in adapting itself to the rapidly changing market; it did not produce enough of its popular compact cars to meet consumer demand; and it had an overstock of larger vehicles.

The corporation reported a US$4 million loss in 1969 and was operating at only 68 percent of its capacity; the previous year, it had earned profits of US$122 million. Car prices were substantially reduced, but this did little to solve the underlying problems. John J. Riccardo, an accountant, succeeded to the presidency and immediately set about reducing expenses. Salaries, workforce, and budget were all cut, and the company experimented with the marketing of foreign-made cars.

Approaching Bankruptcy in the 1970s

Unfortunately, Chrysler seemed incapable of reading the public mood: it narrowed and shortened Dodge and Chrysler models to bring prices down, but sales also tumbled; it continued to make Imperials long after Cadillacs and Lincolns had demonstrated their superiority in the luxury market; and it greeted the 1973–74 Arab oil embargo with a large inventory of gas-guzzlers. Losses in 1974 totaled a massive US$52 million, and the next year's deficit was five times that amount.

The company experienced a brief respite in 1976 and 1977. Its trucks were in demand and foreign subsidiaries turned in good results, but domestic car sales remained a problem. Riccardo further consolidated North American operations and increased manufacturing capacity for compact cars. By the time Chrysler became a significant contender in that market, however, American car buyers were showing a distinct preference for the reliable and relatively inexpensive Japanese compacts. The days of U.S. manufacturing hegemony appeared to be over.

A loss of US$205 million in 1978 led many industry watchers to wonder if Chrysler's rollercoaster finances could rebound from this latest big dip. The syndicate of banks (with Manufacturers Hanover Trust in the vanguard), which for years had been pouring money into Chrysler, panicked. Incredibly, many of the smaller banks had agreed to virtually unlimited lines of credit on the assumption that the company would never need to use them.

But complex and highly charged negotiations eventually saved Chrysler from bankruptcy. The federal government agreed to guarantee loans up to US$1.5 billion, provided Chrysler raised US$2 billion on its own. Politicians could not justify such a massive bailout, however, without changes in Chrysler's management. Riccardo, who had diligently fought against heavy odds, had to go.

It was left to the charismatic Lee Iacocca, who took over in 1978, to preside over Chrysler's comeback. An ex-Ford man with a flair for marketing and public relations, Iacocca took Chrysler's problems to the people, explaining that the company's failure would mean the loss of hundreds of thousands of jobs and could seriously damage the economy of the state of Michigan. Despite popular mythology and the near-adulation of Iacocca in some quarters, many observers suggested that Riccardo was in large part responsible for forging the agreement that gave Chrysler a new lease on life. In any event, the Chrysler Loan Guarantee Bill passed the U.S. Congress on December 27, 1979 and guaranteed US$1.2 billion in loans to Chrysler.

Difficult Recovery in the 1980s and Early 1990s

During the early 1980s, Iacocca's skills as a superb television salesman were of crucial importance as Chrysler lost nearly US$1.8 billion in 1980—the largest loss ever for a U.S. company—and another US$475 million in 1981, before returning to the black in 1982. In August 1983 Chrysler was able to pay off the government loan guarantees seven years early, with the government making a US$350 million profit on its investment. Chrysler's road to recovery was a difficult one, demanding the closure of several plants and the reduction of the company's workforce. In late 1987, Chrysler announced the temporary layoff of employees at two assembly plants, then in 1988 closed an assembly plant in Wisconsin. Two additional plants were closed the following year, coinciding with a companywide restructuring that cost Chrysler US$577 million and left it with US$359 million in net earnings for the year, significantly lower than the US$1.05 billion recorded the year before. Once restructured, Chrysler scrapped its plans to diversify and divested the Gulfstream Aerospace unit it had purchased five years earlier, selling it to a New York investment firm for US$825 million in early 1990. Two other units in the company's Chrysler Technologies subsidiary—Electrospace Systems and Airborne Systems—were slated for divestiture as well, which underscored Iacocca's intent to create a leaner, more sharply focused company. Meanwhile, there were two key developments in the 1980s that helped form the foundation for the 1990s resurgence: the introduction of the minivan in 1984 and the acquisition three years later of American Motors Corporation and its Jeep brand for US$1.2 billion.

Reorganized as such, Chrysler entered the 1990s braced for a full recovery, but the economy did not cooperate. The decline in automotive sales during the fourth quarter of 1989—the company's first fourth quarter decline since 1982—portended a more crippling slump to come, as an economic recession gripped businesses of all types, both domestically and abroad. Net income in 1990 slipped to US$68 million, then plunged to a US$795 million loss the following year, US$411 million of which was attributable to losses incurred by the company's automotive operations. The precipitous drop in earnings for 1991 was the latest in a nearly decade-long series of declines that saw Chrysler's earnings fall each year from the US$2.3 billion generated in 1984 to 1991's disappointing loss. Mired in an economic downturn, Chrysler appeared destined for more of the same, rather than headed toward recovery as Iacocca had hoped, but part of the reason for 1991's losses also led to the company's first step toward genuine recovery.

Partly to blame for the US$795 million loss in 1991 were the high preproduction and introduction costs associated with Chrysler's new Jeep Grand Cherokee and increased production costs at the company's St. Louis minivan plant. These two types of vehicles—minivans and sport utility vehicles—represented the key to Chrysler's recovery. The popularity of these vehicles, coupled with significant price advantages over Japanese models, fueled Chrysler's resurgence. In 1992, when Chrysler's rival U.S. manufacturer Ford registered a US$7.38 billion loss, Chrysler turned its US$795 million loss the year before into a US$723 million gain. It was a signal achievement, accomplished in Iacocca's last year as CEO. Taking over during 1992 was Robert Eaton, who was hired away from General Motors, where he was head of European operations.

Aside from the stifling economic conditions, there were challenges unique to Chrysler that needed addressing before the company's management could be optimistic. In the first quarter of 1993, Chrysler recorded a US$4.4 billion charge for retiree health benefits, which led to a US$2.5 billion loss for the year, a staggering financial blow but one irrespective of the company's ability to successfully sell automotive vehicles. That ability was demonstrated in the first quarter of 1994, when Chrysler posted US$938 million in profits, the most recorded in the company's history and the greatest amount since the US$801 million recorded in the second quarter of 1984. Chrysler went on to enjoy its most successful year ever, with 1994 earnings of US$3.7 billion on revenues of US$52.2 billion.

The good news at Chrysler continued into the late 1990s, after the company managed to fend off a US$22 billion buyout proposed by billionaire investor Kirk Kerkorian in 1995. The long prosperity and low gasoline prices of the middle to late 1990s created a huge demand for large vehicles, and Chrysler was producing hot models in each of the hottest segments: the Dodge Ram pickup truck; the Town & Country minivan; and several sport utility vehicles—the Jeep Grand Cherokee, the Jeep Wrangler, and the Dodge Durango. Questions about the quality of Chrysler products continued to pop up, but the company's share of the U.S. auto market reached as high as 16.7 percent in 1996, the highest level since 1968 and a huge gain from the 1991 level of 12.2 percent. Sales reached US$61.4 billion in 1996, more than double the level of 1991. Also in 1996, Chrysler dedicated its new headquarters in Auburn Hills, Michigan.

Late 1990s and Beyond: The Creation and Early Years of DaimlerChrysler

Daimler-Benz Chief Executive Jürgen Schrempp had concluded as early as 1996 that his company's automotive operations needed a partner to compete in the increasingly globalized marketplace. Chrysler's Eaton was drawing the same conclusion in 1997 based on two factors emerging around the same time: the Asian economic crisis, which was cutting into demand, and worldwide excess auto manufacturing capacity, which was looming and would inevitably lead to industry consolidation. With annual global overcapacity as high as 18.2 million vehicles predicted for the early 21st century, it became clearer that Daimler-Benz and Chrysler could survive only as strong regional players if they continued to go it alone.

After several months of negotiations, Daimler-Benz and Chrysler reached a merger agreement in May 1998 to create DaimlerChrysler AG in a US$37 billion deal. The deal was consummated in November 1998, forming an auto behemoth with total revenues of US$130 billion, factories in 34 countries on four continents, and combined annual unit sales of 4.4 million cars and trucks, placing the company in fifth place worldwide. The two companies fit well together geographically, Daimler strong in Europe and Chrysler in North America, and in terms of product lines, with Daimler's luxurious and high-quality passenger cars and Chrysler's line of low-production-cost trucks, minivans, and sport utility vehicles. Although this was ostensibly a merger of equals and the company set up ''coheadquarters'' in Stuttgart and Auburn Hills, as well as cochairmen in the form of Eaton and Schrempp, it soon became clear that the Germans were taking over the Americans. DaimlerChrysler was set up as a German firm for tax and accounting purposes, and the early 2000 departures of Thomas Stallkamp, the initial head of DaimlerChrysler's U.S. operations, and Eaton (who was originally slated to remain until as late as November 2001) left Schrempp in clear command of the company.

During 1999 DaimlerChrysler concentrated on squeezing out US$1.4 billion in annual cost savings from the integration of procurement and other functional departments. The company organized its automotive businesses into three divisions: Mercedes-Benz Passenger Cars/smart, the Chrysler Group, and Commercial Vehicles; in November 1999 DaimlerChrysler announced that it would begin phasing out the aging Plymouth brand. The Debis services division was merged with Chrysler's services arm to form DaimlerChrysler Services, while DASA was renamed DaimlerChrysler Aerospace. Late in 1999 the company reached an agreement to merge DaimlerChrysler Aerospace with two other European aerospace firms, the French Aérospatiale Matra and the Spanish CASA, to form the European Aeronautic Defence and Space Company (EADS). DaimlerChrysler would hold a 30 percent stake in EADS, which would be the largest aerospace firm in Europe and the third largest in the world. Through each of the EADS partners' holdings in Airbus Industrie, EADS would hold an 80 percent stake in Airbus, which trailed only the Boeing Company in the manufacture of commercial aircraft. EADS would also be the world's leading helicopter manufacturer through its 100 percent ownership of Eurocopter. DaimlerChrysler also retained its other industrial businesses from the Daimler side: the TEMIC automotive electronics operation, the MTU diesel engines unit, and the ADtranz rail systems venture. During 1999 DaimlerChrysler gained full control of ADtranz by acquiring the 50 percent held by ABB for US$472 million. There was also one significant disposal during 1999. The company sold 90 percent of debitel, a mobile telephone subsidiary that had formed part of the services sector, to the public and to Swisscom, recording a gain of US$1.1 billion from an initial investment, nine years previous, of only US$9 million.

In early 2000, DaimlerChrysler set an ambitious goal for itself: become the number one automaker in the world within one to three years. The auto industry had already seen a number of takeovers and alliances that followed in the wake of the merger of Daimler-Benz and Chrysler, so DaimlerChrysler needed to move quickly to reach this goal. The company's most pressing needs were to bolster its presence in Asia, where less than four percent of the company's overall revenue was generated, and to gain a larger share of the small car market in Europe. Filling both of these bills was DaimlerChrysler's planned purchase of a 34 percent stake in Mitsubishi Motors Corporation for US$2 billion, a deal announced in late March. A key part of the agreement was the transformation of Mitsubishi's European manufacturing operation, Netherlands Car B.V., into a 50–50 joint venture responsible for developing small cars for the European market. DaimlerChrysler gained three seats on the Japanese company's ten-person board and veto power over board decisions, but did not gain full control of the company. DaimlerChrysler was likely to pursue other alliances in its attempt to unseat GM as the world leader in automobiles, with speculation centering on Hyundai Motor Company of South Korea. In another key early 2000 development, DaimlerChrysler agreed to join with GM and Ford to create an Internet-based global business-to-business supplier exchange. This would potentially create the world's largest virtual marketplace, although the Federal Trade Commission quickly opened a preliminary antitrust inquiry into the plan.

Principal Subsidiaries

MERCEDES BENZ PASSENGER CARS & SMART: Micro Compact Car smart GmbH; Mercedes-Benz U.S. International, Inc.; Mercedes-Benz India Ltd. (86%); DaimlerChrysler South Africa (Pty.) Ltd. CHRYSLER GROUP: DaimlerChrysler Corporation (U.S.A.); DaimlerChrysler Canada, Inc.; Eurostar Automobilwerk GmbH & Co. KG; DaimlerChrysler Transport, Inc. (U.S.A.); DaimlerChrysler de Mexico S.A. de C.V. COMMERCIAL VEHICLES: EvoBus GmbH; Mercedes-Benz Lenkungen GmbH; Mercedes-Benz España S.A. (Spain); NAW Nutzfahrzeuge AG; Freightliner Corporation (U.S.A.); Mercedes-Benz Mexico S.A. de C.V.; Mercedes-Benz do Brasil S.A. (Brazil); Mercedes-Benz Argentina; Mercedes-Benz Group Indonesia (95%); Mercedes-Benz Türk A.S. (Turkey; 66.9%). VEHICLE SALES ORGANIZATION: Mercedes-Benz USA, Inc.; DaimlerChrysler France S.A.S.; DaimlerChrysler Belgium S.A./N.V.; DaimlerChrysler Nederland B.V. (Netherlands); Mercedes-Benz (United Kingdom) Ltd.; DaimlerChrysler Danmark AS (Denmark); DaimlerChrysler Sverige AG (Sweden); Mercedes-Benz Italia S.p.A. (Italy); Mercedes-Benz (Switzerland) AG; Mercedes-Benz Hellas S.A. (Greece); DaimlerChrysler Japan Co. Ltd.; DaimlerChrysler (Australia/Pacific) Pty. Ltd. SERVICES: DaimlerChrysler Ser-

vices (debis) AG; debis Systemhaus GmbH; Mercedes-Benz Finanz GmbH; Mercedes-Benz Leasing GmbH; Mercedes-Benz Credit Corporation (U.S.A.); Chrysler Financial Company L.L.C. (U.S.A.); Chrysler Capital Company L.L.C. (U.S.A.); Chrysler Insurance Company (U.S.A.). AEROSPACE: DaimlerChrysler Aerospace AG; DaimlerChrysler Aerospace Airbus GmbH; Dornier GmbH (57.6%); Dornier Satellitensysteme GmbH; Eurocopter S.A. (France; 75%); Eurocopter Deutschland GmbH; MTU Motoren- und Turbinen-Union München GmbH; LFK Lenkflugkörpersysteme GmbH (70%); Nortel Dasa Network Systems GmbH & Co. KG (50%). OTHER BUSINESSES: DaimlerChrysler Rail Systems GmbH; TEMIC TELEFUNKEN microelectronic GmbH; MTU Motoren- und Turbinen-Union Friedrichshafen GmbH (88.4%). REGIONAL HOLDING AND FINANCE COMPANIES: DaimlerChrysler North America Holding Corporation (U.S.A.); DaimlerChrysler Nederland Holding B.V. (Netherlands); DaimlerChrysler Schweiz Holding AG (Switzerland); DaimlerChrysler UK Holding plc; DaimlerChrysler France Holding S.A.; DaimlerChrysler Coordination Center S.A./N.V. (Belgium); DaimlerChrysler España Holding S.A. (Spain).

Principal Divisions

Mercedes-Benz Passenger Cars/smart; Chrysler Group; Commercial Vehicles; DaimlerChrysler Services; DaimlerChrysler Aerospace.

Principal Competitors

Bayerische Motoren Werke AG; The Boeing Company; Fiat S.p.A.; Ford Motor Company; General Motors Corporation; Honda Motor Co., Ltd.; Hyundai Motor Company; Isuzu Motors Limited; Mazda Motor Corporation; Navistar International Corporation; Nissan Motor Co., Ltd.; PACCAR Inc.; PSA Peugeot Citroen S.A.; Renault S.A.; Saab Automobile AB; Siemens AG; Suzuki Motor Corporation; Toyota Motor Corporation; Volkswagen AG; AB Volvo.

Further Reading

Abodaher, David, *Iacocca,* New York: Macmillan, 1982.

Aeppel, Timothy, "Daimler-Benz Discloses Hidden Reserves of $2.45 Billion, Seeks Big Board Listing," *Wall Street Journal,* March 25, 1993, p. A10.

"Backbiting at Daimler," *Business Week,* August 7, 1995, p. 45.

Ball, Jeffrey, "DaimlerChrysler Fights to Retain Minivan Dominance," *Wall Street Journal,* January 11, 2000, p. B4.

——, "Eaton Retires As Co-Leader of Daimler," *Wall Street Journal,* January 27, 2000, pp. A3, A8.

Ball, Jeffrey, and Scott Miller, "DaimlerChrysler Aims to Be No. 1 Auto Maker," *Wall Street Journal,* January 14, 2000, pp. A2, A6.

Bellon, Bernard P., *Mercedes in Peace and War: German Automobile Workers, 1903–1945,* New York: Columbia University Press, 1990.

Breer, Carl, *The Birth of Chrysler Corporation and Its Engineering Legacy,* Warrendale, Penn.: Society of Automotive Engineers, 1995.

Browning, E.S., and Helene Cooper, "States' Bidding War Over Mercedes Plant Made for Costly Chase," *Wall Street Journal,* November 24, 1993, pp. A1, A6.

Choi, Audrey, "Daimler-Benz Plans Job Cuts of 13,500 in '95," *Wall Street Journal,* April 13, 1995, pp. A3, A4.

——, "For Mercedes, Going Global Means Being Less German," *Wall Street Journal,* April 27, 1995, p. B4.

——, "Mercedes-Benz Sets Restructuring Plans in Wake of Vehicle Units' Difficulties," *Wall Street Journal,* January 27, 1994, p. A10.

——, "Mercedes to Cut German Force by 14,000 Jobs," *Wall Street Journal,* August 25, 1993, p. A6.

Cole, Jeff, "Boeing Faces European Competition in Effort to Build Small Plane for Asia," *Wall Street Journal,* May 8, 1995, p. B2.

Flint, Jerry, "Chrysler Has the Hot Cars: More Important, It Has a Smart, Disciplined Management Team," *Forbes,* January 13, 1997, pp. 82+.

Gardner, Greg, "Chrysler: The Cat with Nine Lives," *Ward's Auto World,* May 1996, p. 67.

——, "The Cloud Over Chrysler," *Ward's Auto World,* June 1996, pp. 25–28.

"Gentlemen, Start Your Engines," *Fortune,* June 8, 1998, pp. 138+.

Gordon, Maynard M., *The Iacocca Management Technique,* New York: Dodd Mead, 1985.

Gregor, Neil, *Daimler-Benz in the Third Reich,* New Haven, Conn.: Yale University Press, 1998.

Gumbel, Peter, "Daimler to Pay $900 Million to ABB As They Merge Railroad Operations," *Wall Street Journal,* March 17, 1995, p. A6.

Gumbel, Peter, and Audrey Choi, "Germany Making Comeback, with Daimler in the Lead," *Wall Street Journal,* April 7, 1995, p. A10.

Iacocca, Lee, with William Novak, *Iacocca: An Autobiography,* New York: Bantam, 1984.

Kerwin, Kathleen, "The Big Three Are Learning to Hold a Lead," *Business Week,* April 26, 1993, p. 29.

Kimes, Beverly Rae, *The Star and the Laurel: The Centennial History of Daimler, Mercedes, and Benz, 1886–1986,* Montvale, N.J.: Mercedes Benz of North America, 1986.

Kindel, Stephen, "Sweet Chariots: How Chrysler, Said to Be at Death's Door Just Two Years Ago, Became Detroit's Profit Leader," *Financial World,* January 18, 1994, pp. 46–49, 52, 54.

Kisiel, Ralph, "D/C Turns 1: Bigger ... But Better?," *Automotive News,* November 15, 1999, p. 1.

Klebnikov, Paul, "Mercedes-Benz's Bold Niche Strategy," *Forbes,* September 8, 1997, p. 68.

Kujawa, Duane, *International Labor Relations Management in the Automotive Industry: A Comparative Study of Chrysler, Ford, and General Motors,* New York: Praeger, 1971.

Langworth, Richard M., and Jan P. Norbye, *The Complete History of Chrysler Corporation, 1924–1985,* New York: Beekman House, 1985.

Marshall, Matt, and Joseph Kahn, "Mercedes Wins China Minivan Project," *Wall Street Journal,* July 13, 1995, p. A2.

Miller, Karen Lowry, and Joann Muller, "The Auto Baron," *Business Week,* November 16, 1998, pp. 82+.

Miller, Scott, and Norihiko Shirouzu, "Daimler to Take Controlling Stake in Mitsubishi for $1.95 Billion," *Wall Street Journal,* March 27, 2000, p. A21.

——, "Mitsubishi Deal Isn't a Cure-All for Daimler," *Wall Street Journal,* March 28, 2000, pp. A21, A24.

Moritz, Michael, and Barrett Seaman, *Going for Broke: The Chrysler Story,* Garden City, N.Y.: Doubleday, 1981.

Nelson, Mark M., "Daimler-Benz AG Makes Way In-House," *Wall Street Journal,* September 24, 1993, p. B11.

Palmer, Jay, "Shake-Up Artist: Daimler-Benz Chairman Juergen Schrempp Has Knocked the Dust Off Mercedes, Restoring Hope for European Manufacturing," *Barron's,* March 23, 1998, pp. 35–36, 38–40.

Pomice, Eva, "Can Detroit Hold On?," *U.S. News and World Report,* April 15, 1991, p. 51.

Reed, Stanley, "Backbiting at Daimler," *Business Week,* August 7, 1995, p. 45.

Reich, Robert B., and John D. Donahue, *New Deals: The Chrysler Revival and the American System,* New York: Times Books, 1985.

Schmid, John, "Daimler-Benz Reports First-Ever Loss, Reflecting New Accounting, Lower Sales," *Wall Street Journal,* September 20, 1993, p. A10.

Schweer, Dieter, *Daimler-Benz: Innenansichten eines Giganten,* Düsseldorf: Econ, 1995.

Simison, Robert L., "Love Your Big, Luxurious Mercedes? German Car Maker Is Thinking Small," *Wall Street Journal,* December 12, 1994, p. B8.

Simison, Robert L., Fara Warner, and Gregory L. White, "Big Three Car Makers Plan Net Exchange," *Wall Street Journal,* February 28, 2000, pp. A3, A16.

Simison, Robert L., Gregory L. White, and Deborah Ball, "GM's Linkup with Fiat Opens Final Act of Consolidation Drama for Industry," *Wall Street Journal,* March 14, 2000, pp. A3, A8.

Soo-Mi, Kim, "Ssangyong Places Hopes on Accord with Mercedes AG," *Wall Street Journal,* December 18, 1992, p. A5.

Steinmetz, Gene, "BellSouth and Thyssen Join to Compete in German Telecommunications Market," *Wall Street Journal,* May 9, 1995, p. A14.

Taylor, Alex, III, "Blue Skies for Airbus," *Fortune,* August 2, 1999, pp. 102–4, 106, 108.

——, "Can Iacocca Fix Chrysler—Again?," *Fortune,* April 8, 1991, p. 50.

——, "Chrysler: Sandbagged by Its Biggest Shareholder," *Fortune,* May 15, 1995, p. 44.

——, "Chrysler's Great Expectations," *Fortune,* December 9, 1996, pp. 101–02, 104.

——, "The Germans Take Charge," *Fortune,* January 11, 1999, pp. 92–94, 96.

——, "Iacocca's Last Stand at Chrysler," *Fortune,* April 20, 1992, p. 63.

——, "Is the World Big Enough for Jürgen Schrempp," *Fortune,* March 6, 2000, pp. 140+.

——, " 'Neutron Jürgen' Ignites a Revolution at Daimler-Benz," *Fortune,* November 10, 1997, pp. 144–46+.

——, "The New Golden Age of Autos," *Fortune,* April 4, 1994, p. 50.

——, "Will Success Spoil Chrysler?," *Fortune,* January 10, 1994, pp. 88–92.

Templeman, John, "The New Mercedes," *Business Week,* August 26, 1996, pp. 34+.

——, "The Shocks for Daimler's New Driver," *Business Week,* August 21, 1995, pp. 38–39.

——, "Upheaval at Daimler," *Business Week,* February 5, 1996, pp. 14+.

Thomas, Charles M., "Big 3 Picture Brightens After '89 Plunge," *Automotive News,* February 19, 1990, p. 1.

Treece, James B., and David Woodruff, "Crunch Time Again for Chrysler," *Business Week,* March 25, 1991, p. 92.

Vlasic, Bill, "Can Chrysler Keep It Up?," *Business Week,* November 25, 1996, pp. 108+.

Vlasic, Bill, and Kathleen Kerwin, "Fighting Bob: Chrysler's Eaton Takes Off the Gloves with Kerkorian & Co.," *Business Week,* pp. 88+.

Vlasic, Bill, et al., "The First Global Car Colossus," *Business Week,* May 18, 1998, pp. 40+.

Warner, Fara, "Mercedes Goes Hollywood and High-Tech," *Wall Street Journal,* January 24, 1995, p. B6.

Washington, Frank S., "Merger? What Merger?," *Ward's Auto World,* November 1999, pp. 66–67.

Whitney, Glenn, and Timothy Roth, "Daimler's U.S. Listing May Be Sign of Change in German Equities Market," *Wall Street Journal,* March 29, 1993, p. B6.

Zellner, Wendy, "Chrysler's Next Generation: An Heir Apparent and New, Upscale Cars," *Business Week,* December 19, 1998, p. 52.

—Taryn Benbow Pfalzgraf and Jeffrey L. Covell
—updated by David E. Salamie

DeLaRue

De La Rue plc

De La Rue House
Jays Close
Viables
Basingstoke, Hampshire RG22 4BS
United Kingdom
Telephone: (01256) 329122
Fax: (01256) 351323
Web site: http://www.delarue.com

Public Company
Incorporated: 1896 as Thomas De La Rue
Employees: 9,753
Sales: £737.9 million (US$1.2 billion) (1999)
Stock Exchanges: London
NAIC: 323119 Other Commercial Printing; 322121 Paper
   (Except Newsprint) Mills; 333311 Automatic Vending
   Machine Manufacturing; 333313 Office Machinery
   Manufacturing; 334119 Other Computer Peripheral
   Equipment Manufacturing; 334514 Totalizing Fluid
   Meter and Counting Device Manufacturing; 541430
   Graphic Design Services

The world's largest commercial banknote printer and banknote paper manufacturer, De La Rue plc has a presence in literally the four corners of the earth. With 90 percent of its sales outside the United Kingdom, the company's security paper and print division is active in about 150 countries worldwide. Its customers include commercial banks, central banks, and other financial institutions. In security printing, De La Rue provides total solutions—including products and services—to governments and retailers needing secure printed products, such as checks, traveler's checks, passports, vouchers, tickets, and revenue, postage, and other types of stamps. At the forefront of the move to automate retail banking processes, De La Rue's cash systems division is a leader in payment systems, producing cash handling equipment, cash dispensing machines (including ATMs), banknote sorting machines, counting products, and cash processing software systems. De La Rue also holds a 26.7 percent stake in the Camelot Group, operator of the national lottery in the United Kingdom, and a half interest in De La Rue Giori, a maker of banknote printing machinery. A company founded on and fueled by innovation, De La Rue has had a colorful and eventful history.

19th-Century Origins

Thomas de la Rue was born in a small village in Guernsey, the Channel Islands, in 1793. A boy of little formal education but much ingenuity, he was apprenticed at the age of nine to a newspaper printer in Guernsey's capital, St. Peter Port. Immediately after his term of service ended in 1811, de la Rue entered into a partnership with Englishman Tom Greenslade to produce their own weekly "journal politique et littéraire," the *Publiciste.* After only 13 editions, however, de la Rue, whose burning ambition was matched by an equally fiery temper, fell out with his partner and independently set up *Le Miroir Politique,* a forum from which he energetically attacked Greenslade and the other publishers in town.

From the beginning, however, de la Rue was more interested in publishing processes than in editorial content, and by the time he was 25 he had determined that provincial Guernsey offered too restricted a scope and moved to London. In order to support his family, de la Rue began his London career as a manufacturer of straw hats, but all the while he was experimenting with paper surfaces and printing processes. In 1829 he produced a deluxe edition of the New Testament, 25 copies of which were printed with pure gold powder. The result was universally admired, and book lovers judged it a marvel, but unfortunately, with a price tag of £15, only one copy was sold.

The foundation of the De La Rue company, which was initially named Thomas De La Rue, came in 1830, when de la Rue first went into the playing card business. Two years later de la Rue patented his "Improvements to Playing Cards" and produced the first modern cards. His printing technique, electrotyping on enameled paper, represented a notable achievement not only in playing cards but in the history of color printing. Within a few years De La Rue was acknowledged as the premier maker of playing cards in Britain. Although cards remained the backbone of the business until the 1850s, during the 1830s and 1840s De La Rue branched out into all aspects of the stationery business, establishing a brisk trade in elaborately designed Victorian stationery, visiting cards, wedding cards, fancy menus, and railway tickets (a handy way of using up odd pieces of pasteboard). In 1843 De La Rue established its first overseas trade, as de la Rue's brother Paul traveled to Russia to advise on the making of playing cards.

Meanwhile the burgeoning postal system was to supply De La Rue with its next major business avenue. In 1840 the system of prepaid postage was first introduced, and with it the idea of the envelope. The earliest envelopes were sold flat and unfolded; later they were cut and folded, but the whole laborious process was done by hand. In 1846 de la Rue's son Warren, an inventor like his father and in his later years a well-respected amateur scientist and astronomer, designed the first envelope-making machine, able to produce 2,700 envelopes in an hour. This proved to be a tremendous boost to De La Rue, particularly after 1851 when it caught international attention and acclaim at the Great Exhibition at the Crystal Palace in Hyde Park.

Two years later De La Rue scored another coup when it won a four-year contract from the Inland Revenue to produce adhesive fiscal stamps on drafts and receipts. The company's main competitor in this area, Perkins Bacon & Co., might have seemed the logical choice for this contract as it was already making Britain's first postage stamps, but De La Rue was pioneering a new method; instead of the old line engraved system, whereby each sheet was printed from a transferred plate, De La Rue's new process was typographical, or surface printed. The system was more economical and practical, and De La Rue promised, in addition, that they could provide a special "fugitive" ink which would disappear if anyone attempted to clean the stamps to reuse them.

De La Rue's first foray into security printing was thus a tremendous success. By 1855 the company was producing its first British postage stamp, the Fourpenny Carmine, and had begun supplying stamps to the East India Company. This was the start of a hugely lucrative contract; within a few years the company was supplying the entire colony with all its postal requirements.

A rival's bad luck and the uncertain temperament of a government official provided De La Rue's next big break. In 1858 Perkins Bacon inadvertently offended the Agent General in charge of the British colonies' stamps to such a degree that the Agent General relieved that company of the contracts for the Cape of Good Hope, Mauritius, Trinidad, Western Australia, Ceylon, Saint Helena, the Bahamas, Natal, and St. Lucia and awarded them all to De La Rue. This in turn led to another profitable avenue for De La Rue, as the same official contracted the firm to print the paper currency for Mauritius, giving De La Rue its first banknote printing contract, in 1860. Success in the

British colonies bred success at home, and by 1880 De La Rue had completely cornered the domestic postal market.

During the middle decades of the 19th century, De La Rue became an international force in security printing. As new countries emerged or different governments came to power, De La Rue was there to offer its expertise in postal and currency printing. During the U.S. Civil War, De La Rue was hired by the Confederacy to produce the only American stamp ever printed abroad: the Five Cents Blue, adorned with the head of Jefferson Davis. The business expanded into Italy, Portugal, Uruguay, and Ecuador, and as it expanded Thomas de la Rue and his sons Warren and William continued to make improvements in paper and processes.

Early 20th-Century Difficulties

In 1896 Thomas De La Rue converted from a family partnership to a private company. Now under third-generation leadership, the firm seemed to lose those qualities of ambition and innovation that had caused it to flourish under Thomas and his sons, and entered a long period of stagnation and decline. The company did enjoy a brief success with its Onoto pen, the first practical fountain pen. As its eccentric inventor George Sweetser enthused of his creation: "It can not only be filled in a flash and written with, but could be used to syringe your ears, spray the geraniums with insecticide, and it is ideal for ''ink-splashers' as it will carry across the road." Fueled by a £50,000 advertising campaign (an enormous sum at the time), the Onoto was a big success in the early years of the 20th century, though not big enough to save the faltering fortunes of De La Rue.

As early as 1888 there had been some concerns expressed in Parliament about De La Rue's monopoly of the British postage stamp market. That incipient storm had blown over largely because De La Rue was able to convince the government that it was, simply, the best company for the job. By 1910, however, suspicions were rekindled, not least because, although production costs had gone down, De La Rue's prices remained as high as ever. The company was, in fact, making colossal profits and had grown complacent. The Inland Revenue proposed to split the contract between De La Rue and another firm, Harrisons. Reportedly, Thomas de la Rue's grandson, Thomas Andros de la Rue, was so incensed by this proposal that he stormed out of a meeting with the secretary of the Post Office after shouting that De La Rue would have the entire contract or it would have none of it. Thus De La Rue lost a contract it had held for 30 years. The consequences for the company were grave, with idle factories and redundant workers the result. Loss of face was added to loss of profits only months later when Thomas Andros de la Rue died and the rumor went around that De La Rue's workers were each to benefit by his will. The widely publicized rumor proved to be untrue, and De La Rue sank even further in the public's estimation.

With the outbreak of World War I, the company's fortunes were briefly revived with an important government commission to print one and ten shilling notes, but on the whole fourth-generation management fared no better than had third-generation. Indeed, the company started the war with £90,000 to its credit, and ended it £90,000 in debt. Part of the problem stemmed from Stuart de la Rue's too-eager embrace of the

Key Dates:

1830: Thomas de la Rue begins printing playing cards.

1855: De la Rue's company begins producing its first British postage stamp and starts supplying stamps to the East India Company.

1860: Company gains its first banknote printing contract, for Mauritius.

1896: Thomas De La Rue is incorporated as a private company.

1921: Company goes public.

1940: Company's London factories at Bunhill Row are destroyed in the Blitz.

1958: Thomas De La Rue changes its name to De La Rue Company Limited.

1961: De La Rue acquires a longtime printing rival, Waterlow and Sons.

1965: Company enters into a Switzerland-based joint venture called De La Rue Giori, which specializes in the manufacture of banknote printing machinery.

1968: The Rank Organisation Plc makes a takeover bid for De La Rue.

1969: The Monopolies Commission rejects the Rank bid as being against the public interest; De La Rue sells its playing card business to John Waddington.

1974: Crosfield Electronics, maker of banknote handling systems, is acquired.

1989: Crosfield, now a supplier of prepress equipment for the printing and publishing industries, is sold; Norton Opax attempts takeover of De La Rue, but the bid fails when Norton is itself acquired by Bowater; Jeremy Marshall becomes the first outsider named chief executive and launches a restructuring.

1991: Company changes its name to De La Rue plc.

1992: Inter Innovation, a Swedish maker of automated currency handling machines, is acquired.

1993: De La Rue joins Camelot Group plc consortium, taking an initial 22.5 percent stake.

1994: Camelot is awarded the license to operate the U.K. national lottery.

1995: De La Rue acquires Portals Group, a maker of banknote paper.

1998: Marshall is forced into early retirement. Reorganization of banknote business begins. Ian Much is appointed the new chief executive.

1999: De La Rue sells its card-reading terminals business and most of the remainder of its card systems division, in two separate transactions. The cash systems division undergoes a major overhaul.

2000: Services and solutions division is formed.

wartime government's suggestions that manufacturing firms should diversify. De La Rue diversified into everything from cricket bats to motor cars with mostly disastrous results. On one occasion, in a bid to prove De La Rue's security printing superiority, Stuart de la Rue forged one of the company's competitor's banknotes, successfully presented it to his bank, and triumphantly informed the government, only to be nearly imprisoned for counterfeiting.

By 1921, when the company went public, it was nearly ruined. Once at the forefront of new technologies and developing research, De La Rue's factories were degenerating into a jumble of antiquated machinery and outdated processes. Stuart de la Rue, as chairman, was the only family member left in the firm. When the government proposed that the company fulfill India's printing requirements on location rather than in London, Stuart refused to do so, with the result that within a few years the entire Indian contract—a mainstay of the business—was lost.

In 1923, Stuart de la Rue unwisely revealed that De La Rue had a secret private agreement with its competitor Waterlows over stamp interests. De La Rue held a monopoly on domestic and colonial stamps, Waterlows on foreign stamps. If the "wrong" tender were accepted, one company paid compensation to the other. There was a great public outcry at this revelation, and although Stuart received only a public admonishment in the inquiry that followed, the company's reputation was further discredited. Stuart de la Rue's own reputation was in tatters. It is said that, in desperation, he asked his employees what had gone wrong with the company, and one of them, Bernard Westall, a junior clerk who later became managing director, responded, "You." Stuart de la Rue left the company soon thereafter.

It took some time for De La Rue to recover from its troubles, but recover it did. Instrumental in the company's revival was its 1930 entry into the vast and lucrative Chinese market, which was to be for nearly 20 years a mainstay for De La Rue. Operations were frequently fraught with cloak-and-dagger style intrigue as international hostilities heightened and World War II drew near. A factory was secretly built in the French settlement of Shanghai with a backup plant constructed in Rangoon, Burma, as a precaution against Japanese aggression. When France fell, De La Rue succeeded in moving its operations to Rangoon, and when Rangoon fell, to Bombay, India.

De La Rue's London factories at Bunhill Row were destroyed in the Blitz in December 1940, and the old ways of commercial printing were finished forever. De La Rue, however, quickly made arrangements to resume printing elsewhere by offset lithography and was able to honor all commitments.

Postwar Acquisitions, Expansions, and Divestments

Following the war, De La Rue embarked on a half century of acquisitions, developments, and expansions. In a strong postwar position, the company grew, establishing interests in Pakistan, Ireland, and Brazil. In 1958 the company set up Formica Ltd. (with 40 percent participation by American Cyanamid) and within a few years its factories were established in France, Germany, Australia, New Zealand, and India. Security Express, a carrier of valuables, was created the following year. In 1958 the parent company changed its named to De La Rue Company Limited, reflecting its status as a classic conglomerate.

In 1960 De La Rue's growing involvement in bank automation was signaled by its creation of a subsidiary, De La Rue Instruments. The following year the company acquired the de la Rue family's old printing rivals, Waterlow and Sons. The 150th anniversary of Thomas de la Rue's first edition of his own newspaper *Le Miroir Politique* coincided with the company's registration in New York as a security and financial printer to the New York Stock Exchange. The company entered into a Switzerland-based joint venture in 1965 called De La Rue Giori, which specialized in the manufacture of banknote printing machinery. In 1968 the Rank Organisation Plc made a bid for De La Rue but this was rejected the following year by the Monopolies Commission as being against the public interest. In 1969 the early foundation of De La Rue, the playing card business, was finally sold, to John Waddington.

The 1970s and 1980s were busy years of acquisitions and sales, with De La Rue divesting itself of interests that were not part of its core businesses (such as the sale of Formica to American Cyanamid in 1977, which brought the company's conglomerate phase to a close) and consolidating its position in its chosen ventures. Among the acquisitions of the period was the 1974 purchase of Crosfield Electronics, maker of banknote handling systems. In 1975 De La Rue Instruments and Crosfield were merged to form De La Rue Crosfield, the forerunner to the cash systems division of De La Rue. Another key acquisition came in 1982, that of the U.S. payment card firm Faraday National Corporation. Also during the 1980s some of De La Rue's banknote export factories were opened, including those in Singapore and Hong Kong. Most significantly, however, the company moved increasingly into the area of payment systems, among other ventures, forming De La Rue Garny in Germany in 1983 and acquiring the Scottish-based Fortronic in 1987. The German joint venture was transformed in 1989, when De La Rue acquired a 95 percent stake in Garny AG.

The late 1980s brought additional challenges for De La Rue. In late 1987 publishing magnate Robert Maxwell purchased a 15 percent holding in the company, later increased to almost 22 percent. Although Maxwell never gained a seat on the company board, he cast a long shadow over the company's operations. This was most noticeable in 1989 when De La Rue decided to sell the troubled Crosfield manufacturing operation, which by this time specialized in prepress equipment for the printing and publishing industries. Maxwell opposed a proposed sale of Crosfield to a joint venture of Du Pont and Fuji, backing a rival bid by Israel-based Scitex, which was 27 percent owned by a Maxwell-controlled firm. Shareholders sided with management, voting in favor of the sale to Du Pont/Fuji, and Maxwell sold his De La Rue shares in late 1990. Just two weeks after the approval of the sale of Crosfield, De La Rue faced another takeover bid, this time by security printing and publishing rival Norton Opax PLC. De La Rue's independence was saved only after Norton itself was swallowed by Bowater PLC.

Strong Upturn in the Early 1990s

In November 1989, soon after the Norton Opax takeover was narrowly avoided, Jeremy Marshall was named chief executive, becoming the first outsider so appointed. Marshall managed the company through a very successful period in the early 1990s, shaking up what had been a rather insular organization. Finding the structure overly decentralized, Marshall reorganized the company into three main divisions: payment systems, currency, and security printing. Marshall also continued and strengthened the trend toward concentration on these strong core areas, selling off loss-making subsidiaries and concerns not

directly related to the firm's principal ventures. He also initiated a program of strategic acquisitions to bolster these areas.

De La Rue profited as well from political events. The breakup of the Communist bloc resulted in some 26 countries requiring new currency. De La Rue got the lion's share of the business. Boosted by these new markets, the company's currency division remained strong in the early 1990s. Of the world's countries whose governments did not print their own currency, De La Rue had 60 percent of the market share. The company regained its traditional lead in technological innovation: specialized presses were continually being developed and marketed by its associated company, De La Rue Giori. Its patented computer-aided design system, Durer, was able to produce banknote designs in half the time formerly required.

Research and development were also keystones of De La Rue's security printing division in the early 1990s: it supplied the Bank of Scotland with debit cards incorporating laser-engraved photographs, and in partnership with a Dutch electronics company, Philips, developed microchip "smart cards." Plastic payment cards, checks, passports, traveler's checks, and bonds all played a part in De La Rue's security printing business, and the company was expanding into related ventures, moving increasingly into printed materials for elections and for national registration and identity card schemes.

De La Rue's payment services division was the company's fastest growing area of business in the early 1990s. As banking became increasingly automated, De La Rue was at the forefront of technological development and sought out acquisitions to gain a larger portion of this rapidly expanding market. In 1992 the company paid £94.7 million for Inter Innovation, a Swedish maker of automated currency handling machines, including automated cash dispensers, and physical security products, such as safes and vaults. Meanwhile, the company changed its name to De La Rue plc in 1991.

By 1993 Marshall had succeeded in increasing revenues 60 percent, to £559.6 million, and in turning a 1990 pretax loss of £50.6 million into profits of £104.7 million. During 1993 De La Rue joined a consortium called Camelot Group plc, which was formed to make a bid for the license to run the new U.K. national lottery. De La Rue took an initial 22.5 percent stake in Camelot (later raised to 26.7 percent), contributing its security printing expertise to the venture. In 1994 Camelot was awarded the license.

During much of 1994, De La Rue was occupied pursuing a bid for Portals Group PLC, a producer of paper used in making currencies and one of De La Rue's main suppliers. Portals had a history even longer than that of De La Rue. The company traced its origins to 1712 when Henry Portal, a French Huguenot who had fled to England to escape religious persecution, began making stationery paper at a mill in Whitchurch, Hampshire. The quality of his paper became so renowned that he was asked to make paper for the Bank of England. Deals with other banks followed, including the Bank of Ireland and the General Bank of India. After banknote forgery emerged as a major problem in the early 19th century, the company began making paper with elaborate watermarks. In 1855 Portals made the paper for the first Bank of England note containing a shaded watermark. In

1880 Portals supplied paper for the first U.K. Postal Orders, and five years later began making paper for the Bank of Scotland. The early 20th century saw the company rapidly expand its base of international customers. During World War I, Portals began making paper for the Indian rupee, then in 1921 began making banknote paper for Chile. Quickly following the latter were orders from Australia, South Africa, Persia, Danzig, Portugal, Greece, and Argentina. By 1929 Portals was making paper for 41 banknote issues around the world. Building security features into its paper became a specialty of Portals. In 1940 the company pioneered in weaving a fine security thread of special composition into its paper, a procedure that became standard industry practice. Throughout this entire history a member of the Portal family had headed the company, but that tradition ceased shortly after the company went public in 1947.

De La Rue's acquisition of Portals was completed in early 1995 for £682 million (US$1.1 billion). De La Rue was not just interested in gaining control of one of its suppliers. Portals also brought to De La Rue a host of new customers or potential customers—state-owned printers that produced their own banknotes. About 88 percent of the world's banknotes were produced by state-owned printers, and Portals held about half of that market. De La Rue was also interested in gaining Portals' expertise in anticounterfeiting. Concern about forgeries was on the rise in the 1990s as cheaper and higher-quality copiers, scanners, and printers provided counterfeiters with increasingly sophisticated tools of the trade. By controlling both the papermaking and printing stages, De La Rue hoped to offer integrated security features in its banknotes and other products, including watermarks, special inks, and holograms.

Declining Fortunes in the Later 1990s

De La Rue made a number of other acquisitions in 1995 and 1997. During the latter year, the company acquired the French-based smart card business of Philips for £54.2 million. By that time, however, the glory days of the early 1990s had given way to a serious downturn. Profit growth flattened out in the 1996 fiscal year, then profits began to decline. As the company kept issuing profit warnings, its stock tumbled, from a high of more than £10.50 in early 1995 to less than 200p in late 1998. Its market value declined by 80 percent during the same period, from about £2 billion to little more than £400 million. De La Rue was afflicted by a host of difficulties. Its security printing division was hurt by a slowdown in demand and by decreased margins due to the maturing of the market. The cash systems division suffered first from a spate of bank mergers in the United States, then from decreased sales of its newest cash-handling machinery stemming from the Asian financial crisis that erupted in 1997; Asia had been seen as one of the main markets for these new machines. De La Rue's fastest growing unit, the card systems division, was busy developing new smart cards and other technologies, but the payback for these large investments was still in the future. A strong British pound did not help matters. Moreover, analysts also blamed management for responding slowly and inadequately to the growing crisis.

In February 1998, with a turnaround nowhere in sight, Marshall was forced to take an early retirement. While a search for a replacement was conducted, De La Rue began restructuring its operations with a reorganization of its banknote business,

including a 25 percent reduction in printing capacity. Noncore activities began to be jettisoned, starting with the exit from the physical security business (vaults and safes) through the sale of Garny and other units, the last of which was sold in October 1998. During the prior month, Ian Much, a former chief executive of T&N plc, was appointed the new chief executive. Much immediately began shaking things up by forcing out the head of the cash systems division, which he then assumed direct control of. In February 1999 De La Rue sold its card-reading terminals business to Ingenico SA. Next came a major overhaul of the cash systems division, which was restructured in March 1999 into three business streams: desktop products, branch cash solutions, and cash processing. De La Rue also announced that an expensive and complex information technology system then under development was being scrapped and that 500 jobs would be cut from the division (representing one-sixth of the division's workforce).

For the fiscal year ending in March 1999, De La Rue reported a net loss of £7.4 million, stemming from its cash systems division, which was in red for the year, and from £64.5 million in exceptional charges, including £48.5 million in restructuring costs. The company's revamp then continued, with the sale in October 1999 of the bulk of its card systems division, including its smart cards operations, to François-Charles Oberthur Fiduciaire of France for £200 million (US$317.9 million). De La Rue sold the business, its fastest growing sector, after having concluded that it lacked sufficient scale and would require too much additional investment. The company's plan for the early 21st century, then, was to focus on its two core divisions—cash systems and security paper and print—and to develop a third division called services and solutions. Created in April 2000, this division focused on brand protection, electronic security, and other services related to its core customers; several existing businesses in holographics, identity systems, transaction services, and other areas formed the initial core of the new division. De La Rue thus appeared to have returned to its history of innovation; it seemed that Thomas de la Rue, that shrewd businessman and inventor, would surely applaud the latest strategies of the company he founded so long ago.

Principal Subsidiaries

De La Rue Holdings; De La Rue International; Portals Group; Portals Property; The Burnhill Insurance Company; Camelot Group plc (26.7%); De La Rue Giori (Switzerland; 50%); De La Rue Smurfit Limited (Ireland; 50%); De La Rue Cash Systems GmbH (Germany); IMW Immobilien AG (Germany; 95.7%); De La Rue Security Print Inc. (U.S.A.).

Principal Divisions

Cash Systems; Security Paper and Print; Services and Solutions.

Principal Competitors

Ambient Corporation; American Banknote Corporation; Bowne & Co., Inc.; Crane & Co., Inc.; Cummins-American Corporation; Dai Nippon Printing Co., Ltd.; Deluxe Corporation; Diebold, Incorporated; Drexler Technology Corporation; Frisco Bay Industries Ltd.; John H. Harland Company; MDC Corporation Inc.; Merrill Corporation; NCR Corporation; Oki Electric Industry Company, Limited; Quebecor Inc.; Toppan Printing Co., Ltd.; Transaction Systems Architects, Inc.; Triton Systems, Inc.; VeriFone, Inc.; Visage Technology, Inc.

Further Reading

Bilefsky, Dan, ''Restructuring Leads to Losses at De La Rue,'' *Financial Times,* June 2, 1999, p. 22.

Bolger, Andrew, ''De La Rue to Raise £160m for Acquisition,'' *Financial Times,* October 23, 1991, p. 23.

——, ''Maxwell Shadow Still Dogs De La Rue,'' *Financial Times,* July 26, 1990, p. 22.

''De La Rue Is Secret Bidder for Portals,'' *London Times,* May 15, 1994, sec. 3, p. 1.

''De La Rue's Future Looks Secure,'' *Management Today,* June 1991, p. 38.

''Excellent Results from World Leader,'' *Investors Chronicle,* June 4, 1993.

Hill, Andrew, ''Maxwell Places De La Rue Shares,'' *Financial Times,* October 10, 1990, p. 23.

Houseman, Lorna, *The House That Thomas Built: The Story of De La Rue,* London: Chatto & Windus, 1968, 207 p.

''In Line to Make a Mint,'' *Mail on Sunday,* April 4, 1993.

''The Lex Column: De La Rue,'' *Financial Times,* June 2, 1993.

Marsh, Peter, ''Public or Private: Two Ways to Make Money,'' *Financial Times,* November 28, 1997, p. 20.

Marsh, Virginia, ''De La Rue Found Lacking in Currency,'' *Financial Times,* February 20, 1998, p. 26.

——, ''Much Ado About Reworking De La Rue's Shocking Performance,'' *Financial Times,* November 21, 1998, p. 20.

Mitchell, Richard, ''Throwing Down the Gauntlet,'' *Credit Card Management,* January 1996, pp. 18–19.

Price, Christopher, ''De La Rue in Smart Card Buy,'' *Financial Times,* May 16, 1997, p. 28.

——, ''De La Rue Wins Portals for £682m,'' *Financial Times,* December 21, 1994, p. 17.

Rivlin, Richard, and Virginia Marsh, ''De La Rue in Advanced Talks to Sell Cards Division,'' *Financial Times,* July 3, 1999, p. 22.

Syedain, Hashi, ''De La Rue Strikes a New Note,'' *Management Today,* October 1993, pp. 50–54.

''UK Company News: Ex-Communists Help De La Rue Rise 34 Percent,'' *Financial Times,* June 2, 1993.

Waller, David, ''The Not-So-Profitable License to Print Money,'' *Financial Times,* February 16, 1989, p. 33.

Whitney, Glenn, ''De La Rue Seeks to Acquire Portals in $1.1 Billion Pact,'' *Wall Street Journal,* December 21, 1994, p. A11.

—Robin DuBlanc
—updated by David E. Salamie

Department 56, Inc.

One Village Place
6436 City West Parkway
Eden Prairie, Minnesota 55344
U.S.A.
Telephone: (612) 944-5600
Toll Free: (800) 548-8696
Fax: (612) 943-4500
Web site: http://www.d56.com

Public Company
Incorporated: 1984
Employees: 324
Sales: $245.9 million (1999)
Stock Exchanges: New York
Ticker Symbol: DFS
NAIC: 421920 Toy and Hobby Goods and Supplies
  Wholesalers; 421990 Other Miscellaneous Durable
  Goods Wholesalers

Department 56, Inc. is a leading designer, importer, and distributor of hand-crafted collectibles, giftware, and holiday merchandise. The company is perhaps best known for its collection of ceramic and porcelain miniature villages. Also popular, however, are other holiday and home decorative accessories, which include a line of porcelain and pewter figurines known as Snowbabies. In fact, Department 56's product line consists of more than 3,000 different items; the company typically introduces approximately 600 new items each year, while discontinuing items from previous seasons, a practice that enhances the collectibility of Department 56 products. Most of the manufacturing of Department 56 items is contracted to facilities in Asia—particularly in China, Taiwan, and the Philippines—with occasional imports from India and Europe. More than 90 percent of the company's sales are made to about 17,500 independent gift retailers across the United States; the remainder of sales are made to department stores and mail-order houses.

Early Years

Department 56 was founded by Edward R. Bazinet, who worked in the early 1970s as a manager at Minneapolis-based Bachman Holdings, Inc., a retailer of floral, gift, and garden items. Bazinet was in charge of a wholesale gift imports department at Bachman Holdings, which, for accounting purposes, was dubbed Department 56. When Bazinet decided to form his own company in 1976, he named it Department 56. Bazinet served as chairman and chief executive officer, and Todd L. Bachman was named president and vice-chairman. Headquarters were established in Eden Prairie, Minnesota.

Appealing to collectors of Christmas decor, the new company's first offerings centered on its Original Snow Village Collection, which was introduced in 1977. The Original Snow Village comprised small, hand-painted, ceramic pieces nostalgically recollecting small-town American winter scenes. Some of the little buildings and houses featured miniature electric lights inside, the wires for which were meant to be hidden underneath blankets of plastic snow. The unique design and quality of each piece in the Village series appealed to customers, who spotted them in gift and department stores and began acquiring them to recreate entire miniature villages in their homes.

Over the next seven years, the popularity of Department 56 gift items increased steadily, and in 1984, the company was formally incorporated as Department 56, being owned and operated by Bachman Holdings and ed bazinet international, inc. That year, the company introduced a variation on its Snow Village theme: the Heritage Village Collection. The first pieces in this collection became known as the Dickens Village and comprised porcelain homes, buildings, and accessories for recreating a Victorian Christmas village. Porcelain, as opposed to ceramic, allowed for greater detail, and porcelain's translucence gave a warmer visual effect to the pieces when lit. The Dickens Village series also offered tiny figurine representatives of characters from Dickens's *A Christmas Carol.* Moreover, Department 56 obtained a license from the Dickens estate to use the famous Charles Dickens signature initials on some of the products. With the addition of finer detail and quality, the collectibility of Department 56 products rose dramatically.

The year 1986 was an important one for new product introduction at Department 56. That year, two new series were added to the Heritage Village Collection: the New England Village (with such pieces as covered bridges, town halls, and sleighs, recalling winter scenes in rural American towns) and the Alpine Village (with farmhouses, churches, and clock towers reminiscent of hamlets in the Swiss Alps).

Another important introduction in 1986 was that of the Snowbabies. Snowbabies were figurines of toddlers bundled in fuzzy-looking snowsuits; they were made entirely of porcelain bisque, which was also hand-applied onto the little snowsuits, creating the impression that snow crystals had fallen on the babies as they played outdoors in the snow.

The Snowbabies series reportedly took six years for designers Kristi Jensen Pierro and Bill Kirchner to perfect, and the concept could be traced back to the late 1800s. Although some collectors disagree on their origin, two theories have emerged. One is that the concept originated with explorer Admiral Robert Peary and his wife Josephine. The couple, residing in Greenland in 1893, had a daughter, whom the Eskimos referred to as "Ad-Poo-Mickaninny," or "snow baby," because of her white skin. The child was named after an Eskimo woman friend, who made the baby a one-piece snowsuit. Josephine Peary later wrote two children's books about a snow baby, and, as an adult, daughter Marie Peary published an autobiography in 1934 entitled *The Snowbaby's Own Story*. Others, however, trace the snow baby to 19th-century Germany, where "tannenbaumkonfekt"—small dolls made from sugar, flour, and a gum thickener—were a popular holiday decoration. The candy figurines became so popular that commercial confectioners could not keep up with the demand. One confectioner reportedly commissioned a German company to create "snow babies" out of hand-whipped bisque, and other German manufacturers were quick to adapt the designs. The bisque figurines remained popular in Germany through the 1930s.

Department 56 Snowbabies represented considerable craftsmanship and labor on the part of the company's overseas manufacturers. Each design was transformed into a clay model, from which several molds were cast. The final production mold was then filled by hand with a hand-blended mixture of clay and water. All accessories, such as backpacks, wings, and stars were then attached to the dried, hardened figurine by hand, as were the fine grains of bisque known as snow crystals. Finally, facial features and coloring were applied by hand to each figurine. The popularity of the Snowbabies later prompted Department 56 to publish a hardbound book featuring poetry and stories on the adventures of the Snowbabies.

From 1988 to 1991, Department 56 focused primarily on expanding designs and production within their popular collections. Toward that end, it began issuing specialized pieces that would appeal to the vocations and hobbies of consumers. For example, the company introduced a vet and pet shop model for pet owners and veterinarians, a bank or brokerage house for those with financial interests, and a post office that might appeal to mail carriers. Moreover, the Snowbabies collection was expanded to include tree ornaments, picture frames, music boxes, and water globes featuring the popular characters. Snowbabies also became available in pewter. Finally, the company enhanced the Heritage Village Collection (first offering the Christmas in the City and Little Town of Bethlehem series of collectibles in 1987 and the North Pole series in 1990) and introduced such new lines of collectibles as Mercury Glass tree ornaments, Winter Silhouette figurines, and Merry Makers porcelain monk figures.

Department 56 relied on independently owned foreign manufacturers, located primarily in the Pacific Rim, for the manufacture of their collectibles. To oversee quality control and the export of products, the company formed a wholly owned subsidiary, Department 56 Trading Co., Ltd., based in Taiwan. The company believed that its relationship with its foreign manufacturers was crucial to its competitive position in the industry, enabling it to develop and produce detailed, high-quality products, while keeping prices affordable for customers.

Emerging As a Public Company in the Early 1990s

In the early 1990s, Department 56 went through a period of reorganization. In October 1992, the company entered into an agreement to acquire all outstanding stock held by Bachman Holdings, Inc. and ed bazinet international, inc. Department 56 was then organized and acquired by a private investment firm, Forstmann Little & Co. for $270 million. The following year, Forstmann Little and the company's management took Department 56 public, with an initial offering of 5.29 million shares at $18 each. Leadership throughout the reorganization remained with Bazinet and Bachman.

Early in 1994, a second public offering was made of 5.8 million shares at a little more than $27 each. The company was clearly thriving. In fact, since 1989 the company had experienced average annual net sales growth of 25 percent, while net profits averaged a 39 percent annual growth rate.

The financial success of Department 56 was attributable to several factors. First, the company had a large number of repeat sales. In a study conducted by the company, it was learned that 60 percent of Department 56 customers received their first Village piece as a gift. Of these, 70 percent continued to build their collection, acquiring two to three new pieces each year. In fact, Department 56 had built a following of an estimated 200,000 collectors. In addition, the company regulated the availability of its products, creating greater demand. While many Department 56 products were available in the mid-1990s through approximately 19,000 gift retailers, mail houses, and department stores, only 6,000 retailers were authorized to distribute the Village Series and Snowbabies products.

Success also was heightened by the collectors' market the company was helping to foster. As Village Series and Snowbabies designs were retired, they began trading in secondary markets at prices higher than the original retail prices. Although Department 56 did not participate as a purchaser or seller in the secondary market, the company certainly benefited from the publicity and the potential collectibility of its new lines. According to a 1993 article in *Fortune* magazine, one of the most highly prized Department 56 items became a miniature mill produced in a limited quantity of 2,500 and originally selling for $35 in the mid-1980s; a little more than ten years later, the mill sold on the collectors' market for as much as $6,500. To ensure authenticity, each Department 56 item was clearly marked with the series name, title, year of introduction, and company logo.

In 1994, Bachman left Department 56, returning to Bachman's Inc. to serve as chairman and CEO. He was replaced by Susan Engel, who assumed the positions of president and chief operating officer at Department 56. A graduate of Cornell University and Harvard Business School, Engel had extensive experience in marketing and management, which she gained through employment at J.C. Penney Company, Inc. and Booz, Allen and Hamilton, before becoming president and CEO of the Champion Products division of Sara Lee Corporation. It was Bazinet's hope that Engel would help Department 56 build its lead in the giftware market. Commenting on her move to Department 56 in a 1995 *Gifts & Decorative Accessories* magazine article, Engel observed, "It's hard to look at this company and not get really excited about it. . . . Both the products and the displays were so inviting, I knew this was something I could do."

Gaining licenses from Coca-Cola and Walt Disney Co. in the mid-1990s, Department 56 began offering collectibles incorporating these popular logos and themes. Soon consumers were able to build collections from the Disney Parks Village Series, including Mickey's Christmas Shop, antique shops, a fire station, and other Mickey and Minnie Mouse accessories. Longtime collectors of the Snow Village series were offered a new Coca-Cola bottling plant and delivery truck to add to their villages. Moreover, by concealing motors in the bases of village accessories, Department 56 began offering "animated" pieces, including the Village Animated Skating Pond, with skating figures gliding over a "frozen pond," and the Village Animated All Around the Park, with adults and children strolling through a snowy, tree-lined park. In 1994 the Snowbunnies line of collectible figurines made its debut.

To promote its items and raise money for charitable causes, Department 56 held a national holiday decorating program called "Homes for the Holidays" in 1995. There, retailers of Department 56 items offered decorating ideas, free seminars, and demonstrations for decorating the home during the holiday season. In conjunction with this event, Department 56 raised money for Ronald McDonald Houses through corporate contributions, fund-raising raffles, and auctions. Olympic skater Dorothy Hamill was chosen as the event's national hostess, being a loyal collector of Department 56 items herself.

Although giftware and decorative accessories was a highly fragmented and seasonal industry—with most sales occurring around major holidays, especially Christmas, and thousands of companies competing in the industry with a wide variety of products—it also represented a promising niche market, with estimated growth of ten to 14 percent annually. In the mid-1990s Department 56 maintained an enviable position in the market, holding an eight percent share of the collectibles segment, in which the industry leader held about a 16 percent share. Revenues were continuing to increase smartly, reaching $252 million in 1995, an increase of nearly 16 percent over the previous year.

Struggling in the Late 1990s

At the same time that the company announced the good news about 1995, however, it also warned that its 1996 results were not likely to be nearly as rosy. When this announcement was made in February 1996 the company's stock plummeted by more than 40 percent in one day. The difficulties were traced to the dealer distribution system. Some dealers were discounting Department 56 pieces in violation of company policy. About 50 dealers were terminated for such discounting, including Dillard Department Stores, Inc. Other dealers were maintaining excess inventory, some possibly hoarding older pieces, waiting for their retirement; excess inventory also led to the temptation of discounting and price wars between dealers. In response, Department 56 began implementing an inventory management system and deliberately limited new product introductions; this resulted in reduced orders during 1996 as inventories were brought back into balance. Department 56 also developed new ways of communicating with its dealers that year, including a bimonthly newsletter and a web site that included both product information and a dealer locator feature. The company also experimented with several nontraditional sales channels, including incentive programs, the corporate gift market, and television home shopping. In November 1996 Engel was promoted to CEO, with Bazinet remaining as chairman. Sales for

1996 ended up declining to $228.8 million while net income also fell, to $45.9 million, $5 million less than one year earlier.

The inventory reduction effort continued in 1997, leading to a further decrease in revenues and earnings. By late that year the company appeared to have rectified its inventory problems, leading to a 1998 rebound, when earnings were reported at $46.5 million on revenues of $243.4 million. In September 1997 Bazinet stepped down as chairman and Engel was named chairwoman and CEO. More frugal than her predecessor, Engel quickly made one large cost-cutting move by selling the corporate jet. New product introductions picked up steam, highlighted by the firm's first new village series in five years, the Seasons Bay Collection, which debuted in 1998. Based on a late 19th-century American resort town, Seasons Bay was the first village with a ''year-round'' theme. The village series also began featuring a number of new brand names in the late 1990s through new licensing deals, including Ford, Harley-Davidson, McDonald's, and Hershey's. Department 56 also attempted to increase its sales in Canada by offering its full product line to its Canadian dealers in 1997 and by establishing a direct sales force in that country in 1998.

Unfortunately, Department 56 suffered a setback in 1999 in part from Y2K-related problems. The company had difficulty implementing an enterprise-wide computer system that was installed to make the company Y2K compliant. Some orders were lost while others were duplicated in error, all leading to a general productivity decline for the sales force. As a result, revenues for 1999 increased only slightly and net income showed a small decline. Initiatives that year included the debut of a new village series based on the Monopoly board game, the launching of national print advertising in part to boost recognition of the Department 56 name, and the opening of the first corporate retail store, located in the Mall of America in Bloomington, Minnesota. The company was also experimenting with the sale of its products through e-commerce retailers and began implementing a business-to-business Internet system as an avenue for more efficient relationships with its dealers. Although Department 56's products retained their popularity with collectors, the company faced a key challenge as it entered the 21st century: regaining the rapid growth of its initial years as a public company.

Principal Subsidiaries

Department 56 Retail, Inc.; Department 56 Sales, Inc.; Can 56, Inc.; FL56 Intermediate Corp.; D 56, Inc.; Department 56 Trading Co., Ltd.; Browndale Tanley Limited (Hong Kong).

Principal Competitors

The Boyds Collection, Ltd.; Enesco Group Inc.; Roll International Corporation; Ty Inc.

Further Reading

Alexander, Steve, ''Department 56 Encounters a Y2K Problem,'' *Minneapolis Star Tribune,* June 11, 1999, p. 3D.
Apgar, Sally, ''Ceramics Dynamics: Department 56 Produces Villages for Collectors, Lots of Cash for Its Owners,'' *Minneapolis Star Tribune,* December 22, 1995, p. 1D.
——, ''Engel Will Take Over for Bazinet As CEO of Department 56,'' *Minneapolis Star Tribune,* November 14, 1996, p. 1D.
——, ''February Again Turns Ugly for Department 56,'' *Minneapolis Star Tribune,* February 22, 1997, p. 1D.
——, ''Wall Street Hammers Department 56 Stock,'' *Minneapolis Star Tribune,* February 13, 1996, p. 1D.
''Forstmann Little to Acquire Collectibles Firm,'' *HFD—The Weekly Home Furnishings Newspaper,* October 19, 1992, p. 85.
Gibson, Richard, ''Department 56 Sees Its Shares Splinter on Inventory Woes,'' *Wall Street Journal,* February 13, 1996, p. A4.
Labate, John, ''Department 56,'' *Fortune,* December 12, 1994, p. 243.
Moore, Janet, ''Collecting More Cash from Company's Name,'' *Minneapolis Star Tribune,* August 26, 1999, p. 1D.
''People Watching,'' *HFD—The Weekly Home Furnishings Newspaper,* September 26, 1994, p. 71.
Regan, Shawn, ''Dept. 56 Lends Helping Hand to Right Itself,'' *Corporate Report-Minnesota,* June 1998, pp. 28+.
Werner, Holly M., ''Meet Susan Engel,'' *Gifts & Decorative Accessories,* June 1995, p. 158.

—Beth Watson Highman
—updated by David E. Salamie

Dover Publications Inc.

31 East Second Street
Mineola, New York 11501
U.S.A.
Telephone: (516) 294-7000
Fax: (516) 742-6953
Web site: http://www.doverpublications.com

Private Company
Incorporated: 1942
Employees: 118
Sales: $28 million (1997 est.)
NAIC: 51113 Book Publishers

Dover Publications Inc. publishes paperbacks, many of them reissued out-of-print works whose copyright has expired. Dover has been called ''the L.L. Bean of books,'' for its appeal to mail-order customers, who provide the company with a significant share of its revenues. The publisher is also respected for the high quality of its paper, printing, covers, and binding, despite charging prices lower than other publishers for comparable works. It protects the paper covers with laminated plastic coating and stitches the signatures together tightly instead of merely gluing them, a shoddy practice engaged in even by some hardcover publishers.

Hayward Cirker graduated from the City College of New York during the Depression, with a background in the arts and sciences but no specific skills to win him a well-paying job. Attracted to publishing, he started at the bottom—as a $15-a-week shipping clerk for Crown Publishers Inc. Two years later, having helped Crown establish a mail-order division, he was a salesman at $50 a week. In 1941 he and his wife Blanche opened Dover Publications, with their savings of a few hundred dollars, as a buyer of remaindered scholarly books which were then sold by mail order, originally working out of their own apartment in New York City's borough of Queens. The company name was not the result of a bookseller's Anglophilia but came from the name of their apartment house.

Art, Music, and Science Books: 1943–87

Dover, which soon moved to tiny but cheap quarters on Manhattan's lower Fifth Avenue, published its first book, *Tables of Functions with Formulas and Curves,* during World War II. The German copyright of this out-of-print reference work for physicists, mathematicians, and engineers had been voided by the federal government because of the war. To avoid paying a typesetter, Cirker photographed the pages and had the work printed by the offset process. It seemed unlikely to become a best-seller but was still in print 47 years later, by which time some 60,000 copies had been sold. Cirker quickly displayed a penchant for profiting from similar overlooked, esoteric works.

The success of this work inspired Cirker to root out other scientific classics. In order to reprint a woodcut-illustrated Renaissance-era Latin mineralogy work, *De Re Metallica,* he obtained permission from the translator, former president Herbert Hoover, who warned him he was going to lose money. The work was still in print in 1987, its publisher having sold 40,000 copies. In addition, Cirker persuaded Albert Einstein to allow Dover to reprint *The Principle of Relativity,* overcoming the physicist's objection that the work was obsolete. It proved one of the firm's best sellers and was still in print more than 35 years later. By 1978 Dover had published works by some 62 Nobel prizewinners.

Dover came out with its first nonscientific book in 1946, Clarence Hornung's *Handbook of Designs and Devices,* a collection of geometric shapes still in print 40 years later. This was followed, over the next 35 years, by hundreds of other reproductions of design books that made Dover an essential reference source for graphic artists seeking (noncopyrighted) ideas. Dover also began reissuing art books—for as little as $5— among them large, quarto-size collections of graphics by Gustave Doré, Albrecht Dürer, Francisco José de Goya, Giambattista Piranesi, and James McNeill Whistler. These books tended to be oversized in format because Cirker was determined to keep the reproduced matter true in scale. Dover eventually would claim to hold the world's largest collection of copyright-free art.

Key Dates:

1941: Dover is founded to sell remaindered books by mail order.
1943: The company publishes its first book.
1951: Dover begins publishing in the trade paperback format.
1960: Juvenile books are introduced and prove a lucrative line.
1983: Dover is turning out 170 new titles a year.
1990: Dover introduces $1 paperbacks of classic works.
2000: The publisher's catalogue lists more than 7,000 titles.

Beginning in 1955, Dover also reprinted classic works on photography that had fallen into neglect, including an abridged version of Eadweard Muybridge's pioneering *Human and Animal Locomotion*. In 1979 the publisher offered this nearly century-old, 781-plate classic in full, at a price of $100. Other photographers represented in the Dover catalogue included Bernice Abbott, Andreas Feininger, Lewis Hine, and Man Ray. Reprints of music scores of classical composers became a mainstay of the firm about 1970. Its 200 music titles in 1987 ranged from Elizabethan keyboard scores to ragtime rarities and full-score versions of all the operas in Richard Wagner's *Ring* cycle.

Making a decision to reprint a work was only the first step; finding the right copy to reproduce often posed a problem. "Sometimes we have to wait to find a library that will lend us a rare edition," editor-in-chief Stanley Applebaum told Daniel Cohen of *Smithsonian* in 1987. Dover corresponded with dozens of museums and collectors to find what it wanted. "We once reproduced a pre-first edition volume of Goya etchings, then valued at $100,000, from a Harvard library," Applebaum added. "We drove it to the printer and stayed while they did it." Applebaum added that he obtained movie stills from the old Astoria Studios in Queens, Piranesi drawings from the Morgan Library, and rare advertising posters from the New York Historical Society.

A Potpourri of Titles: 1951–87

Dover contributed to the transformation of the book industry in 1951 by issuing some of the earliest standard-sized paperbacks, a format that came to be called trade paperback. At that time paperbacks were pocket-sized mass-market items typically placed by magazine distributors in wire-frame drugstore displays selling for 25 cents and featuring sexy and/or lurid cover artwork even for classic works. Dover proved it could sell quality paperbacks for $1 or even $2 and eventually abandoned hardcover publishing almost entirely. It did not concentrate on bookstore sales, refusing—unlike the rest of the industry—to accept unsold returns from retailers. Nevertheless, by 1980 most bookstores had some Dover books, and many even had a special Dover corner. Moreover, Cirker was willing to fill any order, even for a single copy.

Everett F. Bleiler joined Dover in 1955 as advertising manager. A Harvard-educated anthropologist/archeologist familiar with at least a dozen languages, Bleiler was presumably, as he later told Michele Slung of *Publishers Weekly,* "the only ad man in New York with two years of Sanskrit." In addition to supervising direct mail and writing all the advertising copy, he helped Cirker with cover designs and choice of art works. In his "spare" time Bleiler also began editing, and writing forewords, for the line of Dover fiction reprints that he introduced. He anticipated the counterculture in reissuing classic tales of the supernatural by such writers as Algernon Blackwood, Lord Dunsany, E.T.A. Hoffman, M.R. James, J. Sheridan LeFanu, and H.P. Lovecraft.

Bleiler also sponsored the resurrection of musty Victorian horror writers such as Amelia Edwards, Vernon Lee, G.W.M. Reynolds, Mrs. J.H. Riddell, and J.M. Rymer. Sensing an interest in early detective fiction, he also reintroduced R. Austin Freeman, Jacques Futrelle, J.C. Masterman, and Arthur Morrison to the public. Many of the above works were published in facsimile editions.

Cirker's own uncanny antennae for the trendy enabled him to further anticipate the counterculture of the 1960s by reprinting popular editions of such classic works as the *I Ching* and the *Egyptian Book of the Dead.* By the early 1980s Dover's reprint of Howard Carter's 1920s book on the unearthing of the treasure of the pharaoh Tutankhamen ("King Tut") was selling about 100,000 copies a year. Dover also foresaw the growing interest in American folk crafts, republishing Marguerite Ickis's *Standard Book of Quilt Making and Collecting* in 1960 and introducing pattern books for needlepoint enthusiasts the following year. He reprinted ragtime scores in advance of the revival of Scott Joplin's reputation, published chess texts from 1957, well before Bobby Fischer spawned a new generation of fans, and issued books on sci-fi films prior to the making of *Star Wars.* But Cirker confessed to missing the boat on such 1960s cult figures as Marshall McLuhan—who offered his first book to Dover—and Buckminster Fuller.

In 1959 Dover moved its quarters to Varick Street, in an industrial area on the west side of lower Manhattan that would only 20 years later emerge as part of fashionable TriBeCa. Dover was unique among major New York publishers in having a printing plant on its premises, used for its covers, catalogues, flyers, brochures, posters, and other mailings. The Varick Street offices also housed a bookstore carrying every Dover book in stock and regularly offering half-price sales on damaged books. The actual shipping came to be performed in a warehouse in Mineola, a Long Island suburb. By 1983 all operations except editorial had been moved to Mineola.

Dover began publishing original works in the early 1960s, and they represented about 60 percent of Dover's list by the early 1980s. Among the most popular authors was paper-doll artist Tom Tierney, whose 40 cut-out volumes began with figures of 1930s movie stars and continued with Marilyn Monroe and Rudolph Valentino dolls outfitted from their best-known roles before progressing to theater, opera, sports, fashion, and politics celebrities as well. Many submissions came unsolicited, with all given careful consideration, according to the staff, except for poetry, which was automatically returned. Dover's editorial vice-president said in 1981 that recent trends included a marked increase in craft books, including woodworking, dolls and dollhouses, and stained glass. Where a trend was spotted—such as children's coloring books—Dover would commission books. Dover kept its costs low by paying authors a flat fee rather than royalties. This fee was as low as $1,000 in some cases.

Business Practices: 1975–2000

Like the reprints, Dover's original books were not intended to be best-sellers, and no print run was ever higher than 7,000. About 1975 Dover, while continuing its no-returns policy, began courting bookstores by offering a 40 percent cash-with-order (COP) discount on shipments and free delivery on such orders over $35. This offer was an instant success, and by the summer of 1981, 6,000 of Dover's 14,000 accounts were COPs. Dover's 15 commissioned sales representatives were visiting 1,000 stores regularly, with the rest of the accounts serviced by mail. The firm had annual revenue of $15 million by the 1980s.

By 1983 Dover was turning out 170 new titles a year, had 3,000 books on its list, and was shipping six to seven million books annually. "You can do as few as 1,500 or 2,000 of a distinguished title if you can reach the right market," Blanche Cirker told John F. Baker of *Publishers Weekly* in 1983. "And once a book is published, it's our philosophy to keep it in print as long as possible," Haywood Cirker added. Dover's special interest free catalogues listed from 100 to 300 titles each in such categories as art instruction, chess, cookbooks, fiction, juvenile works (beginning in 1960), music, nature (starting in 1951), photography, pictorial archives, social science, and New York subjects (from about 1970). Some 15 to 20 percent of its sales were coming from abroad. The Cirkers usually visited the annual Frankfurt international book fair, looking for books to reprint, such as complete sets of music scores.

Readers sometimes went ballistic when Dover finally lost patience with a slow-selling title and allowed it to fall out of print. During the 1960s it quietly dropped some titles, including its reprint of Arthur Cleveland Bent's 26-volume *Life Histories of North American Birds*. "We immediately got a flood of mail from discomfited bird watchers," reprints editor John Grafton recalled to Daniel Cohen of *Smithsonian* in 1987. Dover, which restocked the missing works, made penance by publishing *A Natural History of the Ducks* in 1986. Published in two hardbound volumes, this 1920s opus, long out of print, was priced at $100. Another deluxe undertaking—at least for Dover—was its clothbound editions of the works of Henry David Thoreau.

The main mailing list of 500,000 names—culled from persons who received a catalogue, answered an advertisement, or filled in a coupon—had been computerized since 1974. These names were divided into dozens of groups according to the subjects they purchased. At least one-third of all sales were being made through direct mail and, taking into account store sales inspired by the buyer having read the catalogue or seen an advertisement, were perhaps as high as 50 percent. In order to save mailing costs, Dover often stuffed its outgoing envelopes with a variety of flyers, self-mailers, and other pieces. Mailings ranged from about 5,000 for specialized items to the full 500,000 and went out virtually every day except for the three weeks just before Christmas, when such an effort was considered a waste of time.

Dover introduced a new series of $1 paperbacks, Thrift Editions, in 1990. It included such classics as Stephen Crane's *The Red Badge of Courage,* Joseph Conrad's *Heart of Darkness,* and Oscar Wilde's *The Importance of Being Earnest.* Some 100 or more titles were expected within four years. Dover planned to publish 300 titles of all kinds in 1990. These releases and the firm's backlist of 4,000 titles were selling for at least 30 percent below comparable books in the retail market. The company was debt free and had a pretax profit of about ten percent on revenues of around $25 million in 1989. Sales came to about $28 million in 1997. Dover's catalogue had more than 7,000 titles in early 2000, when Hayward Cirker died at the age of 82.

Principal Competitors

Harcourt General, Inc.; The McGraw-Hill Companies, Inc.; Random House Inc.

Further Reading

Baker, John F., "What's Doing at Dover," *Publishers Weekly,* August 14, 1981, pp. 20–22, 24–26.

Cohen, Daniel, "How to Succeed in Publishing with Nary a Best-Seller," *Smithsonian,* July 1987, pp. 83–86, 88, 90, 92.

"From Durer to the *Kin-der-Kids*," *Art News,* January 1982, pp. 20, 22.

Kalmus, Yvonne, "Dover, a Rich Source of Photohistorical Books at Reasonable Prices," *Popular Photography,* August 1983, pp. 28, 30.

McKinley, Jesse, "Hayward Cirker, 82, Who Made Dover a Paperback Powerhouse," *New York Times,* March 11, 2000, p. A13.

Meeks, Fleming, "Mom-and-Pop Publishing," *Forbes,* September 17, 1990, pp. 70, 74.

Poli, Kenneth, "Critical Focus," *Popular Photography,* January 1980, pp. 8, 126–27.

Slung, Michele, "E.F. Bleiler," *Publishers Weekly,* May 1, 1978, pp. 16–18.

Tebbel, John, *A History of Book Publishing in the United States.* New York: R.R. Bowker, 1981, Vol. 4, pp. 403–04.

Van Gelder, Lawrence, "A Bookseller's Tale and How It Grew," *New York Times,* October 9, 1983, Sec. 21 (Long Island), p. 2.

"The White Clips of Dover," *Time,* March 27, 1978, pp. 97–98.

—Robert Halasz

Ecolab Inc.

370 North Wabasha Street
Saint Paul, Minnesota 55102-1390
U.S.A.
Telephone: (651) 293-2233
Fax: (651) 293-2092
Web site: http://www.ecolab.com

Public Company
Incorporated: 1923 as Economics Laboratory
Employees: 12,007
Sales: $1.89 billion (1998)
Stock Exchanges: New York Pacific
Ticker Symbol: ECL
NAIC: 325611 Soap and Other Detergent Manufacturing;
325612 Polish and Other Sanitation Good
Manufacturing; 325999 All Other Miscellaneous
Chemical Product and Preparation Manufacturing;
333319 Other Commercial and Service Industry
Machinery Manufacturing; 561710 Exterminating and
Pest Control Services; 561990 All Other Support
Services

Ecolab Inc. is a leading supplier of cleaning, sanitizing, and maintenance products and services for the institutional, hospitality, healthcare, and industrial markets. The company's institutional division, which is its largest unit, provides cleaners and sanitizers for washing dishes, glassware, utensils, and other kitchen equipment and for laundering needs to restaurants, lodgings, and educational and healthcare institutions. Other Ecolab units offer water and wastewater treatment programs, commercial pest elimination and prevention, and kitchen equipment repair services. The company operates in virtually every country in the world either directly, or through distribution and licensing agreements, or via its Henkel-Ecolab joint venture with the German firm Henkel KGaA. Through its "Circle the Customer—Circle the Globe" strategy, Ecolab aims not only to be a worldwide operator but also to offer a full range of products and services to its core customers.

Early Decades

For the first 60 years of its existence Ecolab was managed by members of the Osborn family. Merritt J. Osborn, founder of the original Economics Laboratory, abandoned his occupation as a salesman and organized a specialty chemical manufacturer in 1923. The company's first product was a rug cleaner for hotels. Its first key product, however, was Soilax, a chemical detergent for mechanical dishwashers. Economics Laboratory entered the equipment sector in 1928 with the introduction of its first product dispenser; this marked the beginning of the company's "systems" approach to meeting its customers' needs. In the 1930s the company began a nationwide expansion. Sales passed $500,000 by the end of the decade, then reached $5.4 million by the end of the 1940s.

In the 1950s the company's product line grew to include consumer detergents and institutional cleaning specialties for restaurants, food processors, and dairies. This area of business came to represent the cornerstone of the company's success; between the years 1970 and 1980 the chemical specialties business quadrupled, generating $640 million by the end of the ten-year period. Yet early in its history the company actively pursued customers outside of the consumer and institutional markets.

By purchasing the Magnus Company in the early 1950s, Economics Laboratory gained access to the industrial specialty market. Magnus's primary business, the selling of cleaning and specialty formulas to numerous industries, including pulp and paper, metalworking, transportation, and petrochemical processing, contributed $12.1 million in sales during 1973.

Meanwhile, international expansion began in the 1950s, with the establishment of the company's first overseas subsidiary in Sweden in 1956. The company grew large enough by 1957 to become a public corporation. Earnings per share rose higher than an average 15 percent annually for the next 20 years. The mid-1960s marked a high point in the company's history as earnings grew 16 percent every year. This was exceeded only by a three-year performance between 1974 and 1977, in which profits eventually reached a 19 percent growth rate. By 1973 Economics Laboratory was divided into five divisions. The Magnus division produced items for the industrial market, while the institutional division manufactured dishwasher products and sanitation formulas. In the consumer division, home dishwasher detergent as well as coffee filters, floor cleaners, and laundry aids were produced. The Klenzade division provided specialty detergents to the food processing industry (Klenzade had been acquired in 1961). Overseas sales were controlled by the international division, founded by future chairman and chief executive officer Fred T. Lanners, Jr., who, it was said, paid his first employees out of his own expense account.

Of all the company's products, detergents for household dishwashers became its bestseller. Second only to Procter & Gamble's automatic dishwasher detergent in domestic sales, Economics Laboratory's detergents were preeminent in overseas markets. In the early 1970s, despite the fine company performance, Economics Laboratory attempted to expand its business by offering several new service and equipment packages. One such package offered on-premise laundry services for hospitals and hotels. This business was strengthened by the purchase of three subsidiaries all engaged in the laundry industry. Another package offered sanitation and cleaning service to the food industry. The company's dishwashing operation service, for example, addressed every aspect of the procedure from selecting the detergent to training the employees.

This trend toward offering services to supplement specialty chemical products represented Economics Laboratory's new market strategy. According to Fred Lanners, then president of the firm, service activity was indispensable to building markets and the single most important asset to offer customers. Prospective company employees were hired according to whether they had the ability to give an impression of total commitment to the needs of clients. Aside from laundry and sanitation, future plans included offering a comprehensive cleaning service to food establishments and a chemical surveillance service to food manufacturers and handlers. The ideas for the structure and implementation of these service packages emerged from Economics Laboratory's research and development department. The increasing importance of this department resulted in a staff of 200 by 1973.

Late 1970s and Early 1980s: A Time of Change

In 1978 the company underwent a number of changes as the profit margin dipped to ten percent. Sales of dishwashing detergent had slowed and the expansion of international operations had a temporary adverse effect on profits. Both causes for the reduced profit gains appeared easily correctable and no major reorganization was in order. Yet the disappointing figures happened to occur at the same time new executives filled positions in Economics Laboratory's management.

E. B. Osborn, son of the founder Merritt J. Osborn, ended his long tenure as chief executive officer in 1978 so that Lanners, the first nonfamily member to achieve such high executive status, could assume the new title. Lanners began at Economics Laboratory in the research and development department, becoming first the chief scientist and then the assistant to the research and development director. At the time of the management shift, E.B. Osborn's experience at the company covered 50 years. The third-generation descendant, S. Bartlett Osborn, stepped up to the positions of executive vice-president and chief operating officer.

By 1979 business had resumed at an accelerated pace. Sales increased 16 percent and earnings per share rose 16.6 percent over the previous year. International sales now increased at a faster pace than domestic sales. Profits, however, did not substantially increase; the unimpressive 6.6 percent was traceable to the effects of a large hiring campaign. The 130 new employees in marketing represented the firm's largest sales personnel increase ever in the course of one year.

The hiring of new staff marked only one tactic in management's strategy for growth. In addition to a larger sales force and continued expansion into foreign markets, Economics Laboratory announced plans to use some of its supply of cash to acquire Apollo Technologies for $71.2 million. This manufacturer of chemicals and pollution-control equipment was purchased in 1979 to improve the company's industrial market share. As the company's traditional lines of business in consumer and institutional products neared the limits of market penetration, Economics Laboratory looked for ways to supplement the operations of the Magnus division. Company management hoped that the acquisition of Apollo could offer that supplement.

At first the subsidiary served this function well, and both companies found the relationship mutually beneficial. Apollo gained the financial backing necessary to enter new markets, particularly overseas, and Economics Laboratory broadened its business in the industrial sector. The Apollo subsidiary now held the responsibility for selling all Economics Laboratory's industrial chemical specialties. In addition to marketing coal additives, catalysts, and dust-control products to the electrical utility and mining industries, Apollo's sales staff was given the added task of selling lubricants, pulp-processing compounds, and temperature reducers to the metal processing and paper industries.

The major advantage Apollo's business activities held for its parent company was the ability to raise the industrial service operations to the same level of success as the Economics Laboratory's institutional services. Prior to the acquisition, Economics Laboratory's industrial business suffered from an inability to offer comprehensive services to its customers. With the purchase, Economics Laboratory acquired not only a company, but also technical service engineers to supervise product implementation.

In 1981 Philip T. Perkins assumed the title of president and chief operating officer. The new top executive had joined Economics Laboratory in 1968 as vice-president of the company's

Key Dates:

1923: Merritt J. Osborn founds Economics Laboratory as a specialty chemical manufacturer.
1957: Company goes public.
1978: Fred T. Lanners, Jr., is named CEO.
1979: Apollo Technologies is acquired.
1982: Richard C. Ashley is named CEO but soon after is killed in a car accident.
1983: Pierson M. "Sandy" Grieve is named CEO; Apollo subsidiary is shut down.
1986: Company changes its name to Ecolab, Inc.
1987: Company sells its consumer dishwashing detergent unit, and purchases lawncare servicer ChemLawn for $376 million.
1991: Ecolab and Henkel KGaA form Henkel-Ecolab European joint venture.
1992: ChemLawn is sold to Service Master L.P. for $103 million.
1994: Kay Chemical, maker of cleaning and sanitizing products for the fast-food industry, is acquired.
1995: Allan L. Schuman is named CEO.
1997: Company acquires Australia-based Gibson Chemical Industries Limited for $130 million; company enters the commercial car wash cleaning products sector.
1998: GCS Service Inc., provider of repair services for commercial kitchen equipment, is acquired.

consumer division. As a graduate of Michigan State University, Perkins used his self-created bachelor's degree in food distribution to assume a number of positions in consumer operations both at Economics Laboratory and other companies. His experience in Economics Laboratory's consumer division attracted the attention of his colleagues; after three years of employment he was chosen as the company's most valuable employee. Prior to becoming president and chief operating officer, Perkins held the position of executive vice-president and chief operating officer of the international division.

As a new top executive, Perkins was considered particularly useful in overseeing the international operations. Before assuming his new title he had developed a plan to consolidate the program into a highly efficient network. His plan was credited with helping to maintain the division's impressive growth rate. Aside from continuing to expand international operations, Perkins planned to increase research and development spending by 25 percent.

The last remaining promotion entitled to Perkins was the advancement to chairman and CEO. Although it was generally assumed that Perkins was being prepared for this final promotion, tradition at the company protected the incumbency of its older chairmen. For this reason, no one expected the 62-year-old Lanners, then chairman and chief executive officer, to be relinquishing his duties in the near future.

Perkins's promotion, however, never materialized. In a surprise move Economics Laboratory recruited and hired its new top executive from outside the company. This abrupt shift in 1982 was said to have been management's response to a sharp decline in sales of pollution-control chemicals. In attempting to remedy the situation, operating units were restructured and a new leader was sought with a strong background in chemistry and experience in the industrial sector. The recruitment process singled out Richard C. Ashley, former president of Allied Chemical and a group vice-president of the parent company. Ashley's degree in chemistry and his successful experience in the chemical field met the company's qualifications.

Ashley's talents were expected to be particularly useful in addressing the ailing Apollo subsidiary. Sales, dropping precipitously to $5 million, had been adversely affected by the depressed industrial sector and by revisions in the Clean Air Act. The move to realign operating units represented the first in a series of steps devised to increase Apollo's business. Soon after assuming his new position, however, Ashley was tragically killed in a car accident.

Mid-to-Late 1980s: Restructuring and ChemLawn Acquisition

Once again Economics Laboratory recruited outside the company for a new chairman and CEO. Early in 1983 Pierson M. "Sandy" Grieve, a 55-year-old executive from the consumer goods company Questor, filled the position. Grieve's experience in acquisitions and corporate planning, as well as his aggressive and articulate management style, were his most valuable assets.

Just a week after assuming his new title, Grieve displayed his talent for decisive strategic planning; the Apollo subsidiary was to be shut down. The closing of the operation caused a $43 million writeoff but eliminated the possibility of continuing adverse effects on profits. Grieve's next strategic move involved reorganizing the Magnus division, issuing ultimatums on sales performance for certain foreign markets not up to standards, and hiring 100 new salespeople to market expanded product lines. Although sales had reached $670 million, ranking the company fourth among the top manufacturers of domestic cleaning products, debts over the past years had accumulated, and the institutional market, representing Economics Laboratory's largest customer base, had shrunk.

Grieve's decision to close Apollo was just one of the many major decisions required early in his tenure. Only months later, a significant attempt by an industry competitor to replace the nation's top dishwashing detergents caused Economics Laboratory's product to slip from second to third place. Lever Brothers, a large consumer product company, released its Sunlight brand detergent and captured a sizeable portion of the market. To prevent any further erosion of the company's market share, Grieve issued a plan to develop new products internally. Moreover, for the first time in ten years, he increased allocations for product promotion by adding $5 million to the soap products' advertising budget.

A final cause for concern emerged with the aggressive maneuvers of the Molson Companies Ltd., a Canadian brewing concern. In an attempt to capture a share of Economics Laboratory's U.S. institutional and industrial markets, Molson purchased the Diversey Corporation, a specialty chemical company. Diversey successfully increased Molson's presence in the United States and in five years the company tripled its sales.

Despite these concerns, Grieve's strategy to regain certain markets appeared effective. By 1986 $55 million in assets had been sold, including the pulp and paper division, the domestic portion of Magnus, the coffee filter business, and several plants. Other consolidation measures involved the laying off of employees and the implementation of new packaging processes. Long-term debt was reduced by an equivalent of $10 million and the company once again controlled a comfortable amount of cash. With the acquisition of Lystads, an exterminating service, and ICE, a pest control operation, Economics Laboratory attempted to broaden its customer base in its institutional division. Similarly, with the purchase of Foussard Associates, a laundry product and service operation, the company sought to augment growth in its institutional division. In 1986, the company also changed its name to Ecolab Inc.

Although its institutional and industrial customers had always comprised Ecolab's core markets, the consumer market had also figured into the product mix. In 1987, Grieve would take the company in two directions at the same time in regard to the consumer market. The firm abandoned its battle with Procter & Gamble and other dishwashing detergent makers, selling its dishwashing unit because it simply could no longer compete. About the same time, Ecolab purchased the lawncare servicer ChemLawn for $376 million, a move that would prove to be the biggest disappointment of Grieve's years at the company's helm.

Industry analysts contended that Ecolab paid too much to acquire ChemLawn, which set off an unfortunate chain of events. In its initial couple of years under Ecolab, ChemLawn was unable to generate enough revenue to pay back the costs of the acquisition. Ecolab management decided to increase revenues through price increases, hoping its focus on delivering a quality service would mitigate any negative effects. But ChemLawn's customers turned out to be much more price-sensitive than expected. Grieve later noted that part of this sensitivity stemmed from consumers considering lawncare a discretionary purchase. Moreover, he observed, an increase in environmental awareness in the late 1980s hit the industry just after Ecolab acquired ChemLawn. Overall, the ChemLawn acquisition was eventually regarded as an ill fit. In fact, after losing money under Ecolab, ChemLawn bounced back to profitability under Service Master L.P., which purchased ChemLawn in 1992 for $103 million. With the sale, Ecolab had to take a $263 million writeoff against 1991 earnings.

Late 1980s and Beyond: "Circle the Customer—Circle the Globe"

Ecolab was able to recover from its ChemLawn disaster through a program that Grieve began in the late 1980s during the initial stages of the ChemLawn debacle. This strategy, eventually known as "Circle the Customer—Circle the Globe," brought the firm to its strong position of the early 21st century. The "Circle the Globe" part of the program emphasized Ecolab's intention to become a worldwide leader in its core businesses. Initially the firm concentrated on the Asia-Pacific region, moving into the area in the late 1980s—one of the first

U.S. firms to do so in a concerted way. Ecolab also significantly increased its presence in Latin America, Africa, and the Middle East, particularly in the early 1990s. Growth was achieved through setting up operations in these regions, or via distribution and licensing agreements.

Ecolab then entered into a joint venture with the German firm Henkel KGaA. Established in mid-1991 and called Henkel-Ecolab, the 50–50 joint venture initially experienced some difficulties as a result of a poor European economy, but in a few short years became the leader in Europe in institutional and hospitality cleaning, sanitizing, and maintenance. The joint venture operated throughout Europe, including Russia and other former republics of the Soviet Union. The agreement between Ecolab and Henkel creating this joint venture also transferred ownership of Henkel's Latin American and Asian cleaning and sanitizing operations to Ecolab. By 1994, 22 percent of Ecolab's net sales originated outside the United States.

Ecolab's "Circle the Customer" strategy was intended to maximize its investment in its core businesses by broadening the range of products and services it offered its customers. By concentrating on the institutional, industrial, and hospitality industries, which it knew best, Ecolab extended its base of core customers in an incremental fashion, most notably with its late 1994 acquisition of Kay Chemical. Ecolab was already a leader in cleaning and sanitizing products for the full-service restaurant industry and added, through this acquisition, the leader in this area for fast-food restaurants—an industry experiencing rapid worldwide growth. A similar expansion occurred through the late 1994 formation of the water care division, which was built through a series of acquisitions and offered water treatment programs to Ecolab's institutional and industrial customers.

Ecolab enjoyed steady growth in net sales and net income in the early 1990s, culminating in 1994 sales of $1.21 billion and $90.5 million in net income—evidence that Grieve's focus on the firm's core businesses and worldwide expansion had begun to pay off. The health of the firm was also evidenced by the smooth transition to new leadership in 1994 and 1995 brought on by Grieve's retirement after 12 years in charge. Allan L. Schuman—who had been president and chief operating officer—became president and CEO early in 1995. Michael E. Shannon—who had served as vice chairman and chief financial officer—became chairman of the board at the beginning of 1996. The two essentially acted as dual leaders, an arrangement that evolved more by accident than by design, based on Schuman and Shannon's strong achievements in their previous positions, complementary personalities and skills, and ability to work as a team.

Under the new leadership team, Ecolab continued with its Circle strategy, expanding its product and service offerings and its geographic reach through several late 1990s acquisitions. In February 1996 Ecolab purchased Huntington Laboratories, Inc. of Huntington, Indiana, a supplier of janitorial products to the healthcare and education markets. When added to Ecolab's janitorial division, Huntington doubled the annual revenues of the division, which was soon renamed the professional products division. Ecolab's second largest division, food and beverage, was similarly bolstered through the purchase of two makers of cleaning products for the North American food processing industry. In August 1996 the company bought the Monarch division of H.B. Fuller Company, then one year later acquired the Chemidyne Marketing division of Chemidyne Corp.; Monarch had annual sales of $30 million, while the Chemidyne operations generated about $17 million. In October 1997 Ecolab acquired Melbourne, Australia-based Gibson Chemical Industries Limited for about $130 million. A maker and marketer of cleaning and sanitizing products for the Australian and New Zealand institutional, healthcare, and industrial markets, Gibson had fiscal 1996 sales of $122 million. Ecolab hoped that Gibson would provide it with a base from which to gain a larger share of the Asia-Pacific market.

Starting in late 1997, Ecolab's institutional division rapidly gained, through acquisition, a significant share of the market for commercial car wash cleaning products. This was a logical extension of the division's dishwasher cleaning product offerings; Schuman, in fact, told *Chemical Market Reporter* that a car wash is "really nothing but a big dishwasher." Two key acquisitions in this area were the December 1997 purchase of the specialty chemical business of Grace-Lee Products Incorporated, which had sales of $16 million, and the February 1999 purchase of Blue Coral Systems, a subsidiary of the Pennzoil-Quaker State Company with sales of about $30 million. Ecolab next moved into the repair of commercial kitchen equipment through the July 1998 acquisition of Danbury, Connecticut-based GCS Service Inc., which reported 1997 sales of $48 million. Ecolab intended to turn GCS Service, which became a division of Ecolab, into a national service company for its commercial foodservice customers. Ecolab aimed to grow both its car wash and equipment repair businesses into $100 million-per-year operations by about 2004.

At year-end 1999, Shannon retired. Schuman was elected by the company board to the additional post of chairman to replace him. Ecolab continued to post record results, with revenues exceeding $2 billion for the first time in 1999, while the company also reported its 19th consecutive quarter of double-digit earnings per share increases and paid common stock dividends for the 63rd straight year. Ecolab continued to churn out successful new products, such as a line of water filters for use in ice machines, juice machines, and coffee makers. The company was also investigating potential new areas of early 21st-century growth, such as selling its institutional products to apartment buildings and complexes. By continually evolving and expanding its array of products and services as well as seeking out new customers for its offerings, Ecolab appeared to have hit upon a strategy for unending success.

Principal Subsidiaries

Ecolab S.A. (Argentina); Ecolab Australia Pty Limited; Ecolab Finance Pty Limited (Australia); Ecolab Pty Limited (Australia); Gibson Chemical Industries Limited (Australia); Gibson Chemicals Limited (Australia); Gibson Chemicals (NSW) Pty Limited (Australia); Gibson Chemicals Fiji Pty Limited (Australia); Gibson Chemicals Great Britain Pty Limited (Australia); Intergrain Timber Finishes Pty Limited (Australia); Leonard Chemical Products Pty Limited (Australia); Maxwell Chemicals Pty Limited (Australia); Nippon Thermochemical Pty Limited (Australia; 60%); Puritan/Churchill Chemical Holdings Pty Ltd. (Australia); Vessey Chemicals (Holdings) Pty Limited

(Australia); Vessey Chemicals Pty Limited (Australia); Vessey Chemicals (Vic.) Pty Limited (Australia); Ecolab Limited (Bahamas); Ecolab (Barbados) Limited; Kay N.V. (Belgium); Ecolab Quimica Ltda. (Brazil); Ecolab Ltd. (Canada); Ecolab S.A. (Chile); Ecolab Colombia S.A. (Columbia); Ecolab Sociedad Anonima (Costa Rica); Ecolab, S.A. de C.V. (El Salvador); Ecolab S.A. (France); Ecolab GmbH (Germany); Ecolab Export GmbH (Germany); Ecolab, Sociedad Anonima (Guatemala); Quimicas Ecolab, S.A. (Honduras); Ecolab Limited (Hong Kong); P.T. Ecolab Indonesia (80%); Ecolab Export Limited (Ireland); Ecolab Co. (Ireland); Ecolab Limited (Jamaica); Ecolab K.K. (Japan); Ecolab East Africa (Kenya) Limited; Ecolab Korea Ltd.; Ecolab Lebanon S.a.r.l.; Ecolab Sdn. Bhd. (Malaysia); Ecolab S.A. de C.V. (Mexico); Ecolab Holdings Mexico, S.A. de C.V.; Ecolab Morocco; Ecolab Finance N.V. (Netherlands Antilles); Ecolab International B.V. (Netherlands); Ecolab Limited (New Zealand); Ecolab Nicaragua, S.A.; Ecolab S.A. (Panama); Gibson Chemicals (PNG) Pty. Limited (Papua New Guinea); Ecolab Chemicals Ltd. (People's Republic of China; 85%); Ecolab Philippines, Inc.; Ecolab Pte. Ltd. (Singapore); Klenzade South Africa (Proprietary) Ltd.; Ecolab Ltd. (Taiwan); Ecolab East Africa (Tanzania) Limited; Ecolab Limited (Thailand); Ecolab East Africa (Uganda) Limited; Ecolab Foreign Sales Corp. (U.S. Virgin Islands); Ecolab S.A. (Venezuela; 51%); BCS Sales Inc.; Kay Chemical Company; Kay Chemical International, Inc.; Ecolab Finance (Australia) Inc.; Ecolab Manufacturing Inc.; Ecolab Holdings Inc.; Ecolab Investment Inc.; Ecolab Foundation; Ecolab Leasing Corporation; FastSource Leasing, Inc.; GCS Service, Inc.; Jackson MSC Inc.; Puritan Services Inc.

Principal Divisions

Institutional; Food and Beverage; Kay; Pest Elimination; Textile Care; Professional Products; Water Care; GCS Service.

Principal Competitors

ABM Industries Incorporated; ARAMARK Corporation; Chemed Corporation; Colin Service Systems, Inc.; CPAC, Inc.; Healthcare Services Group, Inc.; ISS-International Service System A/S; Katy Industries, Inc.; National Service Industries, Inc.; Rollins, Inc.; The ServiceMaster Company; SYSCO Corporation; The Tranzonic Companies; Unicco Service Company; Unilever PLC/Unilever N.V.; Unisource Worldwide, Inc.

Further Reading

Byrne, Harlan S., "Ecolab Inc.: Controversial Acquisition Is Poised for a Move," *Barron's,* October 15, 1990, pp. 49+.
"Cleaning-Products Company Set to Acquire Kay Chemical," *Wall Street Journal,* November 4, 1994, p. A6.
Davis, Riccardo A., "St. Paul, Minn.-Based Ecolab Acquires Industrial Cleaning Products Maker," *St. Paul Pioneer Press,* November 4, 1994.
Feyder, Susan, "Ecolab Still Trying to Revive ChemLawn," *Minneapolis Star Tribune,* May 22, 1989, p. 1D.
——, "Twist of Fate Left Destiny of Ecolab in His Hands," *Minneapolis Star Tribune,* January 11, 1998, p. 1D.
Fredrickson, Tom, "ChemLawn Blooms Under New Owners," *Minneapolis-St. Paul Citybusiness,* July 22, 1994.
——, "Ecolab to Have One CEO in Name, Two in Practice," *Minneapolis-St. Paul Citybusiness,* October 15, 1993.

Harvilicz, Helena, ''Ecolab Makes a Name for Itself by Diversifying Its Operations,'' *Chemical Market Reporter,* August 16, 1999, p. 33.

Kapner, Suzanne, ''Allan Schuman: President, Ecolab, St. Paul, Minnesota,'' *Nation's Restaurant News,* January 1995, pp. 189–90.

Kaufman, Jonathan, ''Heavy Duty: For Latter-Day CEO, 'All in a Day's Work' Often Means Just That,'' *Wall Street Journal,* May 3, 1999, pp. A1+.

Kurschner, Dale, ''With Henkel Deal Near Completion, Ecolab Eyes Income Boost,'' *Minneapolis-St. Paul Citybusiness,* April 1, 1991, p. 2.

Lanners, Fred T., Jr., *Products and Services for a Cleaner World: The Story of Economics Laboratory, Inc.,* New York: Newcomen Society in North America, 1981, 24 p.

Meyers, Mike, ''Ecolab on New Turf with ChemLawn Purchase,'' *Minneapolis Star Tribune,* June 29, 1987, p. 1M.

Miller, James P., ''Ecolab Decision to Shed Lawn-Care Unit Cheered by Investors,'' *Wall Street Journal,* March 3, 1992, p. A5.

Peterson, Susan E., ''Confident Departure: Retiring Executive Sandy Grieve Turned Ecolab from Trouble to Road to Recovery,'' *Minneapolis Star Tribune,* December 25, 1995, p. 1D.

——, ''Ecolab Selling ChemLawn Subsidiary After Five Years of Trying to Turn It Around,'' *Minneapolis Star Tribune,* March 3, 1992, p. 1D.

——, ''Ecolab to Buy Manufacturer of Fast-Food Cleaning Supplies: Kay Chemical Will Be Acquired in $95 Million Deal,'' *Minneapolis Star Tribune,* November 4, 1994, p. 1D.

Schafer, Lee, ''Defending His Turf,'' *Corporate Report-Minnesota,* March 1, 1990, p. 34.

——, ''An Interview with Ecolab's Sandy Grieve,'' *Corporate Report-Minnesota,* July 1, 1994, pp. 44+.

Schmitt, Bill, ''Ecolab: Awash in Growth Prospects,'' *Chemical Week,* January 27, 1999, pp. 48–49.

—updated by David E. Salamie

Federal Prison Industries, Inc.

320 1st Street, N.W.
Washington, D.C. 20534
U.S.A.
Telephone: (202) 305-3500
Fax: (202) 305-7340
Web site: http://www.unicor.gov

Government-Owned Company
Incorporated: 1934
Employees: 20,966
Sales: $566.2 million (1999)
NAIC: 92214 Correctional Institutions; 337211 Wood
    Office Furniture Manufacturing; 337214 Office
    Furniture (Except Wood) Manufacturing; 337127
    Institutional Furniture Manufacturing (pt); 323114
    Quick Printing (pt); 315211 Men's and Boys' Cut and
    Sew Apparel Contractors (pt); 314912 Canvas and
    Related Product Mills (pt); 335931 Current-Carrying
    Wiring Device Manufacturing; 323116 Manifold
    Business Forms Printing (pt)

Federal Prison Industries, Inc., which is known by the trade name UNICOR, is a federal government-owned corporation that employs federal prisoners to manufacture and provide a variety of products and services, primarily to agencies of the U.S. government. More than 20,000 inmates are employed by UNICOR and work in a network of nearly 100 factories in 64 prisons in 30 states. Among the products made and sold by UNICOR are furniture, including office furniture and furniture for college dormitories; clothing and textiles, such as military uniforms; electronics equipment; and plastic and metal goods, including eyewear and traffic signs. UNICOR also offers services, such as data entry, printing services, and bulk mailing. According to federal law, the U.S. government is required to purchase UNICOR products before turning to the private sector.

Putting Inmates to Work: 1930s–60s

Federal Prison Industries, Inc. (FPI) was formed in 1934 during a period when social reform and economic recovery were priorities in the United States. At the time, federal prisoners were unproductive and inactive, and officials in the Department of Justice were concerned that this idleness was creating an increasingly dangerous federal prison system. To occupy the inmates' time and also to teach them job skills and a work ethic that would prove valuable upon their release, the Department of Justice lobbied for a program that allowed men and women incarcerated in federal prisons to manufacture goods for government use. Because President Franklin D. Roosevelt's New Deal included the creation of a number of new agencies and programs and thus an expansion of the government, the Department of Justice argued that the federal prisoners would be filling a necessary niche.

Congress thus voted for the establishment of FPI, providing it with starting funds of $4 million. This seed money was the first and only appropriation the corporation received from the government, as FPI was set up as a self-supporting entity, functioning as part of the Federal Bureau of Prisons, which operated within the Department of Justice. Under provisions established by Congress, the corporation was guaranteed customers because government agencies were required to order and buy merchandise from FPI if the corporation manufactured the needed items. The corporation then invested any profits generated from the sale of products back into operations.

FPI grew slowly and steadily after its inception. Within its first two years of operation, FPI opened a number of factories, including mattress factories, clothing factories, wooden and metal furniture factories, and broom factories. By World War II FPI had a product line that included more than 70 categories and operated 25 shops and factories. FPI also had increased the number of federal inmates it employed. When FPI first began operating, in 1935, it employed about 2,000 prisoners, or 13 percent of the federal prison population. By 1940, FPI was able to employ about 18 percent of the population, and sales reached almost $5.4 million.

The corporation ramped up production during World War II, and 95 percent of the goods made during these years were for the war effort and included parachutes and weapons. Although FPI continued to employ about 3,500 inmates, production during the war tripled. During the 1950s and 1960s FPI expanded greatly and focused on construction projects. Inmate employees

157

Company Perspectives:

It is the mission of the Federal Prison Industries to employ and provide skills training to the greatest practicable number of inmates in federal correctional facilities necessary to ensure the safe and secure operation of such institutions, and in doing so, to produce market priced, quality goods in a self-sustaining manner that minimizes potential impact on private business and labor.

---

worked on the construction and renovation of buildings at more than half of the 31 federal prisons.

Growth in the 1970s and 1980s

Although little-known FPI continued to function as a self-supporting corporation, it was forced to operate as a relatively unstreamlined and unproductive business because of its mission to employ as many inmates as possible. In addition, the corporation opted for labor-intensive practices, which were less efficient than modern manufacturing processes. Still, FPI maintained growth and worked to modernize operations, and in 1974 regional sales offices were established to better serve its customers. Three years later, in 1977, FPI adopted the trade name UNICOR.

By the mid-1980s the federal prison system had grown to include 47 prisons housing more than 32,000 inmates across the United States, up from a federal prison population of 23,566 in 1975. UNICOR operated 75 factories and employed about 9,000 inmates. Inmates were required to apply for jobs with UNICOR and undergo employment interviews before getting hired. UNICOR focused on four product divisions: textiles and leather goods; data and graphics; electronics; and metals, wood, and plastics. Among the products manufactured by UNICOR were street signs that adorned the streets of the U.S. Capitol Mall, canvas bags for the U.S. Postal Service, executive office furniture for agency leaders, electronic circuit boards for U.S. Air Force guided missiles, and bookcases for the law library in the White House. In 1983 UNICOR reported revenues of $161 million and net income of about $7 million. The following year sales increased 23 percent to reach $210.8 million, and net income grew nearly 163 percent, to $18 million.

With the inmate population increasing rapidly, and with no signs that the trend would reverse, UNICOR adopted a more aggressive growth strategy in the 1980s, including a $50 million expansion program to build and expand UNICOR facilities. George M. Farkas, UNICOR's chief operating officer in 1985, explained the drive behind the expansion program in the *Washington Post* and said, "The biggest problem that's facing prisons today is idleness, and idleness breeds management problems, particularly when prisons are overcrowded. One of the best ways we know to reduce idleness is to employ inmates, so that's where prison industries play a significant role."

In 1983 the corporation contracted with Booz-Allen & Hamilton Inc. to conduct a research study to assess the marketing needs of UNICOR and to help set up a corporate marketing department that would explore untapped markets and seek new products appropriate for UNICOR to manufacture. In particular, the mar-

keting division sought products that were in great demand from agencies and that would be labor intensive to produce. To meet this objective, UNICOR formed the Innovation and Technology Program in 1984. Working with the Department of Energy's Energy-Related Invention Program and the Department of Commerce's Office of Small Business Technology, UNICOR's program was designed to provide inventors with federal funding and the resources to actualize their ideas while providing a means for UNICOR to expand its product lines.

Increasing Competition in the 1990s

In 1990 the population of federal prisons reached 47,331, compared with 24,252 inmates a decade earlier, and the numbers continued to swell. In 1995 the population grew to 89,964 federal inmates. Prison population was predicted to reach about 120,000 by 2004, and 28 additional federal prisons were slated to open by 2000, creating demand for additional UNICOR inmate jobs. UNICOR operations grew as a result, and sales of furniture alone grew dramatically, from $155.9 million in 1992 to $178.1 million in 1995. The only year during which furniture sales to government agencies declined was 1994; revenues were $146.4 million, down from $169.6 million in 1993. UNICOR offered a wide array of products, and in 1995 the corporation reported that it had manufactured and sold products or services that included 32 different types of office furniture and spanned 133 industry classification codes. The corporation's board of directors, which consisted of six volunteers appointed by the President, voted in 1995 to allow for the expansion of UNICOR's systems furniture sales by 81 percent by the year 2000, and plans to increase sales of seating products and case goods were underway as well.

With UNICOR's growth, however, came increasingly vociferous protests and criticisms from the private sector. Private industry had long claimed that UNICOR held an unfair advantage with its preferential status and low labor costs—UNICOR's inmate employees were exempt from minimum wage laws and the Fair Labor Standards Act and made from less than 25 cents per hour to $1.15 hourly in the 1990s—but the complaints grew stronger as UNICOR's expansion inched closer to the businesses of private companies. In the mid-1990s a number of organizations rallied against UNICOR's preferred status as the mandatory vendor of products to the federal government. In 1996 the U.S. Chamber of Commerce, which represented a membership base that included more than 200,000 businesses, 3,000 state and local chambers of commerce, 1,200 professional and trade organizations, and 76 overseas chambers of commerce, jumped on the bandwagon to support a legislative bill that would revoke UNICOR's status. R. Bruce Josten, senior vice-president of the U.S. Chamber of Commerce's Membership Policy Group, explained the organization's stand in a letter to U.S. Representative Jan Meyers, a co-sponsor of the bill: "We recognize the importance of the productive training and employment of our nation's inmate population; however, we believe that there are other substantial sources of work available to inmates that would not infringe upon the private sector's opportunities to compete for government contracts. Clearly, a balance must be struck between these two competing goals."

Other organizations and companies that supported the withdrawal of UNICOR's preferred status included the Business &

Key Dates:

1934: Federal Prison Industries is established during the administration of Franklin D. Roosevelt.
1974: Corporation sets up regional sales offices.
1977: Federal Prison Industries adopts the trade name UNICOR.
1996: UNICOR launches an online product catalog.
1999: Corporation begins offering services to the private sector.

Institutional Furniture Manufacturers Association (BIFMA), based in Grand Rapids, Michigan, a hotbed of office furniture manufacturing. BIFMA represented more than 250 makers of office furniture as well as industry suppliers. The U.S. Small Business Administration, Printing Industries of America, National Association of Manufacturers, American Apparel Manufacturers Association, and Indiana Furniture Industries also publicly decried UNICOR's status and claimed the corporation was taking business away from the private sector. BIFMA said that UNICOR had become the tenth largest manufacturer of office furniture by the mid-1990s.

Despite the outcry, UNICOR steadfastly contended that the criticism was overly exaggerated and that its mandatory treatment was justified. Steve Schwalb, chief operating officer of UNICOR and assistant director of the Federal Bureau of Prisons in the 1990s, stated in his testimony before the House Small Business Committee that UNICOR did not operate as a private business might. Private companies generally offered a limited product line and attempted to streamline operations by keeping overhead and staffing levels as low as possible. UNICOR, in contrast, had a wide-ranging product line and sought to maximize employee levels to provide as many inmates as possible with job training. Another reason UNICOR offered a wide variety of products, Schwalb maintained, was to minimize its impact on private industry. UNICOR's preferred status, therefore, served a purpose. "In order to overcome the constraints inherent in meeting FPI's statutory mandates as a correctional program," Schwalb explained in his testimony, "Congress provided FPI with its designation as a mandatory source of procurement for federal agencies. . . . [T]he mandatory source provision is a mechanism that creates sales opportunities for FPI." In addition, federal agencies were allowed to request waivers to purchase products from private industry vendors; UNICOR stated that it granted 80 to 90 percent of the waivers requested in 1995.

Controversy concerning UNICOR did not end as the corporation passed into the second half of the decade. Private businesses continued their protest of UNICOR's preferred status, with many citing lost governmental contracts. Knoxville Glove Co. noted that what used to be a staff of more than 300 employees in the 1950s had dwindled to a group of 40 staff members. Although the company conceded that much of its business had gone to foreign competitors, Knoxville claimed UNICOR had honed in on its business. Knoxville's Rod Townsend told the *News Sentinel* that about 30 to 35 percent of its business formerly had originated from glove contracts with the

Department of Defense. By the 1990s, however, the business had dwindled down to only occasional "emergency" contracts. "We haven't done a major government contract in the last five years," Townsend said, "and this can be directly attributed to the FPI invasion of the defense industry market." Knoxville joined with other glove makers to form the Coalition of Federal Glove Contractors, hired an attorney to look after its interests, and allied itself with the Union of Needletrades, Industrial and Textile Employees (UNITE), another organization fighting against UNICOR.

While UNICOR faced challenges from the private sector, it also battled problems within the federal government. Although UNICOR insisted that quality control was of utmost priority within its factories, many agencies disagreed. A 1993 report that evaluated the quality of electric cable sold by UNICOR to the U.S. Army between 1986 and 1990 indicated that quality problems arose in nearly twice as many UNICOR contracts as private industry contracts. In the mid-1990s further reports and studies found quality problems with UNICOR. John Hagan, Master Chief Petty Officer for the U.S. Navy, testified before the House National Security Committee that UNICOR's "product is inferior, costs more and takes longer to procure. UNICOR has, in my opinion, exploited their special status instead of making changes which would make them more efficient." Deputy commissioner George Allen of the Defense Logistics Agency reported that UNICOR's prices were 13 percent higher, on average, than the prices of commercial businesses and that 42 percent of UNICOR orders were delivered delinquently, compared with an industry-wide average of six percent. Many government agencies believed that UNICOR's performance would improve if it were allowed to compete with commercial companies.

In response to the allegations of poor operations, UNICOR implemented changes to improve product quality, price, and service. One new policy guaranteed delivery of goods within 30 days. UNICOR's turnaround was quickly apparent to many in the federal government. Deputy Commander Peter Isaacs of the U.S. Army's family and support center said in *Government Executive,* "They are as reliable as any vendor, and their prices are comparable or cheaper."

In 1996 UNICOR launched its product catalog online, with merchandise that covered five primary product groups: clothing and textiles; furniture, which accounted for about 40 percent of UNICOR's sales; electronics, plastics, and remanufacturing; metals; and graphics and services, such as printing, data entry, laundry, recycling, and equipment repair. Sales continued to rise, from $495.5 million in 1996 to $534.3 million in 1998. The question of UNICOR's status remained, however, and in 1997 the Senate authorized a study designed to discover ways to make UNICOR more competitive. UNICOR attempted to counter the criticism by exploring new avenues for expansion, ones that would minimize the impact on U.S. companies as much as possible. One idea was to offer services—UNICOR was allowed to provide services to the private sector but not products—that companies generally parceled out to foreign countries because of low wage requirements. UNICOR thus began to provide data entry and bulk mailing services.

In 1999 two bills were introduced that could change the status and operations of UNICOR considerably. One bill, supported by a number of business organizations and the U.S. Chamber of Commerce, proposed an open bidding process for government contracts, which would force UNICOR to compete against commercial companies and remove its preferential status. The other bill, known as the Prison Industries Reform Act, was introduced by Representative Bill McCollum of Florida, who served as the chair of the House Judiciary Subcommittee on Crime. McCollum, a strong supporter of inmate work programs, proposed that UNICOR should compete openly for government contracts and also be allowed to bid on private contracts. McCollum's legislation also allowed for private companies to propose and establish businesses in federal prisons, proposed phasing out UNICOR's preferred status over seven years, and called for minimum wage pay for inmate employees.

As UNICOR rounded the bend into a new century, it faced many challenges and new frontiers. At the end of 1999 UNICOR operated 99 factories in 64 prisons in 30 states and employed more than 20,000 worker inmates, or 25 percent of eligible prisoners. The corporation had sales of $566.2 million in 1999 and net income of $16.6 million. As legislation that could irreversibly alter UNICOR's course was slated to undergo Congressional consideration, the future of FPI seemed uncertain. What was guaranteed, however, was that the federal prison population would continue to grow and UNICOR would strive to offer productive work opportunities for a good portion of these inmates.

Principal Competitors

Steelcase Inc.; U.S. Office Products Company; SCI Systems, Inc.

Further Reading

Erlich, Jeff, "Competing with Convicts," *Government Executive,* June 1997, p. 30.

Geisel, Amy, "Manufacturer Fights Inmate Competition," *News Sentinel,* April 27, 1997, p. D1.

Ghering, Mike, "Prison Industry Trends Combated," *Grand Rapids Business Journal,* September 9, 1996, p. 1.

Lewis, Diane E., "The Rise of Prison Inc.," *Boston Globe,* September 26, 1999, p. G1.

Rast, Bob, "Prison Work Program to Incubate Inventions," *Washington Post,* January 21, 1985, p. 1.

Roberts, John W., *Factories with Fences,* Washington, D.C.: Federal Prison Industries, Inc., 1996.

Ryan, Richard A., and Lisa Zagaroli, "Furniture Makers: Prisons Cutting Sales," *Detroit News,* August 7, 1997, p. A3.

Sator, Darwin, "Prisons Lock Up Federal Contracts," *Dayton Business Reporter,* December 9, 1996, p. 1.

Scherer, Ron, "Jailhouse Capitalism Stirs Revolt," *Christian Science Monitor,* November 10, 1998, p. 1.

Steel, Michael A., "Inmate Labor Program Draws Fire, Praise," *Florida Today,* November 1, 1999, p. E3.

—Mariko Fujinaka

FENWICK & WEST LLP

Fenwick & West LLP

Two Palo Alto Square
Palo Alto, California 94306
U.S.A.
Telephone: (650) 494-0600
Fax: (650) 494-1417
Web site: http://www.fenwick.com

Limited Liability Partnership
Founded: 1972
Employees: 500
Sales: $100 million (1999 est.)
NAIC: 54111 Offices of Lawyers

Although Fenwick & West LLP provides legal services for a variety of clients, its practice focuses on serving high-technology companies. "Lawyering for the Information Age" is the self-described motto of this Silicon Valley-based law firm. It helps firms get started, obtain venture capital, go public, acquire or be acquired, deal with tax and antitrust issues, handle litigation, and protect their interests involving trademarks, patents, and other intellectual property issues. Having celebrated its 25th anniversary in 1997, Fenwick & West is a young but very fast growing law firm, a reflection of its clients. In the late 1990s it represented Apple Computers, Intel Corporation, Sun Microsystems, Cisco Corporation, Amazon.com, AirTouch, Corel Corporation, Silicon Graphics, Xerox Corporation, the American Electronics Association, and many other major clients. Whether providing counsel to hardware, software, electronic commerce, or other types of firms, Fenwick & West attorneys in Palo Alto, San Francisco, and Washington, D.C. serve clients in the United States and many other nations.

Origin and Early Practice in the 1970s

While a student at the Vanderbilt University School of Law, William Fenwick began working with computers to help support his family and in1968 wrote his dissertation called "Automation and the Law." In New York City he represented such large corporations as Pan American Airways and American Smelting.

In 1972 Fenwick teamed up with Henry West and two other attorneys to form a new partnership in Palo Alto, California, where they set up office on one floor of a ten-story building in Palo Alto Square. The new firm decided to move to Palo Alto after surveying the prospects for new high-tech firms in that area and also in Florida and Chapel Hill, North Carolina.

The new firm's first big client was Pioneer Electronics, which provided about 85 percent of the new partnership's work in its first four years. "Pioneer was really the angel for our firm," said Fenwick in a July 6, 1999 interview in the *Recorder*. "They had us involved in litigation in 26 to 28 states. We were involved in mergers and acquisitions."

In 1976, when his law firm employed about 15 lawyers, Fenwick was approached by two young men, Steve Jobs and Steve Wozniak, seeking advice on incorporating to sell a computer kit called Apple I. Jobs and Wozniak knew a sister of one of Fenwick's partners. In the 1999 interview, Fenwick recalled that, "I got the Apple situation simply because my partners' friends thought that if you knew a little bit about computers that you were an oddity as a lawyer."

Fenwick had read about home computers (later called personal computers), but he initially thought the two "pretty scruffy looking" men probably could not do what they desired. Because he thought they did not have money, Fenwick did not charge Jobs and Wozniac to incorporate Apple Computers, a move that launched the personal computer revolution.

German physicist Hans Queisser wrote about the significance of those events. "With a good dose of courage, the Apple Computer Company took the lead. . . . Public demand was so great that Apple could scarcely keep up. The big firms soon jumped on the bandwagon of personal computers. . . . Wozniak and Jobs became millionaires and symbols of high-tech success. The computer had finally shed its aura of inapproachability and of government centralization and control. This change in attitude was important, for in the early days, computers were still thought of in George Orwell's Big Brother imagery. . . ."

Fenwick & West's early history also included spending most of a week with 19-year-old Bill Gates to help him get a license

Company Perspectives:

Fenwick & West is a leading "Silicon Valley" law firm which has represented hundreds of growth-oriented companies from inception. Many of these have become major public companies. It also represents institutional investors and venture capital firms, and has been a leader in structuring new financing vehicles for start-up companies.

for the Microsoft Basic computer language and helping IBM get licensing for VisiCalc, the first spreadsheet designed for the IBM Personal Computer.

From its origins in the 1970s, Fenwick & West tended to have an egalitarian corporate culture. Instead of a hierarchical structure found in other firms, the attorneys created a more open and informal firm with values similar to those found in many computer and other high-tech companies. Such values and also questioning of or skepticism toward establishment authority were part and parcel of America's hippy movement or counterculture. In other words, the rise of Silicon Valley was influenced by its proximity to the University of California at Berkeley, the home of the free speech movement and campus radicals. Dr. Thomas Parke Hughes, a prominent historian of science and professor emeritus at the University of Pennsylvania, made the same point about the similar qualities of the counterculture and high-tech computer firms.

Developments in the 1980s

The decade began with Apple Computers in 1980 choosing Wilson Sonsini Goodrich, another Palo Alto law firm, for its IPO, a decision that was very disappointing for William Fenwick. At the time, Wilson Sonsini already had completed a few IPOs, while Fenwick & West had no IPOs to its record. In the years to come, Apple continued to rely on both Wilson Sonsini and Fenwick & West for many of their legal needs.

In 1981 the partnership hired Gary Reback, a 1974 Stanford Law School graduate who became one of the firm's leading intellectual property and antitrust lawyers in the 1980s.

In 1984 the firm represented XMR Inc. when it was acquired by Amoco. Other clients in the 1980s included Forte Communications when it was acquired in 1987 by Digital Communications, Qronos Technology when it was acquired by IBM in 1989, and Nevada Western Supply when Thomas & Betts acquired it for $20 million in 1988.

One year after ECAD, later renamed Cadence Design Systems Inc., was formed in 1983, it hired Fenwick & West as outside counsel. By 1991 the law firm had assisted Cadence in acquiring eight companies, including San Jose's Valid Logic Systems Inc. in a deal worth $200 million.

Beginning in 1987, Fenwick & West represented Symantec Corporation as it acquired 19 firms by 1996, including the acquisition of Delrina Corporation in 1995 for $450 million.

Major Growth in the 1990s

In October 1991 Fenwick & West lost Gary L. Reback, described in the September 9, 1994 *San Francisco Daily Journal* as "one of its principal rainmakers," when he joined Wilson Sonsini. With the leader of its intellectual property practice gone, Fenwick & West turned to David L. Hayes, who had earned electrical engineering degrees before graduating from Harvard Law School in 1984.

In 1991 the firm's IP practice brought in $3.6 million, 13 percent of firm revenues. Under Hayes's leadership, in 1993 the IP practice accounted for $8.5 million. "The IP practice has exploded," said William Fenwick in the *San Francisco Daily Journal*. "We have one of the largest software patent groups in the U.S. and maybe in the world. The licensing group has grown, and the copyright group is very well respected."

Redwood City-based Excite Inc. chose Fenwick & West as its outside counsel when it was incorporated in 1994. It retained the law firm as it grew and needed help with employee issues, stock matters, acquisitions, and then being acquired in May 1999 by @Home for $7.2 billion. Excite's general counsel Chris Vail praised Fenwick & West for quickly serving any client needs. In the *Business Journal* of February 26, 1999, Vail also said, "They have absorbed the entrepreneurial spirit their clients have."

In addition to such new clients, Fenwick & West continued to represent some long-term clients, especially Apple Computers. For example, in the summer of 1996 the law firm assisted Apple as it tried to reverse its poor financial record by closing a plant in Elk Grove near Sacramento and challenging the Internal Revenue Service's tax assessments.

Serving both long-term such as Apple and new start-ups like Excite helped Fenwick & West prosper in the 1990s. It worked on 22 acquisitions worth about $670 million in 1993. That increased to 52 acquisitions valued at approximately $4.3 billion in 1997, 71 acquisitions valued at over $27 billion in 1999, and 25 acquisitions in 2000 worth more than $38 billion.

Some of Fenwick & West's larger transactions in the 1990s included representing Intuit Inc. in 1993 when it acquired ChipSoft Inc. for $280 million; Cooper & Chyan Technology, Inc. when it was acquired by Cadence Design Systems in 1997; and VERITAS Software Corporation when it acquired OpenVision Technologies for $375 million in 1997. The law firm also represented Intuit when Microsoft failed to buy it in a deal projected at more than $1 billion.

The law firm's financial success, however, did not prevent the loss of some of its attorneys, especially since its high-tech clients sometimes offered stock options and the chance to make much more money. A good example was Fenwick & West partner Mark Stevens, a 15-year veteran at the law firm before he accepted Excite's offer to become its vice-president of business affairs. "The most significant issue is losing good lawyers to clients," said Fenwick & West Chairman Gordon Davidson in the *Business Journal* of February 26, 1999.

Fenwick & West's litigators helped their clients win intellectual property cases in the 1990s. In 1996 the firm represented

ReSource/Phoenix, Inc. when it was sued by Gemisys Corporation. On March 18, 1999 the U.S. District Court dismissed all of Gemisys' copyright infringement and trade secret charges. The law firm in 1999 also gained a favorable ruling for its client Scenix Semiconductor, Inc. in its ongoing patent infringement battle with Microchip Technology.

In addition to high tech firms, Fenwick & West in 1998 and 1999 represented biotechnology, biomedical, and pharmaceutical companies such as Baxter International, Foundation Health Systems, Medical Science Systems, Origin Medsystems, and Mountain View Pharmaceuticals. Other major clients during that time included American Airlines, Andersen Consulting Group, Chrysler Corporation, Fannie Mae, and Harrah's Entertainment.

One of the new challenges faced by law firms in the 1990s was the growing demand that legal documents be written in plain English instead of the convoluted legalese characterized by long paragraphs and legal jargon. The U.S. Securities and Exchange Commission on October 1, 1998 began requiring that plain English be used in all forms submitted for IPOs, other stock offerings, mergers, and acquisitions. Moreover, that agency actually enforced the new rules, much to the chagrin of some attorneys.

Although all companies were subject to the new regulations, one SEC official said Internet and high-tech firms were more scrutinized for plain English compliance. "They have a hard time stepping back and taking on the vocabulary of a retired teacher in Iowa when they work in Silicon Valley," said Shelley Parratt in the *Asian Wall Street Journal* of July 6, 1999. Thus when Fenwick & West helped its client MarketWatch.com go public in 1999, the SEC required that its IPO statements had to be revised twice to comply with the plain English rules.

In 1997 Fenwick & West celebrated its 25th anniversary at San Jose's Tech Museum of Innovation, a most appropriate setting since William Fenwick was one of the museum's original directors and later was replaced by one of the other partners.

The *National Law Journal* in its annual listing of the largest U.S. firms ranked Fenwick & West as number 200 in 1997 based on its 164 attorneys. In 1998 the firm moved to number 171. By 2000 it had expanded to over 250 lawyers, partly because of a booming economy, and was one of the fastest growing law firms in California, not to mention the nation. Although Fenwick & West faced numerous competitors, including several other law firms and also the Big Six accounting firms that hired more tax attorneys, it seemed well prepared for its future challenges.

Principal Operating Units

Intellectual Property; Corporate; Litigation; Tax; Employment and Labor Law; International Transactions.

Principal Competitors

Wilson Sonsini Goodrich & Rosati; Brobeck Phleger & Harrison; Morrison & Foerster; Cooley Godward Castro Huddleson & Tatum; Gray Cary Ware & Freidenrich; Pillsbury Madison & Sutro; Townsend and Townsend Khourie and Crew.

Further Reading

Abate, Tom, "Apple to Shut 1 Plant Near Sacramento Company Continues Restructuring by Cutting 250 Jobs, Raising $575 Million Through Junk Bonds," *San Francisco Examiner*, June 5, 1996, p. B1.

"Andiamo Announces Successful First Round Funding from Veterans of the High-Tech Industry and a Leading Silicon Valley Law Firm," *PR Newswire*, November 2, 1999, p. 1.

Becker, Allison, "Counsel, Silicon Client Have Grown Together," *Recorder*, October 24, 1991.

Bekey, Michelle, "Lawyers Turned Investors," *Venture*, September 1984, p. 98.

"Court Rules for Scenix Semiconductor in Dispute with Microchip; Scenix Architecture, Instruction Set, Never an Issue in Patent Claims," *Business Wire*, February 25, 1999, p. 1.

"Dawn of the Valley," *Recorder*, July 6, 1999.

Deger, Renee, "Nice Guys Finish First," *Recorder*, June 10, 1999.

"Domain Name Disputes Likely to Be Arbitrated," *Denver Business Journal*, October 22, 1999, p. 24A.

Evans, James, "With Practice Floundering, Young Leader [David Hayes] Sets It Afloat," *San Francisco Daily Journal*, September 9, 1994.

"Fenwick & West Handles Three Symantec Deals," *California Law Business*, September 30, 1991.

Hazlewood, Sara, "Fenwick & West Earns Distinction As a Great Employer," *The Business Journal*, February 26, 1999, p. 3.

Madison, Mary, "East-West Relations," *Peninsula Times Tribune*, August 5, 1991.

O'Brian, Bridget, "In New York: U.S. SEC Delays IPOs in Its Zeal for Plain English," *Asian Wall Street Journal*, July 6, 1999, p. 13.

Queisser, Hans, translated by Diane Crawford-Burkhardt, *The Conquest of the Microchip*, Cambridge, Mass.: Harvard University Press, 1988.

"ReSource/Phoenix Wins Lawsuit Against Gemisys Corporation," *Business Wire*, April 15, 1999, p. 1.

Schaefer, Henry O., "High-Tech Law Takes Off Silicon Valley's Success a Jackpot for Attorneys 1995," *San Francisco Examiner*, April 24, 1995, p. D19.

Slind-Flor, Victoria, "Document Exchange by Disk," *National Law Journal*, November 18, 1991.

—David M. Walden

FLUOR

Fluor Corporation

One Enterprise Drive
Aliso Viejo, California 92656-2606
U.S.A.
Telephone: (949) 349-2000
Fax: (949) 349-5271
Web site: http://www.fluor.com

Public Company
Incorporated: 1924 as Fluor Construction Company
Employees: 53,561
Sales: $12.42 billion (1999)
Stock Exchanges: New York Chicago Pacific
   Amsterdam London Swiss
Ticker Symbol: FLR
NAIC: 212111 Bituminous Coal and Lignite Surface
   Mining; 213113 Support Activities for Coal Mining;
   233310 Manufacturing and Industrial Building
   Construction; 233320 Commercial and Institutional
   Building Construction; 234110 Highway and Street
   Construction; 234930 Industrial Nonbuilding Structure
   Construction; 234990 All Other Heavy Construction;
   235950 Building Equipment and Other Machinery
   Installation Contractors; 421520 Coal and Other
   Mineral and Ore Wholesalers; 421810 Construction
   and Mining (Except Petroleum) Machinery and
   Equipment Wholesalers; 532412 Construction,
   Mining, and Forestry Machinery and Equipment
   Rental and Leasing; 541310 Architectural Services;
   541330 Engineering Services; 811310 Commercial
   and Industrial Machinery and Equipment (Except
   Automotive and Electronic) Repair and Maintenance

Fluor Corporation is one of the world's largest engineering and construction companies. Fluor Daniel, the company's largest unit, provides design, engineering, procurement, construction, and other services for a broad range of industries. Fluor Global Services provides an array of services outside of those offered by Fluor Daniel, including construction and industrial equipment rental, sales, and service (through American Equipment Company); staffing services—temporary, contract, and direct hire; operations, maintenance, and consulting services; and services for the governmental and telecommunications sectors. Through the A.T. Massey Coal Company unit, Fluor also has considerable investments in the coal industry, producing steam coal for the electric generating industry and metallurgical coal for the steel industry.

Early Decades of Foundation Building

Fluor's story begins with a Swiss émigré who, upon arriving in the United States knew only one English word—"hello." Born in 1867, John Simon Fluor was a carpenter who had gained engineering experience while serving in the Swiss army. Fluor left his native country in 1888 at the age of 21, joining his two older brothers who had settled in Oshkosh, Wisconsin. The three pooled their money in 1890 to start a saw and paper mill called Rudolph Fluor & Brother. J. Simon Fluor's contribution was $100; he served as manager at the mill.

In 1903 the company name changed to Fluor Brothers Construction Company, with J. Simon Fluor as president. Nine years later he traveled on his own to California and started a general construction business in Santa Ana under his own name. With innovative methods and precise work, Fluor built his venture's reputation quickly. The Southern California Gas Company asked him to build an office and numerous meter shops in 1915, and afterward Fluor received a contract for a compressor station from Industrial Fuel Supply Company. Fluor recognized that the emerging California petroleum industry held enormous potential, so in 1921 he began to tailor his engineering and construction work to meet the demands of the field.

Fluor received a contract to erect a cooling tower in 1921. Believing that those in use at the time were inefficient and wasteful, he designed the "Buddha tower," a radical advancement which not only cooled water more efficiently but reduced water loss. The name came from the tower's resemblance to Buddhist shrines. Fluor soon began manufacturing the towers. The oil and gas companies quickly recognized the Buddha towers' merit, and used them at many installations.

Fluor incorporated his business as Fluor Construction Company in 1924 with a capital investment of $100,000. He began manufacturing large engine mufflers, expanding the company from strictly engineering to engineering and construction. After outgrowing two different facilities, Fluor built new quarters in Los Angeles and consolidated all general offices in one building in 1927.

In the mid-1920s, Fluor started involving his sons in the family business. He retained the presidency until 1943, although his sons ran the company. Fluor's eldest son, Peter Earl, became executive vice-president and general manager. Peter Fluor seemed to be a born salesman, and associates called him ''the company engine.'' He led Fluor's development through the Great Depression and World War II.

Fluor's business continued increasing until the stock market crashed in October 1929. Between 1924 and 1929 annual sales grew from $100,000 to $1.5 million. In need of additional capital in 1929, the company reincorporated and changed its name to Fluor Corporation, Ltd. to reflect its involvement in fields outside construction. At the time of the reincorporation, Peter Fluor and his brother J. Simon Fluor, Jr., encouraged company employees to take advantage of the company's success by offering them Fluor stock at one dollar per month per share. The brothers initiated many employee benefit programs and were considered enlightened employers.

Until 1930 Fluor operated primarily within California. That year, Peter Fluor pushed for expansion, contrary to his father's wishes, and sold Fluor's services to the Panhandle Eastern Pipeline Company. The contract was for construction of compressor stations on an oil pipeline from Texas to Indiana. The company also opened a Kansas City office. Fluor's expansion got another boost later that year when the Shell Oil Company hired the firm to build a $100,000 refining unit in Illinois. It was the company's largest refining contract to date and helped establish Fluor as a major competitor in the refining construction field.

Fluor's business decreased sharply during the Depression years, but the company's leadership wanted to keep its skilled personnel on the payroll. Thus many Fluor employees with sophisticated expertise worked as laborers until business improved. Also during the Depression, Fluor registered patents on two of the company founder's inventions. They were the Fluor aerator tower, patented in 1932; and the Fluor air-cooler muffler, patented in 1938.

The pressures and energy needs of World War II led Fluor into more new work areas. Early in the war years, Fluor had only a few months to develop facilities and personnel capable of producing high-octane gasoline and synthetic rubber. Later, Sinclair Oil Company selected Fluor to design and build a sulfuric alkylation plant at its California refinery. Between 1940 and 1943, Fluor facilities produced more than a third of all 100 percent octane gasoline in the United States, and the Fluor staff developed three patented procedures to improve oil and gas processing.

International Expansion in the Postwar Era

In 1944 J. Simon Fluor died. Peter Fluor succeeded him as president, and J. Simon Fluor, Jr., became executive vice-president. Peter Fluor died unexpectedly in 1947 at age 52. An interim officer followed him in the presidency, and in 1949 the permanent successor, Donald Darnell, took over. The following year, the company's stock began trading over the counter. After a few years of declines in business, Fluor turned to the U.S. government for contracts in the early 1950s, and thus entered another new area of work. The company participated in construction of a large materials testing reactor for the Atomic Energy Commission in Arco, Idaho. Many more assignments in the nuclear field followed.

The immediate postwar years were a time of significant international expansion for the company; the firm secured contracts for refineries and natural gas plants in Canada and Venezuela. In 1946 a contract for a grassroots refinery in Montana solidified Fluor's reputation as a refinery engineering firm and helped lead to an assignment to expand the Aramco facilities in Saudi Arabia. The company formed its Gas-Gasoline Division in Houston in 1948.

By the time the Korean War created massive petroleum product needs in 1950, Fluor's reputation was so widespread that it was a natural choice for many energy-producing projects. In the first half of the decade, Fluor actively diversified its operations, contracting work for the U.S. Air Force at Dhahran Air Base and for refineries in Puerto Rico. In the early 1950s Fluor introduced a new technique that has since become standard in the industry: using scale models in the design of process facilities. The models helped Fluor staff become specialists in lifting large vessels at job sites. More projects followed, including designing and building plants for the petrochemical industry in Canada, Scotland, Australia, and South Africa. A London office opened in 1957. In the late 1950s Fluor's expertise in building helium plants gained the company contracts with Britain's Bureau of Mines and Office of Saline Water.

During this period of rapid expansion and large international contracts, Darnell became chairman of the company, J. Simon Fluor, Jr., became president and chief executive officer, and J. Robert Fluor, grandson of the founder, became executive vice-president.

As the company grew, Fluor's leadership recognized the critical value of recruiting a staff trained in the most current, sophisticated construction methods. Because the marketplace during the 1950s was short of workers with the skills Fluor demanded, the company established in-house training and college tuition reimbursement programs, both of which are still in use. Meanwhile, in 1957, the company's stock began trading on the New York and Pacific exchanges.

Diversification into Offshore Oil and Mining in the 1960s and 1970s

In 1962 J. Robert Fluor, an engineer and former U.S. Air Force pilot who bred thoroughbred horses, became president and chief executive officer of the company. His tenure was significant for Fluor Corporation in four major ways: internationalization, computerization, acquisitions in the offshore oil drilling industry, and mining acquisitions. In the first case, Fluor built refineries in Korea and Iran, extending its operations into two more nations. In the computerization area, the company began using computers throughout its offices for both engineering projects and management needs during the 1960s.

Fluor's extensive diversification into offshore drilling began in 1967 with the merger of five companies into Fluor under the divisional name Coral Drilling. Around the same time Fluor established a new subsidiary called Deep Oil Technology for deep-ocean recovery of oil. In 1968 the company created Fluor Ocean Services, an umbrella management company headquartered in Houston. Ocean Services quickly became a worldwide company. Fluor's largest offshore drilling acquisition occurred in 1969, when the company took over the Pike Corporation of America. Pike's operations had been consolidated under three separate companies—Western Offshore Drilling and Explora-

tion Company, Republic Supply Company of California, an equipment distributor, and the specialty tubing and pipe distributor Kilsby Tubesupply.

Fluor's involvement with the mining and metals industry also began in 1969. The company purchased Utah Construction and Mining Company, forming the subsidiary Fluor Mining & Metals, Inc. Fluor Australia, another mining interest, was set up soon afterward. In later years mining would become a significant interest for Fluor. In the meantime, Fluor consolidated its engineering and construction activities into Fluor Engineers and Constructors, Inc. in 1971.

The company's activities in the 1970s focused heavily on the international natural resources industries: oil, gas, and nuclear power. Fluor also set up subsidiaries and management organizations in Europe, Indonesia, South Africa, Alaska, and Saudi Arabia, the last being a $5 billion gas program. In 1973 Fluor consolidated its oil and gas activities to form Fluor Oil and Gas Corporation. It completed the world's largest offshore facility for natural gas in Java in 1976.

The financial figures for three consecutive years demonstrate the rate of the company's expansion: 1973, $1.3 billion; 1974, $4.4 billion; 1975, $9 billion. New corporate offices opened in Houston and Irvine to accommodate the company's rapidly growing staff. Fluor executives attributed a large part of the company's success to its task force management concept, under which every Fluor project received all the tools, personnel, and resources to get the job done, and the project director had full authority and responsibility for the entire project.

In the late 1970s the Saudi Arabian minister of industry asked company president J. Robert Fluor to help improve Saudi Arabia's poor image in the United States. At that time Fluor chaired the board of trustees at the University of Southern California. He asked executives of 40 major companies that dealt with the Saudis to fund a $22 million Middle East Studies Center at the university. The center was to be run by a former oil company employee and controlled by the donors. The university faculty and the Los Angeles Jewish community blocked the project because of the irregularity of its intended relationship with its fund sources. Fluor Corporation's public relations department claimed the affair had been distorted by the "Jewish Press."

Along with Fluor's extensive and sometimes controversial international involvement, the company also made a significant domestic expansion by acquiring the Daniel International Corporation in 1977. Daniel was an industrial contractor with revenues over $1 billion a year that in many ways complemented the Fluor portfolio. Daniel's operations were primarily based in the United States, whereas Fluor worked largely overseas. The two had different client lists and were involved in different kinds of projects. Most Fluor employees were members of labor unions, but most of Daniel's employees were not. Despite, and in some cases because of, their differences, the two companies integrated efficiently.

Restructuring in the 1980s

This was not the case, however, with the purchase of St. Joe Minerals Corporation in 1981. The acquisition happened at a time when Fluor had a healthy cash flow from its growing engineering and construction sectors. Management knew about the mining industry from its experience building facilities for mines. Fluor executives determined that metals prices ran counter-cyclically to the market variations in the construction industry, making mining the perfect complement to building. Thus the company successfully bid $2.2 billion for St. Joe, which included A.T. Massey Coal Company, Inc.

In the next several years Fluor posted significant losses. The company was not prepared for the crash in metals prices of the early 1980s. The fall was compounded by a deep recession, a reduced inflation rate, and a collapse in petrochemical plant building because of the oversupply of oil. From a high of $71 in 1981, Fluor stock fell to lower than $20 by 1985, and the company accumulated $724 million in debt.

After J. Robert Fluor's death in 1984, David S. Tappan, Jr., moved up from the Fluor presidency to become chief executive officer. Tappan brought a great deal of international experience to the position and looked for ways to ease the company's dependence on oil contracts. As the company continued to lose money from 1983 through 1986, it earnestly sought a return to profitability, finally deciding it must divest some of its holdings and restructure the entire enterprise. Fluor sold all the oil properties and some of the gold affiliated with its St. Joe Minerals operation, all its offshore drilling facilities, and some of the corporate offices it had built during the 1970s.

The company also divested its South African operations in 1986. Fluor's stated political position on the issue was that the company "still believes sanctions and withdrawal of U.S. firms from South Africa are counterproductive to achieving a peaceful solution to the problems of racial inequality. But as uncertainties of continued operation in South Africa escalate, we felt that an orderly transfer of ownership at this time would be in the best interests of all concerned." Fluor retained a repurchase option on the divested South African assets.

Concurrent with Fluor's divestiture of its South African operations in 1986, the company underwent extensive restructuring. The dramatic losses incurred throughout the early 1980s had convinced Tappan that Fluor's survival would not be assured if the company remained almost entirely dependent upon the cyclical oil industry for its business. The collapse of oil prices in the beginning of the decade marked the end of Fluor's $1 billion-plus contracts to construct oil refineries and petrochemical facilities, and the company began to suffer disastrous losses, recording its largest at $633 million in 1985. In order to lessen its dependence on the oil market and to develop a more diversified clientele, Tappan decided in 1986 to merge Daniel International with Fluor Engineers and Constructors to create Fluor Daniel Inc. Operating as the major subsidiary of Fluor Corporation, Fluor Daniel enabled the company to capitalize on the industrial business that had been Daniel's strength. Instead of almost exclusively constructing facilities for the petroleum industry, Fluor now began to contract for plant modernizations, chemical plant constructions, factory retrofits, and high-tech plant construction. To further strengthen its move toward diversification, Tappan reorganized Fluor into five market sectors: process, power, industrial, hydrocarbon, and government.

The transformation proved successful. After losing $60 million in 1986, Fluor posted a profit the following year of $26 million and by the end of the decade had bolstered its earnings to $147 million, on over $7 billion in sales. Although Fluor continued to construct petroleum refineries for $1 billion and upwards—most notably in Saudi Arabia—the company's recovery was due to the diversity of its clientele. Fluor now designed, constructed, and maintained buildings and equipment in more than 30 industries.

Broad Expansion, Then Retrenchment: 1990s

This diverse customer base served Fluor well in the early 1990s when a recession crippled many construction companies. The company increased its operating profit throughout the downturn, benefiting from a $5 billion contract to manage and construct the production facilities of Saudi Aramco and other work in the Middle East resulting from the destruction of petroleum facilities during the war in the Persian Gulf.

In 1992, under the stewardship of Leslie G. McCraw, a former vice-president of Fluor who replaced Tappan a year earlier, Fluor continued to increase its profits in the engineering and construction business and augment its investment in the coal industry. For the fifth consecutive year Fluor Daniel recorded an operating profit, increasing 15 percent from 1991 to $191 million. Revenues for the year were buoyed by a $4 billion U.S. Department of Energy contract to manage the cleanup and dismantling of a plutonium plant in Fernald, Ohio. The company's coal mining concern, A.T. Massey Coal Company, increased its reserves of high-quality, low-sulfur coal to nearly one billion tons, ranking it among the five largest U.S. coal companies. While Fluor's coal business thrived, generating an operating profit of $80 million, the company's lead concern, the Doe Run Company, suffered from a considerable drop in the price of lead. By the end of the year, McCraw decided to end Fluor's presence in the lead industry, designating the Doe Run operation as a discontinued operation. He was finally able to sell the unit in April 1994.

McCraw also oversaw a speeding up of the diversification program started by his predecessor, with 1994 standing out as a key turning point. That year Fluor Daniel aggressively expanded into new industry markets and geographic regions; by early 1995 the unit had operations in more than 80 countries and in 25 industry areas. The corporation also created a new unit, the Diversified Services Group, which began providing a variety of engineering- and construction-related services, including procurement, temporary staffing, and equipment rental and sales. Revenues subsequently soared, from $7.85 billion in 1993 to $11.02 billion in 1996 (an increase of more than 40 percent), while net income climbed from $166.8 million to $268.1 million over the same period (more than 60 percent). Among the major projects that Fluor Daniel was contracted to build during this period—either alone or through a consortium—were a $1 billion petrochemical complex in Kuwait; a $5 billion cleanup effort at a former U.S. Department of Energy plutonium production facility in Hanford, Washington; the $1.6 million Batu Hijau copper and gold mining project in Indonesia; and a $4.8 billion high-speed rail system in Florida.

The big expansion push engineered by McCraw hit a snag in early 1997 when Fluor's profits began suffering from a spate of low-margin contracts and increased competition stemming from industry overcapacity. In February 1997 the company announced that it would take a $140 million pretax charge to cover cost overruns on two major contracts and would launch a restructuring aimed at cutting $100 million out of its bloated overhead, which had reached nearly $700 million because of McCraw's worldwide expansion. A number of new overseas offices that had been opened were shuttered and more than 100 executives left the company. As 1997 continued, however, Fluor's situation worsened thanks to the Asian economic crisis that erupted that summer. In late 1997 the company announced another restructuring. Continuing to pull back from the diversification program, Fluor Daniel was reorganized into four market-focused segments: energy and chemicals; government, environment, and telecommunications; industrial; and mining and minerals. It also began to be more selective about the projects it took on. In early 1998 McCraw took early retirement for health reasons.

After several months of management by an executive committee, Fluor installed a new chairman and CEO in July 1998, Philip J. Carroll, who became the first outsider named chairman in company history. Carroll took the position after a company policy requiring top executives to retire at age 60 forced him to leave his job as president and CEO of Shell Oil Company, the U.S. unit of Anglo-Dutch petroleum giant Royal Dutch/Shell Group. The appointment of an outsider surprised many observers, but Carroll's experience turning Shell around appeared key. In October 1998, soon after Carroll came on board, Fluor abandoned its attempt to sell American Equipment Company, its equipment rental and sales unit, having announced its intention to divest the unit only the previous March. The decision followed the collapse of negotiations with the leading bidder.

Carroll then initiated a much more significant restructuring, which was announced in March 1999. Fluor was reorganized into five semiautonomous business units, the three most important of which were: Fluor Daniel, A.T. Massey Coal, and Fluor Global Services. The last of these was a successor to the Diversified Services Group, and included American Equipment, staffing services, operations and maintenance services, consulting services, and services for the governmental and telecommunications sectors. The restructuring also involved a large-scale overhaul of the Fluor Daniel unit. In order to slash an additional $160 million from Fluor's still bloated overhead, 15 of Fluor Daniel's 75 domestic and overseas offices were closed and about 5,000 jobs were eliminated from the workforce. While not abandoning any existing contracts, Fluor Daniel planned to concentrate on five core areas in the future: chemicals and process (including pharmaceuticals and biotechnology); oil, gas, and power; infrastructure (transportation); mining; and manufacturing (particularly consumer products, food and beverage, microelectronics, and light metals). Fluor Daniel aimed to focus on its 200 largest customers and those industries in which its projects achieved the largest profit margins. For the fiscal year ending in October 1999, a $130 million charge contributed to a 56 percent drop in profits, to $104.2 million. Revenues fell for the second straight year, reflecting the narrowing scope of the company's engineering and construction operations.

Early results of the latest revamp were encouraging though tentative. Revenues continued their expected decline but net income was on the increase, resulting in a clear improvement in profit margins. The spike in oil prices during 2000 boded well for Fluor Daniel's energy unit, and the economic recovery in several key markets provided additional early 21st-century optimism for the still globally active Fluor Corporation.

Principal Subsidiaries

ADP Marshall Contractors Inc.; American Equipment Company, Inc.; A.T. Massey Coal Company, Inc.; Fluor Constructors International, Inc.; Fluor Daniel Inc.; Fluor Daniel Williams Brothers; Fluor Daniel Pty. Ltd. (Australia); Fluor Daniel Brasil; Fluor Daniel Canada Inc.; Fluor Daniel Wright Limited (Canada); Fluor Daniel Chile, S.A.; Fluor Daniel China, Inc.; Fluor Daniel India Private Limited; Fluor Daniel Eastern, Inc. (Indonesia); Fluor Daniel (Malaysia) Sdn. Bhd.; ICA Fluor Daniel (Mexico); Fluor Daniel B.V. (Netherlands); Fluor Daniel Consultants B.V. (Netherlands); Fluor Daniel Sucursal del Peru; Fluor Daniel Pacific Inc. (Philippines); Fluor Daniel Eurasia Inc. (Russia); Fluor Daniel Arabia Limited (Saudi Arabia); Fluor Daniel Engineers & Constructors Ltd. (Singapore); Fluor Daniel South Africa Pty. Ltd.; Fluor Daniel España, S.A. (Spain); Fluor Daniel Group Inc. (United Arab Emirates); Fluor Daniel International Limited (U.K.); Fluor Daniel Limited (U.K.); Tecnofluor Inc. (Venezuela).

Principal Operating Units

Fluor Daniel; Fluor Global Services; Fluor Signature Services; A.T. Massey Coal; Fluor Constructors International.

Principal Competitors

ABB Ltd.; AGRA Inc.; Ansaldo; ARCADIS NV; Arch Coal, Inc.; Bechtel Group, Inc.; Black & Veatch; Bouygues S.A.; CH2M Hill Companies, Ltd.; Day & Zimmermann, Inc.; Foster Wheeler Corporation; Groupe GTM; Halliburton Company; Hyundai Group; J.S. Alberici Construction Co., Inc.; Kajima Corporation; Kvaerner ASA; McDermott International, Inc.; Ogden Corporation; Peter Kiewit Sons', Inc.; Philip Services Corp.; Philipp Holzmann Group; Raytheon Company; Samsung Corporation; Stone & Webster, Incorporated; Technip.

Further Reading

"After McCraw, Fluor Changes Tack," *Engineering News Record,* December 22, 1997, p. 12.

Byrne, Harlan S., "Fluor Corp.," *Barron's,* October 21, 1991, pp. 51–52.

"Doe Run: How to Clean Up on the Cheap," *Fortune,* December 16, 1991, p. 102.

Emshwiller, John R., "Fluor Plans New Round of Cutbacks," *Wall Street Journal,* March 10, 1999, p. B16.

Fluor, J. Robert, *Fluor Corporation: A 65-Year History,* New York: Newcomen Society, 1978, 30 p.

"Fluor: Ready to Capitalize on the Hidden Assets in St. Joe," *Business Week,* April 27, 1981, pp. 104+.

Galluccio, Nick, "The Growth Engineer," *Forbes,* March 30, 1981, p. 62.

Jefferson, David J., "Global Reach: Biggest Builder, Fluor, Sees Kuwaiti Contracts As a Mixed Blessing," *Wall Street Journal,* April 18, 1991, pp. A1+.

McCraw, Leslie G., "Developing Global Strategies at Fluor Corp.," *Site Selection,* April 1990, pp. 391–92.

O'Dell, John, ''Fluor Taps Shell Oil President As CEO,'' *Los Angeles Times,* April 16, 1998, p. D1.

——, ''Irvine's Fluor to Cut Units, Lay Off 5,000,'' *Los Angeles Times,* March 10, 1999, p. A1.

Perry, Nancy J., ''Flush Times for Fluor,'' *Fortune,* November 6, 1989, p. 113.

Poole, Claire, ''Construction,'' *Forbes,* January 7, 1991, pp. 126–28.

Ramirez, Anthony, ''The Big Chill at Fluor,'' *Fortune,* May 13, 1985, pp. 42+.

Reingold, Jennifer, ''No Respect: What Do Rodney Dangerfield and Fluor's Les McGraw Have in Common?,'' *Financial World,* March 14, 1995, pp. 36–38.

Rose, Frederick, ''Fluor, After Touting Big Expansion, Tightens Its Belt,'' *Wall Street Journal,* May 5, 1997, p. B4.

——, ''Fluor, Faced with Sliding Profits, Plans to Re-engineer,'' *Wall Street Journal,* November 18, 1997, p. B4.

——, ''Fluor Plans Restructuring and Retains Search Firm to Find a Chief Executive,'' *Wall Street Journal,* December 12, 1997.

——, ''Fluor's Gloomy Prediction Sends Stock Tumbling,'' *Wall Street Journal,* November 4, 1997, p. A3.

Schine, Eric, ''Cleaning Up at Fluor,'' *Business Week,* October 5, 1992, pp. 112+.

Wrubel, Robert, ''Transforming Fluor,'' *Financial World,* May 30, 1989, pp. 28–29.

—Jeffrey L. Covell
—updated by David E. Salamie

Ford Foundation

The Ford Foundation

320 East 43rd Street
New York, New York 10017
U.S.A.
Telephone: (212) 573-5000
Fax: (212) 599-4584
Web site: http://www.fordfound.org

Foundation
Incorporated: 1936
Employees: 580
Total Assets: $11 billion (1999 est.)
NAIC: 813211 Grantmaking Foundations

Created in 1936 with gifts from Henry and Edsel Ford, The Ford Foundation is one of the top four philanthropic organizations in the United States, and has awarded nearly $10 billion in grants and loans to groups and individuals around the world "to create political, economic, and social systems that promote peace, human welfare, and the sustainability of the environment on which life depends." With a diversified portfolio and assets worth over $11 billion, The New York City-based foundation has offices in Beijing; Bangkok; Cairo; Hanoi, Vietnam; Jakarta, Indonesia; Johannesburg; Lagos, Nigeria; Manila; Mexico City; Nairobi, Kenya; New Delhi; Rio de Janeiro; Moscow; Santiago, Chile; and Windhoek, Namibia.

The Ford Family: 1936–79

American philanthropy dates back to at least 1638, when John Harvard bequeathed his library and half of his estate to the newly founded Harvard University in Cambridge, Massachusetts. He was followed by such people as Benjamin Franklin and Thomas Bond, who donated gifts in 1751 to create Pennsylvania Hospital, the first general hospital in America; American admirer James Smithson, a Brit, who donated gifts to the United States in 1846, creating The Smithsonian Institution and its numerous libraries and museums; Andrew Carnegie and John D. Rockefeller, who donated money in the 1910s and 1920s for foundations that, in turn, funded colleges, libraries, and projects which bear their names.

Automaker Henry Ford was not to be left behind. While he did not believe in giving charity, Ford did believe in helping people help themselves. He already was paying better-than-average wages to his employees and was hiring blacks and disabled workers at a time when few others would. In 1936, the businessman gave his son Edsel $25,000 in cash to establish The Ford Foundation as an independent, nonprofit, non-governmental organization. The following year, Henry donated to the foundation 250,000 shares of nonvoting stock in The Ford Motor Company, beginning nearly 70 years of funding for worthwhile projects.

For roughly the first 15 years, the foundation focused its efforts mainly in the State of Michigan, operating as a local-area philanthropic group. Some of its early projects included The Henry Ford Hospital and The Ford Museum in Dearborn. When Edsel died in 1943, followed by Henry in 1947, the foundation suddenly was the owner of 90 percent of the auto company's nonvoting stock, making the total endowment of the group approximately $474 million, the largest in the country at the time. The Ford family stayed involved in the foundation until 1979, when grandson Henry Ford II stepped down from the board of directors.

New Directions and Expansion: Hoffman and Gaither: 1950s–60s

In 1951, The Foundation brought in Paul Gray Hoffman (former Studebaker Corporation executive as well as administrator of The Economic Cooperation Administration) as president, and Robert Maynard Hutchins (former Yale Law School dean, as well as president and chancellor of The University of Chicago) as associate director. Under their direction, the foundation made broad commitments to the promotion of world peace, the strengthening of democracy, and the improvement of education. Also that year, the foundation provided funding to create The Radio and Television workshop, an early indication of the organization's enduring support of public television. Some of the early education program grants from the foundation, overseen by Hutchins and totaling some $100 million between 1951–53, assisted in establishing significant programs throughout the world, such as the Harvard Center for International Legal Studies and the National Merit Scholarships.

One of the foundation's early creations was the fund for the Republic. The idea for the fund germinated in 1950, when the foundation recognized that pressures from the political and cultural right threatened to restrict basic freedoms. In an effort to ''support activities directed toward the elimination of restrictions on freedom of thought, inquiry and expression in the United States, and the development of policies and procedures best adapted to protect these rights,'' the foundation created the fund. In October 1951, the foundation donated $1 million to open offices, gather a board of directors, and hire attorneys to establish it as a legal organization, which was incorporated in the State of New York on December 9, 1952, as a nonprofit membership corporation. David Freeman was loaned to the fund as temporary president and secretary until 1953, when Hoffman stepped down from the Ford Foundation and became the fund's chairman (where he served briefly before becoming chairman of the board at The Studebaker-Packard Corporation) and New Jersey congressman Clifford Case, the fund's president. The latter was followed by Hutchins, who left the foundation and served at the fund from 1954 until his death in 1977, additionally founding The Center for the Study of Democratic Institutions in Santa Barbara, California, in 1959. He died in 1977, and two years later, the fund was absorbed into the University of California, Santa Barbara.

After Hoffman stepped down from the Ford Foundation's helm, prominent San Francisco lawyer H. Rowan Gaither, Jr., took over as president, and later chairman. During his tenure in the 1950s, the Ford, Rockefeller, and Carnegie Foundations came under intense scrutiny by Communist-hunter Senator Paul McCarthy, and took heavy criticism for their funding projects. To counter McCarthy's allegations, the foundation, in 1956, sold 22 percent of its Ford shares on the public market and awarded $550 million of the proceeds to ''noncontroversial'' recipients such as 600 liberal arts colleges, 3,500 nonprofit hospitals, and 44 private medical schools. Gaither would go on to become a public figure during the Cold War, chairing a committee of leading scientific, business, and military experts—called the Gaither Committee—that prepared a top-secret report for President Eisenhower which, according to David Snead's book, *the Gaither Committee, Eisenhower, and The Cold War*, ''emphasized the inadequacy of U.S. defense measures designed to protect the civilian population and the vulnerability of the country's strategic nuclear forces in the event of a Soviet attack.''

During the 1950s, international work began in Asia and the Middle East (1950) and extended to Africa (1958) and Latin America (1959). Most of these projects were focused on education and rural development. The foundation also supported the Population Council and research in high-yield agriculture with the Rockefeller Foundation.

After the Cold War: Bundy, 1960s–70s

In the early 1960s, the foundation targeted innovative approaches to employment and race relations. McGeorge Bundy (formerly the youngest dean of faculty, 1953–61, at Harvard and special assistant for national security, 1961–66, to Presidents Kennedy and Johnson), became president in 1966, and increased the activist trend with grants for direct voter registration, the NAACP, the Urban League, public-interest law centers, and housing for the poor. Under Bundy's direction in the 1970s, the Ford Foundation supported black colleges and scholarships, child care, and job training for women but, by 1974, inflation, weak stock prices, and overspending had eroded the foundation's assets. Programs were cut, but continued support for social justice issues led Henry Ford II to quit the board in 1976, and Bundy stepped down in 1979.

Worldwide Reach: From 1979 Forward

Lawyer Franklin Thomas, who replaced Bundy in 1979, becoming the first black to lead the Ford Foundation. Under his direction, the foundation established the nation's largest community development support organization, called Local Initiatives Support. Additionally, he more than tripled the foundation's endowments, from $2 billion to $7.7 billion. In the mid-1980s, Thomas was responsible for setting up the first-ever meeting between the African National Congress (ANC) and the South African government, while Nelson Mandela was still imprisoned and the ANC leaders were in exile.

Thomas retired from the foundation in 1996, and Executive Vice-President Susan V. Berresford filled the top spot, becoming the first woman at the helm. After graduating from Vassar College in 1965, Berresford worked briefly for the Neighborhood Youth Corps and the Manpower Development Agency before joining the Ford Foundation in 1970 as a researcher, moving through the ranks to become project assistant for national affairs, officer in charge of women's programs, and vice-president for U.S. and international affairs. She also served on the boards of the Council of Foundations and Chase Manhattan Bank. Trying to get a better focus on the foundation's projects, Berresford consolidated the foundation's grant programs into its three main areas: asset building and community development (which included subcategories such as agricultural productivity, community revitalization, international economics and development, land and water management, and welfare and teen pregnancy); peace and social justice (which included subcategories such as access to social justice/legal services, civic participation, international human rights law, philanthropy, refugees and migrants rights, and U.S. foreign policy); and education, media, arts, and culture (including cultural preservation, vitality, and interpretation; education, knowledge, and religion; media, arts, and culture; and teaching and scholarship). Despite criticism from both the right and the left, in 1997 the foundation announced its largest project ever, the allocation of $50 million to focus on increasing international grants and programs to help people help themselves.

By 1997, drugmaker Eli Lilly donated $12.7 billion to the Lilly Endowment, pushing Ford, then with $9.4 billion, to the number two spot, for the first time in 30 years. The following year, Ford dropped to number four, behind the David and

Key Dates:

1936:　Ford Foundation is established by Henry and Edsel Ford.
1943:　Edsel Ford dies.
1947:　Henry Ford dies; Ford Foundation holds 90 percent of Ford stock
1950s:　International funding begins.
1979:　Franklin Thomas becomes the first African American to head the Foundation.
1996:　Susan V. Berresford becomes the first woman to head the Foundation.

Lucile Packard Foundation, the Lilly Endowment, and the newly created Bill and Melinda Gates Foundation.

By 2000, the Ford Foundation had awarded nearly $10 billion in loans and grants worldwide, and its diversified portfolio was managed to provide a perpetual source of support for the foundation's programs and operations through the 21st century.

Principal Divisions

Asset Building and Community Development; Peace and Social Justice; Education, Media, Arts, and Culture.

Principal Competitors

The Carnegie Corporation of New York; The John D. and Catherine T. MacArthur Foundation; The Rockefeller Foundation; The Lilly Endowment; The Bill and Melinda Gates Foundation; The W.K. Kellogg Foundation; The J. Paul Getty Trust; The Robert Wood Johnson Foundation; The Pew Charitable Trusts; The Robert W. Woodruff Foundation; The Anneberg Foundation; The David and Lucile Packard Foundation.

Further Reading

"Appraising the State of Business Reporting," *Broadcasting*, June 15, 1987, p. 59.

Baker, Denise, "Ford-Kennedy Awards Honor Ten for Innovation," *Nation's Cities Weekly*, October 5, 1992, p. 1.

"Business News Put Under a Microscope," *Broadcasting*, June 8, 1987, p. 63.

Carlino, Bill, "RA Steers Ford Foundation to Top Echelons of B & I Dining: Well-Known for Their Big Name NYC Restaurant Ventures, Restaurant Associates Uses Ford Foundation As an Example of What Its Non-Commercial Arm Can Do," *Nation's Restaurant News*, November 11, 1991, p. 35.

Castro, Janice, "Back to First Principles; The Ford Foundation Boosts Academics at Community Colleges," *Time*, September 19, 1983, p. 60.

"CDHR Holds Constitutional Conference," *Africa News Service*, March 6, 2000, p. 1008041u6953.

Cooper, Hartley W., "Three Local Governments Take Top Honors in Ford-Kennedy Innovation Awards," *Nation's Cities Weekly*, October 25, 1999, p. 4.

Doherty, Ed, "Investing for The Ford Foundation," *Financial World*, August 31, 1983, p. 25.

"Ford Foundation Funds Arts-Technology Symposia," *Back Stage*, June 25, 1999, p. 41.

"Ford in Its Future, Again," *Crain's Detroit Business*, December 7, 1998, p. 31.

Garcia, Guy D., "Hope Stirs in the Ghetto; Improving Big-City High Schools Get Ford Foundation Awards," *Time*, April 25, 1983, p. 95.

Gattuso, Greg, "Ford Foundation Releases $250,000 to NAACP," *Fund Raising Management*, January 1995, p. 9.

Guskind, Robert, "United We Stand: A New Housing Program Is a Sign That America's Largest Charity Is Trying to Keep Up with the Times," *Planning*, July 1993, p. 10.

"Innovations in Government Finalists Named," *Nation's Cities Weekly*, September 21, 1998, p. 2.

Lansner, Kermit, "On to the Sixties," *Financial World*, June 13, 1989, p. 108.

Levere, Jane, "Analysts' Panel Gazes at Deregulation Impact; Wall Streeters Say Carrier Managements Are Still Learning How to Cope with Change," *Travel Weekly*, January 30, 1985, p. 124.

"The Lilly Endowment Ranks As Nation's Top Private Foundation," *Fund Raising Management*, March 1998, p. 6.

Mayer, Milton, *Robert Maynard Hutchins: A Memoir,* Berkeley: University of California Press, 1993.

Millman, Joel, "The Safety of Phony Turf," *Technology Review*, November-December 1984, p. 70.

Reiss, Alvin H., "National Foundations Give Big Boost to Arts," *Fund Raising Management*, January 1992, p. 59.

Scheinbart, Betsy, "America's Richest Foundations Give to Arts," *Back Stage*, August 27, 1999, p. 2.

Seligman, Daniel, "A Kind Word for Thom McAn, Female Equality in Michigan, Ford Foundationism, and Other Matters," *Fortune*, June 19, 1989, p. 195.

Snead, David L., *The Gaither Committee, Eisenhower, and The Cold War*, Columbus: University of Ohio Press, 1999.

"University of Buffalo School of Law," *Business First of Buffalo*, December 10, 1990, p. 38.

Wooster, Martin Morse, *The Great Philanthropists and the Problem of Donor Intent,* Washington, D.C.: Capital Research Center, 1994.

—Daryl F. Mallett

Frank J. Zamboni & Co., Inc.

15714 Colorado Avenue
Paramount, California 90723
U.S.A.
Telephone: (562) 633-0751
Fax: (562) 663-1650
Web site: http://www.zamboni.com

Private Company
Incorporated: 1949
Employees: 60
Sales: $50 million (1999 est.)
NAIC: 339999 All Other Miscellaneous Manufacturing

Frank J. Zamboni & Co., Inc. manufactures a well-known line of equipment used to smooth and resurface ice rinks. The various models of the Zamboni ice resurfacer, which are assembled by hand, one at a time, enjoy a remarkable following in the United States and in the 60 countries where the machine is sold. The family-owned and -operated company capitalizes on the widespread popularity of its ice resurfacers through its subsidiary, Zamboni Merchandising Co., Inc., which sells toys, accessories, and apparel under the Zamboni brand name. While the company's main manufacturing plant is located in Paramount, California, a second production facility operates in Brantford, Ontario. Moreover, to assist with overseas sales efforts, there is a company branch office in Zurich, Switzerland.

1920s: The Zamboni Family Arrives

Southern California was the birthplace of the most widely recognized ice resurfacing machine in the world, a machine that would enjoy a cult following among skating and hockey enthusiasts, as well as among many of those who never stepped onto or sat outside an ice rink. The Zamboni ice resurfacer was created in Paramount, California, where the Zamboni brothers—children of Italian immigrants—settled in the early 1920s.

George Zamboni was the first to arrive in Paramount. He opened his own auto repair shop and soon invited his younger brothers, Frank and Lawrence, to join him in Paramount to help him with his business. Frank and Lawrence arrived in 1922 to join the family business. However, entrepreneurial inclinations in the Zamboni family ran deep, and Frank and Lawrence soon set out on their own, establishing an electrical service business. The younger Zambonis started their company to serve the local dairy industry, for which the pair built and installed large refrigerator units designed to keep milk cool.

For Frank Zamboni, whose education stopped after the ninth grade, a lack of schooling proved no hindrance to his success in the business world. His mechanical skills provided an adequate means of financial support as a young adult, enabling him to establish himself in Paramount. Once settled in his new hometown, his penchant for invention gained full expression, providing the backdrop for his signal achievement, the Zamboni ice resurfacer.

Before Frank Zamboni made the leap from refrigeration equipment to ice resurfacing equipment, his partnership with his brother Lawrence took a fateful turn. The brothers' business grew as the dairy industry it served grew, and it expanded as the local demand for refrigeration equipment expanded. When agricultural companies needed refrigeration equipment, they turned to the Zamboni brothers, who broadened their operational scope by building a plant capable of producing block ice. Frank and Lawrence supplied the ice to wholesalers who used it to pack their produce in rail cars shuttling across the country. The Zambonis' business expanded, supported by both the growing dairy and produce industries, but the brothers' success soon came shuddering to a halt. Improvements in refrigeration technology quickly rendered block ice obsolete, forcing the Zambonis to look for other areas to exploit their newfound expertise with ice.

1940: Zamboni-Owned Ice Rink Opens and Creates a Pressing Need

The Zamboni brothers struck out in a surprising new business direction; they decided to open an ice skating rink in southern California. Ice skating was growing in popularity during this time, and there were few rinks in operation in the area. Frank and Lawrence Zamboni, with the help of a cousin, began

Company Perspectives:

In the early 1940s, Frank Zamboni had an idea. Now, nearly 50 years later, his name is synonymous with the machine he invented. In fact, ice resurfacers like the one he developed for his own rink in Southern California have had a tremendous impact on skating and ice sports throughout the world. And Frank Zamboni's belief in ongoing product improvement and innovation lives on today in the company he founded.

building one of the country's largest skating rinks in Paramount in 1939, opening the Iceland Skating Rink in January of the following year. The rink was designed to hold up to 800 skaters at a time, who could skate throughout 20,000 square feet of ice under the sun-filled skies of a Paramount afternoon.

The intriguing dichotomy of ice skating during a perpetual summer, however, soon lost its attraction to the effects of hot sun and arid desert winds. In response, the Zamboni's open-air facility was soon covered with a domed roof, but the improvement in the surface conditions of the ice was only temporary. The uppermost ice sheet in the rink, grooved and worn by the skaters' blades, required periodic maintenance to regain its smoothness. During the early 1940s, rejuvenating the ice sheet was a laborious process requiring a tractor that pulled a scraper. As the scraper shaved off the tracked ice, three or four workers trailed behind the scraper, gathering the leavings. Once the worn surface had been removed, the workers sprayed water over the rink, cleaned it with a squeegee, and waited for the film of water to freeze. The entire process took an hour to complete, which stirred the inventive nature of Frank. In his mind, the resurfacing process was too cumbersome, prompting him to search for a more efficient solution. Zamboni's search called upon his days tinkering with cars while working for his brother George, his experience developing refrigeration equipment, and his indefatigable energies as an inventor. Eventually, the result was the first Zamboni ice resurfacer.

Frank began his search in March 1942, when he purchased a tractor and started experimenting. Failure followed: Zamboni incorporated a scraping mechanism into a sled pulled by a tractor that neither smoothed the rutted ice nor cleared the shavings adequately. He continued to experiment with his prototype, spending the next five years trying to fashion his tractor-sled design into a workable model. Meanwhile, the laborious process of resurfacing the ice at Iceland Skating Rink continued. Skating crowds were growing, but the hour-long resurfacing process meant less available time for skaters in the rink and less money for the Zamboni family business. Frank pressed ahead with what was becoming his life's challenge.

By 1947, Zamboni had abandoned the tractor-sled concept for a design incorporating the chassis of a used a World War II surplus Jeep. The finished model, dubbed Prototype No. 3, featured all aspects of the resurfacing process in one vehicle, including an elevated tank designed to hold all the scrapings and snow gathered in a single resurfacing. Again, the design was unsuccessful, but parts from Prototype No. 3 were eventually

used to construct an ice resurfacer that met Zamboni's performance criteria. In the summer of 1949, more than seven years after he had begun his quest to build an efficient ice resurfacer, Zamboni at last had a machine capable of consistently producing a clean sheet of ice. At Iceland Skating Rink, he unveiled the "Model A Zamboni Ice Resurfacer," featuring four-wheel drive and four-wheel steering, an in-tank snow melting system, and a patented "Wash Water" system that ensured a pristine sheet of new ice.

Zamboni had labored throughout the 1940s to satisfy his need for a competent resurfacer, and though he considered himself primarily an ice rink operator, not a budding manufacturer, his course would change shortly after he had finished work on the Model A. In 1950, he sold his first ice resurfacer, the $5,000 Zamboni Model B, to the nearby Pasadena Winter Garden. Also that year he would gain world renown, becoming unofficial spokesperson for his pioneering machine. The time had come for Zamboni to regard himself as a full-fledged manufacturer.

Zamboni's Resurfacer Goes Global in the 1950s

In 1950, ice skating's most influential ambassador, three-time Olympic gold medalist Sonja Henie, arrived in Paramount. Henie, winner of the women's singles title in 1928, 1932, and 1936, had spent her post-Olympic career starring in her own traveling ice show, which stopped at Zamboni's Iceland Skating Rink to practice between tour dates. When Henie saw Zamboni's novel ice resurfacer rejuvenate the rink's surface, the Norwegian skater was immediately won over. She asked Zamboni if he would make one for her for an upcoming performance in Chicago. The deadline was tight, but Zamboni could not refuse.

He reportedly spent day and night getting a Model B ready for Henie. He loaded the resurfacing parts into a U-Haul trailer and hitched it to the Jeep that would serve as the chassis for the Model B. Zamboni drove the Jeep to Chicago and assembled the ice resurfacer in time for the opening performance of the Sonja Henie Ice Review. The following year, Henie ordered another Model B and took one of the ice resurfacers with her on tour to Europe, giving Zamboni invaluable exposure overseas. In 1952, the Ice Capades purchased the last Model B Zamboni made, a machine that later found a permanent home in the Hockey Hall of Fame. By this time, Zamboni had turned his ice resurfacing invention into a full-time business and was ready to move on toward the next generation of Zamboni ice resurfacers.

Zamboni continued to operate the Iceland Skating Rink, but as the orders for the Model B came in one after another, he decided to form a separate company to oversee his manufacturing activities. Initially, he wanted to call his company the Paramount Engineering Company, but that name was already in use, so he chose a corporate title that was sure to be original: his own name. Frank J. Zamboni & Co., whose manufacturing site was established down the block from the Iceland Skating Rink, began its corporate life just as the U.S. economy began to show signs of enormous postwar growth.

During these halcyon years of robust economic expansion, Americans embraced the concept of leisure time as they never

Key Dates:

1940: Zamboni family's Iceland Skating Rink opens in Paramount, California.

1942: Frank Zamboni tries to build his own machine to resurface ice.

1949: The Model A Zamboni Ice Resurfacer debuts at Iceland Skating Rink.

1964: The HD Series is introduced, with technological innovations that set the standard for the industry.

1978: The release of the 500 Series marks the advent of the modern ice resurfacer.

1988: Frank Zamboni's death triggers transition to the second generation of family management.

1997: Subsidiary Zamboni Merchandising Co., Inc. is established.

had before, fueling, among myriad other pursuits, the popularity of ice skating and increasing the number of ice rinks in the country. Although he could not have known it when he first began experimenting with a new ice resurfacer, Zamboni's timing was perfect. His revolutionary machine was already beginning to gain widespread notice just as a wave of new ice rinks were opening up across the country. Zamboni worked diligently to supply the growing community of ice rink operators with improved versions of his original ice resurfacer. Some of his alterations worked, while others produced no improvement in performance and were scrapped, but all the changes represented evolutionary steps in the development of the founder's signature line of machines.

Zamboni's next series of ice resurfacers featured an elevated driver's seat, giving the operator a clearer view over the snow tank. After the debut of the Model C in 1952, Zamboni introduced the Model D with a redesigned dump tank, but the alteration did little to improve performance, prompting Zamboni to abandon the design concept and move quickly to the Model E. Introduced in 1954, the Model E was the first Zamboni ice resurfacer designed for mass production. Within two years, 20 of the Model E machines were sold, including one to the Boston Garden. Following the success of the Model E series, Zamboni turned his attention to addressing the particular requests of his customers. Ice rink operators, whose ranks were growing steadily by the mid-1950s, clamored for greater snow and water capacity, which led Zamboni to make fundamental changes in the Model F, introduced in 1956. Instead of using a complete Jeep, Zamboni stripped away much of the vehicle, providing for increased water and snow capacity. After this initial spree of new model releases, Zamboni waited eight years before making any substantial changes to his invention, and when the next version debuted, its characteristics set the standard for the industry for the remainder of the 20th century.

1960s–70s: Development of the Modern Ice Resurfacer

The Model HD, introduced in 1964, was the first Zamboni ice resurfacer devoid of any remnants of a Jeep chassis. The machine also featured a revamped system to carry snow from the ice surface to the snow tank and it was equipped to discharge snow from the tank at a significantly faster rate than previous models. The next innovative leap in the Zamboni ice resurfacer occurred in 1978, when the 500 Series was introduced. The 500 Series, produced by Zamboni & Co. for the remainder of the 20th century, replaced the air-cooled engines of its predecessors with a liquid-cooled engine. The Model 552 used new battery technology to give customers the first electric ice resurfacer, which along with the Model 500 developed into the most popular ice resurfacers made by Zamboni. For the legions of admirers who transformed Zamboni's bulky-looking invention into a cultural icon, the 500 and the 552 were most commonly the objects of their tributes.

Although Frank J. Zamboni & Co. succeeded as an enterprise largely because of the pioneering work of its founder, the widespread popularity of the machine among the general, non-buying public played an instrumental role in the company's success. In the minds of many of those who watched it in action, the Zamboni ice resurfacer transcended its existence as a piece of athletic equipment to become an object of adoration. Zamboni ice resurfacers appeared in Charles Schulz's hugely popular ''Peanuts'' comic strip, debuting in January 1980 and making more than 50 appearances during the ensuing 20 years. People wrote songs about the Zamboni ice resurfacer, a race horse was named after the machine, and celebrities such as Disney chief Michael Eisner, country singer Garth Brooks, and race-car driver Richard Petty used their influence to get behind the wheel of the famed ice resurfacer. The machines were featured in films, advertising campaigns, and in popular television shows such as the situation comedy ''Cheers,'' in which a reccurring character was killed by a Zamboni ice resurfacer traveling at its top speed of nine miles per hour. Perhaps the ultimate recognition of the ice resurfacer's fixed position in the mindset of the nation occurred in the mid-1990s, when Zamboni appeared as a proper noun and brand name in *Webster's Collegiate Dictionary.*

Supported by successive waves of improved models and by what amounted to a fan base that stretched across the globe, Frank J. Zamboni & Co. attained startling prominence in an otherwise insignificant industry niche. By the late 1990s, more than 6,500 machines had been sold to customers in 60 countries, with the standard model selling for approximately $50,000 and the most inexpensive model—an ice resurfacer designed for backyard use—retailing for roughly $7,000. The decades of unbridled success during the company's first half-century of business enabled the Zamboni family to establish a second manufacturing facility in Brantford, Ontario, as well as a branch office in Zurich, Switzerland.

As the company's 50th anniversary approached, the second generation of Zamboni management was in place. Frank's death in 1988 forced the company to make its first significant change in management—often a stumbling block for family-operated companies–and continued success ensued under the leadership of Frank's son, Richard Zamboni. In the late 1990s, Richard's own son, Frank, headed the Brantford manufacturing operations, auguring a third generation of Zamboni management. Perhaps the most notable achievement in the decade following Frank's death was the establishment of a merchandising subsidiary, Zamboni Merchandising Co., in 1997 that produced toys, apparel, and accessories under the Zamboni brand name. The addition of a merchandising arm, which promised to provide a significant stream of revenue, coupled with the entrenched market appeal of the company's ice resurfacers, created a powerful business combination at the century's end, one that promised to exude strength in the century ahead.

Principal Subsidiaries

Zamboni Merchandising Co., Inc.

Principal Competitors

Resurface Corporation; Jimbini Manufacturing Company.

Further Reading

Hillburg, Bill, "California's Zamboni Co. Makes Ice-Rink Machines, Stays in the Family," *Knight-Ridder/Tribune Business News,* June 13, 1997.

Miller, Jeff, "Slow Ride," *Orange Country Register,* December 19, 1999, p. D1.

—Jeffrey L. Covell

SEARLE

G. D. Searle & Co.

5200 Old Orchard Road
Skokie, Illinois 60077
U.S.A.
Telephone: (847) 982-7000
Fax: (847) 470-1480
Web site: http://www.searlehealthnet.com

Wholly Owned Subsidiary of Monsanto Company
Incorporated: 1908
Employees: 9,400
Sales: $3.92 billion (1999)
NAIC: 325412 Pharmaceutical Preparation Manufacturing

Skokie, Illinois-based G.D. Searle & Co. is a mid-sized pharmaceutical firm owned entirely by chemical producer Monsanto Company. Searle concentrates on developing, manufacturing, and marketing pharmaceuticals in five main areas: arthritis, insomnia, cancer, cardiovascular disease, and women's reproductive health. Its top-selling product is the arthritis drug Celebrex, which was introduced in early 1999 and became the most successful pharmaceutical launch in U.S. history, with 19 million prescriptions written in the first 12 months. Over its more than 100-year history, Searle has developed a number of well-known products, including the laxative Metamucil, motion-sickness treatment Dramamine, the first birth control "pill," high-blood-pressure medication Aldactone, and the artificial sweetener aspartame (brand name NutraSweet). Four generations of the Searle family guided the company through much of its development. In October 1985 Monsanto acquired Searle, which then operated as a wholly owned subsidiary. In December 1999 Monsanto agreed to a merger with Pharmacia & Upjohn Inc., a development that signalled the likely end of Searle's existence as an operating company.

Early History

Gideon D. Searle founded his namesake company in 1888 in Omaha, Nebraska. Searle was a young druggist who decided to become a full-time pharmaceutical manufacturer. In 1890 he relocated the company to the corner of Ohio and Wells streets in Chicago. He formally incorporated his venture as G.D. Searle & Co. on April 10, 1908. Initially the small firm sold a wide variety of products to doctors throughout the Midwest who dispensed medications directly to their patients rather than sending them to a drugstore. Claude Howard Searle, son of Gideon and a practicing physician, took over as president of the company following his father's death in 1917.

Under Claude Searle's leadership, the company continued his father's marketing strategy but—like other pharmaceutical companies who saw their supply of drugs from Germany cut off with the start of World War I—also began to emphasize research and development in the late 1910s and 1920s. During the latter decade Searle developed an American version of a European treatment for syphilis. Aminophyllian, a treatment for cardiac and respiratory disorders, was introduced in 1930.

Helping to steer the company through the difficult environment of the Great Depression was John G. Searle, son of Claude, who became general manager in 1931, then president and CEO in 1936. John Searle reduced the company's product line to highly specialized and profitable items, with a particular emphasis on filling niches left by other pharmaceutical firms.

An early example of the new strategy was the 1934 introduction of Metamucil, the first effective but nonirritating laxative. Metamucil went on the become the top selling laxative in the United States. In 1941 company headquarters were moved to Skokie, a northern Chicago suburb. Eight years later, one of Searle's most successful products—Dramamine, the first motion-sickness pill—was discovered. In 1966 Dramamine remained a leader in motion-sickness medications; by the 1980s the drug had become a household staple. Also successfully introduced in the years following World War II was a treatment for peptic ulcers. During the 1950s Searle began an international expansion, which took the company into Europe, Latin America, Asia, and Africa.

1960s: The "Pill" and Diversification

The company's reputation as a manufacturer of quality drugs corresponded to its growing profits. Increasing sales by $1 million to $2 million annually, the company had sales of $37 million

Company Perspectives:
[Searle's] mission is to bring to the market innovative, value-added healthcare products that satisfy unmet medical needs.

by 1960. Searle's former successes, however, offered no indication of the large profits to come with the introduction of one of the most revolutionary drugs of the decade—an oral contraceptive. Under the direction of Dr. Albert L. Raymond, head of Searle's research department since the 1930s, pioneering work with synthetic hormones in 1951 led to Searle's development of Enovid, the first contraceptive of its kind to reach the market. Within four years of the introduction of "the pill" in 1960, Searle's sales increased 135 percent to $87 million, with a 38 percent return on stockholder's equity. Moreover, almost half of the company's $73 million in total assets existed in cash and marketable securities, long-term debts were virtually nonexistent, and Searle stock traded at 34 times earnings.

Notwithstanding three stock offerings between the years 1950 and 1966, the Searle family maintained a 46 percent share of their namesake enterprise. Upon John G. Searle's death in January 1978, the family had become one of Chicago's wealthiest, with an estimated net worth of $250 million. John Searle's descendants were not only destined to become wealthy men, but his two sons would eventually assume positions of company leadership. Interestingly enough, however, in early 1963 a proposed merger between G.D. Searle and Abbott Laboratories, arranged by the two companies' presidents, was said to be inspired by John Searle's lack of confidence in his offsprings' business acumen. The golfing partners arrived at a tentative agreement over drinks in Chicago's exclusive Old Elm golf club. According to the arrangement, no plans were made to include top management positions for John Searle's sons.

The proposed merger never occurred. One explanation cited John Searle's realization that the amount of bickering on the golf course between him and Abbott's George Cain was an indication of how poorly they would get along as business partners. A more likely explanation pointed to the complications arising from the younger Searles's sizable holdings in the merged company. At any rate, John Searle went into semiretirement during 1966 in the wake of the aborted merger; he assumed the title of chairman and his two sons moved into executive positions. William L. Searle became vice-president of marketing while his older brother, Daniel Searle, a Harvard Business School graduate, succeeded his father as president with the additional title of chief operating officer. Daniel now inherited the leadership of one of the most profitable pharmaceutical companies in the industry.

Yet even before the leadership had changed, a number of industry developments foreshadowed an era of growing problems. Competition from other manufacturers producing birth-control pills, including Upjohn and Johnson & Johnson, reduced Searle's share of the market. Furthermore, a concern about side effects associated with oral contraceptives slowed management's decision to increase production and prolonged

the Food & Drug Administration's market approval of Searle's Ovulen, a second-generation contraceptive. Finally, the increasing cost of research, coupled with its unpredictable results, meant that company scientists were unable to bring to fruition a new product line. By 1965 earnings decreased to $23.2 million, down from $24.2 million the previous year; while industry competitors posted net profit increases of 19.4 percent, Searle's dropped 4.4 percent.

It was under these circumstances that Daniel Searle initiated an ill-fated policy of acquisition. Purchasing a dozen small companies with a wide variety of products, including nuclear instrumentation, medical electronics, and veterinary and agricultural products, Searle diversified into unfamiliar waters. While industry competitors made similar purchases outside the business of ethical drugs, few companies were less fortunate in their choices. By 1977 Searle reported a $95 million write-off; sales had increased to $844 million, but return on equity dropped from 50 percent to 11 percent. The acquisitions outside the area of pharmaceuticals accounted for 57 percent of sales but only 13 percent of profits, and G.D. Searle's profitability decreased sharply.

In addition to a new generation of family executives, 1966 brought Dr. Raymond's tenure as director of the research department to an end. Dr. Thomas P. Carney, former director of research at Eli Lilly, succeeded Raymond as head of the Searle laboratories. Carney's background in both chemical engineering and organic chemistry, as well as his success in developing profitable agricultural chemicals for Lilly, promised to facilitate the development of new innovative drugs for Searle. Aldactone and Aldactazide, two diuretics used in the treatment of hypertension, and Flagyl, a drug to cure reproductive tract infections, awaited and received FDA approval.

1970s and Early 1980s: Publicity Woes and the Battle over Aspartame

By 1971 an estimated 80 percent of company profits resulted from sales of pharmaceuticals other than oral contraceptives. The previous year's profits had actually risen 12 percent, but only on the company's ability to use its Puerto Rican operations as a tax shelter; while profits before taxes actually fell $5 million, Searle's tax bill was reduced by $9 million. Long-term debt was now reported at $49 million.

By 1973 sales of Aldactone and Aldactazide alone contributed 18 percent of annual revenues, surpassing sales generated from the birth control pill for the first time. Research expenditures at Searle laboratories increased 33 percent and led to the development of a new artificial sweetener, aspartame. Aspartame's unique structure resulted from the combination of two naturally occurring amino acids. While the company awaited approval to market the product as a food additive, production was planned using the expertise of Ajinomoto Co., Inc., a Japanese company experienced in the manufacture of amino acids. With cyclamates removed from the market and questions circulating about the safety of saccharin, Searle's new product represented the possibility of a large market share. In addition to developing the sweetener, the company moved into new areas of birth control. A copper intrauterine contraceptive was introduced in England and awaited market approval in the United States.

Key Dates:

1888: Gideon D. Searle, a young druggist, founds a pharmaceutical manufacturing concern in Omaha, Nebraska.
1890: Searle relocates his company to Chicago.
1908: Searle formally incorporates his venture as G.D. Searle & Co.
1917: Claude Howard Searle, son of the founder, takes over as president following his father's death.
1934: The laxative Metamucil is introduced.
1936: John G. Searle, son of Claude, is named president and CEO.
1941: Company headquarters are moved to Skokie, Illinois.
1949: Searle introduces Dramamine, the first motion sickness pill.
1950: The company goes public.
1963: A proposed merger between Searle and Abbott Laboratories is called off.
1965: Searle R&D discovers aspartame, an artificial sweetener.
1966: Daniel Searle succeeds his father as president of the company.
1973: Searle merges with Will Ross, bringing Vision Centers (later Pearle Vision Centers) into the company fold.
1977: Donald H. Rumsfield, former U.S. secretary of defense, is named president and CEO, becoming the first outsider to lead the company.
1981: The FDA approves aspartame (branded NutraSweet) for use as a table top sweetener.
1983: The FDA approves aspartame for use in carbonated beverages.
1985: Divestment of Pearle Vision Centers is completed; Monsanto Company acquires Searle for $2.7 billion, making Searle a wholly owned subsidiary of Monsanto.
1995: Roche Holding's Syntex women's healthcare product line is acquired for $250 million.
1999: Arthritis drug Celebrex is introduced in the United States and becomes the most successful pharmaceutical launch in U.S. history; Monsanto agrees to merge with Pharmacia & Upjohn, likely marking the end of Searle's existence as an operating company.

The July 1981 FDA approval of aspartame's use as a table top sweetener, as well as a food additive in a number of items, resulted in a minor victory for Searle. Sugar prices had recently tripled and the market for low calorie products began expanding significantly. Furthermore, aspartame lacked the bitter aftertaste of saccharin and eliminated 95.5 percent of the calories of sugar. Yet several disadvantages in the new product caused industry analysts to remain cautious in their assessment of aspartame's future. The projected cost for the new sweetener was many times greater than that of saccharin, and its short shelf life—it lost its sweetness after several months—precluded any speedy acceptance in the profitable soft drink market. Bottlers would resort to a more stable, less expensive product before they would turn to aspartame. Nevertheless, Searle persevered

in the test marketing of Equal, the consumer brand name for its new product.

Despite such hopeful products emerging from Searle laboratories, many industry analysts remained skeptical about the company's future. Diluted earnings, resulting in part from the company's numerous acquisitions, aspartame's unclear future, and the expiration of a number of important patents all contributed to this attitude. Yet, apart from these problems, Searle management could never have been prepared for the series of blows dealt them in a televised hearing involving an FDA challenge to their reputation. In July 1975 a Senate subcommittee on health, headed by Edward Kennedy, sought to investigate allegations about questionable research surrounding the safety of both Aldactone and Flagyl. A 1972 article in the *Journal of the National Cancer Institute,* with the support of numerous subsequent independent studies, cited an increased incidence of lung tumors in mice treated with Flagyl. Similar cancer risks, not evident in Searle's research data, appeared in tests of Aldactone.

While conceding that "clerical errors" had occurred, Searle categorically denied any suppression of lab tests. The company did embark on a public relations campaign to improve its image of social responsibility. The price of company stock, however, dropped from around $25 to $15 per share as analysts estimated that sales of Flagyl, Aldactone, and Aldactazide would be reduced by half its previous volume. With a new strategy of public relations, Searle's problems were hardly over. In December 1975, in an unprecedented move, the FDA suspended permission to market aspartame based on an audit of Searle's new drug applications filed since 1968.

The FDA actions resulted in more delays than actual damage. While labels warning about cancer risks appeared on the investigated products, sales for Aldactone and Aldactazide actually rose 24 percent on the last quarter of 1975; Flagyl's increased 12 percent. Aspartame remained under investigation, only to receive market approval six years later. The $29 million already invested in its production was left in abeyance.

While the assault on Searle's corporate integrity marred the company's public image, internal problems threatened to disrupt its very operations. By 1977 money borrowed in the United States against the $420 million saved in the Puerto Rican tax shelter translated into an interest payment of $24 million; earnings from this same tax haven amounted to only $17 million. This, in turn, had some effect on overall company earnings so that shares gaining $1.56 in 1975 gained only $.57 in 1977.

To remedy the situation, an outsider was called in to assume control of the company. Donald H. Rumsfeld, a former congressman, presidential aide, and defense secretary, agreed in 1975 to step in as president and chief executive officer, thus ending four generations of family management. Daniel Searle, who advanced to chairman, had met Rumsfeld 15 years earlier and supported him in his congressional election bid. Their friendship gave impetus to Rumsfeld's midlife career change. While refusing to state he had given up public life for good, the accomplished politician rose to the challenge of correcting the company's numerous problems.

Searle's turnabout was almost immediate. By repatriating Puerto Rican dollars, bringing in new staff, selling unprofitable divisions, and announcing a massive write-off, Rumsfeld cleared the way for major changes in the company. From 1977 to 1983 Searle divested businesses with aggregate sales of almost $500 million. An optical retailing business, under the name Vision Centers, represented a profitable new subsidiary; it had been acquired as part of a 1973 merger with Will Ross. In 1978 this retailer of eyeware contributed $91 million; a five-year estimate placed contributions at $400 million. While long-term debt now stood at $350 million, Vision Center's profits were necessary to improve the company's performance.

By 1981 Searle reported the second highest profit margin among 30 leading U.S. drug firms. Furthermore, an FDA announcement ended aspartame's years-old struggle to win market approval. Rumsfeld's revitalization of the research department through the infusion of $100 million promised a new line of pharmaceuticals from anti-ulcer medication to treatments for herpes. An aggressive policy of licensing and joint ventures generated income to supplement the research costs. Long-term debt was reduced to $89 million as the renamed Pearle Vision Centers moved to the top of the optical retailing business.

In 1983 a 39 percent drop in earnings during the first quarter prompted a decision to sell the eyecare subsidiary. In September 1983 Searle sold 55 percent of Pearle to the public through an IPO; two years later, the remaining stake was sold to GrandMet USA, Inc., a unit of U.K. food and alcohol giant Grand Metropolitan PLC. It was hoped that income generated from the sale would help improve pharmaceutical research which had not produced an extremely lucrative "blockbuster" drug in several years. Drug research, however, did not bring the sought after profits; instead, industry analysts were surprised as sales of aspartame reached record-breaking figures. As a tabletop sweetener and a food additive in cold cereals and dry drink mixes, sales between 1981 and 1982 increased from $13 million to $74 million. As the product was ready to enter into the immensely profitable soft drink market, Searle invested $25 million to expand production in the United States. Once Searle received the expanded FDA approval in 1983, carbonated drink companies lined up to secure contracts. By the end of 1983 virtually all major bottlers became Searle customers, and with the marketing plan to print the consumer name on all products using the sweetener, NutraSweet became a household name.

Despite this expansion after 17 years of testing, fears of aspartame's side effects were not completely dispelled. One study noted changes in behavior after large quantities of carbohydrates and aspartame had been ingested. Woodrow Monte, director of the Food Sciences & Nutrition Laboratory at Arizona State University, along with several consumer groups, challenged NutraSweet's safety by pointing to its production at high temperatures of methanol, a compound associated with poisoning. The FDA reasserted aspartame's safety by pointing to the existence of methanol in fruit juices.

While sales of aspartame reached $336 million in 1983, the continuing question of its safety was not the only issue to concern Searle management. The sweetener's patent was scheduled to expire in 1987; forthcoming competition threatened the sales figure. Even more disturbing was the lack of new pharma-

ceuticals. One observer facetiously predicted that the company, like its new campaign to sweeten sodas exclusively with Nutra-Sweet as opposed to a combination with saccharin, was in danger of itself becoming 100 percent NutraSweet.

As sales of NutraSweet edged towards maximum market potential the Searle family, still holding a 34 percent interest, announced a decision to liquidate part of their stake. Industry analysts, noting the timing of this announcement, predicted that the family could collect as much as $75 per share. Four months after the announcement, not one company had tendered an offer. The financial burden of running NutraSweet's huge operations, as well as an Internal Revenue Service investigation into allegedly deficient taxes paid by the Puerto Rican subsidiary, deterred potential suitors. Liability for the contested taxes was estimated at $381 million.

1985–2000: The Monsanto Era

Only two months later, the announcement to withdraw the offer to sell Searle seemed to indicate a new effort to remain independent. The company purchased 7.5 million of the Searle family shares, reducing their holdings to 21 percent. Rumsfeld succeeded Daniel as chairman, which further solidified independent management. No sooner had these events taken place than Monsanto Co., a chemical firm, announced it planned to purchase Searle for an agreed-upon $2.7 billion. For Monsanto the acquisition represented an end to its long search for an ethical drug company that could generate the income necessary to boost its maturing agricultural chemical products. Monsanto also hoped to benefit from Searle's experienced marketing and sales staff, its biotechnological expertise, and the attractive market potential of new products like the antiulcer drug, Cytotec. Following the completion of the acquisition in October 1985, Searle became a wholly owned subsidiary of Monsanto.

Along with Searle's attractive qualities, Monsanto also accepted the drug company's tax dispute liabilities. What the new parent company did not expect, however, was to become embroiled in a new controversy. Searle's Copper 7, the most widely used intrauterine contraceptive device (IUD), was suddenly accused of causing pelvic infections and infertility. Even more disturbing was a major business magazine's disclosure that the company distorted information surrounding the IUD's safety. The final version of the company's lab results did not state that some cells in the test monkeys developed "premalignant transformations," but only referred to cell modification. Similarly, Searle's human test results may not have accurately reported the rate of pelvic inflammatory disease developed by users. On January 3, 1986, facing 305 pending lawsuits out of a total 775 claims, Searle withdrew the Copper 7 from the market. While continuing to defend the product's safety, the company acted to preempt growing litigation costs; Searle's defense had already cost $1.5 million. The specter of events surrounding the Dalkon Shield, an IUD manufactured by A.H. Robins, undoubtedly expedited Searle's removal of the IUD from the market. Litigation costs surrounding alleged infections and ailments suffered by users of the Dalkon Shield eventually caused A.H. Robins to seek protection under Chapter 11 of the Bankruptcy Code.

The Copper 7 crisis continued to unfold in the late 1980s, as hundreds of new claims—including shareholders charging the company with failing to inform them of the IUD suits—were filed against Searle. Although a jury ordered Searle to pay $8.2 million for damages related to the Copper 7 IUD in 1988, the company appealed the decision.

Apparently undaunted by the ongoing litigation, Monsanto established a new strategy for Searle, combining research and development goals with performance objectives, and promoting those efforts with aggressive marketing initiatives. By the mid-1990s, the company planned to average one important new product introduction each year, annual sales of $3 billion, and a standing among the world's top 15 drug companies. Monsanto also turned Searle into a pure pharmaceutical company, placing Searle's artificial sweetener business into a separate subsidiary called the NutraSweet Company.

Launched in 1987, Searle's "Patient Promise" marketing program made it the first pharmaceutical firm in America to extend refunds on any of its products that proved ineffective. The program successfully promoted Searle's blood pressure treatment, Calan SR, to the leading position among such "calcium channel blockers." By 1990, the drug had captured one-fifth of that market in spite of competition from at least three similar medicines, and had become Searle's leading product. According to an article published in *Forbes* magazine that year, Calan SR was the catalyst that changed Searle's financial losses into profits.

Searle countered burgeoning governmental and popular criticism of the U.S. pharmaceutical industry with a separate special public relations campaign. The company's "Rx Partners" program set up interviews wherein top executives of pharmaceutical firms could offer their perspectives on such divisive issues as pricing, marketing, and research and development.

Led by Sheldon G. Gilgore in the early 1990s, Searle underwent an admittedly "difficult" restructuring in 1992, as the company fought to achieve consistent profitability. The reorganization focused on three primary areas: rationalizing capacity; consolidating global research and development efforts; and reducing the administrative workforce by nearly 2,000 employees. Savings from this effort helped make possible a massive $305 million investment in research and development (20 percent of sales). Although Calan SR was still Searle's leading product, by this time it had lost its patent protection and was under competition from generics. Pinning its future on new patented drugs, Searle launched three products in 1993: Daypro and Arthrotec, two nonsteroidal anti-inflammatory drugs (NSAIDs) specially formulated for treatment of arthritis, and Ambien, an insomnia treatment. Daypro became Searle's first product to exceed over $100 million in sales within the first year of its U.S. introduction. Heavy investment in research and development put several promising drugs in Searle's pipeline as well.

In late 1994 Richard U. De Schutter, a 20-year Monsanto veteran, was named CEO of Searle. Philip Needleman became head of Searle R&D. Over the next several years, the focus of Needleman's R&D efforts would be in five main areas: arthritis, insomnia, cancer, cardiovascular disease, and women's reproductive health. Searle entered the last of these fields in 1995 when it purchased Roche Holding Ltd.'s Syntex women's healthcare product line for $250 million. In addition to focusing

the company's research more narrowly, Needleman also instituted a ruthless policy of quickly ending research on a new drug if it failed an early acid test. In this way—given that Searle was a relatively small pharmaceutical firm—he was able to save precious resources.

By 1996 earnings for Searle were a healthy $200 million on sales of $2 billion. By this time, annual sales of both Daypro and Ambien were nearing the $300 million mark. Sales increased to $2.4 billion in 1997. During the following year, Monsanto reached an agreement with American Home Products Corporation on a $35 billion merger. Combining the research laboratories of Searle and American Home would have created a pharmaceutical entity on a par with the industry's leaders, Pfizer Inc. and Merck & Co., Inc. But late in 1998 Monsanto and American Home called off the merger, having failed to agree on a number of major issues.

On December 31, 1998—soon after the merger's demise—the FDA approved a new Searle drug, Celebrex, for the treatment of arthritis pain and inflammation. This was the first of a new category of pain drugs, dubbed Cox-2 inhibitors, to be approved. Cox-2, an enzyme present in various diseases, was blocked by the new drugs. As a treatment for arthritis, Celebrex was noted for being effective and for not irritating the stomach. Searle partnered with Pfizer for the global marketing and distribution of Celebrex. Launched in the United States in February 1999, Celebrex became the most successful pharmaceutical launch in U.S. history, with 19 million prescriptions written in the first 12 months; sales during 1999 alone exceeded $1.4 billion. With 43 million Americans suffering from arthritis, and hundreds of millions worldwide, sales of Celebrex were predicted to reach $3 billion annually by 2002. The development of rival Cox-2 inhibitors, however, had the potential to dampen sales of the blockbuster new drug. In December 1999 the FDA approved Celebrex for a second use, that of treating a particular genetic disease that almost always results in colorectal cancer.

Also in December 1999 Monsanto and Pharmacia & Upjohn Inc., a major pharmaceutical company based in Peapack, New Jersey, announced an agreement to merge via a deal initially valued at $27 billion. The merger would create a new company, to be called Pharmacia Corporation, which would be one of the global giants in pharmaceuticals with annual sales of $17 billion and an annual pharmaceutical R&D budget of more than $2 billion. Within the new company, Monsanto's agricultural operations would be deemphasized, with a partial IPO planned for the unit, which would retain the Monsanto name. Searle, meantime, would no longer exist as a separate company, but its name would be retained to designate one of Pharmacia's sales divisions. It thus appeared that the firm known as G.D. Searle & Co. would end its history soon after introducing its most successful product ever.

Principal Subsidiaries

Continental Pharma Inc. (Belgium); Searle do Brasil Ltda. (Brazil); Searle PRC (China); Searle European Inc. (Czech Republic); Sanitas, a.s. (Czech Republic); Heumann Pharma GmbH (Germany); Searle Vianex (Greece); Searle Hong Kong Ltd.; Searle & Co. Ltd. (Ireland); Searle Malaysia Sdn. Bhd.; Searle de Mexico S.A. de C.V.; Searle (Nederland) B.V. (Netherlands); Searle Philippines Inc.; Searle Farmaceutical Ltda. (Portugal); Searle & Co. (Puerto Rico); Searle (South Africa) PTY, Ltd.; Searle Ciba-Geigy Korea, Ltd. (South Korea); Searle Iberica S.A. (Spain); Searle S.A. (Switzerland); Searle Pharma Ltd. (Taiwan); Searle U-Liang Co., Ltd. (Taiwan); Searle Thailand Ltd.; Searle de Venezuela, C.A.

Principal Competitors

Alpharma Inc.; AstraZeneca PLC; Biomatrix, Inc.; Bristol-Myers Squibb Company; Centocor, Inc.; Cypress Bioscience, Inc.; Hi-Tech Pharmacal Co., Inc.; IVAX Corporation; Merck & Co., Inc.; Novartis AG; Sanofi-Synthelabo; Schering AG; SmithKline Beecham plc.

Further Reading

Barrett, Amy, and Richard A. Melcher, "Why Searle Is Feeling No Pain," *Business Week,* February 15, 1998, p. 36.

Burton, Thomas M., "A Pharmaceutical Plum in Monsanto's Basket," *Wall Street Journal,* June 2, 1998, p. B1.

Bylinsky, Gene, "The Battle for America's Sweet Tooth," *Fortune,* July 26, 1982, pp. 28+.

Deogun, Nikhil, Robert Langreth, and Thomas M. Burton, "Pharmacia & Upjohn, Monsanto Boards Approve $27 Billion Merger of Equals," *Wall Street Journal,* December 20, 1999, p. A3.

Ellis, James E., "Monsanto and the Copper-7: A 'Corporate Veil' Begins to Fray," *Business Week,* September 26, 1998, p. 50.

Ellis, James E., Ellyn E. Spragins, and Jane Sasseen, "Why Monsanto Is Bucking the Odds," *Business Week,* August 5, 1985, pp. 75+.

"The FDA Gives Searle a Series of Shocks," *Business Week,* December 22, 1975, p. 20.

"G. D. Searle: A Transfusion of Funds to Revive Its Drug Business," *Business Week,* July 4, 1983, p. 87.

"G. D. Searle Replaces a Tainted Image," *Business Week,* September 8, 1975, p. 62.

Glaberson, William B., "Did Searle Close Its Eyes to a Health Hazard?," *Business Week,* October 14, 1985, pp. 120+.

Heller, Linda, "Troublesome Side Effects?," *Barron's,* November 16, 1987, pp. 44+.

Klimstra, Paul D., "Integrating R&D and Business Strategy," *Research-Technology Management,* January/February 1992, pp. 22–28.

Langreth, Robert, "Pharmacia Says Combining Drug Units Validates Planned Monsanto Merger," *Wall Street Journal,* December 23, 1999, p. A4.

Levine, Joshua, "Selling Hard Without Hype," *Forbes,* December 10, 1990, pp. 202, 204.

McMurray, Scott, "Monsanto Pressed to Rewrite Drug Unit's Prescription," *Wall Street Journal,* October 14, 1992, p. B4.

Oloroso, Arsenio, Jr., "Deal Talk Buzzes About G.D. Searle," *Crain's Chicago Business,* September 25, 1995, p. 4.

Ostrowski, Helen, "Pharmaceutical Giants Tell Their Story," *Public Relations Journal,* October 1993, p. 20.

"Searle: Rallying a Drug Company with an Injection of New Vitality," *Business Week,* February 8, 1982, pp. 98+.

Somasundaram, Meera, "With Mega-Merger Off, Searle Must Regroup," *Crain's Chicago Business,* October 26, 1998, p. 4.

Stodghill, Ron, II, "How G.D. Searle Got Off Its Sickbed," *Business Week,* February 24, 1997, p. 134.

Strazewski, Len, "NutraSweet Tells a Sweet Story for Searle," *Advertising Age,* September 27, 1984, pp. 16+.

Teitelman, Robert, "Bittersweet," *Forbes,* August 27, 1984, pp. 36+.

Winslow, Ron, "Heart-Failure Patients Get New Hope, Thanks to a Forgotten Drug," *Wall Street Journal,* November 3, 1999, pp. A1+.

—April Dougal Gasbarre
—updated by David E. Salamie

General Electric Company

3135 Easton Turnpike
Fairfield, Connecticut 06431-0001
U.S.A.
Telephone: (203) 373-2211
Fax: (203) 373-3131
Web site: http://www.ge.com

Public Company
Incorporated: 1892
Employees: 293,000
Sales: $111.63 billion (1999)
Stock Exchanges: New York Boston London
Ticker Symbol: GE
NAIC: 233310 Mfg. & Industrial Building Construction;
325211 Plastics Material & Resin Mfg.; 333415 Air-Conditioning & Warm Air Heating Equip. & Commercial & Industrial Refrigeration Equip. Mfg.; 333611 Turbine & Turbine Generator Set Unit Mfg.; 334290 Other Communications Equip. Mfg.; 334510 Electromedical & Electrotherapeutic Apparatus Mfg.; 334515 Instrument Mfg. for Measuring & Testing Electricity & Electrical Signals; 335110 Electric Light Bulb & Part Mfg.; 335121 Residential Electric Lighting Fixture Mfg.; 335122 Commercial, Industrial, & Institutional Electric Lighting Fixture Mfg.; 335222 Household Refrigerator & Home Freezer Mfg.; 335224 Household Laundry Equip. Mfg.; 335311 Power, Distribution, & Specialty Transformer Mfg.; 335312 Motor & Generator Mfg.; 335313 Switchgear & Switchboard Apparatus Mfg.; 335912 Primary Battery Mfg.; 335931 Current-Carrying Wiring Device Mfg.; 336321 Vehicular Lighting Equip. Mfg.; 336412 Aircraft Engines & Engine Parts Mfg.; 336510 Railroad Rolling Stock Mfg.; 512110 Motion Picture & Video Production; 512120 Motion Picture & Video Distribution; 513120 Television Broadcasting; 513210 Cable Networks; 522210 Credit Card Issuing; 522220 Sales Financing; 522291 Consumer Lending; 522292 Real Estate Credit; 523920 Portfolio Management; 524113 Direct Life Insurance Carriers; 524126 Direct Property & Casualty Insurance Carriers; 524130 Reinsurance Carriers; 532420 Office Machinery & Equip. Rental & Leasing; 532490 Other Commercial & Industrial Machinery & Equip. Rental & Leasing; 541330 Engineering Services; 561790 Other Services to Buildings & Dwellings

The history of General Electric Company is a significant part of the history of technology in the United States. General Electric (GE) has evolved from Thomas Edison's home laboratory into one of the largest companies in the world, following the evolution of electrical technology from the simplest early applications into the high-tech wizardry of the turn of the millennium. The company has also involved into a conglomerate, with an increasing shift from technology to services, and with ten main operating units: GE Aircraft Engines, the largest producer of small and large jet engines for commercial and military aircraft in the world; GE Appliances, one of the world's leading appliance manufacturers; GE Capital Services, which provides its clients with an array of financial services, including various types of insurance, mutual funds and annuities, consumer and commercial financing, credit services, and equipment management; GE Industrial Systems, a leading supplier of products related to electrical power and equipment; GE Lighting, a preeminent global maker of lighting products for consumer, commercial, and industrial customers; GE Medical Systems, a world leader in medical diagnostic imaging technology and services; National Broadcasting Company, one of the four major U.S. broadcast television networks, which has interests in numerous other media ventures; GE Plastics, a specialist in high-performance engineered plastics used in the office equipment, automotive, building and construction, and high-tech industries; GE Power Systems, which is a world leader in gas, steam, and hydroelectric turbines and generators for power production and other applications; and GE Transportation Systems, the number one maker of diesel freight locomotives in North America. GE operates in more than 100 countries worldwide, and generates approximately 43 percent of its revenues outside the United States.

Late 19th Century: The Edison Era

Thomas Edison established himself in the 1870s as an inventor after devising, at the age of 23, an improved stock ticker. He subsequently began research on an electric light as a replacement for gas light, the standard method of illumination at the time. In 1876 Edison moved into a laboratory in Menlo Park, New Jersey. Two years later, in 1878, Edison established, with the help of his friend Grosvenor Lowry, the Edison Electric

Light Company with a capitalization of $300,000. Edison received half of the new company's shares on the agreement that he work on developing an incandescent lighting system. The major problem Edison and his team of specialists faced was finding an easy-to-produce filament that would resist the passage of electrical current in the bulb for a long time. He triumphed only a year after beginning research when he discovered that common sewing thread, once carbonized, worked in the laboratory. For practical applications, however, he switched to carbonized bamboo.

Developing an electrical lighting system for a whole community involved more than merely developing an electric bulb; the devices that generated, transmitted, and controlled electric power also had to be invented. Accordingly, Edison organized research into all of these areas and in 1879, the same year that he produced an electric bulb, he also constructed the first dynamo, or direct-current generator.

The first application of electric lighting was on the steamship *Columbia* in 1880. In that same year, Edison constructed a three-mile-long trial electric railroad at his Menlo Park laboratory. The first individual system of electric lighting came in 1881, in a printing plant. But the first full-scale public application of the Edison lighting system was actually made in London, at the Holborn Viaduct. The first system in the United States came soon after when Pearl Street Station was opened in New York City. Components of the system were manufactured by different companies, some of which were organized by Edison; lamps came from the parent company, dynamos from the Edison Machine Works, and switches from Bergmann & Company of New York. In 1886 the Edison Machine Works was moved from New Jersey to Schenectady, New York.

While these developments unfolded at Edison's company, the Thomson-Houston Company was formed from the American Electric Company, founded by Elihu Thomson and Edwin Houston, who held several patents for their development of arc lighting. Some of their electrical systems differed from Edison's through the use of alternating-current (AC) equipment, which can transmit over longer distances than DC systems. By the early 1890s the spread of electrification was threatened by the conflict between the two technologies and by patent deadlocks, which prevented further developments because of patent-infringement problems.

By 1889, Edison had consolidated all of his companies under the name of the Edison General Electric Company. Three years later, in 1892, this company was merged with the Thomson-Houston Electric Company to form the General Electric Company. Although this merger was the turning point in the electrification of the United States, it resulted in Edison's resignation from GE. He had been appointed to the board of directors but he attended only one board meeting, and sold all of his shares in 1894, though he remained a consultant to General Electric and continued to collect royalties on his patents. The president of the new company was Charles A. Coffin, a former shoe manufacturer who had been the leading figure at Thomson-Houston. Coffin remained president of General Electric until 1913, and was chairman thereafter until 1922.

In 1884, Frank Julian Sprague, an engineer who had worked on electric systems with Edison, resigned and formed the Sprague Electric Railway and Motor Company, which built the first large-scale electric streetcar system in the United States, in Richmond, Virginia. In 1889 Sprague's company was purchased by Edison's. In the meantime, the two other major electric-railway companies in the United States had merged with Thomson-Houston, so that by the time General Electric was formed, it was the major supplier of electrified railway systems in the United States.

One year after the formation of General Electric, the company won a bid for the construction of large AC motors in a textile mill in South Carolina. The motors were the largest manufactured by General Electric at the time and were so successful that orders soon began to flow in from other industries such as cement, paper, and steel. In that same year, General Electric began its first venture into the field of power transmission with the opening of the Redlands-Mill Creek power line in California, and in 1894 the company constructed a massive power-transmission line at Niagara Falls. Meanwhile the company's electric-railroad ventures produced an elevated electric train surrounding the fairgrounds of the Chicago World's Fair in 1893. Electrification of existing rail lines began two years later.

Early 20th Century: Bolstering Electrification Operations and Moving Beyond Them

By the turn of the century General Electric was manufacturing everything involved in the electrification of the United States: generators to produce electricity, transmission equipment to carry power, industrial electric motors, electric light bulbs, and electric locomotives. It is important to any understanding of the evolution of GE to realize that though it was diverse from the beginning, all of its enterprises centered on the electrification program. It is also worth noting that it operated in the virtual absence of competition. General Electric and the Westinghouse Electric Company had been competitors, but the companies entered into a patent pool in 1896.

In 1900 GE established the first industrial laboratory in the United States. Up to that point, research had been carried out in universities or in private laboratories similar to Edison's Menlo Park laboratory. Initially, the lab was set up in a barn behind the house of one of the researchers, but the lab was moved in 1900 to Schenectady, New York, after it was destroyed in a fire. The head of the research division was a professor from the Massachusetts Institute of Technology. The importance of research at General Electric cannot be underestimated, for GE has been awarded more patents over the years than any other company in the United States.

Key Dates:

1878: Thomas Edison establishes the Edison Electric Light Company.

1889: Edison has, by this date, consolidated all of his companies under the name of the Edison General Electric Company.

1892: Edison's company merges with the Thomson-Houston Electric Company to form the General Electric Company (GE).

1894: Edison sells all his shares in the company, remaining a consultant to GE.

1900: GE establishes the first industrial laboratory in the United States.

1903: Stanley Electric Manufacturing Company of Pittsfield, Massachusetts, a manufacturer of transformers, is acquired.

1906: The first GE major appliance, an electric range, is introduced.

1918: GE merges with Pacific Electric Heating Company, maker of the Hotpoint iron, and Hughes Electric Heating Company, maker of an electric range; and forms the Edison Electric Appliance Company to sell products under the GE and Hotpoint brands.

1919: GE, AT&T, and Westinghouse form the Radio Corporation of America (RCA) to develop radio technology.

1924: GE exits from the utilities business following government antitrust action.

1930: Company sells its holdings in RCA because of antitrust considerations.

1938: GE introduces the fluorescent lamp.

1943: General Electric Capital Corporation is established.

1949: Under antitrust pressure, the company is forced to release its light bulb patents to other companies.

1955: The U.S. Navy launches the submarine *Seawolf*, which is powered by a GE nuclear reactor.

1957: GE receives a license from the Atomic Energy Commission to operate a nuclear power plant; an enormous appliance manufacturing site, Appliance Park, in Louisville, Kentucky, is completed.

1961: The company pleads guilty to price fixing on electrical equipment and is fined nearly half a million dollars.

1976: GE spends $2.2 billion to acquire Utah International, a major coal, copper, uranium, and iron miner and a producer of natural gas and oil.

1981: John F. (Jack) Welch, Jr., becomes chairman and CEO.

1986: Company acquires RCA, which includes the National Broadcasting Company (NBC), for $6.4 billion; Employers Reinsurance is also acquired for $1.1 billion, as well as an 80 percent stake in Kidder Peabody.

1994: Company liquidates Kidder Peabody.

1998: Revenues surpass the $100 billion mark.

During the early decades of the 20th century General Electric made further progress in its established fields, and also made its first major diversification. In 1903 General Electric bought the Stanley Electric Manufacturing Company of Pittsfield, Massachusetts, a manufacturer of transformers. Its founder, William Stanley, was the developer of the transformer.

By this time GE's first light bulbs were in obvious need of improvement. Edison's bamboo filament was replaced in 1904 by metalized carbon developed by the company's research lab. That filament, in turn, was replaced several years later by a tungsten-filament light bulb when William Coolidge, a GE researcher, discovered a process to render the durable metal more pliable. This light bulb was so rugged and well suited for use in automobiles, railroad cars, and street cars that it was still employed in the 1990s. In 1913, two other innovations came out of the GE labs: Irving Langmuir discovered that gas-filled bulbs were more efficient and reduced bulb blackening. To this day virtually all bulbs over 40 watts are gas-filled.

The first high-vacuum, hot-cathode X-ray tube, known as the "Coolidge tube," was also developed in 1913. Coolidge's research into tungsten had played an important role in the development of the X-ray tube. The device, which combined a vacuum with a heated tungsten filament and tungsten target, has been the foundation of virtually all X-ray tubes produced ever since, and its development laid the foundation for medical technology operations at General Electric.

Perhaps GE's most important development in the early part of this century was its participation in the development of the high-speed steam turbine in conjunction with English, Swedish, and other inventors. Until this invention, all electricity (except hydroelectric) had been produced by generators that turned at no more than 100 rpm, which limited the amount of electricity a single unit could produce. An independent inventor had come up with a design for a very-high-speed steam turbine before the turn of the century, but it took five years of research before GE could construct a working model. By 1901, however, a 500-kilowatt, 1,200-rpm turbine generator was operating. Orders for the turbines followed almost immediately, and by 1903 a 5,000-kilowatt turbine was in use at Chicago's Commonwealth Edison power company.

Such rapid progress led to rapid obsolescence as well, and the Chicago units were replaced within six years. As a result, GE shops in Schenectady were soon overflowing with business. By 1910 the volume of the company's trade in turbine generators had tripled and GE had sold almost one million kilowatts of power capacity. At the same time, General Electric scientists were also researching the gas turbine. Their investigations eventually resulted in the first flight of an airplane equipped with a turbine-powered supercharger.

In the early days of electric power, electricity was produced only during evening hours, since electric lighting was not needed during the day and there were no other products to use electricity. GE, as the producer of both electricity-generating equipment and electricity-consuming devices, naturally sought to expand both ends of its markets. The first major expansion of the General Electric product line was made in the first decade of the 20th century. Before the turn of the century, light bulbs and electric fans were GE's only consumer product. One of the first household appliances GE began to market was a toaster in 1905. The following year the company attempted to market an electric range. The unwieldy device consisted of a wooden table top equipped with electric griddles, pans, toasters, waffle irons, pots, and a coffee maker, each with its own retractable cord to go into any one of 30 plugs. The range was followed by a commercial electric refrigerator in 1911 and by an experimental household refrigerator six years later.

At the same time two other companies in the United States were producing electric devices for the home. The Pacific Electric Heating Company produced the first electric appliance to be readily accepted by the public: the Hotpoint iron. The Hughes Electric Heating Company produced and marketed an electric range. In 1918 all three companies were prospering, but to avoid competition with one another, they agreed upon a merger. The new company combined GE's heating-device section with Hughes and Pacific to form the Edison Electric Appliance Company, whose products bore either the GE or the Hotpoint label.

GE's first diversification outside electricity came with its establishment of a research staff to investigate plastics. This occurred primarily at the prompting of Charles P. Steinmetz, a brilliant mathematician who had been with the company since the 1890s. All of the initial work by this group was devoted to coatings, varnishes, insulation, and other products related to electrical wiring, so that even this diversification was tied in to electrification.

A more radical branching of GE's activities occurred in 1912, when Ernst Alexanderson, a GE employee, was approached by a radio pioneer looking for a way to expand the range of wireless sets into higher frequencies. Alexanderson worked for almost a decade on the project before he succeeded in creating electromagnetic waves that could span continents, instead of the short distances to which radios had been limited. In 1922, General Electric introduced its own radio station, WGY, in Schenectady. In 1919, at the request of the government, GE formed, in partnership with AT&T and Westinghouse, the Radio Corporation of America (RCA) to develop radio technology. GE withdrew from the venture in 1930, when antitrust considerations came to the fore. General Electric also operated two experimental shortwave stations that had a global range.

Other developments at General Electric contributed to the progress of the radio. Irving Langmuir had developed the electron tube. This tube, necessary for amplifying the signals in Alexanderson's radio unit, was capable of operating at very high power. Other important developments by scientists at General Electric included the world's first practical loudspeaker and a method for recording complex sound on film that is still in use today.

Developments continued apace at GE in the electric motor field. In 1913 the U.S. Navy commissioned General Electric to build the first ship to be powered by turbine motors rather than steam. In 1915 the first turbine-propelled battleship sailed forth, and within a few years, all of the navy's large ships were equipped with electric power. General Electric also owned several utility companies that generated electrical power, but in 1924 GE left the utilities business when the federal government brought antitrust action against the company.

During the Great Depression the company introduced a variety of consumer items such as mixers, vacuum cleaners, air conditioners, and washing machines. GE also introduced the first affordable electric refrigerator in the late 1920s. It was designed by a Danish toolmaker, Christian Steenstrup, who later supervised mechanical research at the GE plant in Schenectady. In addition, GE introduced its first electric dishwasher in 1932, the same year that consumer financing of personal appliances was introduced.

Also in 1932 the first Nobel Prize ever awarded to a scientist not affiliated with a university went to Irving Langmuir for his work at GE on surface chemistry, research that had grown out of his earlier work on electron tubes. The years that followed witnessed a steady stream of innovation in electronics from the GE labs. These included the photoelectric-relay principle, rectifier tubes that eliminated batteries from home receivers, the cathode-ray tube, and glass-to-metal seals for vacuum tubes. Many of these developments in electronics were crucial to the growth of radio broadcasting.

The broadcasting division of General Electric achieved a breakthrough in the late 1930s. The company had been developing a mode of transmission known as frequency modulation (FM) as an alternative to the prevailing amplitude modulation (AM). In 1939 a demonstration conducted for the Federal Communications Commission proved that FM had less static and noise. GE began broadcasting in FM the following year.

Of course, the light bulb was not forgotten in this broadening of research activity at General Electric. The world's first mercury-vapor lamp was introduced in 1934, followed four years later by the fluorescent lamp. The latter produced light using half the power of incandescent bulbs, with about twice the lifespan. Less than a year after the introduction of the fluorescent light, General Electric introduced the sealed-beam automotive headlight.

Even though production of convenience items for the consumer halted during World War II, the war proved profitable for General Electric, whose revenues quadrupled during the war. The president of General Electric at the time, Charles Wilson, joined the War Production Board in 1942. GE produced more than 50 different types of radar for the armed forces and over 1,500 marine power plants for the navy and merchant marine. The company, using technology developed by the Englishman Frank Whittle, also conducted research on jet engines for aircraft. The Bell XP-59, the first U.S. jet aircraft, flew in 1942 powered by General Electric engines. By the end of the war this technology helped General Electric develop the nation's first turboprop engine.

Postwar Growth and Difficulties

When production of consumer goods resumed immediately after the war, GE promptly found itself in another antitrust battle. The government discovered that GE controlled 85 percent of the light bulb industry—55 percent through its own output and the other 30 percent through licensees. In 1949 the court forced GE to release its patents to other companies.

In this period the first true product diversifications came out of GE's research labs. In the 1940s a GE scientist discovered a way to produce large quantities of silicone, a material GE had been investigating for a long time. In 1947 GE opened a plant to produce silicones, which allowed the introduction of many products using silicone as a sealant or lubricant.

Meanwhile, as research innovation blossomed and postwar business boomed, the company began an employee relations policy known as ''Boulwarism,'' from Lemuel Boulware, the manager who established the policy. The policy, which eliminated much of the bargaining involved in labor-management relations, included the extension by GE to union leaders of a non-negotiable contract offer.

During the late 1940s General Electric embarked on a study of nuclear power and constructed a laboratory specifically for the task. Company scientists involved in an earlier attempt to separate U-235 from natural uranium were developing nuclear power plants for naval propulsion by 1946. In 1955 the navy launched the submarine *Seawolf*, the world's first nuclear-powered vessel, with a reactor developed by General Electric. In 1957 the company received a license from the Atomic Energy Commission to operate a nuclear-power reactor, the first license granted in the United States for a privately owned generating station. That same year GE's consumer-appliance operations got a big boost when an enormous manufacturing site, Appliance Park, in Louisville, Kentucky, was completed. The flow of new GE products—hair dryers, skillets, electronic ovens, self-cleaning ovens, electric knives—continued.

Other innovations to come from GE labs during the 1950s included an automatic pilot for jet aircraft, Lexan polycarbonate resin, the first all-transistor radio, jet turbine engines, gas turbines for electrical power generation, and a technique for fabricating diamonds.

Antitrust problems continued to vex the company throughout the postwar years. In 1961 the Justice Department indicted 29 companies, of which GE was the biggest, for price fixing on electrical equipment. All the defendants pleaded guilty. GE's fine was almost half a million dollars, damages it paid to utilities who had purchased price-fixed equipment came to at least $50 million, and three GE managers received jail sentences and several others were forced to leave the company.

During the 1960s and 1970s GE grew in all fields. In 1961 it opened a research center for aerospace projects, and by the end of the decade had more than 6,000 employees involved in 37 projects related to the moon landing. In the 1950s General Electric entered the computer business. This venture, however, proved to be such a drain on the company's profits that GE sold its computer business to Honeywell in 1971.

By the late 1960s, GE's management began to feel that the company had become too large for its existing structures to accommodate. Accordingly, the company instituted a massive organizational restructuring. Under this restructuring program, the number of distinct operating units within the company was cut from more than 200 to 43. Each new section operated in a

particular market and was headed by a manager who reported to management just beneath the corporate policy board. The sections were classified into one of three categories—growth, stability, or no-growth—to facilitate divestment of unprofitable units.

When this reorganization was complete, General Electric made what was at the time the largest corporate purchase ever. In December 1976 GE paid $2.2 billion for Utah International, a major coal, copper, uranium, and iron miner and a producer of natural gas and oil. The company did 80 percent of its business in foreign countries. Within a year Utah International was contributing 18 percent of GE's total earnings.

The divestiture of its computer business had left GE without any capacity for manufacturing integrated circuits and the high-technology products in which they are used. In 1975 a study of the company's status concluded that GE, one of the first U.S. electrical companies, had fallen far behind in electronics. As a result, GE spent some $385 million to acquire Intersil, a semiconductor manufacturer; Calma, a producer of computer-graphics equipment; and four software producers. The company also spent more than $100 million to expand its microelectronics facilities.

Other fields in which GE excelled were in trouble by the mid-1970s, most notably nuclear power. As plant construction costs skyrocketed and environmental concerns grew, the company's nuclear-power division began to lose money. GE's management, however, was convinced that the problem was temporary and that sales would pick up in the future. When by 1980 General Electric had received no new orders for plants in five years, nuclear power began to look more and more like a prime candidate for divestment. GE eventually pulled out of all aspects of the nuclear-power business except for providing service and fuel to existing plants and conducting research on nuclear energy.

Though General Electric's growth was tremendous during the 1970s and earnings tripled between 1971 and 1981, the company's stock performance was mediocre. GE had become so large and was involved in so many activities that some regarded its fortunes as capable only of following the fortunes of the country as a whole.

1981 and Beyond: The Jack Welch Era

GE's economic problems were mirrored by its managerial reshuffling. When John F. (Jack) Welch, Jr., became chairman and CEO in 1981, General Electric entered a period of radical change. Over the next several years, GE bought 338 businesses and product lines for $11.1 billion and sold 232 for $5.9 billion. But Welch's first order of business was to return much of the control of the company to the periphery. Although he decentralized management, he retained predecessor Reginald Jones's system of classifying divisions according to their performance. His goal was to make GE number one or two in every field of operation.

One branch of GE's operations that came into its own during this period was the General Electric Credit Corporation, founded in 1943. Between 1979 and 1984, its assets doubled, to $16 billion, due primarily to expansion into such markets as the leasing and selling of heavy industrial goods, inventories, real estate, and insurance. In addition, the leasing operations provided the parent company with tax shelters from accelerated depreciation on equipment developed by GE and then leased by the credit corporation.

Factory automation became a major activity at GE during the early 1980s. GE's acquisitions of Calma and Intersil were essential to this program. In addition, GE entered into an agreement with Japan's Hitachi to manufacture and market Hitachi's industrial robots in the United States. GE itself spent $300 million to robotize its locomotive plant in Erie, Pennsylvania. Two years later GE's aircraft-engine business also participated in an air force plant-modernization program and GE later manufactured the engines for the controversial B-1B bomber.

In 1986 General Electric made several extremely important purchases. The largest was the $6.4 billion purchase of the Radio Corporation of American (RCA), the company GE had helped to found in 1919. RCA's National Broadcasting Company (NBC), the leading U.S. television network, brought GE into the broadcasting business in full force. Although both RCA and GE were heavily involved in consumer electronics, the match was regarded by industry analysts as beneficial, since GE had been shifting from manufacturing into service and high technology. After the merger, almost 80 percent of GE's earnings came from services and high technology, compared to 50 percent six years earlier. GE divested itself of RCA's famous David Sarnoff Research Center, since GE's labs made it redundant. In 1987 GE also sold its own and RCA's television-manufacturing businesses to the French company Thomson in exchange for Thomson's medical diagnostics business.

GE justified the merger by citing the need for size to compete effectively with large Japanese conglomerates. Critics, however, claimed that GE was running from foreign competition by increasing its defense contracts (to almost 20 percent of its total business) and its service business, both of which were insulated from foreign competition.

In 1986 GE also purchased the Employers Reinsurance Corporation, a financial services company, from Texaco, for $1.1 billion, and an 80 percent interest in Kidder Peabody and Company, an investment banking firm, for $600 million, greatly broadening its financial services division. Although Employer's Reinsurance contributed steadily to GE's bottom line following its purchase, Kidder Peabody lost $48 million in 1987, in part due to the settlement of insider trading charges. Kidder Peabody did come back in 1988 to contribute $46 million in earnings, but the acquisition still troubled some analysts. GE owned 100 percent of Kidder Peabody by 1990.

General Electric's operations were divided into three business groups in the early 1990s: technology, service, and manufacturing. Its manufacturing operations, traditionally the core of the company, accounted for roughly one-third of the company's earnings. Still, GE continued to pour more than $1 billion annually into research and development of manufactured goods. Much of that investment was directed at energy conservation— more efficient light bulbs, jet engines, and electrical power transmission methods, for example.

In 1992 GE signaled its intent to step up overseas activity with the purchase of 50 percent of the European appliance business of Britain's General Electric Company (GEC). The two companies also made agreements related to their medical, power systems, and electrical distribution businesses. Welch said that his aim was to make GE the nation's largest company. To that end, General Electric continued to restructure its existing operations in an effort to become more competitive in all of its businesses. Most importantly, the company launched an aggressive campaign to become dominant in the growing financial services sector.

GE's aggressive initiatives related to financial services reflected the fact that the service sector represented more than three-quarters of the U.S. economy going into the mid-1990s. Furthermore, several service industries, including financial, were growing rapidly. GE's revenues from its giant NBC and GE Capital divisions, for example, rose more than 12 percent annually from about $14.3 billion in 1988 to more than $25 billion in 1994. Encouraged by those gains, GE's merger and acquisition activity intensified. For example, in 1994 the company offered a $2.2 billion bid for Kemper Corp., a diversified insurance and financial services company (it retracted the bid in 1995). GE's sales from services as a percentage of total revenues increased from 30 percent in 1988 to nearly 45 percent in 1994, and neared 60 percent by 1996. The troubled Kidder Peabody unit remained a drag on GE's services operations, leading to the company's late 1994 decision to liquidate the unit. As part of the liquidation, GE sold some Kidder Peabody assets and operations to Paine Webber Group Inc. for $657 million.

In contrast to its service businesses, GE's total manufacturing receipts remained stagnant at about $35 billion. Nevertheless, restructuring was paying off in the form of fat profit margins in many of its major product divisions. Importantly, GE made significant strides with its Aircraft Engine Group. Sales fell from $8 billion in 1991 to less than $6 billion in 1995, but profit margins rose past 18 percent after dipping to just 12 percent in 1993. Reflective of restructuring efforts in other GE divisions, the company accomplished the profit growth by slashing the engineering workforce from 10,000 to 4,000 and reducing its overall Aircraft Engine Group payroll by about 50 percent, among other cost-cutting moves.

Despite a global economic downturn in the early 1990s, GE managed to keep aggregate sales from its technology, service, and manufacturing operations stable at about $60 billion annually. More importantly, net income surged steadily from $3.9 billion in 1989 to $5.9 billion in 1994, excluding losses in the latter year from Kidder Peabody operations. In 1994, in fact, General Electric was the most profitable of the largest 900 U.S. corporations, and was trailed by General Motors, Ford, and Exxon. Revenues reached $70 billion by 1995, the same year that the company's market value exceeded $100 billion for the first time.

The late 1990s saw General Electric reach a number of milestones. In 1996 the company celebrated its 100th year as part of the Dow Jones Index; GE was the only company remaining from the original list. That year, NBC joined with Microsoft Corporation in launching MSNBC, a 24-hour cable television news channel and Internet news service. Overall revenues exceeded the $100 billion mark for the first time in 1998, while the continuing stellar growth at GE Capital led that unit to generate nearly half of GE's revenues by the end of the decade.

Acquisitions in the late 1990s centered on two of the company's growth initiatives: services and globalization. In 1996 the GE Appliances division acquired a 73 percent interest in DAKO S.A., the leading manufacturer of gas ranges in Brazil. GE Capital Services expanded in Japan through the 1996 purchase of an 80 percent stake in Marubeni Car System Co., an auto leasing firm; the 1998 acquisitions of Koei Credit and the consumer finance business of Lake Corporation; and the 1998 formation of GE Edison Life following the purchase of the sales operations of Toho Mutual Life Insurance, which made GE Capital the first foreign company involved in the Japanese life insurance market. In early 1999 GE Capital made its largest deal in Japan to date with the purchase of the leasing business of Japan Leasing Corporation, a business with $7 billion in leasing assets. Then in late 1999 GE Capital agreed to purchase the remaining assets of Toho Mutual for ¥240 billion (US$2.33 billion); Toho had collapsed during 1999 after suffering huge losses from the thousands of old, unprofitable policies in its portfolio, and a large portion of its liabilities were to be covered by Japan's life insurance association. Expansion also continued in Europe for GE Capital, highlighted by the 1997 acquisition of Woodchester, one of the largest financial services companies in Ireland. Overall, GE spent some $30 billion during the 1990s in completing more than 130 European acquisitions.

Under Welch's leadership, General Electric in the late 1990s also adopted "six sigma," a quality control and improvement initiative pioneered by Motorola, Inc. and AlliedSignal Inc. The program aimed to cut costs by reducing errors or defects. GE claimed that by 1998 six sigma was yielding $1 billion in annual savings. The company also continued to restructure as necessary, including taking a $2.3 billion charge in late 1997 to close redundant facilities and shift production to cheaper labor markets. During 1999 General Electric adopted a fourth growth initiative, e-business (globalization, services, and six sigma being the other three). Like many longstanding companies, GE reacted cautiously when the Internet began its late 1990s explosion. But once he was convinced of the new medium's potential, Welch quickly adopted e-commerce as a key to the company's future growth. Among the early ventures was a plan to begin selling appliances through Home Depot Inc.'s web site, a move aimed at revitalizing lagging appliance sales.

In late 1999 Welch announced that he planned to retire in April 2001 but he did not name a successor. At the time, General Electric was one of the world's fastest growing and most profitable companies, and boasted a market capitalization of $505 billion, second only to Microsoft. Revenues for 1999 increased 11 percent to $111.63 billion while net income rose 15 percent to $10.72 billion. These figures also represented huge gains since Welch took over in 1981, when the company posted profits of $1.6 billion on sales of $27.2 billion. According to *Barron's,* $100 invested in GE stock in 1981 would have been worth $4,676 in early 1999. GE and Welch were consistently mentioned as among the most admired companies and managers, respectively, in the world. It appeared likely that Welch, only the eighth CEO in GE's long history, would leave his successor a mighty challenge: continuing one of the most remarkable periods of achievement for a company in all of business history.

Principal Subsidiaries

Caribe General Electric Products, Inc.; GE Aircraft Engines Maintenance Services, Ltd. Wales (U.K.); GE Appliances Parts LLC; GE Energy Parts, Inc.; GE Engine Services Distribution, LLC; GE Fanuc Automation North America Inc. (55%); GE Information Services, Inc.; GE Lighting Tungsram RT (Hungary); GE Plastics Pacific Pte. Ltd. (Singapore); GE Power Systems Licensing Inc.; GE Quartz Inc.; GE Superabrasives Ireland (Bermuda); GE Yokogawa Medical Systems, Ltd. (Japan; 75%); General Electric Canadian Holdings Limited (Canada); General Electric Capital Services, Inc.; General Electric Capital Corporation; GE Global Insurance Holding Corporation; General Electric International, Inc.; General Electric Plastics B.V. (Netherlands); National Broadcasting Company, Inc.; Nuovo Pignone SpA (Italy; 92%); RCA Thomson Licensing Corporation (96%).

Principal Operating Units

GE Aircraft Engines; GE Appliances; GE Capital Services; GE Industrial Systems; GE Lighting; GE Medical Systems; National Broadcasting Company; GE Plastics; GE Power Systems; GE Transportation Systems.

Principal Competitors

ABB Ltd.; Agilent Technologies, Inc.; American International Group, Inc.; Alstom S.A.; Bank of America Corporation; Caterpillar Inc.; CIGNA Corporation; Cooper Industries, Inc.; Electrolux AB; General Motors Corporation; General Re Corporation; GTE Corporation; Hitachi, Ltd.; ITT Industries, Inc.; Johnson Controls, Inc.; Koninklijke Philips Electronics N.V.; Matsushita Electric Industrial Co., Ltd.; Maytag Corporation; Mitsubishi Group; Mitsui Group; The News Corporation Limited; Polaroid Corporation; Raytheon Company; Rockwell International Corporation; Rohm and Haas Company; Rolls-Royce plc; Siemens AG; Textron Inc.; Thyssen Krupp AG; Time Warner Inc.; Toshiba Corporation; United Technologies Corporation; U.S. Industries, Inc.; Viacom Inc.; The Walt Disney Company; Whirlpool Corporation.

Further Reading

Banks, Howard, "General Electric: Going with the Winners," *Forbes,* March 26, 1984, pp. 97+.

Bernstein, Aaron, Susan Jackson, and John Byrne, "Jack Cracks the Whip Again," *Business Week,* December 15, 1997, pp. 34–35.

Bongiorno, Lori, "Hot Damn, What a Year!," *Business Week,* March 6, 1995, pp. 98–100.

Brady, Diane, "How GE Locked Up That Boeing Order," *Business Week,* August 9, 1999, pp. 72, 74–75.

Byrne, John A., "Jack' A Close-up Look at How America's #1 Manager Runs GE," *Business Week,* June 8, 1998, pp. 90–95, 98–99, 102, 104–6, 110–11.

Byrne, John A., and Jennifer Reingold, "Who Will Step into Jack Welch's Shoes?," *Business Week,* December 21, 1998, pp. 37–38.

Carley, William M., "Power Ranger: GE Taps Trains Chief in Effort to Shore Up Troubled Energy Unit," *Wall Street Journal,* May 6, 1996, pp. A1+.

Carlson, W. Bernard, *Innovation As a Social Process: Elihu Thomson and the Rise of General Electric, 1870–1900,* New York: Cambridge University Press, 1991, 377 p.

Colvin, Geoffrey, "The Ultimate Manager," *Fortune,* November 22, 1999, pp. 185–87.

"A Conversation with Roberto Goizueta and Jack Welch," *Fortune,* December 11, 1995, pp. 96–99, 102.

Cox, James A., *A Century of Light,* New York: Benjamin, 1979, 224 p.

Curran, John, "GE Capital: Jack Welch's Secret Weapon," *Fortune,* November 10, 1997, pp. 116–20, 124, 126, 130, 132, 134.

Farrell, John, "GE Cuts Number in Layoff Plans," *Capital District Business Review,* October 31, 1994, p. 5.

Finn, Edwin A., Jr., "General Eclectic," *Forbes,* March 23, 1987, pp. 74+.

"GE Monkeys with Its Money Machine," *Fortune,* February 21, 1994, p. 81.

"GE: Not Recession Proof, but Recession Resistant," *Forbes,* March 15, 1975, p. 26.

Grant, Linda, "GE's 'Smart Bomb' Strategy," *Fortune,* July 21, 1997, pp. 109–110.

Griffiths, Dave, "GE + RCA = A Powerhouse Defense Contractor," *Business Week,* January 27, 1986, pp. 116+.

Grover, Ronald, and Mark Landler, "NBC Is No Longer a Feather in GE's Cap," *Business Week,* June 3, 1991, pp. 88+.

Hammond, John Winthrop, *Men and Volts: The Story of General Electric,* Philadelphia: Lippincott, 1941, 436 p.

Harris, Marilyn A., et al., "Can Jack Welch Reinvent GE?," *Business Week,* June 30, 1986, pp. 62+.

"Jack Welch's Lessons for Success," *Fortune,* January 25, 1993, p. 86.

Koenig, Peter, "If Europe's Dead, Why Is GE Investing Billions There?," *Fortune,* September 9, 1996, pp. 114–18.

Laing, Jonathan R., "Riding into the Sunset: Can Jack Welch's Successor at General Electric Hope to Inherit His Magic Touch?," *Barron's,* February 15, 1999, pp. 23–24, 26–27.

McClenahen, John S., "CEO of the Decade," *Industry Week,* November 15, 1999, p. 38.

Miller, John Anderson, *Men and Volts at War: The Story of General Electric in World War II,* New York: McGraw-Hill, 1947, 272 p.

Mitchell, Russell, "Jack Welch: How Good a Manager?," *Business Week,* December 14, 1987, pp. 92+.

Morrison, Ann M., "Trying to Bring GE to Life," *Fortune,* January 25, 1982, pp. 50+.

Murray, Matt, "GE Chairman Sets His Departure Date for 2001: Successor Remains Unclear," *Wall Street Journal,* November 3, 1999, p. B12.

——, "Late to the Web, GE Now Views Internet As Key to New Growth," *Wall Street Journal,* June 22, 1999, p. B1.

Norman, James R., "General Electric Is Stalking Big Game Again," *Business Week,* March 16, 1987, pp. 112+.

O'Boyle, Thomas F., *At Any Cost: Jack Welch, General Electric, and the Pursuit of Profit,* New York: Knopf, 1998, 449 p.

Pare, Terence P., "GE As a Service Company," *Fortune,* April 18, 1994, p. 16.

——, "Jack Welch's Nightmare on Wall Street," *Fortune,* September 5, 1994, p. 40.

Petre, Peter, "What Welch Has Wrought at GE," *Fortune,* July 7, 1986, pp. 42+.

Schatz, Ronald W., *The Electrical Workers: A History of Labor at General Electric and Westinghouse, 1923–1960,* Urbana: University of Illinois Press, 1983, 279 p.

Sherman, Stratford P., "Inside the Mind of Jack Welch," *Fortune,* March 27, 1989, pp. 38+.

Slater, Robert, *The New GE: How Jack Welch Revived an American Institution,* Homewood, Ill.: Business One Irwin, 1993, 295 p.

Smart, Tim, "GE's Money Machine," *Business Week,* March 8, 1993, pp. 62+.

——, "Jack Welch's Cyber-Czar," *Business Week,* August 5, 1996, pp. 82–83.

——, "Jack Welch's Encore," *Business Week,* October 28, 1996, pp. 154–60.

——, "Just Imagine If Times Were Good," *Business Week,* April 17, 1995, pp. 78–79.

Smart, Tim, Pete Engardio, and Geri Smith, "GE's Brave New World," *Business Week,* November 8, 1993, pp. 64+.

Stewart, Thomas A., "GE Keeps Those Ideas Coming," *Fortune,* August 12, 1991, pp. 40+.

——, "See Jack. See Jack Run Europe," *Fortune,* September 27, 1999, pp. 124–27, 130, 132, 136.

Tichy, Noel M., and Stratford Sherman, *Control Your Destiny or Someone Else Will: How Jack Welch Is Making General Electric the World's Most Competitive Corporation,* New York: Doubleday, 1993, 384 p.

Vogel, Todd, "Big Changes Are Galvanizing General Electric," *Business Week,* December 18, 1989, pp. 100+.

Wise, George, *Willis R. Whitney, General Electric, and the Origins of U.S. Industrial Research,* New York: Columbia University Press, 1985, 375 p.

—Dave Mote
—updated by David E. Salamie

Gilbane, Inc.

7 Jackson Walkway
Providence, Rhode Island 02903
U.S.A.
Telephone: (401) 456-5800
Fax: (401) 456-5936
Web site: http://www.gilbaneco.com

Private Company
Incorporated: 1873
Employees: 1,100
Sales: $2.2 billion (1999 est.)
NAIC: 233320 Commercial and Institutional Building
Construction

Gilbane, Inc., located in Providence, Rhode Island, is a privately owned company that has been in the same family for over 125 years. Gilbane is one of the oldest and largest building companies in the United States and has two subsidiaries: Gilbane Building Company and Gilbane Properties, Inc. Together these businesses serve the industrial, institutional, and commercial markets, offering everything from financing and planning to development, management, and construction. A member of the *Forbes* 500 list of private companies, Gilbane also ranks as the fifth largest general building contractor in the nation.

1873 to the 1960s: Small Beginnings to Big Growth

In 1873 William Gilbane was an Irish immigrant and a talented carpenter. He used his talents to work for others until he decided to begin a company of his own. Unknown to him, that decision secured a future for the next four generations of his family. He founded Gilbane, Inc. in Providence, Rhode Island, as a small family-run carpentry and general contracting business serving the local area.

The company grew steadily and passed to the second and then third generation of the Gilbane family. The third generation of the family, brothers Thomas and William, helped the company to greater expansion during their tenure. Both 1933

graduates of Brown University, they led the company through a tremendous expansion period.

During World War II, Gilbane prospered, like many other U.S. companies, because of the war effort. For Gilbane, the growth came in the form of Navy contracts, and that growth spurred on additional success in the coming years.

1970s–80s: Diversifying for Success

In 1970 Gilbane, Inc. established Gilbane Properties (GPI) as the subsidiary to handle project development, financing, and real estate. GPI was designed to work with customers from start to finish on building projects. The subsidiary's specialties included alternative capitalization financing, needs analysis, negotiation of economic incentives, ownership transactions, debt/equity underwriting, and build-to-suit options. The corporation's other subsidiary, Gilbane Building Company, continued to be a part of high profile projects such as the National Air and Space Museum in Washington, D.C., in 1976, and the 1980 Winter Olympics facilities in Lake Placid, New York.

In 1981, Thomas F. Gilbane died at the age of 70, leaving his brother, William to lead the company through the next years. The firm helped build everything from skyscrapers to memorials and sometimes even helped build a bridge to better communication. In 1983, Gilbane assisted in a major economic summit conference in Williamsburg, Virginia. Seven heads of state, some 1,500 guests, and up to 6,000 members of the media met to discuss the economy, and the Gilbane Building Company set up the press facilities for the event at William and Mary College.

1990s: Recession and Recovery

The early part of the 1990s were a difficult time for the building industry, due to the interrelated causes of recession and loss of building contracts. Yet by 1992, though the building industry was still struggling to recover, Gilbane Building Company saw a substantial increase in new business, partially due to high-profile projects such as the international terminal at O'Hare International Airport and the renovation project at Chicago Public Schools. In an interview with *Crain's Chicago*

Company Perspectives:

Gilbane: An organization of superior employees dedicated to providing quality construction, real estate development and related services.

Business, Joseph F. Clare, vice-president of Gilbane Building Company noted that competition was more intense than a decade before, but Gilbane succeeded in weathering the increased level of competition.

In 1996, 26 years after the death of his brother and business partner, Thomas Gilbane, William Gilbane, Sr., chairman and former CEO of Gilbane, Inc., died. He was 87 years old. The reins of the company passed to yet another descendant of the company's founder, Paul J. Choquette, Jr. Choquette joined the company in 1969 and had graduated from Brown University and Harvard Law School.

By 1997 the building market had finally recovered and contractors were enjoying a growth period. From 1995 to 1996, there was an increase of 15.7 percent in revenues in the industry. In 1996, Gilbane was listed fourth on the list of the top 50 U.S. general building contractors, behind Centex Construction Group, The Turner Corporation, and Bovis, Inc.

Gilbane Building Company Senior Vice-President Alfred K. Potter was quoted in an article in *Engineering News-Record* about the industry's recent growth. "I'm optimistic about the future because the market has the fundamentals—economics, corporate profitability, demographics—to continue with strength for the next couple of years," he said.

One of the major challenges for the Gilbane Building Company was communication. In 1995, Gilbane did not even have voice-mail in the corporate offices. However, when it came time to evaluate and plan a state-of-the-art communication system, Gilbane explored the options and then partnered with other companies to come up with an innovative solution to connectivity.

With 21 offices across the nation and 150 different job sites each year, Gilbane needed a way for employees and customers to communicate effectively. The company partnered with another Rhode Island corporation, Atrion Networking Corp., to meet its needs. With the installation of the new system, job site managers now had easy access to PCs and could swiftly send and receive everything from voice to forms to Computer Aided Design (CAD) drawings.

In 1997, Gilbane Building Company received the Build America Award from the Associated General Contractors of America for its work on the Baltimore Convention Center in Baltimore, Maryland. The next year, Gilbane was awarded the prize again for the design and construction of the Wallens Ridge State Prison.

In 1999, Gilbane Building Company, with $2.2 billion in revenues, was ranked fifth on the annual list of general building contractors as selected by *Engineering News Record.* In the same magazine, the company was ranked first in the pharmaceutical plants and research and development laboratory

market, second in education and corrections, and in the top ten in several other areas, including sports facilities and government offices.

Also in 1999, Gilbane was again awarded the Build America Award by the Associated General Contractors of America. The award honored the company for work on the historic renovation of the New Jersey Statehouse dome.

2000: High Profile Projects Continue

In 2000, Robert V. Gilbane was president of Gilbane Properties (GPI). The subsidiary continued to focus on helping businesses plan commercial real estate needs. Gilbane Building Company had a variety of projects planned and focused on several aspects of construction, including pharmaceutical, healthcare, and educational facilities.

In an article on Gilbane's web site, Chairman and CEO Paul J. Choquette, Jr., said, "Making a positive impact on the communities where we work is a driving force for Gilbane employees. Having an impact on the schools that will educate this country's next generation is a very satisfying feeling." Gilbane Building Company was involved with construction projects for 31 school districts, integrating the buildings with networks for the information age.

Gilbane continued to work with the nation's leading businesses, and its client list included eight of the most prominent *Fortune* 500 companies, namely General Motors Corporation, Exxon Corporation, General Electric Company, IBM, AT&T Corp., Mobil Corporation, Chrysler Corporation, and Pfizer, Inc. The company also worked with government agencies, universities, and sports organizations to offer innovative solutions to construction needs.

Gilbane, Inc. remained involved in all sectors of the construction and real estate industries including industrial, institutional, and commercial. The company had a history of steady growth and innovation, and could be expected to meet whatever challenges loomed ahead in the new century.

Principal Subsidiaries

Gilbane Building Company; Gilbane Properties, Inc.

Principal Divisions

Advanced Technologies Sector; Relocation Management Group.

Principal Competitors

McCarthy; Turner Corporation; Whiting-Turner; Centex Construction Group; Bovis, Inc.

Further Reading

Alexander, Erin, "Builders Feeling Pinch of Economy's Squeeze," *Crain's Chicago Business*, November 5, 1990, p. 23.

"Contractor Passes Reins to Parent Firm," *Richmond Times-Dispatch*, November 2, 1998.

"Contractor's Chairman William Gilbane Dies," *Engineering News Record*, January 15, 1996, p. 13.

"County Chooses Company to Oversee Building Reds Stadium," *Associated Press*, April 3, 2000.

"Gilbane Fights DBE Charge," *Engineering News-Record*, April 24, 1986, p. 64.

"Gilbane Fraud Suit Dropped," *Engineering News-Record*, November 6, 1986, p. 111.

Holsendolph, Ernest, "Summit Caterer: Big Business," *New York Times*, March 31, 1983, p. D1.

Long, Timothy, "Building the Foundation for Connectivity's Future," *Enterprise Partner*, April 12, 1999, p. 34.

Mendez, Adolfo, "Building Contractors Mirror Slow Economy," *Crain's Chicago Business*, November 2, 1992, p. 21.

Parrillo, Bill, "Bill Gilbane, Sr.: A Builder of the Tangible and Intangible," *Providence Journal-Bulletin*, January 10, 1996, p. 1C.

"Thomas Gilbane Dies; Industry Leader," *Engineering News-Record*, December 17, 1981, p. 143.

Tulacz, Gary J., and Angelo, William J., "Builders Finding Modest-Sized Jobs in Immodest Quantities," *Engineering News-Record*, May 26, 1997, p. 90.

—Shawna Brynildssen

Griffon Corporation

100 Jericho Quadrangle
Jericho, New York 11753
U.S.A.
Telephone: (516) 936-6644
Fax: (516) 938-5644
Web site: http://www.griffoncorp.com

Public Company
Incorporated: 1959 as Waldorf Controls Corp.
Employees: 5,400
Sales: $1.03 billion (fiscal 1999)
Stock Exchanges: New York Boston Chicago
    Philadelphia
Ticker Symbol: GFF
NAIC: 321911 Wood Window and Door Manufacturing;
    322221 Coated and Laminated Packaging Paper and
    Plastics Film Manufacturing; 326199 All Other
    Plastics Product Manufacturing; 332321 Metal
    Window and Door Manufacturing; 33429 Other
    Communications Equipment Manufacturing; 44411
    Home Centers; 44419 Other Building Material
    Dealers; 56179 Other Services to Buildings and
    Dwellings

Griffon Corporation is a diversified manufacturing company with operations in four business segments: garage doors, installation services, specialty plastic films, and electronic information and communication systems. The company name stands for a mythical beast—half-eagle, half-lion—and symbolizes the combined strength of its varied operations.

Booming Conglomerate: 1959–70

Griffon was founded in 1959 as Waldorf Controls Corp. but took the name Instrument Systems Corp. before the year was out. Located in College Point, Long Island, it made electronic and electromechanical products for military and government markets and was 25 percent-owned by Emerson Radio & Phonograph Corp. Sales and profits picked up after Edward J.

Garrett became chairman and president in 1964, and two younger brothers took high executive posts. The Garretts closed deficit-ridden plants and began seeking civilian markets while also successfully seeking government research-and-development contracts. Sales increased from $7.3 million in fiscal 1964 (the year ended September 30, 1964) to $25.76 million in fiscal 1967. The loss of $170,000 in the former year had been transformed into net income of $1.02 million in the latter.

In 1968 Instrument Systems, now headquartered in Huntington, Long Island, began selling shares on the American Stock Exchange. It now had 18 subsidiaries with plants throughout the United States and Canada. Among its notable acquisitions had been Telephonics Corp. Dating from 1934, this company, purchased in 1961, became the nucleus of the parent corporation's Electronics Group, which, besides making electronic devices for industry and defense, also produced other electronic equipment, audio equipment, motors, and even teaching machines. The Automotive Group manufactured special purpose trucks and trailers, automotive and hardware tools, and batteries and battery chargers. The Home Products Group made juvenile and outdoor furniture and decorative glassware and giftware. The Packaging Group designed and manufactured plastic packaging, plastic bags, and polystyrene-foam film and sheet materials. The Business Machine Group made calculators and data processors. The Building Products Group produced lighting fixtures and sheet-metal building products.

After receiving a $47 million contract from Boeing, Instrument Systems established a division to develop the technology for a mutliplex entertainment system for airline passengers. This system went into production in 1969 for the Boeing 747 with channels for music and movie audio. The system was also adopted for the Lockheed L-1011 and, later, for the Douglas DC-10. A heavy user of integrated circuits, Instrument Systems created a semiconductor division in 1970 and announced plans to build its own microelectronics manufacturing plant in Huntington. The company's Phonplex Corp. subsidiary was seeking customers for a proposed computer with voice-response capability. ''All it takes is a computer, a push button telephone and a solid-state memory bank of 'phonemes,' '' Edward Garrett told Gene Smith of the *New York Times* in 1971.

Shedding Unprofitable Divisions: 1974–83

Instrument Systems' ambitious plans were all but halted as the go-go 1960s turned into the recessionary 1970s. Wall Street soured on conglomerates, and the company's military business fell victim to budget cutbacks following the end of U.S. participation in the war in Vietnam. Profits peaked at $8.05 million in fiscal 1969 and net sales at $233.25 million in fiscal 1974. The company raised some money by selling one-fifth of its building products group, which became Buildex Inc., to the public. The plastics and packaging divisions—combined into a subsidiary, Plascor Inc., in 1974—were sold in 1976 for $13.3 million.

In 1975 the Garretts ran into resistance from recalcitrant shareholders, who repudiated $1.2 million in ten-year, uncollaterized company loans made to them in 1972 to finance their purchases of company stock. The loans, which were interest-free for the first five years, also provoked two stockholder lawsuits. Although these dissidents were seeking to punish management for poor results, ironically repudiation of the loans benefited the Garretts since they had bought company stock at prices that subsequently dropped sharply in the markets. Instrument Systems lost money in fiscal 1976 and 1977.

Edward Garrett suddenly fired his brothers in December 1978 and 33 other executives the following month. A lawsuit—later dropped—charged that Garrett had instituted a ''reign of terror'' because of a personality change following heart surgery. Instrument Systems, which moved its headquarters from Huntington to nearby Jericho in fiscal 1980, fell victim to the severe recession of 1980–82, losing $41.3 million during this period. Garrett responded by selling nine money-losing divisions and consolidating others. The company also converted debentures into stock five times in order to help reduce long-term debt from $72.2 million to a more manageable $16 million. Garrett died in 1982 and was succeeded as chairman by his son-in-law, Harvey Blau. Robert Balemian became president.

Branching Out Again in the 1980s and 1990s

Instrument Systems emerged from this ordeal leaner but profitable. Leading the way was Telephonics, which in 1981 received a five-year order worth about $100 million to supply the central integrated test system for Rockwell International

Corp.'s B-1B bomber. Telephonics was also developing integrated communications and radio control systems for the Navy's anti-submarine S-3A aircraft and LAMPS MK III helicopters and a new advanced audio communications system for NASA's Space Shuttle Orbiter Vehicle. Other businesses that remained under the parent company's corporate umbrella were the home furnishings and furniture-related operations, a specialty stainless steel hardware unit, and three companies providing aluminum lockboxes and bulk-mail containers to the U.S. Postal Service.

A shrewd acquisition was the 1986 purchase of Cincinnati-based Clopay Corp. in 1986 for about $40 million, including expenses. This company had been founded in 1859 as a wholesaler of paper and allied products and originally incorporated in 1889 as Seinheiser Paper Co. It acquired plastic films in 1952 and garage doors in 1966. By 1992 Clopay was the nation's leading manufacturer and retail supplier of residential garage doors, and also the leading supplier of plastic liners for diapers, surgical gowns, and drapes, and films and laminates for disposable surgical instruments. Clopay's operations accounted for 70 percent of the parent company's $50.1 million in operating income in fiscal 1991.

Telephonics was still Instrument Systems' largest business in the late 1980s. It was deriving about half its sales from internal communications systems for U.S. military aircraft and about another third from international operations. A subsidiary was making integrated circuits used by Ford Motor Co. for automatic window controllers in automobiles. Instrument Systems entered another business sector in 1984 when it acquired Oneita Knitting Mills, Inc., a New York company that dated from 1893, for about $15 million. This producer of T-shirts and clothing for newborns was renamed Oneita Industries. Instrument Systems began selling pieces of the business in 1988 and disposed of it entirely in 1993.

Instrument Systems changed its name to Griffon in 1995. Growing in sales each year and solidly profitable, the company was now worth about $9 a share, compared to only $1 a share in 1989. Clopay was now by far the parent company's largest entity, while Telephonics was reducing its dependence on military projects and soliciting commercial and nondefense governmental business. It retained, however, significant contracts to provide communications equipment for a U.S. military plane known as JSTARS and in 1997 won a contract worth more than $100 million to supply communications equipment to upgrade British Royal Air Force antisubmarine airplanes known as Nimrods. Also in 1997, Telephonics won a $26 million contract to supply wireless communications equipment for 1,080 New York City subway cars.

In 1996 Clopay formed Finotech, a joint venture with German-based Corovin GmbH, to manufacture specialty plastic film and laminate products in Europe. Clopay took a 60 percent stake in the company. Clopay also acquired Bohme Verpackungsfolien GmbH & Co., a German manufacturer of plastic packaging and specialty films, in 1998. Griffon sold the specialty hardware portion of its business in 1997. That year it acquired Holmes-Hally Industries, a manufacturer and installer of residential garage doors and related hardware, for about $35 million. Holmes-Hally had annual sales of approximately $80 million at this time.

Griffon continued to increase its sales in the late 1990s, surpassing the $1 billion mark in fiscal 1999. Net income remained over $20 million—as it had in every year since 1991—although dropping from the record of $33.2 million in 1997. The company's stock was, however, in 1999 trading at about half the $17 a share reached in late 1997 and early 1998. Some analysts suggested that a company like Griffon, with three widely different product lines, was hard for investors to assess. While perhaps true, company officials were quick to point out the underlying logic of such a strategy. "It's worked for us," Blau told James Bernstein of *Newsday* in 1997. "If one of our divisions has a slight growth problem, the other takes over. The key to our business style is independent management. We do not have layers of management and guys running around with clipboards." Griffon bought back 20 percent of its outstanding shares between 1993 and 1996.

Griffon in 1999

In 1999 Griffon's Garage Doors segment was designing and manufacturing garage doors for use in the residential and commercial building markets. The Installation Services segment was selling, installing, and servicing garage doors, garage-door openers, manufactured fireplaces, floor coverings, cabinetry, and a range of related building products, primarily for the residential housing markets. The Specialty Plastic Films segment was developing, producing, and selling plastic films and film laminates for use in infant diapers, adult incontinence products, feminine hygiene products, and disposable surgical and patient-care products. The Electronic Information and Communication Systems segment was designing, manufacturing, and providing logistical support for communication and radar systems, information and command and control systems, and custom mixed-signal large-scale integration circuits.

Company-owned Telephonics manufacturing plants were located in Farmingdale and Huntington, Long Island. Manufacturing plants for films were in Nashville; Augusta, Maine; Fresno, California; and Aschersleben and Dombuhl, Germany. Plants for garage doors were in Los Angeles; Nesbit, Maine; Russia, Ohio; Auburn, Washington; and Baldwin, Wisconsin. A plant for garage doors and installation service was in Tempe, Arizona. Company headquarters remained in Jericho.

Of Griffon's $1.03 billion in revenues from external customers in fiscal 1999, garage doors accounted for 41 percent, installation services for 23 percent, specialty plastic films for 19 percent, and electronic information and communication systems for 17 percent. In terms of geographical area, the United States accounted for 81 percent, Germany for six percent, the United Kingdom for four percent, and others for nine percent. Of Griffon's operating profit of $57.8 million, garage doors accounted for 49 percent, electronic information and communication systems for 27 percent, specialty plastic films for 13 percent, and installation services for 11 percent. Net income

was $20.2 million. Griffon had a long-term debt of $135.3 million at the end of fiscal 1999. KMR Corp. owned 8.8 percent of the stock and Blau 6.9 percent at the end of the calendar year.

Principal Subsidiaries

Clopay Corp.; Holmes-Hally Industries; Lightron Corporation; Standard-Keil Industries, Inc.; Telephonics Corp.

Principal Operating Units

Electronic Information and Communication Systems; Garage Doors; Installation Services; Specialty Plastic Films.

Principal Competitors

Anderson Corporation; General American Door Co.; Harris Corporation; Honeywell Inc.; Industrial Coatings Group Inc.; Lockheed Martin Corporation; Morgan Products Ltd.; Northrup Grumman Corporation; Overhead Door Corporation; Raytheon Company; Tomkins Industries Inc.; Woodgrain Millworks Inc.

Further Reading

Bernstein, James, "Defense Contractor Rides the Rails," *Newsday,* September 9, 1992, p. 41.

——, "Surviving with Success," *Newsday,* December 1, 1997, p. C8.

——, "Telephonics Wins $100M Contract," *Newsday,* March 4, 1997, p. A35.

Berrell, D.J., "Spiraling Growth Rate Starts to Worry Instrument Systems," *Investment Dealers' Digest,* July 1, 1968, pp. 32–33.

Bolton, Douglas, "Clopay Fortunes Up: Specialty Plastics Unit Giving Garage Door Maker a Big Lift," *Cincinnati Post,* October 13, 1992, Business section.

Byrne, Harlan S., "Instrument Systems," *Barron's,* March 8, 1993, pp. 43–44.

Demery, Paul, "Telephonics Steers Toward Automakers," *LI Business News,* February 18, 1991, p. 3.

"Instrument Systems Corp.," *Wall Street Transcript,* April 27, 1981, p. 61,424.

"ISC Charts Semicon Production Plan," *Electronic News,* February 9, 1970, p. 25.

Martorana, Jamie, "Griffon Beefs Up Staff, Facility in $130M Sales Jump," *LI Business News,* July 20, 1998, pp. 1A+.

Molotsky, Irvin, "Company Shake-Up on L.I. Pits 3 Brothers in a Dispute," *New York Times,* February 5, 1979, pp. B1, B4.

Mulqueen, John, "Smaller and Better," *Barron's,* February 6, 1984, pp. 48–49.

"Multiplex Joining Big Leagues," *Electronic News,* June 2, 1969, Part II, p. 10.

Schmedel, Scott R., "Instrument Systems Holders to Resolve Dilemma Over Firm's Loans to Officers," *Wall Street Journal,* May 20, 1975, p. 15.

Shabad, Theodore, "U.S. Turns to Eastern Europe to Help Alleviate Shortages," *New York Times,* December 13, 1973, pp. 73, 79.

Smith, Gene, "Chatting Via Computer," *New York Times,* September 12, 1971, Sec. 3, p. 6.

Wax, Alan J., "Doors, Diapers and Defense," *Newsday,* March 20, 1995, pp. C1, C5.

—Robert Halasz

Grupo Gigante, S.A. de C.V.

Avenida Ejercito Nacional 769-A
11520 Mexico, D.F.
Mexico
Telephone: (525) 269-8369
Fax: (525) 269-8308
Web site: http://www.gigante.com.mx

Public Company
Incorporated: 1983
Employees: 21,192
Sales: 19.07 billion pesos (US$2.04 billion) (1998)
Stock Exchanges: Mexico City OTC (ADRs)
Ticker Symbols: GIGANTE; GBGTY
NAIC: 44511 Supermarkets and Other Grocery Stores;
45299 All Other General Merchandise Stores;
5551112 Offices of Other Holding Companies; 72211
Full-Service Restaurants

Grupo Gigante, S.A. de C.V. is a holding company that, through its subsidiaries, constitutes one of the largest retailers in Mexico. The company's Tiendas Gigante, Bodegas Gigante, and Super G chain stores sell both groceries—including Gigante's own line of private-label goods—and general merchandise. Grupo Gigante also owns the Cafeteria Toks restaurant chain and operates Office Depot and Radio Shack stores in joint ventures with these respective U.S. companies. Grupo Gigante opened two Gigante supermarkets in the Los Angeles metropolitan area in 1999.

Growing by Acquisition: 1962–92

Angel Losada Gomez was born in Spain in 1908 and came to Mexico at the age of 15. He started his business career in Tulancingo, a town about 100 miles northeast of Mexico City, in 1948 with a store selling groceries, beer, and garden seeds. It was not until 1962 that, at the age of 54, he founded his first Gigante (Spanish for giant) store, in Mexico City with seven partners. Appropriately named, it was the largest commercial establishment in Latin America—about 320,000 square feet in size, with 64 departments selling not only supermarket items but also clothing, shoes, household appliances, books, records, gifts, and even automobiles. All but one of the partners sold out after losing a third of their investment in the first year, and the remaining partner soon gave up, too, but Losada eventually made Gigante a paying proposition.

In 1971 Losada opened the first unit of his Cafeteria Toks chain (which, in spite of the English interpretation of the name, is not self-service). In 1975 Gigante's sales came to 2.29 billion pesos ($183.2 million), placing it second among Mexican self-service chains to Aurrera, S.A. (which later became Cifra, S.A. de C.V.). There were 12 Gigante outlets by 1978, when Losada purchased the Hemuda retail chain in Guadalajara, Mexico's second largest city. These were placed under the Gigante banner and increased the chain's revenues from 3.45 billion pesos (about US$150 million) in 1977 to 6.25 billion pesos (about US$275 million) in 1979, when Gigante was the nation's third largest retail chain, with 21 units. By 1986 nearly a third of Gigante's 60-odd stores were in Guadalajara.

In 1987 Losada added the 23-store Astra chain to his holdings. This acquisition, which buttressed Gigante's position in northern Mexico, was the first to require significant borrowing, a practice that Losada previously had sought to avoid. With the Astra purchase, Losada's 82-unit Gigante chain now had 500,000 square meters of selling space. There were 19 Cafeteria Toks restaurants, the majority in Mexico City. Also under the corporate umbrella were three auto agencies and—together with Spanish interests—an outlet for pharmaceutical and drugstore items plus a factory for making sweets. Gigante had no less than 7,500 suppliers, was selling 65,000 items, and was serving 105 million customers a year.

Grupo Gigante was still Mexico's third largest retailer in 1991, when it had 97 stores in more than 20 cities. It made its initial public offering in July 1991, selling ten percent of the company to new shareholders. Net sales came to 5.64 billion pesos (US$1.82 billion) and net income to 293 million pesos (US$94.7 million) that year. These figures (in new pesos) retrospectively included the 1992 93.6 percent acquisition, for US$30 million, of Blanes, S.A. de C.V., owner of 89 Blanco Sucesores supermarkets. The purchase made Gigante Mexico's largest retailer in number of stores. Business observers, however, described Blanco as a drag on profits, especially since Gigante assumed its debt of 400 million pesos (about US$130 million). Writing in *Forbes,* Ronald Fink called Blanco's operations "a basket case, even by Latin American standards, with most of its stores in the poorest areas of the country." Fink added that, unlike rival Cifra, Gigante still lacked a sophisticated computer system.

Grupo Gigante sold one Blanco store and transferred to other operators the leases of 23 stores in outlying areas—the Yucatan Peninsula and the Gulf Coast state of Tamaulipas. Some 32 others were placed under the Gigante banner, and another became a Toks coffee shop. Another 30 stores were converted into a new store group, Bodegas Gigante, which stocked a wider variety of apparel and other nonfood items. Of these, 20 were in central Mexico, with ten within 100 miles of the capital.

Counting on Joint Ventures: 1992–94

By March 1992 there were 109 stores under the Gigante banner in 25 Mexican cities. The chain was especially strong in the Guadalajara area, where 24 outlets had a market share of about 70 percent. The 20 Monterrey stores had a market share of 50 to 55 percent. In Mexico City, 24 stores had a market share of 20 percent. Gigante stores averaged about 58,000 square feet of space and featured up to six specialty departments, including pharmacies and bakeries. They stocked apparel as well as perishables and grocery items. The chain had seven distribution and storage centers with a total of 630,000 square feet of space.

In 1993 Gigante introduced in Guadalajara the first of an upscale line of supermarkets called Super G.

In 1991 Cifra formed an alliance with Wal-Mart Stores Inc., and Grupo Gigante's other big competitor, Comercial Mexicana, signed a similar pact with Price Co. Losada countered in 1992 by agreeing to join Fleming Cos. in a joint venture to establish a chain of 40,000- to 55,000-square-foot supermarkets stocking 10,000 to 14,000 items, mostly branded ones. Investment analysts were hopeful that Fleming's expertise would lead to technology transfer and a consequent improvement in Gigante's inventory control.

The first of the joint venture outlets was opened under the SuperMart name at a former Blanco site in San Juan del Rio in December 1992. Three more opened in early 1993, one at a former Blanco location and the other two newly constructed. They carried a wide assortment of dry goods and perishables, with most packaged goods national brands from both Mexico and the United States. Losada's son Angel Losada Moreno was chairman of the joint venture, named Gigante Fleming, S.A. de C.V. He was kidnapped for ransom in 1994 and held for more than three months until released after an undisclosed payment by his family.

These SuperMarts were the first of a projected chain of 50 price-impact stores that Gigante Fleming planned to open over the next five years, but the number peaked at five. It became clear in 1994 that customers preferred the wider variety of clothing and other nonfood items that Grupo Gigante was offering under its bodega format. Consequently, the joint venture stores were converted to the Bodegas Gigante name and integrated into that group. Only three remained when Fleming sold its 49 percent share in the joint venture to Grupo Gigante in 1998.

In 1994 Grupo Gigante established a second joint venture, this time with Carrefour S.A., a French mass marketer. Plans called for the establishment, under Carrefour management, of a chain of "hypermarkets" of more than 8,000 square meters (86,000 square feet) each, selling both groceries and general merchandise. This European-style format, which had not proven successful in the United States, started with a Mexico City Hiper G outlet that included 40,000 items.

In 1993 Grupo Gigante also established a joint venture with Tandy Corporation, which opened 18 Radio Shack stores that year and 30 more in 1994. At the end of 1993 there were 135 Gigante supermarkets and 32 Toks coffee shops. There were also 33 Bodega Gigante stores, four Gigante-Fleming Super-Marts, the Hiper G, and two Super G's. In 1994 Grupo Gigante signed an agreement with Office Depot, Inc. to establish Office Depot outlets in Mexico.

Grupo Gigante's profits were not keeping up with the company's expansion, however, falling 77 percent in 1992 and then sliding to only 79.1 million pesos (about US$25 million) in 1993. In 1994 it dropped from second to third among self-service chains, falling behind Comercial Mexicana.

Restructuring in the Late 1990s

Like other retailers, Gigante suffered from the national recession that followed the peso devaluation of late 1994. Sales dropped 25 percent the following year. Its problems were aggravated by demands from the owners of the acquired Blanco chain for payments due. In addition, federal agents accused Losada Gomez of selling pirated goods. Grupo Gigante dismissed some 6,000 workers and closed some of its stores. To pay its debts it borrowed money at high rates of interest and sold 20 percent of its shares to two banks: Banamex and Inbursa. The founder of Gigante retained a fortune valued at US$800 million, but this sum was down from US$1.3 billion in 1993.

Grupo Gigante gradually recovered from the crisis. Sales rose from 11.8 billion pesos in 1995 (about US$1.8 billion) to 19.07 billion pesos (US$2.04 billion) in 1998. Profits, which dipped to a low of 270 million pesos (US$41.3 million) in 1995, increased each year to 870 million pesos (US$93 million) in 1998. There were 13 Hiper G stores when Grupo Gigante sold its share of the joint venture in 1998 to Carrefour for 1.76 billion pesos (US$188.27 million), a sum it badly needed to modernize its stores and pay down its short-term debts. Gigante had been unable to properly finance its share of the undertaking and also had come to feel Carrefour was acting as a rival rather than a partner.

The largest unit of the Grupo Gigante empire in 1999—located in 51 cities of 28 states—remained the 116 Tiendas Gigante stores, establishments selling food items, general merchandise, and articles for the home in Mexico City and the states of Baja California Norte, Jalisco, and Nuevo Leon. These stores, aimed at middle-class and upper-middle-class consumers, accounted for almost 70 percent of the company's total sales in 1998. The 42 Bodegas Gigante outlets were located in Mexico City and the central and southern areas of the country. Accounting for 18 percent of sales, they were generally smaller and less well appointed than the Tiendas Gigante stores, catered to lower-income consumers, and sold mainly food items, general merchandise, and clothing. Each of these chains made about two-thirds of its sales in food and the remaining third in general merchandise.

The 26 Super G stores, located in Mexico City and the states of Jalisco and Nuevo Leon, were smaller in size but catered to an upper- and upper-middle-income clientele, selling groceries and perishable food items. They accounted for seven percent of the company's sales, and 79 percent of that was in food. For all three chains, the company's private-label Marca Gigante line of 650 products accounted for seven percent of total sales. The 39 Toks coffee shops—all in Mexico City—accounted for only two percent of Grupo Gigante's sales in 1998. The 37 Office Depot stores, in Mexico City and Nuevo Leon, accounted for three percent, and the 45 Radio Shack outlets for .6 percent. Grupo Gigante was also operating 47 real estate companies that owned land where company stores were located. There were two big warehouses in Mexico City, responsible for 75 percent of the chain's deliveries to its stores. A joint Gigante-Banamex credit card was introduced in 1998.

Grupo Gigante was, according to analysts, continuing to suffer a competitive disadvantage because of overcentralization and a low level of technology. Its sales of 30,700 pesos (about US$3,285) per square meter in 1998 were the lowest in the self-service field. A strategic plan adopted in 1998 called, by the end of 2000, for the chain to deploy optical-reading cash registers in the stores and software intended to reduce inventory turnover from 54 to 44 days, measures intended to save US$30 million in labor costs. The technological gains also would make it easier for Grupo Gigante to identify its most salable items, target its campaigns of discounting and promotion, and reorder and deploy merchandise from its suppliers.

On the succession of Angel Losada Moreno, the founder's son, to the position of chief executive officer in 1998, Grupo Gigante entered a period of more professional management. He hired as director general of the firm Robert Salvo, a top executive of the rival Cifra-Wal-Mart joint venture, introduced a discounting campaign to match the competition, and intended to preside over, by late 2000, the renovation of 80 percent of Gigante's stores with better illumination and wider aisles.

Although more cautious than his father about assuming new obligations, Losada Moreno authorized the opening of Grupo Gigante's first U.S. store in May 1999, in Pico Rivera, a community in the greater Los Angeles area. The new 60,000-square-foot outlet was promptly picketed by members of the United Food & Commercial Workers, who contended it would threaten union jobs at nearby supermarkets. A second outlet opened in the metropolitan area's San Fernando Valley before the end of the year, and a third was planned for Covina.

Principal Subsidiaries

Bodega Gigante, S.A. de C.V.; Cafeteria Toks, S.A. de C.V.; Controtiendas, S.A. de C.V.; Gigante, S.A. de C.V.; Gigante-Fleming, S.A. de C.V.; Gigante Holding International (U.S.A.); Office Depot de Mexico, S.A. de C.V. (50%); Servicios Gigante, S.A. de C.V.; Servicios Toks, S.A. de C.V.

Principal Competitors

Cifra, S.A. de C.V.; Controladora Comercial Mexicana, S.A. de C.V.

Further Reading

Fink, Ronald, "Manana?," *Forbes,* September 1, 1982, pp. 60–62.

"Fleming Selling Stake in Mexican Venture," *SN/Supermarket News,* January 19, 1998, p. 4.

Hope, Maria, "Las huellas de Gigante," *Expansion,* April 13, 1988, pp. 31, 33–35.

"Mexico Chain to Rename Acquired Stores," *SN/Supermarket News,* November 9, 1992, p. 11.

Pettersson, Edvard, "Mexican Chain Ires L.A. Union," *Los Angeles Business Journal,* May 10, 1999, pp. 3 +.

Ramirez Tamayo, Zacarias, "El nuevo rastro de un Gigante," *Expansion,* December 22, 1999, pp. 48–50.

Ruiz, Yolanda, "La ultima tentacion de un apostador," *Expansion,* August 4, 1999, pp. 166–67, 169–70, 172, 174–75.

Santiago, Jaime, "Angel Losada Gomez," *Expansion,* April 10, 1996, p. 15.

Tosh, Mark, "Fleming Cos. in Mexican Store Pact," *SN/Supermarket News,* March 2, 1992, pp. 1, 53.

Zwiebach, Elliot, "Fleming, Grupo Gigante Open Their 1st Price-Impact Store," *SN/Supermarket News,* December 21, 1992, p. 6.

—Robert Halasz

Heineken N.V.

Tweede Weteringplantsoen 21
1017 ZD Amsterdam
The Netherlands
Telephone: (20) 523 92 39
Fax: (20) 626 35 03
Web site: http://www.heinekencorp.nl

Public Company (50% Owned by Heineken Holding N.V.)
Incorporated: 1873 as Heineken's Bierbrouwerij Maatschappij N.V.
Employees: 36,733
Sales: EUR 7.15 billion (US$6.9 billion) (1999)
Stock Exchanges: Amsterdam Brussels Luxembourg
NAIC: 312120 Breweries; 312110 Soft Drink Manufacturing; 422810 Beer and Ale Wholesalers; 422820 Wine and Distilled Alcoholic Beverage Wholesalers; 422490 Other Grocery and Related Products Wholesalers

Heineken N.V. owns and operates one of the largest and most respected network of breweries in the world, producing the popular Heineken and Amstel brands of beer (which rank number one and number two, respectively, in Europe), as well as Murphy's Irish Stout, all of which the company markets internationally. The company's beer portfolio also includes a large number of national and regional brands, including Tiger, the number one regional brand in Asia. Heineken ranks second in the world beer market (trailing only Anheuser-Busch Companies, Inc.), selling beer in 170 countries and brewing beer at more than 110 company-owned breweries in more than 50 countries. Run by the Heineken family for most of its existence, the business built a solid reputation early in its history for maintaining high standards for its beer, standards the company continues to adhere to more than 135 years later. Moreover, Heineken is also the single largest exporter of beer in the world. The company has operations in many countries outside its base in the Netherlands, though it has no brewing facilities in the United States, by far the company's largest export market;

Heineken beer is the number two imported beer in the United States (behind Grupo Modelo, S.A. de C.V.'s Corona). In parts of Europe, Heineken N.V. owns beverage wholesalers, which, in addition to handling beer, also supply soft drinks and spirits to restaurants and taverns; some of these soft drinks are manufactured in Heineken factories. Although no longer involved in day-to-day management, the Heineken family retains influence over the company it founded through its 50 percent ownership of Heineken Holding N.V., which holds a 50 percent stake in Heineken N.V.

Birth and Early Development

In 1864 Gerard Adriaan Heineken convinced his mother that there would be fewer problems with alcoholism in Holland if the Dutch could be induced to drink beer instead of gin, and, moreover, that beer brewed in Holland was of such poor quality that he felt a personal obligation to produce a high-quality beer. Heineken's mother bought him an Amsterdam brewery known as De Hooiberg (The Haystack) which had been established almost 300 years before, in 1582. Heineken was only 22 when he assumed control of De Hooiberg, one of Amsterdam's largest breweries. He was so successful that after four years he built a new, larger brewery and closed the original facility. His business continued to grow rapidly, and after six more years, in 1874, he purchased a Rotterdam brewery to add to his operation. Heineken incorporated his company as Heineken's Bierbrouwerij Maatschappij N.V. (Heineken's Beer Brewery Company) in 1873.

During this time, using a new cooling technique developed by Carl von Linde, Heineken gained the ability to brew year round at a consistent quality level. Heineken was thus one of the first breweries in the world to eliminate the brewer's traditional dependence on seasonal natural ice. In 1879 Heineken hired Dr. Elion, a former student of Louis Pasteur, to research yeast. Over the next 13 years Elion systematically bred and selected a specific yeast cell for Heineken, which came to be known as the ''Heineken A-yeast'' (yeast being the source of alcohol and carbon dioxide in beer). The Heineken A-yeast would continue in use into the 21st century and would eventually be shipped from Holland to all breweries owned or operated by the com-

Company Perspectives:

As in every industry, today's international beer market is characterised by increasing globalisation. The world is growing smaller in many ways—but that doesn't mean the diversity of local culture will diminish as a result.

At Heineken, we believe the opposite is true. The more we learn about each other—and experience the variety of life at first hand—the more we value our differences. Heineken is a global company in every sense—but we are wholeheartedly committed to servicing local tastes and attitudes. Our business is global—but many of our brands are rooted in the cultures of individual markets. And although our heritage is Dutch, our working methods are multinational.

It is this unique combination—combined with the guaranteed quality of all our products—that makes Heineken the success it is today: the world's preferred brewer of quality beers.

pany, providing for a uniformity in taste among Heineken products, regardless of the different climates in which they were produced or consumed.

Heineken began to export just 12 years after the De Hooiberg purchase, with regular shipments to France. Exporting to the United States began soon after the founder's son, Dr. H.P. Heineken, assumed control of the company in 1914. Traveling on the Dutch liner *Nieuw Amsterdam* to New York, he met Leo van Munching, the liner's bartender. Impressed by van Munching's knowledge of beer, Heineken offered him a position as the company's importer in New York. The bartender quickly accepted. Van Munching distributed Heineken beer to the finer restaurants, taverns, and hotels in the New York area until Prohibition forced him to stop in 1920.

1930s Through Mid-1960s: Accelerating International Expansion

After the repeal of Prohibition in 1933, Heineken was the first beer imported into the United States. World War II once again brought importing to a temporary halt while van Munching served in the U.S. Navy. When he returned in 1945, he formed Van Munching and Company, Inc. and established a nationwide distribution system to expand the beer's market beyond the New York area.

Beginning in the 1940s, the U.S. market became extremely important to Heineken, eventually becoming the beer's largest market outside the Netherlands. Through Van Munching's distribution system, Heineken became the dominant beer import in most of the United States. While many imports were available only in metropolitan areas or other limited geographical regions, by the 1980s Heineken was available in 70 percent of the nation's retail outlets handling alcoholic beverages. The majority of Heineken beer destined for the United States was brewed at the company's Hertogenbosch brewery, where special production lines accommodated the varied labeling requirements of the different states. Heineken beer also became the leading import in Japan, Canada, and Australia. Moreover, currency

fluctuations had little effect on the company itself, largely because Heineken sold its beer to Van Munching, which paid the brewer in guilders and thereby assumed all currency risks.

In 1931 the company entered the first of many joint brewing ventures in countries to which it had previously exported. That year Malayan Breweries was formed in Singapore in association with a local partner. This was followed closely by participation in a brewery in Indonesia. In 1949 the company built the first of four breweries in Nigeria; the fourth opened in 1982. Between 1958 and 1972 the company also built four breweries and two soft drink plants in Zaire. Heineken had breweries in Rwanda, Chad, Angola, the People's Republic of Congo, Ghana, Madagascar, and Sierra Leone as well.

During the late 1940s H.P. Heineken sent his son Alfred to New York to learn about Van Munching's marketing operation. The young Heineken took advertising and business courses in the evening and spent his days canvassing New York on foot with Van Munching's sales staff. His return to Holland in 1948 marked the beginning of a new era in the company's marketing strategy. Alfred Heineken had been impressed with the changes in the U.S. lifestyle brought about by electrical refrigerators and modern supermarkets, and he foresaw the eventual impact of modern conveniences on the Dutch way of life. He prompted the company to implement marketing techniques that capitalized on these habits. Recognizing the importance of the take-home market, for instance, the company began selling beer in grocery stores (with store displays designed by Alfred Heineken). In addition, Heineken began advertising its beer on the radio. Previously, advertising had been considered unnecessary because tavern owners were tied to specific breweries.

In the 1960s the company institutionalized its meticulous quality control efforts under its technical services group, Heineken Technisch Beheer, or H.T.B., which was formed in 1963. High quality was always the company's hallmark. The brewing process of medium-quality beers usually took three days and aging lasted a week at most. Heineken, however, brewed its beer for eight days and aged it for six weeks. The H.T.B. unit operated out of the company's laboratory at Zoeterwoude in the Netherlands and provided laboratory services, research on raw materials, project engineering, and other services for all breweries associated with the company. There was also a tasting center at the Zoeterwoude laboratory. Samples of all beers brewed under Heineken supervision were shipped there each month to be tested by panels of taste experts. The tests at Zoeterwoude augmented the taste testing that was carried out at each individual brewery.

Late 1960s Through 1980s: Product Diversification and Continued Growth

Product diversification began relatively late in Heineken's history, because the company's emphasis had been on expanding its markets. In 1968, however, the company purchased the Amstel Brewery, Holland's second largest, founded by Jonkheer C.A. de Pesters and J.H. van Marwijk Kooy in 1870 and the first in Holland to brew lager beers. Amstel's export market was firmly established by the time Heineken purchased the operation. Through its acquisition of Amstel, Heineken gained interests in breweries in Surinam, the Netherlands Antilles, Jordan, Lebanon, and Greece. In 1980 Heineken eventually

Key Dates:

1592: An Amsterdam brewery known as De Hooiberg (The Haystack) is established.
1856: Murphy's Irish Stout is first brewed in Cork, Ireland.
1864: Gerard Adriaan Heineken assumes control of De Hooiberg.
1870: Jonkheer C.A. de Pesters and J.H. van Marwijk Kooy establish Amstel Brewery.
1873: Heineken incorporates his company as Heineken's Bierbrouwerij Maatschappij N.V.
1876: Company begins exporting, with regular shipments to France.
1900: Beer volume reaches 200,000 hectoliters.
1914: Dr. H.P. Heineken, son of the founder, takes control of the company.
1931: Company enters into its first joint brewing venture, Malayan Breweries.
1933: Heineken is the first beer imported into the United States following the repeal of Prohibition.
1968: Heineken acquires Amstel.
1970: Company acquires the James J. Murphy brewery and its Murphy's Irish Stout brand; beer volume reaches 11.3 million hectoliters.

1971: Alfred Heineken, grandson of the founder, is appointed chairman.
1972: Company changes its name to Heineken N.V.
1980: Amstel Light makes its debut.
1991: Heineken purchases Van Munching & Company; expansion into Eastern Europe begins with the purchase of a majority stake in Hungary-based Komáromi Sörgyár RT.
1994: Company acquires stakes in Poland's Zywiec Brewing and Bulgaria's Zagorka Brewery.
1995: Interbrew Italia S.p.A. and a majority stake in Slovakia's Zlatý Bazant A.S. are acquired.
1996: Heineken takes over France's Fischer Group and Italy's Birra Moretti S.p.A.
1998: Heineken increases its stake in Zywiec to 75 percent, then combines Zywiec with Brewpole, emerging with a 50 percent stake in the new Zywiec, now Poland's largest brewer.
1999: Beer volume reaches 90.9 million hectoliters.
2000: Grupo Cruzcampo S.A., Spain's largest brewer, is acquired.

entered the low calorie beer market with Amstel Light; by the 1980s Amstel beers were sold in more than 60 countries.

In 1971 Alfred Heineken was appointed chairman. The following year, the company changed its name from Heineken's Bierbrouwerij Maatschappij N.V. to Heineken N.V. The company's remarkable success outside the Netherlands led management to emphasize Heineken's international presence rather than casting it as a Dutch company with significant international operations. In fact, the company looked upon all of Europe as its domestic market. Heineken Holland had headquarters at the Zoeterwoude brewery. Its various breweries contracted with Heineken World to supply worldwide beer shipments. Heineken World headquarters remained in Amsterdam and were housed in an addition to the Heineken family home.

In 1970 Heineken entered the stout market by buying the failing James J. Murphy brewery in Cork, Ireland. In addition to Murphy's Irish Stout, which dated back to 1856, the brewery produced Heineken light lager brew under license. Wines, spirits, and soft drinks were also becoming increasingly important Heineken products. Soft drinks were made at Bunnik by Vrumona B.V., and the company bottled PepsiCola and 7Up under license. Heineken and its affiliates also sold Royal Club, Sisi, Sourcy, and B3 soft drinks; Royal Club and Green Sands shandies; and nonalcoholic beers such as Amstel Brew. Spirits and wines included Bologna, Hoppe, Coebergh, Glenmark, Grand Monarque, and Jagermeister brands. In 1971 Heineken purchased the Bokma distillery. Bokma Genever was Holland's most popular gin. The distillery at Zoetermeer was the headquarters of Heineken's Netherlands Wine and Spirits Group B.V.

The French market proved the most challenging to Heineken, and since entering France in 1972 through the purchase of a

majority stake in the third largest brewing group, Heineken had only one profitable year there by the mid-1980s. The situation was considered so bleak that in 1986 the company and its French partner cut 500 jobs and closed down three breweries and a bottling plant in France, offering displaced employees retraining and outplacement. From 1983 to 1986 Heineken invested significantly in Sogebra S.A. (Société Générale de Brasserie), trying to sustain the company's French activities.

Heineken continued its international expansion throughout the 1970s and 1980s. Through license agreements, Heineken beer began to be produced in Sierra Leone and Trinidad (1972), Jamaica (1973), Norway and Sweden (1975), St. Lucia and Tahiti (1976), Haiti (1977), Ireland (1978), Italy (1979), Morocco (1980), Greece and South Korea (1981), Japan (1983), and Spain (1988). The company also purchased stakes in numerous foreign brewers, including: a minority stake in Cervejarias Kaiser S.A., a leading Brazilian brewing group, in 1983; a minority stake in El Aguila S.A., a leader in Spain, in 1984 (increased to 51.2 percent in 1986); and a minority stake in Quilmes International (Bermuda) Ltd., which had interests in Argentina, Uruguay, and Paraguay and later expanded into Chile.

In the 1980s the company was a victim of a series of criminal incidents. In 1982 two unsuccessful blackmail attempts were made against the brewery, followed the next year by an extortion attempt. The most serious incident was the November 1983 kidnapping of the company chief, Alfred Heineken, and his chauffeur. The two were held for 21 days and released after the company paid out an estimated 30 million guilders for their return (though the actual amount was never made public).

Heineken spent tens of millions of guilders each year to bolster its image as a prestigious import. The company's refusal to brew in the United States, even though its beer is brewed under license in many other countries, was in part attributable to a need to maintain the image. Löwenbräu's experience was not lost on Heineken; when Miller Brewing Company began brewing Löwenbräu under license in the United States the German brand lost a major portion of its market share. It appeared that Americans enjoyed the exclusivity of an import. The premium price they paid for Heineken beer lent credence to the image.

Heineken was unquestionably a powerful force in the brewing industry in the 1980s. In revenues it ranked fifth in the world behind Anheuser-Busch, Miller Brewing, Britain's Allied Domecq PLC, and Japan's Kirin Brewery Company, Limited. Its share of the world beer market increased from 2.61 to 2.82 percent between 1977 and 1981.

Management policies at Heineken changed little over the years. The family retained control over virtually all aspects of the company, which was managed by a small team selected by the head of the family. The group was kept small in order to prevent factions from developing. As in the past, however, the family head of the company was involved in Heineken's day-to-day functions. Alfred Heineken, grandson of the founder and owner of 50 percent of the shares in the company, directly supervised research and development, finance, and public relations in the mid-1980s. Though Alfred Heineken officially retired in 1989, he kept close ties with the company well into the 1990s, serving as chairman and delegate member of the supervisory council (until 1995) and as chairman of the board of Heineken Holding N.V., which held a 50 percent stake in Heineken N.V.

1990s: Expanding Aggressively into Emerging Markets

As the company entered the 1990s, Gerard Van Schaik took over as chairman. When Van Schaik joined the company in 1959, he was responsible for export sales to the United States, which then, as in the 1990s, was the most important source of profits for Heineken. U.S. sales represented just 2.6 percent of the company's total, but contributed 23 percent of the company's US$435 million in pretax profits in 1991; a 24-bottle case of Heineken sold on average for about 50 percent more than a case of the domestic favorite Budweiser.

Van Schaik focused on expanding the company's presence in Germany, by far the world's top consumer of beer. Emphasizing Heineken as a premium beer, the company invested in costly advertising, targeting in particular young Germans who, it was hoped, might find a foreign, imported beer appealing. Van Schaik also oversaw an important U.S. acquisition in 1991, when Heineken purchased Van Munching & Company, the U.S. operation that had handled the Heineken import business in the United States for six decades. This business then became officially known as Heineken USA, the U.S. arm of subsidiary Heineken Worldwide. Expansion into former communist markets began in 1991 with the acquisition of a 50.3 percent interest (increased to 100 percent in 1994) in Komáromi Sörgyár RT, a Hungarian brewer.

In the 1990s specialty beers remained very strong among the U.S. beer-drinking public as many consumers began drinking less and drinking better beers. Heineken was able to take advantage of this trend, offering a more full-bodied, European beer that many consumers desired. In fact, Heineken became the leading imported beer in the United States and brought the entire Heineken USA portfolio double-digit growth in 1994. During this time, more than one out of every five imports in the United States was a Heineken.

According to a 1992 *Forbes* magazine article, worldwide annual beer consumption had increased to about 30 billion gallons, equivalent to more than ten six-packs of beer per person per year, with especially strong volume in Latin American and Asia. In accordance with this trend, Heineken announced in 1992 that it had signed a joint agreement to become the first foreign beer producer in Vietnam. A US$42.5 million brewery located near Ho Chi Minh City began producing beer under the Heineken and Tiger labels. In 1993 Heineken also moved into China, which in 1994 represented the world's second largest beer market, after the United States. By 1994, Heineken had three export offices and three breweries in China.

Karel Vuursteen became Heineken's chairman in 1993 and continued to expand the company's international presence focusing on Latin America, the Far East, Scandinavia, and Middle Europe. To facilitate the introduction of Heineken in Poland, Heineken paid US$40 million for a 25 percent stake in Poland's Zywiec Brewing in 1994 (the stake was increased to 31.8 percent later in 1994). That same year, the company moved into Bulgaria through the purchase of 40 percent of the state-owned Zagorka Brewery A.D., which was based in Stara Zagorka and held 20 percent of the country's beer market. Also in 1994, Heineken entered into ventures to build new breweries in China (to brew Tiger beer) and in Cambodia (to brew Tiger and ABC Stout). The company also sold the bulk of its spirits and wine business that year.

In early 1995 Heineken acquired Interbrew Italia S.p.A., whose brands included Stella Artois and Classica von Wunster, from Interbrew S.A. of Belgium, increasing Heineken's Italian market share from 25 to 30 percent. Interbrew Italia was merged into Heineken Italia S.p.A. In October 1995 Heineken acquired a 66 percent stake in Zlatý Bažant A.S., the largest brewery in Slovakia. That year, Heineken also ventured into Myanmar through a joint venture that began constructing a new brewery to produce Tiger beer. Heineken's Indonesian subsidiary broke ground in 1995 at the site of a new brewery near Surabaja.

Heineken's aggressive acquisition drive continued in 1996. Early that year the company acquired the fourth largest brewer in France, the Fischer Group, and the third largest Italian brewery, Birra Moretti S.p.A., which produced the Moretti and Sans Souci brands. Heineken thereby gained the number two position in France, with 35 percent market share, and the top spot in Italy, with 38 percent of the market—although at the price of a short-term reduction in profits due to high integration costs. Also in 1996, the company withdrew from its Myanmar venture, concerned about the human rights situation there and the impact its presence there might have on the company's reputation.

The late 1990s continued to provide conditions ripe for consolidation in the global beer industry. Growth was slowing not only from the maturation of developed markets but also from the financial crises that rocked such emerging areas as Asia and Latin America. Heineken remained at the forefront of the consolidation trend, enhancing its position as the most international brewing group in the world through additional dealmaking. Poland was the focus during 1998. That year Heineken increased its stake in Zywiec to 75 percent, then merged Zywiec with Brewpole, the largest brewing group in the country and maker of the popular EB brand. Heineken held a controlling 50 percent stake in the enlarged Zywiec, which commanded 38 percent of the Polish market. Also in 1998 Heineken gained a 25 percent stake in Pivara Skopje A.D., the leading beer maker in Macedonia with a market share of 70 percent. In June 1999 Heineken reached an agreement to acquire Grupo Cruzcampo S.A., Spain's largest brewer, from Diageo plc. Spanish regulators, concerned about the purchase because of Heineken's majority stake in El Aguila, forced the company to cut about one-sixth of its Spanish production and storage facilities before the deal was consummated in January 2000. Heineken immediately began integrating Cruzcampo into El Aguila.

Heineken's position of international preeminence at the dawn of the 21st century was attributable to its two-pronged strategy of exporting its key global brands—Heineken, Amstel, and Murphy's—and acquiring or building from scratch foreign breweries with strong local or regional brands. Heineken thereby had attained leading positions in several markets in Europe and elsewhere and the number two position in Africa, behind South African Breweries plc (SAB). The company did occasionally bypass expansion opportunities, as it did in early 1999 when it decided not to bid for a controlling stake in SAB. But another cropped up a year later when Bass PLC of the United Kingdom began exploring the sale of its brewing operations and Heineken showed keen interest. It faced a potential battle, however, from several rivals, including SAB itself, Anheuser-Busch, and Denmark's Carlsberg A/S.

Principal Subsidiaries

Heineken Nederlands Beheer B.V.; Heineken Brouwerijen B.V.; Heineken Nederland B.V.; Heineken Internationaal Beheer B.V.; Heineken Technical Services B.V.; Amstel Brouwerij B.V.; Amstel Internationaal B.V.; Vrumona B.V.; Inverba Holland B.V.; Brouwerij De Ridder B.V.; B.V. Beleggingsmaatschappij Limba; Brand Bierbrouwerij B.V.; Beheer-en Exploitatiemaatschappij Brand B.V.; Sogebra S.A. (France); El Aguila S.A. (Spain; 71.3%); Heineken Italia S.p.A. (Italy); Athenian Brewery S.A. (Greece; 98.8%); Murphy Brewery Ireland Ltd.; Amstel Sörgyár RT (Hungary); Zywiec S.A. (Poland; 50%); Zlatý Bažant A.S. (Slovakia); Pivovar Corgon S.R.O. (Slovakia; 59%); Calanda Haldengut A.G. (Switzerland; 99.7%); Mouterij Albert N.V. (Belgium); Ibecor S.A. (Belgium); Heineken USA Inc.; Antilliaanse Brouwerij N.V. (Netherlands Antilles; 56.3%); Commonwealth Brewery Ltd. (Bahamas; 53.2%); Windward & Leeward Brewery Ltd. (St. Lucia; 72.7%); 'Bralima' S.A.R.L. (Democratic Republic of the Congo; 94.3%); Brasseries et Limonaderies du Rwanda 'Bralirwa' S.A. (70%); Brasseries et Limonaderies du Burundi 'Brarudi' S.A.R.L. (59.3%); Brasseries de Bourbon S.A. (Réunion; 85.4%); Ghana Breweries Ltd. (75.6%); Brasseries du Logone S.A. (Tsjaad); P.T. Multi Bintang Indonesia Tbk. (84.5%).

Principal Competitors

Adolph Coors Company; Allied Domecq PLC; Anheuser-Busch Companies, Inc.; Companhia Antarctica Paulista Industria Brasileira de Bebidas e Conexos; Asahi Breweries, Ltd.; Bass PLC; Bavaria S.A.; Brauerei Beck & Co.; Canandaigua Brands, Inc.; Carlsberg A/S; Companhia Cervejaria Brahma; Diageo plc; Fomento Economico Mexicano, S.A. de C.V.; Foster's Brewing Group Limited; The Gambrinus Company; Genesee Corporation; Groupe Danone; Grupo Modelo, S.A. de C.V.; Interbrew S.A.; Kirin Brewery Company, Limited; Miller Brewing Company; Molson Inc.; S&P Company; San Miguel Corporation; Scottish & Newcastle plc; South African Breweries plc; Taiwan Tobacco & Wine Board; Whitbread PLC.

Further Reading

Boland, Vincent, "Heineken Aims to Refresh Parts of Slovakian Brewer," *Financial Times,* August 30, 1996, p. 19.

Brown, Andrew C., "A Dutch Challenge to the King of Stout; Heineken, the Masterly European Marketer of Light Lagers, Has Moved Boldly into Guinness's Backyard," *Fortune,* February 3, 1986, p. 75.

Dawson, Havis, "Brand Brewing," *Beverage World,* October 1995, p. 50.

"Empire Builder," *Beverage World,* April 1995, p. 20.

Flynn, Julia, "Heineken's Battle to Stay Top Bottle," *Business Week,* August 1, 1994, pp. 60+.

Fuhrman, Peter, "Make Haste Slowly," *Forbes,* November 9, 1992, p. 44.

Hagerty, Bob, "Heineken Fights to Remain Green Giant: European Push Mounted to Maintain No. 1 Status," *Wall Street Journal,* April 26, 1991, p. A9A.

"Heineken Buys into Polish Brewer," *Advertising Age,* March 14, 1994, p. 41.

"Heineken's Gift to Cambodia," *Beverage World,* December 1994, p. 20.

"Heineken Three Ways," *Beverage World,* May 1992, p. 16.

"Heineken to Open Vietnam Brewery," *Nation's Restaurant News,* January 6, 1992, p. 54.

Korthals, H.A., and J.A., Emmens, *Korte geschiedenis der Heineken's Bierbrouwerij Maatschappij N.V., 1873–1948,* Amsterdam: C.V. Allert de Lange, 1948, 429 p.

Oram, Roderick, "Heineken Finds Strong Global Brew," *Financial Times,* February 7, 1996, p. 26.

Prince, Greg W., "The Green Standard," *Beverage World,* February 1995, p. 30.

Raghavan, Anita, and Keith Johnson, "Heineken Nears Deal to Acquire Spanish Brewing Unit of Diageo," *Wall Street Journal,* June 10, 1999, p. A18.

Tinnin, David B., "The Heady Success of Holland's Heineken," *Fortune,* November 16, 1981, pp. 158+.

Van Munching, Philip, *Beer Blast: The Inside Story of the Brewing Industry's Bizarre Battles for Your Money,* New York: Times Business, 1997, 309 p.

——, "Show Us Your Badge," *Beverage World,* September 15, 1998.

Willman, John, and Gordon Cramb, "Outsider at Heart of Family Brewer," *Financial Times,* January 18, 1999, p. 13.

Willman, John, and Ian Bickerton, "Heineken Wins Race for Spain's Largest Brewer," *Financial Times,* June 11, 1999, p. 23.

The World of Heineken, Amsterdam: Heineken International Beheer, May 1995, 34 p.

—Beth Watson Highman
—updated by David E. Salamie

Henkel KGaA

Henkelstraße 67
40191 Düsseldorf
Germany
Telephone: (211) 797-3533
Fax: (211) 798-2484
Web site: http://www.henkel.de

Public Company
Incorporated: 1876 as Henkel & Cie
Employees: 56,400
Sales: EURO 11.4 billion (US$12.1 billion) (1999)
Stock Exchanges: Düsseldorf Frankfurt
NAIC: 551112 Offices of Other Holding Companies;
    325211 Plastics Material and Resin Manufacturing;
    325320 Pesticide and Other Agricultural Chemical
    Manufacturing; 325411 Medicinal and Botanical
    Manufacturing; 325412 Pharmaceutical Preparation
    Manufacturing; 325520 Adhesive Manufacturing;
    325611 Soap and Other Detergent Manufacturing;
    325612 Polish and Other Sanitation Goods
    Manufacturing; 325613 Surface Active Agent
    Manufacturing; 325620 Toilet Preparation
    Manufacturing; 325999 All Other Miscellaneous
    Chemical Product and Preparation Manufacturing

Based in Germany, Henkel KGaA is one of the world's largest chemical companies. It has five main operating sectors: adhesives (22 percent of overall sales), where it holds the number one position in the world; cosmetics/toiletries (16 percent), where it is number three in Europe; detergents/household cleansers (23 percent), where it ranks second in Europe; industrial and institutional hygiene/surface technologies (16 percent), which includes a joint venture with Ecolab Inc. that is a European market leader in hygiene products, and which also is the world leader in products for the chemical surface treatment of metals; and chemical products (23 percent), a unit that is contained within an independent, but wholly owned, subsidiary called Cognis, which is the world leader in oleochemical products. In addition to its joint venture

with Ecolab, Henkel also holds a 21.8 percent stake in that St. Paul, Minnesota-based supplier of cleaning, sanitizing, and maintenance products and services. Henkel owns a 24.7 percent interest in the Clorox Company, a maker of consumer products based in Oakland, California; and is involved in detergent joint ventures in the United States and Mexico with Scottsdale, Arizona-based Dial Corporation. With operations in more than 70 countries, Henkel derives more than 70 percent of its sales outside of Germany, making it one of the most internationally active German companies. Descendants of the founding Henkel family maintain an 80 percent stake in the company.

Late 19th-Century Roots

Henkel's roots go back to September 26, 1876, when Fritz Henkel founded Henkel & Cie, a three-man company based in Aachen, engaged in making a "Universal Detergent." Henkel was from the Hesse region and was then 28. Two years later, the company launched one of the first German consumer products to bear a brand name. This was Henkel's Bleaching Soda. The packet bore the company's early trademark, a benevolent-looking lion in front of a halo of sunbeams. The same year, 1878, saw the young firm's move to a new factory in Düsseldorf, where the company still has its headquarters. The actual site changed in 1899, when Henkel transferred production to a much larger plant at Düsseldorf-Holthausen. Convenient for transporting goods either by railway or on the Rhine, this was to be Henkel's permanent home. (Over the years, however, it would grow from 600,000 square feet to 16.2 million square feet.) In 1877 and 1879 Fritz Henkel bought out his two cofounders, and from then on control was kept firmly in the family.

From the start Henkel appreciated the power that the control of raw materials confers. Not only does such control insulate the manufacturer from the vagaries of third-party suppliers; it also puts control of ingredient quality into its hands. Sodium silicate, or water glass, was one of the main ingredients of Henkel's detergents; accordingly in 1884 Henkel acquired the Rheinische Wasserglasfabrik and started to make its own water glass. Already the importance of research and development was appreciated; the process for making water glass was improved upon to the point where, in 1898, Henkel was to patent its own process.

The drive to control as much of the production process as possible continued to be apparent. In 1908 and 1909 Henkel opened soap factories for detergent production and a fat-splitting plant for fatty acid production, which in turn went into the soap. In 1910 came a plant to process glycerol, a byproduct of the manufacture of fatty acids.

In 1893 Fritz Henkel had welcomed his elder son, 18-year-old Fritz Henkel, Jr., into the firm as an apprentice. In due course, Fritz was to play a key role in developing the company's innovative policy of marketing under brand names. Fritz Henkel Jr.'s brother, Hugo Henkel—a trained chemist—joined the family firm 12 years later. While contributing to the company's technological side in particular, he helped Henkel to diversify into the well-rounded chemical business we know today.

Persil, World War I, and Diversification

At the turn of the century, Henkel was already demonstrating a forward-looking concern for the welfare of its 80 employees: it provided free staff lunches from 1900. A few years later Henkel became involved in a building cooperative providing rental housing for workers' families and low-cost mortgages for executives. Recreational facilities such as gyms were supplied by the firm, as were the washrooms, which factory workers needed in order to comply with the company stipulation that they bathe at least once a week. Some early staff benefits may strike the modern reader as overly paternalistic: for example, female workers who announced their intention of getting married were offered a trousseau and a cookery and domestic-science course to be taken at the firm's expense.

The year 1907 was exceptionally important for product development. It marked the launch of Henkel's arguably most famous brand, the revolutionary detergent Persil. The name came from two of its most important ingredients, a perborate and a silicate. The product, Henkel's own invention, was almost simultaneously invented by two Stuttgart chemists. To be on the safe side, Henkel acquired the chemists' patent but never used it. Three years later, after further intensive research on Henkel's part, the product was registered as Persil. The product was a breakthrough in labor-saving since no rubbing or bleaching was required to clean clothes.

Since those early days, the brand name Persil has caused some confusion. In 1909, the English firm of Joseph Crosfield acquired the patent rights and trademarks of Persil for the United Kingdom and various British, Dutch, and Danish colonies. Crosfield was later absorbed by Lever Brothers, which in turn became part of Unilever. Today both Henkel and Unilever continue to market a product named Persil. In Western Europe, for example, Unilever owns the trademark Persil in Britain and France, while Henkel has Germany, Belgium, Luxembourg, the Netherlands, Italy, and Denmark.

In the early 1900s, Henkel's use of brand names was innovative. Its products were easy to spot by their packaging and were widely distributed. Henkel felt that there was more to be gained by informative advertising than from what would now be called hype. The objectives were to make the Henkel name synonymous with quality and reliability, and to keep reminding the public of Henkel's presence by having its goods and name on display everywhere. As early as 1911, motorized delivery vans bearing the Henkel livery were to be seen in Düsseldorf. There was a famous slogan, ''Persil bleibt Persil'' (''Persil remains Persil''). By 1914, Henkel had 120 salesmen out in the field.

Henkel had been quick to set up marketing operations in Germany's neighbor countries. In 1913 Henkel opened a foreign subsidiary, the first of many, at Basel-Pratteln in Switzerland, a country whose appetite for Persil and bleaching soda had already proved particularly healthy. Four years later it was to acquire another subsidiary, this time German, when it bought Matthes & Weber of Duisburg.

Henkel played a patriotic part in World War I. Jobs of workers who went to the defense of their country were kept open for their return—though 71 never returned. A hospital was set up for the employees who were wounded. Henkel employees fighting in the German trenches continued to receive not only food parcels but also copies of the company newspaper, which had begun to be published in 1914.

Rationing of oils and fats made it necessary in 1916 to bring in a low-soap version of Persil. In general, the war had less effect on Henkel's business than did the Allied occupation of the Rhineland from 1919 onwards. Some of the effects of the occupation were positive. The danger that the Holthausen plant would be cut off from its customer base led to the construction of a new factory at Genthin in central Germany, which opened in 1921. The extra capacity would be valuable later on.

The war was followed in Germany by a period of hyperinflation. At its peak, in November 1923, a packet of Persil cost 1.25 billion marks. Once this situation was brought under control, Henkel's expansion continued apace, in line with a general Western European trend towards higher standards of living, and in particular of personal and domestic hygiene. In Germany, soap products were becoming affordable, and thanks in part to Henkel's advertisements, their virtues were well known. For most of its first half-century the company had focused on the manufacture of detergent and cleaning products. A period of vigorous diversification began in the 1920s under the guidance of Hugo Henkel, now supported not only by his sons but by a board of eight directors. This activity continued throughout the interwar period, but the stimulus to diversify again came from the occupation of the Rhineland. In 1923, fearing that the occupying forces would restrict the supply of the adhesives it needed for detergent packaging, Henkel started to manufacture its own glues. With characteristic opportunism, it was soon putting the glue department's products on the market.

Key Dates:

1876: Fritz Henkel founds Henkel & Cie in Aachen.
1878: Company moves to Düsseldorf and introduces its first consumer brand, Henkel's Bleaching Soda.
1907: Henkel introduces the revolutionary detergent Persil.
1913: The first foreign subsidiary is established, in Switzerland.
1924: Marketing of institutional cleaning products begins.
1930: Acquisition of Thompson-Werke takes Henkel into the production of household care products.
1947: Production of personal hygiene and cosmetic products begins.
1960: First U.S. company, Standard Chemical Products, is acquired.
1974: Henkel patents Sasil, a phosphate substitute later used in detergents; the company purchases a minority stake in the Clorox Company.
1975: Henkel KGaA is established as the holding company for the Henkel Group.
1982: Dixan, the first phosphate-free detergent, is introduced.
1985: Company goes public through an offering of preferred, nonvoting shares.
1996: Novamax Technologies is acquired; the company lists its common, voting shares on the stock exchange for the first time.
1997: Hostile takeover of Loctite Corporation is completed.
1999: Chemical operations are spun off into a new, Henkel-owned entity called Cognis.

Henkel's next move, in 1924, was to start marketing cleaning products aimed at institutional and industrial markets. In 1929 the P3 phosphate-based cleaning agents were added to Henkel's product lines for industrial machinery and food production. By buying Thompson-Werke in 1930 and Deutsche Hydrierwerke in 1932, it acquired an interest in the market for household care products, such as polishes and scouring powders, and increased its capacity to manufacture the fatty alcohols needed for its detergents.

Henkel's acquisition of Böhme-Fettchemie, Chemnitz, in 1935, followed the latter's launch of a new type of detergent named Fewa. This synthetic product, designed to wash delicate fabrics, was the first of its kind. The same year saw the foundation by Henkel of a German whaling association which sent a fleet to the Antarctic Ocean three times in the prewar years. The fleet's catches were of relevance to oleochemical production. By 1939 Henkel could boast of 15 European plants in addition to the main factory in Düsseldorf.

Henkel's expansion of its product range between the wars meant more research and development. A laboratory had existed since the early 1900s, but in 1920 a test department for new products was set up. At first the focus was inorganic chemistry, but later on other branches of chemistry were included. Further new laboratories were built and equipped during the 1930s, culminating in a major laboratory which opened on the Deutsche Hydrierwerke site at Rodleben, shortly before the outbreak of World War II, designed to support all of Henkel's products. Cash-starved Germany could ill afford to import natural fats and so one important object of research was the development of soapless washing powders. By 1936 Henkel was producing powders using fatty acids derived from coal. Meanwhile, improvements had been made in the manufacturing process: packaging of detergents became fully automatic in 1926. Always keen to take advantage of new technology in management as well as production, Henkel installed an automatic telephone exchange in 1928, and in 1935 became the first subscriber to the Düsseldorf teleprinter service.

Alongside its policy of expansion and diversification in the interwar period, Henkel maintained an imaginative approach to advertising. Skywriting planes emblazoned the name of Persil far above the heads of astonished German spectators, and in an interesting variation on the sandwich board, six men carried through the streets snow-white umbrellas bearing the name "Persil." Henkel continued to forge ahead in the field of staff management and welfare. First-aid facilities, the precursor of today's Henkel staff medical centers, had arrived in 1912. A pension plan began three years later. In 1925 a training structure for specialist staff was established, and two years later Henkel became the first member of the German chemical industry to appoint a safety engineer to reduce the risk of accidents.

Jost Henkel, son of Hugo Henkel, had joined the company in 1933, and it was under his leadership that Henkel weathered World War II. The war itself had relatively little impact on the Düsseldorf works, although 259 employees were lost in action, prison camps, and air raids. Henkel had to abandon Persil in favor of basic, state-approved products during wartime. Once again the aftermath of war was more serious. The occupying British forces removed the Henkel family from the head of the firm, and did not allow it to return until 1947. The Genthin plant was expropriated by the communists in 1946. In line with the German economy, which began to recover at that time, Henkel was able to get back on a level footing in time for its 75th anniversary in 1951.

Postwar Growth

After World War II, Henkel, under first Jost Henkel and then his brother Konrad Henkel, who took over in 1961, did not simply set about rebuilding what it had before, but entered one new market after another, diversifying its products through innovation and acquisition, and gaining representation in parts of the world not previously penetrated. In 1946, the Düsseldorf factory started to manufacture chemical products for use in the textile and leather industries, and the Poly hair-care brand was launched. The following year, personal hygiene and cosmetic products were added to the range. During this period, Henkel's production facilities for oil-related chemicals were brought together at the Düsseldorf-Holthausen plant, giving a greatly increased capacity for the manufacture of ingredients for soaps, detergents, cosmetics, and pharmaceutical products. In 1951 Pril dishwashing liquid was introduced. During the 1950s, the company set up manufacturing plants in Japan and Brazil, gaining its first footholds in the East Asian and South American marketplaces.

The first acquisition of a U.S. company, Standard Chemical Products, Inc., in 1960, heralded the two decades of Henkel's most dramatic expansion (Standard, a maker of chemicals for the textile industry, was renamed Henkel Corporation in 1971). To give a solid foundation to its growth program, the Henkel Group opened a state-of-the-art research center in 1962 at the main Düsseldorf plant. This laboratory complex had been in phased construction since 1959 and was not completed until 1967. Pritt, the solid glue in a cylindrical tube, was launched in 1969, contributing to Henkel's lead in the European adhesive market.

By the 1970s, there was mounting concern about the environmental impact of the chemical industry in general, and specifically about the use of phosphates in detergents. In 1974 Henkel patented a compound known as Sasil, which was to prove a good substitute for the offending phosphates. Now there could be a phosphate-free Persil; Henkel introduced Dixan, the first phosphate-free detergent, in 1982. The discovery of Sasil helped Henkel gain the leading position in the European detergent market. Henkel also began collecting license fees from other users of Sasil or related products.

A biological institute was added to Henkel's group of laboratories in 1974. The scientists and technologists who worked there concentrated on the protection of the consumer and the environment. Also in 1974, Henkel purchased a minority stake in the Clorox Company, a U.S.-based consumer products firm; Clorox in turn gained access to Henkel's research-and-development capabilities and acquired manufacturing and marketing rights to Henkel-developed products in the United States, Canada, and Puerto Rico. In 1975 Henkel KGaA was established as the holding company for the Henkel Group. Seven years later, the group's U.S. activities were concentrated within Henkel Corporation.

When the founder, Fritz Henkel, died in 1930, ownership of the company had been divided between the families of his three children. By 1985, control was held by 66 family members who in that year decided, together with president Helmut Sihler, that it was time to go public. Thus Henkel shares were issued at last to an eager market. At the same time steps were taken to guard against excessive outside interference; the issue was of nonvoting preferred shares, and all ordinary shares were to belong to the family at least until the year 2000.

Expansion continued apace through the 1980s, most notably with the acquisition of Union Générale de Savonnerie in France, and of Parker, maker of metal surface treatments; Oxy Process Chemicals; and Emery Group, a base-materials and chemicals company, in the United States. Emery, based in Cincinnati, was the leading maker of oleochemicals in the country. An important new production plant opened in Malaysia in 1984. Three years later, Henkel acquired a minority stake in Hartford, Connecticut-based Loctite Corporation, a leading adhesives and sealants firm. By the end of the 1980s, the expansion in the United States was particularly noteworthy, having led to a quadrupling of revenues over just the last few years of the decade.

Henkel succeeded in maintaining a sound balance sheet throughout all its acquisition activities. Although outsiders sometimes regarded the group as overdiversified, its management was satisfied with the mix. It had clear rules for acquisition: not to diversify through acquisition, to retain acquired

companies' existing management, and to purchase companies that complied with their profit requirements. Unprofitable companies, or those that do not fit in, were rejected. Strategic relationships are formed, and minority shareholdings bought as the least risky and cheapest way of getting a foothold in a new market. The *Wall Street Journal,* on November 25, 1988, described Henkel's business approach as "a blend of America's short-term emphasis on profit and West Germany's long-term emphasis on the future." Certainly, Henkel's consistently healthy results gave credibility to its strategies.

In its research and development, Henkel continued to target environmental and consumer protection issues. DM 282 million was spent on this area in 1989 alone, while DM 30 million was earmarked for related capital expenditure. In addition to measures to develop safer and more environmentally sound products in all ranges, there were programs to minimize the pollution generated by the manufacturing plants. Henkel claimed that environmental damage caused by its parent plant had been reduced by between 50 and 75 percent between 1984 and 1990.

On the marketing and production front in the late 1980s, Henkel was preparing intensively for the planned single European market. It was designing its branding concepts with Europe in mind and was reviewing its distribution and production facilities. Management development programs too were being specifically targeted at international business. Language classes were offered to staff throughout the group.

1990s and Beyond

Konrad Henkel, the grandson of founder Fritz Henkel, continued as chairman of the supervisory board and shareholders' committee until the end of 1990, when Albrecht Woeste, great grandson of the founder, replaced him. Taking over as president and CEO in July 1992 was Dr. Hans-Dietrich Winkhaus. Woeste and Winkhaus were thereby in charge for most of the 1990s, a decade in which Henkel's revenues nearly doubled and its international presence deepened through a number of acquisitions and joint ventures. Henkel also improved its profitability in the 1990s through streamlining and restructuring efforts, including the divestiture of noncore units and workforce layoffs.

The decade began, however, with the company's return to Eastern Germany following the reunification of the country. In 1990 Henkel repurchased the laundry detergent plant in Genthin that had been expropriated in 1946. The following year Henkel and St. Paul, Minnesota-based cleaning and maintenance company Ecolab Inc. combined their European cleaning and sanitizing businesses into a new 50–50 joint venture, Henkel-Ecolab. Henkel also received a 19 percent stake in Ecolab, while the U.S. firm acquired Henkel's cleaning and sanitizing operations in Latin America and Asia. The joint venture experienced some initial difficulties as a result of a poor European economy, but in a few short years became the leader in Europe in institutional and hospitality cleaning, sanitizing, and maintenance. Henkel-Ecolab, which was based in Düsseldorf, operated throughout Europe, including Russia and other former republics of the Soviet Union.

In 1992 Henkel purchased the consumer goods division of Nobel Industries of Sweden, gaining its first foothold in Scandinavia. Asia became a main focus for the company in 1993 and 1994, with a particular emphasis on China, where Henkel had eight joint ventures in place by late 1994. Sales in China were about US$100 million in 1994. A key step came in 1995 when Henkel established a Beijing-based holding company for its growing operations there, Henkel (China) Investment Co Ltd., thereby enabling it to directly hire Chinese managers. Also in 1995 Henkel became a leading supplier of hair care products in Europe through the purchase of a 77 percent stake in Hamburg-based Hans Schwarzkopf GmbH from Hoechst AG. Two years later Henkel purchased the remaining shares in Schwarzkopf from the founding family.

The company bolstered its surface technologies operations through the 1996 acquisition of Novamax Technologies Inc., an Atlanta-based specialist in products and systems for the treatment of metal surfaces. In November 1996 Henkel began a hostile takeover bid for the 65 percent of Loctite it did not already own. When Henkel increased its bid to US$1.3 billion, Loctite agreed to be taken over, with the deal finalized in January 1997. This was the largest acquisition in company history. To help finance it, Henkel sold its 16 percent stake in Degussa, a German metals and chemical group, to German utility firm Veba for DM 1.3 billion. Meanwhile, in an alteration to the Henkel family's 1985 agreement, the company listed its common, voting shares on the stock exchange for the first time in 1996. Nevertheless, the founding family continued to own 80 percent of the common stock into the early 21st century.

Acquisitions were again at the forefront in 1998, with the two most significant being U.S. firms: Manco Inc., a US$111 million purchase, and DEP Corporation, for US$93 million. Manco, a private company based in Avon, Ohio, had sales of US$160 million and provided Henkel a much enhanced presence in the U.S. consumer adhesives market. With the purchase of DEP, a financially troubled firm based in Los Angeles with sales of US$117 million, Henkel entered the U.S. personal care market for the first time and furthered its goal of fully globalizing its cosmetics/toiletries sector. Among DEP's brands were DEP, L.A., Looks, Agree, Halsa, and Lilt in hair care; Theorie, Porcelana, Cuticura, and Le Systeme in skin care; and Lavoris and Topol in dental care.

In 1999 Henkel spun off its chemicals unit—including the oleochemicals, care chemicals, and organic specialties operations—into a standalone, but fully Henkel-owned entity called Cognis. The separation was intended to provide Cognis with additional flexibility in regard to forming joint ventures, entering into mergers, or raising funds through an IPO. Cognis also gained the freedom to sell its products to competitors of Henkel in such areas as detergents and adhesives. Henkel intended to indefinitely retain at least a majority stake in Cognis.

Henkel entered into another significant joint venture in 1999. Marking a further move by Henkel into the U.S. consumer market, the company and Dial Corporation formed a 50–50 venture to create new laundry detergent products under Dial's Purex brand. In early 2000 the two companies entered into a second detergent joint venture in Mexico, where they purchased an 80 percent stake in Fabrica de Jabon Mariano Salgado, S.A. de C.V., a leading maker of detergents and soaps in that country. Henkel's aggressive U.S. expansion helped

make the company one of the most globally active German companies, with more than 70 percent of sales being generated outside the home market. This geographical balance, coupled with strong positions in both consumer and industrial sectors, provided Henkel with a portfolio that appeared capable of counteracting the typically cyclical nature of the chemical industry.

Principal Subsidiaries

DORUS Klebetechnik GmbH & Co. KG; Grünau Illertissen GmbH; Hans Schwarzkopf GmbH & Co. KG; Henkel Bautechnik GmbH; Henkel-Ecolab GmbH & Co. OHG (50%); Henkel Fragrance Center GmbH; Henkel Genthin GmbH; Henkel Klebstoff GmbH; Henkel Oberflächentechnik GmbH; Henkel Teroson GmbH; Henkel Waschmittel GmbH; Henkos Cosmetic GmbH; Kepec Chemische Fabrik GmbH; Lang Apparatebau GmbH (50%); Loctite Deutschland GmbH; Neynaber Chemie GmbH; OptiMel Schemlzguatechnik GmbH & Co. KG; Pritt Produktionsgesellschaft mbH; Schwarzkopf & Henkel Production Europe GmbH & Co. KG; Sichel-Werke GmbH; Stalo Chemicals GmbH; Thompson-Siegel GmbH; Henkel Argentina S.A.; Henkel Australia Pty. Ltd.; Schwarzkopf Pty. Ltd. (Australia); Henkel Central Eastern Europe Gesellschaft mbH (Austria); Henkel Benelux Group (Belgium/Netherlands); Henkel S.A. Indústrias Químicas (Brazil); Henkel Canada Ltd.; Loctite Canada Inc.; Henkel Chile S.A.; Henkel Asia-Pacific Ltd. (China); Henkel (China) Investment Company Ltd.; Henkel China Ltd.; Henkel Ecolab AS (Denmark; 50%); Henkel Finland Oy; Henkel France S.A.; Loctite France S.A.; Produits Chimiques du Sidobre-Sinnova S.A. (France); Henkel Hellas AE (Greece; 98.69%); Henkel Centroamericana S.A. (Guatemala); P.T. Henkel Indonesia (66.85%); Henkel Ireland Ltd.; Loctite (Ireland) Ltd.; Loctite Overseas Ltd. (Ireland); Henkel SOAD Ltd. (Israel; 50%); Henkel SpA (Italy); Loctite Italia SpA (Italy); Henkel Chemicals (Caribbean) Ltd. (Jamaica); Henkel Japan Ltd.; Loctite (Japan) Corporation; Henkel Korea Ltd.; Henkel Lebanon SAL (50%); WK Participations S.A. (Luxembourg); Henkel Chemicals (Malaysia) SDN BHD (50%); Henkel Kimianika (Malaysia) SDN BHD (50%); Henkel Mexicana S.A. de C.V. (Mexico); Henkel Maroc S.A. (Morocco; 93.76%); Henkel Ecolab B.V. (Netherlands; 50%); Henkel Oleochemicals Nederland B.V. (Netherlands); Henkel New Zealand Ltd.; Henkel Nopco AS (Norway); Henkel Philippines Inc.; Era AG (Russia; 94.3%); OOO Henkel Sued (Sovhenk) (Russia); Henkel South Africa (Pty) Ltd. (50%); Henkel Ibérica S.A. (Spain; 80%); Henkel Norden AB (Sweden); Henkel & Cie AG (Switzerland); Laesser Klebstoffe AG (Switzerland); Henkel Taiwan Ltd.; Henkel Thai Ltd. (Thailand); Türk Henkel A.S. (Turkey); Henkel Turyag A.S. (Turkey); Henkel Bautechnik (Ukraine; 66%); Henkel Ltd. (U.K.); Loctite UK Ltd.; Henkel of America Inc. (U.S.A.); Henkel Corporation (U.S.A.); Loctite Corporation (U.S.A.); Manco Inc. (U.S.A.); Schwarzkopf & DEP Corporation (U.S.A.); Henkel Venezolana S.A. (Venezuela; 44.9%).

Principal Operating Units

Adhesives; Cosmetics/Toiletries; Detergents/Household Cleansers; Industrial and Institutional Hygiene/Surface Technologies; Chemical Products (Cognis).

Principal Competitors

Akzo Nobel N.V.; Alusuisse Lonza Group Ltd.; American Home Products Corporation; Avon Products, Inc.; BASF Aktiengesellschaft; Bayer AG; Beiersdorf AG; The BFGoodrich Company; Burmah Castrol plc; CK Witco Corporation; Colgate-Palmolive Company; Cosmair, Inc.; Degussa-Hüls AG; The Dial Corporation; The Dow Chemical Company; E.I. du Pont de Nemours and Company; Elf Atochem; The Esteé Lauder Companies Inc.; H.B. Fuller Company; Hercules Incorporated; Imperial Chemical Industries PLC; Illinois Tool Works Inc.; Koor Industries Ltd.; L'Oréal; MacAndrews & Forbes Holdings Inc.; Minnesota Mining and Manufacturing Company; PPG Industries, Inc. The Procter & Gamble Company; Rohm and Haas Company; S.C. Johnson & Son, Inc.; Shiseido Company, Limited; Unilever PLC/Unilever N.V.

Further Reading

Alperowicz, Natasha, "Henkel to Separate Chemicals, Will Consider Mergers, IPO," *Chemical Week,* February 17, 1999.

Bowtell, Maurice, "Henkel: 75 and Going Strong," *Adhesives Age,* May 30, 1998.

Brockinton, Langdon, "Betting on a New U.S. Strategy at Henkel," *Chemical Week,* January 25, 1989, pp. 20+.

——, "For Emery, It's Henkel," *Chemical Week,* March 22, 1989, pp. 8+.

"Dial and Henkel Form North American JV for Laundry Detergents," *Chemical Market Reporter,* April 26, 1999, p. 3.

1876–1976 Hundert Jahre Henkel, Düsseldorf: Henkel, 1976.

"European Trimming Fills Henkel's China Sails," *Chemical Week,* February 9, 1994, pp. 20+.

Fisher, Andrew, "Hoechst Sells Hair Care Arm to Henkel," *Financial Times,* August 12, 1995, p. 11.

Gibson, W. David, "Henkel Tightens Up Its U.S. Operations," *Chemical Week,* February 5, 1986, pp. 22+.

Goosmann, Cornelia, *Ein Jahrhundert Wasserglas von Henkel,* Düsseldorf: Henkel, 1985, 76 p.

"Henkel Enters US Personal Care Market," *Chemical Market Reporter,* July 20, 1998, p. 3.

Henkel—Specialist in Applied Chemistry, Düsseldorf: Henkel, 1989.

Kerber, Ross, "Loctite Accepts New Henkel Offer of $1.3 Billion," *Wall Street Journal,* December 6, 1996, p. A12.

Kiesche, Elizabeth S., "In the U.S., Henkel Achieves Critical Mass, Focuses on Productivity," *Chemical Week,* February 9, 1994, pp. 20–21.

Layman, Patricia L., "A Rejuvenated Henkel Looking for New Markets," *Chemical and Engineering News,* February 10, 1986, p. 15.

Lipin, Steven, "Loctite Sought by Henkel in Hostile Step," *Wall Street Journal,* November 6, 1996, p. A3.

Marcial, Gene G., "Clorox' Uneasy Alliance," *Business Week,* November 7, 1988, p. 162.

Marsh, Peter, "The Secret Is in the Mix for Germany's Brightest," *Financial Times,* December 7, 1988.

Marshall, Matt, "Henkel Leaves German Fold to Go Global," *Wall Street Journal,* December 9, 1996, p. A9.

McCoy, Michael, "Henkel CEO Is Cautious on Outlook," *Chemical Marketing Reporter,* March 22, 1993, p. 9.

O'Boyle, Thomas F., "Henkel Makes Mark with Acquisitions," *Wall Street Journal/Europe,* November 25, 1988.

Schöne, Manfred, *Stammwerk Henkel 80 Jahre in Düsseldorf-Holthausen,* Düsseldorf: Henkel, 1981, 148 p.

——, *Von der Leimabteilung zum grössten Klebstoffwerk Europas,* Düsseldorf: Henkel, 1979, 68 p.

Scott, Alex, "Henkel Shows Rivals a Green Pair of Heels," *Chemical Week,* January 19, 2000, p. 45.

Walsh, Kerri, "Free to Serve Henkel's Rivals," *Chemical Week,* September 8, 1999, p. 53.

—Alison Classe and Olive Classe
—updated by David E. Salamie

Hermès International S.A.

24, rue de Faubourg Saint Honoré
F-75008 Paris 08
France
Telephone: (40) 17 47 17
Fax: (40) 17 47 18

Public Company
Founded: 1837
Employees: 4,096
Sales: FFr 6.08 billion (US$1 billion)(1999)
Stock Exchanges: Paris
Ticker Symbol: HRMS
NAIC: 315999 Other Apparel Accessories and Other
Apparel Manufacturing; 316991 Luggage
Manufacturing; 316992 Women's Handbag and Purse
Manufacturing; 32562 Toilet Preparation Manufactur-
ing; 315992 Glove and Mitten Manufacturing; 332211
Cutlery and Flatware (Except Precious)
Manufacturing; 44815 Clothing Accessories Stores

Known as "one of the world's most elegant businesses," Hermès International S.A. is a manufacturer and marketer of upscale luggage, apparel, and accessories. From a 19th-century foundation in leather goods, the company (pronounced "air-may") diversified into silk goods, ready-to-wear clothing, and perfume. Its ongoing dedication to family ownership and management, impeccable craftsmanship, and careful protection of the brand's mystique set Hermès apart from many of its French luxury goods compatriots. With or without the venerable trademark, Hermès products are distinguished by their uncompromising quality, a concept summarized in a family credo: "Que l'utile soit beau" ("That the useful be beautiful").

Founding a Luxury Dynasty in the 19th Century

Hermès's trademark calèche, or horse-drawn carriage (based on a drawing by Alfred de Dreux), harkens back to its origins as a wholesale saddlery business. Founded in 1837 by Thierry Hermès, the firm gained renown as a producer of one-of-a-kind saddlery for European noblemen. It was rumored that coronations were sometimes postponed for years until Hermès could create original carriage designs.

The functional and decorative "saddle stitch" used by Hermès craftsmen to join pieces of leather together would come to represent the branded goods' quality and simple elegance. When executed by hand (as it was throughout Hermès's history), the technique involved punching holes through multiple layers of leather, then alternating needles at either end of a beeswaxed linen thread through the holes in a figure-eight pattern. The company continued to custom-make saddles, investing 20 to 40 hours in each, throughout the 19th and 20th centuries.

Thierry Hermès's son Emile-Charles moved the family business to 24, rue du Faubourg St. Honoré—a site that would become one of Paris's most prized pieces of real estate—and launched retail sales sometime before the turn of the 20th century. He sold his stake in the business to brother Emile-Maurice in 1922.

Faced with the ascent of the automobile and corresponding obsolescence of the carriage, Emile-Maurice Hermès began to diversify into travel- and sport-related leather goods. Still, he never abandoned Hermès's "horsey heritage," though saddlebags would give way to luggage, wallets, and handbags. The famous Hermès "Kelly" bag, named in the 1950s after Princess Grace (née Kelly) of Monaco, who was often photographed with the accessory, started out as a specialty 19th-century saddlebag and was reintroduced as a handbag in the 1930s. The attention to detail that had become a family hallmark was applied to every new Hermès product. The construction of each Kelly bag, for example, required 18 hours of work by a single artisan. The association with royalty and celebrities—the Hermès "Constance" purse was a favorite of Jacqueline Kennedy Onassis—helped burnish the brand image. Although the company introduced a dozen new handbag styles each year, these two designs–the Kelly and the Constance–would remain in consistent demand.

Another company innovation under the leadership of Emile-Maurice Hermès was his purchase of a two-year patent on a Canadian invention, the *fermeture éclair*, or zipper, which he

Company Perspectives:

Over the course of the following years, Hermès will pursue its strategy based on the creativity and quality of its products, the reinforcement of its know-how in each of its markets, as well as the development of new client areas.

brought back to France. The closure became so closely associated with Hermès products (handbags, jockey silks, and leather gloves) that Frenchmen came to call it a *fermeture Hermès*. One oft-repeated "zipper story" finds the Prince of Wales, a well-known fashion maven, requesting a zippered leather golfing jacket, thereby inaugurating the Hermès line of leather apparel. The family launched ready-to-wear clothing, leather-banded watches, and leather gloves in the 1920s as well.

Emile-Maurice Hermès passed the family business on to his son-in-law, Robert Dumas, who would direct the design and production of the first Hermès *carré,* or scarf, in 1937. The custom-ordered silk accessory featured a print of white-wigged ladies playing a popular period game in a design the company entitled *Jeu des Ombinus et Dames Blanches.* Over the years the Hermès scarves became ingrained in the French culture as a traditional heirloom. Although scarf production slackened in the mid-20th century, by the mid-1980s Hermès would be unveiling a dozen new designs each year.

Like the production of leather goods, Hermès's scarf-making process was totally dedicated to the pursuit of quality. Vertical integration was an important factor in that cause. Hermès oversaw the entire process, from the purchase of the raw Chinese silk at auction, its spinning into yarn, and its weaving into a fabric twice as strong and heavy as that found in most scarves. Hermès scarf designers would spend years composing new prints, which were individually screen-printed with vegetable dye. In the process, each color is allowed to dry for one month before the next is applied. Hermès artisans would choose from a palette of over 200,000 colors; the most complicated design featured 40 colors. Hand-rolling and -hemming the scarves, which consumed a half-hour each, completed the process.

Despite this painstaking work, Hermès managed to put out two new scarf collections a year in the 1990s. Some were limited designs, part of annual themes, like "the road" (1994) or "the sun" (1995), while other perennial favorites remained in circulation for decades. Scarf motifs ranged from germane—the French Revolution, French cuisine—to the unexpected, including the flora and fauna of Texas. Some considered the scarves collectible works of art. Overall scarf production volume would multiply from 250,000 in 1978 to 500,000 in 1986 and 1.2 million in 1989.

The Hermès union of quality materials and time-consuming handcraftsmanship was reflected in its high retail prices. By the mid-1990s one Hermès scarf commanded US$245, a tie cost US$115, and a Kelly purse set its owner back about US$3,500. High demand added another element to the cost: customers were known to wait more than a year for orders to be filled.

Over the decades Hermès also earned a reputation for creating unique custom articles. Urging clients to *faites nous rêver* (make us dream), Hermès designers and craftsmen fashioned unusual special orders. The custom items ranged from the functional, such as a calfskin fly-fishing tackle box, to the frivolous, including an ostrich-skin Walkman case. These limited-edition novelties did not come cheap either; indulgences such as US$175 chewing-gum holders made of leather, US$1,000 silk kites, US$20,000 alligator golf bags, and US$12,500 mink jogging suits were out of reach for most of the world's consumers.

Turnaround in the 1980s

During the 1970s some analysts suspected that the profitability of Hermès was being sacrificed on the altar of quality. The company's dedication to modest styles and classic, natural materials (silk and leather) clashed with the era's penchant for newer man-made materials—like plastic and polyester—as well as sexy fashions. During this time, the company's five percent annual sales growth rate lagged France's 15 percent inflation rate, and at one point, the company's workrooms—known familiarly as *la ruche* (the beehive)—fell silent during a two-week lapse in orders.

When Robert Dumas died in 1978, his son, Jean-Louis Dumas, assumed the company's top post. The younger Dumas had worked as a buyer for Bloomingdale's before returning to the family firm in 1964, and this "outside" experience may have been the catalyst for the sweeping turnaround he engineered in the 1980s.

Dumas's multifaceted strategy expanded and revitalized the product line, strengthened the brand's youth appeal, extended vertical integration, and targeted the United States and Asia as fertile ground for growth. Dumas hired two young clothing designers, Eric Bergére and Bernard Sanz, to revive the apparel line, and together they added unusual new garments such as python motorcycle jackets and ostrich-skin jeans, which they characterized as "a snazzier version of what Hermès has been all along." A 1979 French advertising campaign that featured a young, denim-clad woman accessorized with an Hermès scarf introduced the branded goods to a new generation of consumers. As one observer noted, "Much of what bears the still-discreet Hermès label changed from the object of an old person's nostalgia to the subject of young peoples' dreams." By 1990 Hermès had expanded its array of merchandise to include 30,000 different items.

Dumas also revived the Hermès passion for vertical integration, which brought quality control at all phases of production under the family's watchful eyes. For example, Hermès had launched a line of "art de vivre"—giftware and home furnishings—in 1954. In the 1980s Dumas strengthened the company's hold on its suppliers, acquiring major stakes in such prestigious French glassware, silverware, and tableware manufacturers as Puiforcat, St. Louis, and Perigord. These tactics positioned tableware as one of Hermès's most promising business segments for the 1990s.

The company's explosive growth—annual sales multiplied from about US$50 million in 1978 to US$460 million by 1990, and its net profit grew even faster—had as much to do with

Key Dates:

1837: Company is founded, by Thierry Hermès, as a maker of saddles for horses.

1920: Company launches a line of clothing, watches, and gloves.

1930s: Leadership passes to Robert Dumas, son-in-law of Emile-Maurice Hermès; company introduces handbags and enters the U.S. market.

1937: The first Hermès scarf debuts.

1954: A line of giftware and home furnishings is launched.

1978: Jean-Louis Dumas takes over leadership of the company.

1990: Total Hermès stores, company-owned as well as franchised, reaches 225.

1993: Company goes public.

1996: An Hermès store is opened in Beijing, China.

1999: Company acquires a 35 percent interest in Groupe Jean-Paul Gaultier.

changing consumer values as with Dumas's revitalization. The trend of the 1960s and 1970s toward synthetic materials reversed, and a wave of conspicuous consumption engrossed consumers, especially Japanese and U.S. "nouveau riche." Although demand for luxury goods stalled somewhat in the early 1990s, the global market surged overall from US$4 billion in 1988 to nearly US$6 million in 1994, according to France's luxury trade group, the Comité Colbert.

Dumas took advantage of the resurgence in Hermès's popularity by boosting locations and licensed boutiques in the United States, Japan, Asia, and the Pacific Rim. The number of Hermès-owned stores quadrupled from 15 in 1978 to 60 in the early 1990s, as the total number of outlets worldwide grew to more than 225.

In the United States, sales tripled from US$20 million in 1986 to nearly US$60 million in 1988 under the direction of Chrysler Fisher, an American. Hermès had first entered the U.S. market in the 1930s, when its products were offered at Lord & Taylor's New York store. The company later pulled out of the United States, only to relaunch a line of ties at Neiman-Marcus in the 1960s. Fisher, a former Neiman-Marcus executive, tailored Hermès to the convenience-oriented U.S. consumer with the addition of a toll free number, a customer service department, and direct mail. When Fisher resigned in 1993, Laurent Mommeja, a sixth-generation Hermès descendant, would take over leadership of American operations and announce plans to double U.S. sales by 1998.

Growth in the 1990s

Jean-Louis Dumas continued to head Hermès as it experienced on even greater growth in the 1990s. Stanley Marcus, chairman emeritus of Neiman-Marcus, called Dumas "one of the brightest retailers in the world." Credited with building Hermès's worldwide retailing empire by directing an intense program of geographic expansion, Dumas helped shift the com-

pany's sales from its reliance on Europe to the United States and Asia/Pacific regions. Although more than 50 percent of annual sales were still generated in Europe in the early 1990s, the Asia/Pacific region contributed nearly one-third of annual revenues, and the United States pitched in 11 percent of yearly turnover. Hermès enjoyed average annual sales increases of 23 percent from 1984 to 1994 but expected that heady growth to slow to single-digit percentages in the mid- to late 1990s.

Under pressure from some factions in the extended family, Hermès made its first public stock offering in June 1993. The equity sale generated more excitement than the semiannual sales at Hermès's flagship store: the 425,000 shares floated at FFr 300 (US$55) each were oversubscribed by 34 times. Dumas told *Forbes* magazine that the equity sale helped lessen family tensions by allowing some members to liquidate their holdings without squabbling over share valuations among themselves. By 1995 the shares were trading at FFr 600. The Hermès family nonetheless maintained tight control; some 80 percent of the company's stock remained in the family, earning Jean-Louis Dumas and family a place on the *Forbes* list of billionaires. Such tight familial control prompted Mimi Tompkins of *U.S. News & World Report* to dub the company "one of Paris' best-guarded jewels."

Perfume was one of the few Hermès ventures to struggle. This business segment had been launched by Jean Guerrand, a son-in-law of Emile-Maurice, in 1951 with the introduction of "Eau d'Hermès." The business was elevated to subsidiary status in 1961 concurrent with the introduction of "Calèche" perfume, named for the company's carriage trademark. By 1993 this Comptoir Nouveau de la Perfumerie subsidiary was generating about FFr 200 million (US$40 million) in annual sales. Although the company's line of fragrances for men and women had captured seven percent of global perfume sales, its annual losses mounted in the early 1990s. This segment's sales peaked at FFr 254 million in 1990 and declined to FFr 200 million by 1994, while losses rose from FFr 1.4 million in 1992 to about FFr 30 million by 1994.

The very nature of the product provided some insight into Hermès's struggle to make it viable in the 1990s. While the vast majority of Hermès products were carefully fashioned to endure a lifetime of use, perfume was a mass-produced product with a decidedly ephemeral effect. Nevertheless, the company remained in the perfume business, launching "24, Faubourg," a scent named for the address of the company's flagship store, in 1995. Hermès hoped that the light, fresh fragrance would appeal to a younger customer than its more traditional perfumes and recapture the essence of luxury that had infused its perfume business with success in the 1950s and 1960s. In the meantime, the company sought to achieve profitability by contracting its excess manufacturing capacity to others in the mid-1990s. Hermès continued to introduce new fragrances through the end of the 1990s, and would achieve considerable success with "Hiris," launched in 1999.

Hermès's 1994 revenues totaled FFr 3.43 billion, 20 percent more than the previous year's mark, and net income increased 38 percent to FFr 290 million. A growing advertising budget was partially credited with sales spurts in leather goods, scarves, and other silk products. Same-store sales grew a whopping 16 percent during the period.

In the mid-1990s, Dumas planned to boost profits by reducing the number of Hermès ''concessionaires'' or franchisees. Specifically, he planned to cut Hermès's total number of venues from 250 to 200 and to expand the number of company-owned stores from 60 to 100. This strategy would bring more control of venue under family hands. Although this move was expected to cost the company FFr 200 million in the short term, it would increase long-term profit potential. With over FFr 500 million in cash on hand, Hermès could afford the investment. Among the company's new targets was China, where the company opened its first store in Beijing in 1996. Another unique, innovative move on the part of Dumas was to hire Martin Margiela, a modernist designer, to head up women's ready-to-wear operations at Hermès.

In the late 1990s, Hermès maintained its course of reducing the number of franchised stores; in 1999, for example, the company bought up franchises in Marseilles, Padua, and Berlin, while at the same time opening new non-franchised stores, including locations in Las Vegas and Atlanta. A new store on New York's Madison Avenue was scheduled to open in 2000; in that year the company also expected to add four new Hermès stores in Lisbon, Santiago, Barcelona, and Taiwan, while also opening its first John Lobb footwear store in New York. Meanwhile, the company had already begun renovation of its Tokyo Ginza-district store and the opening of a branch in Moscow. In September 1999, Hermès raised fashion eyebrows when it paid FFr 150 million for a 35 percent stake in the Jean-Paul Gaultier fashion house. The move, seen as part of a consolidation in the luxury goods market, was greeted nonetheless as a positive development both for the relatively small Gaultier group and for Hermès.

Principal Subsidiaries

Groupe Jean-Paul Gaultier (35%); John Lobb.

Principal Competitors

Chanel S.A.; Gucci Group N.V.; LVMH Moët Hennessy Louis Vuitton SA; Christian Dior S.A.

Further Reading

Berman, Phyllis, ''Mass Production? Yech!,'' *Forbes,* September 22, 1986, p. 182.

Brubach, Holly, ''The Hunger for Hermès,'' *Atlantic,* December 1986, p. 92.

Drawbaugh, Kevin, ''Hermès-Gaultier Fires Luxury Deals Talk,'' *Reuters,* July 9, 1999.

Dryansky, G.Y., ''Hermès: Quality With a Kick,'' *Harper's Bazaar,* April 1986, p. 218.

Fawcett, Karen, ''France's Hermes Counts on American Risk-Takers,'' *USA Today,* December 4, 1996, p. 5.

''Hermès Sales Leap in '99,'' *Women's Wear Daily,* February 11, 2000, p. 14.

Hornblower, Margot, ''As Luxe As It Gets: The Bold Scion of Hermès Gives an Old World Firm Fresh Pizazz,'' *Time,* August 6, 1990, p. 52.

Michael, Jane Wilkens, ''Family Ties,'' *Town & Country Monthly,* June 1992, p. 53.

Reynolds, C.P., ''Hermès,'' *Gourmet,* February 1987, p. 42.

Rotenier, Nancy, ''Tie Man Meets Queen of England,'' *Forbes,* September 13, 1993, p. 46.

''Scarves Everywhere,'' *New Yorker,* January 30, 1989, p. 24.

Thomas, Dana, ''Gaultier Goes for Growth,'' *Newsweek International,* July 19, 1999, p. 23.

Tompkins, Mimi, ''Sweatshop of the Stars,'' *U.S. News & World Report,* February 12, 1990, p. 51.

Weisman, Katherine, ''Bag War: Hermès Must Pay Bugatti for Use of Its Name,'' *Women's Wear Daily,* January 30, 1995, p. 9.

——, ''Hermès: Scents Were Off in Otherwise Robust '93,'' *Women's Wear Daily,* June 1, 1994, p. 16.

——, ''Hermès Sees Growth Slowing After Strong '94,'' *Women's Wear Daily,* June 1, 1995, p. 2.

—April Dougal Gasbarre
—updated by M.L. Cohen

The Hockey Company

3500 Boulevard Maisonneuve West
Suite 800
Westmount, Quebec H3Z 3C1
Canada
Telephone: (514) 932-1118
Fax: (514) 932-6043

Public Company
Incorporated: 1991 as SLM International Inc.
Employees: 1,756
Sales: US$190.6 million (1999)
Stock Exchanges: NASDAQ
Ticker Symbol: THCX
NAIC: 339920 Sporting and Athletic Goods
   Manufacturing; 421910 Sporting and Recreational
   Goods and Supplies Wholesalers; 315223 Men's and
   Boys' Cut and Sew Shirt (Except Work Shirt)
   Manufacturing (pt); 315299 All Other Cut and Sew
   Apparel Manufacturing (pt); 316219 Other Footwear
   Manufacturing

The Hockey Company is the world's largest manufacturer of hockey equipment, producing and distributing hockey products such as hockey skates, sticks, uniforms and apparel, and protective gear. The company also makes inline skates and holds licensing agreements to make and market apparel and other products with the National Hockey League (NHL) logo. In addition to its flagship brand CCM, The Hockey Company sells merchandise under the brand names Canadien, Heaton, Jofa, Koho, and Titan. The Hockey Company was formerly known as SLM International Inc. and emerged from Chapter 11 in 1997.

Falling into Hockey: Mid-1970s

What eventually became The Hockey Company began as somewhat of a chance occurrence. The Zunenshine family was well known in Montreal for its commercial real estate business Belcourt Inc., which it began in the 1950s. In 1976 an interest in diversification and a tax-loss credit prompted chairman David Zunenshine to purchase GC Knitting, a manufacturer of polyester hockey jerseys. Though Zunenshine had no intention of expanding into sporting goods, GC Knitting was performing strongly, and thus Zunenshine decided to keep the business and make a go of it.

The Zunenshine family moved more decisively into the hockey realm in 1983 with the purchase of the hockey assets of CCM Inc., which had been making ice hockey skates since 1905. CCM commanded strong brand awareness, but the company fell into bankruptcy in the early 1980s. With the CCM purchase the Zunenshines also acquired the Tacks brand of skates. Also in the early 1980s the Zunenshines bought Sandow Sports Knit, which provided them with the license to make and market NHL jerseys, and in 1985 the Zunenshines purchased St. Lawrence Manufacturing Canada Inc., the primary supplier of ice skate blades for CCM. St. Lawrence, like CCM, faced financial troubles.

Using the initials of St. Lawrence, the Zunenshines called their company SLM Canada and worked to revitalize the ailing companies, financing their efforts with real estate resources. The purchase of St. Lawrence gave the Zunenshine family additional manufacturing capabilities and more plastic injection molding capacity than the company required. To take advantage of the resources, the Zunenshines bought equipment specifically designed to manufacture toboggans and plastic sleds and imported the gear from Scandinavia.

Foray into Toys Sparks Growth in the Late 1980s and Early 1990s

One problem SLM faced was that its business was largely seasonal, with most of the company's products geared toward winter sports and activities. As a result, the company's factories were relatively unproductive during the summer months. To tackle the dilemma, the Zunenshines acquired Coleco Industries, a toy manufacturer, in 1988 when Coleco went bankrupt. Coleco was known for producing Cabbage Patch dolls but also made swimming pools and other plastic goods for children. The Zunenshines hoped the purchase would round out SLM and boost productivity throughout the year.

Company Perspectives:

The Hockey Company's strategy is based on superior product technology and brand leadership. The hockey equipment market is driven by new product innovation and the Company manages a portfolio of the world's leading brands—CCM, Koho, and Jofa—that market these new technologies. Each brand is focused on a different consumer segment and multiple channels of distribution. The strategy is intended to allow the Company to fully penetrate all viable hockey markets with products it develops, manufactures and markets. The Company believes it can achieve annual revenue growth at a higher rate than the expected growth of the world-wide hockey market.

The Zunenshines expanded further into the toy market in 1990 when they acquired another financially troubled company—Buddy L Corp., a 70-year-old manufacturer of steel and plastic toy cars and trucks based in the United States. The method of growth through the acquisition of bankrupt companies caught up with the Zunenshines, however, and the family found itself struggling to keep SLM afloat. To help manage the financially beleaguered network of companies, the Zunenshines hired Earl Takefman to head SLM's toy division in 1990. Takefman was a Montreal entrepreneur who had recently resigned his post as president of Charan Industries Inc., a toy, gift, and sporting goods company that had gone from success to disaster. Takefman, who was named co-CEO with Howard Zunenshine, founder David Zunenshine's son, vowed not to repeat past mistakes and set about turning SLM around.

The year 1990 was not a good one financially for SLM. The toy division, still in the midst of reorganization, posted an operating loss of US$2.2 million, and the company overall reported a net loss of US$3.2 million. The toy segment quickly began to improve sales, however, when the company obtained the licensing rights to reproduce such popular characters as the Little Mermaid, Big Bird, and Cookie Monster on toy swimming pools. The industrywide rise in toy sales in 1991 also helped SLM, and the company reported net income of US$6.3 million for fiscal 1991.

Motivated by the rapid turnaround, SLM sought additional avenues for growth, and in November 1991 the company went public, adopted the new name SLM International Inc., and set up headquarters in New York. By February 1992 the company's stock had increased 71 percent, and SLM was one of the fastest-growing toy companies in the United States. Industry analysts gave SLM glowing reviews and projected strong growth. Takefman believed the toy division was the key to SLM's success and anticipated further growth and expansion, particularly in overseas markets.

By the early 1990s the hockey division, despite steady performance, was no longer the mainstay of SLM; in fact, hockey equipment accounted for less than 25 percent of sales in 1991. Expansion continued to drive the company, and in 1992 SLM purchased Kevin Sports Toys International Inc., the maker of the Wayne Gretzky NHL hockey game; Norca Industries Inc., a

plastic toy manufacturer of such products as swimming pools, sleds, and sandboxes; and Innova-Dex Sports Inc. of Montreal, a bicycle helmet manufacturer. SLM also sold fitness equipment through its SLM Fitness division. Products included the Superstep aerobic portable platform, Heavy Hands exercise weights, and Gravity Edge exercise unit, which were marketed through television infomercials featuring sports celebrities, including Olympian Bruce Jenner.

Innovation also drove SLM, and the company planned to introduce a number of new products, including the Voice Command Vehicle, a voice-activated toy truck, and a line of inline skates featuring "Pump" air-bladder technology licensed from Reebok International Ltd. Another pioneering product SLM readied for the retail market brought the company much publicity—in early 1993 SLM announced it would introduce the Super Charger, a recharger designed to renew the life of disposable alkaline batteries. While battery manufacturers, particularly market leader Duracell International, maintained that alkaline batteries were not designed to be recharged and that attempting to do so was potentially dangerous, SLM stated that its recharger had been tested rigorously and was safe. Though SLM hoped the recharger would significantly boost sales, the company contended that its future was not contingent upon the recharger's success. "We're not a battery-charger company. We're a toy company," Earl Takefman said in the *Asian Wall Street Journal*. "We're not going to sink or swim on this product."

Success certainly seemed to have hit SLM. Revenues for fiscal 1992 reached a record US$231.4 million, a 41 percent increase over 1991, and profits rose from US$6.2 million in 1991 to US$16.3 million. Toy sales alone grew 26 percent, to US$118.1 million, and SLM's market share in the toy industry was on the rise. In 1992 SLM's trucks powered past the Tonka brand to capture 27 percent of the market. SLM ranked second in the wheeled preschool toy market and was selected by retail giant Toys "R" Us as "vendor of the year" for three years running. SLM's sporting goods segment also performed strongly, with sales up 61 percent in 1992 compared to 1991 sales.

SLM appeared unstoppable as revenues and profits continued to climb. Since its IPO in late 1991, SLM had posted eight successive quarters of record revenues and earnings. The company continued to grow through acquisitions, and in 1994 SLM bought #1 Apparel Inc., a manufacturer of licensed sports apparel, particularly hats and outerwear. SLM had plans to expand its hockey and toy operations and penetrate the European market. Howard Zunenshine, who headed SLM's sporting goods division, explained SLM's strategy in *Sporting Goods Business* and said, "Our theory is it's easier to buy than build. . . . If you have cash in your pocket and you can buy shelf space, you're in. That's the way to go."

Things Fall Apart: Mid-1990s

SLM's success seemed to fade as quickly as it had appeared, and by late 1994 the company appeared to be in financial straits. The Zunenshine family's Belcourt Inc. went bankrupt in 1994, and in August Earl Takefman left the company, leaving with a severance package worth $1.5 million. SLM, of which the Zunenshines owned 42 percent in late 1994, reported a loss of

US$52 million for the third quarter ended October 1, 1994. The company's stock, which had reached a high of $30 in late 1993, plunged to less than $3 a share by late 1994. At the beginning of October SLM reported a deficit in working capital of US$5.8 million, compared to a surplus of $84 million just a year earlier. The company also disclosed that it had breached its loan agreements with its lenders.

Howard Zunenshine, who became sole CEO after Takefman's departure, attributed many of the company's problems to the toy division, which he said had "run amok." The expense of producing infomercials for toys and fitness equipment proved costly and caused SLM's selling and general and administrative expenses to nearly double in the first nine months of 1994. The Buddy L Super Charger did not perform to the company's expectations, and after continued controversy and a negative review by *Consumer Reports* magazine, the product was pulled from the market. Despite SLM's difficulties, Howard Zunenshine remained optimistic about the company's future. The sporting goods division managed to perform well during the first nine months of 1994, with sales increasing 44 percent, and new management was placed in the toy division. Zunenshine told the *Gazette (Montreal),* "We're not in dire straits by any stretch of the imagination. . . . We've had better years, . . . but we're optimistic."

Optimistic or not, the Buddy L toy division filed for Chapter 11 bankruptcy protection in early 1995, and SLM's lenders attempted to force four SLM units—Toy Factory Inc., Consumer InfoMarketing Inc., Maska U.S. Inc., and #1 Apparel Inc.—into bankruptcy. SLM's shares were then delisted from the NASDAQ exchange in May because they failed to meet NASDAQ's minimum net worth requirement. For fiscal 1994 SLM reported a net loss of US$112 million on sales of $181 million, and the following year the company's net loss was $77.5 million on sales of $161 million.

In July 1995 SLM exited the toy industry when it sold its Buddy L toy division to Empire of Carolina, Inc., for US$3.75 million and 757,000 shares of stock. The company also sold its fitness equipment business to a group consisting of former SLM Fitness management. SLM planned to refocus its efforts on its flagship hockey equipment division. In October SLM International and its subsidiaries filed for Chapter 11, noting debt of US$184.6 million. Though operations continued, SLM's status as a leader in the hockey realm was in question. CCM's exclusive contract with the NHL to produce apparel ended in 1995 when the NHL formed licensing agreements with other companies, beginning with Starter Corp., which in about half a year gained more than half of the market share in NHL jerseys.

Rebuilding and Return to Hockey: Late 1990s

In April 1997 SLM emerged from bankruptcy with new management in place and a reorganization plan. New York-based investment bank Wellspring Associates LLC, which specialized in buying financially troubled companies, became the primary shareholder of SLM, and the Zunenshine family was no longer part of the company. The company's new common stock began trading under the symbol "THCX" on the OTC Bulletin Board. The company's new CEO, drawn out of retirement by SLM's lenders, was Gerald Wasserman, who had been the president and CEO of SLM competitor Canstar Sports Inc. and a key player in Canstar's turnaround in the early 1990s. Canstar, acquired by NIKE, Inc. in 1995 and renamed Bauer Inc., was headed by a former colleague of Wasserman's.

Wasserman planned to take advantage of the booming hockey industry, estimated to be worth more than US$600 million in the United States alone, and leverage the strength of the CCM brand. Wasserman closed SLM's New York offices and moved the headquarters to Montreal. Operations were consolidated, several facilities were closed, and subsidiary Mitchel & King Skates Limited was sold. His executive team included several people Wasserman managed to lure away from Bauer. Wasserman intended to invest more in research and development, believing that innovation and technology were key components of success in the hockey industry. Though the new team felt confident in SLM's future and possibilities, it faced many challenges, particularly from Bauer. Of the hockey skates and hockey gear sold in North America in the mid-1990s, SLM and Bauer accounted for 95 percent. And though 40 percent of NHL players used CCM's Tacks brand of skates, the Bauer brand was stronger among the general public, commanding twice the market share.

In 1998 SLM became the largest hockey company in the world when it acquired Montreal-based Sports Holding Corp., a manufacturer of hockey equipment. Sports Holding's brands included Finnish Koho, Titan, Swedish Jofa, Canadien, and Heaton. The acquisition significantly boosted SLM's presence in Europe, as Sports Holding was the leading hockey equipment company in Central Europe and Scandinavia. In addition, the company was a market leader in hockey sticks and protective gear, sold under the Jofa and Koho brands. The combined company was estimated to have sales of about US$200 million a year.

In early 1999 SLM changed its name to The Hockey Company. Wasserman commented on the new name in a prepared statement and said, "Our new name reflects the leadership position that our company enjoys in the hockey industry. The Hockey Company possesses the most widely recognized hockey brands in both Europe and North America, as well as product lines and geographic strengths that are highly complementary.'' The Hockey Company secured a ''Center Ice'' licensing agreement with the NHL which permitted the company to make and market apparel with NHL logos. The company also made protective equipment under license from the NHL. The Hockey Company's share of the NHL licensed apparel trade increased in 1999 as well, as Starter Corp. and NIKE both withdrew from the replica jersey industry.

Sales in fiscal 1999 grew 4.1 percent compared to 1998 figures to reach US$190.6 million. Revenues were supported by an increase in apparel sales, in the selling price of goaltender equipment, and in hockey stick sales. The Hockey Company reported a net loss of US$1.8 million, slightly down from a net loss of US$2.0 million in 1998. The ultimate fate of The Hockey Company was unknown, and the company had certainly experienced its share of ups and downs. With the popularity of hockey still growing, an experienced and knowledgeable team managing the company, and a host of new and innovative products readied for launch, the odds seemed to be in The Hockey Company's favor.

Principal Subsidiaries

Maska U.S., Inc.; Sport Maska Inc.; SLM Trademark Acquisition Corp.; SLM Trademark Acquisition Canada Corporation; Sport Maska Europe S.A.R.L.; Maska H.K. Limited; Sports Holding Corp.; KHF Finland Oy; KHF Sports Oy; WAP Holding Inc.; JOFA Holding AB; JOFA AB; JOFA Norge A/S; J.W. Verwaltungsgesellscahft mbH; Solte Kunstoffverarbeltungsgesellschaft mbH; 2867923 Canada Inc.

Principal Competitors

NIKE, Inc.; Rawlings Sporting Goods Company, Inc.; Riddell Sports Inc.

Further Reading

Bernstein, Andy, ''Starter, Others Cutting into NHL Pie As CCM Sorts Out Troubles,'' *Sporting Goods Business,* January 1, 1996, p. 28.

Hadekel, Peter, ''After Belcourt Bankruptcy, Zunenshines Take Beating in Toy Department,'' *Gazette (Montreal),* November 29, 1994, p. D1.

Ingram, Mathew, ''U.S. Insurers Seek SLM Bankruptcy,'' *Globe and Mail,* March 7, 1995, p. B15.

Leitch, Carolyn, ''SLM Hopes to Rebuild CCM Line,'' *The Globe and Mail,* January 9, 1997, p. B8.

Levingston, Steven E., ''SLM Sparks Controversy As It Launches Product,'' *Asian Wall Street Journal,* February 8, 1993, p. 10.

McEvoy, Christopher, ''SLM International,'' *Sporting Goods Business,* February 1, 1994, p. 76.

Millan, Luis, ''Ice Follies,'' *Canadian Business,* June 1, 1997, p. 126.

Morris, Kathleen, ''SLM International: A Buy in Toyland,'' *FW,* July 21, 1992, p. 16.

Reguly, Eric, ''Toymaker SLM Playing with Big Boys,'' *Financial Post,* June 26, 1993, p. 14.

Shalom, Francois, ''CCM Is Back in the Game,'' *Gazette (Montreal),* February 17, 1997, p. C12.

——, ''SLM Laces Up Merger,'' *Gazette (Montreal),* October 9, 1998, p. E1.

——, ''SLM Subsidiary Upbeat Despite Parent Firm's Problems,'' *Gazette (Montreal),* October 25, 1995, p. D8.

Strauss, Gary, ''SLM Skating Toward Big Growth,'' *USA Today,* February 25, 1992, p. B3.

Toomey, Craig, ''Fun and Games,'' *Gazette (Montreal),* March 30, 1992, p. B8.

Weinberg, Neil, ''One Thing Led to Another,'' *Forbes,* October 25, 1993, p. 206.

—Mariko Fujinaka

Hyder plc

PO Box 295
Alexandra Gate
Rover Way
Cardiff CF2 2UE
United Kingdom
Telephone: (+44) 1222 500-600
Fax: (+44) 1222 585-600
Web site: http://www.hyder.co.uk

Public Company
Incorporated: 1989 as Welsh Water
Employees: 9,400
Sales: £1.29 billion (US$2.1 billion) (1999)
Stock Exchanges: London
Ticker Symbol: WW.A
NAIC: 22111 Electric Power Generation; 221210 Natural Gas Distribution; 221310 Water Supply and Irrigation Systems

Many-headed Hyder (the Welsh word for confidence; rhymes with rudder) plc provides integrated water, electricity, and gas services to some three million customers in Wales and throughout the United Kingdom. More than three million water customers, one million electricity customers, and over 400,000 gas customers have helped Hyder plc claim its status as Wales's largest publicly listed company, with more than 9,000 employees and annual turnover of nearly £1.3 billion. In April 2000, however, Hyder prepared to leave the London Stock Exchange when it agreed to be purchased by Japanese bank Nomoru. While the company's new owners pledged to keep Hyder's name and especially its Cardiff location, the company continues a restructuring of its operations begun in 1999, including the shedding of more than 1,000 jobs and the jettisoning of its SWALEC (South Wales Electric Company) retail electricity company, in a sale to British Electric finalized in February 2000. The streamlined Hyder will continue to provide water services, including an ambitious investment program and beach cleaning and other related water supply operations. Hyder also provides infrastructure consulting services for such major con-

struction projects as highways and roads, tunnels, bridges, railways, shipping ports, and airports, while extending its infrastructure component to design, build, and operate onsite water and waste management and utility systems for major corporations. Further lessening the company's dependence on the increasingly competitive—yet still tightly price-controlled—utilities sector is Hyder's increasing investments in the services market. In this sector the company provides a range of services, such as call centers and payroll management to both private companies and government agencies.

19th-Century Sources

Hyder surfaced from two centuries of water provision in Wales. The first private water companies in the United Kingdom appeared in the 18th century, often established by local communities. By the end of the 18th century, the United Kingdom's water supplies were handled by a large number of small, generally locally based companies. This situation began to change in the early years of the 19th century, as the Industrial Revolution transformed the United Kingdom's economic and social landscapes. More and more people were moving to the cities to seek work in the new economy, placing growing pressures on each city's infrastructure.

Water supply—especially the need to build the pipelines, lay the water mains, and construct other elements of the water supply infrastructure—quickly became a government responsibility. By 1848, the first legislation had been passed giving the government control over the water supply industry. Further legislation—the Health Act of 1875—gave the government full control of the United Kingdom's water utility sector. While the industrialization of the British economy required a reliable water supply, the increasing recognition of the key role of clean, drinkable water in the maintenance of good health had, by the beginning of the 20th century, also brought the issue of water supply into the sphere of national importance.

In 1924, the government took steps to reform the water industry. In that year, the United Kingdom's water industry was reorganized into a number of regional water councils. Over the next 50 years, the national government increased its position in the country's water supply, bringing its operation more and more under centralized oversight at the national level. This process was completed in 1973, when the Water Act of that year created a network of ten regionally operating water authorities. One of these new bodies was the Welsh Water Authority, based in Cardiff.

Nationalized control lasted only as long as the Labour Party-led government. The rise to power of the conservative government led by Margaret Thatcher introduced a new wave of privatization, as many of the country's hitherto government-operated industries and companies were turned out into the private sphere. Welsh Water's turn came in 1989, when the Water Industry Act of that year transformed the United Kingdom's water utility operators into private companies. These companies, with oversight from the government's Office of Water Services, were granted protection from any takeover attempts, as well as relatively high water rates, which seemed at the time to guarantee a healthy and highly profitable future. However, the Water Industry Act also contained provisions requiring the new private water utilities to maintain an ongoing infrastructure investment program.

Drying Up in the 1990s

Welsh Water began its new life with an optimistic plan to expand beyond water supply to become one of the country's first multiple-utilities providers. Taking the lead of the company was Graham Hawker. A Welsh native, Hawker came from a family that had long worked the region's mines—Hawker's grandfather, father, and brother had all been miners. When the local mine closed, Hawker had already taken a different path, attending school. After dropping out at the age of 16, Hawker took a position as a clerk in the community wage office. From there, Hawker, who in the meantime had earned an accountant's degree, moved to a post with the predecessor to Welsh Water. Rising through the ranks, Hawker had been named finance director when Welsh Water was privatized. In that same year, Hawker helped take Welsh Water public on the London Stock Exchange. The company became Wales's largest publicly listed corporation.

Taking over as CEO in 1993, Hawker launched Welsh Water on an ambitious program to diversify its holdings and extend its interests beyond water supply—which remained subject to strict government controls. The first step of the company's expansion was taken that same year, when Welsh Water acquired Acer Consultants, transforming the company into an internationally operating concern.

Acer Consultants had been formed in 1987 from the merger of two of the United Kingdom's most prominent infrastructure

specialists, Freeman Fox & Partners and John Taylor & Sons. Freeman Fox & Partners, one of the world's first infrastructure consultants, was formed in 1857 by Sir Charles Fox, one of the founders of the British railway system. Fox's career began in the 1820s, when he helped design one of the earliest steam locomotives. Fox opened a building and railways contracting firm, Mssrs. Fox and Henderson, and, in 1851, oversaw the construction of the famed Crystal Palace for that year's Great Exhibition in London. One of the first buildings to pioneer modern large building techniques, it was this structure that earned Fox his knighthood.

In 1857, Fox established a consultants firm, and became responsible for the building of a number of important railways, including London's Central Line, the State Railway in Hyderabad, India. Beyond the British Empire, Fox's firm oversaw the construction of more than 8,500 kilometers of railway in North and South America and in Africa. The company also became a leading bridge specialist, with early projects including the Tower Bridge of London.

By the 1930s, Fox's firm, renamed Freeman Fox & Partners in 1938, was one of the world's most reputable names in the building of bridges. Among the world landmarks attributed to the firm were the Humber Bridge, then the world's longest suspension bridge, the Sydney Harbour Bridge in Australia, and the Bosporus Bridges between Europe and Asia. With the rise of the automobile in the 20th century, Freeman Fox & Partners also became leading designers of roadways, including such projects as the M5 Motorway in England, and the Bangkok and Kuwaiti expressways. Freeman Fox also continued its tradition as a railway builder, with the construction of the Hong Kong Mass Transit Railway, begun in 1967 and completed in 1995. By then, Freeman Fox & Partners had merged with John Taylor & Sons, which had specialized in the design of water distribution and sewer treatment systems since its founding in 1869. John Taylor & Sons had been responsible for such major projects as the sewer system in Leningrad and the water supply system for Shanghai. Welsh Water's Acer Consultants unit was renamed Hyder Consulting in 1996.

By then, the United Kingdom was in the middle of an extended drought, placing the water industry under extreme pressure. While Welsh Water—in traditionally rain-heavy Wales—was in less dire straits, the company nonetheless started to feel the heat, and began to look elsewhere to shore up its profits. The delegislation of the United Kingdom's electric power industry seemed a likely bet for Welsh Water, which sought to offer a full package of utilities—water, electricity, and gas—to Wales. In 1996, the company bought SWALEC, the South Wales Electricity Company, paying £900 million, with the purchase financed largely by debt.

In its move beyond water supply, Welsh Water changed its name to Hyder, using the Welsh word for confidence, while playing on the Greek "hydro," for water. The SWALEC acquisition appeared a sound investment—the company quickly signed on more than 400,000 customers for its gas supply business, some four times more than its original projections. SWALEC also added nearly one million electricity customers to its three-million strong water supply base. In 1998, Hyder reformed its water, gas, and electricity supply businesses into a new subsidiary, Hyder Utilities. Yet the heavy debt brought on by the SWALEC purchase quickly led Hyder into trouble—and moves by the new Labour government were to bring Hyder to its knees.

Labour's long threat of a windfall tax, designed to retrieve some of the massive profits made by the United Kingdom's water suppliers, came into reality, hitting Hyder for some £300 million. At the same time, the government's new ministers overseeing the country's utilities clamped down on prices, with water rates reduced between 15 and 20 percent. Hyder's debt, and its obligation to continue infrastructure investments, including cleaning up the beaches of its South Wales region, as well as bond obligations scheduled to come due in the first years of the new century, soon brought the once high-flying Hyder down to earth.

The company's initial attempt to fend off financial disaster involved the shedding of some 1,200 jobs from 1999, a move that was criticized as pandering to the company's shareholders. With its stock price plummeting, Hyder ended that year by cutting its dividends. The company was also actively seeking to shed its electric utility business and exit the retail sales sector. In June 1993, Hyder agreed to sell the retail activities of SWALEC to British Energy, for a price of £105 million. That sale was completed in February 2000.

By then, Hyder had already announced that it had run out of financing, and that it expected to run out of capital within 15 months. The company put itself up for sale. Initial attempts to find a single buyer were unsuccessful—and Hyder was forced to consider a breakup, with an offer of £1.73 billion for Welsh Water from Barclays Capital, and a separate offer from U.S.-based South Western Electricity, a subsidiary of Pennsylvania Power and Light, of £600 million for the power distribution wing of SWALEC.

Instead, Hyder finally found a buyer for the whole company. In April 2000, Hyder announced its agreement to be purchased by Principal Finance Group, the London-based arm of Japan's Nomura Bank, which had already built up substantial holdings in the United Kingdom, including the Thorn rental chain, some 5,000 pubs, the Angel Trains railway leasing firm, and the William Hill bookmaker company. While Nomura's bid of £402 million was lower than the combined total of the two separate offers—leading to disagreement among Hyder's board of directors—the Hawker's backing of the Nomura offer won the day.

The Nomura purchase, which included assumption of Hyder's 1.9 billion in debt, for a total price of £2.3 billion, was expected to clear regulatory approval. The purchase also brought in a new chief executive, Mike Kinski, formally chief executive with the Stagecoach rail and bus company. Despite the sale of Wales's largest publicly held company to a foreign firm, the purchase was greeted with enthusiasm. Not only was Hyder guaranteed the needed financial backing, Nomura pledged to keep the Hyder name and the company's Cardiff location, thus restoring confidence in Hyder's future.

Principal Subsidiaries

Hyder Consulting Group Limited; Hyder Industrial Limited; Hyder Infrastructure Management Limited; Hyder Investments Limited; Laing Hyder plc; UK Highways M40 (Holdings) plc; (40%); Dwr Cymru Welsh Water Ltd.; Hyder Utilities (Operations) Limited (50%); South Wales Electricity plc; SWALEC Gas Limited.

Principal Competitors

Anglian Water; Centrica plc; Kelda Group; National Power PLC; Northern Electric; Pennon Group; PowerGen PLC; ScottishPower plc; Severn Trent PLC; Thames Water plc; Tractebel S.A.; United Utilities.

Further Reading

Callus, Andrew, and Dan Lalor, "Hyder Marks Low Tide for Water Stocks," *Reuters*, December 9, 1999.

Gribben, Roland, "Downstream Ride for Water Groups," *Daily Telegraph*, December 10, 1999, p. 36.

Minton, Ann, "Hyder Says Cut in Water Prices Is Impossible," *Independent*, June 4, 1999, p. 21.

Pickard, Jim, "Welsh Dragon No Longer Roars," *Financial Times*, April 19, 2000.

Rankine, Kate, "Hyder Divided but Nomura Bid Accepted," *The Scotsman*, April 19, 2000.

——, "Water Chief with a Spring in His Step," *Daily Telegraph*, June 13, 1998, p. 33.

—M. L. Cohen

IDT Corporation

190 Main Street
Hackensack, New Jersey 07601
U.S.A.
Telephone: (201) 928-1000
Toll Free: (800) 225-5438
Fax: (201) 928-1057
Web site: http://www.idt.net

Public Company
Incorporated: 1990 as International Discount
    Telecomunications Corporation
Employees: 1,271
Sales: $732.18 million (1999)
Stock Exchanges: NASDAQ
Ticker Symbol: IDTC
NAIC: 51331 Wired Telecommunications Carriers; 51333
    Telecommunications Resellers; 514191 On-Line
    Information Services

IDT Corporation is a leading provider of long-distance telephone access, Internet access, and global Internet telephony services. Its telecommunications activities include wholesale carrier services and prepaid calling cards. Launched as International Discount Telecommunications Corporation, the company pioneered international callback telephone service with a technology allowing anyone around the world to bypass the high cost of placing international calls from countries outside the United States.

International Telephone Callback Service: 1990–93

A native of New York City's borough of the Bronx, Howard Jonas graduated from Harvard in 1978. During the next decade he built a small brochure-distributing and publishing business into an enterprise with revenue exceeding $1 million a year, running it from a converted Bronx funeral home that he shared with his father's insurance brokerage. Shocked by the massive phone bills incurred by staffers who opened a company sales office in Israel, Jonas began thinking of ways to cut this cost of business. After a few months, and with the help of a computer engineer, he had, at an expense of $1,200, a working automatic-dialing device.

In 1990 Jonas entered the telecommunications industry with International Discount Telecommunications (IDT) Corporation, which introduced international call-reorganization service. This service capitalized on the often-prohibitive rates charged for long-distance telephone calls in certain highly regulated international markets. Subscribers calling a designated number from a foreign carrier's standard international calling service contacted an IDT node in Hackensack, New Jersey, transmitting a dial tone and hanging up after the first ring. The node was equipped with custom-designed call processors programmed to recognize such a call, routing it into the U.S. public switched telephone network and thereby enabling the client to place the call through the usually cheaper international calling service of the U.S. carrier chosen for this purpose.

For calls to the United States from such countries as Brazil, Italy, Spain, and the Soviet Union, the customer typically saved half the cost—sometimes more—by having these calls re-originated in the United States. IDT billed its customers at rates high enough to cover its operational costs and make a profit. (Before long, however, the company began leasing its processors so that clients could avoid this markup.) Because touch-tone phones were not readily available abroad, subscribers had to use hand-held dialers to generate the dual-tone multifrequency tones needed to enter access codes and telephone numbers into IDT's call processors. As part of the $250-a-month service, International Discount Telecommunications gave such callers a small electronic box with an automatic dialer and a device to coordinate conference calls. Each box could handle about 100 calls.

The company's first customer was NBC, which needed to be in frequent contact with a three-man team in Barcelona, Spain, preparing for the 1992 Summer Olympic Games. By the end of 1991 the company had 150 customers, some of them *Fortune* 500 firms, such as PepsiCo, Inc. Few, if any, were foreign enterprises, because they were fearful of angering their national telephone companies—most of them government-owned monopolies. France Telecom threatened legal action, for example, before reducing its own rates so much that Jonas pulled IDT out of the country.

Key Dates:

1990: Howard Jonas founds International Discount Tele-communications as an overseas callback service.
1993: IDT becomes a wholesale carrier for domestic customers.
1994: The company begins offering dial-up Internet access.
1995: Company is renamed IDT Corporation.
1996: IDT goes public; PC2Phone connects PCs and telephones over the Internet.
1997: IDT's Net2Phone enables calls to be made over the Internet using standard telephones.
1999: IDT earns its first annual profit.

In 1992 International Discount Telecommunications relocated its headquarters in the windowless, two-story, cement-block Hackensack building where it had placed the call receptors. Jonas sold 14 percent of IDT that year to an investor group for $1.4 million and bought new equipment, also hiring a couple of Bell Laboratories engineers to improve the technology. By the spring of 1993 Jonas claimed that his company was taking in $400,000 a month in revenue from more than 1,000 customers in about 60 countries.

Internet and Other Services: 1993–98

International Discount Telecommunications used the expertise derived from, and the calling volume generated by, its call-reorigination business to enter the domestic long-distance business in late 1993 by reselling the long-distance services of other carriers to its domestic customers. As a value-added service for these customers, the company began offering Internet access in early 1994. IDT also introduced an international fax service, offering a new, brand-name machine to any customer who would commit to sending $500 worth of such calls over the next two years and promising free e-mail and Internet access as well. Some 7,000 small businesses had signed up by midyear. The company also got a boost when the Federal Communications Commission denied AT&T Corp.'s 1992 petition to ban call-back services.

In May 1994 International Discount Telecommunications, in collaboration with the London-based Index on Censorship and other human rights groups, began publishing articles by political dissidents on the Internet. Its "Digital Freedom Network" web site offered a variety of material banned by various governments. The company's free-access policy extended to pornography—which raised some eyebrows, since Jonas was an Orthodox Jew and father of six. While other Internet providers were shutting down access to some sites, radio host Barry Farber, as part of a $10 million-a-year ad campaign, was promoting IDT's $15.95-a-month ($29.95 with images as well as text), no-time-limit service with the words, "I access *all* Internet services. I said *all* Internet services—get that naughty smirk off your face." By early 1996 IDT, seeking to survive the inevitable shakeout among the 1,350 or so U.S. Internet-access providers, had 65,000 subscribers.

International Discount Telecommunications had revenue of $3.17 million in fiscal 1994 (the year ended July 31, 1994), about half from domestic long-distance service. The company lost $289,000 but had no long-term debt. Revenue more than tripled in fiscal 1995, to $10.8 million, but rising expenses resulted in a loss of $2.15 million. Shortly after reincorporating as IDT Corporation, the company went public in February 1996, taking in $42.78 million by selling about 20 percent of its common stock at $10 a share. Jonas retained a 54 percent stake in the company. Revenue shot up fivefold in fiscal 1996, reaching $57.69 million, of which Internet, rather than telephone, service accounted for about 40 percent. IDT's costs rose even more rapidly, however, resulting in a net loss of $15.76 million for the fiscal year.

Under strain from its rapid expansion, IDT found itself flooded with mounting complaints from customers concerning technical problems, overbilling, and false or misleading advertising claims. At least some of the technical problems stemmed from IDT having become a national Internet provider without establishing a national infrastructure, instead contracting with more than 200 smaller service providers and thereby running the risk of incompatibility between carriers. In early 1997 IDT agreed to offer refunds to unhappy customers and to refrain from misleading and false statements in its advertising. (The company had, for example, neglected to inform Internet subscribers that they had to sign on for long-distance telephone as well as Internet service to qualify for the $15.95 rate.)

IDT also agreed to pay $100,000 to settle claims that it was using unlicensed software. At this point the company had 150,000 Internet subscribers but was losing money on the service because of the growing cost of seeking new customers. It began deemphasizing its Internet-access service, and its revenue from this segment of its business peaked at $32.9 million in fiscal 1997.

International Discount Telecommunications was offering Internet access to some 10,000 corporate clients in 80 countries in late 1995, when it announced that international computer users could soon use its links to make telephone calls to the United States or Great Britain over the Internet for the price of local calls.

In August 1996 the company introduced PC2Phone, which it called the first commercial telephone service to connect calls between personal computers and telephones over the Internet. There were about 350,000 customers for that service in late 1997, when IDT introduced Net2Phone Direct, which enabled users to make both international and domestic calls over the Internet using standard telephones. The company began marketing prepaid calling cards in January 1997.

IDT's revenues doubled in fiscal 1997, to $135.19 million, and its loss decreased to $3.84 million. Revenue soared to $335.38 million in fiscal 1998, during which the company lost $6.4 million. At the end of that fiscal year IDT was selling prepaid debit and rechargeable calling cards providing access to more than 230 countries and territories. The cards were being marketed to retail outlets throughout the United States through Union Telecard Alliance, LLC, a joint venture company in which IDT owned 51 percent of the equity. Customers were primarily members of ethnic communities in the United States who made calls to specific countries where IDT had favorable agreements. The cards also were being marketed to similar customers in Great Britain, France, and The Netherlands.

IDT sold another 4.6 million shares of stock to the public in January 1998 at $24.88 a share. It spun off Net2Phone as a separate business in August 1999, completing an initial public offering of the stock that yielded $85.3 million in net proceeds to the parent company, which retained 56 percent of the shares. In March 2000 Net2Phone Inc. had a market value of $2.6 billion—about twice that of IDT itself. That month Liberty Media Group purchased almost ten percent of IDT's common stock for about $130 million, or $34.50 a share.

IDT in 1999

IDT earned its first profit in fiscal 1999, when it had net income of $2.92 million on revenue of $732.18 million—more than double the previous year's sum. Of this total, telecommunications accounted for 94 percent, Net2Phone for four percent, and Internet service for two percent. International sales accounted for 13 percent of revenue (compared with a high of 25 percent in fiscal 1997). The company had long-term debt of $112.97 million at the end of the fiscal year. Jonas held 32.2 percent of the stock in December 1999. IDT had offices in London, Paris, Mexico City, and Rotterdam, The Netherlands. Its headquarters remained in Hackensack.

IDT was delivering its telecommunications service over a network of 70 switches in the United States and Europe, and it owned and leased capacity on 16 undersea fiber-optic cables. It was obtaining additional transmission capacity from other carriers. The company also was operating a domestic Internet dial-up network consisting of multiple leased lines.

By acting as a ''carrier's carrier,'' IDT was providing wholesale carrier service to about 125 domestic and international customers. Wholesale carrier sales represented 39.5 percent of the company's total consolidated revenues in fiscal 1999. Sales of prepaid calling cards—some 50 million in the fiscal year—generated even more money, amounting to 49.7 percent of total consolidated revenues. IDT's rechargeable cards, distributed primarily through in-flight magazines, allowed users to place calls from 43 countries through international toll free services.

IDT was also still offering international retail services to clients outside the United States, mainly through call re-origination. In 1999 it launched DebitalK, its first prepaid call-back phone card. The company had more than 50,000 call-reorganization customers in 170 countries during the fiscal year. Certain long-distance services were being marketed directly to retail customers in the United States as a value-added bundled service with dial-up Internet access for $15.95 a month plus a minimum of long-distance billings of $40 a month. In 1999 IDT offered a plan with five-cent-a-minute calls for a $3.95 monthly fee that it believed made it the lowest-cost long-distance domestic provider in the United States.

IDT had three primary Internet-access and online services: dial-up access for individuals and businesses, direct-connect dedicated Internet services for corporate customers, and Genie online entertainment and information services. A basic dial-up Internet service was being offered for $19.95 a month and a premium service for $29.95 a month, both fully graphical accounts that included e-mail. An e-mail account only was available at $7.95 a month. Bundled customers who maintained monthly telephone billings of at least $150 a month could get basic Internet access for free. Internet customers also could receive e-mail by telephone, using text-to-speech technology. There were about 65,000 dial-up retail customers and nearly 500 large and medium businesses using IDT Internet access.

Principal Subsidiaries

Genie Interactive Inc.; IDT America, Corp.; IDT Debit Card Limited; IDT Europe B.V.; IDT Global Ltd.; IDT International Corp.; IDT Internet Services, Inc.; InterExchange, Inc.; Internet Online Services, Inc.; Media Response, Inc.; Net2Phone, Inc. (56%); Nuestra Voz Direct Inc.; Rock Enterprises, Inc.; Union Telecard Alliance, LLC (51%); Yovelle Renaissance Corporation.

Principal Competitors

Pacific Gateway Exchange, Inc.; Star Telecommunications Inc.; Telegroup Inc.

Further Reading

Berreby, David, ''Absolute Internet,'' *New York,* May 22, 1995, pp. 30, 35.

Coughlin, Kevin, ''Internet Firm Dials Up Refunds and Layoffs,'' *Newark Star-Ledger,* February 13, 1997, p. 43.

Crockett, Barton, ''Start-Up Undercuts Foreign PTTs' Prices,'' *Network World,* June 24, 1991, p. 25.

Goetz, Thomas, ''Down with IDT,'' *Village Voice,* May 21, 1996, pp. 24–25.

Jonas, Howard, *On a Roll: From Hot Dog Buns to High-Tech Billions,* New York: Viking, 1998.

Lee, Jeanne, ''How IDT Hopes to Upend the Phone Biz,'' *Fortune,* November 9, 1998, p. 284.

Marshall, Jonathan, ''New Long-Distance Service Uses the Net,'' *San Francisco Chronicle,* November 27, 1997, pp. E1, E5.

Meeks, Fleming, ''David 1, Goliath 0,'' *Forbes,* June 20, 1994, p. 92.

——, ''Dial H for Hustle,'' *Forbes,* May 24, 1993, pp. 62, 64.

Ramirez, Anthony, ''Hot-Wiring Overseas Telephone Calls,'' *New York Times,* January 9, 1992, pp. D1, D6.

Schiesel, Seth, ''IDT Says Liberty Media Will Buy Stake,'' *New York Times,* March 27, 2000, p. C8.

Weber, Thomas E., ''Tiny IDT, an IPO, Bucks Trend Against Internet Porn,'' *Wall Street Journal,* March 22, 1996, p. B4.

—Robert Halasz

Instinet Corporation

875 Third Avenue
New York, New York 10022
U.S.A.
Telephone: (212) 310-9500
Fax: (212) 832-5055
Web site: http://www.instinet.com

Wholly Owned Subsidiary of Reuters Group PLC
Incorporated: 1967 as Institutional Networks Corp.
Employees: 1,379
Sales: £525 million (US$845.25 million) (1999)
NAIC: 52312 Securities Brokerages; 52321 Securities &
Commodities Exchanges; 52393 Investment Advice

Instinet Corporation operates the largest of a number of privately owned electronic communications networks (ECNs) that act as alternatives to traditional stock exchanges. Officially a broker-dealer, it is a member of many exchanges in North America, Europe, and Asia. Known for its low trading costs, Instinet allows clients to enter orders onscreen and trade anonymously with fund managers, market makers, and exchange specialists nearly 24 hours a day in more than 40 markets around the world. It also offers a variety of advanced electronic research and analytic services to its clients.

Institutional Networks: 1967–85

Instinet was founded by Jerome M. Pustilnik and Herbert R. Behrens and was incorporated in 1967 as Institutional Networks Corp. The founders aimed to compete with the New York Stock Exchange by means of computer links between major institutions such as banks, mutual funds, and insurance companies, with no delays or intervening specialists. Through this Instinet system, which was operating by 1970, the company provided computer services and a communications network for the automated buying and selling of equity securities on an anonymous, confidential basis. It also acted as a securities information processor, supplying professional-level market data systems containing last sale, quote, and size information. Institutional Networks received income from commissions on the trades and

from the rental of the Instinet terminals located in the offices of its clients.

By early 1971 Institutional Networks had more than 30 clients, including the Chase Manhattan, First National City, Morgan Guaranty, Manufacturers Hanover, Wells Fargo, Bank of America, and Bank of New York banks, United States Trust Company, and the Prudential, Metropolitan Life, All-State, and Aetna Life insurance companies. Other clients were mutual funds, self-administered trusts that corporations operated for their employees, and "third-market makers" who did not trade on exchange floors. An Institutional Networks subsidiary, INC Trading Corp., was, in 1983, a member of the Boston, Cincinnati, and Pacific stock exchanges and was also a member of the National Association of Securities Dealers, the operator of NASDAQ.

Institutional Networks lost money every year until 1981, although its revenue nearly tripled between 1978 and 1980, from $548,000 to $1.59 million. In 1983 Instinet still had no more than 110 institutional clients. "Pension-plan sponsors thought of market makers and specialists almost like sharks," one of the original designers of the system later told *Institutional Investor* in 1987. "They didn't want the buy side against them, even thought the trades were supposedly anonymous." (A market maker buys and sells stocks on exchanges, earning a fee from the difference, or spread, between bid and ask prices.)

In 1983 William Lupien, who succeeded Pustilnik as president, and some partners invested $5 million in the company in return for slightly more than 20 percent of the stock. Lupien decided to market the system wholesale through market makers, specialists, and broker-dealers of over-the-counter stocks as well as institutional investors. By the fall of 1984 the Instinet system was carrying bids and offers on 3,500 stocks on every exchange in the United States, and by the following spring it was connecting some 500 broker-dealers—including 19 of the 20 largest—specialists, and financial institutions. In 1984 four big U.S. brokerage houses purchased 14 percent of Institutional Networks for $11.2 million, including warrants to buy another 11 percent of the company.

Instinet's clients could call up a stock on a video terminal screen and check the price quotes, market by market. If the client decided to make a trade in an unlisted stock, it was carried out instantly; if in a listed stock, there was a 30-second delay while the information was transmitted to other broker-dealers. Large institutional trades were carried out through a terminal-conducted negotiation between buyer and seller.

Institutional Networks was renamed Instinet in 1985. By late 1986 its subsidiary, INC Trading Corp., had added the American, Midwest, and Philadelphia stock exchanges and the Chicago Board Options Exchange to its membership roster, and over-the-counter trading accounted for 20 percent of its average daily volume of 2.7 million shares in 1985. Revenues grew rapidly, reaching $16.4 million in 1986, but expenses increased faster, and Instinet lost money during 1983–86—a record $3.7 million in 1986.

Growing Reuters Subsidiary: 1987–94

One company that saw a bright future for Instinet was the British news-gathering agency Reuters, which in 1985 had negotiated an agreement to offer in all countries outside North America Instinet's automated trading system for U.S. equities, American Depositary Receipts, and options. Reuters also purchased six percent of Instinet's stock. In November 1986 Reuters Holdings PLC announced it would seek to buy all Instinet shares it did not already own, an offer valued at $102 million. Instinet joined the London Stock Exchange that year.

Reuters held a 49 percent interest in May 1987, when Instinet shareholders approved a proposed merger with Reuters, under which Instinet became a subsidiary of the British company but remained based in New York City. Lupien resigned as chairman and chief executive officer shortly before the end of 1987. A Reuters spokesman attributed his resignation, and that of Murray Finebaum, president and chief operating officer, to "differences of management style," according to a *Wall Street Journal* reporter. The spokesman added that the departing executives "were not particularly happy to be part of a management structure required for a large company such as Reuters." Michael Sanderson succeeded Lupien as chief executive officer.

After the 1987 Wall Street crash, even more institutions gravitated to the system as a way of cutting costs. "Too many money managers found themselves chasing too few pension dollars and focused on the cost of their business, especially the cost of trading," an Instinet executive told Michael Peltz of *Institutional Investor* in 1995. Still, proprietary trading systems such as Instinet accounted for only a few percentage points of trading volume. To stimulate further growth, Instinet, in December 1987, introduced Crossing Network, an after-hours trading system that matched buy and sell orders at the day's closing price. Participants were divided into four categories kept separate by personnel and computer linkup to assure each client that its traders would not be dealing with other traders—

such as market makers and specialists, for example—who might have superior information.

By 1990 the Instinet network was beginning to make an impact on trading in Europe. A member of the International Stock Exchange, Instinet UK catered to British market makers and institutional investors and, in May 1990, added selected leading European stocks to its trading network.

In 1991 Instinet introduced Market Match, a new electronic equities trading system that used a volume-weighted-average system. This pricing method was based on the dollar value of a stock's daily trading volume divided by the number of shares traded that day on the consolidated tape and NASDAQ. The service was aimed at individual investors as well as managers of large index funds, marking the first time an electronic trading system had targeted retail investors, although such individuals did not have direct access.

It was the increasing power of institutional investors, however, that fueled Instinet's growth. By late 1995 the network had 5,200 terminals around the world and was reportedly handling 70 to 80 million shares a day. It accounted for about 20 percent of NASDAQ's daily trading volume and an amazing 60 percent of the trades in NASDAQ's 100 largest stocks. Revenues rose from $57 million in 1991 to $279 million in 1994. Much of this business came from customers who preferred the anonymity of the electronic system to trading through NASDAQ's 500 or so market makers, who mostly transacted their business by telephone before entering the trades into the exchange's SelectNet computers. Moreover, Instinet posted completed trades immediately, while there was a 90-second delay on NASDAQ screens. Furthermore, Instinet had a bottom-line advantage; a 1994 survey found Instinet to be the cheapest means of executing trades.

Instinet also offered related products, not only after-hours trading but also an order management system and a research and analytic package. Its New York and London offices included personnel called "facilitators" who helped new customers learn to use the system and notified clients when stocks in which they had shown an interest became active. Instinet bought members of the Paris, Frankfurt, and Zurich stock exchanges in 1993, and also acquired Thamesway, a broker with sizeable operations in Asia. Trading outside the United States was accounting for only 15 percent of the company's revenues, however.

Responding to Competition: 1995–99

Instinet's revenues reached $327.1 million in 1995. It was the third largest U.S. market—busier than the American Stock Exchange—and accounted for 18 percent of the trades of over-the-counter stocks. Douglas Atkin succeeded Sanderson as chief executive officer in 1998. By this time Instinet was a member of 17 exchanges and had eight offices worldwide. During Atkin's six years in charge of international operations, revenues outside the United States had grown three times as fast as sales within the country, where Instinet was facing pressure from competitive electronic systems such as Island, Terranova, and Trade Book, some of them even faster and cheaper. In September 1999 Island outstripped Instinet, for the first time, in quantity of NASDAQ trades. Fears that Instinet was losing its

Key Dates:

1967: Company is incorporated as Institutional Networks Corp.
1970: The Instinet system is operating by this year.
1981: Institutional Networks is profitable for the first time.
1983: Broker-dealers as well as institutions now use Instinet.
1987: Instinet becomes a subsidiary of Reuters Holdings PLC .
1995: Instinet trades make up 18 percent of NASDAQ's volume.
1999: About 12 percent of its trades are outside market hours.

long-secure market led to a sudden 15 percent drop in Reuters stock in October 1999.

To drum up more business, Instinet signed a 1999 agreement to allow E*Trade Group Inc.—the nation's second largest Internet broker—to trade on its system for 2½ hours after the New York Stock Exchange and NASDAQ closed at 4 p.m. Instinet was conducting about 12 percent of its trades before and after regular market hours. The company had recently won approval from the Securities and Exchange Commission to serve as a broker-dealer to individual investors.

In 1999 Instinet took a 16.4 percent stake in Archipelago Holdings LLC, a smaller electronic communications network that was applying to become a full-fledged stock exchange and thereby compete with the New York Stock Exchange. Atkin said that Instinet would likely eventually shift some business from the New York Stock Exchange and NASDAQ to Archipelago. Earlier in the year, Instinet had joined with some of the same financial services companies that invested in Archipelago to acquire Tradepoint Financial Networks PLC, a struggling British electronic stock exchange registered to trade British stocks in the United States. Instinet also took an 11.4 percent share in W.R. Hambrecht + Co., a San Francisco-based operator of online auctions for initial public offerings (IPO) of stock.

The Hambrecht acquisition indicated that Instinet intended to enter the IPO trading market. It was also expected, during the first half of 2000, to begin offering trading to retail investors, with related services such as mutual funds, credit cards, and mortgages, and also to begin handling trades in bonds and other fixed-income securities. The retail operation was not expected to compete with online deep discounters such as E*Trade on commission costs but rather to serve, at a premium price, active and professional traders willing to pay for performance. Reuters was also said to be considering a possible initial public offering for Instinet.

Instinet's revenue increased from £446 million (US$740.3 million) in 1998 to £525 million (US$845.25 million) in 1999. U.S. equities accounted for nearly 80 percent of total revenue in 1999, but international revenue grew by 39 percent. Its operating income fell from £155 million (US$257.28 million) to £129 million (US$207.69 million), however.

Principal Subsidiaries

Instinet Australia Limited); Instinet Canada Ltd.; Instinet France SA; Instinet Japan Limited; Instinet Pacific Limited (Hong Kong); InstinetGmbH (Germany); Instinet(Schweiz) AG (Switzerland); InstinetUK Limited (U.K.).

Principal Competitors

Bloomberg LP; Datek Securities Inc.

Further Reading

Buckman, Rebecca, "E*Trade Group, Instinet Set Deal to Extend Trading," *Wall Street Journal,* August 18, 1999, p. C13.

"Bypassing the Street," *Institutional Investor,* April 1987, pp. 133–34.

Currie, Antony, "A Pioneer Under Pressure," *Euromoney,* November 1999, pp. 79–82.

Hamilton, Walter, "Instinet Seeks to Court Small Traders Online," *Los Angeles Times,* December 29, 1999, p. C5.

"Instinet Corp. Accepts Offer from Reuters After It Is Sweetened," *Wall Street Journal,* November 11, 1986, p. 22.

"Instinet Holders Approve Merger Plan with Reuters," *Wall Street Journal,* May 13, 1987, p. 23.

"Instinet: Towards a Global Market," *Banker,* May 1985, p. 93.

Ip, Greg, "Instinet May Invite Everyone to 'After-Hours,' " *Wall Street Journal,* May 5, 1999, pp. C1, C19.

——, "Instinet to Invest in an ECN," *Wall Street Journal,* July 28, 1999, pp. C1, C15.

Jones, Stacy V., "Network Lets Investors Bypass Brokers," *New York Times,* April 10, 1971, p. 28.

Labate, John, and James Harding, "Instinet May Be Floated to Unlock Hidden Value," *Financial Times,* December 22, 1999, p. 16.

Lax, Hal, "Instinet Plans Marketing Push to Retail Investors," *Investment Dealers' Digest,* December 16, 1991, pp. 5–6.

Lee, Peter, "An Exchange in All but Name," *Euromoney,* June 1990, pp. 13–14.

Messina, Judith, "Leaving His Trading Stamp," *Crain's New York Business,* October 5, 1998, p. 41.

Peltz, Michael, "Instinet's Identity Crisis," November 1995, *Institutional Investor* (national edition), pp. 53–56, 58.

Stern, Richard L., "What's in It for Your Broker?" *Forbes,* September 26, 1983, p. 96.

"Top Officers Resign Posts at Reuters' Instinet Unit," *Wall Street Journal,* Decmeber 21, 1987, p. 25.

Williams, Manci Jo, "Why the Big Players Want a Piece of Instinet," *Fortune,* August 19, 1985, p. 145.

Winder, Robert, "The Final Days of the Trading Floor," *Euromoney,* October 1984, pp. 82–83.

—Robert Halasz

Iwerks Entertainment, Inc.

4540 West Valerio Street
Burbank, California 91505
U.S.A.
Telephone: (818) 841-7766
Fax: (818) 840-6188
Web site: http://www.iwerks.com

Public Company
Incorporated: 1986
Employees: 115
Sales: $34.86 million (1999)
Stock Exchanges: NASDAQ
Ticker Symbol: IWRKD
NAIC: 512111 Motion Picture and Video Production;
512131 Motion Picture Theaters (Except Drive-Ins);
51121 Software Publishers

Iwerks Entertainment, Inc. designs and manufactures high-technology, software-based entertainment attractions. The company's products combine advanced theater systems with entertainment or educational software to create multi-sensory attractions found at location-based entertainment centers, theme parks, movie theaters, museums, science centers, shopping centers, casinos, resorts, and various other locations. With the largest library of ride simulation films in the industry, Iwerks Entertainment specializes in ride simulation theater systems using sophisticated hardware and company-produced films to give the viewer the physical and visual impression that he or she is actually experiencing the action onscreen. The company has installed more than 250 theaters and touring attractions in 38 countries.

Origins

The story behind Iwerks' incorporation in the mid-1980s began more than a half-century earlier in Kansas City, Missouri, at the Pesman-Rubin Studios. It was there that two of the most renowned innovators in the entertainment industry worked side by side as young adults, struggling to forge their careers. At Pesman-Rubin, Walt Disney and Ub Iwerks worked amid a clutter of wooden desks, busily creating artwork for local newspaper advertisements and theater programs. Disney and Iwerks spent only a month together at Pesman-Rubin, but their brief association developed into a partnership when, after being laid off, the pair formed the Disney-Iwerks Company in Kansas City. The entrepreneurs subsisted on a trickle of business before financial pressures forced them to abandon their partnership and seek work elsewhere. Iwerks remained in Kansas City, while Disney, attracted by opportunities in the West, packed his belongings and moved to Los Angeles.

Disney realized his first success with Laugh-O-Grams, brief cartoons that he sold to movie theaters. At the time, animation was a novel art form with few adept practitioners, but Disney knew of one skilled animator, his former partner Iwerks. Iwerks joined Disney in Los Angeles, bringing together the two creative minds that helped make Walt Disney Companies a multibillion-dollar entertainment conglomerate. Iwerks was credited with pioneering several of the technological advancements underpinning modern animation, as well as playing a critical role in the technological development of the hugely popular Disney theme parks. His impressive achievements became a legacy, a wealth of experience and knowledge that he passed on to his son, Don Iwerks. Don Iwerks followed his father's example and joined the Disney organization in 1951, beginning a tenure of service that would span three decades. Like his father, Don Iwerks made a reputation for himself as a creative trailblazer, ultimately finding his niche among a team of Disney executives who designed and manufactured the film systems employed at Disneyland and Disney World. In 1986, after 35 years working for Walt Disney Companies, Don Iwerks set out on his own and formed Iwerks Entertainment, a company whose background was steeped in Disney tradition and whose future drew its promise from two generations of Iwerks innovation.

From its inception, Iwerks Entertainment took its cue from Don Iwerks's work at Walt Disney Companies. The high-technology, cinematic attractions at Disneyland and Disney World were proven winners, convincing Don Iwerks that the attractions could stand on their own and attract lines of customers outside the borders of sprawling theme parks. Further, Iwerks reasoned, the high-technology attractions could draw even larger audiences if presented at more conveniently accessible locations than Disneyland and Disney World. By penetrating more markets, Iwerks could expect larger audiences, but the strategy also depended on a vast amount of capital. Financing the design and manufacture of high-tech attractions was not a major problem within the immensely wealthy Disney organization; it would prove to be a perennial problem for the independent Iwerks Entertainment. Nevertheless, Don Iwerks was convinced he could develop the world's premier location-based entertainment (LBE) company. He began in 1986 to muster the creative and financial resources he would need to establish a network of LBE attractions.

International Growth During the Late 1980s and Early 1990s

Iwerks Entertainment secured its toehold in the business world overseas. The company's first three sales, consisting of its proprietary large format film projection product, were in Asia, one in South Korea and the other two in Japan. The initial success in international markets established a trend that intensified as the company progressed through its formative years. Overseas markets, particularly in the Far East, were more receptive to multimedia attractions than the U.S. market, which at the time was more inclined to invest in what were commonly referred to as ''hard'' rides, the traditional concrete-and-steel attractions such as roller-coasters. An Iwerks Entertainment research program revealed as much, prompting the beginning of ''very concentrated efforts'' in the Far East in 1989, according to a company executive quoted in the March 15, 1993 issue of *Amusement Business.* Following its findings, the company became involved in a series of projects in the Far East, as well as in other international markets. In 1990, Iwerks Entertainment served as a subcontractor for a project at the Osaka World Expo in Japan, which led to its role as the major contractor for three pavilions at the Universal Exposition of Seville in Spain in 1992 and an identical role for five pavilions at The Taejon International Exposition in South Korea in 1993. Other major projects in 1993 typified the company's focus on the Far East: Iwerks Entertainment large format film systems debuted in China, Japan, Taiwan, and Malaysia.

Although Iwerks Entertainment was involved in numerous other projects during the late 1980s and early 1990s, the company's involvement in major expositions during the early 1990s figured prominently as a revenue contributor. The company's exposition projects also set a dangerous precedent. In 1992 and 1993, Iwerks Entertainment earned 50 percent and 40 percent, respectively, of its total revenues from sales of attractions to world expositions, which loomed as an alarming portion of the company's business as executives looked toward the future and noted that no major expositions were scheduled to open in 1994

and 1995 (the next major exposition was the Specialty Exposition: The Oceans in Portugal in 1998). Clearly, it was time for a change in strategy. Unless company officials were willing to forsake roughly half of their business, some other markets needed to be explored to replace the sales derived from expositions.

Aside from pressing financial vulnerabilities, other factors pointed to a need for new strategic direction in the early 1990s. In the early part of the decade, the LBE industry was still trying to define itself, still struggling to determine exactly what it should offer to the public and how companies within the industry should operate. Among the handful of competitors in the industry, there were competing strategies and visions of the future that all generally revolved around technological issues. As a whole, the industry had not settled on determining its identity largely because the technologies it used were constantly changing. At Iwerks Entertainment, where the company began with its proprietary large format film projection product, the currents of technological innovation had diversified the company's expertise into a variety of new multimedia formats, including ride simulation, 360 degree video, group interactive, and three-dimensional attractions. With the addition of these new capabilities, coupled with the imminent departure of any major exposition customers, the question facing Iwerks Entertainment executives was how to best utilize new and emerging technologies in the marketplace and, thereby, become the model of how a successful LBE company should operate.

Iwerks Entertainment's new strategy hinged on what it called Cinetropolis entertainment centers, the single solution for delivering its growing portfolio of products to the marketplace. The Cinetropolis concept, which Iwerks Entertainment management began developing in 1992, combined the company's various attractions with restaurants and retail establishments, all tailored in a highly themed environment. Touted as the theme park of the 1990s, Cinetropolis emerged as the multimedia vehicle to compensate for the lack of exposition projects, becoming the central focus of the company's corporate strategy. Considerable effort and finances were directed toward bringing the concept to life, resulting in the debut of the first Cinetropolis entertainment complex at the Foxwoods Casino in Connecticut in January 1994. The Cinetropolis operation, developed in partnership with Foxwoods, was intended to lure families to the casino complex, where they could immerse themselves in a variety of film-based attractions. Included within the first Cinetropolis were a 350-seat giant screen theater, a 360 degree theater presenting an Iwerks-produced film called *Dinosaur Adventure,* and a 48-seat Turbo Ride Theater, offering a variety of simulated adventures.

The opening of the Connecticut Cinetropolis marked the beginning of an exceptionally busy year for Iwerks Entertainment, its first year as a publicly traded concern. The company's initial public offering (IPO) had been completed in October 1993, when Iwerks Entertainment stock debuted at $18 per share. By the following day, the company's share price had soared to $37, its rise fueled by investors' desire to latch on to the promising trend toward multimedia entertainment. In the wake of the resoundingly successful IPO, the Connecticut Cinetropolis had emerged as the company's direction for the future, with construction of a second Cinetropolis, slated to open in Chiyu, Japan, in November 1994, underway.

Key Dates:

1986: Don Iwerks leaves Walt Disney Companies to start Iwerks Entertainment.
1993: Company completes initial public offering of stock.
1994: Omni Films International Inc. is acquired.
1998: Proposed merger with Showscan Entertainment Inc. is blocked by Iwerks Entertainment shareholders.
2000: After retiring, Don Iwerks rejoins the company as chairman and interim chief executive officer.

The company was also moving stridently forward in other directions, showing no fear of over-expansion. Construction was underway for a 450-seat Iwerks Entertainment theater just outside Utah's Zion National Park, expected to be completed in May 1994, and roughly a dozen projects were being completed in the Far East; but the biggest news of the year arrived a few weeks after the Connecticut Cinetropolis opened. In February 1994, the company announced it had signed a definitive agreement to acquire Florida-based Omni Films International Inc., a movie-based entertainment company regarded as Iwerks Entertainment's second largest competitor. The acquisition, completed in May 1994, established the company's Attractions and Technology Division as the single dominant force in the high-growth ride simulation industry, giving it simulation theaters in approximately 50 sites throughout the world and the largest single simulation film library.

Mid-1990s: Change in Strategy

Although the progress achieved in 1994 was meaningful, it came at a cost, enveloping Iwerks Entertainment in financial difficulties. As the company rapidly expanded its operations— too quickly, a company official later conceded—earnings plunged and analysts grew wary. From its celebrated high of $37 per share, the company's stock value began to fall precipitously, dropping to one-third of its per share price in a six-month period. The resultant turmoil at company headquarters led to a change in management, a corporate-wide reorganization, and a change in its strategic direction. Citing a "lack of market response" to the Cinetropolis concept in its annual filing to the Securities and Exchange Commission in 1996, Iwerks Entertainment declared it would redirect its focus on less capital intensive projects and no longer regard the ownership and operation of its own attractions as its first priority strategically.

Despite the setback, Iwerks Entertainment emerged from the mid-1990s as arguably the strongest contender in the LBE industry. Profitability was restored after the sweeping changes, enabling executives to genuinely celebrate the company's tenth anniversary. During the late 1990s, the company's strategic focus was settled on the ride simulation attraction business. In 1997, the company made a bid to greatly increase its interests in ride simulation by announcing a merger with Showscan Entertainment Inc., a competitor with 70 motion simulation theaters and a film library of 28 titles. The deal was scotched, however, when a group of Iwerks Entertainment shareholders voted against the merger in 1998, claiming it would dilute the value of their holdings.

On the international front, Iwerks Entertainment's heavy presence in the Far East incurred a decisive blow during the late 1990s when a pernicious economic crisis crippled many Asian markets. The company, which continued to derive roughly 40 percent of its revenue from across the Pacific, stepped up its involvement in Chinese markets to compensate for the loss in business. The push into China, relatively unaffected by the depressed economic climate surrounding it, was applauded by outside observers, who saw a wealth of opportunities in China for Iwerks Entertainment.

As Iwerks Entertainment exited the 1990s, it occupied an entrenched market position in an industry it had helped to create. The company ranked as the second largest provider of large format theater systems in the world, behind Imax Corporation, and as the industry leader in ride simulation attractions. In an industry defined by technological sophistication, Iwerks Entertainment's success depended greatly on continued innovation, something the company paid strong attention to throughout its history, despite the numerous hiccups along the way. As the company charted its course for the beginning of the 21st century, effective and stable leadership stood as the company's most pressing problem. After numerous and frequent executive management changes during the 1990s, the company named Don Iwerks as its chairman and interim chief executive officer in February 2000. To Iwerks, who came out of retirement to take charge of the company, fell the critical task of successfully managing and executing Iwerks Entertainment's legacy of innovation.

Principal Subsidiaries

Iwerks Film Production.

Principal Competitors

Cinema Ride, Inc.; Imax Corporation; Showscan Entertainment Inc.

Further Reading

Berger, Robin, "Interactive Entertainment Form's Stock Gets Rattled," *Los Angeles Business Journal,* May 16, 1994, p. 8.

Johnson, Stephen S., "Take a Ride on Iwerks," *Forbes,* November 18, 1996, p. 290.

Kanter, Larry, "All Eyes on China," *Los Angeles Business Journal,* February 23, 1998, p. 1.

Langberg, Mike, "Virtual Reality Interactive Systems Profiting in Theme Parks," *Knight-Ridder/Tribune Business News,* May 17, 1994, p. 05170178.

Medina, Hildy, "Marriage in Motion," *Los Angeles Business Journal,* August 11, 1997, p. 14.

O'Brien, Tim, "Iwerks' Efforts in Far East Pay Off," *Amusement Business,* March 13, 1993, p. 18.

Ray, Susan, "Iwerks' First Cinetropolis Premieres in Connecticut," *Amusement Business,* January 31, 1994, p. 20.

——, "Kinsey: Software-Driven Attractions to Fit Entertainment Needs in Future," *Amusement Business,* July 18, 1994, p. 40.

Spring, Greg, "Iwerks Forecasts $3 Million Loss for the Year," *Los Angeles Business Journal,* September 4, 1994, p. 5.

——, "Iwerks Reports Its First Profit in Two Years," *Los Angeles Business Journal,* December 18, 1995, p. 10.

Waddell, Ray, "Showscan and Iwerks Announce Plans to Merge," *Amusement Business,* August 11, 1997, p. 1.

Zoltak, James, "Two New Iwerks Attractions Open," *Amusement Business,* January 27, 1997, p. 23.

—Jeffrey L. Covell

J. Crew Group, Inc.

770 Broadway
New York, New York 10003
U.S.A.
Telephone: (212) 209-2500
Fax: (212) 209-2666
Web site: http://www.jcrew.com

Private Company
Incorporated: 1947 as Popular Merchandise, Inc.
Employees: 5,400
Sales: $824.2 million (1999)
NAIC: 454110 Electronic Shopping and Mail-Order
  Houses; 448140 Family Clothing Stores

J. Crew Group, Inc. markets several lines of casual men's and women's clothing through distinctive catalogs, a chain of retail stores, and the company web site. Each year the company issues 24 editions of the J. Crew catalog, distributing more than 80 million copies. Its retail stores include 127 units in the United States, 45 of which are factory outlets, and 76 locations in Japan, which are operated under license by ITOCHU Corporation. J. Crew Group was owned by the Cinader family for most of its existence, but in October 1997 investment firm Texas Pacific Group Inc. purchased a majority stake in the firm. By the year 2000, Texas Pacific held an approximate 62 percent stake, a group of J. Crew managers held about ten percent, and Emily Woods, the chairman of J. Crew and founder of the J. Crew brand along with her father, Arthur Cinader, held most of the remainder.

1980s: Creation of a Famous Brand

Popular Merchandise, Inc., doing business as Popular Club Plan, was founded in 1947 by Mitchell Cinader and Saul Charles to sell low-priced women's clothing through in-home demonstrations. By the early 1980s, the owners of Popular Club Plan (which was by then under the direction of Mitchell Cinader's son, Arthur) watched as catalog retailers of clothing, including Lands' End, Talbots, and L.L. Bean, reported booming sales. In an effort to duplicate the success of these companies, Popular Club Plan initiated its own catalog operation.

The company focused on leisurewear for upper-middle-class customers, aiming for a Ralph Lauren look at a much lower price. Accordingly, Popular Club situated its merchandise in the niche between Ralph Lauren, on the high end, and the Limited, on the lower end. In an effort to connote a "preppy" spirit, Popular Club Plan dubbed this operation "J. Crew." The first J. Crew catalog was mailed to customers in January 1983. Instrumental in orchestrating the J. Crew look was Arthur Cinader's daughter Emily Cinader (later Woods), who joined the company after graduating from college.

Over the next several years, J. Crew's catalog evolved a distinctive look featuring young, attractive models having fun in a variety of appealing settings. The pictures in the catalog appeared to be photographs from a house party of old friends, all of whom happened to be gorgeous and outfitted by J. Crew. Their catalogs often showed the same garment in more than one picture, worn by different models and coordinated with other products. As a result, customers could get a sense of how the garment looked on the body, how it hung and draped, and how it could be used with various items of clothing. In addition, J. Crew included close-up shots of the fabrics from which its products were made, helping to validate its claims of quality.

J. Crew closely controlled the production of its catalog, selecting images from more than 8,000 rolls of film shot each year and having all catalog copy written in-house. Catalogs with more than 100 glossy pages were mailed to customers 14 times a year. The company also maintained an in-house design staff to develop its products and carefully controlled the manufacturing process, hiring factories to produce garments to its specifications.

Throughout the mid-1980s, sales from J. Crew's catalog operations grew rapidly, as the catalog retailing industry as a whole experienced strong growth. During this time, J. Crew continued to refine its presentation and increase the number of people receiving its catalog. "Growth was explosive—25 to 30 percent a year," Cinader later recollected in the *New York Times*. Annual sales grew from $3 million to more than $100 million over five years.

Key Dates:

1947: Popular Merchandise, Inc. is founded by Mitchell Cinader and Saul Charles to sell low-priced women's clothing through in-home demonstrations.
1983: The first J. Crew catalog is mailed to customers.
1985: Clifford & Wills women's clothing catalog is launched.
1989: Company changes its name to J. Crew Group, Inc. The first J. Crew retail outlet opens; deal to sell Popular Club Plan falls through.
1991: Catalogs are sent to Canada for the first time.
1993: Through a joint venture, J. Crew retail stores begin appearing in Japan.
1997: Texas Pacific Group Inc. acquires a majority stake in the company.
1998: Popular Club Plan is sold to Fingerhut Companies.
2000: Clifford & Wills is sold to Spiegel Inc.

With the success of its first catalog operation, J. Crew launched a second catalog program in 1985. Dubbed ''Clifford & Wills,'' this operation sold women's clothing that was more affordable than the J. Crew line. In 1986 Emily Cinader was promoted to president of the J. Crew operation.

Despite the phenomenal success of J. Crew, and the prominent profile that the J. Crew catalog soon attained, internal management of the company was less than smooth. Both Cinaders, father and daughter, were reputed to be difficult to work with, and employee turnover was high. In 1987 the company suffered a setback when two high-level executives left to start their own catalog operation, Tweeds, which drew on the lessons learned and example established by the J. Crew operation. With a more European look, Tweeds was soon competing successfully with J. Crew.

Although J. Crew's sales continued to be strong throughout the fall season of 1988, when the company reaped annual sales of $100 million, by the end of the 1980s growth was beginning to slow in the catalog market as a whole. By 1989 rumors had begun to circulate in the apparel industry that J. Crew was in trouble and that the company might be up for sale.

Though these rumors were vociferously denied, it was clear that J. Crew would have to implement changes to sustain its vigorous growth. To begin with, the company undertook a number of steps to focus its attention on its most important and profitable units. In 1989 the company changed its name from Popular Merchandise, Inc.—a holdover from the 1940s, when the Popular Club Plan was the company's main business—to J. Crew Group, Inc. In February 1989, the company announced that the Popular Club Plan would be sold to International Epicure, a direct-marketing food company. With the proceeds from this sale, J. Crew planned to help finance a broadening of its J. Crew enterprises, and to compensate, in part, for the fact that its operations were less solidly financed than those of many of its catalog competitors.

J. Crew also planned to expand into retail. In opening stores, J. Crew hoped to capitalize on the strong brand identity it had established through its catalogs, and also to tap the significant number of customers that did not shop through catalogs (company research suggested that 60 percent of clothes buyers did not shop by mail, and that only 15 percent of apparel customers bought a significant number of items from catalogs).

To avoid compromising its existing catalog operations, J. Crew set up its new retail branch as a separate unit within the company. The Cinaders hired Arnold Cohen, who had previously worked for Gucci, to head a new management team that would be in charge of a chain of J. Crew stores. The start-up staff for this arm of the company, dubbed J. Crew Retail, numbered 22. In order to minimize cannibalization of its catalog operations, J. Crew planned to make 60 to 70 percent of the goods offered in its stores unavailable through its catalogs. In March 1989 the first J. Crew retail outlet opened, in the South Street Seaport in Manhattan. With 4,000 square feet of selling space, this store was designed to appeal to the many members of the New York financial community who frequented the seaport. The company planned to open 45 stores in its first push into retail.

Five months after the opening of its first store, J. Crew added two new catalog lines: ''Classics'' and ''Collections.'' ''Collections'' used more complicated designs and finer fabrics to create dressier and more expensive items, while ''Classics'' featured clothes that could be worn both to work and for leisure activities, and acted as a bridge between the products J. Crew had originally offered and its ''Collections'' items. With these lines, J. Crew hoped to further differentiate itself from its catalog competitors.

In the fall of 1989, J. Crew opened three new stores, each larger than the first, in Chestnut Hill, Massachusetts; San Francisco, California; and Costa Mesa, California. J. Crew chose these locations because they were in markets where catalog sales had historically been strong. Each of these openings was supported by print ads in local newspapers and magazines that featured images from the catalogs, with a line indicating the store's location. In November 1989, J. Crew also launched a national magazine advertising campaign. By the end of the year, this had helped to produce retail sales of nearly $10 million.

Despite 1989 revenues that were estimated at $320 million, J. Crew suffered a setback when its agreement to sell its Popular Club unit collapsed at the end of that year. In addition, rumors circulated that the company's Clifford & Wills low-priced women's apparel catalog was doing badly. J. Crew began to delay payments to its suppliers and lay off staff members.

Expanding Internationally in the Early 1990s

J. Crew embarked on an attempt to win greater sales from its existing catalog customers, noting that its expansion was limited by the relatively small segment of the population that served as its customer base, estimated at seven to ten percent of the population. J. Crew's target customer was young, educated, and affluent, with a median age of 32, some postgraduate education, and an annual household income above $62,000. ''I don't know if there are 20 people left in the country who are prime J. Crew prospects who haven't seen the catalog 10 or 20 times,'' Cinader went on. ''So . . . I think most increases will come from increased sales per person.'' To bring this about, J. Crew broadened its line of merchandise even further, adding sleepwear, outerwear, working clothes, and versatile jackets. In this way, the company hoped to supplement its sales of low-priced items—such as its most offerings, T-shirts and socks—with higher-ticket purchases.

J. Crew saw revenues reach $400 million in 1990, but reported that its four existing stores had not yet started producing enough profits to cover their overheads. ''We're working on improving merchandise selection and we're working on strengthening the visual image,'' J. Crew president Arnold Cohen told the *New York Times*. The next phase of store openings included outlets in Philadelphia, Cambridge, and Portland. The company scaled back its plans for opening retail stores from 45 stores to 30 or 35.

In early 1991 the company hired a director of new marketing development and began efforts to expand their sales across the Canadian border. In an effort to simplify the complications of doing business internationally, J. Crew ''Canadianized'' its catalogs, including information on the payment of taxes and duties, the Canadian Goods and Services Tax, and customs requirements.

In April 1991, J. Crew mailed 75,000 J. Crew catalogs and 60,000 Clifford & Wills catalogs to potential customers in Ontario. Response rates to this effort were slightly lower than in the United States, but each order, on average, was higher. Clifford & Wills received an especially warm response, and a second mailing of 120,000 copies of this catalog took place in September 1991. The company benefitted from the relative paucity of catalog retailers in Canada, which made its brochure stand out better, but also made collecting names of potential customers much more difficult.

In the following year, J. Crew intensified its push into international markets by hiring a new vice-president for international development. The company already mailed hundreds of catalogs to customers in Japan and Europe, most of whom had become acquainted with J. Crew while traveling or living in the United States. In early 1992, J. Crew conducted a feasibility study to explore avenues for marketing its goods to customers overseas on a larger scale. In February 1993, the company completed an agreement with Japanese retailers ITOCHU and Renown, Inc., to open 46 stores in Japan, with estimated annual sales of $68 million.

Despite the economic recession at home, J. Crew racked up $70 million in retail sales in 1992, a strong increase from previous years. The company discovered that opening stores did not significantly hurt its catalog sales; in New York, in fact, opening a store increased catalog sales. But in 1993 the domestic retail expansion was once again curtailed because of a tougher retailing climate and the resignation of Cohen, who was the chief proponent of the retailing push. The following year, the head of the company's retail division, Gary Scheinbaum, resigned as well. Cohen's position as president was not filled for nearly a year, before Robert Bernard was named president in 1994.

Late 1990s: Texas Pacific Group and a Retailing Expansion

A turn of events came during 1994 when an increase in postal rates was soon followed by a sharp increase of 40 percent in paper costs. The catalog operations suddenly seemed quite vulnerable. A renewed retail push thereby emerged. In May 1995 David DeMattei was hired away from Banana Republic to head up J. Crew's retailing operations. At the time, there were fewer than 30 retail outlets in the United States. A dozen more were soon added, bringing the total to around 40 by late 1996. But J. Crew still lagged behind other cataloger-turned-retailers, such as Talbot's and Eddie Bauer, while the Gap, which perhaps had the product line most similar to J. Crew's, was operating 226 stores nationwide by the end of 1996. Even more troubling was the continued turnover among the company's most senior managers. Bernard resigned in 1996, with Cinader taking over his duties. Observers placed at least part of the blame for the management turmoil at the laps of Cinader and Woods, both of whom had reputations as micromanagers.

By mid-1997, with the company's retailing arm running 47 stores, J. Crew entered into negotiations with investment firm Texas Pacific Group Inc. regarding a leveraged buyout. The deal was completed in October 1997, with Texas Pacific emerging with about 85 percent of the company and Woods with the remaining 15 percent. Texas Pacific invested about $560 million in J. Crew to gain its stake, while the leveraged nature of the buyout increased J. Crew's debt from $86.8 million to $283.9 million. Texas Pacific planned to bolster J. Crew's retailing operations and eventually take the company public. The management situation was potentially improved following the retirement of Cinader. Woods became chairman, then in February 1998 the CEO slot was handed to Howard Socol, who was a former chairman of Burdines, a unit of Federated Department Stores. Meanwhile, J. Crew's mail-order operation felt a negative impact from the 1997 strike at United Parcel Service of America Inc., as customers curtailed their catalog purchasing. J. Crew laid off 100 employees in early 1998 as a consequence of the 1997 difficulties.

Also during 1998 J. Crew began to divest its noncore catalog operations, with the November sale of Popular Club Plan to Fingerhut Companies. Mid-year, Clifford & Wills was put on the block as well. The retail expansion continued in 1998 as 14 new stores opened their doors, bringing the total in the United States to 65. In January 1999, however, Socol resigned suddenly following ongoing disagreements with Woods over company strategy. Hired on as the new CEO was Mark Sarvary, who had headed up the frozen foods unit of Nestlé USA. By early 2000 Sarvary was given full day-to-day operational control over J. Crew, lessening the role of Woods and perhaps signaling an end to the management turnstile. As it prepared for a likely IPO in the early years of the 21st century, J. Crew continued expanding on the retail side, increasing the number of U.S. stores to 82 by early 2000. The company was also running 45 J. Crew factory outlets and had expanded into e-commerce backed by the company's first ever network television advertisements in December 1999. The retail expansion and the move into e-commerce was helping to reignite revenue growth but J. Crew's earnings were being hurt by high marketing costs and the burden of servicing still hefty debt.

Principal Subsidiaries

J. Crew Operating Corp.; J. Crew Inc.; Grace Holmes, Inc.; H.F.D. No. 55, Inc.; J. Crew International, Inc.; J. Crew Services, Inc.

Principal Divisions

J. Crew Mail Order; J. Crew Retail; J. Crew Factory Outlets.

Principal Competitors

AnnTaylor Stores Corporation; Benetton Group S.p.A.; Calvin Klein Inc.; Dillard's Inc.; Federated Department Stores, Inc.; The Gap, Inc.; Guess?, Inc.; Hartmarx Corporation; Intimate Brands, Inc.; J.C. Penney Company, Inc.; L.L. Bean, Inc.; Lands' End, Inc.; The Limited, Inc.; Liz Claiborne, Inc.; Loehmann's, Inc.; Marks & Spencer p.l.c.; The May Department Stores Company; The Men's Wearhouse, Inc.; Nautica Enterprises, Inc.; The Neiman Marcus Group, Inc.; Nordstrom, Inc.; Polo Ralph Lauren Corporation; Saks Incorporated; Sears, Roebuck and Co.; Spiegel, Inc.; The Talbots, Inc.; Target Corporation; Tommy Hilfiger Corporation.

Further Reading

Bongiorno, Lori, "J. Crew Plays Dress-Up," *Business Week,* May 5, 1997, p. 127.

Bounds, Wendy, "Dressed for Change, J. Crew Reaches Crossroads," *Wall Street Journal,* August 22, 1997, p. B1.

——, "J. Crew Catalog Retail Empire Discusses Its Own Sale to Texas Pacific Group," *Wall Street Journal,* August 21, 1997, p. A4.

——, "Texas Pacific Buys Majority Interest in J. Crew Group," *Wall Street Journal,* October 20, 1997, p. B4.

Chevan, Harry, "J. Crew: Building on Its Brand," *Catalog Age,* September 1993, p. 7.

Curan, Catherine, "Fast Fix at J. Crew: Key Investor Ousts CEO at Debt-Heavy Cataloger," *Crain's New York Business,* January 11, 1999, p. 1.

Cyr, Diane, "King Arthur's Crew," *Catalog Age,* January 1997, pp. 1, 52–54.

Del Franco, Mark, "J. Crew to Sell Clifford & Wills," *Catalog Age,* July 1998, p. 5.

Gault, Ylonda, "J. Crew Unfurling Its Sales: Cataloger Revisits Retail with an Eye on New York," *Crain's New York Business,* November 25, 1996, p. 1.

——, "New Exec Tailors J. Crew Comeback," *Crain's New York Business,* April 27, 1998, p. 4.

Graham, Judith, "Cataloger Tried Retail Units," *Advertising Age,* August 21, 1989.

Haggin, Jeff, and Bjorn Kartomten, "Product Photography: Glamour or Benefit?" *Catalog Age,* June 1989.

"J. Crew, CW Score High in Ontario," *Catalog Age,* October 1991, p. 8.

"J. Crew to Launch Catalog in France with 3 Suisses," *Daily News Record,* November 30, 1993.

Kamen, Robin, "New Opportunity Seen Overseas by J. Crew's VP," *Crain's New York Business,* March 16, 1992.

Kleinfeld, N.R., "Even for J. Crew, the Mail-Order Boom Days Are Over," *New York Times,* September 2, 1990, p. 5.

Moin, David, "Howard Socol Leaves CEO Post at J. Crew After Less Than a Year," *Women's Wear Daily,* January 5, 1999.

Morgenson, Gretchen, "Storm Warnings," *Forbes,* December 11, 1989, pp. 140–48.

Quick, Rebecca, "J. Crew CEO Savary Broadens Control As Chairman Curbs Day-to-Day Role," *Wall Street Journal,* February 10, 2000, p. B7.

Steinhauer, Jennifer, "J. Crew Caught in Messy World of Finance As It Sells Majority Stake," *New York Times,* October 18, 1997, p. D1.

—Elizabeth Rourke
—updated by David E. Salamie

JDS Uniphase Corporation

163 Baypointe Parkway
San Jose, California 95134
U.S.A.
Telephone: (408) 434-1800
Fax: (408) 954-0540
Web site: http://www.jdsunph.com

Public Company
Incorporated: 1999
Employees: 8,200
Sales: $587.9 million (1999)
Stock Exchanges: NASDAQ Toronto
Ticker Symbols: JDSU; JDU (Toronto)
NAIC: 334413 Semiconductors and Related Device
    Manufacturing; 334417 Electronic Connector
    Manufacturing

JDS Uniphase Corporation is a high technology company that designs, develops, manufactures, and distributes a wide range of products for the growing fiberoptic communications market. The company's fiberoptic components and modules are used by system manufacturers worldwide to develop advanced optical networks for the telecommunications and cable television industries.

Fiberoptic systems work by turning digitized information into rapid-fire pulses of invisible infrared light generated by a laser beam. To increase bandwidth, researchers developed new systems that could split light into many more wavelengths, each carrying a separate stream of data. This technology, known as wavelength division multiplexing (WDM), is what JDS Uniphase specializes in. Riding the demand for more bandwidth that has been fueled by the growth of the Internet and electronic commerce, JDS Uniphase stock has been extremely popular with investors. For 1999 its stock rose 814 percent, then added another 77 percent by mid-March 2000.

JDS Fitel Inc.: 1981–98

JDS Fitel Inc. was formed in 1981 by Jozef Strauss and three coworkers at Bell-Northern Research Ltd., the now-defunct re-

search arm of what became Nortel Networks Corporation, in Canada. As employees of Bell Northern, they were part of a team of physicists and engineers assigned to design components for Nortel's first generation of fiberoptic systems. Strauss and his coworkers decided to establish their own business making components for fiberoptic networks. They called it JDS, using the last-name initials of the cofounders Philip Garel-Jones, Gary Duck, William Sinclair, and Strauss.

By 1990 JDS Fitel had grown to 70 employees and $7 million a year in sales. Demand for fiberoptics, which had been predictably linear during the 1980s, would grow exponentially following the creation of the World Wide Web in 1990. By making it possible to combine text with graphics, which typically require more bandwidth, the Web stimulated demand for more bandwidth, or network capacity. With the addition of video and audio files, even more bandwidth was needed. Demand began to soar following the introduction of the first commercial Web browser in 1994, Netscape Navigator.

In March 1996 JDS Fitel completed its initial public offering (IPO) and raised C$93.6 million before underwriting expenses. Following the IPO the Furukawa Electric Co. Ltd. of Japan retained a majority interest in JDS Fitel of about 55 percent. For fiscal 1996 ending May 31 JDS Fitel had C$74.8 million in revenues, up 21.5 percent from fiscal 1995, and net income of C$12.9 million compared to net income of C$10.4 million in fiscal 1995.

In February 1997 JDS Fitel entered into a strategic alliance with Optical Coating Laboratory Inc. (OCLI) to capitalize on the growing opportunities in the dense wavelength division multiplexing (DWDM) business. Revenues rose substantially in fiscal 1997 to C$115 million, while net income more than doubled to C$8.3 million. In November 1997 the company raised net proceeds of C$118.4 million through a secondary public offering.

In May 1998 the company acquired a 68 percent interest in FITEL-Photomatrix (Canada) Inc. from The Furukawa Electric Co. Ltd. for C$20.4 million. FITEL-Photomatrix designed and manufactured WDM and related products. Later in the year JDS Fitel acquired the remaining 32 percent of the company for

---

Company Perspectives:

Every time you make a long-distance phone call, watch a cable television program, use a cell phone or surf the net, you have more than likely used components and modules designed and produced by JDS Uniphase. Our lasers, modulators, multiplexers, amplifiers, switches and other products form the fiberoptic foundation for these and other types of communications.

C$13.6 million. For fiscal 1998 sales nearly doubled to C$227.2 million, while net income more than doubled to C$22.5 million.

In November 1998 JDS Fitel acquired the Akzo Nobel Photonics business unit from Netherlands-based Akzo Nobel N.V. Akzo Nobel Photonics was a world leader in waveguide technology for optical switching.

Uniphase Corporation: 1990s

Uniphase Corporation became a public company in 1993. It manufactured red helium and blue argon gas lasers for printing, biomedical, and other applications. Its helium neon lasers were used in bar code readers. The company then developed a new automatic defect classification system for semiconductor wafers that it called Ultrapointe. During the semiconductor boom of 1994–96 Ultrapointe helped the company grow. The assets of the Ultrapointe business were sold to Tencor Instruments in December 1996.

In 1995 Uniphase acquired the United Technologies Photonics Division, which became the core of Uniphase Telecommunications Products (UTP). It made lithium niobate-based modulators that are used to convert electronic signals to optical. UTP also made optical transmission equipment. UTP grew so fast over the next two years that Uniphase became focused entirely on the communications market. In 1996 Uniphase bought a U.K. laser packaging company that formed the base of its operations there. For fiscal 1996 ending June 30, Uniphase reported sales of $69 million compared to $42.3 million in fiscal 1995. Net income for fiscal 1996 rose to $2.8 million from $735,000 in fiscal 1995.

In 1997 Uniphase acquired Australian-based Indx, a leader in fiberoptic reflection filters for wavelength division multiplexing (WDM), and renamed it the Uniphase Fiber Components division. Indx was managed by Dr. Simon Poole, a co-inventor of the erbium-doped fiberoptic amplifier (EDFA).

In March 1997 Uniphase acquired the laser diode manufacturing unit of IBM, located in Zurich, Switzerland, and renamed it Uniphase Laser Enterprise AG. Uniphase moved its European laser research to Zurich and subsequently closed Uniphase Lasers Ltd. in Rugby, England. In March 1998 the company opened its European semiconductor laser fabrication plant in Zurich at a cost of about $20 million. In June 1998 Uniphase acquired Philips Optoelectronics B.V., the Netherlands-based laser operations of Philips Electronics N.V., and renamed it Uniphase Netherlands. These developments made Uniphase the dominant supplier of transmitter lasers used in fiberoptic networks for the telecommunications and cable television industries.

For the fiscal year ending June 30, 1998, Uniphase reported net sales of $185.2 million, up from $107 million in fiscal 1997, and a net loss of $19.6 million compared to a net loss of $18.9 million in fiscal 1997. JDS Fitel had sales of C$227.2 million (US$162.2 million) and net income of C$47.6 million (US$34 million) in fiscal 1998. In November 1998 Uniphase acquired Broadband Communications Products, which became Uniphase Broadband Products, Inc.

Creating a Fiberoptic Powerhouse, the JDS Fitel and Uniphase Merger: 1999

In 1998 Jozef Straus approached Uniphase CEO Kevin Kalkhoven. Uniphase was a leading supplier of active fiber components, including lasers, to leading telecommunications equipment providers such as Nortel, Lucent Technologies, and Alcatel SA of France. JDS Fitel specialized in so-called passive components. Together, JDS and Uniphase would be able to supply customers with a full range of fiberoptic hardware. When the merger was announced in January 1999, it was valued at C$6.1 billion (US$4.7 billion).

On June 28, 1999, the stockholders of JDS Fitel Inc. and Uniphase Corporation approved the merger of the two companies to form JDS Uniphase Corporation. While they had little overlap in products, the two companies shared a tremendous overlap in customers. The merger created an independent supplier with a broader portfolio of components and modules for modern communications systems.

Kevin Kalkhoven became co-chairman and CEO, while Jozef Straus became co-chairman, president, and chief operating officer (COO). Shares of JDS Uniphase began trading on the NASDAQ under the symbol JDSU, while shares of JDS Uniphase Canada Ltd. began trading on the Toronto Stock Exchange under the symbol JDU. The two companies began combined operations starting July 1, 1999, the start of its new fiscal year.

For the fiscal year ending June 30, 1999, the company reported pro forma combined sales of $587.9 million and net income of $124.9 million. Separately, Uniphase Corporation reported net sales of $282.8 million and a net loss of $171.1 million. The loss was due in part to a reevaluation of the cost of acquired research and development in connection with the Uniphase Netherlands acquisition. JDS Fitel, Inc. reported sales of C$456 million (US$305.7 million) and net income of C$99 million (US$66.4 million) for its fiscal year ending May 31, 1999.

Acquiring Several High-Tech Companies: 1999–2000

In August 1999 JDS Uniphase raised $602.8 million through a public offering of more than nine million shares of common stock of JDS Uniphase and more than 500,000 exchangeable shares of JDS Uniphase Canada. The U.S. shares were priced at $82.625 a share. In September 1999 the company acquired AFC Technologies, a Quebec-based developer of optical amplifiers and broadband instruments. In October 1999 it acquired Ramar Corporation, a Massachusetts-based developer of lithium niobate-based integrated optical components. JDS Uniphase planned to integrate Ramar into its modulator business, which produced lithium niobate modulator components for the telecommunications industry.

Key Dates:

1981: JDS Fitel Inc. is formed by former employees of Bell-Northern Research Ltd. in Canada.
1993: Uniphase Corporation completes its initial public offering (IPO).
1996: JDS Fitel completes its IPO.
1999: JDS Fitel Inc., located near Ottawa, Canada, and Uniphase Corporation of San Jose, California, merge to form JDS Uniphase Corporation.

In November 1999 JDS Uniphase announced a merger with Optical Coating Laboratory, Inc. for about $2.8 billion in stock. The two companies had operated a successful joint venture since 1997. OCLI was a leading manufacturer of optical thin film coatings and components used to control and enhance light propagation to achieve specific effects. This technology, essential in the fiberoptic telecommunications industry and other important markets, was becoming increasingly important as the demand for bandwidth continued to drive system manufacturers to increase the number of wavelengths in their wavelength division multiplexing (WDM) systems. The merger would enable JDS Uniphase to expand its product lines, speed up product development, and obtain access to a key technology for building the optical telecommunications networks of the future. The merger was completed in February 2000, with OCLI continuing to operate as a wholly owned subsidiary of JDS Uniphase.

At the same time JDS Uniphase completed its acquisition of EPITAXX, Inc., a New Jersey-based supplier of optical detectors and receivers for fiberoptic telecommunications and cable television networks, for approximately 2.2 million shares of common stock valued at $400 million.

In December 1999 the company completed its acquisition of SIFAM Ltd., a United Kingdom-based maker of fused component products that are used to split, combine, and filter light in optical fiber, for £60 million. Many of SIFAM's products were critical components in optical amplifiers.

Responding to high levels of demand for its fiberoptic products, JDS Uniphase announced plans at the end of 1999 to invest $125 million to expand its production capacity by adding 600,000 square feet and related capital equipment to its global operations. The largest single expansion would take place in Ottawa, Canada, where the company would begin construction of the third phase of its main campus facility, consisting of about 360,000 square feet of additional R&D, manufacturing, and office facilities. The remaining 240,000 square feet would be added to operations around the world in Sydney, Australia; Chalfont, Pennsylvania; Bloomfield, Connecticut; West Trenton, New Jersey; Melbourne, Florida; and Torquay, England. The expansions would bring the company's total square footage to more than 2.1 million square feet.

Positioning for the Future

At the start of 2000 JDS Uniphase announced a merger with E-TEK Dynamics Inc. for $15 billion in stock. E-TEK had 2,450 employees and was headquartered in San Jose, California. It was a leader in the design and manufacture of high quality passive components and modules for fiberoptic systems, including wavelength division multiplexers (WDMs) that increased the capacity of new and existing fiberoptic networks. The company also made components such as isolators, couplers, and integrated optics that were important in enabling optical communications systems. Following the merger E-TEK would operate as a wholly owned subsidiary of JDS Uniphase.

JDS Uniphase announced it would introduce more than 30 new products at OFC 2000, a major fiberoptics show taking place in March 2000. It was the broadest array of new products introduced by JDS Uniphase to date and represented intense new product development activities. The new optical components and modules would serve a wide range of applications in the telecommunications and cable television industries, including optical transmission, amplification, dense wavelength division multiplexing (DWDM), switching and network control, data communications, and optical instrumentation.

The acquisitions continued in 2000 as the company announced an agreement to acquire Cronos Integrated Microsystems, Inc., a North Carolina-based provider of optical MEMS (micro-electro-mechanical systems) devices to the telecommunications industry, for $750 million in stock. MEMS technology was expected to play a key role in future generations of optical components. Before the year was out, the company was expected to command a workforce in excess of 12,000, a phenomenal increase, considering it listed fewer than 100 just a decade earlier.

Principal Subsidiaries

E-TEK Dynamics Inc.; Optical Coating Laboratory, Inc.; Uniphase Laser Enterprise AG (Switzerland); Uniphase Broadband Products, Inc.; Uniphase Netherlands.

Principal Operating Units

Active Products Group; Transmission and Test Group; Laser Subsystems Group.

Principal Competitors

Corning Inc.; Fujitsu America Inc.; Lucent Technologies Inc.

Further Reading

Austen, Ian, "Supplier to the Stars," *Canadian Business,* May 29, 1998, p. 81.
Donlon, J.P., "Photon Man," *Chief Executive (U.S.),* May 1999, p. 30.
Gilder, George, "Paradigm Party," *Forbes,* August 24, 1998, p. S95.
Laver, Ross, "An Empire Built on Light," *Maclean's,* March 27, 2000, p. 46.
Slocum, Kevin C., "The Making of a Powerhouse," *Electronic News (1991),* April 3, 2000, p. 48.
"Uniphase Corp.," *CDA-Investnet Insiders' Chronicle,* May 16, 1994, p. 16.
"Uniphase Selling Ultrapointe Business to Tencor," *Electronic News (1991),* December 16, 1996, p. 32.

—David P. Bianco

Jockey International, Inc.

2300 60th Street
Kenosha, Wisconsin 53140
U.S.A.
Telephone: (262) 658-8111
Fax: (262) 658-0036
Web site: http://www.jockey.com

Private Company
Incorporated: 1876 as S.T. Cooper & Sons
Employees: 5,400
Sales: $545.5 million (1998 est.)
NAIC: 315192 Underwear and Nightwear Knitting Mills;
   315221 Men's and Boys' Cut and Sew Underwear
   and Nightwear Manufacturing; 315231 Women's and
   Girls' Cut and Sew Lingerie, Loungewear, and
   Nightwear Manufacturing

Jockey International, Inc. is one of the oldest and best-known U.S. underwear manufacturers. The company markets a broad range of underwear for men, women, and children, along with related products. Its products are primarily sold under the flagship Jockey brand, but the company also produces products under license agreements, such as those with Tommy Hilfiger and Liz Claiborne. Jockey International's manufacturing facilities include about a dozen plants in Costa Rica, Honduras, Jamaica, the United Kingdom, and the southern United States, and it licenses and distributes its products in more than 120 countries worldwide. Within the United States, the Jockey brand is distributed through more than 14,000 department and specialty stores. Privately owned since its inception, Jockey began by making socks and branched out to make innovative designs in men's underwear, pioneering the marketing of the brief.

Early History

Jockey got its start in 1876, when Samuel T. Cooper purchased six hand-operated knitting machines. Along with his sons Charles, Henry, and Willis, he used this equipment to found S.T. Cooper & Sons, a hosiery manufacturer located in the small town of Ludington, Michigan. Cooper sold heavy wool socks to general stores, which in turn sold them to customers.

Cooper soon expanded its line from wool socks to men's underwear, adding union suits, the only men's underwear then manufactured. The union suit was a long-sleeved, long-legged knit garment that buttoned up the front. At the turn of the century, Cooper moved its operations from Ludington, Michigan, to the slightly larger town of Kenosha, Wisconsin, which became its headquarters. In addition Cooper changed its name to Cooper's Underwear Company. In 1910, Cooper's introduced a new design for its union suits which eliminated the need for buttons down their fronts. The "Kenosha Klosed Krotch" consisted of two overlapping pieces of fabric that could be drawn apart to create an opening. Cooper's patented this design innovation, and trademarked the "Kenosha" name.

In the following year, Cooper's undertook the first national advertising campaign for a line of men's underwear when it took out an ad in the *Saturday Evening Post*. The company hired a well-known illustrator named Leyendecker for the magazine to produce a series of color renderings of Cooper's products. The first of these promotional spots ran in the May 6, 1911, edition of the journal. Three years later, a Leyendecker rendering of a "man on the bag" became a staple of the Cooper's brand identity.

With the entry of the United States into World War I, large numbers of men were inducted into the armed services for the first time in a generation. In the army, servicemen were given woven shorts to wear as underwear in the summer, as opposed to the long johns typically worn in civilian life. After the war ended in 1918, many demobilized soldiers continued to prefer the greater comfort and convenience of boxer shorts, shunning the union suit. By the early 1920s, the more traditional kind of garment had fallen into disfavor. Despite this decline in popularity, Cooper's did not dramatically change its product offerings throughout the 1920s. In 1926, the company briefly changed its name to Cooper's, Inc., and two years later, Cooper's created an export department to facilitate the eventual marketing of its products outside the United States.

1930s and Early 1940s: Jockeys and Briefs

At the end of the decade, Cooper's introduced a new product line, a variation on the union suit called the "Jockey Singleton.'' This sleeveless, one-piece garment was made of Durene yarn, and came only to the knees. The company called the snug-fitting underwear ''Jockey'' to suggest athleticism and flexibility. Cooper's trademarked this name and the construction of the garment, and sold a high volume of this product throughout the 1930s. Three years after the introduction of the singleton, Cooper's rolled out another new product line when it began to sell knit pajamas. In 1934, Cooper's expanded its line of knit products once again, when it started marketing knit sports shirts to retailers.

In 1934, Cooper's made its most important innovation in underwear when it designed the brief. This idea came about after a senior vice-president of Cooper's saw a picture of men on the French Riviera wearing a new type of bathing suit. He saw this garment as a potential prototype for a new kind of men's support underwear. In September 1934, Cooper's produced an experimental prototype, brief style #1001. In response to its introduction, competitors labeled the new underwear style a fad. On January 19, 1935, Marshall Field and Company, the premier Chicago department store, unveiled a window display featuring the new brief. On that day, Chicago was experiencing a severe blizzard, and the skimpy men's underwear in the window made a stark contrast to the wintry conditions outside. Under these circumstances, Marshall Field's managers gave the order to take the brief out of the window display. When the workers who were to carry out this order were delayed, however, the new underwear style stayed on display, and prompted an unexpected surge of demand for the product. More than 600 briefs were sold before noon, at a price of 50 cents apiece.

The brief's popularity remained strong in the following days. Over the next week, more than 12,000 of the new underwear style were sold. In its first three months of sales, Marshall Field's rang up more than 30,000 pairs of the red-hot item. With this runaway success, the brief garnered widespread attention in the underwear industry. In August 1935, Cooper's Underwear Company received a patent on the construction principles of the Y-front brief from the U.S. Patent Office.

Building on the strength of its new underwear style, Cooper's introduced another new line in 1935, when it began to sell a Junior set of products for boys. The first items offered were a brief and an athletic shirt. Cooper's also became the first company to sell men's underwear in packages in that year. In 1936, Cooper's began to market its products outside the United States for the first time when it signed a contract for a Canadian firm to manufacture and sell its styles under license. In an effort to

further enhance the sales of its brief, Cooper also unrolled an advertising campaign designed to point out the disadvantages of boxer shorts. Called the ''stop squirming'' promotion, this campaign went on to win awards in its field.

Following these efforts, Cooper's in 1937 brought a greater degree of structure to the retail underwear business. In that year, the company introduced a model program for retailers to use in controlling their inventory of Cooper's underwear products, and also produced a manual called ''New Era for Underwear Selling'' that was designed to instruct retailers in the most effective marketing of Cooper's wares. In addition, the company began to offer special mannequins for use in displaying Cooper's products in stores.

Cooper's move toward greater retailing sophistication continued in February 1938, when the company mounted an innovative display at the National Association of Retail Clothiers and Furnishers Convention in Chicago. The company presented the first underwear fashion show, which it called the ''Cellophane Wedding.'' The display consisted of a male and female model, each dressed in evening clothes, as if for a wedding. The trick to the display, however, was that half of the man's coat and pants, and half of the woman's gown, were made of cellophane, displaying the couple's underwear underneath. The woman wore fashionable undergarments of the day, and the man wore a brief and a t-shirt. This fashion show caused a sensation at the convention, and pictures of the couple appeared in every major newspaper and magazine, winning Cooper's a bonanza of free publicity.

Also in 1938, Cooper's introduced another promotional device, the Jockey hip tape. This was used to insure a proper fit for underwear. The company received its second patent on the brief, this one for the ''Classic'' style #1007, with Y-front construction, on January 2, 1938.

In the following year, Cooper's enhanced its display systems for retailers when it designed a table-top dispenser for its products that customers could use themselves. In the late 1930s and early 1940s, Cooper's also employed a number of sports celebrities to endorse its products, including Babe Ruth, Yogi Berra, Bart Starr, and others. As the 1940s began, Cooper's also introduced a new trademark, the Jockey Boy statue, which it used to differentiate its products from those of its competitors.

To reinforce the consistent impression made by the Jockey Boy trademark, Cooper's introduced a slide and sound film on how to sell underwear in 1941. At the end of that year, the United States entered World War II, and Cooper's, like the rest of the country's industry, switched over to wartime production. The company manufactured flare parachutes and underwear for the armed forces for the duration of the war.

Rapid Postwar Expansion

At the cessation of hostilities, the U.S. economy entered a period of rapid expansion. In order to help its market share grow, Cooper's began to use radio advertising to push its products in selected major cities in 1948. That year, the company also came up with a new way to make its briefs appealing to customers, when it began offering underwear made out of fabrics that had been decorated with novelty prints. These promotions went under the name ''fancy pants.'' By 1953, Cooper's had expanded its ''fancy pants'' line by adding its

---

Key Dates:

1876: Samuel T. Cooper purchases six hand-operated knitting machines and with his sons founds S.T. Cooper & Sons, a hosiery manufacturer located in Ludington, Michigan.

c. 1900: Company relocates to Kenosha, Wisconsin, and changes its name to Cooper's Underwear Company.

1911: Cooper's undertakes the first national advertising campaign for a line of men's underwear with an ad in the *Saturday Evening Post.*

1929: The Jockey brand is first used for a one-piece garment called the "Jockey Singleton."

1934: Cooper's designs and introduces a new underwear style, the brief.

1938: Company presents the first underwear fashion show at an industry convention.

1948: Cooper's begins to use radio advertising to push its products; the company also moves toward the positioning of its products as fashion items with a line of underwear decorated with novelty prints.

1954: Company begins to promote underwear as a gift item by packaging its products in a special Christmas box.

1955: Television advertising is added, with the first spots airing on NBC's "Home Show."

1971: Harry Wolf, a company consultant, purchases Cooper's.

1972: Company is reincorporated as Jockey International, Inc.

1978: Wolf dies and ownership passes to his three children; Donna Wolf Steigerwaldt holds controlling interest and becomes chair and CEO.

1980: Baltimore Orioles pitcher Jim Palmer becomes sole spokesperson for the company.

1982: The Jockey for Her line of cotton panties is introduced.

1985: Company establishes its own in-house advertising agency.

1988: Company purchases Nantucket Mills, a hosiery manufacturer.

1993: Steigerwaldt buys out her sister's share to become sole owner of Jockey.

1994: Jockey begins making and marketing a Tommy Hilfiger line of underwear.

1995: Edward C. Emma is named president and COO.

1998: The men's and women's divisions are consolidated into a single unit called Jockey Brand; the Jockey for Her label is replaced by Jockey Intimates; the "Let 'em know you're Jockey" ad campaign is launched.

2000: Under a license agreement, Jockey launches Liz Claiborne Intimates, a line of bras, panties, daywear, foundations, and related accessories.

---

most popular item, animal prints. Among the animal skin designs were leopard, tiger, and zebra.

Cooper's also expanded its line of non-underwear products in 1950, when it began to offer men's sportswear. Two years later, the company began to market products for women for the first time, introducing a feminine version of the Jockey short called the "Jockette." The company also stepped up its efforts to sell underwear for boys, taking out advertisements for its Jockey Junior line in *Parent's Magazine.* In a further promotional effort, Cooper's produced two new training tools for salespeople, how-to films entitled "All I Can Do" and "The Big Little Things."

Also in 1953, Cooper's introduced a new fabric which, like the design for the brief, had originated in France. Called "tricot," the French word for "knit," this material was originally made of pure silk thread, knitted into a soft, supple fabric. Cooper's adapted this substance for the U.S. market, manufacturing tricot out of nylon. In addition, the company moved beyond basic white, offering products made of tricot in a full range of colors.

With the introduction of animal prints and colored tricot underwear, Cooper's moved away from the conception of underwear as a plain, functional item toward a conception of its product as a fashion item, with style and novelty value that extended beyond its basic utility. This process continued in 1954, when the company began to promote underwear as a gift item, packaging its products in a special Christmas box. This trend was expanded to a second holiday in the following year, when Cooper's introduced a special fashion brief as part of a Valentine's Day promotion.

In the following year, Cooper's again expanded the number of fabrics out of which its products were sewn when the company began to offer a line of woven boxer shorts. The company also took another step in its promotional efforts, when it began to advertise underwear on television, running spots on NBC's "Home Show." In addition to these advances, Cooper's notched yet another patent in its field after it developed a unisized hosiery package.

In 1957, Cooper's continued its promotional innovations when it proclaimed the first "National Long Underwear Week." In a further effort in this area, the company became a sponsor of the "Jack Parr Show" on NBC, which later became known as the "Tonight Show." Two years later, Cooper's scored another underwear fad when it introduced "Skants," smaller cut briefs with a no-fly front. In addition, the company extended its line of sportswear and also began to sell men's hosiery, returning to its original roots as a sock manufacturer.

In the 1960s, Cooper's continued to adjust the design of its products to keep pace with current trends in fashion. In general, the company's knit and woven underwear became shorter, tighter fitting, and were offered in more bright colors and patterns. Despite the broad variety of offerings, however, 97 percent of the company's sales still came from white underwear. In 1964, Cooper's rolled out "Life," a Lo Rise fashion underwear collection. At the same time, the company began to make its products out of Suprel, a trade name for a blend of polyester and combed cotton.

In the late 1960s, Cooper's returned to its earlier practice of using sports stars and other celebrities to endorse its products.

The company's new line of golf sportswear, for instance, was promoted by Bert Yancey and Tom Weiskopf, and ads for Jockey brand products were run on the "Wide World of Sports" television program. For these efforts, Cooper's was named "Brand Names Manufacturer of the Year" in 1969.

1970s and 1980s: New Ownership, Jim Palmer, and Jockey for Her

Three years later, the Cooper's Underwear Company was purchased by Harry Wolf, who had previously worked as a consultant to the company. At that time, the company was renamed for its trademark, which Cooper's had promoted aggressively over the decades. On May 1, 1972, the company was reincorporated under the new name Jockey International, Inc. In the following year, Jockey expanded its product line further by merging two similar categories of garment, the bathing suit and the brief, into a product called the "DP." In 1974, the company took another step away from strict utility and toward fashion when it hired a New York designer, Alexander Sheilds, to design its sportswear.

When Wolf died in 1978, ownership of Jockey passed on to his three children. Within five years, Wolf's son sold his interest in the firm to his sisters, and Donna Wolf Steigerwaldt, who held a controlling interest in the company, became chair and chief executive officer of Jockey.

Jockey's promotional efforts received a big boost in 1980, when the company selected Jim Palmer, a handsome pitcher for the Baltimore Orioles and an experienced Jockey model, to be sole spokesperson. The image of Palmer wearing a Jockey "Elance" brief became so popular that it was manufactured and distributed as a poster. In 1982, Jockey stepped up its marketing of women's underwear, when it rolled out a new "Jockey for Her" line of cotton panties at a formal fashion show in New York. The company launched the line with three styles, and soon added fashion colors and stripes, and matching tops. Two years later, Jockey added a fourth style, the "French Cut" brief, and in 1985 a line of "Queen Size" underwear for taller and larger women.

Also in 1985, Jockey established its own in-house advertising agency to handle all of its promotional campaigns and marketing activities. In that year, the company began to feature "real people," such as a construction worker, an executive vice-president, and a mother, in its advertising, a strategy that won Jockey praise from women's groups.

Three years later, Jockey purchased Nantucket Mills, a hosiery manufacturer. Following this acquisition, the company began to market "Sheer & Comfortable," a collection of women's hosiery with four styles. This line was soon expanded to include "Sheerest Ever" and "Ultra Sheer" products. To promote its hosiery products, the company sponsored a nationwide "Legs Search" for real people to model its stockings.

1990s and Beyond

Jockey continued to expand its line of product offerings in the early 1990s, adding new styles and fabrics, as well as related products, such as socks. In 1993 Donna Wolf Steigerwaldt bought out her sister's share of Jockey, and so became its sole owner. That year, and continuing into 1994, the company also worked to address the problem of excess capacity in its manufacturing operations through plant closings. Four U.S. manufacturing plants were closed, including its last factory in Wisconsin. A distribution center in Kenosha was also shuttered, leaving only the corporate headquarters in the town. Nearly 1,000 jobs were eliminated from the company workforce in connection with these closures. These moves culminated a several years long shift of production to lower-wage areas in the southern United States and in offshore areas in Central America and the Caribbean.

In mid-1994 Jockey began manufacturing and marketing, through a license agreement, a new line of underwear under the Tommy Hilfiger brand. The line consisted of cotton briefs, cotton boxer shorts, athletic boxer shorts, and knit boxer shorts. It proved successful enough that the original three-year deal was extended in 1997.

In May 1995 Edward C. Emma was named managing director and chief operating officer of Jockey International, assuming responsibility for the company's day-to-day operations. He replaced Thomas J. Bienemann, who had been hired in 1993 to lead the downsizing and restructuring effort. Emma joined Jockey in 1990 as director of the Jockey Menswear division, then was promoted to senior vice-president of retail operations in 1993. In the latter post Emma spearheaded the opening of 37 Jockey retail and manufacturer's outlet stores, a move intended to counter the increasingly difficult task of selling underwear and related items through department stores. In October 1995 Emma was promoted to president and COO. In January of the following year the company reorganized its operations into five independent units—men's, women's, special markets, retail, and international—each of which had its own president reporting to Emma.

In late 1996 Jockey announced that it would purchase from Courtaulds Textiles a long-running licensee operation in the United Kingdom, which manufactured Jockey brand underwear at a plant in northern England and distributed the products in the United Kingdom and Scandinavia. Jockey made another purchase in early 1997 with the acquisition of the Formfit seamless panties division of I. Appel Corp. In mid-1997 Jockey entered into another licensing agreement, this one with Russell Corporation for the launch of a line of sports underwear for the mass market called Jerzees Sport.

Further reorganizing came in early 1998 when the company consolidated its men's and women's divisions into a single unit called Jockey Brand. At the same time, the company gradually began to phase out the Jockey for Her label in favor of Jockey Intimates, paralleling the Jockey Men's appellation. With designer brands grabbing increasing shares of the underwear market, and with the company fighting an image as an old-fashioned, uptight maker of white underwear, Jockey aimed to capture younger consumers while keeping its longstanding customers through the introduction of new, more fashionable products and a hipper marketing campaign. In March 1998 Jockey, with the help of its new ad agency, Grey Advertising, launched a campaign dubbed "Let 'em know you're Jockey." Among the products pushed were a new line called Jockey Sport featuring such items as boxer briefs in bright colors. In the ads, male and female models dropped their trousers to show the world that they proudly wear Jockey underwear. David Drescher, vice-president for marketing and advertising, told the *New York Times,* ''We want to spark Jockey with a new spirit, breathe new life into the Jockey name, get Jockey talked about.'' The campaign was the subject of much media attention.

In addition to its new ad campaign, Jockey International also worked to expand through licensing agreements. Most notable was an agreement with Liz Claiborne whereby Jockey would make and market bras, panties, daywear, foundations, and related accessories under a new brand called Liz Claiborne Intimates, which was launched in early 2000. This was Jockey's first license in women's wear. Other turn of the millennium initiatives included the launching in the spring of 1999 of the first line of Jockey bras, an increased use of outside sourcing, and the shift of more operations offshore, specifically packaging facilities.

Principal Competitors

Calvin Klein Inc.; Danskin, Inc.; Donnkenny, Inc.; Fruit of the Loom, Ltd.; Oneita Industries, Inc.; Sara Lee Corporation; Tultex Corporation.

Further Reading

Abend, Jules, ''Jockey Colors Its World,'' *Bobbin,* February 1999, pp. 50–54.

Backmann, Dave, ''Emma, 40, Named to Lead Jockey,'' *Kenosha News,* May 16, 1995, p. 1.

——, ''Jockey in National Spotlight,'' *Kenosha News,* March 5, 1998, p. C6.

——, ''Jockey Park Dedicated: Time Capsule Buried During Ceremony,'' *Kenosha News,* May 22, 1993.

Elliott, Stuart, ''Jockey Tries to Update the Image of Its Underwear Line,'' *New York Times,* March 4, 1998, p. D6.

Feitelberg, Rosemary, ''Jockey Revamp Splits It into Five Separate Firms,'' *Women's Wear Daily,* October 9, 1995, p. 11.

Friedman, Arthur, ''Liz Claiborne, Jockey Sign Pact for Innerwear,'' *Women's Wear Daily,* September 24, 1998, p. 4.

Gray, Jacquelyn, ''Jockey: Kenosha Firm's History Makes a Splash in New York, *Milwaukee Journal,* June 21, 1992, p. G6.

Guilford, Roxanna, ''Understanding the Challenges of Underwear,'' *Apparel Industry Magazine,* November 1999, pp. 50, 52–53.

Hajewski, Doris, ''In Brief, Jockey Aims for Fun,'' *Milwaukee Journal Sentinel,* April 5, 1998, p. 1.

Hart, Elena, ''Hilfiger Launches Ad Campaign and New Underwear Collection: Line Is Licensed to Jockey International, *Daily News Record,* June 28, 1994, p. 8.

——, ''Tommy Hilfiger Licenses Jockey for Underwear Line for '94,'' *Daily News Record,* September 22, 1993, pp. 2+.

''In This Suit, Lawyers Will Argue About Briefs,'' *New York Times,* June 3, 1993, p. D4.

''Jockey's Field Is Widening in Merchandise Mix,'' *Daily News Record,* March 17, 1989, p. 7.

Lloyd, Brenda, ''Jerzees—Labeled for Undercover Action: Jockey Licenses Russell's Brand for Sports Briefs Line,'' *Daily News Record,* June 30, 1997, p. 12.

McKinney, Melonee, ''Jockey Gallops into Global Marketing: Company Also Set to Battle Designer Lines As Level of Underwear Fashions Rise,'' *Daily News Record,* January 16, 1998, pp. 4+.

Monget, Karyn, ''Jockey Acquires Appel's Formfit Seamless Panties,'' *Women's Wear Daily,* January 8, 1997, p. 23.

——, ''Jockey Sizes Up a New Line of Bras,'' *Women's Wear Daily,* March 8, 1999, p. 28.

Munde, Jeannine, ''Jockey's Golden Success Story: The Cotton Brief,'' *Daily News Record,* September 17, 1984, p. 8.

Palumbo, Sandra, ''Women's Line Is Blooming for Jockey As Division Builds Toward 40% of Firm,'' *Women's Wear Daily,* February 12, 1987, pp. 10+.

Parr, Jan, ''The Woman's Touch,'' *Forbes,* October 27, 1986, pp. 332+.

Sandler, Larry, ''Jockey Will Close Plant in Kenosha,'' *Milwaukee Sentinel,* October 23, 1993, p. 1A.

Sharoff, Robert, ''Jockey Gallops into Mass Market Riding New Brands,'' *Daily News Record,* December 17, 1990, pp. 18+.

Smarr, Susan L., ''Chairman Holds a Steady Rein,'' *Bobbin,* September 1988, pp. 178+.

——, ''Thoroughbred Takes Jockey to the Winner's Circle,'' *Bobbin,* September 1988, pp. 170+.

''Why Jockey Switched Its Ads from TV to Print,'' *Business Week,* July 26, 1976, p. 140.

—Elizabeth Rourke
—updated by David E. Salamie

The John D. and Catherine T. MacArthur Foundation

140 S. Dearborn Street
Chicago, Illinois 60603
U.S.A.
Telephone: (312) 726-8000
Fax: (312) 920-6284
Web site: http://www.macfound.org

Private Foundation
Founded: 1978
Employees: 200
Total Assets: $4 billion (1999 est.)
NAIC: 813211 Grantmaking Foundations

The John D. and Catherine T. MacArthur Foundation, one of the largest grantmaking foundations in the United States, is most widely known for its "genius" awards—the MacArthur Fellows Program which awards grants to creative individuals in any field. In addition to the Fellows Program, the Foundation's grantmaking programs are the Program on Human and Community Development, the Program on Global Security and Sustainability, and the General Program. Through these programs, the Foundation funds research, education, and policy development on such topics as U.S. energy efficiency, public school reform, arms reduction, biodiversity, and youth development.

From Rascal to Millionaire: 1897–1945

John Donald MacArthur was born in 1897, in eastern Pennsylvania, the youngest of seven children. His father, William, left the coal mines to become a traveling evangelist, eventually rising to national prominence. John dropped out of school in the eighth grade, where, according to Foundation literature, he was bright but "extremely mischievous." One story had it that he was expelled from school for a week for climbing into a girls' dormitory. He headed for Chicago a few years later and went to work as a salesman at his brother's insurance company. He obviously found his niche—when he was 19, he sold $1 million in policies in one year.

When the United States entered World War I, MacArthur wanted to see action. He joined the U.S. Navy but left when he was not sent overseas. The same thing happened when he joined the Royal Canadian Air Force. Eventually he was caught trying to stow away on a troop ship headed for Europe.

MacArthur tried his hand at journalism, working as a cub reporter for the *Chicago Herald and Examiner,* and then turned to small business ventures. In 1919, he married Louise Ingalls, with whom he had two children, Roderick and Virginia, and whom he later divorced. MacArthur returned to the insurance industry following his business attempts, working for an annual salary of $10,000.

In 1928, at age 30, he went into business for himself, buying the Marquette Life Insurance Company, which had assets of $15.31. He met and married Catherine Hyland, a secretary at his brother's insurance company. Unlike John, Catherine was detail-oriented, and she quickly became part of his business, handling the books. Their small office was in Chicago's South Loop, in an old building now owned by the Foundation.

In 1935, during the Depression, MacArthur borrowed $2,500 and bought Bankers Life and Casualty Company of Chicago, whose assets consisted of a box of papers. MacArthur first sold policies door-to-door, but then hit on a novel means of selling insurance—by mail. He put ads in newspapers and mailed out thousands of flyers. Within five years, Bankers had assets of over $1 million. The company expanded nationwide, with a sales force of "ordinary people," clerks, truck drivers, firemen. In 1942, at age 45, MacArthur became a millionaire.

Real Estate and Land Development: 1950s–70s

Bankers continued to grow through the 1950s, as MacArthur bought up small, struggling insurance companies. In 1958, the MacArthurs moved to Florida, where they and their two poodles lived in an old resort hotel John bought in the Palm Beach area. John, who worked out of the hotel's coffee shop, became interested in real estate and at one point was the largest landowner in the state, owning 100,000 acres of Florida. But business ventures were not the only things he got involved in. In 1965, he ransomed the Delong Ruby from underworld jewel cutters for $25,000. The ruby had been stolen from the Ameri-

Company Perspectives:

The John D. and Catherine T. MacArthur Foundation is a private, independent grantmaking institution dedicated to helping groups and individuals foster lasting improvement in the human condition. The Foundation seeks the development of healthy individuals and effective communities: peace within and among nations; responsible choices about human reproduction; and a global ecosystem capable of supporting healthy human societies. The Foundation pursues this mission by supporting research, policy development, dissemination, education and training, and practice.

can Museum of Natural History in New York City—John recovered it in a telephone booth.

In addition to the land and 12 insurance companies, MacArthur owned shopping centers, development companies, 19 commercial buildings in New York City, pulp and paper companies, radio and television stations, 6,000 apartments in Manhattan, and several publishing enterprises. "I'm not rich," he often said. "I just work for companies that are rich as hell. And I happen to own the companies." In the 1970s, MacArthur became a billionaire, one of two in the country. Bankers was the largest privately owned insurance company in the country and John MacArthur was the only stockholder.

Establishing a Foundation: 1978

MacArthur did not believe that children should inherit great wealth, so he placed 92 percent of his fortune in charitable trusts. All the stock of Bankers went into a trust to fund a nonprofit charitable entity to be called the John D. and Catherine T. MacArthur Foundation. Catherine received half of the remaining $70–$80 million and their children, Roderick and Virginia, each received a quarter in life estates. When John MacArthur died in 1978, the Foundation received assets worth approximately $700 million.

MacArthur left no instructions to the Foundation's board as to how he wanted the organization run or as to what types of activities it should fund. "I know of a number of foundations where the donors tried to run them from their graves," he wrote in a letter. "I have guaranteed the trustees that when I am gone, they can run the show."

A Rocky Beginning: 1978–84

The first board of directors included Catherine and J. Roderick MacArthur, both the president and the vice-chairman of Bankers Life and Casualty Company, the news commentator Paul Harvey, whose broadcasts were sponsored by Bankers, and two business associates of John MacArthur's. In addition to determining the direction of the Foundation, they had to deal with the MacArthur businesses. Tax-exempt foundations were not allowed to own more than 20 percent of an active business; the board had five years to sell Bankers and diversify the Foundation's assets.

Both of the board's responsibilities caused conflict, usually pitting Roderick MacArthur against the other board members. A

millionaire in his own right, Roderick wanted to spend 80 percent of the available funds (some $30 million a year) to support "MacArthur Researchers," giving outstanding individuals multi-year grants with no strings attached. "We'll fund Michelangelo," Roderick told *Forbes*. The other board members liked the idea generally but questioned the magnitude. As that option was being debated, the Foundation made its first awards. Amnesty International received $50,000, as did the California League of Cities to study the effect of Proposition 13, which froze property taxes in that state. The third recipient was the Better Government Association, a "good government" organization based in Chicago that used the money to begin nationwide studies of government corruption.

In 1980, the foundation's grants totaled $42 million. While $9–$10 million continued to support good government and education "general grants," the foundation began focusing on one of its major areas, mental health, which received $8 million that year. It also donated 1.5 miles of oceanfront property in Palm Beach (worth $18.3 million) as a public park and spent $1 million to rescue *Harper's* magazine.

In June 1981, the foundation announced the first 21 recipients of its "genius" award. Paid over a period of five years, the prize amounts ranged from $24,000 to $60,000. Later that year, Catherine T. MacArthur died.

The other major conflict had to do with the Foundation's assets. Roderick wanted to sell the Bankers stock quickly and over the next few years accused the other members of conflicts of interest because of their close ties with Bankers and sued several for mismanaging the foundation's assets and paying themselves excessive fees. In 1979, the board added seven new members, people not associated with the insurance empire. John E. Corbally, former president of the University of Illinois, was elected the Foundation's first president. Other new members included Jonas Salk, inventor of the polio vaccine, and William Simon, former Secretary of the Treasury.

In 1984, the board sold Bankers Life and Casualty Co. to ICH Corp., a Louisville-based holding company, for a total of $482 million. Later that year, Roderick dropped a lawsuit seeking to liquidate the foundation and soon afterwards died of cancer.

Program Directions (Mental Health, Parasitic Diseases, World Environment, and More): 1979–88

The foundation concentrated on a limited number of fields. Its objective was to make investments where a small amount of money could have widespread implications and possibly effect long-term change. Mental health was one such field. Funding for research to prevent and treat mental illness had fallen substantially in the 1970s. But lack of money was not the only problem the foundation saw. The little research being done was very fragmented and tended to focus on curing mental illness; there were few studies about mental health.

What was needed, according to the foundation, was support for "intellectual networking"—interdisciplinary research that involved scientists and other researchers from a variety of fields examining the developmental process across the lifespan. This approach supported, for example, researchers at Yale, Colum-

Key Dates:

1935: John D. MacArthur buys Bankers Life and Casualty for $2,500.

1950s: Bankers Life and Casualty ranks as largest private insurance company in United States.

1978: John D. MacArthur dies, leaving $700 million in stock to fund the John D. and Catherine T. MacArthur Foundation.

1988: Foundation's assets grow to $2.5 billion

1991: Creation of MacArthur Fellows Program, the "genius" awards; Catherine T. MacArthur dies.

1998: With assets of $4 billion, Foundation is distributing $170 million in grants each year.

bia, and London's Institute of Psychiatry working to determine whether adult and childhood depression were the same disease or were developmentally linked. In another example, interdisciplinary research led the shift in gerontology to focus on biological and psychosocial characteristics of successful aging. By the end of 1987, the foundation had committed more than $71 million to the mental health field and was the single largest supporter of research on mental health outside the federal government.

In 1983, the foundation began a five-year, $20 million initiative for the study of parasitic diseases. It established an international consortium of 11 research groups, recruiting specialists inside and outside the field of parasitic biology—geneticists, immunologists, and cellular and molecular biologists. Grants also supported graduate students working at the research centers, a summer course at the Marine Biology Lab at Woods Hole, Massachusetts, and related programs of the World Health Organization.

In 1982, the foundation established the World Resources Institute to develop ecologically sound public policies. The Institute was seen as a bridge between scientists and key policy makers and conducted studies of world energy needs, global warming, and acid rain; generated an international plan to stop the destruction of tropical forests; and examined how the World Bank, global corporations, and other institutions could improve resource management in developing nations.

Gradually, the foundation focused its environmental efforts on endangered tropical ecosystems and how to reconcile conservation and development in tropical regions. Grants ranged from funds to purchase portions of tropical forests in Costa Rica, Florida, and Hawaii, to strengthening local and regional conservation organizations in 20 developing countries, to educational efforts in support of conservation.

In 1984, the foundation initiated its Program on Peace and International Cooperation with the objective of increasing the understanding of the forces that lead to international conflict. To accomplish this, it worked to bring new talent into the field and to involve disciplines other than peace and security. The foundation funded research and graduate fellowships for scholars and analysts; and established fellowships for research and writing that related peace, security, and international cooperation to

diverse issues, including the introduction of computer technology in the Soviet Union. Grants also went to National Public Radio for coverage of peace and security issues and for teleconferences between journalists from different countries.

Chicago received support from the foundation to address neighborhood problems and to build the capacity of local groups to cope with urban problems. A 1987 grant of $11.3 million established the Fund for Community Development for economic and housing development projects. Between 1979 and 1988, the foundation awarded an additional $48 million to cultural organizations in the city. Palm Beach also received significant resources from the foundation in addition to the John D. MacArthur Beach State Park created in 1980.

Initially, the foundation gave grants to universities and colleges to establish endowed professional chairs. By the end of its first decade, it had shifted its focus to children ages four through 14 and to involving families in local education. Grants supported adult literacy efforts, Reading is Fundamental, the application of successful models and curricula, and a study of the National Assessment of Education Progress. The foundation was also very involved in the decentralization and reform of Chicago's schools.

New Directions: 1989–98

In 1989, John Corbally stepped down as president of the foundation. Adele Simmons, president of Hampshire College in Massachusetts and a native Chicagoan, assumed that post in 1990. The foundation had $3.4 billion in assets, with an annual budget of $140 million.

Simmons began her tenure by committing $40 million over the next ten years to parent and community groups in Chicago involved in reform of the local schools and pushing for greater collaboration among foundations. In 1991, MacArthur joined the Pew Charitable Trusts and the Rockefeller Foundation in establishing the Energy Foundation to promote energy efficiency and alternative energy sources such as wind and solar power.

"It's hard to remember or realize that the MacArthur Foundation is a very young foundation," Simmons told the *Chronicle of Philanthropy* in 1998. "When I came, all the programs had really just been put in place. So it was first an opportunity to nurture and encourage those programs and help build linkages among them, and ultimately to restructure the existing programs."

The restructuring, which occurred in 1996–97, integrated the foundation's six program areas into two large, interdisciplinary programs. Domestically, the Program on Human and Community Development funded organizations, researchers, and scientists working in the areas of economics opportunity, community capacity building, child and youth development, and mental health. The Program on Global Security and Sustainability provided grants internationally to address three global issues: arms reduction and security, ecosystem conservation, and population. Both programs stressed linkage and collaboration among researchers, practitioners, and policy analysts. In addition, the foundation's General Program supported work in telecommunications policy and in media, along with areas of special interest. Meanwhile, the MacArthur Fellows Program continued.

The MacArthur Fellows program was derided for over a decade by many on the left for "discovering the already discovered," according to a *New York Times* article. Complaints focused on the demographics of the winners, who were primarily white, male, and well established. Things changed in 1993 when a new director was named. Within two years, women comprised 60 percent of the awardees, and political conservatives complained that many awardees were selected for their political correctness.

1999 to the Present

In September 1999, Jonathan Fanton succeeded Adele Simmons as president of the foundation. Fanton was president of the New School for Social Research in New York City. The foundation's first new initiative under its new leader was announced in April 2000, a collaboration with three other foundations to spend $100 million to support improvement of universities and academic associations in several African countries.

Simmons summarized the foundation's efforts in her final president's letter: "A long-term approach, investments in efforts to understand problems, coordinated application of a variety of approaches, collaboration with other funders, and tolerance for occasional failure—these make for effective grantmaking in the face of complexity."

Principal Competitors

The Ford Foundation; The Carnegie Corporation of New York; The Rockefeller Foundation; The Lilly Endowment; The Bill and Melinda Gates Foundation; The W.K. Kellogg Foundation; The J. Paul Getty Trust; The Robert Wood Johnson Foundation; The Pew Charitable Trusts; The Robert W. Woodruff Foundation; The Anneberg Foundation; The David and Lucile Packard Foundation.

Further Reading

Dunejerski, Marina, "After a Decade at the Helm, Head of MacArthur Fund to Step Down," *Chronicle of Philanthropy*, May 21, 1998, p. 17.

"Foundations Launch $100 Million Initiative Supporting African Higher Education," *U.S. Newswire*, April 24, 2000.

"Grantmaking Guidelines," Program on Global Security and Sustainability, John D. and Catherine T. MacArthur Foundation, http://www.macfound.org/programs/gss/gss_guidelines.htm.

"Grantmaking Guidelines," Program on Human and Community Development, John D. and Catherine T. MacArthur Foundation, http://www.macfound.org/programs/hcd/hcd_guidelines.htm.

"John D. and Catherine T. MacArthur," http://www.macfound.org/aboutfdn/john_cath.htm.

John D. MacArthur: The Man and His Legacy, Chicago: John D. and Catherine T. MacArthur Foundation, 1988.

"Jonathan F. Fanton Is Named President of the John D. and Catherine T. MacArthur Foundation," *PR Newswire*, December 10, 1998.

"Manna from MacArthur," *Forbes*, July 20, 1981, p. 12.

"The New Insurance Empire That's Raising Eyebrows," *Business Week*, June 11, 1984, p. 143.

"1998 Grants Essay," General Program, John D. and Catherine T. MacArthur Foundation, http://www.macfound.org/grants/gen_essay.htm.

Scott, Janny, "MacArthur 'Genius' Grants Get Some Heat and a New Head," *New York Times*, December 9, 1997, p. G5.

Simmons, Adele, "President's Essay, Accepting Complexity: Thoughts at the End of a Decade," The John D. and Catherine T. MacArthur Foundation, http://www.macfdn.org/aboutfdn/presmessage.htm.

Tamarkin, Bob, "Bitter Charity," *Forbes*, June 11, 1979, p. 113.

Teltsch, Kathleen, "Foundation Leader Charting New Paths," *New York Times*, May 25, 1991, p. 10.

—Ellen D. Wernick

Korn/Ferry International

<table>
<tr><td>

1800 Century Park East, Suite 900
Los Angeles, California 90067
U.S.A.
Telephone: (310) 843-4100
Fax: (310) 553-6452
Web site: http://www.kornferry.com

Public Company
Incorporated: 1969 as Korn/Ferry Enterprises
Employees: 1,600
Sales: $373.16 million (1999)
Stock Exchanges: New York
Ticker Symbol: KFY
NAIC: 541612 Human Resources & Executive Search
    Consulting Services

</td></tr>
</table>

Korn/Ferry International is the number one executive recruitment firm in the world, with more than 70 offices in 40 countries. The company's clients include large corporations, nonprofits, and other organizations. Fees are typically equivalent to 30 percent of the salary a new executive receives, although the company also works on a contractual basis for a number of clients. In 1998 an Internet-based middle management recruitment service, Futurestep, was launched in conjunction with the *Wall Street Journal.* The company, briefly public in the early 1970s, issued stock for a second time in 1999.

Beginnings

Korn/Ferry International was founded by a pair of restless partners at Peat Marwick Mitchell & Co. (later KPMG Worldwide). Lester Korn had earned his M.B.A. from UCLA in 1960 and had begun work on a Ph.D. at Harvard Business School when he left to join "Big 8" accounting firm Peat Marwick as a management consultant. In 1963 he was asked to run the company's executive search department on the West Coast and several years later was made a partner. Richard Ferry, from Ohio, had earned a degree in accounting from Kent State University and had worked for several accounting firms, including one that he cofounded, before joining Peat Marwick in 1965.

He, too, soon moved into the executive search field there, eventually succeeding Korn as West Coast search department manager. He made partner in 1969. Despite the success of both men within the company, each found himself chafing at the constraints encountered in working for a large firm. In November 1969 they made the decision to form their own personnel consulting agency, Korn/Ferry Enterprises.

The initial scope of Korn/Ferry (whose name was soon changed to Korn/Ferry International) included a range of personnel consulting services, only one facet of which was executive search. The two founders' strong backgrounds in this area and its relatively untapped market on the West Coast, however, led them to concentrate in it. The new partners started out sharing all the work, but over the next several years they hired additional employees, including several from Peat Marwick.

Korn/Ferry was put together in a more rigorously organized manner than the typical search firm of the era, which often worked as more of an "old boys' network" than a systematically run business. Lester Korn, the more public member of the team, took on the job of promoting the firm to both clients and potential candidates. He hired public relations agencies to get the word out and also came up with the idea of performing surveys of executive vacancies for distribution to the media, which resulted in free publicity. Richard Ferry, working more in the background, specialized in developing methods for running the company efficiently, which included using a research staff to handle many aspects of the search process, keeping careful records of time spent on each search, and creating a clear hierarchy of duties. Many other recruitment firms left the entire work load to a single person whose job included seeking out clients as well as tracking and "cold calling" prospective candidates. Ferry's systems parceled these tasks out to support staffers, leaving the senior members of the firm free to concentrate on keeping in touch with clients and conducting interviews of final candidates. An innovation during the company's first year was the creation of a specialty division dedicated to real estate.

The first several years of business were highly successful for Korn/Ferry, which soon opened offices in a number of cities including New York, Houston, and Chicago. By its third year the company's annual revenues had risen to $1.8 million and its

Company Perspectives:

Korn/Ferry International is the worldwide market leader in executive recruitment through the utilization of a seamless global network of the most competent professionals in our business. We provide our clients the highest quality, most innovative and professional counsel and services in a collegial, stimulating work environment.

staff had grown to more than 40. Specialty divisions now included petrochemicals/energy and financial services, in addition to real estate. Expansion into Europe was accomplished in 1972 by a merger with the British search firm G.K. Dickinson Ltd., and the company also opened an office in Japan a few months later.

In 1972 the company's founders decided to take the firm public, selling ownership of a quarter of the business on the over-the-counter market for slightly less than a million dollars. Although highly profitable, and with annual sales growth of nearly 100 percent in 1973 and more than 40 percent in 1974, the stock value dropped from $8 to slightly more than $5. Finding that they were spending large amounts of their time dealing with the responsibilities of being publicly owned, Korn and Ferry decided to buy back the outstanding stock for $7 a share.

Growing in the 1970s

The company's growth continued at a rapid clip throughout the 1970s. The 1977 purchase of 49 percent of Latin American search firm Hazzard and Associates took Korn/Ferry south of the border, and the company expanded to Australia two years later with the acquisition of Guy Pease Associates. By the end of 1979, as it celebrated its tenth anniversary, Korn/Ferry had made partners of 59 of its senior recruiters. In 1980 the company was declared to be the number one search firm in the world by industry observer *Executive Recruiter News*.

The early 1980s saw more strong years for the firm, and by 1985 Korn/Ferry boasted 106 partners, 11 specialty divisions, and revenues of an estimated $58 million. The company employed more than 400 and operated 36 offices worldwide. Income from overseas recruiting accounted for about a quarter of revenues, with a significant amount also derived from the financial services specialty. Korn/Ferry was now performing 1,500 searches per year for executives earning salaries of more than $75,000. The firm's staff profited from its success, receiving performance-based bonuses that sometimes equaled 50 percent or more of their annual salaries.

The company had several high-profile success stories to its credit, including the recruiting of Peter Ueberroth to head the 1984 Olympic Committee and the placement of CEOs at corporations such as Storage Technology, Seafirst, and Nissan USA. It had also suffered embarrassment when a managing partner, David H. Charlson, resigned after he was discovered to have padded his resumé with a fictional M.B.A. degree from Stanford. Several other Korn/Ferry recruiters also left after they were found to be making exaggerated claims about their education.

The search business was becoming increasingly competitive during these years, with clients seldom remaining loyal to a single firm and staging "shootouts" where competing recruiters had to make pitches to win a search. The financial rewards were great, however, as executive salaries were spiraling upward and search firms' one-third commissions, based on first-year salary, were increasing proportionately. Revenues also were being fed by a widespread erosion of employee loyalty and by the many companies that had poor internal systems for developing management talent. Although the majority of open positions were filled by the companies themselves, they were forced to rely on executive recruitment firms when internal candidates and advertising for applicants did not pan out. Executive recruiters, known somewhat sarcastically as headhunters, were sometimes seen as shady operators who brazenly called unsuspecting employees to offer them positions at rival companies. The reality was that recruiters provided a necessary service, as they offered a discreet way for a company to woo needed staff away from competitors. Attention from recruiters became a sign of success for executives, who would wonder what they were doing wrong if they did not regularly receive a certain number of calls from headhunters.

Changing Times in the 1990s

Korn/Ferry's business had grown to an estimated $103.3 million in fiscal 1989, but the U.S. economy was leveling off and executive hiring, especially in the financial services area, began to decline. Revenues had shrunk to $97.3 million two years later, and the company reportedly trimmed its staff by 20 percent between 1990 and 1992. Korn/Ferry also took other steps to remain competitive, including reducing fees charged to clients, pushing up the pace of searching, and even guaranteeing that its candidates would perform well for up to a year from date of hire. Times were tough industrywide, with an estimated one-sixth of the 2,300 firms active in 1989 having closed their doors just three years later.

Founder Lester Korn, who had temporarily left the firm to serve as a representative to the United Nations in 1987 and 1988, departed for good in early 1991, and his ownership stake was purchased by Korn/Ferry's 140 partners. Richard Ferry added Korn's job of chairman to his own roles of president and CEO. With the economy on the mend in the early 1990s, the search business picked up and the company again began to look toward growth. In a move that greatly boosted its European presence, in 1993 Korn/Ferry purchased Carre Orban International of England for $20 million. The move paid off, as international recruiting soon became the company's largest growth area, amounting to half its revenues within four years. New offices were opened in such far-flung locales as Russia, India, and Asia.

By the mid-1990s the company also had begun pursuing a strategy of signing long-term agreements with major corporations. These recognized Korn/Ferry as the client's primary search firm, which helped reduce the dreaded "shootouts," but also limited the company's ability to recruit executives from its clients, which included AT&T, Johnson & Johnson, and General Electric. The deals typically guaranteed Korn/Ferry a minimum of $1 million a year in business, with the company promising lower fees and better service as part of the bargain. Korn/Ferry reported that it was realizing 20 percent of its revenues

Key Dates:
1969: Company is founded by Lester Korn and Richard Ferry.
1970: First specialty division is created for real estate recruiting.
1972: Merger with G.K. Dickinson Ltd. of England; initial public offering.
1974: Return to private ownership.
1977: Merger with Hazzard and Associates extends presence to Latin America.
1980: Korn/Ferry ranks as number one search firm, according to *Executive Recruiter News.*
1991: Founder Lester Korn leaves.
1993: Merger with Carre Orban International.
1998: Formation of Futurestep online recruitment service.
1999: Company goes public for the second time.

from such arrangements in 1995 and expected this share to double by 2001.

Going Online in the Late 1990s

In 1997 the company began to offer an Internet-based recruitment service in California, initially called Korn/Ferry: Careerlink. This targeted middle management executives, an area that Korn/Ferry had previously ignored. The trial run proved successful, and the company quickly moved to expand it nationally under a new name, Futurestep. The service, which was provided with assistance from the *Wall Street Journal* (which took no ownership stake), asked prospective candidates to register online. If they were being considered for a specific job, they would be interviewed later by a Korn/Ferry staffer. The number of people who chose to put their resumés online grew to more than 500,000 within the first 18 months.

Korn/Ferry had begun contemplating going public again and, after a slight delay, issued stock on the New York Stock Exchange in 1999. Following a disappointing start, by year's end Internet-dazzled investors had bid up the company's stock price significantly. Korn/Ferry later issued a "tracking stock" for subsidiary Futurestep, Inc. Following the public offering, the company began a round of acquisitions, purchasing Amrop International Australasia of Australia, Hofmann Herbold & Partner of Germany, and Crist Partners of Chicago. A number of other acquisitions were also reportedly in the works. Co-founder Richard Ferry still held the title of chairman, with former COO Windle Priem now filling the roles of president and CEO. He had replaced Michael Boxberger, who succeeded Ferry at those jobs in the mid-1990s.

As it passed the 30-year mark, Korn/Ferry International looked to be in good health. The company's successful Internet-based recruitment service and ongoing international expansion were strong additions to what was already a solidly run operation. Korn/Ferry appeared likely to retain the position of number one recruitment firm for some time to come.

Principal Subsidiaries

Amrop International Australasia (Australia); Avery & Associates, Inc.; bgu Beratungsgesellschaft fur Unternehmensentwicklung AG (Switzerland); Carre Orban & Partners, Ltd. (U.K.); Continental American Management Corp.; Crist Partners; Didier, Vuchot et Associes (France); DRF-Beteiligungs AG (Switzerland); DR-Miro AG (Switzerland); Hofmann Herbold & Partner (Germany); Korn/Ferry International Futurestep, Inc.; Korn/Ferry Worldwide, Inc.; Pintab Associates Ltd. (U.K.); Postgraduados y Especialistas, S.A. de C.V. (Mexico); REMCO Research & Management Consulting Services S.A. (Switzerland). The company has other subsidiaries in Argentina, Australia, Brazil, Canada, Chile, China, the Czech Republic, Denmark, Finland, France, Germany, Greece, Hong Kong, Hungary, India, Indonesia, Italy, Japan, Korea, Malaysia, Mexico, The Netherlands, Norway, Peru, Poland, Romania, Singapore, Slovakia, Spain, Sweden, Switzerland, Thailand, Turkey, the United Kingdom, and Venezuela.

Principal Competitors

TMP Worldwide, Inc.; Heidrick & Struggles International, Inc.; Christian & Timbers; Russell Reynolds Associates, Inc.; Spencer Stuart Management Consultants N.V.; Egon Zehnder International; Electronic Data Systems Corp.; FMR Corp.; StaffMark, Inc.

Further Reading

Bodovitz, Katherine, "Headhunters Face Off in Shootout As Search Industry Consolidates," *Crains New York Business,* October 13, 1986, p. 17.

Breznick, Alan, "Korn/Ferry Searches for Profits," *Crains New York Business,* December 7, 1992, p. 3.

Byrne, John A., *The Headhunters,* New York: MacMillan, 1986.

Eadie, Alison, "Masters of the Round-The-World Choose Headhunting," *Daily Telegraph London,* January 28, 1998, p. 65.

Finch, Camilla, "Recruiter Must Don Founder's Big Shoes," *Crains New York Business,* May 11, 1992, p. 13.

Gabriel, Frederick, "Korn/Ferry Turns Clients into Partners with Deals," *Crains New York Business,* July 29, 1996, p. 17.

Hagerty, Bob, and Joann S. Lublin, "Internet Putting Added Pressure on Headhunters," *Wall Street Journal,* February 14, 1997, p. A9D.

Newman, Morris, "Korn/Ferry International Founder Runs $64-Million Job Search Firm," *Los Angeles Business Journal,* February 22, 1988, p. 1.

Peltz, James F., "Stock Spotlight: Earnings, Economy Help Korn/Ferry Get Ahead," *Los Angeles Times,* January 18, 2000, p. C1.

Sarkisian, Nola L., "Korn/Ferry Now Flies High After Getting a Slow Start," *Los Angeles Business Journal,* October 11, 1999, p. 60.

Taub, Daniel, "Global Recruiting: Richard Ferry Helped Take Korn/Ferry International from Two-Man Office to World's No. 1 Executive Search Firm," *Los Angeles Business Journal,* December 16, 1996, p. 15.

Temes, Judy, "International Focus Pays Off at Korn/Ferry," *Crains New York Business,* April 15, 1996, p. 16.

Vrana, Debora, "Executive Recruiter Korn/Ferry to Launch Long-Delayed IPO," *Los Angeles Times,* February 8, 1999, p. C1.

——, "Korn/Ferry IPO Gets Mixed Reviews," *Los Angeles Times,* August 24, 1998, p. D1.

—Frank Uhle

Leiner Health Products Inc.

901 East 233rd Street
Carson, California 90745-6204
U.S.A.
Telephone: (310) 835-8400
Toll Free: (800) 533-VITA; (800) 533-8482
Fax: (310) 835-6615
Web sites: http://www.leiner.com
          http://www.yourlifevitamins.com

Private Company
Founded: 1973
Employees: 2,111
Sales: $626.9 million (1999)
NAIC: 325412 Pharmaceutical Preparations
    Manufacturing, 422210 Botanicals Wholesaling

Leiner Health Products Inc. regards itself as the world's largest manufacturer of vitamin supplements and herbs. With manufacturing and packaging/distribution plants in both the United States and Canada, the company produces over 25 billion tablets annually of its Your Life brand of supplements as well as manufacturing private label brands for mass retailers, drugstores, supermarkets, convenience stores, military outlets, and warehouse clubs. Over 64,000 retail establishments, including 52,000 in the United States, sell supplements made by Leiner. Among Leiner's retail customer base, Wal-Mart Stores and Costco have the largest share, commanding 30 and 11 percent, respectively, of 1999 sales. Leiner claims the distinction of being the first company to make supplements according to the strict standards of the United States Pharmacopoeia (USP) Convention. In addition to nutritional supplements, Leiner sells branded and private label nonprescription pharmaceuticals, such as pain medications and cold remedies, and also the Bodycology brand of skin and hair care products. With the contribution of companies it acquired in the late 1990s, Leiner Health Products plays a major role in the growing self-help movement by providing nutritional supplements and nonprescription products to consumers.

1970s–90s: Early Incarnations

In 1973 P. Leiner & Sons, America, Inc. started a new vitamins division that two years later began producing Your Life Vitamins, its most prominent brand name. In 1979, a group of P. Leiner managers and Booker PLC, a food conglomerate based in the United Kingdom, purchased the vitamin division, renaming it P. Leiner Nutritional Products Corporation. According to company literature, this predecessor firm in 1980 was the first company to introduce a line of natural vitamins that had no sugar, salt, artificial colors, or preservatives. Other industry firsts occurred in 1982 with the introduction of outer cap safety seals for vitamin containers and the use of nutritional data directly on labels. In 1984 P. Leiner Nutritional Products became the first to offer single-serving multivitamin packages for convenience stores. In 1986 P. Leiner continued to innovate by introducing to chain drugstores the first vitamin/drug interaction program. Two years later the firm began offering customers the first toll free hotline for vitamin products, the kind of service more consumers appreciated and even expected as part of the self-help movement.

While the Leiner products gained popularity, its own corporate structure was somewhat mercurial. In 1984 P. Leiner Nutritional Products went public, trading on the American Stock Exchange. That year management had agreed that Booker would own no more than a 49 percent stake in P. Leiner. By 1989, however, P. Leiner had lifted that restriction, and Booker proceeded to buy up stock that by 1991 would give it 60 percent ownership of P. Leiner.

In late 1991 Booker informed P. Leiner that it intended to sell its entire 60 percent ownership; it planned to leave the health products industry as part of a reorganization to reduce its debt. Booker offered P. Leiner first choice in buying its 3.2 million shares out of a total of 5.3 million common shares outstanding. However, P. Leiner CEO Michael Leiner turned down the offer in order to avoid further debt himself. For the fiscal year ending March 31, 1991, P. Leiner earned net income of $5.4 million from revenues of $135.3 million.

In January 1992 new owners based in New York took over P. Leiner. A New York company called AEA Investors Inc. set up Leiner Health Products Group Inc. in Delaware, and in May 1992 Leiner Group became a holding company by paying Booker about $90.9 million to purchase P. Leiner Nutritional Products. The same month Leiner Group spent $24.7 million to acquire XCEL Laboratories, Inc., a private firm that made over-the-counter pharmaceuticals under private-label contracts. In 1993 XCEL was merged into P. Leiner Nutritional Products, which then changed its name to Leiner Health Products Inc.

When Leiner's management decided to expand the company in 1993, they received tax, relocation, and job-training incentives to move to Arizona, Nevada, and Colorado. However, they chose to stay in Carson, California, purchasing two vacant 250,000-square-foot warehouses in the area. The local government funded a $600,000 conveyer bridge to connect the two buildings, and the state government offered some tax credits. Leiner President Gale Bensussen related in the July 28, 1994 *Los Angeles Times* that, ''We didn't really think anybody in the government would care if we packed up our bags and left. Pleasantly, we were dead wrong.'' Government incentives prompted Leiner to buck a recent trend among companies leaving the state in droves. (In 1992, 140 companies and about 18,000 jobs left southern California; 44 firms and 7,100 jobs left the following year.)

With its upgraded and expanded facilities, Leiner Health Products was able to meet voluntary standards set by the U.S. Pharmacopeia (USP) Convention. In the summer of 1994, Your Life Vitamins became the first vitamins meeting these voluntary standards for solid dosages (tablets or capsules), including disintegration/dissolution times, weight variations, strength limits, and limits to control harmful bacteria. While USP's role was not to verify that Leiner or other companies actually complied, the standards helped ensure that vitamin and other health product companies would not be found guilty of false advertising through inaccurate labeling.

Other challenges to the industry came from special interest groups. For example, after testing calcium supplements and calcium-containing antacids from over 20 companies, the nonprofit Natural Resources Defense Council (NRDC) found that most of those products exceeded the California legal state limit of 0.5 micrograms of lead per 1,000 milligrams of calcium. Thus in the fall of 1996 the NRDC sent notice to several California companies that it intended to sue them for violating California's law. In early 1997 Leiner Health Products, the nation's largest manufacturer of calcium supplements at the time, agreed to a settlement with NRDC to avoid a legal battle. Leiner decided to use chelation, an existing technology, to remove virtually all lead from its calcium supplements sold under the Your Life brand or sold as private label brands in large retail chains.

Following Leiner's action, the NRDC and the California Attorney General negotiated with several other calcium manu-

facturers, which also agreed to reduce the amount of lead in their supplements and antacids. These developments were significant given the possible dangers of lead poisoning, especially to pregnant and nursing women and their fetuses or young infants. Moreover, The National Academy of Sciences in 1997 recommended that adults under age 50 should increase their daily calcium intake from 800 to 1,000 milligrams and those over 50 should consume 1,200 milligrams. With few Americans getting even the old daily recommendation, the use of supplements was expected to increase.

Expansion Through Acquisition in the Late 1990s

In January 1997, Leiner Health Products purchased Vita Health Company Ltd., a Canadian firm that manufactured about 350 different kinds of nutritional supplements. Its five main products were vitamin C, vitamin E, multivitamins, glucosamine, and herbal products, although it also made OTC pharmaceuticals, including pain relievers and items to treat coughs and colds. Vita Health operated a 100,000-square-foot manufacturing and distribution plant in Winnipeg, Manitoba. In 1998 the firm changed its name to Vita Health Products Inc., and VH Holdings Inc. was set up as a subsidiary of Leiner Health Products to oversee Vita Health Products.

By 1999, Leiner Health Products was operating two main manufacturing plants in the United States. Its 138,500-square-foot facility in Garden Grove, California, made most of the firm's vitamins, while its 51,250-square-foot plant in Kalamazoo, Michigan, produced most Leiner over-the-counter pharmaceuticals. At Leiner's Carson, California, headquarters, the company ran a distribution and packaging center. In an effort to consolidate some of its operations, Leiner closed packaging/distribution centers in Ohio, Wisconsin, and New York, choosing to house those operations at a new facility in Fort Mill, South Carolina. By April 1999 the 680,000-square-foot Fort Mill plant was completely operational, including its tableting and laboratory capabilities.

Leiner Health Products in December 1999 announced it had completed its purchase of almost all assets of Granutec, Inc., a subsidiary of Ontario, Canada-based Novopharm, Ltd. With manufacturing/distribution plants in Largo, California, and Wilson, North Carolina, Granutec was the ''fourth-largest distributor of private label, over-the-counter (OTC) pharmaceutical drugs,'' in the United States, according to a Leiner press release. ''With this acquisition, Leiner will become the nation's second largest supplier of private label OTC products,'' management asserted. Such products accounted for $2.6 billion in the consumer-driven self-help movement. However, Leiner CEO Robert M. Kaminski added that expired patents of $12.6 billion worth of prescription drugs in 2002 would expand the private-label OTC market even more. In addition to acquiring Granutec's private-label products, Leiner also benefited from Granutec's expertise using the ''Abbreviated New Drug Application'' process to convert prescription drugs to over-the-counter items.

Through its subsidiary Vita Health Products Inc., Leiner also purchased substantially all assets of Stanley Pharmaceuticals, Ltd., a Vancouver, Canada-based subsidiary of Novopharm that made and distributed private label OTC drugs and vitamins. At the same time Leiner began a partnership with Novopharm's 200 research and development scientists.

Key Dates:

1973: P. Leiner & Sons, America, Inc. launches a vitamin products division.
1975: P. Leiner begins production of Your Life brand vitamins.
1984: P. Leiner Nutritional Products Corporation goes public.
1992: Leiner ownership changes hands and company acquires XCEL Laboratories, Inc.
1994: Leiner's Your Life supplements become the first vitamins to meet USP standards.
1997: Company acquires Vita Health Company Ltd. of Canada.
1998: Company starts consolidating its packaging and distribution at its new Fort Mill, South Carolina, plant.
1999: Leiner purchases Granutec, Inc. and Stanley Pharmaceuticals Ltd.

Leiner Health Products sold basically three types of supplements under its flagship Your Life brand. First, it sold a complete line of specific vitamins and minerals, multivitamins, and various combinations. Second, it offered its trademarked Body Benefits Paks intended to help consumers with particular needs. That included a choice of two core multivitamin Paks plus a choice of various supplements in the company categories of Bones & Joints, Immune Booster, Circulatory & Heart, Energy, Memory, and Healthy Moods. Third, Leiner sold over 30 kinds of herbal products, including ginseng, echinacea, St. John's Wort, cranberry, garlic, papaya, kava kava, and ginkgo biloba. It sold a total of over 500 vitamin and herbal products in more than 10,000 stock keeping units (SKUs), whether in its own Your Life brand or private labels. In addition, Leiner marketed over 100 over-the-counter products in about 2,000 SKUs for relief of pain, cough, cold, or digestive problems

Leiner was selling most of its products through mass market retailers, unlike competing supplement firms, such as Twinlab Corporation, which sold primarily to health food stores. Leiner estimated that it made 20 percent of all vitamins sold through mass retailers in the United States and over 50 percent of private label brands sold by mass retailers. Leiner sold its vitamins to America's ten largest drugstores, including American Drug Stores, Walgreen Company, Eckerd Corporation, CVS Corporation, and Rite Aid Corporation. It also sold to eight of the ten major supermarket chains, such as Winn-Dixie Stores, Albertson's, A&P, Lucky Stores, and Safeway.

Leiner Health Products recorded net sales of $626.9 million in 1999, up from $502.1 million the year before. It also ended the year with net income of $10.3 million, compared to a net loss of $17.4 million in 1998.

As it prepared for a new century in the vitamin business, Leiner entered the electronic commerce field, becoming the main supplier of a Web-based retailer called HealthQuick.com. With America Online owning five percent of its equity, HealthQuick.com offered over 1,000 SKUs of various supplements and also healthcare and bath and skin care products. Founder Herbert Haft had set up this new business to offer discount prices and no shipping fees for orders over $20.

Under the executive team of Gale K. Bensussen, Robert M. Kaminski, Kevin J. Lanigan, and Charles F. Baird, Jr., Leiner enjoyed good times; consumers were buying more vitamins and nutritional supplements than ever before, in spite of some critics who alleged that many if not most vitamins were unnecessary with a good diet and otherwise were overpriced.

In any case, the big boom came in the sale of herbal products. For example, in 1997 consumers spent over $12 billion on natural supplements, almost double what they spent in 1994. In addition, more studies indicated the possible benefits of vitamin supplements and herbal products. The federal government established an agency to study alternative healing, including herbalism, during this time.

Challenges, however, came in the form of increased competition. Upstarts entered the supplement industry because of the increasing consumer demand and also because most vitamins and herbal products could not be patented, unlike prescription drugs. Leiner in 2000 faced some tough challenges, especially as much larger firms for the first time entered the vitamin and herbal arena.

Principal Subsidiaries

VH Holdings Inc.

Principal Competitors

Rexall Sundown, Inc.; NBTY, Inc.; Perrigo Company; American Home Products Corporation; Bayer A.G.; Bristol-Myers Squibb Company; Twinlab Corporation; Murdock Madaus Schwabe; Nature's Sunshine; Weider Nutrition International Inc.

Further Reading

"Booker PLC to Sell 60% in P. Leiner Nutritional Products," *Wall Street Journal*, November 6, 1991.

"California; Leiner to Lower Lead in Calcium Tablets," *Los Angeles Times*, January 28, 1997, pp. D2–3.

Freeman, Laurie, "Bringing Credibility to Herbals," *Supermarket Business*, April 1999, pp. 75–77.

Greenwald, John, "Herbal Healing," *Time*, November 23, 1998, pp. 59–68.

"Leiner Expands Bodycology Line," *Supermarket News*, June 26, 1995, p. 48.

Myers, David W., "California, Here We Stay: More Businesses Are Finding Reasons to Remain in the State," *Los Angeles Times*, July 28, 1994, p. D1.

"No Bones About It: NRDC Scores a Major Public Health Victory in California on Lead in Calcium Supplements," *Amicus Journal*, Spring 1997, p. 53.

"P. Leiner Nutritional Agrees to End Limit on British Firm's Stake," *Wall Street Journal* (Eastern Edition), May 30, 1989, p. 1.

"Rapid Expansion Continues at Leiner," *MMR*, November 24, 1997, p. 27.

Rock, Andrea, "Vitamin Hype: Why We're Wasting $1 of Every $3 We Spend," *Money*, September 1995, p. 82.

Rosendahl, Iris, "USP Designation Appears on Vitamin Labels," *Drug Topics*, July 25, 1994, p. 37.

Tosh, Mark, "Drug Store Industry's Haft Goes Online with HealthQuick.com," *Drug Store News*, August 2, 1999, p. 3.

—David M. Walden

London Stock Exchange Limited

London EC2n 1HP
England
Telephone: (+44) 171 797 1372
Fax: (+44) 171 410 6861
Web site: http://www.londonstockexchange.com

Private Company
Founded: 1773 as The Stock Exchange
Employees: 536
Operating Revenues: £149.8 million (US$93.19 million) (1999)
NAIC: 52321 Securities and Commodity Exchanges

The London Stock Exchange Limited (LSE) is the world's oldest stock exchange and one of the top three stock exchanges in the world, after the New York and Tokyo exchanges. Founded in 1773 and reincorporated as a private limited company in 1986, the LSE is also the world leader in international share trading. The LSE operates a number of market products, including the main board listing, featuring more than 3,000 companies and including over 500 international companies, as well as the secondary AIM (Alternative Investment Market), established in 1995 as a vehicle for trades in small, high-growth companies. More than 70 companies are listed on the AIM board. After launching the Stock Exchange Electronic Trading Services (SETS) in 1997, the LSE introduced a new listing, techMARK, tailored to the specific needs of the high-technology sector and designed to compete with the NASDAQ index. With a total equity turnover value of more than £3.5 billion, the LSE achieved gross revenues of £149.8 million in 1999. The LSE is led by Chairman John Kemp-Welch and CEO Gavin Casey.

A World's First in the 18th Century

Founded in 1773, the LSE reflects more than 200 years of the development of share-based enterprise. The world's first joint-stock company was created in the mid-16th century. Traditionally, companies were either owned by a single individual or through a partnership with two or more owners. While this arrangement sufficed for smaller businesses and stable market sectors, direct financial responsibility for riskier endeavors—such as the great trade exploration voyages of the period—were judged too precarious for an individual or limited group of investors. The organization of such a venture, that of a voyage to trace a northern sea route to the Far East from London in 1553, introduced the world's first shareholder-based company. Selling shares to a larger number of investors reduced the financial risk for each individual investor, while enabling the company itself to raise the capital needed to fund its operations.

This first joint-stock company failed to find a northern sea route to the Far East. However, a meeting with Russian tsar Ivan the Terrible brought the company the exclusive rights to trade between Russia and England. The Muscovy Company, as it came to be called, became a commercial success, rewarded its shareholders with large profits, and inspired the creation of new investment ventures. The Muscovy Company served as the model for future shareholder-based companies. Investors contributed capital funding, while direction of the company's operations remained in the hands of its management. The investors, who were allowed to sell their holdings or buy more shares, were given dividends according to the company's profits.

As more companies were set up following the Muscovy model, a new profession came into being, that of the broker, who acted as a middleman for trades of shares, helping to boost not only the number of joint-stock companies but also the number of investors. Adding impetus to this movement was the foundation of the Bank of England as a joint-stock company by King William III in order to provide funding for England's military campaign against France at the end of the 17th century. The shareholder system was given further support by legislation to limit and punish brokers for malpractice.

By the 18th century, a flourishing "market" for shares was in place—so much so that the period marked the first stock market crash in 1720. While trading took place at the Royal Exchange through the middle of the century, the rowdy behavior—itself to become something of a tradition on the market floor—of certain brokers led to their exclusion. Instead of leaving the business, these brokers began meeting at Jonathan's Coffee House and other coffee shops in the Threadneedle Street area of London. In 1760, some 150 brokers founded their own

Company Perspectives:

Developing our Markets: *Our task is to ensure that we continue to win business for our markets and for London. Our portfolio of markets, designed to meet U.K. and international needs, provides the infrastructure which enables companies and investors to prosper, as well as meeting the needs of securities firms.* Regulating our Markets: *To maintain investor protection, as well as a fair and efficient marketplace for issues, we keep our rules and procedures under regular review, remaining responsive to customers' needs and to changes in the business environment.* Delivering our Markets: *In delivering our services, we aim for the best possible combination of responsiveness, reliability, functionality and cost. We are committed to providing a consistently high level of service to all our customers—whatever the conditions prevailing in the market.*

club to buy and sell stock at Jonathan's. The following decade, in 1773, the members of the club changed its name to the Stock Exchange.

As the individual broker members of the Stock Exchange began to establish brokerage firms, and the number of markets expanded, the Stock Exchange saw a need for new quarters. In 1801, the Stock Exchange began construction on a new building at what was to become its permanent London location. The following year, the Stock Exchange published a Deed of Settlement, formally outlining the operating rules and procedures of the stock market.

If the original joint-stock companies were formed to provide funding for the many voyages of discovery, overseas trading, and foreign military campaigns, the shareholder-based company structure showed itself easily adaptable to the changing economic landscape of the 19th century. The Industrial Revolution, coupled with such major infrastructure undertakings as the building of a national railroad system, provided the basis for the modern period of shareholder-based corporations. The appearance of a great many new companies exploiting a greater number of materials, products, and markets prompted the formation of some 20 other stock exchanges operating in the United Kingdom. Nonetheless, the London Stock Exchange remained the United Kingdom's most important stock exchange. New technologies, such as the telegraph, brought such stock market innovations as the ticker tape—the first, launched in 1872 by the London Stock Exchange, was capable of an output of six words per minute—which in turn enabled trades to take place elsewhere than the market floor. London's position as the world's financial center placed the LSE at the top of the world's stock markets.

20th-Century Evolution

At the end of the 19th century, the LSE revised its charters. Changes in the Deed of Settlement in 1875 created a more corporate-based entity for the Exchange, which now operated on behalf of its owner-members—as opposed to being operated by its members—while members remained responsible for the company's debts and operational obligations. A further evolu-

tion occurred in 1890, when the country's stock exchanges were linked together for the first time, under an Association of Stock Exchanges. The individual exchanges continued to operate independently, however. At the beginning of the 20th century, a new set of guidelines refined the Stock Exchange's member lists into "broker" and "jobber" classes.

Disruption in European trade caused by the outbreak of World War I led to the closure of the continent's stock exchanges. The LSE was forced to follow suit, suspending trades in July 1914, the last of the European exchanges to close. The Exchange's members quickly joined the war effort, creating the Stock Exchange Battalion of Royal Fusiliers, which succeeded in raising more than 1,600 volunteers. After it became evident that the war was to be a protracted one, the LSE reopened at the beginning of 1915. Normal trading conditions were not restored, however, until the end of the war in 1918, when the British government introduced a highly successful series of "Victory Bonds."

If the British market was largely spared the brunt of the New York stock market crash of 1929, the LSE was nonetheless forced to end trading in U.S. shares. While the buildup to World War II enabled the world's stock markets to regain their momentum, the devastation of the European economy brought on a vast change in the world economic and stock market landscape. The rise of the United States as the world's preeminent economic force saw the New York Stock Exchange outpace the LSE as the world's busiest and richest exchange. The rise of Japan as an economic power beginning in the 1960s and especially into the 1970s and 1980s saw the Tokyo Stock Exchange take over the number two position.

Nonetheless, London remained the center of the European community's financial markets, and the LSE gained increasing importance in the market for international stocks. London was also to figure prominently as the undisputed financial center of the then-forming European Union. Meanwhile, the stock markets were attracting larger numbers of investors, and especially investments from private individuals. The Exchange's member firms saw the need to expand their broker staff to accommodate the new influx of investors as well as the new investment products being introduced at the time. The increasing activity led to the need for new quarters; in 1972, the new LSE building, featuring a new 23,000-square-foot trading floor and a 26-story office building, was completed on the site where the Exchange had operated since 1801. In the same year, women were granted the right to become stockbrokers for the first time.

Increasing competition and technological development had also brought about both the need and the potential to consolidate the United Kingdom's many stock exchanges. The cooperation that had begun under the Association of Stock Exchanges had led to closer coordination among the United Kingdom's stock exchanges, and particularly among the more than 20 exchanges operated outside of London. The new market realities of the late 20th century were increasingly challenging the viability of these smaller exchanges. In 1973, moves were taken to combine the United Kingdom's smaller provincial exchanges into a single national exchange under the LSE.

The year 1986 marked a new era for the LSE. Changes in the legislation governing the United Kingdom's investment busi-

<table>
<tr><td colspan="2">**Key Dates:**</td></tr>
<tr><td>**1553:**</td><td>The world's first joint-stock company is founded.</td></tr>
<tr><td>**1694:**</td><td>The Bank of England is formed as a joint-stock company.</td></tr>
<tr><td>**1697:**</td><td>Legislation governing brokers is introduced.</td></tr>
<tr><td>**1760:**</td><td>A stock broker's club convenes at a coffee house in London.</td></tr>
<tr><td>**1773:**</td><td>The stock broker's club adopts a new name: The Stock Exchange.</td></tr>
<tr><td>**1801:**</td><td>A permanent exchange site is constructed.</td></tr>
<tr><td>**1872:**</td><td>The ticker tape is introduced.</td></tr>
<tr><td>**1890:**</td><td>Association of Stock Exchanges is founded.</td></tr>
<tr><td>**1929:**</td><td>Wall Street crash ends the Exchange's trading in U.S. stocks.</td></tr>
<tr><td>**1972:**</td><td>A new Stock Exchange building is opened.</td></tr>
<tr><td>**1973:**</td><td>England's provincial exchanges are combined; women are allowed on trading floor for the first time.</td></tr>
<tr><td>**1986:**</td><td>The Exchange reorganizes as a private limited company; electronic trading is initiated.</td></tr>
<tr><td>**1998:**</td><td>An alliance with Germany's Frankfurt Exchange is forged.</td></tr>
<tr><td>**2000:**</td><td>An alliance with eight European exchanges is finalized.</td></tr>
</table>

nesses, as part of the Companies Act of 1985, enabled the LSE to restructure its operations the following year as a private limited company (plc) with its member broker firms becoming shareholders. Under the company's articles of incorporation, these shareholders were not eligible to receive distribution of any profits. Instead, all profits were to be returned to the company for infrastructure and other development costs.

On October 27, 1986, the LSE underwent a still more visible transformation. Known thereafter as the "Big Bang" of the London financial scene, that day saw the implementation of several changes to the LSE's operations. For one, the company's member firms were now allowed to be purchased by outsider corporations, enabling these brokerages to increase their own capital resources in order to compete with increasingly powerful firms overseas. Another change was the abolition of minimum commission charges; stock exchange member firms were now free to negotiate their commissions with clients. At the same time, the individual members of the exchange no longer held voting rights. Moreover, marking the end of centuries of tradition, trading was moved off the trading floor to so-called "dealing-rooms," where trades were no longer conducted face-to-face but by computer and telephone. The days of the "rowdy" broker were done, at least in London. The introduction of computer technology, which enabled instantaneous pricing displays anywhere in the United Kingdom—or even the world—also allowed brokers to operate offices beyond London. The appearance of new commercial brokerage branch offices soon became commonplace across the United Kingdom.

The LSE's Deed of Settlement, in place since 1885 and originally introduced in 1802, was finally replaced by a Memorandum and Articles of Association in 1991. Under the new articles, the LSE's governing body, the Council of the Exchange, was replaced by a board of directors drawing not only from the Exchange's own management but also from its member and client base.

Changing Financial Climate in the 1990s and Beyond

The LSE faced rising pressures to adapt to the changing nature of the stock market in the 1990s. On the one hand, new technologies–particularly electronic trading systems that were rapidly rendering obsolete the Exchange's reliance on telephone confirmations—were stepping up the pace of trading and enabling trading to continue nonstop around the world; as Western markets closed for the day, their Far Eastern counterparts were just beginning trading. On the other hand, playing the stock market was becoming popular among larger portions of the population, with resulting pressures to make trading more accessible.

At the same time, a new breed of company was making evident the need for a new type of stock exchange. The roaring success of so-called "start-up" companies, that is, high-technology specialists that often went from zero to enormous market capitalization in brief periods of time, gave new impetus to exchanges, such as the NASDAQ, that were able to offer the flexibility these new companies, which often had yet to show a profit, required. In 1995, the LSE responded to this new market with the creation of AIM, the Alternative Investment Market, created specifically for startups and smaller companies. By the end of the decade, AIM had managed to attract nearly 400 companies.

In 1997, the LSE undertook another new venture with the introduction of the Stock Exchange Electronic Trading Service (SETS), which replaced—at least for some brokers and trades—traditional techniques with an electronic interface. Meanwhile, the LSE was preparing to confront the new realities of the European Market, as the EC prepared for the launch of the Euro, the single European currency. With Frankfurt winning the position as the site of the European Central Bank, London suddenly found its position as European financial leader under attack. In order to defend its position, the LSE quickly entered into a partnership agreement with the Deutsche Börse in Frankfurt.

Momentum among high-technology stocks continued to build in the waning years of the century, when much of the world began preparations to enter into a new economic landscape, the so-called Internet Economy. In 1999, in order to provide a more appropriate vehicle for this new breed of stock, the LSE launched the techMark exchange. This new exchange, modeled directly on the NASDAQ and the Neuer Markt of Germany, provided still more flexible listing conditions for high-tech and startup companies.

As the LSE entered its fourth century of trading, it continued to show the willingness to evolve and embrace new economic realities that had enabled it to maintain its position as not only the world's oldest stock exchange, but one of the world's leading exchanges. In early 2000, the LSE began reviewing a number of its policies—including allowing anonymous electronic trades for certain companies—meant to bring London in line with the policies of a new alliance among exchanges in Amsterdam, Brussels, Frankfurt, Paris, Madrid, Milan, and Zurich, scheduled to begin trading in November 2000.

Principal Competitors

New York Stock Exchange, Inc.; Paris Bourse SA; Tokyo Stock Exchange.

Further Reading

Andrew, John, ''Understanding Stock Markets: Deals Were Done,'' *Independent,* November 1, 1997, p. 5.

Garfield, Andrew, ''London Stock Exchange to Launch Rival to NAS-DAQ,'' *Independent*, August 21, 1999, p. 15.

Jagger, Suzy, ''Exchange Overhaul Attacked by Dealers,'' *Daily Telegraph* (London), January 3, 2000, p. 1.

''London's Quiet Revolution,'' *Economist*, October 18, 1997.

''London Under Threat,'' *Economist*, November 21, 1998.

—M. L. Cohen

Lucent Technologies
Bell Labs Innovations

Lucent Technologies Inc.

600 Mountain Avenue
Murray Hill, New Jersey 07974-0636
U.S.A.
Telephone: (908) 582-3000
Toll Free: (888) 4-LUCENT; (888) 458-2368
Fax: (908) 582-2110
Web site: http://www.lucent.com

Public Company
Incorporated: 1995
Employees: 153,000
Sales: $38.3 billion (1999)
Stock Exchanges: New York
Ticker Symbol: LU
NAIC: 334413 Semiconductors and Related Device
Manufacturing; 334417 Electronic Connector Manufac-
turing; 541512 Computer Systems Design Services

Lucent Technologies Inc. is the corporate descendant of
AT&T's Western Electric manufacturing division, which AT&T
bought in 1881. For most of the 20th century it was Western
Electric that made telephones in nothing but black. Over the years
it manufactured other products, including network boxes for telecommunications carriers, PBXs (private branch exchanges) for
offices, and semiconductors. Bell Laboratories is also under the
Lucent umbrella. Headquartered in Murray Hill, New Jersey, and
formed in 1925, Bell Laboratories has a long history of innovations, from synchronizing sound and film in the 1920s to inventing the transistor in the 1940s and the laser in the 1950s. In
1999 Lucent introduced 128 products that originated in Bell
Labs, and researchers there claimed more than 1,000 patents
during the year—their highest number of patents ever. Lucent
has complemented its Bell Labs innovations by acquiring numerous high-tech companies. From 1997 to 1999 Lucent spent more
than $32 billion on some 30 acquisitions.

In 1999 the company realigned its businesses into four main
groups, plus Bell Labs, which supports the other Lucent units by
providing basic research and product and service development.

Service Provider Networks included optical networking, switching and access solutions, wireless networks, and communications
software, plus business focused on serving cable TV operators
and other service providers. Enterprise Networks was responsible
for voice and data solutions for business and government enterprises and included Business Communications Systems and Government Solutions. NetCare Professional Services offered services for the life cycle of a network, including planning, design,
implementation, operations, maintenance, education, and software. Microelectronics and Communications Technologies consisted of the company's microelectronic business, network products, new ventures, and intellectual property. Its products include
integrated circuits, optoelectronic components, power systems,
optical fiber, cable, and connectivity solutions.

Beginning with $20 Billion
in Annual Sales: 1995–96

At the beginning of October 1995 AT&T Chairman Richard
Allen announced that AT&T would break into three separate
companies. AT&T would continue as a telecommunications company offering long-distance service and wireless communications.
The second company would be Global Information Solutions,
which would make automated teller machines, bar-code scanners,
and other computerized systems. The third would be Lucent
Technologies, a company focused on network equipment, switching devices, and business communications hardware.

Lucent was incorporated in Delaware in November 1995. In
February 1996 AT&T began the process of making Lucent a
stand-alone company by transferring assets and liabilities related to its business. Lucent was formed from the systems and
technology units that were formerly part of AT&T Corp., including the Bell Laboratories. Its core was AT&T's Network
Systems Group, which manufactured complex telephone
switches, semiconductors, and consumer telephone equipment.
Lucent also included the former AT&T Microelectronics.
Lucent would begin business with more than $20 billion in
annual revenues and a workforce of 137,000 employees.

In April 1996 Lucent completed the initial public offering
(IPO) of its stock. The IPO raised more than $3 billion, making

Company Perspectives:

Lucent's strategy is to meet its customers' needs by offering an end-to-end solutions platform. This strategy brings together the core products of switching, transmission, software, messaging and optoelectronics (including microelectronic componentry) with the new portfolio offerings obtained through strategic acquisitions as well as the research and development of Bell Laboratories.

it the largest IPO at the time in U.S. corporate history. On September 30, 1996, Lucent became independent of AT&T when AT&T distributed to its shareowners all of its Lucent shares. Once Lucent was separated from AT&T, it began to win large equipment contracts from telecommunications carriers who were AT&T's rivals. In October 1996 Lucent sold its interconnect products and Custom Manufacturing Services (CMS) businesses.

Lucent formed its New Ventures Group in 1996 to nurture small companies, make venture capital investments, and spin out entrepreneurial firms that could later go public. The New Ventures Group was instrumental in determining which Bell Labs inventions became marketable products. Between 1996 and the end of 1999 Lucent New Ventures created 11 companies and created syndicates of investors to spread the risk involved. At the beginning of 2000 Lucent said it planned to launch at least five new companies each year.

Series of Acquisitions and Mergers Beginning in 1997

Richard McGinn succeeded Lucent's CEO Henry Schacht in October 1997 following Schacht's retirement. McGinn had joined the old AT&T's Illinois Bell as a salesman in 1969. By 1993 he was in charge of AT&T's Network Systems Group. When Lucent was separated from AT&T in 1996, the AT&T board selected Schacht, former head of Cummins Engine and a favorite of Wall Street, over McGinn. Until Schacht's retirement, McGinn served as number two under Schacht.

Under McGinn, Lucent began a series of acquisitions and mergers that continued through 2000. Through early 2000 Lucent spent $32 billion in stock and cash to acquire or merge with 30 companies. McGinn also sold off some of Lucent's businesses and refocused the semiconductor unit on digital signal processors instead of commodity chips.

Lucent's first acquisition since becoming an independent company took place in September 1997, when the company acquired Octel Communications Corporation, a provider of voice, fax, and electronic messaging technologies, for $1.8 billion in stock. In December 1997 Lucent acquired Livingston, a global provider of equipment used by Internet service providers (ISP) to connect their subscribers to the Internet, for $650 million.

In October 1997 Lucent contributed its Consumer Products business to a new venture formed by Lucent and Philips Electronics N.V. in exchange for a 40 percent interest in the venture, which was called Philips Consumer Communications. The venture was formed to create a worldwide provider of personal communications products. A year later Lucent and Philips announced their intention to end the venture, which was terminated in late 1998. In December 1998 Lucent sold certain assets of its wireless handset business to Motorola. Since then, Lucent has continued to look for opportunities to exit the consumer products business.

During 1998 Lucent acquired the following companies: Prominet, a participant in the emerging Gigabit Ethernet networking industry, for $200 million in stock; Optimay GmbH, a German-based software developer for chip sets to be used for Global Systems for Mobile Communications cellular phones, for $65 million; Yurie, a provider of asynchronous transfer mode (ATM) access technology and equipment for data, voice, and video networking, for $1 billion; SDX, a U.K.-based provider of business communication systems, for $200 million; MassMedia, a developer of next-generation network interoperability software that manages connections across data, voice, and video networks; LANNET, an Israel-based supplier of Ethernet and ATM switching solutions, for $117 million; JNA, an Australian telecommunications equipment manufacturer, reseller, and system integrator; Quadritek, a start-up developer of next-generation Internet protocol (IP) network administration software solutions, for $50 million; and Pario Software, a maker of network security software. By acquiring a large number of data-network equipment and software companies, Lucent was positioning itself to compete with companies such as Cisco Systems in building multiservice networks that could support voice, video, and data traffic.

Lucent continued to acquire similar companies in 1999: WaveAccess, an Israel-based developer of high-speed systems for wireless data communications, for $54 million; Kenan Systems Corp., a software developer for third-party billing and customer care, for $1.48 billion in stock; Sybarus, a semiconductor design company; the Ethernet LAN component business of Enable Semiconductor for $50 million; and Ascend Communications, a developer, manufacturer, and seller of wide area network (WAN) solutions, for more than $20 billion in stock. With the acquisition of Ascend Communications in 1999, Lucent became the leader in both voice and data for service providers. An estimated 70 percent of the world's Internet traffic traveled over Ascend equipment in 1999.

Additional acquisitions in 1999 included: Nexabit, a developer of high-speed switching equipment and software that directs traffic along telecommunications networks, for $900 million; Mosaix Inc., a provider of software that links a company's front and back office operations to help them deliver more efficient customer service, for $145 million in stock; 61 percent interest in SpecTran Corporation, a designer and manufacturer of specialty optical fiber and fiber-optic products; International Network Services (INS), a global provider of network consulting and software solutions, for $3.7 billion in stock; Excel Switching Corp., a provider of open switching solutions for telecom carriers, for $1.7 billion in stock; and Xedia Corporation, a developer of high-performance Internet access routers for wide area networks (WAN), for $246 million.

Continued Profitability: 1996–2000

From 1995 to 1999 Lucent's revenues rose from $21.7 billion to $38.3 billion. After reporting a net loss in 1996 of

```
┌─────────────────────────────────────────────┐
│                                             │
│              Key Dates:                     │
│                                             │
│  1995:  Company is incorporated in November.│
│  1996:  Structural transformation is com-   │
│         pleted when Lucent Technologies is  │
│         formed from the systems and tech-   │
│         nology units, including Bell Labor- │
│         atories, that were formerly part of │
│         AT&T; IPO occurs in April.          │
│  1997:  After reporting a loss in 1996,     │
│         Lucent becomes profitable with net  │
│         income of $150,000.                 │
│  1999:  Amidst numerous acquisitions, the   │
│         merger with Ascend Communications   │
│         ranks as the company's largest to   │
│         date and catapults Lucent into the  │
│         leadership position for providing   │
│         voice and data to Internet service  │
│         providers.                          │
│                                             │
└─────────────────────────────────────────────┘
```

$230,000, Lucent improved its profitability over the next three years with net incomes of $150,000 (1997), $340,000 (1998), and $1.52 million (1999).

For fiscal 1999 revenues improved across all segments for Lucent. For Service Provider Networks revenues rose 23.3 percent, or $4.45 billion, to $23.56 billion; revenues from Enterprise Networks rose 7.6 percent, or $605 million, to $8.56 billion; revenues from Microelectronics and Communications Technologies rose 17.2 percent, or $796 million, to $5.42 billion.

Since its initial public offering in 1996, Lucent stock increased 11 times its original value, or 1,100 percent, by the end of 1999. It had surpassed AT&T to become the United States' most widely held stock, with 4.6 million shareholders. When the company's first quarter results for fiscal 2000 fell short of analysts' expectations, however, its stock lost 28 percent of its value in one day, January 5, 2000, reducing the company's market capitalization by approximately $65 billion.

In the following months the stock regained much of its value. The company reported, however, that it was aware of at least 12 class-action lawsuits filed on behalf of persons who purchased Lucent's common stock between late October 1999 and January 6, 2000, claiming that Lucent and certain of its officers misrepresented Lucent's financial condition and failed to disclose material facts that would have an adverse effect on Lucent's future earnings and prospects for growth.

Lucent attributed its shortfall for the first quarter of 2000 to its inability to meet demand for new optical networking products and delays in customers deploying their new network equipment. Analysts noted that Lucent had misread the shift in demand to fiber optics, which provided more bandwidth, and then reacted too slowly to stop its customers from defecting to chief competitor Nortel Networks.

Analysts were mixed in their outlook for Lucent. Neil Weinberg of *Forbes* wrote, "Lucent is well poised to help lead an optical revolution that will whip information around the globe at a fraction of today's cost." He noted that big mergers such as America Online and Time Warner would only increase the demand for Lucent's products and services. Although the company's reputation had been sullied by its first quarter results,

analysts foresaw a surge in spending on telecommunications equipment over the next four years. Meanwhile, Lucent was investing heavily to increase its fiber-optic production capacity.

As part of Lucent's strategy to focus on high-growth markets, the company announced at the end of February 2000 that it would spin off its private branch exchange (PBX), cabling, and LAN (local area network) business segments later in 2000 into a new company that would be headed by Lucent CFO Donald Peterson. Those segments represented Lucent's slower-growing corporate networking businesses. Although those business segments were profitable and exceeded growth rates in their markets, they did not fit Lucent's aggressive growth profile. The new company would include most of Lucent's enterprise equipment, and Lucent's channel partners supported the concept of being able to deal with a smaller business entity.

Continued Acquisitions in 2000

In the first quarter of 2000 Lucent acquired Agere Inc., an Austin, Texas-based maker of programmable network processors, for about $415 million. It also acquired Ortel Corporation, the second largest producer of lasers used for video in cable TV networks, for about $2.95 billion in stock. Lucent planned to use Ortel to supply interactive television equipment to large cable operators, such as AT&T, to enable them to transform one-way broadcasting systems into interactive two-way communications networks.

Although Lucent was best known for its networking products, the company also was involved with other emerging technologies. In the field of digital music Lucent developed the ePAC (enhanced perceptual audio coder) to deliver high-quality sound in a safe and secure environment. Lucent was one of the founding members of the Secure Digital Music Initiative, an industry group of more than 140 companies and organizations that worked to support the rights of content owners who wished to deliver music securely over the Internet. Lucent licensed its ePAC technology to a wide range of music companies, from record labels to makers of downloadable players.

Internet video was another new field in which Lucent was active. In March 2000 Lucent formed a new company called GeoVideo Networks, which was 40 percent owned by Lucent New Ventures Group, to create the first video network designed for the Internet. The network would allow users to share video between remote locations. GeoVideo planned to stream high-definition TV, a much higher-quality video than was presently available over the Internet.

Principal Divisions

Service Provider Networks; Enterprise Networks; NetCare Professional Services; Microelectronics and Communications Technologies; Bell Laboratories.

Principal Competitors

Alcatel USA Inc.; Bay Networks Inc.; Cisco Systems Inc.; Fujitsu America Inc.; JDS Uniphase Corporation; Nortel Networks Corporation; Siemens Corporation; Sycamore Networks Inc.

Further Reading

Auerbach, Jon, "AT&T Spins Off Lucent Technologies Inc. to Investor Enthusiasm," *Knight-Ridder/Tribune Business News,* April 5, 1996.

"Big Deals," *Electronic News (1991),* August 16, 1999, p. 4.

Caisse, Kimberley, "Cisco, Lucent Each Make Acquisition," *Computer Reseller News,* August 31, 1998, p. 76.

Church, George J., "Just Three Easy Pieces," *Time,* October 2, 1995, p. 38.

Cook, William J., "Dialing for Dollars," *U.S. News & World Report,* October 2, 1995, p. 59.

Cope, James, "Lucent to Spin Off Corporate Networking," *Computerworld,* March 6, 2000, p. 12.

D'Amico, Mary Lisbeth, "Lucent Can Consolidate GSM Technology via Optimay Deal," *InfoWorld,* April 27, 1998, p. 62.

Gibbs, Lisa, "Don't Hang Up on Lucent," *Money,* March 1, 2000, p. 52.

Green, Stephanie, "Breaking Up May Be Easy to Do for Lucent," *Computer Reseller News,* March 6, 2000, p. 2.

Haber, Carol, "Lucent Arrives—in Style," *Electronic News (1991),* April 8, 1996, p. 1.

Hersch, Warren S., "Network Pairings May Spark Trend," *Computer Reseller News,* August 16, 1999, p. 114.

"Kenan Systems: The Quieter Buy for Lucent," *America's Networks,* February 15, 1999, p. 10.

Korzeniowsi, Paul, "Unleashing Lucent," *America's Networks,* May 1, 1996, p. 34.

Lawson, Stephen, "Lucent Buys Multiservice Vendor," *InfoWorld,* August 3, 1998, p. 44.

"Lucent-Ascend Merger OK'd," *Electronic News (1991),* April 19, 1999, p. 37.

"Lucent Buys Chipmaker," *Computer Reseller News,* January 24, 2000, p. 2.

"Lucent Buys Livingston," *Computerworld,* October 20, 1997, p. 32.

"Lucent Buys Pario Software," *PC Week,* December 7, 1998, p. 152.

"Lucent Does It Again," *Israel Business Today,* November 30, 1998, p. 23.

"Lucent Does It for Lannet," *Israel Business Today,* July 15, 1998.

"Lucent Enters New Wireless Data Space," *Telephony,* December 7, 1998.

"Lucent to Buy Enable's Ethernet Biz," *Electronic News (1991),* March 8, 1999, p. 4.

"Lucent to Buy IP Company," *Computer Reseller News,* October 12, 1998, p. 2.

Murphy, Chris, "Capacity Problems Hurt Lucent's Revenue, Earnings," *InformationWeek,* January 24, 2000, p. 123.

Niccolai, James, "Ascend Falls into Place," *InfoWorld,* July 19, 1999, p. 46.

Ohlson, Kathleen, "Lucent Bids for Access to Europe," *InfoWorld,* June 15, 1998, p. 68.

Perone, Joseph R., "Lucent Buys Laser Producer for Interactive Television Technology," *Knight-Ridder/Tribune Business News,* February 7, 2000.

——, "Lucent Unit Spins Off Big Inventions into Profitable Small Businesses," *Knight-Ridder/Tribune Business News,* January 12, 2000.

——, "New Jersey-Based Lucent Completes Octel Acquisition," *Knight-Ridder/Tribune Business News,* September 30, 1997.

——, "New Jersey-Based Lucent Technologies Takes $60 Billion Beating," *Knight-Ridder/Tribune Business News,* January 6, 2000.

Presti, Ken, "Lucent to Acquire Start-Up Prominet," *Computer Reseller News,* December 15, 1997, p. 14.

Robinson, Sara, "Nortel Acquisition Fortifies Lead in Optical-Networking Field," *Knight-Ridder/Tribune Business News,* March 21, 2000.

Schaff, William, "Lucent's Networking Splash," *InformationWeek,* May 4, 1998, p. 206.

Semilof, Margie, "Lucent Buys Nexabit in $900M Deal," *Computer Reseller News,* July 19, 1999, p. 64.

——, "Lucent Buys Switch Maker for $1.7B," *Computer Reseller News,* August 23, 1999, p. 30.

Thyfault, Mary E., "Lucent to Buy Maker of CRM Software," *InformationWeek,* April 12, 1999, p. 191.

Traiman, Steve, "A Century of Audio Innovation," *Billboard,* January 29, 2000, p. L1.

Weinberg, Neil, "Wired and Restless," *Forbes,* February 7, 2000, p. 90.

—David P. Bianco

marchFIRST, Inc.

311 S. Wacker Drive, Suite 3500
Chicago, Illinois 60606-6621
U.S.A.
Telephone: (312) 922-9200
Toll Free: (800) 426-7767
Fax: (312) 913-3020
Web site: http://www.marchfirst.com

Public Company
Incorporated: 2000
Employees: 8,500
Sales: $1.13 billion (1999 pro forma)
Stock Exchanges: NASDAQ
Ticker Symbol: MRCH
NAIC: 541810 Advertising Agencies; 541512 Computer
   Systems Design Services; 541611 Administrative
   Management and General Management Consulting
   Services; 541613 Marketing Consulting Services

marchFIRST, Inc. was created on March 1, 2000, by the merger of two firms that provide electronic commerce and information technology (IT) consulting services, Whittman-Hart Inc. of Chicago and USWeb/CKS of San Francisco. Upon its formation, marchFIRST had 8,500 employees in 64 cities and 14 countries worldwide. For 1999 it had pro forma revenues of $1.13 billion.

Specializing in Information Technology and E-Business Solutions: 1984–99

Robert Bernard established Whittman-Hart Inc. in 1984 to provide computer services related to IBM's mid-range computers. Throughout the 1980s and 1990s, the company developed an expertise in business systems integration. It eventually became a leading provider of IT (information technology) and e-business solutions. It focused on mid-size companies and divisions of larger companies, a niche market where it faced less competition. The company was organized into five business units: solutions strategy, network enabled solutions, interactive solutions, packaged software solutions, and custom applications.

At the end of 1997 Whittman-Hart employed more than 1,900 consultants, up from 844 at the end of 1996. Nonetheless, it was facing a shortage of high-quality consultants and programmers. For fiscal 1997 the company had $173.5 million in revenue. For fiscal 1998 Whittman-Hart had sales of $307.6 million, a 69 percent increase over 1997. Earnings rose 88 percent to $18.8 million compared to 1997. During the year it opened new branch offices in Atlanta and Minneapolis and completed four acquisitions. At the end of 1998 the company's workforce had grown to 3,000 employees.

In March 1999 Whittman-Hart acquired Waterfield Technology Group, based in Boston. In May it acquired POV Partners Inc. of Columbus, Ohio. The company was pursuing a strategy of opening new branch offices every 90 to 180 days. During 1999 it opened offices in St. Louis and Pittsburgh. Each branch that Whittman-Hart opened grew quickly.

In October 1999 Novell Inc. announced it would invest $100 million in Whittman-Hart for a six percent ownership interest. Novell hoped the alliance would increase the use of Novell Directory Services (NDS) in e-commerce and other tasks by the 2,000 small and midsize companies that were Whittman-Hart's clients. Under the alliance Whittman-Hart would develop custom solutions using NDS software, which managed and directed traffic on computer networks.

During 1999 the company's revenues benefited from more demand for its e-business services, including front-office applications and customer-relationship management systems on the Web. It acquired several companies to strengthen its e-business services, including Four Points Digital LLC, Fulcrum Solutions Ltd., and BALR Corp. By the end of 1999, 90 percent of the company's projects were related to electronic commerce. In 1999 Robert Bernard, 38, made *Fortune*'s first list of the "40 Richest Americans under 40."

Company Perspectives:

In the new economy, sustaining industry leadership and competitive advantage requires a radically new level of business integration. marchFIRST leads this revolution by combining the disciplines necessary to win the digital economy with the global scale and reach needed to take on leading-edge challenges worldwide. At the core of marchFIRST is a multidisciplinary focus that helps clients build visionary business models, brands, systems, and processes.

USWeb, Focusing on Web Site Design and E-Commerce: 1995–99

USWeb was founded in 1995 by three former executives of Novell Inc.—Joe Firmage, Tobey Corey, and Sheldon Laube—to provide Internet-related services. They raised $14 million in venture capital and went public in December 1997. The firm was headquartered in Santa Clara, California.

USWeb needed to grow quickly to take advantage of the opportunities in electronic commerce and the World Wide Web. Before going public the company enlisted existing Web-design firms as affiliates to operate under the USWeb brand. By mid-1997 USWeb began buying its affiliates and grew to more than 1,000 employees at the end of 1997. Over the next two years USWeb acquired more than 35 smaller companies.

Late in 1998 USWeb merged with the CKS Group Inc., an advertising and marketing firm based in Cupertino, California, that USWeb acquired for stock valued at more than $540 million. In November 1998 Robert Shaw, former executive vice-president for worldwide consulting services at Oracle, replaced USWeb cofounder Joe Firmage as CEO of the new company to be formed by the merger of US Web and the CKS Group Inc. The new company was originally to be called Reinvent, but the name USWeb/CKS was used instead. It had about 1,800 employees when the merger was completed in December 1998. For fiscal 1998 the company reported a loss of $188.3 million on revenue of $228.6 million, compared to a loss of $50.7 million on revenues of $114.3 million in 1997.

Firmage, who was to be the new company's chief strategist, stepped down after his beliefs that space aliens have influenced modern technology became known. Firmage revealed he was working on a book about how modern technology was reverse-engineered from an alien space ship recovered at Roswell, New Mexico, in 1947. He also set up a web site called Kairos and invested $3 million to establish a nonprofit group, the International Space Sciences Organization. In 1999 Firmage formed a start-up Web development company called Intend Change with USWeb/CKS president Tobey Corey and other former USWeb/CKS executives. USWeb/CKS was one of several backers of the new company and would provide its technology as part of the partnerships Intend Change hoped to establish with other Internet start-up companies. Intend Change also hoped to partner with *Fortune* 500 companies seeking to establish Web-based subsidiaries and divisions.

Among the projects USWeb/CKS handled in 1999 were a new ad campaign for Fujitsu PC Corp. for its LifeBook notebook computers; the development and launch of Jenny Craig's web site; and the launch of Walgreen Co.'s full-service e-commerce web site that included an online pharmacy.

In early 1999 USWeb/CKS launched a new e-services division for outsourced application services covering electronic commerce, communications and knowledge management, customer relationship management, and back office. These applications, which ranged from entry-level to enterprise-level, could be integrated into a company's existing business systems. They were offered on a subscription basis.

In the second quarter of 1999 USWeb/CKS acquired international technology consultant Case Consult, which added 140 employees in Belgium, Luxembourg, and the Netherlands. Case Consult specialized in building Internet applications for businesses. USWeb/CKS had acquired five Internet services companies in Europe and established its own office in Norway. The company was seeking to expand its worldwide business development efforts and had more than 550 employees in eight European countries. Meanwhile, USWeb/CKS moved its headquarters from Santa Clara to San Francisco in the summer of 1999. For the second quarter of 1999 USWeb/CKS exceeded $100 million in quarterly revenue for the first time.

Around this time Rick Markovitz, former senior vice-president and general manager of BBDO Worldwide's interactive division, joined USWeb/CKS as a partner for integrated marketing communications. Through integrated marketing communications, USWeb/CKS offered its clients the opportunity to develop their brands through interactive advertising and marketing campaigns.

In September 1999 USWeb/CKS acquired Mitchell Madison Group for about $300 million in stock. Mitchell Madison was a consulting firm with about 550 consultants specializing in banking, investments, and communications. Following the merger, Mitchell Madison cofounder Tom Steiner became president and chief operating officer of USWeb/CKS and a member of its board of directors. He replaced USWeb cofounder Toby Corey, who remained as a strategic consultant.

In October 1999 Microsoft announced it would invest $67.5 million in USWeb/CKS over the next three years and purchased a $15 million warrant to buy one million USWeb/CKS shares over the next five years. The two companies planned to open a technology-development lab in Redmond, Washington, later in 1999. As part of the agreement, USWeb/CKS would develop, host, and manage custom e-commerce, knowledge management, customer-relationship management, and back-office application using a software infrastructure called iFrame based on Microsoft's Digital Internet Architecture (DNA) 2000. Microsoft would receive royalties on sales of the iFrame platform. For the third quarter of 1999 USWeb/CKS revenues reached $138.9 million, more than double the same period in 1998.

In December 1999 USWeb/CKS introduced IAMcommerce (Internet Application Management), a set of consulting, strategy, hosting, and integration services for enterprises that wanted to set up e-commerce sites. Customers would pay a $25,000 base fee and a monthly subscription fee based on the

Key Dates:
1984: Robert Bernard establishes Whittman-Hart Inc. to provide computer services to mid-sized companies.
1995: USWeb is founded by former executives of Novell Inc. to provide Internet-related services.
1998: USWeb merges with the CKS Group to form USWeb/CKS.
2000: marchFIRST is created by a merger of Whittman-Hart Inc., based in Chicago, and USWeb/CKS, located in San Francisco.

amount of processing required. As a customer's e-business expanded, it would pay a larger monthly fee, an approach dubbed "pay-as-you-grow." The applications could be customized for individual customers and integrated with back-end systems. The service was expected to be available in mid-2000.

At the end of 1999 USWeb/CKS had a market capitalization of $3.1 billion, less than six times revenues. The company's stock was relatively depressed, due to a complex equity structure resulting from nearly 50 acquisitions—many of them involving stock deals—over the past three years.

Creation of marchFIRST Through Merger: 2000

When the proposed merger of USWeb/CKS and Whittman-Hart was announced in December 1999, investors were taken by surprise. The market capitalization of the two companies, initially around $5.88 billion, lost a combined $2 billion following the announcement, a drop of almost 23 percent. Whittman-Hart's stock plunged 31 percent, while USWeb/CKS's shares fell almost 14 percent.

On March 1, 2000, the merger was completed. Robert Bernard, chairman and CEO of Whittman-Hart, became the new company's president and CEO. Robert Shaw would serve as chairman. The new Internet professional services firm had more than 8,500 employees in 64 cities and 14 countries worldwide. A formal brand launch for marchFIRST was planned for the summer of 2000.

In addition to providing professional services related to electronic commerce and the Internet, marchFIRST introduced other initiatives. One was the launch of Bluevector, a venture capital organization that would invest in new companies and new technologies. The second was a new global practice, the Corporate Partnership Practice, that would seek out clients and build partnerships among Global 2000 companies and executives.

The market for e-commerce services in North America alone was projected to grow to $80 billion by 2003. With its global network of offices organized into five geographic operating units, marchFIRST was positioned to capitalize on the growth opportunities of the Internet and e-commerce services market. Its clients represented a wide range of industries, including manufacturing, distribution, healthcare, transportation, financial and business services, retail, and communications.

Principal Competitors

KPMG Peat Marwick; EDS; Andersen Worldwide; McKinsey Consulting & Co.; Scient Corp.; Razorfish Inc.; Proxicom Inc.; Sapient Corp.; iXL Enterprises Inc.; AppNet Systems Inc.; US Interactive Inc.; Viant Corp.; Cambridge Technology Partners Inc.; Keane Inc.; MPL2.com Inc.

Further Reading

Andrews, Whit, "Oracle Exec Steps in As US Web CEO," *Internet World,* November 9, 1998, p. 8.

Booker, Ellis, "Integrators Pair up for E-Biz," *InternetWeek,* December 20, 1999, p. 9.

Boulton, Guy, "Novell to Buy $100 Million Stake in Chicago Consulting Company," *Knight-Ridder/Tribune Business News,* October 1, 1999.

"B2B2C: The Next Wave," *InternetWeek,* January 31, 2000, p. 19.

Caulfield, Brian, "Newsmaker," *Internet World,* January 18, 1999, p. 6.

——, "USWeb/CKS Execs Form VC Firm for Startups, Spinoffs," *Internet World,* June 21, 1999, p. 43.

"CRN Business Close-Up: An Interview with Robert Bernard," *Computer Reseller News,* March 20, 2000, p. 96.

Daniels, Steve, "Chicago Internet Giant: Can Bob Make It Work?," *Crain's Chicago Business,* December 20, 1999, p. 1.

"Digest," *PC Week,* March 1, 1999, p. 55.

Feuerstein, Adam, "New Giant USWeb/CKS Making Big Push into Europe," *San Francisco Business Times,* May 7, 1999, p. 5.

Goldfisher, Alastair, "USWeb/CKS Moves HQ North to Multimedia Gulch," *Business Journal,* March 26, 1999, p. 5.

Hersch, Warren S., "Whittman-Hart Acquires QCC," *Computer Reseller News,* April 6, 1998, p. 38.

Hibbard, Justin, "Jenny Craig Offers Virtual Health Aid," *InformationWeek,* March 22, 1999, p. 38.

Jastrow, David, "Analysts, Investors Skeptical," *Computer Reseller News,* April 3, 2000, p. 42.

——, "Consolidation on Tap for New Year," *Computer Reseller News,* January 3, 2000, p. 29.

——, "Overcoming Obstacles," *Computer Reseller News,* June 28, 1999, p. 69.

——, "Partnership Extended—USWeb/CKS, Microsoft Sign iFrame Development Deal," *Computer Reseller News,* October 18, 1999, p. 89.

——, "USWeb/CKS Completes Acquisition," *Computer Reseller News,* September 13, 1999, p. 36.

——, "USWeb/CKS' E-Commerce Strategy: Pay As You Grow," *Computer Reseller News,* December 6, 1999, p. 198.

——, "USWeb/CKS Wants to MarchFIRST," *Computer Reseller News,* March 27, 2000, p. 96.

——, "Walgreen Teams up with USWeb/CKS to Create New Internet Pharmacy," *Computer Reseller News,* July 12, 1999, p. 73.

——, "Web Integrators' Revenue Soars—Sector Earnings Continue to Fall Short," *Computer Reseller News,* July 26, 1999, p. 6.

Jastrow, David, and Sandy Portnoy, "Web Integrators Miss the Profit Boat," *Computer Reseller News,* November 1, 1999, p. 164.

Kaiser, Rob, "Chicago-Based Technology Consultant's Stock Drops After Merger News," *Knight-Ridder/Tribune Business News,* December 14, 1999.

Kelly, Jane Irene, "USWeb/CKS Quick on the Draw for Fujitsu PC," *Adweek Western Advertising News,* February 22, 1999, p. 5.

Madden, John, "MarchFirst Steps Out," *PC Week,* March 27, 2000, p. 14.

——, "USWeb Pushes Services," *PC Week,* December 6, 1999, p. 1.

Mateyaschuk, Jennifer, "Services Companies See E-Business Benefit," *InformationWeek,* July 19, 1999, p. 117.

——, "USWeb Readies Its Move into the ASP Market." *Informa-tionWeek,* December 6, 1999, p. 203.

Morrison, Mary E., "BBDO Exec Joins USWeb/CKS," *Business Mar-keting,* July 1, 1999, p. 9.

Murphy, H. Lee., "Snubbing Y2K Boosts Whittman-Hart," *Crain's Chicago Business,* June 7, 1999, p. 113.

Nee, Eric, "An E-Consultant Cleans up Its Room," *Fortune,* December 6, 1999, p. 172.

O'Brien, Chris, "San Francisco-Based Internet Consultants to Merge, Move to Chicago," *Knight-Ridder/Tribune Business News,* December 13, 1999.

Orenstein, David, "Deal Gets USWeb/CKS to Use Win 2000," *Com-puterworld,* October 4, 1999, p. 6.

"Outsource Internet Solutions," *Industry Week,* May 17, 1999, p. 9.

Pape, William R., "Virtual Manager," *Inc.,* March 16, 1999, p. 27.

Pugh, Angela M., "Net Managers from Mars?," *Data Communica-tions,* March 7, 1999, p. 14.

Ricadela, Aaron, and Clinton Wilder, "Microsoft Takes Stake in USWeb/CKS," *InformationWeek,* October 4, 1999, p. 182.

"Robert Bernard," *Fortune,* November 22, 1999, p. 366.

Rogers, Amy, "Keep It Simple," *Computer Reseller News,* April 10, 2000, p. 126.

Rosa, Jerry, "Whittman-Hart Speeds to Internet with New Alliances," *Computer Reseller News,* December 13, 1999, p. 55.

Schaff, William, "Whittman-Hart Set to Soar," *InformationWeek,* March 30, 1998, p. 141.

"USWeb's Bold Buy of Mitchell Madison," *Future Banker,* September 1999, p. 10.

—David P. Bianco

Mayo Foundation

200 First Street SW
Rochester, Minnesota 55905
U.S.A.
Telephone: (507) 284-2511
Fax: (507) 284-0161
Web site: http://www.mayo.edu

Nonprofit Company
Incorporated: 1919 as Mayo Properties Association
Employees: 32,531
Sales: $2.37 billion (1998)
NAIC: 622110 General Medical and Surgical Hospitals;
541710 Research and Development in the Physical,
Engineering, and Life Sciences; 611310 Colleges,
Universities, and Professional Schools; 621491 HMO
Medical Centers

The nonprofit Mayo Foundation oversees the largest and most renowned private medical center in the world, the Mayo Medical Center of Rochester, Minnesota. The heart of the center is the Mayo Clinic, a research and treatment leader in cardiology, endocrinology, gynecology, neurology, oncology, orthopedics, urology, and a number of other disciplines. The Mayo Clinic, however, is virtually inseparable from two nearby, highly reputed hospitals, Saint Marys and Rochester Methodist, both of which are entirely owned and governed by the Mayo Foundation. Since the mid-1980s, the Mayo Foundation has spearheaded a program to extend the unique Mayo medical system of total patient care far beyond southern Minnesota. Mayo Clinic Jacksonville (in Florida) and Mayo Clinic Scottsdale (in Arizona), both linked via satellite to Mayo Clinic Rochester, are two major outcomes of this nationwide expansion program. The Mayo Foundation also supports the Mayo Graduate School of Medicine, Mayo Medical School, the Mayo School of Health-Related Sciences, and the Mayo School of Continuing Medical Education. The foundation-owned Mayo Health System is a network of 14 community-based clinics and medical centers providing healthcare services to 54 communities in Minnesota, Iowa, and Wisconsin.

To visit the 12-building, pedestrian subway-linked Mayo "campus" in Rochester—a city of around 70,000 whose local economy is dominated by the healthcare, hospitality, and computer industries (a major IBM plant is located on the outskirts of the city)—is to understand just how completely the dreams of Mayo's founder, William Worrall Mayo, have been realized. Each year, about 400,000 patients and their families flock to this medical mecca. Some do so for geographic reasons (85 percent of all Mayo patients are from the Upper Midwest); others, out of long-established habit (former U.S. Supreme Court Justice Harry Blackmun, for example, revisited Mayo each summer for a checkup from the 1950s, when he served as the clinic's general counsel, until his death at the age of 90 in 1999); and still others, because of a high recommendation from a relative or acquaintance. (Although Mayo still bears the image of a hospital for the elite, it requires no physician referrals or lengthy admissions process; more than 95 percent of its patients consistently report that they are "satisfied" or "very satisfied" with the care they have received.) All, without question, visit Mayo secure in the knowledge that it is home to some of the most advanced medical technology and one of the most respected groups of physicians in the world.

Mayo and Sons in Private Practice in the Late 19th Century

Mayo's long, rich history of excellence in medicine extends back to 1863, when Dr. William Worrall Mayo of Le Sueur, Minnesota, was appointed examining surgeon of Civil War enlistees for the state's southern district. The district's headquarters were located in Rochester, then a ten-year-old pioneer settlement with a population of less than 3,000. Born and raised in England, Mayo arrived in the United States in 1845 at the age of 26. His first job was that of chemist for Bellevue Hospital in New York City. A string of nonmedical jobs intervened before Mayo became apprenticed to a doctor in Lafayette, Indiana. Harold Severson noted that Mayo studied at the Indiana Medical College in LaPorte. "This put him in a special category, for until the 1860s—and in some sections long afterward—a frontier doctor was almost any man who had the audacity to advertise himself as one."

A bout with malaria in 1854 convinced Mayo that he needed to move to a more congenial climate. Ultimately, the doctor chose St. Paul, although his wife, Louise, was at first hesitant to relinquish her thriving Indiana millinery business. Once the move was completed, however, she quickly launched a new shop that was equally prosperous. Mayo, on the other hand, resisted settling or committing to one line of employment, for he was an inveterate explorer and jack-of-all-trades. Nonetheless, his medical calling resurfaced within a year or so, and he decided to become a country doctor in the picturesque town of Le Sueur. Louise agreed to sell her business and follow him.

Mayo supplemented his small and unstable income by farming, running a ferry boat, and serving as local veterinarian and justice of the peace. "All these divergent activities," wrote Helen Clapesattle, "were not such deviations from the Doctor's professional path as they might appear; they helped immeasurably to spread his name and acquaintance up and down the Minnesota Valley." Although always faced with competition, Mayo was able to expand his regular practice across three counties, earning himself in the process a reputation as a skilled and caring doctor.

Despite the attractions of Le Sueur, Mayo perceived more fertile prospects in Rochester after working there for a year, and, in 1864, he again relocated his family. This move marked the end of Mayo's itinerant path and the beginning of Rochester's development into a center for modern U.S. medical knowledge and treatment. Mayo staked his private, home-visit practice upon his own ingenuity, experience, and energetic personality. The clinical thermometer had yet to be invented, and the use of the stethoscope, not to mention anesthetics, was still in its infancy. Antisepsis, the technique of preventing infection, was a lofty and far-off goal; surgery of any kind was a procedure best avoided, if at all possible. Despite such handicaps, the medical profession was on the brink of rapid advancement and Mayo, according to Philip K. Strand, shortly became "one of the most respected physicians in Minnesota." This was in no small part due to Mayo's drive for excellence. "A perfectionist who would not tolerate sloppy medicine," says Strand, "[Mayo] went to great lengths to increase his own medical knowledge." After barely five years of successful doctoring in Rochester, he realized that his training was inadequate for the high standards he wished to maintain. Therefore, he chose to take several months off from his practice to study in New York with some of the country's top surgeons. Upon his return, Mayo abandoned his primitive microscope in favor of the latest model, which he purchased by mortgaging his house.

In 1880 Mayo attempted his first critical operation, the surgical removal of an ovarian tumor. Only a handful of doctors in the East were then attempting and succeeding at this particular operation. It soon became Mayo's forte. Although still teenagers, Mayo's sons, William Mayo and Charles Mayo, were assisting in the operating room by this time. Dr. Will and Dr.

Charlie, as they were later affectionately known, were to become the very essence of the Mayo Clinic. It was their partnership, as much as that with their father, that brought the term Mayos' Clinic into common usage by the turn of the century. There is no doubt that W.W. Mayo greatly guided and influenced his sons to follow in his footsteps. However, wrote Harriet W. Hodgson, "Some think Louise Mayo deserved equal credit for Will and Charlie becoming physicians. An intellectual in her own right, she pursued interests in astronomy and botany, assisted her husband with surgery, applied splints, and listened to patients' complaints when Dr. W.W. was out on a call. . . . Her medical education was gleaned from on-the-job training and persistent study of her husband's textbooks."

1880s Through Early 1900s: Creation of the Mayo Clinic and the Multispecialty Group Practice

Aside from the maturation of the Mayo boys into full-fledged physicians during the 1880s, the decade also marked the beginning of hospitalized care in Rochester. On August 21, 1883, a tornado struck the town, causing widespread injury and havoc. In the aftermath, Mayo sought a place to house and care for the wounded. The most likely spot was the convent operated by the Sisters of Saint Francis, a local teaching order. With poorly trained, volunteer nurses and virtually no management structure, the improvised hospital was chaotic but nonetheless served its immediate purpose. It served another purpose as well: that of convincing convent head Mother Alfred that a permanent hospital should be built by the order to serve the Rochester area. Prior to the tornado, Mother Alfred actually had been approached by St. Paul Bishop John Ireland about founding a hospital, but at the time she rejected the idea because her nuns were educators and not nurses. Now, after witnessing a citywide emergency and seeing the capable response of W.W. Mayo and scores of volunteers, Mother Alfred became a strong proponent of the plan and beseeched Mayo to oversee the hospital upon its completion. Interestingly, she had difficulty convincing Mayo, for he was keenly aware of the public's perception of hospitals as places where the sick and indigent succumbed to death. Finally, Mayo agreed to the plan, with the stipulation that the Sisters should allot $40,000 for construction expenses. Six years later the first hospital in Rochester—and only the eighth in the entire state—was completed.

A three-story building with 27 beds, this was the original Saint Marys Hospital that, after numerous additions and modernizations, grew by its centennial into a 1,000-plus-bed facility in which an average of 130 surgeries were performed daily. During its first full year of operation, Saint Marys hospitalized some 300 patients while maintaining an enviably low death rate, attributable in large part to the diligent practice of Dr. Joseph Lister's technique of wet antisepsis. "Eventually," wrote Clapesattle, "the message began to spread throughout the Midwest: Saint Marys Hospital is a place where people go to be healed."

The original Mayo group practice quickly evolved into one in which Dr. Will Mayo (who received his medical degree in 1883) and Dr. Charlie Mayo (who received his five years later) served as the two attending surgeons while Dr. W.W. Mayo functioned as the consulting physician. Of the three, Will demonstrated the greatest ability and concern for handling the clinic's financial and administrative matters, which from the inception of Saint Marys

Key Dates:

1863: Dr. William Worrall Mayo takes a job in Rochester, Minnesota, as an examining surgeon for the Union Army.

1864: Mayo locates permanently in Rochester.

1883: A tornado hits Rochester, leading the Sisters of Saint Francis to persuade Mayo and his physician sons to build and staff a hospital.

1889: Saint Marys Hospital opens in Rochester with 27 beds.

1914: Construction of the first building bearing the Mayo Clinic name and the first in the world designed specifically for a group medical practice.

1915: The Mayo brothers establish the Mayo Foundation for Medical Education and Research (later called the Mayo Graduate School of Medicine), the world's first graduate training program for physicians.

1919: The Mayo brothers transfer the assets of the Mayo Clinic to a nonprofit foundation, initially called the Mayo Properties Association.

1964: The Mayo Properties Association is renamed the Mayo Foundation.

1972: The Mayo Medical School opens.

1973: The Mayo School of Health-Related Sciences opens.

1983: The *Mayo Clinic Family Health Book* and the *Mayo Clinic Health Letter* are first published.

1986: The Mayo Clinic, Saint Marys Hospital, and Rochester Methodist Hospital are integrated to form Mayo Medical Center, the largest nonprofit medical concern in the country; Mayo Clinic Jacksonville opens, marking the foundation's first endeavor outside Minnesota; subsidiary Mayo Management Services, Inc. (MMSI) is created to operate a Minnesota-based HMO, Mayo Health Plan; Mayo Medical Ventures is formed.

1987: Mayo Clinic Scottsdale opens and St. Luke's Hospital in Jacksonville is acquired.

1992: Foundation begins building a regional network of community-based clinics and medical centers, the Mayo Health System.

1995: MMSI enters the commercial market, offering and administering a variety of customized, self-insured health plans.

1998: Mayo Clinic Hospital opens in Phoenix, near Scottsdale; foundation partners with Winn-Dixie Stores, Inc. to install Mayo Clinic health information kiosks in more than 600 grocery stores and pharmacies.

1999: Foundation enters into a joint venture with the Shansby Group to develop an interactive healthcare web site.

were remarkably sound. So successful was the Mayo enterprise that two other physicians in the area opened a rival group named Riverside Hospital in 1892. Although it, too, thrived, the Riverside practice was moved to St. Paul within a few years. Around this same time, the Mayo Clinic began attracting outside medical talent. By the turn of the century, the practice numbered eight doctors, two of whom were women.

The tradition of Mayo innovation was already alive during these early days, for W.W. Mayo had instilled in his sons a strong emphasis on continuing medical education and scientific experimentation. This, in turn, resulted in the hiring of uniquely gifted and motivated colleagues who could extend the clinic's areas of expertise. In effect, the original group of partners assembled by the Mayo brothers represented a new concept in medicine, the multispecialty group practice. Will Mayo concentrated on diagnosing and treating pelvic and abdominal problems and Charlie Mayo focused on eye, ear, nose, and throat ailments. No member of the group was more brilliant, eccentric, or esteemed than Dr. Henry Plummer, a former intern at St. Marys who joined the clinic in 1901. Considered "no less than a genius" by Dr. Will Mayo for his work with iodine solutions to treat thyroid disease, Plummer is equally revered by Mayo historians for his lasting contributions to the day-to-day operations of the clinic and Saint Marys. These include such inventions as a compressed air system to transport internal records; an intraclinic phone system; an envelope-coding system; and the system of underground walkways that link the Mayo Campus; as well as his architectural masterpiece, the Plummer Building.

By the early 1900s, W.W. Mayo had effectively retired to pursue his abiding interests of research, politics, and travel. He died in 1911, just a few months before his 92nd birthday and was paid tribute by the town he had helped to build. Saint Marys was now one of the largest and most advanced hospitals in the United States; more operations were being performed there each year than at any other facility in the country, including the prestigious Johns Hopkins in Maryland. The Mayo Clinic's reputation was now truly international, with famous physicians from Paris, Leipzig, Edinburgh, and elsewhere having made the trek to Rochester to learn firsthand from the "country doctors" Will and Charlie Mayo, luminaries in their own right. Both men researched, wrote, and lectured extensively throughout their careers. In 1905 Will Mayo was named president of the American Medical Association; a decade later, Charlie received the same honor. Although vastly different in personality, the two formed a close bond, holding the same ideals of dedicated service and commitment championed by their father.

1919 Through Early 1980s: Early Decades As a Foundation

In 1914 the brothers oversaw the construction of the first building to bear the Mayo Clinic name and the first in the world designed specifically for a group medical practice. Now 75 strong, the Mayo partners were seeing an average of 30,000 patients annually. The following year the independently wealthy Mayo brothers, in an effort to preserve the education and research tradition they had founded, established a nonprofit endowment through the University of Minnesota, which they named the Mayo Foundation for Medical Education and Research. This foundation was funded by nearly $2 million from the brothers' personal savings. Eventually renamed the Mayo Graduate School of Medicine, this organization was the world's first formal graduate training program for physicians. Then in 1919, "in an act without precedent in American medicine," according to *Mayo Clinic,* "the two brothers transferred all of the assets of the Mayo Clinic into an endowment to advance medical science (originally named the Mayo Properties Association, this endowment became the Mayo Foundation in 1964). Thus began Mayo's tradition of giving, an essential part of our position in world medicine." Since the foundation was nonprofit, Mayo physicians from this point forward would be paid a salary and would not share directly in the proceeds of their practice. Funds left over after operating expenses were met were contributed to education, research, and patient care.

From 1919 until 1939, Dr. Will Mayo served as president of the foundation. Among the highlights of this era were the construction in 1922 of a state-of-the-art surgical pavilion, which doubled the capacity of Saint Marys; the beginning of air transportation to Rochester in 1928; and the public donation of Mayo Foundation House, the former residence of Dr. Will and his wife, so that it might be used as "a meeting place for the exchange of ideas for the good of mankind."

With the deaths of Charles in May and Will in July 1939, an enormous loss was felt around the country. Harold Severson reported that "messages of condolences poured in from people in all walks of life—from President and Mrs. Franklin D. Roosevelt to a little old woman in Texas who sent a potted plant and a note to Mrs. Charlie Mayo expressing her deep sorrow on the death of the man who had been so kind to her years ago." Harry Harwick, chief administrative officer since 1908, assumed the chairmanship of the foundation upon Will's death. He presided over a thrilling era of Mayo's development, which included the creation of the first post-anesthesia room (a forerunner of modern intensive care units) in 1942 and the awarding of the Nobel Prize in 1950 to two Mayo researchers for their synthesis of cortisone. Later, the foundation opened two more medical schools: the Mayo Medical School in 1972 and the Mayo School of Health-Related Sciences, which specialized in training students in allied health programs, in 1973. Other medical advances—too numerous to chronicle—continued to keep the Mayo name in the spotlight of world medicine into the early 21st century.

Mid-1980s and Beyond: Merging and Expanding in a More Competitive Era

Until the mid-1980s, the structure of the Mayo Foundation, including its longstanding alliance with Saint Marys Hospital, remained essentially unchanged. With improvements in healthcare, concurrent declines in patients' average hospital stays, rising medical costs, and tighter governmental controls, however, there was a much more pressing need for conserving resources and maintaining revenue levels. Therefore, the Mayo Foundation, Saint Marys, and a third entity, Rochester Methodist Hospital, entered into negotiations about integrating. On May 28, 1986, their organizational merger was complete and the newly expanded Mayo Medical Center was now the largest nonprofit medical concern in the country. At the time of the merger, combined revenues exceeded half a billion dollars, with pooled assets listed at around $1 billion. One proviso of the agreement was that Saint Marys would retain its separate legal identity as a Catholic hospital and continue to receive support from the Sisters of St. Francis.

Also in 1986, the Mayo Foundation began expanding outside of Minnesota. The Mayo Clinic Jacksonville opened in Florida that year, and Mayo Clinic Scottsdale opened in Arizona the following year. The foundation acquired St. Luke's Hospital in Jacksonville in 1987, thereby gaining the clinic-hospital pairing that worked so well in Rochester. Also in 1987 the original Mayo Clinic in Rochester went smoke-free, becoming one of the first medical facilities in the country to do so.

In addition to its expansion, Mayo also found new sources of income by providing specialized lab services to outside doctors and hospitals (through a unit called Mayo Medical Laboratories) and by launching such commercial enterprises as the *Mayo Clinic Family Health Book* and the *Mayo Clinic Health Letter* (which now carries 385,000 subscribers worldwide)—both of which were first published in 1983. In 1986 the foundation created another new unit, called Mayo Medical Ventures, which in addition to assuming responsibility for the publishing ventures, managed technology transfer agreements, patent applications, and licensing deals, and created pharmacies and a medical supply outlet in Rochester. In addition, Mayo began actively soliciting charitable contributions, whereas previously it operated as a self-funding organization. By 1992 outside philanthropy to Mayo totaled more than $58 million, approximately the same amount that was spent separately by the foundation on education and research.

The mid-1980s also saw the Mayo Foundation begin to participate in the burgeoning managed healthcare sector, which was bringing profound changes to the industry. In 1986 the foundation created a subsidiary called Mayo Management Services, Inc. (MMSI) to operate a Minnesota-based health maintenance organization (HMO) called Mayo Health Plan. Two years later, MMSI entered the plan administrative services sector when it began providing claims administration for St. Luke's Hospital in Jacksonville. In somewhat of a return to its general practice roots, the Mayo Foundation in 1992 began building a regional network of community-based clinics and medical centers—called the Mayo Health System—with the acquisition of Decorah Medical Associates in northeastern Iowa. By the late 1990s this system included 500 physicians, 7,600 allied health staff, and 13 hospitals with nearly 900 beds and was providing healthcare services to 54 communities in Minnesota, Iowa, and Wisconsin. The Minnesota portion of the Mayo Health System served as the core of the Mayo Health Plan HMO. Strategically, the Mayo Health System served in part as a conduit to the Mayo Clinic, since the primary care physicians in Mayo's new network were the doctors referring patients to its specialized facilities. The network's regional makeup also made sense as half of the patients who went to the Mayo Clinic lived within 120 miles of Rochester. In 1995 MMSI entered the commercial market, offering and administering a variety of customized, self-insured health plans. With the Mayo Health System as its core network, supplemented by providers outside the system, MMSI began managing health plans for such regional employers as Hormel Foods Corporation and the Ashley Companies.

The pressure on the Mayo Foundation to find alternative revenue sources was highlighted in 1993 when the foundation had an operating loss of $6.2 million, its first year in the red since the Great Depression. Contributing to the loss were higher patient care costs and lower Medicare reimbursement levels. In early 1994 the Mayo Clinic announced that it would cut 450 jobs in an effort to save $18.5 million. Through the remainder of the 1990s, the Mayo Foundation's earnings suffered from the growing number of patients who were covered either by Medicare or a managed care plan. Earnings fell 50 percent in 1998 from the previous year, to $86 million, in large part as a result of an estimated $85 million loss on Medicare patients. Meantime, during 1998, the Scottsdale operations were augmented with the opening in nearby Phoenix of Mayo Clinic Hospital, a five-story facility with 178 beds and complete emergency room/urgent care services. The Scottsdale system thereby included both a clinic and a hospital, as well as a regional network of seven primary care centers similar to the Mayo Health System.

As the 21st century neared, the Mayo Foundation continued to seek out alternative ways of generating revenue and of simply making the Mayo Clinic name more widely known. In 1998 the foundation partnered with Winn-Dixie Stores, Inc. to begin installing Mayo Clinic kiosks featuring free health information in more than 600 grocery stores and pharmacies owned by the Jacksonville-based chain. The two organizations had a long-standing relationship, highlighted by Winn-Dixie having donated the land on which the Mayo Clinic in Jacksonville was built. Also in 1998, in a partnership with a leading housewares retailer, the *Mayo Clinic/Williams-Sonoma Cookbook* was published. By this time the Mayo Foundation also had established a web site, the Mayo Clinic Health Oasis, to provide specialized medical information to consumers. The site generated strong traffic but little revenue because advertising and sponsorship opportunities were not being aggressively pursued. In late 1999, however, the foundation entered into a joint venture with a San Francisco-based private equity company, the Shansby Group, to develop an interactive web site that was intended to compete more aggressively in the burgeoning online healthcare sector. The aim was not to practice medicine on the Internet; Dr. Patricia Simmons, chair of the foundation's Internet steering committee, told the *Minneapolis Star Tribune*, "I'd look at this as an activity that will fill the gap between having an encyclopedia of health information and having a real thorough medical visit with a physician. We will tailor the information to help people manage their own health." The joint venture, of which Mayo retained majority control, was the foundation's first major for-profit venture. Having stayed on the cutting edge of the medical field for more than 100 years, it now appeared that the Mayo Foundation was not willing to let the electronic revolution pass it by.

Principal Subsidiaries

Mayo Management Services, Inc.; Mayo Medical Laboratories; Mayo Medical Ventures.

Principal Operating Units

Mayo Clinic Rochester; Mayo Clinic Jacksonville; Mayo Clinic Scottsdale; Saint Marys Hospital, Rochester; Rochester Methodist Hospital; St. Luke's Hospital, Jacksonville; Mayo Clinic Hospital, Phoenix; Charter House, Rochester; Mayo Health System.

Principal Competitors

Allina Health System; Ascension Health; Catholic Health Initiatives; Catholic Healthcare Partners; Columbia/HCA Healthcare Corporation; Detroit Medical Center; Health Management Associates, Inc.; HEALTHSOUTH Corporation; Henry Ford Health System; The John Hopkins Health System; Memorial Sloan-Kettering Cancer Center; Mercy Health Services; Methodist Health Care System; New York City Health and Hospitals Corporation; Rush System for Health; Scripps; SSM Health Care System Inc.; Tenet Healthcare Corporation; UCSF Stanford Health Care; Universal Health Services, Inc.

Further Reading

"America's Best Hospitals: 1998 Annual Guide," *U.S. News & World Report,* July 27, 1998.

Berss, Marcia, "Mayo's Dilemma," *Forbes,* October 25, 1993, pp. 72, 74–75.

Bischoff, Dan, "Mayo Whistles Dixie," *Modern Healthcare,* May 11, 1998, p. 46.

Braasch, William F., *Early Days in the Mayo Clinic,* Springfield, Ill.: Thomas, [1969].

Clapesattle, Helen, *The Doctors Mayo,* Minneapolis: University of Minnesota Press, 1941, 2nd ed., 1963.

Cope, Lewis, "Shuttle Deploys Satellite for Mayo 'Telemedicine,' " *Minneapolis Star Tribune,* September 13, 1993, pp. 2A, 4A.

Gelbach, Deborah L., "Mayo Clinic," *From This Land: A History of Minnesota's Empires, Enterprises, and Entrepreneurs,* Northridge, Calif.: Windsor Publications, 1988.

Gonzales, Angela, "Mayo Clinic Wants Cut of HMO Industry," *Phoenix Business Journal,* January 10, 1997, pp. 1+.

Herrera, Stephan, "Name-Dropper," *Forbes,* June 14, 1999, p. 158.

Herrmann, John, "The New Mayo Clinic," *Health Systems Review,* July/August 1994, p. 14.

Hodgson, Harriet W., *Rochester: City of the Prairie,* Northridge, Calif.: Windsor Publications, 1989.

Jacobson, Gary, "The Healthcare Biz: Alive and Kicking at the Mayo Clinic," *Management Review,* September 1989, pp. 10+.

Japsen, Bruce, "Rockford, Mayo to Affiliate, Not Merge," *Modern Healthcare,* September 8, 1997, p. 16.

Johnson, Victor, *Mayo Clinic: Its Growth and Progress,* Bloomington, Minn.: Voyageur Press, 1984.

Lerner, Maura, "Mayo Clinic, Group of Private Investors to Expand Web Site," *Minneapolis Star Tribune,* December 7, 1999, p. 1D.

Mayo Clinic, Rochester, Minn.: Mayo Foundation, 1990.

Nissen, Todd, "A Glimpse of the Might of Mayo," *Corporate Report-Minnesota,* August 1993, p. 30.

Severson, Harold, *Rochester: Mecca for Millions,* Rochester, Minn.: Marquette Bank & Trust Company, 1979.

Solberg, Carla, "Mayo Reaches Out in a Prescription for Managed Care," *Minneapolis-St. Paul Citybusiness,* August 26, 1994, p. 3.

Strand, Philip K., *A Century of Caring, 1889–1989,* Rochester, Minn.: Saint Marys Hospital, 1988.

Winslow, Ron, "Mayo Clinic to Form Internet Firm with a Private-Equity Investor," *Wall Street Journal,* December 6, 1999, p. B8.

Zemke, Ron, and Dick Schaaf, "The Mayo Clinic and Hospitals," *The Service Edge: 101 Companies That Profit from Customer Care,* New York: New American Library, 1989, pp. 153–56.

—Jay P. Pederson
—updated by David E. Salamie

McKechnie plc

Leighswood Rd.
Aldridge Walsall
West Midlands WS9 8DS
United Kingdom
Telephone: (+44) 1922 743887
Fax: (+44) 1922 451045
Web site: http://www.mckechnie.co.uk

Public Company
Incorporated: 1915 as McKechnie Brothers Limited
Employees: 1,346
Sales: £525.6 million (US$788 million) (1999)
Stock Exchanges: London OTC
Ticker Symbol: MKNE
NAIC: 339999 All Other Miscellaneous Manufacturing;
    33429 Other Communications Equipment
    Manufacturing

Once nicknamed "Widget plc"—because of its myriad of low-margin, high-volume commodity products, such as the plastic fittings that make bottled beer taste like draft beer—McKechnie plc has reinvented itself as an international specialist engineering and plastics group. Since the end of the 1990s, McKechnie has divested the large majority of its low-margin products, including its entire consumer products division, to focus on high-margin components for several key markets: Aerospace, Automotive, Mobile Telecommunications, and Retail Materials Handling. The company's Specialist Products division, which included subsidiaries Arger Enterprises and Valley Todeco in the United States, Linread Northbridge in the United Kingdom, and Dzus in Germany and France, designs and manufactures component products for the automotive and aerospace industries, with an emphasis on the company's core fasteners expertise. Specialist products also include components for the mobile telephone and portable computer markets, with major clients such as Nokia and Compaq including the company's fasteners in their product designs. While the company's Engineered Plastics division continues to churn out widgets for Guinness and other bottled beer manufacturers, this division has increasingly specialized in high-margin products, such as returnable plastic container systems, surgical implants, including components for pacemakers, wheel trim and molding, hubcaps, components for braking systems and other automotive components, and components for missiles and other military applications. In October 1999, McKechnie sold off its Consumer Products division, which included such brand names as Harrison Drape, Spur, Douglas Kane, and Homelux, to U.S. giant Newell Rubbermaid for £83 million. That division represented some 20 percent of the company's 1999 sales of £525.6 million. More than half of the company's sales are generated by acquisitions completed between 1997 and 2000. The transformed McKechnie continues to seek opportunities to boost its strong market positions, announcing a war-chest of some £200 million for the start of the new century.

From Metal Smelter to Widget Maker in the 19th Century

Founder Duncan McKechnie opened his first factory—collecting, smelting and recycling scrap metals—in St. Helens in 1871. McKechnie was joined by sons Alexander and Daniel, who opened an additional factory in Widnes in 1891 and assumed the leadership of the family business. As the business grew, the brothers formalized their partnership as a limited company, McKechnie Brothers Limited, in 1915. By then, the company was already preparing to diversify. Recognizing the value of the chemical byproducts of the smelting process, McKechnie Brothers began collecting and separating these byproducts for sale.

The McKechnie family continued to control the company through the first half of the 20th century, expanding operations throughout the United Kingdom. At the end of World War II, McKechnie Brothers began to move onto the international stage, turning to a Europe devastated by the war and needing to rebuild, and to the United States, flush with victory and preparing to enter a new period of economic growth. The company also moved into the Australian and New Zealand markets. In order to fuel its own growth, McKechnie Brothers went public in 1953. The McKechnie family maintained its majority in the company's voting rights.

The newly buoyant marketplace in the United Kingdom and elsewhere gave McKechnie Brothers the impetus to move deeper into the manufacturing end, and the companies production activities gradually replaced its smelting operations. The company also recognized the transition of many products from metal and other materials to plastics. McKechnie Brothers too joined this trend, adding plastics in the 1960s. The company also moved into the consumer products market during this time.

While McKechnie Brothers' diversification effort proved successful, the McKechnie family itself was losing its majority status among the company's shareholders. The conversion of a portion of ordinary shares into shares with voting rights spelled the end of the McKechnie family's control in 1971. The company's new shareholder base encouraged the continued diversification of McKechnie Brother's product line, which also began to see a stronger engineering component. Among the company's products of the time were heat-resistant materials, using ceramics and fiberglass, needed to replace the huge installed base of asbestos, which by the late 1970s had been recognized as exceedingly dangerous and the use of which had been placed on tight restrictions.

Selling a minority share in its McKechnie Refractory Fibres subsidiary enabled McKechnie Brothers to open into new territory, with the acquisition of Ever Ready Tool & Engineering in 1981. The company moved more steadily into engineering products during the 1980s. In 1984, the company dropped the "Brothers" from its name, adopting the name McKechnie plc.

Transformation into Engineering Specialist in the 1990s

Through the 1980s McKechnie continued to boost its engineering component. In 1986, the company added the manufacture of fasteners—later to become a core product—with the acquisition of PSM International. The following year, McKechnie boosted its plastics operations with the purchase of Precision Molded Plastics and Trent Valley Plastics.

These acquisitions were joined by McCourtney Plastics one year later. Consumer goods were also taking on a prominent role, as the company added such products as curtain components and extended into the booming do-it-yourself (DIY) market with such brands as Harrison Drape, Spur, Nenplas, Douglas Kane, and Windoware. The move into DIY coincided with the downturn in the housing market and the entry into the lengthy recession of the 1990s. In the early 1990s, the company also added DIY manufacturer Savage, for £47 million, a move designed to enable the company to profit from the slow recovery of the housing market in the United Kingdom.

The company also added to its plastics capacity with the purchase of a majority share of Charter Supply Corporation in the United States, adding that company's packaging and containers products in 1989. The company's containers were to become a key product category for the company, especially among the United Kingdom's large supermarket chains. McKechnie began designing custom-engineered container systems for such chains as Marks & Spencers, Great Mills, and Asda, replacing traditional cardboard containers.

Entering the 1990s, McKechnie began to focus its direction beyond its diversified operations to new product areas, including the automotive and aerospace industries. The company moved into automobile components in 1989 with the purchase of Conex Union BV of the Netherlands, which added that company's extruded plastic hoses and other products. The Conex acquisition was joined by those of Barrington Products and Injection Moulded Plastics, increasing McKechnie's automotive components capacity in the U.K. and European markets. Injection-molded plastics were quickly to become an important growth area in the automotive industry, as automakers sought means to decrease the weight of vehicles—in part to help meet tightening pollution restrictions—and the costs of vehicle production.

After the automobile market, McKechnie took the leap into the aerospace industry. In 1994, the company made its first aerospace industry acquisition, of Linread plc and its trading name of Linread Northridge. That purchase, which, in particular, gave the company a place among suppliers to the European aerospace consortium Airbus, was quickly followed by the acquisition of Valley Todeco, which enabled the company to enter the aerospace market in the United States.

In the mid-1990s, McKechnie began to step up the growth of its automotive and aerospace production. In 1996, the company formed its Motor Vehicle Components USA division for acquisitions of businesses including Thompson International, adding wheel trims and hubcaps. Plastics-based wheel trim became something of a company specialty in the late 1990s, as car manufacturers began replacing traditionally metal-based hubcaps with plastics. In the late 1990s, also, McKechnie began increasing its market position in another area of the automotive market, that of fuel- and fluid-handling systems, for such manufacturers as Ford, Daimler-Chrysler, and General Motors.

The design and engineering of fasteners—with applications ranging from door latches for military aircraft to hinges for mobile telephones—took on a greater share of the company's turnover and profits in the 1990s, particularly with the acquisition of fastener specialist Dzus in 1996, which added that company's latching systems and quarter-turn fasteners. By then, however, the heavily diversified McKechnie had begun to face

Key Dates:

1871: Duncan McKechnie opens scrap metal smelting factory in St. Helens.
1891: Sons Alexander and Daniel take over factory's operations; new factory opens in Widnes.
1915: Business incorporates as McKechnie Brothers Limited and begins selling chemical byproducts from smelting process.
1953: Completes public offering.
1971: McKechnie family loses control of company.
1981: Acquisition of Ever Ready Tool & Engineering.
1984: Name changes to McKechnie plc.
1996: MVC is acquired, representing entry into U.S. automotive market.
1998: Plastic blow molded packaging operations are sold.
1999: Consumer Goods division is sold to Newell Rubbermaid; Western Sky Industries is acquired.

criticism—particularly among stock market analysts—for its lack of product focus. With the company's share price slipping (and with the increasing shareholder's position of insurance industry giant Prudential, which had acquired nearly 20 percent of McKechnie's stock by the late 1990s), the company's then-CEO Michael Ost found himself under pressure. In 1997, Ost resigned, replaced by Andrew Walker.

Walker immediately led McKechnie on a massive restructuring program, seeking to transform the company from a diversified manufacturer of primarily low-margin, high-volume commodity items to a highly specialized engineering and plastics group with the emphasis on the production of high-margin products. One of Walker's first moves was to sell off the company's blow-molded plastic packaging and products operations, a move taken in March 1998. Several months later, the company's entire holdings in low-margin, cyclical products in Australia and New Zealand were sold off, thereby exiting one of the company's oldest markets. The company's streamlining continued into 1999, when, in October of that year, McKechnie sold its entire Consumer Products division—which by then had been reduced to just 20 percent of sales—to U.S.-based Newell Rubbermaid for £83 million.

That sale significantly changed McKechnie's profile. Entering the 21st century, McKechnie had now reorganized around its newly refocused Specialty Products and Engineered Plastics divisions. The company's focus had also turned more solidly to the aerospace industry—and particularly the aerospace aftermarket, less vulnerable to cyclical downswings. By the beginning of the year 2000, some 40 percent of McKechnie's sales were generated through the aerospace industry.

The company continued to enhance its aerospace operations with the acquisitions of PTM International Inc. of Miami, Florida, adding to the company's aerospace aftermarket penetration, and Western Sky Industries, the U.S.-based maker of bolts and fasteners, for US$260 million. These acquisitions helped to consolidate McKechnie's new strategic direction. They also pointed toward similar acquisitions in the near future: at the end of 1999, McKechnie announced its intention to spend up to £200 million on acquisitions in the next year.

Principal Subsidiaries

Arger Enterprises, Inc (U.S.A.); Burnett Polymer Engineering; DFS International, Inc (U.S.A.); Dzus Fasteners; Dzus Fasteners GmbH (Germany); Dzus France SA; Eachairn Investments SARL (Luxembourg) Fijaciones Industriales PSM SA (Spain); Hartwell Corporation (U.S.A.); Jesse Industries, Inc (U.S.A.); Linread plc; McKechnie Espana SA; McKechnie Nederland BV; McKechnie Plastic Components, Inc (U.S.A.); McKechnie Vehicle Components; McKechnie Vehicle Components North America, Inc (U.S.A.); PSM Fastener Corporation (U.S.A.); PSM Fixation SA (France); PSM International; PSM Metall-und-Kunststoff Verbindungssysteme (Germany); Valley Todeco, Inc (U.S.A.); Western Sky Industries (U.S.A.).

Principal Divisions

Specialist Products; Engineered Plastics; Consumer Products.

Principal Competitors

AlliedSignal Inc.; PMC Global; Arvin Industries, Inc.; Summa Industries; The BFGoodrich Company; Tenneco Automotive; Cooper Industries, Inc.; Triple S Plastics; Formosa Plastics Corporation; Tuscarora Inc.; General Electric Company; Wyman-Gordon Company; ITT Industries.

Further Reading

Anderson, Simon, "McKechnie Scoops US Bolt Maker," *Daily Telegraph*, May 26, 1999.
Anderson, Simon, and Roberts, Dan, "McKechnie Leads Share Fightback in Engineering, *Daily Telegraph*, October 7, 1998.
Larsen, Peter Thal, "McKechnie's Widgets Resist the Slowdown," *Independent*, October 7, 1998, p. 25.
Trefgarne, George, "Hopes Rise at Refocused McKechnie," *Financial Times*, January 22, 2000.
——, "McKechnie Has £200m to Spend on Acquisitions," *Daily Telegraph*, April 1, 1999.
——, "McKechnie Makes US Acquisition," *Financial Times*, May 26, 1999.

—M. L. Cohen

Meggitt PLC

6 Poole Road
Wimborne
Dorset BH21 1JH
United Kingdom
Telephone: (1202) 847847
Fax: (1202) 842-478
Web site: http://www.meggitt.com

Public Company
Incorporated: 1947 as Willson Lathes
Employees: 4,200
Sales: £346.5 million (1999)
Stock Exchanges: London
Ticker Symbol: MGGT.L
NAIC: 54171 Research and Development in the Physical,
Engineering, and Life Sciences; 334511 Search,
Detection, Navigation, Guidance, Aeronautical, and
Nautical System and Instrument Manufacturing;
336399 All Other Motor Vehicle Parts Manufacturing;
336411 Aircraft Manufacturing; 336413 Other
Aircraft Parts and Auxiliary Equipment Manufacturing

From obscure origins, Meggitt PLC has grown into a global aerospace supplier. Its subsidiaries manufacture instrumentation and other products found in a wide spectrum of military and civil aircraft. The company's purchase of U.S.-based Whittaker in 1998 has given it a significant aftermarket business as well. Meggitt also produces remote-operated target aircraft for the military, sensors for the automobile industry, energy industry equipment, ticketing systems, and point-of-sale systems for fuel stations.

Engineering Origins

Meggitt PLC began as a small, family-owned engineering firm in Dorset, England. Willson Lathes, a publicly listed machine tool manufacturer based in Halifax, acquired the company in a reverse takeover in 1964. Willson Lathes had gone public in April 1947.

Eventually, Meggitt began to flounder. It lost £180,000 on sales of less than £4 million in 1983. Nigel McCorkell and Ken Coates, directors at nearby Flight Refuelling Ltd., came to see the company as a prospective launching pad for future acquisitions. Together with the investment group 3i (Investors in Industry), they accumulated a 29.9 percent share in Meggitt in a management buy-in.

McCorkell and Coates soon turned around the demoralized, money-losing firm. Coates, an engineer himself, had run a number of different companies. McCorkell was a chartered accountant and former merchant banker. They sold off stockpiled product and invested in expanding Meggitt's metal fabricating business as they aimed for growth sectors in the engineering field. Removal of management constraints allowed the gas filtration business to streamline itself. Meggitt posted a profit of £354,000 for fiscal 1984 after three years of losses.

Then the acquisition spree began. Meggitt bought Insley, a cutting tools distributor, for £2.5 million in stock and cash in September 1984. A sale and leaseback arrangement sweetened the deal. Soon after, Meggitt paid just £1 for the insolvent engineering firm Filtration & Transfer, for which it had previously offered £1 million.

This series of acquisitions, including that of the diversified aerospace engineering firm Negretti, magnified Meggitt's stock value and competitive profile. The Negretti deal cost £16 million in shares. Although the company was a large catch, Negretti's process control operation was losing money, and the profitable Negretti units lacked sufficient financial controls. McCorkell and Coates focused the firm on its core business, aircraft instrumentation, and set out to restore profitability to the process control line. Expansion into U.S. markets was another key point in the recovery plan.

Meggitt Holdings announced profits of more than £2 million for the fiscal year ending October 31, 1985, on turnover of £28 million. Towards the end of 1985, Meggitt bought Holsworthy for £3.5 million in cash and stock. Holsworthy produced film circuitry; the purchase increased Meggitt's sales by 75 percent.

Taking Over Bestobell in 1986

In 1986, Meggitt Holdings acquired the Bestobell engineering group, which had three times Meggitt's annual sales, for £86 million in a hostile takeover. Coates and McCorkell were joined by Sir Owen Green, whose giant BTR plc industrial conglomerate had been stuck with a 29 percent minority holding after a failed £29 million takeover bid in 1979. Owen received 18 percent of the new Meggitt in exchange for his share of Bestobell.

After taking over Bestobell, Coates and McCorkell cut unprofitable operations in remote locations, such as Africa. Consistent with its emphasis on U.S. sales, Meggitt acquired two American firms for its Bestobell subsidiary. The company spent $40 million in 1988 to buy Plastic Fabricating of Kansas and New York's Ragen Data Systems.

Meggitt Holdings posted pretax profits of £16 million for the year ending December 1987. Turnover fell to £167 million as a result of selling off most of Bestobell's overseas assets. Aerospace and defense, the largest division, accounted for £73 million, boosted by a major U.S. Department of Defense contract for Negretti Aviation. At the time, Meggitt was arranged in four divisions: engineering distribution, aerospace and defense systems and components, energy and petrochemical industry equipment, and electronic components and circuitry. Controls would be the fifth.

In September 1988, Meggitt acquired Microsystems Group for £33 million, guiding the electronics business into the higher margins of ticketing machines, taxi meters, and telephone-logging systems. It quickly disposed of its unprofitable Raitel subsidiary, which manufactured security telephones. Meggitt bought well established German controls installer Sunvic, while it allowed management to buy out the traditional machine tools line.

The USH Fiasco of 1989

A failed attempt to buy United Scientific Holdings (USH) in the fall of 1989 left a lingering chill in the minds of analysts. USH was best known for its Alvis subsidiary, the armored vehicle manufacturer based in Coventry. The deal would have been even larger than the Bestobell takeover. Meggitt canceled at the last minute, bringing its motives into question. USH manufactured night vision equipment and armored vehicles; perhaps Meggitt thought twice about prospects in the limited defense market. A profits warning from USH, though, may have been enough cause for Meggitt to abandon its hostile takeover bid. USH's Avimo Taunton plant was locked into money-losing contracts to supply the Ministry of Defence with sight systems.

On the day Meggitt's bid was launched, USH announced it planned to sell its U.S.-based Optic-Electronic Corporation (OEC) subsidiary to Imo Industries of New Jersey. Meggitt opposed the sale and U.S. regulators blocked it on competition grounds. However, OEC's proxy board—required when overseas companies own defense suppliers in the United States— had secretly established $2.5 million (£1.6 million) worth of

golden parachutes for themselves. In addition, USH's share price fell well below the value of Meggitt's offer.

Meggitt did complete a smaller acquisition in November 1989. It bought Swindon-based automotive supplier Citec from BICC, an international cables and construction group, for £5 million in cash.

Meggitt posted pretax profits of £23.5 million on sales of £302 million in 1991. Both figures were flat from the year before in spite of the recession. Its most profitable division was Aerospace, while Controls survived in a highly fragmented market.

Meggitt cut nearly 1,200 jobs in 1991 and 1992. A rights issue in November 1991 gave the company plenty of cash for acquisitions. Meggitt arranged to buy U.S.-based sensor manufacturer Endevco from Allied-Signal for US$53 million (£29 million). It bought Micrelec, an unprofitable maker of electronics for the energy industry in the spring of 1992 for £17 million and also acquired the lucrative gas processing equipment manufacturer Howmar.

BTR sold its 17.2 percent stake in Meggitt in April 1993. During their six-year relationship beginning with the Bestobell takeover, Meggitt's sales increased from £28 million to £327 million, although earnings had been flat for a few years.

Sir Owen and BTR bailed out just in time. By 1994, the vagaries of the defense market had caught up with Meggitt. Intense competition in the commercial aerospace market also depressed sales. The company continued to trim its workforce, to under 6,000, and sold off or integrated many of its subsidiaries, eradicating any lack of focus among its somewhat diversified holdings. The company sought to leave the energy sector entirely. Sales were £345.5 million in 1994, producing profits of just £14.8 million. Plastic Fabrication, a U.S.-based subsidiary, had a particularly disastrous year. It lost its accreditation from Boeing. Meggitt fired the entire management team and began looking for a buyer.

Restructuring in 1995

As Ken Coates stepped back due to ill health, Mike Stacey moved from managing the Aerospace and Electronics divisions to becoming group managing director. The TT Group, a conglomerate also known for its acquisitive ways, bought a 4.2 percent stake in Meggitt in February 1995, raising the threat of a takeover. However, TT disposed of the stake by October.

Meggitt restructured in 1995, closing or selling 16 companies and arranging the rest into special business units (SBUs) led by "Stacey's Boys," managers appointed by new CEO Mike Stacey. Nigel McCorkell resigned as deputy chairman in January 1996, although the timing, said some, "was not of his choosing." By the summer, he had taken a position as chairman at newly created Cork Industries.

Profits at the controls division rose considerably in 1995, though, thanks in large part to write-offs, Meggitt lost £21.5 million on sales of £358.2 million. This was reversed in 1996 with profits of £24.3 million on sales of £256.3 million. Aerospace profits rose 40 percent.

Key Dates:

1947: Machine tool manufacturer Willson Lathes begins trading shares publicly.
1964: Willson Lathes accomplishes reverse takeover of the Meggitt firm.
1983: Nigel McCorkell and Ken Coates lead management buy-in.
1984: Meggitt begins acquisition spree.
1986: With help of BTR, Meggitt accomplishes hostile takeover of much larger Bestobell.
1989: Aborted bid for USH chills analysts.
1993: BTR sells its stake in Meggitt after a few years of lackluster results.
1995: New management, led by Mike Stacey, is appointed as Meggitt restructures.
1998: Whittaker buy bolsters Meggitt's prospects.

In the fall of 1996, Meggitt bought Cartwright Electronics, a U.S.-based electronic target scoring systems manufacturer. The acquisition immediately boosted sales at Meggitt's Target Systems Division. Meggitt, now firmly oriented toward the U.S. market, had become Boeing's main supplier of elastomeric seals for its 777 aircraft. Forty percent of its products were manufactured in the United States. Meggitt's new Secondary Flight Display System (SFDS), which combined attitude, altitude, and air speed indicators in a single liquid crystal display, found acceptance in a variety of U.S. military cargo aircraft. Production of SFDS systems reached 2,000 in February 2000.

Meggitt started 1998 with a $100 million order for such backup instrumentation from Boeing. It then expanded that market to small aircraft. Pretax profits had risen 30 percent to £31.5 million in 1997 as sales rose four percent to £265 million. Although hurt by exchange rates, the electronics division was also strong, particularly in sensors for pacemakers.

In 1998, Meggitt bought Vibro-Meter SA, a complement to its Endevco business. Vibro-Meter was strong with Airbus, while Endevco had enjoyed good relations with Boeing. Pre-tax profits for the year reached £35.4 million on sales of £293.9 million.

Meggitt bought Whittaker Corporation for US$380 million (£237 million) in June 1999. Whittaker was a NYSE-listed diversified aerospace supplier to virtually every Western aircraft manufacturer. In addition to greater access to markets and the potential for millions of dollars of savings in synergies, Whittaker offered a strong aftermarket parts business as a buffer during cyclical down times, and helped the company remain relevant in the face of impending consolidation among smaller aerospace suppliers.

In the first half of 1999, delivery of 6,000 ticket machines to London Transport boosted profits in the electronics division 60 percent, while Boeing's cancellation of the MD90 program dampened aerospace results. Industrial controls also saw sales fall due to declining oil industry spending. The company's Vibro-Meter unit won a contract to outfit U.S. Army helicopters in conjunction with BF Goodrich Aerospace. Meggitt sold off its money-losing Mobrey industrial controls business to Roxboro Group PLC for £22.3 million in cash. True to its predictions, results improved in the last half of 1999, resulting in (preliminary) pretax profits of £50.7 million for the year on a turnover of £346.5 million.

Principal Divisions

Aerospace; Electronics.

Principal Operating Units

Aerospace Systems; Aerospace Equipment; Meggitt Defence Systems; Electronic Sensors; Heatric; Electronic Systems.

Principal Competitors

Cobham plc; Honeywell Inc.; Sextant Avionique; Smiths Industries PLC.

Further Reading

Batchelor, Charles, "Sir Owen Deals a Strong Hand," *Financial Times,* July 16, 1986, p. 22.
Bolger, Andrew, "In Defence of a Strategic Withdrawal," *Financial Times,* November 21, 1989, p. 31.
——, "Meggitt and USH Call a Truce over £104 Million Takeover Battle," *Financial Times,* November 2, 1989, p. 30.
——, "A Victory Within Sight But Doubts Abound," *Financial Times,* November 1, 1989, p. 32.
Burt, Tim, "Engineering a Recovery Story," *Financial Times,* October 4, 1995, p. 25.
——, "Write-Offs Push Meggitt into Loss," *Financial Times,* March 27, 1996, p. 26.
Foster, Geoffrey, "A Small Spanner in the Works," *Management Today,* June 1992, pp. 66–70.
Gourlay, Richard, "BTR Sells Its 17.2 Percent Stake in Meggitt," *Financial Times,* April 22, 1993, p. 26.
Harris, Clay, and Andrew Bolger, "Hostilities Begin at Defence Contractor," *Financial Times,* September 12, 1989, p. 24.
"Insley Deal Initiates Meggitt Growth Plan," *Financial Times,* August 24, 1984, p. 16.
Jackson, Dominique, "Busy Year for Meggitt As Profits Advance to £16 Million," *Financial Times,* March 24, 1988, p. 29.
Jones, Adam, "Aerospace Minnows Emerge from Niches to Make Profits," *Times,* Bus. Sec., January 20, 1998.
Kennedy, Carol, "50 and Still Nifty," *Director,* October 1997, pp. 30–36.
Larsen, Peter Thal, "Meggitt Expects Pick-Up in Aerospace Division," *Financial Times,* September 9, 1999, p. 26.
——, "Meggitt in $380 Million Aerospace Deal: Acquisition of Whittaker Will Boost Parts Supplier's Influence As Industry Consolidates," *Financial Times,* June 10, 1999, p. 23.
Maughan, Ray, "3i Backing New Team in Meggitt Diversification," *Financial Times,* November 11, 1983, p. 30.
"Meggitt Seen Gaining Strong Position in Sector After Vibro-Meter Buy," *AFX News,* August 20, 1998.
"Meggitt Tops £2 Million and Seeks Cash to Expand," *Financial Times,* February 8, 1986, p. 8.
Morrocco, John D., and Carole A. Shifrin, "Meggitt Restructuring Shows Promising Returns," *Aviation Week & Space Technology,* April 14, 1997, p. 42f.
Peel, Michael, "Meggitt Sets Sights on Private Jets," *Financial Times,* March 12, 1999, p. 24.
Reed, David, "Fuel Injection," *Marketing Week,* February 4, 1999, pp. 37–42.

Southey, Caroline, "Defence Uncertainties Catch Up with Meggitt," *Financial Times,* September 16, 1994, p. 21.

Taylor, Roger, "Meggitt 'Gaining Share in Aerospace Markets,'" *Financial Times,* March 25, 1998, p. 41.

Travers, Nicolas, "The Irresistible Rise of Meggitt," *Director,* December 1986, pp. 30–32.

Wilkinson, Terence, "Meggitt Prepares for Acquisition," *Independent,* April 8, 1992, p. 31.

——, "Meggitt Sees Little Sign of Improvement," *Independent,* September 17, 1992, p. 33.

—Frederick C. Ingram

Menard, Inc.

<table>
<tr><td>

4777 Menard Dr.
Eau Claire, Wisconsin 54703
U.S.A.
Telephone: (715) 876-5911
Fax: (715) 876-5901

Private Company
Incorporated: 1972
Employees: 7,000
Sales: $4 billion (1999 est.)
NAIC: 44419 Other Building Material Dealers

</td></tr>
</table>

Menard, Inc. is the nation's third largest home improvement supply chain. A rarity among retailers, Menards (as the company's stores are called) also operates its own manufacturing facility. The cost-saving measure is representative of founder and owner John Menard's penchant for keeping prices low. The regional chain faces increased market pressure as Home Depot and Lowe's continue to build their presence in the Midwest.

Founder's Values, a Bedrock for Business: 1950s–80s

John Menard, the eldest of eight children, worked his way through the University of Wisconsin-Eau Claire by building pole barns with some fellow students. In college, he majored in business, math, and psychology, but his work philosophy was influenced by his upbringing. "Menard remains a farm boy at heart, anchored by a few simple beliefs," the *National Home Center News* (NHCN) stated in a 1996 profile. His parents, both teachers and dairy farmers, instilled in him "the principles of frugality and, in Menard's words, common sense."

Alert to opportunity, Menard expanded the boundaries of his late-1950s construction business. He began buying wood in bulk and then resold it to builders scrambling to find materials on the weekends: a time when lumberyards typically were closed. In 1960, Menard added to his building supply line. A decade later, when the building supplies generated a majority of his revenues, Menard sold the construction end of the business.

He founded Menard, Inc. in 1972, just in time to catch the building wave of do-it-yourselfers.

Deviating from the standard lumberyard format, Menards stores featured wide aisles, tile floors, and easy to reach shelves—a design similar to mass merchandisers. During the 1970s and 1980s, Menard opened building supply stores in a five-state area: Wisconsin, Iowa, North and South Dakota, and Minnesota. Menard snapped up vacated retail sites, which were inexpensive but well-situated. Seconds, overstocks, and close-out items were peppered among the product mix. By 1986, Menards ranked 15th among the top home improvement chains, with estimated sales from the 34 outlets approaching the half billion mark.

Early 1990s Expansion

To support the growing company, in the early 1990s Menard opened a huge warehouse/distribution center and a manufacturing plant. Menard moved into Nebraska in 1990, the Chicago area in 1991, and Indiana and Michigan in 1992. The economic downturn in the early 1990s slowed home turnover and boosted sales on the home repair and improvement front.

By the fall of 1993, 12 Menards stores served suburban Chicago and were in direct competition with the 28-unit, Illinois-based Handy Andy, as well as Builders Square and HomeBase. Anticipating the arrival of Atlanta's Home Depot, Menard announced a major expansion drive. The company planned to open up to 18 additional stores in three different formats.

The regional chain ended 1993 with a total of 88 stores and $1.7 billion in revenues. The $9 billion home improvement supply leader, Home Depot, entered the Chicago market in September 1994.

John Menard, meanwhile, based on a net worth of close to $400 million, qualified for the *Forbes* Four Hundred list. His personal wealth allowed him to finance a longtime hobby. In 1979, along with two friends, Menard bought a $65,000 racer which Herm Johnson drove in the Indianapolis 500. Team Menard cars became perennial entries in the event; Menard spent millions on car and engine development. In 1994, Menard qualified two out of the three cars he sponsored for the Indy 500 and placed 8th and 20th. "He'll need to do a lot better than that to succeed in Chicago," wrote Frank Wolfe for *Forbes* magazine in June 1994.

By the end of 1995, Menard operated 115 outlets and produced $2.7 billion in sales. The company's rapid growth in the Chicago area played a significant role in the demise of Handy Andy and Courtesy Home Centers according to *NHCN*. The privately held Menard funded its growth through cash flow generated by the stores: "That cash flow is sustained by aggressive cost containment policies that come directly from its president, whom vendors will describe as 'tenacious,' 'frightening,' 'entrepreneurial' and 'paranoid,' all in the same breath," reported *NHCN* in May 1996.

Keeping Prices Low: Mid-1990s

Opinion aside, sole owner John Menard's business practices served the company well: Menard, Inc. claimed the 44th spot on the *Forbes* list of the largest private U.S. companies in 1996 and held third place in the home improvement industry.

In spite of the company's ever increasing size, Menard retained the flavor of a family business. One of John Menard's brothers, a daughter, a son, and a nephew held prominent management positions, and day-to-day policies reflected the owner's world view.

Employees put in six-day work weeks, both in stores and at the 600-plus-acre corporate headquarters in Eau Claire. Store workers built gondolas, bulk displays, and checkout counters. Scrap wood was used for store signage, and carpet remnants covered displays. The company's buyers played hard ball with suppliers when negotiating allowances, discounts, and price increases.

Menard tenaciously held to his low price strategy, even in head-to-head competition with super-sized Home Depot. Even when it meant slim margins. Staple products such as studs and paint sold consistently below Home Depot's price, sometimes just by a penny.

Conversely, Menards was trying to upgrade its image in order to draw in more middle and upper income shoppers. In the familiar 120,000-square-foot format, Menards stores were reminiscent of 1970s discount stores, but in upscale neighborhoods the company needed to cater to customers more concerned with quality than cost.

Menards shelved better quality product lines in areas such as kitchen and bath; more employees walked the sales floor. In 1996, a new 165,000-square-foot format was introduced although the department store-like design was retained. Menards also upped its advertising expenditures and offered its first private label credit card that year. Changes aside, the dominant advertising theme remained the same: "Save Big Money at Menards."

Menards stores, furthermore, were considered a rarity among retailers by depending on vertical integration as a cost-saving measure, according to *NHCN*. The products Menard manufactured in its plant accounted for about a quarter of items sold. In-house production cut an estimated ten percent off the cost of going through a supplier for a steel door. Among others items, Menards stores offered its own line of Formica countertops, dog houses, and picnic tables. The company had $45 million invested in the state-of-the-art manufacturing facility, according to a 1997 *Forbes* article.

Menard's across-the-board control helped him produce highest sales per employee ratio among industry leaders. On the other hand, Menard's penchant for being in charge generated lawsuits from disgruntled ex-employees, as well as customers and suppliers. Few, though, could ignore his bottom line, 1996 after-tax profits were $93 million, up 15 percent from 1995, according to *Forbes*. The 128 Menards stores produced $3.1 billion in sales on the year.

Pressure Building at Century's Close

The onslaught of larger players had brought other home improvement concerns to their knees while Menard flourished. Kmart closed its five Minneapolis area Builders Square stores when Home Depot entered the market. By contrast, Menard's properties produced higher per square foot sales than Home Depot's Midwest offerings.

In a February 1997 *Forbes* article, James Samuelson said John Menard attributed part of his success against Home Depot to the sheer size of the industry leader's stores. "He believes that many do-it-yourselfers, especially the weekenders, feel pressed for time and are put off by Home Depot's cavernous, cement-floored superstores, where the merchandise is stacked high in the air." Menards offered a comparable number of items, an average of 50,000 per store, in a smaller space by rapidly restocking shelf items from ample warehouse and stockroom space adjacent to each store.

The Menards chain distinguished itself from Home Depot via advertising as well. While Home Depot's promotions had some glitz, Menards' television ads, shot in the flagship store, had a down-home feel. "The spots feature a 70-year-old Ray Szmanda, a longtime employee from Eau Claire who simply goes on the air to point out Menards' low prices on hammers and shower curtains and other household gear that appeals to local do-it-yourselfers," wrote Samuelson. Menards used its Midwest roots to encourage customer loyalty.

In the latter half of 1997, rumors circulated regarding Menard's future as an independent entity. Some Wall Street analysts suggested the number two home improvement retailer was interested in buying Menard to gain a foothold in the Midwest. North Carolina-based Lowe's Companies Inc. operated 402 stores and reported 1996 sales of $8.6 billion. At the time, number one Home Depot had sales of $19.5 billion. Both of the industry leaders were in expansion drives. John Menard denied the rumors.

Also in 1997, Menard received a fine of $1.7 million for violating Wisconsin laws regulating the disposal of hazardous waste. The company had also been fined in 1989 and 1994. In other legal action, Menard faced off against fellow contenders in the $150 billion home improvement market over advertising claims. Sears sued Menard and Menard in turn sued Home Depot.

Home Depot entered another one of Menard's Midwest strongholds in 1998. The four Milwaukee area Menards stores, thanks to its regional roots, held market leadership. A number of independent retailers also had a strong following among area consumers. Menard planned to add more Milwaukee stores in response to Home Depot's challenge.

In 1998, Home Depot's 888 stores earned nearly $40 billion; Lowe's 550 stores produced sales of about $16 billion; and number three Menard's 139 stores followed behind with $4 billion in sales.

In 1999, number two Lowe's entered the Chicago market with plans to open 20 to 30 stores. Menard had 25 Chicago outlets. Home Depot operated 31 units and was poised to add ten to 20 more. Lowe's' entry was expected to spark a price war in the nation's largest hardware market. Menard had cut prices ten percent during a 1998 price war with Home Depot.

Lowe's pending entry into the Chicago area rekindled some speculation about a merger with Menard, according to a December 1999 *Crain's Chicago Business* article. " 'John Menard hasn't been intimidated by Home Depot in the past,' says John Caulfield, executive editor of *National Home Center News* in New York. 'So, it's unlikely he'll be intimidated by Lowe's. The two companies might not make a good merger fit anywhere, since Menard's lays out its stores differently and focuses on lower-priced goods,' " reported H. Lee Murphy.

Menard celebrated the opening of its 150th store in early 2000. At the time, Christopher Menard, vice-president of distribution, announced that the company would be phasing out the sale of products made out of wood cut from endangered forests.

Menard followed the action of other home improvement dealers such as Home Depot.

Just as the industry had been under pressure by environmentalists, Menard felt the squeeze of market leaders Home Depot and Lowe's. Industry observers generally agreed that only two big chains could thrive in a particular market. Given John Menard's competitive nature it was likely he would fight to hang on to his share of the Midwest home improvement scene.

Principal Competitors

The Home Depot, Inc.; Lowe's Companies, Inc.

Further Reading

"Builders Square Closing 34 Units," *Chicago Tribune,* February 11, 1999.

Demaster, Sarah, "Depot's Entry Did Not Shake Rivals in Milwaukee Market," *National Home Center News,* May 3, 1999, pp. 9+.

Freeman, Laurie, "Menards John Menard," *Advertising Age,* June 30, 1997, p. S23.

"Home Center Mogul Keeps a Low Profile," *St. Paul Pioneer Press,* September 3, 1997, p. 7B.

"John Menard," *National Home Center News,* December 16, 1996, pp. 57+.

Klobuchar, Jim, "Disabled Girl's Dad Loses Job by Building House with Ramps," *Star Tribune* (Minneapolis), June 3, 1992, p. 3B.

McAuliffe, Bill, "FYI: The Menards Guy Is Calling It Quits," *Star Tribune* (Minneapolis), November 17, 1998, p. 1B.

"Menard Has No Trouble Playing with the Giants," *National Home Center News,* May 20, 1996, p. 68.

"Menard Prepares for Aggressive Chicago Push," *Building Supply Home Centers,* October 1993, p. 20.

"Menards Hops onto Eco Bandwagon," *National Home Center News,* February 21, 2000, p. 4.

"Menards Is Fined for Mishandling Hazardous Waste," *Star Tribune (Minneapolis),* December 11, 1997, p. A6.

Moore, Janet, "Menard Discounts Speculation About Buyout by Lowe's," *Star Tribune (Minneapolis),* September 11, 1997, p. D1.

Murphy, H. Lee, "Lowe's Builds for Area Expansion: Hardware Retailer Aims to Nail Menard's, Home Depot," *Crain's Chicago Business,* December 20, 1999, p. 3.

"The NHCN Top 10: A Five-Year Perspective: Menard Inc.," *National Home Center News,* May 25, 1998, p. 84.

"The NHCN Top 10: A Five-Year Perspective: Menard Inc.," *National Home Center News,* May 24, 1999, p. 58.

"No. 3: Menard," *National Home Center News,* May 26, 1997, p. 80.

Reusse, Patrick, "The Right Stuff," *Twin Cities Business Monthly,* August 1999.

Samuelson, James, "Tough Guy Billionaire," *Forbes,* February 24, 1997, pp. 64, 66.

Wolfe, Frank, "Rearview Mirror," *Forbes,* June 20, 1994, p. 138.

—Kathleen Peippo

Merck & Co., Inc.

One Merck Drive
P.O. Box 100
White House Station, New Jersey 08889-0100
U.S.A.
Telephone: (908) 423-1000
Toll Free: (800) 613-2104
Fax: (908) 423-1043
Web site: http://www.merck.com

Public Company
Incorporated: 1927
Employees: 62,300
Sales: $32.71 billion (1999)
Stock Exchanges: New York Boston Cincinnati
    Philadelphia Pacific
Ticker Symbol: MRK
NAIC: 325412 Pharmaceutical Preparation
    Manufacturing; 325199 All Other Basic Organic
    Chemical Manufacturing; 325411 Medicinal and
    Botanical Manufacturing; 325413 In-Vitro Diagnostic
    Substance Manufacturing; 325414 Biological Product
    (except Diagnostic) Manufacturing; 422210 Drugs and
    Druggists' Sundries Wholesalers; 454110 Electronic
    Shopping and Mail-Order Houses; 541710 Research
    and Development in the Physical, Engineering, and
    Life Sciences

Merck & Co., Inc. is one of the largest pharmaceutical companies in the world. Among the company's most important prescription drugs are Vioxx, a painkiller used to treat arthritis; Zocor and Mevacor, used to modify cholesterol levels; Cozaar, Prinivil, and Vasotec, hypertension medications; Fosamax, for the treatment and prevention of osteoporosis; Pepcid, an ulcer medication; Primaxin and Noroxin, antibiotics; Crixivan, a protease inhibitor used in the treatment of HIV; Singulair, an asthma treatment; Cosopt, Timoptic, and Trusopt, all used to treat glaucoma; Propecia, a hair loss remedy; and several vaccines, including M-M-R II, chicken pox vaccine Varivax, and hepatitis B vaccine Recombivax HB. Merck also develops, manufactures, and markets pharmaceuticals through a number of joint ventures, including: a partnership with Johnson & Johnson that concentrates on designing and commercializing over-the-counter versions of prescription medications, such as Pepcid AC; a venture with Aventis A.G. focusing on the European vaccine market; and another partnership with Aventis, this one concentrating on animal health and poultry genetics. Nearly half of the company's revenues are generated by Merck-Medco Managed Care, a pharmacy benefit management subsidiary principally involved in selling prescription drugs through managed prescription drug programs. Merck spends more than $2 billion each year on pharmaceutical research and development. About 40 percent of the company's human health product sales are generated outside the United States.

German Origins

Merck's beginnings can be traced back to Friedrich Jacob Merck's 1668 purchase of an apothecary in Darmstadt, Germany, called "At the Sign of the Angel." Located next to a castle moat, this store remained in the Merck family for generations.

The pharmacy was transformed by Heinrich Emmanuel Merck into a drug manufactory in 1827. His first products were morphine, codeine, and cocaine. By the time he died in 1855, products made by his company, known as E. Merck AG, were used worldwide. In 1887 E. Merck sent a representative, Theodore Weicker, to the United States to set up a sales office. Weicker (who would go on to own drug powerhouse Bristol-Myers Squibb) was joined by George Merck, the 24-year-old grandson of Heinrich Emmanuel Merck in 1891. In 1899, the younger Merck and Weicker acquired a 150-acre plant site in Rahway, New Jersey, and started production in 1903. Weicker left the firm the following year.

The manufacture of drugs and chemicals at this site began in 1903. This same location housed the corporate headquarters of Merck & Co. and four of its divisions, as well as research laboratories and chemical production facilities, into the 1990s. Once known as "Merck Woods," the land surrounding the original plant was used to hunt wild game and corral domestic

Company Perspectives:

The mission of Merck is to provide society with superior products and services—innovations and solutions that improve the quality of life and satisfy customer needs—to provide employees with meaningful work and advancement opportunities and investors with a superior rate of return.

animals. In fact, George Merck kept a flock of 15 to 20 sheep on the grounds to test the effectiveness of an animal disinfectant. The sheep became a permanent part of the Rahway landscape.

The year 1899 also marked the first year the *Merck Manual of Diagnosis and Therapy* was published. In 1983, the manual entered its 14th edition. A *New York Times* review rated it "the most widely used medical text in the world."

In 1917, upon the entrance of the United States into World War I, George Merck, fearing anti-German sentiment, turned over a sizable portion of Merck stock to the Alien Property Custodian of the United States. This portion represented the company interest held by E. Merck AG, thereby ending Merck & Co.'s connection to its German parent. At the end of the war, Merck was rewarded for his patriotic leadership; the Alien Property Custodian sold Merck shares, worth $3 million, to the public. George Merck retained control of the corporation, and by 1919 the company was once again entirely public-owned.

1920s Through 1950s: Growth Through Mergers and R&D

By 1926, the year George Merck died, his son George W. Merck had been acting president for more than a year. The first major event of the younger Merck's tenure—which would last 25 years—was the 1927 merger with Philadelphia-based Powers-Weightman-Rosengarten, a pharmaceutical firm best known for antimalarial quinine. Following the merger, Merck incorporated his company as Merck & Co., Inc. The merger enabled Merck & Co. to increase its sales from $6 million in 1925 to more than $13 million in 1929. With the resultant expansion in capital, Merck initiated and directed the Merck legacy for pioneering research and development. In 1933, he established a large laboratory and recruited prominent chemists and biologists to produce new pharmaceutical products. Their efforts had far-reaching effects. En route to researching cures for pernicious anemia, Merck scientists discovered vitamin B_{12}. Its sales, both as a therapeutic drug and as a constituent of animal feed, were massive.

The 1940s continued to be a decade of discoveries in drug research, especially in the field of steroid chemistry. In the early 1940s, a Merck chemist synthesized cortisone from ox bile, which led to the discovery of cortisone's anti-inflammation properties. In 1943, streptomycin, a revolutionary antibiotic used for tuberculosis and other infections, was isolated by a Merck scientist.

Despite the pioneering efforts and research success under George W. Merck's leadership, the company struggled during the postwar years. There were no promising new drugs to speak

of, and there was intense competition from foreign companies underselling Merck products, as well as from former domestic consumers beginning to manufacture their own drugs. Merck found itself in a precarious financial position.

A solution was found in 1953 when Merck merged with Sharp & Dohme, Incorporated, a drug company with a similar history and reputation. Sharp and Dohme began as an apothecary shop in 1845 in Baltimore, Maryland. Its success in the research and development of such important products as sulfa drugs, vaccines, and blood plasma products matched the successes of Merck. The merger, however, was more than the combination of two industry leaders. It provided Merck with a new distribution network and marketing facilities to secure major customers. For the first time, Merck could market and sell drugs under its own name.

At the time of George W. Merck's death in 1957, company sales had surpassed $100 million annually. Although Albert W. Merck, a direct descendant of Friedrich Jacob Merck, continued to sit on the board of directors into the 1980s, the office of chief executive was never again held by a Merck family member.

1960s Through Mid-1980s: Diversifying, Reemphasizing Research, Surviving Various Difficulties

Henry W. Gadsen became CEO in 1965 and, as was fashionable at the time, initiated a program of diversification. Among the businesses acquired in the late 1960s and early 1970s were Calgon Corporation, a supplier of water treatment chemicals and services; Kelco, a maker of specialty chemicals; and Baltimore Aircoil, a maker of refrigeration and industrial cooling equipment. Many of these businesses were quickly divested after it was discovered that profits were hard to come by, but Calgon and Kelco remained part of Merck into the early 1990s. Under Gadsen's emphasis on diversification, Merck's pharmaceutical operations suffered.

In 1976, John J. Honran succeeded the 11-year reign of Gadsen. Honran was a quiet, unassuming man who had entered Merck as a legal counselor and then became the corporate director of public relations. But Honran's unobtrusive manner belied an aggressive management style. With pragmatic determination Honran not only continued the Merck tradition for innovation in drug research, but also improved a poor performance record on new product introduction to the market.

This problem was most apparent in the marketing of Aldomet, an antihypertensive agent. Once the research was completed, Merck planned to exploit the discovery by introducing an improved beta-blocker called Blocadren. Yet Merck was beaten to the market by its competitors. Furthermore, because the 17-year patent protection on a new drug discovery was about to expire, Aldomet was threatened by generic manufacturers. This failure to beat its competitors to the market is said to have cost the company $200 million in future sales. A similar sequence of events occurred with Indocin and Clinoril, two anti-inflammation drugs for arthritis.

Under Honran's regime, the company introduced a hepatitis vaccine, a treatment for glaucoma called Timoptic, and Ivomac, an antiparasitic for animals. In addition, while Honran remained

---

Key Dates:

1668: Friedrich Jacob Merck purchases an apothecary in Darmstadt, Germany.

1827: Heinrich Emmanuel Merck transforms the pharmacy into a drug manufactory.

1887: The German firm, E. Merck AG, sets up a sales office in the United States.

1891: George Merck, grandson of Heinrich Merck, joins the U.S. branch, known as Merck & Company.

1899: The *Merck Manual of Diagnosis and Therapy* is first published.

1903: U.S. production begins at a site in Rahway, New Jersey.

1917: Entrance of United States into World War I leads to severing of relationship between Merck & Co. and E. Merck AG.

1925: George W. Merck takes over as president, succeeding his father.

1927: Company merges with Powers-Weightman-Rosengarten and is incorporated as Merck & Co., Inc.

1940s: Merck's laboratories make a series of discoveries: vitamin B_{12}, cortisone, streptomycin.

1953: Company merges with Sharp & Dohme, Incorporated.

1965: Henry W. Gadsen is named CEO and launches an ill-advised diversification program.

1976: John J. Honran succeeds Gadsen and reemphasizes drug research.

1979: Company begins marketing Enalapril, a high-blood-pressure inhibitor whose annual sales eventually reach $550 million.

1982: Merck enters into a partnership with Astra AB to sell that company's products in the United States.

1985: Dr. P. Roy Vagelos takes over as CEO; Vasotec, a treatment for congestive heart failure, is introduced.

1988: Vasotec becomes Merck's first billion-dollar-a-year drug.

1989: Over-the-counter medication joint venture is created with Johnson & Johnson.

1992: Zocor, a cholesterol-fighter, is introduced and eventually becomes a blockbuster.

1993: Medco Containment Services Inc., a drug distributor, is acquired for $6.6 billion.

1994: Raymond V. Gilmartin is named chairman and CEO, becoming the first outsider so named.

1995: Company divests its specialty chemicals businesses.

1999: Astra pays Merck $1.8 billion stemming from a joint venture between the companies and from Astra's merger with Zeneca; arthritis medication Vioxx makes its debut.

---

strongly committed to financing a highly productive research organization, Merck began making improvements on research already performed by competitors. In 1979, for example, Merck began to market Enalapril, a high-blood-pressure inhibitor, similar to the drug Capoten, which was manufactured by Squibb. Sales for Enalapril reached $550 million in 1986. Honran also embarked on a more aggressive program for licensing foreign products. In 1982 Merck purchased rights to sell products from Swedish firm Astra AB in the United States; a similar arrangement was reached with Shionogi of Japan. Two years later the Merck-Astra agreement was transformed into a joint venture, Astra Merck Inc.

Honran's strategy proved very effective. Between 1981 and 1985, the company experienced a nine percent annual growth rate, and in 1985 the *Wall Street Transcript* awarded Honran the gold award for excellence in the ethical drug industry. He was commended for the company's advanced marketing techniques and its increased production. At the time of the award, projections indicated a company growth rate for the next five years of double the present rate.

In 1984, Honran claimed Merck had become the largest U.S.-based manufacturer of drugs in the three largest markets—the United States, Japan, and Europe. He attributed this success to three factors: a productive research organization; manufacturing capability that allowed for cost-efficient, high-quality production; and an excellent marketing organization. The following year, Honran resigned as CEO. In 1986, his successor, Dr. P. Roy Vagelos, a biochemist and the company's former head of research, also was awarded the ethical drug industry's gold award.

Although Merck's public image was generally good, it had its share of controversy. In 1974, a $35 million lawsuit was filed against Merck and 28 other drug manufacturers and distributors of diethylstilbestrol (DES). This drug, prescribed to pregnant women in the late 1940s and up until the early 1960s, ostensibly prevented miscarriages. The 16 original plaintiffs claimed that they developed vaginal cancer and other related difficulties because their mothers had taken the drug. Furthermore, the suit charged that DES was derived from Stilbene, a known carcinogen, and that no reasonable basis existed for claiming the drugs were effective in preventing miscarriages. (A year before the suit, the Federal Drug Administration, or FDA, banned the use of DES hormones as growth stimulants for cattle because tests revealed cancer-causing residues of the substance in some of the animals' livers. The FDA, however, did not conduct public hearings on this issue; consequently, a federal court overturned the ban.)

Under the plaintiffs' directive, the court asked the defendants to notify other possible victims and to establish early detection and treatment centers. More than 350 plaintiffs subsequently sought damages totaling some $350 billion.

Merck was not beleaguered by the DES lawsuit only. In 1975, the company's name was added to a growing list of U.S. companies involved in illegal payments abroad. The payoffs, issued to increase sales in certain African and Middle Eastern countries, came to the attention of Merck executives through the investigation of the Securities and Exchange Commission. While sales amounted to $40.4 million for that year in those areas of the foreign market, the report uncovered a total of $140,000 in bribes. Once the SEC revealed its report, Merck initiated an internal investigation and took immediate steps to prevent future illegal payments.

Later, Merck found itself beset with new difficulties. In its attempt to win hegemony in Japan, the second largest pharmaceutical market in the world, Merck purchased more than 50 percent of the Banyu Pharmaceutical Company of Tokyo. Partners since 1954 under a joint business venture called Nippon Merck-Banyu (NMB), the companies used Japanese detail men (or pharmaceutical sales representatives) to promote Merck products.

When NMB proved inefficient, however, Merck bought out its partner for $315.5 million—more than 30 times Banyu's annual earnings. The acquisition was made in 1982, and Merck was still in the process of bringing Banyu into line with its more aggressive and imaginative management style in the early 1990s.

Problems in labor relations surfaced during the spring of 1985 when Merck locked out 730 union employees at the Rahway plant after failing to agree to a new contract. For three months prior to the expiration of three union contracts, involving 4,000 employees, both sides negotiated a new settlement. When talks stalled, however, the company responded by locking out employees. The unresolved issues involved both wages and benefits.

By June 5, all 4,000 employees participated in a strike involving the Rahway plant and six other facilities across the nation. In West Point, Virginia, operations were halted when union picketers prevented nonstriking employees from entering the plant. Merck, however, was able to win a court-ordered injunction limiting picketing.

The strike proved to be the longest in Merck's history; but after 15 weeks an agreement was finally reached. A company request for the adoption of a two-tier wage system that would permanently pay new employees lower wages was rejected, as was a union demand for wage increases and cost-of-living adjustments during the first year. Nevertheless, Merck's reputation as an exceptional, high-paying workplace remained intact, and its subsequent contract agreements were amicable. In fact, Merck was ranked as one of the "100 Best Companies to Work for in America" and one of *Working Mother* magazine's "100 Best Companies for Working Mothers" since that ranking's 1986 inception.

Late 1980s and Early 1990s: Blockbuster Drugs, Joint Ventures, Medco

During the late 1980s, double-digit annual sales increases catapulted Merck to undisputed leadership of the pharmaceutical industry. CEO Vagelos's research direction in the 1960s and 1970s laid the foundation for Merck's drug "bonanza" of the 1980s. Vasotec, a treatment for congestive heart failure, was introduced in 1985 and became Merck's first billion-dollar-a-year drug by 1988. Mevacor, a cholesterol-lowering drug introduced in 1987, and ivermectin, the world's top-selling animal health product, also contributed to the company's impressive growth. In the late 1980s, Merck was investing hundreds of millions of dollars in research and development—ten percent of the entire industry's total. Over the course of the decade, Merck's sales more than doubled, its profits tripled, and the company became the world's top-ranked drug company as well as one of *Business Week*'s ten most valuable companies.

The company also was recognized for its heritage of social responsibility. In the 1980s, Merck made its drug for "river blindness"—a parasitic infection prevalent in tropical areas and affecting 18 million people—available at no charge. In 1987, the company shared its findings regarding the treatment of human immunodeficiency virus (HIV) with competitors. These efforts reflected George W. Merck's assertion: "Medicine is for the patients. It is not for the profits. The profits follow, and if we have remembered that, they have never failed to appear. The better we have remembered it, the larger they have been."

Growth did slow in the early 1990s, however, as Merck's drug pipeline dried up. Although the company maintained the broadest product line in the industry, its stable of new drugs was conspicuously absent of the "blockbusters" that had characterized the previous decade, with one exception. In 1992 Merck introduced Zocor, a cholesterol-fighting drug that eventually surpassed $1 billion in annual sales and became the company's top-selling drug and one of the most successful pharmaceuticals in history.

In the meantime, Merck entered into a number of joint ventures that created alternative avenues of product development. In 1989 Merck joined with Johnson & Johnson in a venture to develop over-the-counter (OTC) versions of Merck's prescription medications, initially for the U.S. market, later expanded to Europe and Canada. Two years later Merck and E.I. du Pont de Nemours and Company formed a joint venture to research, manufacture, and sell pharmaceutical and imaging agent products. Merck and Connaught Laboratories, Inc. (later part of Aventis S.A.) jointly agreed in 1992 to develop combination vaccines in the United States. In 1994 Merck created a venture with a related company, Pasteur Merieux Connaught (which was also later part of Aventis S.A.), to market combination vaccines in Europe.

In 1993 Merck acquired Medco Containment Services Inc. for $6.6 billion. Medco was a mail-order distributor of drugs that was previously acquired by Martin Wygod in the early 1980s for $36 million. With the help of infamous investment banker Michael Milken, Wygod built Medco into a mass drug distribution system with $2.5 billion in revenues and $138 million in profits by 1992. The acquired company soon was renamed Merck-Medco Managed Care.

The wisdom of the purchase was debated among analysts. On one hand, it was regarded as making Merck more competitive in a U.S. healthcare industry dominated by cost-cutting managed care networks and health maintenance organizations. On the other hand, some observers noted that Merck's newest subsidiary would necessarily distribute competitors' drugs and that it had been a major proponent of discounting, which threatened to cut into Merck's R&D funds.

The Medco acquisition also complicated Vagelos's plans for a successor. Vagelos's choice, Richard J. Markham, resigned unexpectedly in mid-1993, just months before the CEO's anticipated retirement. Some observers speculated that 54-year-old Wygod, with his cost-cutting tendencies and marketing forte, was a likely successor, but he, too, resigned in March 1994. In the end, other internal candidates were bypassed as well in favor of the company's first outsider in Merck history to take the top job, Raymond V. Gilmartin. Named CEO in June 1994 and chairman in November of that year, Gilmartin had helped turn around medical equipment maker Becton Dickinson & Co. as that firm's chairman and CEO.

Mid-1990s and Beyond

Although Vagelos had built Merck into its position of industry preeminence by the time of his retirement, the entire pharmaceutical sector was in upheaval stemming from the growth of managed care. Sales and earnings growth were on the decline. Industry pressure resulted in large mergers that created Glaxo Wellcome plc and Novartis AG and toppled Merck from its position as the world's biggest drugmaker to a tie for third place with Germany's Hoechst Marion Roussel. Merck also was suffering from the difficult 18 months it took to find Vagelos's successor and the "turf-conscious, defection-ridden" culture (so described by *Business Week*'s Joseph Weber) that Vagelos left behind. One of Gilmartin's first major tasks, then, was to restructure the company's management team. In September 1994 he set up a 12-member management committee to help him run the company and plot strategies for growth. The management team included sales executives in Europe and Asia, the heads of the veterinary and vaccine divisions, the president of Merck-Medco, and executives from the research, manufacturing, finance, and legal areas. The creation of this committee helped to streamline and flatten Merck's organizational structure, fostered a greater degree of company teamwork, and halted the exodus of top managers that occurred during the Vagelos succession.

One of the management committee's first acts was to create a mission statement for Merck, which affirmed that the company was primarily a research-driven pharmaceutical company. Gilmartin then launched a divestment program, which jettisoned several noncore units, including a generic-drug operation and a managed mental-health care unit. In 1995 Merck sold its Kelco specialty chemicals division to Monsanto Company for $1.1 billion, and its other specialty chemicals unit, Calgon Vestal Laboratories, went to Bristol-Myers Squibb Company for $261 million. These sales also helped Merck pay down the debt it incurred in acquiring Medco, a unit that Gilmartin retained.

There were also two significant divestments in the late 1990s. In July 1997 Merck exited from the agribusiness sector when it sold its crop protection unit to Novartis for $910 million. In July 1998 Merck sold its half-interest in its joint venture with E.I. du Pont to its partner for $2.6 billion. Merck also restructured its animal health unit by combining it with that of Rhone-Poulenc S.A. to form Merial, a stand-alone joint venture created in August 1997. At the end of the 1990s Merial stood as the world's largest firm focusing on the discovery, manufacture, and marketing of veterinary pharmaceuticals and vaccines. By that time, Merck's partner in Merial was Aventis S.A., which had been formed from the late 1999 merger of Rhone-Poulenc and Hoechst A.G.

Another joint venture—the one formed with Astra in 1982—was restructured in the late 1990s. This venture's big-

gest success came with the December 1996 approval of Prilosec for the treatment of ulcers and heartburn. Prilosec went on to become a blockbuster. In July 1998 Merck and Astra agreed to transform the joint venture into a new limited partnership in which Merck would have no management control but would hold a limited partnership interest and receive royalty payments. This gave Astra more flexibility in terms of seeking a merger partner, and in April 1999 the company merged with Zeneca Group Plc to form AstraZeneca AB. Stemming from this merger and the 1998 agreement between Merck and Astra, Merck received from Astra two one-time payments totaling $1.8 billion.

From 1995 through 1999, Merck introduced a total of 15 new drugs. Gilmartin helped bring these new products to market, but credit for developing them fell to Dr. Edward M. Scolnick, the research chief under Vagelos who stayed with the firm even though he had vied to succeed Vagelos. Within 18 months of Gilmartin's arrival, Merck had launched a record eight drugs, including Crixivan, a protease inhibitor used in the treatment of HIV; Fosamax, used to treat osteoporosis; and hypertension medication Cozaar. The eight drugs accounted for more than $1 billion in sales in 1996, about ten percent of the company's total drug sales. Through its joint venture with Johnson & Johnson, Merck also received U.S. approval in April 1995 for the antacid Pepcid AC, an OTC version of Merck's Pepcid.

As the 1990s continued, Merck faced the specter of the expiration of patent protection for some of its biggest-selling products—Vasotec and Pepcid were slated to expire in 2000, Mevacor and Prilosec in 2001. These five drugs generated $5.2 billion in U.S. sales in 1997. Under intense pressure to replace this—at least potentially—lost revenue, Merck continued its torrid pace of product debuts. In 1998 the company introduced a record five drugs: Singulair for asthma, Maxalt for migraine headaches, Aggrastat for acute coronary syndrome, Propecia for hair loss, and Cosopt for glaucoma. Merck managed only one drug introduction in 1999, but it was a blockbuster. Making its U.S. debut in May 1999, Vioxx was part of a new category of pain drugs, dubbed Cox-2 inhibitors. Cox-2, an enzyme present in various diseases, was blocked by the new drugs. As a treatment for arthritis, Vioxx was noteworthy for being effective while not irritating the stomach. Despite being second to market behind G.D. Searle & Co.'s Celebrex, Vioxx had a remarkable first seven months in which U.S. physicians wrote more than five million prescriptions. The new medication was expected to have sales in 2000 of more than $1 billion, a rapid rise to that level.

Merck headed into the uncertainty of the early 21st century riding a triumphant 1999 wave. In addition to its successful introduction of Vioxx, the company was heartened by the continued strength of its top-selling drug, Zocor, which was gaining market share despite intense competition, particularly from Warner-Lambert Company's Lipitor. Zocor was likely to have worldwide sales of more than $5 billion in 2000. Overall sales in 1999 increased 22 percent, reaching $32.71 billion, while net income increased 12 percent to $5.89 billion. Merck's worldwide pharmaceutical sales totaled $12.55 billion in 1999, placing the company in the number one position. This ranking was unlikely to last, however, thanks to two proposed mergers expected to close in 2000: the U.K. marriage of Glaxo Wellcome plc and SmithKline

Beecham plc, and the U.S. coupling of Pfizer Inc. and Warner-Lambert. Merck's Gilmartin stated that he had no interest in such a merger, despite the looming patent expirations. One apparent reason for Gilmartin's go-it-alone approach was the company's rapidly growing Merck-Medco unit, which achieved 1999 sales of $15.23 billion. The unit had established the world's biggest Internet-based pharmacy, merckmedco.com, and formed an alliance with CVS Corporation in 1999 to sell OTC medicines and general health products through this site. Merck-Medco also was helping enhance the sales of Merck drugs, although the FDA launched an investigation in the late 1990s into the practices of pharmacy-benefit management (PBM) firms, including whether any illegalities were taking place in regard to the PBMs steering patients to drugs made by a particular firm. Another reason for optimism about the future of Merck was its continued R&D commitment, represented in 2000 by a $2.4 billion budget. The company's pipeline included a potential blockbuster drug for the treatment of depression and anxiety, which could reach the market by 2001, in addition to several others in various stages of testing.

Principal Subsidiaries

Chibret A/S (Denmark); Hangzhou MSD Pharmaceutical Company Limited (China); International Indemnity Ltd. (Bermuda); Johnson & Johnson-Merck Consumer Pharmaceuticals Company; Laboratorios Prosalud S.A. (Peru); MCM Vaccine Co.; Merck and Company, Incorporated; Merck Capital Investments, Inc.; Merck Capital Resources, Inc.; Merck Enterprises Canada, Ltd.; Merck Foreign Sales Corporation Ltd. (Bermuda); Merck Hamilton, Inc.; Merck Holdings, Inc.; Merck Investment Co., Inc.; Merck Liability Management Company; Merck-Medco Managed Care, L.L.C.; Merck Resource Management, Inc.; Merck Sharp & Dohme (Europe) Inc.; Merck Sharp & Dohme Industria Quimica e Veterinaria Limitada (Brazil); Merck Sharp & Dohme (New Zealand) Limited; Merck Sharp & Dohme Overseas Finance N.V. (Netherland Antilles); Merck Sharp & Dohme (Panama) S.A.; Merck Sharp & Dohme Peru S.C.; Merck Sharp & Dohme (Philippines) Inc.; Merial Limited; MSD International Holdings, Inc.; MSD (Japan) Co., Ltd.; SIBIA Neurosciences, Inc.; The O'Hare Group, Inc.

Principal Competitors

Abbott Laboratories; American Home Products Corporation; Amgen Inc.; Baxter International Inc.; Bayer AG; Boehringer Ingelheim; Bristol-Myers Squibb Company; Eli Lilly and Company; Express Scripts, Inc.; Glaxo Wellcome plc; Monsanto Company; Novartis AG; Pfizer Inc.; Pharmacia & Upjohn, Inc.; The Procter & Gamble Company; Roche Holding Ltd.; Schering-Plough Corporation; SmithKline Beecham plc; Warner-Lambert Company.

Further Reading

Baldo, Anthony, "Merck Plays Hardball," *Financial World,* June 26, 1990, pp. 22+.

Barrett, Amy, "Can Merck Grow Without a Megamerger?," *Business Week,* June 22, 1998, p. 40.

Byrne, John A., "The Miracle Company," *Business Week,* October 19, 1987, pp. 84+.

Cloud, David S., "Pharmacy-Benefit Management Firms Got Subpoenas in Drug-Marketing Probe," *Wall Street Journal,* March 7, 2000, p. B7.

Eklund, Christopher S., and Judith H. Dobrynski, "Merck: Pouring Money into Basic Research to Replace an Aging Product Line," *Business Week,* November 26, 1984, pp. 114+.

Galambos, Louis, and Jane Eliot Sewell, *Networks of Innovation: Vaccine Development at Merck, Sharp, & Dohme, and Mulford, 1895–1995,* New York: Cambridge University Press, 1995.

Gannes, Stuart, "Merck Has Made Biotech Work," *Fortune,* January 19, 1987, p. 58.

Harris, Gardiner, "Cold Turkey: How Merck Intends to Ride Out a Wave of Patent Expirations," *Wall Street Journal,* February 9, 2000, pp. A1, A8.

Koberstein, Wayne, "The Inner Merck: Chairman Ray Gilmartin Charts Pace-Setting Growth," *Pharmaceutical Executive,* January 2000, pp. 44–48+.

Langreth, Robert, "Merck Raises Its Estimate of Astra Sum," *Wall Street Journal,* December 10, 1998, p. B7.

"Mercky Waters," *Economist,* May 24, 1997, pp. 59–61.

Nossiter, Daniel D., "Blue Chip Bet on Research: Merck to Launch Raft of New Products," *Barron's,* November 8, 1982, pp. 16+.

O'Reilly, Brian, "Why Merck Married the Enemy," *Fortune,* September 20, 1993, pp. 60–64.

Reingold, Jennifer, "Mercky Waters," *Financial World,* January 17, 1995, pp. 28–29.

Robertson, Wyndham, "Merck Strains to Keep the Pots Aboiling," *Fortune,* March 1976, p. 134.

Rudnitsky, Howard, "Anticipating Hillary," *Forbes,* August 30, 1993, pp. 44–45.

Scheibla, Shirley Hobbs, "Merck's Main Man: He Sees New Drugs Sparking Continued Growth," *Barron's,* November 11, 1985, pp. 13+.

Seiden, Carl, "Why Merck Has to Run Just to Stay in Place," *Medical Marketing and Media,* August 1998, pp. 38–40, 42, 44, 46.

Smith, Lee, "Merck Has an Ache in Japan," *Fortune,* March 18, 1985, pp. 42+.

Tanouye, Elyse, "Drug Makers' PBM Strategy Produces Uneven Results," *Wall Street Journal,* February 11, 1998, p. B4.

——, "Gilmartin, Merck's New CEO, Expected to Try Approaches He Used at Becton," *Wall Street Journal,* June 13, 1994, p. B6.

——, "Merck's Competition in Key Markets Pressure Earnings," *Wall Street Journal,* July 24, 1998, p. B4.

Tanouye, Elyse, and Stephen D. Moore, "Novartis to Pay $910 Million for Merck Business," *Wall Street Journal,* May 14, 1997, p. A3.

Warren, Susan, "DuPont Is Paying Merck $2.6 Billion to Buy Out 50% Stake in Drug Venture," *Wall Street Journal,* May 20, 1998, p. A4.

Weber, Joseph, "Merck Is Showing Its Age," *Business Week,* August 23, 1993, pp. 72–74.

——, "Merck Needs More Gold from the White Coats," *Business Week,* March 18, 1991, pp. 102+.

——, "Merck Wants to Be Alone—But with Lots of Friends," *Business Week,* October 23, 1989, p. 62.

——, "Mr. Nice Guy with a Mission," *Business Week,* November 25, 1996, pp. 132+.

——, "Suddenly, No Heir Is Apparent at Merck," *Business Week,* July 26, 1993, p. 29.

Weber, Joseph, et al., "Merck Finally Gets Its Man," *Business Week,* June 27, 1994, p. 22.

"What the Doctor Ordered," *Time,* August 18, 1952.

Willatt, Norris, "Merck's Unlimited Medicine," *Management Today,* May 1981, pp. 82+.

—April Dougal Gasbarre
—updated by David E. Salamie

Minnesota Power, Inc.

30 West Superior Street
Duluth, Minnesota 55802-2093
U.S.A.
Telephone: (218) 722-2641
Fax: (218) 723-3996
Web site: http://www.mnpower.com

Public Company
Incorporated: 1906 as Duluth Edison Electric Company
Employees: 8,000
Sales: $1.13 billion (1999)
Stock Exchanges: New York
Ticker Symbol: MPL
NAIC: 221122 Electric Power Distribution

Minnesota Power, Inc., a broadly diversified utility, remains one of the lowest-cost electric producers in the country. Throughout its long history, the company's fortunes have been closely linked to the development of the considerable natural resources in the Arrowhead region of Minnesota. Approximately half of the company's total electric sales go to big industrial customers, particularly taconite and wood products plants. Proportionally, Minnesota Power holds the greatest number of industrial customers among investor-owned electric utilities. To offset this historically beneficial yet potentially limiting dependency, the utility entered into a variety of non-regulated ventures beginning in the 1980s and gained national attention in the process. Minnesota Power's holdings range from ADESA Corporation, one of the country's largest vehicle auction networks, to Lehigh Acquisition Corp., a Florida-based real estate company.

Forerunners: 1880s–1910s

Minnesota Power's roots go back to the late 1880s when small electric utilities were sprouting up across the nation. These early entrepreneurial ventures competed with each other to provide service to growing urban industrial and commercial areas. Duluth, Minnesota, at the southwestern tip of Lake Superior, was a port town receiving timber from the white pine forests of northeastern Minnesota and grain from the Red River Valley to the west. The electric utilities were eager to serve the lumber and shipping businesses on the shore of the big lake and the city itself. To do so, they needed to create an infrastructure to carry the electricity to their customers—a difficult task in a city built on rock.

Alexander W. Hartman was one of the people who was instrumental in electrifying Duluth. As was typical with early utilities ventures, Hartman's efforts materialized in many mergers and acquisitions, ending with the formation of Duluth Edison Electric Company in 1906. The electric power retailer would be one of the principal companies that merged with other regional electric utilities to form Minnesota Power & Light Company (MP&L).

While Hartman and other electric retailers were creating the systems of power lines to deliver the electric power, other visionaries were developing hydroelectric power from the area's abundant water resources. Investment banker Jay Cooke helped lay the groundwork for the construction of a dam on the lower St. Louis River which ran into Lake Superior. The Thomson Hydroelectric Station was constructed in 1907 by Great Northern Power Company, the second of the regional utilities which would form MP&L.

General Light and Power Co. in Cloquet, about 20 miles from Duluth, and the smallest of the four utilities to later form MP&L, had a history that is representative of the physical difficulties of electrifying the region. In Duluth, the utilities had trouble installing electric poles because of the rock bed on which the city was built. The Cloquet utility's problem with nature was the abundance of pine and aspen forests and the occurrence of devastating forest fires. Two such fires, one in the late 19th century and another in the early 20th century, destroyed entire systems of lines and caused more than a thousand deaths. Nature, in northeastern Minnesota, brought disaster on the one hand and on the other provided plentiful resources that served the growing utility industry.

The last decade of the 19th century was marked by the discovery of rich iron ore deposits in northeastern Minnesota. The Minnesota Utilities Company was created in 1917 from smaller utilities vying to serve the booming mining industry; it ranked as the state's third largest supplier of electricity. Usage of electric power by iron mines quadrupled from 1918 to 1924 and quadrupled again by 1929. In 1922, the year before its consolidation with MP&L, the Minnesota Utilities Company was earning a profit on revenues of $544,000.

Political and Economic Climates Shape Utilities: 1920s–40s

On October 23, 1923, Minnesota Power & Light was consolidated by Electric Bond and Share, a subsidiary of the Eastern electrical equipment manufacturer General Electric. The manufacturer, through its subsidiary, had been financially tied to small electric utilities in the area since the 1890s. By 1922, Electric Bond and Share Co., which provided capital for the small utilities, owned most of Duluth Edison Electric Co. and had a controlling interest in the Great Northern Power Company. Minnesota Utilities and General Light and Power entered into agreements with Electric Bond and Share that year. The consolidation of the four utilities was financed with 125,000 shares of preferred stock of American Power and Light Co., a holding company subsidiary, at a par value of $12.5 million. The sale was a complex one which would later be brought under federal scrutiny.

The federal government had encouraged the consolidation of utilities such as MP&L due to the massive needs of World War I, which helped foster the concept of the holding company, as well as the need to link up utility systems in order to provide an adequate supply of power. Herbert Hoover, as secretary of commerce in the early 1920s, promoted this "super power" idea, the networking of electric utilities. In addition, the 1920 Federal Power Act had given electric utilities the right of eminent domain in building and operating hydroelectric dams on rivers.

Not surprisingly then, the 1920s were years of expansion for the newly created Minnesota Power & Light Co. Construction of three dams and the linkage of the four existing utility systems by transmission lines highlighted the decade. Total capitalization rose from about $41 million at the time of consolidation to $70 million at the end of the decade. In those early years, MP&L sold the bulk of its electricity to northeastern Minnesota industries—mines, paper mills, and coal shipping docks. In 1927, 66 percent of its kilowatt hours (kwh) went to industrial customers, and over 50 percent of revenues were derived from fewer than 200 customers. The company ended the decade with $6 million in annual sales.

The Great Depression of the 1930s brought with it social and economic change, and, with the election of Franklin Delano Roosevelt in 1932, the climate for the electric utility holding companies was drastically altered. Legislation created the Tennessee Valley Authority and the Rural Electrification Administration, which were intended to bring power to distressed areas and farmers. In effect, the federally financed projects directly competed with the utilities. The Public Utilities Holding Company Act was also passed, calling for the breakup of the holding companies. In Minnesota, in the region served by MP&L, a movement of local governments emerged to create publicly owned utilities in order to curb costs of electrifying their cities.

In spite of political and economic stresses brought on by the Depression and the accompanying recession in the iron and steel industries, MP&L survived the decade. Electric utilities were a growing industry at the time, and both commercial and residential use increased throughout the 1930s. Stock dividends were down and operations and wages cut back during the worst times, but by the end of the decade MP&L was back up to its 1929 revenue level.

The Roosevelt-era movement to change the face of electric utilities was put on hold in December 1941 when the United States entered World War II. As Bill Beck noted in *Northern Lights: An Illustrated History of Minnesota Power & Light,* "The Sherman tanks rolling off assembly lines in Detroit, the airplanes being assembled in the California plants, the aircraft carriers sliding down the ways in East Coast shipyards—all were dependent upon the soft, red iron ore of the Mesabi Range."

When the war ended, MP&L focused on recapitalization of its stock and reclassification of its accounts. The recapitalization was due to the 1935 Public Holding Company Act, which required subsidiaries to be separated from their holding companies. The reclassification was the result of other federal action in the 1930s. During an investigation of electric holding companies, MP&L was found to have overvalued stock at the time of consolidation. The decade was also marked by MP&L's decision to move from hydroelectric generation of power to coal-fired steam generation. Coincidentally, the region was facing the worst drought in decades. Nevertheless, MP&L weathered the turmoil and finished the 1940s financially strong while setting new records for power usage.

Independent Yet Interconnected: 1950s–70s

MP&L entered the 1950s by terminating its affiliation with American Power and Light as its holding company. Thus Minnesota Power began the new decade as a small utility serving the seasonal needs of the iron ore industry, with 58 percent of its power coming from hydroelectric sources and 42 percent through steam generation. It was a decade of increased defense needs due to the Korean War and a rapid increase of residential use due to widespread home modernization. MP&L's speedy construction of steam generating stations resulted in the first rate increase in its history. Economic diversification of the region helped MP&L grow. The St. Lawrence Seaway connected Duluth with the Atlantic Ocean, paper production in the city was expanded, and commercial ventures were on the rise. The 1950s also saw the advent of atomic power in utilities.

The 1960s marked the end of MP&L's relative isolation from other utilities when the company linked with the two other large utilities in the state, Northern States Power and Otter Tail

Power. MP&L expanded its power pooling and transfer of bulk power through a regional grid when the Minnesota utilities joined those in Iowa and Wisconsin to form the Upper Mississippi Valley Power Pool in 1961. In 1963, the Midcontinental Area Power Planners linked 22 power suppliers in ten states and Canada.

The decade also proved a politically charged one for the utility, as it fought the expansion of federally funded electric cooperatives and pressure from Minnesota Senator Hubert H. Humphrey regarding MP&L's own rates. However, the company benefited from the passage of Minnesota's taconite amendment, which would revitalize the fading iron ore industry in the Arrowhead region. In 1968, the company decided to shift from high-sulfur Eastern coal to low-sulfur Western coal and began initiating extensive plant construction and adaptation of existing plants.

The 1970s was a growth decade for MP&L and the taconite industry, which unlike the iron ore industry demanded electric power 24 hours a day throughout the year. Revenues went from $50 million to $281 million in the ten-year period. As the taconite plants grew MP&L kept pace by adding additional coal-fired generating stations. According to Beck, "During the latter half of the decade, MP&L was perhaps the fastest growing electric utility in the United States." During the decade, the company also increased its power supply through a cooperative project with a utility in North Dakota. The Square Butte Electric Cooperative offered access to the area's vast lignite coal reserves through a 400,000 kilowatt mine-mouth generating plant and sent power to Minnesota via a state-of-the-art AC/DC transmission line. On the political front MP&L was entering the era of federal and state environmental regulation. The 1970s also marked the end of a 40-year trend toward lower rates. The low point of 2.26 cents per kwh in 1967 doubled to 4.51 cents in 1979.

In 1980, the company changed its name to Minnesota Power and began the decade with legal proceedings, fighting a 30 percent severance tax on Montana coal and a 62 percent rate increase by Burlington Northern Railroad, its sole rail shipper. More foreboding for the utility, however, was the national economic recession. The recession hit the taconite industry hard and production of the low-grade ore fell 40 percent from 1979 to 1982. In an effort to cut costs the utility trimmed 15 percent of its workforce between 1980 and 1985. Anthony Carideo, in an article for a November 1984 edition of the *Minneapolis Star Tribune,* observed that "Five years ago, Minnesota Power looked like a candidate for the poor house. Strapped with an $850 million construction program, the Duluth-based utility was at the door of the Minnesota Public Utilities Commission (PUC) for rate increases every year except one between 1976 and 1981. Faced with a nearly insolvent utility, state regulators allowed the company to bill consumers for millions of dollars in construction costs before the work was finished, a concession it had never made before to any utility and has allowed only once since." The company comeback was also served by the take-or-pay contracts it had entered into with the taconite companies when the industry was booming and they were building plants to keep up with the demand for power. Under such contracts, the companies had agreed to pay for a certain level of use each month whether they used it or not. However, by the mid-1980s, the taconite producers wanted out of the contracts.

Drive Toward Diversification: 1980s–Early 1990s

Fortunately, Minnesota Power had by then built a profitable investment portfolio (stocks and bonds of other utilities) and had formed a subsidiary, Topeka Group, Inc., which owned a five-state telephone firm and a water and wastewater treatment company in Florida. The utility was also embarking on a joint venture with St. Paul-based Pentair, Inc. to build a high-tech supercalender paper plant in Duluth. The plan was to keep investments in regulated and core support industries. Minnesota Power had used the post-construction cash buildup it had beginning in 1981 for its investments rather than give large stockholder dividends. By 1985, the company was looking at a 44 percent market return (stock movement plus dividends) according to Standard and Poor's, while the industry average was 25 percent. The company also exceeded the industry's five-year compound earnings growth and dividend growth with increases of 13 and eight percent, respectively. A December 1989 *Forbes* article reported that Minnesota Power had the second lowest electric utility rates in the country at 4.2 cents per kwh yet was among the most profitable with a five-year average return on equity of 15.8 percent. *Forbes* also reported that by the end of 1989 the utility had sold its telephone investment for three times the purchase price, expanded its water and wastewater ventures, and purchased a coal mining venture to serve its North Dakota power generation interests. Minnesota Power also sold about 100 megawatts of surplus capacity—a problem since the taconite industry downturn—to a group of Wisconsin municipal utilities. The company still gained 57 percent of its $460 million in operating revenue from electric sales to industrial customers, compared with a 30 percent utility industry average.

The 1990s marked a change in the company's approach to its largest customer, the taconite industry. Jack Rowe, who led the company during the taconite hey days, had stood firm on the take-or-pay contracts. With Arend "Sandy" Sandbulte at the helm, the company began to renegotiate rates to the remaining taconite plants, giving a 20 to 30 percent decrease in rates and shortening the length of contracts. The company continued to look toward a future that was less dependent on the taconite industry with a goal of accelerating the contributions of non-electric businesses to over 60 percent of total revenue by the year 2000.

The 1990s also saw increased involvement by Minnesota Power in the economic development of the Arrowhead region. Minnesota Power not only provided funding for start-up businesses but offered financial support as part of a state package to attract a Northwest Airlines' maintenance base and reservations center to Duluth and the Iron Range. In another move to create usage for its core business of electric power, Minnesota Power created Synertec, a waste paper reclamation subsidiary. In partnership with four competing paper mills, Synertec opened a $76 million paper recycling plant in Duluth, named Superior Recycled Fiber Industries.

In spite of Minnesota Power's move toward decreased dependency on the taconite industry, the company's financial strength was still clearly tied to it. When National Steel Co., one of its largest customers, shut down its Keewatin plant indefinitely in the fall of 1993, Minnesota Power experienced a more than $2 a share fall on the stock market. The utility responded by actively working with other stakeholders in the taconite industry to facilitate the restarting of the Japanese-owned plant. By mid-1994, new corporate management at National's subsidiary had recommitted to fully integrated steel operations and was prepared to end the deadlock and resume operations, following various concessions and the approval of union steelworkers. National Steel Pellet and Minnesota Power arrived at a new electric rate deal in July 1994.

In January 1994, Minnesota filed for a rate increase of up to 25 percent for residential and commercial customers. The last rate increase Minnesota Power had filed for was in 1987, one which was successfully fought by the Minnesota Senior Federation's Northeastern Coalition. Subsequently, rates for homes and businesses had not risen in 12 years. The utility asserted in the filing that industrial users had been carrying an unfair share of the company's costs; the Minnesota Public Utilities Commission granted the company a residential retail rate increase.

Also during this time, the company faced more changes on the regulatory front. The state of Minnesota began to require that utilities include environmental costs—such as air emissions of coal-burning plants—in the estimate of the costs of future plants.

In terms of the bottom line, a downturn in its usually strong investment portfolio, losses by the company's hydraulic lifting equipment company, Reach All, Inc., and heavy rainfall in Florida which depressed water utility revenue, all conspired to drop Minnesota Power's earnings to its lowest point in a decade.

Risky Route for Utility: Mid- to Late 1990s

In early 1995, Minnesota Power earned the scorn of some market analysts when the utility announced its intention to purchase North America's third largest auto auction company. Indianapolis-based ADESA Corporation sold 400,000 vehicles in 1994, up from 112,000 two years earlier, and netted $7.7 million.

"I think this is a negative for shareholders," Eric Elverkrog, an analyst with Chicago-based Duff & Phelps, said in a January

1995 *Duluth News-Tribune* article. "Buying an auto auction business is not a good strategic fit for Minnesota Power." Elverkrog questioned the utility's ability to successfully negotiate the twists and turns of a rapid-growth industry.

About mid-year 1995, Minnesota Power pulled out of Lake Superior Paper, the joint venture with Pentair, and sold Reach All, freeing up resources for its other pursuits. Following the acquisition of an 80 percent share in ADESA in July, the company moved to bolster its real estate holdings. Minnesota Power had entered the Florida market in 1991 with the purchase of Lehigh Acres, a home site development near Fort Myers. In September 1995, Minnesota Power bought into Sugarmill Woods Communities, a development north of Tampa and, in April 1996, closed a deal to purchase nearly one-third of Palm Coast, a planned community south of St. Augustine.

Meanwhile, skepticism regarding the auto auction investment led Standard and Poor's to lower Minnesota Power's bond rating early in 1996. ADESA's earnings performance proved to be weaker than expected during its first few quarters under Minnesota Power majority ownership. Responding to the situation, the utility sped up the time table for acquiring the last shares of the company from the founder and remaining executives and gained 100 percent ownership in August 1996.

Elsewhere, Minnesota Power was fine-tuning its core electric operations. The utility negotiated long-term contracts with some of its large industrial customers, including an 11-year agreement with USX Corporation's Minntac iron ore processing plant, one of the top electric users in the country. By and large, previous long-term contracts with large customers had been tied to lender stipulations on new plant construction, but the move toward deregulation of the electric industry prompted Minnesota Power to stabilize those important relationships. One scenario in the restructuring of electric utility markets foresaw a time when Minnesota Power would be required to give transmission line access to competitors and therefore vie for the business of long established customers.

In the same vein, Minnesota Power launched a new power marketing division, MPEX, in 1996. The utility had been involved in group buying and selling of energy for 25 years, but the move further positioned the company to take advantage of opportunities in the wholesale power market which had largely been deregulated by state and federal lawmakers. Bulk power sales were the main contributor to the 14 percent increase in electric sales during 1996.

Developments in the water services segment included a name change for the Florida water utility affiliate. Southern States Utilities was renamed Florida Water Services. Minnesota Power also purchased a Florida-based predictive, preventive, and corrective maintenance company, Instrumentation Services, Inc., (ISI), which served clients such as Coca-Cola, Amoco, and the city of Houston. The utility largely pulled out of South Carolina, blaming the difficult regulatory environment, but it continued to push for regulatory relief in Florida operations, seeking the right to charge higher rates.

As Minnesota Power's auto auction business began to significantly contribute to earnings, analysts changed their tune about the utility's endeavor. "This was for years the stock that everyone loved to hate,'' said David Thickens, a Dain Bosworth analyst, in a June 1997 *Knight-Ridder/Tribune News* article. The Minnesota-based investment firm rated Minnesota Power a good buy during a time when utility stocks in general were sagging due to deregulation uncertainties. Minnesota Power, in addition to making gains with ADESA, was a solidly positioned, low-rate utility without the burdens related to nuclear power plants.

In 1997, Minnesota Power established a new telecommunications subsidiary, MP Telecom. Through MP Telecom, the utility sold bandwidth off its fiber optic network, a system established in the early 1970s to link far-flung substations and power plants. Minnesota Power's was the first utility-owned network in the nation. The company planned to offer system access to high volume users such as long distance phone companies, large businesses, and internet providers—the Telecommunications Act of 1996 had opened the door to this market.

Also in 1997, the utility added two new subsidiaries to the water services division: U.S. Maintenance and Management and America's Water Services, providing, respectively, predictive maintenance services and water and wastewater services. Elsewhere, ADESA's Automotive Finance Corp. (AFC) began providing dealer financing at independent auto auctions in the United States and Canada, expanding for the first time outside the ADESA. AFC wrote short-term inventory loans for wholesale and retail car dealers buying vehicles at those various auction sites.

The 1998 annual report touted ADESA as the fastest-growing automotive remarketing company in North America, and reported AFC had doubled in size every year since the 1995 purchase. In spite of the impressive gains, electric operations continued to produce the lion's share of Minnesota Power's operating revenues. On the year, profitability continued upward, and operating revenue topped $1 billion for the first time in company history.

1999/2000: Charging Up for an Electric Future?

Early in 1999, Minnesota Power moved to gain a toehold in the Chicago market as it signed an agreement to purchase electricity from a power plant to be constructed 30 miles southwest of the city. While electric consumption was stagnant in the company's retail service area, Chicago utilities needed to purchase excess power through the wholesale market, especially during the hot summer months. Down in Florida, Minnesota Power expanded its real estate holdings, buying about 2,500 acres of Cape Coral residential, commercial, and recreational properties for $45 million. North Carolina-based Heater Utilities acquired Mid-South Water Systems, Inc. in 1999 and was ranked as that state's largest investor-owned water business.

Faring less well in another area of its investments, Minnesota Power took a non-cash charge of $36.2 million against 1999 net operating income due to events related to the sale of Capital Re Corporation to ACE Ltd. The 21 percent interest Minnesota Power held in the reinsurance company represented a key component of its investment portfolio. Capital Re's value begun to plummet in the second half of 1998 due in part to extraordinary claims generated by a bankrupt client.

As automotive services continued to grow, so did the expectation that the segment would overtake Minnesota Power's electric business as the largest producer of net income early into the 21st century. ADESA operated 29 vehicle auction sites and was poised to enter the hot Los Angeles market. Other Minnesota Power automotive businesses offered customers such options as transport and information services. On the whole, automotive net income jumped 57 percent in 1999; electric operations net income declined.

Minnesota Power entered 2000 exclaiming, ''Now, more than ever, Minnesota Power is more than Minnesota . . . and more than power.'' While seemingly well positioned to negotiate the changing electric utility landscape, future growth was clearly tied to relatively new endeavors, particularly the automobile auction business. Stockholders and analysts alike would be sure to keep a watchful eye on Minnesota Power's progress on both fronts.

Principal Subsidiaries

ADESA Corporation; Lehigh Acquisition Corp.; Automotive Finance Corporation; Minnesota Power Telecom, Inc.; BNI Coal, Ltd.; Florida Water Services Corporation.

Principal Operating Units

Automotive; Water; Investments; Electric.

Principal Competitors

Alliant Energy Corporation; Copart, Inc.; Northern States Power Company; Otter Tail Power Company.

Further Reading

Adams, Paul, ''Minnesota Power Aims to Use Its Fiber Optic Network to Enter Telecom Market,'' *Duluth News-Tribune*, January 27, 1998.
——, ''Minnesota Power Rated a Good Buy,'' *Knight-Ridder/Tribune Business News*, June 5, 1997.
——, ''Minnesota Power Swaps Stake in Capital Re for Stake in ACE,'' *Knight-Ridder/ Tribune Business News*, January 4, 2000.
Beck, Bill, ''Do You Know Your Company Roots?,'' *Electric Perspectives,* Winter 1986, pp. 63–64.
——, *Northern Lights: An Illustrated History of Minnesota Power,* Duluth: Minnesota Power, 1986.
Breimhurst, Henry, ''Bundling Utilities,'' *Minneapolis/St. Paul City-Business*, January 16, 1998, pp. 19, 22.
Brissett, Jane, ''Minnesota Power Passages,'' *Corporate Report Minnesota,* April 1988, pp. 115–16.
Brochu, Ron, ''Minnesota Utility Attributes Net-Income Increase to Diversification,'' *Knight-Ridder/Tribune Business News*, October 18, 1999.
Carideo, Anthony, ''Blindsided in Duluth,'' *Star Tribune* (Minneapolis), October 21, 1993, p. 1D.
——, ''LSPI's New Plant: A Thriving 1-Year-Old,'' *Star Tribune* (Minneapolis), March 20, 1989, p. 1D.
——, ''Minnesota Power Is Busy Generating Revenues,'' *Star Tribune,* November 11, 1984, p. 1D.
Cook, James, ''Deft Management,'' *Forbes,* December 11, 1989, pp. 96, 100, 105.
''Corporate Capsule: Minnesota Power & Light Co.,'' *Minneapolis/St. Paul CityBusiness*, May 12, 1995, p. 24.

DeSilver, Drew, "Minnesota Power Fuels Up on Real Estate," *Minneapolis/St. Paul CityBusiness*, April 12, 1996, p. 2.

"Duluth-Based Minnesota Power to Make Stock Swap," *Duluth News-Tribune*, May 28, 1999.

"Duluth, Minn.-Based Power Company Enters Illinois Market," *Duluth News-Tribune*, March 19, 1999.

Egerstrom, Lee, "Minnesota Power Signs Major Electricity Pact with Inland Steel Co.," *St. Paul Pioneer Press*, February 6, 1997.

——, "Pentair, Minnesota Power Agree to Sell Duluth-Based Lake Superior Paper," *St. Paul Pioneer Press*, May 10, 1995.

"The Good, The Bad, and Minnesota Power," *Corporate Report Minnesota*, March 1981, pp. 26–30.

"How Minnesota Power Deals with the Dreaded "D Word," *Electrical World*, December 1990, pp. 20–21.

Lappen, Alyssa A., "Gene's Dream," *Forbes*, May 30, 1988, pp. 212–15.

Marcotty, Josephine, "Minnesota Power Charging Ahead," *Star Tribune* (Minneapolis), June 8, 1987, p. 1M.

Marx, Patrick, "Railroad Issue Threatens Utility's Coal Future," *Star Tribune* (Minneapolis), November 9, 1980, p. 1D.

Mattson, Beth, "Strategic Alliances," *Minnesota Business & Opportunities*, March 1997, pp. 28–29.

McDonnell, Lynda, "Utility Navigates New Route," *Pioneer Press & Dispatch* (St. Paul), February 10, 1986, pp. 1, 10–11.

Meersman, Tom, "PUC Says Utilities Must Start Tallying Ecological Costs of Power Plants," *Star Tribune* (Minneapolis), February 5, 1994, p. 1B.

Miller, Joe, "Utility's Auto Division May Over Power Its Parent," *Automotive News*, May 17, 1999, p. 32.

"Minnesota Power Posts 47% Drop in Quarterly Earnings," *Star Tribune* (Minneapolis), April 23, 1994, p. 2D.

"Minnesota Power Subsidiary Buys Vibration Correction Services in Duluth," *Duluth News-Tribune*, June 18, 1998.

"Minnesota Power Subsidiary to Acquire Florida Properties," *Knight-Ridder/Tribune Business News*, May 6, 1999.

"Minnesota Utility Promotes Top Executive, Focuses on Deregulation," *Knight-Ridder/Tribune Business News*, January 9, 2000.

Morse, Mary, "Pulp Romance," *Corporate Report Minnesota*, June 1986, pp. 80–83.

——, "There's No Place Like Home," *Corporate Report Minnesota*, April 1992, pp. 50–54.

Oakes, Larry, "Duluth Utility Requests Rate Increase," *Star Tribune* (Minneapolis), January 5, 1994, p. 2B.

——, "9-Month Deadlock, 3-Day Solution; New Management Key to Keewatin Plant Agreement," *Star Tribune* (Minneapolis), June 28, 1994, p. 5B.

——, "Officials Promise Iron Range Placement Assistance," *Star Tribune* (Minneapolis), October 23, 1993, p. 1B.

——, "U.S. Union Leaders to Appeal to Tokyo Firm," *Star Tribune* (Minneapolis), January 15, 1994, p. 2B.

"People," *Electrical World*, September 1988, p. 29.

Peterson, Susan E., "New Paper Out of Old," *Star Tribune* (Minneapolis), October 6, 1993, p. 1D.

Vazzano, Sheri, "Aspen Aerials of Duluth, Minn., Buys Division of Defunct Reach All," *Duluth News-Tribune*, June 23, 1995.

——, "Minnesota Power Sells Plant, but Jobs Remain in Duluth, Minn.," *St. Paul Pioneer Press*, April 26, 1995.

——, "Minnesota Power to Acquire Majority of Shares in Indiana's ADESA," *Duluth New-Tribune*, January 6, 1995.

Welbes, John, "Minnesota Power Buys ADESA Car Auction Firm, to Name New Chief," *Duluth News-Tribune*, August 22, 1996.

——, "Minnesota Power Hopes Offbeat Electrical Products Will Popularize Store," *Duluth News-Tribune*, November 8, 1996.

—Jay P. Pederson
—updated by Kathleen Peippo

ROLEX

Montres Rolex S.A.

Rue Francois-Dussaud 3
Case Postale 92
1211 Geneva 24
Switzerland
Telephone: 41 22 308-2200
Fax: 41 22 300-2255
Web site: http://www.rolex.com

Private Company
Incorporated: 1905 as Wilsdorf & Davis
Employees: 2,800
NAIC: 334518 Watch, Clock, and Part Manufacturing;
    42194 Jewelry, Watch, Precious Stone, and Precious
    Metal Wholesalers; 81149 Other Personal and
    Household Goods Repair and Maintenance

Montres Rolex S.A. is the best known of the premier producers of fine watches in the world. Recognized as an innovator in technology and marketing, the company is credited with establishing the widespread popularity of the wristwatch in the early 20th century. Rolex watches are prized for their precision timekeeping, durability, functionality, and distinctive design. Rolex's mystique as a closely held private company and its carefully cultivated image continue to strengthen the watch's desirability as a status symbol as well as a precision instrument. Based in Geneva, Switzerland, where the company opened a new headquarters in 1995, Rolex has become closely linked with a number of major events in such sports as yachting, equestrian riding, golf, and tennis. Rolex watches—available in stainless steel, gold, and platinum, and with or without custom-set precious stones on the dial, crystal, or band—retail anywhere from $2,400 to over $100,000.

Developing the Wristwatch: Late 1800s and Early 1900s

The company's founder, Hans Wilsdorf, was born in Kulmbach, Bavaria, on March 22, 1881. One of three children, Wilsdorf was orphaned at the age of 12. He was raised by his uncles, who encouraged him to be independent and self-reliant at a very early age. According to Osvaldo Patrizzi, author of *Orologi Da Polso Rolex,* Wilsdorf later attributed his success to that early upbringing. As a teenager, Wilsdorf studied mathematics and languages at school and apprenticed with a prominent exporter of artificial pearls. At 19 he went to work as an errand boy and English translator for Cuno Kourten, a major clock and watch exporter in La Chaux de Fonds, Switzerland, which, along with Geneva, formed the hub of the high-quality watchmaking industry at the time. There, Wilsdorf was exposed to the most influential people and practices in watchmaking, which would later be an important asset in the founding and success of Rolex.

In 1903 Wilsdorf moved to London, where he worked for a large watch store. Two years later, he borrowed money from his sister and brother-in-law to establish his own company, Wilsdorf & Davis, with his brother-in-law a partner in the venture. Wilsdorf chose London for his new enterprise at least in part because of its position at the time as the world's economic center. Its colonial holdings gave England tremendous wealth as well as a network of trade avenues that would later be advantageous in Rolex's international business.

Wilsdorf soon distinguished his company from its many successful competitors in two essential ways. First, he was tireless and methodical in pursuit of perfection in his products. Second, he specialized in unusual items, most notably the wristwatch. Pocket watches were still the accepted timepiece, with wristwatches considered inelegant and useful only for specialty purposes, such as sporting activities, where it was impractical to consult a pocket watch. The association of the wristwatch with hard physical work gave it a rough reputation that was distasteful to the genteel consumer. In his book *Timeless Elegance— Rolex,* George Gordon noted that men of the time were heard to say they would ''sooner wear a skirt than a wristwatch!''

The wristwatch also presented logistical difficulties, including ensuring accuracy in so small a device and avoiding damage in the watch's unprotected position on the outside of the wrist: unlike a pocket watch, a wristwatch was exposed to blows, moisture, and dust. Shipments of wristwatches sent abroad were often found to have rusted by the time they arrived from exposure to dampness.

Company Perspectives:

Ever since its creation, Rolex has consistently focused on establishing the renown of the Rolex brand worldwide, ensuring that the Oyster is far more than a passing trend. To safeguard its reputation for quality and reliability, Rolex has created a global network of specialists who alone are qualified to guarantee Rolex owners worldwide of the authenticity of their watch and the dependability of the features which ensure its longevity.

These obstacles were a galvanizing force for Wilsdorf, who cast a shrewd eye to the future. He calculated that resistance to the wristwatch would wane as its usefulness grew with the changing times. The wristwatch was already becoming more popular with young people and with the fashion world, which appreciated its ornamental value.

The wristwatch was also becoming more suitable for an increasingly active and mobile society. Technological innovations made travel to distant shores available to a significant number of people. People also began to appreciate a variety of new sports that required rugged, specialized equipment, of which the wristwatch became an indispensable part. Flying expeditions, car racing, mountain climbing, and sea exploration grew in popularity and caught the public imagination. Rough and tumble sports began to take on a reputation as romantic and adventurous. Rolex would capitalize on these associations and promote this image heavily in its marketing materials.

Early in his venture, Wilsdorf demonstrated his nature as a risk-taker and innovator by making a large investment in small caliber lever escapement wristwatches. He spent several hundred thousand Swiss francs, five times the capital of his firm, on the first order. Wilsdorf purchased the internal mechanisms from the Swiss firm of Herman Aegler, a manufacturer whose reputation for quality Wilsdorf knew from his time as an apprentice. The mechanisms were machine-made and so were available at a reasonable price; they were also durable and precise.

To house the mechanisms, Wilsdorf supplied the cases, which he purchased from well-known English manufacturers. The cases were made in sterling silver and three types of gold in a wide array of styles for dress, casual, or sportswear. The watches sold briskly in England and abroad, including the Far East. Working in concert with Aegler on logistical aspects of production, Wilsdorf developed a line of immensely popular watches.

Introducing the Rolex: 1908

The next several years saw many changes and innovations at Wilsdorf & Davis. In 1906 Wilsdorf introduced the expandable metal watch strap. This style of strap, made to match the watch case, would become a signature Rolex look continuing to the present day. The next year, Wilsdorf opened a technical office at La Chaux de Fonds, Switzerland. Wilsdorf delegated the management of that office, obtained British citizenship, and settled in London, marrying a short time later. In 1908 he coined the name ''Rolex'' to establish a signature brand that would distin-

guish his product from other watches that may even have contained the same parts. Wilsdorf reportedly settled on the name Rolex because it was easy to pronounce in different languages and short enough to show clearly on a watch face.

This move demonstrated Wilsdorf's farsightedness. Although it later became common practice to use one brand name for the entire watch, this was a new idea at the time. As watch parts came from different manufacturers and distributors, it was the retailer's name that appeared on the watch face and internal movements. Wilsdorf justified his desire to use his own trade name by maintaining that the watches he sold had to meet more stringent quality criteria than either the manufacturer or the other suppliers required. Initially, Wilsdorf met with great resistance from retailers. By placing only a small number of watches with the name ''Rolex'' on the face with the other watches in an order, Wilsdorf was able to convince retailers to take the Rolex-brand watches along with the ones stamped with the retailer's name. He gradually introduced the Rolex name in the marketplace by increasing the proportion of Rolex watches in his shipments over time. An intensive marketing campaign later solidified the name recognition of Rolex. By establishing an identity separate from that of the retailer, Wilsdorf had shifted the balance of control in his favor, and retailers came to rely on the Rolex name as a customer draw as much as Wilsdorf relied on the retailers for market exposure.

At the time that Wilsdorf established the Rolex brand name, he began to focus in earnest on the production of wristwatches with the accuracy of a chronometer. Two milestone awards were bestowed on his timepieces in 1910 and 1914. In 1910 Wilsdorf & Davis was given the world's first certificate of a first-class chronometer for a wristwatch from the School of Horology at Bienne, Switzerland. In 1914 a Rolex wristwatch was awarded a Class A certificate by the distinguished Kew Observatory in England, the first given to a wrist chronometer. The certificate required passing a series of tests over 45 days. The watch was tested in five different positions and three different temperatures, including ambient (65 degrees Fahrenheit), oven-hot, and refrigerator-cold. After earning its Class A certificate, the company insisted that all Rolex watches would be required to meet chronometer standards, and none would be sold without a certificate. In fact, self-imposed standards were applied to all of the internal mechanisms received from outside suppliers. If the movements did not meet the standards after seven days of rigorous testing, they were rejected. The reputation of the Rolex as a quality instrument continued to grow.

Postwar import tax increases prompted Wilsdorf to move his company headquarters to Switzerland in 1919. He established Montres Rolex S.A. in Geneva and retained the London office as a branch office. In the 1920s, Wilsdorf established Rolex's image as a sportsman's technological tool. He tackled the problems of moisture, dust, and heat resistance and began working toward an automatic winding mechanism. He introduced new styles that were waterproof, lightweight, and durable. He also began a series of innovative marketing events showcasing Rolex watches in real-world action. As he introduced new models, he would link them to events generating new records in sporting and technological achievement. In particular, he focused on sports events requiring considerable daring and, most often, considerable means. The elite sporting associations made

Rolex popular not only with sportsmen but also with wealthy spectators as the watch became a status symbol. In 1925 Rolex registered the crown trademark, a symbol of its elite aspirations.

Rolex introduced the Rolex Oyster, the world's first waterproof, airtight wristwatch in 1926. He patented the twinlock and triplock screw-down crown and the waterproof case. The following year marked the first of many record-setting marketing events. Mercedes Gleitz swam the English Channel in the record time of 15 hours and 15 minutes, wearing a Rolex watch. When she emerged, the watch had kept perfect time. To capitalize on the event, Rolexes were often displayed in aquariums in jewelers' windows. By 1927, "Rolex" was printed on the case, movement, and dial of all Rolex watches. The following year saw the introduction of the Rolex Prince, an elegantly styled timepiece that gained a reputation as a gentleman's watch.

Technological Innovations in the 1930s

In 1931 Rolex introduced the Rolex Oyster Perpetual, the first waterproof, self-winding wristwatch. The rotor automatic winding mechanism, invented by Rolex's technical chief, was semicircular and able to turn both clockwise and counterclockwise, so that the movement of a wrist could wind it. The watch was even more accurate than a traditional watch, since the tension put on the mechanism by constant winding was greater than that provided by winding done once a day. In another marketing coup, in 1935 a Rolex Oyster went over 300 miles per hour on the wrist of Sir Malcolm Campbell as he set the world land-speed record in his race car at Salt Lake Flats.

The 1940s were a significant decade for the future of Rolex. In 1944, Wilsdorf's wife died after a four-day illness. The couple had no children, and Wilsdorf was determined to protect the business he had created, even after his death. He set up the Hans Wilsdorf Foundation and transferred his interest in Rolex to the foundation, creating a governing council and detailing precisely how he wanted the funds handled. His specifications included large donations to charity, horological institutions, universities, and professional schools.

Rolex achieved an industry record in 1945 with 50,000 certificates for wrist chronometers. The company introduced four new models over the next few years, the Date Just in 1945, the Rolex Moonphase in 1947, and the Rolex Day/Date/Month and the Oyster Day/Date/Month in 1949.

In 1953 Rolex enjoyed another marketing coup when the British Himalayas Expedition reached the summit of Mount Everest wearing Rolex Oyster Perpetuals—which lost no accuracy in extreme weather and rough handling. A new Day/Date model was introduced in 1956 that had the day written in full in one of 26 languages. The first automatic waterproof watch, the Submariner, was introduced in 1953, with resistance to 100 meters' depth, and the GMT Master, a watch for pilots that tracked time in two different time zones simultaneously, was introduced in 1955.

In early 1960, Rolex performed its most astonishing feat when the bathyscaphe Trieste emerged from 35,798 feet with a special Oyster attached to its outside still running perfectly. The watch had been exposed to a pressure of almost seven tons per square inch.

Later that year Hans Wilsdorf died at the age of 78, and in 1963 André Heiniger assumed leadership of the company. Heiniger, born in 1921 at La Chaux de Fonds, continued to guide the firm in much the same way Wilsdorf had. During Heiniger's tenure, however, tradition became more the focus than innovation. Rolex continued to do well by keeping quality high and production relatively low, maintaining a steady course through fluctuations in the economy, explosions in the price of components such as gold, and the flood of electronic parts into the watchmaking industry.

In 1971 Rolex introduced the Oyster Perpetual "Sea Dweller," the first diving watch with a helium valve for saturation diving, which was waterproof to 2,000 feet. In 1975 six divers won the world diving record off the Labrador coast in Canada, reaching 350 meters wearing Rolex Sea Dwellers. In 1978 Rolex introduced a quartz movement Oyster, waterproof to 165 feet and resistant to magnetic pull up to 1,000 oersted. The same year, a Rolex Oyster Quartz reached the top of Mount Everest, as Reinhold Messner made a significant climb without an oxygen mask. In 1973 Tom Shepperd crossed the Sahara wearing a Rolex Oyster GMT Master, which was unimpaired by exposure to extreme heat or sand storms.

Success Symbol: The 1980s and Beyond

During the 1980s, Rolex introduced improved versions of its traditional styles. The Rolex Oyster Perpetual Chronograph Chronometer Daytona with tachometer was introduced in 1988, and by 1989 over half of all the Swiss chronometers certified by the Swiss Institutes for Chronometers had been produced by Rolex. The year 1990 marked the manufacture of ten million chronometers. New models such as the Oyster Perpetual Yachtmaster built on Rolex's reputation for creating instruments for the elite sporting set, and advertising targeted such upscale magazines as *Gourmet* and *Outside,* showing Rolex watches in action with such elite performers as the U.S Equestrian Team and the U.S. Sailing Team.

From the early 1960s through the mid-1990s, Rolex's sales increased by approximately 20 percent a year, while the production of about 500,000 watches a year, well short of demand, kept the price high. In fact, Rolex was so successful in creating a status icon that counterfeiting became a major issue for the company. To deter counterfeiters, Rolex invested in an anti-counterfeiting device that was not reproducible. Equally inimitable was the quality built into each timepiece; in the 1990s Rolex remained one of only a few Swiss manufacturers still doing a majority of hand building, carefully guarding its niche as a producer of durable luxury chronometers.

In the 1990s, Rolex introduced two new models, each the result of some five years of development. The first of these debuted in 1992, as the Oyster Professional Yacht-Master. The second, introduced in 2000, was directed at the women's market and extended the company's Oyster Daytona range, with the Oyster Perpetual Daytona for women. In 1992, Rolex's board of directors appointed Patrick Heiniger to lead the company into the next millennium. Heiniger continued the company's association with the high-end sports bracket, placing the Rolex name on such prestigious sporting events as the U.S. PGA Championship tournament, The U.S. and British Masters golf tournaments, the Rolex International Polo and Equestrian Championship, as well as events in the professional tennis and yachting sports circuits. In 1995, Rolex moved into new headquarters, known as Rolex VII, located on the outskirts of Geneva and housing some one-third of the company's employees. There, the company remained committed to its tradition of excellence and quality.

Principal Subsidiaries

Rolex Watch U.S.A., Inc.; The Rolex Watch Co., Ltd. (U.K.).

Principal Competitors

LVMH Moët Hennessy Louis Vuitton SA; Movado Group, Inc.; Compagnie Financiere Richemont AG; The Swatch Group SA; TAG Heuer International SA.

Further Reading

Aehl, John, "Rolex Presents Its Big Moments in Time," *Wisconsin State Journal*, October 29, 1993, p. 1.

Gordon, George, *Timeless Elegance—Rolex*, Hong Kong: Zie Yongder Co., Ltd., 1989.

Jardine, Cassandra, "Timeless Mystique of the Rolex," *Business-London*, February 1988, pp. 114–17.

Patrizzi, Osvaldo, *Orologi Da Polso Rolex*, Milano: Antiqorum Italia Srl, 1992.

"Rolex Plans $10 Million Site Near Lititz; Ultra-Secretive Maker of Ultra-Expensive Watch to Build Service Center," *Lancaster (Pennsylvania) New Era*, February 19, 2000.

Sasseen, Jane, "Consumer Products: Stop Thief," *International Management*, September 1990, pp. 48–51.

Schnorbus, Paula, "Tick Tock," *Marketing & Media Decisions*, October 1988, pp. 117–32.

—Katherine Smethurst
—updated by M.L. Cohen

Motorola, Inc.

1303 East Algonquin Road
Schaumburg, Illinois 60196
U.S.A.
Telephone: (847) 576-5000
Toll Free: (800) 262-8509
Fax: (847) 576-5372
Web site: http://www.motorola.com

Public Company
Incorporated: 1928 as Galvin Manufacturing Corporation
Employees: 133,000
Sales: $30.9 billion (1999)
Stock Exchanges: New York Midwest London
Ticker Symbol: MOT
NAIC: 334210 Telephone Apparatus Manufacturing;
334220 Radio and Television Broadcasting and
Wireless Communications Equipment Manufacturing;
334290 Other Communications Equipment
Manufacturing; 334413 Semiconductor and Related
Device Manufacturing; 334418 Printed Circuit
Assembly (Electronic Assembly) Manufacturing;
334419 Other Electronic Component Manufacturing;
336322 Other Motor Vehicle Electrical and Electronic
Equipment Manufacturing

Electronic communications pioneer Motorola, Inc. is a leading designer and manufacturer of cellular phones, cordless phones, two-way radios, pagers, cable modems, broadband set-top boxes, and other communications products and systems. The company is the world's number two maker of mobile phones (trailing Nokia Corporation), with a market share of about 17 percent, and is number one worldwide in two-way radios. Through its Semiconductor Products Sector, Motorola is also the world's leading producer of embedded processors, with an emphasis on such high-growth areas as wireless communications, transportation, and Internet networking. Additionally, Motorola's Integrated Electronic Systems Sector designs and manufactures a wide variety of electronic components and sys-

tems for the automotive, computer, industrial, transportation, navigation, energy, consumer, and lighting markets. Nearly 60 percent of Motorola's sales are generated outside the United States. Motorola has gained recognition over the years for its emphasis on quality, for which it garnered the first annual Malcolm Baldrige National Quality Award in 1988, and for its innovative employee welfare and training programs.

Origins in Radio Technology

The story of Motorola is that of a U.S. classic. It begins during the 1920s, when a small-town Illinois boy, Paul Galvin, went to Chicago to seek his fortune. Galvin had returned from World War I with an interest in the technological changes of the time. In 1920 he worked for a Chicago storage-battery company, and one year later he opened his own storage-battery company with a hometown friend, Edward Stewart. After two years of rocky operations, the government closed the business for nonpayment of excise taxes.

The former partners, undaunted by this setback, joined forces again three years later when Galvin bought an interest in Stewart's new storage-battery company. But with the rise of electric power, batteries lost popularity with the public. To keep their business afloat, Stewart created a device that allowed a radio to be plugged into an ordinary wall outlet, aptly named the "battery eliminator." Once again, the storage-battery company failed, though Galvin was able to buy back the eliminators at the company's public auction. Joe Galvin joined his brother Paul at this time to peddle the eliminators to various retail distributors, such as Sears, Roebuck and Company. In 1928 Paul formed the Galvin Manufacturing Corporation with five employees and $565, and continued making battery eliminators.

During the Great Depression, Galvin Manufacturing Corporation found itself burdened by inventory that it could not sell because of restricted market conditions and underselling by other manufacturers. To rectify this situation, Galvin began experimenting with the virtually untouched automobile-radio market. Before this time, automobile radios had been deemed impractical because they had very poor reception. The first commercially successful car radio came out of Galvin Manufacturing in 1930 under the brand name Motorola. The name, coined by Galvin, was a hybrid of "motor" and "victrola." The units sold for about $120 including accessories and installation, which compared favorably with the $200–$300 custom-designed units then available.

During the 1930s the company also established its first chain of distributorships (Authorized Motorola Installation Stations), began advertising its products in newspapers and on highway billboards, and started to research radios to receive only police broadcasts. The market for police radios appeared so promising that the company formed a police radio department. In 1937 Galvin Manufacturing entered the home-radio market, introducing the first push-button tuning features.

In 1936, after a tour of Europe with his family, Galvin returned home convinced that war was imminent. Knowing that war could provide new opportunities, he directed the company's research into areas he felt could be useful to the military. The Handie-Talkie two-way radio and its offspring, the Walkie-Talkie, resulted. Used by the U.S. Army Signal Corps, these were among the most important pieces of communications equipment used in World War II.

Galvin was always concerned with the welfare of his employees, and in 1947 he instituted a very liberal profit-sharing program that was used as a model by other companies. By this time, the company employed around 5,000 people and had formed an early human relations department. The company's good labor relations enabled it to remain nonunion throughout its history. After Galvin's son Robert and Daniel Noble, an engineer who would eventually have a tremendous impact on the future of the company, joined the company in 1947, its name was officially changed to Motorola, Inc.

The first Motorola television was introduced that same year. It was more compact and less expensive than any competing models—Motorola charged $180, while its nearest competitor charged more than $300. The Motorola "Golden View" set became so popular that within months of its introduction the company was the fourth largest seller of televisions in the nation.

Later in 1947, Motorola bought Detrola, a failing automobile-radio company that had manufactured car radios for the Ford Motor Company. The purchase was made on the condition that Motorola retain Detrola's contract with Ford. This deal greatly strengthened the company's automobile-radio business. Motorola subsequently supplied 50 percent of the car radios for Ford and Chrysler as well as all of the radios for American Motors.

Postwar Shifting of Emphasis to Electronics

The creation of the transistor in 1948 by Bell Laboratories marked a major turning point for Motorola. The company had concentrated on the manufacture of consumer products, and Paul Galvin felt that the company was unequipped to enter the transistor and diode field. With his son Robert and Dan Noble advocating the company's expansion into this new market, however, a semiconductor development group was formed. The first Motorola product to result from this effort was a three-amp power transistor, and later a semiconductor plant was constructed in Arizona. Following this expansion, Motorola supplied transistors to other companies for use in products that Motorola also manufactured. In effect, Motorola found itself in the awkward position of supplying its competitors with parts.

During the 1950s, Motorola became involved in the Columbia Broadcasting System's failed entry into the color television industry. Motorola used the CBS-designed and produced color tubes in its color television sets. After a convoluted struggle for approval from the Federal Communications Commission (FCC), the CBS system was rejected in favor of a system developed by the Radio Corporation of America (RCA). Despite this setback, Motorola pioneered many new features in television technology, including a technique for reducing the number of tubes in black-and-white sets from 41 to 19.

By the middle of the decade, Paul Galvin realized that the company had become too large for one man to continue making all the decisions. He granted divisional status to various businesses, giving each its own engineering, purchasing, manufacturing, and marketing departments and regarding each as an individual profit center. This was the beginning of Motorola's famous decentralized management scheme. As part of this reorganization, Robert Galvin became president and each divisional manager, an executive vice-president. Paul Galvin became chairman of the board and CEO, which he remained until his death in 1959, whereupon Robert Galvin took over the company leadership. Beginning in 1958, Motorola became involved in the U.S. space program. Virtually every manned and unmanned space flight since that time utilized some piece of Motorola equipment.

Motorola made several acquisitions during the 1960s that left observers baffled. It purchased, and sold almost immediately, Lear Inc.'s Lear Cal Division, which manufactured aircraft radios. This was followed by the purchase and subsequent divestment of the Dalberg Company, a manufacturer of hearing aids. Acquisitions were also considered in the fields of recreation, chemicals, broadcasting, and even funeral homes. This trend continued into the 1970s and constituted a period of real adjustment for Motorola. Nevertheless, three very important corporate strategies grew out of this floundering.

First, the company began to expand operations outside the United States, building a plant in Mexico and marketing Motor-

Key Dates:
1928: Paul Galvin forms Galvin Manufacturing Corporation, initially making "battery eliminators."
1930: Company introduces the first commercially successful car radio under the brand name Motorola.
1947: Company institutes a very liberal profit-sharing program, introduces its first television, and changes its name to Motorola, Inc.
1959: Robert Galvin, son of Paul, takes over company leadership upon the death of his father.
1974: Motorola sells its consumer products division, including Quasar television; unveils its first microprocessor, the 6800; and launches an innovative employee training and involvement program.
1977: Codex Corporation, a data communications company, is acquired.
1978: Universal Data Systems is acquired.
1982: Company acquires Four-Phase Systems, Inc., a maker of computers and terminals and a software designer.
1983: Company makes its last car radio; Motorola's first cellular telephone network begins commercial operation.
1988: Motorola is awarded the first annual Malcolm Baldrige National Quality Award; George Fisher succeeds Galvin as CEO.
1993: Gary L. Tooker takes over as CEO.
1997: Christopher Galvin, son of Robert, is named CEO.
1998: Motorola undergoes major restructurings, creating a new divisional organization, consolidating operations, cutting the workforce by about ten percent, and taking a $1.95 billion charge.
1999: The $5 billion Iridium satellite phone venture enters bankruptcy protection.
2000: Company acquires General Instrument Corporation, the leading maker of broadband set-top boxes, in a $17 billion stock swap.

ola products in eight countries, including Japan. An office in Japan was opened in 1961, and in 1968 Motorola Semiconductors Japan was formed to design, market, and sell integrated circuits. Second, Robert Galvin instituted several progressive management policies. In 1974 the company launched an employee training and involvement program that emphasized teamwork and empowered workers at all levels to make decisions. Such policies laid the groundwork for Motorola's much-touted quality and efficiency gains of the 1980s. Third, in the late 1970s, Motorola gradually began to discontinue its consumer-product lines in favor of high-tech electronic components.

Motorola's radio and television interests were the first to go. In 1974 Motorola sold its consumer products division, which included Quasar television, to the Matsushita Electric Industrial Company of Japan. That year Motorola also unveiled its first microprocessor, the 6800. Three years later the company acquired Codex Corporation, a data-communications company based in Massachusetts. In 1978 Universal Data Systems was added. Motorola began phasing out its car-radio business at the

end of the decade, and made its last car radio in 1983. These maneuvers were intended to concentrate Motorola's activities in high technology.

1980s: Four Phase, Cellular Phones, and TQM

Motorola's largest acquisition theretofore—and one of the most important in company history—came in 1982 with its purchase of Four-Phase Systems, Inc. for $253 million. A California-based manufacturer of computers and terminals, Four-Phase also wrote software for its own machines. The purchase puzzled observers because Four-Phase was in serious trouble at the time. Though Four-Phase did quite well in the 1970s, by the end of that decade its product line was aging, its computer-leasing base had grown too large, and its debt was tied to the rising prime rate. These problems had their origin in the company's insistence upon manufacturing its own semiconductors instead of purchasing commercially available components—an insistence that consumed time and money, and also meant that new product developments at Four-Phase were slow in coming. Motorola, however, was looking for a custom-computer manufacturer and was impressed with the sales force at Four-Phase: Motorola's grand strategy was to branch into the new fields of office automation and distributed data processing.

Distributed data processing involved the processing of data through computers that were geographically distributed. The purchases of both Four-Phase and Codex made perfect sense when viewed in light of Motorola's intent to enter this field. The plan was simple: data processing provided by Four-Phase computers would be linked by data-communications equipment provided by Codex, and Motorola proper would provide the semiconductors and much of the communications equipment for the operation. The goal was to create a fully mobile data-processing system that would allow access to mainframe computers from a pocket unit. Motorola also figured that its experience in portable two-way radios and cellular remote telephone systems would prove valuable in this endeavor. Although Motorola was able to turn Four-Phase around temporarily, Four-Phase lost more than $200 million between 1985 and 1989.

The cellular remote telephone system was developed by American Telephone and Telegraph's Bell Laboratories in the early 1970s. The system functioned by dividing an area into units, or cells, each with a low-level transmitter that had 666 channels. As a driver using a phone moved from cell to cell, his call was carried on the transmitter in each successive cell. After he left a cell, the channel he was using became available for another call in that cell. (Earlier remote systems relied on a powerful transmitter covering a large area, which meant that only a few channels were available for the whole area.) Motorola aided in the design and testing of the phones and supplied much of the transmission-switching equipment. In 1983 the company's first cellular telephone network began commercial operation, following 20 years and $200 million in development.

Motorola's early estimates of the cellular phone market seemed astronomical—one million users by the early 1990s—though in fact there were more than four million users by 1989. However, the system developed major problems. There were massive licensing and construction problems and delays. Added to this were complaints about the quality and reliability of

Motorola's phones compared to Japanese-manufactured remote phones. A surplus of phones, coupled with the desire to capture a large market share, soon prompted Japanese companies to cut their prices radically—some by as much as half. Motorola went straight to the U.S. government to request sanctions against the Japanese companies. In 1986 the Commerce Department declared that eight Japanese companies were in fact "dumping" their products (selling at a below-cost price) and were liable to pay special duties. This gave Motorola a new edge in the cellular-phone market—it soon became the world's top supplier of cellular phones, though the competition remained intense.

Motorola's relations with Japanese companies has been checkered. In 1980 it formed a joint venture with Aizu-Toko K.K. to manufacture integrated circuits in Japan. Two years later Motorola acquired the remaining 50 percent interest in the company from Aizu-Toko and created Nippon Motorola Manufacturing Company, a successful operation run along Japanese lines mostly by Japanese. Also in 1982, Motorola received a $9 million order for paging devices from Nippon Telegraph and Telephone. These ventures were followed by vigorous pleas from Robert Galvin for the U.S. government to respond in kind to Japan's trade tactics. In fact, Galvin was a founder of the Coalition for International Trade Equity. This organization lobbied Congress for legislation that would impose tariffs on foreign companies subsidized by their governments. Motorola further called for a surcharge on all imports to reduce the U.S. trade deficit. Other major companies in the United States (Boeing and Exxon among them) rejected these measures on the grounds that they would spark trade wars that would damage the position of U.S. companies doing business with Japan.

In 1986, Motorola made a groundbreaking deal with Japan's Toshiba to share its microprocessor designs in return for Toshiba's expertise in manufacturing dynamic random access memories (DRAMs). Prior to this arrangement, the Japanese had driven Motorola, along with nearly every other U.S. semiconductor company, out of the DRAM market.

In 1988, Motorola took on the Japanese in another way: that year its Boynton Beach, Florida, plant began producing the company's Bravo model pocket pager in a fully automated factory. The prototypical facility used 27 small robots directed by computers and overseen by 12 human attendants. The robots could build a Bravo within two hours of the time an order was received at corporate headquarters in Schaumburg, Illinois; the process normally would take three weeks.

Motorola's adoption of "Total Quality Management" (TQM) principles during the 1980s furthered that push for quality and earned it the admiration of analysts and competitors alike. Building on the foundation laid by his employee empowerment programs of the 1970s, Robert Galvin was able to instill a drive for continuous quality improvement in his teams of workers. From 1981 to 1986, Motorola reduced its defect rate by 90 percent. By 1992, the company had achieved "six sigma quality": less than 3.4 mistakes per million. The corporation did not sacrifice productivity for these quality improvements, either: from 1986 to 1994, sales per employee increased 126 percent, in spite of a net increase in the workforce. Some divisions had achieved such high quality rates that they were striving to reduce error rates to defects per *billion* in the 1990s.

The corporation's ongoing goals were to reduce error rates tenfold every two years and simultaneously reduce production time tenfold every five years. Motorola's campaign for quality was highlighted by its 1988 receipt of the first annual Malcolm Baldrige National Quality Award. That year, George Fisher succeeded Robert Galvin as CEO, becoming the first non-Galvin to head the company.

In 1989 Motorola introduced the world's smallest portable telephone, but soon found that its new product was excluded from the Tokyo and Nagoya markets, two cities that together represented more than 60 percent of the $750 million Japanese cellular phone market. When Motorola cried foul, the Japanese government agreed to allow adapted Motorola phones in Tokyo, but only for use in automobiles. This excluded the 90 percent of portable phones used on trains. In response to these restrictions, Motorola led the push to impose trade sanctions on certain Japanese imports. Then-President George Bush publicly accused Japan of being an unfair trading partner and threatened to take punitive action if the Japanese did not remove barriers to free trade.

The growth of the computer industry provided both opportunities and challenges for Motorola. Throughout the 1980s, the company's most popular 68000 family of microchips powered personal computers (PCs) and workstations built by Apple Computer, Inc., Hewlett-Packard Company, Digital Equipment Corporation, and Sun Microsystems, Inc., among others. Upstart competitor Intel Corporation, whose chips were the cornerstone of International Business Machines Corporation (IBM) and IBM-compatible PCs, launched a successful campaign to capture the microchip market. Intel combined ever-increasing power and speed with aggressive marketing to win the semiconductor market from Motorola. Undaunted, Motorola teamed up with industry giants Apple and IBM to develop the PowerPC in the 1990s. Throughout most of the 1990s, Motorola maintained the number three ranking among the world's semiconductor manufacturers, behind Intel and Japan's NEC Corporation.

1990s and Beyond: Communications Coming to the Fore

In many respects, however, Motorola's computer chip operations were eclipsed by its communications interests during the 1990s. The company's 45 percent leading share of the global cellular phone market and whopping 85 percent of the world's pager sales forced it to place an increased emphasis on consumer marketing in the early 1990s. Accordingly, Motorola recruited market specialists from General Electric, Black and Decker, Apple, and (as *Fortune* put it in a 1994 article) "even Mattel." The company began selling its pagers at mass merchandisers and offering them in a variety of colors. Evidence of its reentry into the consumer market after nearly 20 years came in the form of a 1993 television and print campaign targeted at women (especially mothers).

Over the course of the 1980s, Motorola's sales and profits tripled, to $9.6 billion and $498 million, respectively, in 1989. By 1993, sales vaulted more than 56 percent to $16.96 billion and earnings more than doubled to over $1 billion. The company underwent its third transfer of power that year, when Robert Galvin "retired" to the office of chairman of the board's executive committee at the age of 71, at the same time that Fisher left to take the top spot at Eastman Kodak. Gary L. Tooker, former president and chief operating officer, advanced to the chief executive office, and Galvin's son Christopher assumed Tooker's responsibilities.

Although some analysts worried that Motorola, like many other large, successful corporations, would fall into complacency, that fear did not seem well founded. The company earned a reputation for "self-obsolescence" that seemed likely to keep it in the vanguard of wireless communication. For example, the Motorola Integrated Radio Service (MIRS) combined features of cellular phones, pagers, and two-way radios in a system that could rival all three. Motorola hoped to undermine the cellular "duopolies" organized by the Federal Communications Commission by operating the system over Specialized Mobile Radio (SMR) frequencies that had been limited to use by taxis and tow trucks. Motorola also continued work on its multibillion-dollar "Iridium" project (launched in 1990 then spun off as a limited partnership), a plan to wirelessly interconnect the entire globe through a system of low-earth-orbiting satellites (LEOS), with a projected completion date of 1998.

Continuing globalization at Motorola focused on Asian, Eastern European, and Latin American markets in the early 1990s. In 1993, the company announced "Corporate America's biggest manufacturing venture in China": two plants for the manufacture of simple integrated circuits, pagers, and cellular phones. By 1995 sales in China and Hong Kong had almost doubled, reaching $3.2 billion, nearly 12 percent of overall Motorola revenues.

The good times at Motorola lasted through 1995, a year in which the company posted profits of $1.78 billion on sales of $27.04 billion. The latter figure was nearly triple the company's 1989 revenue figure. Then, seemingly, Motorola took a sudden downturn. Revenue growth slowed dramatically and profits fell. In 1997 the company reported net income of $1.18 billion on sales of $29.79 billion. There were numerous reasons for the downturn, including price wars in and declining sales of cellular phones, slumps in the semiconductor and paging industries, troubles at Apple Computer which impacted sales of the PowerPC chip, and the Asian economic crisis which began in 1997. Perhaps most importantly, however, Motorola seemed to have lost its ability to stay on the cutting edge of technology, particularly in the wireless telephone field. Motorola had dominated the wireless world in the analog era, but it was not fully prepared when the switch to digital technologies began in the mid-1990s. Because it hung onto its cellular technology for too long, its share of the U.S. wireless phone market plunged from 60 percent in 1994 to 34 percent in early 1998.

In the midst of these travails came another leadership change. In January 1997 Tooker moved into the chairmanship, while Christopher Galvin took over as CEO. The appointment of Galvin, whose background was in marketing and management rather than engineering, was well-timed; a number of observers had concluded that Motorola's troubles stemmed at least in part from its inability to listen to its customers. The company's autonomous divisions were creating products—many of them innovative—without first determining if the market desired them. The autonomous structure created further problems. Motorola's pag-

ing, cellular, two-way radio, and satellite communications units operated as separate divisions, and in the company's decentralized structure did not collaborate with each other, despite the increasing amount of overlap in these technologies. Galvin attempted to address these problems through a 1998 restructuring that merged all of the company's communications operations into a new entity called the Communications Enterprise. Within this organization were created several customer-focused sectors, with the three main ones being: personal communications, which served the consumer market and included wireless phones, pagers, and some two-way radios; network solutions, which served telecommunications providers and concentrated on wireless-telephone infrastructure and satellite communications; and a commercial, government, and industrial solutions group which was created to design and build communications systems for large organizations.

Motorola's semiconductor and integrated circuit operations were also restructured in the late 1990s; these units were reorganized into two areas: the Semiconductor Products Sector, which adopted a concentration on embedded semiconductors, and the Integrated Electronic Systems Sector, which focused on embedded electronic systems for various industrial markets. Motorola began winding down its involvement in the general-purpose semiconductor sector, a process that culminated in 1999 with a management buyout, led by Texas Pacific Group, of the Semiconductor Components Group. As part of the transaction, Motorola received $1.6 billion in cash and a ten percent stake in the new company, renamed ON Semiconductor. Galvin's restructuring efforts also included the launch in mid-1998 of a 12-month program of factory consolidation, divestments of underperforming units, and asset writedowns; as well as the elimination of 15,000 workers from the company payroll, a ten percent workforce reduction. Motorola took a $1.95 billion charge related to the restructuring, leading to a net loss for 1998 of $962 million; sales fell one percent from the previous year, to $29.4 billion, as a result of the divestments.

It appeared that 1999 might be considered a turnaround year for Motorola, as revenues surpassed the $30 billion mark for the first time, despite the divestment of the commodity semiconductor business; the company also returned to profitability. Motorola finally began selling substantial numbers of digital cellular telephones during the year, although sales were hampered by shortages of certain components. The company was also returning to the cutting edge through its attempt to develop a new technology to deliver voice, data, and video from the Internet to wireless devices. This endeavor was telling in that Motorola, an historically go-it-alone company, was partnering with Cisco Systems Inc. and Sun Microsystems Inc. In addition to forging alliances, Motorola was also working to shift from being strictly a maker of hardware to being a software designer as well. For example, the company was working to equip all of its cellular telephones with an Internet browser.

Motorola also turned to the acquisition route in 1999, in a very large way, with the announcement of a $17 billion stock swap for General Instrument Corporation, the leading maker of broadband set-top boxes. Completed in early 2000, this was the largest acquisition in Motorola history, and it gave the company a significant presence in the emerging broadband telecommunications sector. Broadband visionaries spoke of a dramatic convergence whereby all the main telecom services—telephony, cable television, video, e-mail, high-speed Internet access, and interactive gaming—would be delivered to a television via a single set-top box. Following the completion of the acquisition, General Instrument became the new broadband communications sector within the Communications Enterprise. This new sector also included Motorola's existing cable modem operations. General Instrument also brought to Motorola its 67 percent stake in Next Level Communications, a supplier of the emerging digital subscriber line (DSL) technology. With DSL, basic copper telephone wires were able to be used for high-speed Internet access.

A dark cloud hanging over Motorola as the 21st century began was the Iridium satellite phone system, which began operation in late 1998 following $5 billion in development costs. Iridium immediately began having technological glitches and, even though it allowed its users to use their cellular phones anywhere on the planet, suffered from low demand because of its extremely high rates (e.g., $3 per minute calls). In August 1999 Iridium LLC, in which Motorola held an 18 percent stake, began operating under bankruptcy protection. Motorola subsequently took a $740 million charge related to Iridium in late 1999, leaving it with a $460 million cash exposure to the venture. In early 2000 Motorola also faced a possible $3.5 billion lawsuit from a group of Iridium bondholders. Despite these setbacks, Motorola was moving forward with another, even larger satellite venture, Teledesic L.L.C., in which it was the chief contractor and held a 26 percent stake. A $10 billion project, Teledesic aimed to create, by 2004, a low-orbit satellite system for the delivery of voice, data, and high-speed Internet access to handheld devices. Motorola's prominent involvement in the satellite and broadband ventures, however risky they might be, provided ample evidence that the company was back on the technological cutting edge.

Principal Subsidiaries

Motorola Argentina, S.A.; Motorola Gesellschaft M.B.H. (Austria); S.A. Motorola N.V. (Belgium); Motorola de Bolivia S.A.; Motorola do Brasil LTDA. (Brazil); Starfish Software, Inc.; Indala Corporation; Motorola Canada Limited; Motorola (China) Electronics Ltd.; Motorola de Colombia Limitada; Motorola International Capital Corporation; Motorola International Development Corporation; Motorola Credit Corporation; Motorola Lighting, Inc.; Motorola International Network Ventures; Motorola del Ecuador S.A.; Motorola Limited (U.K.); Motorola Semiconducteurs S.A. (France); Motorola S.A. (France); Motorola G.m.b.H. (Germany); Motorola A.E. (Greece); Motorola Finance B.V. (Netherlands); Motorola Asia Limited (Hong Kong); Motorola Semiconductors Hong Kong Limited; Motorola Hungary Communications Limited Liability Company; Motorola (India) Limited; Motorola Ireland Limited; TCS Insurance Company of Ireland Limited; Motorola Israel Limited; Motorola Semiconductor Israel Limited; Motorola Israel Information Systems Limited; Motorola S.p.A. (Italy); Motorola Japan Limited; Motorola Korea Limited; Motorola Malaysia Sdn. Bhd.; Motorola Semiconductor Sdn. Bhd. (Malaysia); Motorola Electronics Sdn. Bhd. (Malaysia); Motorola de Mexico, S.A.; North African Cellular Investments, Ltd. (Morocco); Motorola del Paraguay S.A.; Motorola Portugal Comunicacoes,

Lda; Motorola Communications SRL (Romania); Motorola A.O. (Russia); Motorola Electronics Pte. Limited (Singapore); Motorola South Asia Pte Limited (Singapore); Motorola Asia Treasury Pte. Ltd (Singapore); Motorola Southern Africa (Proprietary) Ltd. (South Africa); Motorola España S.A. (Spain); Telcel S.A. (Spain); Motorola (Suisse) S.A. (Switzerland); Motorola Electronics Taiwan, Limited; Motorola (Thailand) Ltd.; Motorola Komunikasyon Ticaret Ve Servis Limited Sirketi (Turkey); Motorola de los Andes, C.A. (Venezuela); Motorola Foreign Sales Corporation (Virgin Islands).

Principal Operating Units

Semiconductor Products; Integrated Electronic Systems.

Principal Competitors

ADC Telecommunications, Inc.; Advanced Micro Devices, Inc.; Agilent Technologies, Inc.; Alcatel; Analog Devices, Inc.; Casio Computer Co., Ltd.; Cisco Systems, Inc.; Fujitsu Limited; General Electric Company; Harris Corporation; Hitachi, Ltd.; Hyundai Group; Intel Corporation; International Business Machines Corporation; ITT Industries, Inc.; Koninklijke Philips Electronics N.V.; Kyocera Corporation; LG Group; Lucent Technologies Inc.; Marconi plc; Matsushita Electric Industrial Co., Ltd.; Micron Technology, Inc.; Mitsubishi Group; National Semiconductor Corporation; NEC Corporation; Nokia Corporation; Nortel Networks Corporation; Oki Electric Industry Company, Limited; QUALCOMM Incorporated; Racal Electronics Plc; Robert Bosch GmbH; Samsung Group; Scientific-Atlanta, Inc.; Siemens AG; Sony Corporation; Telefonaktiebolaget LM Ericsson; Texas Instruments Incorporated; Thomson S.A.; 3Com Corporation; Toshiba Corporation.

Further Reading

Alster, Norm, "A Third-Generation Galvin Moves Up," *Forbes,* April 30, 1990, pp. 57+.

Barboza, David, "Motorola Rolls Itself Over: After a Bad Year, Almost Everything Is Coming Up Rosy, and Wireless," *New York Times,* July 14, 1999, p. C1.

Bettner, Jill, " 'Underpromise, Overperform,' " *Forbes,* January 30, 1984, pp. 88+.

Brown, Kathi, *A Critical Connection: The Motorola Service Station Story,* Rolling Meadows, Ill.: Motorola University Press, 1992, 253 p.

Cauley, Leslie, "Motorola Corp. Unveils Deal for $11 Billion," *Wall Street Journal,* September 16, 1999, p. B10.

——, "Motorola Profit Meets Estimates, Despite Iridium Woes, Shortages," *Wall Street Journal,* January 18, 2000, p. B6.

Coy, Peter, and Ron Stodghill II, "Is Motorola a Bit Too Patient?," *Business Week,* February 5, 1996, pp. 150–51.

Crockett, Roger O., "Has Motorola Found Its Cable Guy?," *Business Week,* September 27, 1999, p. 50.

——, "Motorola Girds for a Shakeup," *Business Week,* April 13, 1998, p. 33.

——, "Motorola: Slow and Steady Isn't Winning Any Races," *Business Week,* August 10, 1998, p. 62.

Crockett, Roger O., and Catherine Yang, "Why Motorola Should Hang Up on Iridium," *Business Week,* August 30, 1999, p. 46.

Crockett, Roger O., and Peter Elstrom, "How Motorola Lost Its Way," *Business Week,* May 4, 1998, pp. 140+.

Dreyfack, Kenneth, "It's Now or Never for Motorola Computers," *Business Week,* September 15, 1986, pp. 184J+.

Elstrom, Peter, "Did Motorola Make the Wrong Call?," *Business Week,* July 29, 1996, p. 66.

Elstrom, Peter, Gail Edmondson, and Eric Schine, "Does This Galvin Have the Right Stuff?," *Business Week,* March 17, 1997, pp. 102 +.

Feder, Barnaby J., "Some Humbling Times for a High-Tech Giant," *New York Times,* October 13, 1996, sec. 3, p. 1.

Galarza, Pablo, "Keep the Faith," *Financial World,* January 30, 1996, pp. 30–32.

Galvin, Robert W., *The Idea of Ideas,* Rolling Meadows, Ill.: Motorola University Press, 1993.

Hardy, Quentin, "Galvin's Task: Make Motorola Scary Again," *Wall Street Journal,* March 7, 1997, p. B8.

——, "Higher Calling: How a Wife's Question Led Motorola to Chase Global Cell-Phone Plan," *Wall Street Journal,* December 16, 1996, pp. A1 +.

——, "Motorola Prepares Major Restructuring," *Wall Street Journal,* March 31, 1998, p. A3.

——, "Motorola Selects Christopher Galvin, Grandson of Firm's Founder, as CEO," *Wall Street Journal,* November 15, 1996, p. A3.

——, "Motorola Unveils a Major Reorganization," *Wall Street Journal,* July 10, 1998, p. B5.

——, "Next Leader in the Motorola Dynasty Faces Task of Reshaping Corporation," *Wall Street Journal,* November 18, 1996, p. B10.

——, "Unsolid State: Motorola, Broadsided by the Digital Era, Struggles for a Footing," *Wall Street Journal,* April 22, 1998, pp. A1 +.

Harris, Nicole, "Motorola Sees Strong Growth This Year," *Wall Street Journal,* January 19, 2000, p. B6.

Henkoff, Ronald, "Keeping Motorola on a Roll," *Fortune,* April 18, 1994, pp. 67–68 +.

——, "What Motorola Learns from Japan," *Fortune,* April 24, 1989, pp. 157 +.

Hill, G. Christian, and Don Clark, "Motorola to Slash Staff, Take Big Charge," *Wall Street Journal,* June 5, 1998, p. A3.

McWilliams, Gary, "Microprocessors Are for Wimps," *Business Week,* December 15, 1997, p. 134.

"Motorola's New Strategy," *Business Week,* March 29, 1982, pp. 128 +.

Naik, Gautam, "Motorola Still Is Struggling in Europe," *Wall Street Journal,* February 11, 2000, p. A12.

——, "Nokia Widens Lead in Wireless Market While Motorola, Ericsson Fall Back," *Wall Street Journal,* February 8, 2000, p. B8.

Petrakis, Harry Mark, *The Founder's Touch: The Life of Paul Galvin of Motorola,* New York: McGraw-Hill, 1965; 3rd. ed., Chicago: Motorola University Press/J.G. Ferguson, 1991, 242 p.

Roth, Daniel, "Burying Motorola: From Poster Boy to Whipping Boy," *Fortune,* July 6, 1998, pp. 28–29.

——, "Motorola Lives!," *Fortune,* September 27, 1999, pp. 305–6.

Schoenberger, Karl, "Motorola Bets Big on China," *Fortune,* May 27, 1996, pp. 116–18 +.

Schonfeld, Erick, "Hold the Phone: Motorola Is Going Nowhere Fast," *Fortune,* March 30, 1998, p. 184.

Slutsker, Gary, "The Company That Likes to Obsolete Itself," *Forbes,* September 13, 1993, pp. 139 +.

Tetzeli, Rick, "And Now for Motorola's Next Trick," *Fortune,* April 28, 1997, pp. 122–24 +.

Therrien, Lois, "Motorola Sends Its Work Force Back to School," *Business Week,* June 6, 1988, pp. 80 +.

——, "The Rage to Page Has Motorola's Mouth Watering," *Business Week,* August 30, 1993, pp. 72 +.

——, "The Rival Japan Respects," *Business Week,* November 13, 1989, pp. 108 +.

Thurm, Scott, Joann S. Lublin, and Leslie Scism, "Galvin Must Show a Motorola Recovery Before Dismissal Pressure Grows Intense," *Wall Street Journal,* June 8, 1998, p. A3.

Upbin, Bruce, "Motorola Inside," *Forbes,* May 31, 1999, pp. 51–52.

Upbin, Bruce, and Michael Ozanian, "Analytic Myopia," *Forbes,* June 1, 1998, pp. 42–43.

Yee, David, "Motorola: More Than Chips," *Financial World,* fall 1994, p. 14.

Zajac, Andrew, "Technical 'Convergence' at Heart of Motorola Merger," *Chicago Tribune,* September 15, 1999.

—April Dougal Gasbarre
—updated by David E. Salamie

Nissan Motor Co., Ltd.

17-1, Ginza 6-chome
Chuo-ku
Tokyo 104-8023
Japan
Telephone: (3) 5565-2147
Fax: (3) 3546-2669
Web site: http://global.nissan.co.jp

Public Company (37 Percent Owned by Renault S.A.)
Incorporated: 1933 as Jidosha Seizo Company, Ltd.
Employees: 131,260
Sales: ¥6.58 trillion (US$54.38 billion) (1999)
Stock Exchanges: Tokyo Osaka Niigata Nagoya Kyoto
    Fukuoka Sapporo Frankfurt NASDAQ (ADRs)
NAIC: 336111 Automobile Manufacturing; 336112 Light
    Truck and Utility Vehicle Manufacturing; 336120
    Heavy Duty Truck Manufacturing; 336211 Motor
    Vehicle Body Manufacturing; 421110 Automobile and
    Other Motor Vehicle Wholesalers; 522291 Consumer
    Lending; 532111 Passenger Cars Rental; 532112
    Passenger Cars Leasing; 551112 Offices of Other
    Holding Companies

Established in 1933, Nissan Motor Co., Ltd. was a pioneer in the manufacturing of automobiles. Nearly 70 years later, Nissan has become one of the world's leading automakers, with annual production of 2.4 million units, which represented 4.9 percent of the global market. Domestically, the company sells 774,000 vehicles on an annual basis, placing it second behind Toyota Motor Corporation. About 35 percent of Nissan's vehicles are sold in Japan, 25 percent in the United States, and 20 percent in Europe. In the North American market, the company's top models include the Infiniti, Maxima, Altima, and Sentra passenger cars, the Quest minivan, the Frontier pickup truck, and the Pathfinder sport utility vehicle. After losing money for most of the 1990s, Nissan entered into a global alliance with Renault S.A. in March 1999, with the French company taking a 37 percent stake in Nissan. A massive restructuring was then launched.

Early History

In 1911 Masujiro Hashimoto, a U.S.-trained engineer, founded the Kwaishinsha Motor Car Works in Tokyo. Hashimoto dreamed of building the first Japanese automobile, but lacked the capital. In order for his dream to come true, he contacted three men—Kenjiro Den, Rokuro Auyama, and Keitaro Takeuchi—for financial support. To acknowledge their contribution to his project, Hashimoto named his car DAT, after their last initials. In Japanese, "dat" means "escaping rabbit" or "running very fast."

Debuting in 1914, the first DAT was marketed and sold as a ten horsepower runabout. Another version, referred to as "datson" or "son of dat," was a two-seater sports car produced in 1918. One year later, Jitsuyo Jidosha Seizo Company, another Nissan predecessor, was founded in Osaka. Kwaishinsha and Jitsuyo Jidosha Seizo combined in 1926 to establish the Dat Jidosha Seizo Company. Five years later, the Tobata Imaon Company, an automotive parts manufacturer, purchased controlling interest in the company. Tobata Imaon's objective was to mass-produce products that would be competitive in quality and price with foreign automobiles.

In 1932, "Datson" became "Datsun," thus associating it with the ancient Japanese sun symbol. The manufacturing and sale of Datsun cars was taken over in 1933 by the Jidosha Seizo Company, Ltd., which was established in Yokohama that year through a joint venture between Nihon Sangyo Company and Tobata Imaon. In 1934 the company changed its name to Nissan Motor Co., Ltd., and one year later the operation of Nissan's first integrated automobile factory began in Yokohama under the technical guidance of American industrial engineers.

Datsun cars, however, were not selling as well as expected in Japan. Major U.S. automobile manufacturers, such as General Motors Corporation (GM) and the Ford Motor Company, had established assembly plants in Japan during this time. These companies dominated the automobile market in Japan for ten years, while foreign companies were discouraged from exporting to the United States by the Great Depression of 1929.

With the advent of World War II in 1941, Nissan's efforts were directed toward military production. During wartime, the

Company Perspectives:

Nissan's challenge is to enhance its corporate value and to build a corporate foundation that will enable the Company to win out in the competitive environment of the 21st century. The management team is also keenly aware of its responsibility to meet the expectations of shareholders by reinstating dividend payments as soon as possible. We will do our utmost to achieve a new corporate consciousness and to implement sweeping improvements in our corporate structure. We look forward to the continuing support and guidance of our shareholders as we strive to attain these goals.

Japanese government ordered the motor industry to halt production of passenger cars and, instead, to produce much needed trucks. Nissan also produced engines for airplanes and torpedo boats.

Postwar Recovery and Overseas Expansion

After World War II, the Japanese auto industry had to be completely recreated. Technical assistance contracts were established with foreign firms such as Renault, Hillman, and Willys-Overland. In 1952 Nissan reached a license agreement with the United Kingdom's Austin Motor Company Ltd. With American technical assistance and improved steel and parts from Japan, Nissan became capable of producing small, efficient cars, which later provided the company with a marketing advantage in the United States.

The U.S. market was growing, but gradually. Nonetheless, Nissan felt that Americans needed low-priced economy cars, perhaps as a second family car. Surveys of the U.S. auto industry encouraged Nissan to display its cars at the Imported Motor Car Show in Los Angeles. The exhibition was noticed by *Business Week*, but as an analyst wrote in 1957, "With over 50 foreign car makers already on sale here, the Japanese auto industry isn't likely to carve out a big slice of the U.S. market for itself."

Nissan considered this criticism as it struggled to improve domestic sales. Small-scale production resulted in high unit costs and high prices. In fact, a large percentage of Datsun cars were sold to Japanese taxi companies. Yet Kawamata, the company's new and ambitious president, was determined to increase exports to the United States. Kawamata noted two principal reasons for his focus on exports: "Increased sales to the U.S.A. would give Nissan more prestige and credit in the domestic markets as well as other areas and a further price cut is possible through mass producing export cars."

By 1958 Nissan had contracted with two U.S. distributors, Woolverton Motors of North Hollywood, California, and Chester G. Luby of Forest Hills, New York. Nevertheless, sales did not improve as quickly as Nissan had hoped. As a result, Nissan sent two representatives to the United States to help increase sales: Soichi Kawazoe, an engineer and former employee of GM and Ford; and Yutaka Katayama, an advertising and sales promotion executive. Each identified a need for the develop-

ment of a new company to sell and service Datsuns in the United States. By 1960 Nissan Motor Corporation, based in Los Angeles, had 18 employees, 60 dealers, and a sales total of 1,640 cars and trucks. The success of the Datsun pickup truck in the U.S. market encouraged new dealerships.

Datsun assembly plants were built in Mexico and Peru during the 1960s. In 1966 Nissan merged with the Prince Motor Company Ltd.—gaining the Skyline and Gloria models—and two years later Datsun passenger cars began production in Australia. During 1969 cumulative vehicle exports reached one million units. This was a result of Katayama and Kawazoe's efforts to teach Japanese manufacturers to build automobiles comparable to U.S. cars. This meant developing mechanical similarities and engine capacities that could keep up with American traffic.

The introduction of the Datsun 240Z marked the debut of foreign sports cars in the U.S. market. Datsun began to receive good reviews from automotive publications in the United States, and sales began to improve. Also at this time, the first robotics were installed in Nissan factories to help increase production.

1970s and 1980s: From Economy Cars to Luxury Sedans

In 1970, Japan launched its first satellite on a Nissan rocket. Only five years later, Nissan export sales reached $5 million. But allegations surfaced that Nissan U.S.A. was "pressuring and restricting its dealers in various ways: requiring them to sell at list prices, limiting their ability to discount, enforcing territorial limitations," according to author John B. Rae. In 1973 Nissan U.S.A. agreed to abide by a decree issued from the U.S. Department of Justice that prohibited it from engaging in such activities.

The 1970s marked a slump in the Japanese auto industry as a result of the oil crisis. Gasoline prices started to increase, and then a number of other difficulties arose. U.S. President Richard Nixon devalued the dollar and announced an import surcharge: transportation prices went up and export control was lacking. To overcome these problems, Nissan U.S.A. brought in Chuck King, a 19-year veteran of the auto industry, to improve management, correct billing errors, and minimize transportation damages. As a result, sales continued to increase with the help of Nissan's latest model, the Datsun 210 "Honeybee," which was capable of traveling 41 miles on one gallon of gas.

In 1976 the company began the production of motorboats. During this time, the modification of the Datsun model to U.S. styling also began. Additions included sophisticated detailing, roof racks, and air conditioning. The new styling of the Datsun automobiles was highlighted with the introduction of the 1980 model 200SX.

During the 1980s Nissan established production facilities in Italy, Spain, West Germany, and the United Kingdom. An aerospace cooperative agreement with Martin Marietta Corporation also was concluded, and the Nissan CUE-X and MID4 prototypes were introduced. In 1981, the company began the long and costly process of changing its name from Datsun to Nissan in the U.S. market.

Key Dates:	

Key Dates:

1911: Masujiro Hashimoto founds the Kwaishinsha Motor Car Works in Tokyo.
1914: Hashimoto introduces his first car, the DAT.
1918: The Datson model is first produced.
1932: The Datson brand is changed to Datsun.
1933: The manufacturing and sale of Datsun cars is taken over by the Jidosha Seizo Company, Ltd.
1934: Jidosha Seizo changes its name to Nissan Motor Co., Ltd.
Early 1940s: During World War II, the company makes military trucks and engines for airplanes and torpedo boats.
1951: Nissan becomes a publicly traded company.
1952: Nissan enters into a license agreement with U.K.-based Austin Motor Company Ltd.
1958: Export of cars to the U.S. market begins.
1966: The company merges with Prince Motor Company Ltd.
1981: The company begins changing its name from Datsun to Nissan in the U.S. market.
1989: The Infiniti line of luxury automobiles is introduced.
1992: The company posts the first pretax loss in its history as a public company; Nissan introduces the Altima small luxury sedan and the Quest minivan, the latter a joint development with Ford Motor Company.
1994: Nissan posts a loss of nearly US$2 billion.
1999: Nissan and Renault S.A. enter into a global alliance, with Renault taking a 37 percent stake in Nissan. A massive restructuring begins.

The new generation of Nissan automobiles included high-performance luxury sedans. They featured electronic control, variable split four-wheel drive, four-wheel steering, an ''intelligent'' engine, and a satellite navigation system, as well as other technological innovations. Clearly, the management of Nissan had made a commitment to increase expenditures for research and development. In 1986 Nissan reported that the company's budget for research and development reached ¥170 billion, or 4.5 percent of net sales.

During the late 1980s, Nissan evaluated future consumer trends. From this analysis, Nissan predicted that consumers would prefer a car with high performance, high speed, innovative styling, and versatile options. All of these factors were taken into account to form ''a clear image of the car in the environment in which it will be used,'' said Yukio Miyamori, a director of Nissan. Cultural differences also were considered in this evaluation. One result of this extensive market analysis was the company's 1989 introduction of its Infiniti line of luxury automobiles.

The use of robotics and computer-aided design and manufacturing reduced the time required for computations on aerodynamics, combustion, noise, and vibration characteristics, enabling Nissan to have an advantage in both the domestic and foreign markets. The strategy of Nissan's management during the late 1980s was to improve the company's productivity and thus increase future competitiveness.

Sustained Difficulties in the 1990s

By the start of the next decade, however, Nissan's fortunes began to decline. Profits and sales dropped, quelling hopes that the 1990s would be as lucrative as the 1980s. Nissan was not alone in its backward tumble, however: each of the major Japanese car makers suffered damaging blows as the decade began. The yen's value rose rapidly against the dollar, which crimped U.S. sales and created a substantial price disparity between Japanese and U.S. cars. At the same time, the United States' three largest automobile manufacturers showed a surprising resurgence during the early 1990s. According to some observers, Japanese manufacturers had grown complacent after recording prolific gains to surpass U.S. manufacturers. In the more cost-conscious 1990s, they allowed the price of their products to rise just as U.S. manufacturers reduced costs, improved efficiency, and offered more innovative products.

In addition, the global recession that sent many national economies into a tailspin in the early 1990s caught Nissan with its resources thinly stretched as a result of its bid to unseat its largest Japanese rival, Toyota Motor Corporation. Toyota, much larger than Nissan and possessing deeper financial pockets, was better positioned to sustain the losses incurred from the global economic downturn. Consequently, Nissan entered its ninth decade of operation facing formidable obstacles.

The first financial decline came in 1991, when the company's consolidated operating profit plummeted 64.3 percent to ¥125 billion (US$886 million). Six months later, Nissan registered its first pretax loss since becoming a publicly traded company in 1951—¥14.2 billion during the first half of 1992. The losses mounted in the next two years, growing to ¥108.1 billion in 1993 and ¥202.4 billion by 1994, or nearly US$2 billion. To arrest the precipitous drop in company profits, Nissan's management introduced various cost-cutting measures—such as reducing its materials and manufacturing costs—which saved the company roughly US$1.5 billion in 1993, with an additional US$1.2 billion savings realized in 1994. Nissan also became the first Japanese company to close a plant in Japan since World War II and cut nearly 12,000 workers in Japan, Spain, and the United States from its payroll. Nissan also was staggering under a debt load that reached as high as US$32 billion and threatened to bankrupt the company. Only intervention from Nissan's lead lender, Industrial Bank of Japan, kept the company afloat.

There were some positive signs in the early 1990s to inspire hope for the future. Nissan's 1993 sales increased nearly 20 percent, vaulting the car maker past Honda Motor Co., Ltd. to reclaim the number two ranking in import sales to the all-important U.S. market. Much of this gain was attributable to robust sales of the Nissan Altima, a replacement for its Stanza model, which was introduced in 1992 and marketed in the United States as a small luxury sedan priced under $13,000. To the joy of Nissan's management, however, the Altima typically was purchased with various options added on, giving the company an additional $2,000 to $3,000 per car. Nissan also was encouraged by strong sales of its Quest minivan, which was introduced in the United States in 1992 and had been developed jointly with Ford Motor, which marketed its own version, the Ford Windstar.

Nissan's losses continued through the fiscal year ending in March 1996, cumulating to US$3.2 billion over a four-year span. The company's return to profitability in fiscal 1997 came about in part because of the cost-cutting program and in part from the yen's dramatic depreciation against the dollar. Despite the return to the black, Nissan remained a troubled company. From its 1972 peak of 34 percent, the company's share of the Japanese auto market had fallen to 20 percent by early 1997. Competition from the more financially stable Toyota and Honda played a factor in this decline, but Nissan also hurt itself by failing to keep pace with changing consumer tastes both in Japan and in overseas markets. For example, Nissan was behind its rivals in adding minivans and sport utility vehicles to its product lineup, having for years dismissed these sectors as passing fads. Meanwhile, minivans, sport utility vehicles, and station wagons accounted for half of all passenger car sales in Japan by early 1997, up from just more than ten percent in 1990. In the U.S. market, the Altima lost ground to two midsized rivals, the Honda Accord and the Toyota Camry, because Nissan's model was smaller and thus less desirable. In the luxury car sector, Toyota's Lexus line became the hot brand in the United States, triumphing over the Infiniti. Because of these and other factors, Nissan returned to the red for fiscal years 1998 and 1999. Although the losses were not as large as earlier in the decade, the company's continued sky-high debt load—which stood at US$19.7 billion in late 1998—did not bode well for Nissan's future.

1999 and Beyond: The Renault Era

The late 1990s was a period of intense consolidation in the auto industry, stemming from rapid globalization, the increasing cost of developing ever more sophisticated vehicles, and worldwide automotive production overcapacity. The November 1998 merger of Daimler-Benz AG and Chrysler Corporation that formed DaimlerChrysler AG was the largest partnership created in this period, but there were a number of smaller mergers, acquisitions, and strategic alliances as well. Both Nissan and Renault S.A. of France were eagerly looking for a partner in order to compete in the 21st century. Nissan was rebuffed by both DaimlerChrysler and Ford and Renault was turned away by other Japanese automakers, before the two companies reached an agreement on a global alliance in March 1999. The combination of Nissan and Renault made strategic sense in that the companies' main sales territories and production locales were complementary. In vehicle sales, Nissan was strongest in Japan and other parts of Asia, the United States, Mexico, the Middle East, and South Africa, while Renault concentrated on Europe, Turkey, and South America. The production side followed a similar pattern. On a global basis, the two companies held just more than a nine percent market share, which would position the combination number four in the worldwide auto industry.

As part of the agreement, Renault pumped US$5.4 billion into cash-hungry Nissan in exchange for a 37 percent stake in Nissan Motor and a 22.5 percent stake (later raised to 26 percent) in Nissan Diesel Motor Co., a heavy truck unit. Although it did not secure complete control of Nissan, Renault gained veto power over capital expenditures and installed Carlos Ghosn (rhymes with ''bone'') as Nissan's chief operat-

ing officer (he became president as well in 2000). The Brazilian-born Ghosn was an executive vice-president at Renault and had engineered a rapid turnaround there after joining the company in 1996. French newspapers tagged him with the nickname ''le cost killer'' because of his tenacious approach to cost cutting—his Renault restructuring slashed US$3.5 billion in costs over a three-year period.

The capital injection from Renault quickly reduced Nissan's debt load to ¥1.4 trillion (US$13 billion). Ghosn rapidly began implementing a massive restructuring of Nissan. Nonautomotive operations began to be divested, including mobile and car telephone operations and the aerospace division. Nissan's forklift unit was likely to be sold and Nissan Diesel was a candidate for sale as well, given that Nissan Motor had declared that making cars and light trucks was its core business. In early 2000 Nissan sold a stake it held in Fuji Heavy Industries Ltd. As for the automotive operations, Ghosn in October 1999 laid out a tough cost-containment program slated to be completed by 2002. The program included: a 14 percent workforce reduction—representing 21,000 jobs, primarily in Japan—through attrition, early retirement, and noncore business spinoffs; the closure of five production plants in Japan in 2001 and 2002; the slashing of ¥1 trillion (US$9.5 billion) in annual costs, including a 20 percent reduction in purchasing costs and a 20 percent cut in overhead, the latter to include the elimination of one-fifth of Japanese Nissan dealers; and a 50 percent reduction in debt, to ¥700 billion (US$6.5 billion). Ghosn also began tackling the crucial need for a revitalization of Nissan's bland line of vehicles by substantially increasing capital spending, toward a goal of speeding new products to market four times faster than before. Although such a restructuring was by this time routine in the United States and becoming more commonplace in Europe, Ghosn's plan ran counter to many established business practices in Japan. The biggest question was whether Ghosn could implement the plan without resorting to large-scale layoffs in Japan, which would likely face fierce opposition from workers and labor unions and even from leaders of other Japanese firms. Perhaps to underscore the seriousness of his mission and his determination to turn Nissan around, Ghosn also announced that he would resign if Nissan was not profitable by March 2001.

Principal Subsidiaries

Autech Japan, Inc.; JATCO Corporation; NDC Co., Ltd.; Nissan Altia Co., Ltd.; Nissan Car Leasing Co., Ltd.; Nissan Finance Co., Ltd.; Nissan Koe Co., Ltd.; Nissan Kohki Co., Ltd.; Nissan Motor Car Carrier Co., Ltd.; Nissan Texsys Co., Ltd.; Nissan Trading Co., Ltd.; Nissan Transport Co., Ltd.; Rhythm Corporation; Tachi-S Co., Ltd.; Tennex Co., Ltd.; Vantec Corporation; Nissan Sunny Tokyo Motor Sales Co., Ltd.; Nissan Prince Tokyo Motor Sales Co., Ltd.; Tokyo Nissan Motor Sales Co.; Aichi Nissan Motor Co., Ltd.; Nissan Capital of America, Inc. (U.S.A.); Nissan CR Corporation (U.S.A.); Nissan Design International, Inc. (U.S.A.); Nissan Finance of America, Inc. (U.S.A.); Nissan Forklift Corporation, North America (U.S.A.); Nissan Motor Acceptance Corporation (U.S.A.); Nissan Motor Corporation in Guam; Nissan Motor Corporation in Hawaii, Ltd. (U.S.A.); Nissan North America, Inc. (U.S.A.); Nissan Research & Development, Inc. (U.S.A.); Nissan Textile Machinery Corporation in U.S.A.; Nissan Canada, Inc.; Nissan Canada Finance, Inc.; Nissan Mexicana, S.A. de C.V. (Mexico); Nissan European Technology Centre Ltd. (U.K.); Nissan International Finance (Europe) PLC (U.K.); Nissan Motor (GB) Ltd. (U.K.); Nissan Motor Manufacturing (UK) Ltd.; Nissan Europe N.V. (Netherlands); Nissan Finance, B.V. (Netherlands); Nissan International Finance (Netherlands) B.V.; Nissan Motor Netherland B.V.; Nissan France S.A.; Nissan Bank GmbH (Germany); Nissan Design Europe GmbH (Germany); Nissan Motor (Schweiz) AG (Switzerland); Nissan Motor Iberica, S.A. (Spain); Nissan Financiacion, S.A. (Spain); Nissan Motor España, S.A. (Spain); Nissan European Technology Centre España, S.A. (Spain); Nissan Italia S.p.A. (Italy); Nissan Finanziaria S.p.A. (Italy); Nissan Motor Co. (Australia) Pty, Ltd.; Nissan Datsun Holdings Ltd. (New Zealand); Nissan Middle East F.Z.E. (United Arab Emirates); Nissan Motor (China) Ltd.

Principal Competitors

Bayerische Motoren Werke AG; DaimlerChrysler AG; Fiat S.p.A.; Ford Motor Company; Fuji Heavy Industries Ltd.; General Electric Company; General Motors Corporation; Honda Motor Co., Ltd.; Hyundai Group; Isuzu Motors Limited; Kia Motors Co., Ltd.; Mazda Motor Corporation; Mitsubishi Group; Outboard Marine Corporation; PSA Peugeot Citroen S.A.; Saab Automobile AB; Suzuki Motor Corporation; Toyota Motor Corporation; Volkswagen AG; AB Volvo; Yamaha Corporation.

Further Reading

Armstrong, Larry, "Can Nissan Regain Its Youth?," *Business Week,* July 13, 1998, p. 132.

Beatty, Sally Goll, "Mixed Message: Nissan's Ad Campaign Was a Hit Everywhere But in the Showrooms," *Wall Street Journal,* April 8, 1997, pp. A1+.

Chang, C.S., *The Japanese Auto Industry and the U.S. Market,* New York: Praeger, 1981.

Chrysler, Mack, "Tackling a Big Turnaround: Nissan Chief Says Automaker's Suffering Is Solvable," *Ward's Auto World,* December 1998, p. 14.

Crate, James R., "Japan's Big Five Atone for Sins of Late '80s: Drive to Cut Costs Focuses on Proliferation of Parts," *Automotive News,* May 17, 1993, p. 19.

——, "Nissan Posts $273 Million Loss," *Automotive News,* November 1, 1993, p. 8.

Diem, William, "The Renault Nissan Deal," *Ward's Auto World,* May 30, 1999.

Edmondson, Gail, and Emily Thornton, "He Revved Up Renault. Will Nissan Be Next?," *Business Week* (international ed.), April 12, 1999, p. 23.

Edmondson, Gail, et al., "Dangerous Liaison: It Could Take 10 Years for Renault-Nissan to Yield a Return," *Business Week* (international ed.), March 29, 1999, p. 22.

Gross, Ken, "Doomed to Niches?," *Automotive Industries,* May 1992, p. 13.

——, "Learning from Mistakes," *Automotive Industries,* March 1994, p. 64.

Inaba, Yu, "Nissan Motor Company: Aiming for the Top Spot," *Tokyo Business Today,* December 1988, pp. 50+.

——, "Nissan's Management Revolution," *Tokyo Business Today,* October 1989, pp. 38+.

Johnson, Richard, "Nissan Loss Widens to Nearly $2 Billion," *Automotive News,* June 6, 1994, p. 6.

Maskery, Mary Ann, "Nissan Gets First Taste of Red Ink," *Automotive News,* November 9, 1992, p. 6.

Miller, Karen Lowry, and Larry Armstrong, "Will Nissan Get It Right This Time? After a Decade of Trouble, the Carmaker Is Making Major Changes," *Business Week,* April 20, 1992, p. 82.

"Nissan Earnings Dive 64.3 Percent," *Automotive News,* June 3, 1991, p. 4.

Sapsford, Jathon, "A Tuned-Up Nissan Takes on Its Rivals," *Wall Street Journal,* August 12, 1997, p. A10.

Shirouzu, Norihiko, "Nissan Calls Truck Unit Noncore, Possibly Signaling Eventual Sale," *Wall Street Journal,* February 18, 2000, p. A12.

——, "Nissan's Revival Relies on Operating Chief's Agility," *Wall Street Journal,* October 18, 1999, p. A37.

Simison, Robert L., "Nissan's Crisis Was Made in the U.S.A.," *Wall Street Journal,* November 25, 1998, p. B1.

Simison, Robert L., and Norihiko Shirouzu, "Nissan Unveils Tough Program to Cut Costs," *Asian Wall Street Journal,* October 19, 1999, p. 1.

Sobel, Robert, *Car Wars: The Untold Story,* New York: Dutton, 1984.

Strom, Stephanie, "Can Nissan Turn on a Centime: Trying to Revamp a Company and a Corporate Culture," *New York Times,* October 14, 1999, p. C1.

——, "No. 2 and Not Enjoying the Ride: Nissan Announces New Losses and Sweeping Changes," *New York Times,* May 21, 1998, p. D1.

Taylor, Alex, III, "The Man Who Vows to Change Japan Inc.," *Fortune,* December 20, 1999, pp. 189–90+.

Thornton, Emily, "Remaking Nissan," *Business Week* (international ed.), November 15, 1999, pp. 38+.

Thornton, Emily, and Kathleen Kerwin, "Back in the Mud: Nissan's Makeover Hasn't Jump-Started Profits," *Business Week* (international ed.), November 2, 1998, p. 26.

Thornton, Emily, and Larry Armstrong, "Nissan's Slow U-Turn: Its Recovery Is Far from Complete," *Business Week,* May 12, 1997, p. 54.

Thornton, Emily, et al., "A New Order at Nissan," *Business Week,* October 11, 1999, p. 54.

Updike, Edith, et al., "Japan Is Back," *Business Week,* February 19, 1996, pp. 42.+

Weinberg, Neil, "Member of the Pack," *Forbes,* May 19, 1997, p. 65.

Woodruff, David, "Cultural Chasm: Renault Faces Hurdles in Bid to Turn Nissan Around," *Asian Wall Street Journal,* March 31, 1999, p. 1.

—Jeffrey L. Covell
—updated by David E. Salamie

NORTEK

Nortek, Inc.

50 Kennedy Plaza
Providence, Rhode Island 02903
U.S.A.
Telephone: (401) 751-1600
Fax: (401) 751-4610
Web site: http://www.nortek-inc.com

Public Company
Incorporated: 1967
Employees: 12,200
Sales: $1.99 billion (1999)
Stock Exchanges: New York
Ticker Symbol: NTK
NAIC: 332322 Sheet Metal Work Manufacturing; 333415
   Air Conditioning and Warm Air Heating Equipment
   and Commercial and Industrial Refrigeration
   Equipment Manufacturing; 335228 Other Major
   Household Appliance Manufacturing

Nortek, Inc., founded in 1967 by Ralph R. Papitto, is a leading international, diversified manufacturer and distributor of building products for residential, light commercial, and commercial applications. From its headquarters in Providence, Rhode Island, Nortek manages over 30 wholly owned subsidiaries that operate within three principal segments: Residential Building Products; Air Conditioning and Heating (HVAC) Products; and Windows, Doors, and Siding Products. These subsidiaries manufacture and sell—primarily in the United States, Canada, and Europe—a wide variety of building products in key categories, such as kitchen range hoods and other spot-ventilating products, heating and air conditioning systems, wood and vinyl windows and doors, vinyl siding products, indoor air-quality systems, and specialty electronic products. Nortek products are designed to meet the needs of professionals in the manufactured home, new construction, and remodeling markets as well as those of individual contractors, wholesalers, and do-it-yourself customers. Nortek is the world's number one manufacturer of kitchen range hoods and bath fans; it is also North America's leading manufacturer of residential products for the quality of interior air; custom-designed HVAC equip-

ment; and HVAC equipment for the manufactured-housing market.

Shifting Business Structures, Fluctuating Economy: 1956–68

Ralph R. Papitto began his career as an entrepreneur in 1956 by founding Glass-Tite Industries, Inc., later known as GTI Corporation, a manufacturer of electronic semiconductor components. On July 24, 1967, Papitto founded Nortek, Inc. (named in part after Norma, his first wife) in Cranston, Rhode Island, and took the company public in September. His purpose, as stated in Nortek's 1967 annual report, was to form "an alliance of companies with long records of successful growth." Within a Nortek alliance, Papitto believed these companies could operate from "a larger perspective . . . and better cope with technical, financial, production, and marketing problems." In other words, Papitto based his business philosophy on "strong internal growth and external growth with strong companies in carefully selected industries."

Papitto quickly implemented this business philosophy. On November 20, 1967, Nortek purchased Kinetic Instrument Corp. and Kaybe Machine and Instrument Corp.; in December he acquired Nursery Plastics, Inc. and Young Designs, Inc. Kinetic produced high-performance elements—such as small gears, gyroscope yokes, wave guides, and microwave insulators for space-age technologies. Kaybe was a recognized manufacturer of large multiple-needle stitching machines and the innovator of quilting patterns used by textile firms. Nursery Plastics and Young Designs, on the other hand, worked with educators, pediatricians, and child psychologists to manufacture items for developing the coordination, association, and memory retention of small children.

During 1968, Nortek acquired four organizations. The first two were Vitta Corporation, originator of a new dry-plating method that used flexible tapes in the electronics industry primarily to transfer thin layers of precious metals to surfaces without causing any molecular change; and Providence, Rhode Island-based Domestic Credit Corporation, which conducted several banking activities. In December Nortek purchased American Flexible Conduit Co., Inc. and its two associated

Company Perspectives:

Nortek's mission is to broaden its offerings of high-quality building products; profitably grow its businesses both domestically and internationally; make strategic acquisitions, and assimilate these into its operations; and continue to build shareholder value.

companies (all of which Papitto bought after his retirement). Nortek also acquired the Massachusetts-based Duro Group of seven companies engaged in dyeing, finishing, printing, and distributing textiles. By year-end 1968, Nortek reported net revenues of $23.70 million compared to revenues of $13.62 million in fiscal 1967. Internal growth of operating units during 1968 averaged 15 percent, compared to a growth of nine percent in the Gross National Product Index of that year.

In an interview included in Nortek's 1968 annual report, Chairman Papitto told financial analyst James D. Kilpatrick that Nortek's rapid growth was largely due to the application of the multi-market company concept. Most medium-sized companies in the United States, said Papitto, were "convinced of the merits of becoming public companies" but feared that lack of sufficient resources would prevent them from performing successfully as public companies responsible to shareholders. Papitto persuaded companies to join multi-market Nortek, a parent organization that would give them the resources for meeting public company responsibilities of growth through new opportunities for "planning, research, risk-taking, and expansion." Papitto explained that Nortek's business strategy was one of "planned growth through balanced diversification."

Diversification, Energy Crisis, Recession, and Inflation: 1969–79

In 1969 Nortek was listed on the American Stock Exchange and was one of the most actively traded issues of that year. Initially, the company focused on three major areas: land sales and development; consumer and industrial products, and financial services. Nortek purchased Vermont-based Rock of Ages Corporation and its granite quarries. Rock of Ages was the leader of the memorialization industry (monuments, markers, mausoleums, memorials) in North America. In Nortek's 1969 annual report, Papitto quoted data from *U.S. News & World Report* indicating that from 1959 to 1969 land prices "soared 95 percent while common stocks, by contrast, rose only 18 percent in the same period, in terms of the Dow Jones Industrial average."

In sync with the trend to buy land, Nortek acquired the Webb Realty Group of five associated companies that were among the fastest-growing organizations in the land development business in Florida (where they created planned communities) and also acquired large acreage for community developments in New England, Arizona, Nebraska, and Michigan. The growth of consumer reliance on installment credit fostered Domestic Credit Corp.'s diversification into financing and mortgaging services. Net sales and operating revenues for fiscal 1969 totaled $43.75 million, compared to $23.70 million (as restated for pooling of interests) in fiscal 1968.

The Webb Realty Group sold mobile homes and reported record revenues. In 1971 Domestic Credit Corp. relocated to Cranston, Rhode Island and offered all financial services, except checking and trust functions. Domestic's operations complemented those of the Webb Group; financial services were a necessary dimension for full-service land sales and development, including the financing and development of mobile home communities. Nortek also acquired Arizona-based Mastercraft Homes, Inc.—which had a strong growth record as a builder of homes. Despite the soft economy that prevailed in 1971, Nortek reported revenues of $30.81 million for that fiscal year.

During 1972–73, Nortek reduced overhead costs, raised selling prices, and increased sales. Substantial debt was eliminated by the company's withdrawal from real estate and land development activities. Nortek divested itself of both Nortek Properties, Inc. (formerly the Webb Group) and Mastercraft Homes, Inc., continued to nurture the growth of its other subsidiary companies, and strengthened corporate management. Richard J. Harris joined the company as manager of corporate accounting, thereby initiating a career path that would bring him to serve as vice-president, treasurer, and chief financial officer beyond the year 2000. At the end of fiscal 1973, Nortek reported net earnings of $1.43 million, compared to $1.14 million in 1972.

An energy crisis, shortages of raw materials, high interest rates, government controls, and accelerating inflation created an adverse economic environment during 1974–75. Nortek strengthened its senior management team with the appointment of Richard L. Bready (who became president and CEO in 1990) as vice-president and treasurer. A growing demand for Duro Group's fabrics allowed it to recover from the 1974 turndown of the textile industry. Rock of Ages continued to upgrade its procedures and, according to Nortek's 1975 annual report, "was particularly proud of the unique 27-x30-foot bas-relief granite sculpture completed for installation on the facade of the giant Libby Dam in Montana." For fiscal 1975, Nortek posted net sales of $62.42 million, an increase of 28 percent over 1974.

Although net sales for 1976 peaked at $72.71 million, net earnings—reduced by settlement of litigation for a seven-year-old lawsuit and reorganization of Nortek's Cable and Wire Division—dropped to $82,000. Nortek sold its marginally profitable finance subsidiary, Domestic Credit Corporation, and merged its new acquisition—Minnesota-based Manufacturers Systems, Inc.—into a Nortek subsidiary. MSI manufactured and distributed a wide variety of metal products for heating and cooling systems. During 1977, harsh winter weather severely impacted the quarrying operations of Nortek's Rock of Ages subsidiary and the worldwide oversupply of copper caused continued erosion in the selling prices and gross profit margins of the Cable and Wire Division. Nevertheless, despite adverse economic conditions in many of Nortek's primary markets, none of Nortek's operating divisions experienced losses during 1978–79. Net sales for fiscal 1979 rose to $117.96 million while net earnings grew to $3.75 million.

Rebounding Economy, Rise and Decline of Housing Market, High Leverage and Downturn: 1980–89

The 1980s, according to Kingwood College Library's web site, was "an era of hostile takeovers, leveraged buyouts, and

---

Key Dates:

1967: Ralph R. Papitto founds Nortek, Inc.
1969: Nortek is listed on the American Stock Exchange.
1971: Nortek subsidiary reports record sales of mobile homes.
1980–81: Nortek enters building-products industry.
1985: Nortek relocates its headquarters to Providence, Rhode Island.
1989: Housing starts drop sharply for the third consecutive year.
1990: Chairman Papitto retires in favor of Nortek President Richard L. Bready.
1993: Nortek management restructures operations and revises its business strategy.
1995–96: Nortek restructures its product segments.
1998–99: Nortek sells eight businesses and acquires seven major companies.
1999: Nortek posts record sales.

---

mega-mergers that spawned a new breed of billionaires.'' For many people, binge buying and running up credit were the order of the day during this decade, which began with double-digit inflation. President Reagan (1981–89) ''obtained legislation to curb inflation, stimulate economic growth, increase employment, strengthen the military and renew national self confidence.'' The recession of 1981–82 slowly gave way to relative prosperity as corporations adapted to a changing economy.

Higher prices for supplies and raw materials, rising wage levels, additional fringe benefits, and other costs that Nortek could not completely pass along to customers had a negative impact on net earnings. Furthermore, reduced demand for exports of higher-margin rough granite and price fluctuations in copper adversely affected the profitability of Rock of Ages and of the Cable and Wire Division.

It was at this time that Nortek, with subsidiaries in various types of business, entered the building products industry with the acquisition of Miami-based Glassalum Engineering Corp. and of Glassalum Installations, Inc. These companies engineered, manufactured and installed glass and aluminum exteriors for multi-story commercial buildings and condominiums—and brought in a $16 million backlog of orders. In January 1981, Nortek further strengthened its position in the building products industry by acquiring Wisconsin-based Broan Mfg. Co., Inc., a manufacturer of built-in home products, and the largest manufacturer of kitchen-range hoods; Broan products were used in new construction and in renovation projects.

Nortek's investment in building products did not pay off immediately but did serve as the seed from which Nortek would grow. High interest rates on mortgages slowed down the demand for housing in 1981–82. In the mid-1980s, however, according to Carl Horowitz's analysis of housing in the 1980s, the United States ''had 102.7 million dwellings in 1987, a 49.5 percent increase over the 68.7 million dwellings in 1970.'' The increase was due in part to a recovering economy and a shift in population brought on by baby boomers who, ''by the close of the 1980s,

were in the 35–54 age group, had established their own households''—and were not seeking housing for the first time.

''During the 1980s,'' according to the April 29, 1990 issue of the *Boston Globe,* Nortek ''bought or sold more than a dozen companies, including makers of aerospace fasteners, bicycle spokes, aircraft landing gear, brass nuts and plastics.'' Nortek continued to diversify through acquisitions, mainly Linear Corporation and Nordyne Inc. At first, Nortek financed acquisitions with commercial bank debt. Early in the 1980s, however, ''the company was introduced to a different way of raising money: selling high-yield, high-risk debt, known as junk bonds,'' according to Neil Downing in the *Providence Journal-Bulletin.* These bonds gave Nortek millions of dollars for acquisitions. ''Nortek issued junk bonds to help pay for one or two big acquisitions, which never materialized. While searching for deals, Nortek invested a lot of the proceeds from the bond sales in other companies' junk bonds or in junk-bond mutual funds,'' Downing noted. At the end of the decade, the company's profits suffered from the 1987 stock market crash, which devastated Nortek's junk-bond portfolio. For several years after early 1988, Nortek made no significant material acquisitions.

Furthermore, by 1989, Nortek had other problems. Housing starts had begun to plummet in 1986 and by 1989 were down for the third consecutive year nationwide and at their lowest level since the 1981–82 recession. ''Resales of existing homes were at a five-year low,'' wrote Biddle for the *Boston Globe.* Nortek had to settle two court cases and resolve allegations brought by the Securities and Exchange Commission. For fiscal 1989, the company posted a $12.5 million loss on sales of $1.08 billion, the company's largest net loss and, ironically, its largest net sales in about ten years. But all was not gloom and doom: Nortek had begun to evolve as a manufacturer of building products, to cut operating costs, and to restructure.

Lean Years and an Upturn: 1990–94

Since its founding in 1967, Nortek had owned a granite quarry, a land development company, and a lamp manufacturer. It had bought and sold dozens of companies, including those involved in textiles, toys, banking, and aerospace. A significant number of acquisitions made in a relatively short time rapidly increased the company's debt. Relatively high interest rates, problems in the savings-and-loan industry, and a sudden downturn in the housing market slowed sales of building products. Nortek found it difficult to service its debt on a continuing basis. By 1990, Nortek shares had plunged to $2.875 per share, compared to a range before the October 1987 crash of $12–$16 per share.

In November 1990, Papitto retired in favor of his longtime associate, Nortek President Richard L. Bready, who succeeded him as the company's chief executive officer. Bready came into his new position to face $350 million in short- and long-term debt, including $170 million in junk bonds. Nortek's stock had dropped down to less than $2 a share.

Nortek's growth had been generated largely by strategic acquisitions and mergers, and by the success of its product groups. The profitability of these groups was significantly impacted between 1986 and 1991 by a decline of 43.8 percent in new housing starts as well as by harsh economic conditions, particularly in the Northeast, California, and Canada. Construction of residential housing increased about 20 percent during 1990–94 but remained below the levels of the mid-1980s. President and CEO Bready led Nortek management through a restructuring of operations and a revision of Nortek's business philosophy. The company reduced production costs and overhead levels, improved the efficiency and productivity of its operations, and showed operating earnings despite a slow economy. Net sales decreased to $744.11 million in 1993 but net losses that had spiraled to $38.1 million in 1990 were down to $20.8 million in fiscal 1993, although 1993 sales were $55.87 million lower than those of the preceding year.

During an interview with Don DeMaio for the *Providence Business News,* Chairman Bready commented that since 1990, Nortek had sold nine businesses, reduced the workforce by 15 percent, and "cost-reduced the entire delivery system. . . ." Bready explained Nortek's revised business philosophy: "We want to have one of the best products in the industries that we're in and the lowest delivered cost. You have to have continuous improvement in both the product and your costs. If you don't have that, somebody else will," he emphasized. At year-end 1994, Nortek posted net earnings of $17.8 million and had accumulated $100 million in cash reserves.

As a diversified manufacturer of residential and commercial building products, in 1995 Nortek operated within three principal product sections: the Residential Building Products Group; the HVAC Products Group; and the Plumbing Products Group. To strengthen the Residential Building Products Group, during the last quarter of 1995, Nortek acquired Texas-based Rangaire Company (kitchen-range hoods and lighting fixtures); the capital stock and related entities of Italy-based Best S.p.A. (kitchen-range hoods); and the stock of Venmar Ventilation Inc. (continuous ventilation systems and energy-recovery ventilators), headquartered in Quebec, Canada. These acquisitions expanded Nortek's product lines, advanced its indoor air-quality technology, and moved the company into new global markets.

In mid-1994 Nortek had experienced significant increases in the cost for raw materials as well as fewer demands for building products. Although these negative factors increased in fiscal 1995 Nortek posted net earnings of $15 million on sales of $776.21 million. In 1996 Nortek's operations were stimulated by an increase in housing starts throughout the United States and Canada. Cost increases subsided and Nortek began to reap increased benefits from the turnaround strategy that Chairman Bready and his team had set in place in the early 1990s; namely, development of a strong core group of businesses; divestiture of units that did not fit the core; reduction of debt-servicing costs; and initiation of a rigorous but realistic system of cost reductions and controls. Nortek became one of the largest suppliers of custom-designed commercial HVAC products in the United States. Fiscal 1996 net sales grew to $969.80 million and net earnings to $22 million.

1996 and Beyond

Because of continuing losses in the Plumbing Products Group, in 1997 Nortek adopted a plan to discontinue this Group and reorganized the company into three segments: Residential Building Products; Air Conditioning and Heating Products; and Windows, Doors, and Siding. The August acquisition of New York-based Ply Gem Industries, Inc., a leading manufacturer and distributor of specialty building products for the home-improvement industry and a major supplier to national do-it-yourself retail home centers, represented a quantum leap in growth for the company and raised it to national leadership ranks in the building products industry. Ply Gem operated two principal product groups targeting the residential and light-commercial markets: Windows, Doors, and Siding; and Specialty Products and Distribution; Ply Gem was phased into one of Nortek's wholly owned subsidiaries. Nortek's sales for fiscal 1997 peaked at $1.13 billion and net earnings were $21.2 million.

During 1998 Nortek sold eight businesses, some of which were considered non-strategic assets that had come with the purchase of Ply Gem. In July, from London-based Williams Plc, Nortek acquired Ohio-based NuTone, Inc., which specialized in intercom systems and home theater systems. In October Nortek acquired Pennsylvania-based Napco Inc., which owned factories—within a few miles of each other—for the production of quality vinyl siding, aluminum building products, and vinyl windows. Napco's siding business was combined with Nortek's Variform siding subsidiary, and Napco's window fabrication operations were merged with Nortek's Great Lakes Window Inc. subsidiary, according to the September 7, 1998 issue of *Plastic News.* All of Nortek's core businesses were profitable in fiscal 1998, principally as a result of acquisitions and higher sales for superior-level, built-in ventilation products in North America. Net sales for fiscal 1998 rose to $1.74 billion, a 53 percent increase over those of 1997; net earnings increased to $35 million, a 65 percent rise over those for 1997.

During 1999 the company acquired seven companies, among which was Webco, Inc.—a designer and manufacturer of custom air-handling equipment for industrial, institutional, and commercial customers. To expand its presence in the windows and doors marketplace, Nortek also purchased three businesses from United Kingdom-based Caradon plc: Georgia-based Peachtree Doors and Windows, a national supplier of premium residential windows, entry doors and patio doors that targeted custom and high-end home markets; Pennsylvania-based Thermal-Gard, which made premium replacement windows, patio doors and sunrooms; and Alberta, Canada-based CWD Windows and Doors, a leading provider of complete window and door systems for new homes in western Canada.

Next came Nortek's purchase of Multiplex Technologies, Inc., a manufacturer of high-performance, multi-room video distribution equipment for the home. In October Nortek acquired Kroy Building Products, Inc., a market leader in vinyl fencing, railing profiles and vinyl decking systems for residential and commercial applications. In early December Nortek acquired Xantech Corporation, a manufacturer of residential infrared remote-control systems for extending control of VCR, cable, satellite, and stereo systems to multiple rooms throughout an entire household.

Fiscal 1999 was the second consecutive year for which Nortek reported record financial results. Net sales for the year rose to $1.99 billion, a 15 percent increase from the $1.74

billion for 1998. Net earnings peaked at $49 million, a 41 percent increase from the $35 million reported for 1998.

As the year 2000 unfolded, Chairman Bready commented, in a letter to Nortek shareholders, that Nortek was poised ''to benefit from generally favorable economic conditions. Low inflation, near full employment, strong liquidity and strong consumer confidence continued to help Americans fulfill their dream of home ownership and improved home amenities through extensive home remodeling and expansion.''

In short, Nortek had known lean years—but judging from its history and a strong trend to new homes and renewed emphasis on home renovation—the company had good reason to believe in its near-term and longer-term prosperity as an international leader of the building products industry.

Principal Subsidiaries

Best S.p.A. (Italy); Broan-NuTone LLC; Broan-NuTone Canada Inc.; CWD Windows and Doors (Canada); Elektromec S.p.A. (Italy); Goverenair Corporation; Great Lakes Window, Inc.; Hoover Treated Wood Products, Inc.; Kroy Building Products, Inc.; Linear Corporation; Mammoth, Inc.; Napco, Inc. Nordyne Inc.; NuTone Inc.; Peachtree Doors & Windows, Inc.; Rangaire LP; Richwood Building Products, Inc.; SNE Enterprises, Inc.; Temtrol, Inc.; Thermal-Gard, Inc.; Variform, Inc.; Venmar Ventilation Inc. (Canada); Venmar Aston (Canada); Venmar CES (Canada); Ventrol Air Handling Systems, Inc.; Webco, Inc.

Principal Operating Units

Residential Building Products; Air Conditioning and Heating (HVAC) Products; Windows, Doors, and Siding Products.

Principal Competitors

American Standard Companies; Carrier Corporation; Goodman Holding Company; Lennox International Inc.; York International Corporation, Inc.

Further Reading

''American Cultural History: 1980–89,'' http://www.kingwoodcollege library.com/subjects.html#history.

Biddle, Frederic M., ''Why Wall Street Doesn't Believe Nortek Anymore,'' *Boston Globe*, April 29, 1990, p. 69.

Davis, Paul, ''Nortek Eyes New Strategy After Loss of $19.9 Million,'' *Providence Journal-Bulletin*, November 4, 1992.

DeMaio, Don, ''Bready: Improve Product and Cost = Nortek Success,'' *Providence Business News,* September 15, 1995.

Downing, Neil, ''Parting Shots: Nortek's Feisty Founder Defends Junk Bonds, Calls Company Sound,'' *Providence Journal-Bulletin*, November 4, 1990, p. F1.

——, ''Trouble at Nortek: A Predator's Fall; Nortek Growth Strategy Flounders in Red Ink,'' *Providence Journal-Bulletin,* April 29, 1990.

Horowitz, Carl F., ''Washington's Continuing Fiction: A National Housing Shortage,'' August 22, 1990, http://www.heritage.org/library/categories/healthwel/#bg 783.html].

Urey, Craig, ''Consolidation & Merger of Corporations: Napco, Inc.; Nortek, Inc.,'' *Plastic News*, September 7, 1998.

—Gloria A. Lemieux

O'Sullivan Industries Holdings, Inc.

<table>
<tr><td>

1900 Gulf Street
Lamar, Missouri 64759-1899
U.S.A.
Telephone: (417) 682-3322
Fax: (417) 682-8104
Web site: http://www.osullivan.com

Public Company
Incorporated: 1954
Employees: 2,350
Sales: $379.6 million (1999)
Stock Exchanges: New York
Ticker Symbol: OSU
NAIC: 337211 Wood Office Furniture Manufacturing;
   33712 Household and Institutional Furniture
   Manufacturing

</td></tr>
</table>

O'Sullivan Industries Holdings, Inc. is the third largest maker of ready-to-assemble furniture in the United States. O'Sullivan is the tenth largest manufacturer of furniture overall and is publicly traded. The company manufactures desks, credenzas, computer workcenters, entertainment centers, kitchen accessories, and other products for homes and offices. The products are sold through department stores, office superstores, and home centers in North America and the United Kingdom. O'Sullivan Industries operates manufacturing facilities in South Boston, Virginia; Cedar City, Utah; and Lamar, Missouri, where the company is headquartered. In 1999 O'Sullivan reported $379.6 million in sales and employed 2,350 people.

1954 and the Early Years: Television Original Inspiration

At a July 4th picnic, Thomas O'Sullivan listened to his host's complaints about the new television he had purchased. The television was supposed to be portable, but the owner found it to be extremely difficult to move. That small problem was all the inspiration that Thomas O'Sullivan needed. He returned home to his machine shop and created a solution—a cart designed to move a television easily. The design, perhaps the very first TV cart, was the original product of Sullivan Industries. Television manufacturers, including RCA and General Electric, were among the first customers.

Founded as Sullivan Industries, the company changed its name to O'Sullivan Industries in 1957. Also in 1957, the growth of the business dictated that a new facility was needed, and the company moved from its founding location in Japan, Missouri, to Owensville, Missouri. Just seven years later, in 1964, the company moved once again, this time to the site of its newest plant in Lamar, Missouri.

Merger and Expansion: 1960s–80s

In 1969, five years after O'Sullivan Industries moved to Lamar, Thomas O'Sullivan decided to merge the company with fellow furniture manufacturer Conroy. The merger allowed for greater competitiveness in the marketplace, but the O'Sullivan family no longer had a controlling interest in the company with their name.

In 1979, the business was growing at such a rate that O'Sullivan Industries decided to expand the facilities in Lamar, Missouri. The location continued to serve as the corporate headquarters, but boasted an increased capacity in the manufacturing facility.

In 1983, Conroy sold O'Sullivan Industries to Tandy Corporation, an electronics retailer. Though O'Sullivan Industries was mostly profitable at the time, Tandy Corporation faced many challenges, especially with its flagship company, Radio Shack. Tandy experienced poor stock performance because of its lack of profitability.

When founder Thomas O'Sullivan retired in 1986, his son Daniel was named CEO and president of O'Sullivan, which remained a subsidiary of Tandy Corporation. In 1988, O'Sullivan was still growing and an additional plant was built in South Boston, Virginia.

Company Perspectives:

O'Sullivan's corporate mission has been to become the unquestioned leader in ready-to-assemble furniture. Our path to success has been to focus on having the most innovative product designs, being a low cost producer and empowering our employees to continually improve product quality and customer service. The dedication to this mission is shared by everyone at O'Sullivan.

Going Public: 1990s

In 1994, Tandy Corporation offered O'Sullivan as a public company. The sale, though prompted by Tandy's ailing profitability, was itself a success for the parent company. The public offering brought in $350 million, four times Tandy's original investment.

O'Sullivan family members and management bought shares but were short of obtaining a controlling interest. However, the O'Sullivan family continued in the company's leadership. Also in 1994, the company forged a licensing agreement with Fisher-Price to make a line of infant and juvenile furniture. The furniture line helped to meet the need for affordable and attractive children's furniture.

In 1995, an additional distribution center and manufacturing facility in Cedar City, Utah was built. In 1996 O'Sullivan's top five customers accounted for 51 percent of sales. The office superstore Office Depot was responsible for 16 percent of sales while Office Max accounted for 13 percent of sales. Despite the stability represented by these major customers, O'Sullivan faced challenges as a niche furniture manufacturer in the coming years.

In the mid- to late 1990s, prices for wood products such as particleboard and packing materials were on the rise, and this situation caused profits for the company to decline. The volatile retail industry also had an effect as bankruptcies and mergers in that area caused a decline in O'Sullivan's customer base. In 1996, Best Products filed for bankruptcy, and in 1997 another major customer, Montgomery Ward, filed for Chapter 11 reorganization.

In response to declining profits, O'Sullivan restructured its business by cutting jobs and streamlining its product line. In 1996, for the first time in the company's history, the president of the firm did not carry the O'Sullivan name. While Daniel O'Sullivan remained chairman and CEO, Richard D. Davidson, a former Sunbeam executive, was named president of the company.

In 1998 O'Sullivan's sales grew by only 5.6 percent and net income was down 9.1 percent. Many one-time factors contributed to the decrease, according to the company, including the installation of a new, fully integrated software package designed to tie together all levels of activities at the company's three manufacturing facilities. Capital improvements were a factor as well, as the facility in South Boston, Virginia, was upgraded to meet the standards of the rest of the company.

In 1999 O'Sullivan was purchased for about $350 million by investment group OSI Acquisition, an affiliate of Brockman,

Rosser, Sherrill & Co., L.P. (BRS). BRS was a private investment firm located in New York. The group included O'Sullivan executives, but the company's preferred shares were still publicly traded. After the announcement of the merger, a lawsuit was filed by O'Sullivan stockholders against O'Sullivan, the directors of O'Sullivan, and BRS. The class-action lawsuit alleged that the directors of O'Sullivan had breached their fiduciary duties in approving the transaction. Tandy Corporation and its subsidiary, TE ELECTRONICS INC, filed an unrelated lawsuit dealing with the initial public offering and the interpretation of an existing tax sharing agreement.

Despite the two lawsuits, the merger moved forward and was completed in November 1999. Of the two companies, O'Sullivan was the surviving corporation following the merger. After the merger, members of O'Sullivan's management team owned almost 30 percent of the company while BRS owned the remainder of the stock.

Trending Towards Increased Growth: 2000s

O'Sullivan Industries enjoyed a growth period at the end of the 1990s. Sales grew 11.8 percent to $379.6 million in 1999. Along with fiscal growth, the company increased its employee base by 17.5 percent to 2,350 at the three facilities in Lamar, Missouri; South Boston, Virginia; and Cedar City, Utah.

Daniel O'Sullivan retired as CEO in 2000 though remained chairman, while Richard D. Davidson became both CEO and president of the company. The company began the year 2000 with other internal promotions as well. Thomas M. O'Sullivan, Jr., was named senior vice-president-sales, and Michael P. O'Sullivan was named senior vice-president-marketing. The founding O'Sullivan family remained well represented on the company's roster.

In regard to his retirement, Daniel O'Sullivan said in the 1998 annual report, "A vital aspect of O'Sullivan's growth has been the willingness to accept and even encourage change. During my tenure with the company, we have evolved from a maker of metal TV stands to simple wood furniture to a fully automated manufacturer of a line of highly diverse furniture products. Embracing this philosophy of change was a primary factor in my decision to retire as Chairman and Chief Executive Officer."

The first quarter of fiscal 2000 showed continued growth for the company, with sales rising 16.3 percent to $102 million. "First quarter results reflected the positive effects of the significant capital investments we have been making for the past several years, as well as the increasing capabilities of our employees in all three plant locations," said Richard D. Davidson in a corporate press release. "Profits were positively impacted on virtually every level over the first quarter of last year. ..."

In the second quarter, the upward trend continued with sales rising 13.5 percent. Growth in major customer channels led to the record sales numbers. "We expect continued growth for the rest of the fiscal year," said Davidson. "It should be at a more moderate pace. We remain focused on providing superior customer service and product development in order to become the vendor of choice of the major RTA (ready-to-assemble) retailers."

Key Dates:

1954: Sullivan Industries is founded in Japan, Missouri.
1957: Name changes to O'Sullivan Industries; company moves to Owensville, Missouri.
1964: O'Sullivan Industries moves to Lamar, Missouri.
1969: O'Sullivan Industries merges with Conroy.
1979: Expansion begins on O'Sullivan's Lamar facilities.
1983: Conroy sells O'Sullivan Industries to Tandy Corp.
1986: Tom O'Sullivan retires; Dan O'Sullivan is named CEO and president.
1988: South Boston, Virginia plant is built.
1994: Tandy orchestrates IPO of O'Sullivan Industries.
1995: Cedar City, Utah plant is built.
1999: O'Sullivan executives, as part of an investment group, purchase O'Sullivan Industries.
2000: Dan O'Sullivan retires; Rick Davidson is named CEO and president.

The continued growth in home offices remained a positive factor for O'Sullivan Industries. As the demand for home office furniture such as desks, computer workstations, and credenzas increased, O'Sullivan adapted its product offerings to meet its customer's needs. The popularity of all ready-to-assemble furniture increased as well and was offered in a variety of superstore-type locations, including Wal-Mart, Home Depot, Office Depot, and Sears.

One of the ways that O'Sullivan met the growing demand for attractive, easy to assemble, and affordable furniture was by offering a wide selection of designs for consumers. One of its trademarked designs, Intelligent Designs, was created to give the consumer stylish furniture at an affordable price.

While many ready-to-assemble furniture designs featured sharp corners, the Intelligent Designs line was designed with rounded, profiled edges and with the goal of emulating hand-crafted furniture. The designs were targeted for both homes and home offices.

As O'Sullivan prepared for the future, its three facilities represented two million square feet of manufacturing, distribution, and office capacity. Both sales and employee numbers were increasing, and changes in ownership and management augured well for the company.

Principal Competitors

Bassett Furniture Industries, Inc.; Bush Industries, Inc.; Furniture Brands International; HON Industries Inc.; IKEA International A/S; Knoll Group Inc.; LifeStyle Furnishings International; Sauder Woodworking; Steelcase; WinsLoew Furniture.

Further Reading

Anderson Forest, Stephanie, "Promises, Promises at Tandy," *BusinessWeek,* June 15, 1997.
Gump, Warren, "Comparing Furniture Makers," *Motley Fool,* February 2, 1999.
"Office Furniture: O'Sullivan Industries Holdings," *Motley Fool,* September 19, 1997.
"O'Sullivan Industries Announces Promotions of Senior Executives," *PR Newswire,* January 28, 2000.
"O'Sullivan Industries Reports Continued Record Sales and EBITDA After One-Time Charges for Second Quarter," *PR Newswire,* January 25, 2000.

—Shawna Brynildssen

Olivetti S.p.A.

Via Jervis 77
10015 Ivrea (TO)
Italy
Telephone: (0125) 52-00
Fax: (0125) 52-2524
Web site: http://www.olivetti.it

Public Company
Incorporated: 1908 as Ing. C. Olivetti & C., S.p.A.
Employees: 132,000
Sales: L 48 trillion (US$28 billion) (1999 est.)
Stock Exchanges: Milan Brussels Frankfurt London
Ticker Symbol: OLVTY
NAIC: 513310 Wired Telecommunications Carriers;
513322 Cellular and Other Wireless
Telecommunications; 513340 Satellite
Telecommunications; 333313 Office Machinery
Manufacturing; 333315 Photographic and
Photocopying Equipment Manufacturing; 334119
Other Computer Peripheral Equipment Manufacturing;
334210 Telephone Apparatus Manufacturing

Olivetti S.p.A. (also known as Olivetti Group), through its majority ownership of Telecom Italia S.p.A., is Italy's leading telecommunications company. Telecom Italia is the former Italian phone monopoly, which was privatized in 1997 then taken over by Olivetti in a 1999 hostile takeover. In addition to its fixed-line telephone operations, Telecom Italia also holds majority control of Telecom Italia Mobile, which specializes in cellular telephone services. Olivetti's emergence as a leading telecommunications player marked a dramatic shift in the company's history. Olivetti was long a world leader in the manufacture and sale of typewriters, before its 1980s plunge into the information technology market, where it became a top European maker of computers and computer systems. However, the company nearly went bankrupt in the 1990s as losses in its computer operations mounted; the company eventually divested its personal computer (PC) division. Though primarily focused on telecommunications as it approached the 21st century, Oli-

vetti maintained some information technology interests, including Olivetti Lexikon, which continues the company's office products tradition through the manufacture of fax machines, photocopiers, printers, and other products.

Typewriter Beginnings

Olivetti was founded in 1908 in the small northern Italian town of Ivrea, not far from Milan. Camillo Olivetti had been much impressed, on his various trips to the United States, with the typewriter, already well established in U.S. offices but still largely unknown in his native Italy. Olivetti pulled together a modest capital fund of L 350,000 and, in Ivrea, Italy, opened his own typewriter manufacturing plant—the country's first—employing 20 workers.

In 1911 he exhibited the first Italian typewriter, the Olivetti M1, at the Turin Universal Exposition. The M1 was not significantly more advanced than the U.S. machines on which it was modeled. However, as Olivetti commented at the time, "the aesthetic side of the machine has been carefully studied." The M1's "elegant and serious" design was typical of Olivetti. As the company grew, this preoccupation with design developed into a comprehensive corporate philosophy, which embraced everything from the shape of a space bar to the color scheme for an advertising poster. Many years later the Museum of Modern Art in New York City would recognize Olivetti's enduring commitment to design by mounting an exhibition of its products and honoring the company as the leading design firm in the western world.

During Olivetti's first 20 years, Italy suffered the effects of World War I, uncontrolled inflation, political instability, and finally the crash and Great Depression of 1929. Olivetti itself, however, enjoyed remarkable and lasting success in the relatively immature Italian industrial economy. The little plant in Ivrea expanded rapidly, adding both floor space and employees as fast as they could be assimilated; yearly machine production shot up tenfold between 1914 and 1929, from 1,300 to 13,000 typewriters. As the company added new models to its line—the M20 in 1920 and M40 ten years later—it opened sales offices in six foreign countries, originating Olivetti's consistently international approach to business. In 1928 Camillo Olivetti's son Adriano had opened the company's first advertising office, which soon employed some of Europe's leading artists to communicate Olivetti's commitment to aesthetics as well as efficiency. Adriano Olivetti, born in 1901, gradually took on more of the company's management, becoming general manager and effectively head of the firm in 1933.

During this time, the Olivettis took an active interest in the welfare, particularly the living conditions, of their workers. The company began building housing for its workers in 1926, and made an effort to create a corporate environment designed as a haven for its employees. As Adriano Olivetti gradually gained control of the family business during the 1930s, he embarked on an ambitious plan for the entire town of Ivrea, building schools, housing, roads, and recreation facilities in addition to regularly expanding the Olivetti plant itself. Olivetti founded a magazine and later a publishing house to further his social ideals, and remained a leading force in European industrial philosophy until his death.

Providing the wherewithal to support such philanthropy was Olivetti's continuing success in the marketplace. The company increased typewriter production threefold between 1929 and 1937, at which later date some 40 percent of its machines were of the new, portable variety introduced in 1933. Other new products were added during these years as well—office furniture, adding machines, and teleprinters—presaging the company's eventual emergence as a diversified office-products manufacturer. Olivetti went public in 1932, initially capitalized at L 13 million and managed to maintain its profitability through the worst years of the Depression. Within ten years, corporate capital had tripled, employees numbered 4,700, and Olivetti machines were being exported to over 22 countries.

As World War II dragged on, however, the position of the Olivetti family, which was Jewish, became untenable. Adriano Olivetti was forced to flee the country shortly after his father's death in 1943; when he returned at war's end, he was able to pick up the pieces quickly and join the postwar economic boom.

Postwar Growth

Olivetti enjoyed unprecedented growth in the years following the war. The company expanded its export business to include the entire industrialized world. It also acquired Underwood, the U.S. typewriter manufacturer, in 1959, and built new plants in southern Italy, Spain, Brazil, Argentina, Mexico, and the United States. Its growing collection of office products all exhibited the aesthetic sensitivity that had made

Olivetti famous in the world of design, and Adriano Olivetti pursued his vision of an industrial giant responsive to the needs of both consumer and worker.

In 1959, in addition to its line of typewriters, adding machines, teleprinters, and office furniture, Olivetti unveiled the Elea 9003, Italy's first computer. This room-sized machine was built with an eye toward eventual competition with IBM and the other early computer developers. However, within a few years Olivetti realized that it could not match strides with the more advanced U.S. products and abandoned the mainframe market.

Adriano Olivetti's death in 1960 brought to an end the Olivetti family's direct management of the corporation. The company employed some 40,000 people, less than half of whom worked in Italy, in 1960, and its capital had reached L 40 billion. Despite an impressive list of awards and international acclaim, the company entered a period of falling profits and gradual insolvency. Olivetti found itself in need of outside capital and management, and in 1964 it was rescued by a consortium of Italian banks and industrial concerns. Bruno Visentini was made president.

While Olivetti left the mainframe market during the early 1960s, it did not ignore the electronic revolution then just beginning. In addition to converting its adding machines to what we now call calculators, the firm began manufacturing electronic typewriters, banking terminals, and telecommunications equipment. Olivetti also entered two new markets, offering the Copia 2000 line of copiers and an increasing array of industrial-automation systems, including robots and precision machine tools. Most significantly, the company continued to produce smaller computers, and by 1965 was selling both minicomputers and an early version of the desktop micro. Olivetti thus survived a period of technological change and international competition that proved to be too much for many other long-established machine manufacturers.

Late 1970s–80s: De Benedetti and the Shift to Computers

Olivetti survived the challenge, but it did not prosper. By the end of the 1970s the firm employed a peak of 62,000 individuals, and had L 1.55 trillion in sales in 1978; but with corporate debt at an alarming level, Olivetti turned once again to the financial markets for help. Carlo and Franco De Benedetti, young entrepreneurial brothers, acquired 14 percent of the company for a bargain price of US$17 million. Carlo De Benedetti, who took over as chief executive, brought to Olivetti more than an infusion of capital; he pushed the company to drop its traditional corporate style. Despite the recent electronic overhaul, the company had remained relaxed and rather friendly. For years Olivetti had supported various artistic and philanthropic projects, building day-care centers for its employees as well as beautiful typewriters for its customers, but it had not been especially concerned with efficiency and profit. De Benedetti realized that such a business would not survive the challenge posed by Asian international competitors.

Olivetti continued its expansion in the information technology market, but with new vigor, efficiency, and aggressiveness. Olivetti accordingly added new products, such as cash registers,

Key Dates:

1908: Camillo Olivetti founds Ing. C. Olivetti & C., S.p.A., the first Italian typewriter manufacturer.

1911: Olivetti exhibits the first Italian typewriter, the Olivetti M1, at the Turin Universal Exposition.

1932: Company goes public.

1933: Adriano Olivetti, son of Camillo, becomes general manager.

1959: Company acquires Underwood, a U.S. typewriter manufacturer; Olivetti unveils the Elea 9003, Italy's first computer.

1978: Carlo De Benedetti acquires stake in Olivetti and takes over as chief executive.

1983: Company enters into a computer alliance with AT&T, following the introduction of the M24, an IBM-compatible personal computer.

1991: Olivetti posts its first loss in 13 years, resulting from troubled computer operations.

1995: Olivetti-led Omnitel begins offering cellular service; Olivetti also forms Infostrada, a fixed-line telephone start-up.

1996: De Benedetti resigns under pressure; Roberto Colaninno takes over as chief executive.

1997: Company exits the PC business; telecom operations are placed under a new holding company, owned jointly by Olivetti and Mannesmann.

1999: Olivetti acquires a majority stake in Telecom Italia S.p.A.; company sells holdings in Omnitel and Infostrada.

automated teller machines (ATMs), and advanced copiers, to its line of electronics systems and made a major commitment to its micro- and mini-computer divisions. The company's 1982 personal computer, the M20, was widely recognized as a solid machine, but it was not IBM compatible. The following year Olivetti pushed into production the M24, which was not only IBM compatible but an attractive enough product to bring De Benedetti the international trading partner he had hoped to find. AT&T offered to sell Olivetti micros under its own name in the United States, while Olivetti would sell AT&T minis outside the United States. In addition, AT&T agreed to buy 22 percent of Olivetti, retaining an option on a further 18 percent.

The deal was signed in December 1983 and was an immediate success. AT&T sold the Olivetti machines as fast as it could get them, distributing some 200,000 units in 1986 alone, while Olivetti produced more modest but acceptable sales figures with the AT&T minis. De Benedetti made the cover of *Time* as Olivetti sales reached L 7.3 trillion and profits hit L 565.5 billion. Olivetti, however, was late on several key innovations in 1987. As a result, AT&T's sales fell off drastically, bringing with them Olivetti profits, and the two partners nearly ended relations in April 1988. Amid mutual recriminations, De Benedetti reaffirmed his faith in Olivetti by upping his share in the company to 20 percent, which also made a takeover by AT&T less likely. Profits continued to fall nevertheless, to a 1988 low of L 356 billion, as Olivetti's stock price and market share both took a beating in the tightening computer race.

De Benedetti took decisive action in the beginning of 1989. He and Vittorio Cassoni, the new managing director of Olivetti, completely revamped the firm's lines of command, creating four new and separate companies under the ownership of Olivetti. In order of decreasing sales, these companies were: Olivetti Systems and Networks, which handled the production and marketing of all professional level personal computers (PCS) and minicomputers; Olivetti Office, which managed the bulk of the company's traditional business in fields such as typewriters and calculators, as well as PCS, photocopiers, and facsimile machines for home and office; Olivetti Information Services, which offered a wide variety of information services, including software, large-scale integration projects, and custom-tailored information networks for large users; and the Olivetti Technologies Group, a collection of 24 smaller companies engaged in the ancillary computer hardware field and the development and management of large-scale industrial projects. De Benedetti and Cassoni hoped that the new organization would provide a more efficient format for Olivetti's extremely wide variety of products and technologies.

1990s: Computers Out, Telecommunications In

Despite the late 1980s revamp, Olivetti's fortunes continued to worsen in the first half of the 1990s. Much of the company's difficulties still stemmed from its troubled PC business, which lost its main partner in 1989 when the alliance with AT&T ended. Within the larger environment of a weak European economy and an even weaker Italian economy, the PC industry became increasingly competitive in the 1990s, with prices plunging and U.S. companies invading Olivetti's European turf with low-priced PCs that were at least initially superior to Olivetti's. Consequently, the company posted its first loss in 13 years in 1991, a US$401 million net loss, then stayed in the red through 1996, with the darkest days coming in 1995, which produced a net loss of US$1.01 billion on sales of US$6.21 billion. Numerous restructurings were attempted to turn the tide, including massive reductions which cut the workforce by more than half, from 53,700 in 1990 to 26,300 in 1996. During this period, De Benedetti was also embroiled in legal difficulties. In 1992 he was convicted in connection with the fraudulent bankruptcy of Milan-based Banco Ambrosiano in 1982. Upon appeal, De Benedetti, initially sentenced to six years and four months in prison, succeeded in having the sentence reduced to four years and six months in 1996, and then in having the conviction tossed out entirely in 1998. Further problems came in 1993 when Olivetti came under investigation as part of the nationwide crackdown on corruption. De Benedetti voluntarily appeared before magistrates in Milan and admitted that Olivetti had paid bribes to political figures to gain contracts; he was never charged in connection with this widespread probe.

Although it was little noted at the time, the seeds of Olivetti's revival lay in the 1989 formation of Omnitel, the company's first foray into telecommunications. Specializing in the burgeoning cellular phone market, Omnitel did not become operational until late 1995 following its successful bid for a license early that same year—a license purchased for a hefty US$500 million. The wireless start-up was led by Olivetti, which held a 36 percent stake, in partnership with U.S. firms AirTouch Communications, Bell Atlantic Corporation, and Cellular Communications International; with Germany's Mannesmann AG; and with Sweden's Telia. Although it faced stiff competition from the state-owned Telecom Italia Mobile, Omnitel saw its subscriber base increase rapidly after launch, reaching 713,000 by the end of 1996. Olivetti also ventured into the fixed-lined telephone sector through the formation of Infostrada, which began competing head-on with Telecom Italia in the wake of the deregulation of the Italian telecommunications industry.

Already analysts were calling Olivetti's telecommunications ventures its most important assets, but the company continued to be saddled with its flagging PC operations. Under pressure from foreign investors clamoring for change, De Benedetti resigned as chairman in late August 1996 although he remained a powerful figure through his stake in the company of about 14.5 percent. Francesco Caio, who had led the successful launch of Omnitel, took over the helm but was ousted in mid-September amidst management chaos. A more permanent successor was soon found in Roberto Colaninno, a man with ties to De Benedetti—making investors suspicious about who was really in charge—who nonetheless, according to *Euromoney,* proclaimed, ''I took this job on three conditions, that De Benedetti is considered a normal shareholder, with the same rights as any other; that my job is to relaunch this business as a profitable company and that I be given enough power to do all this.''

Under Colaninno's leadership, Olivetti launched a sweeping reorganization, highlighted by the April 1997 sale of the PC business to U.K. venture capitalist firm Centenary Corporation. Olivetti's telecommunications operations were strengthened—as was its balance sheet—through an enhanced alliance agreement with Mannesmann reached in September 1997 whereby Mannesmann gained a 49 percent stake in a newly formed holding company for Olivetti's telecom interests in exchange for two payments totaling US$1.36 billion. Another key development came in March 1998 when Wang Laboratories Inc. (later Wang Global) acquired Olivetti's computer services business for about US$430 million, with Olivetti emerging from the deal with a 16 percent stake in Wang Global. Other, smaller divestments were also made, leading Olivetti to be primarily a telecommunications firm by the end of 1998. Omnitel's subscriber base reached 6.2 million by that time, making it the third largest mobile phone operator in Europe. In the summer of 1998 Infostrada and its fiber-optic network became fully operational, with the upstart firm gaining more than 900,000 customers for its voice services by year-end, more than 750,000 of which were residential. Infostrada was also involved in Internet services, data transmission, and international telephone cards.

Colaninno was not done yet, however. In February 1999 he launched a hostile bid to take over Olivetti's chief domestic telecommunications rival, Telecom Italia S.p.A., which had been privatized in 1997 and was five times the size of Olivetti. Telecom Italia was not only the number one telecommunications firm in Italy, it was also the sixth largest in the world, with interests in or joint ventures with companies in Spain, France, Greece, Argentina, Brazil, Chile, and elsewhere. The company also held majority control over the largest cellular phone operator in Europe, Telecom Italia Mobile (TIM), and was involved in satellite systems and services through its Telespazio unit. Telecom Italia attempted to fend off the Olivetti bid first by proposing a merger with TIM, then seeking to merge with Deutsche Telekom, but Colaninno's bold gambit prevailed in the end, at least in part because it kept Telecom Italia in Italian hands. In June 1999 Olivetti completed its tender offer, securing 52.12 percent of Telecom Italia's shares for US$34.8 billion. By October of that year, it had raised its stake to 55 percent. To fund the takeover, as well as secure antitrust approval, Olivetti sold its holdings in Omnitel and Infostrada to Mannesmann; it also took on more than US$14.7 billion in debt. Additional funds were raised in August 1999 when Olivetti sold to Wang Global its 80.1 percent stake in Olivetti Ricerca, a specialist in research and development activities in the field of information technology and telecommunications.

Olivetti had completed its acquisition of Telecom Italia through a publicly traded subsidiary, Tecnost S.p.A., which was 70 percent owned by Olivetti. Tecnost had been a maker of automation systems and gambling machines, but these operations were sold to Olivetti in early February 2000. Tecnost thereby became purely a holding company for Olivetti's telecommunications activities. As part of its plan to reduce its heavy debt load, Olivetti attempted in late 1999 to transfer control of the highly valued TIM from Telecom Italia to Tecnost. Olivetti abandoned this maneuver, however, following fierce resistance from minority shareholders and institutional investors who considered it detrimental to Telecom Italia. They had been expecting Tecnost and Telecom Italia to merge, which had been Olivetti's original plan.

This shareholder revolt was a setback for the new Olivetti, but it was unclear how serious a one it was. Tecnost remained saddled with a huge debt load. Telecom Italia was in desperate need of restructuring, and plans to cut the workforce by as much as 13,000 were already beginning to incur union resistance. At the same time, the telecommunications industry in Europe and abroad was in the midst of its greatest wave of consolidation yet, including Vodafone's blockbuster hostile bid for Mannesmann, which some analysts claimed had its roots in Olivetti's takeover of Telecom Italia. Olivetti itself appeared vulnerable to a takeover, although the Italian government, which maintained a 3.95 percent stake in Telecom Italia, would take a dim view of the fall of the former phone monopoly into foreign hands and had the ability to block major decisions affecting the company.

Principal Subsidiaries

Tecnost S.p.A. (72.8%); Telecom Italia S.p.A. (55%); Olivetti Lexikon S.p.A.; O.i.S. Italia S.p.A.; Olivetti Multiservices S.p.A.

Principal Competitors

Alcatel; Autostrade—Concessioni e Costruzioni Autostrade S.p.A.; British Telecommunications plc; Canon Inc.; Deutsche Telekom AG; ENEL Societa per Azioni; France Telecom; Italgas—Societa Italiana per il Gas S.p.A.; Mannesmann AG; MCI WorldCom, Inc.; Mediaset SpA; Nokia Corporation; Oce N.V.; Pitney Bowes Inc.; Ricoh Company, Ltd.; Telefonaktiebolaget LM Ericsson.

Further Reading

"Alone at Last?," *Economist,* November 30, 1996, pp. 67–68.

"AT&T and Olivetti Unsheathe a Strategy to Win Europe," *Business Week,* July 16, 1984, pp. 41 +.

Auerbach, Jon G., "Wang to Buy Computer-Services Unit of Olivetti for as Much as $340 Million," *Wall Street Journal,* March 2, 1998, p. B10.

Ball, Deborah, "Olivetti's Religion Finally Gets Disciples," *Wall Street Journal,* January 16, 1998, p. B21D.

——, "Olivetti's Win May Reshape Telecom Industry," *Wall Street Journal,* May 24, 1999, p. A22.

Ball, Robert, "A Confident Capitalist Redesigns Olivetti," *Fortune,* October 22, 1979, p. 78.

Betts, Paul, "The Engineer Sets Sail for Calmer Waters," *Financial Times,* March 9, 1998, p. 11.

Bostico, Mary, "Olivetti Keys in to Electronic Age," *International Management,* January 1974, p. 14.

Cane, Alan, and Haig Simonian, "Olivetti Pins Survival Hope on Specialisation," *Financial Times,* February 20, 1993, p. 12.

Design Process: Olivetti, 1908–1983, Ivrea, Italy: Ing. C. Olivetti & C., S.p.A., 1983.

Edmondson, Gail, John Rossant, and David Fairlamb, "Olivetti: Back to the Bad Old Ways?," *Business Week,* October 18, 1999, p. 172.

"The Four Horsemen of the Italian Apocalypse," *Economist,* April 2, 1988, pp. 55 +.

Graham, Robert, "Colaninno to Replace PCS with People," *Financial Times,* October 4, 1996, p. 24.

Hansen, James, "Olivetti: Hardware the Hard Way," *Europe,* April 1995, p. 14.

Hill, Andrew, and Peter Martin, "The Engineer on the Line," *Financial Times,* December 19, 1995, p. 15.

Jewkes, Stephen, "Olivetti Stuns Italians with Telecom Takeover," *Europe,* October 1999, pp. 31–32.

Klebnikov, Paul, "Fallen Hero," *Forbes,* April 27, 1992, p. 110.

Kline, Maureen, "Olivetti Chairman De Benedetti Quits," *Wall Street Journal,* September 4, 1996, p. A3.

Lee, Peter, "The Man Who Won't Quit Centre Stage," *Euromoney,* November 1996, pp. 44–50.

"Meet the Mechanic," *Economist,* May 29, 1999, p. 68.

Naik, Gautam, "Bold Stroke: Olivetti Reinvents Itself Once More, This Time As a Telecom Giant," *Wall Street Journal,* February 22, 1999, p. A1.

Ochetto, Valerio, *Adriano Olivetti,* Milan, Italy: A. Mondadori, 1985, 331 p.

"Olivetti and Bribes: Carlo Goes to Confession," *Economist,* May 22, 1993, p. 81.

"Olivetti Is Reaching Out for the Apple," *Euromoney,* September 1986, pp. 393 +.

"On the Ropes," *Economist,* May 20, 1995, p. 60.

Peterson, Thane, "How Olivetti Cloned Its Way to the Top," *Business Week,* June 16, 1986, p. 82.

Peterson, Thane, and Frank J. Comes, "Is De Benedetti's Far-Flung Empire Stretching Thin?," *Business Week,* May 2, 1988, pp. 44 +.

Piper, Allan, "Olivetti's Carlo De Benedetti: Facing the Realities of Global Alliances," *International Management,* April 1986, pp. 22 +.

Rosenbaum, Andy, "Olivetti Hedges Its Bets While Gambling on High Tech," *Electronic Business,* May 15, 1989, pp. 91 +.

Rossant, John, "Now, Maybe Olivetti Can Find Its Way," *Business Week,* September 16, 1996, p. 62.

Rossant, John, Kerry Capell, and Jack Ewing, "Raiders at the Gate," *Business Week,* March 8, 1999, p. 50.

Solomon, Steven, "Conglomeration Italian Style," *Forbes,* March 23, 1987, pp. 36 +.

Sturani, Maria, "Olivetti, Nearly Free of Its PC Division, Now Must Turn Around Core Business," *Wall Street Journal,* January 24, 1997, p. A9A.

Symonds, William C., et al., "Dealmaker De Benedetti," *Business Week,* August 24, 1987, pp. 42 +.

——, "De Benedetti Is Bloodied but Unbowed," *Business Week,* July 11, 1988, p. 41.

Taggiasco, Ronald, "Olivetti and AT&T: An Odd Couple That's Flourishing," *Business Week,* March 4, 1985, pp. 44 +.

Taggiasco, Ronald, Todd Mason, and Charles Gaffney, "At Olivetti, Success Just Fuels Ambition," *Business Week,* June 17, 1985, pp. 76 +.

Trofimov, Yaroslov, "Olivetti Is Looking More Like a Takeover Play As Stock Plunge Follows About-Face in Strategy," *Wall Street Journal,* November 4, 1999, p. A25.

——, "Olivetti Splits Off Cellular Operations from Telecom Italia in Big Revamp," *Wall Street Journal,* September 29, 1999, p. A19.

Turner, Graham, "Inside Europe's Giant Companies: Olivetti Goes Bear-Hunting," *Long Range Planning,* April 1986, pp. 13 +.

Willatt, Norris, "The Ordeals of Olivetti," *Management Today,* January 1980, p. 74.

Willoughby, Jack, "Skeleton in the Closet," *Forbes,* December 31, 1984, pp. 78 +.

—Jonathan Martin
—updated by David E. Salamie

Opus Group

10350 Bren Road W.
Minnetonka, Minnesota 55343
U.S.A.
Telephone: (952) 656-4444
Fax: (952) 656-4529
Web site: http://www.opuscorp.com

Private Company
Founded: 1953 as Rauenhorst Construction Company
Employees: 1,400
Sales: $806 million (1999 est.)
NAIC: 23332 Commercial and Institutional Building
    Construction

Opus Group ranks among the top ten U.S. design-build commercial construction firms. The vertically integrated enterprise operates in the industrial, retail, and office markets. Working nationwide through six independent regional operating companies, Opus builds custom facilities for purchase or lease, develops business parks, and maintains an inventory of space for immediate occupancy.

Simple Beginning/Solid Construction: 1950s–60s

Gerald Rauenhorst founded his own construction business in 1953. The farm boy from Olivia, Minnesota, earned a degree in economics from St. Thomas University in St. Paul, and one in civil engineering from Michigan's Marquette University, where he taught for a year. Rauenhorst put in another two years as a construction engineer before striking out on his own. His first solo project, which got off the ground thanks to a loan from his brother, was the construction of the Zion Lutheran Church in his hometown of Olivia. Rauenhorst Construction built a number of other buildings for religious organizations during its first years of operation.

In 1957, Rauenhorst moved his business out of the breezeway of his suburban Minneapolis home into a small Bloomington office building and, by renting out the adjacent office space, established a leasing business.

By 1960, Rauenhorst Construction held a solid position in the Twin Cities design-build market. The next year, two significant developments occurred. One was the completion of the company's first "turnkey" project: the design, engineering, and construction of a 157,000-square-foot office and manufacturing facility for the Toro Company. Secondly, the company purchased 200 acres of undeveloped land in the southwest Minneapolis suburbs. Shortly thereafter, Rauenhorst contracted to build Control Data's headquarters on the property and thus launched what would be Rauenhorst Construction's first business park development, Normandale Center Industrial Park. The growing company built itself new headquarters in 1963 and changed its name to Rauenhorst Corporation in 1965.

Changing Skylines: 1970s to Mid-80s

In the 1970s, Rauenhorst Corporation moved beyond the Twin Cities, opening an office in Milwaukee in 1972 and one in Chicago in 1978. The decade was also marked by the construction of the company's first office tower. Construction volume for the privately held company was an estimated $75 million in 1977. In addition, the regional developer had more than 500 construction projects newly contracted or in progress, totaling in excess of $250 million. The company concentrated its efforts on smaller growing cities spread throughout the eastern two-thirds of the nation.

A 1970s diversification drive was less successful. Rauenhorst tried manufacturing concrete walls and floor planks as well as fiberglass parts, toys, and heavy equipment. Losing money on such efforts, the company dropped the businesses by mid-decade.

Rauenhorst, meanwhile, had another more engaging concept in mind. He envisioned a suburban development encompassing ponds and green space, commercial and industrial facilities, and housing, all served by a dual roadway system to cut down pollution from exhaust fumes. In 1974, the company broke ground on Opus II, located on some prime property at the convergence of three major thoroughfares less than ten miles from the center of downtown Minneapolis.

Just as the ambitious project was started, an economic recession hit, creating some uneasy days. "As it happened, even the timing worked out to Rauenhorst's ultimate advantage. The recession reduced the competition for one thing. And more important, when the upturn finally occurred Opus II was well underway and ready to meet the rejuvenated demand for commercial and industrial building,'' wrote William Swanson in a 1977 *Corporate Report Minnesota* article.

About the same time, Rauenhorst delegated responsibility for the real estate and construction ends of the business, in effect moving the company from an entrepreneurial to a corporate structure and creating more time for his many family and community commitments.

Rauenhorst Corporation opened an office in Phoenix in 1980. Then, reflecting the ongoing growth and expansion, the company changed its name to Opus Corporation in 1982. The same year, the company moved into new headquarters located in the Opus II mixed-use development project and purchased a Florida-based construction company, creating a presence in the southeastern United States. During the early 1980s, the company reorganized based on its geographic locations.

Opus Corporation's entry into the downtown Minneapolis market in 1984, via the development of a 25-story tower, depicted the changes taking place within the company. "Five years ago, the Minnetonka-based firm was known as a builder of sound if unimaginative, one story warehouse, manufacturing plants and office buildings in suburban Minneapolis, Milwaukee and Chicago,'' wrote Eric Wieffering for *Minneapolis/St. Paul CityBusiness* in 1985.

The Minneapolis endeavor, the company's first speculative project in a highly competitive downtown market, moved the company into a new submarket, an accomplishment Rauenhorst pointed to with pride. In the early 1970s, architects were both derisive and threatened by Rauenhorst's design-build niche. The developer had moved outside the norm of the day by taking on all elements of a project: finance, design, and construction. But by the mid-1980s, according to a 1987 *Star Tribune* profile by Sharon Schmickle, the two ends of the spectrum were "barely distinguishable'' from one another. Rauenhorst now paid more attention to design, and architectural firms had begun adding engineering and construction services.

"Rauenhorst and company continue to exploit one distinguishing feature of the design-build approach: the ability to move quickly. Opus can start a project as soon as it finds a tenant and finance it later because it maintains lines of credit backed by its real estate assets,'' wrote Schmickle.

Founder and Chairman Gerald Rauenhorst was the driving force for his company's long-term growth as others handled the day-to-day operations. William Tobin served as president and COO. He had succeeded longtime employee and board vice-chair Robert Dahlin.

Mixed Reviews: Late 1980s Through Mid-1990s

By 1987, Opus had created more than 1,000 buildings. Annual construction surpassed $200 million, placing the company among the top 100 in *Engineering News-Record*'s ranking of leading U.S. contractors.

Opus decentralized in 1988, forming a holding company, Opus U.S. Corp., for the regional operating companies. Mark Rauenhorst, son of the founder, was named president and COO of the holding company in 1990. The younger Rauenhorst joined Opus in 1982, after earning a degree in finance and an M.B.A. and gaining seven years of work experience outside the family business. Opus further decentralized operations in 1990 by creating Opus Architects and Engineers, Inc. as a subsidiary of Opus U.S. Corp.: the entity provided architectural and engineering services to affiliate companies.

"Rauenhorst describes the overall operation as 'opportunistic,' adding that 'we are always looking for the right opportunity for development,' '' wrote Barbara Knox for *Corporate Report Minnesota* in 1990. Speculative industrial development represented a major piece of Opus U.S. Corp.'s business. Keith Bednarowski served as chairman and CEO of the company, which was based in Minnesota but operated primarily outside the state.

Opus weathered a late 1980s industry downtown and in 1991 ranked among the top 15 developers in the U.S., producing a combined construction volume of more than $300 million. The company received its industry's highest honor in 1992: Developer of the Year by the National Association of Industrial Office Properties (NAIOP).

Nevertheless, Opus faced challenges in the early 1990s. Internally, the company was moving toward the succession of one generation of leadership to the next. Three of Gerald Rauenhorst's sons, including Mark, held top management positions. Externally, the Tampa and Phoenix markets were in a downturn, prompting workforce layoffs in those regions. A new affiliate, Opus Investments, Inc. was formed to acquire, develop, and remarket distressed properties. The Chicago market, on the other hand, was growing, and Opus had long-established customers and a high rate of repeat business.

In 1995, the *National Real Estate Investor* ranked Opus the nation's largest developer, based on 8.3 million square feet under construction nationwide. Gerald Rauenhorst, over four decades, had guided his business from a one-wheelbarrow operation to a national design-build and real estate concern. His accomplishment was no small feat in an industry hit by four or five downturns during his many years in business.

In fact, during the 1990s Opus was still feeling the pinch of the late 1980s Minneapolis office glut. Wieffering wrote for *Corporate Report Minnesota* in 1995, "Gerald Rauenhorst made his name and fortune in the suburbs southwest of Minneapolis by guessing where the people were going to be, and buying land in

<table>
<tr><td colspan="2">Key Dates:</td></tr>
<tr><td>1953:</td><td>Gerald Rauenhorst undertakes first solo construction project.</td></tr>
<tr><td>1957:</td><td>Rauenhorst Construction moves into first headquarters.</td></tr>
<tr><td>1961:</td><td>Company completes its first ''turnkey'' project.</td></tr>
<tr><td>1972:</td><td>Expands beyond Twin Cities metropolitan area.</td></tr>
<tr><td>1982:</td><td>Changes name to Opus Corporation.</td></tr>
<tr><td>1984:</td><td>Builds first office tower in major downtown market.</td></tr>
<tr><td>1988:</td><td>Decentralizes into regional operating companies.</td></tr>
<tr><td>1992:</td><td>Opus is named developer of the year by industry association.</td></tr>
<tr><td>2000:</td><td>Founder retires as chairman of company.</td></tr>
</table>

advance of their arrival. Once he brought his company, Opus Corporation, to downtown Minneapolis in the early 1980's, he applied the same strategy. Though the results have so far been mixed, it's one reason why Opus owns more potential development sites in downtown Minneapolis than anyone else.''

In 1998, Opus lost a two-year legal battle with the city of Minneapolis over some of that property. The city condemned an Opus-owned site on the Nicollet Mall for a subsidized development slated to be built by a competitor.

Concurrently, Gerald Rauenhorst prepared for his eventual exit from the business—something he'd been planning for since the mid-1980s. In addition to bringing in the best personnel he could find, Rauenhorst added four outsiders to the seven member board of the holding company and relinquished more control to the management team lead by Bednarowski. In a 1996 *Star Tribune* article Sally Apgar reported that Bednarowski was ''also charged, say insiders, with helping to educate the next generation.''

Construction Ahead: Late 1990s into the 21st Century

As a merchant builder, Opus had sold almost everything it built. During 1998, the company changed gears, raising nearly $250 million from investors for two real estate investment funds. '' 'It's an unbelievable mechanism,' '' Tom Crowley of Chicago-based Heitman Financial told Dirk Deyoung in a 1999 *Minneapolis/St. Paul CityBusiness* article. ''Opus is already one of the most respected, well-capitalized developers in the nation. Now it's building a 'great machine' that can efficiently swallow, digest and eventually divest the huge volume that it manufactures, he said. 'It's a perfect strategy for Opus.' ''

On another front, Opus pushed to win more national accounts. Local or regional projects compromised much of the company's business due to the limitations of its decentralized structure. A national accounts group was created in the late 1990s to pursue clients, pull together resources from the regional offices, and assist the regional companies in taking current customers to the multiple development level.

Gerald Rauenhorst retired as chairman of the company in 2000, although he remained on the board of directors.

Bednarowski succeeded him as chair, and Mark Rauenhorst was named president and CEO. National Real Estate Investor had named Gerald Rauenhorst one of the 40 most influential people in real estate in 1998, and over the years, Rauenhorst had received frequent recognition for his principled conduct in business and for his contributions to his community.

The organization Rauenhorst built planned to develop more than 28 million square feet of new commercial space in 2000, ranging from speculative and build-to-suit office buildings to distribution and warehousing facilities, retail complexes, and institutional facilities. Opus had completed about 1,800 commercial projects in more than 35 states. The independent operating companies included: Opus East, Opus North, Opus Northwest, Opus South, Opus West, and Opus National. All in all, the company appeared well prepared for the winds of change certain to again buffet the real estate industry.

Principal Subsidiaries

Opus East L.L.C.; Opus North L.L.C.; Opus Northwest L.L.C.; Opus South L.L.C.; Opus West, L.L.C.; Opus National, L.L.C.; Opus Architects & Engineers, Inc.; Opus Properties, L.L.C.; Opus Northwest Management, L.L.C.(Minneapolis); Opus North Management Corporation; Opus West Management Corporation; Normandale Properties South Corporation.

Principal Competitors

IDI; Hines Interests; Duke Weeks Realty Corp.

Further Reading

Apgar, Sally, ''Opus Corp. Heading Down a New Path: Multiple Transitions Pending,'' *Star Tribune* (Minneapolis), October 19, 1992, p. 1D.
——, ''Setting the Stage,'' *Star Tribune* (Minneapolis), February 5, 1996, p. 1D.
Bloomfield, Craig, ''Opus Targets National Accounts,'' *Commercial Property News,* November 1, 1999.
Deyoung, Dirk, ''Opus Raises $250M As Part of Strategic Shift,'' *Minneapolis/St. Paul CityBusiness,* January 8, 1999. pp. 1+.
Diaz, Kevin, ''Minnesota Supreme Court Lets City's Target Store Deal Stand,'' *Star Tribune* (Minneapolis), November 3, 1998, p. 1A.
Knox, Barbara, ''Mark Rauenhorst: Moving Up in His Father's Company,'' *Corporate Report Minnesota,* September 1990, p. 82.
Levy, Melissa, ''Gerald Rauenhorst Retires As Chairman of Opus,'' *Star Tribune* (Minneapolis), April 11, 2000, p. 3D.
Mundale, Charles I., ''The Opus Culture,'' *Corporate Report Minnesota,* January 1983, p. 154.
Schmickle, Sharon, ''Opus Chief's Business Dealings Reflect the Man,'' *Star Tribune* (Minneapolis), August 31, 1987, p. 1M.
Sundstrom, Ingrid, ''New Opus President Says Firm Will Continue to Expand,'' *Star Tribune* (Minneapolis), March 25, 1991, p. 2D.
Swanson, William, ''Rauenhorst's Song of the Suburbs,'' *Corporate Report Minnesota,* July 1977, pp. 29–31, 64–68.
Wieffering, Eric, ''Opus' Interests in Downtown Development,'' *Corporate Report Minnesota,* February 1995, pp. 8–10.
——, ''Opus Makes Its Mark on Downtown, *Minneapolis/St. Paul CityBusiness,* August 28, 1985, pp. 34, 36.
——, ''Opus Not Telling Plans for Powers,'' *Minneapolis/St. Paul CityBusiness,* August 28, 1985, p. 34.

—Kathleen Peippo

Otto Versand (GmbH & Co.)

Wandsbeker Strasse, 3-7
22179 Hamburg
Germany
Telephone: (040) 64 61-0
Fax: (040) 64 61-85 71
Web sites: http://www.otto.de
        http://www.shopping24.de

Private Company
Incorporated: 1949
Employees: 50,055
Sales: EURO 14.07 billion (US$15.57 billion) (1999)
NAIC: 454110 Electronic Shopping and Mail-Order
   Houses; 421430 Computer and Computer Peripheral
   Equipment and Software Wholesalers; 442110
   Furniture Stores; 442299 All Other Home Furnishings
   Stores; 452910 Warehouse Clubs and Superstores;
   492110 Couriers; 522110 Commercial Banking;
   561510 Travel Agencies

While Otto Versand (GmbH & Co.) is the world's largest mail-order company with subsidiaries and affiliates in Europe, Asia, South America, and the United States, it remains very much a family concern, being majority-owned and operated by the Otto family. Based in Hamburg, Otto Versand's numerous catalog businesses in 20 countries include Grattan and Freemans in the United Kingdom, 3 Suisses in France, and Heine, Schwab, and the flagship Otto in Germany. Otto Versand offers its customers a variety of ordering methods, including print and CD-ROM catalogs as well as options via online services and the Internet. The company is also involved in several non-mail-order businesses in Germany, including the Actebis Group, a distributor of computers and peripherals; Fegro/Selgros GmbH & Co., a cash-and-carry chain offering 50,000 food and nonfood items; several travel agencies; Hanseatic Bank, a 24-branch, full-service regional bank; and Hermes, the company's delivery and customer service unit which also offers its services to third parties. In the United States, Otto Versand holds a majority stake in Euromarket Designs Inc., which operates the Crate & Barrel chain of home furnishings stores. In the early 1980s Otto Versand acquired Spiegel, Inc., known for its flagship Spiegel catalog, but soon transferred that ownership from Otto Versand (GmbH & Co.) to the separate Otto family enterprise known as Otto Versand Combined Group.

Early Years

Otto Versand (GmbH & Co.) was founded in 1949—the same year as the West German nation—in Hamburg by Werner Otto, a refugee from Communist East Germany; it followed the country's rising fortunes from occupied state to reunification. Otto was one of a generation of extremely successful German entrepreneurs after World War II that included such famous names as Max Grundig, Axel Springer, and Heinx Nixdorf. These men rose to prominence after the currency reforms of June 1948 that restored confidence to consumers in the U.S., British, and French zones of occupied Germany. After three years of severe shortages, Germans had no faith in the money issued by the occupation powers. Cigarettes were a more popular parallel currency, and the black market was thriving. Nevertheless, Ludwig Erhard, director of the economic council for the joint Anglo-U.S. occupation zone, persuaded the Western Allies to accept his currency reform plan, which required the population to exchange a limited amount of the old currency for the new deutsche mark. Goods suddenly appeared as if by magic and Germans went on a buying spree, first for food, then household goods, and finally clothes, which were to become the mainstay of the Otto Versand mail-order empire. In this new market, Otto's formula was to offer low-cost fashion garments and cheap credit. For the first time, German customers were invoiced, rather than required to pay upon delivery. Later, in 1969, Otto Versand acquired its own Hanseatic Bank and offered three-, six-, and nine-month payment plans.

In retrospect, the mail-order market was ripe for development when 300 hand-bound copies of Otto's first, 14-page shoe catalog were distributed in 1950. In the then-new West Germany, retail distribution was still badly dislocated by World War II. Rationing and shortages meant that many goods had been unavailable for years in local shops and the range of choice was poor. City commercial centers had been heavily bombed, and the absence of Jews left a noticeable gap in retail distribution, as in many other fields where Jews had been successful and innovative before the

Key Dates:

1949: Company is founded by Werner Otto.
1950: The first catalog, featuring 14 pages of shoes, is distributed.
1963: Telephone ordering service is introduced.
1969: The Hanseatic Bank is acquired.
1972: Hermes Paketschnelldienst, a proprietary delivery service, is launched.
1981: Michael Otto succeeds his father as chairman.
1982: U.S. mail-order giant Spiegel is acquired.
1984: Ownership of Spiegel is transferred to the Otto family.
1987: Otto Versand becomes the world's largest mail-order group.
1990: Otto Versand becomes the first mail-order company to open an order center in the former East Germany.
1993: Company acquires the largest Italian mail-order firm, Postalmarket.
1995: Company launches e-commerce site www.otto.de.
1998: A majority stake in Crate & Barrel is acquired; Postalmarket is divested.

rise of the Nazis. By 1950, however, West Germany had restored most of its postal and telephone systems, which were a relatively low-cost way to facilitate the distribution of goods in a country in which many store locations were still in ruins. German shop hours were restrictive, giving working people little opportunity to shop. All shops closed at 6:30 p.m. on weekdays. Retailers closed at 2:00 p.m. on Saturday afternoons, except on the first Saturday of the month, and were closed all day on Sundays. These hours were zealously protected by the shopworkers' union. In fact, the only way Otto Versand was later able to offer 24-hour ordering was to establish its telephone bank in Denmark and hire German-speaking operators.

In 1949 Ludwig Erhard became economics minister of the new Federal Republic of Germany and pushed through further reforms that, along with Marshall Plan aid, helped create the famous Wirtschaftswunder, or German economic miracle. Rationing and price controls were ended, duties on imports were lowered, and tax on overtime work was abolished. Erhard encouraged production of consumer goods to stimulate employment and economic revival. The boom lasted into the early 1990s and the wealth spread downward to lower-paid workers. By 1953 living standards were higher than in 1938, and by 1961 Germany was one of the world's largest industrial powers. German incomes tripled between 1950 and 1965. In this rising tide of prosperity, mail order bridged gaps between supply and demand. At the turn of the millennium, Germany remained by far Europe's largest annual per capita spender on mail order with annual sales of DM 43.5 billion. Seventy percent of all German households received at least one catalog, and mail order accounted for 4.6 percent of all retail sales—surpassing the 3.3 percent figure in the United States.

By 1951, Otto's sales had already reached DM 1 million, generated by 1,500 catalogues of 20 pages each. In 1952, Werner Otto's next major innovation was to introduce a system whereby customers ordered through agents or representatives who forwarded the orders to the company's main office in Hamburg. Werner Otto believed that his company owed its early success to this form of personal contact. It also enabled the company to keep costs and prices low through lower catalog numbers. By 1953, Otto Versand had more than 100 employees, and the company's catalog had grown to 82 pages. A total of 37,000 copies were distributed, and sales reached DM 5 million.

Unlike Werner Otto's archrival, Quelle, whose market strategy included a safety net of retail stores as well as a mail-order empire, Werner Otto concentrated on mail-order catalogs and representatives throughout the 1950s. From the 1960s onward telephone ordering to Otto's regional centers began to replace representatives.

In the United States, the United Kingdom, and several other countries, mail order had in the past appealed only to low-income bargain hunters or people living in remote rural areas, far from centers of population. By the mid-1950s, however, German consumers began to demand higher quality goods, and Otto Versand discovered that all kinds of potential customer groups could be targeted. The company became most successful by going against the grain of conventional mail-order wisdom. Otto Versand developed a methodical, computerized approach and gained knowledge of preferred customers in highly concentrated urban areas. Catalogs such as Otto Heimwerker targeted specific groups such as home enthusiasts, while Post Shop offered the latest styles to fashion-oriented youth. When the company later began its overseas expansion, areas such as Scandinavia, with its widely dispersed population, were ignored in favor of more urbanized, densely populated countries such as Holland and Belgium.

By the end of Otto's first decade in business, the company had more than 1,000 employees and sales of DM 150 million. In the early 1960s, Otto Versand became one of the first German companies to install integrated data-processing equipment. Otto Versand used this equipment to become, in 1963, the first mail-order company to offer telephone ordering.

The 1966 Otto Versand catalog had 828 pages and was now the largest in Germany. It had moved upmarket, featuring designers such as Pierre Balmain, Jean Patou, Nina Ricci, and Christian Dior. In 1972 Otto Versand launched Hermes Paketschnelldienst, a proprietary delivery service named for the mythic Greek messenger. *Stores* magazine called this operation ''a significant competitive edge, since it can offer domestic deliveries within 24 hours and free pickup of returned items.'' By the end of 1972, only 50 percent of all Otto Versand shipments were being handled by the German Federal Post Office.

Mid-1970s and Forward: International Expansion

By 1974, the year of the company's 25th anniversary, Otto Versand felt strong enough to begin a period of international expansion, which intensified in the 1980s. The company's first move was into France, where it acquired, in 1974, 50 percent of 3 Suisses, the second largest mail-order firm in France. In 1979, Otto Versand founded Otto B.V., which grew to become one of the largest mail-order companies in the Netherlands. Otto Versand formed partnerships with Venca, the largest Spanish mail-order company, and Austria's 3 Pagen. In 1974 Otto Versand acquired an interest in Heinrich Heine, a German company specializing in luxury clothing and household goods. At the same time Otto Versand continued to expand within Germany, acquiring Schwab in 1976, Alba Moda in 1982, the linen and home textiles company Witt Weiden in 1987, and a holding in Sport-Scheck in 1988.

Michael Otto succeeded his father as chairman in 1981. Having set up his own financial and real estate business, the second-generation leader had joined his father's company in 1981, advancing from textile purchasing through the corporate ranks. Michael Otto pushed his family's company to undertake its riskiest venture to date when it seized an opportunity to buy the Spiegel catalog sales company in the United States in 1982. Although Spiegel was still a U.S. household name, its fortunes had been declining for years. Like the early Otto Versand company, it had concentrated on low-cost women's fashions. Otto Versand realized that the U.S. mail-order market had changed and gambled by taking the entire operation upmarket. The image makeover was accompanied by a thorough fiscal reorganization and productivity enhancements.

Spiegel's sales quadrupled within its first two years under its new management, and it had become the largest U.S. mail-order company by the end of the decade. In the meantime, however, the ownership of Spiegel was restructured. In 1984 all of the capital stock was transferred from Otto Versand to members of the Otto family, resulting in common ownership for Otto Versand and Spiegel but no direct financial or legal link between the two. What the family called the Otto Versand Combined Group included both Otto Versand and the so-called Spiegel Group. The latter name was adopted to reflect Spiegel's acquisitions of outdoor clothing specialist Eddie Bauer in 1988 and of Newport News, a catalog offering women's apparel and home furnishings, in 1993.

Otto Versand entered the 1990s as the world's largest mail-order firm, a position it had gained in 1987. German reunification took center stage in the early 1990s, and Otto Versand did not want to be outdone by its rivals in the former East Germany. By March 1990, three months before formal economic unification, Otto Versand had opened mail-order centers in Leipzig, Dresden, and the former East Berlin—becoming the first mail-order company to open an order center in the former East Germany. By July of that year, Otto Versand was the only mail-order house to boast a comprehensive distribution network in all five of the new federal states, the result of an earlier agreement with an East German association of consumer cooperatives. Sales in these new states exceeded DM 1.1 billion, more than double the company's original forecast, and more than 1,000 order centers were soon established throughout the former East Germany.

Initially, the company was less interested in the other former communist countries in Eastern Europe, but moves by Quelle and other competitors rapidly changed Otto's outlook. With the formation of Otto-Epoka mbH, Warsaw, a joint venture, Otto Versand entered the Polish market in May 1990. Order centers were established in Czechoslovakia, Hungary, and the Soviet Union. At the same time, Otto Versand worked to strengthen its presence in Western Europe in anticipation of the unified European market. In 1988 Otto Versand acquired a 75 percent stake in Euronova S.R.L., the third largest Italian mail-order house. Five years later, Otto Versand acquired the largest Italian mail-order company, Postalmarket. Meanwhile, the company continued to bolster its customer service: in 1990, introducing 24-hour express delivery service, and in 1991, launching 24 hours a day, seven days a week telephone sales.

Otto Versand had wanted to expand into the United Kingdom for many years before its well publicized £165 million bid for a majority stake in Grattan, the mail-order arm of the troubled Next retailer, finally succeeded in March 1991. In 1986, it had been outbid by Next, which paid £300 million, but in 1991 it was prepared to pay a premium of £15 million above a rival £150 million bid by Sears plc, which controlled the Freemans mail-order house, to secure this U.K. base. Grattan—the fourth largest U.K. mail-order firm—had a computerized warehouse system, a huge customer base, and 13 percent of the U.K. mail-order market, but it had been devastated by the recession of the early 1990s and a postal strike. Its parent company, Next, desperately needed to refinance a convertible bond issue. Otto Versand had already begun to enter the U.K. market in a joint venture with Fine Art Developments Ltd., a greeting card company. In December 1988 Otto Versand launched Rainbow Home Shopping Ltd., a Bradford mail-order firm, and announced that Rainbow would join forces with Grattan, also Bradford-based.

Otto Versand also made significant inroads into largely untapped Asia, forming a joint venture with Sumitomo Corporation, Otto-Sumisho Inc., in 1986. The German company hoped to develop this market, which boasted many of the characteristics of markets in which it had been successful elsewhere, namely urban concentrations of the newly affluent and fashion-conscious. In 1993, Otto Versand, through the Otto-Sumisho joint venture, and Eddie Bauer formed a joint venture to sell the Eddie Bauer line through retail stores and catalogs in Japan. From its Japanese base, Otto Versand developed similar markets on the Pacific Rim, including a 1994 strategic alliance with Burlingtons' in India known as Otto-Burlingtons Mail Order Pvt. Ltd. Initial results were encouraging.

The company did not shy away from new technology or new business opportunities in the early 1990s, becoming the first mail-order firm to offer an interactive CD-ROM catalog in 1994, for example. Having dabbled in the travel industry since the early 1980s, Otto Versand stepped up its efforts in this segment with the 1993 acquisition of a controlling interest in Reisland GmbH's 60 travel agencies. The company also partnered with Rewe in a 1990-created joint venture, Fegro/Selgros GmbH & Co., which established a cash-and-carry chain offering more than 50,000 food and nonfood items. Otto Versand bought two British collection agencies in 1994.

Retail industry analysts remained divided about the impact of the single European market on the prospects for mail-order firms. Companies such as Otto Versand were expected to achieve economies of scale with pan-European operations, and the development of satellite networks increased opportunities for home shopping, but mail-order firms still had to cope with problems of distance and national distribution networks. Proposed European Community directives also threatened the use of mailing lists. With 25 percent of the European Community market, Otto Versand was also concerned not to breach competition laws. In recognition of this situation, Otto Versand announced that it would continue its policy of operating through national subsidiaries and allowing a degree of freedom to local subsidiaries familiar with local customs and markets.

In his 14 years at Otto Versand's helm, Michael Otto built his father's company into an international retail colossus and garnered high praise from analysts and competitors alike in the process. His ''green'' side was evinced by environment-friendly business policies such as reducing energy consumption and selecting environmentally sensitive products. He was named Environment Manager of the Year in 1991 and created the Michael Otto Foundation for the Environment in 1993. In 1988, Otto Versand introduced employee equity ownership through participation rights. By 1990 participation rights capital increased by DM 4 million to DM 10 million, and one-third of employees were participating in the profit-sharing scheme. Michael Otto's combination of business sense and social awareness helped win him 1995's National Retail Federation International Award.

These progressive strategies did not preclude growth or profitability. Annual sales increased 17.2 percent from DM 16.42 billion in 1992 to DM 19.25 billion in 1994, and net income increased 32 percent from DM 369.83 million to DM 488.07 million during the same period. By the mid-1990s Otto Versand was represented by 36 mail-order firms on three continents and in a total of 16 countries.

Late 1990s and Beyond

Probably the most significant development during the late 1990s for the entire global mail-order industry was the emergence of the Internet as a new selling channel. Otto Versand was quick to set up a web site, www.otto.de, in 1995 from which it began selling the flagship Otto line as well as specialty catalog lines. Two years later the company set up a second web site, www.shopping24.de, a ''virtual mall'' featuring a much wider range of products and services from Otto Versand's various companies and joint ventures, including fashion items, furniture, books, CDS, posters, travel services, insurance, and a parcel service (from Hermes). Also featured were computers and other high-tech goods stemming from the company's 1995 investment in Actebis, Germany's second largest distributor of computers. By 1997 sales through the CD-ROM and Internet channels had already reached DM 435 million (US$247 million).

Otto Versand also continued its aggressive late 20th century expansion through its usual assortment of joint ventures and acquisitions. The company's partnership with Eddie Bauer, which had begun in Japan in 1993, broadened via additional joint ventures, first to Germany in 1995, then to the United Kingdom in 1996. In Asia, Otto Versand partnered with local firms to set up joint venture catalog and Internet shopping endeavors in Shanghai, China, in 1996, and in both Taiwan and South Korea in 1997. The late 1990s financial difficulties in the region provided these ventures with a difficult launch environment. Italy was also having economic troubles in this period, which particularly affected that country's mail-order sector,

leading Otto Versand to sell its Postalmarket stake in 1998 and to concentrate on the Euronova business.

In April 1998 Otto Versand made another bold move into the U.S. market when it acquired a majority stake in Crate & Barrel, which primarily sold through its chain of more than 60 home furnishings stores but which also sold via catalog. Crate & Barrel, whose legal name was actually Euromarket Designs Inc., agreed to the deal in order to tap into the deep pockets of its new parent for expansion; it also hoped that Otto Versand's mail-order expertise could bolster its catalog operation. For Otto Versand, the addition of Crate & Barrel further widened its product range.

Also serving to diversify Otto Versand's activities were several other late 1990s developments. In 1997 that company launched a new mail-order company in Germany called Otto Büro & Technik, which offered a wide range of office products, including furnishings and electronics and telecommunications goods. The following year the travel services unit was bolstered through the purchase of 25 travel offices from American Express Germany. In early 1999 Actebis, the computer distributor, was enlarged through the purchase of a competing firm, Peacock AG.

In April 1999 Otto Versand paid about £150 million to acquire the Freemans U.K. mail-order business from Sears plc. The acquisition increased Otto Versand's share of the U.K. catalog market from eight percent to 15 percent, making it the number three player, trailing only Great Universal Stores P.L.C. and Littlewoods Organisation.

This was the last major acquisition of the 20th century for a company that was clearly on the rise heading into the new millennium. Sales had more than doubled during the 1990s, and net income was on the increase as well. During 1999 Otto Versand celebrated its 50th anniversary and could also celebrate its position as the preeminent company in the global mail-order market.

Principal Subsidiaries

Schwab Versand GmbH; Josef Witt GmbH; Baur Versand GmbH & Co. (49%); Handelsgesellschaft Heinrich Heine GmbH; Alba Moda GmbH; Sport-Scheck GmbH; Eddie Bauer GmbH & Co. (60%); Zara Deutschland GmbH; Bon Prix Handelsgesellschaft mbH; Otto Büro & Technik Handelsgesellschaft mbH & Co. KG; Otto Reisen GmbH; Reiseland GmbH & Co. KG (75%); KG Maris Reisen GmbH & Co. (51%); KG Travel Overland Flugreisen GmbH & Co. (75%); FCB Freizeit-Club Betreuungs-GmbH & Co. (50%); OHG Fegro/Selgros Gesellschaft für Grosshandel mbH & Co. (50%); Actebis Holding GmbH; Peacock AG; Otto Versand GmbH (Austria); Otto B.V. (Netherlands); Otto Katalogusaruhaz Kft. (Hungary); Jelmoli Versand AG (Switzerland; 65%); Crate & Barrel Holdings, Inc. (U.S.A.; 50%); Together Ltd. (U.K.); Selgros Sp. z o.o. (Poland; 50%); Euronova S.R.L. (Italy); Otto Sp. z o.o. (Poland); Grattan PLC (U.K.); Tesco Home Shopping Limited (U.K.; 40%); Eddie Bauer (UK) Ltd. (60%); Arcadia International S.A. (Spain); Arcadia Holding S.A. (Chile; 50%); Shanghai Otto-Cheer Mailorder Co., Ltd. (China; 80%); Otto-Doosan Mail Order Ltd. (Korea; 75%); Otto-Chailease Mailorder Co.

Ltd. (Taiwan; 55%); Otto-Sumisho Inc. (Japan; 51%); Eddie Bauer Japan Inc. (70%); Otto-Burlingtons Mail Order Pvt. Ltd. (India; 74%); 3 Suisses International S.A. (France; 50%); 3 Suisses France S.C.S. (France; 92%); Civad S.A. (France); 3SH S.N.C. (France); Senior & Cie S.A. (France; 99%); XPL S.A. (France); Beaute Createurs S.A. (France; 50%); Becquet S.A. (France); Jm. Bruneau S.A. (France; 62%); Saint Brice S.A. (Belgium); 3 Pagen Versand und Handelsgesellschaft mbH; La Cite Numerique S.N.C. (France; 92%); C.I.F.D. S.A. (Spain); VPC Portugal Lda.; Motive Ltd. (U.K.); Cidal S.N.C. (France); Club Createurs Beaute Japon Inc. (80%); Hermes General Service GmbH; KG Hermes Versand Service G.m.b.H. & Co.; Shopping 24 GmbH; Corso Handelsgesellschaft mbH; Oktavia Gesellschaft für Bekleidung mbH; Media Handelsgesellschaft mbH; Otto Versand International GmbH; Hanseatic Versicherungsdienst GmbH; I.V.K. Industrie-Versicherungskontor GmbH & Co.; Northside Insurance Company Ltd. (Guernsey); Hanseatic Bank GmbH & Co.; Cofidis S.A. (France; 80%); Banque Covefi S.A. (France; 66%); Cofidis S.A. (Belgium; 85%); Cofidis Hispania EFC S.A. (Spain; 85%); Vecofin S.p.A. (Italy; 85%); Cofidis Ltd. (U.K.; 85%).

Principal Competitors

DAMARK International, Inc.; The Great Universal Stores P.L.C.; Hammacher Schlemmer & Company; Hanover Direct, Inc.; Karstadt Quelle AG; L.L. Bean, Inc.; Lands' End, Inc.; Lillian Vernon Corporation; Littlewoods Organisation; METRO AG; Pinault-Printemps-Redoute SA; Schickedanz-Holding AG & Co. KG; Vendex KBB N.V.

Further Reading

Berner, Robert, "Crate & Barrel Sells a Majority Stake to German Mail-Order Firm Versand," *Wall Street Journal,* February 13, 1998, p. B20.

Dowling, Melissa, "Translating from the German," *Catalog Age,* February 1995, pp. 53–55.

Hollinger, Peggy, "Green Starts to Unbundle Sears," *Financial Times,* April 8, 1999, p. 29.

Krienke, Mary, "Michael Otto," *Stores,* January 1995, p. 150.

"Marketinglektionene aug dem Versandweg" ("Marketing Lessons the Mailorder Way"), *Absatzwirtschaft* (Düsseldorf), October 1982, pp. 24+.

Miller, Karen L., "Otto the Great Rules in Germany," *Business Week,* January 31, 1994, p. 70J.

Miller, Paul, "Following Otto's Lead," *Catalog Age,* March 15, 1999, p. 10.

Otto, Werner, *Die Otto-Gruppe: Der Weg zum Grossunternehman,* Düsseldorf: Econ, 1982, 319 p.

Paine, Mandi, and Suzanne Bidlake, "Catalogues Face a New Order," *Marketing,* January 31, 1991, p. 2.

Tyson, Laura, "German Mail-Order Group in Asia Push," *Financial Times,* September 17, 1997, p. 21.

—Clark Siewert
—updated by April Dougal Gasbarre
and David E. Salamie

Outback Steakhouse, Inc.

2202 North Westshore Boulevard
5th Floor
Tampa, Florida 33607
U.S.A.
Telephone: (813) 282-1225
Fax: (813) 282-1209
Web site: http://www.outback.com

Public Company
Incorporated: 1987 as Multi-Venture Partners, Inc.
Employees: 40,500
Sales: $1.65 billion (1999)
Stock Exchanges: NASDAQ
Ticker Symbol: OSSI
NAIC: 722110 Full-Service Restaurants

Outback Steakhouse, Inc. runs one of the largest casual steakhouse chains in the United States, Outback Steakhouse. The chain consists of more than 600 Australian-themed restaurants in 47 states and several countries. The dinner-only restaurants serve moderately priced entrees such as seasoned steaks, prime rib, chicken, seafood, and pasta. The chain's signature, however, is an appetizer, the "Bloomin' Onion." The company also runs the Carrabba's Italian Grill chain, which includes about 70 dinner-only restaurants offering moderately priced Italian cuisine in a casual atmosphere. Outback Steakhouse, Inc. is also involved in two emerging restaurant chains: an upscale steakhouse called Fleming's Prime Steakhouse and Wine Bar, and another upscale chain called Roy's Restaurants, which features "east-west" cuisine and was founded by celebrated chef Roy Yamaguchi.

Creating the Concept and Achieving Quick Success

The enterprise—originally called Multi-Venture Partners, Inc.—was founded in Florida in 1987 by three partners, Tim Gannon, Bob Basham, and Chris Sullivan, all of whom had experience in the restaurant industry. Both Sullivan and Basham had worked at the Steak & Ale restaurant chain, which pio-

neered the salad bar and other popular concepts in the American restaurant industry. Following this experience, the two moved to a Steak & Ale's competitor, Bennigan's, and then returned to work with Steak & Ale's founder to open outlets of his new chain, Chili's, in Florida. Gannon also worked at Steak & Ale and in other restaurants in New Orleans.

By the late 1980s, all three men were anxious to launch a new endeavor. "Here are three guys who have always worked for other people and always said, 'God, if we had our own, we would do it a little bit different,' " Gannon later recounted to *Restaurants and Institutions* magazine.

Despite conventional wisdom, which said that Americans were moving away from meat and toward healthier, lighter food, Gannon, Sullivan, and Basham observed that restaurants specializing in steak, from inexpensive eateries such as Ponderosa to high-priced restaurants such as Ruth's Chris, were doing well. "Our research had really showed us that beef and prime rib were still the No. 1 thing people went out to eat," Basham remarked to *Restaurants and Institutions* magazine. He and his partners decided to open a steak restaurant that served the middle of the market, featuring high-quality food, a casual atmosphere, and an average dinner bill of $15 to $20.

All the partners needed was a theme that would give their restaurant concept a memorable identity. At the time, the 1986 movie *Crocodile Dundee* had recently been released and become a big hit. Despite the fact that none of the restaurant's founders had ever been to Australia, the trio decided to give their venture an Australian theme. In this way, they would be tapping into the traditional "western" association with steak, but with a twist. "Most Australians are fun-loving and gregarious people, and very casual people," Basham later told *F&B Magazine*. "We thought, 'That's exactly the kind of friendliness and atmosphere we want to have in our restaurants.' Then it was just a matter of coming up with an Australian name that worked for us. The Outback was kind of the wild, wild west of Australia. So there you go for the western theme. But instead of United States western, it's Australian western."

Initially, the group had modest plans for their venture. Rather than planning nationwide expansion, they hoped to open half a dozen outlets, and earn a nice living. "We figured if we divided up the profits with what we thought we could make out of five or six restaurants, we could have a very nice lifestyle and play a lot of golf," Basham told *F&B*.

However, opening night for the first Outback restaurant, in March 1988 in Tampa, Florida, did not look promising. In keeping with the Australian theme, the restaurant's decor featured boomerangs hung on paneled walls, kangaroo posters, shark jaws, stuffed koalas, and surfboards. The menu, however, was free of Australian influence, containing all American food, with specially seasoned steaks as its centerpiece. This split was deliberate, as was the group's refusal to visit Australia in the course of developing the restaurant's theme. "I might have tried to bring back authentic Australian food, which Americans don't generally like," Sullivan told *Fortune*. "Our company sells American food and Australian fun."

The company was not selling either on Outback's debut night. "We opened our doors, and it was very quiet," Gannon later told *F&B*. "Hardly anybody came. We had to call people over for dinner. No one had ever heard of Outback except our friends. And they were our only customer base."

Business began to pick up as the partners increased promotion—including cooking at radio stations and other local events—and as they received favorable reviews from restaurant critics. Outback's timing coincided with growing interest in more traditional, so-called "comfort" foods such as beef. Within 15 months, five more restaurants had been opened, and the chain was off to a fast start.

Outback's quick takeoff attracted the notice of other people in the restaurant industry. "We had guys who came to us and said: 'Listen—we're either going to franchise from you or we're going to rip you off. Take your choice.' Their point was they really loved our concept and they wanted to be a part of it," Gannon related to *F&B*. Faced with this kind of interest, Outback's founding partners agreed to an expansion of their concept.

Through franchise agreements and joint ventures, Outback's founders introduced their restaurant idea to areas outside Tampa in the late 1980s and early 1990s. After takeover talks with Chili's petered out in late 1989, Outback opened locations in

Orlando and Jacksonville, Florida; Louisville, Kentucky; Houston and Dallas, Texas; Indianapolis, Indiana; and Washington, D.C. By the end of 1990, the company was operating 23 restaurants. In the following year 26 more locations opened for business, for a total of 49 restaurants.

Early 1990s: Expansion As a Newly Public Company

Late in 1991, Outback's three founders, whose ownership stakes totaled 40 percent each for Sullivan and Basham, with the remaining 20 percent held by Gannon, decided to go public. With the $23.5 million raised by Outback's offering on the NASDAQ, the company began a gradual process of consolidating its ownership of the Outback locations. At this time, the company's name was changed to Outback Steakhouse, Inc.

The number of Outback restaurants continued to expand in 1992, as a total of 36 new restaurants were opened. Overall, the company had 52 outlets that it owned outright, 15 joint-venture operations, and 18 franchised locations, for a total of 85 Outback restaurants. In May 1992, Outback was named the third best small company by *Business Week* magazine.

Outback's rapid growth was fueled by several key tenets held by the company's founders. As a result of their extensive experience in the restaurant industry, Outback's owners believed in decentralized management. "We've been in their shoes as regional supervisors," Gannon remarked to *F&B*. "We've worked for companies and said, 'If you guys would just leave us alone and let us do our jobs, we would be so much more efficient.' We know that." Outback required that certain standards be met and retained final approval over plans for expansion, but otherwise let local managers run things as they saw fit.

Outback also gave its managers a stake in the company's overall well-being by allowing them to purchase a ten percent interest in their stores, and other employees had the right to purchase stock in the company. In addition, the company took steps to maintain positive working conditions for its employees, so that they would provide cheerful service to the restaurant's patrons. "If you worry about your employees and their environment and their ability to do the job, and you make sure they're happy, you don't have to worry about the guest," Gannon said. Accordingly, wait staff were responsible for only three tables apiece, and the company devoted 40 percent of the space at each location to the kitchen so food preparers would not be crowded. "We understand from having been managers, waiters, cooks, what they feel like," Gannon told *F&B*. "We know what the heat of the kitchen is like—personally."

The Outback menu featured items such as "Kookaburra Wings," "Aussie Cheesefries," and "Jackaroo Chops," and the company's signature appetizer, the "Bloomin' Onion." This item, which Gannon codeveloped with a chef in New Orleans, was a Spanish onion with its center removed, which had been sliced into wedges so that it fanned out like a flower, and deep-fried. The onion was served on a plate with a bowl of sauce at the center for dipping, as an alternative to onion rings. "We had to figure how to get the center out, how to fry it, how to make it work as an appetizer where each petal could be pulled out individually," Gannon recounted to *F&B*. "Then the idea was to apply New Orleans seasonings to the onion, so that not only did you have something pretty, but you also had something with an exciting flavor profile. And the recipe for the seasoning on ours, that's my recipe.''

Outback's steaks, the centerpiece of its menu, also featured a New Orleans flavor, being seasoned with 18 herbs and spices. To help them cope with the enormous cuts of meat that the restaurant served, Outback gave its diners oversized flatware as well, including a steak knife that more closely resembled a saber.

While American food ruled Outback's menu, the Australian theme reasserted itself at the bar, where each restaurant typically earned 17 percent of its revenues. About three-fifths of the company's beer sales, and four-fifths of its wine sales, were generated by Australian brands, including Foster's, Rosemount, and Black Opal. Much of the bar business came from customers waiting for tables—the restaurants were so popular that there was typically a 30-minute wait for dinner. To meet this demand, Outback began to build larger restaurants in the early 1990s, expanding from its prototype 160-seat design to a 200-seat design. The company also switched from paging waiting customers to a quieter beeper system, which helped cut down on the tumult that came to characterize the Outback experience.

In marketing its concept, Outback targeted people between the ages of 35 and 54 with annual incomes exceeding $50,000. To distinguish its restaurants, Outback developed a huge red neon sign that fronted its buildings. In addition, the company signed on to sponsor the nationally televised college football Gator Bowl, which was played each year in Jacksonville, Florida. Outback also devised a ''No Rules'' advertising campaign, focusing on the theme that diners could get what they wanted— good food and prompt, cheerful service—at Outback. Customers were assured that they could order items not on the menu and that the kitchen would strive to fulfill their wishes.

One wish Outback did not set out to fulfill, however, was a diner's desire to eat there for lunch. Because a lunch shift complicated restaurant operations, and rarely brought in profits, the company opened only for dinner. ''There's not much money in lunch, and it burns out employees,'' Sullivan explained to *Fortune*. This policy also allowed Outback to save on real estate for the restaurants it built, since locations near where people worked were more expensive than areas where people lived.

By the end of 1992, these policies had pushed Outback's systemwide restaurant sales to $195 million. Rapid growth both in revenues and number of restaurants continued in the following year. Outback added 35 company-owned outlets and 26 new franchised restaurants in 1993. The chain passed the 100-restaurant mark in March of that year, having expanded into 15 states. Overall, Outback had reported 147 percent annual growth over its first three years as a public company.

Mid-1990s and Beyond: Adding Carrabba's and Other Concepts to the Menu and Expanding Internationally

Outback began to test a second restaurant concept in March 1993, entering into a joint venture with a Houston restaurant group to develop Carrabba's Italian Grill restaurants, which featured Italian cuisine in a casual setting. For $2 million, Outback acquired a half interest in two existing restaurants, and

the company agreed to invest an additional $8 million in the construction of new restaurants. The company added two new locations in Houston in 1993, and laid plans to open six to eight more in Texas and Florida in the following year.

The Carrabba's concept was similar to the original Outback restaurant in many ways. Its average diner's check was somewhat higher, and alcohol made up nearly one quarter of sales, versus 17 percent at Outback. Overall, however, food costs at Carrabba's were lower. By opening this second front in the restaurant wars, Outback hoped to guarantee continued growth as the market for Outback steakhouses became saturated.

Outback continued its brisk pace of expansion in 1994. The company opened 68 new Outback steakhouses and eight new Carrabba's Italian Grill locations. Financial returns also remained robust, as the company continued to report increasing sales and revenues. The company was making steady progress in its transformation from a regional restaurateur to a national presence in the hospitality industry. By the end of 1995 there were a total of 297 Outback steakhouses and 23 Carrabba's. Revenues for 1995 reached $664 million, more than double the figure of two years earlier. Net income stood at $53.7 million, a 37 percent increase over the previous year.

International expansion of the Outback concept began in 1996 with the opening of the first unit in Canada. Over the next few years, Outbacks were opened in Aruba, Brazil, China, Guam, Mexico, the Philippines, and South Korea. By decade's end, there were about 40 of the steakhouses operating outside the United States. The results were mixed, with Brazil and Asia showing the most promise; the company therefore planned to add 20 to 30 international restaurants per year in the early 21st century, focusing mainly on those two markets. At the same time, the Outback chain neared its maturity in the U.S. market; at the end of the 1990s there were about 575 domestic units, with the company projecting a ceiling of 700 to 750. Domestic expansion, therefore, was slowed; rather than adding 60 to 70 units per year, the company planned for an additional 40 to 50. The late 1990s also saw the rollout of the Curbside Take-Away program, a takeout concept conceived by an Outback restaurant manager in Florida that involved running orders out to cars as they pulled into the parking lot. After some fine-tuning, the program proved quite successful.

The Carrabba's chain, meantime, was not doing nearly as well as the company flagship, and was suffering from the fierce competition in the casual Italian dining sector. In late 1997 nine underperforming Carrabba's were closed, and the expansion of the chain was slowed to six to eight units per year (there were 72 chainwide by the end of the decade). This pullback was followed by a reconceptualizing of the Carrabba's concept and the launching of a chainwide remodeling effort.

As it became clearer that the Carrabba's chain would not be the growth vehicle the company's management had hoped for, Outback Steakhouse began searching for new opportunities. Realizing it would be difficult to develop another breakout concept like Outback, the company began looking for upscale—but casual—concepts with higher per-person checks than Outback and the potential to eventually generate about $500 million in annual revenue from a smaller number of units than the Outback chain. Three concepts were emerging at the end of the 1990s, one of which was being developed in-house: a Creole restaurant slated to be launched in 2000. In August 1999 Outback Steakhouse entered into a joint venture with acclaimed chef-restaurateur Roy Yamaguchi for the further development of Roy's Restaurants, an upscale east-meets-west concept with a per-person check average of about $35. There were already 20 Roy's in Hawaii, California, New York, and Tokyo, and Outback agreed to help open and operate at least 100 new units worldwide. Outback went even further upscale one month later when it entered into another joint venture, this one for the operation and development of Fleming's Prime Steakhouse and Wine Bar, which had existing units in Newport Beach, California, and Scottsdale, Arizona; and a unit under development in La Jolla, California. Fleming's featured prime cuts of meat and a selection of 100 premium wines by the glass; its average per-person tab approached $50.

The continued success of the Outback Steakhouse chain propelled the company past the $1 billion revenue mark in 1997 and, by 1999, to $1.65 billion, a 21 percent increase over the previous year. In terms of the value of its stock, the company stood at the dawn of a new century as one of the six largest publicly traded U.S. restaurant firms. To continue this heady growth beyond 2000, Outback Steakhouse was focusing on international expansion, the development of additional restaurant concepts, and experimentation with smaller versions of its flagship chain which would be located in alternative locations such as airports.

Principal Subsidiaries

Outback Steakhouse of Florida, Inc.; Carrabba's Italian Grill, Inc.; Outback Steakhouse International, Inc.; OS Pacific, Inc.; OS Prime, Inc.; Outback Sports, LLC.

Principal Competitors

Applebee's International, Inc.; Brinker International, Inc.; Carlson Restaurants Worldwide Inc.; Chart House Enterprises, Inc.; Darden Restaurants, Inc.; Family Steak Houses of Florida, Inc.; Ground Round Restaurants, Inc.; Investor's Management Corp.; Landry's Seafood Restaurants, Inc.; Lone Star Steakhouse & Saloon, Inc.; Metromedia Company; Morton's Restaurant Group, Inc.; RARE Hospitality International, Inc.; The Riese Organization; Ruth's Chris Steak House; Ryan's Family Steak Houses, Inc.

Further Reading

"The Best Small Companies," *Business Week,* May 25, 1992, p. 97.

Chaudhry, Rajan, "Outback's Bloomin' Success," *Restaurants & Institutions,* December 15, 1993, pp. 34–55.

Frumkin, Paul, "Outback, Yamaguchi Forge Pact for Global Growth of Roy's," *Nation's Restaurant News,* August 16, 1999, pp. 1, 11+.

——, "Roy's Deal Encore: Outback, Fleming's Ink Pact," *Nation's Restaurant News,* October 11, 1999, pp. 1, 128.

George, Daniel P., "Australia, American-Style," *F&B Magazine,* November/December 1993, pp. 20–24.

Hayes, Jack, "Outback's Founders Blaze New Trails by Rewriting the Rules," *Nation's Restaurant News,* March 27, 1995, pp. 51+.

Janofsky, Michael, "On the Menu, Steak Bucks Trend," *New York Times,* January 25, 1993.

Kapner, Suzanne, "Bob Basham," *Nation's Restaurant News,* March 27, 1995, pp. 80+.

——, "Robert Basham," *Nation's Restaurant News,* October 14, 1996, pp. 148, 150.

Kronsberg, Jane, "Outback's Specialties Outsized," *Charleston Post and Courier,* May 5, 1994, p. 14D.

McLaughlin, Mary-Beth, "Toledo Says ''G'day Mate' to New Outback Steakhouse," *Toledo Blade,* March 13, 1993.

Michels, Antony J., and John Wyatt, "Managing," *Fortune,* August 9, 1993, p. 40.

Papiernik, Richard L., "Avery and Merritt: Outback's Prexy, CFO Put Aussie-Influenced Chain on Map for the Mainstream to Enjoy," *Nation's Restaurant News,* January 2000, pp. 22, 24.

Ruggless, Ron, "Outback Fine-Tunes Carrabba's As Fast-Track Growth Vehicle," *Nation's Restaurant News,* March 27, 1995, pp. 78+.

—Elizabeth Rourke
—updated by David E. Salamie

Parsons Brinckerhoff, Inc.

One Penn Plaza
New York, New York 10119
U.S.A.
Telephone: (212) 465-5000
Toll Free: (800) 877-7754
Fax: (212) 465-5096
Web site: http://www.pbworld.com

Private Company
Incorporated: 1975
Employees: 7,900
Sales: $945 million (1999 est.)
NAIC: 23411 Highway and Street Construction; 23412
    Bridge and Tunnel Construction; 54133 Engineering
    Services; 551112 Offices of Other Holding Companies

Parsons Brinckerhoff, Inc. is the holding company for one of the world's leading engineering consulting firms, involved in the design and construction of transportation, power, building, and telecommunications systems. While the company has long been the leading consulting engineer firm for transportation projects in the United States, it also has a presence in nearly 80 countries. Originally organized as a partnership, Parsons Brinckerhoff incorporated in 1975, with all of its shares being employee-owned.

Transportation Specialist: 1885–1956

The history of Parsons Brinckerhoff may be traced to 1885, when William Barclay Parsons, the company founder, opened an office as a consulting engineer in lower Manhattan. Parsons' had earned an engineering degree from Columbia University in 1882. Business steadily grew, and in 1900 he was awarded a major project: design and engineering of the New York City subway. By 1904, the first stage of the project was opened, offering transportation from Manhattan to Harlem. Eugene Klapp and Henry M. Brinckerhoff joined Parsons in 1906 in what would become known as the firm of Barclay Parsons and Klapp by 1909. Brinckerhoff would gain fame as integral to the

invention of the "third rail," a concept that would revolutionize rapid transit. Another associate, Walter J. Douglas, joined the firm in 1908. During this time, Parsons and Brinckerhoff were responsible for transportation projects, while Klapp and Douglas focused on building bridges. In addition, Douglas and Parsons oversaw power plants and dam projects.

In 1914, Parsons was named chief engineer in the construction of the Cape Cod Canal. Following the completion of that project, however, Parsons scaled back his involvement in the engineering firm in order to focus on the war effort. Parsons founded and led a special regiment during World War I known as "the fighting engineers." First, he was instrumental in organizing the First Reserve Engineer Regiment, and then he went abroad, being among the first to land in Europe, where he studied and made recommendations for improving railway systems, ports, shipping terminals, and the like. At war's end, at the age of 60, Parsons was detached from his engineering corps and returned to New York, where he resumed his work at the firm while also authoring several books on engineering and serving as trustee for such prominent organizations as Columbia University, the New York Public Library, and the Carnegie Institute.

While Parsons had served abroad, Brinckerhoff had remained on the home front, directing the construction of naval dry docks to support the war effort. Brinckerhoff and Douglas were eventually made partners after the war, and the firm became known as Parsons Klapp Brinckerhoff & Douglas. Between 1920 and 1939 the firm completed more than $50 million of work, including railroad and harbor terminals and manufacturing plants.

Parsons died in 1932 and was succeeded as senior partner of the firm by Douglas; the company would, however, continue to bear the name of its famous founders, even after the passing of Brinckerhoff. After the completion of the Detroit-Windsor Tunnel linking Michigan and Ontario in 1930 and a tunnel under the Scheldt River for Antwerp, Belgium, completed in 1931, the firm fell upon lean times due to the Great Depression.

Between 1936 and 1940 net income totaled only $293,010. Still, the company managed to secure important projects, among them construction of the network of roads for the 1939

Company Perspectives:

Parsons Brinckerhoff will: Provide quality, cost-effective consulting services for public and private infrastructure worldwide. Infrastructure includes transportation, energy, environmental and building facilities. Consulting services encompass planning design, project management, construction management and facility operation, maintenance and management; Commit to performing its services in a socially, ethically and environmentally responsible manner and to high professional standards; Provide a stimulating stable and rewarding work environment and attract, retain and develop employees as leaders in the business of providing professional services to its clients; Perpetuate the company as an employee-owned firm, providing a reasonable return on shareholders' investments and appropriate benefits to all employees; and Continue to make meaningful contributions to the advancement of its profession.

World's Fair in New York. This project was headed up by Brinckerhoff and John P. Hogan, who became senior partner that year. In 1943, Hogan and Eugene Macdonald replaced Klapp and Douglas—both now deceased–as name partners in the firm. During World War II virtually the entire staff worked on designing the U.S. Navy's fixed and floating drydocks, including those for the Brooklyn Navy Yard.

Hogan retired in 1947 and was succeeded as senior partner by Macdonald. Projects in the immediate postwar years included tunnels, bridges, airports, and highways, culminating in New Jersey's 173-mile-long Garden State Parkway, for which Parsons Brinckerhoff served as the general engineering consultant. This project was completed in 1955 at a cost of $330 million. Also noteworthy was the firm's construction of the first Hampton Roads Bridge-Tunnel, completed in 1957. Upon his retirement in 1956, Macdonald was succeeded as managing partner by Maurice Quade, who was assisted by Walter S. Douglas, son of Walter J. Douglas. The firm now became Parsons Brinckerhoff Quade & Douglas.

Four Decades of Growth: 1957–95

During the ensuing years the firm designed and supervised the construction of the headquarters for the Air Force's North American Air Defense (NORAD) Command Center, which was completed in 1964. This facility was built underground, beneath Cheyenne Mountain in Colorado. By 1965 the firm had branch offices in four cities and field offices in nine. A joint venture of Parsons Brinckerhoff Quade & Douglas and Tudor Engineering Co. had begun work on a public rail system centered around San Francisco and Oakland for the Bay Area Rapid Transit District (BART). This undertaking included nine miles of subway, 14 miles of single-bore tunnel, a three-mile twin rock tunnel, and a 3.5-mile tube tunnel under San Francisco Bay that was, at the time, the longest underwater tunnel in the world. The $1.6-billion, 71-mile system was not completed until 1974—five years behind schedule. The same joint venture constructed a rapid-transit system for the Atlanta metropolitan area that opened in 1979.

Parsons Brinckerhoff Quade & Douglas had been incorporated in the early 1950s to meet the licensing requirements of certain states, but it continued to operate as a partnership until 1975, when it transformed itself into an employee-owned corporation in order to foster further growth and to meet increased competition and combat rising costs. Shares were offered annually to middle and senior managers, based on nominations made to a corporate committee, with the shares accumulated to be sold back to the company over a ten-year period following the employee's departure or retirement. There were 83 shareholders in 1982.

The change from partnership to corporation affected company culture as well as organization. Henry Michel, the firm's president in 1983, told *Management Review:* "The partnership structure endowed individual partners, each of whom specialized in one technical area, with absolute decision-making power in their respective fields of expertise. . . . The partners were almost controlling little fiefdoms." Under the new corporate structure, however, the partners found their power somewhat diminished. The company felt that sharing the decision-making controls allowed, according to Michel, "the best technicians and the best managers to concentrate on what they do best." Of the new employee-ownership status, Michel noted that employee-owners were more likely to keep an eye out for cost overruns, as witnessed by a 350 percent increase in business since 1974. The change to corporate status also allowed Parsons Brinckerhoff to retain earnings and thus ease the borrowing needed for expansion.

Parsons Brinckerhoff Inc. (PB) was established in 1979 as the holding company for several subsidiaries. Parsons Brinckerhoff Quade & Douglas (PBQD) continued to be responsible for the firm's traditional transit, highway, and bridges and tunnels projects. Parsons Brinckerhoff International was charged with servicing clients abroad and also acted as a holding company for foreign subsidiaries. In addition, PB oversaw Parsons Brinckerhoff Construction Services and Parsons Brinckerhoff Development Corporation. By 1982 20 percent of the company's business was coming from overseas, including projects in Singapore and Hong Kong. PB also established a subsidiary for the alternative-energy facilities that the company was designing, building, and operating for third-party clients, including cogeneration, hydroelectric, and waste-to-energy projects in New England and California.

In 1985, PB's centennial year, the company was at work on no fewer than 14 subway systems and won nine of the 11 major projects on which it had made proposals. It was also designing and managing construction of the Fort McHenry Tunnel in Baltimore Harbor—at 8,000 feet in length and eight lanes in width the largest underwater tunnel in the world at the time. PBQD, along with Morrison Knudsen Corporation and CRSS Inc., won a contract valued at $1.6 billion in 1990 to design and build the tunnels, service areas, roads, campus, utilities, and experimental facilities for the world's largest atom smasher. (This Texas-based high-energy-physics project was later canceled, however.)

In fiscal 1993 (the year ended October 31, 1993) PB reported operating income of $13.9 million on revenues of $343.1 million, both company records. The number of employees—3,575—was also a record. The four major operating subsidiaries were in charge of infrastructure, construction services, facil-

Key Dates:

1885: William Barclay Parsons opens an engineering office in New York City.
1900: Parsons breaks ground for his New York City subway system project.
1906: Henry Brinckerhoff joins the firm.
1916: Parsons founds and leads the Eleventh Engineer Regiment of World War I; on the homefront, the firm constructs facilities to support the war effort.
1930: The firm completes the Detroit-Windsor Tunnel.
1939: Brinckerhoff and the firm design the road network for the New York World's Fair.
1964: Firm completes the NORAD underground command center for the Air Force in Colorado.
1974: In a joint venture PB completes the Bay Area transit system.
1975: The firm converts from a partnership to a corporation.
1979: Parsons Brinckerhoff is established as a holding company.
1987: PB, in a joint venture, begins work on a Boston transportation project that becomes the most expensive in the world.
1998: Staff grows by 45 percent after four acquisitions.

ities, and international work. The second largest of the company's more than 80 offices was in Hong Kong, and a Shanghai office also was opened in 1993. By late 1996 one-fifth of PB's workforce was based in five East Asian offices. PB also had clients in eastern Europe and had recently formed a Madrid-based transportation company with a Spanish partner. In seeking to gain access to Asia's lucrative and developing private-power market, PB acquired Merz & McLellan Holdings Ltd., a British-based power consultant, in 1994. The company also opened a Vienna office that year.

Projects of the Late 1990s

When work began in 1996 on the 2,400-megawatt Sabiya power plant in Kuwait—one of the largest in the world—Merz & McLellan was responsible for the design, project management, and site supervision. PBQD was in charge of project management services for the H-3 highway, the largest construction project in Hawaii history, completed in 1997. That year it won a contract, with CH2M Hill Ltd., for the planning, design, construction, and project management of a $6 billion deep-tunnel sewage collection, treatment, and disposal system in Singapore. PBQD was the prime engineering consultant for the construction of Pearl Harbor Naval Station's Ford Island Bridge, which opened in 1998. It was managing the construction of Cairo's subway, which began in 1986 and was scheduled for completion in 2003.

PB's revenues reached a record $698 million in fiscal 1998. Net income came to nearly $9 million, and the company enjoyed its 23rd consecutive year of increased value per share of stock. Its number of employees grew by 45 percent, to 7,700. Four new acquisitions were made during the year, including Booker Associates Inc., a St. Louis-based engineering and

architectural firm, and Kennedy & Donkin Group, a British engineering firm. In addition to the aforementioned undertakings, the projects in which PB was taking part at this time included London's $1.4 billion Heathrow Airport Terminal 5; Saudi Arabia's $1.2 billion Ghazlan II Power Station; and Brazil's $500 million Castello-Raposo, Lot 12 toll road.

PB's main job—and its biggest headache–in the 1990s was its work with Bechtel Group, Inc. as project manager for Boston's Central Artery/Third Harbor Tunnel project, the largest civil engineering project in U.S. history. Authorized in 1987 as a mile-long portion of Interstate 93 that would run through downtown Boston underground, it was also intended to link the Massachusetts Turnpike (Interstate 90) to Logan Airport by means of a third tunnel through Boston's inner harbor. The "Big Dig" was originally planned for completion in 1994 and the cost estimated at $2.5 billion. By the time the 1.6-mile Ted Williams Tunnel opened in late 1995, the estimate had reached nearly $8 billion. A report by an independent consultant charged that Bechtel/PB managers had allowed costs to spiral needlessly by not delegating authority to area managers in a position to control spending. The project had already fallen behind schedule and over budget because managers had failed to test the soil properly before designing the tunnel. The next part of the job involved establishing a link between the turnpike and the tunnel. In just 1,150 feet, nine lanes of highway had to be threaded under eight sets of railroad tracks bringing 40,000 people into South Station each working day, and just inches above 81-year-old tunnels through which ran a rapid-transit line. By early 2000, cost estimates had reached $12.2 billion, with completion of the project not expected until 2005.

This domestic challenge notwithstanding, PB was widely recognized as the leader in American transportation engineering and by the late 1990s was truly a global concern with offices in Europe, South Africa, China, Australia, and South America. Achieving such prominence in servicing all types of infrastructure, in addition to its flagship transportation services, remained its goal for the next century.

Principal Subsidiaries

Parsons Brinckerhoff Quade & Douglas Inc.; Parsons Brinckerhoff Construction Services Inc.; Parsons Brinckerhoff Energy Services; Parsons Brinckerhoff FG Inc.; Parsons Brinckerhoff International; Parsons Brinckerhoff Services PC; PB Farradyne Inc.; PB Kennedy & Donkin Group (U.K.); Merz & McLellan Holdings Ltd. (U.K.).

Principal Competitors

CH2M Hill Ltd.; The Parsons Corporation.

Further Reading

"Acquisition Puts PB in World Power Play," *ENR/Engineering News-Record,* October 24, 1994, p. 24.
"BART District Sues for Damages of $237.8 Million," *Wall Street Journal,* November 20, 1974, p. 15.
Bobrick, Benson, *Parsons Brinckerhoff: The First 100 Years,* New York: Van Nostrand Reinhold, 1985.
"Employee Ownership As a Corporate Strategy," *Management Review,* June 1983, pp. 4–5.

Gersten, Alan, "US Group to Run Singapore Sewer Project," *Journal of Commerce,* July 31, 1997, p. 6A.

Green, Peter, "Money Flows Through Boston Aorta," *ENR/Engineering News-Record,* July 21, 1988, pp. 22–23.

Howe, Peter J., "Threading the Needle," *Boston Globe,* May 20, 1996, pp. 45, 48.

Korman, Richard, "Taking a Lot More 'Prudent Risks'," *ENR/Engineering News Record,* June 13, 1994, pp. 34–37.

Kosowatz, John J., "A-E and Management Team Named for Superconducting Supercollider," *ENR/Engineering News-Record,* March 1, 1990, pp. 10–11.

Palmer, Thomas C., Jr., "Mismanagement Blamed for Costs, Delays in Big Dig," *Boston Globe,* December 12, 1995, pp. 1, 18.

"Parsons Brinckerhoff Builds on Project Expertise," *Project Finance,* October 1998, p. 8.

"Parsons Brinckerhoff's High Stakes Players," *ENR/Engineering News-Record,* September 30, 1982, pp.22–24.

"Providing Careers Prospects for Engineers and Technicians," *Management Review,* February 1981, pp. 29–31.

Yamin, Rebecca, "Pioneering Transit Engineering Firm Celebrating Centennial Year," *Mass Transit,* January 1985, pp. 8–10, 26–27.

Zutell, Irene, "Parsons Engineering New Blueprint in Asia," *Crain's New York Business,* November 14, 1994, p. 17.

—Robert Halasz

Pier 1 imports®

Pier 1 Imports, Inc.

301 Commerce Street
Suite 600
Fort Worth, Texas 76102
U.S.A.
Telephone: (817) 252-8000
Toll Free: (888) 807-4371
Fax: (817) 878-7883
Web site: http://www.pier1.com

Public Company
Founded: 1962 as Cost Plus
Employees: 12,600
Sales: $1.14 billion (1999)
Stock Exchanges: New York
Ticker Symbol: PIR
NAIC: 442110 Furniture Stores; 442299 All Other Home
 Furnishings Stores; 453220 Gift, Novelty, and
 Souvenir Stores

Pier 1 Imports, Inc. is a leading specialty retailer, operating more than 800 casual home furnishing stores in 48 U.S. states, two Canadian provinces, and in Mexico, Puerto Rico, the United Kingdom, and Japan. The vast majority operate under the Pier 1 Imports name, while the U.K. units are known as ''The Pier'' and the operations in Mexico and Puerto Rico consist of ''store within a store'' outlets in Sears stores. The U.S. and Canadian stores are typically freestanding units of about 7,500 square feet located near major shopping centers or malls. They offer a wide selection of merchandise, including more than 5,000 items imported from more than 60 countries worldwide (the bulk coming from Asia), with the principal categories consisting of furniture, decorative accessories, dining and kitchen goods, bath and bedding accessories, and seasonal items. Sales through the company's proprietary credit card account for more than 28 percent of overall sales.

1960s: The Early Years

Charles Tandy and Luther Henderson opened the precursor to Pier 1 shops in 1962 under the name Cost Plus. Henderson was serving as treasurer for Tandy's burgeoning Tandy Corpo-

ration, which became best known for its Radio Shack chain. Pier 1 was inspired by the owner of a rattan furniture importer and wholesaler in San Mateo, California, who was having credit problems. To help liquidate costly inventory, the shop owner opened a liquidation outlet in 1958 called Cost Plus. Impressed by the shop's success, Tandy offered the owner of Cost Plus a loan to start a retail Cost Plus outlet. At the same time, Tandy secured the rights to open and operate additional stores under the Cost Plus name.

The concept behind Tandy's Cost Plus chain plan was relatively simple: a strong U.S. dollar would allow him to import items, including rattan furniture, brass candlesticks, specialty textiles, and other items, at rock bottom prices from countries such as Mexico, India, and Thailand. Even with large markups the goods would seem relatively cheap in the United States. Furthermore, items that did not sell well could be easily liquidated by cutting their price to near cost. Although most of the merchandise was second-rate in comparison to U.S. or European-made goods, it was popular with the large baby-boom generation, most of whom were first-time buyers of furnishings.

Tandy opened 16 Cost Plus retail outlets between 1962 and 1965. By 1966, however, Tandy's growing Radio Shack enterprise began to take much of his attention away from his Cost Plus venture. On February 10, 1966, a group of 30 investors led by Henderson bought Tandy's Cost Plus operation. They changed the name to Pier 1 Imports to reflect the store's import emphasis and embarked on a mission to expand the concept nationally. The original Cost Plus outlet remained under separate ownership and eventually grew into the nationwide Cost Plus chain of the early 21st century, one of Pier 1's competitors.

By 1967, Pier 1's sales had already reached $4.5 million annually, and growth accelerated throughout the remainder of the decade. By 1969, the chain had grown to 42 stores and demand for Pier 1's goods was increasing. Pier 1 went public in 1970 to raise money for continued expansion. The company's stock was initially listed on the American Stock Exchange, before moving to the New York Stock Exchange two years later. Pier 1 had multiplied its chain to 123 stores, which represented sales growth of more than 100 percent since 1968. Among Pier 1's shops were stores that had been opened in Australia and England in 1971. During the following two years

Company Perspectives:

Pier 1 Imports offers distinct, casual home furnishings at a good value. Our ever-changing collections are presented in a sensory environment that encourages customers to have fun shopping for their homes. Pier 1 is a socially conscious company that conducts business with personal and professional integrity. We employ committed, caring associates whose first priority is responding to the needs of our customers.

the chain also branched out into France, West Germany, the Netherlands, and Belgium.

Pier 1 prospered during the late 1960s and early 1970s by focusing on the baby boom generation, members of whom were looking for interesting, exotic goods such as love beads, incense, leather sandals, and serapes. "You could characterize a lot of our customers as flower children," recounted Pier 1 chief executive officer Clark Johnson in the *Dallas-Fort Worth Business Journal*. "Our stores had the look of an old grocery store . . . and, at that time, the appeal was heavily toward cost." As the "flower children" rushed to Pier 1 to decorate their dormitory rooms, bedrooms, and apartments, company sales rose to $68 million and earnings to $3.8 million by 1973.

Mid-1970s to Early 1980s: Reorganizing and Restructuring

After an explosive decade of growth, Pier 1's fortunes began to change in the mid-1970s. Importantly, global inflation and exchange rate fluctuations exposed Pier 1's unique vulnerability to worldwide financial changes. Foreign goods became much more expensive, thus diminishing Pier 1's important cost advantage. Furthermore, other retail chains and department stores began to vie for some of Pier 1's market share by offering many of the same imported goods. To make matters worse, the core group of customers upon which Pier 1 had focused its energy was changing; baby boomers were becoming more sophisticated by the mid- and late 1970s and were increasingly interested in more mainstream goods. According to some critics, Pier 1 lost touch with its patrons and failed to change its inventory to meet market demands.

In an attempt to buoy sales and profits, Pier 1 mounted several reorganization campaigns and new marketing strategies during the mid-1970s. The company even tested different types of stores, including specialty retail outlets, art supply centers, rug stores, and fabric shops. Pier 1 also diversified into several wholesale operations such as Singapore Candle Company, Southwestern Textile Company, Rug Corporation of America, and Pasha Pillows. Many of its retail and wholesale experiments languished, and Pier 1 eventually jettisoned most of them.

Although the company failed to sustain the rampant growth it had achieved during its first ten years, Pier 1's balance sheet had improved slightly by the late 1970s. By 1979, the chain included approximately 300 stores worldwide, while sales and profits had stabilized. Pier 1 merged with Cousins Mortgage and Equity Investments (CMEI) in 1979 in an effort to boost its

capital. Then, in 1980, the board of directors brought in Robert Camp to help improve the company's performance.

Camp had successfully operated his own chain of Pier 1 stores in Canada and had a knack for retailing. Camp forced Pier 1 to reevaluate its buying operations and store location strategies. He also focused on improving visual merchandising techniques. During 1981 and 1982, Pier 1 consolidated its retail import operations, closed marginal stores, opened larger outlets in more profitable locations, and shifted from novelty items to higher quality goods. Investors were impressed by Camp's initiatives. Within two years, sales increased 41 percent to $165 million and operating income jumped 66 percent, to $6 million. Pier 1's stock price quickly rose from about $1 in 1980 to more than $7 by 1982.

Mid-to-Late 1980s: Refocus on the Customer

Just as Pier 1 began to build momentum under the direction of Camp, control of the company changed hands. Under the leadership of Charles (Red) Scott, La Jolla, California-based Intermark, Inc., a billion-dollar holding company with a reputation for turning ailing companies around, bought a majority interest in Pier 1. Camp eventually left, and Scott hired Clark Johnson to run Pier 1 in 1985. Johnson, who was known as an aggressive and sociable businessman, had a varied background that included experience in both the furniture and sporting goods industries. He had also managed lumberyards and had partnered with Jack Nicklaus to run MacGregor Golf Co. As president of Wickes Furniture he had engineered the turnaround of that company during the mid-1970s. Likewise, he boosted sales at MacGregor from $17 million to $50 million in just five years.

Like Camp, Johnson initiated numerous changes within the Pier 1 organization. He immediately sold Pier 1's two major subsidiaries, Sunbelt Nursery Group Inc. and Ridgewood Properties Inc. He also jettisoned the mail-order business, which lost more than $1 million in 1985 alone. In addition, Johnson developed plans to modernize Pier 1's computer information systems, upgrade advertising and marketing programs, and consolidate its North American management offices. Furthermore, between 1985 and 1989 he closed more than 60 marginal stores and refurbished most of the company's existing outlets at an average cost of $190,000 each. More aggressive managers were brought in and given the freedom to make critical decisions.

Perhaps Johnson's most notable strategic contribution during the mid-1980s was improving Pier 1's attentiveness to its customer base. "It was clear that there was a huge audience out there which had once felt a tremendous allegiance to Pier 1," recalled Johnson in *Adweek's Marketing Week,* adding "I believed we could rekindle that allegiance if we showed them that we were in tune with their new values." Johnson retained New York PR agency Makovsky & Company to conduct what it termed "the most comprehensive study of the American home ever undertaken."

The study was designed with two goals in mind: (1) to determine whether or not Pier 1 was on track with the values it was emphasizing in its stores, and (2) to generate publicity as the sponsor of the study. Among other statistics, survey findings indicated that 92 percent of college-educated Americans were

Key Dates:

1962: Charles Tandy and Luther Henderson open their first Cost Plus store.

1966: A group of investors led by Henderson buys Tandy's Cost Plus operation and changes the name to Pier 1 Imports.

1970: Company goes public.

1971: International expansion begins with the opening of stores in Australia and England.

1979: Chain includes approximately 300 stores worldwide.

1985: Intermark purchases a majority interest in Pier 1; new efforts are made to win back customer base and reposition the company.

1989: Number of stores exceeds 550.

1991: Intermark sells its stake in Pier 1, returning Pier 1 to true public ownership.

1993: Pier 1 "stores within a store" are launched in Mexico; partnership is forged to operate "The Pier" chain in England.

1997: Company enters into a joint venture to open stores in Japan.

1999: For the fiscal year ending in February, net sales exceed $1 billion for the first time.

satisfied with their homes; 86 percent decorated their homes themselves; 57 percent believed that their homes were nicer than what they had grown up in; and an overwhelming majority described their home interior as casual. As hoped, the media reported the survey's findings and brandished Pier 1's name on the cover of major national newspapers and on television screens.

Confident of his strategy to win back Pier 1's customer base and reposition the company, Johnson embarked on an aggressive program of growth in 1986. He set a goal of doubling the total number of Pier 1 outlets by 1990 and increasing the average floor space and annual sales of the stores. Pier 1 achieved its goal one year early. By 1989 the company had doubled its chain to include more than 550 outlets worldwide. In addition, profit margins increased and the average ticket value of store items rose to $25 (from just $5 in the early 1980s), aided by the 1988 introduction of the Pier 1 Preferred Customer Card, the chain's proprietary credit card. As a result, sales leapt from $173 million in 1985 to $517 million by 1990. More importantly, profits soared from $60 million to $210 million during the same time period.

Encouraged by Pier 1's success, Johnson boldly proposed expansion plans for the next decade. "The best way to predict the future is to create it," Johnson stated in *Adweek's Marketing Week*. He continued: "Pier 1 Imports has a vision of the kind of company it would like to become. By the year 2000 Pier 1 will operate more than 1,000 stores, producing more than $1.25 billion in sales and serving more than 10 million customers."

Early 1990s: Stumbling Through the Recession

Despite these grand plans, Johnson was forced to slow Pier 1's pace in 1990 after seven years of expansion. Economic

sluggishness in the United States forced the slowdown. Although sales swelled to $562 million in 1991, net income shrunk as retail markets became increasingly competitive. Pier 1 repurchased Sunbelt Nursery Group late in 1990 in an effort to diversify and reduce its total dependence on retail markets. By early 1991, its chain included more than 650 stores, but Johnson planned to open only a few new stores during 1991 and to close several as part of a company consolidation plan. Pier 1 trimmed its home office staff, reorganized management, and brought its advertising activities in-house to save money. Johnson explained that the company was shifting its focus from growth to more acute management of its existing operations.

Although it stumbled in the early 1990s, Pier 1 was the bright spot on its parent's list of company holdings. Intermark's other major holdings consisted of many different kinds of companies, including Dynamark (a manufacturer of mag wheels), Liquor Barns (liquor stores), and Western Sizzlin (restaurants). Intermark's stock price plunged during 1991 from $12 to $1.37 per share as the company posted a loss of $67 million (on the heels of a $10 million loss in 1990). To avert disaster, CEO Scott was forced to sell Pier 1, making Pier 1 a public company. Scott's responsibilities at Intermark were reduced as the company slid into debt-induced jeopardy. Intermark would declare bankruptcy in 1992, emerging in June 1993 as Triton Group Inc.

Economic sluggishness continued to hurt Pier 1 during 1992 and 1993. Although its growth in comparison to the late 1980s was meager, the company managed to sustain moderate revenue gains and to stabilize profits. Net income surged to about $25 million annually during 1992 and 1993 as sales climbed to $629 million. Unfortunately, Pier 1's long-term debt obligations also increased, from about $92 million in 1990 to $147 million by 1993. As part of a reorganization strategy, Pier 1 repositioned itself as "The Place to Discover" in 1992. It also decentralized operations to better serve its 600 stores. In an effort to generate capital, Pier 1 again sold its interests in Sunbelt Nursery.

Although Johnson's efforts at Pier 1 were generally lauded by industry observers, some critics characterized his management style as "glad handling," while citing his salary as inflated. Moreover, some criticized Pier 1's financial condition. Of concern to analysts was Pier 1's excessive debt, which had multiplied fivefold since Johnson's arrival. In addition, Pier 1's operating costs had increased, significantly reducing the company's overall profitability compared to leaner retailers competing in the same market. Other criticisms addressed Pier 1's selection of inventory and marketing strategy.

Buffeting criticism, however, was a history of strong growth and relatively steady earnings. In addition, Pier 1 had boosted its image through charitable donations, which included a $785,000 gift to UNICEF in 1992. Pier 1 had started donating to UNICEF after Johnson's arrival in 1982 and had supplied over $3.3 million to the organization between 1985 and 1992 from the sale of greeting cards in Pier 1 outlets. The extremely successful fundraiser was established by Marvin J. Girouard (pronounced "Gerard"), a Pier 1 veteran who was named president and chief operating officer of the company in 1988.

Mid-1990s and Beyond

Pier 1's sales surged to $685 million in 1994, an increase of about eight percent over the previous year, which helped allay doubts about the company's overall approach. Pier 1 opened 48 new stores and closed 17 during 1994, bringing the total size of its international chain to 636. Pier 1's reach extended into most of the United States, with an emphasis on Florida, California, New York, Texas, and Ohio. It operated 30 stores in Canada and was active in several joint ventures, particularly in Mexico and the United Kingdom.

Pier 1 continued to emphasize imports from low-cost producers in the mid-1990s. China, its largest supplier, contributed about one-third of its inventory in the early 1990s. Other major suppliers included India, Indonesia, Thailand, and the Philippines. Sales of furniture and kitchen goods each represented about one-quarter of the company's revenues in 1994. Textiles and jewelry each comprised about 13 percent of sales, and the remainder was attributable to miscellaneous gifts and accessories.

As revenues continued to increase in early 1995, Johnson reaffirmed his intent to pursue the ambitious growth plans he had proffered in 1989. He still wanted to build the Pier 1 chain to more than 1,000 stores by the turn of the century and to push sales past the $1 billion mark. Toward that end, Pier 1 was pursuing growth through a multifaceted strategy in the mid-1990s that highlighted international expansion. Johnson hoped to open 100 foreign stores by the end of the decade by buying into existing retail chains or setting up joint ventures. Pier 1 was already operating two Pier 1 "stores within a store" in Mexico through a joint venture with Sears de Mexico S.A. which was launched in 1993. In addition, the company entered into a partnership with a chain of ten retail import stores in the United Kingdom called "The Pier," a venture that began in 1993.

Pier 1 was also striving to boost sales through its credit card, which was reportedly used in about 14 percent of store purchases in 1994 (totaling $100 million), as well as through the creation of smaller, more conveniently located stores. To that end, Pier 1 was bucking the retail trend toward giant warehouse stores and was initiating a program of building multistore locations that provided a better shopping experience (better parking and customer service, and a more pleasant atmosphere). In addition, the company was experimenting with new advertising media, including television, in an effort to lure younger buyers. Pier 1 launched its first national television ads in July 1995.

Sales continued to increase in 1995 and 1996, reaching $810.7 million in the latter year. Aiding the increase was further tinkering with the product mix, most notably a cutting back on space devoted to the sluggish apparel category. By 1996 apparel accounted for only six percent of overall sales, and the following year the category was discontinued altogether. Management also continued to push the chain's remaining product offerings upmarket, as the household income of its average customer reached about $60,000 by 1996, compared to $26,600 a decade earlier. As an example of the upscaling of Pier 1, Johnson told *HFN* in 1996 that the chain's most expensive basket sold for $129, compared to $4.95 in 1985. The average customer ticket total in mid-1996 was $44, a huge increase over the 1980 figure of $5.25.

Unfortunately, the earnings picture was not nearly as bright as that of revenues. To wind down its investment in Sunbelt Nursery, Pier 1 was forced to take writeoffs totaling $37.3 million, including a $14 million charge during the 1996 fiscal year. That same year the company suffered a large trading loss. Capital Insight, a firm Pier 1 had hired to invest its excess cash and short-term funds, lost $19.3 million making risky futures investments that went sour. Following 1995 net income of just $22.1 million, the financial setbacks led to a decline to $10 million in net income the following year. The trading loss also led to the firing of Pier 1's longtime CFO, Robert G. Herndon, who was responsible for overseeing the investments. The company also pursued legal action to attempt to recover its loss, and subsequently received an $11 million settlement during the 1998 fiscal year.

International expansion continued in the late 1990s, although the company's Mexican operations suffered from the devaluation of the peso. During fiscal 1996 Pier 1 entered into an agreement with Sears Roebuck de Puerto Rico, Inc. to develop Pier 1 "stores within a store" in Sears outlets located in Puerto Rico, an arrangement similar to the one in Mexico. By early 1999 seven Sears Puerto Rico stores were offering Pier 1 merchandise. In 1997 Pier 1 entered into a joint venture with Akatsuki Printing Co., Ltd. and Skylark Group to open stores in Japan. By early 1999 there were 18 Pier 1 stores in that country. Also during this time, the company purchased an Omaha, Nebraska-based national bank, which was soon renamed Pier 1 National Bank and which held the credit card accounts for the company's proprietary card. The Pier 1 credit card was responsible for 28 percent of sales by the end of the decade.

Pier 1's earnings decline appeared to be only temporary, as the company rebounded by fiscal 1998 to post profits of $78 million on record sales of $1.08 billion. This also marked the first time sales had exceeded the $1 billion mark. In June 1998 Girouard was appointed CEO, taking over from the retiring Johnson. Girouard added the chairmanship as well in February of the following year. Although sales grew again in 1999, reaching $1.14 billion, this represented an increase of only 5.6 percent over the previous year, compared to the 13 to 17 percent increases of the previous three years.

With markets for new Pier 1 stores in the United States at a minimum, and with competition increasing from fast-growing discounters such as Cost Plus and such upscale housewares chains as Pottery Barn and Crate and Barrel, Pier 1 Imports appeared to be hitting a plateau, prompting Girouard to investigate alternative avenues of growth. He first considered opening a second chain which would offer discount merchandising, before deciding that the upscale markets had more potential. In mid-1999 the company entered negotiations to purchase the privately held Z Gallerie, a retail chain offering high-end home furnishings. The deal, however, fell apart in August, leading to the immediate departure of another CFO, Stephen F. Mangum, who had championed the acquisition. In the aftermath, the company's stock plunged 33 percent in one day. Girouard subsequently abandoned plans to open or acquire a second chain, deciding instead to concentrate on revitalizing the Pier 1 concept by cutting prices, opening stores in smaller markets, and experimenting with larger formats. A 1,000-item online catalog was also being developed.

Principal Subsidiaries

Pier 1 Assets, Inc.; Pier 1 Licensing, Inc.; Pier 1 Imports (U.S.), Inc.; Pier 1 Funding, Inc.; Pier Lease, Inc.; Pier-SNG, Inc.; PIR Trading, Inc.; Pier International Limited (Hong Kong); Pier Alliance Ltd. (Bermuda); The Pier Retail Group Limited (U.K.); The Pier (Retail) Limited (U.K.); Pier Direct Limited (U.K.); Pier-FTW, Inc.; Pacific Industrial Properties, Inc.; Pier Group, Inc.; Pier 1 Holdings, Inc.; Pier 1 Services Company; Pier 1 National Bank.

Principal Competitors

The Bombay Company, Inc.; Cost Plus, Inc.; Euromarket Designs Inc.; Garden Ridge Corporation; HomePlace of America Inc.; IKEA International A/S; Lechters, Inc.; Michaels Stores, Inc.; MJDesigns, Inc.; Spiegel, Inc.; Williams-Sonoma, Inc.

Further Reading

Byrnes, Nanette, and Stephanie Anderson Forest, "Goldinger: He's Not the Man with the Midas Touch," *Business Week,* January 15, 1996, p. 34.

"Capital Insight's Bad Bets Caused Losses of Over $36 Million for Pier 1, Others," *Wall Street Journal,* December 28, 1995, p. A3.

Chatham, Laura, "Pier 1 Inc. Well-Positioned to Appeal to Baby Boomers," *Dallas-Fort Worth Business Journal,* April 21, 1986, p. 2A.

Erlick, June Carolyn, "The Trade Winds Are Up at Pier 1: Or How a Chain Turned a Five-Buck Sale into $130," *HFN—The Weekly Newspaper for the Home Furnishing Network,* July 22, 1996, p. 1.

Feldman, Amy, "But Who Is Minding the Store?," *Forbes,* November 22, 1993, p. 47.

Forest, Stephanie Anderson, "At Pier 1, a Search for Lost Cachet," *Business Week,* November 1, 1999, pp. 109, 112–13.

——, "Pier 1's Ship Comes In: Even a $20 Million Trading Loss Won't Spoil a Boffo Year," *Business Week,* January 22, 1996, p. 45.

Helliker, Kevin, "Pressure at Pier 1: Beating Sales Numbers of Year Earlier Is a Storewide Obsession," *Wall Street Journal,* December 7, 1995, p. B1.

Henderson, Barry, "Pier 2?," *Barron's,* November 16, 1998, pp. 19–20.

Howell, Debbie, "Pier 1 Contemplates Upscale Expansion Through Acquisition," *Discount Store News,* May 24, 1999.

"Intermark's CEO Actually Thrives on Failure," *San Diego Business Journal,* January 19, 1987, p. 1.

Lee, Louise, "Pier 1 Fires Financial Chief Herndon over Loss Tied to Goldinger's Collapse," *Wall Street Journal,* February 12, 1996, p. B4.

——, "Pier 1 Restates Net, Reflecting Investment Loss," *Wall Street Journal,* January 17, 1996, p. B5.

——, "Pier 1 to Take Charge on Money-Manager Trades," *Wall Street Journal,* December 27, 1995.

Lockwood, Herbert, "Has Intermark Bottomed Out? Scott Says So," *San Diego Daily Transcript,* July 30, 1991, p. A1.

Pasztor, Andy, Louise Lee, and Fred Vogelstein, "Goldinger's Bet on Rates Led to Losses of Up to $100 Million, Associates Say," *Wall Street Journal,* January 2, 1996, p. 3.

The Pier 1 Imports Story, Fort Worth: Pier 1 Imports, Inc., 1992.

Sain, Ariane, "Pier 1's Ship Has Finally Come in As Baby Boomers Mature," *Adweek's Marketing Week,* January 9, 1989, p. 43.

Schnurman, Mitchell, "Chief Executive of Pier Next in Line for Departure," *Fort Worth Star-Telegram,* May 21, 1998, p. 1.

——, " 'Pier 1 Had Everything I Wanted': Loyalty, Persistence Paid Off for Firm's New Chief Executive," *Fort Worth Star-Telegram,* June 29, 1998, p. 1.

——, "Pier 1 Plans 2nd Chain with Upscale Goods," *Fort Worth Star-Telegram,* June 25, 1999, p. 1.

"A 60's Store Passes Pier Review; Pier 1 Imports Plays Catch Up with Its Customers," *Adweek's Marketing Week,* May 29, 1989, p. S8.

—Dave Mote
—updated by David E. Salamie

PILKINGTON

Pilkington plc

Prescot Road
St. Helens WA10 3TT
United Kingdom
Telephone: (01744) 28882
Fax: (01744) 692660
Web site: http://www.pilkington.com

Public Company
Incorporated: 1894 as Pilkington Brothers Ltd.
Employees: 31,000
Sales: £2.71 billion (US$3.98 billion) (1999)
Stock Exchanges: London Frankfurt
Ticker Symbol: PILK
NAIC: 327211 Flat Glass Manufacturing; 327212 Other
    Pressed and Blown Glass and Glassware
    Manufacturing

Pilkington plc is one of the largest glassmakers in the world, specializing in the flat glass and safety glass sectors. With about 85 percent of its sales originating outside the United Kingdom, the company operates 23 float glass plants in 11 countries—Finland, Italy, Germany, Poland, Sweden, the United Kingdom, the United States, Argentina, Brazil, Chile, and Australia—and has interests in ten more. Pilkington invented the float glass process, which is the standard method for producing high-quality flat glass. About half of Pilkington's sales come from glass products for buildings, with 45 percent from automotive glass products and the remainder from technical products, such as very thin float glass for the electronics industry and for solar energy panels. Pilkington's rise to international preeminence occurred during the mid-to-late 20th century.

19th-Century Roots: Becoming the U.K. Glass Leader

The St. Helens Crown Glass Company—to give Pilkington its original name—was formed in 1826 at St. Helens, then a small town at the heart of a coal-mining area of about 10,000 people. Cheap coal had already attracted a number of furnace industries, including glass. Of the six local men who became

partners in the new crown—or window—glass business, two already owned a glassworks in the district. One of the others, the son of a leading coal owner in the area, became the new company's bookkeeper and was joined by the local solicitor. The other two, originally brought in only for their capital, were William Pilkington, son of a local doctor who had done well in distilling, and his brother-in-law Peter Greenall, who was in charge of the local brewery. When the two technical men had to withdraw from the glassmaking venture because of an attempt to evade paying excise duty on their flint glass, William Pilkington—who had been apprenticed to a Liverpool distiller, ran the family distillery, and was already considered an astute business man—was called in to take charge. William's elder brother, Richard Pilkington, was brought in when it was discovered that the bookkeeping partner was not keeping the books properly. The local solicitor chose this critical moment to withdraw from the venture. Thus, almost by accident, the Pilkington brothers found themselves landed with a tiny, struggling glassworks, much less profitable than the family distillery.

Skilled glass blowers, drawn mainly from Dumbarton, Scotland, where a glass manufacturer had gone bankrupt, provided the necessary technical expertise, and Peter Greenall—a partner in Parr's Bank at Warrington—saw to it that the struggling young business (which was renamed Greenall & Pilkington in 1929) received an overdraft far larger than its size warranted. William Pilkington, as salesman, traveled through Great Britain and Ireland seeking orders while his brother stayed at home and looked after the works and office. Business grew with the increasing demand for glass for the many new houses being built. A second furnace was built in 1834 and a third in 1835. Peter Greenall, who became a member of Parliament in 1841, remained an important, but sleeping, partner in the business, until his death in 1845, when the firm became Pilkington Brothers (PB).

Once the company was in operation, progress was determined partly by a willingness to accept technical change and partly by the initiative and drive of the new generations. The founders each had six sons, and two from each side became partners.

The taxation system for glass manufacturers favored crown glass against its more efficiently produced rival, sheet glass.

PB's willingness to venture into sheet glass in the early 1840s stood it in good stead a few years later when the duties on glass were removed. Cheaper sheet glass from continental Europe, and especially from Belgium, drove out of business those U.K. manufacturers who had clung to crown glass. By the 1850s there were only three U.K. survivors: Chance Brothers of Smethwick near Birmingham; James Hartley & Son of Sunderland in the northeast, which had previously been the center of the industry in the United Kingdom; and PB, which thrived in this more competitive climate. Between 1849 and 1854 PB's labor force rose sharply from 450 to 1,350.

The second generation, whose influence began to make itself felt from the later 1860s as the founders retired, embarked upon a vigorous export drive. In the early 1870s, PB surpassed its two remaining U.K. rivals by replacing pot furnaces—which necessitated 24-hour intervals between week-long glassmaking campaigns while the pots were recharged and reheated—with Siemens's glassmaking tanks, which allowed continuous round-the-clock production and much more cost-effective eight-hour shifts. PB also chose the very profitable years of the early 1870s to build a new factory for the manufacture of polished plate glass, used in larger windows and mirrors. Intensive foreign competition soon drove the other longer-established U.K. plate glass manufacturers out of business, but PB survived, because it alone had another profitable product to sustain it. In 1903 it emerged as the sole U.K. producer of plate glass. By then Hartley & Son had gone out of business and Chance Brothers, which had failed in its attempt to enter plate glass manufacturing and had delayed in introducing tank furnaces for sheet, was very much a runner-up. PB had emerged as the undisputed leader in flat glass manufacture in the United Kingdom, though it was still subject to continued fierce competition from European producers. Between 1874 and 1894 the firm's capital had grown more than ninefold, from £150,000 to £1.4 million. In 1894, the business was then made a private limited company, Pilkington Brothers Ltd., with £800,000 in ordinary shares and £600,000 in five percent debentures. There were then ten family shareholders, three of the four senior partners having each brought in two of their sons.

Even during the hard years between 1874 and 1896, PB managed to flourish. Despite reinvestment of £1.25 million, £725,000 was distributed among the family. Between 1894 and 1914, the company did even better: nearly £3 million was reinvested and approximately £2.3 million distributed. The four Pilkingtons of the second generation reaped the financial rewards of their success on a scale far greater than did their fathers.

Early 20th Century: Saving Itself from Near Disaster

The third generation, which took over in the Edwardian period, did not match its predecessors' impressive performance.

This may have been due to unexpected family losses. One son was killed in the Boer War. Another died of tuberculosis, and his twin brother, Austin Pilkington, who was himself an able manager, fell ill with tuberculosis in 1907 and, in a last attempt to save his life, was sent from the smoke and chemical fumes of St. Helens to live in the dry, thin air of Colorado, where he recovered. Another son, who became company chairman in 1914, died in 1921 at the age of 50, and at about the same time another decided to retire, mainly on grounds of ill health, at the age of 42. In the 1920s the main responsibility for running the company and earning profits upon which the growing number of non-executive family members depended, fell to the fully recovered Austin Pilkington, together with his younger brother Cecil, a natural sciences graduate from Oxford who became the firm's technical director. They were joined by Edward Cozens-Hardy (Lord Cozens-Hardy after his elder brother's death in 1924), formerly a partner in the London electrical engineering consultancy of O'Gorman and Cozens-Hardy, whose sister, Hope, had married Austin Pilkington. Cozens-Hardy had moved north and taken Austin Pilkington's place at PB in 1908, but had stayed on after his brother-in-law's return.

Just before World War I, this weakened third generation made two decisions which were to lead to much subsequent trouble. Having moved into the continuous melting of sheet glass in the 1870s, it made the mistake of opting for drawn cylinder machinery. This machinery replaced glass blowers but not the flatteners who had to reheat the cylinders and slit them open in order to produce the panes of glass. The large cylinders blown by machine could only be made one at a time. Instead the company should have opted for either the Libbey-Owens-Ford (LOF) or the Fourcault process which drew the sheet of glass directly from the tank. Although these flat drawn processes were still being developed, preference for the compromise deprived PB of what was soon to prove the better alternative and nearly caused it to abandon sheet glass manufacture altogether during the 1920s. The decision also involved PB in a disastrous sheet glass venture in Canada in order to protect its drawn cylinder process rights. Secondly, having sensibly acquired, as a defense against European competitors, an interest in a small plate glassworks at Maubeuge in northern France in the 1890s, it unwisely decided to put down a second plate glassworks in the United Kingdom near the east coast, fearing that European competitors might establish their own factories on British soil if it did not do so. This factory, decided upon just before World War I, was built near Doncaster at great cost during the postwar boom. It swallowed up not only many of the vast reserves accumulated before and during that war but also £1 million of new capital, which had to be raised from the family in 1920.

PB saved itself by taking a world lead in plate glass manufacture at St. Helens. In the early 1920s, in collaboration with the Ford Motor Company of Detroit, it developed a new process which enabled a roughly cast ribbon to be cast continuously by pouring the molten glass out of the tank, instead of having to be ladled from pots to form a single plate of glass at a time, each side of which had to be ground and polished separately. Associated with the continuous flowing of the glass ribbon was a long series of grinding and polishing heads under which the ribbon was passed to produce the high-quality glass with more perfect parallel surfaces than had previously been possible. It was this extraordinarily costly process which float glass was to replace, but, being to a large degree continuous—a twin grinder was developed which ground both sides of the ribbon simultaneously, but not a twin polisher—it was less costly than the intermittent processes it replaced. Such high-quality polished plate glass, being thicker than the sheet glass then made, and more lustrous, commanded high prices which would not only cover the costs but also bring in good rates of profit. Sheet had saved plate at Pilkington in the later 19th century. Now the situation was reversed.

Having managed to save its sheet glass production during the 1920s, thanks to plate glass profits, PB then had a stroke of good fortune. The U.S. plate glass manufacturer Pittsburgh

Plate Glass Company (PPG) developed its own method of drawing sheet glass directly from a tank which was superior to that of LOF or Fourcault. PB secured a license for this process in 1929. PPG machines, installed at St. Helens in the early 1930s and subsequently improved there, enabled the company to regain some of its market. The flat glass industry fared better in the United Kingdom because it supplied two markets, the building and motor trades, which survived the depressed years of the 1930s better than most others. There was also money to be made out of raw glass, particularly plate glass, when it was processed into safety glass. PB acquired a majority share in a factory built just outside St. Helens by Triplex (Northern) Limited, which came into production in 1930. Soon afterward it also became involved in safety glass processing plants in Canada, South Africa, and Australia. In 1936, an agreement was reached with Chance Brothers whereby PB would buy its old rival over a number of years. By 1939 it had already acquired nearly half of Chance's shares. It completed the takeover in 1952.

Austin and Cecil Pilkington retired from day-to-day management of the company at a critical moment in 1931, when PB recorded its first loss. Control passed to an executive committee which Cozens-Hardy set up with himself as chairman. His right-hand man was Ronald Weeks, who had been recruited from Cambridge in 1912 and had played a notable part in the management of the plate glass factory, subsequently marrying into the Pilkington family. Ronald Weeks was to gain a national reputation during World War II as General Weeks, deputy chief of the Imperial General Staff and afterward as chairman of Vickers and director of other companies. He became Lord Weeks in 1956. It was under this regime during the early 1930s that the fourth generation of the family began to play a greater part. Geoffrey Langton Pilkington, who was much older than his cousins, had been a director since 1919 and served as company chairman from 1932 to 1949. The others, some of whom had entered the business from university in 1927, served a rigorous probation; one of them did not make the grade. Harry Pilkington and Douglas Phelps, the son of a Pilkington daughter, reached the executive committee in 1934; Roger Percival, the son of another Pilkington daughter, followed in 1936, and Peter Cozens-Hardy in 1937. By then Lawrence Pilkington—Harry Pilkington's brother—and Arthur Pilkington, after five years as a regular officer in the Coldstream Guards, had entered the company and joined the executive committee in the 1940s, followed by a much younger member, David Pilkington, born in 1925. This team was to succeed more spectacularly than any of its predecessors.

When PB closed its Maubeuge factory in 1935, as part of the general rationalization of the European plate glass industry which followed an agreement between the European and U.S. manufacturers reached the previous year, it ceased to manufacture any glass outside the United Kingdom. It was soon, however, the major participant in the establishment of a window glass factory built at Llavallol outside Buenos Aires, a joint European venture to safeguard the Europeans' Argentine market. This factory had hardly come into production when World War II broke out and the Pilkington management there had to struggle hard to maintain and extend it during the war years, when communication between Llavallol and St. Helens was difficult and technical assistance from the parent company was unobtainable.

Postwar Era: The Float Glass Process and Diversification

Lord Cozens-Hardy retired in 1939 and Sir Ronald Weeks did not return to the company after the war. With Douglas Phelps as chairman of the executive committee from 1947, succeeded by Arthur Pilkington in 1965, and Harry Pilkington, the future Lord Pilkington, as company chairman from 1949, the fourth Pilkington generation saw the company's assets grow from £12.5 million in 1949 to £206 million in 1973, when Lord Pilkington retired from the chairmanship. This growth was due to the outstanding success of the float glass process and also to diversification into what were, for PB, new branches of the glass industry.

In some respects, change was forced on the company rather than welcomed by it. Manufacture of sheet glass in South Africa in 1951, for instance, came about because the South African government, determined to develop a manufacturing industry in that country, proposed to allow a rival to build a sheet glass factory if PB did not do so. PB's interests would have been best served by exporting as much U.K. glass as possible and thus keeping its machines at home working at full capacity. For similar reasons, PB sheet glass manufacture had to be started in Canada in the same year and in India, with local as well as Pilkington capital, in 1954. In Australia, where Australian Window Glass (AWG) had a financial stake in Pilkington's safety glass processing plants, PB took a share in AWG when PB helped to modernize AWG's obsolete sheet glass factory in 1960. A few years later, PB and AWG took over an aspiring local manufacturer in New Zealand who had attempted to make sheet glass but soon had failed. PB's window glass operations in Argentina, started just before World War II, were developed and led in due course to the acquisition of a sheet glass works in Brazil. Although PB sacrificed sheet glass exports to these factories, it never lost those of plate glass: maintaining a plate glass factory in these countries would have been far too costly. Manufacture of higher quality glass overseas had to await the development of the less costly float glass process, which tipped the scales further in the direction of manufacture abroad rather than at home.

The float glass process was invented by Alastair Pilkington in 1952. In this process, molten glass was poured onto one end of a bath of molten tin at about 1,000 ° C and formed into a ribbon which floated, frictionless and in a controlled atmosphere, down the bath through a temperature gradient falling to about 600 ° C at the other end. At this temperature the ribbon, fire finished, was cool enough to be taken off on rollers without marking the surface. This revolutionary new method of glassmaking produced polished plate glass much more cheaply by removing the large fixed capital investment in grinding and polishing machinery and by cutting working costs. To obtain perfectly parallel, distortion-free surfaces, the polished plate glass process required 20 percent of the original rough-cast glass to be ground off by many grinding and polishing machines, with vast expenditure of electrical energy. Having experimented with the new process and developed a full-scale production plant during the 1950s, PB began to sell its own float glass before the decade was out and licensed the process to other glass manufacturers from 1962, with PPG being the first licensee. Plate glass could no longer compete at the quality end

of the market nor, from the early 1970s, when float technology had progressed further, could the cheaper sheet glass. Pilkington built more float lines at St. Helens, and manufacturers elsewhere in the world sought Pilkington licenses and expertise. Its growing industrial muscle and rising license income led to Pilkington building its own float plant in Sweden in the mid-1970s. Others came on stream in overseas markets which it already dominated: Australia in 1973, and a second in 1988; South Africa in 1977; and Argentina in 1989. Its factories in Brazil were operated jointly with Saint-Gobain and in China with the People's Republic. It also acquired a majority, in Flachglas AG, the leading German producer, in 1980, followed by the 1986 purchase of the glassmaking interests of Libbey-Owens-Ford (LOF), second in this field in the United States.

Alastair Pilkington, who invented the float glass process, was unrelated to the St. Helens glassmaking family and was a mechanical sciences graduate from Cambridge University. Although not a member of the Pilkington family, he came to St. Helens as a family trainee in 1947. By the time the float process was being developed, he was already on the board pleading its case. He became a Fellow of the Royal Society in 1969 and was knighted the following year. Between 1973 and 1980 he was chairman of the company.

PB was brought into glass fibers and optical glass as a result of its acquisition of Chance Brothers in the years after 1936. The latter had acquired the U.K. and British Empire rights to glass fiber manufacture from 1930 and had long specialized in optical glass. Glass Fibres Ltd. was formed jointly by PB and Chance Brothers in 1938. A glass fiber factory was built at St. Helens after the war, and others followed at home and abroad to make glass silk for weaving and fibers for insulation and reinforcement. In the late 1980s Pilkington Reinforcements Limited stood as the world's leading supplier of special reinforced belting for engines and machinery, that is, for power transmission.

Chance Brothers' interest in optical glass went back to the 19th century and its world-renowned lighthouse department. During World War II Chance Brothers and Pilkington operated a shadow plant—a duplicate located away from the original factory as a precaution against bombing—at St. Helens and continued to undertake defense contracts afterwards. Beginning in 1957, on the initiative of Lawrence Pilkington, optical and ophthalmic glass began production at a specially built works at St. Asaph in north Wales, which soon became the largest producer of unpolished spectacle discs in Europe. In 1966 PB and Perkin-Elmer, a subsidiary of the U.S. multinational Perkin-Elmer Corporation, joined forces at St. Asaph to make optical and electro-optical systems. The joint venture became Pilkington P.E. in 1973, when Pilkington acquired the U.S. company's stake in the business. This side of the business was strengthened greatly by later acquisitions, notably the purchase of Barr and Stroud, the Scottish optical and precision engineers, in 1977; Sola Holdings of Australia in 1979; Syntax Ophthalmic Inc. in 1985; and Revlon's Barnes-Hind and Coburn Vision Care companies in 1987. At the end of the 1980s, the business was divided into Pilkington Visioncare, its ophthalmic side, which was growing throughout the world, including China and Japan, and Pilkington Optronics, the electro-optical side, which supplied the U.K. defense industry, primarily through Barr & Stroud and Pilkington P.E.

The fourth Pilkington generation oversaw this vast expansion overseas and diversification at home as well as the development of float glass and many other activities. They were served loyally by senior managers who acted like proconsuls on their behalf abroad and by others at home who accepted greater responsibility as the business grew and its committee system was expanded. From the mid-1960s, when Arthur Pilkington became chairman of the executive committee, much of the company's business devolved to the five divisional boards. One or two outstanding managers had joined the executive committee from the 1930s. Now a few more followed Alastair Pilkington to the top. Harry Pilkington, the company's chairman, was a businessman with a remarkable head for figures, a clear, analytical brain, limitless energy, and a great devotion to work. In addition to his demanding corporate responsibilities, he managed to fit in the presidency of the Federation of British Industries in London and the chairmanship of a royal commission.

The Pilkington family influence persisted for some years after the company went public in 1970. Lord Pilkington, created honorary life president when he retired in 1973, used to come into the office regularly until shortly before his death in 1983, and the fourth generation was represented on the board until 1985 when the youngest, David Pilkington, retired. In 1985 Pilkington Brothers Ltd., became Pilkington Brothers plc, and in 1987 the company dropped ''Brothers'' entirely from its official name. Pilkington became a holding company for a number of major subsidiaries, of which there were 45 in 1990. Economy and efficiency became the watchwords, especially in the difficult years of the early 1980s, when nearly £100 million was spent in redundancy payments in the U.K. alone. While this changed the atmosphere at St. Helens, it revived the company's fortunes and enabled it to ward off a takeover bid from the London-based conglomerate BTR in 1986. As the company entered the 1990s, only one Pilkington remained on the board—the chairman, Sir Antony Pilkington, son of Arthur Pilkington, knighted for his service to U.K. business in 1990.

1990s: Refocusing on Glass and Restructuring

Pilkington entered a traumatic period in the early 1990s. Competition in the glass sector had intensified in the 1980s following the entrance of U.S. and Japanese glassmakers into the European market and the expansionary moves of French archrival Compagnie de Saint-Gobain. Pilkington was also buffeted by the effects of the deep recession that began in the late 1980s and continued into the early 1990s, with two of the company's main markets—the automotive and building sectors—being particularly hard hit. Compounding the situation was Pilkington's ill-timed, if not ill-conceived, diversification into eyecare products. In hindsight, the purchase of Barnes-Hind was particularly troublesome. Barnes-Hind specialized in hard contact lenses and solutions, a part of the eyecare market that—soon after Pilkington bought into it—was eclipsed by the rapid growth of soft and disposable lenses. The combination of all of these negatives led revenues to decline from £3 billion in 1989 to £2.6 billion in 1993, and pretax profits to slump from £300 million to £41 million over the same period. The bottom line for 1993 was an actual loss.

According to Andrew Lorenz, writing in *Management Today,* Pilkington's difficulties in this period also stemmed from its corporate culture, which had not yet fully transitioned from that of

a family firm to that of a public company. It was more than symbolic, then, that in 1992 Roger Leverton become the first outsider named Pilkington chief executive. Antony Pilkington remained chairman but retired in 1995 and was succeeded by Nigel Rudd, the first non-Pilkington chairman; Rudd took the position as a nonexecutive chairman, leaving Leverton the distinct head of operations. During this leadership transition, Pilkington made the clear decision to refocus on its core flat and safety glass operations, to bolster these operations through new investment and acquisitions, and to begin disposing of noncore activities. Among the first operations jettisoned were the cement and rubber reinforcement businesses, insulation contracting, and the company's holdings in South Africa. A 50 percent interest in Pilkington Optronics was also quickly sold off, but the troubled eyecare business—Pilkington Visioncare—proved harder to divest. In 1993 Coburn Optical was divested, then Sola was sold that same year for £200 million. Two more Visioncare businesses were sold in 1995—the lens care operations of Pilkington Barnes Hind and Paragon Optical—and the exit from opthalmics was completed the following year with the sale of the Pilkington Barnes Hind contact lens business to Wesley Jessen Corporation.

On the acquisitions front, Pilkington moved into the eastern European market for the first time in 1992 with the purchase of a 45 percent stake in International Glass Poland, a processor and distributor of glass building products, as well as the establishment of a joint venture, 40 percent owned by Pilkington, for the purpose of constructing that country's first float glass plant. Back home, the company moved toward vertically integrating its U.K. operations through the 1993 acquisition of the glass processing and distribution business of Heywood Williams for £95 million. Also in 1993 Pilkington formed a joint venture with an Italian firm, Techint Finanziaria, to acquire Societa Italiana Vetro SpA (SIV), the state-owned glassmaker which the Italian government had decided to privatize. Pilkington paid about £43 million for its share. Two years later the company bought out its partner for £128 million to take full control of SIV, which was a market leader in vehicle glass for such manufacturers as Fiat S.p.A., Volkswagen AG, Renault S.A., and PSA Citroen S.A. Through its acquisition of SIV, Pilkington increased its share of the European automotive glass market from 16 percent to 34 percent. Growth in 1994 came through expansion in the emerging markets of China, Brazil, and Chile, and by the purchase of full control of the company's Finnish float glass subsidiary, Lahden Lasitehdas OY. In 1995 Pilkington acquired the Interpane Group's glass processing and distribution businesses in Switzerland, Denmark, and Norway for £58 million.

By early 1996 Leverton's efficiency drive led to annual cost savings of £230 million. The workforce was reduced by 15 percent, to 36,000, and productivity was increased by 32 percent. Also, Pilkington's management structure in Europe was overhauled, beginning in 1995. Previously the European operations were organized geographically on a country-by-country basis. Leverton reorganized Pilkington Europe into three business lines: automotive products, building products, and technical glass products, which included specialized mirrors, solar energy panels, and glass for the electronics industry. Leverton then followed up with a series of major restructuring programs to further improve efficiencies in various operations.

But in May 1997, in the wake of dismal results for the 1997 fiscal year, the board of directors concluded that the pace of the restructuring was proceeding too slowly and ousted Leverton. Paolo Scaroni was promoted to chief executive from his position as head of the company's worldwide automotive products operations. Scaroni had previously led a rapid restructuring of SIV, and had once served as global head of the glassmaking operations of Saint-Gobain.

Aiming to make Pilkington the world's most efficient glassmaker, Scaroni immediately quickened the restructuring pace, launching a two-year overhaul that cut a further 7,500 jobs from the workforce and shuttered 70 distribution and fabrication operations in Europe. The restructuring led Pilkington to take £225 million (US$376 million) in writeoffs for the 1998 fiscal year, leading to a net loss of £186 million (US$303 million) for the year. In late 1998 Pilkington announced another 1,500 job cuts spread across its worldwide operations, then in mid-1999 announced plans for an additional 2,500 job cuts, this time with an emphasis on Germany and North America. By this time Pilkington had improved its competitiveness in Europe, and now began turning its attention to improving the profitability of its U.S. operations. At the same time Scaroni began seeking opportunities for growth through acquisition and the establishment of joint ventures, following the company's return to profitability in the 1999 fiscal year. In early 2000, then, Pilkington doubled its holding in a Chinese affiliate, Shanghai Yaohua Pilkington, to 16.7 percent; increased its stake in Pilkington Sandoglass Sp.z o.o., a Polish float glass subsidiary, to 75 percent; and formed a joint venture with German glass processor Interpane International Glas to build the world's first integrated float glass manufacturing, laminating, and coating plant.

Principal Subsidiaries

EUROPE: Pilkington United Kingdom Limited; Pilkington Automotive UK Limited (80%); Flachglas AG (Germany; 95%); Flachglas Automotive GmbH (Germany; 95%); Flabeg GmbH (Germany; 95%); Pilkington EOMAG AG (Austria); Pilkington Norge AS (Norway); Interpane Glas AG (Switzerland); Pilkington Floatglas AB (Sweden); Pilkington Bilglas AB (Sweden); Pilkington Lamino OY (Finland); Pilkington Lahden Lasitehdas OY (Finland); Pilkington France SA; Pilkington Danmark A/S (Denmark); Pilkington Aerospace Limited; Pilkington IGP SA (Poland); Pilkington Sandoglass Sp.z o.o. (Poland; 75%); SIV SpA (Italy); Pilkington Micronics Limited; Pilkington Special Glass Limited. NORTH AMERICA: Libbey-Owens-Ford Co. (U.S.A.; 80%); Libbey-Nippon Holdings Inc. (U.S.A.; 40%); L-N Safety Glass, SA de CV (Mexico; 40%); Pilkington Aerospace Inc. (U.S.A.). REST OF THE WORLD: Pilkington (Australia) Limited; Vidrieria Argentina SA (51%); Vidrios Lirquen SA (Chile; 26%); Santa Lucia Cristal S.A.C.I.F. (Argentina); Pilkington Vidros Limitada (Brazil); Blindex Vidros De Seguranca Limitada (Brazil); Pilkington (New Zealand) Limited; Guilin Pilkington Safety Glass Co Limited (China; 60%); Changchun Pilkington Safety Glass Co Limited (China; 51%). HOLDING AND FINANCE COMPANIES: Pilkington Holdings Inc. (U.S.A.); Pilkington Nederland Holdings BV (Netherlands); Pilkington International Holdings BV (Netherlands); Pilkington Nederland (No 2) BV (Netherlands); Pilkington Australasia Limited (Australia); Pilkington Finance Limited; Pilkington (Forex) Limited; Pilkington Channel Islands Limited (Jersey; 66%); Pilkington Deutschland GmbH (Germany); Dahlbusch AG (Germany; 99%).

Principal Competitors

Apogee Enterprises, Inc.; Asahi Glass Company, Limited; Compagnie de Saint-Gobain; Corning Incorporated; Donnelly Corporation; Glaverbel Group; Guardian Industries Corp.; Nippon Sheet Glass Company, Limited; Oberland Glas AG; PPG Industries, Inc.; Safelite Glass Corp.; Schott Glas; Vitro, S.A. de C.V.

Further Reading

Arbose, Jules, et al., "Why Once-Dingy Pilkington Has That Certain Sparkle," *International Management,* August 1986, pp. 44 + .

Barker, T.C., *An Age of Glass: The Illustrated History,* London: Boxtree, 1994, 144 p.

——, *The Glassmakers,* London: Weidenfeld & Nicolson, 1977, 557 p.

——, *Pilkington Brothers and the Glass Industry,* London: Allen & Unwin, 1960, 296 p.

Caulkin, Simon, "Pilkington After BTR," *Management Today,* June 1987, pp. 42 + .

Dawkins, William, and Charles Leadbeater, "People in Glass Houses Start to Throw Stones," *Financial Times,* May 8, 1990, p. 21.

Graham, George, and Andrew Taylor, "Pilkington Drops Licensing Policy: Glassmaker Bows to Pressure As US Steps Up Anti-Trust Battle," *Financial Times,* May 27, 1994, p. 18.

Gresser, Charis, "Make or Break Time for Pilkington," *Financial Times,* October 30, 1997, p. 18.

——, "A Real Test of Endurance: Is Pilkington Fit Enough to Stay the Course," *Financial Times,* November 1, 1997, p. 5.

Gresser, Charis, and Sheila Jones, "Pilkington to Shed 6,000 Jobs in Restructuring," *Financial Times,* October 30, 1997, p. 17.

Guthrie, Jonathan, "Pilkington Sheds Flab but Makeover Is Incomplete," *Financial Times,* October 30, 1998, p. 22.

——, "Pilkington's Purge Fails to Cut Much Ice," *Financial Times,* June 5, 1998, p. 26.

Leadbeater, Charles, and Ian Hamilton Fazey, "Pilkington Integrates European Operations," *Financial Times,* October 9, 1991, p. 17.

Lorenz, Andrew, "Pilkington Picks Up the Pieces," *Management Today,* March 1996, pp. 37–40.

Lorenz, Christopher, "Transparent Move to European Unity," *Financial Times,* July 24, 1992, p. 15.

Morais, Richard C., "Glassmaker to the World," *Forbes,* January 22, 1996, p. 48.

Novak, Viveca, "U.S. Wins Accord with British Firm on Glass Factories," *Wall Street Journal,* May 27, 1994, p. A12.

"Pilkington: Facing Up to a Cruel World," *Economist,* October 12, 1991, p. 78.

Pretzlik, Charles, "Pilkington to Cut More Jobs," *Financial Times,* June 4, 1999, p. 23.

Salmans, Sandra, "Pilkington's Progressive Shift," *Management Today,* September 1980, p. 66.

Tieman, Ross, "Cracking Start by Scaroni," *Financial Times,* May 23, 1997, p. 25.

——, "Singing Sweet Music to Analysts and Shareholders," *Financial Times,* June 6, 1997, p. 29.

Urry, Maggie, "Pilkington Hopes for a Clear Recovery," *Financial Times,* June 18, 1993, p. 17.

——, "Pilkington Hopes to Put a Shine on Its Prospects," *Financial Times,* December 10, 1992, p. 21.

Wagstyl, Stefan, "Pilkington Cuts 1,900 Jobs in Restructuring," *Financial Times,* March 28, 1996, p. 21.

Wighton, David, "Recovery Reflects Cost Cutting at Pilkington," *Financial Times,* November 23, 1994, p. 32.

Wilsher, Peter, "A Right Moving Story," *Management Today,* December 1991, p. 27.

—T. C. Barker
—updated by David E. Salamie

P I X A R

Pixar Animation Studios

1001 W. Cutting Blvd.
Richmond, California 94804
U.S.A.
Telephone: (510) 236-4000
Fax: (510) 236-0388
Web site: http://www.pixar.com

Public Company
Incorporated: 1986
Employees: 430
Sales: $121 million (1999)
Stock Exchanges: NASDAQ
Ticker Symbol: PIXR
NAIC: 512110 Motion Picture Production

Pixar Animation Studios burst onto the big screen with the release of *Toy Story*, the first ever feature-length animated film created solely through computerized graphics. Yet Pixar's background is one of considerable pedigree, from roots at the University of Utah and the New York Institute of Technology before becoming part of George Lucas's Lucasfilm Ltd. of San Rafael, California. Purchased in 1986 by computer wunderkind Steven P. Jobs, cofounder of Apple Computer and NeXT Inc., the newly independent company was named after its primary product, the Pixar computer. After several one-of-a-kind, award-winning computer graphics and animation software packages (including the patented RenderMan, Ringmaster, Marionette, and CAPS), Pixar's creative geniuses produced some memorable television commercials before joining forces with Walt Disney to design and produce feature-length animated films. These works, *Toy Story* and its successor, *Toy Story 2*, as well as *A Bug's Life*, were huge hits for both Disney and Pixar, beloved by audiences and critics alike. Pixar's talent lineup has been the recipient of nine Academy Awards to date.

Origin of the Species: 1970s–80s

Pixar's tenuous evolution began in the 1970s when millionaire Alexander Schare, then president of the New York Institute of Technology (NYIT), was looking for someone to create an animated film from a sound recording of *Tubby the Tuba*. Enter a computer scientist named Ed Catmull with a Ph.D. from the University of Utah, who along with several others set up house (at Schare's expense) at NYIT's Long Island campus to work with computer graphics. Though *Tubby the Tuba* was never made, the team successfully produced video artwork. When creative mogul George Lucas proposed moving the team to the West Coast in 1979 as part of Lucasfilm Ltd., the breeding ground of the original *Star Wars* trilogy, Catmull and his colleagues agreed.

Over the next few years, Catmull and his ensemble created innovative graphics programs and equipment for Lucas, including an imaging computer called the "Pixar." The Pixar was then used to develop high-tech graphics and animation sequences for Lucasfilm projects. Unlike other computers, Pixar's software constructed high-resolution, three-dimensional color images of virtually anything, from buildings and cars to tornadoes and aliens. Remarkably, Pixar was also capable of helping medical professionals at Johns Hopkins diagnose diseases from 3D renderings of CAT-scans and x-rays; giving weather technicians new images from satellites; and even helping prospectors locate oil from enhanced seismic readings—all at a speed some 200 times faster than previous computer programs.

In 1984, John Lasseter, who had met Catmull at a computer graphics conference and was employed by Walt Disney Studios, visited Lucasfilm for a month-long stint. Lasseter, who had graduated from the California Institute of the Arts where he had won two Student Academy Awards for animated film, decided to stay. Meanwhile, after spinning off a joint venture called Droid Works, George Lucas started shopping around Pixar with hopes of a second spinoff. Pixar caught the interest of several companies, including EDS, then a division of General Motors, Philips N.V., and computer whiz-kid Steve Jobs, cofounder and chairman of Apple Computer Inc. Unable to convince Apple's board of directors to invest in or purchase the fledgling graphics company, Jobs reluctantly abandoned his hopes for Pixar.

Yet circumstances changed drastically for Jobs in 1985. Stripped of his responsibilities and deposed from his Apple kingdom (at about the same time the first Pixar computer went on the market for $105,000), Jobs sold the majority of his Apple stock and started over. Plunging $12 million into a new computer enterprise named NeXT Inc., specializing in personal computers for colleges and universities, Jobs approached Lucas in 1986 and paid $10 million for the San Raphael-based Pixar and created an independent company. Though Catmull, Lasseter, and crew regarded Jobs as kin in their quest for high-tech fun and games given his laidback reputation and status as a computer wonder boy—the new boss instructed them to put aside their dreams of animation and film and to instead concentrate on technical graphics they could sell.

Highs and Lows: Late 1980s to 1991

"If I knew in 1986 how much it was going to cost to keep Pixar going, I doubt if I would've bought the company," Jobs later told *Fortune* magazine. "The problem was, for many years the cost of the computers required to make animation we could sell was tremendously high." Luckily, Pixar's crew came up with several software innovations, which they used to create a myriad of products. In 1986 came the first of many Oscar nominations from the Academy of Motion Picture Arts and Sciences for a short animated film called *Luxo Jr.* Next came *Red's Dream* in 1987, then the development of RenderMan, for which the company applied for and received a patent. A revolutionary graphics program that allowed computer artists to add color and create texture to onscreen 3D objects, RenderMan produced stunningly realistic photo images almost indistinguishable from actual photographs. RenderMan's brand of images paid off when *Tin Toy,* written and directed by Lasseter as the first computer-generated animation, won an Academy Award as Best Animated Short Film in 1988.

As CEO of Pixar, Jobs expanded the company's leading edge graphics and animation capabilities by joining forces in July 1989 with the San Francisco-based Colossal Pictures, a live action, animation, and special effects studio, for collaboration purposes and to broker Pixar for television commercials and promotional films. With Colossal's background and experience in broadcast media and Pixar's unique computer capabilities, the partnership was poised for tremendous success. By 1990 when more than a dozen RenderMan products were introduced, RenderMan licensing fees finally began to pay off. Not only were many hardware and software packagers incorporating the graphics program into their products, but RenderMan was endorsed by such industry heavyweights as Digital Equipment, IBM, Intel Corporation, and Sun Microsystems. In addition, Pixar created two commercials in its association with Colossal. The second commercial, for Life Savers "Holes" bite-size

candies (which took 12 weeks to produce using RenderMan's software), aired in March and was a hit with audiences.

In April 1990 Pixar signed a letter of intent to sell its valuable yet stagnating hardware operations, including all proprietary hardware technology and imaging software, to Vicom Systems of Freemont, California. The move, which included the transfer of 18 of Pixar's 100 employees, was finalized several weeks later and allowed Pixar to devote the company's full energy to further development of its rendering capabilities. Before the end of the year, Pixar moved from San Rafael to new $15 million digs in the Point Richmond Tech Center of Richmond, California, and reached revenues of just under $3.4 million, though still not reporting a profit.

While Jobs's other company, NeXT Inc., seemed to prosper and was expected to reach $100 million in computer sales, Pixar still struggled to make ends meet in 1991. In February, 30 employees were laid off, including President Charles Kolstad. Jobs, sometimes criticized as a mercurial spinmeister with too little substance to back up his visions and words, was brought to task in the media for the shortcomings of both companies. Yet salvation came to Pixar in the name of *Toy Story,* the first full-length computer-animated feature film, as a collaboration between Pixar and Lasseter's old stomping grounds, Walt Disney Studios. Signing a contract to produce quality "digital entertainment," Pixar was responsible for the content and animation of three full-length films; Disney provided the funding for production and promotional costs, owning the marketing and licensing fees of the films and their characters. Though Disney retained the lion's share of revenue and profit, Pixar negotiated for a slice of the gross revenues from the box office and subsequent video sales. At this juncture, neither Disney nor Pixar knew the potential of their alliance—one that proved successful beyond their wildest expectations.

The Right Mix of Magic and Mastery: 1992–95

In 1992, the joint project between Pixar and Disney, called CAPS (computer animated production system) was another stellar development, winning Pixar's second Academy Award (shared with Disney). The following year, Jobs's NeXT Inc., like Pixar before it, was forced to lay off workers and sell its hardware division to concentrate on software development and applications. Yet 1993 was a banner year for Pixar, with RenderMan winning the company's third Academy Award and a Gold Clio (for advertising excellence) for the funky animated Listerine "Arrows" commercial. The next year, Pixar won its second Gold Clio for the Lifesavers "Conga" commercial, a colorful romp with a contagious beat. Despite such heavy accolades from critics and peers, Pixar still had not managed a profit since its spinoff in 1986, and reported a loss of $2.4 million on revenue of $5.6 million for 1994.

The following year, in 1995, Pixar was wrapping up its work on *Toy Story* and everyone was anxious for the finished result to hit theaters in November. Tom Hanks, Tim Allen, Don Rickles, and Annie Potts had signed on to voice major characters, and Randy Newman was composing the film's musical score. By the end of the third quarter with more than 100,000 copies of RenderMan sold and a huge licensing deal with Bill Gates and

---

Key Dates:

1979: George Lucas brings Ed Catmull and associates from the New York Institute of Technology to the West Coast as part of Lucasfilm Ltd.

1984: John Lasseter leaves Disney for Lucasfilm.

1986: Lucas spins off Pixar computer graphics unit, which is bought and incorporated by Steve Jobs; first Academy Award nomination for *Luxo Jr.*

1988: Company receives first Academy Award for *Tin Toy.*

1992: CAPS (Computer Animated Production System) wins joint Academy Award for Pixar and Disney.

1993: Pixar earns third Academy Award, for RenderMan.

1995: *Toy Story* debuts and conquers box office; fourth Academy Award, for digital scanning technology, is received.

1997: *A Bug's Life* opens at the box office; company garners two more Academy Awards for Marionette 3D Animation Systems and animated short film *Geri's Game.*

1999: *Toy Story 2* debuts and breaks box office records; Pixar claims a ninth Academy Award for Technical Achievement.

2000: Company moves to new headquarters in Emeryville, California.

Microsoft, Pixar announced its first-ever profit of $3.1 million on revenues of $10.6 million.

For Pixar, 1995 was a string of accelerating successes: first came *Toy Story's* pre-Thanksgiving release, grossing over $40 million its first weekend, with rave reviews from critics and families alike. Leading box office receipts, both Disney and Pixar hoped *Toy Story* could best *Pochahontas's* $140 million take earlier in the year. Next came Pixar's IPO of 6.9 million shares in November on the NASDAQ; the market closed at $22 per share, up from its initial offering of $12 to $14 each, giving Pixar a market value of some $800 million. Jobs, who since his purchase of Pixar for $10 million had sunk an additional $50 million into the enterprise, recouped a handsome paper profit of more than $600 million for his 80 percent stake (the shares eventually hit a high of $45.50 on November 30th).

Another boon came when *Toy Story* garnered several award nominations, including Randy Newman's score for two Golden Globes and an Oscar; an Oscar for Catmull and Thomas Porter, director of effects animation or digital scanning technology; and an additional Special Achievement Oscar for Lasseter's writing, direction, and technical wizardry for *Toy Story.*

Multiple Lightning Strikes: 1996–99

After the release of *Toy Story* while part of Pixar's crew worked on a CD-ROM game of the animated film, others were busy working on several Coca-Cola commercials for the Creative Arts Agency, hired by Michael Ovitz. Pixar was also immersed in its next Disney film, *A Bug's Life*, which was scheduled for release in two years. By February 1996, *Toy Story* had grossed over $177 million at the box office and in March

Lasseter attended the Academy Awards to receive his Oscar. He brought along Woody and Buzz Lightyear, who were part of several sketches and fodder for running gags during the live telecast. Pixar completed the year with a huge leap in revenues, up to $38.2 million (from 1995's $12.1 million), extraordinary net income of $25.3 million, and stock prices hitting a high of $49 per share in the fourth quarter.

Though it had been said by Bob Bennett of Autodesk, Inc., a client and competitor of Pixar, that "Pixar is the best in the world at what it does," continued advances in computer and graphics technology brought considerable competition. Everyone it seemed—from Digital Domain and Industrial Light & Magic to Microsoft and Silicon Graphics—was trying their hand at graphics software development. After the stellar success of *Toy Story*, all the major motion picture studios were creating computerized animation, including DreamWorks SKG, Turner Broadcasting, Warner Bros., and even Disney.

Other developments surrounded Jobs, as Apple stumbled horribly and the company came close to financial ruin. Still attached to the company he had cofounded and brought to enormous success, Jobs came to its rescue in 1997 shortly after Apple bought his NeXT Inc. Few doubted Jobs's ability to juggle both Pixar and Apple, and they were right. Not only did Jobs bring Apple back to the forefront of the computer industry with the flashy iMac, but Pixar went on to rule the box office with *A Bug's Life*. During the magic "holiday" window of October, November, and December 1997, *A Bug's Life* was up against four animated films, including another insect-related story by Dreamworks SKG, entitled *Antz.* Dreamworks had also released *The Prince of Egypt* and Nickelodeon brought *The Rugrats Movie* to the big screen as well. Yet Pixar beat the pack and went on to ring up over $360 million in worldwide box office receipts, even topping *Toy Story.*

Once again Pixar was nominated for and won big at the Academy Awards: two separate awards for Scientific and Technical Achievement (for the Marionette 3D Animation System, and for digital painting), as well as another for Best Animated Short Film (*Geri's Game*). Pixar also finally received a sizeable financial boost in 1997, as revenues and net income reached $34.7 million and $22.1 million, respectively. The box office and critical triumphs of both *Toy Story* and *A Bug's Life* also brought a new deal with Disney to produce an additional five pictures within the next ten years, with both companies as equal partners. The agreement eclipsed the previous deal; the former's remaining two films became the first two of the new five-picture negotiation. Lastly, Pixar would sell Disney up to five percent of its common stock at $15 per share.

In early 1998 *A Bug's Life* was released on video and DVD simultaneously and Pixar's top guns worked feverishly on the sequel to *Toy Story,* slated for release in November. The sequel was a gamble, since only one animated feature film had ever spawned a theater-released follow-up, Disney's *The Rescuers Down Under.* Most sequels or prequels were released directly to video; Pixar was ready to buck the trend. Dollars from its venture with Disney continued to slowly trickle in and Pixar finished the year with $14.3 million in revenue and net earnings of $7.8 million.

The last year of the century brought more kudos for Pixar: David DiFrancesco won the company's ninth Academy Award (for Technical Achievement), *Toy Story 2* opened in November to sweeping box office dominance (even higher receipts than *Star Wars: The Phantom Menace*'s first few weeks of release the year before), and the company celebrated its fifth consecutive profitable year, with revenues of $121 million and earnings topping $50 million.

The New Century: 2000 and Beyond

Pixar was as busy as ever in the 21st century: the company was preparing to move into its new 225,000-square-foot headquarters in Emeryville, California, due for completion in mid-2000 and were hard at work on its next full-length animated film in collaboration with Disney. The new feature was scheduled for release in 2001, under the working title of ''Monsters, Inc.'' The company's fifth film was tentatively slated for release in 2002, was a top-secret project to be directed by Andrew Stanton, who had worked on both *Toy Story* and *A Bug's Life*. Despite a slow, financially difficult beginning, Pixar Animation Studios had landed on the fast track and was known throughout the world. With its technological breakthroughs and brilliantly crafted animated films, the sky was the limit in the coming decade and beyond. As stated in its 1996 annual report, Pixar succeeded because it was well aware of the pitfalls of filmmaking: ''Though Pixar is the pioneer of computer animation, the essence of our business is to create compelling stories and memorable characters. It is chiseled in stone at our studios that no amount of technology can turn a bad story into a good one.''

Principal Competitors

DreamWorks SKG; Fox Entertainment; Lucasfilm, Ltd.; Warner Bros.

Further Reading

Baker, Molly, and Thomas R. King, ''Pixar Share Offering, Hyped by *Toy Story*, Is Looking Good,'' *Wall Street Journal,* November 29, 1995, pp. C1,C2.

Bernard, Diane, ''Pixar to Bring 3-D Rendering to the Macintosh,'' *PC Week,* February 12, 1990, pp. 33–34.

Brown, Ivy, ''The Man Behind the (Computer) Mouse,'' *Los Angeles Times,* November 13, 1996, p. F1.

Carlsen, Clifford, ''Pixar Corp. to Sell Hardware Division to Vicom Systems,'' *San Francisco Business Times,* April 30, 1990, pp. 1,13.

Cortino, Judy, ''Pixar Expects Profits to Rise with Success of Graphics Program,'' *PC Week,* January 8, 1990, p. 120.

Deutschman, Alan, ''Into Every Life a Little Rain,'' *Fortune,* May 6, 1991, p. 111.

Gelman, Eric, et al., ''Showdown in Silicon Valley,'' *Newsweek,* September 30, 1985, pp. 46–50.

Giles, Jeff, and Corie Brown, ''This Bug's for You,'' *Newsweek,* November 16, 1998, pp. 79–80.

Goldrich, Robert, ''Colossal, Pixar Ink Production/Sales Agreement,'' *Backstage,* July 14, 1989, pp. 1, 25.

——, ''Pixar Produces Its First Commercial, for Life Savers Holes and FCB/Leber Katz,'' *Backstage,* March 23, 1990, pp. 6, 34.

''The Great Leap of Computer Graphics,'' *Fortune,* April 27, 1987, p. 7.

Krantz, Michael, ''Animators, Sharpen Your Pixels,'' *Time,* November 30, 1998, pp. 109–10.

Lohr, Steve, ''Woody and Buzz, the Untold Story,'' *New York Times,* February 24, 1997.

Markoff, John, ''Apple Computer Co-Founder Strikes Gold with New Stock,'' *New York Times,* November 30, 1995, pp. A1, D7.

Patterson, William Pat, ''Out to Pasture at 30,'' *Industry Week,* June 24, 1985, p. 22.

Reeves, Scott, ''Pixar's Initial Offering Gives Investors a Chance to Bet on Animated Films,'' *Wall Street Journal,* November 3, 1995, p. A9E.

Schlender, Brent, ''Steve Jobs' Amazing Movie Adventure,'' *Fortune,* September 18, 1995, pp. 154–72.

Schlender, Brent, and Steve Jobs, ''The Three Faces of Steve Jobs,'' *Fortune,* November 9, 1998, p. 96.

Siwolop, Sana, ''Picture Perfect,'' *FW,* February 6, 1990, pp. 76–77.

Tracy, Eleanor John, ''Droids for Sale,'' *Fortune,* August 5, 1985, pp. 63–64.

''Two Cheers for Apple,'' *Fortune,* February 17, 1986, p. 9.

—Nelson Rhodes

Polk Audio, Inc.

5601 Metro Drive
Baltimore, Maryland 21215
U.S.A.
Telephone: (410) 358-3600
Toll Free: (800) 377-7655
Fax: (410) 764-5266
Web site: http://www.polkaudio.com

Private Company
Incorporated: 1972
Employees: 124
Sales: $71.81 million (1999)
NAIC: 33431 Audio and Video Equipment Manufacturing

Polk Audio, Inc. is one of the largest manufacturers of home and automotive loudspeakers in the United States. Polk products have traditionally been sold through specialized stereo shops, but in recent years the company has sought distribution through large electronics chains such as Best Buy and Circuit City, as well as overseas. Publicly traded since 1986, the company's founders led Polk's return to private status in 1999.

Beginnings

Polk Audio was founded in 1972 by two young graduates of Johns Hopkins University in Baltimore, Maryland. Matthew Polk, a physics major, and George Klopfer, a student of history, had built public address systems for fiddlers' conventions, and the pair decided they would start a business making audio speakers. The new company, which was formed with only $200 in capital, was named after Polk because his name was easier to pronounce. Initially working out of an unheated garage, the two founders set as their goal speakers which would combine the airy, crisp sound of European designs with the bassier, more powerful style of American ones.

The company's initial contract was to build private-label speakers for a Washington, D.C. stereo shop, but when that order was canceled, Polk and Klopfer were left with unsold inventory which they were forced to market themselves. Assisted by new partner Sanford Gross, they redesigned the cabinets

and managed to successfully find buyers for their wares. The new company's speakers received a positive response from both consumers and critics, and within a short period of time the partners were able to move the company's operations to a large Victorian house in Govans, Maryland.

In 1976 Polk Audio, now with 12 employees, secured a $75,000 loan from the U.S. Small Business Administration to help increase production, and revenues grew fourfold the next year, to over $1 million. Two additional SBA loans followed. Annual revenues hit $3.6 million in 1980, with the company now boasting over 100 employees and production of more than 1,000 speakers a week. As a measure of its success, Polk was named to Inc. magazine's list of the 100 fastest growing private companies in the United States.

Going Public

Polk's growth continued at a fast pace during the early 1980s. Improved speaker designs were continually being introduced, and the company's annual sales reached $14 million in 1986. At that time Polk had over 200 employees and was manufacturing its speakers at a 68,000-square-foot factory in Baltimore. Sales of compact disc players were contributing to a robust home audio equipment marketplace, and Polk, seeking an influx of capital, made an initial public offering of 700,000 shares of stock on the NASDAQ exchange in the summer of 1986. The following year Polk shareholders voted to reincorporate the company in Delaware, and an agreement was also made for distribution of Polk products in Japan.

A top-of-the-line Polk speaker from this era utilized what was called Stereo Dimension Array. This was a sophisticated system of sending copies of the left and right audio signals to their opposite speakers at lower volume levels, slightly delayed in time, so that they effectively ''canceled out'' the sound each speaker produced that reached the opposing ear, thus creating a more expansive stereophonic effect. A Polk model using this design, the SDA-SRS-2, was priced at $1,990 per pair and measured 50 inches high by 20 inches wide.

The late 1980s saw Polk fend off several attempts to unionize its workforce, as well as the departure from the company of Sanford Gross, who sold his 15 percent ownership stake. In

1988 some manufacturing operations were also shifted to a plant in Tijuana, Mexico, through a subcontracting agreement with Cal-Pacifico, Inc. By the end of fiscal 1990 the company's sales had grown to $27.5 million, with profits of $1.9 million. Polk's various lines of speakers were priced at between $200 and $3,500 per pair.

At this time Polk began negotiations to purchase a British concern, AGI Ltd. AGI was a holding company which owned speaker manufacturer KEF Electronics and audio component maker Boothroyd-Stuart, Ltd. Both had similar reputations to Polk for quality. The deal was expected to greatly open up Polk's marketing possibilities in Europe, and would also double the company's size. The negotiations went slowly, however, and after Polk had invested $3.4 million in an initial phase of the deal, things began to go sour for AGI. By the spring of 1992 the merger was off after AGI was placed into receivership by its principal lender. Polk lost only some $800,000 on the deal, however, being spared further damage by the tough British bankruptcy laws. Subsequently, former AGI head Peter Gaskarth was hired to serve as Polk's managing director for Europe.

Polk's sales growth slowed in the early 1990s, with earnings for 1992 dipping to $321,000. The market for speakers had become much more competitive, and the resulting lowering of prices and profit margins was putting a squeeze on revenues. Nevertheless, the company's products continued to be well received with the public, with several successful new models introduced, including a line of inexpensive bookshelf speakers.

In late 1993 Polk sued New York-based mail-order company 6th Avenue Electronics for allegedly obtaining its speakers fraudulently from authorized dealers. Polk had first sent a cease and desist letter to the retailer in January 1992, but initiated a lawsuit when the practice continued. The company asserted that 6th Avenue was removing original serial numbers and substituting false ones to cover up the source of the merchandise. The suit was later settled out of court. Polk speakers were sold through a network of 350 authorized resellers, which were typically service-oriented, high-end stereo shops that charged premium prices, and the company feared that their availability from a mail-order discounter would damage its relationship with these loyal dealers.

Moving Manufacturing to Mexico

In 1995 Polk announced that it would be moving most of its manufacturing operations to Tijuana, leaving only the assembly of its high-end speakers in Baltimore. Until this time, the company's products had been assembled there from components largely made in Mexico. A distribution center was also located in San Diego,

California. The move eliminated 34 jobs in Baltimore, though over 100 remained there in administration and engineering. The company cited the savings it would realize by paying wages seven to eight times lower than those of the United States, as well as through reduced shipping costs due to the proximity of the assembly and component manufacturing facilities.

By this time a promising new market was developing for Polk in the realm of home theater equipment. With the U.S. economy again booming, and with the growing popularity of lavish television and video playback systems, the market for audio speakers which could replicate the sound of a Dolby Stereo movie soundtrack at home was creating a new opportunity for the company. The spring of 1995 saw the debut of Polk's Signature Reference Theater (SRT) system, which was expected to come to market later in the year with a retail price of $6,500 or more. The company had also been making speakers for use in cars since the early 1990s. These were sold as aftermarket equipment to customers who wished to supplement or replace factory-installed systems.

In June 1995 Polk announced the formation of a wholly owned subsidiary, Eosone, Inc. Eosone would manufacture home theater speakers for sale exclusively in the 213-store Best Buy discount electronics chain. The speakers would be designed by a company based in Vail, Colorado, named Genesis Technologies, Inc. Polk also announced the expansion of manufacturing in Tijuana, with the opening of a new $2 million speaker cabinet plant. Half the company's cabinets were to be made there, with the rest produced by outside contractors. In the fall of 1995 further lawsuits were started against unauthorized dealers. 6th Avenue Electronics was again named, as were two other companies which were owned by a New York businessman.

Winter 1995: Restructuring

Things had been changing rapidly for Polk in many areas, and the company, after undergoing a review by an outside consultant, took steps to more formally structure its operations. A senior executive of four years, James Herd (formerly with competitor Bose) was appointed president, while Matthew Polk continued in his role as chairman and George Klopfer remained Chief Executive. The two founders had shared the president's duties until this time. The company was also divided into four operating units which consisted of Polk Home Entertainment Products, Polk Automotive Products, Eosone International, and Polk Manufacturing. The latter included both production and design activities.

Polk's stock had never attracted much attention among investors, and in June 1996 the company moved its listing from the NASDAQ to the American Stock Exchange (AMEX) in an attempt to increase its appeal. Polk also hired The Levin Group to help promote the stock. Early in 1997 additional restructuring activities took place, and 16 Baltimore area workers were laid off when warehousing and service operations there were relocated to San Diego. The last manufacturing jobs, those related to the top-of-the-line SRT series speakers, were also moved to Tijuana.

Although the company had signed new deals to license its designs for use in Hewlett-Packard computers and Samsung televisions, its profits again began to slide during 1997. This was partly due to a delayed rollout of new models and the

Key Dates:

1972: Company is founded by Matthew Polk and George Klopfer.
1976: Polk receives first Small Business Administration loan for expansion.
1986: Initial public offering is completed on the NASDAQ.
1995: Eosone subsidiary is formed; restructuring occurs and most production is moved to Mexico.
1998: Eosone interests are sold.
1999: Company goes private.

"destocking" of Polk products by Best Buy and other retailers. In December a major new deal was announced with electronics giant Circuit City to sell Polk home and automotive speakers in its chain of nearly 550 stores. Polk products were also being more widely distributed overseas, with the brand now available in 50 countries. At the same time Polk announced a deal to acquire Genesis Technologies of Colorado. An initial investment of $500,000 was made, with the option to purchase the rest of the company over three years. Genesis was a maker of even higher-end speakers than Polk, with some of its models costing as much as $90,000 per system.

Faltering sales continued to be a problem, however, and in March 1998 Polk announced a "unilateral minimum resale price policy." This meant that Polk would refuse to sell stock to dealers who undercut its minimum prices, and represented a further attempt to eliminate the problem of "free riders," or sales by companies who undercut the full-service, high-end stores Polk relied upon. Later in the year, the company announced it was selling its Eosone brand name and its interest in Genesis Technologies to The Providers, Inc. of Vail, Colorado. The barter agreement gave Polk a package of promotional services in lieu of cash.

Going Private

In the spring of 1999 Polk management took another major step to right the company's ship. Their repeated attempts to boost interest in the stock among investors had not borne fruit, and the company's board approved a full stock buyout, with AMEX trading halted in May. An effort to find an outside buyer for the company prior to this had not been successful. Polk expected to realize savings of several hundred thousand dollars per year in costs related to operating as a public company, and also gained greater privacy for strategic decision-making. Additionally, management would not have to worry about the impact every decision would have on share price, a factor which was cited as one of the main reasons for pulling out of the market.

The now private Polk, still guided by its founders, appeared to have resolved many of the problems that had given it difficulties in the 1990s. As it approached the end of its third decade in business, the company was still following its original goal of producing high quality speakers at a reasonable price.

Principal Subsidiaries

Brittania Investment Corp.; Polk Audio Europe, Inc.; Eosone International, Inc.

Principal Divisions

Polk Home Entertainment Products; Polk Automotive Products; Polk Manufacturing.

Principal Competitors

Bang & Olufsen Holding a/s; Bose Corporation; Boston Acoustics, Inc.; Cambridge SoundWorks, Inc; Carver Corporation; Denon Electronics; Harman International Industries, Inc.; Koss Corporation; Matsushita Electric Industrial Co. Ltd.; Pioneer Electronic Corporation; Recoton Corporation; SANYO North America Corporation; Yamaha Corporation.

Further Reading

Ariano, Alexis, "Polk Cranks Up Speaker Volume," *Daily Record (Baltimore)*, December 26, 1997, p. 1.
——, "Polk Invests $500,000 in Partner," *Daily Record (Baltimore)*, January 5, 1998, p. 3.
Benjamin, Jeff, "It Doesn't Get Tweeter Than This," *Daily Record*, July 31, 1996, p. 3.
——, "Polk Audio Founders Paying Greater Mind to What Sound Management Can Produce," *Warfield's Business Record*, August 19, 1996, p. 5.
——, "Polk Audio Launches New Subsidiary Making Speakers for Best Buy Stores," *Daily Record*, June 7, 1995, p. 5.
——, "Polk Scores on Mexico Move," *Daily Record*, May 9, 1995, p. 1.
——, "Polk Sounds Off As Earnings Soar," *Daily Record*, May 15, 1996, p. 3A.
Browning, Graeme, "Polk to Sell Its Sound Overseas," *Baltimore Sun*, November 25, 1990, p. 1C.
Fantel, Hans, "Speakers Extend Limits of Left and Right," *San Diego Union-Tribune*, August 30, 1987, p. E3.
Frye, Lori, "George Klopfer, CEO of Polk Audio" [Interview], *Dow Jones Investor Network*, June 17, 1996.
Gold, Herbert, "The Joy of Low Tech," *Forbes*, June 2, 1986, p. 220.
Hetrick, Ross, "Polk Opens New Plant in Mexico," *The Baltimore Sun*, August 1, 1995, p. 10C.
Ketchum, Bradford W., Jr., "The Inc. Private 100," *Inc.*, December, 1981, pp. 35–48.
Knight, Jerry, "Polk Audio Trades a Public Life for a Private One," *Washington Post*, May 24, 1999, p. F7.
Myers, Randy, "Polk Audio Hopes New Speaker Lines Will Be Music to Wall Street's Ears," *Warfield's Business Record*, May 28, 1993, p. 5.
"Polk Audio Going Private," *Consumer Electronics*, March 29, 1999.
"Polk Defends New Minimum Price Policy," *Audio Week*, March 16, 1998.
"Polk Shifting Some Baltimore Speaker Production to Mexico," *Audio Week*, April 3, 1995.
"Polk Sues N.Y. Merchants on Array of Trade Charges," *Audio Week*, August 21, 1995.
"Q & A: WBR Talks with George M. Klopfer," *Warfield's Business Record*, September 24, 1993, p. 55.
Shelsby, Ted, "Polk Audio to Restructure, Names New President," *The Baltimore Sun*, December 19, 1995, p. 2C.
Somerville, Sean, "Polk Audio Cuts Back in City," *The Baltimore Sun*, April 8, 1997, p. 1C.
Warren, Rich, "Polk Speakers Play the Middle Against Both Ends," *Austin American-Statesman*, November 14, 1992, p. 23.

—Frank Uhle

Potlatch

Potlatch Corporation

601 West Riverside Avenue, Suite 1100
Spokane, Washington 99201
U.S.A.
Telephone: (509) 835-1500
Fax: (509) 835-1555
Web site: http://www.potlatchcorp.com

Public Company
Incorporated: 1903 as Potlatch Lumber Company
Employees: 6,800
Sales: $1.68 billion (1999)
Stock Exchanges: New York Pacific Chicago
Ticker Symbol: PCH
NAIC: 113310 Logging; 321113 Sawmills; 321212
   Softwood Veneer & Plywood Manufacturing; 321219
   Reconstituted Wood Product Manufacturing; 322110
   Pulp Mills; 322121 Paper (Except Newsprint) Mills;
   322130 Paperboard Mills; 322291 Sanitary Paper
   Product Manufacturing

Potlatch Corporation—a mid-sized manufacturer of wood products, printing paper, and other pulp- and paper-based products—has its roots in the mountainous, evergreen forests of northern Idaho. Established there in 1903, it has since grown to be a national, billion-dollar-plus enterprise, with about 1.5 million acres of timberland in Idaho, Arkansas, and Minnesota. The company is among the country's market leaders in high-quality coated paper, oriented strand board, bleached paperboard, and, in the western United States, private label household tissue products. Potlatch sells its products mainly in the United States, but is a major international supplier of bleached paperboard.

Early History

The early history of Potlatch is closely tied to the more general history of the U.S. logging industry. In the United States logging began in New England, where forests were cleared, often carelessly, to make room for the country's first towns and farms and to provide lumber for buildings, fuel, and furniture.

Once thought to be a virtually inexhaustible resource, these forests were nearly depleted by the mid-1800s, and logging companies thus began to spring up in the Midwest, especially in the "North Woods" of Wisconsin, Michigan, and Minnesota. By the 1890s much of these vast Midwestern pine forests also were cleared, forcing lumbermen to look to the South and to the far Northwest for new regions of forested land.

Also in the 19th century the railroads were spreading their tracks to the outer edges of the nation. The Utah Northern extended its line in 1874 just across the southern Idaho border and several years later began to lay additional tracks to reach the mining communities farther north. By 1883 Northern Pacific had built a line from St. Paul, Minnesota, to Tacoma, Washington, which wound its way through such towns in northern Idaho as Bonner's Ferry and Sandpoint. Without the railroads to carry logs and lumber products, dreams of harvesting Idaho's evergreen forests would never have been realized.

As the railroads brought settlers to the Western frontier, stories of the land's riches were carried back east. Northern Idaho, cut off from the southern part of the state by the deep gorge of the Salmon River, was uncharted for the most part, but many Midwestern timbermen began to hear of the area's towering stands of white pine and other valuable trees. Frederick Weyerhaeuser of St. Paul, Minnesota—a powerful lumber capitalist and one of the founders of Potlatch—saw an exhibit of Idaho timberland at Chicago's 1893 World's Fair, and it was he who led the charge of Midwest lumber companies to the Northwest. He did this with the help of the "Weyerhaeuser syndicate," a group of Midwestern businessmen who had long worked together to secure timber for their individual mills. In 1900 his syndicate bought an astonishing 900,000 acres of timberland in the Pacific Northwest, thus forming Weyerhaeuser Timber Company, and that year Weyerhaeuser himself toured on horseback northern Idaho's stands of white pine. Soon the syndicate was buying additional Northwest timberland from railroads, state auctions, and homesteaders; other Midwestern companies, trusting Weyerhaeuser's judgment, quickly followed.

In northern Idaho's Palouse, Potlatch, and Elk River basins, thousands of acres of timberland were being purchased by Midwestern companies, but most went to just two men—

William Deary of Northland Pine Company, a firm established by the Weyerhaeuser syndicate, and Henry Turrish of Wisconsin Log & Lumber Company. Although competitors, Deary and Turrish were by 1902 buying land together, in part for convenience but also to keep land prices lower. The owners of Northland and Wisconsin Log & Lumber soon recognized the value of this collaboration, and the following year they decided to merge their Idaho timberland under a new firm, which they called Potlatch Lumber Company. When the company was formed it owned more than 100,000 acres, but it quickly gained additional land, as well as two mills, when it bought nearby Palouse River Lumber Company and Codd Lumber Company in 1903 and 1904, respectively.

Backed with an initial $3 million in capital, Potlatch Lumber Company was established with great hopes but with little recognition of the difficulties posed by the area's rugged environment. Its name—derived from the northwest Indian word *patshatl,* which referred to an elaborate ceremony of gift-giving—was selected because the Potlatch River cut through the company's land. The first president of Potlatch was Weyerhaeuser's son, Charles, and the vice-president was Turrish, but the dominant personality of the company was Deary, who was appointed general manager. One of the first goals of Potlatch was to plan and build a magnificent new sawmill, which Deary decided to place along the Palouse River about 15 miles north of Moscow, Idaho. Opened on September 11, 1906, the structure was some 300 feet long, 100 feet wide, and 70 feet tall, and its giant Corliss engine gave the mill an annual capacity of 135 million board feet. Production began with 125 employees.

To house these employees, the company decided to build a town on two hills overlooking the sawmill. By the mill's opening day there were already 128 completed homes, and soon there was also a hotel, two churches, a large general store, and an elementary and high school. Called Potlatch, this attractive, well-designed town was a great source of pride for the company but also a considerable drain on funds. The company continued to own and maintain the town until the 1950s.

Another major investment by the early company was its 45-mile railroad line, which, when completed in 1907, ran from Palouse, Washington, east through Potlatch and other towns, ending in Bovill, Idaho. It was used to carry logs from the company's timberland to the new mill, as well as to transport finished lumber to connecting railroads at Palouse and Bovill.

Despite Potlatch Lumber Company's high-quality timber, modern sawmill, and new railway, its early years were disappointing and often marked by losses. The first dividend was not paid until 1911, and even that was just three percent, a low

figure in the high-risk lumber business. A few years later the company was paying ten percent, but the average dividend from 1903 to 1923—when the company's holdings had reached some 170,000 acres—was just 3.6 percent. Before his death in 1914, Frederick Weyerhaeuser reportedly said the company was appropriately called Potlatch because he had given it so much money with little return. Other Idaho timber companies had similarly poor records.

The company's tree-cutting policy contributed to this shaky financial picture. Instead of selectively cutting the area's white pine, ponderosa pine, and Douglas fir—the species most in demand—the company cut all trees in its path, even those, such as tamarack, that often cost more to harvest than sell. Other problems included the company's high capital costs (for the railway, mill, and town), rugged terrain and inaccessible timber areas, deep winter snow, the relatively few trees per acre, and heavy state taxes. The 1914 opening of the Panama Canal had an especially harsh impact on Potlatch and other Idaho timber companies. Before the canal's opening, Potlatch benefited from rail costs cheaper than those paid by its Pacific Coast rivals, who were hundreds of miles farther from the major Eastern markets. After 1914 companies located on the Pacific Coast were able to send their timber to these markets by boat, at a cost one-third cheaper than rail, thus undercutting the price of lumber sold by Potlatch and other Idaho timber firms.

Great Depression: Crisis and Merger

As early as 1926 the entire Northwest lumber industry was suffering from overproduction and declining prices. When the Great Depression hit the country in 1929, causing a precipitous drop in new building construction, Potlatch found itself facing potential bankruptcy, as did northern Idaho's other major timber companies, Clearwater Timber Co. and Rutledge Timber Co., which had been established in 1900 and 1902, respectively, by the Weyerhaeuser syndicate. The Clearwater mill was located just south of Potlatch in the town of Lewiston, and the mill of Edward Rutledge was found farther north in Coeur d'Alene.

After considerable debate among stockholders, the financial crisis was resolved by merging the three companies into an organization called Potlatch Forests, Inc. The new corporation, headquartered in Lewiston, was headed initially by John Philip Weyerhaeuser, Jr., a grandson of Frederick Weyerhaeuser, and later, in 1935, by the older Rudolph M. Weyerhaeuser, one of the founder's sons. Effective April 29, 1931, the merger did not remove the companies' common problem of a weak market but did provide for better efficiency. Some timber in the Clearwater land, for example, could be taken more cheaply to the Potlatch mill. Expensive machinery could be shared between the three concerns. The merger also allowed for a more ambitious attempt at selective cutting, which Clearwater had begun in 1929. The goal of selective cutting was to fell only mature or diseased trees, allowing the younger, healthy ones to stand for future generations of logging. Reforestation, however, did not begin until 1954.

Despite these gains, the Depression remained a difficult period for Potlatch, which was forced to cut its prices and the wages of its workers. The Coeur d'Alene mill was closed for some time beginning in 1932, and that year its operations in the town of Potlatch were open only to ship lumber held in storage.

Key Dates:

1903: William Deary and Henry Turrish merge their Idaho timberland in a new company called Potlatch Lumber Company.
1906: Potlatch opens a new sawmill with an annual capacity of 135 million board feet.
1931: Potlatch merges with Clearwater Timber Co. and Rutledge Timber Co. to form Potlatch Forests, Inc.
1950: Company pioneers in the production of bleached paperboard from wood waste.
1956: Company merges with Arkansas-based Southern Lumber Company.
1964: Company expands into Minnesota with the acquisition of Northwest Paper Company.
1965: Headquarters are moved to San Francisco.
1971: Richard B. Madden becomes CEO and begins trimming the company to concentrate on four core areas and initiates a capital expenditure program.
1973: Company changes its name to Potlatch Corporation.
1981: Company builds the first U.S. plant to make oriented strand board.
1994: John M. Richards is named chairman and CEO.
1997: Corporate headquarters are relocated to Spokane, Washington.
1999: A deal with Anderson-Tully Company to form Timberland Growth Corporation, a timber-based REIT, falls apart; L. Pendleton Siegel is named chairman and CEO.

Losses were reported in all but two years of the 1930s, resulting in a total deficit of $8.7 million for the decade. During this period, however, the company did develop an important new product, Pres-to-logs, a slow-burning, virtually smokeless fuel made of compressed sawdust, wood chips, and splinters. The logs were ideal for fireplaces located in homes or on railcars, where smoke had to be kept to a minimum. A first in the industry, Pres-to-logs were made by a process involving extreme heat, high pressure, and moisture.

Postwar Era: New Products and Geographic Expansion

World War II brought increased demand for lumber to build houses, military camps, and other facilities for soldiers, and Potlatch, benefiting from booming lumber orders, gained badly needed profits. From 1940 to 1945 the company's after-tax profits surpassed $5 million, of which $1.2 million was placed in a reserve fund for future upgrading of its mills and machinery and for introducing new products. By the war's end, the company was poised for strong, sustained growth, which would be overseen by George F. Jewett, a grandson of the founder, who became president of Potlatch in 1946. Three years later Jewett was elected the company's first chairman of the board, a position that was filled later by Edwin Weyerhaeuser Davis, another grandson, in 1957 and then by Benton R. Cancell in 1962.

The company's profitable postwar era was distinguished by its large number of new products. The first to be introduced was

veneer, or thin sheets, of white pine, which Potlatch hoped would be popular for home paneling. To make this product, giant logs of white pine had to be peeled and then made into rolls. In 1949, after three years of developing the process, the company began making white pine veneer, but the project quickly came to be too expensive and problematic. By 1952 the operations were successfully converted to make a different product, plywood, which was made from layers of Douglas fir, white pine, ponderosa pine, or larch.

An especially important new product for Potlatch was paperboard—a thick paper with a variety of uses, such as making milk cartons and other containers. To manufacture the product, the company in 1950 built a new bleach kraft pulp and paper mill, located in Lewiston, which was the first in the United States to produce bleached paperboard from sawmill wood waste, namely chips. Within the next few years Potlatch introduced "Lock-Deck" laminated decking, "Pure-Pak" cartons for milk, and additional paperboard items, such as paper plates and meat trays. By the early 1960s the company had also purchased a mill for folding paperboard and entered a new line of products by acquiring Clearwater Tissue Mills, Inc.

To obtain the raw materials for these new products, Potlatch began to expand its timber reserves. In 1956 it merged with Southern Lumber Company, an Arkansas firm founded by the Weyerhaeuser syndicate in 1882. With the subsequent purchase of Bradley Lumber Company, also located in Arkansas, Potlatch controlled more than 100,000 acres of Arkansas timberland, mostly of southern yellow pine, oak, and other hardwoods. Directing its sights to Minnesota, Potlatch merged in 1964 with another Weyerhaeuser creation, Northwest Paper Company, a producer of printing and writing paper. Established in 1898, Northwest owned about 220,000 acres of forested land in Minnesota, where jack pine, aspen, red pine, and balsam fir were the most common species. With these mergers, Potlatch had become a national company, and the small town of Lewiston subsequently proved to be a difficult place from which to manage its new holdings. As a result, the company's headquarters were moved to San Francisco in 1965, and a few years later, in 1973, the company changed its name from Potlatch Forests, Inc. to Potlatch Corporation.

The Madden Era, 1971–94: Refocusing and Capital Expenditures

By 1971, when Richard B. Madden became CEO, the company had diversified into some 20 separate product lines—including modular housing and corrugated boxes—and its sales had reached $356 million. Potlatch also was investing millions of dollars to reduce its air and water pollution. Not simply taking over the reins, Madden spent much of his first year developing what became the company's guiding business philosophy: "Potlatch will be a company characterized by a growing profit and reasonable rate of return that is achieved by talented, well-trained, and highly motivated people. It will be a company that is properly supported by a sound financial structure and will feature a keen sense of social responsibility."

Using this simple statement, Madden then initiated an intensive review of the company's many components. The result was a decision to sell off its less profitable activities and to concentrate on just four product lines: wood products (lumber, plywood, and particle board), printed papers, pulp and paperboard, and tissue products. Moreover, the company decided to focus on "higher-value-added" products, or those that had a relatively high value compared with the cost of the raw materials. Such products tended to be less affected by recurring business cycles. In printed papers, for example, Potlatch concentrated on high grades of coated paper, the type commonly used for annual reports and advertising brochures.

Beginning in the mid-1970s and extending into the 1980s and 1990s, the company combined these shifting priorities with a new program of capital expenditures. In 1981, for example, Potlatch built in Minnesota the first U.S. plant to make oriented strand board (OSB). An alternative to plywood, OSB was a multilayered board made from strands of aspen "oriented" in various directions; the strands were held together by a mixture of wax and resin and compressed under intense heat. By 1991 the company was making more than a billion square feet of OSB in two varieties: Oxboard, with five layers, and Potlatch Select, with three. Although capital projects were curtailed during the recession of the early 1980s, by the late 1980s Potlatch was again spending large sums of money to retool its plants and machinery. Projects completed by the early 1990s included a $40 million upgrade of the Lewiston sawmill and log processing center; a $400 million modernization of the Lewiston pulp and paperboard mill; a new, $27 million lumber mill in Warren, Arkansas; and, as part of a $107 million upgrade of its tissue operations, a new "twin wire" tissue machine in Lewiston. In 1993 Potlatch completed construction of a new $25 million tissue complex in North Las Vegas, Nevada, to service the Southwestern market; that year, the company also began a three-year, $500 million expansion of its pulp mill in Cloquet, Minnesota.

This program of capital expenditures was reflected in the company's skyrocketing sales and healthy profit margins. Total sales jumped from $356 million in 1971, the year Madden became chairman of the board, to $504 million in 1975, $820 million in 1980, $950 million in 1985, and $1.37 billion in 1993, Madden's last full year as chairman. Even during the down years of the cyclical forest products industry, Potlatch managed to stay in the black. In the early 1990s earnings were highest in its wood products, such as lumber and oriented strand board, and, owing to difficult market conditions, considerably lower in printing paper and pulp and paperboard.

Mid-1990s and Beyond

In May 1994 John M. Richards, president and COO, was named to replace Madden as chairman and CEO. L. Pendleton Siegel was promoted to Richards's former position. Capital expenditures continued in 1994, as Potlatch opened a new $27 million sawmill in Warren, Arkansas. Also in 1994, Potlatch expanded into northeastern Oregon when it began developing a 22,000-acre plantation for the growing of hybrid poplar trees, which could be harvested in six years, rather than the usual 50 to 70 years. The trees were slated to supply the bleached pulp mill in Lewiston—beginning in the early 21st century—and were viewed as a method to reduce the company's dependence on outside fiber sources. In December 1995 the company filed suit against Beloit Corporation alleging that Beloit had installed a defective pulp washer system at the Lewiston pulp mill. In June 1997 a jury awarded Potlatch damages of $95 million but the judgment was thrown out by the Idaho Supreme Court in 1999. An out-of-court settlement was expected to be reached between the two parties.

In a cost-saving move, Potlatch in 1997 relocated its corporate headquarters to Spokane, Washington, the closest city to Lewiston with a major airport. The following year Potlatch began planning a complex merger of its Arkansas timberland with that of Anderson-Tully Company located in Mississippi and Arkansas into a newly formed real estate investment trust (REIT) called Timberland Growth Corporation. This deal fell apart during 1999, however, following the weakening of markets in Asia and the United States.

In mid-1999 Richards retired as chairman and CEO, with Siegel taking over those positions. Richard L. Paulson was named president and COO. Potlatch thus entered the 21st century under new leadership and with a 15-year, $2 billion capital improvement program behind it. The forest products industry had been plagued in the late 1990s by overcapacity stemming from the Asian financial crisis, but at the turn of the millennium markets in Asia seemed to be on the upswing. With prospects for the industry brightening and the capital improvement program laying the groundwork for greater efficiency and profitability, Potlatch was poised to improve upon the results it posted in 1999: net earnings of $40.9 million on net sales of $1.68 billion.

Principal Subsidiaries

Duluth & Northeastern Railroad Co.; Prescott & Northwestern Railroad Co.; St. Maries River Railroad Co.; Warren & Saline River Railroad Co.

Principal Operating Units

Wood Products Group; Pulp and Paper Group; Resource Management Group.

Principal Competitors

Abitibi-Consolidated Inc.; Boise Cascade Corporation; Champion International Corporation; Georgia-Pacific Corporation; International Paper Company; The Mead Corporation; Pope & Talbot, Inc.; Smurfit-Stone Container Corporation; Weyerhaeuser Company; Willamette Industries, Inc.

Further Reading

"At Potlatch, Caution Is the Key," *Business Week,* January 11, 1988, p. 72.

Blackman, Ted, "Team Concept Involves Crews in All Aspects of Mills," *Forest Industries,* November 1991, p. 14.

Caldwell, Bert, "The REIT Stuff: Complex Potlatch Deal Represents 'New Approach to Doing Business,' " *Spokesman Review,* March 1, 1998, p. A12.

Hansen, Dan, "Groups Threaten Suit Over Pollution Permit: Activists Say Potlatch's Discharge Endangers Fish," *Spokesman Review,* August 13, 1998, p. B2.

Harrison, Andy, "Potlatch Expands in Major Market Sectors," *Pulp and Paper,* February 1995, pp. 34–35.

Hidy, Ralph W., Frank Ernest Hill, and Allan Nevins, *Timber and Men: The Weyerhaeuser Story,* New York: MacMillan, 1963.

Jones, Grayden, "Potlatch Picks Spokane for Corporate HQ," *Spokesman Review,* May 20, 1997, p. A1.

Koncel, Jerome A., "Potlatch Keeps It Simple to Achieve Solid Successes," *American Papermaker,* June 1990, pp. 26–29.

Louis, Arthur M., "Potlatch Moving Out of S.F.: New Headquarters Will Be in Spokane," *San Francisco Chronicle,* May 20, 1997, p. C1.

McCoy, Charles, "Potlatch Corporation Expects Earnings Recovery to Take Root: Concern's Timber Holdings Are Largely Immune to Spotted-Owl Controversy," *Wall Street Journal,* April 13, 1992, p. B4.

Mehlman, William, "Leverage, Spotted Owl Seen Pulling Hard for Potlatch," *Insiders' Chronicle,* August 19, 1991, pp. 1, 14–15.

Nelson, Warren, and Marc Lerch, "Potlatch Mill Saves Energy Costs by Using Wide-Gap Heat Exchanger," *Pulp and Paper,* March 1990, pp. 212–13.

Petersen, Keith C., *Company Town: Potlatch, Idaho, and the Potlatch Lumber Company,* Pullman, Wash.: Washington State University Press, 1987.

Read, Paul, "A Look Inside Potlatch Corp.," *Journal of Business,* December 4, 1997, p. A1.

——, "Potlatch Positioned for Payoff," *Journal of Business,* May 20, 1999, p. A1.

Wiegner, Kathleen K., "To Make Your Company Raider-Proof, Run It Right," *Forbes,* November 3, 1986, pp. 106+.

—Thomas Riggs
—updated by David E. Salamie

Prodigy Communications Corporation

Prodigy Communications Corporation

44 South Broadway
White Plains, New York 10601
U.S.A.
Telephone: (914) 448-8000
Toll Free: (800) 213-0992
Fax: (914) 448-3467
Web site: http://www.prodigy.com

Public Company
Incorporated: 1996 as Prodigy Inc.
Employees: 313
Sales: $189.04 million (1999)
Stock Exchanges: NASDAQ
Ticker Symbol: PRGY
NAIC: 514191 On-Line Information Services; 51331
   Wired Telecommunications Carriers

Prodigy Communications Corporation provides its subscribers with Internet access and related value-added services, such as Prodigy-branded Internet content powered by Excite. With some 1.5 million billable subscribers at the end of 1999, Prodigy users included small and mid-sized businesses as well as individual consumers. Moreover, the company's services were available in Spanish as well as English versions. After a successful initial public offering in 1999, Prodigy planned to partner with SBC Communications, Inc., the largest regional telephone company in the United States. When finalized, the partnership would make Prodigy the exclusive retail Internet service provider for SBC's 650,000 small-business and residential consumers. This would also elevate Prodigy's subscriber base to just over two million, making it the third largest Internet service provider in the United States.

IBM-Sears Joint Venture: 1984–96

Prodigy had its origins in a joint venture. In 1984 IBM, Sears, and CBS established a joint venture, named Trintex, to offer videotex services. In this pre-Internet era, Videotex was a system enabling subscribers to obtain information and perform other functions, such as banking or shopping, through a home terminal or specially equipped television set hooked up to a telephone.

Plans called for the service to supply subscribing PC-owners with information, news, home shopping, and catalogs. Other videotex ventures, most notably Knight-Ridder's Viewtron, had foundered, and CBS dropped out of the Trintex project in 1986. IBM and Sears persevered, however, and by the fall of 1988 had invested $450 million in start-up costs. Their Prodigy Services Co. was established to oversee the Trintex enterprise, and in June 1988 the entire venture became known as Prodigy. Its product became the world's first consumer-focused online service that year.

Prodigy was aimed at the estimated five million homes with IBM-compatible computers powerful enough to operate the fledgling service's sophisticated software. First available in Atlanta, San Francisco, and Hartford, Connecticut, in May 1988, Prodigy offered a $149.95 start-up kit that consisted of a modem, software, and three months of free service. After purchasing the start-up kit, subscribers paid a monthly subscription fee of $9.95. Prodigy was supported by a national advertising campaign, including TV spots, direct mail, and the distribution of point-of-purchase materials in computer stores, software stores, and department stores. By the end of 1988 Prodigy had expanded its geographic scope to include Los Angeles, Sacramento, San Diego, and Santa Barbara, California.

By mid-1989 more than nine million home computers were theoretically capable of using the Prodigy network, but only 65,000 households were signed up. The service had added New York City during this time but was still only available in 13 markets covering a total of 30 percent of the potential subscribers. Households that did subscribe were receiving hundreds of news stories a day, complete with graphics, from reporters and editors based in Prodigy's White Plains, New York, headquarters.

Prodigy's subscribers also had access to the reservations system of American Airlines for airline, hotel, and car-rental reservations, and they could order merchandise from Sears, J.C. Penney, and some 45 other direct-shipping merchants. New York's

Manufacturers Hanover Trust Bank offered banking transactions, and Wall Street's Donaldson, Lufkin & Jenrette, stock purchases by computer. A package of improved financial services was later made available at additional cost. Prodigy also offered low-fee electronic mail, and a grocery-shopping service was also introduced but later dropped for lack of interest.

Prodigy was available nationwide by September 1990 and claimed 635,000 customers by the end of the year, ranking it second in its field to H & R Block's (eventually America Online's) CompuServe Inc. In addition to its monthly fee (now $12.95), Prodigy was earning revenue from add-on features and also from advertisements that appeared onscreen. However, analysts noted that after an investment estimated at between $500 million and $1 billion, Prodigy was still years away from earning a profit. One industry observer, Robert F. Kleiber, described the service to Eben Shapiro of the *New York Times* as a "black hole," adding, "It does not provide the fundamental capability that people are really looking for in an on-line service," which he described as an easy way to communicate with other members.

Although Prodigy offered both electronic mail and electronic bulletin boards, it was censoring messages that it called "obscene, profane or otherwise offensive," a practice the company defended by saying that Prodigy was a family service. When Prodigy imposed an add-on fee at the beginning of 1991 for more than 30 electronic-mail messages a month, disgruntled subscribers called the charge a violation of the original subscription agreement.

Prodigy claimed 1.75 million subscribers in October 1992 but was still losing money. Reviewing the service in the *Wall Street Journal,* Walter S. Mossberg called it "seriously flawed. Its navigation system is unusual and confusing, its text is clunky and moves at a snail's pace, its content promises more than it delivers. . . . It is organized more like a broadcast network than a common carrier of information . . . and access to software downloads costs extra—in some cases doubling the monthly fee." The monthly fee did increase, to $14.95, in November 1992. Prophetically, Mossberg described much-smaller America Online Inc. as "the sophisticated wave of the future among such services."

Prodigy could boast some improvements in 1993; during the fall of the year it introduced Windows-based software and e-mail gateway to the Internet. The service's customer base peaked at about two million in 1994. Although Prodigy was available on Macintosh computers, in mid-1994 Mac users still could not receive Internet electronic mail. Indeed, with the exception of e-mail functions, Prodigy did not offer general access to the Internet until October of that year, when it made available unrestricted access to the bulletin boards known as Usenet (and also a new chat-line service) for $3.60 an hour.

In 1995, new leadership came to Prodigy, with Edward Bennett joining the company as CEO. Bennett had come to Prodigy after heading up television's VH-1 music channel for Viacom; he hoped to turn Prodigy around. Indeed, that year Prodigy became the first consumer online computer network to test and implement its own web browser to enhance user access to the World Wide Web. By the summer of 1995 the company boasted one million subscribers and was claiming it was on the road to profitability for the first time in its existence. However, Prodigy's Internet service quickly fell behind America Online and CompuServe in subscriber volume. Prodigy's losses continued to be heavy throughout this period. Prodigy lost $60 million on total revenues of $195.2 million in 1993; $52 million on $211 million in 1944; and $34.6 million on $243.4 million in 1995.

Internet Service Provider: 1996–98

After incurring at least $1.3 billion in losses, IBM and Sears sold their Prodigy Services Co. in May 1996 to International Wireless Inc., and about 40 executives from Prodigy, for $78.12 million in cash and notes. By this time there were said to be less than one million subscribers. Renamed Prodigy Inc., the company's new management de-emphasized the company's original services in favor of becoming what it described as a "value-added" Internet service provider by means of Prodigy Internet, introduced in October 1996.

Along with online Internet access, Prodigy Internet offered a variety of proprietary-content subject areas, such as business- and education-oriented web sites, chat rooms, instant messaging, and a lineup of computer games. A financial area, Prodigy Investor, included personal portfolio tracking, access to financial news, links to online brokers, and a database of mutual funds. Like Prodigy Internet, Prodigy Classic offered unlimited monthly Internet access and cost the same $19.95 a month for unlimited service, but it was not as strong technologically as Prodigy Internet, the first major access service to be programmed in HTML, or Hyper Text MarkUp Language, the programming language for Web pages.

In September 1997 Prodigy split into three divisions: the core domestic online service division, a software development unit, and international operations. While eschewing Europe, already well accommodated by other Internet service providers, Prodigy had an online presence in six African countries and had introduced service in China in two languages. A move into Mexico was imminent.

In March 1998, Prodigy dropped its monthly fee to $15.75 and promised a new interface designed with Excite providing the gateway, plus a new digital 56k network. At this time the company claimed 830,000 subscribers for Prodigy Classic (which it was seeking to phase out) and Prodigy Internet. The actual number of billable subscribers was only 613,000, however, at the end of 1997, far short of the estimated 1.5 million needed for the company to break even. Moreover, Prodigy's losses continued to mount, from $90.8 million on revenues of $98.91 million in 1996 to $132.78 million on revenues of $134.19 million in 1997.

Going Public and Allying with SBC in 1999

Prodigy's billable subscribers increased to 671,000 in 1998, with the number of Internet customers rising from 221,000 to 505,000. However, revenues, at $136.14 million for the year, were little changed, and the net loss, although pared, remained a severe $65.08 million. Despite this woeful result, the company—renamed Prodigy Communications Corporation in August 1998—was able to attract investors after going public in February 1999. More than $160 million was raised by selling stock at $15 a share, and, in the hot Wall Street market for Internet stocks, the price rose as high as $50 a share during the year.

Mexico's Carso Global Telecom S.A. de C.V., which had been a major investor in International Wireless, controlled, directly or through its Telefonos de Mexico (Telmex) holding, more than 60 percent of Prodigy after the initial offering. Reflecting this orientation, Prodigy launched the first-ever fully bilingual Spanish-language Internet-access service in the United States in April 1999, offering all-you-can-surf access to Hispanic customers at the same $19.95 a month as the English-language service. The company also formed a joint venture with Telmex to manage the subscriber base of Prodigy Internet de Telmex, Mexico's largest Internet service provider. Prodigy sold Africa Online, Inc. in 1998 for $2.81 million.

In November 1999 Prodigy announced plans to form a limited partnership with SBC Communications Inc., the nation's largest local telephone company. The transaction, pending federal regulatory approval, would make Prodigy the exclusive retail Internet service provider for the 650,000 small-business and residential consumers in SBC's service area, thereby bringing Prodigy's subscriber base to just over two million and making it the third largest Internet service provider. (Prodigy had acquired rival FlashNet Communications, Inc. earlier in the month for $113 million, thus adding 244,000 new members.)

SBC also pledged to deliver an additional 1.2 to 1.3 million online customers to Prodigy over a three-year period, drawn from its service-area base of some 100 million residents. In return, Prodigy gave SBC a 43 percent stake in the partnership and the right to convert that stake into a direct equity interest in Prodigy for about $1.6 billion. In addition to adding subscribers, Prodigy would benefit from the deal because it would allow the service to begin offering high-speed digital subscriber lines, in which SBC had been investing heavily.

Prodigy had revenues of $189.04 million in 1999, of which Prodigy Internet accounted for 82 percent. The number of billable subscribers reached 1.5 million at the end of the year. Still, the company incurred a net loss of $80.49 million for 1999. Through its alliance with SBC, however, Prodigy hoped to realize its role as a competitive Internet provider and turn a profit in the process.

Principal Subsidiaries

Comstar Cellular S.A.

Principal Competitors

America Online, Inc.; Compuserve Interactive Services, Inc.; AT&T Corp.; EarthLink Network Inc.; Microsoft Corporation; MindSpring Enterprises Inc.

Further Reading

Arenson, Karen W., "CBS, I.B.M., Sears Join in Videotex Venture," *New York Times,* February 15, 1984, p. D4.

Chakravarty, Subrata N., and Evan McGlinn, " 'This Thing Has to Change People's Habits'," *Forbes,* June 26, 1989, pp. 118, 122.

Graham, Judith, "Linkup: IBM, Sears, Set Ads for Videotex Venture," *Advertising Age,* May 23, 1988, pp. 1, 93.

Jensen, Kris, "Prodigy Poised to Leap Forward in Changing Industry," *Atlanta Constitution,* December 11, 1994, p. H1.

Lewis, Peter H., "Prodigy Developing a Service for Internet," *New York Times,* September 29, 1994, p. D4.

——, "Prodigy Leads Its Peers onto the World Wide Web," *New York Times,* January 18, 1995, p. D7.

Lohr, Steve, "Prodigy to Get New Owners And Strategy," *New York Times,* May 13, 1996, pp. D1, D4.

McDermott, Michael J., "Upstart Getting Upper Hand in Data Wars," *Crain's New York Business,* December 10, 1990, p. 20.

Mehta, Stephanie N., "SBC, Prodigy to Combine Internet Plans," *Wall Street Journal,* November 23, 1999, pp. A3, A6.

Miller, Michael W., "Prodigy Computer Network Bans Bias Notes from Bulletin Board," *Wall Street Journal,* October 24, 1991, p. B6.

Mossberg, Walter S., "Prodigy Has Promise, But America Online May Be the Prodigy," *Wall Street Journal,* October 18, 1992, p. B1.

Petersen, Andrea, "Prodigy Plans Internet Service for Spanish Speakers in the U.S.," *Wall Street Journal,* p. B6.

Revkin, Andrew C., "A Test Case of Internet Exuberance," *New York Times,* January 31, 1999, Sec. 3, p. 9.

Shapiro, Eben, "Can Prodigy Be All Things to 15 Million PC Owners?," *New York Times,* June 2, 1991, Sec. 3, p. 4.

Tedesco, Richard, "Prodigy Tries Three-Part Approach," *Broadcasting & Cable,* September 29, 1997, p. 73.

Walsh, Mark, "Purchase Buoys Prodigy in Consolidating Industry," *Crain's New York Business,* December 6, 1999, p. 4.

Warner, Bernhard, "Prodigy Aims to Boost Subs with New Games, Areas," *Brandweek,* September 22, 1997, p. 24.

—Robert Halasz

The Quaker Oats Company

Quaker Tower
Post Office Box 049001
Chicago, Illinois 60604-9001
U.S.A.
Telephone: (312) 222-7111
Toll Free: (800) 494-7843
Fax: (312) 222-8323
Web site: http://www.quakeroats.com

Public Company
Incorporated: 1901
Employees: 11,860
Sales: $4.73 billion (1999)
Stock Exchanges: New York Midwest Pacific London
Ticker Symbol: OAT
NAIC: 311211 Flour Milling; 311212 Rice Milling;
311230 Breakfast Cereal Manufacturing; 311340
Nonchocolate Confectionery Manufacturing; 311423
Dried and Dehydrated Food Manufacturing; 311822
Flour Mixes and Dough Manufacturing from
Purchased Flour; 311823 Dry Pasta Manufacturing;
312111 Soft Drink Manufacturing; 312112 Bottled
Water Manufacturing

The product of a rocky union between three 19th-century millers, The Quaker Oats Company maintains a portfolio of strong branded products within the food and beverages sectors. Although the company originally centered around oats, it is the Gatorade sports drink—acquired in 1983 as part of Stokely-Van Camp—that has become the company's largest single brand, accounting for more than 38 percent of overall sales. Quaker's other main brands include Quaker oatmeal; Cap'n Crunch, Life, and other ready-to-eat cereals; Quaker rice cakes and Quaker Chewy granola bars; Rice-A-Roni, Pasta Roni, and Near East flavored rice and pasta side dishes; and Aunt Jemima mixes and syrups. Of total U.S. sales, 92 percent are derived from brands that are number one or two within their product categories. Quaker's overseas sales efforts are centered around Latin America, Europe, and China, generating about 18 percent of total revenues.

Oatmeal Battles in the 19th Century

Ferdinand Schumacher undertook an ambitious project in 1856 when he organized his German Mills American Oatmeal Factory in Akron, Ohio. His mission was to introduce steel-cut oats to the American table at a time when oats were considered an inappropriate food for anything but horses. German and Irish immigrants were his initial customers, since they were accustomed to eating oats and unused to the high cost of American meat. Oat milling was a low-cost operation, and competitors quickly appeared as oats gained acceptance as a food.

One competitor with an innovative approach to business was Henry Parsons Crowell of nearby Ravenna, Ohio. Crowell purchased the Quaker Mill in Ravenna, gave his oats the Quaker name, and packed them in a sanitary, two-pound paper package with printed cooking directions. He also advertised in newspapers with German, Scottish, and Irish readers, a practice which was at that time associated with disreputable showmen. Crowell became the first marketer to register a trademark for cereal, registering his Quaker symbol in 1877. (The Quakers—that is the Society of Friends Christian sect—played no role in the development of the Quaker Oats Company.) Soon Crowell's success impinged on Schumacher's business, with urban customers often specifically requesting Quaker brand oats.

Another competitor, Robert Stuart, emigrated with his father from Embro, Ontario, to establish a mill in Cedar Rapids, Iowa, in 1873. Eventually he helped finance the building of a new oatmeal mill in Chicago and expanded the original mill. Under the same label the two mills established markets throughout the Midwest, especially in Chicago, Milwaukee, and Detroit, carefully avoiding territories dominated by Schumacher or Crowell.

In 1885 Crowell and Stuart joined forces in a price war against Schumacher's larger operation. An attempt to form the Oatmeal Millers Association that year failed when Schumacher refused to join. One year later Schumacher's largest mill burned to the ground; Crowell reacted by immediately raising his prices. Because Schumacher had been uninsured, he finally

---

Company Perspectives:

Our goal is to be the undisputed leader in the food and beverage industry. We intend to do this by making Quaker a winning company—a place where talented people have opportunities and are rewarded for contributing to an exciting, profitable growth story. Winning means that our products will be those for which consumers hunger and thirst. Winning also means that we outpace our competitive set with consistently strong financial results.

---

agreed to join Stuart and Crowell in their venture. Crowell became president of the Consolidated Oatmeal Company, Stuart was vice-president, and Schumacher, the former oatmeal king, was treasurer.

Consolidated, however, only made up half of the trade, and the other half was determined to destroy it. Competitors built mills they did not want, knowing Consolidated would purchase them simply to keep them out of production. Half of Consolidated's earnings were spent this way, and in 1888, under financial and legal pressure, it collapsed.

A third and finally successful attempt at consolidation came that same year, when seven of the largest American oat millers united as the American Cereal Company. Schumacher ended up with a controlling interest, and he appointed himself president and Crowell vice-president. The company doubled production in two years by consolidating operations into the two major mills at Cedar Rapids and Akron, Ohio. The concentration of facilities gave them the strength to survive the depression of the 1890s.

Crowell promoted Quaker Oats aggressively during the decade. Schumacher, however, insisted that his own brand, F.S. Brand, be sold alongside Quaker, blunting the success of the better-selling Quaker. Then Stuart crossed Schumacher, the company's treasurer, by purchasing two food companies at bargain prices and investing in machinery for the Cedar Rapids mill. Opposed to both actions, Schumacher requested and secured Stuart's resignation in 1897. The following year he also voted Crowell out of the organization.

The ousted Crowell and Stuart, who together owned 24 percent of American Cereal, quietly began to buy available shares. In 1899, after a proxy fight, Schumacher lost control of the company to Stuart and Crowell. Stuart immediately built new facilities and diversified the product line while Crowell increased promotional efforts. Quaker was now producing wheat cereals, farina, hominy, cornmeal, baby food, and animal feed.

Early Years As Quaker Oats

In 1901 American Cereal became the Quaker Oats Company, with sales of $16 million. Twenty years of growth followed, including a wartime peak of $123 million in sales in 1918. With the 1911 acquisition of Mother's Oats, Quaker owned half of all milling operations east of the Rocky Mountains. (The federal government filed a suit against the purchase, but eventually withdrew its last appeal in 1920, when national interest in trust-busting had faded.) An interest in finding a use

for discarded oat hulls led to the establishment of a chemical division in 1921. Although a profitable use for furfural (a chemical produced from oat hulls that has solvent and other properties) did not appear until World War II, postwar sales of the product would exceed oatmeal sales into the 1970s.

Also in 1921 the company weathered a grain-surplus crisis; dealers had been caught with an oversupply and prices fell rapidly, leading that year to the company's first reported loss. Stuart's eldest son John became president of Quaker the following year. John Stuart immediately changed Quaker's retail sales strategy to one of optimum, rather than maximum, sales. The growth of the grocery chains helped to encourage a system of fast turnover rather than bulk purchasing.

Early in the century Crowell and Stuart invested in foreign markets by establishing self-supporting overseas subsidiaries. These subsidiaries operated mills in Europe and sold oats in South America and Asia. Under John Stuart's company reorganization in 1922, foreign operations became a corporate division. Approximately 25 percent of Quaker's sales were derived abroad. During John Stuart's 34 years as CEO, the company increased its toehold on the growing market of ready-to-eat cereals with Puffed Wheat and Puffed Rice. Quaker further diversified its product line by purchasing name brands that were already established, such as Aunt Jemima pancake flour in 1925. Similarly, the company entered the pet food industry through the purchase of Ken-L-Ration in 1942. Internal attempts to develop a cat food failed, and the company eventually purchased Puss 'n Boots brand cat food in 1950.

In 1942 sales reached $90 million. Wartime demand for meat and eggs pumped new life into the sagging animal-feed division as well as boosting sales of the company's grains and prepared mixes. Quaker's furfural became important in the manufacture of synthetic rubber, and during the war Quaker built and ran a bomb-assembly plant for the government.

Postwar Growth and Diversification

In the years that followed World War II, Quaker's sales grew to $277 million generated by 200 different products, a broad product line requiring heavy promotion. John Stuart's younger brother, R. Douglas Stuart, studied under Crowell and assumed control of promotions when John Stuart became CEO. After World War II he adopted the then-radical policy of using more than one advertising agency. The Stuart brothers recognized that the grocery industry would continue to expand into pet foods, convenience products, and ready-to-eat cereals, and matched the company's product line and promotions accordingly.

The company's first outside manager, Donald B. Lourie, rose to CEO in 1953. Under Lourie, Quaker retained the atmosphere of a family company with personal leadership; the company needed external support, however, for its increasingly complex marketing decisions. National advertising for the Aunt Jemima brand came at a price of $100,000. The cost of introducing Cap'n Crunch in 1963 was $5 million.

For many food companies, the 1960s were a period of automatic growth as consumer demand for convenience increased and brand recognition grew. For Quaker, however, sales rose just 20 percent and profits only ten percent as long-term

<table>
<tr><td colspan="2">Key Dates:</td></tr>
<tr><td>1856:</td><td>Ferdinand Schumacher organizes the German Mills American Oatmeal Factory in Ohio.</td></tr>
<tr><td>1873:</td><td>Robert Stuart establishes an oatmeal mill in Iowa.</td></tr>
<tr><td>1877:</td><td>Henry Parsons Crowell—owner of the Quaker Mill in Ravenna, Ohio—becomes the first marketer to register a trademark for cereal: the Quaker symbol.</td></tr>
<tr><td>1886:</td><td>Schumacher, Stuart, and Crowell join forces as the Consolidated Oatmeal Company.</td></tr>
<tr><td>1888:</td><td>Seven of the largest American oat millers—including the Consolidated principals—unite as the American Cereal Company.</td></tr>
<tr><td>1899:</td><td>Schumacher loses control of American Cereal to Stuart and Crowell, who diversify the product line.</td></tr>
<tr><td>1901:</td><td>American Cereal changes its name to Quaker Oats Company; sales stand at $16 million.</td></tr>
<tr><td>1911:</td><td>Mother's Oats is acquired, giving Quaker ownership of half of all milling operations east of the Rocky Mountains.</td></tr>
<tr><td>1925:</td><td>The Aunt Jemima brand is acquired.</td></tr>
<tr><td>1942:</td><td>Company enters pet food industry through purchase of Ken-L-Ration brand.</td></tr>
<tr><td>1963:</td><td>The Cap'n Crunch cereal brand is introduced.</td></tr>
<tr><td>1969:</td><td>Fisher-Price Toy Company is acquired.</td></tr>
<tr><td>1979:</td><td>William D. Smithburg is named CEO; overall sales reach $2 billion.</td></tr>
<tr><td>1983:</td><td>Quaker acquires Stokely-Van Camp, maker of Gatorade sports drink.</td></tr>
<tr><td>1986:</td><td>Quaker acquires Golden Grain Macaroni Company, maker of Rice-A-Roni.</td></tr>
<tr><td>1991:</td><td>Fisher-Price is spun off.</td></tr>
<tr><td>1993:</td><td>Company acquires the Near East rice and pasta product brand.</td></tr>
<tr><td>1994:</td><td>Snapple Beverage Corporation is acquired for $1.7 billion.</td></tr>
<tr><td>1995:</td><td>U.S. and European pet food operations are divested.</td></tr>
<tr><td>1997:</td><td>Snapple is sold to Triarc Companies, Inc. for $300 million; Robert S. Morrison replaces Smithburg as CEO.</td></tr>
</table>

development absorbed earnings. Quaker expanded in the industry's fastest-growing areas: pet foods, convenience foods, and ready-to-eat cereals. By the end of the decade growth rates had increased, but not as much as hoped. Robert D. Stuart, Jr., became CEO in 1966. The decade's slow growth and a general corporate trend toward diversification prompted him to make acquisitions outside the food industry for the first time since 1942. Many of these acquisitions were eventually sold, but Fisher-Price Toy Company, purchased in 1969, was held for more than two decades and grew beyond expectations. Within ten years, it made up 25 percent of Quaker's total sales.

Late in 1970 Stuart restructured Quaker's organization around four decentralized businesses: grocery products, which now included cookies and candy; industrial and institutional foods, which contained the newly acquired Magic Pan restaurants; toys and recreational products; and international. Sales in 1968 had been frustratingly low at $500 million, but with

Stuart's acquisitions, the company reported $2 billion in sales by 1979.

Economic recession during the 1970s kept sales down. A second toy company, Louis Marx Toys, was purchased in 1972. During 1974 and 1975, Marx, which was purchased as a "recession-proof" company, drove earnings per share from $2.04 to $1.45. Magic Pan Restaurant's profits fell for four consecutive years. The chemical division reported a net loss of $7 million when a cheaper substitute for furfural came onto the market. This introduction took the company by surprise, as it expected earnings from that division to climb steadily.

Looking to expand its foreign market in grocery and pet foods, Quaker made seven acquisitions of foreign companies during the decade. But while the company focused on diversification, product development slipped. Between 1970 and 1978, only one new major product, 100 Percent Natural Cereal, was introduced. Shelf space in major grocery chains did not increase. Stuart had successfully lessened the company's dependence on grocery products, but profits also dropped, to a low of $31 million in 1975.

By the end of the decade, however, a turnaround was in sight. Quaker's least profitable areas were limited to its smallest divisions, and since the entire industrial and restaurant industries had been weakening, the company was already preparing to divest its holdings in that field.

William D. Smithburg replaced Stuart as CEO in late 1979. Smithburg aggressively increased Quaker's sales force and advertising budget, improvements that were badly needed. The company also refocused on its core food business. Quaker had two new successes as the 1980s dawned: Ken-L-Ration's Tender Chunks became the second best-selling dog food in its first year, and Corn Bran had a commendable 1.2 percent share of the ready-to-eat cereal market. In addition, Fisher-Price sales had increased tenfold since 1969, to $300 million. Quaker planned to expand the division by building plants in Europe, raising its target age group, and lowering unit selling prices.

By 1979 Quaker had a return on invested capital of 12.3 percent—higher than the industry average, but well below competitor Kellogg's 19.4 percent. The company still needed to divest its interests in companies that absorbed profits.

Gatorade and Golden Grain Come Aboard in the 1980s

In the first half of the decade, Quaker sold Burry, a cookie maker; Needlecraft; Magic Pan restaurants; its Mexican toy operations; and its chemical division. During the same period, the company made several acquisitions. Like many food companies at the time, Quaker entered specialty retailing, with such purchases as Jos. A. Bank Clothiers, the Brookstone mail-order company, and Eyelab, all purchased in 1981; all would be sold in late 1986. By then, Smithburg had decided that the price for retail chains was inflated and that Quaker could get a better return on food. He proved himself right. By 1987 Quaker's return on shareholder equity matched Kellogg's. Quaker confirmed its new path with its 1983 acquisition of Stokely-Van Camp, the maker of Gatorade sports drink and Van Camp pork and beans. By expanding Gatorade's geographic market, Quaker made the drink its top seller in 1987.

Quaker's revival came about through the strong potential of its low-cost acquisitions. Golden Grain Macaroni Company, the maker of Rice-A-Roni, gave the company a base to expand further into prepared foods. Anderson Clayton & Company, purchased in late 1986, gave Quaker a 15 percent share of the pet-food market with its Gaines brand, effectively challenging Ralston Purina's lead in that market.

With the purchase of Anderson Clayton, financed by the sale of its unwanted divisions, Smithburg managed to strengthen Quaker's position in existing markets and improve its product mix without overloading the company with specialty products. Products with leading market shares made up 75 percent of 1987 sales and over half came from brands that Quaker had not owned six years earlier.

The late 1980s tempered that success, however. Pet food sales were flat throughout the industry, and Quaker took $112 million in charges related to its recently expanded pet division. The corporation was a rumored takeover candidate because of its high volume of shares outstanding and its strong branded products. In response, the company announced in April 1989 that it would repurchase seven million of its nearly 80 million outstanding shares, and that July, Smithburg reassigned some managerial duties. The company also decreased its advertising and marketing expenses.

Refocusing on Food and Beverages in the 1990s

Despite some setbacks, Quaker entered the 1990s with 14 years of unbroken sales growth. The company concentrated on three major divisions: American and Canadian grocery products; international grocery products; and Fisher-Price toys. Still, Quaker continued to streamline its operations into the early 1990s, spinning off Fisher-Price Toys in 1991, a move which made Quaker solely a packaged-food company for the first time in over 20 years. Sales that year hit a record $5.5 billion, and over 70 percent of the products in Quaker's portfolio held either the first- or second-share position in their segments. Quaker's international sales continued to be a significant percentage of the company's total, and in 1991, the company restructured both its European and Latin American operations to focus marketing on a continental, as opposed to a country-by-country, basis.

As it divested itself of its nongrocery products, Quaker continued to expand its packaged foods portfolio. Its concentration was on healthful food brands, such as Near East rice and pasta products, Chico-San rice cakes, and Petrofsky's bagels, all acquired in 1993. The buying spree continued through 1994 and into 1995 with the acquisitions of Proof & Bake frozen bagels, Maryland Club coffee, Arnie's Bagelicious Bagels, and Nile Spice Foods, a maker of dried soups, pasta, and beans.

Quaker's largest acquisition was its 1994 purchase of Snapple Beverage Corporation, a maker of ready-to-drink juice beverages and teas, for $1.7 billion. Some industry experts considered the price too high for this upstart company with annual sales just below $1 billion, but the purchase boosted Quaker's share of the non-alcoholic beverage market signifi-

cantly. With combined sales of over $2 billion, Quaker was now the nation's third largest producer of non-alcoholic beverages.

On the international front, Quaker continued its aggressive Gatorade marketing drive, and by 1994 the beverage was available in 25 countries across Latin America, Asia, and Europe. The company also strengthened its foothold in the Latin American food products market with the 1994 acquisition of Adria Produtos Alimenticios, Ltd., Brazil's top pasta manufacturer. Although much of Quaker's expansion was through acquisitions, the company also sought to grow its products portfolio internally, especially in its historically strong rice and grains category. Between 1992 and 1995, volume in that category tripled with the addition of new products such as Quaker chewy granola bars and flavored rice cakes. Companywide sales in 1994 hit $5.95 billion, a record high for the 19th consecutive year.

Despite its record sales figures, Quaker's overall financial outlook was not so bright as it entered 1995. Due to the acquisition of Snapple, Quaker held a high debt to total capitalization ratio and felt it necessary to divest itself of a number of businesses in early 1995. In March, H.J. Heinz Company acquired Quaker's U.S. and Canadian pet foods operations for $725 million. The following month, Quaker's European pet foods division was sold to Dalgety PLC for $700 million. Other 1995 divestitures included a Mexican chocolates business and the Wolf/VanCamps bean and chili businesses. The selloff continued in 1996 with the sale of the company's U.S. and Canadian frozen food business to Van de Kamp's for $185.8 million.

While Quaker worked to pay down debt incurred with the Snapple acquisition, it also almost immediately found that it had paid dearly for a faltering brand. In hindsight, it became clear that Quaker had bought Snapple just as the brand reached its peak. Imitators were quick to enter the tea drink market, including Arizona Iced Tea, Mystic, and Nantucket Nectars. Even worse, soft drink giants Coca-Cola Company and PepsiCo, Inc. entered the sector through alliances with Nestea and Lipton, respectively. By the end of 1996 Lipton had claimed 33 percent of the market and Nestea 18 percent, while Snapple was left with only a 15 percent share. In addition to the increased competition, Snapple was also hurt by distribution problems and failed marketing campaigns.

By early 1997 Quaker Oats had suffered Snapple-related losses and charges of more than $100 million. Unable to turn the brand around, and facing pressure from angry shareholders, Quaker sold Snapple to Triarc Companies, Inc., owner of RC Cola and the Arby's restaurant chain, for $300 million. It also took a $1.4 billion pretax charge—essentially the difference between the purchase and selling prices. This led to a net loss for the year of $930.9 million. The Snapple debacle also led to the departure of Smithburg, who was replaced as chairman, president, and CEO by Robert S. Morrison, a former head of Kraft Foods' North American operations, in October 1997.

Almost immediately, Morrison took several decisive measures. Feeling that for a relatively small food company Quaker had an overall complex management structure, Morrison eliminated an entire layer of top management then elevated ten managers to head the company's main brands, with each reporting directly to the new CEO. He also initiated a number of restructuring moves, including a consolidation of U.S. sales operations, a streamlining of the worldwide supply chain, and the realigning of Quaker's overseas units. These and other moves led to $65 million in savings during 1998. Morrison also took a hard-line approach to the company's brand portfolio, jettisoning those product lines identified as underperforming. Four such brands were sold during 1998 for a total of $192.7 million: Ardmore Farms juice, Continental Coffee, Nile Spice, and Liqui-Dri foodservice biscuits and mixes. The sale of the troubled Adria pasta brand followed in 1999.

While some analysts predicted that Morrison was getting Quaker Oats in shape for a sale, such a turn of events was not in the immediate offing. Morrison planned to center the company around the fast-growing Gatorade brand, which accounted for about 38 percent of overall sales in 1999, a figure the company expected to increase to more than 50 percent by about 2004. Approaching the turn of the millennium, Quaker Oats appeared to be a company on the rebound, with net income increasing from $284.5 million in 1998 to $455 million in 1999. In late 1999 the company announced a ten percent workforce reduction, equivalent to about 1,400 employees, as part of a cost-saving plan centering around Quaker's slower growing cereal operations. At the same time the company said it would increase production capacity for Gatorade through a $230–$245 million expansion program. In addition, as part of revitalized new product development initiatives, Quaker Oats in early 2000 was planning the introductions of a Gatorade-branded bottled water called Propel (which included some of the beneficial nutrients featured in Gatorade but with one-fifth the calories), Gatorade energy bars, and a juice drink dubbed Torq, which was heavier in carbohydrates and calories than Gatorade.

Principal Subsidiaries

The Gatorade Company; Gatorade Puerto Rico Company; Golden Grain Company; Grocery International Holdings, Inc.; QO Coffee Holdings Inc.; Quaker Oats Asia, Inc.; Quaker Oats Europe, Inc.; Quaker Oats Holdings, Inc.; Quaker Oats Music, Inc.; Quaker Oats Philippines, Inc.; Quaker South Africa, Inc.; Quaker Spain, Inc.; Stokely-Van Camp, Inc.; SVC Equipment Company; SVC Latin America, Inc.; SVC Latin America, LLC.

Principal Competitors

Borden, Inc.; Campbell Soup Company; The Coca-Cola Company; ConAgra, Inc.; ERLY Industries Inc.; General Mills, Inc.; The Hain Food Group, Inc.; H.J. Heinz Company; International Home Foods, Inc.; Kellogg Company; Kraft Foods, Inc.; Malt-O-Meal Company; Mars, Inc.; McKee Foods Corporation; Nabisco Holdings Corp.; Nestlé S.A.; PepsiCo, Inc.; Ralcorp Holdings, Inc.; Unilever plc.

Further Reading

Balu, Rekha, "Like Oatmeal, Morrison Proves Good for Quaker," *Wall Street Journal,* October 27, 1998, p. B1.

"A Big Spender—That's What Quaker Oats Has Become, and It Should Pay Off," *Barron's,* January 7, 1985, pp. 45+.

Burns, Greg, "Crunch Time at Quaker Oats," *Business Week,* September 23, 1996, p. 70.

——, "Will Quaker Get the Recipe Right?," *Business Week,* February 5, 1996, p. 140.

Campbell, Hannah, "The Story of Quaker Oats," *Country Living,* December 1988, p. 146.

Day, Richard Ellsworth, *Breakfast Table Autocrat: The Life Story of Henry Parsons Crowell,* Chicago: Moody Press, 1946, 317 p.

Dreyfack, Kenneth, "Quaker Is Feeling Its Oats Again," *Business Week,* September 22, 1986, pp. 80+.

Franz, Julie, "Quaker Adapts: Smithburg Puts His Brand on Company," *Advertising Age,* January 19, 1987, pp. 3+.

——, "Quaker Strategy Is to Buy Small, Think Big," *Advertising Age,* June 23, 1986, pp. 6+.

Gibson, Richard, "At Quaker Oats, Snapple Is Leaving a Bad Aftertaste," *Wall Street Journal,* August 7, 1995, p. B4.

——, "Quaker Oats Sets Broad Realignment, Takes Charge of As Much As $130 Million," *Wall Street Journal,* May 17, 1994, p. A2.

——, "Quaker Oats to Spin Off Fisher-Price Unit," *Wall Street Journal,* April 25, 1990, p. A4.

Helliker, Kevin, "Gatorade Set to Stir the (Bottled) Waters with 'Propel'," *Wall Street Journal,* December 10, 1999, p. B4.

Leonhardt, David, "Stirring Things Up at Quaker Oats," *Business Week,* March 30, 1998, p. 42.

Manring, M.M., *Slave in a Box: The Strange Career of Aunt Jemima,* Charlottesville: University Press of Virginia, 1998, 210 p.

Marquette, Arthur F., *Brands, Trademarks and Good Will: The Story of the Quaker Oats Company,* New York: McGraw-Hill, 1967, 274 p.

McCarthy, Michael J., "Quaker Oats Posts $1.11 Billion Quarterly Loss," *Wall Street Journal,* April 24, 1997, p. A3.

——, "Quaker Oats to Buy Snapple for $1.7 Billion," *Wall Street Journal,* November 3, 1994, p. A3.

McCarthy, Michael J., Richard Gibson, and Nikhil Deogun, "Quaker to Sell Snapple for $300 Million," *Wall Street Journal,* March 28, 1997, p. A3.

McManus, John, "Quaker Matrix Management Models for Turbulent Future," *Brandweek,* May 23, 1993, p. 16.

Moukheiber, Zina, "He Who Laughs Last," *Forbes,* January 1, 1996, p. 42.

Murray, Matt, and Christina Duff, "Heinz Agrees to Acquire Quaker Oats' North American Pet-Food Operations," *Wall Street Journal,* February 7, 1995, p. A3.

Palmeri, Christopher, "Opportunities Lost," *Forbes,* July 20, 1992, pp. 70+.

Rockford: The Pet Food Story, 1923–1987, Rockford, Ill.: Rockford Pet Foods Division, Quaker Oats Company, 1987, 98 p.

Saporito, Bill, "How Quaker Oats Got Rolled," *Fortune,* October 8, 1990, pp. 129+.

Thackray, John, "The Crunch at Quaker," *Management Today,* October 1983, pp. 82+.

Thornton, Harrison John, *The History of the Quaker Oats Company,* Chicago: University of Chicago Press, 1933, 279 p.

Upbin, Bruce, "Breaking a Sweat: Streaking Past the Snapple Debacle and with a New Guy at the Helm, Quaker Oats Is a Growth Company Again," *Forbes,* December 27, 1999, p. 68.

Vogel, Jason, "How Sweet It Isn't: Snapple Shareholders Made a Killing Selling Out to Quaker. What about Quaker Shareholders?," *Financial World,* July 4, 1995, p. 36.

Whitford, David, "The Gatorade Mystique," *Fortune,* November 23, 1998, pp. 44+.

—updated by Maura Troester
and David E. Salamie

Radio Flyer Inc.

6515 Grand Avenue
Chicago, Illinois 60707
U.S.A.
Telephone: (773) 637-7100
Toll Free: (800) 621-7613
Fax: (773) 637-8874
Web site: http://www.radioflyer.com

Private Company
Incorporated: 1923 as Liberty Coaster Wagon Company
Employees: 100
Sales: $26.5 million (1998 est.)
NAIC: 339932 Game, Toy, and Children's Vehicle
   Manufacturing

Radio Flyer Inc. is the world's leading manufacturer of children's toy wagons. Its principal product is an icon of American childhood, the classic little red wagon. The company is named after its most famous model, the Radio Flyer, a much-beloved article depicted in scores of advertisements and films. Although other companies, too, make red wagons, Radio Flyer has trademarked the shape of its classic model, and the exact red paint the company uses is a formula known only to itself. In addition to classic steel wagons, Radio Flyer also manufactures wooden and plastic wagons. The company makes wagons in varying sizes as well, including products sized for stuffed animals, and miniatures used as key chains. In total the company makes more than 50 wagon models. Radio Flyer also manufactures a line of wagon accessories such as seats, umbrellas, cooler packs, and handle extensions. Though a small company, Radio Flyer dominates the wagon industry, controlling approximately 70 percent of the U.S. market.

Early Years

Radio Flyer Inc. was founded by Italian immigrant Antonio Pasin. Pasin's family had been fine woodworkers for generations, specializing in furniture and cabinetry. Pasin grew up working in wood as well. But he longed to leave his small town outside of Venice and make a new start in the United States. His family backed his plan, selling their mule to raise money for Antonio's ticket. He arrived in Chicago in 1914. Here he hoped to work as a cabinetmaker, but at first he could only find unskilled work, beginning as a water boy for a crew of sewer diggers. Eventually Pasin found a job that used his woodworking skills, finishing pianos in a piano factory. By the time he had been in the United States for three years, he had saved enough to buy his own woodworking tools and to rent one room to use as a shop. In the evenings, Pasin worked alone, crafting children's wooden wagons. During the day, he walked the streets of Chicago peddling his samples. Pasin worked tirelessly and alone until 1923, when his wagon business had picked up enough that he was able to hire helpers. He incorporated his business as the Liberty Coaster Wagon Company, fondly naming it after the Statue of Liberty that had greeted him when he arrived in his new country.

Mass Production in the 1930s

Although Pasin's background was in woodworking, he soon became enamored of a new technology, metal stamping. Henry Ford had used metal stamping in his automobile factories, where huge machines stamped identical pieces out of sheets of steel. Pasin believed the automotive method could be used for his wagons, enabling him to mass-produce a cheap, well-built product. By the late 1920s, Pasin had refitted his factory for metal stamping, and Liberty Coaster began putting out stamped steel wagons. Pasin named a 1927 model the ''Radio Flyer,'' capturing the excitement of the burgeoning radio industry. In 1930, Liberty Coaster changed its name to the Radio Steel & Manufacturing Company. This new name made note of both the new metal technology and the popular Radio Flyer model.

Pasin consciously studied Ford's factory method. His aim was not only to adapt metal stamping to toy wagons, but to produce a quality product along efficient lines. Radio Steel grew to be a major employer, putting out at least 1,500 wagons a day in the 1930s. Even though this was the depth of the Great Depression, Pasin provided steady work to scores of people, mostly Italian-Americans like himself. The motto for Radio Steel's wagons was ''For every boy. For every girl.'' This rang true, as the wagon was a basic toy that provided years of fun for

Company Perspectives:

Located on Chicago's Far West Side, Radio Flyer is the world's leading wagon maker, manufacturing high-quality products for children since 1917. The makers of the original little red wagon, Radio Flyer is the only company to produce plastic, steel and wood wagons. Radio Flyer is one of the oldest remaining national toy companies still owned and operated by the founding family.

all kinds of kids, not a fad product or something that appealed only to a niche group. Radio Steel churned out its thousands of identical red wagons just like Ford had produced the Model T, and Pasin won for himself the nickname "Little Ford."

Already by the year 1930, Radio Steel was the world's largest producer of children's coaster wagons, and it set the standard for what a wagon should look like. Despite the Depression, which idled many other industries, Radio Steel worked at full capacity throughout the 1930s. Although the company made its mark with the classic, simple red coaster wagon, it also made more sophisticated products, such as the Streak-O-Lite of 1934, a wagon with control dials and working headlights. Another popular 1930s model was the Zep, which imitated the streamlined styling of the day's fancy automobiles. Pasin passed on his success to his workers, initiating generous programs such as English language tutoring within the factory. He also provided interest-free loans to his workers so they could build houses, contributing to the stability of the mostly Italian neighborhood around the factory on Chicago's West Side.

World War II and Beyond

When the United States entered World War II, many industries converted to making wartime products. Radio Steel halted its production of wagons to manufacture so-called blitz cans. These were five-gallon containers used for either fuel or water, mounted on tanks, trucks, and jeeps. Radio Steel's blitz cans saw service in Europe, the Pacific, and Africa.

After the war, the factory went back to making wagons and developed several new models in tune with the times. In the era of the station wagon, Radio Steel began producing its Radio Rancher Convertible, a high-capacity wagon with removable steel stake sides. Beginning in 1957, the company branched out, for the first time making garden carts. These were not toys, but metal carts designed to haul yard waste, perhaps a shrewd line extension in view of the growth of suburbia and suburban gardens. Soon the company also began making wheelbarrows.

Yet the classic little red wagon continued to be the company's mainstay. Radio Steel continued production unabated, even though the toy industry in the United States began to change. In the 1970s, the industry consolidated, with many small, private firms being bought out by bigger competitors. These large firms, including Mattel and Hasbro, made inroads into the wagon market with branded products of their own. By the 1980s, the market had swayed away from simple, classic toys to increasingly high-tech items like video games. Big toy companies also poured money into faddish toys and toys that could be marketed through

licensing tie-ins to movies and television shows. Despite these developments, Radio Steel plugged away in much the same way it always had. In 1977, the company improved its core product with several patented safety features. These included a new ball joint between the wagon handle and the undercarriage in which fingers could not get pinched, and a controlled turning radius to prevent accidental tipping. It also deployed new toys, such as the Fireball 2000, a 1970s children's car. The company also made bicycles and tricycles.

Changes in the 1990s

In 1987, Radio Steel & Manufacturing changed its name for a third time, to Radio Flyer Inc. This name immediately brought to mind its most popular product. By this time, the company was a distinct anomaly in the U.S. toy industry, because it had remained privately owned and was still run by the family of its founder. Mario Pasin had succeeded his father Antonio, and Mario's sons Robert and Paul also were involved in the firm. Larger companies had made competitive inroads in the wagon business. One competitor was Rubbermaid, mostly known for its kitchenware, but which produced a line of plastic wagons through its Little Tikes division. In the 1990s, Radio Flyer worked to expand its product line and step up its marketing to maintain its market share. It used the Radio Flyer name on toy bicycles, such as the Totally Rad Flyer Bicycle. Its name received wide press in 1992 with the release of a movie called "Radio Flyer," the story of the imaginary journeys of two boys in their Radio Flyer wagon. The wagon image also was used extensively in advertising, and the Radio Flyer was featured in advertisement campaigns by car makers Porsche and Chevrolet and in ads for the insurance company Northwestern Mutual Life.

In 1996, Antonio Pasin's grandsons Robert and Paul took over management of the company from their father, with Robert succeeding as president and Paul as executive vice-president. The third generation of the Pasin family moved aggressively to build new types of wagons. In addition to classic red tricycles and steel wagons of various sizes, the company put out plastic wagons with updated designs. In 1996, Radio Flyer introduced the Voyager wagon and the Trailblazer, two plastic wagons that retained the classic red color but were otherwise quite different from the company's standard product. The trailblazer was a very sturdy wagon, ten percent larger than competitors' similar models, but with unique features that made it easy and compact to store. The Voyager was a wagon shaped more like a little car, with an asymmetrical body. It had two seats, one rear- and one front-facing, accessed by a hinged side door. The Voyager also featured a built-in storage compartment and an arched canopy roof. Radio Flyer acted to protect its new wagon features with patents. In 1996 Little Tikes, the wagon division of Rubbermaid, challenged a patent issued to Radio Flyer for a storage system it used. Both companies had wagons with similar storage systems, but only Radio Flyer held a patent. In all, Radio Flyer held 30 patents on various aspects of wagon design, and it had even trademarked the shape of its classic Radio Flyer.

In 1997, Radio Flyer marked 80 years in the wagon business. For a promotional celebration, the company produced what it billed as the "World's Largest Wagon," a 27-foot-long, 15,000-pound behemoth that then visited cities across the United States. Radio Flyer stepped up its marketing at this time. In 1999 it

---

Key Dates:

1917: Italian immigrant Antonio Pasin begins producing and selling children's wooden wagons in Chicago.
1923: Pasin founds the Liberty Coaster Wagon Company.
1930: Company is renamed Radio Steel & Manufacturing.
1941: Radio Steel converts to wartime manufacturing.
1957: Firm extends product lines beyond toys, to garden carts.
1987: Radio Steel changes name again, to Radio Flyer Inc.
1994: Company begins producing new line of plastic wagons.

---

introduced a new model plastic wagon, which it called "the most innovative wagon ever created." This was its Quad Shock, a plastic vehicle shaped much like the classic Radio Flyer, but mounted on steel wheels served with four heavy-duty shock absorbers. The company followed the Quad Shock with a Radio Flyer Sport Utility Wagon, capitalizing on the popularity of the Sport Utility Vehicle among suburban families. Radio Flyer also entered licensing agreements with other toymakers. In partnership with Enesco, it produced a series of Christmas ornaments featuring teddy bears and other animals seated in Radio Flyer wagons. It made Radio Flyer train cars, key chains, and refrigerator magnets, and in partnership with Danbury Mint, it produced miniature wagons to go with that company's line of collectible porcelain dolls. Radio Flyer also worked with Mattel, one of the two largest American toy companies, licensing its name on the popular Hot Wheels brand of toy cars to make what appeared to be a souped-up race car-type wagon. Other licensed products included a toy Radio Flyer wagon that held a stuffed toy of the beloved Curious George monkey, and another similar toy with a Gund brand stuffed bear.

Aware that the company was a rarity in the fiercely competitive toy business, the company announced at the 2000 International Toy Fair that it would step up its licensing plans to spread its well-known brand name. The company had plans in 2000 to build two new model tricycles, and it conceded that it was considering launching a series of children's books. President Robert Pasin remarked in a February 15, 2000 interview in the *Chicago Tribune* that the company had stayed true to its original product line while nevertheless responding to changing tastes. He said: "When consumers wanted big air tires on their wagons, we gave it to them. When they wanted plastic wagons with cup holders, we produced that. We've continued to innovate, while staying close to the consumer." Although still a relatively small company, Radio Flyer had managed to maintain its position since 1930 as the world's largest producer of children's toy wagons. In spite of increased competition, the company still held an estimated 70 percent of the wagon market as of the year 2000. Under the leadership of the third generation of the Pasin family, the company seemed ready to adapt to further challenges.

Principal Competitors

Rubbermaid Incorporated; Mattel, Inc.

Further Reading

Chiem, Phat X., "Blazing a New Wagon Trail," *Chicago Tribune,* February 15, 2000, pp. B1, B4.
Frankston, Janet, "Radio Flyer Inc., Little Tikes Co. in Toy Patent Dispute," *Knight-Ridder/Tribune Business News,* August 1, 1996, p. 8010045.
Neville, Lee, "Toy Story," *U.S. News & World Report,* October 20, 1997, p. 12.
"Product Recalls," *Consumers' Research Magazine,* November 1992, p. 36.
"Radio Flyer Rolls Out New Wagons," *Playthings,* July 1996, p. 46.

—A. Woodward

RCM Technologies, Inc.

2500 McClellan Avenue, Suite 350
Pennsauken, New Jersey 08109-4613
U.S.A.
Telephone: (856) 486-1777
Fax: (856) 488-8833
Web site: http://www.rcmt.com

Public Company
Incorporated: 1971 as RCM Corporation
Employees: 4,550
Sales: $313.4 million (1999)
Stock Exchanges: NASDAQ Pacific
Ticker Symbol: RCMT
NAIC: 541330 Engineering Services; 541411 Custom
Computer Programming Services; 541512 Computer
Systems Design Services; 541513 Computer Facilities
Management Services; 541519 Other Computer
Related Services; 561310 Employment Placement
Agencies; 561320 Temporary Help Services

RCM Technologies, Inc. provides information technology (IT) and professional engineering services through consultation, project management, and temporary staffing. RCM employee skills in IT include software development, network communications, systems analysis and design, database design, client/server development, web-based technologies, systems integration, and technical support. Professional engineering services involve analysis, design, and drafting and encompass mechanical, chemical, environmental, aeronautical, architectural, civil/structural, electrical, and electronic engineering, as well as field services. RCM seeks out government contracts in most areas of its technical capacities. The company also offers temporary staffing for light industrial, clerical, and office positions, including specialty healthcare. With more than 65 offices in the United States and Canada RCM promotes itself as ''The Source of Smart Solutions.''

A Variant Early History

RCM Technologies began as an environmental technology company through the consolidation of small engineering firms in Los Angeles. The original entity, RCM Corporation, was formed in 1971 for the purpose of developing pollution control systems, such as the patented Clean Coal Technology Process. Preliminary testing of the process revealed that 99 percent of sulfur dioxide (SO_2) could be cleaned from the exhaust gases generated by power stations burning coal with a high sulfur content. RCM's trademarked Novaspar compound assisted removal of impurities from molten steel. The economic difficulties of the steel industry and later importation of cheap, foreign steel led RCM to halt research and development activities related to Novaspar in the early 1980s.

An initial public offering of stock in 1981 enabled RCM to broaden the company's services to temporary staffing of professional engineers and technical personnel. RCM Corporation adopted the name RCM Technologies to reflect the change in July 1981 and completed the acquisition of Intertec Design, Inc., of Camden, New Jersey, a month later. Through Intertec, RCM provided engineering, design, drafting, and other types of technical personnel to the aerospace, electronics, energy, chemical, and marine industries. With 25,000 resumés on file, Intertec engaged individuals at an hourly rate for contracts that averaged nine months, ranging from four months to over three years.

Intertec became the center of revenue growth as sales at RCM increased from under $1 million in 1980 to $6.7 million in 1982. More than 70 percent of revenues came from staffing government-related projects. Intertec had been providing engineers and technicians to the Sikorsky Aircraft Division of United Technologies since 1978. In the early 1980s the value of similar contracts increased along with government spending on national defense. In 1986 more than 56 percent of RCM's revenues came from United Technologies, which designed and built the Blackhawk and Seahawk helicopters for the U.S. military through Sikorsky Aircraft. In 1983 a $1.2 million contract involved technical writing services for revision of specification manuals and drawing of maintenance manuals. Contracts with Lockheed Aircraft also contributed significantly to revenues, at 15 percent in 1984 and 19.9 percent in 1985, with total RCM revenues at $14 million and $17.9 million, respectively.

Other government-related revenues derived from the U.S. Navy. Intertec Marine Corporation (IMC) formed in 1982 to provide ship repair technicians to the U.S. Navy, which had

---

Company Perspectives:

RCM's mission is to be in a leadership position in its industry by providing responsive, high-quality, reliable, technologically advanced, cost-effective services that enable our customers to meet their business objectives, allow RCM to enhance shareholder value, and offer its employees the opportunity to realize their professional and personal goals. We support this mission with dedication, resources, and expertise.

---

begun a major fleet overhaul and expansion. IMC opened a facility in Norfolk, Virginia, near the Navy's major marine facilities, where the company also provided technical personnel for the U.S. Coast Guard and foreign military contracts. In 1983 the company employed 275 ship repair technicians, but losses led RCM to discontinue IMC in 1984.

RCM formed the Marine and Mechanical Services Corporation (MMS) in 1983 to provide technicians for commercial marine operators as well as for asbestos removal and re-insulation. As ship repair service contracts ended in 1985, asbestos removal became the subsidiary's focus of operations. MMS obtained contracts from the U.S. Navy, the Veterans Administration, school districts in Pennsylvania and New Jersey, the Atlantic City Improvement Authority, and others. With 75 contracts valued at more than $2.5 million, MMS employed between 70 and 100 people, providing the government-required five-day training. By 1987 MMS began to reject business that did not offer an adequate markup over cost, however, and RCM discontinued operations after the fulfillment of active contracts in 1989.

Research and development of RCM's flue gas desulfurization process continued with testing at a demonstration facility completed in Camden, New Jersey, in 1985. The test model involved a modified coal-fired boiler with a heating capacity of two million BTUs per hour and the necessary emission control equipment including SO_2 detector tubes. RCM conducted the tests in accordance with the U.S. Environmental Protection Agency standards, and an independent research laboratory, the Franklin Research Center of Philadelphia, confirmed the results in February 1987.

The first test examined methodology; a second test involved a chemical analysis of sample gases taken from the entrance and exit of the test chamber and from the test stack. Chemical analysis showed that gas entering the system contained 160 parts per million of SO_2, while gas exiting the system contained 0.25 parts per billion, a 99 percent removal rate. Similar tests in June 1987 employed nitrogen dioxide (NO_2) detector tubes and found that the process removed 70 to 99 percent of NO_2 from emissions. RCM filed a patent application as tests indicated enhancements to the basic patent.

As the general public became more aware of the problems of acid rain, caused by high levels of SO_2 and NO_2 in the air, RCM viewed the technology as a potentially low-cost, efficient remedy. The best technology available to the electric utility industry involved costly equipment and proved insufficient for coal with

a high sulfur content. In addition, the unique dry process eliminated land and water pollution—the sludge—generated from wet processes. In anticipation of stricter clean air regulations, RCM formed a new subsidiary in 1989, RCM Industries Corporation, to handle the commercial aspects of the new technology. The next stage involved building equipment for commercial use on a small scale.

Focusing on Commercial Staffing: 1990s

In the late 1980s the focus of operations at RCM began to shift away from government-related technical services to temporary staffing services as well as from engineering and technical services to commercial enterprises. Through a new division of Intertec, RCM expanded its services to temporary staffing for office, computer, retail, and manufacturing positions. In 1987 the company acquired small temporary agencies and renamed them IDI Temps. IDI's four offices in the Los Angeles area generated $2.5 million in revenues the first year in operation. By 1990 IDI grew to $11.8 million in revenues through the employment of 4,396 temporary personnel serving 835 clients. IDI clients included Kmart, Saks Fifth Avenue, Honeywell, IBM, Westinghouse, Columbia Pictures, Reebok International, Sony, Marriott, Sunkist, and other large corporations.

RCM diversified for economic stability and necessity as the federal government's reduction of defense-related spending motivated the shift toward commercial staffing services. By 1991 only 25 percent of RCM's revenues originated with contracts to businesses serving government needs, the amount equal to its business from United Technologies. The federal government had terminated the Blackhawk and Seahawk Helicopter program, but affected companies gained some reprieve with the 1991 Light Helicopter program. Indicative of the shift toward commercial staffing, contracts with Dow Corning, of Midland, Michigan, accounted for 12.9 percent of RCM revenues in 1985, but comprised 28 percent by the early 1990s. Offices in Milford, Connecticut; Midland, Michigan; Camden, New Jersey; Louisville, Kentucky; and five offices in the greater Los Angeles area engaged technical and engineering personnel on state and local government projects as well as commercial projects.

The economic recession brought about by reduction in government spending adversely affected overall business. Revenues at IDI Temps fell to $9.2 million, with 683 clients, in 1991, resulting in the closure of two offices. As insurance premiums skyrocketed to 168 percent, the company dissolved business relationships with clients found to have filed excessive worker compensation claims. IDI rebounded in 1992 with a $5 million contract. In the area of engineering staffing services, RCM sought to remain competitive by maintaining up-to-date skills and invested in equipment with capabilities for IBM's new Computer-Aided Design drafting system.

With a newly elected board of directors and new management, including Leon Kopyt as president, RCM sought to reshape company operations. RCM endured net losses through most of the 1980s and RCM Industries continued to absorb operating profits, with more than $600,000 spent on research and development each year since 1985. RCM employed the United Engineers and Constructors to conduct a comprehensive

Key Dates:

1971: Company incorporates.
1981: Expands into engineering and technical temporary staffing.
1987: Forms IDI Temps.
1990: Federal cuts in defense spending spur diversification.
1992: Clean air technology program is terminated.
1996: Growth through acquisition strategy is accelerated.
1998: Company integrates subsidiaries under RCM Technologies name.
2000: Wireless business solutions unit is established.

review of the clean air technology in 1992. The report stated that the process was not technically feasible or commercially viable on a large scale, so the board of directors voted to cease operations immediately. At the suggestion of Kopyt, RCM repositioned itself for entrance into professional staffing services for the growing computer and electronics industries. In addition to providing stability for a company now reliant on three clients for 75 percent of revenues, diversification into Information Technology (IT) offered a higher profit margin and higher growth potential.

Coming of Age in the Mid-1990s with Information Technology

RCM pursued its goal of expansion into IT staffing and services with existing resources as well as through acquisition. The company's strategy involved the purchase of several small engineering and IT staffing services with annual revenues from $5 million to $30 million. These companies were too small to become public entities, but wanted to grow. In addition, large competitors tended to ignore small companies as targets for acquisition, so RCM had less competition in pursuing acquisitions. This strategy enabled RCM to expand geographically with companies small enough to integrate easily into its corporate structure. RCM completed its first acquisition in December 1994 with Great Lakes Design, a professional engineering firm based in Grand Haven, Michigan, which accrued $3.9 million in annual revenues; RCM purchased the company for $200,000.

The two transactions that followed involved mergers with much larger companies. RCM merged with Cataract, Inc., a professional engineering company in Newtown, Pennsylvania, for $3.2 million in cash and stock and gained potentially $20.4 million in annual revenues through seven office locations. Cataract merged with RCM and then formed a new legal subsidiary, also named Cataract. In February 1996 RCM merged with The Consortium in a $6.5 million stock transaction. The Fairfield, New Jersey company operated five offices and counted 700 temporary employees, including general staffing, IT staffing, and staffing for the healthcare industry. The Consortium generated $26 million in revenues in 1995.

RCM experienced a realignment in shareholder ownership as two new large shareholders provided financial capital for further acquisitions. Limeport Investment LLC acquired 1.3

million shares off the open market and Heartland Advisors, Inc. acquired 1.4 million shares, together providing more than $2 million in capital. To attract more investors and bring the company's stock value in line with actual assets, RCM applied to the Securities and Exchange Commission for a 5-to-1 reverse stock split. RCM's stock valued at 0.875 cents per share in February 1996; the reversal changed the value to nearly $5 per share.

With the seven acquisitions that followed in 1996 and 1997, RCM expanded primarily into IT staffing services and geographic expansion occurred primarily in the East and the upper Midwest. Most companies acquired generated less than $10 million in annual revenues, with the exception of Camelot Contractors Limited of Manchester, New Hampshire, which garnered $16.2 million in 1996. The January 1997 acquisition of Programming Alternatives of Minnesota, Inc. yielded RCM a staff of IT consultants with crucial client-server skills. In addition, the acquisition of Programming Resources Unlimited, Inc. of Philadelphia brought such high-profile clients as CIGNA and Core States Bank.

Supported by a $50 million stock offering, expansion accelerated in 1998 with the acquisition of ten IT staffing and service companies in the East, upper Midwest, and California. Prominent acquisitions included Global Technology Solutions, Inc. of Sacramento, which provided IT personnel to large corporations, such as IBM, Bank of America, Walt Disney, Hewlett-Packard, and the State of California. Software Analysis & Management, Inc. of Orange, California, provided specialized IT services in software and system engineering through ten offices nationwide. That company's $20 million in revenues stemmed from customers in aerospace, satellite communications, and defense, including ballistic missiles.

RCM's strategy of growth entailed certain risks, which the company controlled through its agreements with new subsidiaries. RCM compensated for the risk of paying too much for a company by shifting some of the risk to the seller. Agreements required owners to remain with the company for two to three years, while a portion of the payment depended on achieving earnings goals. In addition, RCM completed integration of a newly acquired company within 90 days. RCM assumed control of administrative functions, including payroll, employee benefits, invoicing, hiring, and training. The acquired company had complete autonomy in improving sales and service as it gained access to RCM's database of contract opportunities nationwide. RCM integrated literature and marketing plans as the last step. Of the 30 acquisitions RCM completed between December 1994 and October 1999, the revenues of 23 companies ranged from $1 million to $10 million; the small size of these companies eased integration.

By the end of fiscal 1998 the composition of RCM's business had shifted dramatically. In 1995 general staffing services represented 51 percent of revenues and professional engineering the remaining 49 percent. In 1998 general staffing and specialty healthcare accounted for 12 percent and two percent of revenues, respectively, professional engineering accounted for 24 percent, and IT realized 62 percent of revenues. The hourly billing of services greatly increased as well. General staffing charged $8 to $18 per hour, specialty healthcare rates ranged from $40 to $70 per hour, engineering rates ranged from $50 to

$75 per hour, and project management or consultation rates ranged from $110 to $155 per hour. Billing rates for IT ranged from $60 to $85 per hour for normal staffing and $125 to $185 per hour for project management or consultation.

Through acquisition RCM expanded its range of professional abilities and gained clients in public utilities, government agencies, manufacturing, finance, and *Fortune* 500 companies. In 1998 purchase orders, as well as occasional contracts for complex projects, originated from 53 branch offices in 21 states and generated revenues of $201.5 million and net income of $9.8 million. RCM began to integrate its subsidiaries under the RCM Technologies name for brand recognition as well as for simplicity on the company's new web site.

In 1999 RCM completed ten acquisitions that extended the company's reach into Texas, North Carolina, Alabama, and eastern Canada and strengthened markets already served. Revenues of newly acquired companies ranged from $1 million at Mu-Sigma Engineering Consultants of Toronto to $10 million at A.R.I.S. E. International of Houston. RCM planned to target future acquisitions in the range of $75 million to $125 million and to seek opportunities nationally and internationally, especially in Europe.

21st-Century Business Solutions

With the company's later acquisitions RCM expanded further into providing business solutions and more complex IT services. These capabilities included Enterprise Resources Planning implementation and post-implementation support, redesigning business processes, Enterprise Application Integration, and Lawson software implementation. Through the acquisition of Business Support Group of Michigan, Inc., RCM acquired the license to represent QAD software to mid-level clients in industrial electronics and the automotive industry. New clients included Denso Manufacturing, SPX Aftermarket Tool & Equipment Group, and EPI Printers. Although 30 percent of IT service revenues originated from business solutions services, RCM planned to increase that proportion to 50 percent with an emphasis on project management.

RCM's shift toward business solutions led to close collaboration with its customers on web site development. With Pace Global Laboratory Resources (Pace GLR) RCM created an Internet-based application that provided analytical services to companies with insufficient technological capacities, primarily companies in the industrial sector. Introduced in March 1999, the service connected customers who needed analytic capacity with corporate laboratories that possessed excess capacity or specialized capabilities. RCM completed a similar project a year later with LabSeek.com. RCM developed a web-based service to provide for the exchange of scientific measurements and knowledge.

RCM's strategy to provide business solutions extended to wireless communications through in-house development. In March 2000 the company formed the RCM Wireless Business Unit and opened a facility at Morristown, New Jersey, the Wireless Technology Competency Center. RCM planned to develop new applications to provide remote access to desktop tools, such as e-mail, contact lists, and calendars, via wireless, Internet-ready technology, including wireless telephones, Personal Digital Assistants, and two-way pagers. RCM planned to include management and operation of servers and web portals in its wireless integration services.

Principal Subsidiaries

Business Support Group of Michigan, Inc.; Camelot Contractors, Limited; Cataract, Inc.; Constellation Integration Services; Global Technology Solutions, Inc.; Encompass Business Solutions; Insight Consulting Group, Inc.; Intertec Design, Inc.; Northern Technical Services, Inc.; Procon, Inc.; Programming Alternatives of Minnesota, Inc.; Software Analysis & Management, Inc.; Solutions Through Data Processing, Inc.; The Consortium.

Principal Competitors

Alternative Resources Corporation; Metamor Worldwide, Inc.; Modis Professional Services, Inc.

Further Reading

"Austin Nichols Technical Sells Division to New Jersey Concern," *Knight-Ridder/Tribune Business News*, November 20, 1997, p. 1120B1026.

Baker, Nancy Croft, "Two Sludgeless Scrubbing Methods Eyed by Utilities," *Environment Today*, April 1991, p. 1.

Brubaker, Harold L., "Acquisitions Are Helping RCM, But Not Its Share Price, Grow," *Philadelphia Inquirer*, August 17, 1999, p. D5.

"Business Brief—RCM Technologies Inc.: Gas-Control System Work Terminated; Stock Plunges," *Wall Street Journal*, July 7, 1992, p. B8.

"Coronato Quits Posts As Chairman, Chief of RCM Technologies," *Wall Street Journal*, August 20, 1992, p. B2.

Jacobs, Chip, "Engineering Company Foresees Big Profits in System to Cut Pollution Causing Acid Rain," *Los Angeles Business Journal*, May 28, 1990, p. 6.

"PCX Lists Six New Options Issues," *PR Newswire*, December 4, 1998, p. 1478.

"RCM Changes Year," *Philadelphia Business Journal*, February 4, 2000, p. 17.

"RCM Technologies Expects to See Profits As It Shifts Emphasis," *Wall Street Journal*, September 17, 1990, p. 9A.

"RCM Technologies Inc.," *Los Angeles Business Journal*, August 20, 1990, p. 54.

"RCM Technologies, Inc.—Company Report," *Investext*, July 1, 1997, p. 1.

"RCM Technologies RCMT," *CDA-Investnet Insider's Chronicle*, July 20, 1998, p. 16.

"RCM Technologies Reports Earnings for Year to Oct. 31," *New York Times*, February 23, 1984, p. D5.

"RCM Technologies Wants to Become an IT Services Powerhouse, One Company at a Time," *IT Services Business Report*, September 1999.

Webber, Maura, "RCM Technologies Inc. Bets on Corporate Austerity," *Philadelphia Business Journal*, February 26, 1996, p. 3S.

Wilen, John, "RCM Gobbles Up Another Company," *Philadelphia Business Journal*, January 16, 1998, p. 11.

—Mary Tradii

Ritz Camera Centers

6711 Ritz Way
Beltsville Maryland 20705
U.S.A.
Telephone: (301) 419-0000
Fax: (301) 419-2995
Web site: http://www.ritzcamera.com

Private Company
Incorporated: 1918
Employees: 6,500
Sales: $650 million (1998 est.)
NAIC: 812922 One-Hour Photofinishing; 812921
    Photofinishing Laboratories (Except One-Hour)

Ritz Camera Centers is the nation's largest photo-specialty chain with more than 1,000 stores. The stores are located in 47 states and the District of Columbia. A privately held company, Ritz Camera Centers is ranked 369th on the list of the *Forbes* Private 500. The company reported 1998 sales of $650 million and employed over 6,500 people. Located in Beltsville, Maryland, the company is led by President and CEO David Ritz.

Small Beginnings: 1918

Not until the late 19th century did photography become accessible to everyday people. What had formerly been the photographic options of the wealthy became available to everyone with portable cameras.

In 1918 another advancement began quietly in Atlantic City, New Jersey, and the future of cameras and photo developing experienced another step ahead. The first Ritz Camera Centers began with a single studio on the Atlantic City boardwalk. At the studio, customers could have their photos taken as well as their film developed. Started and still operated by the Ritz Family, that first store was founded by Edward Ritz and introduced a concept that had plenty of growth potential.

Slow and Steady Growth: 1930s–80s

As Ritz Camera Centers expanded from that one location in Atlantic City, the firm reached out to nearby states, especially Maryland, where a Baltimore store was added in the 1930s. As stores were added, so were services and retail goods. Not just a place to have a photo taken or have a photo developed, the stores became one-stop shops for all photographic needs. From cameras to photographic equipment, accessories, and service, Ritz Camera Centers offered it all.

The company enjoyed ongoing success, but as a new generation of the Ritz family took over the business, change was on the horizon. David Ritz became president and CEO of Ritz Camera Centers in 1978. He helped launch the next era in the company's history, a time of careful planning and controlled expansion. By the mid-1980s, Ritz Camera Centers had grown from that one Atlantic City store to nearly 100 locations.

Diversifying the Company: 1980s

In the late 1980s, Ritz Camera Centers diversified into the marine retail business with the addition of Boater's World. A division of Ritz Camera, Boater's World also began with a single location. Boater's World was a full service boating and fishing accessories superstore, located in some of the hot-spots for boating and fishing along the East Coast from Maine to Florida as well as the Gulf of Mexico, the shores of the great lakes, and the West Coast. Boater's World was the second largest company in the marine accessory industry. With fishing equipment representing one of the largest specialties at Boater's World, the company carried a vast selection of lures, baits, nets, line, hooks, and tackle.

In addition to the smaller stores, Boater's World also added two superstores in Fort Lauderdale, Florida, and Warwick, Rhode Island. These two larger stores carried a wide variety of all types of equipment and accessories. They also offered motor parts for common marine engines.

Boater's World had two divisions of its own: Outer Banks Outfitters and Chicago Yacht and Navigation rigging shop. Outer Banks Outfitters was one of the mail-order leaders for marine outfitting and fishing. The Chicago Yacht and Navigation rigging shop took care of all of the sailing rigging for Boater's World.

Ritz Camera Centers also added, in its own retail stores, a diversified line of merchandise. Although most were photo-related, the stores also offered such items as binoculars and cellular phones. The stores also offered the still-popular 1-hour Ritz "Big Print."

Besides the headquarters and merchandise distribution center in Beltsville, Maryland, Ritz Camera also operated a second distribution center in Topeka, Kansas. Together, the centers stocked over 4,000 products for delivery to the store locations.

Full Speed Ahead: 1990s

In the 1990s, Ritz expanded Boater's World as well, adding inland Boater's World stores in Tulsa, Oklahoma; Pittsburgh, Pennsylvania; Nashville, Tennessee; Atlanta, Georgia; Kansas City, Missouri; and Topeka, Kansas.

In 1997, Ritz Camera Centers acquired one of its biggest competitors, Kits Camera Inc. of Seattle, Washington. This move strengthened the company's presence in the West Coast market, providing broader coverage of the entire nation. The purchase of Kits Camera Inc. gave Ritz 140 more retail stores. Located in eight western and southwestern states, Kits Camera Stores continued to operate under their own name as part of the purchase agreement between the two companies.

In an interview with the *Baltimore Sun,* Ted Fox, the operations officer with the Photo Marketing Association International at the time of the purchase, said, "They've been growing steadily for some time . . . it was a strategic acquisition which opened up the West Coast for Ritz. Ritz has had a presence in the West Coast, but with 140 stores of Kits, they really get market penetration."

As in many of the acquisitions of the 1990s, the owners of smaller chains or individual stores were ready to move on and were not interested in investing in the new technology and equipment of the retail photographic business.

In 1998, Ritz acquired 83 more stores from affiliates of Fuji Photo Film USA, Inc., and in 1999, Ritz Camera Centers continued its expansion with the purchase of The Camera Shop, Inc., a 72-store chain.

The Camera Shop was, until the purchase, the nation's third largest camera retailer, behind Ritz and Wolf Camera. The Camera Shop stores, purchased by Ritz, were located in Maryland, Pennsylvania, New Jersey, Delaware, and New York. As a part of the agreement, former Camera Shop President John Bogosian agreed to serve in an advisory capacity to Ritz, and his daughter, Karen Bogosian, became Ritz's regional manager.

While Ritz Camera Centers was aggressively buying smaller chains and stores, there were some critics, leery of the larger company becoming such a massive force in the industry. When Ritz Camera Centers purchased Sam Bass Camera in Raleigh, North Carolina, in 1998, the local newspaper, the *News & Observer,* reported that area photographers were concerned about the buyout. The local store had served the professional photographers of the area, and customers were used to very personal and individualized attention. Juan Mendez, a Ritz Camera executive, was quoted in the article that the emphasis of the store would remain the same and that even the Sam Bass name would remain. "We don't plan on changing anything," Mendez said, "except we may add more inventory."

Besides acquisitions, Ritz Camera Centers also opened new stores throughout the nation. During the 1990s, Ritz remained the leading specialty photo retailer, but Wolf Camera, a Georgia-based retailer, was quickly acquiring companies and going head-to-head with Ritz in many markets across the nation. One of Wolf's largest purchases was in 1998 with the acquisition of Eastman Kodak's 450-store Fox Photo Chain. Despite the substantial addition to Wolf's stores, Ritz Camera Centers continued to lead the industry.

Embracing New Technology: 2000s

As the company embraced the year 2000, the photographic industry was in the midst of big changes. There were new advances everywhere: from the way pictures were taken to the way they were stored. In fact, it was the cost of some of those changes that prompted smaller camera shops and chains to sell to large companies such as Ritz in the 1990s.

Ritz Camera Centers approached the new millennium by implementing new technology in photographic equipment, on the Web, and with e-commerce. The retail web site, introduced in late 1999, was offered as a premier online shopping source for photographic products and equipment. An e-commerce web site was also created, in partnership with phobo.com (a privately held company founded in 1999 and closely affiliated with Ritz).

Other Ritz companies such as Boater's World and Outer Banks Outfitters also offered phobo.com web sites and e-commerce. Phobo.com had an exclusive arrangement with Ritz Camera Centers for its e-commerce sites, which had the potential of reaching companies with a combined total of more than $30 billion in sales. David Ritz, president and CEO of Ritz Camera Centers, also served as chairman of phobo.com.

The Ritz retail web site was also used as a marketing and education tool, offering consumers photographic tips and advice. In early 2000, ritzcamera.com announced that it would add auctions as a part of the web site. The auctions were planned to feature new and used cameras, hard-to-find accessories, and other photographic items.

Key Dates:

1918: Ritz Camera Centers starts in Atlantic City with a single portrait studio.
1997: Adding 140 more stores, Ritz Camera Centers purchases Kits Camera, Inc. of Seattle, Washington.
1998: Ritz Camera Centers acquires 83 retail photographic stores from Fuji.
1999: Ritz Camera Centers purchases The Camera Shop, Inc., the third largest photofinishing chain with 72 stores and 500 employees; adds e-commerce web site.
2000: With more than 1,000 stores, Ritz Camera is the nation's largest photo specialty store.

Ritz Camera Centers offered technological advances in its retail stores as well. Digital photography became more popular, and Ritz Camera Centers offered products and support for new users. Free promotional CDs on using digital photography were offered through early 2000.

"Through the CD, consumers can access information and services to help them expand their knowledge about photography. And, with the click of a button, consumers can access the vast array of photographic products and services available at ritzcamera.com," said Andre Brysha, chief marketing officer for ritzcamera.com, in a company press release.

In April 2000, Ritz Camera announced a partnership with America Online (AOL) to offer Ritz products through AOL channels. As a part of the five-year agreement, AOL would also market its services through Ritz Camera Centers and its web site. Bob Pittman, President and Chief Operating Officer of AOL, said in a company press release, "Our new marketing alliance with Ritz and phobo.com will make it easy and convenient for our members to find Ritz's wide selection of photographic equipment and services."

Ritz Camera Centers started as a one-store operation in 1918 and had expanded to become the leading photographic specialty store in the nation. As Ritz continued to acquire stores and expand services, more growth could be expected in the future. With new technology constantly on the horizon, Ritz Camera Centers had proven that it would embrace change and use it to help the company grow.

Principal Subsidiaries

Boater's World; Outer Banks Outfitters (division of Boater's World); Chicago Yacht and Navigation Rigging Shop (division of Boater's World).

Principal Competitors

Wolf Camera; Walgreen Co.; West Marine, Inc.

Further Reading

Evans, Sandra, "Top 15 Private Companies," *Washington Post,* April 26, 1999.
Mirabella, Lorraine, "Ritz Camera Snaps up a Rival," *Baltimore Sun,* November 26, 1997, p. 1C.
Obermayer, Joel B., "Snapshot of Industry Trend: Sam Bass Camera Sold," *News & Observer,* April 23, 1998.
Von Bergen, Jane M., "Merger Enters Picture," *New York Daily Record,* July 28, 1999, p.6.

—Shawna Brynildssen

RMC Group p.l.c.

RMC House
Coldharbour Lane
Thorpe
Egham, Surrey TW20 8TD
United Kingdom
Telephone: (01932) 568833
Fax: (01932) 568933
Web site: http://www.rmc-group.com

Public Company
Incorporated: 1930 as Ready Mixed Concrete Limited
Employees: 35,000
Sales: £4.70 billion (US$7.57 billion) (1999)
Stock Exchanges: London
NAIC: 212312 Crushed and Broken Limestone Mining
    and Quarrying; 212313 Crushed and Broken Granite
    Mining and Quarrying; 212319 Other Crushed and
    Broken Stone Mining and Quarrying; 234110
    Highway and Street Construction; 234990 All Other
    Heavy Construction; 324121 Asphalt Paving Mixture
    and Block Manufacturing; 327310 Cement
    Manufacturing; 327320 Ready-Mix Concrete
    Manufacturing; 327331 Concrete Block and Brick
    Manufacturing; 327332 Concrete Pipe Manufacturing;
    327390 Other Concrete Product Manufacturing;
    327410 Lime Manufacturing; 327420 Gypsum
    Product Manufacturing; 327999 All Other
    Miscellaneous Nonmetallic Mineral Product
    Manufacturing; 444110 Home Centers; 562111 Solid
    Waste Collection; 562212 Solid Waste Landfill

RMC Group p.l.c. is among the world's leading suppliers of building materials. It is the world's largest supplier of ready-mixed concrete and of aerated concrete products; the latter includes construction materials, such as building blocks and horizontal load-bearing beams. The company is also among the world leaders in cement and aggregates (sand, gravel, and crushed stone). Other construction-related activities include coated roadstone, lime, and mortar. In its home base of the United Kingdom, RMC is a leader in waste management and disposal through a subsidiary called Hales Waste Control Limited, and owns the nationwide 94-unit Great Mills chain of do-it-yourself superstores. About 25 percent of RMC's revenues are generated domestically, 27 percent in Germany, 26 percent in the rest of Europe, 18 percent in the United States, and the remaining four percent elsewhere.

Struggling Early Years

Before World War II builders doubted that ready-mixed concrete could be successfully delivered to construction sites, although ready-mixed is more convenient than mixing on the spot. Their skepticism stemmed partly from the failure of ready-mix ventures in the United States—in the days before self-agitating cement trucks the concrete was often rock hard by the time it arrived at the site. When a truck mixer that inhibited crystallization was invented in the United States in 1926, Danish engineer Kjeld Ammentorp invested in the new industry in England.

Ammentorp built his first plant at Bedfont, in a pit on land owned by the builders' suppliers Hall and Company. With money from friends in Denmark, Ammentorp incorporated his business, Ready Mixed Concrete Limited, in July 1930. The Bedfont location was ideal not only because it was close to London, where new construction was booming, but also because supplies of aggregates, the raw materials needed for mixing concrete, were abundant in the area. By building the plant directly in the pit, Ammentorp eliminated the need to haul materials.

Building the plant took more time than expected. Permission to build was slow in coming, and the first concrete to pave the yard and the loading bay was not poured until February 1931. Further delays occurred when parts had to be imported from Scandinavia. The completed structure was primitive. Gravel had to be hauled by chain-and-bucket elevators that broke down often. Early workers recalled working through the night with only the warmth of whiskey and rum to spur them on. The production process itself was crude—as one employee recalled in *The Readymixers,* weighing and measuring sand, ballast, and cement and adding water was a hit-or-miss process.

378

Demand for the new product was not high since the public was not yet convinced the ready-mix method worked. Government road-improvement projects set up to ease the unemployment caused by the stock market crash and ensuing Great Depression gave Ready Mixed Concrete some work. As profits slowly increased, Ammentorp increased the size of his truck fleet by buying agitators from Denmark.

World War II brought RMC's growth almost to a halt. Although there were a few new contracts for air-raid shelters and emergency construction work, general construction declined. When Ammentorp and other members of the staff were called up for military duty, operations nearly ceased until the end of the war.

Postwar Growth

The war's devastation of Europe offered many opportunities for the construction industry and those businesses that serviced it. Before taking advantage of the situation, however, Ammentorp had to deal with three challenges: replacing worn-out equipment, overcoming the increasing number of competitors, and building up the supplies of cement that had been depleted by wartime rationing. Ammentorp's salesmanship produced a pretax profit of £9,000 by 1950, when work began on a new Bedfont plant. A year later, Ready Mixed Concrete increased its output by 50 percent and its profit by 100 percent.

About the time that Ammentorp was leaving his business to become a soldier, an Australian accountant named Sam Stirling met Bill Freeman, a lawyer from Sydney, on a plane ride in New Guinea. The two men eventually became partners in a venture to supply and deliver ready-mixed concrete in Australia. The company was registered in 1939 as Ready Mixed Concrete Limited of Australia, and Stirling designed the bright orange diamond-shaped logo that is still in use today.

Like its counterpart in Great Britain, Ready Mixed of Australia suffered a series of losses until 1946. Then Stirling began to think about expanding overseas, in Europe. Stirling was a charismatic man who favored a seat-of-the-pants management style. He appreciated the same traits in other people as well. Bryan Kelman, a young British engineer who had worked with Ready Mixed of Australia on a project in Canberra, came upon Stirling adjusting some of the company's equipment one day when he was visiting the office. Not knowing that Stirling was the owner, Kelman demanded that he leave the equipment alone and leave the premises. Even when Stirling assured Kelman that he did indeed belong there, Kelman held his ground. Impressed, Stirling convinced Kelman to work for him at twice his current pay and sent him to Great Britain to assess the ready-mix market.

After arriving in England in April 1951, Kelman opened a company bank account and met with John Gauntlett, a corporate lawyer in the firm of Linklaters and Paines, to draw up the papers for the formation of Stirling Readymix Concrete. Gauntlett became an important link between the new company and the London business community and eventually became deputy chairman. When Kelman could not find investors for the new company, Stirling came to London himself. But even his charisma and business acumen could not convince British financiers that ready-mixed concrete could be a viable industry. Stirling had to get funds from the Australian business community.

With the new funding, Kelman purchased a plant in Liverpool and moved it to Poplar, where operations began in April 1952. Stirling assigned Kelman to convince Ammentorp to sell the now-prosperous Ready Mixed Concrete to the Australian company. Early in 1952, Ammentorp sold his company to Stirling for £92,500, and Stirling Readymix Concrete became Ready Mixed Concrete, based in Great Britain. Ammentorp stayed on as a board member for six years and then left England and the company he had founded.

Kelman returned to Australia, and Stirling sent for Norman Davis, Frank Nugent, and Alf Smith from the Australian operation to sell ready-mixed concrete to still-skeptical customers in England. Ammentorp had not always been prompt in his deliveries and Stirling wanted to change public perception as soon as possible. An opportunity to do so came when the engineering department of a local council hired RMC to fill miles of scrapped tram lines. This new account provided daily work for the company for four years, and the orange trucks became a familiar sight running from the plant to the tram lines.

While Alf Smith remained in London as the chief executive and Davis was put in charge of the Poplar plant, Nugent was busy in the Midlands, setting up the company's first production plant at Queslett, about five miles from Birmingham. While there, he hired a civil engineering graduate named John Camden. When Nugent was sent to Rio de Janeiro to supervise international expansion there, Camden was left in charge of the Queslett operation.

Building licenses and controls in the United Kingdom were lifted in 1954, and the postwar reconstruction intensified. RMC grew, often purchasing the plants and equipment of failed competitors. Jim Owen, a Welsh site engineer, and Norman Grant, a technical engineer, joined the company during this time. Both would become RMC executives in the future.

Also in the early 1950s, RMC expanded to continental Europe, although the move was not planned. A deal had been struck with Kellogg, an American contracting firm, for RMC-Australia to pour concrete in Tasmania. While the RMC engineers were waiting for specially ordered equipment to be delivered, Kellogg backed out of the deal. Since the equipment was in transit in West Germany, RMC management in Sydney decided to set up shop there. John Camden established a plant in Düsseldorf. Although postwar Germany was a natural market for the construction industry, exceedingly harsh winters meant little work for RMC. It was four years before the company was ready to build another German plant, this one north of Düsseldorf.

Key Dates:

1930: Danish engineer Kjeld Ammentorp founds Ready Mixed Concrete Limited and begins construction of its first plant in Bedfont, England.

1939: Ready Mixed Concrete Limited of Australia is founded by Sam Stirling and Bill Freeman.

1952: Ammentorp sells his company to Ready Mixed Concrete of Australia.

1962: RMC goes public, raising needed capital.

1963: The company's Australian shareholders are bought out, and Ready Mixed Concrete regains its independence.

1965: John Camden begins long reign as chief executive.

1966: RMC expands into Ireland.

1968: Hall and Ham River, a leading U.K. supplier of aggregates, is acquired.

1979: RMC opens the Thorpe Park amusement park; expands into the United States through the establishment of a holding company, RMC Industries Corporation, and the acquisition of Piedmont Concrete and Ewell Industries; and enters the do-it-yourself retailing sector with the purchases of Great Mills Superstores and Regent Warehouses.

1982: Company changes its name to RMC Group p.l.c.; RMC enters the roadstone sector through the acquisition of Derbyshire-based Peakstone.

1998: RMC sells several noncore assets: Thorpe Park amusement park, builders' supplier Hall & Co., and its interest in the Chaufourneries lime joint venture.

2000: RMC acquires the Rugby Group PLC, the number three U.K. cement firm, for US$1.45 billion.

In 1955, Alf Smith returned to Australia and Bryan Kelman was named chairman and chief executive of RMC. A strong proponent of expansion, Kelman aggressively sought mergers with other companies. For part of 1959, RMC opened one new plant in the United Kingdom every ten days. The company expanded just as dramatically in West Germany, where each new plant that opened was formed into a separate company, and also moved into Jamaica in 1959 and Austria in 1961.

Also in 1961, a lawyer named Hermann Warmke joined the company to handle contracts, personnel, and insurance. Amazed at the lack of organization, Warmke set up regular working hours and a holiday schedule.

A move into Italy was RMC's first unsuccessful expansion. The company closed a production plant in Milan when operating problems mounted, and when a construction job was repeatedly stalled because contractors hit buried Roman ruins, RMC sold or closed its other Italian interests too.

Another less than satisfactory venture was RMC's partnership with two German firms, Rheinisch Kalksteinwerke Wulfrath (RKW), a ready-mix producer, and Dyckerhoff, a major supplier of cement, an important component of concrete. Under the name Beton Union, the three companies built 30 plants, set up so as not to compete with each other. Eventually, this arrangement cut into everyone's profit, and in 1964 RMC pulled out of the union over strategy disagreements. RKW followed suit in 1968. Dyckerhoff then entered the ready-mix market, forcing RMC to invest in the cement business to protect its own supplies. Cement was not a profitable part of the corporation, however; stiff competition and stringent pollution-control regulations kept Readymix Zementwerke from producing at capacity.

During the 1960s, ready-mix technology improved. RMC engineer Norman Grant developed the Cusum production method that allowed concrete to be tested within 24 hours rather than days. The company also developed and patented a hydraulic driving device for truck mixers. To ensure its future growth, RMC began to explore sea dredging as an alternate source of gravel as resources were depleted.

In May 1962 the rising cost of operations forced RMC to become a public company. The following winter was a difficult one: below-freezing weather curtailed production and a fire destroyed the Vienna plant. In addition, Sam Stirling's health was failing rapidly. Nevertheless, RMC expanded into Israel, a move that eventually added £11 million annually to company profit. By the end of 1962, RMC had 19 subsidiary companies and 80 plants in the United Kingdom that were supplying a quarter of the country's ready-mixed concrete. The company payroll listed over 800 employees, approximately 300 of whom were owner-drivers. When their self-employed status was challenged, England's High Court decided in RMC's favor and the drivers remained independent.

By 1963 tension between the Australian and British factions of the company peaked. The Australian directors believed that management in Great Britain had become too independent, and set about making plans to sell their shares to another company. In a boisterous board meeting, Kelman offered to top the Australians's asking price by selling 2.8 million shares to institutions and investors instead of to a single buyer. The shares brought £7.5 million.

Under Kelman's chairmanship, the newly independent Ready Mixed Concrete continued to expand. Plants were opened in Northern Ireland and Wales in the early 1960s. During 1963, RMC completed eight corporate acquisitions and formed a partnership with SOPEAL, a small company in Paris, to gain a foothold in France. The company even made an unsuccessful bid for the original Australian company. As the decade wore on, however, the British Labour Party's opposition to firms taking business outside the country made foreign expansion difficult.

In 1965 Bryan Kelman decided to accept an offer to work for the Australian firm that had acquired Ready Mixed Concrete of Australia. After extensive discussions, the board of directors brought John Camden back from Europe and appointed him chief executive. Bob Northcott took Kelman's place as chairman of the board.

As the top executive, Camden's style was very different from Bryan Kelman's; he conducted business more formally. Camden's first objective was to move the company away from its centralized management and give more responsibility to the regional managers. Under Camden's plan, the United Kingdom was divided into regions, and each company was run by general and departmental managers. The result was that local operating companies kept their own identities, and the central office became less involved in their daily operations. The reorganization was unpopular with some senior officers, who resigned.

In 1966 RMC moved into the Republic of Ireland with a ready-mixed concrete plant at Palmerston, to the northwest of Dublin. Despite continuing strife in the country, RMC's business interests thrived and the company acquired other Irish businesses. In Great Britain, during 1967, RMC acquired a 50 percent stake in St. Alban's Sand and Gravel. The company also moved into Berlin, where it eventually bought out the city's largest producer of ready-mix concrete.

In 1968 an explosion in a high-rise apartment building that had been built by RMC's joint-venture subsidiary, Taylor Woodrow-Anglian, killed several people. RMC's industrial work ceased until new design criteria for such buildings were approved by the British Ministry of Housing. Litigation stemming from the accident lasted well into the 1980s, and in 1985 RMC sold its shares to Taylor Woodrow. Founder Sam Stirling died in 1968 and was buried in his native Australia.

Early in the same year, RMC entered a takeover fight for Hall and Ham River, a builders' merchant and the biggest supplier of aggregates in southeastern Great Britain. Redland, a major building materials group, made numerous offers to purchase Hall and Ham. RMC executives watched from the sidelines until Redland eventually gave up. The weakened Hall and Ham accepted an offer from RMC, which made the company the leading producer of concrete aggregates in the United Kingdom. Although the purchase was worthwhile because of the aggregates it brought to RMC, management spent many hours cleaning up the disarray in Hall and Ham's operations.

As part of the Hall and Ham deal, RMC acquired a large home called ''the Grange at Thorpe'' in Surrey. In 1969, the Grange was turned into a technical and training center with Joe Dewar as its first director. The first class included 1,000 Hall and Ham employees who were retrained in RMC methods. The Grange was eventually expanded to include a group training center and a laboratory complex.

Toward the end of the decade, RMC formed a consortium with several other concrete aggregate companies to speed up the excavation of the Queen Mary Reservoir in Sunbury. For the first time, management acknowledged public concern about the industry's effects on the environment. At a shareholders' meeting, Chairman of the Board Bob Northcott warned that RMC would have to start restoring excavation areas even though it would be time-consuming and expensive. Acquisitions during this time included an aggregate business and a ready-mix company in Germany that were then combined to form Ready Mix Kies.

Diversified in the 1970s and 1980s

By the 1970s, RMC was the world's largest producer of ready-mix concrete, and highly profitable. The construction industry had accepted not only ready-mixed concrete, but also higher prices for it, and no expensive new plant-building projects were planned.

One of the people who had come to RMC with the Hall and Ham River merger, Tim Hartwright, took Northcott's concerns about the restoration of gravel pits seriously. Hartwright suggested building a safari and water park at one of the worked-out pits. After he and several others visited theme parks in the United States, the company constructed Thorpe Park near the Grange. RMC's financial director, Alan Endsor, was especially pleased with the new venture since he had been recommending that the company begin to diversify its interests. Although RMC encountered some public resistance to the idea at first and a period of low sales in ready-mixed concrete kept the cash flow down, Thorpe Park finally opened in 1979 and went on to become one of Great Britain's top ten tourist attractions.

In 1972, RMC commissioned a new ten-story corporate office on London Road in Staines and opened a plant in Hong Kong. Bob Northcott retired in 1973 and John Camden became chairman of the board while retaining his position as chief executive. Soon afterward, the economic recession fueled by the oil shortage hit the construction industry. At the same time, the British government placed restraints on business in an attempt to curb inflation. In 1973 Anthony Barber, the Conservative chancellor, introduced an emergency budget designed to slow what he is quoted in *The Readymixers* as calling the building industry's ''obscene gains.'' A miners' strike and the imposition of a three-day work week exacerbated RMC's financial problems. West German operations were also hard-hit by the recession. Industrywide, ready-mix production slumped by 12 percent. Competition became so fierce that some suppliers were selling concrete at prices below cost. To reduce some of its short-term loan commitments, RMC decided to sell the recently completed corporate office in Staines for £9 million.

By 1976 RMC's finances had improved slightly, and the company began to look for other markets and products that were not as dependent on the construction industry. At the same time, the company explored the possibilities of expansion to the American ready-mix market. Peter L. Young, RMC's director for corporate planning, was directed to spend five years appraising available growth options. Young looked at three options: first, RMC could continue to use its current business plan; second, the company could expand its conventional businesses; or third, the company could move into new geographical areas and new product markets. Young concluded that RMC would be best advised to expand its traditional business into new geographical areas and expand into new products at home. RMC had already experimented with some diversification. One of its subsidiaries, Hall Containers, disposed of dry and liquid industrial waste. Depleted gravel pits at Kingsmead had been turned into a fishing project, and the theme park at another site, at Thorpe, had proven to be successful.

Young's recommendations were put into action immediately. RMC moved into the United States with the purchase of Piedmont Concrete in North Carolina in 1979, and eight months later RMC bought Ewell Industries in Lakeland, Florida. The company entered another new market in March 1979 when it bought the Katelise Group, a do-it-yourself home-improvement business that operated 14 Great Mills Superstores in the southern and southwestern sections of England. By the end of 1979, RMC had also bought the Regent Warehouses chain. RMC entered the service industry when it purchased a 51 percent share in C. Rowbotham & Sons, an insurance brokerage, that same year. RMC acquired the remainder of the company in 1983. In December 1979, RMC purchased Lander Alarm Company, an electronic security and alarm business in Scotland. The company also joined an oil exploration consortium led by Arpet Petroleum, a subsidiary of Atlantic Richfield Company.

Diversification on a large scale came when RMC's readymix business was under fire by the government. During the early years of the recession, RMC and other ready-mix companies had made secret agreements to share business in order to keep themselves afloat. When this practice was discovered in an Office of Fair Trading investigation, the companies were brought before the Restrictive Practices Court. The businesses involved were reprimanded and future agreements were banned. A few years later, a Monopolies and Mergers Commission investigation caused more concern. At the time, RMC controlled one-third of the market and company executives were prepared for the worst. The commission concluded, however, that while RMC's business did constitute a monopoly, it was not harmful to public interest.

Although effects of the recession were still being felt during the early 1980s, RMC continued to acquire new businesses. The company moved into Spain through a merger with Asland SA that produced Readymix Asland. Acquisitions in Florida also continued. In February 1981, RMC's management was restructured into four sectors: concrete and aggregates, trading and environmental, services and financial, and general industries. The following year, the company changed its name from Ready Mix Concrete to RMC Group p.l.c.

By 1982 RMC's profits reached £55 million despite some problems. Expansion of the do-it-yourself chain was slower than expected, and business in West Germany and Austria slumped. Government restraints caused a construction lag in France, and RMC plants in Ireland registered their first losses. Although the British and European construction industries remained slow throughout the decade, RMC increased its profits through the aggregate business and its U.S. plants. The insurance subsidiary and some other new acquisitions were also profitable. Efforts to restore its gravel pits led RMC to new profit-making ventures, including growing grapes for wine and evening primroses in a joint venture with Germplasm Resource Management, for their oil.

At the end of 1982, RMC entered the roadstone business through the acquisition of Peakstone, a limestone producer in Derbyshire. The following year proved to be the company's best in a long time as the West German businesses finally started to prosper. A road-building program in the United Kingdom resulted in lucrative contracts for RMC, and the company's security and alarm subsidiaries in Scotland continued to thrive. In 1984 a modern ready-mix concrete plant was built in Birmingham, and the old plants in Bordesley and Queslett were closed. In the United States, RMC took over Metromont Materials in South Carolina and moved into Atlanta, Georgia, in 1985. In 1986, Jim Owen replaced John Camden as group managing director. Camden remained chairman of the board.

In the latter 1980s several events put RMC in an unfavorable light. In the summer of 1989, at least 60 people were killed when an RMC dredger rammed a pleasure boat on the Thames River. In February of the same year, Anthony Hulett, an area manager, and Tony Lewis, a plant manager, were indicted by the Office of Fair Trading for violating the bans on unlawful agreements. Plans for RMC to excavate the Test Valley in Hampshire brought an outcry by prominent environmentalists.

1990s: Expanding in Eastern Europe and Beyond

The early 1990s were marked by RMC's expansionary moves in the newly opened markets of eastern Europe. RMC had first entered the eastern European market in 1989 with the opening of a ready-mixed concrete plant in Budapest, Hungary. The following year saw the company venture into eastern Germany with the purchase of a rundown cement plant in Rüdersdorf, near Berlin. Its activities in eastern Germany were initially organized under a joint venture holding company called Readymix Berlin GmbH. In 1993 Readymix Berlin was merged into RMC's existing German subsidiary, Readymix AG. Two years later RMC gained full control of Readymix—which by that time was one of the leading suppliers of construction materials on the European continent—by buying out its German partners in the venture. In September 1995 RMC launched a £459 million rights issue to fund the buyout. Meantime, RMC in 1991 acquired Germany-based Ytong AG, one of the world's leading producers of aerated concrete, with operations in Bulgaria, Croatia, Germany, Slovakia, the Netherlands, and Hungary. In 1993 RMC's German lime and limestone operations were combined with those of the Belgian Lhoist Group in France and the Czech Republic to form a 50–50 joint venture, Chaufourneries de Hergenrath S.A.

RMC in 1995 expanded within the United Kingdom through the acquisition of Hargreaves Quarries Limited, and in Austria with the purchase of a 24.9 percent stake in Kies-Union Vereinigte Kieswerke AG, that country's leading aggregate producer. In 1996 RMC bolstered its Austrian interests by increasing to 72 percent its stake in Kies-Union, which was then rechristened Readymix Kies-Union AG. That year, Peter Young was named chief executive.

In the later 1990s, with its large German operations being severely affected by a depressed construction market, RMC expanded aggressively outside of Europe. In 1996 RMC entered India for the first time with the creation of RMC Readymix (India) Limited, in which RMC held a 50 percent stake. The company also expanded into Jordan with the opening of a ready-mixed concrete plant in Amman through the newly formed Al-Ramz Concrete Industries Limited, a venture 75 percent owned by RMC. Entry into Croatia was gained in 1997 through the purchase of 51 percent of Dalmacijacement d.d., a cement supplier, while Indonesia fell into the group's orbit that same year with the acquisition of a 90 percent stake in a Jakarta-based ready-mixed concrete producer, which was renamed PT. RMC Readymix Indonesia. Expansion continued in 1998 with the establishment of a joint venture in the United Arab Emirates and the acquisition of a ready-mixed concrete company in Malaysia. The following year RMC entered the South American market for the first time through the creation of Readymix Argentina S.A. RMC also made a number of acquisitions in the United States during this period; by decade's end, RMC Industries Corporation, its U.S. holding company, had operations in

13 states, was the country's largest producer of ready-mixed concrete, and had major positions in aggregates and concrete products.

The continuing struggles in Germany led to revenue and profit declines in 1998. That year the company initiated a cost-cutting program, emphasizing Germany and the United Kingdom, and disposed of some noncore assets, including the Thorpe Park amusement park and builders' supplier Hall & Co. RMC also sold to its partner its interest in the Chaufourneries lime joint venture. RMC bolstered its position in Germany in 1998 through the acquisition of Wülfrather Zement for £156 million. On the negative side, RMC's German operations became the subject of a 1999 antitrust probe by the German Cartel Office, which in November 1999 fined the RMC subsidiaries a total of DM 102 million (£34 million).

In late 1999 RMC failed in a bid to acquire Scancem, a Swedish building materials firm; this prize instead went to Heidelberger Zement, one of RMC's chief German rivals. On the heels of this failure, RMC aggressively pursued an acquisition of the Rugby Group PLC, which was completed in January 2000 in a US$1.45 billion deal. Rugby, the third largest maker of cement in the United Kingdom and also a manufacturer of lime, had its main operations in the United Kingdom, Australia, and Poland, with smaller operations in the Czech Republic and Jamaica.

RMC's profits before taxation increased 15 percent in 1999, to £347.7 million, while revenues were up almost seven percent. The improvement stemmed mainly from the group's operations in the robust U.S. market and in European markets outside the United Kingdom and Germany—particularly France and Spain. Following the Rugby acquisition, RMC faced the early 21st century with confidence. It also faced it under new leadership, following the mid-2000 retirement of Young after nearly 40 years of company service. Taking over as chief executive was Stuart Walker, who had joined RMC in 1971 and had most recently been responsible for the group's mainland European operations.

Principal Subsidiaries

Great Mills (Retail) Limited; Hales Waste Control Limited; RMC Readymix East Anglia Limited (50%); RMC Readymix South West Limited (51%); RMC Aggregates (UK) Limited; RMC Building Products (UK) Limited; RMC Finance Limited; RMC Group Services Limited; RMC Readymix Limited; RMC (UK) Limited; Rombus Insurance Brokers Limited; Rombus Leasing Limited; The Rugby Group PLC; Readymix AG für Beteiligungen (Germany); Readymix Beton AG (Germany); Readymix Kies GmbH (Germany); Readymix Zement GmbH (Germany); Ytong AG (Germany); Readymix Betonbauteile GmbH (Germany); RGS-Holding GmbH (Germany); Readymix Kies-Union AG (Austria; 72%); Lieferbeton GmbH (Austria); Kies-Union GmbH (Austria); N.V. Readymix-Belgium SA; Dalmacijacement d.d. (Croatia; 51%); Readymix CR s.r.o. (Czech Republic; 70%); 4K-Beton A/S (Denmark); RMC France SA; Béton Rationnel Controlé (France); Sablières et Enterprises Morillon Corvol SA (France); Danubiusbeton Kft (Hungary); Broceni A/S (Latvia; 72%); RMC Holdings B.V. (Netherlands); Readymix Nederland N.V. (Netherlands); Readymix plc (Republic of Ireland; 63%); Readymix Asland SA (Spain; 50%); Cementownia Rudniki S.A. (Poland; 96%); RMC Industries Corporation (U.S.A.); Allied Readymix Inc. (U.S.A.); Ewell Industries Inc. (U.S.A.); Krehling Industries Inc. (U.S.A.); Metromont Materials Corp. (U.S.A.); Piedmont Concrete Co. (U.S.A.); Singletary Concrete Products Inc. (U.S.A.); RMC LONESTAR (U.S.A.); RMC Topmix LLC (United Arab Emirates; 49%); RMC Readymix (India) Limited (50%); PT. RMC Readymix Indonesia (90%); Readymix Industries (Israel) Limited (67.55%); Al-Ramz Concrete Industries Limited (Jordan; 75%); RMC Concrete (Malaysia) Sdn.Bhd.

Principal Competitors

Apasco, S.A. de C.V.; Browning-Ferris Industries, Inc.; Blue Circle Industries PLC; Cemex, S.A. de C.V.; Centex Construction Products, Inc.; Franz Haniel & Cie. GmbH; Hanson PLC; Heidelberger Zement AG; "Holderbank" Financiere Glaris Ltd.; J Sainsbury plc; Lafarge S.A.; SITA; Tarmac plc; Vulcan Materials Company; Waste Management, Inc.

Further Reading

Batchelor, Charles, "Vertical Integration Sets Building Material Debate: Continental Trend Reaches UK Shores and Threatens to Upset Traditional Industry Relationships," *Financial Times*, December 17, 1999, p. 26.

Bolger, Andrew, "RMC Signs First Deal in East German Growth," *Financial Times*, October 9, 1990, p. 26.

Cassell, Michael, *The Readymixers*, London: Pencorp Books, 1986.

Guthrie, Jonathan, "RMC in German Cement Purchase," *Financial Times*, May 22, 1998, p. 22.

——, "RMC Warns of Severe Slowdown in East Germany," *Financial Times*, September 18, 1998, p. 22.

London, Simon, "Germany Causes Decline at RMC," *Financial Times*, September 20, 1996, p. 22.

Minton, Anna, "German Cartel Watchdog Hits RMC with £34m Fine," *Financial Times*, November 2, 1999, p. 31.

——, "RMC Builds Up 19.9% Rugby Stake in Dawn Raid," *Financial Times*, November 9, 1999, p. 30.

Pretzlik, Charles, "Hard Times for Concrete Group," *Financial Times*, March 27, 1999, p. 2.

——, "RMC Expands in US via $117m Purchases," *Financial Times*, April 1, 1999, p. 30.

——, "RMC in German Cartel Probe," *Financial Times*, August 10, 1999, p. 16.

——, "RMC to Move on Rugby in £990m Deal," *Financial Times*, November 8, 1999, p. 24.

Taylor, Andrew, "RMC Launches £459m Rights Issue," *Financial Times*, September 8, 1995, p. 15.

Waples, John, "RMC Seeks to Cement £800m Rugby Takeover," *London Sunday Times*, November 7, 1999.

—Mary F. Sworsky
—updated by David E. Salamie

The Rockefeller Foundation

420 Fifth Avenue
New York, New York 10018-2702
U.S.A.
Telephone: (212) 869-8500
Fax: (212) 764-3468
Web site: http://www.rockfound.org

Foundation
Incorporated: 1913
Employees: 150
Sales: $388.3 million (1998)
NAIC: 813219 Other Grantmaking & Giving Services

One of the oldest and largest private charitable organizations in the world, The Rockefeller Foundation supports programs focused on making the world a better place for all humanity. The New York-based organization provides grants and fellowships as well as support for conferences; the foundation disbursed more than $170 million in 1999. Among the numerous programs and fields supported by the foundation are agricultural initiatives designed to reduce hunger by helping farmers in developing nations increase crop yields, arts and humanities projects, equal opportunity programs, global vaccination endeavors, environment studies, and family planning and population studies. As the foundation entered the 21st century, it modified its mission to adopt a more global approach and to focus more heavily on food security, creativity and culture, world health, and working communities.

Pioneering Philanthropy: Early 1900s

The founder of The Rockefeller Foundation, John D. Rockefeller, displayed an interest in philanthropy from an early age. During his teen years, Rockefeller, an avid member of the Baptist church, saved money from his first job to donate to his church. As the years passed Rockefeller expanded his charitable donations, regularly giving to Sunday schools, churches, and an orphanage.

In 1870 Rockefeller and his business partners founded Standard Oil of Ohio. The business was so successful that Rockefeller soon became one of the wealthiest men in the United States. With this prosperity came an increase in Rockefeller's interest in charitable giving. Rockefeller also was influenced by steel industry magnate and fellow philanthropist Andrew Carnegie. In an essay, "The Gospel of Wealth," Carnegie wrote, "The day is not far distant, when the man who dies leaving behind him millions of available wealth, which was free for him to administer during life, will pass away unwept, unhonored, and unsung." This essay had a profound effect on Rockefeller, who read it in 1889 and then wrote to Carnegie to assure him that "the time will come when men of wealth will more generally be willing to use it for the good of others."

Rockefeller then seriously committed himself to the task of philanthropy, beginning with a donation that helped to found the University of Chicago. Rockefeller gifted a total of about $36 million over the course of 25 years to help build the university. In 1901 Rockefeller established The Rockefeller Institute for Medical Research, which later became Rockefeller University. Two years later, to promote education, particularly of African Americans in the South, Rockefeller started the General Education Board. Continuing with his charitable giving, Rockefeller in 1909 created the Rockefeller Sanitary Commission for Eradication of Hookworm Disease.

Although Rockefeller was prepared to start The Rockefeller Foundation as early as 1909, the organization was not created until 1913. Attempts to secure a federal charter were unsuccessful, and the foundation instead incorporated in New York State on April 24, 1913. Its mission and statement of purpose read, "To promote the well-being of mankind throughout the world." Rockefeller gifted $35 million to the foundation that first year, and the next year he gave $65 million. Despite Rockefeller's ties to the foundation, however, he chose to stay out of the day-to-day business of running the organization and did not attend board meetings. Rockefeller's son, John D. Rockefeller, Jr., was elected president, and the foundation became an organization independent of the Rockefeller family's interests.

Late in 1913 The Rockefeller Foundation made its first grant when it provided $100,000 to the American Red Cross, enabling the Red Cross to acquire property in Washington, D.C., for its national headquarters. The foundation chose to focus on film, American studies, and the preservation of native cultural materials.

In its other divisions, the foundation emphasized economics and social science research, with grants given to such research centers as the London School of Economics, the Social Science Research Council, and the National Bureau of Economic Research. The foundation also began its involvement with agricultural studies with a rural reconstruction program in China. The organization's fight against disease, including schistosomiasis, continued, and the foundation also supported research in biology. In 1935 the foundation successfully developed the first effective vaccine against yellow fever; the importance of this finding was recognized in 1950, when microbiologist Max Theiler of The Rockefeller Foundation Virus Laboratory was awarded the Nobel prize in medicine and physiology for his work on the vaccine.

During the 1940s the foundation provided support for the development of nuclear science research tools, such as the electron microscope, and continued to support the humanities with funding to such activities as language studies, American cultural studies, and library development. The foundation created the Atlantic Awards, which provided grants to help young writers, particularly British writers suffering hardships following World War II. An interest in population studies was recognized with a grant to Princeton University's Office of Population Research, which investigated ties between population and developing countries.

Postwar Shifts: Focus on Agricultural Studies

In the late 1940s The Rockefeller Foundation progressed in its efforts to better the world. To replenish the dwindling resources of the General Education Board, the foundation made its largest gift of 1946 with $7.5 million. The board's focus had shifted to promoting education for blacks and whites in the South. The foundation funded a variety of programs and activities, including the development of the mechanical differential analyzer at the Massachusetts Institute of Technology (MIT), a precursor to the modern computer; a 12-year program in area studies, which included grants to universities across the globe; and support for genetics research, which involved the building of genetics departments at leading universities, including Stanford University, the California Institute of Technology, and MIT. The foundation also was interested in the socioeconomic conditions of developing nations, and in 1948 it launched a research effort that combined the social sciences, health, and natural sciences divisions.

By the 1950s a number of organizations focused on natural sciences and physics had emerged, the United Nation's World Health Organization among them, leading The Rockefeller Foundation to disband its biology division in 1951. In 1952 John D. Rockefeller III became chair of the board of trustees, and the foundation adopted a more concerted interest in agricultural studies. The foundation had supported some agricultural work in Mexico in the 1940s, and it expanded on this work in the ensuing decades. The aim of the agricultural efforts, which later came to be known as the Green Revolution, was to boost crop yields in order to feed the world's inhabitants. In 1950 the foundation created an agricultural development program in Co-

Company Perspectives:

The Rockefeller Foundation is a knowledge-based, global foundation with a commitment to enrich and sustain the lives and livelihoods of poor and excluded people throughout the world.

health and medical education, granting money to Johns Hopkins University to expand its medical school and facilities and providing $25,000 to establish the International Health Commission, its first overseas venture and an offshoot of the Rockefeller Sanitary Commission for Eradication of Hookworm Disease. The foundation also lent financial support to the Bureau of Social Hygiene, which conducted research and provided education on birth control, sex education, and maternal health, and founded the China Medical Board to help develop a modern medicine system in China.

Active during its early years, the foundation also began a program to further the education of future leaders through the provision of international fellowships. The Rockefeller Sanitary Commission for Eradication of Hookworm Disease was integrated into the foundation in 1914, and in addition to researching hookworm, the foundation began studies of malaria and yellow fever. In the late 1910s the foundation became more heavily involved with public health education and the natural sciences. Three schools of public health were endowed by the foundation in the late 1910s and early 1920s—Johns Hopkins University, Harvard University, and the University of Michigan—with plans to establish additional schools around the world. In addition, the foundation set up a Division of Medical Education to fund medical schools and provided funds to the National Research Council for fellowships in the natural sciences, particularly physics and chemistry.

John D. Rockefeller, Jr., stepped down as president in 1917 and became the chair of the board of trustees. George E. Vincent was elected president. The foundation's funds were enhanced by additional gifts from John D. Rockefeller, who gave the foundation a total of more than $182 million. In the 1920s the foundation continued its efforts to promote education by establishing the International Education Board, a counterpart to the U.S. General Education Board, backed with $20 million. In the late 1920s the foundation shifted its interests and reorganized into five core divisions: international health, medical sciences, natural sciences, social sciences, and humanities. Within social sciences the foundation chose to support programs in international relations, economic stabilization, and public administration.

The foundation's early efforts in the humanities included gifts to the American School of Classical Studies, which assisted the progress of the excavation of the Athenian Agora; funding for the Oriental Institute of the University of Chicago, which helped train archaeologists; and support to Harvard University's Fogg Art Museum for the education of curators and art historians. In the 1930s the foundation supported library projects, American regional drama, and Far Eastern studies. It also developed new interests in the humanities, including radio and

---

Key Dates:

1913: John D. Rockefeller establishes The Rockefeller Foundation.

1928: Foundation reorganizes to focus on five core divisions.

1935: The foundation's Virus Laboratory develops a vaccine for yellow fever.

1960: Foundation establishes the International Rice Institute to research new strains of rice.

1970: Rockefeller Foundation scientist Dr. Normal Borlaug receives the Nobel Peace Prize for helping to modernize agriculture.

1990: The Energy Foundation, formed to study sustainable energy sources, is created in a joint venture with other foundations.

1998: British agricultural ecologist Gordon Conway is elected as the foundation's 12th president.

1999: Foundation adopts a new global mission.

---

lombia, where researchers worked with wheat seeds that had been developed through its Mexican projects. Participation in the agriculture program expanded to Chile in 1955 and Ecuador and India in 1956. In 1960 the foundation established the International Rice Research Institute in the Philippines. The institute hoped to develop new strains of rice and methods for increasing crop yields of rice, a staple in many developing countries. In 1966 the foundation lent support to the establishment of the International Maize and Wheat Improvement Center in Mexico, and in 1971 the foundation partnered with the Ford Foundation to set up the Consultative Group on International Agriculture Research. The mission of the group was to develop better food crops for developing nations. The foundation's efforts in agricultural studies in the mid-20th century resulted in increased crop output and several new strains of wheat, rice, and other crops. Its work also led to the awarding of the Nobel Peace Prize in 1970 to Dr. Norman E. Borlaug, a Rockefeller Foundation scientist, for his efforts to modernize agriculture in the developing world.

Despite the foundation's emphasis on agriculture in the mid-1900s, it did not neglect its other divisions. Among the causes supported by the foundation from the 1940s through the 1960s were population studies, including grants to the Population Council and the establishment of population research departments at major universities; the arts, including funding for the American Shakespeare Festival in Stratford and New York's Lincoln Center, as well as grants to novelists, playwrights, and dance companies; and education, which placed emphasis on promoting the education of African American students. In 1963, in fact, the foundation lent support not only to recruit African American students for colleges but to enhance the level of education and training available at historically black colleges and universities. The foundation also began its University Development program, later known as Education for Development and spanning 20 years, which supplied funding to universities all over the world. Also in 1963 the foundation implemented a reorganization to focus on five core concerns: Conquest of Hunger, Population and Health, Education for

Development, Equal Opportunity, and Arts, Humanities, and Cultural Values.

As a result of negative economic conditions in the 1970s, the foundation's assets declined to a low of $732 million in 1977, but this did not deter the organization from providing support to worthy programs and causes. The foundation supported population research, social history projects, and the arts and humanities, including grants to modern dance and ballet groups. In 1974 the foundation provided funds for the formation of the International Agricultural Development Service, which offered assistance in agriculture and rural development to developing nations. Three years later an international network of biomedical research groups was created to investigate key diseases affecting the developing world.

Health initiatives launched in the 1980s included the founding of an international clinical epidemiology network that focused on training physicians in developing countries, a grants program that supported biomedical studies in regard to the introduction of contraception in developing nations, and support for researching the newly discovered AIDS virus. The foundation also turned to the difficulties affecting the poor, launching a program that provided job training to single minority women in the United States in 1981 and creating a national research program to address poverty in U.S. cities in 1987. In agricultural studies, the foundation supported genetic engineering tests of cereal plants and in 1986 researchers developed a pioneering method of regenerating rice plants from rice protoplasts. In the late 1980s the foundation embarked upon three new initiatives—a global environment program, a school reform program in the United States, and an international security program, which addressed issues concerning destructive weapons.

Changing Times: A Global Approach in the Late 20th Century

The Rockefeller Foundation entered the 1990s as one of the largest and oldest charitable organizations in the world, and its aim was to continue addressing critical global issues. The foundation began the decade by forming the Energy Foundation with the John D. and Catherine T. MacArthur Foundation and the Pew Charitable Trusts. Each contributor agreed to gift up to $100 million over the course of a decade to the Energy Foundation, which would explore alternative energy sources. The foundation formed another alliance in 1991 when it partnered with the United Nations Development Programme, UNICEF, the World Health Organization, and the World Bank to establish the Children's Vaccine Initiative, designed to inoculate children all over the world against preventable childhood diseases. Other partnerships included the Partners in Population and Development program, formed with the United Nations Population Fund and designed to promote collaboration regarding family planning and reproductive health issues, and a program providing job training and job opportunities to poor, inner-city residents, developed with the Manpower Demonstration Research Corporation as well as the U.S. Department of Housing and Urban Development and Chase Bank.

The emphasis on the importance of agricultural studies continued, and progress was made. In the mid-1990s scientists succeeded in cloning a gene that was resistant to bacterial blight, a disease that affected rice crops globally. Foundation-funded scientists also discovered, in 1997, that cereal plants were genetically similar, which meant that findings from the rice biotechnology program could be applied to other cereals, such as maize, sorghum, and wheat. Scientists also succeeded in developing a genetic engineering method that incorporated vitamin A and iron, two key nutritional vitamins, in rice.

In 1998 the foundation elected Gordon Conway as its 12th president. Conway, an agricultural ecologist who had pioneered the method known as integrated pest management, was the first ecologist to lead a major charitable organization. The timing could not have been more appropriate, for as the foundation's agricultural studies grew, so did public objections to bioengineered food crops, the research of which the foundation supported. By the late 1990s the foundation found itself wedged between two opposing factions—those against the development of genetically engineered crops and large corporations hoping to cash in on genetically manufactured plants. Conway was equipped to speak to both, since he supported but also disagreed with aspects of each. Conway believed that bioengineered food was necessary to eradicate world hunger, but he also believed that companies in the biotech-food industry were not being responsible in their efforts and were ignoring the needs of farmers in developing countries. Ecologists, farmers, and biotech companies, Conway felt, needed to work together to start the "doubly green revolution," a new agricultural revolution that would increase crop yields in developing nations and do so in an environmentally and socially sound manner. In an attempt to reach effective solutions, Conway set aside $3 million to support activists lobbying for product labeling of genetically engineered food ingredients, to fund the study of the ethical implications of bioengineered food, and to promote constructive and open dialogue between the differing factions.

By the late 1990s the foundation's endowment had a value exceeding $3 billion. The foundation's initiatives had evolved since its founding in 1913, but the organization found itself struggling with too many diverse initiatives. In response, The Rockefeller Foundation adopted a new global mission as it entered a new century. The new focus of the foundation centered on improving the lives of poor people around the world. The foundation's giving would revolve around four themes—creativity and culture, food security, health equity, and working communities, which involved helping poor urban neighborhoods to become effective and safe communities.

Principal Competitors

The Ford Foundation; The Carnegie Corporation of New York; The Lilly Endowment; The Bill and Melinda Gates Foundation; The W.K. Kellogg Foundation; The J. Paul Getty Trust; The Robert Wood Johnson Foundation; The Pew Charitable Trusts; The Robert W. Woodruff Foundation; The Anneberg Foundation; The David and Lucile Packard Foundation.

Further Reading

Brooks, Karen, "Genetically Engineered Rice Stirs Latest Debate on Biotechnology," *Fort Worth Star-Telegram,* January 12, 2000, p. 1.

Chernow, Ron, *Titan: The Life of John D. Rockefeller, Sr.,* New York: Random House, 1998.

Fosdick, Raymond Blaine, *A Philosophy for a Foundation,* New York: Rockefeller Foundation, 1963.

——, *The Story of the Rockefeller Foundation,* New York: Harper, 1952.

Goldin, Milton, "Shaky Foundations: Institutions to Strengthen Society Became Personal and Political Tax Shelters," *Barron's,* July 12, 1999, p. 46.

Lagnado, Lucette, "Raising the Ante: For Those Fighting Biotech Crops, Santa Came Early This Year," *Wall Street Journal,* December 14, 1999, p. A1.

Pennar, Karen, "Gordon Conway, Green Revolutionary," *Business Week,* November 16, 1998, p. 191.

Shaplen, Robert, *Toward the Well-Being of Mankind: Fifty Years of the Rockefeller Foundation,* Garden City, N.Y.: Doubleday, 1964.

Stipp, David, "The Voice of Reason in the Global Food Fight," *Fortune,* February 21, 2000, p. 164f.

—Mariko Fujinaka

Rollerblade, Inc.

One Sportsystem Plaza
Bordentown, New Jersey 08505
U.S.A.
Telephone: (609) 291-5800
Toll Free: (800) 283-6647
Fax: (609) 291-5900
Web site: http://www.rollerblade.com

*Wholly Owned Subsidiary of Benetton Sportsystem USA
(Division of Benetton Group S.p.A.)*
Incorporated: 1982 as Ole's Innovative Sports
Employees: 200
Sales: $150 million (1999 est.)
NAIC: 33992 Sporting and Athletic Good Manufacturing

Rollerblade, Inc., originator of the sport of inline skating, is a leading manufacturer in the ever-evolving inline skate market. Through product innovation and aggressive marketing Rollerblade established a sport and fitness craze that became synonymous with its name. The downside, however, was that Rollerblade had suddenly become a generic term for inline skates and skating, prompting the company to unleash a marketing campaign to protect its name. Despite its phenomenal growth from the 1980s into the mid-1990s, a slump in the late 1990s forced Rollerblade and its rivals to diversify into faster and flashier skates. Sales rebounded and by the 21st century inline skates were still the rage for fun, fitness, and sport—even spawning inline hockey, skating, and even soccer leagues. Rollerblade products are sold in dozens of countries, from the United States and Canada to Colombia, Hong Kong, India, Norway, Switzerland, Saudi Arabia, the United Kingdom, Uruguay, and others.

Something Borrowed, Something New: 1700s to 1981

Rollerblade started the inline skating phenomenon by improving and rejuvenating an existing product. Inline skates were invented in The Netherlands in the early 1700s: a Dutchman looking for a way to skate in the summer months nailed wooden spools to strips of wood and attached them to shoe bottoms. The first patent for skates with wheels in a single line was issued in Paris in 1819 to M. Petitbled. Models of the skate were made in both Europe and the United States, but all were unstable and difficult to turn. Skates with side-by-side wheels or "quad" skates, were developed by American James L. Plimpton in 1863. The new skates were easier to control, and they quickly became popular. Versions of the single-line skates continued to be produced, but roller-skating dominated that segment of recreational sports. Yet a young semipro hockey player and his brothers changed everything when their innovations made single-line skates faster and more maneuverable than roller skates.

With thousands of new sport and recreation products introduced to the market every year, few have had the success and name recognition of the Rollerblade skate developed by Scott Olson and his brothers. Olson, after a successful high school hockey career in Minnesota, went north to play junior level hockey in Brandon, Manitoba. He advanced to the National Hockey League (NHL) system and played with the Winnipeg Jets' minor league teams. In 1978 Olson came upon a pair of ice skates with wheels. He loved the idea of being able to skate year-round and believed other hockey players would enjoy using the skates for off-season training. Olson obtained the distribution rights for Canada and the Upper Midwest from the Los Angeles-based company that sold the skates. In 1980 Olson left professional hockey and began selling the skates full-time. He pitched the skates by wearing them everywhere; he even skated from Minneapolis to Grand Rapids, Minnesota, a distance of about 200 miles, to promote the skates.

Because Olson was constantly on the skates he knew they could use some improvement. He devised a way to make the blade length adjustable and, therefore, more maneuverable and developed a dual-bearing wheel which made the skate faster. The manufacturer, however, was not interested in the innovations. Through a patent search Olson found that Chicago Rollerskate, the largest U.S. manufacturer of roller skates, had an inactive single-line skate which was similar to his design. The 20-year-old Olson went to Chicago to negotiate buying the patent, which he finally obtained in 1981.

Ultimate Highs and Lowest Lows: 1982–85

Olson incorporated Ole's Innovative Sports in 1982. The company started out small, with Olson, his brothers Brennan

Company Perspectives:

Skating is many things to many people. To some, skating is about turning physical exertion into mental exhilaration. To others, it's about the heart racing at the mere smell of freshly laid asphalt. And to others still, it's about hearing music in the throbbing cadence of eight rolling wheels. Rollerblade knows that whether on boardwalks or city streets or the manicured cul-de-sacs of suburbia, skaters are ever striving to build speed and momentum. It's instinctive. The freedom of inline demands not that skaters leave well enough alone; but rather, that they leave it behind.

and Jim, and a few others assembling skates in the Olson family basement. First year sales on Rollerblade skates, which were equipped with a molded polyurethane boot shell for ankle support and a heel brake for stopping, exceeded $300,000. In 1983 the company moved to a facility in Eden Prairie, Minnesota, near the Minnesota Vikings Training Center. By then Olson had a growing company to manage. He also was busy seeking NHL player endorsements, promoting the skates to the media, and convincing sporting goods dealers to carry the skates. He needed more help and brought on a friend to handle the finances, but by the next year the growing business was in financial trouble which Olson attributed to his friend.

Help came from a Twin Cities automobile dealer, Jack Walser, who first put $75,000 into the company to keep it afloat and later offered $300,000 for 50 percent of the business. Robert L. Sturgis, a Minneapolis entrepreneur, was also interested in the company. According to Terry Fiedler in the September 1989 *Corporate Report Minnesota*, "Sturgis told Olson he could raise $1.5 million in a limited partnership for that same half of the company's stock." Olson agreed to the deal, and Sturgis and Robert O. Naegele (president of the investment company Naegele Communications and former owner of his family's billboard concern), extended Olson $100,000 in the form of a note. Sturgis was named CEO of Ole's Innovative Sports, and Scott Olson continued with sales and promotion of the skates. A few months later Sturgis told Olson he was having difficulty raising the $1.5 million and cut the offer in half. By late 1985 the money still had not been raised, and Sturgis and Naegele finally offered to buy out Olson. Unable to pay back the money the investors had put into the company Olson settled for $96,000 over two years and a royalty package. Olson's brothers stayed with the company.

Once out of the company Olson fought for the rights to his product designs, and when his royalties were reduced from two to one percent he filed a suit against Naegele and began a legal battle that lasted six years. Two disparate views of the high-profile Scott Olson were circulated. In one he was portrayed as a business owner without management skills or capital, and that he was fortunate to get as much as he did from the sale of the company. In the other he was cast as too honest and trusting and was forced out of the company he had founded. Dick Youngblood, in April 1993, wrote, "There's no need to mourn for Scott Olson, whose creative genius produced a gold mine called Rollerblade Inc. in 1979—but whose dearth of capital and management expertise cost him control of the company six years later."

In addition to pulling in Rollerblade royalties (which were expected to total about $10 million over the ten-year deal), Olson went into competition with the company he founded. He produced his Switch-It brand skates through Innovative Sports Systems, Inc. (ISS), and then through O.S. Designs Inc., he developed the Nuskate, which he sold in 1993 to CCM Sport Maska, Inc. of Canada. The company Olson first founded went on without him under a new name—as North American Training Corporation before becoming Rollerblade, Inc.—and under new leadership.

A New Era: 1986–91

In 1986, the year financial expert John Sundet and sports marketing veteran Mary Horwath joined Rollerblade Inc., the company was still losing money. The next year Sturgis sold his share of the company to Naegele, and Sundet succeeded him as president. Sundet, along with Horwath, repositioned the company in the marketplace. Rollerblade skates were trimmed down, painted neon colors, and given to beach-side skate rental shops on popular California beaches. The skate took off. "Instead of trying to market inline skates as an adjunct to ice hockey, we focused on selling the product as a leisure sport in and of itself," said Sundet in a February 1995 *Minneapolis Star Tribune* article. Rollerblade sales doubled in 1988, and the company claimed to have 70 to 75 percent of the estimated $10–$12 million market. Another Minnesota-based company, First Team Sports, Inc., was a distant second in the inline skate market.

Top sales for Rollerblade were in the ice skating strongholds of Minneapolis/St. Paul and Boston, but sales in southern California were rising rapidly. By 1990 nearly one-quarter of Rollerblade's business was in California, and the total inline market had grown to about $60 million. The sagging sporting goods industry was getting a boost from sales of inline skates priced from $100 for basic skates up to $330 for five-wheel racing models. Inline skating was no longer only a cross-training sport for hockey players and cross-country skiers; moreover, one-third of the new breed of skaters were female. Demand for Rollerblade skates started to outstrip production. The number of retail outlets selling the skates had grown from 31 in 1984 to 3,000 in 1990. The skates were sold in Canada, Europe, Australia, New Zealand, and Korea, as well as the United States.

In January 1991, Rollerblade doubled its space with a move to new headquarters in Minnetonka. Three months later the world's leading ski boot manufacturer, Nordica, purchased 50 percent of Rollerblade, Inc. from Naegele for an undisclosed amount. Naegele continued in his position as chairman of the newly formed board. Competitors, Scott Olson (then president of ISS) and David G. Soderquist (president of First Team Sports, Inc.), saw the purchase as a positive development for the inline skate industry. Nordica, with consolidated revenues of $450 million, had money available to promote the sport and establish it as more than just a fad.

Fad or not, Rollerblade sales had at least doubled every year from 1987 to 1991, and the competition was heating up. Number-two manufacturer First Team Sports brought NHL hockey superstar Wayne Gretzky aboard to promote its Ultra-Wheels line. Canstar Sports, Inc. was gaining market share with its Bauer Precision InLine Skates. The low end of the market was

---

Key Dates:

1981: Scott Olson buys single-line skate patent and begins making Rollerblade skates.

1982: Olson incorporates Ole's Innovative Sports (later renamed North American Training Corporation).

1984: Money problems force Olson to team up with Robert Sturgis, who becomes CEO.

1985: Olson is forced to sell out to Sturgis and local Minneapolis entrepreneur Robert Naegele.

1987: Sturgis sells his share of Rollerblade to Naegele.

1988: Rollerblade dominates the market with sales nearing $10 million.

1991: Naegele sells 50 percent stake to Nordica.

1993: Rollerblade files patent infringement lawsuits against competitors.

1994: Company introduces award-winning Active Brake Technology (ABT).

1995: Naegele sells the remainder of stake in Rollerblade to Nordica.

---

being tapped by Taiwanese-made skates selling for under $50, but because all but First Team Sports were privately held, market figures for the rapidly growing industry remained sketchy, and claims by the leading manufacturers conflicted with each other.

Competition was not the only threat to Rollerblade's market domination. Because Rollerblade was so successful in establishing the sport of inline skating its trademark was in danger of becoming a generic name—aspirin, linoleum, and cellophane were all once brand names that lost their trademarks to general use. The brand name Rollerblade was being used as a noun (rollerblades or blades) and as a verb (rollerblading or blading), much as the Xerox Corporation found its name synonymous with making copies. In 1990 the company had launched a campaign to protect its identity. Its market strategy shifted from promoting the sport of inline skating to developing brand identification. Print advertising and national TV ads were added to the company's less traditional promotional tool box. Concept shops, which highlighted Rollerblade skates, brightly-colored Blade Gear sportswear, accessories, and protective gear, were opened in sporting goods stores, but the company continued to use the unorthodox promotions that brought them early success.

When Mary Horwath had joined Rollerblade, she relied on "guerilla marketing" tactics that equated inline skating with a fun, active, and sexy lifestyle. With only a $200,000 budget she depended on aggressive and unorthodox yet inexpensive methods to get the skates into the public eye. Rollerblade skates were given to high profile celebrities and athletes who were seen and often photographed wearing the skates. Cross promotional tie-ins paired Rollerblade with large well-known companies that sought to be identified with youthful, athletic activities. Team Rollerblade, a group of elite stunt skaters, traveled around the country on "Rock 'N' Rollerblade Tours," appeared in commercials, and performed at the Super Bowl and at the Olympic games. Perhaps most importantly, the company took the skates out on the streets and gave the public opportunities to try them.

Wherever people gathered—fairs, festivals, theme parks, and college campuses—Rollerblade demonstration vans arrived.

Rivals Gaining Ground: 1992–95

The year 1992 was a time of transition for Rollerblade as it moved further away from its entrepreneurial roots. The inline market and the inline leader were maturing. In an executive overhaul, former Tonka executive John F. Hetterick assumed the roles of president and COO, and other top level positions were filled by people with experience in major corporations. John Sundet resigned as CEO in May 1992 and was succeeded by Hetterick. Mary Horwath, who in 1992 was ranked as one of the nation's 100 top marketing executives by the trade journal *Advertising Age*, left Rollerblade the next year. Rollerblade began to place more emphasis on the efficiency of operations, especially striving to meet shipping dates: late orders had been an ongoing headache for distributors. Twenty-four jobs were cut, mostly in marketing, sales, and finance, and more emphasis was placed on customer service. By the end of 1992 the company was again looking for more space to accommodate its rapid growth. *Corporate Report Minnesota* estimated Rollerblade's average annual growth rate to be 115.5 percent between the years 1987 and 1992.

Rollerblade's growth rate was propelled by a tripling of the number of inline skaters in the United States; however, the *Wall Street Journal* predicted in November 1993 that the industry was headed for a fall: sales growth had slowed, big ski industry concerns had entered the high-end market ($150–$300 range), and low-end skates accounted for 44 percent of total inline sales. Michael Selz of the *Wall Street Journal* wrote, "To cope with competition, skate makers are fighting harder. Rollerblade mounted one of the most aggressive responses, partly because it has the most to lose." In February 1993, Rollerblade filed a patent lawsuit against 33 competitors. Later that year, Rollerblade settled out-of-court with seven of the manufacturers, including the number two maker. First Team Sports, which was ranked 15th on *BusinessWeek*'s 1993 Hot Growth list, had experienced depressed earnings due to the suit.

Rollerblade remained the big name in recreational inline skates, but Bauer and Cooper brands, owned by the largest hockey equipment maker in the world, Canstar Sports, Inc., were the skates of choice for inline hockey. Sunbelt in-line hockey leagues were becoming as popular as Little League, and Canstar banked on brand name recognition and status as official sponsor of a professional league to help them overtake Rollerblade and First Team. Canstar's 1993 inline sales grew to $26 million. Second place First Team had sales of $38.2 million, and Rollerblade planned to challenge Canstar with its own inline hockey skate.

Safety was an ongoing concern for all the manufacturers. As the number of inline skating injuries rose, the Consumer Product Safety Commission issued warnings about the dangers of the sport. The June 1994 issue of the *Journal of the American Medical Association (JAMA)* cited key factors that contributed to inline injuries: cruising speeds of 10–17 miles per hour; sharing the roadways with motor vehicles, bicyclists, pedestrians, and pets; and falling on hard surfaces. Rollerblade encouraged use of safety equipment and lessons for beginners through its "Skate Smart" safety education program and its "Asphalt Bites" campaign. In 1994 Rollerblade introduced Active Brake Technology (ABT), an award-winning innovation which made stopping easier for beginners and improved speed control.

Rollerblade's 1994 sales were estimated by *Newsweek* to be about $260 million or about 40 percent of the $650 million inline market, and its competitors appeared poised to capture more of Rollerblade's market share. In late 1994 Canstar was purchased by Nike Inc., the athletic footwear and clothing giant. Already benefitting from the resurgence of hockey, Canstar received an added boost from Nike's marketing and sales mastery. First Team Sports also was capitalizing on the inline hockey boom and reported sales revenues of $86 million in fiscal 1995. Rollerblade was still relying on its grassroots activities and promotional tie-ins to sell its skates. The company's advertising budget remained modest—$4 million in1995—and was limited to spot markets.

In November 1995—following months of speculation about the company's future—Naegele sold his stake in Rollerblade to Nordica. The *New York Times* said Naegele received at least $150 million for his 50 percent share of the company, though later reports put the figure at $200 million. Nordica, in turn, had sold a minority interest of Rollerblade to an affiliate of Goldman, Sachs & Company. No longer under a dual ownership Rollerblade appeared to be in a better position to capitalize on the financial strength, research and development support, manufacturing capacity, and international distribution capabilities that Nordica offered.

Rollerblade and inline skating had moved into the mainstream of recreational sports, yet had plenty of room for growth with only 14 percent of U.S. households owning inline skates in 1995 as compared with 51 percent owning bicycles. Inline makers were optimistic about growth in the international marketplace, where Rollerblade had a foothold by way of Nordica. According to industry and company estimates Rollerblade still held nearly half of the market in 1995, but it remained to be seen if inline skating would continue to grow or would follow the path of the roller-skate industry and slip into a cycle of boom and bust.

Boom & Bust Indeed: 1996–99

In 1996 inline skating was far more than just a fad and brought revenue to the recreational, fitness, and athletic markets. Statistics from the International Inline Skating Association charted the meteoric rise of inline skating, and cited it as the fastest growing sport in the nation. No longer a radical form of roller-skating, it was instead a burgeoning fitness craze for people of all ages. Rollerblade rode the crest to its peak and, inevitably, the market faltered in 1997. In the obligatory bust all three of the inline skate behemoths lost their footing; Rollerblade still dominated with about 40 percent of the U.S. market and $355 million in sales, yet second and third place producers First Team Sports and K2 Inc. were the worse for wear. According to an October *Forbes* article, First Team experienced an estimated 36 percent falloff in sales while K2 tumbled some 15 percent. All this despite research figures finding in excess of 30 million inline skate owners (divided evenly between men and women) in the United States, and the burgeoning preteen market. According to Rollerblade's web site, nearly two-thirds of all 11-year-olds owned a pair of inline skates in 1997.

Yet while it seemed as if the inline skating boom was over with faltering sales and sports stores slashing prices to move product, Rollerblade's parent company, Benetton Sportsystem (which also owned Nordica) upped the ante by raising prices and bringing fancier models to stores to concentrate on diehard enthusiasts rather than beginners. Then the Benetton family, major shareholders in both the public company and its private subsidiaries, began selling off its shares in the sports-related division to the publicly traded parent company, Benetton Group, in 1998. Benetton Sportsystem was renamed Playlife in Europe and Asia after the transition, and several Playlife megastores were opened in Europe. Subsequently, rather than open such stores in the United States, Benetton instead made a surprising deal with Sears to market both its clothing and sporting goods through the retailer's stores. For many, it was a drastic dressing down to Benetton's image, but the company was soon dumped by Sears. After the debut of another of the parent company's controversial ad campaigns (which had been stirring up debate for several years), this time featuring death row inmates, Sears pulled all Benetton products from its stores in early 2000. Rollerblade's products, it seemed, were lost amid all the chaos.

Though the inline skating industry faltered briefly, Rollerblade and its rivals continued to entice customers with newer and wilder versions of its skates and sales rallied once again. With the increased popularity of "extreme" sports, Rollerblade was there with several new models of skates, as well as accessories (helmets, elbow, wrist, and knee pads, etc.) specifically designed for all age groups. Inline skating reinvented itself and became the impetus for rethinking other sports—from Scott Olson's original use for inline skates, off-season hockey training—came inline basketball and hockey leagues, speed skating, extreme skating (dubbed "aggressive" or "stunt" skating), and even more unusual variations such as inline dancing and even inline soccer. Though growth for the industry was only in the low single-digits, as opposed to huge leaps earlier in the decade (such as 51 percent from 1991 to 1992 and 49 percent from 1993 to 1994, according to Rollerblade's web site), there was still growth. Sales were also subject to weather restrictions, except in fair weather states such as California and Texas (which led the market in sales), but spring and summer always brought a surge in sales.

Inline Skating in the 21st Century and Beyond

The future of inline skating was anyone's guess in the 21st century, but the sport demonstrated serious staying power. For fitness, strapping on a pair of Rollerblade skates was an excellent workout. For skaters both young and old, inline skating was fast fun that burned calories, strengthened muscles, and was less stressful to the body than running. Even *Prevention* magazine had begun recommending inline skating to its readership as a good, low-impact form of exercise and recreation (with proper protective equipment). More and more cities built inline skating trails and paths, and in case anyone was forgetting its name, Rollerblade had donated millions of dollars to be the official inline skate of New York City's parks. With increased emphasis on safety, injuries had fallen nationwide and some parks even favored inline skating patrols to police recreational areas. Rollerblade, meanwhile, eyed continued comfort and flexibility as a key to its market share. Newer innovations included convertible skates (removable shoe-boots on plastic wheel frames, called "Nature" skates), models with shock absorbers for rougher terrains (such as the "Coyote" and "Outback X"), and even "Xtenblade" skates with adjustable framing for the constantly growing feet of children.

Principal Competitors

First Team Sports, Inc.; K2 Inc.; Variflex, Inc.

Further Reading

Alexander, Steve, "Rollerblade, Inc. Settles Out-of-Court with Seven Competitors over Patents," *Star Tribune* (Minneapolis), September 15, 1993, p. 1D.

Benezra, Karen, "Rollerblade Taps Disney, Gatorade," *Brandweek,* October 10, 1994, p. 3.

Beran, George, "Rollerblade, Inc. on a Roll," *Pioneer Press Dispatch* (St. Paul), June 19, 1988.

Brumback, Nancy, "Mega-Deals on Wheels," *Daily News Record,* August 11, 1995, p. 22.

Comte, Elizabeth, "Blade Runner," *Forbes,* October 12, 1992, pp. 114–17.

Crowley, Aileen, "Communication with Consultants Keeps Projects Rolling Along (Case Study of Rollerblade Inc.)," *PC Week,* August 10, 1998, p. 67.

Dendy, Christina, "On a Roll," *Parks & Recreation,* September 1999, pp. 152–59.

Dickinson, Ben, "Skating's Soft Science," *Esquire,* October 1997, p. 130.

Fiedler, Terry, "Rolling with the Punches," *Corporate Report Minnesota,* September 1989, pp. 47–52.

Feineman, Neil, *Wheel Excitement: The Official Rollerblade Guide to Inline Skating,* New York: Hearst Books, May 1991, 143 p.

Ferguson, Tim W., and Josephine Lee Forbes, "Road Rash (Inline Skating Companies' Earnings Decrease)," October 6, 1997, p. 48.

Ferguson, Tom W., and Josephine Lee, "Road Rash," *Forbes,* October 6, 1997, p. 48.

Feyder, Susan, "Nordica Buys 50 Percent of Rollerblade," *Star Tribune* (Minneapolis), March 22, 1991, p. ID.

Goerne, Carrie, "Rollerblade Reminds Everyone That Its Success Is Not Generic," *Marketing News,* March 2, 1992, pp. 1–2.

Greisin, David, "A Fleet No. 2 in the Rollerblade Derby," *BusinessWeek,* May 24, 1993, pp. 67–68.

Gross, David M. "Zipping Along in Asphalt Heaven," *Time,* August 13, 1990, p. 56.

"Growing Pains Afflict In-Line Skate Firms," *CityBusiness* (Minneapolis/St. Paul), May 29, 1992, p. 2.

Horwath, Mary, "Guerrilla Marketing 101," *Working Women,* December 1991, pp. 23–24.

Kaszuba, Mike, "Rollerblade's Success Hasn't Brought Happiness," *Star Tribune* (Minneapolis), March 6, 1991, p. ID.

Krajick, Kevin, "Don't Look Now, But Here Come the Bladerunners," *Smithsonian,* September 1995. pp. 60–69.

Marin, Rick, with T. Trent Gegax, "Blading on Thin Ice," *Newsweek,* December 12, 1994, pp. 64–65.

Matzer, Marla, "A Nice One for the Great One," *Forbes,* May 8, 1995, p. 88.

Merrill, Ann, "Italian Investors Want Piece of Skate Maker Rollerblade," *City Business* (Minneapolis/St. Paul), March 18–24, 1991, pp. 1, 19.

Munk, Nina, "Hockey in the Sun," *Forbes,* August 15, 1994, pp. 95–96.

"Nike to Acquire Canadian Hockey Gear Firm," *Star Tribune,* (Minneapolis), December 15, 1994, p. 7D.

O'Connor, Leo, "From Roller Skates to Rollerblades," *Mechanical Engineering,* August 1995, p. 84.

Pesky, Greg, "Sharpening the Blade," *Sporting Goods News,* August 1992, pp.56–57.

Peterson, Susan E., "Sundet Resigns As Rollerblade CEO," *Star Tribune* (Minneapolis), May 9, 1992, p. 3D.

Porter, Paula, "Key to the Design of the Newest Hot Wheels: Trail and Error," *Design News,* August 2, 1999, p. 73. "Rollerblade Complaint Rocks In-Line Market," *Sporting Goods Business,* March 1993, p. 8.

"Rollerblade Co-Owner Sells Stake to Nordica," *New York Times,* November 14, 1995, p. C3.

Schafer, Lee, "It's Not a Fad," *Corporate Report Minnesota,* April 1992, pp. 31–39.

Schieber, M.D., Richard A.; Christine M. Branche-Dorsey, Ph.D.,MSPH; and George W. Ryan, Ph.D., "Comparison of In-Line Skating Injuries with Rollerskating and Skateboarding Injuries," *JAMA,* June 15, 1994, pp. 1856–1858.

Schott, Susan, "In-Line Skating Boom Breaks the Ice," *Reuter Business Report,* February 8, 1995.

Selz, Michael, "Once-Rolling In-Line Skate Makers Skid Amid Rivalry," *Wall Street Journal,* November 30, 1993, p. 2B.

Smith, Tom, "When Gravity Fails: The State's Fastest Growing Companies," *Corporate Report Minnesota,* May 1993, p. 88.

Therrien, Lois, "Rollerblade Is Skating in Heavier Traffic," *BusinessWeek,* June 24, 1991, pp. 114–15.

—Kathleen Peippo
—updated by Nelson Rhodes

St Ives plc

St Ives House
Lavington St
London SE1 0NX
United Kingdom
Telephone: (+44) 171 928-8844
Fax: (+44) 171 633-9116
Web site: http://www.st-ives.co.uk

Public Company
Incorporated: 1964
Employees: 5,124
Sales: £452.2 million (US$718 million) (1999)
Stock Exchanges: London
Ticker Symbol: SIV
NAIC: 323119 Other Commercial Printing; 323111
    Commercial Gravure Printing

St Ives plc is one of the United Kingdom's leading commercial printers and that country's leading printer of financial documents. St Ives and its subsidiaries provide printing services for book and magazine publishers; the direct response market; multimedia products, including CD and CD-ROM sleeve art; and the financial community. The company specializes in just-in-time and last-minute orders, making it especially popular among magazine publishers. The company prints such well-known U.K. magazines as the *Sunday Telegraph*, the *Economist, Vogue, Heat, Computing,* and *Top Gear.* In all, St Ives prints more than 600 magazine titles for such publishers as VNU, Reed Business, EMAP, and others. Magazine contracts account for some 30 percent of the company's sales. St Ives's strength as a printer for the mergers-and-acquisitions market, IPOs, annual reports, and prospectuses, has enabled the company, through subsidiary Burrups, to capture the lead in the United Kingdom's financial printing market. In the multimedia market, the company has printed the CD sleeve art for such artists as Cher, Madonna, Aerosmith, Tina Turner and Boyzone. While music printing remains a limited part of St Ives's sales, the company has made stronger inroads in printing for the computer and CD-ROM markets. Book printing also plays a key role in the company's

sales, and the company, particularly through subsidiary Clays Limited, prints books for much of the United Kingdom's major publishers, and the company regularly prints such prestigious (and best-selling) titles as the winners of the Booker and Whitbread awards. The fast rising segment of St Ives is its direct-marketing division, which prints leaflets, newspaper inserts and direct-mail products. The company has targeted this division not only for growth in the United Kingdom, boosting its operations with the acquisition of rival Hunters Armley in 1998, but also overseas: St Ives has established strong positions in the U.S. market, particularly through the acquisition of Perlmuter Printing in the mid-1990s, giving the company a base in Florida; and in the German market, with the acquisition of Johler Druck in 1995. Direct-mail printing accounts for approximately one-third of the company's revenues. St Ives' willingness to invest heavily not only in acquisitions but also in modernized technology has long set it apart from its rivals.

The Formative Years: 1960s–80s

St Ives was founded by Robert Gavron in 1964. Gavron, a lawyer and barrister, had entered a small London-based printing company in 1955 as an assistant. By the early 1960s, Gavron's experience led him to make an offer to buy the company. With a loan of £5,000, Gavron bought the company, and renamed it after one of its printing plants, which was located in the seaside resort town of St Ives.

Gavron began building St Ives into a strong regional printer, achieving much of the company's growth internally. In the 1980s, however, Gavron decided to make the leap into the leading ranks of printers. Taking St Ives public in 1985, Gavron raised the capital to begin making a series of acquisitions, buying up many of its smaller rivals in order to build up its market position.

These acquisitions propelled St Ives to the top of its market, making the company the United Kingdom's largest commercial printer. One of the company's most important purchases came in 1986, with the acquisition of the Clays Limited, a strong player in the book printing market located in Bungay. The following year, St Ives added to its printing portfolio when it

Company Perspectives:

We have continued to strengthen our competitive position in our principal markets. This has been achieved through consistent investment in people, systems and equipment to an extent unrivaled by our competitors. The investment planned for the coming years will further consolidate our position. Our commitment to customer service is of paramount importance in retaining and growing our business.

acquired financial printer Burrups Limited, which had been in business since the early 17th century and which counted among the United Kingdom's most prominent financial printers. In this way, St Ives gained a strong share of the bustling financial printing sector—at a time when the financial community was undergoing a wave of mergers and acquisitions.

By the end of the 1980s, St Ives began eyeing other markets, and particularly the vast commercial printing market of the United States. In 1989, the company acquired A.D. Weiss Printing, located in Hollywood, Florida. This acquisition brought the company into the U.S. direct-mail market, a printing category that rapidly grew into one of the company's most important revenue sources. After the purchase, the Florida subsidiary was renamed St Ives Inc. and became the basis for the company's further growth in the United States.

Back home, however, the recession of the early 1990s caught up with the company. By 1991, St Ives was experiencing a cut in its profits. The entire printing industry was under pressure, with many of the company's competitors struggling to stay afloat. Despite its own financial difficulties, St Ives maintained its steady investment program, and began concentrating especially on modernizing its equipment. These investments were later credited with helping the company recover more quickly from the recession than its competitors, enabling St Ives to build an even stronger position in its home markets.

Roughing It in the 1990s

In the meantime, the company continued to face profit pressures. The company's financial printing activities were crimped by the nervousness of the stock market—which saw many IPOs, a primary source of St Ives' financial printing activity, put on hold. At the same time, the worldwide cutback in advertising spending—one of the more immediate results of the recession—led to a sharp decrease in the company's magazine printing business. As publishers cut back on pagination, St Ives' revenues in the sector, one of its largest revenue producers, also began to shrink. The company's troubles in the United Kingdom were mirrored in its operations in the United States, which began losing money in the early 1990s.

Robert Gavron retired from his position as company chairman in 1993, taking a non-executive directorship while still holding a sizable share in the company he had built over 30 years into the foremost U.K. commercial printer. Gavron maintained his shareholding through the middle of the decade, finally selling the majority of his interest in 1998.

Gavron was replaced by Miles Emley, who continued to lead the company into the new century. By 1994, the worst of the recession seemed to have passed. St Ives was once again seeing a rise in its contracts—particularly in the crucial magazine markets, as advertisements once again began to fill out pagination. The company was also helped by the award of contracts to print documents relating to a new round of company privatizations in France. Despite rising paper costs—which caused the magazine sector to stagnate for a time in 1995—St Ives began to see renewed profit growth. The company's strong investment program, which saw St Ives invest more than £125 million over the first five years of the decade, had succeeded in modernizing the company's machine park—allowing them to keep printing costs low.

As St Ives came through the end of the recession in the mid-1990s, it began to take steps to lessen its exposure to the cyclical nature of its core markets—books, magazines and financial printing. The company targeted two new areas for future growth: direct mail, a market which was growing strongly in the United Kingdom at mid-decade; and multimedia, particularly printing the inserts for CDs and CD-ROMs, a sector that saw double-digit growth in the second half of the decade. At the same time, St Ives continued to profit from its ongoing investment program, establishing its leading position for turnaround times—supplying overnight delivery to the new boom in mergers and acquisitions, takeovers, and IPOs.

In 1995, the company stepped into new territory when it acquired Johler Druck, of Germany. This acquisition not only gave St Ives its first entry onto the continent, it also strengthened its direct-mail activities. By the end of the decade, direct mail became one of the company's top revenue regenerators, with as much as one-third of annual sales provided by this sector. Nonetheless, the United Kingdom remained the company's chief base of operations, producing some 75 percent of sales.

One year after the Druck acquisition, the company moved to bolster its U.S. business, acquiring Ohio-based Perlmuter Printing, further strengthening the company's direct-mail position there. Back home, the United Kingdom and Europe as a whole began to see steady increases in the number of mergers and acquisitions, and particularly so-called megamergers, as well as hostile takeovers, as the European Union moved closer toward the single currency market. These developments gave a boost to St Ives in 1997, as it was called on to print many of the related financial documents. The deregulation of the U.K.'s building societies (a form of cooperative banking), which allowed the building societies to convert to publicly listed status, proved a windfall for St Ives, as the company won the contracts to print the documents for some of the largest of the converting building societies.

In the late 1990s, St Ives continued to build its direct marketing business. In 1998, the company acquired rival U.K. printer Hunters Armley. While the move was greeted with acceptance by industry analysts, by the end of the decade the company's increasing reliance on direct marketing had begun to raise flags. The rise of the Internet and growing belief in a coming Internet-based economy suggested that direct mailing would soon become a thing of the past—as more and more marketers turned to the Internet, rather than printed mailings.

```
┌─────────────────────────────────────────────┐
│              Key Dates:                       │
│                                               │
│ 1955:  Robert Gavron joins printing company.  │
│ 1964:  Gavron purchases company, renames it   │
│        St Ives.                               │
│ 1985:  Company completes public offering.     │
│ 1986:  Acquisition of Clays Limited.          │
│ 1987:  Acquisition of Burrups Limited.        │
│ 1989:  Acquisition of A.D. Weiss Printing.    │
│ 1993:  Gavron retires.                        │
│ 1995:  Acquisition of Johler Druck.           │
│ 1996:  Acquisition of Perlmuter Printing.     │
│ 1998:  Acquisition of Hunters Armley.         │
│ 2000:  Company announces two-year, £100 mil-  │
│        lion investment program.               │
└─────────────────────────────────────────────┘
```

If technology appeared to threaten St Ives from one side, it held out promise from another. By the end of the 20th century, St Ives was preparing to move fully to next-generation digital printing systems, promising more flexibility and still quicker turnaround times. Having built a leading position in the rapidly maturing British market, St Ives began to look toward the United States and Europe for future growth, promising new acquisitions in the early years of the century. At the same time St Ives announced its continued commitment to investing in its future, promising some £100 million in investments through the year 2002.

Principal Subsidiaries

Bryer & Spencer Limited; Burrups Limited; Burrups Japan KK; Clays Limited; DisplayCraft Limited; Harlequin Colourprint Limited; Hunters Armley Limited; Johler Druck GmbH (Germany); Red Letter Marketing Services Limited; Smiths Colour Printers Limited; St Ives Data Management Limited; St Ives Graphics Media Limited; St Ives Multimedia BV (Netherlands); St Ives Multimedia Limited; St Ives Inc. (U.S.A.); Sevenoaks Print Finishers Limited; The Perlmuter Printing Company (U.S.A.); Westerham Press Limited.

Principal Competitors

Banta Corporation; Experian Inc.; Bertelsmann AG; Merrill Corporation; Big Flower Press Holdings, Inc.; Quebecor Inc.; Bowne & Co., Inc.; R.R. Donnelley & Sons Company; Times Publishing.

Further Reading

Kar-Gupta, Sudip, "St Ives Boosted by Rise in M&A Activity," *Reuters*, April 18, 2000.

Levi, Jim, "St Ives Arrives Just in Time," *Daily Telegraph*, April 19, 2000, p. 37.

Potter, Ben, "St Ives on an Uncertain Road," *Daily Telegraph*, October 14, 1998, p. 29.

Stevenson, Tom, "St Ives Looks Impressive in Print," *Independent*, October 9, 1996, p. 25.

—M. L. Cohen

The SAS Group

Frosundaviks Alle 1, Solna
S-195 87 Stockholm
Sweden
Telephone: +46 8 797-00-00
Toll Free: (800) 221-2350
Fax: +46 8 797 12-10
Web site: http://www.scandinavian.net

Consortium of SAS Danmark A/S, SAS Norge ASA, and
SAS Sverige AB, Each 50% State-Owned
Incorporated: 1946
Employees: 28,900
Sales: SKr 41.51 billion (1999)
Stock Exchanges: Copenhagen Oslo Stockholm
Ticker Symbols: SASDK; SASB.OL; SAS.ST
NAIC: 481111 Scheduled Passenger Air Transportation;
481112 Scheduled Freight Air Transportation; 481212
Nonscheduled Chartered Freight Air Transportation;
481211 Nonscheduled Chartered Passenger Air
Transportation; 72111 Hotels (Except Casino Hotels)
and Motels

The SAS Group is made up of the Scandinavian Airlines System and SAS International Hotels d.b.a. Radisson SAS Hotels and Resorts. The namesake airline is a unique example of international cooperation between three culturally similar but independent nations. Its charismatic CEO of the 1980s, Jan Carlzon, helped steer the airline through deregulated skies by an uncompromising dedication to business travelers. In spite of seemingly endless rounds of cost-cutting in the 1990s, the airline still satisfies them.

Underground Beginnings

Late in the 1930s three independent Scandinavian airline companies, Det Danske Luftartselskab (DDL) of Denmark, Det Norske Luftfartselskap (DNL) of Norway, and Aktiebolaget Aerotransport (ABA) of Sweden, made plans for a collaborative transatlantic passenger service. But their plans for the Bergen-New York service had to be postponed when Denmark and Norway were invaded by Nazi Germany. During the war the three companies secretly continued to arrange their consortium. Since Sweden remained neutral its investors were relatively free to conduct their own business. The private owner of Sweden's share of SAS, Swedish Intercontinental Airlines (SILA), negotiated to purchase American airplanes when the war ended. They hoped this would give SAS an auspicious start and enable it to begin operations immediately after the war. In 1943, SILA, the purchasing agent for SAS, placed the first order for seven Douglas DC-4s. At great risk the Danes smuggled their share of the down payment to Sweden.

When the war ended SILA purchased a number of American B-17 bombers. These airplanes were acquired by SILA for only one dollar each. The "Flying Fortresses" were converted for passenger service by the Svenska Aeroplan Aktiebolaget (SAAB). On June 27, 1945, barely two months after the fall of Germany, ABA inaugurated their transatlantic service to New York from Stockholm employing the refitted B-17s. A year later the DC-4s went into service. SAS's three-nation flag and logo were created that year, and south Atlantic DC-4 service to Brazil and Uruguay also was inaugurated. The Atlantic services of DDL, DNL, and ABA were combined under SAS, but their European and domestic services continued to operate independently until 1948. That same year SILA acquired all of ABA's privately held stock. In 1951 the European, Atlantic, and domestic services of the three companies were combined, and SAS became the international flag carrier of Norway, Denmark, and Sweden.

DDL, DNL, and ABA were each 50 percent owned by the governments of Denmark, Norway, and Sweden, respectively. Together the three companies formed the SAS Consortium. DDL and DNL each owned two-sevenths of the SAS Consortium and ABA owned three-sevenths. From its inception SAS was operated as an unsubsidized instrument of the Scandinavian trade and commerce.

In 1949 SAS expanded its intercontinental service to Bangkok via Europe and central Asia. Two years later service was extended from Bangkok to Tokyo. In 1954 SAS pioneered a polar route to Los Angeles and, three years later, one to Tokyo.

Company Perspectives:

SAS shall offer competitive flight connections in, between, to and from each of the Scandinavian countries via flights arranged either under its own auspices or together with selected partners. SAS prioritizes absolute safety, maximum punctuality and excellent personal service. SAS makes every effort to design its products and services to meet the market's general requirements, as well as the individual's specific wishes and the need for freedom of choice. SAS's operations shall maintain satisfactory profitability in terms of its owners' requirements for a return on their investments. SAS shall also be perceived as an attractive investment object. SAS is strongly committed to limiting the environmentally harmful effects of aviation. SAS encourages social development through its contributions to cultural life, as well as sports and education.

It was the first airline to fly the Caravelle, a revolutionary French-built jet with its engines mounted on the rear of the fuselage. The airline also ordered special cold weather versions of the DC-8 and DC-9 from Douglas.

About this time SAS was confronted with a basic problem in airline economics. Most of its destinations were European, which meant that most of its flights were of short duration. This, in turn, translated into frequent takeoffs and landings and increased wear on the airplane. Moreover, the cost of preparing an aircraft for another flight was incurred more frequently. There was, therefore, an economic incentive to operate ''long haul'' flights to more distant points. During this period SAS also suffered from overcapacity, or simply having too many airplanes.

A solution to these problems arose when SAS was approached by officials from Thailand who wished to establish their own international airline services. SAS was chosen over other airline companies because Thailand regarded the Scandinavian countries as politically neutral. In 1959 an agreement was reached and a new company called Thai Airways International, Ltd. was formed. Under the agreement SAS contributed 30 percent of that company's total capital of US$100,000. Thai Airways would be sole concessionaire on all routes to foreign destinations for 15 years. SAS would provide the management, support, and flight personnel in addition to leasing the necessary aircraft. Thai Airways began operations in 1960 and recorded its first profit five years later. Today, Thai companies are sole owners of TAI, Ltd. but technical, operational, and commercial cooperation with SAS continues.

Innkeepers in 1960

SAS began a limited related diversification in 1960 when it purchased the Royal Hotel in Copenhagen. Later, SAS established a catering subsidiary and a charter airline called Scanair. In 1965, SAS created the first Europe-wide computerized reservation service (or ''CRS''), providing the company with a significant advantage over its larger European competitors.

In February 1970, SAS formed an inter-airline association with KLM (Royal Dutch Airlines), Swissair, and UTA (Union

de Transports Aeriens of France), known as the KSSU group. Together they established a maintenance pool that offered cooperative operational and technical services. As one unit they were better able to compete with major airlines such as BOAC, Air France, and Lufthansa. SAS spent much of the 1970s expanding its service area and updating its fleet. The combined ''internal'' and ''external'' expansion programs made SAS a major international air carrier by the end of the decade.

After 17 profitable years SAS suffered its first loss in 1980. It was threatened by increased competition from the recently deregulated American airline companies and low-cost operators, including Freddie Laker's transatlantic ''Skytrain.'' Compounding this problem was SAS's overly conservative management style. Not only was there less concern for passengers or service on SAS, but entrenched management was broadening its scope of authority and centralizing the bureaucracy. Indeed, a number of employee responsibilities were taken away. Many changes were needed if SAS was to remain competitive, and the first step was to install more enlightened leadership.

The Carlzon Years: 1981–93

The man chosen by the board of directors in 1981 was Jan Carlzon, formerly the head of Linjeflyg, a domestic Swedish air carrier and subsidiary of SAS. Applying an innovative management style, Carlzon first recommended treating expenses as resources in an effort to find ways of raising efficiency. He declared, ''All three Scandinavian countries can only survive by doing business in foreign markets; business travel is the backbone of SAS traffic; the first purpose of a Scandinavian airline must be to serve business.'' Since SAS failed to consistently attract the business traveler, Carlzon initiated a strong campaign to standardize and improve the company's business class passenger service. As a result, one year later SAS recorded a US$24.6 million profit for the airline operation, and more than doubled that the following year. Moreover, SAS invested millions of dollars in programs for staff training and motivation, urging employees to ''work smarter, not harder.'' Finally, in the effort to bring about changes in management, most of the airline's principal managers were replaced as a new organizational structure was introduced.

Carlzon also launched a campaign aimed at making SAS the most punctual airline in the world. He even had a computer terminal installed in his office so that he was constantly apprised of every flight. When a delay threatened the departure of an airplane he would telephone the crew and investigate the problem personally. On-time efficiency was raised to 90 percent, making SAS the most punctual airline in Europe. Carlzon then took steps to improve flight operations by selling or leasing older jets and purchasing the most recent state-of-the-art equipment. The airports of Copenhagen and Bangkok were designated as the airline's European and Asian hubs. All flights were designed to connect at these hubs to facilitate passenger transfers. Much of Copenhagen Airport's traffic includes passengers flying on to other destinations. The other airports, Oslo's Fornebu and Stockholm's Arlanda, are secondary hubs connecting SAS with smaller domestic services.

In 1984, SAS began operating hovercraft between Copenhagen Airport and the busy southern Swedish port of Malmö. The

---

Key Dates:

1946: SAS consortium is officially formed, though certain services of the three carriers remain independent.

1951: Operations are consolidated and SAS serves as the international flag carrier of Norway, Denmark, and Sweden.

1954: SAS pioneers polar route to Los Angeles.

1960: Purchase of the Royal Hotel in Copenhagen brings the group into the hospitality industry.

1970: KSSU group teams SAS with three continental carriers to save operational costs.

1981: Jan Carlzon chosen to steer SAS through hostile, deregulated skies.

1993: Carlzon leaves after Alcazar alliance crumbles.

1999: "SAS 2000" program is launched to deliver improved service with a Scandinavian flavor.

17-mile trip across the Oresund strait directly to the airplane tarmac in Copenhagen could be made in 30 minutes. The hovercraft (British Hovercraft Corporation AP-188s) were impervious to water, land, and ice. Although owned by DSO (a subsidiary of Danish State Railways), the hovercraft operated under the SAS name and with SAS personnel.

Believing that little more could be done to improve the "air travel" of SAS, Carlzon concentrated on what happened to the customer on the ground. A new service concept called SAS Business Hotels and Destination Service was introduced that enabled passengers to confirm reservations and arrange rental cars and hotel rooms with one phone call. In addition, SAS created Business Travel Systems that expanded the capabilities of its computerized reservations system.

SAS investigated the feasibility of a second teaming arrangement with Sabena of Belgium and Finnair of Finland. An agreement would involve coordination of flight schedules to more efficiently utilize their share of certain highly competitive markets. Because of its size and pragmatic character SAS often was compared with Delta Air Lines in the United States. SAS flew to 90 cities in 40 countries, operating 96 aircraft, including DC-8s, DC-9s, DC-10s, B-747s, and F-27s. The airline planned to receive 16 new aircraft to cover expansion plans for the 1988–90 period. Its air cargo business, with a hub in Cologne, West Germany, was one of the most sophisticated in the world. SAS shopped around the model for this facility's computerized cargo system to airlines that did not compete in the same markets.

The SAS Group operated a number of subsidiaries aside from the airline. These included Vingresor, the largest tour operator in Scandinavia, and Service Partner, a profitable catering service. In addition, the group operated a network of 11 first class hotels in Scandinavia, Vienna, and Singapore. The SAS Group also owned the Olson & Wright air cargo company, the Scanair charter airline service, and an insurance company.

By the end of the decade, a half dozen U.S. carriers had set up routes to Scandinavia. To keep a share of inbound international traffic (most of its passengers were Scandinavian themselves), SAS worked to forge links to other airlines' networks. British Airways PLC thwarted the company's offer to buy British Caledonian Airways Ltd. in 1987. Its attempts to invest in Aerolineas Argentinas were classified a "privatization nightmare." SAS did acquire an 18.4 percent share of struggling U.S. carrier Continental Airlines, which boosted U.S. traffic by 28 percent for SAS in its first year. Another deal with Airlines of Britain, a group of small carriers, gave SAS some rare slots at London's Heathrow Airport.

Cutting Costs and Making Pacts in the 1990s

SAS streamlined its corporate structure in the late 1980s, thinning layers of management as well as reducing the number of employees per plane. Job-cutting and efficiency measures continued into the early 1990s as the Gulf War and a global recession slowed business. SAS lost US$120 million in 1990, after earning US$193 million the year before. It lost more than US$250 million in the next two years. Carlzon launched another US$1 billion cost-cutting program to ensure that SAS would be among the surviving European airlines. Among positive developments, the fall of the Soviet Union opened up a new frontier for SAS, particularly in cargo. In addition to trade with the CIS itself, SAS ferried shipments from Asia through Scandinavia to the United States.

SAS helped pioneer the concept of airline alliances. Although Sabena ditched SAS in favor of British Airways and KLM, SAS was able to strike up a lucrative, long-lived partnership with Swissair. It then formed the European Quality Alliance (EQA) with Swissair and Austrian Airlines (AUA), a means of building up some critical marketing mass. This also allowed the partners to share operating expenses. Finnair joined the EQA in 1989 but left two years later to pursue a looser pact with Lufthansa.

The EQA spawned the Alcazar project, an attempt to merge KLM, Swissair, AUA, and SAS. After spending most of 1993 in discussions, however, the alliance fell apart in November over the choice of a U.S. partner. SAS had naturally insisted upon Continental. Carlzon left SAS after the debacle, and Jan Stenberg became the new CEO.

The next round of cost-cutting saw SAS shedding noncore businesses such as catering (but not hotels). It sold off a 43 percent stake in Lan Chile, practically exiting the South American market. The company also sloughed off the excess desks one might expect a tripartite bureaucracy to accumulate. It even axed the long-running Copenhagen-Los Angeles route as it retrenched itself in its familiar Scandinavian waters.

British Airways was meanwhile making significant inroads in Scandinavia. It teamed with Maersk, Braathens, and Sunair on certain routes and SAS bought a 40 percent share of British Midland. SAS also was able to team with Lufthansa, effectively muscling Finnair out of its alliance with the German carrier. Finnair responded by making a second hub out of Stockholm, literally flying in the face of SAS's administrative center. Both Finnair and SAS entered limited code share agreements with the region's numerous smaller airlines, and SAS joined the United Airlines and Lufthansa-led Star Alliance in 1997.

SAS 2000

Company officials unveiled an extensive corporate make-over in late September 1998. Beyond redesigning uniforms and aircraft liveries, "SAS 2000" also aimed to incorporate the results of the airline's most in-depth study of its customer interactions. It added a number of passenger amenities, such as mirrors in overhead compartment doors and unique, automatically adjustable seating in business class. The carrier emphasized its Scandinavian heritage in new menu items and design elements.

In spite of the improvements, SAS had trouble filling seats in 1999, although it continued to receive high customer satisfaction ratings. The carrier renewed its efforts in intercontinental operations, launching a strategic alliance with Singapore Airlines. It ordered Airbus A330 and A340 aircraft to replace its medium-sized Boeing 767s, and it ordered larger A321s for European service. New Boeing 737s and de Havilland Q400s also were added to the fleet.

Principal Subsidiaries

SAS International Hotels; Scandinavian Airlines Data; SMART; SAS Flight Academy; British Midland PLC (40%); Spanair (49%); Grolandsfly (37.5%); Polygon Insurance (30.8%); Wideroe's Flyveselskap (63.2%); airBaltic (38.2%); Cimber Air A/S (26%); Skyways Holding (25%); Air Botnia.

Principal Divisions

SAS; SAS International Hotels.

Principal Competitors

Finnair Oy; Braathens; Maersk; KLM Royal Dutch Airlines; British Airways plc.

Further Reading

Carlzon, Jan, "The Art of Loving" (interview by George Gendron and Stephen D. Solomon), *Inc.,* May 1989, pp. 34–45.

——, *Moments of Truth* (Reprint Edition), New York: HarperCollins, 1989.

——, "We Used to Fly Airplanes; Now We Fly People," *Business Forum,* Summer 1989, pp. 6–7.

Feldman, Joan M., "The Nordic Airline War," *Air Transport World,* November 1997, pp. 85–89.

Flint, Perry, "Scandinavian and Proud," *Air Transport World,* November 1998, pp. 79, 84.

——, "There's No Place Like Home," *Air Transport World,* November 1995, pp. 44–54.

Gidnitz, Betsy, *The Politics of International Air Transport*, Lexington, Mass.: Lexington, 1980.

Grosse, Robert, "A Privatization Nightmare: Aerolíneas Argentinas," in *Privatizing Monopolies: Lessons from the Telecommunications and Transport Sectors in Latin America,* edited by Ravi Ramamurti, Baltimore and London: Johns Hopkins, 1996.

Kapstein, Jonathan, and Mark Maremont, "Can SAS Keep Flying with the Big Birds?," *Business Week,* November 27, 1989, pp. 142, 146.

Labich, Kenneth, "An Airline That Soars on Service," *Fortune,* December 31, 1990, 94–96.

Lefer, Henry, "How SAS Keeps 'Em Flyin'," *Air Transport World,* November 1991, pp. 68–74.

——, "SAS's Hub Strategy," *Air Transport World,* March 1992, pp. 87–89.

Marcom, John, Jr., "Moment of Truth," *Forbes,* July 8, 1991, pp. 83, 86.

Martinsson, Jan, "The Humbling of Jan Carlzon," *International Management,* March 1988, pp. 34–40.

Nelms, Douglas W., "SAS Aims for Survival," *Air Transport World,* March 1993, pp. 86–87.

——, "SAS on Steady Course," *Air Transport World,* September 1995, pp. 109–10.

—updated by Frederick C. Ingram

Seagate

Seagate Technology, Inc.

920 Disc Drive
Scotts Valley, California 95066
U.S.A.
Telephone: (831) 438-6550
Fax: (831) 438-4127
Web site: http://www.seagate.com

Private Company
Incorporated: 1979
Employees: 82,000
Sales: $6.8 billion (1999)
NAIC: 334112 Computer Storage Device Manufacturing;
334413 Semiconductors and Related Device
Manufacturing; 511210 Software Publishers

Seagate Technology, Inc. has been the world's leading independent manufacturer of rigid magnetic disks and disk drives for computers since the 1980s. The company pioneered the downsizing of mainframe hard disk drives, making them affordable for personal computers. In the 1990s the company expanded into software and presently is the leading provider of technology and products that enable computers to store, access, and manage information, including disk drives, magnetic disks and heads, tape drives, and software. In 2000 Seagate was transitioning from public to private ownership, due to a complex $2 billion buyout.

Producing Hard Disks for Computers: 1979–84

Seagate was established in 1979 in Scotts Valley, California, by a group of businesspeople, including Alan Shugart, who had been an engineer with Memorex for four years after spending 18 years at IBM. Seagate was his second startup after having founded Shugart Associates, the company that made floppy disk drives a standard feature on personal computers. When Shugart Associates was sold to Xerox a year later, Shugart was forced out. Of Seagate's group of four cofounders, another significant member was Tom Mitchell. He had come from Commodore, where he had served as general manager of Commodore business machines, and had previously worked at Bendix, Fairchild Camera, and Honeywell. Shugart became president and CEO of the new company, while Mitchell started out as senior vice-president of operations.

Another cofounder was Finis Conner, who left Seagate in 1984 to form Conner Peripherals. It was Conner who approached Shugart with the idea of installing hard disks in personal computers. After competing with Seagate in hard disks for more than a decade, Conner Peripherals was acquired by Seagate in 1996.

Hard disks are made of one or more magnetic-coated aluminum platters. Data is stored on, retrieved from, and erased off the rapidly rotating disk by a mechanical arm, which moves across the disk. The whole mechanism is called the disk drive, or hard drive, and the technology for the sealed unit, which is also known generically as a Winchester disk, is Seagate's basic product. Hard disk technology allows the storage of more data than a floppy disk, and does it at a faster rate.

Unlike larger mainframe computers, personal computers were originally built with only a floppy disk drive and without hard drives. Therefore, the market was open for an independent company like Seagate to manufacture hard drives and sell them directly to computer manufacturers. They in turn would incorporate the drives into their personal computers as add-on features. Seagate's first client was IBM in 1980, just as the latter was about to introduce its personal computers, which would set the standard for the industry. Seagate's first product, a 5.25-inch hard drive, was very successful. By 1982, with sales of $40 million, Seagate had captured half of the market for small disk drives. The company went public in September 1981, with an initial stock offering of three million common shares.

Seagate made a name for itself by producing the least expensive disk drives in the industry, largely due to Mitchell's successful efforts to procure component parts from vendors at the lowest possible prices. In 1983 Mitchell replaced Shugart as president, though the latter remained chairman and CEO. Mitchell also took on the new position of chief operating officer to direct day to day operations, while Shugart oversaw planning.

By 1984 sales had shot up to $344 million as Seagate became the world's largest producer of 5.25-inch disk drives,

Company Perspectives:

Every time you surf the Internet, hit "send," trade a stock online, click on an ad, watch a Hollywood blockbuster or use an ATM, you access, share and store tremendous amounts of digital information. And for 20 years, we've been developing the technology and manufacturing the products that help make all of that happen. Data storage—Seagate's core business—makes billions of Internet pages, millions of transactions and entire new industries possible. Worldwide demand for storage doubles every 9 months, creating a storage market opportunity that is estimated to reach approximately $100 billion by 2002. Given this growth, most major computer companies are looking to storage as their next area of opportunity. And when they look to storage, they look to Seagate—the world's largest and most technologically rich independent storage company.

with three-fourths of the company's shipments going to IBM. Then in mid-1984 the computer industry entered a slump, and the average price for a wholesale ten-megabyte disk drive fell from $430 to $320 in a matter of days. A number of factors contributed to the situation, including a slowing in the growth of personal computer sales, industrywide falling prices, a glut of disk drive competitors, and rising costs of producing the new generation of drives. Diminished growth of personal computer sales came just as the disk-drive companies were squeezing the last profits from their older product lines. These difficulties were intensified for Seagate, with its reliance on IBM's business, when that company reduced orders and began demanding lower prices. Thus, Seagate's sales for the first quarter of fiscal 1985, at $50.6 million, were half of what they had been for the last quarter of fiscal 1984. Annual sales for fiscal 1985 declined 38 percent to $215 million.

Focusing on Low-Cost, Efficient Manufacturing: 1985–91

Mitchell immediately began looking into ways of manufacturing the drives even more cheaply. Realizing that disk drives, as a commodity product, would become subject to price pressures, he had already decided to begin relocating Seagate's manufacturing operations overseas where labor costs were lower, and the pressures resulting from cutbacks forced quick implementation of the move. In July 1984, 900 of the 1,600 employees in Scotts Valley were laid off, as component production shifted to Singapore. By December most of its drives were being produced there, and plans were underway to open another plant in Thailand. In so doing, Seagate successfully followed the Japanese strategy of using less expensive Southeast Asian labor in manufacturing, which had allowed Japanese companies to dominate the floppy disk drive market. Now, however, with the high value of the Japanese yen, Seagate was able to undercut the prices of Fujitsu, Hitachi, NEC, Toshiba, and others, and dominate the hard disk market.

At the same time, Mitchell made one outlet of sales more secure by extending credit to a small but important client, CMS. The latter was buying stripped-down IBM personal computers, furnishing them with Seagate drives and selling them to retail-

ers at bargain prices. Thus, while Seagate's revenues fell temporarily in 1984–85, the company managed to stay profitable.

Seagate was faced with another problem in the fall of 1984—the replacement of its ten-megabyte drives, which were becoming obsolete as higher capacity drives appeared on the market. Mitchell saw an opportunity to outmaneuver a rival, Computer Memories, which was already providing disks with greater memory, but less reliability, to IBM. He promised IBM a shipment of 20 prototype high-capacity, high-reliability drives by December, before Seagate had even finished designing them. Working long hours, Seagate engineers pulled it off. Although mass quantities could not be delivered by March as originally promised, IBM was satisfied and placed orders for tens of thousands of the disk drives.

Seagate also sought to diversify its clientele in order to be less vulnerable to fluctuations in demand. Seagate began marketing more to value-added resellers (VARs), dealers that package stripped-down computer components and software and resell them as specialized systems. By 1987 such dealers came to represent 47 percent of Seagate's clients, up from zero in 1983, while sales to IBM fell to 24 percent. In that year a deal was also signed to supply drives to Hewlett-Packard, among other new personal computer makers. To expand sales internationally, Seagate set up a European headquarters in Versailles, France, in 1987.

Beginning in 1985 Seagate experienced a phenomenal rise in sales, hitting $1 billion in revenue by 1987, with a record $115.3 million in profits. This reflected the rapid growth of the market for hard drives in desktop computers. In 1984 only 15–20 percent of personal computers had hard drives, while this figure had reached 70 percent by 1987, according to analyst Ronald Elijah at Robertson, Colman & Stephans. As the market grew, Seagate was able to maintain its dominant share by keeping its prices down. It had reduced the costs of storing data by 95 percent since it first went into business.

However, Seagate's concentration on efficient production, while allowing technological innovation to take a back seat, made it vulnerable to the boom and bust cycles of the rapidly changing high technology industry. In 1987 computer manufacturers started demanding the smaller 3.5-inch drives earlier than anticipated. IBM, which was purchasing 30 percent of Seagate's 5.25-inch drives, was now planning to manufacture some of its own 3.5-inch drives. As a consequence, Seagate's profits declined by 39 percent during this product transition period in the second half of 1987, and profits remained low into 1988.

Seagate introduced six models of its first 3.5-inch drives that spring, although 5.25-inch drives continued to dominate its sales. The company had added 32,000 square feet to its Singapore plant, where the 3.5-inch disk drives were made. Meanwhile, it expanded operations in Thailand beyond the manufacture of components and sub-assembling to include the complete assembly process and testing of disk drives. More significantly, Seagate began investing greater amounts on research and development in 1987, double the amount of the previous year, by issuing $250 million in debentures. The company established a new research and development facility in Boulder, Colorado, in addition to the one at its headquarters in Scotts Valley.

The market's growth was less than anticipated, however, and revenue for fiscal 1988 declined 50 percent from the previous year, while inventories of 5.25-inch disks piled up. Seagate blamed the problem on industrywide overproduction, while Shugart moved quickly to lay off nearly 2,200 employees in Singapore and the United States. The company barely stayed in the black for fiscal 1989.

Although Seagate remained the undisputed leader in market share, ups and downs in the demand for the personal computer market were a serious concern. Thus, Seagate's next move was to gain entry into the market for the high capacity drives used in mainframes, by purchasing Control Data's disk-drive subsidiary, Imprimis, in June 1989. In addition, the $450 million acquisition nearly doubled Seagate's sales, to $2.4 billion for fiscal 1990, larger than all its U.S. competitors—Conner Peripherals, Maxtor, Micropolis, and Quantum—combined.

Seagate also had an edge on its competitors in its ability to provide consistently lower priced products, because the company manufactured its own disk drive components. In plants throughout the United States and in Asia, Seagate turned out motors, precision recording heads, and other parts. While the company built many of these factories itself, key component suppliers were also acquired by Seagate. In 1987 the company purchased Integrated Power Semiconductors, Ltd. of Scotland—a longtime Seagate supplier—and Aeon, a Brea, California-based producer of substrates to make thin film magnetic recording media.

On the other hand, Seagate continued to lag behind the competition when it came to introducing new technology. "Seagate has never been that interested in getting products out of the lab first. We wait until we've squeezed every penny of cost out of a product before we bring it to market," Shugart explained in *Forbes* in 1991. "But the product cycles are getting shorter and shorter. Now we can't afford to wait." The latest product on the market was a 2.5-inch disk drive for laptop and notebook computers. Seagate introduced the drive in November 1990, only five months behind competitor Conner Peripherals, as compared with a delay of a year for the 3.5-inch drives.

Emphasizing New Products: 1991–97

Mitchell's emphasis on high volume manufacturing over product innovation was one of the points of contention that led him to resign under pressure from the board in September 1991. Shugart then reasserted his role in running the company by giving up his position as chairman and assuming the posts of president and chief operating officer vacated by Mitchell. Gary Filler, former vice-chairman, replaced Shugart as chairman. This change in management came on the heels of a disappointing year, with the layoff of another 1,650 workers and revenues down 42 percent.

Firmly in charge again, Shugart pursued a strategy of turning out new products as soon as they were designed. He also began focusing on higher profit margins and specific markets, contrary to Mitchell's goal of general large-volume sales. One of Shugart's first products in this regard was the 1480 disk drive introduced at the end of 1991. This 425-megabyte, 3.5-inch drive was successfully targeted at the high-end workstation and minicomputer markets, where profit margins were greater. Seagate beat the competition by introducing the product first, then continuing to outsell its rivals.

Seagate's profits rebounded beyond expectations in early 1992 as sales of lower priced, high-end personal computers took off amid vendor price wars. At the same time, Seagate also benefited from the current PC owner trend toward buying new higher capacity drives to run more powerful programs. The company's large market share ensured that such upswings in personal computer demand would have a definite effect on its sales.

Shugart in turn pumped those profits into more research and development and strategic investments. In early 1993 Seagate invested $65 million in a factory in Londonderry, Northern Ireland, which doubled its capacity to produce a key part used in its hard drives. In addition, Seagate acquired a 25 percent stake in the Sundisk Corporation—another manufacturer of computer data storage products—and together the two companies produced data storage systems for portable computers and other hand-held electronic devices. In April of that year Seagate signed an agreement with Corning, the glass manufacturer, to provide a new glass-ceramic compound for use in disks. The new material allowed Seagate to reduce the distance between a disk and its magnetic read-write head, which enabled a higher capacity for data.

Expanding into Software: 1993–96

Disk drive makers hit a slump in 1993 due to rapidly declining prices. Industry leaders included Seagate, Quantum Corporation, Western Digital Corporation, Conner Peripherals, Maxtor, and Micropolis. For fiscal 1993 Seagate earned $195 million, while its competitors lost a combined $400 million.

Seagate began acquiring software companies in 1994 to establish a position in data-retrieval software. It acquired software developers Palindrome Corporation of Napierville, Illinois, for $69 million, and Crystal Computer Services Inc. of Vancouver, British Columbia, for $18.6 million. It also invested in Dragon Systems Inc. of Newton, Massachusetts. The company was investing in technologies and companies that would be significant for data management in the future. For fiscal 1994 ending June 30 Seagate reported record sales of $3.5 billion and record earnings of $225 million.

Seagate continued to acquire software companies in 1995, including Frye Computer Systems of Boston for $20 million, NetLabs Inc., and Network Computing Inc. In September 1995 Seagate announced it would acquire competitor Conner Peripherals in a deal valued at $1.04 billion. Conner not only manufactured disk and tape drives, it owned software subsidiary Arcada Software. After experiencing component shortages, price pressures, and significant losses, Conner agreed to a merger with Seagate. The deal was completed in February 1996. Together, Seagate and Conner accounted for about 33 percent of all hard-drive units sold in 1995, making the combined company the market-share leader ahead of Quantum Corporation.

In February 1996 Seagate officially formed a new software group, the Seagate Software Storage Management Group, by combining the operations of Palindrome Corporation and Arcada Software. The division became Seagate Software, Inc., later in 1996 and was headquartered in Arcada's home of Lake Mary, Florida. During the year Seagate continued to acquire software companies, including OnDemand Software Inc. for $13 million and Calypso Software Systems for $13 million. Calypso specialized in enterprise systems management software.

Despite complaints from its distributors that Seagate was forcing them to take more inventory, Seagate enjoyed the highest level of sales for high-capacity, mid-size, and small disk drives, according to the annual brand preference survey conducted by *Computer Reseller News*. For fiscal 1996 Seagate reported record sales of $8.59 billion and $213 million in net income.

By 1997 Seagate had evolved beyond its position as the world's largest disk drive and components manufacturer into a leading provider of technology and products that enabled people to store, access, and manage information. The company committed more than $479 million in fiscal 1997 to research and development while formally establishing Advanced Concept Labs to pursue R&D activities related to storage technologies. For fiscal 1997 sales were $8.08 billion while net income tripled to $658 million.

In August 1997 Seagate acquired Quinta Corporation, a developer of optically-assisted Winchester technology designed to integrate optical, magnetic, and telecommunications technologies for use in a new generation of high-capacity disk drive storage devices. After paying $10 million for a 20 percent interest, Seagate completed the acquisition for $230 million and was responsible for an additional $96 million based on Quinta achieving certain performance targets. Seagate also acquired Holistic Systems Ltd., which developed software for large-scale, enterprise-wide management information and decision support systems.

In September 1997 Seagate promoted Stephen J. Luczo from executive vice-president to president and chief operating officer. Luczo joined Seagate in 1993 with a background in investment banking. Shugart remained as chairman and CEO.

Financial Woes and Change in Management: 1997–98

Seagate's financial results worsened significantly in fiscal 1998. At the end of 1997 the company laid off 1,400 workers in Ireland and told analysts its third quarter earnings would be less than half of Wall Street's estimates. For its fiscal year ending June 30, 1998, Seagate reported a net loss of $530 million on declining revenues of $6.8 billion. The poor results were due in part to Seagate losing significant market share in the server market, which accounted for about half of the company's revenues. Weak demand for personal computers and lower disk drive prices also impacted the company's earnings. In July Shugart was removed by the board of directors and subsequently resigned his position on the board. Luczo took over as president and chief executive officer. William Watkins was subsequently promoted to chief operating officer.

Among the problems facing the company were integrating recently acquired Conner Peripherals and speeding up the time it took to bring products to market. The company's worldwide workforce had grown to 100,000 employees, of which 10,000 were cut. In addition, Luczo consolidated the company's design centers from five to three. In mid-1998 Seagate acquired Eastman Software Storage Management Group, Inc., a subsidiary of Eastman Kodak Co., for $10 million.

At the end of 1998 Seagate again led the field in small hard-disk drives, according to the *Computer Reseller News* survey, ahead of Western Digital Corporation and Maxtor Corporation. In the large disk-drive class Seagate also led, ahead of Western Digital Corporation and IBM's Storage Systems Division.

Returning to Profitability: 1998–99

For fiscal 1999 ending July 2 Seagate reported revenues of $6.8 billion and net income of $1.17 billion. While revenues were flat over the previous year, the company improved its profitability in spite of price erosion on disk drive products through extensive cost-cutting and restructuring. During the fiscal year Seagate reduced its workforce from 87,000 to 82,000, of which some 65,000 were employed in Seagate's Far East operations. By the end of 1999 the company's workforce had been reduced to about 71,500 people.

The company's software subsidiary had revenues of $293 million and more than 1,700 employees, making it one of the 50 largest software companies in the world. It was organized in two operating groups, the Information Management Group and the Network and Storage Management Group. In May 1999 the Network and Storage Management Group was sold to Veritas Software Corporation in exchange for 41.6 percent of Veritas's outstanding common stock valued at $3.1 billion.

In the latter half of 1999 Seagate decided to repurchase 50 million of its shares, about 25 percent of the stock outstanding. The previous year it had repurchased 48 million shares. Some analysts considered its stock undervalued, and there were rumors that Fujitsu and IBM were interested in acquiring the company. In December Seagate acquired XIOtech Corp, a storage area network (SAN) vendor, for $360 million in stock.

Going Private: 2000

At the end of the first quarter of 2000 Seagate announced a complex financial deal involving Veritas Software and an investor group led by Silver Lake Partners, in which Seagate would become a privately held company. According to published reports, Seagate decided to go private to get away from the scrutiny of Wall Street investors. Under the terms of the deal, Veritas would acquire all of the Veritas Software shares held by Seagate, while the investor group would acquire Seagate's operating businesses for approximately $2 billion in cash in what was described as a management buyout. The investor group included members of Seagate's management team as well as other investors.

As a private company, Seagate would be able to better focus on strengthening its core storage business. Company executives were more comfortable with their new partners' long-term views, as opposed to Wall Street's shorter-term expectations. Seagate planned to continue to implement its advanced manufacturing technologies, seek operational efficiencies, and position the company to take advantage of increased demand for storage-related technologies and products across multiple markets.

Principal Competitors

Western Digital Corporation; Maxtor Corporation; IBM's Storage Systems Division; Fujitsu Limited; Quantum Corporation.

Further Reading

Bliss, Jeff, "Seagate Steaming Ahead with Acquisition of Conner," *Computer Reseller News,* February 12, 1996, p. 12.

Brandt, Richard, "Seagate Goes East—And Comes Back a Winner," *Business Week,* March 16, 1987, p. 94.

"California-Based Seagate Technology Names Three Executives," *Knight-Ridder/Tribune Business News,* August 25, 1998.

Cote, Michael, "Boulder, Colo.-Based Computer Firm's CEO Outlines Strategy," *Knight-Ridder/Tribune Business News,* November 11, 1998.

"Driven Down," *Forbes,* January 9, 1989, p. 115.

"Drive Woes Continue," *Computerworld,* December 15, 1997, p. 29.

Dubashi, Jaganath, "Seagate Technology: Too Soon to Bet?," *Finance World,* July 10, 1990, pp. 19–20.

Elliott, Heidi, "An Act of Privacy," *Electronic News (1991),* April 3, 2000, p. 1.

Fisher, Lawrence M., "Seagate Trips, Industry Cringes," *New York Times,* August 23, 1988, p. D1+.

Francis, Bob, "Disk Drive Giant Purchases Palindrome," *InfoWorld,* August 1, 1994, p. 8.

——, "Seagate Riding Success Wave," *InfoWorld,* July 18, 1994, p. 8.

Gibson, Stan, "Seagate Nets Frye for Under $20M," *PC Week,* May 15, 1995, p. 101.

Grober, Mary Beth, "The Seagate Saga," *Forbes,* May 4, 1998, p. 158.

Hostetler, Michele, "Hardwaremaker Seagate Wants the Lead in Software Game," *Business Journal,* November 14, 1994, p. 7.

——, "With Seagate-Conner Deal Pending, Quantum Still Tops," *Business Journal,* December 25, 1995, p. 4A.

Howle, Amber, "Large-Drive Sweep by Seagate," *Computer Reseller News,* December 7, 1998, p. I24.

——, "Seagate Leads in Small Drives," *Computer Reseller News,* December 7, 1998, p. I22.

Kindel, Stephen, "Maverick: How Seagate Is Winning the Disc Drive Wars Through Vertical Integration," *Financial World,* January 18, 1994, p. 44.

Kovar, Joseph F., "Hard-Drive Vendor Swims Against IPO Tide," *Computer Reseller News,* April 3, 2000, p. 94.

——, "On the Prowl: Intel, Compaq and Seagate," *Computer Reseller News,* December 13, 1999, p. 196.

Larson, Erik, "Decline in Disk-Drive Demand Puts Squeeze on Many Makers," *Wall Street Journal,* December 3, 1984, p. 4.

Lashinsky, Adam, "Scotts Valley, Calif.-Based Seagate Technology, Inc. Names President," *Knight-Ridder/Tribune Business News,* September 9, 1997.

Leon, Mark, "Seagate Acquires Calypso," *InfoWorld,* May 20, 1996, p. 55.

——, "Seagate Acquires OnDemand Software," *InfoWorld,* April 15, 1996, p. 66.

——, "Seagate Vies for More of LAN Market," *InfoWorld,* February 26, 1996, p. 43.

Longwell, John, "Alan Shugart," *Computer Reseller News,* November 16, 1997, p. 89.

——, "Large-Drive Lead No Surprise," *Computer Reseller News,* December 16, 1996, p. S46.

——, "Seagate Tops in Midsize Drives," *Computer Reseller News,* December 16, 1996, p. S45.

——, "Seagate Wins Big in Drives," *Computer Reseller News,* December 16, 1996, p. S44.

Marks, Don, "Seagate Technology," *Datamation,* June 15, 1992, pp. 49–52.

McCright, John S., "Seagate, Veritas Part Company," *PC Week,* April 3, 2000, p. 14.

Moltzen, Edward F., "Seagate Acquisition of Conner on Track, Hits Homestretch," *Computer Reseller News,* November 27, 1995, p. 33.

Murphy, Chris, "Seagate Goes Private in Veritas Deal," *InformationWeek,* April 3, 2000, p. 169.

Pendery, David, and Ephraim Schwartz, "Big Challenge Ahead for Seagate CEO," *InfoWorld,* July 27, 1998, p. 14.

Pereira, Pedro, "Seagate Looking to Beef up Profits with Stuffing," *Computer Reseller News,* June 17, 1996, p. 2.

Pitta, Julie, "The Survivor," *Forbes,* July 8, 1991, pp. 94–95.

Quinlan, Tom, "Scotts Valley, Calif.-Based Disk-Drive Maker Announces More Job Cuts," *Knight-Ridder/Tribune Business News,* September 14, 1999.

Rae-Dupree, Janet, "Seagate-Conner Merger Puts New Spin on Disk Drive Business," *Knight-Ridder/Tribune Business News,* February 11, 1996.

Rogers, Alison, "Who's Up—and Who's Down—in the Disk Drive Wars," *Fortune,* December 27, 1993, p. 12.

Schmitt, Richard B., "Seagate Technology's Mitchell Resigns As Board Decides to Shift Management," *Wall Street Journal,* September 23, 1991, pp. B4(W), B8(E).

Schroeder, Erica, "Seagate Taps Client/Server Software," *PC Week,* May 23, 1994, p. 171.

"Seagate Dumps Shugart," *PC Week,* August 3, 1998, p. 43.

"Seagate Income Slips," *InformationWeek,* July 20, 1998, p. 26.

"Seagate Revs, Net Slips," *Electronic News (1991),* August 12, 1996, p. 74.

Sullivan, Thomas, "Veritas Acquires Seagate Software Network and Storage Management Group," *ENT,* October 21, 1998, p. 1.

"A Surge at Seagate," *Business Week,* November 22, 1999, p. 191.

Vaughan, Jack, "What Goes on Those Disks, Anyway?" *Software Magazine,* July 1995, p. 26.

Yamada, Ken, "Once-Battered Seagate Gains in Computer Price War," *Wall Street Journal,* June 1, 1992, p. B2.

—Heather Behn Hedden
—updated by David P. Bianco

Select Comfort Corporation

10400 Viking Drive
Minneapolis, Minnesota 55344
U.S.A.
Telephone: (952) 551-7000
Toll Free: (800) 548-7231
Fax: (952) 551-7826
Web site: http://www.selectcomfort.com

Public Corporation
Incorporated: 1987
Employees: 1,520
Sales: $273.8 million (1999)
Stock Exchanges: NASDAQ
Ticker Symbol: SCSS
NAIC: 33791 Mattress Manufacturing

Select Comfort Corporation, the industry leader in air bed technology, designs, manufactures, and markets a line of mattresses with adjustable firmness, mattress foundations, and sleep-related accessories. Through aggressive marketing, Select Comfort carved out a niche for air mattresses but remained well behind the pack of four industry-leading mattress makers.

Seeking Sound Sleep: 1987–91

Seeking a better night's sleep, Minneapolis businessman Robert A. Walker designed a new mattress. On the outside, it looked like a conventional mattress, but the inside was filled with a series of adjustable air chambers instead of steel springs. Walker spent more than a decade, working out of his garage, perfecting the air bed and recruiting friends to test it for comfort. Having worked for a mattress maker in the 1960s, Walker approached bed manufacturers with the product, but they were not interested. Stymied, Walker now had to put some other experience into play. During the 1980s he had helped other inventors bring product to market.

Walker sold his mattresses directly to department stores and other retail outlets, but they proved to be slow movers. First of all, retailers carried the mattresses of a number of name brand manu-facturers, many with multimillion-dollar advertising budgets. Customers asked for those products by name. In addition, salespeople generally were accustomed to pitching low prices, not high customer benefits—Walker's new style of mattress appealed to higher-income people with back problems. From 1987, the founding year of Select Comfort Corporation, to 1991, annual sales remained below the $1 million mark and losses piled up.

On the upside, the mattress received national attention through articles in *Bedroom* and *Playboy* magazines and as a prize offering on the "Wheel of Fortune" game show. On the other end of the spectrum, purchases by the U.S. military for troops fighting in the Gulf War and serving elsewhere overseas provided about 50 percent of sales—the collapsible bed was economical to ship.

Walker, in a February 1991 *Star Tribune* article, touted his mattress as an "evolutionary step in bedding," claiming it provided a better cushioning than either springs or water. Even though the founder remained confident in the quality of his product, the company itself was running out of air. Cash-starved Walker needed to sell more mattresses. They retailed for $400 to $1,000.

Venture Capital Money Broadens Distribution: 1991–93

When Walker realized that Minnesota-based NordicTrack had hit the jackpot through direct marketing, he started looking for backers to make the switch. The cross-country ski exercise machines had cracked a venue traditionally confined to low-price items. Walker felt that his bed, which could be shipped entirely by UPS, would find market success this way as well. After several attempts, Walker finally sold the controlling interest in his company to a group of three venture capital firms. Lead investor Minnesota-based St. Paul Venture Capital Inc., along with Cherry Tree Ventures, also in Minnesota, and Connecticut-based Consumer Venture Partners put down $4.6 million, according to a 1993 *Corporate Report Minnesota* article recounting the 1991 sale.

The new owners hired consumer products manager Mark L. de Naray to run the company; Walker stepped aside as CEO and president but remained on as vice-president of research and development. De Naray had last worked for Canadian-based Magic Pantry Foods and Minnesota-based Pillsbury. "The last thing we needed was someone from the mattress industry who would bring a traditional approach," St. Paul Venture Capital's Patrick A. Hopf recalled in a 1995 *Twin Cities Business Monthly* article. "It's a traditionally sleepy industry used to selling commodity products for low prices. Ours is a product that features a totally new way of sleeping, and our whole marketing thrust is one featuring benefits."

Ads hit national newspapers and magazines in November 1991 and produced an immediate growth spurt. The new management group realized that, despite the positive gains, about half its potential market just would not buy a bed sight unseen, regardless of informational videos and a 90-day return policy. Select needed some retail outlets. At first, upscale mall owners were reluctant to bring in a store selling a single brand of mattress: it just was not done. Beds were sold in furniture stores or department stores. The company opened a kiosk in a suburban St. Paul shopping center in 1992. The test run was a success—the kiosk drew hundreds of shoppers. Additional venture capital money allowed Select to open more kiosks and small retail showrooms, including one in the gigantic Mall of America. Sales well exceeded that elusive million-dollar mark in 1992.

At year end 1993, the number of company-owned retail outlets reached 18, including kiosks. Sales were $13.6 million, or triple the previous year's $4.4 million. Direct marketing accounted for 80 percent of the figure, primarily gleaned through ads in more than 100 consumer magazines, according to a 1994 *Minneapolis/St. Paul CityBusiness* article. To support the growing retail side of the business, Select began looking for its first ad agency. Select faced some barriers to gaining a significant share of the $5 billion mattress market, including perceptions that air beds were merely recreational items for swimming or camping.

Telemarketing and retail sales efforts were supported by strong word-of-mouth referrals. Select encouraged this by offering customers $50 for each referral that resulted in a sale. Referrals accounted for ten percent of annual revenue.

Pumped Up Expansion Drive: 1994–98

Since 1991, nearly $12 million in venture capital—about half from St. Paul Venture Capital—had been pumped into the company. An additional $6 million in venture capital came in during the third quarter of 1994 to help drive expansion. By the end of the year, Select had 35 company-owned permanent stores, and sales had more than doubled to $30 million.

Inc. magazine placed Select in the number 69 slot on its 1994 list of the nation's fastest-growing private companies. Yet Select held less than one percent of the mattress market. Sealy, Simmons, Serta, and Spring Air brands controlled nearly 60 percent. Major air bed competitor Comfortaire, established in 1981, generated sales of nearly $20 million. Other air bed marketers were selling beds originally designed to hold water but then converted to air when the market peaked.

Eager to broaden awareness of its product, Select experimented with a number of marketing techniques. The company displayed beds at the Twin Cities international airport. Bed and breakfasts and small hotels used Select Comfort mattresses and offered customers the chance to view a video about the bed. There were infomercials and radio personality endorsements. Select Comfort "road shows"—displays and presentations in hotels—tested the potential for retail outlets in other cities.

During 1994 and 1995, Select made the move from a small entrepreneurial company to a large business. The board membership was indicative of the direction the company was heading. It included: Ken Macke, former Dayton Hudson CEO; John Scully, former chair of Apple Computer and PepsiCo; Tom Albani, president and CEO of Electrolux; and David Kollat, former president of Victoria's Secret. In addition to opening stores at a rapid pace, Select developed new products and line extensions, such as a wireless remote firmness control system and a lightweight mattress foundation.

Mid-year 1996, Select opened its 100th store. The company held the number six spot on *Inc.*'s fastest-growing list. On the year, sales topped $100 million. For the first time, retail matched direct sales, each at 45 percent; road shows brought in the remaining ten percent. Select Comfort President and CEO De Naray left the company a few months into the new year. Under his leadership, Select Comfort had become the fifth largest U.S. mattress maker, as well as the third largest bedding retailer, operating 145 stores in more than 40 states and employing well more than 1,000 people.

Overall, most of the 800-plus domestic mattress manufacturers remained small, community-based operations, and an estimated 90 to 95 percent of them produced inner spring mattresses. Water beds, futons, adjustable beds, and air mattresses comprised the remaining five to ten percent. The top four manufacturers still controlled about 60 percent of the estimated $7 billion market. Trying to take a bite out of their share of the pie, Select earmarked $28 million for a national ad campaign during 1997. The company also opened a second manufacturing plant. The South Carolina operation was positioned to serve not just the Southeast but the whole East Coast.

Select Goes Public: 1999

Sales leaped to $184 million in 1997 and then to $246 million in 1998. Select stood poised for a public offering. The company planned to use the proceeds to pay down some long-term debt, add retail stores and a third manufacturing/distribution plant, and, possibly, acquire other business operations. Select sold four million shares of stock at $17 per share in the

Key Dates:

1987: Select Comfort Corporation is formed to make and sell air beds.
1991: Inventor/founder sells controlling interest to a venture capital consortium.
1992: Retail stores are added.
1996: Company opens 100th store and tops $100 million in sales.
1999: Initial public offering of Select Comfort stock.

January 1999 initial public offering (IPO). Charles Schwab & Co., as a first time co-manager for an IPO, used its own version of direct mail to bring aboard investors. The brokerage mailed more than a quarter million postcards to Select Comfort customers who also had Schwab accounts. According to a January 1999 *Business Week* article, the technique helped boost the proceeds.

Select Comfort also broke some new ground when it established an e-commerce subsidiary in April 1999, becoming the first major mattress maker to do so. Selectcomfort.com planned links to furnishing stores and health/wellness web sites. In another development, Select was making an entry into Bed Bath & Beyond stores. The lease agreement allowed for up to 150 Select Comfort departments in various superstore locations by the end of 2001. Unfortunately, the feeling of optimism surrounding the company was about to end.

Select Comfort's stock price had risen by 50 percent within a month of its offering. "Analysts love the firm, with a universal 'buy' rating among those who follow it," wrote Adam Weintraub in a 1999 *CityBusiness* article. But Select management changes and aggressive plans to overtake the industry leaders coupled with media reports questioning the validity of Select's "good night's sleep" studies resulted in shareholder jitters. The stock dropped below its offering price by mid-May.

Downplaying the stock woes, Select pushed forward. The company was about to move from six to 16 retail markets. A new sofa sleeper product was on tap—Select had invested $2 million in the manufacturer. But Select Comfort was not going to rest easy. Select stock fell again, to less than half its offering price, after the company announced a drop-off in sales growth and possible second quarter losses. Some stockholders filed lawsuits against the company, claiming management had been aware of the downturn earlier but withheld the information. Select denied the claims.

Making its second top management change in a three-month period, Hopf took over as interim CEO. The company managed to show a slight profit in the second quarter, but overall sales rose by only nine percent, down from 22 percent the previous quarter.

Strategically, Select had begun to depend on advertising to drive sales in the slow growth market—on average people changed homes more often than mattresses. The company spent around $32 million, or an equivalent of about 15 percent of sales, on advertising in 1998. By comparison, Sealy spent $15

million or two percent of its $891 million in sales, according to a 1999 *Star Tribune* article by Susan Feyder. Select projected ad budgets of $45 million for 1999 and $70 million for the year 2000. On a side note, other air bed makers benefited from the product awareness Select created with its advertising dollars.

Select Comfort stock dropped off again in the wake of third quarter losses. The company brought in outside consultants to help turn things around by tackling problems with product positioning, marketing, and distribution. Select also implemented a stock repurchase plan.

New Game Plan for Year 2000

Near year-end 1999, Select was still without a permanent CEO. Hopf said the company was considering offering lower-priced beds through wholesale channels. Although sales of mattresses costing more than $1,000 were on the rise, the high-end segment produced less than 12 percent of total industry sales. The largest manufacturers sold the majority of their product through furniture stores and bedding specialty stores.

Late in December, Select announced a strategic change in business operations and marketing. "I think the realization was that maybe we had the wrong goal," Hopf said in a December 1999 *Star Tribune* article. "Our goal should really be to maximize shareholder value. If we can do that by having slower sales growth but increasing profitability, that's the way we should go."

A slowdown in store openings, some store closures, deemphasis of the slogan "the air bed company," a new focus on technology, plus wholesale distribution comprised key elements of the new game plan. The store openings pullback was of particular significance since rapid expansion had been a key part of the company's goal to overtake the four industry leaders. Select opened 194 outlets in 1997, 54 in 1998, and 47 in 1999. A planned 45 openings were scaled back to 15 for 2000.

Select ended 1999 with stock trading in the $4 to $5 range. The company changed its ticker symbol in early January 2000 to SCSS ("Select Comfort Sleep Solutions") from AIRB to coincide with the change in strategic direction. Net sales of $273.8 million represented an increase of 11 percent over 1998, but the company reported a net loss of $8.2 million or 45 cents a share in 1999. The company netted $5.2 million a year earlier. Store closings and consulting fees contributed to the deficit. Comparable store sales rose an anemic five percent on the year versus 24 percent in 1998.

Keeping a watchful eye on competition—big mattress makers were starting to roll out their own air beds—Select filed a patent infringement lawsuit against Simmons and the maker of an air bed with hand controls. In early 2000, the larger company agreed to end its licensing agreement for the product. Select held 24 issued or pending patents in the United States.

Select Comfort faced the new millennium with 341 retail stores, including 45 leased departments in the Bed Bath & Beyond stores. During 2000, Select planned to expand home delivery and assembly capability, continue the rollout of sleeper sofa products, remodel some existing stores, and possibly expand its online venues. Cris Carter, a six-time pro-bowl player for the Minnesota Vikings, had signed an endorsement agreement—the company had used other sports figures for promotion in the past. Investors, shareholders, and management alike would probably be tossing and turning, waiting to see if the new plan would produce a check in the win column.

Principal Competitors

Sealy Inc.; Serta Inc.; Simmons Co.; Spring Air Co.; Park Place Corporation (Comfortaire).

Further Reading

Barshay, Jill J., "De Nary to Resign at Select Comfort in Favor of More-Experienced Manager," *Star Tribune* (Minneapolis), February 12, 1997, p. 3D.

——, "Select Comfort Plans Big Public Stock Offer," *Star Tribune* (Minneapolis), September 4, 1998, p. 1D.

——, "Select Comfort to Post Loss; Stock Tumbles," *Star Tribune* (Minneapolis), September 18, 1999, p. 1D.

Brauer, David, "No Sleep Lost Over Control of Mattress Company," *Corporate Report Minnesota,* May 1993, p. 21.

"Cris Carter Signs on with Select Comfort," *PR Newswire,* January 6, 2000.

Davis, Riccardo A., "Minneapolis-Based Select Comfort Executive Resigns," *St. Paul Pioneer Press,* February 12, 1997.

De Nary, Mark, "The Misunderstood Mattress," *Ventures,* May 1997, pp. 62–67.

Earley, Sandra, "Select Comfort to Select Ad Firm," *Minneapolis/St. Paul CityBusiness,* May 13–19, 1994, p. 6.

Feyder, Susan, "Select Comfort May Change Its Strategy," *Star Tribune* (Minneapolis), November 8, 1999, p. 2D.

——, "Select Hopes to Plug Its Slow Leak," *Star Tribune* (Minneapolis), December 24, 1999, p. 1D.

——, "Tossing and Turning," *Star Tribune* (Minneapolis), August 2, 1999, p. 1D.

Franklin, Jennifer, "Agency Aims to Put Consumers to Sleep," *Minneapolis/St. Paul CityBusiness,* August 6, p. 11.

Himelstein, Linda, and Leah Nathans, "Schwab's New Net Message: 'You've Got IPOs!,'" *Business Week,* January 11, 1999, p. 49.

Kalstrom, Jonathan, "Sweet Dreams," *Minnesota Ventures,* June 1993, pp. 68–69.

Kunkel, Karl, "Mattress Makers Respond to Shifting Channels," *HFN,* November 8, 1999, p. 10.

Mensheha, Mark, "Your Move," *Minneapolis/St. Paul CityBusiness,* July 9–15, 1993, p. 16.

Miller, Matthew R., "Select Comfort Rests Easy As the Leader in the Air Bed Industry," *Response,* May 1999, p. 12+.

Morris, Jared, "Bed Spread," *Twin Cities Business Monthly,* March 1995, pp. 60–63.

Phillips, Michael M., "Company Takes Comfort in Sales of Its Air Mattresses," *Star Tribune* (Minneapolis), February 26, 1991, p. 1D.

"Select Comfort Exec and Director Plan to Resign," *Star Tribune* (Minneapolis), August 14, 1999, 3D.

"Select Comfort Launches E-Commerce Subsidiary," *HFN,* April 12, 1999, p. 12.

Vincenti, Lisa, "Select Comfort Cozies Up to Sofa Sleeper," *HFN,* June 14, 1999, p. 6.

——, "Select Comfort Reworks Business Plan," *HFN,* January 3, 2000, p. 11.

Weinberger, Betsy, "Investors Lay Down Money for Growing Mattress Firm," *Minneapolis/St. Paul CityBusiness,* July 17, 1992, p. 8.

Weintraub, Adam, "Select Lays Down Stock Challenge," *Minneapolis/St. Paul CityBusiness,* May 17–23, 1999.

Welbes, John, "Columbia, S.C., Company Expands Air Mattress," *Knight-Ridder/Tribune Business News,* October 2, 1997.

Youngblood, Dick, "Select Comfort Corp. Rests Easily on Its Products, Profits," *Star Tribune* (Minneapolis), August 8, 1994, p. 2D.

—Kathleen Peippo

Selfridges Plc

400 Oxford St.
London W1A 1AB
United Kingdom
Telephone: (+44) 171-629-1234
Fax: +44-171-495-8321
Web site: http://www.selfridges.co.uk

Public Company
Incorporated: 1909
Employees: 3,000
Sales: £360 million (US$506.3 million) (1999)
Stock Exchanges: London
NAIC: 452110 Department Stores

One of the grand names in the history of the department store, Selfridges Plc has undergone a facelift in the late 1990s—not only has the company renovated its landmark Oxford Street, London location, but the company itself is undergoing a transformation. In 1997 the company was spun off from former parent Sears Plc (not to be confused with the United States' Sears Roebuck and Co.), taking a listing on the London stock exchange. Selfridges, led by CEO and former Habitat home furnishings chief Vittorio Radice, is also taking the company's famous name on the road. After opening a second store in Manchester, England, in 1998, the company has announced its intention to build up to three new Selfridges. The first of these is scheduled to open in Birmingham's revitalized Bull Ring district in 2003. The company is also looking for suitable locations in Glasgow and Newcastle. More than just a department store, Selfridges has long featured such amenities as a 300-room, four-star hotel; a parking garage with a car wash service; 15 restaurants; shoe shine, pharmacy, and other facilities, in addition to some 54 departments covering some 540,000 square feet of selling space. After spending close to £100 million on an extensive renovation of the Oxford Street flagship store, Selfridges has repositioned itself as a "house of brands." The company has also sharply improved its profitability, posting pre-tax profits of £27 million on sales of £360 million in 1999.

Founding a Department Store: 1909

Selfridges is the brainchild of famed retailer Harry Gordon Selfridge, an American who came to England at the turn of the century. Described as an instinctive retailer, Selfridge belongs to the era of such retailing greats as Marshall Field—indeed, Selfridge started his career with Field, Leitner & Co., which operated the famed Chicago-based department store chain. At Field, Leitner, Selfridge was credited with a number of firsts in the retailing industry. Selfridge proposed the concept of the January sale as a means of reducing stock left over from the holiday season. Selfridge also introduced the "bargain basement" to the American shopper, and was later credited with the famous phrase: "The customer is always right."

However, Field, Leitner was not right for Selfridge. Denied a senior partnership with that company, Selfridge left his job and his country, moving to London at the age of 50. There he bought a piece of property on what was then the "dead end" of Oxford Street, paying £400,000—by the beginning of the 21st century, that same property was valued at more than £324 million. Selfridge devised a logo for his new company by combining the symbols for the U.S. dollar and the British pound.

The Selfridge department store opened in 1909 and represented a revolution in British retailing. While the United Kingdom had been credited with developing the department store concept in the early part of the 19th century, by the turn of that century, British retailing was seen as largely trailing its more innovative counterparts in Europe and the United States. The Selfridge store helped to return England to the forefront of retailing technology. Considered the world's largest department store at the time, Selfridge offered more than simply shopping counters. Inside the huge complex, shoppers found such amenities as a post office, a library, rooms dedicated to foreign visitors, and a department dedicated to selling items for clergymen.

Selfridge, a keen marketer, also had a sense of the visual, adding window displays to the outside of the department store and a rooftop garden. Inside the store, shoppers were treated to lavish displays and decorations. In 1913, the store added another innovation, that of a nursery for caring for customers' children while they shopped. Selfridge also began offering

Christmas puddings to the bus drivers operating the routes past the Oxford Street store, encouraging the buses to stop—and passengers to come into the store.

Buoyed by the store's success, Selfridge took the company public in 1921, and expanded its property holdings, giving the company one of the largest parcels of privately held land in the Oxford Street district of London. Later that same decade, Selfridge became the first department store in the world to open a department dedicated to a new invention: the television. Yet the lavish decorations and upscale trimmings that had made Selfridges one of England's most prominent retailers also became the company's heaviest burden. With the stock market crash of 1929 and the worldwide depression of the 1930s, Selfridges found itself in increasing difficulties. The outbreak of World War II only exacerbated the company's troubles. H. Gordon Selfridge was finally forced to sell his company, to Lewis's Investment Trust, for £3.4 million. Selfridge, however, was to die in poverty.

Slumbering Through the Decades

While Selfridges remained an Oxford Street landmark, it also became a symbol for the dowdy department store by the late 1980s. In the mid-1960s, Selfridges caught the eye of another fast-rising retailing magnate, and the store was sold to Charles Clore in 1965. Clore had been responsible for building up the British Shoe Corporation, as part of his Sears Plc retail empire. While Sears—unrelated to Sears Roebuck & Co. of the United States—built up its shoe division, which, by the late 1980s boasted more than 2,500 stores and accounted for one of every four pairs of shoes sold in the United Kingdom, it also began to invest in Selfridges. In the 1970s, Sears built the four-star Selfridge Hotel behind the department store, added a 500-car parking facility, and expanded its restaurant.

During this period, Selfridges also underwent a series of renovation attempts, which, in keeping with the fashion of the time, aimed to cover up the "old-fashioned" features of the building in order to create a more modern appeal. This trend continued through the 1980s and into the 1990s, as Sears installed artificial ceilings and covered over such features as the huge solid bronze doors at the building's entrance, and removed much of its marble trim. Such decorative moves were nonetheless unable to counter the increasing association of "dowdy" with the Selfridges name.

In the 1990s, Sears began a new round of investments in Selfridges, including expanding its retail floor space, extending its range of restaurants, adding personal shopping services and a beauty salon. Meanwhile, Sears was apparently neglecting its core British Shoe Corporation business. By the early 1990s, consumer shoe tastes and habits had changed, with people opting not only for sneakers instead of shoes, but also eschewing the small specialty shoe shops which made up the bulk of British Shoe Corporation's store chain in favor of buying their shoes in the same store they bought their clothing.

By the mid-1990s, Sears, once a dominant player in the United Kingdom retail market, had earned the prefix "struggling." The company seemed unable to counter its dwindling sales, despite successive reorganizations. By the second half of the 1990s, Sears' management saw no choice but to begin selling its holdings, including breaking up the British Shoe Corporation into its component brands to competitors. The company's Cable & Co. chain was purchased, for example, by the United States' Nine West.

By the time the last of British Shoe Corporation had been sold, Sears had managed to lose more than £240 million on the breakup. Meanwhile, the company, criticized for holding on to Selfridges while shedding its core shoe business, was having troubles there too. Its attempt to move beyond the London city center, notably with the opening of two new stores near Heathrow airport, first in 1995, with the second added in 1996, met with failure. The company was forced to abandon the Heathrow stores in 1997.

A New Look for the New Century

By then, Sears was forced to begin looking for ways to shed the rest of its holdings. In 1997, the company decided to spin off Selfridges, a move which was completed in 1998 when Selfridges returned to a separate listing on the London stock exchange . By then, Selfridges had brought in Vittorio Radice, who had previously worked wonders turning around the Habitat chain of home furnishings stores. Since joining Selfridges in 1996, Radice had already helped push through a massive seven-year, £100 million renovation plan meant to restore the Selfridges building to its previous splendor.

Radice also broke from Selfridges long identification with the single Oxford Street store when he announced plans to build a new £43 million store in Manchester, in the north of England. At one-third the size of the Oxford Street store, the new Selfridges was also moving out of town, to a new £600 million shopping complex. While some observers were initially skeptical about the company's chances at this new location, which opened in 1998, the Manchester Selfridges quickly outpaced its projections, turning profitable by the end of 1999.

The public listing had immediately attracted the attention of British Land Corporation, led by John Ritblatt, which began acquiring stock in Selfridges. From an early position of more than six percent, British Land built up shares worth more than 13 percent of Selfridge's stock by the end of the century. These moves fueled rumors that Selfridges might be taken over, or acquired outright. Radice, however, insisted on the company's determination to maintain its independence.

The renovation of the Selfridges store reached completion in 1999 and immediately proved its worth, as shoppers returned to the store in force, raising company profits and sales. As Radice pointed out to the *Sunday Telegraph:* "Gordon Selfridge used to say this is not a store but a community centre. I believe this. It is not about selling goods but entertaining people." At the same

Key Dates:

1909: Harry Gordon Selfridge opens Oxford Street store.
1913: Adds nursery, window displays, and rooftop garden.
1921: Selfridges goes public.
1928: First dedicated television department.
1965: Acquisition by Sears Plc.
1970s: Adds four-star Selfridge Hotel and Food Hall.
1995: Opens first Heathrow Airport store; begins £100 million renovation of Oxford Street store.
1996: Opens second Heathrow Airport store.
1997: Closes both Heathrow stores.
1998: Selfridges spun off as public company; opens Manchester store.
1999: Oxford Street renovation completed; begins development of Birmingham store.
2000: Announces expansion plans for Oxford Street renovation.

time as entertaining the store's customers, however, Radice also took steps to increase their likelihood of buying. Among the company's initiatives was the introduction of a ''house of brands'' concept, separating departments into a collection of instore boutiques for such famed brand names as Gucci, Calvin Klein, and Yves Rocher. ''What you want is the feeling you get when you walk down Bond Street,'' Radice told the *Independent*, ''You enter the Gucci store there or the Gucci space here and it is the same experience, the same ambience, staff with the same kind of knowledge of the product. But our big advantage is that here, if you want to return a Gucci jumper, you can pick up some Patrick Cox shoes instead.''

With sales rising to £360 million and profits doubling over the previous year to top £27 million in 1999, Selfridges turned buoyantly to the future. By then, the company had started construction on a third store, tagging some £40 million for a venue that would be part of the revitalization of the Birmingham Bull Ring district. Selfridges also announced its intention to expand to as many as five stores, with Glasgow and Newcastle among the company's top choices for its new locations. With the renovation of the Oxford Street store completed by the beginning of 2000, Selfridges immediately announced ambitious plans for that location as well. Seeking a real estate partner—with British Land among the favorites—to provide financing and expertise, Radice announced plans for a radical new extension of the Oxford site. In addition to adding an additional 100,000 square feet of selling space, the new plans called for the construction of an office tower and residential complex above the site, as well as a new hotel and cinema.

Principal Competitors

Arcadia Group plc; Marks and Spencer p.l.c.; Debenhams Plc; Next Plc; Harrods; Sears PLC.

Further Reading

Dickson, E. Jane, ''The Retail Therapist,'' *Independent*, April 24, 1999, p. 14.

Hardcastle, Elaine, ''Selfridges in New Store, Development Plans,'' *Reuters*, February 16, 2000.

——, ''Selfridges' Profits Eclipse Rivals,'' *Reuters*, March 30, 2000.

Potter, Ben, ''Selfridges Lifted by Makeover,'' *Daily Telegraph*, October 1, 1999, p. 37.

Ravlin, Richard, ''Selfridges Relishes Its New Liberty,'' *Sunday Telegraph*, June 21, 1998. p. 6.

Worsley, Giles, ''The Grande Dame of Shopping Gets Sexy,'' *Daily Telegraph*, December 17, 1999, p. 26.

—M. L. Cohen

Stanley Furniture Company, Inc.

1641 Fairystone Park Hwy.
Stanleytown, Virginia 24168
U.S.A.
Telephone: (540) 627-2000
Fax: (540) 629-4085
Web site: http://www.stanleyfurniture.com

Public Company
Incorporated: 1924
Employees: 3,100
Sales: $264.7 million (1999)
Stock Exchanges: NASDAQ
Ticker Symbol: STLY
NAIC: 337122 Nonupholstered Wood Household
    Furniture Manufacturing

Stanley Furniture Company, Inc. is a leading designer and manufacturer of furniture, employing over 3,000 people. The high-quality wood furniture produced by the company is targeted for the upper-medium price range of the residential market. The Stanley line includes furniture for bedrooms, dining rooms, home offices, living rooms, and entertainment rooms. The furniture is manufactured in the United States at facilities in Stanleytown and Martinsville, Virginia, and West End, Robbinsville, and Lexington, North Carolina. Distribution is achieved through a broad domestic and international client base of 3,500 furniture stores, department stores, and regional furniture chains. The company's total sales rose seven percent in 1999 to $264.7 million with net income rising 32.4 percent to $19.2 million.

The Beginning of a Tradition: 1924

At age 33, Thomas Bahnson Stanley had a bright future ahead of him. In fact, his work as an executive at Bassett Furniture Company in Bassett, Virginia, was about to pay off. His employer, J.D. Bassett, was ready to recommend that Stanley be selected as president of the company in January 1924.

Thomas Stanley had a different goal, however. Not content to be president of someone else's company, he was determined to found a company of his own. Consequently, he offered his resignation at Bassett and founded the Stanley Furniture Company. The youngest of seven children and born in Henry County, Virginia, Stanley founded the company in his home county. Two other family members were associated with the company from the beginning, nephew Fred A. Stanley and brother John W. Stanley.

As Thomas Stanley built his first factory, he realized that he would need workers to make his furniture products and that those workers would need homes. As the Stanley Furniture Company took shape so did Stanleytown—streets were laid and some 100 homes were built. The town and factory were built on 150 acres of what had been pasture, and the factory itself was 150,000 square feet. Rent for the brick and frame homes was four to five dollars per month.

Roaring Business for a Roaring Era: 1920s

One year after Thomas Stanley founded the company, the first suite of furniture was introduced: a dining room suite complete with buffet, china closet, server, table, and chairs. As the furniture was introduced in Grand Rapids, Michigan; Chicago, Illinois; and New York, it was met with enthusiasm.

From 1925 through 1928, the company's profits steadily grew, as did the feverish pitch on Wall Street. By the beginning of 1929, the Stanley Furniture Company was debt-free and growing quickly.

Stanley's goal was to manufacture high quality furniture at a price that Americans could afford, and he was succeeding. As sales soared and opportunities rose, Stanley decided to expand. The company doubled its size and production capacity to meet growing demands.

1929: Stock Market Crash

When the stock market collapsed in October 1929, Stanley Furniture Company was in debt from the recent expansion. Banks were closing, factories shutting down, and people everywhere were out of work.

Company Perspectives:

Dreams begin at home . . . home begins with Stanley.

Thomas Stanley promised that no one at Stanley Furniture Company would lose his job. Not willing to send his employees to the breadlines, Stanley asked the 400 employees to work with him to keep the factory open by accepting a pay cut. The employees accepted the cut as well as agreeing to work ten hours of time for nine hours of pay. Stanley himself took a pay cut of 125 percent, cutting his monthly income from $750 to $333.33. The rents in Stanleytown were dropped by 20 percent, and those who were having trouble were allowed to pay when able. The hard work paid off as the Stanley Furniture Company remained open during the Great Depression, operating with a narrow profit margin.

Politics and Business: 1930s–50s

Also in 1929, Thomas Stanley was elected to the Virginia House of Delegates. Despite the hardships his company was facing, Stanley decided to continue in public service and eventually he was elected first as a U.S. representative, then as governor of Virginia (1954–58). While Stanley pursued his political career, he remained dedicated to the company he had founded. Successful in both industry and government, Thomas Bahnson Stanley was respected by his colleagues. When he left the U.S. House of Representatives to become governor of Virginia, then-Majority leader Charles Halleck said, "We who have been trying to attain fiscal integrity in government and reasonable economy where it could be applied, will miss the sound business sense of Tom Stanley. He has been a stalwart warrior in our battle for economy."

Eventually, his sons, Tom Stanley, Jr., and John David Stanley became involved in the business as well. Tom Stanley, Jr., worked his way from the machine room to the presidency of the company while his brother, John, became head of production.

Soon, it became necessary to expand the company again to modernize facilities and increase production. Unlike the first expansion in the late 1920s, the expansion in 1957 was not met with economic disaster.

That year, Stanley announced a $2.7 million expansion program which, by the time it was completed, cost $4 million. The goal of the expansion was to increase automation and bring the production facilities in line with modern capabilities.

Changing Times: 1960s–70s

In 1969, Stanley Furniture Company became part of Mead Corporation. Mead owned the company for ten years. Then, beginning in 1979, the company became part of several leveraged buyouts. Needless to say, this was a time of change and readjustment for the company, and in the late 1980s, it emerged as a wholly owned entity once more.

Key Dates:

1924: Thomas Bahnson Stanley founds Stanley Furniture Company, Inc.
1925: Stanley Furniture offers its first suite of furniture.
1929: Stanley promises no layoffs during Great Depression.
1957: Expansion program is launched.
1969: Company is bought by Mead Corporation.
1979: Mead divests Stanley, which becomes the subject of several leveraged buyouts.
1988: Albert Prillaman is named chairman, CEO, and president.
1993: Company initiates public offering of 1.7 million shares of common stock; fire damages portion of Stanleytown, Virginia, manufacturing facility.
1994: Company introduces its *Saturday Evening Post/ Norman Rockwell* collection and enters the upholstered furniture market.
1998: Company announces phase-out of upholstered product line.
2000: New facility opens in Martinsville, Virginia for the home office line.

1990s and Beyond: Growth and Changing Markets

In November 1992, the company underwent a financial restructuring. A public offering of 1.7 million shares of common stock followed in July 1993. That same year, a fire damaged the Stanleytown plant, temporarily eliminating 12 percent of the company's manufacturing facilities. A new 60,000-square-foot manufacturing facility, designed for maximum efficiency and future expansion, was built adjacent to the damaged plant.

In 1994 the company discontinued production of custom window treatments and bedcoverings and instead introduced upholstered furniture with a popular *Saturday Evening Post/ Norman Rockwell* theme. However, in 1998, the upholstered furniture was phased out to refocus on the company's wood furniture, sales of which were on the rise.

One high growth area had been in the Young America (youth bedroom) product line. The product line had experienced 15 percent growth over the previous five years. Another growth area was in the home office category. In March 2000, the company opened a new facility near Martinsville, Virginia. The 300,000-square-foot building was planned to focus exclusively on the home office line. The company projected that nearly 50 million American households would have home offices by the year 2002. Therefore, the dedicated facility as well as the nearly 200 items in the office collection were planned to meet that growing need. The new $15 million facility was built in Henry County, Virginia, the home county of Stanley's headquarters. Three hundred new jobs were added as a result.

Because of Stanley's continued investment in the Henry County area as well as the state of Virginia, Governor James S. Gilmore approved a grant of $600,000 from the Governor's Opportunity Fund to assist with site preparation.

As the new facility was designed and built, special consideration was given to creating a modern and efficient layout. The company planned to utilize state-of-the-art equipment, computerized routers, and ergonomic design for maximum safety, comfort, and quality with a long-term goal of shipping customer orders in an average of two weeks. ''We believe this new plant will be the largest, most modern manufacturing facility for home office furniture in the United States,'' Prillaman said.

In April 2000, Prillaman commented on the company's long stretch of record earnings. ''We are very pleased with our first quarter performance, especially considering that we were starting up a new factory and lost production due to inclement weather in January,'' he said. ''We continue to experience strong demand for our products including excellent results at the recently completed International Home Furnishings Market in High Point, North Carolina. We believe the high growth potential in our Young America bedroom and home office product categories will allow us to continue to outpace industry sales growth.''

Principal Competitors

Ethan Allen Interiors, Inc.; Furniture Brands International; Life-Style Furnishings International; Bassett Furniture Industries, Inc.; Broyhill Furniture Industries, Inc.

Further Reading

''Governor Gilmore Announces 500 New Jobs in Henry County,'' *Richmond: Virginia Economic Development Partnership*, March 31, 1999.

O'Hara, Terence, ''Did You Hear,'' *Washington Post*, October 25, 1999, p. F3.

''Stanley Furniture Announces Nineteenth Consecutive Quarter of Record Earnings,'' April 18, 2000, http://www.bloomberg.com.

''Stanley Furniture Appreciates EPA Concerns But Questions Formal Allegations,'' *PRNewswire,* July 1999.

''Stanley Furniture Company to Concentrate on Wood Furniture,'' August 7, 1998, http://www.bloomberg.com.

''Stanley Opens Dedicated Facility to Keep Pace with Home Office,'' *PR Newswire,* March 28, 2000.

—Shawna Brynildssen

Starbucks Corporation

2401 Utah Avenue South
Seattle, Washington 98134
U.S.A.
Telephone: (206) 447-1575
Fax: (206) 682-7570
Web site: http://www.starbucks.com

Public Company
Incorporated: 1985 as Il Giornale
Employees: 37,000
Sales: $1.68 billion (1999)
Stock Exchanges: NASDAQ
Ticker Symbol: SBUX
NAIC: 722213 Snack and Nonalcoholic Beverage Bars;
   311920 Coffee and Tea Manufacturing; 312111 Soft
   Drink Manufacturing; 422490 Other Grocery and
   Related Products Wholesalers; 454110 Electronic
   Shopping and Mail-Order Houses

Starbucks Corporation is the leading roaster, retailer, and marketer of specialty coffee in North America. Its operations include upwards of 2,400 coffee shops and kiosks in the United States and Canada, more than 100 in the United Kingdom, and more than 200 in other countries, including China, Japan, Kuwait, Lebanon, New Zealand, Malaysia, the Philippines, Singapore, South Korea, Taiwan, and Thailand. In addition to a variety of coffees and coffee drinks, Starbucks shops also feature Tazo teas; pastries and other food items; and espresso machines, coffee brewers, and other assorted items. The company also sells many of these products via mail order and online at starbucks.com. It also wholesales its coffee to restaurants, businesses, education and healthcare institutions, hotels, and airlines. Through a joint venture with Pepsi-Cola Company, Starbucks bottles Frappuccino beverages and sells them through supermarkets and convenience and drugstores. Through a partnership with Kraft Foods, Inc., the company sells Starbucks whole bean and ground coffee into grocery, warehouse club, and mass merchandise stores. A third joint venture is with Dreyer's Grand Ice Cream. In addition, it distributes Starbucks

premium coffee ice creams to U.S. supermarkets. From a single small store that opened in 1971 to its status as a gourmet coffee giant at the turn of the millennium, Starbucks has led a coffee revolution in the United States and beyond.

Roots in Coffee Retailing and Wholesaling

Starbucks was founded in Seattle, Washington, a haven for coffee aficionados. The city was noted for its coffee before World War II, but the quality of its coffee had declined so much by the late 1960s that resident Gordon Bowker made pilgrimages to Vancouver, British Columbia, to buy his beans there. His point of reference for the beverage was dark, delicious coffee he had discovered in Italy. Soon Bowker, then a writer for *Seattle* magazine, was making runs for friends as well. When *Seattle* folded, two of Bowker's friends, Jerry Baldwin, an English teacher, and Zev Siegl, a history teacher, also happened to be seeking new ventures; the three banded together and literally built their first store—located in Seattle's Pike Place Market—by hand. They raised $1,350 apiece, borrowed another $5,000, picked the name Starbucks—for the punchy "st" sound and its reference to the coffee-loving first mate in *Moby Dick*—then designed a two-tailed siren for a logo and set out to learn about coffee.

Siegl went to Berkeley, California, to learn from a Dutchman, Alfred Peet, who ran Peet's Coffee, which had been a legend among local coffee drinkers since 1966. Peet's approach to coffee beans became the cornerstone for Starbucks' reputation: high-grade arabica beans, roasted to a dark extreme by a trained perfectionist roaster. Starbucks bought its coffee from Peet's for its first nine months, giving away cups of coffee to hook customers. The plan worked. By 1972 the three founders had opened a second store in University Village and invested in a Probat roaster. Baldwin became the young company's first roaster.

Within its first decade, Starbucks had opened stores in Bellevue, Capitol Hill, and University Way. By 1982 the original entrepreneurs had a solid retail business of five stores, a small toasting facility, and a wholesale business that sold coffee primarily to local restaurants. The first of the company's growth versus ethos challenges came here: how does one maintain a near fanatical dedication to freshness in wholesale? Starbucks insisted that the shelf life of coffee is less than 14 days after roasting. As a result, they donated all eight-day-old coffee to charity.

In 1982 Starbucks hired Howard Schultz to manage the company's retail sales and marketing. While vice-president of U.S. operations for Hammarplast, a Swedish housewares company, and working out of New York, Schultz met the Starbucks trio and considered their coffee a revelation. (He had grown up on instant.) He and his wife packed up and drove 3,000 miles west to Seattle to join Starbucks.

There were other changes taking place at Starbucks at the same time. Siegl had decided to leave in 1980. The name of the wholesale division was changed to Caravali, out of fear of sullying the Starbucks name with less than absolute freshness. Blue Anchor, a line of whole-bean coffees being prepackaged for supermarkets, was relinquished. Starbucks learned two lessons from their brief time in business with supermarkets: first, supermarkets and their narrow profit margins were not the best outlet for a coffee roaster who refused to compromise on quality in order to lower prices, and second, Starbucks needed to sell directly to consumers who were educated enough to know why the coffee they were buying was superior.

Mid-1980s: The Shift to Coffee Bars

In 1983 Starbucks bought Peet's Coffee, which had by then become a five-store operation itself. That same year, Schultz took a buying trip to Italy, where another coffee revelation took place. Wandering the piazzas of Milan, Schultz was captivated by the culture of coffee and the romance of Italian coffee bars. Milan had about 1,700 espresso bars, which were a third center for Italians, after work and home. Schultz returned home determined to bring Italian coffee bars to the United States, but found his bosses reluctant, being still more dedicated to retailing coffee. As a result, Schultz left the company to write a business plan of his own. His parting with Starbucks was so amicable that the founders invested in Schultz's vision. Schultz returned to Italy to do research, visiting hundreds of espresso and coffee bars. In the spring of 1986, he opened his first coffee bar in the Columbia Seafirst Center, the tallest building west of Chicago. Faithful to its inspiration, the bar had a stately espresso machine as its centerpiece. Called Il Giornale, the bar served Starbucks coffee and was an instant hit. A second was soon opened in

Seattle, and a third in Vancouver. Schultz hired Dave Olsen, the proprietor of one of the first bohemian espresso bars in Seattle, as a coffee consultant and employee trainer.

A year later, Schultz was thriving while Starbucks was encountering frustration. The wholesale market had been reconfigured by the popularity of flavored coffees, which Starbucks resolutely refused to produce. The company's managers were also increasingly aggravated by the lack of wholesale quality control, so they sold their wholesale line, Caravali, to Seattle businessman Bart Wilson and a group of investors. In addition, Bowker was interested in leaving the company to concentrate on a new project, Red Hook Ale. Schultz approached his old colleagues with an attractive offer: how about $4 million for the six-unit Starbucks chain? They sold, with Olsen remaining as Starbucks' coffee buyer and roaster; the Starbucks stores were merged into Il Giornale. Baldwin remained president of the now separately operated Peet's Coffee and Tea. In 1987 the Il Giornale shops changed their names to Starbucks, and the company became Starbucks Corporation and prepared to go national.

In August 1987 Starbucks Corporation had 11 stores and fewer than 100 employees. In October of that year it opened its first store in Chicago, and by 1989 there were nine Chicago Starbucks, where employees trained by Seattle managers served coffee roasted in the Seattle plant.

Their methods were costly, using high-grade arabica beans and expensive dark roasting, while suffering the financial consequences of snubbing the supermarket and wholesale markets. Nevertheless, Starbucks' market was growing rapidly: sales of specialty coffee in the United States grew from $50 million in 1983 to $500 million five years later.

In 1988 Starbucks introduced a mail-order catalog, and by the end of that year, the company was serving mail-order customers in every state and operating a total of 33 stores. Because the company's reputation grew steadily by word of mouth, it spent little on ads. Schultz's management philosophy, "hire people smarter than you are and get out of their way," fed his aggressive expansion plans. Industry experts were brought in to manage Starbucks' finances, human resources, marketing, and mail-order divisions. The company's middle ranks were filled with experienced managers from such giants as Taco Bell, Wendy's, and Blockbuster. Schultz was willing to lose money while preparing Starbucks for explosive growth. By 1990 he had hired two star executives: Howard Behar, previously president of a leading developer of outdoor resorts, Thousand Trails, Inc.; and Orin Smith, chief financial and administrative officer for Danzas, USA, a freight forwarder.

Starbucks installed a costly computer network and hired a specialist in information technology from McDonald's Corporation to design a point-of-sale system via PCs for store managers to use. Every night, stores passed their sales information to Seattle headquarters, which allowed planners to spot regional buying trends almost instantly. Starbucks lost money while preparing for its planned expansion, including more than $1 million in 1989 alone. In 1990 the headquarters expanded and a new roasting plant was built. Nevertheless, Schultz resisted both the temptation to franchise and to flavor the beans. Slowly, the chain developed near-cult status.

Key Dates:

1971: Gordon Bowker, Jerry Baldwin, and Zev Siegl open the first Starbucks in Seattle's Pike Place Market.

1982: Howard Schultz is hired to manage retail sales and marketing.

1983: Peet's Coffee is acquired.

1985: Schultz leaves the company to found Il Giornale, an operator of coffee bars.

1987: Schultz buys the six-unit Starbucks chain from the original owners for $4 million, merges them into Il Giornale, renames his company Starbucks Corporation, and begins a national expansion by opening stores in Chicago. Baldwin remains president of the now separate Peet's Coffee and Tea business.

1988: A mail-order catalog is introduced.

1992: Company goes public.

1993: First East Coast store opens, in Washington, D.C.

1995: Frappuccino beverages are introduced.

1996: Overseas expansion begins with units in Japan, Hawaii, and Singapore. Partnership with Dreyer's begins selling Starbucks Ice Cream. Partnership with Pepsi-Cola begins selling bottled Frappuccino beverages.

1998: U.K.-based Seattle Coffee Company is acquired. Partnership with Kraft Foods is formed for the distribution of Starbucks coffee into supermarkets.

1999: Pasqua Coffee Co. and Tazo Tea Company are acquired.

2000: Schultz steps aside as CEO to become chief global strategist, while remaining chairman; Orin Smith takes over as CEO.

Rapid Early 1990s Growth As a Public Company

Starbucks also developed a reputation for treating its employees well. In 1991 it became the first privately owned company in history to establish an employee stock option program that included part-timers. Starbucks also offered health and dental benefits to both full- and part-time employees. As a result, the company had a turnover rate that was very low for the food service industry. Employees were rigorously trained, completing at least 25 hours of coursework on topics including the history of coffee, drink preparation, and how to brew a perfect cup at home. The company went public in 1992, the same year it opened its first stores in San Francisco, San Diego, Orange County, and Denver. Its stores totaled 165 by year's end. The company began special relationships with Nordstrom's and Barnes & Noble, Inc., offering coffee to shoppers at both chains.

Growth mandated the opening of a second roasting plant, located in Kent, Washington, by 1993. After 22 years in business, Starbucks had only 19 individuals it deemed qualified to roast coffee. One of the 19 was Schultz, who considered it a tremendous privilege. Roasters were trained for more than a year before being allowed to roast a batch, which consisted of up to 600 pounds of coffee roasted for 12 to 15 minutes in a gas oven. The beans made a popping sound, like popcorn, when ready, but roasters also used sight and smell to tell when the

beans were done to perfection. Starbucks standards required roasters to test the roasted beans in an Agron blood-cell analyzer to assure that each batch was up to standards. If not, it was discarded.

Starbucks' first East Coast store opened in 1993, in a premier location in Washington, D.C. The chain had 275 stores by the end of 1993 and 425 one year later. Sales had grown an average of 65 percent annually over the previous three years (reaching $284.9 million in 1994), with net income growing 70 to 100 percent a year during that time. Starbucks broke into important new markets in 1994, including Minneapolis, Boston, New York, Atlanta, Dallas, and Houston, and purchased the Coffee Connection, a 23-store rival based in Boston, for $23 million, making it a wholly owned subsidiary. Smith was promoted to president and COO and Behar became president, international. Starbucks also announced a partnership with Pepsi-Cola to develop new ready-to-drink coffee beverages. After Starbucks debuted a frozen coffee drink called Frappuccino in its stores in the summer of 1995, resulting in a sales bonanza, the partnership with Pepsi began rolling out a bottled version in grocery, convenience, and drugstores the following year. Starbucks broke into new markets in 1995, including Pittsburgh, San Antonio, Las Vegas, and Philadelphia. That same year, Starbucks began supplying coffee for United Airlines flights and launched a line of Starbucks compilation music CDs which were sold in its coffee houses.

Late 1990s and Beyond: International Expansion and New Ventures

The following year—in addition to continued North American expansion into Rhode Island, Idaho, North Carolina, Arizona, Utah, and Ontario—the company ventured overseas for the first time. Its initial foreign forays were launched through joint venture and licensing arrangements with prominent local retailers. With the help of SAZABY Inc., a Japanese retailer and restaurateur, the first market developed in 1996 was Japan; through other partnerships, Hawaii and Singapore also received their first Starbucks that year. The Philippines followed in 1997. Meantime, Starbucks entered into a partnership with Dreyer's Grand Ice Cream, Inc. in 1996 to develop and sell Starbucks Ice Cream. Within eight months of introduction, the product became the number one coffee ice cream in the United States. Starbucks' expansion into Florida, Michigan, and Wisconsin in 1997 helped the total number of units reach an astounding 1,412 by year-end, more than double the previous two-year total. Sales approached the $1 billion mark that year, while net income hit $57.4 million, more than five times the result for 1994.

As this rapid growth continued, the company began to be needled by late night talk show hosts for its seeming Starbucks-on-every-corner expansion strategy, while a number of owners and patrons of local coffee shops began speaking out and demonstrating against what they considered overly aggressive and even predatory moves into new territory. Critics complained that the company was deliberately locating its units near local coffee merchants to siphon off sales, sometimes placing a Starbucks directly across the street. In 1996 and 1997 residents in Toronto, San Francisco, Brooklyn, and Portland, Oregon, staged sidewalk protests to attempt to keep Starbucks out of their neighborhoods. One of the company's responses to the scattered resistance was to try to enhance its image through stepped-up advertising. Still, like Wal-Mart Stores, Inc. and its reputation in some quarters as a destroyer of Main Street, Starbucks remained the object of snickers from comedians and derision from a vocal minority of protesters. This undercurrent of hostility burst into the spotlight in late 1999 when some of the more aggressive protesters against a World Trade Organization meeting took their anger out on several Starbucks stores in the company's hometown of Seattle, tagging a number of the 26 downtown locations with graffiti and inflicting more serious vandalism on three stores, which were then temporarily closed.

The anti-multinational protesters in Seattle also singled out stores operated by McDonald's Corporation and Nike, Inc. The lumping of the once-modest purveyor of gourmet coffee in with these global giants was in part an outgrowth of the company's aggressive overseas expansion in the late 1990s. Growth in the Pacific Rim continued with the opening of locations in Taiwan, Thailand, New Zealand, and Malaysia in 1998 and in China and South Korea in 1999. By early 2000 the number of Starbucks in Japan had reached 100. The company aimed to have 500 stores in the Pacific Rim by 2003. The Middle East was another target of global growth, with stores opened in Kuwait and Lebanon in 1999, but it was the United Kingdom that was the object of the company's other big late 1990s push. In 1998 Starbucks acquired Seattle Coffee Company, the leading U.K. specialty coffee firm, for about $86 million in stock. Starbucks began rebranding Seattle Coffee's locations under the Starbucks name. Aggressive expansion in the United Kingdom yielded more than 100 units by late 1999. Starbucks hoped to use its U.K. base for an invasion of the Continent, aiming for 500 stores in Europe by 2003.

Growth was not slowing back home either. Areas receiving their first Starbucks in 1998 and 1999 included New Orleans, St. Louis, Kansas City, and Memphis and Nashville, Tennessee. The number of North American locations approached 2,200 by early 2000. Always searching for new revenue streams, Starbucks in 1998 entered into a long-term licensing agreement with Kraft Foods, Inc. for the marketing and distribution of Starbucks whole bean and ground coffee into grocery, warehouse club, and mass merchandise stores. The company also began experimenting with a full-service casual restaurant called Café Starbucks. A further move into food came in early 1999 through the purchase of Pasqua Coffee Co., a chain of coffee and sandwich shops with 56 units in California and New York. Starbucks had already developed its own in-house tea brand, Infusia, but it was replaced following the early 1999 acquisition of Tazo Tea Company, a Portland, Oregon-based maker of premium teas and related products with distribution through 5,000 retail outlets.

Starbucks had also launched a web site featuring an online store in 1998, and Schultz began talking about Starbucks becoming a mega-cybermerchant offering everything from gourmet foods to furniture. To this end, the company attempted, but failed, to acquire Williams-Sonoma, Inc., a specialty retailer of high-end kitchenware. Wall Street analysts began questioning the wisdom of moving so far afield from the company's core coffee business. In mid-1999, following Starbucks' announcement of an earnings shortfall, the company's stock plunged 28 percent, leading Schultz to pull back on his ambitious cyber plans. In early 2000, however, the company did enter into an agreement with Kozmo.com Inc., an operator of an Internet home-delivery service providing its customers with videos, snacks, magazines, books, and other items. Kozmo.com agreed to pay Starbucks $150 million over a five-year period to place drop boxes in Starbucks stores for the return of videos and other items, and to begin delivering Starbucks coffee, Tazo teas, and other items to its customers.

Other developments included an agreement with Albertson's, Inc. to open more than 100 Starbucks coffee bars in Albertson's supermarkets in the United States; and the acquisition of the five-store San Francisco-based Hear Music chain, in an extension of Starbucks' music retailing ventures. Image problems continued to crop up for the rapidly growing company, whose fiscal 1999 revenues of $1.68 billion were nearly six times the figure of five years earlier. In April 2000 a San Francisco-based human rights group called Global Exchange was readying a large protest at Starbucks in 29 cities to publicize its allegations that the coffee company was buying its beans from wholesalers who were paying farmers what amounted to poverty wages. In a preemptive move, which staved off the protests and the resultant bad publicity, Starbucks announced that it would buy more coffee certified as ''fair trade,'' meaning that the farmers who grew it received more than market price for their crop, sometimes as high as three times the 30 cents per pound they typically received.

In the early 21st century, Starbucks was working to achieve Schultz's ambitious goals of 500 stores in both Japan and Europe by 2003, as well as his ultimate goal of 20,000 units worldwide. With about half of that total envisioned to be located outside North America, Schultz decided to spend more time on the company's overseas operations. In June 2000 he stepped down as CEO of the company to become its chief global strategist, while remaining chairman. Schultz would work closely with Peter Maslen, who had taken charge of the international division in late 1999, following the retirement of Howard Behar. Assuming the CEO title was Orin Smith, who retained his previous responsibility for domestic retail and wholesale operations, alliances, and coffee roasting and distribution.

Principal Subsidiaries

The Coffee Connection, Inc.; Starbucks New Venture Company; Starbucks Coffee International, Inc.; Starbucks Holding Company; Starbucks Manufacturing Corporation; SBI Nevada, Inc.; Circadia Corporation; Starbucks U.S. Brands Corporation; Starbucks Asset Management Corporation; Starbucks Foreign Sales Corporation; Starbucks Coffee Holdings (UK) Limited; Starbucks Coffee Company (UK) Limited; Seattle Coffee Company International (U.K.); Torz & Macatonia Limited (U.K.); Tazo Tea Company; Pasqua Inc.; Starbucks Coffee France, EURL; Starbucks Coffee Asia Pacific Ltd.; Starbucks Coffee Company (Australia) Pty Ltd (90%); Tympanum, Inc.

Principal Competitors

ABP Corporation; AFC Enterprises, Inc.; Allied Domecq PLC; BAB Holdings, Inc.; Diedrich Coffee, Inc.; Einstein/Noah Bagel Corp.; Farmer Bros. Co.; Green Mountain Coffee, Inc.; Kraft Foods, Inc.; Nestlé S.A.; New World Coffee-Manhattan

Bagel, Inc.; New York Bagel Enterprises, Inc.; Panera Bread Company; Peet's Coffee & Tea; The Procter & Gamble Company; Sara Lee Corporation; Tully's Coffee Corporation.

Further Reading

Abramovitch, Ingrid, "Miracles of Marketing: How to Reinvent Your Product," *Success,* April 1993, pp. 22–26.

Anders, George, "Starbucks in Pact with Kozmo.com on Using Stores," *Wall Street Journal,* February 14, 2000, p. A34.

Barron, Kelly, "The Cappuccino Conundrum," *Forbes,* February 22, 1999, p. 54.

Brammer, Rhonda, "Grounds for Caution," *Barron's,* August 15, 1994, p. 20.

Browder, Seanna, "Starbucks Does Not Live by Coffee Alone," *Business Week,* August 5, 1996, p. 76.

Cuneo, Alice, "Starbucks' Word-of-Mouth Wonder," *Advertising Age,* March 7, 1994, p. 12.

Fitzpatrick, Eileen, "Starbucks Buy Hear Music Chain," *Billboard,* December 4, 1999, p. 10.

Frank, Stephen, "Starbucks Brews Strong Results Analysts Like," *Wall Street Journal,* July 14, 1994, p. C1.

Gibson, Richard, "Some Meatloaf with That Decaf Latte?," *Wall Street Journal,* March 16, 1999, p. B1.

——, "Starbucks Cyberspace Mission Returns to Earth After Big Bang on Wall Street," *Wall Street Journal,* July 23, 1999, p. B4.

——, "Starbucks Holders Wake Up, Smell the Coffee and Sell," *Wall Street Journal,* July 2, 1999, p. B3.

Hamstra, Mark, "Starbucks' Pasqua Purchase Dovetails with Food-Café Tests," *Nation's Restaurant News,* January 4, 1999, pp. 3, 104.

Harris, John, "Cuppa Sumatra," *Forbes,* November 26, 1990, pp. 213–14.

Jones Yang, Dori, "The Starbucks Enterprise Shifts into Warp Speed," *Business Week,* October 24, 1994, pp. 76–78.

Kaplan, David A., "Trouble Brewing," *Newsweek,* July 19, 1999, pp. 40–41.

Kim, Nancy J., "Starbucks Weighing European Growth Strategies," *Puget Sound Business Journal,* August 20, 1999, p. 9.

Kugiya, Hugo, "Seattle's Coffee King," *Seattle Times,* December 15, 1996, p. 20.

Ordonez, Jennifer, "Starbucks' Schultz to Leave Top Post, Lead Global Effort," *Wall Street Journal,* April 7, 2000, p. B3.

Pressler, Margaret Webb, "The Brain Behind the Beans," *Washington Post,* October 5, 1997, p. H1.

Reese, Jennifer, "Starbucks: Inside the Coffee Cult," *Fortune,* December 9, 1996, pp. 190–92 + .

Robinson, Kathryn, "Coffee Achievers," *Seattle Weekly,* August 2, 1989.

Schultz, Howard, "By Way of Canarsie, One Large Hot Cup of Business Strategy," *New York Times,* December 14, 1994, pp. C1, C8.

Schultz, Howard, and Dori Jones Yang, *Pour Your Heart into It: How Starbucks Built a Company One Cut at a Time,* New York: Hyperion, 1997, 351 p.

Schwartz, Nelson D., "Still Perking After All These Years," *Fortune,* May 24, 1999, pp. 203 + .

Simons, John, "A Case of the Shakes: As Starbucks Cafes Multiply, So Do the Growing Pains," *U.S. News and World Report,* July 14, 1997, pp. 42–44.

Spector, Amy, "Starbucks Launches Lunch Tests in Seven Major Markets," *Nation's Restaurant News,* October 18, 1999, p. 32.

Strauss, Karyn, "Howard Schultz," *Nation's Restaurant News,* January 2000, pp. 162–63.

Weiss, Naomi, "How Starbucks Impassions Workers to Drive Growth," *Workforce,* August 1998.

Whalen, Jeanne, "Starbucks, Pepsi Tackle Coffee Venture," *Advertising Age,* August 1, 1994, p. 44.

—Carol I. Keeley
—updated by David E. Salamie

Stoll-Moss Theatres Ltd.

Manor House, 21 Soho Square
London W1V 5FD
United Kingdom
Telephone: +44 (0) 20-7494-5399
Fax: +44 (0) 20-7494-5156
Web site: http://www.stoll-moss.com

Private Company
Incorporated: 1950s
Sales: £105 million (1999 est.)
NAIC: 71131 Promoters of Performing Arts, Sports, and
Similar Events with Facilities (pt)

With roots dating back to the late 19th century, Stoll-Moss Theatres Ltd. has grown over a century to become one of London's leading theater operators. The venerable theater operator boasts the following storied venues: The Lyric, The Apollo, The Gielgud, The Queen's, The Duchess, The Theater Royal, Drury Lane, The Cambridge, The Garrick, Her Majesty's Theater, and The London Palladium. Early in 2000, Andrew Lloyd Webber's The Really Useful Group agreed to purchase Stoll-Moss and thus ensure that its rich and colorful history as an icon of theatrical entertainment would continue.

Building Theaters: 1860–1942

In the late 19th century, Sir Edward Moss and Sir Oswald Stoll, working independently with such architects as Frank Matcham and C.J. Phipps, began building theaters in Britain. One of the theaters Moss commissioned British architect Matcham (also known for The Blackpool Grand Theater, The Hippodrome, the shopping arcades at Leeds, and The Victoria Theater) to build was The Empire Palace Theater in Ireland in 1892. The 3,000-seat theater burned down in 1911 when illusionist Lafayette accidentally ignited the draperies with a torch.

Stoll—an Australian-born Irishman who had been running his family's music hall in Liverpool since he was 14, and who would go on to become a composer/arranger–in turn, commissioned Matcham to build The Hackney Empire Theater in 1901.

With 2,158 seats, it is still considered one of England's finest proscenium arch Theatres and among Matcham's greatest works. The century-old building was the first all-electric theater and featured opera house acoustics, a vacuum-pump cleaning system, air conditioning via a sliding roof, and a projector box (placing it among the world's oldest cinemas). Charlie Chaplin, Stan Laurel, Liberace and others passed through before the theater became the home of such television shows as "Oh Boy!," "Take Your Pick," and "Emergency Ward 10." Mecca converted the theater into a bingo hall during its ownership, destroying the original oil paintings, gold-leaf decorations, statuary, and terra cotta domes. In 1986, CAST, a small touring group, acquired the building, reopening it as a theater on December 9, 1986, the building's 85th birthday.

In 1904 Stoll commissioned Matcham to build The London Coliseum. London's largest theater—with 2,356 seats—it featured the first revolving stage in Britain, as well as the first lifts, or elevators, to upper levels. In 1931, with vaudeville's decline, The Coliseum turned to musical comedy, which it discontinued in 1968, becoming a cinema. In 1974, The Coliseum became home to The English National Opera, which still performs there. Stoll actively managed his theaters until at least the late 1920s. He died in 1942. During the 1950s, the Stoll and Moss groups combined to become Stoll-Moss Theatres Ltd.

The Stoll-Moss Fold: Acquired Theaters, 1633–1930

The Theater Royal Drury Lane first opened in 1663 with *The Humorous Lieutenant*. Nell Gwynne appeared in *The Indian Queen* (1665), and the theater burned in 1672. The second Drury Lane was attributed to Sir Christopher Wren in 1674. Garrick made his first appearance in 1742 and took over in 1747. Mrs. Siddons debuted there in 1775 and Richard Brinsley Sheridan took over in 1776. *School for Scandal* (1777) and his later plays were produced there. In 1794, Sheridan built a third, larger theater, which burned in 1809. Samuel Whitbread, founder of the Whitbread Brewery, funded the fourth theater, which opened in 1812. The Drury Lane limped along until 1879, when a series of popular melodramas, pantomimes, and spectaculars filled its coffers. One of the theater's unique traditions is The Twelfth Night Cake. Started upon his death in 1794,

Company Perspectives:

Stoll Moss Theatres has its roots in the late 19th century. The last 100 years has seen the company develop into London's leading theater operator. We welcome over 3.5 million visitors to West End Theatres each year.

by actor Robert Baddeley who left money for cake and wine for the guests annually on Twelfth Night, the party still occurs today, over 200 years later. Drury Lane also has its own phantom—''The Man in Grey,'' supposedly the ghost of a man whose bones were found behind a wall of the theater in 1840—said to haunt The Upper Circle, especially during matinees.

The theater at London's Haymarket—now known as Her Majesty's Theater—was built originally in 1705 as Queen Anne's Theater by architect/playwright Sir John Vanbrugh. Renamed The Italian Opera House, it survived a 1789 fire, name changes with monarchs, became The King's Theater, and, finally, Her Majesty's Theater with the accession of Queen Victoria (1837). An 1867 fire closed it for ten years, and lack of success caused its demolition in 1891. The current theater was commissioned by Beerbohm Tree (founder of The Royal Academy of Dramatic Art) and built by Phipps in 1897. The theater was refurbished from 1990–93 without interrupting performances.

The Lyric Theater at London's Shaftesbury Avenue is Stoll-Moss's oldest original building. Funded by composer/arranger Henry Leslie and designed by Phipps, The Lyric was built in 1888—although what is now the dressing room entrance was built back in 1767 as anatomist Dr. William Hunter's home.

The Garrick at Charing Cross Road was designed by Walter Emden and Phipps. The theater opened in April 1889 after two years of work and nearly being abandoned because the deep excavations necessary for the below-ground auditorium unearthed a river which flooded the foundations. *The Notorious Mrs. Ebbsmith* opened in 1895, and a woman named Ebbsmith drowned in the Thames with a ticket for the play in her pocket. In addition, the ghost of former manager Arthur Bourchier reputedly haunts the theater. During the early 1930s, plans to turn the theater into a cinema were scrapped when Wendy Hiller starred in *Love on the Dole* (1935) and saved the venue. Other plays included *Rattle of a Simple Man* (1962), *Stand by Your Bedouin* (1967), and *No Sex Please, We're British!* (1982–87).

The Apollo Theater—commissioned by Henry Lowenfeld and built by architect Lewen Sharp—opened with *The Belle of Bohemia* (1901). The fourth theater to be built on Shaftesbury, the French-façade building with 769 seats featured *Kitty Grey* (1902), *Tom Jones* (1907), *Gaslight* (1939), *Flarepath* (1942–44), *Seagulls over Sorrento* (1950), Sir John Gielgud in *Forty Years On* (1968) and *The Best of Friends* (1988), Albert Finney in *Orphans* (1986), and Hiller in *Driving Miss Daisy* (1988), to name a few.

The Gielgud, also on Shaftesbury Avenue, was built by W.G.R. Sprague and opened as The Hicks in 1906. Renamed The Globe in 1909, it has been directed by some of England's

top managers, including Charles Frohman, Anthony Prinsep, and H.M. Tennent.

The Queen's Theater—named with Queen Alexandra's blessing—was designed by Sprague as a companion to The Globe, opening with *The Belle of Brittany* (1908), followed by *The Apple Cart* (1929); Gielgud as Hamlet (1930); and Margaret Rutherford, Tempest, and Rex Harrison in *Morley's Short Story* (1935). During du Maurier's *Rebecca* (1940), the theater was bombed by the Germans and remained closed until 1959, when Gielgud soloed in *The Ages of Man*. Notable performances include Vanessa Redgrave in Chekhov's *The Seagull* (1964, 1985); Noel Coward in his last stage appearance in his own *Suite in Three Keys* (1966); *Getting On* (1971); *The Dresser* (1980); and *Another Country* (1982). The theater was refurbished in early 1991.

The Palladium–which opened on Boxing Day in 1910—dates back to the 1870s, when circus showman Frederick Charles Hengler housed *Hengler's Grand Cirque* there. It then became The National Skating Palace and a music hall before being rebuilt by Matcham. Rivaling The Hippodrome and The Coliseum in magnificence and size, it is London's second largest theater, with 2,302 seats. Renamed The London Palladium (1934), the venue housed *Peter Pan* every Christmas from 1930–38. *Sunday Night at the London Palladium*, televised live, was one of the ITV's first great successes, and almost every international star has appeared there, from Judy Garland to Bob Hope.

The Duchess, on Catherine Street, was built in 1929 by Ewan Barr and is one of the smallest theaters in London. The first production, in 1930, did not finish opening night, but the theater recovered and went on to produce *Eden End* (1934), *Cornelius* (1934), *Night Must Fall* (1935), *The Corn Is Green* (1938–39), *Murder in the Cathedral* (1936), *Blithe Spirit* (1942), *The Deep Blue Sea* (1952), and *Oh Calcutta!* (1974–80). Stoll-Moss acquired the theater in January 1986.

Designed in 1930 by Wimperis, Simpson, and Guthrie, The 1,283-seat Cambridge Theater on London's Earlham Street has featured Finney in *Billy Liar* (1960s), Ingrid Bergman and Michael Redgrave in *A Month in the Country* (1960s); Maggie Smith in *Hedda Gabler* (1970); Sir Lawrence Olivier as Shylock in *The Merchant of Venice* (1970); and *Return to the Forbidden Planet* (1990s).

New Owners: Australia and Back Again: 1980s–2000

In 1984, Stoll-Moss was purchased by Australia-based Heytesbury Party Ltd. (founded in 1923), at the time led by tycoon Robert Holmes à Court. Upon his death in 1990, his widow Janet inherited everything. In 1994, she announced major changes for the theater group, including renaming The Globe after Gielgud (so there would be only one Globe in London–Shakespeare's) and announcing plans to reopen The Royalty Theater.

In August 1999, Heytesbury suddenly put Stoll-Moss on the market. It was their only European-based asset and Heytesbury wanted to concentrate on projects in Australasia. Before the shocking announcement, it was believed that Stoll-Moss was looking to acquire Associated Capital Theatres, the second

Key Dates:

1866: Sir Oswald Stoll is born.
1901: Stoll and Frank Matcham build The Hackney Empire Theater.
1942: Stoll dies.
1950s: Stoll and Moss groups combine to become Stoll-Moss Theatres Ltd.
1984: Stoll-Moss is purchased by Australia-based Heytesbury Party Ltd.
2000: Sir Andrew Lloyd Webber purchases the company.

largest West End group, with eight theatres, including Wyndhams, Albery, and three Curzon cinemas. The Albery and The Wyndham theatres went to promoter Sir Cameron Mackintosh in late 1999 for about £7 million (US$11.2 million).

Stoll-Moss's availability came on the heels of the £170 million acquisition of The Apollo Leisure Group—Britain's biggest theater operator, with 27 London-based and regional venues, and the US$116 million acquisition of Livent Inc. by SFX Entertainment Inc., the world's largest promoter. Apollo's venues included The Lyceum, The Apollo Victoria, The Dominion, and The Apollo Hammersmith in London; The Opera House, The Palace, and The Apollo in Manchester; The Bristol Hippodrome; The Edinburgh Playhouse; The Old Fire Station and The Apollo in Oxford; The Liverpool Empire; and others in Sheffield and Cardiff. The acquisitions by SFX included Apollo's 50 percent stake in concert and theater production company, The Barry Claymore Corporation. Parties involved in the bidding eventually came to include U.S.-based Shubert Organization Inc.; a consortium led by Sir Michael Grade and Peter Holmes à Court, Janet's producer son; and SFX, whose subsidiary PACE Theatrical sold its 25 percent in The Ambassador Group in November.

In March 2000, The Really Useful Group–repurchased from Seagram in 1999 by founder and famed composer Andrew Lloyd Webber (the creative force behind *Phantom of the Opera, Cats,* and numerous other hit musicals)—bought (with NatWest Equity Partners) Stoll-Moss from Heytesbury for approximately £87.5 million (US$200 million), beating out competitors Mackintosh and American entrepreneur Max Weitzenhoffer. Lloyd Webber already owned The Adelphi, The Palace, and The New London; the acquisition made him one of London's biggest theater owners. In a TV interview with David Frost, Lloyd Webber said he purchased the group to preserve London's theatrical tradition and keep it safe from what he called "the money men." In the interview, he said, "If you were a pen-pusher or a number-cruncher, and you were given a musical about furry animals dressed up as cats, to poems by T.S. Eliot and directed by the then-director of The Royal Shakespeare Company, you would have perhaps said 'I don't think I fancy that.' It's terribly important that for the interest of theater we are willing to take on new ideas and try them out."

Stoll-Moss CEO Richard Johnson and his management team would stay on to run the new company, whose name would likely change to Really Useful Theatres. Lloyd Webber would lose The Gielgud and The Queen's in 2006 when their leases reverted to Mackintosh, who purchased them in 1999 when they were not producing expected revenues. But, with Lloyd Webber's vision and over 3.5 million visitors each year, the Stoll-Moss empire was expected to continue through the 21st century.

Principal Subsidiaries

Select Theater Breaks.

Principal Competitors

SFX Entertainment Inc.; Shubert Organization Inc.; Jujamcyn Theaters.

Further Reading

Barker, Felix, *The House That Stoll Built: The Story of the Coliseum Theater,* London: Muller, 1957, 256 p.

"Mackintosh Buys U.K. Theatres," *Back Stage,* October 8, 1999, p. 2.

McGillivray, David. "West End Power Struggle Rages," *Back Stage,* September 17, 1999, p. 19.

Peers, Martin, and Claude Brodesser, "Britain's Stoll Moss Eyes Livent," *Variety,* February 16, 1999.

"Stoll Moss," *Economist,* August 7, 1999, p. 5.

Thorncroft, Tony, "Lloyd-Webber Pays £87.5M for Theatres; Entertainment Really Useful Group Bids for Stoll Moss's 10 West End Venues," *Financial Times,* January 10, 2000, p. 2.

——, "West End Plays Leading Role in Stage-Managed Profitability: Lord Lloyd-Webber Is Becoming a Leading Light in Theater Ownership As the London Stage Shines, Writes Antony Thorncroft," *Financial Times,* January 11, 2000, p. 5.

"Top London Theatres for Sale," August 2, 1999, http://news.bbc.co.uk/hi/english/entertainment/newsid_409000/409753.stm.

Treadgold, Tim, "Heytesbury's Theater of the Absurd," *Business Review Weekly,* August 13, 1999, p. 41.

Wolf, Matt, "Court Houses on the Mend in West End," *Variety,* August 29, 1994, p. 45.

—Daryl F. Mallett

T. Rowe Price Associates, Inc.

100 East Pratt Street
Baltimore, Maryland 21202
U.S.A.
Telephone: (410) 345-2000
Fax: (410) 345-2394
Web site: http://www.troweprice.com

Public Company
Incorporated: 1950 as T. Rowe Price & Associates
Employees: 3,500
Sales: $1.04 billion (1999)
Stock Exchanges: NASDAQ
Ticker Symbol: TROW
NAIC: 52393 Investment Advice; 523991 Trust,
    Fiduciary, and Custody Activities; 52312 Securities
    Brokerage; 52392 Portfolio Management (pt)

T. Rowe Price Associates, Inc. is a Baltimore-based investment management firm that provides a broad range of mutual funds and other investment services, including retirement planning, discount brokerage, trust, and international investment programs. In addition to serving as investment adviser to the T. Rowe Price family of mutual funds (Price Funds), the firm offers a full spectrum of investment advice on equity, bond, and money market securities. The company's diverse client base ranges from individual investors to institutions.

Providing Financial Advice and Services: 1930s–40s

Thomas Rowe Price, Jr., set the groundwork for his own investment counsel firm in the mid-1930s. Mr. Price's original goal was to provide stock investors with a new and virtually unavailable service, which he called "investment counseling." Price's idea was to recommend investment picks and strategies by applying sound research, basing his fees on expertise, not on standard commission income. With that goal in mind, the young entrepreneur founded Price Associates, a financial counseling business, in 1937; ten years later the partnership was renamed T. Rowe Price & Associates.

If Price's idea to market financial advice was novel, then the growth stock theory of investing that he championed was unheard of. Price was not satisfied with the common treatment of stocks as cyclical investments, which rise and fall in value according to prevalent economic trends and should be bought or sold at the right time to make a profit. Instead, he believed that investor interests were best served by a long-term view of the investment process—one by which a financial advisor helped clients identify stocks in well-managed companies that would grow over a long period of time. Rather than buying and selling stocks for speculative profits, Price emphasized the value of investing in growing businesses and sticking with them "through thick and thin." Price believed that true growth companies—identified with careful research—would enjoy earnings growth that would augment both market value and growth of dividend income over the long haul.

Price's early experience and some of his distinct personality traits helped prepare him for the rigors of starting his own firm—especially one that would initially run against the grain of generally accepted investment practices. After studying for a career as an industrial chemist and landing two short-lived jobs in that field, he decided to turn his energies toward his real passion: investing. Brief stints at a brokerage house and a small bond house in the early 1920s provided him with enough experience to land a more permanent position in finance. In 1925, he became a stockbroker at the Baltimore investment firm Mackubin, Goodrich & Co. (later known as Mackubin, Legg & Co. and ultimately as Legg, Mason & Co. by the late 1980s). There, he climbed the corporate ladder, becoming head of the bond department and, by 1930, head of the investment management department.

By 1934, Price had convinced senior management at Mackubin, Goodrich to let him start up an investment management department at the firm. Several factors, however, worked against Price. First, his growth-stock philosophy met with unusual resistance from many principals at the firm. In addition, the residual effect of the Great Depression still cast somber light on investing in general. Finally, Price was reputed as iron-willed and often difficult to work with, adding some disfavor to his already unprofitable department. By 1937, the principals of

Mackubin, Goodrich decided to phase out the investment management program altogether, prompting Price to set out on his own. Several of Price's closest colleagues joined his entrepreneurial venture. Marie Walper, Isabella Craig, Walter Kidd, and Charles Schaeffer comprised the original "Associates" of the newly established partnership, T. Rowe Price & Associates.

Price's fledgling investment management firm struggled through its early years. Even in the best of financial markets, such a business depended on the time-consuming and uncertain process of winning client confidence. From the late 1930s right through the 1950s, moreover, financial markets were unfavorable. For several years, T. Rowe Price & Associates boasted few individual and no institutional clients. The partners accepted irregular salaries and exchanged actual pay for shares in the new enterprise. Fortunately, Price's wife had the financial resources to bankroll many of the firm's early losses. Even though Price's initial objective—that of building a company with 25 employees and $60 million in assets under management—was reasonable, it remained dubious for nearly the first decade in operation.

By the late 1940s, however, T. Rowe Price's growth-style of investing had started to chalk up a few of the successes that would give the firm forward momentum. The key was careful research, on which T. Rowe Price placed tremendous importance. For example, the firm would only invest in stock of a company whose president had been carefully interviewed by a T. Rowe Price analyst. The result was several winning stock picks between 1938 and 1949: Sharp & Dohme, the pharmaceutical company, jumped 468 percent over that period; Abbott Laboratories (334 percent); USF&G Corporation, the insurance provider (198 percent); Addressograph-Multigraph (140 percent). In the late 1930s and early 1940s, the company's investments in companies such as Minnesota Mining and Manufacturing (later 3M Corp.) and IBM Corp. also proved invaluable.

Despite the tremendous odds facing T. Rowe Price before the end of World War II, the company managed to expand at a reasonable rate. According to records kept by Walter Kidd, director of research, total assets under management increased from $2.3 million in 1938 to $28 million in 1945 and $42 million in 1949. That year marked an important milestone: 12 years after the company's inception, T. Rowe Price finally broke into the black.

Steady Growth and Focus on Mutual Funds in the 1950s and 1960s

The 1950s marked an overall transition into a faster rate of growth and change for the company. In 1950, the firm converted from a three-person partnership to a corporation. Also that year, T. Rowe Price contracted its first institutional client, American Cyanamid, which remained a major account into the 1990s. In 1950, Price also introduced the Growth Stock Fund, the firm's first mutual fund. At that time, mutual funds were still not in vogue. Price regarded the new fund merely as a service to clients who wanted to capitalize on the Uniform Gift to Minors Act. Recently passed by Congress, the act permitted parents to manage trusts for their children and pay taxes at a relatively negligible rate. Moreover, the fund charged no "load," or sales charge, adding extra appeal to its subscribers. Although the Growth Stock Fund began as a low-profile product, it ultimately showcased the success of T. Rowe Price's growth-stock strategy in action; by 1960, Weisenberger's fund-rating service rated it as the country's best performer for the ten-year period.

The success of the Growth Stock Fund through the 1950s reflected an improved investment environment. With the exception of some economic fallout from the Korean War—such as a new Excess Profits Tax—the 1950s was a decade of strong economic growth and low inflation. Growth stocks made a comeback, and Mr. Price stood in the limelight, claiming center stage through a series of articles he contributed to *Forbes* magazine on a regular basis. Meanwhile, a vigorous market for pension funds had taken shape, and T. Rowe Price jumped on the bandwagon. In all, economic recovery and a turnaround in growth stocks set the groundwork for an upcoming decade of new institutional clients and a broader range of mutual fund offerings, including pension funds.

One such fund was the New Horizons Fund, which Price introduced in 1960 in order to capitalize on the growth potential of so-called emerging growth companies, or small, rapidly growing companies in the early stage of corporate development. Some of the first stocks in New Horizon Fund's portfolio of investments included Texas Instruments, Hertz, and Haloid-Xerox, the precursor of Xerox Corp. To manage New Horizons (and a projected progeny of other mutual funds to follow) Price founded Rowe Price Management, which he headed while remaining at the helm of the parent company.

The New Horizons Fund, like T. Rowe Price itself, suffered difficult beginnings. In fact, the fund not only lagged in the 1961 bull market but also when the market turned bearish in 1962: New Horizons dropped by 29 percent, versus a decline of nine percent for the Standard and Poor's (S&P) 500—a common index of leading company performance. Not surprisingly, critics coined derogatory variations on the fund's forward-looking name: "New Horizontal," "Blue Horizons," and "Lost Horizons."

By 1965, yet another market correction worked in favor of small growth companies, and the New Horizons Fund lived up to its real name. The fund's total return leaped 44 percent in one year, compared to 12 percent for the S&P 500. Such success attracted new investors, and both New Horizons and T. Rowe Price snowballed; by the end of 1965, the firm had topped the $1 billion mark. In fact, emerging growth stocks grew so heated that Price decided to temporarily step back. Price thought shareholders might be ill-served if the New Horizons Fund continued to invest new assets in an overvalued growth. From October 1967 to June 1970 and from March 1972 to September 1974, Price closed the fund to new investors. As John Train suggested in *The Money Masters,* Price was clearly not driven by short-term greed

Key Dates:

1937: Thomas Rowe Price, Jr., founds Price Associates.
1947: Price Associates becomes T. Rowe Price & Associates.
1950: Firm converts from a partnership to a corporation and introduces its first mutual fund.
1961: Rowe Price Management, designed to manage new mutual funds, is founded.
1971: Thomas Rowe Price retires; firm launches a fixed-income division.
1979: Firm expands internationally through the formation of a joint venture with London-based Robert Fleming Holdings Ltd.
1986: Firm goes public.
1999: Firm establishes joint venture with Sumitomo Bank Ltd. and Daiwa Securities Co. to serve Japanese investors.

but had the best interest of his shareholders in mind through these maneuvers. Meanwhile, the Growth Stock Fund also rode the wave and would continue to do so into the 1970s. From 1966 through 1972, shares of that fund appreciated 80 percent, assuming reinvestment of dividends and capital gains.

As T. Rowe Price grew in the 1960s, Mr. Price's relationship with the firm loosened and a new generation of leaders began to move toward the helm. Employing roughly 200 personnel and offering new and diverse products and services required a more formal administrative structure. Price's various colleagues gradually moved away from their multiple-chore posts and into more specialized cadres. Mr. Schaeffer gravitated toward public relations and Mr. Kidd became the equivalent of chief operations officer, while other associates such as E. Kirdbride Miller and John Ramsay became senior investment counselors. In 1968, Price relinquished presidency of the Growth Stock Fund, and he resigned as president of New Horizons Fund the following year. In addition, in 1968, he sold the remaining shares of Rowe Price Management (RPM) to T. Rowe Price Associates, which held a controlling interest in RPM since 1966.

Along with his responsibilities at the company, Price's overall economic outlook began to change. He foresaw the onset of a bleak ''new era'' in which the dollar would decline, inflation would rage, natural resources would diminish, and growth stocks would suffer. In near antipathy to his previous growth theories, he told *Forbes* in 1969 that: ''People will not want paper dollars. They will want tangible property: land, natural resources, timber, minerals in the ground. They will want investments in companies that can increase their profits faster than the decline in the value of the dollar.''

To accommodate such a shift, Price founded the New Era Fund in 1969. The fund's portfolio of investments emphasized natural resource companies (gold, silver, uranium, copper, and forest products), while mixing in some technology and a measure of more traditional growth stocks. As was often the case with Price's initiatives, the New Era Fund performed badly at first and eventually proved itself. In the early 1970s, growth stocks held up well, and the New Era Fund lost ground. When the oil embargo aggravated economic recession until the end of 1974, the New Era Fund and its growth-driven cousins all suffered comparable pains. By the late 1970s and early 1980s, however, rampant inflation finally paid off for Price's ''Anti-Inflation Fund,'' as he had originally intended to call the New Era Fund. Between 1978 and 1981—with inflation approaching the 20 percent mark and the price of gold topping $800 an ounce—New Era jumped almost 130 percent. A key lesson that the firm derived from New Era's performance was that its traditional growth strategy could be effectively combined with other strategies to best accommodate economic change.

Diversification in the 1970s and 1980s

Starting in the 1970s—and to a much greater degree in the 1980s and onward—T. Rowe Price Associates began diversifying its strategies and its products. Indeed, Price's retirement in 1971 marked just one of many momentous changes. In 1971, George J. Collins was hired to start a fixed-income division. By the end of 1973, Collins had created New Income Fund, a balanced, fixed-income mutual fund. Though the new bond fund was not an immediate eye-opener, it soared when interest rates increased dramatically in the latter half of the decade; by 1977, New Income ranked as the third largest corporate bond fund in the United States.

When Congress passed legislation permitting tax-free municipal bond funds, Collins launched the Tax-Free Income Fund in 1976. By 1978, that fund boasted $215 million in assets and ranked third among more than 40 rivals. By the early 1990s, T. Rowe Price's lineup of tax-free mutual funds offered nearly every maturity category, as well as an insured fund for investors seeking extra credit protection and a high-yield fund for the more risk-tolerant.

A combination of sociopolitical and technological advances in the late 1970s and early 1980s greatly facilitated international trade and investing, virtually turning the financial world into a global marketplace. In 1979, T. Rowe Price's joint venture with Robert Fleming Holdings Ltd., a London-based merchant bank, rode the wave. Meanwhile, the growing popularity of mutual funds throughout the 1980s gave individual investors the resources to invest globally—through fund managers with the ability to conduct international research, probe credit and currency risk, and employ sophisticated hedging techniques. By 1994, Rowe Price-Fleming International, Inc. had become one of the largest managers of overseas assets in the United States, with approximately $17 billion under management.

In addition to new vigor in the international investment arena, numerous other influences prompted T. Rowe Price to diversify its financial services and products. Entering the 1980s, the rapidly growing firm had struck a delicate balance between its past growth tradition and a wide slew of new investment alternatives. Indeed, in 1984—the year after Mr. Price passed away—George J. Collins stepped up as president. The man who had brought bond investing to the exclusively growth-stock-driven firm 13 years earlier was now in command. Responding to greater competition in the financial services field—largely spurred by deregulation in the early 1980s—the company launched numerous new types of stock and bond funds.

Special emphasis was placed on retirement funds for both large institutional clients and small retail investors. After Congress created tax incentives for individuals to establish retirement accounts, T. Rowe Price correctly anticipated a decline in defined benefit retirement programs—pension plans in which a retired worker was assured a fixed income. Instead, the firm began developing funds geared toward 401(k) plans, funds sponsored by an employer in which workers can invest money tax-free until it is withdrawn after age 59. Although T. Rowe Price barely placed among the top ten mutual fund companies in assets by October 1993, it stood third in the 401(k) market, according to Leslie Wayne in a 1993 *New York Times* article.

In an effort to diversify its services, T. Rowe Price also made available innovative limited partnerships starting in the early 1980s. In 1983, the Threshold Limited Partnership was formed to help finance select private companies expected to go public within 12 to 18 months. T. Rowe Price eventually joined the bandwagon itself; it went public in 1986, and—disregarding a slight dip in 1990—enjoyed steadily rising earnings into the early 1990s. The New Frontier Fund Limited Partnership was also introduced to help non-U.S. clients invest in very small U.S. public companies.

Applying many of the venture-capital techniques from its limited partnership dealings, T. Rowe Price moved into real estate in 1984. That year, it developed the first real estate limited partnership available to investors nationwide with no sales commission. According to the company's 1986 annual report, the real estate business was "an excellent source of diversification and improved long-term returns for all investors." Consequently, a real estate management subsidiary was formed.

A Volatile Market and Heavy Competition in the 1990s

The early 1990s saw continued efforts to diversify in order to compete in an increasingly ferocious investment market. In 1992, for example, the company acquired six mutual funds managed and distributed by USF&G Corporation. Then in 1993, T. Rowe Price, the CUNA Mutual Insurance Group, and the Credit Union National Association & Affiliates formed a joint venture to provide a family of proprietary no-load mutual funds for credit union members.

These and other initiatives called for more effective programs in customer support. By the late 1980s, the company had already implemented a sophisticated computerized telephone system—Tele*Access—with which customers could use a touchtone phone to access their accounts 24 hours a day, or to buy, sell, and exchange shares in the T. Rowe Price fund family. The company also implemented advanced administrative tools, such as PAS, a computerized record keeping system for defined contribution retirement plans.

Meticulously planned marketing campaigns also helped support T. Rowe Price's services into the 1990s. In 1989, the company first introduced its Retirement Planning Kit and Retirees Financial Guide, designed for both employed people planning ahead and retired investors seeking advice. While other financial houses offered similar free guides, Price's stood out for their lucid language and current details on tax and Social

Security laws, according to Susan Antilla in a 1992 *New York Times* article. Accompanying Retirement Planning Kit software was described as "friendly to the point of being verbose, but its price makes it a package to consider," by *PC Magazine.* By 1994, when the company offered new editions, investors had requested more than one million kits.

T. Rowe Price advertising was consistent with a low-key, honest approach. In September 1993, for example, the company introduced its first corporate campaign designed to burnish its corporate image rather than specific products. The broadcast and print campaign, by McCaffrey & McCall New York, carried the slogan, "Invest with confidence." The campaign was intended to correspond with the company's product-oriented promotions, which have been consistently noted for their lucidity and usefulness by such independent rating agencies as Morningstar, Inc.

As T. Rowe Price entered the mid-1990s, the firm introduced several new funds, including Emerging Markets Stocks and Health Sciences, in 1995. The following year, George Collins, who had headed the firm since 1984, retired, passing on the CEO position to George Roche. Roche began working at T. Rowe Price in 1968 and had developed a reputation as a detail-oriented and conservative manager. Prior to taking over as president and CEO in April 1997, Roche had served as the firm's CFO.

Conservative investing continued to guide T. Rowe Price in the late 1990s, and the policy proved to be a bit of a hindrance as the market remained highly volatile. Risky investments often outperformed low-risk alternatives, but T. Rowe Price managed to boost revenues nonetheless, helped by growing numbers of clients putting money into mutual funds. By mid-1997, T. Rowe Price was the 25th biggest mutual fund company in the nation. The firm's revenues had more than doubled between 1992 and 1997, and net income had nearly tripled to reach $98.5 million. Industry analysts voiced confidence in T. Rowe Price's financial future. Alexander Brown Inc. analyst John Hall told the *Baltimore Sun,* "Their numbers have been great. . . . I think the growth prospects from a long-term perspective are pretty good."

T. Rowe Price counted on its investors to focus on long-term growth as the unpredictable market continued to pose challenges. Many investors began to shy away from stock funds because of the poor performance by international and small stocks, opting instead to invest in more stable money market and bond funds. T. Rowe Price's net sales of stock and bond funds declined from $9 billion in 1997 to about $3.5 billion in 1998. Still, the firm managed to generate record revenues of $886.1 million in 1998, and assets under management increased from $124.3 billion to $147.8 billion. Of the total assets under management, the majority, $94 billion, consisted of mutual funds. Rose Price-Fleming International also performed well, increasing its assets under management by $2.9 billion to end the year at $32.9 billion.

Maintaining strength and remaining competitive were priorities for T. Rowe Price in the late 1990s, and the firm introduced new funds and undertook new ventures to ensure the company's growth. In early 1999, T. Rowe Price announced it would form an asset management company with Sumitomo Bank Ltd. and

Daiwa Securities Co. to serve retail and institutional investors in Japan. T. Rowe Price planned to acquire ten percent of the joint venture, known as Daiwa SB Investments, for about $15 million. Though Japan had not yet recovered from a recession, the country had ample potential in the eyes of U.S. financial firms—Japan's pension market was undergoing deregulation, and the nation had about $11 trillion in household savings. T. Rowe Price also said it would form a joint venture with Robert Fleming Holdings designed to manage the non-Japanese security investments of Japanese clients.

Also in 1999, T. Rowe Price opened a customer service call center in a leased building in Colorado Springs, Colorado, and made plans to further expand its operations in Colorado. The firm agreed to purchase 31 acres in a business development area in Colorado Springs and said it intended to build a new call center and, if warranted, a second building. Work also continued on the expansion of its headquarters, including the completion of two office buildings and parking facilities in Owings Mills, Maryland.

In October, T. Rowe Price received a boost when its common stock was added to the S&P 500 index. News of the announcement sent its share price up 12.8 percent in one day. The firm's share price was also affected by rumors that T. Rowe Price was a prime target for acquisition. Not only had other mutual fund firms, such as Pimco Advisors, been purchased by foreign companies, but some industry analysts stated their opinions that T. Rowe Price would make a fine acquisition for a foreign business trying to break into the United States. Though CEO Roche said the firm, which by 1999 was the seventh largest mutual fund company in the United States, was not for sale, speculation caused the stock price to rise 4.9 percent in one day.

The year 1999 proved to be a standout one for T. Rowe Price, and the firm reported record revenues of more than $1 billion, up 17 percent from the previous year. Net income rose 37 percent from 1998 to reach $239 million, and for the first time in the company's history, three of its funds had returns of at least 100 percent. T. Rowe Price International Discovery, which was heavy on foreign, small company stocks, achieved a total one-year return of 155 percent. T. Rowe Price Japan was up 112.7 percent, and T. Rowe Price Science & Technology was up 101 percent. Despite such outstanding performance, however, the firm advised investors to temper their expectations, as such continued growth was not sustainable over the long term. In addition, some analysts continued to criticize T. Rowe Price's conservative approach. With a long and dependable history of steady growth, however, few could question T. Rowe Price's abilities to survive. T. Rowe Price vice-chairman James Riepe told the *Wall Street Journal,* "We've got to stick to our principles, even though those principles might hurt us in the short term. We have discipline, and we'll keep on doing this for a long time."

Principal Subsidiaries

T. Rowe Price Investment Services, Inc.; T. Rowe Price Investment Technologies, Inc.; T. Rowe Price Retirement Plan Services, Inc.; T. Rowe Price Services, Inc.; T. Rowe Price Stable Asset Management, Inc.; TRP Finance, Inc.; T. Rowe Price (Canada), Inc.; Daiwa SB Investments (Japan; 10%); Rowe Price-Fleming International, Inc. (50%); TRP Suburban Second, Inc.

Principal Competitors

FMR Corp.; The Vanguard Group, Inc.; Merrill Lynch & Co. Inc.

Further Reading

Antilla, Susan, "Does Little Pay off a Lot? T. Rowe Price Does," *New York Times,* June 17, 1992, p. C15.

Atkinson, Bill, "Staying on Course," *Baltimore Sun,* July 20, 1997, p. D1.

Brown, Ken, "T. Rowe Price to Offer Funds with Fees," *Wall Street Journal,* February 3, 2000, p. C21.

Eliott, Stuart, "To a Company That Sells Mutual Funds, a Return on Its Image Is the Goal of a New Campaign," *New York Times,* September 7, 1993, p. C6.

"History of T. Rowe Price," Baltimore: T. Rowe Price Associates, 1987.

McGough, Robert, and Patrick McGeehan, "Market Gyrations Prompt Nervous Investors to Cut Back on Stock of Mutual-Fund Firms," *Wall Street Journal,* February 24, 1999, p. C3.

Michaels, James W., "Thomas Rowe Price 1898–1983," *Forbes,* November 21, 1983, p. 51.

Rulison, Larry, "Takeover Talk Fuels Price Stock," *Baltimore Business Journal,* November 5, 1999, p. 1.

Tam, Pui-Wing, "T. Rowe Price Joins Japanese Venture," *Wall Street Journal,* January 26, 1999, p. C27.

Tam, Pui-Wing, and Aaron Lucchetti, "T. Rowe Price Pays High Price for Avoiding Tech Craze," *Wall Street Journal,* March 6, 2000, p. R1.

Train, John, *The Money Masters,* New York: Harper & Row, 1979, p. 139.

Trivette, Don, "T. Rowe Price Retirement Planning Kit (Software Review)," *PC Magazine,* November 24, 1992, p. 596.

Wayne, Leslie, "T. Rowe Price Sticks with Its Niche," *New York Times,* October 18, 1993, p. C1.

—Kerstan Cohen
—updated by Mariko Fujinaka

Taylor Nelson Sofres plc

Westgate
London W5 1UA
United Kingdom
Telephone: (+44) 20 8967 0007
Fax: (+44) 20 8967 4060
Web site: http://www.tnsofres.com

Public Company
Incorporated: 1997
Employees: 6,000
Sales: £380.9 million (US$571.4 million) (1999)
Stock Exchanges: London
Ticker Symbol: TNN
NAIC: 541910 Market Research Services

London-based Taylor Nelson Sofres plc is the world's fourth largest market research specialist, with 150 offices in over 40 countries. The company, which leads the United Kingdom and French markets, has extended its reach to a further 20 countries through a series of strategic partnerships. Taylor Nelson Sofres provides customized market research and analysis to many of the world's leading multinational corporations; the company has also developed a series of branded research products and services, including the Miriad information system; the customer commitment and loyalty scale Conversion Model; Needscope, used for understanding the customer-brand relationship; FoQus2, for measuring customer satisfaction; and Optima, for the management of brand portfolios. The combination of Taylor Nelson AGB and Sofres in 1997 created a global market research company specializing in such categories as consumer panels, a segment in which the company is worldwide leader; television audience measurement, using the viewer ratings system PeopleMeter to challenge industry leader A.C. Nielsen; the automotive, healthcare, and telecommunications industries; media monitoring; and information technology. In 2000, the company moved to increase its position in the growing Internet market, with the US$88 million acquisition of Competitive Market Research from rival VNU Marketing Information, Inc. The company's move into the Internet market has been further bolstered by the creation of a dedicated Internet division. Taylor Nelson Sofres has grown strongly since the last half of the 1990s, building its revenues from just £80 million in 1995 to more than £380 million in 1999. Most of that growth has come from acquisitions: in 1999 alone, the company made some ten acquisitions. Taylor Nelson is led by Tony Cowling as executive chairman, and Pierre Weill as managing director.

Boom Years for Pollsters in the 1960s

One of the first examples of the predictive power of modern market research techniques was seen during the 1936 U.S. presidential elections. A straw poll conducted among some two million readers of the *Literary Digest* gave contender Alf Landon the presidential victory. But a new service, formed by George Gallup, chose instead to use a representative sample—in other words, an attempt to recreate American society on a small scale—of only 4,000 people to make its prediction on the outcome of the race. Gallup's poll correctly forecast Franklin Roosevelt as the winner—and gave rise to the modern era of market research.

Politicians flocked to the use of polls and other market research techniques, and continued to feature among the largest users of market researchers into the next century. Corporations, and especially those producing consumer products, also rapidly saw the value of the new techniques, which promised to enable a company not only to measure the effectiveness of an advertisement campaign, but also to help direct their advertising budget and even to develop the product range itself. Market research companies began developing new and more sophisticated tools for "reading" the consumer public. The rise of television created another new market—measurements of audience viewing levels permitted broadcasters to attract more (or fewer) advertisements, establish per-minute fees, and also to target specific audiences for specific products.

The market research phenomenon rapidly became a global industry, as each country developed its own services. In France, for example, the Institut Français de l'Opinion Publique, that country's first polling organization, showed that a majority of the country had agreed with the signing of the Munich Treaty in

---

Company Perspectives:

We have identified four key elements to our strategy, which we believe will lead to continued, profitable growth: To extend the Taylor Nelson Sofres global network; To develop business in our chosen specialist sectors; To increase the volume of syndicated and tracking services and develop branded research solutions; To use high-tech solutions to collect, analyse and present quality information.

1938. It was no surprise, however, that the conducting of polls was an activity banned in the Nazi-occupied countries during World War II.

The economic boom years of the postwar period, which gave rise to a new and accelerated consumer culture, also proved a boom to the market research industry. Where a handful of players had shared a relatively limited terrain up to the 1960s, a new breed of market researchers, often specializing in single industries, appeared. These companies in turn helped to transform the marketplace, and particularly the relationship between consumers and manufacturers.

The founding companies of what later became Taylor Nelson Sofres were formed in the first half of the 1960s. The first of these, Intersearch, was founded in the United States in 1960, followed two years later by London-based Audits of Great Britain, which later simplified its name to AGB. In France, Pierre Weill formed Sofres in 1963. In Australia, the company Frank Small and Associates was founded in 1964. Lastly, Elizabeth Nelson, already a market research specialist, and Tony Cowling, who played a principal role in expanding the company, joined with investor Steward Taylor to form Taylor Nelson in London in 1965.

During the 1960s, AGB won the right to measure audience levels for the BBC networks in the United Kingdom. The contract gave AGB the boost it needed to go public, listing on the London Stock Exchange in 1970. AGB went on to challenge the A.C. Nielsen Company's longtime dominance of the television audience measuring market in the United States in the mid-1980s, developing its interactive PeopleMeter system. Nielsen responded, however, with its own, similar system. After sinking some £50 million into establishing a foothold in the U.S. market, AGB was forced to abandon the attempt. By 1988, AGB had been bought up by Pergamon Professional and Financial Services, a unit of the sprawling, 1980s-era empire of Robert Maxwell. Pergamon paid more than US$230 million for AGB.

Taylor Nelson had meanwhile gone public in 1985, only to find itself snapped up by Addison Page in that company's attempt to diversify its operations. Addison Page bundled Taylor Nelson with its other market and media research holdings and formed the Addison Consultancy division. Following the market crash of 1987, however, Addison Page was forced to shed a number of its businesses, and Addison Consultancy was spun off as part of a management buyout led by founding Taylor Nelson member Tony Cowling. Cowling took the chief executive's position in 1989.

Consolidation in the 1990s

While a number of players loomed large on the international market research scene—including Nielsen in the United States, Sofres in France, and Addison Consultancy in the United Kingdom, the industry remained highly fragmented, with few companies operating at any kind of international level. The 1990s saw the industry transform itself, consolidating into a limited number of global heavyweights.

Under Pierre Weill, Sofres had already begun to build up its dominant position in France. At the end of the 1980s, Sofres went on a buying spree, moving beyond its domestic market to establish itself as one of Europe's leading market research companies. Among the companies acquired by Sofres at this time were Belgium's Sobemap, Italy's Abacus, Emnid of Germany, and Sofemasa and Demoscopia of Spain. By 1991, Sofres had succeeded in transforming itself into one of the most dynamic of the international market research companies, with 60 percent of its sales achieved outside of France. At home, Sofres took on the French market's leading position, especially after its 1992 acquisition of Secodip, a specialist in conducting consumer panels with strong positions in the French, Spanish, and Portuguese markets. A year later, Sofres had gained a dominant position in the Spanish market, taking control of that country's television measuring contracts.

By then, AGB had changed hands. The death of Robert Maxwell led to the swift unraveling of his media empire. By 1991, AGB was up for sale—and was snapped up by Addison Consultancy for less than US$25 million. The purchase made Addison Consultancy—which shortly renamed itself Taylor Nelson AGB—the largest market researcher in the United Kingdom.

Taylor Nelson AGB spent the first half of the 1990s solidifying its position in its home market and extending its range of products and services, especially through the acquisition of companies such as Teledynamics, a telemarketing specialist, and John Richardson Computers. By mid-decade, the wave of domestic consolidations began to wash across Europe's borders, as the market research industry, which has traditionally been country-specific, began to transform itself. As more and more of market researchers' customers had begun operating on a multinational and global basis, the market research industry too began to move toward a globally operating industry.

Sofres fired the first shot, moving into the United Kingdom market in 1994 with the acquisition of Harris Research Centre. Sofres also acquired France's Louis Harris, while increasing its position in Belgium with the acquisition of Dimarso. In 1995, Sofres moved even farther afield, buying up Frank Small & Associates (FSA), which over 30 years had established itself not only as a leader in the Australian and New Zealand markets, but also as the Asian Pacific region's second largest market researcher, with offices in ten countries in the region. The year following the FSA acquisition brought Sofres into the Japanese market, through a joint-venture with that country's Japan Statistics Research. Sofres also entered Vietnam, and began to prepare its launch into India as well.

By then, Taylor Nelson AGB joined the internationalization drive, launching a subsidiary, Taylor Nelson AGB Media Facts,

Key Dates:

1960: Intersearch is formed.
1962: Audits of Great Britain (later AGB) is founded.
1966: AGB wins U.K. television measurement contract.
1963: Sofres is founded.
1964: Frank Small & Associates is founded.
1965: Taylor Nelson is formed.
1970: AGB lists shares on the London Stock Exchange.
1985: Taylor Nelson is listed on the London Stock Exchange; AGB launches PeopleMeter.
1987: Addison Page acquires Taylor Nelson, which is renamed Addison Consultancy.
1988: Pergamon acquires AGB; Addison Consultancy is spun off in management buyout.
1991: Addison Consultancy acquires AGB, which is renamed Taylor Nelson AGB; Sofres acquires Sofemasa.
1997: Taylor Nelson AGB acquires Gallup A/S (Denmark); Taylor Nelson merges with Sofres and forms Taylor Nelson Sofres.
1998: Taylor Nelson Sofres acquires Chilton Research Services.
1999: Company buys Market Development, NIPO, Scher International, and QCR.
2000: Company acquires Competitive Media Reporting.

in the Czech Republic. Media Facts quickly opened new branches in Poland, Russia, and Romania. These moves were followed by Taylor Nelson's purchase of Gallup A/S, of Denmark. Meanwhile, in 1997, Sofres moved into the U.S. market, buying up Intersearch. Yet, a few months later, Taylor Nelson AGB bought out Sofres, paying £119 million.

The acquisition led the company to change its name to Taylor Nelson Sofres, in order to reflect the merging of its operations. The two company's complementary operations combined to produce one of the world's top five market research firms. Tony Cowling was named chairman of the new industry heavyweight, with Pierre Weill given the chief executive's chair.

Taylor Nelson Sofres immediately began to broaden its position not only in its core European and Asian market, but also in the huge U.S. market. In 1998, the company picked up Reed Elsevier's Chilton Research Services; the following year, the company, which went on a buying spree, picked up two more U.S. companies, Market Development and QCR. Throughout 1999, Taylor Nelson Sofres made numerous acquisitions, including Scher International, WHF, and Customer Satisfaction Surveys of the United Kingdom; NIPO of the Netherlands; and Lit Tout of France.

An agreement to partner with Facta Research of Mexico in September 1999 brought Taylor Nelson Sofres onto the South

American continent—a vast market of more than 500 million people. The Facta partnership added to the company's acquisition of San Diego, California-based Market Development, which specialized in the U.S. and Latin American Latino markets. Taylor Nelson Sofres continued to build up its U.S. position in early 2000, buying Competitive Media Reporting, based in New York, from VNU Marketing Information, Inc.

While Taylor Nelson Sofres continued to solidify its international operations, offering a one-stop shop to the world's global companies with its own multinational operations, the company was also moving into the extra-national sphere: by the end of the century, the company's attentions had turned to developing its activities on the Internet. Developing a next-generation set of tools for measuring Internet and web site traffic, Taylor Nelson Sofres sought to extend its leadership position into what promised to soon become one of the largest market research markets.

Principal Subsidiaries

: Abacus Spa (Italy); Central Pentru Studierea Opinieri Si Pietei SRL (Romania; 48%); CVSC Sofres Media Co Ltd (China; 40%); D Mas A Documentacion Y Analisis SA (Spain); Demoscopia SA (Spain; 40%); Dimarso SA (Belgium); Dympanel SA (Spain); Dympanel SA (Argentina; 51%); EM-NID GmbH & Co Kg (Germany; 78%); Gallup A/S (Denmark); GI Consulting (29%); GIE Audiepub (France; 33%); Market Research Bureau of Ireland (85%); Mode Research (India; 30%); Norske Gallup Institutt A/S (Norway); OBOP Sp zoo (Poland; 60%); SC Arema International SRL (Romania); Secodip SA (France); Sobemap SA (Belgium); Sofres AM Liban (Lebanon; 49%); Sofres AM SA (Spain); Sofres Modus Kft (Hungary; 51%); Sofres SA (France); Taylor Nelson AGB Media Facts sro (Czech Republic); Taylor Nelson Sofres Asia Pacific Pty (Australia; 75%); Taylor Nelson Sofres BV (Netherlands); Taylor Nelson Sofres Intersearch (U.S.A.); TRC (Hong Kong; 26%).

Principal Competitors

A.C. Nielsen Company; Audits & Surveys; Boron, LePore & Associates; Ceridian Corporation; IMS Health; Information Resources, Inc.; M/A/R/C; NFO Worldwide, Inc.; NPD Group; VNU Marketing Information, Inc.; WPP Group plc.

Further Reading

Larsen, Peter Thal, "Taylor Nelson Choose the Global Media Path," *Independent*, September 22, 1998, p. 21.
——, "Taylor Nelson Quashes Fears on Merger," *Independent*, January 13, 1999 p. 19.
Newman, Cathy, "Taylor Nelson in Merger with French Rival," *Independent*, November 19, 1997, p. 26.
"Taylor Nelson on Shopping Spree," *Daily Telegraph*, September 22, 1998.
"US Election to Bolster Taylor Nelson," *Financial Times*, March 21, 2000.

—M. L. Cohen

TEXTRON

Textron Inc.

40 Westminster Street
Providence, Rhode Island 02903-2596
U.S.A.
Telephone: (401) 421-2800
Fax: (401) 421-2878
Web site: http://www.textron.com

Public Company
Incorporated: 1923 as Special Yarns Corporation
Employees: 68,000
Sales: $11.58 billion (1999)
Stock Exchanges: New York
Ticker Symbol: TXT
NAIC: 336411 Aircraft Manufacturing; 336112 Light
 Truck & Utility Vehicle Manufacturing; 33636 Motor
 Vehicle Seating & Interior Trim Manufacturing;
 336399 All Other Motor Vehicle Parts Manufacturing

Textron Inc. has made so many changes in its corporate identity that any characterization of it is subject to revision on rather short notice. It has, however, consistently earned a profit for its stockholders. For that reason, many investors may not care what it does so long as it keeps generating a profit for them. Textron, involved in many industries, has limited its areas of investment since the 1970s. Through its Bell Helicopter and Cessna subsidiaries, Textron remains an important United States aerospace manufacturer.

Birth of a Conglomerate

The man behind the success of Textron, Royal Little, graduated from Harvard in 1919. He then sought practical business experience as an unpaid apprentice at a textile mill before working for the Franklin Rayon Yarn Dyeing Corporation. There, he recognized the drawbacks of producing a product in a business vulnerable to volatile market cycles. As far back as the 1920s, Little advocated diversification as a means to insulate a company from occasional slumps in certain lines of business. Specifically, Little advocated ''non-related'' diversification,

that is, simultaneous operation of totally unrelated businesses. The system had to be unrelated so that heavy losses in one business would not affect the profitability of related industries.

Little founded the Special Yarns Corporation in Boston, Massachusetts in 1928. With first year revenues of $75,000, these were modest beginnings for the world's first conglomerate. By World War II, the company had been renamed the Atlantic Rayon Corporation. The textile business boomed during the war, but by 1943, Little was already looking to the civilian market. At this time, the company changed its name to Textron. The name comes from ''textiles'' and the ''-tron'' suffix of synthetic fabrics such as Lustron. (It is hard to imagine a global conglomerate named ''Señorita Creations,'' but that was the advertising agency's first choice.)

Revenues reached $67.8 million in 1949. Neither Little nor his company, however, were in a position to implement a general diversification until 1952. Little later recalled in his book *How to Lose $100,000,000 and Other Valuable Advice* that a banker refused to back his acquisitions until he proved that he could run a textile business. Little successfully completed a hostile takeover of American Woolen in 1955 in what *Fortune* magazine called ''the stormiest merger yet.'' Little's policy for successful takeover bids was to ''be sure to pick a company whose board of directors isn't smart enough'' to fight back with a counter-takeover.

In 1956 Royal Little hired a Providence banker, Rupert Thompson, to oversee what he admitted were his irrepressible impulses to acquire more companies. Thompson made sure that Textron's acquisitions were ''balanced,'' or sufficiently spread out so that a depression in any one market would not severely affect the company as a whole. Based on this strategy, Little and Thompson established what has (arguably) been declared the world's first conglomerate. Notable acquisitions in the 1950s included Homelite, Camcar, and CWC.

Airborne in the 1960s

Textron entered the aerospace industry in 1960 when it purchased the Bell Aircraft company. Bell was best known for its helicopters, but first gained wide recognition shortly after

---

Company Perspectives:

Textron's Vision is to be: One of the World's Best Managed Companies; Excellent Managers of Shareholder Resources; A Multi-Industry Company with Global Leadership Positions in Each of Our Businesses.

World War II when it built the XP-59 Airacomet, which was the first American jet aircraft. During the war, Bell was a major supplier of aircraft parts to the Army Air Corps. Its founder, Lawrence D. Bell, worked as an engineer for Glenn Martin and later for Donald Douglas. Under the protection of Textron's financial umbrella, the Bell division was able to invest more money into longer-term research and development of helicopters and their new specialty, rockets.

Royal Little retired from Textron in 1962 and relinquished his seat on the board of directors. Thompson maintained a strict policy toward Textron's various divisions. The company would sell a particular division at the first sign of adverse performance. Such was the case for Textron's last textile holding in 1963; Amerotron was sold when it "failed to perform."

Rupert Thompson was described as having combined Alfred Sloan's management strategy for General Motors and Little's strategy of growth through acquisition. Textron maintained a consistency for meeting production and financial targets, demanding a 20 percent return on equity after taxes for the company's various divisions. Thompson was the manager of a company that, perhaps, was better described as an asset portfolio, or "management concept."

Rupert Thompson left Textron in 1968 after he was diagnosed as having cancer. The man he appointed to take his place was the company's president, G. William Miller. The company Miller took over was a well-diversified manufacturer of tools, industrial machines, consumer goods, plastics, appliances and, of course, helicopters.

Only months after he assumed the leadership of Textron, Miller attempted a takeover of United Fruit. When the attempt was thwarted Textron returned to less ambitious acquisitions of small firms, particularly zipper and fastener manufacturers. By 1971 Textron was ready for another ambitious takeover, this time of the Kendall Company, which would have placed Textron in the healthcare business. The attempted takeover of Kendall failed when another company outbid Textron.

Miller's most ambitious takeover attempt came shortly afterward when he tried to engineer a 45 percent controlling interest in the larger but nearly bankrupt Lockheed Corporation. Lockheed resisted the bid and later brought pressure from Wall Street upon Miller to abandon the takeover.

Miller's attempt to enter into the oil and gas business was cut short when he left the company in 1977 to take a position with the Carter administration as Federal Reserve chairman, and then later as secretary of the Treasury. One of Miller's best qualities was his insightful recognition of the fact that the United States was rapidly transforming itself into a service-oriented economy.

He brought Textron into financial services by acquiring insurance and other financial service companies.

A New Strategy for the 1970s

The man who replaced Miller was Joseph Collinson. Collinson's tenure was short-lived; he retired from the company in 1979. He was succeeded by Bob Straetz as chairman and Beverly Dolan as president. (Dolan had started E-Z-Go, the golf cart manufacturer, in his garage. He joined Textron when it bought the company in 1960.) The new men in charge were quicker to sell divisions that were performing poorly. One of the first to be sold was Polaris, the snowmobile manufacturer.

Straetz and Dolan later divested Textron of divisions not related to aerospace or technology. In effect, Textron was being reconverted into an operating company. They professed impatience with subsidiaries that did not "perform" and promised to "dump" them without a grace period. Straetz told *Fortune* magazine, "Some of that concept of non-related diversification still exists, but we're trying to make Textron a more focused company." The company operated principally around Bell Aerospace, which accounted for about one quarter of Textron's sales.

Bell's UH-1 Huey helicopter was used extensively during the American involvement in the Vietnam war. After Vietnam, Textron cultivated a strong market for Bell helicopters in Iran. This $875 million market was lost, however, with the fall of the Shah. From this turn of events, Straetz and Dolan learned the importance of maintaining a diverse group of customers. They tried next to establish a lucrative commercial market for Bell.

Bell produced a number of light helicopters, characterized by their dragonfly appearance. It competed with Boeing's Vertol and, particularly, with the Sikorsky division of United Technologies. Sikorsky manufactured larger, heavy-duty helicopters, but competed intensely with Bell in the medium-sized section of the market. Typical of many recent Pentagon contracts, Sikorsky and Bell were teamed to jointly develop a "VTOL," or vertical takeoff and landing airplane.

Bell was the division most responsible for Textron's identity as an aerospace company. That identity was preserved by the continuing success of Bell. Whereas Bell's products were of good quality, however, a unique management structure also must be credited for the general success of the division and its parent.

Unlike most other firms, an unusual amount of authority was vested with Textron's vice-presidents. A vice-president was thereby enabled to specialize in a certain area of the operation with the full authority of his office behind him. This also encouraged good communication within the top management echelon and allowed the president and chief executive officer to concentrate on more general matters, such as acquisitions and divestitures. Many American corporations have admitted to copying this style of management.

In 1984 Textron was the object of a hostile takeover bid by Chicago Pacific Corporation. It was the third unsolicited bid for Textron, which had become a target because of its large debt. Chicago Pacific was one-sixth the size of Textron. It had emerged from bankruptcy only months before the bid, selling all its railroad capital, including engines, track, and traffic rights. The company had a large amount of cash and was embarking on an acquisition program. Textron, however, mounted a defense that rather easily foiled the takeover bid.

Shortly thereafter, Dolan completed Textron's $3 billion acquisition of Avco. Avco was formerly the Aviation Corporation of the Americas, one of the three large aeronautic combines of the 1930s and the company that launched Pan Am and American Airlines. Over the years Avco gradually sold most of its aircraft interests until, by 1985, it was primarily a financial institution centered around the insurance business. (It did continue to manufacture sections of large military aircraft, however.) Avco already was threatened by a takeover from a smaller company when Textron, Avco's preferred suitor, made its own bid. With the success of the Avco acquisition, Dolan replaced Bob Straetz as chief executive officer.

In 1985 Textron surprised its stockholders by offering to sell its main operating division, Bell Aerospace. Upon closer inspection the stockholders voted in favor of the proposed sale, but it marked a serious change in Textron's stated intention to convert itself from a conglomerate into an operating company. The sale of Bell was intended to raise stockholders' return on equity and eliminate the corporate debt that made it an attractive takeover target.

The sale was postponed following an improvement in the company's financial position. Bell ultimately was retained and reorganized into two operating units: Bell Aerospace, which continued to handle the aeronautic business; and Textron Marine Systems, for marine projects.

Still Flying After the Cold War

By the late 1980s, the hounds of peace could be heard over the Steppes. The end of the Cold War hurt defense company stocks, and as one analyst explained in *Forbes,* conglomerates generally suffered according to their lowest common denominator. At the time, Textron's 32 operating companies made up three groups: aerospace, commercial products, and financial services. In the last category, the company's Paul Revere Insurance helped lift Textron's balance sheet. Still, aerospace, with 1988 sales of $3.6 billion, remained the largest division (the other two had sales of less than $2 billion each).

Textron had high hopes in the $25 billion V-22 tilt-rotor aircraft program. Developed by Bell and Boeing for the U.S.

Marine Corps, the fusion of helicopter and fixed-wing aircraft was expensive to fly. Faced with few possible users in the United States, the company resorted to asking Japan and West Germany for funding for a civilian variant. Fortunately, the market for civilian helicopters was up, and Avco Corp., now the Aerostructures division, had entered the booming airliner market, making wings for Airbus. Textron's automotive businesses also were generally lucrative.

One strategic priority was regaining an overseas presence, lost with the sale of Ex-Cell-O Corp.'s machine tool businesses in the mid-1980s. In 1989, however, U.S. regulators blocked Textron's $250 million purchase of Avdel, a British manufacturer of industrial fasteners. Textron was able to make progress through a manufacturing venture in The Netherlands with Ford and a helicopter distribution arrangement in Japan (Mitsui). Textron had revenues of $7.4 billion in 1989.

Textron acquired Cessna Aircraft from General Dynamics for $605 million in early 1992. The company had made 6,500 small planes a year in its heyday, but this business had been crippled by an industrywide wave of airplane crash lawsuits. When Textron bought it, Cessna was devoted to manufacturing its popular line of Citation business jets. Legislation in 1994 to limit manufacturers' liability on planes more than 18 years old, however, made making single-engined, propeller-driven aircraft feasible again, and the company resumed production on the small trainers that made it famous. Cessna's revenues were $783 million in 1993.

Revenues reached $8.3 billion in 1992. Aerospace contributed more than a third of the company's profits, in spite of the reliance on military contracts. The financial segment accounted for 43 percent of income; commercial, 20 percent. James F. Hardymon became CEO in 1992 after joining Textron as president and chief operating officer three years earlier. (He had previously held those two positions at Emerson Electric.)

Textron bought Acustar, Chrysler's plastics operations, for $139 million in 1993. The same year, it sold the public a 16.7 percent stake in Paul Revere Insurance, the star of Textron's financial services portfolio. The unit suffered heavy disability claims in 1994, which led Hardymon to consider selling the remainder of the company. Homelite, a maker of lawn care equipment, was divested in 1994, as was piston aircraft engine manufacturer Lycoming. These sales took in $495 million. After several years, Textron finally was able to gain control of Avdel. In the mid-1990s, the fastener and automotive businesses were merged into Textron Fastening Systems and Textron Automotive Company, respectively. In late 1994, Bell did win a $2.5 billion contract to make just six V-22 aircraft for the U.S. military, although a V-22 crash soured the Pentagon on a full-scale production contract.

Hardymon retired in July 1998, succeeded by Lewis B. Campbell. Like his predecessor, Campbell had grown up in the rural South and studied engineering before working in sales, marketing, and management positions. Campbell formed his career at GM, rather than Emerson Electric, like Hardymon. He joined Textron in 1992 and became president and chief operating officer within two years. Campbell also became board chairman in February 1999.

By the late 1990s, more than 30 percent of Textron's revenues came from abroad. The company posted record results in 1999 as revenues increased 20 percent. Textron acquired 18 business and entered two joint ventures while selling Avco Financial Services for $2.9 billion. A fatal crash of a Marine V-22 Osprey in April 2000, however, raised doubts about the viability of the program.

Principal Subsidiaries

Bell Helicopter Textron; Cessna Aircraft Company; Textron Automotive Company; Textron Fastening Systems; Textron Industrial Products; Textron Turf Care and Specialty Products.

Principal Divisions

Aircraft; Automotive; Industrial; Finance.

Principal Competitors

General Electric Corporation; Learjet Inc.; United Technologies Corporation.

Further Reading

Banks, Howard, "Being a Conglomerate Is Not All Bad," *Forbes,* December 11, 1989, pp. 40–41.

Byrne, Harlan S., "Lifting Off," *Barron's,* March 27, 1995, pp. 17–18.

"Case Study in Diversification," *Forbes,* June 7, 1993, p. 14.

Eisenhauer, Robert S., *Textron—From the Beginning,* Providence, R.I.: Textron Inc., 1979.

Little, Royal, *How to Lose $100,000,000 and Other Valuable Advice,* Boston: Little Brown, 1979.

Simon, Jane, "With Its Second Billion-Dollar Buy, a Remodeled Textron Eludes Easy Definition," *New England Business,* September 15, 1986, pp. 37–39.

Wrubel, Robert, "Lost Innocence," *Financial World,* August 11, 1987, pp. 20–22.

Zipser, Andy, "Into the Wild Blue Yonder," *Barron's,* August 15, 1994, p. 14.

——, "The Text on Textron," *Barron's,* June 14, 1993, pp. 32–33.

—updated by Frederick C. Ingram

The Thomson Corporation

Toronto Dominion Bank Tower, Suite 2706
P.O. Box 24
Toronto-Dominion Centre
Toronto, Ontario M5K 1A1
Canada
Telephone: (416) 360-8700
Fax: (416) 360-8812
Web site: http://www.thomcorp.com

Public Company
Incorporated: 1977
Employees: 30,000
Sales: US$5.75 billion (1999)
Stock Exchanges: Toronto Montreal London
Ticker Symbol: TOC
NAIC: 511110 Newspaper Publishers; 511120 Periodical
    Publishers; 511130 Book Publishers; 511140 Database
    and Directory Publishers; 514199 All Other
    Information Services; 551112 Offices of Other
    Holding Companies; 611710 Educational Support
    Services

As it prepares to enter the 21st century, The Thomson Corporation is completing its transformation from a media, information, and travel empire into a focused information powerhouse primarily serving the business and professional markets. The company is also concentrating on providing electronic—particularly Internet-based—information services and solutions, with half of revenues being generated from electronic media. The markedly decentralized Thomson is organized into four main groups, each of which is among the market leaders in its field: Thomson Legal & Regulatory, which accounts for about 43 percent of overall sales, serves law, tax, accounting, intellectual property, corporate finance, and human resources professionals; Thomson Financial, which accounts for 26 percent, serves financial communities worldwide; Thomson Learning, which accounts for 17 percent, is a publisher of college and higher education textbooks and of career information with a focus on technology, trades, healthcare, and cosmetology; and

Thomson Scientific, Reference & Healthcare, which accounts for 14 percent, serves researchers and other professionals in segments of the healthcare, academic, scientific, business, and governmental markets. Among the specific market leading positions of Thomson units are: West Group, number one in the U.S. legal sector; Derwent Information, the world's leading patent information provider; Law Book Company, number one in the Australian legal market; and Gale Group, leading provider to the U.S. library reference market. Thomson also continues to own the *Globe and Mail,* the self-described "national newspaper of Canada," which is part of Thomson Financial. Control of the company has long rested in the hands of founder Roy Thomson's son, Kenneth, Canada's richest man and heir to his father's title, Lord Thomson of Fleet. The Thomson family owns 73 percent of the company's stock.

Early Years: From Radio to Newspapers to Television

Born in Toronto in 1894, Roy Thomson left school at 14 to become a bookkeeper and, later, branch manager of a cordage company. After a brief, unsuccessful attempt at farming in Saskatchewan, he returned to Ontario in 1920 to establish an automotive parts distributorship, which also proved unsuccessful. Finally, in 1930, Thomson agreed to a franchise arrangement to sell radios in the remote town of North Bay. As Susan Goldenberg reported in *The Thomson Empire:* "Only someone with Thomson's optimism, stamina and ebullient salesmanship would have accepted such an assignment under the odds he faced. In addition to the Depression and poor radio reception, the single transmitter in North Bay was decrepit." Thomson solved the predictable problem of feeble radio sales by opening his own radio station, CFCH, in 1932 on borrowed money. Roy Thomson's avowed ambition was to become a millionaire by the time he was 30 but, nearing the age of 40 now, he was nearly penniless. His decision to capitalize on advertising revenue in his current venture, however, helped him to belatedly achieve his goal several hundred times over. Within two years of CFCH's debut, Thomson had bought additional stations in Kirkland Lake and Timmins. This latter purchase coincided with Thomson's entry into newspaper publishing, another source of advertising revenue and what would soon be the

---

Company Perspectives:

Thomson's mission is to achieve superior shareholder value by empowering our people to help customers become more successful by providing them with indispensable information, insight and solutions.

---

cornerstone of his empire, via the *Timmins Press,* a paper whose offices were in the same building as his newest station. By 1944 his holdings included five newspapers and eight radio stations. Newspapers became Thomson's main concern, while Jack Kent Cooke, with whom he went into partnership in 1940, assumed management of the radio end of the business. Their partnership ended in 1949, just as Thomson began buying newspapers outside Ontario.

In 1952 he bought his first non-Canadian newspaper, the *Independent* of St. Petersburg, Florida, to add to the 12 he already owned. A turning point came in 1953, when Thomson moved to Great Britain, leaving his North American operations under the control of Kenneth, then 30. Thomson's first U.K. acquisition was the *Scotsman,* a prestigious Scottish daily that had been founded in 1817 but was suffering financially. Owning Scotland's leading newspaper put Thomson in an excellent position to make his successful bid for a commercial television franchise covering central Scotland when it became available in 1957. Famous for his frugality as well as for his quotes on the topic of wealth, he called this coup ''a license to print money.'' The enormous profits from Scottish Television (STV) made it possible for him to buy London's leading Sunday paper, the *Sunday Times,* as well as 17 other local newspapers, from the Kemsley family in 1959. This was the first ''reverse takeover'' in U.K. business history. Kemsley Newspapers bought Thomson's STV company in return for Kemsley shares, which gave Thomson majority control of the group and allowed it indirectly to retain STV as well, with 70 percent control of the total business. Later, stricter government controls led to a forced reduction in Thomson's holding and the company sold its remaining interest in 1977.

1960s–70s: Adding Publishing, Travel, and Petroleum

Presciently, Thomson did not restrict himself to newspapers and television. Thomson Publications, the forerunner of what became Thomson's largest and most profitable group, Thomson Information/Publishing, was established in 1961 to publish books and magazines. This subsidiary began with the acquisition of the Illustrated London News Company, which owned not only the magazine of that name and the *Tatler,* but also the trade book publisher Michael Joseph. To this base Thomson Publications added in the first half of the 1960s the educational publisher Thomas Nelson & Sons; George Rainbird, specializing in illustrated books; Hamish Hamilton in trade books; and Derwent Publications in scientific and technical information. The company moved into consumer, professional, and business press publishing in the United Kingdom, Australia, and southern Africa. It also revamped the regional newspaper group; launched four newspapers; started new magazines, including

Family Circle and *Living,* to be distributed only through supermarkets (a novel concept that proved highly successful in the United Kingdom); and started the *Sunday Times* color magazine, which by 1963 was an unqualified success. In addition, Thomson Publications created a paperback imprint, Sphere, in 1966, aiming its titles at confectioners, news agents, and tobacconists rather than established bookshops. This venture suffered losses, in part because it could not secure the paperback rights of books published by other Thomson companies, since most of these had already been bought by rival paperback publishers.

In 1964 Roy Thomson made it clear that Britain rather than Canada was now his base by taking British citizenship and accepting a seat in the House of Lords as Lord Thomson of Fleet, an honor sponsored by prime minister Harold Macmillan. From television, newspapers, books, and magazines, Thomson next extended his empire into the travel business starting in 1965, when foreign travel was just beginning to become a popular activity in Britain. Three existing package tour companies and a small airline, Britannia Airways, were bought and formed the basis for Thomson Travel. After an initial period of good profits, the company encountered intense competition in the early 1970s, which resulted in the failure of several competing companies. Thomson Travel survived as the largest operator due to a reconstruction of its management, organizational, and commercial policies.

In 1972 the group moved into travel retailing with the acquisition of Lunn Poly. Thomson introduced Yellow Pages to the United Kingdom as a long-term profit venture. Once he had won the contract from the Post Office to sell advertising in its telephone directories, Thomson persuaded the agency of the need for a classified directory for all 64 telephone regions. From this enterprise the company learned the constraints and difficulties of working in a commercial venture with a public utility. In 1980 International Thomson would relinquish the Yellow Pages contract and start its own local directory operation in partnership with the American firm Dun & Bradstreet.

Thomson had been looking for a national daily newspaper to put together with the *Sunday Times,* and in 1966 he bought the *London Times* and its associated weeklies, *Times Literary Supplement* and *Times Educational Supplement,* from the Astor family. Thomson described the acquisition as the summit of a lifetime's work, and the man who admitted that he was ''tighter than any Scot'' cheerfully bore the continuing financial losses as his one extravagance. At the time of his death, the *Times'* American counterpart, the *New York Times,* reported that ''Lord Thomson poured at least £10 million into rescuing the *Times,* expanding the newspaper's staff, introducing a business supplement, promoting the daily issues, livening up the stolid paper . . . and seeking to give it a new informal style.'' Yet, ''the newspaper itself, now plagued by spiraling newsprint costs coupled with the impact of the stagnating British economy, remains in somber financial shape.'' It would be left to his son to sell this prized possession. Perhaps even more to his credit than his financial commitment was Roy Thomson's well-known pledge, applicable as much to the *Times* as any of his other holdings, that the editorial support of his newspapers was not for sale to anyone, that the organization's headquarters would not guide the policies of the papers, and that the papers' editors would be free and independent.

Key Dates:

1932: Roy Thomson begins operating a radio station in North Bay, Ontario.
1934: Thomson acquires his first newspaper, the *Timmins Press.*
1949: Thomson exits from the radio field to concentrate on newspapers.
1952: Thomson buys his first non-Canadian newspaper, the *Independent* of St. Petersburg, Florida, and expands into the United Kingdom the following year.
1966: The *London Times* and its associated weeklies are acquired.
1978: International Thomson Organisation Ltd. (ITOL) is established and corporate headquarters are moved to Toronto.
1980: Thomson Newspapers Ltd. acquires a group of Canadian newspapers, including the *Globe & Mail.*
1981: Times Newspapers division is sold to Rupert Murdoch.
1989: ITOL and Thomson Newspapers merge to become The Thomson Corporation.
1994: Thomson acquires database specialist Information Access Company (IAC) and healthcare database firm Medstat Group.
1995: Company divests its remaining U.K. newspaper holdings.
1996: Legal publisher West Publishing Co. is acquired, while 43 daily newspapers in the United States and Canada are sold.
2000: Company announces intentions to divest its remaining newspaper interests, with the exception of the flagship *Globe and Mail;* Kenneth R. Thomson announces his decision to step down as chairman within two years.

In 1971 Thomson went into its single most profitable area of business when it joined with Occidental Petroleum, Getty Oil, and Allied Chemical as the sole U.K. partner in a bid for licenses to explore for oil in the North Sea. The consortium's first strike, in 1973, was in the Piper field, containing more than 800 million barrels of oil. Thomson rejected the U.S. partners' offer to buy his 20 percent stake, and his investment turned out even wiser than had been expected when a second strike, in the Claymore field in 1974, brought the consortium another 400 million barrels. Within a decade the International Thomson Organisation was gaining most of its overall profits from North Sea oil on the basis of an initial stake of just $5 million and a series of bank loans using the oil itself as collateral. In 1977 International Thomson showed a trading profit of almost $190 million, compared with less than $20 million in 1971.

Late 1970s–80s: Expansion Through Acquisition

When Kenneth Thomson succeeded his father in 1976, he inherited control of a $750 million media monolith. British government policy on monopolies prevented expansion of newspaper holdings in the United Kingdom, and exchange controls—since abolished—would have made overseas investment from a base in London very costly. The decision was made to concentrate on expanding in North America by investing oil profits into publications and publishers with proven records. In 1978 International Thomson Organisation Ltd. (ITOL) was established and corporate headquarters were moved back to Toronto. ITOL's philosophy, according to a 1988 *Forbes* article, became: "Buy the market leader, even in a specialized field, and then you can afford to pay for the acquisition."

In 1979 ITOL's first acquisition in North America was the U.S. college textbook publisher Wadsworth Inc., quickly followed by others in business and professional publishing and information services, such as Callaghan & Company, Van Nostrand Reinhold, Research Publications, and Warren, Gorham & Lamont, as well as numerous business magazines. By 1983, 25 percent of ITOL's sales were to the United States and nearly 20 percent of its workforce was employed there. Acquisitions continued over the next several years, bringing in such companies as Gale Research (eventual parent company of St. James Press); American Banker/Bond Buyer; South-Western Publishing Co.; and Mitchell International.

Back in the United Kingdom, Times Newspapers had become a source of continual trouble for the group. By 1978 strikes over pay and conditions were seriously disrupting the publication of both titles. The situation continued to deteriorate until the company suspended publication for 11 months. Not long after the papers' operations resumed, International Thomson gave up the unequal struggle to introduce new technology on terms acceptable to the company and, in 1981, sold the titles to Australian media magnate Rupert Murdoch for £12 million; the trading losses and losses on disposal for the previous year were an estimated US$36 million.

The Canadian company Thomson Newspapers Ltd., which was separate from ITOL, had long restricted itself to owning small Canadian and U.S. newspapers with circulations below 20,000; the strategy was in keeping with Roy Thomson's drive to contain costs while nonetheless being assured of near monopolies in local advertising. During the 1950s under Kenneth Thomson, the group published the largest number of newspaper titles in Canada. In the following decade a bold U.S. acquisition program was launched. In 1967 the company acquired 16 daily and six weekly newspapers, mainly from the purchase of the Brush Moore Newspaper, Inc., and was publishing more daily newspapers in the United States than in Canada. By 1974 the group owned more than 100 newspapers.

In 1980 its profile was transformed through the acquisition of FP Publications and its chain of newspapers in most of the big cities of Canada, including Toronto's *Globe and Mail,* which Thomson attempted to turn into a national newspaper along U.K. lines. Soon afterward Thomson closed down one of the FP papers, the unprofitable *Ottawa Journal.* Simultaneously a rival newspaper chain, Southam, closed down its Winnipeg paper and bought Thomson's shares in two newspaper firms in Montreal and Vancouver, while Thomson closed down the FP News Service.

By the 1980s Thomson Travel ranked as the largest inclusive tour operator based in the United Kingdom (about three times the size of its nearest rival), owned the country's biggest charter airline, and was one of the largest travel retailers. Within a few years of entering the U.S. market it became one of the top three U.S. tour operators, although by 1988 it had withdrawn completely in order to concentrate on its activities based in the United Kingdom. This same year Thomson strengthened its U.K. leadership in tour operating, charter airlines, and travel retailing with the acquisition of the Horizon Travel Group, which had been one of its major competitors.

For ITOL, expansion continued throughout the 1980s in Britain and the United States alike. With the 1986 acquisition of South-Western, the largest American publisher of business textbooks for schools and colleges, ITOL became second overall in U.S. college textbook publishing. The following year saw one of ITOL's biggest British purchases, when it acquired Associated Book Publishers (ABP), a group including the legal publisher Sweet & Maxwell and the academic publisher Routledge, Chapman & Hall. Purchased for US$323 million, ABP represented a major advance for ITOL in legal, scientific, technical, and academic publishing in the United Kingdom, North America, and Australia.

This trend toward what Laura Jereski called "high-profit publishing niches," was orchestrated by Thomson's right-hand man, Gordon Brunton, and furthered by then-president Michael Brown; both were keenly aware that ITOL's oil holdings were rapidly becoming depleted. The 1986 fall in oil prices dragged the North American petroleum subsidiaries into overall losses and both were sold off in 1987. In 1989 ITOL finalized its move away from oil and gas by selling its remaining British interests. Although the immediate cause was the major accident on the Piper Alpha oil rig in 1988, the longer-term rationale was that the company had been less and less dependent on North Sea oil revenue, which had fallen both absolutely and as a proportion of ITOL's business since its peak in 1982. At that time it had provided about 75 percent of ITOL's profits, but by 1985, when the Scapa field in which it had invested came onstream, this proportion had fallen to just over 50 percent.

By leaving the petroleum industry altogether ITOL was able to concentrate even more resources and attention on its core activities of publishing and information services. In 1988, for instance, subsidiary Thomson & Thomson launched a database containing over 300,000 trademarks and logos; Mitchell International developed further its involvement in the computerizing of motor car building and repairs; and ITOL acquired 36 free newspapers in Britain. By the end of 1988, after 54 years of growth, Thomson Newspapers was publishing 40 daily and 12 weekly newspapers in Canada, and 116 daily and 24 weekly newspapers in the United States, representing the largest number of daily newspapers of any newspaper publishing group in either country. The daily circulation exceeded three million.

In March 1989, to remain competitive in a dawning era of mega-mergers among media conglomerates (Time Inc. and Warner Communications Inc. had proposed such a landmark merger, which was completed in early 1990), ITOL and Thomson Newspapers announced preparations to merge as The Thomson Corporation, a $4.7 billion entity which began operations a few months later. Thus empowered, the new company then bought the Lawyers Cooperative Publishing Company for $815 million, at the time the largest acquisition ever by a

Thomson company. In 1990 Thomson Newspapers purchased five daily newspapers and several associated weekly publications in the United States, its largest ever single purchase. Eight more Canadian local papers and the *Financial Times of Canada* were also bought. Thomson newspapers were now being published in 32 of the 50 American states and in eight of the ten Canadian provinces.

1990s: Transition to a Single Focus on Information

From 1990 to 1992, Thomson saw its revenues and profits rise from $5.36 billion to $5.98 billion; its operating profits, however, stumbled from $726 million to $692 million, before partially rebounding to its 1992 figure of $714 million. Two straight years of double-digit profit declines for Thomson Newspapers, caused by recession-influenced decreases in advertising, explained this trend. According to Thomson's 1992 annual report, however, U.S. circulation increased slightly and overall market share remained strong. In addition, more than 400 new products were introduced, including the first corporation-generated project, an entertainment weekly entitled *CoverSTORY,* whose circulation, primarily through Thomson newspapers, approached one million. Consequently, the division faced the future optimistically and expected to renew its growth track with the economic recovery.

Writing in 1984, Goldenberg had claimed that "The Thomson empire has been in the vanguard among media empires in branching into nonpublishing ventures, but it is a member of the pack, not the leader, in today's mecca for the press lords—information services." Yet, by 1992, Thomson had gone far toward quelling such criticism, for it could by then boast ownership of 190 online services, 161 CD-ROM products, and a large number of other software offerings, all part of The Thomson Information/Publishing Group (TIPG). In April 1992 Thomson accelerated its entry into information services with the $210 million purchase of New York-based JPT Publishing; according to *Publishers Weekly* and Thomson's chief financial officer, the deal was struck primarily to acquire data provider Institute for Scientific Information (ISI). ISI enjoyed over 300,000 customers worldwide and was believed to be generating healthy annual profits estimated at $15 million.

During the mid-1990s Thomson completed several more acquisitions, three of which were particularly important. In 1994 the company paid about US$465 million for Foster City, California-based Information Access Company (IAC), a former division of Ziff-Davis Communications Co. IAC was a leading provider of reference and database services for academic and public libraries, corporations, hospitals, and schools. Also in 1994 Thomson added to its healthcare information portfolio with the US$339 million purchase of the Medstat Group, but lost out to rival Reed Elsevier plc in the bidding for a leading information database, Lexis-Nexis. Two years later Thomson completed the largest acquisition in its history when it paid US$3.4 billion for Eagan, Minnesota-based legal publisher West Publishing Co., maintainer of more than 6,000 electronic databases on law, medicine, and insurance. Thomson and West were the two largest U.S. legal publishers, which prompted close antitrust scrutiny and objections from competitors in the field, most notably Reed Elsevier plc. To gain antitrust approval, Thomson and West had to sell off more than 50 legal publications, while resolution of a lawsuit filed by Reed Elsevier was reached when Thomson agreed to sell some of these legal publications—about $50 million worth—to the Anglo-Dutch firm. (In early 1997 West and Thomson Legal Publishing were merged as West Group.) Meanwhile, Thomson's newspaper holdings grew smaller still through the 1995 divestment of its remaining U.K. newspaper holdings and through the 1996 disposal of 43 daily newspapers in the United States and Canada.

Michael Brown was named deputy chairman in 1998, replacing longtime adviser to Kenneth Thomson, John Tory; Brown was in turn replaced as president and CEO by Richard Harrington. The early 1998 acquisition of Computer Language Research Inc. for about US$325 million bolstered Thomson's existing tax and accounting information operations, which centered on its Research Institute of America Group. By this time, Thomson's information services operations were the core of the company, with overall information revenue increasing by more than 75 percent over a five-year period, to US$4.8 billion. The company took another major step that furthered its focus on information in May 1998, when it spun off Thomson Travel through a public offering that generated net proceeds of US$2 billion. As a result, more than 83 percent of 1998 revenues were derived from Thomson's information businesses.

Perhaps even more dramatically, given the company's historic roots, Thomson announced in mid-February 2000 that it intended to sell off all of its remaining newspaper interests, with the exception of the flagship *Globe and Mail*. Thomson Newspapers included 55 daily newspapers and more than 75 nondaily newspapers and generated US$810 million in 1999 revenues. Proceeds from the sale—perhaps as much as US$2.5 billion— were expected to be used to further bolster Thomson's growing portfolio of electronic databases. Acquisitions remained a key company strategy, as evidenced by the March 2000 purchase of the Prometric business of Sylvan Learning Systems Inc. for US$775 million. Prometric, which became part of Thomson Learning, was a global leader in computer-based testing and assessment services. Prometric was a prime example of the type of company Thomson intended to pursue: one that was electronic and global—not print and local.

The future of Thomson—that of an electronic information powerhouse—seemed clear at the beginning of the 21st century. By 2005 the company aimed to generate 80 percent of its revenue from the electronic distribution of information (compared to the 50 percent figure of early 2000) and, more specifically, between 35 and 50 percent from the delivery of data and services over the Internet. (Only seven percent of overall revenues were Internet-based in early 2000.). The company was spending US$600 million per year on technology and the creation of Web platforms for Internet delivery. To achieve its ambitious Internet growth, however, Thomson would need to rely on an increased penetration of high-speed Internet hookups in businesses and homes—particularly because the company's databases were typically on the large side. Another issue for Thomson in the new century was the preparation for a leadership transition. That issue was at least partially resolved in May 2000, when Chairman Kenneth R. Thomson announced his decision to retire within two years. The septuagenarian leader requested of the board that they consider his son David Thomson, then 42 and a fellow director, to be his replacement.

Another Thomson heir, David's brother Peter, age 35, was also being groomed for executive office in the coming years.

Principal Subsidiaries

Thomson Learning Inc.; Institute for Scientific Information, Inc.; The Gale Group, Inc.; Jane's Information Inc.; Derwent Inc.; Thomson Publishing Corp.; Medical Economics Company Inc.; Micromedex, Inc.; The MEDSTAT Group Inc.; Medical Economics Data Inc.; Thomson Information Services Inc.; First Call Corporation; Intelligence Data Inc.; E*Link Corporation; Thomson Bankwatch Inc.; Sheshunoff Information Services Inc.; Thomson Global Markets Inc.; Thomson Institutional Services Inc.; Thomson Proxy Services Inc.; West Publishing Corporation; Compu-Clerk, Inc.; Thomson & Thomson, Inc.; Thomson Professional & Regulatory Inc.; PPC's Financial Advisory Services, Inc.; Thomson Newspapers Inc.; Thomson Canada Limited.

Principal Operating Units

Thomson Legal & Regulatory; Thomson Financial; Thomson Reference, Scientific & Healthcare; Thomson Learning.

Principal Competitors

Bell & Howell Company; Bloomberg L.P.; Bridge Information Systems, Inc.; Dow Jones & Company, Inc.; The Dun & Bradstreet Corporation; FinancialWeb.com, Inc.; Gannett Co., Inc.; HCIA-Sachs; The Hearst Corporation; Hollinger Inc.; Hoover's, Inc.; InfoUSA Inc.; John Wiley & Sons, Inc.; Knight Ridder; LEXIS-NEXIS; The McGraw-Hill Companies, Inc.; The News Corporation Limited; Pearson plc; Reed Elsevier plc; Reuters Group PLC; Southam Inc.; The Times Mirror Company; Torstar Corporation; Tribune Company; United News & Media plc; W.W. Norton & Company, Inc.; Wolters Kluwer NV.

Further Reading

Berss, Marcia, "Greener Pastures," *Forbes*, October 23, 1995, p. 56.
Braddon, Russell, *Roy Thomson of Fleet Street*, London: Collins, 1965, 396 p.
Coffey, Michael, "Thomson Pays $210M for Electronic Database, Journals," *Publishers Weekly*, April 20, 1992, p. 6.
Craig, Susanne, "Thomson and Globe Shift Gears: Flagship Publication Will Be Centre of Information Powerhouse," *Globe and Mail*, February 16, 2000, p. A1.
Daneshkhu, Scheherazade, "Thomson to Float Travel Business Valued at £1.5bn," *Financial Times*, March 19, 1998, p. 25.
Fabrikant, Geraldine, "2 Thomson Companies in a Proposal to Merge," *New York Times*, March 16, 1989, p. D22.
Faustmann, John, "Buying Legal History: Thomson's Biggest Takeover Draws Mixed Reaction," *Maclean's*, March 11, 1996, p. 36.
Goldenberg, Susan, *The Thomson Empire*, New York: Beaufort Books, Inc., 1984, 260 p.
Greenberg, Larry M., "Thomson Pushes to Get Customers to Use Online Data," *Wall Street Journal*, March 9, 2000, p. B14.
Heinzl, Mark, "Thomson Decides to Stop the Presses," *Wall Street Journal*, February 16, 2000, pp. A3, A6.
Jereski, Laura, "Profits by the Numbers," *Forbes*, September 19, 1988, pp. 104–06.
Lipin, Steven, Raju Narisetti, and Solange De Santis, "Thomson to Purchase West Publishing for $3.43 Billion," *Wall Street Journal*, February 27, 1996, p. A3.

''Lord Thomson Dies; Built Press Empire,'' *New York Times,* August 5, 1976, pp. 1, 32.

Lord Thomson of Fleet, *After I Was Sixty: A Chapter of Autobiography,* London: Hamilton, 1975, 224 p.

''Mid-Life Makeover,'' *Canadian Business,* June 26–July 10, 1998, pp. 85–88.

Milner, Brian, and Susanne Craig, ''Thomson Targets New Media,'' *Globe and Mail,* February 16, 2000, p. B1.

Morantz, Alan, ''The Power Elite: Kenneth Roy Thomson,'' *Canadian Business,* November 1989, pp. 49–51.

Moskowitz, Milton, et al., ''Thomson,'' in *Everybody's Business: A Field Guide to the 400 Leading Companies in America,* New York: Doubleday, 1990.

Newman, Peter C., ''Celebrating Success—Very, Very Privately,'' *Maclean's,* June 1, 1998, p. 48.

——, ''The Private Life of Canada's Richest Man,'' *Maclean's,* October 14, 1991, pp. 44–52.

Pritchard, Timothy, ''Thomson Jumps Head First into an Electronic Future,'' *New York Times,* February 21, 2000, p. C11.

Rudolph, Barbara, ''Good-bye to All That,'' *Forbes,* March 2, 1981, p. 108.

Schachter, Harvey, ''Information Overlord,'' *Canadian Business,* November 1995, pp. 34–38+.

Sheppard, Robert, ''No News Here,'' *Maclean's,* February 28, 2000, p. 44.

Smith, Desmond, ''Thomson: Media's Quiet Giant,'' *Advertising Age,* May 14, 1984, pp. 4, 74.

Symonds, William C., ''Lord of the Cyberpress: Thomson Charges Online with His West Publishing Purchase,'' *Business Week,* March 11, 1996, p. 36.

''Thomson Set to Buy Sylvan's Prometric in $775 Million Deal,'' *Wall Street Journal,* January 27, 2000, p. B21.

Wickens, Barbara, ''Highway Patrol: Thomson Gathers Speed on the Infobahn,'' *Maclean's,* November 14, 1994, p. 86.

—Jay P. Pederson and Patrick Heenan
—updated by David E. Salamie

3Com Corporation

3Com Corporation is the world's number two provider of computer networking products, systems, and services, trailing only Cisco Systems, Inc. A pioneering networking company, particularly in the area of Ethernet network adapters, 3Com offers products and services for local area networks (LANs), wide area networks (WANs), and the Internet. The company also is aggressively targeting emerging areas for future growth, including home networks, wireless products, broadband cable, digital subscriber line (DSL) services, and Internet telephony. Some of its key product areas include switches, network hubs (central switching devices for network communication lines), internetworking routers (devices that automatically select the most effective routes for data being transmitted between networks), remote access systems, network management software, network interface cards, and modems. 3Com also owns about 95 percent of Palm, Inc., the number one maker of handheld computer devices, which 3Com planned to completely spin off to shareholders in late 2000.

Ethernet Origins

3Com Corporation was founded in 1979 by Robert M. Metcalfe as a consulting firm for computer network technology. The name 3Com was derived from its focus on computers, communication, and compatibility. Bob Metcalfe, an M.I.T.-educated engineer, originally established the firm as a consultancy because the market for computer network products had not yet emerged. Six years earlier at Xerox's Palo Alto Research Center, Metcalfe had led a team that invented Ethernet, one of the first local area network (LAN) systems for linking computers and peripherals (printers, scanners, modems, etc.) within a building. In 1979, after attending an M.I.T. alumni seminar on starting one's own business, the 32-year-old Metcalfe quit Xerox to start his own consulting firm. Later that year, he incorporated 3Com, with the participation of college friend Howard Charney, an engineer turned patent attorney, and two others as cofounders.

In 1980, the group of four decided the time was ripe to convert their company into a LAN equipment manufacturing business using the Ethernet technology. It was at this time, following Metcalfe's encouragement, that Xerox had decided to share its Ethernet patent with minicomputer manufacturer Digital Equipment Corporation and microprocessor manufacturer Intel Corporation to establish Ethernet as a LAN industry standard. As a manufacturer, 3Com was still a little ahead of its time; although there were very few enterprises that had multiple computers, most having only one mainframe or at most a couple of minicomputers, Metcalfe foresaw that personal computers would someday become commonplace.

The group began approaching California venture capital firms in October 1980 for financing to begin developing products. 3Com's business plan emphasized a strategy of letting market demand determine its rate of growth, taking the risk that the market might run away, and focusing on long-term growth, rather than short-term market share. Despite the initial slow growth predictions, three venture capitalists contributed a total of $1.1 million in the first round of financing, in large part on the strength of its founders' reputations.

In March 1981, Metcalfe recruited L. William Krause, who then was general manager of Hewlett-Packard's General Systems Division, to become 3Com's president. Metcalfe retained the positions of chief executive officer and chairperson and assumed the additional title of vice-president of engineering. Bill Krause also was given a nine percent share in the company, second in size only to Metcalfe's 21 percent. 3Com then had only nine employees, but Krause had visions of a much larger company. Also that month, 3Com began shipping its first hardware product, its first Ethernet transceiver and adapter. Krause soon hired a vice-president of sales and a vice-president of marketing, and, a few months later, he hired someone else to assume Metcalfe's position of vice-president of engineering.

Krause had a conservative, risk-averse management style. When sales of 3Com's interim product were not as high as expected in the summer of 1981 and a cash flow problem loomed, Krause initiated a survival plan that involved a hiring freeze, a pay cut for all employees and officers, and a specific list of objectives. Even so, 3Com was not in serious difficulty. Sales for the year ending May 31, 1982 were $1.8 million. A second round of financing totaling $2.1 million came in January 1982. At the June 1982 board meeting, the board compelled Metcalfe to relinquish his title of CEO to Krause, who had really been in charge since he came to 3Com. Metcalfe then took on a new, more active role in the position of vice-president of sales and marketing.

3Com's sales took off in the summer months of 1982, not long after IBM introduced its 16-bit personal computer. The young company became profitable in 1983, and, in March 1984, 3Com went public, raising $10 million. By then it was expanding by approximately 300 percent annually, having grown from $4.7 million to $16.7 million in sales for the fiscal year ending May 1984. Earnings that year were $2.3 million, and the company had a 15 percent operating profit. Two years later, for the fiscal year ending May 31, 1986, revenues reached $64 million.

The company was doing well selling adapter cards to value-added resellers and to original equipment manufacturers, which were large computer manufacturing companies. The market was rapidly maturing, however, as computer manufacturers, including IBM and Digital Equipment, were beginning to integrate their own networking functions into their computers. In 1986, 3Com held eight percent of the LAN market, while computer manufacturer IBM had captured 28 percent of the market by including LAN hardware and software within its computers.

Mid-to-Late 1980s: Providing More Complete Computer Network Systems

In response to the trend, 3Com decided to move in the direction of providing more complete computer network systems. In 1984, Metcalfe had started a new software division to develop advanced network software, and the company shipped its first network operating system software, 3+, two years later. Also during this time, 3Com began marketing its own computer called the 3Server to function as a network server, a computer on a network whose data is accessed by multiple desktop computers in a configuration known as client-server. By the spring of 1986, servers accounted for 32 percent of 3Com's sales. To complete the system, 3Com also wanted to offer computers that functioned as clients. Therefore, in early 1986, it pursued a merger with Convergent Technologies Inc., which manufactured UNIX-based workstations. Two days before the scheduled shareholder approval in March 1986, however, 3Com's investment banker advised against being acquired by Convergent. On its own, 3Com then began selling systems that included modified personal computers, referred to as network stations, which operated only within its networks.

In 1987, 3Com began marketing itself more as a workgroups computing company that made and marketed PC-network systems. As such, it emphasized products that improved the productivity of workgroups. Several product introductions were made that year, including new network servers, software, and industry-standard network adapter cards. With this market strategy, however, 3Com was running into competition with Novell, Inc., which offered similar products. One important difference, however, was that 3Com targeted niche markets of more sophisticated users.

In September 1987, 3Com made a significant acquisition by purchasing Bridge Communications Inc. for $151 million. Bridge was a provider of internetwork gateways and multiple-protocol bridges, devices that link different networks together on a corporate level. Thus Bridge's products complemented 3Com's, and the largest independent networking manufacturer at that time was formed.

Integration of the two companies, however, was not without difficulties. Bridge was completely merged into 3Com by March 1988, but it was not until the end of 1989 that its new internetworking products were introduced. Bridge cofounder William Carrico was appointed president of 3Com, with Krause remaining as CEO, but differences in management styles and corporate cultures prompted Carrico to resign in May 1988, and Krause regained the presidency. At the same time, Bridge Communications Division General Manager Judy Estrin, another cofounder of Bridge, also resigned.

The integration of the sales forces also caused problems, since 3Com had focused on value-added resellers, whereas Bridge was more involved in direct sales. Therefore, a Cooperative Selling Program was launched whereby sales representatives earned commissions on sales to value-added resellers just as they did for direct sales. The buildup of a direct sales force, however, angered some of 3Com's traditional dealers, and sales of LAN Manager suffered.

Key Dates:

1979: 3Com Corporation is founded by Robert M. Metcalfe as a consulting firm for computer network technology.
1981: Company ships its first hardware product, an Ethernet transceiver and adapter.
1984: 3Com goes public, raising $10 million, and introduces its first network operating system.
1986: Revenues reach $64 million.
1987: Bridge Communications Inc. is acquired for $151 million.
1990: Implementation of a "New Renaissance Plan" begins, in effort to refocus the company away from client-server networking; Eric Benhamou is named president and COO.
1994: Company acquires Synernetics Inc., Centrum Communications Inc., and NiceCom Ltd.
1995: 3Com acquires Chipcom Corporation, a maker of high-speed switches, for $775 million.
1997: 3Com acquires U.S. Robotics Corporation—maker of modems, remote access devices, and handheld computing products—for $8.5 billion.
2000: Spinoff of Palm, Inc. begins with an $874 million IPO, which includes about five percent of Palm stock.

Also in 1987, 3Com had entered into a joint effort with Microsoft Corporation to develop and market LAN Manager network software for the OS-2 operating system. 3Com sold LAN Manager under a license agreement with Microsoft and, beginning in 1988, it also marketed 3 + Open, its own version of LAN Manager. LAN Manager, however, was a direct competitor of Novell's product, NetWare, and OS-2 eventually proved less popular an operating system than expected.

3Com's sales for the year ending May 31, 1988 were $252 million, up from $156 million in the previous year, and earnings had risen from $16.2 million to $22.5 million. By 1988, 3Com was the leading company specializing in computer networks. As a provider of networks, it was second only to Digital Equipment and was ahead of IBM.

Then, in the summer of 1989, revenue growth began to slow seriously for the first time, in part due to the poor sales of LAN Manager. 3Com had its first annual drop in earnings for the year ending May 1990. The company also was losing in its battle against rival Novell's NetWare, which by 1990 had 65 percent of the network operating system market share. In 1989, 3Com shipped 14,000 copies of its 3 + and 3 + Open software, whereas Novell shipped 181,000 copies of NetWare. Meanwhile, internetworking products, the specialty of the acquired Bridge Communications, were being neglected.

Early 1990s: Focusing on the Networks Themselves

Krause responded by implementing a "New Renaissance Plan" beginning in January 1990 to reorganize and refocus the company. 3Com began marketing itself as a "network integra-

tor" and a "network systems supplier," as a single source for network hardware and applications software compatible with multiple vendors' systems. Client/server networking was de-emphasized, and the focus shifted to comprehensive networking and internetwork connections. 3Com thus gave up going head to head against Novell, and 3Com's hardware henceforth supported both LAN Manager and its former competitor, NetWare. The marketing of LAN Manager, meanwhile, was left to Microsoft.

Krause also centralized the company by reducing the number of divisions from five to three: product development, internal operations, and sales. New executive vice-presidents were named to head each division, replacing the authority of Metcalfe's vice-presidency. Krause then removed himself from daily operations and began looking for someone else to replace him as CEO.

In April 1990, 3Com appointed Eric Benhamou, who had been the new executive vice-president of product development, as president and chief operating officer. Benhamou had been one of the cofounders of the acquired Bridge Communications company. A month later, founder Metcalfe resigned from his posts as vice-president of marketing and board member, after being passed over for the position of president. In August 1990, Krause himself resigned as CEO of 3Com, and Benhamou assumed that post as well. Krause remained only as chairman of the board, leaving management satisfied with his accomplishments in building 3Com into a significant company of 2,000 employees.

Benhamou continued the process of refocusing the company along the lines of Krause's Renaissance plan. 3Com began investing more in technically innovative products such as network adapters, software, network management, and internetworking. Increasing emphasis was put on the cohesiveness of its products. To that end, in November 1990 two new divisions were created to replace four previous product-oriented groups. A Network Adapter Division was created to sell the company's Ethernet cards, replacing the former Transmission Systems Division, and a Network Systems Division, headed directly by Benhamou, assumed the responsibilities of the former Enterprise Systems Division, Distributed Systems Division, and the Management, Messaging and Connectivity Division. Some mid-level managers were removed in the process.

In January 1991, 3Com further redefined its business objectives. The company completely gave up the network operating system software business, which had been providing the software packages LAN Manager, 3 +, and 3 + Open, since the LAN Manager royalty contract with Microsoft had become a financial burden. Under the contract, 3Com had to pay Microsoft royalties even if the computer servers it sold did not include LAN Manager but 3Com's 3 + Open instead. Moreover, when LAN Manager was sold independently, not bundled with 3Com hardware, 3Com still had to pay the expense of customer support for LAN Manager and thus was losing money. 3Com's exit from the network operating system business freed the company from its royalty contract with Microsoft, and all marketing and support of LAN Manager was turned over to Microsoft. 3Com's LAN operating system, which had been losing market share to Novell's NetWare for the past three years, held only 14 percent of the market when the company dropped out.

The restructuring also involved steering away from providing client and server computers in order to focus on the networks themselves. Benhamou's redirection and reorganization of the company also involved putting two businesses up for sale. Communications Solutions Inc., a manufacturer of connectivity products beyond LANs that had been acquired in 1988, was sold to Attachmate Corporation. The workgroup business, that which sold servers and workstations, however, could not find a buyer and was gradually eliminated. Whereas workgroup-related hardware and software had contributed $113 million, almost one quarter of 3Com's revenues, in 1990, this figure had dropped to 11 percent in 1991. The reorganization also involved laying off 234 employees, or 12 percent of the workforce, and a $67 million restructuring charge.

Thereafter, the company refocused on its successful LAN adapter line and internetworking products, such as bridges, hubs, adapters, and routers. 3Com had begun to depend increasingly on sales from its internetworking business, that of the acquired Bridge Communications company, after neglecting it for three years. 3Com had seen its market share in bridges and routers fall from 29 percent in 1988 to 19 percent in 1990, although it was still the third ranking company in the field, following Cisco Systems, Inc. and Vitalink Communications Corporation Network adapters, meanwhile, came to account for 72 percent of sales in the second half of 1991. 3Com further concentrated on improving its core adapter product line with the development of adapters for wireless notebook computers and adapters for higher speed network systems.

The initial results of the restructuring included lower revenues due to fewer product lines. For calendar year 1991, sales declined 15 percent to $370 million, and the company suffered a loss of $33 million, compared with a $24 million profit the previous year. Lower profits also were caused in part by the more competitive nature of the LAN adapter market that had emerged in the early 1990s. By the end of 1991, 14 percent of the company's workforce had been laid off, leaving a total of 1,676 employees. By 1992, however, the company was back on track, with sales rebounding to $423.8 million for the fiscal year ending May 31, 1992 and earnings becoming positive at $7.96 million.

For its other LAN components, 3Com came to rely increasingly on licensing or acquiring third-party technology. The company bolstered its hub business by acquiring the Data Networks business of U.K.-based BICC PLC, one of Europe's largest hub manufacturers, in January 1992. This gave 3Com the LinkBuilder ECS, an Ethernet chassis hub. In September 1992, 3Com introduced LinkBuilder 3GH, a high-end switching hub licensed from Synernetics Inc., a manufacturer of LAN switches. In a move to expand beyond Ethernet LAN structures, in 1993 3Com acquired Star-Tek Inc., which produced hubs for the Token-Ring network architecture. 3Com introduced a multifunction hub, LinkBuilder MSH, which could support both Ethernet and Token-Ring LANs in the spring of 1993. In December of that year, 3Com purchased wireless communications technology from Pacific Monolithics Inc. Early in 1994, 3Com acquired Synernetics, a manufacturer of LAN switches, and Centrum Communications Inc., which provided products for remote network access. In September 1994, 3Com purchased ATM innovator NiceCom Ltd., a subsidiary of Nice Systems based in Tel Aviv, Israel. 3Com rounded out its acquisitions spree in late 1995 with the $775 million purchase of

Chipcom Corporation, a maker of multifunction high-speed switches for large computer networks. This acquisition not only gave 3Com its first presence in the large corporate systems segment, it also propelled 3Com into second place among the world's networking companies, behind only Cisco Systems. 3Com's product strategy and acquisitions under Benhamou helped the company reach $2.33 billion in sales for the fiscal year ending in May 1996, nearly six times that of four years prior. Reflecting its rising stature, while at the same time representing an attempt to make the company better known to the general public, 3Com paid $3.9 million to the city of San Francisco to change the name of Candlestick Park, where the Giants played major league baseball, to 3Com Park, a move that angered many baseball fans.

Late 1990s: U.S. Robotics and Palm

Despite its diversification efforts, 3Com remained primarily a maker of network adapters in the mid-1990s, a period in which the emergence of the Internet heightened demand for networking products of all sorts. While market leader Cisco Systems concentrated mainly on the devices that formed the backbone of the Internet, 3Com focused on the Internet edge with its products that connected personal computers to networks—both LANs and WANs and to the Internet, and those that welded together local area networks. 3Com's key acquisition in its emerging Internet strategy was that of U.S. Robotics Corporation, which was completed in June 1997. Dallas-based U.S. Robotics was the leading maker of low-cost modems, which were used to connect personal computers to the Internet and to other remote networks. The company also had a leading presence on the other end of the modem, that is in the remote access devices that were the entry points into Internet service providers and corporate networks for users dialing in through a modem. U.S. Robotics was particularly strong in the area of corporate remote access devices. In 1995 the company also had acquired Palm Computing, a pioneer in the field of handheld computing devices.

Following the acquisition of U.S. Robotics, 3Com derived more than half of its revenues from the low end of the networking segment, that which included network adapters and modems. Overall revenues reached $5.42 billion for the 1998 fiscal year but the company was barely profitable thanks to merger-related and other charges totaling $253.7 million. Integrating U.S. Robotics into 3Com proved more difficult than anticipated, in part because of the geographic and cultural divide between Silicon Valley and Texas oil country. An inventory backlog also developed for U.S. Robotics modems for a time while an industry standard was being adopted for another increase in analog modem speed, this time to 56 kilobits per second. In fact, with faster alternative access technologies—such as cable modems and digital subscriber lines (DSL)—being developed, many analysts were predicting the demise of the analog modem and questioned the wisdom of the U.S. Robotics acquisition. Although the analog modem proved longer lasting than anticipated, and new access technologies were slow to be adopted, 3Com was forced to contend with a number of shareholder lawsuits stemming from the U.S. Robotics purchase and the company's plummeting market value.

For the 1999 fiscal year, 3Com posted net income of $403.9 million on sales of $5.77 billion, representing a vast improvement in profitability but only a slight revenue gain. The company was suffering from intense competition and sagging prices, particularly in its core network adapters and modems segment, where revenues were actually on the decline. The brightest spot was Palm Computers, which had captured 70 percent of the handheld computer market. But by late 1999 3Com management had concluded that Palm had become a distraction away from the company's networking core. 3Com, therefore, announced that it would spin off Palm during 2000. In early March of that year 3Com sold about five percent of the common stock of the newly named Palm, Inc. in an initial public offering that raised $874 million—an IPO conducted in the midst of a technology stock frenzy on Wall Street. 3Com next planned to distribute the remaining Palm stake to 3Com shareholders later in 2000.

As the 21st century began, speculation continued that 3Com would itself become an acquisition target or would be broken up through further spinoffs. But Benhamou was insisting that the company would remain independent and had the right mix of networking products. 3Com was counting on being a key player in such emerging areas as home networks, wireless products, broadband cable, DSL services, and Internet telephony. To facilitate this, the company was forging alliances, such as a partnership with Microsoft to develop home networking products. In addition, 3Com continued to make strategic acquisitions, such as the March 1999 $87.8 million purchase of NBX Corporation, a company specializing in Internet telephony systems that integrated voice and data communications over small business LANs and WANs.

Principal Subsidiaries

Palm, Inc. (95%); 3Com Asia Limited (Hong Kong); 3Com Asia Pacific Rim PTE Limited (Singapore); 3Com Australia Pty. Ltd.; 3Com (Austria) GesmbH; 3Com Benelux B.V. (Netherlands); 3Com Bilgisayer Ticaret A.S. (Turkey); 3Com Bulgaria EOOD; 3Com Canada Inc.; 3Com Corporation Zagreb (Croatia); 3Com Costa Rica S.A.; 3Com Credit Corporation; 3Com do Brasil Servicos Ltda. (Brazil); 3Com de Chile S.A.; 3Com de Mexico, S.A. de C.V.; 3Com Denmark AS; 3Com Development Corporation; 3Com Engineering Limited (U.K.); 3Com Europe Limited (U.K.); 3Com Far East Limited (Cayman Islands); 3Com GmbH (Germany); 3Com Holdings Limited (Cayman Islands); 3Com Hungary Kft; 3Com Iberia S.A. (Spain); 3Com International, Inc.; 3Com International (New Zealand) Limited; 3Com IFSC (Ireland); 3Com India Pte. Ltd.; 3Com Ireland Technology Limited (Cayman Islands); 3Com Israel Limited; 3Com Japan K.K. (Japan); 3Com Korea Limited; 3Com Limited (U.K.); 3Com Mediteraneo S.r.l. (Italy); 3Com Nordic AB (Sweden); 3Com Pension Scheme (1996) Trustees Limited (U.K.); 3Com Philippines Inc.; 3Com Polska sp. z.o.o. (Poland); 3Com Russia OOO; 3Com S.A. (France); 3Com (Schweiz) A.G. (Switzerland); 3Com Slovakia s.r.o.; 3Com South Asia PTE. Ltd. (Singapore); 3Com Technologies (Cayman Islands); 3Com (Thailand) Co. Ltd.

Principal Competitors

Casio Computer Co., Ltd.; Cisco Systems, Inc.; Compaq Computer Corporation; Com21, Inc.; Conexant Systems, Inc.; General Electric Company; General Instrument Corporation; Hewlett-Packard Company; Intel Corporation; Koninklijke Philips Electronics N.V.; Lucent Technologies Inc.; Microsoft Corporation; Motorola, Inc.; Nortel Networks Corporation; Olivetti S.p.A.; Psion PLC; Sharp Corporation; Siemens AG; Sony Corporation; Xircom, Inc.

Further Reading

Alpert, Bill, "The Future Is 3Com," *Barron's,* December 1, 1997, pp. 15–16.

Barney, Cliff, "Sales and Profit Gains Ease the Pain of the 3Com/Bridge Merger," *Electronic Business,* November, 15, 1988, pp. 54–56.

Bransten, Lisa, and Scott Thurm, "For Palm Computers, an IPO and a Flashy Rival," *Wall Street Journal,* September 14, 1999, p. B1.

Burke, Steven, "3Com Recharts Networking Course," *PC Week,* January 14, 1991, pp. 1, 8.

Burrows, Peter, "3Com Is Showing a Lot of Hustle," *Business Week,* October 2, 1995, pp. 130, 132.

Doler, Kathleen, "Eric Benhamou, Chairman and CEO of 3Com Corp.," *Upside,* May 1999, pp. 106–12, 114, 116+.

Duffy, Jim, "3Com Captain Remains Calm Despite Stormy Forecasts," *Network World,* July 5, 1999, pp. 1, 57.

Epstein, Joseph, "Showtime: 3Com Has Finally Made It into the Big Leagues," *Financial World,* October 24, 1995, p. 29.

Flynn, Laurie, "As Networks of Computers Grow, 3Com Stock Surges," *New York Times,* August 31, 1994, pp. C1, C4.

Franson, Paul, "Challenging Perceptions," *Electronic Business,* June 1999, pp. 74–80+.

Goldstein, Mark L., "Bill Krause Changes Course," *Industry Week,* June 1, 1987, p. 55.

Gomes, Lee, and Evan Ramstad, "3Com Agrees to Acquire U.S. Robotics," *Wall Street Journal,* February 27, 1997, p. A3.

Hill, G. Christian, and William M. Bulkeley, "3Com to Buy Chipcom for $775 Million," *Wall Street Journal,* July 28, 1995, p. A3.

Kerr, Susan, "3Com Corp.," *Datamation,* June 15, 1992, p. 141.

Lewis, Jamie, "3Com's Pulse Strong After Years of Change," *PC Week,* January 25, 1993, p. 64.

Moad, Jeff, "On the Road Again," *Datamation,* May 1, 1986, pp. 31–37.

Ould, Andrew, "3Com Reorganizes Divisions; Key Executive Departs," *PC Week,* November 5, 1990, p. 181.

Reinhardt, Andy, "Palmy Days for 3Com?," *Business Week,* March 16, 1998, p. 104.

——, "Why 3Com Is Handing Off Palm," *Business Week,* September 27, 1999, p. 48.

Richman, Tom, "Growing Steady," *Inc.,* September 1984, pp. 69–81.

——, "Who's in Charge Here?," *Inc.,* June 1989, pp. 36–46.

Roth, Daniel, "3Com Tries to Solve Its Palm Problem," *Fortune,* October 11, 1999, pp. 167–68.

Schonfeld, Erick, "The Avis of Networking," *Fortune,* May 11, 1998, pp. 164, 168.

Shao, Maria, "3Com's 'New Renaissance' Hasn't Ended Its Dark Ages," *Business Week,* April 23, 1990, pp. 118–19.

Thurm, Scott, "3Com Faces Challenges in Developing New Lines," *Wall Street Journal,* March 25, 1999, p. B6.

——, "3Com Tops Expectations But Warns on Growth," *Wall Street Journal,* December 22, 1999, p. B6.

Young, Jeffrey, "Underdog Strategy," *Forbes,* November 3, 1997, pp. 364+.

—Heather Behn Hedden
—updated by David E. Salamie

The Topps Company, Inc.

One Whitehall Street
New York, New York 10004-2109
U.S.A.
Telephone: (212) 376-0300
Fax: (212) 376-0573
Web site: http://www.topps.com

Public Company
Incorporated: 1947 as Topps Chewing Gum, Inc.
Employees: 400
Sales: $229.41 million (1999)
Stock Exchanges: NASDAQ
Ticker Symbol: TOPP
NAIC: 311340 Nonchocolate Confectionery
    Manufacturing; 511120 Periodical Publishers; 511199
    All Other Publishers

The Topps Company, Inc. is one of the most recognized makers and marketers of trading cards and bubble gum in the world. With products sold in more than 50 countries, a variety of entertainment licenses including exclusive arrangements with virtually all the players in Major League Baseball, the National Football League, the National Basketball Association, and the National Hockey League, and trading card sales in the millions, the company that introduced baseball cards as premiums to sell gum has become part of Americana. Topps's popular Bazooka Bubble Gum is almost as familiar to consumers as its trading cards; in fact, Bazooka's aroma was one of those most frequently cited in a study of smells that elicit memories. Besides trading cards and bubble gum, Topps has marketed high-quality color comic books, collectibles such as sticker and album collections, and candies. Among its most successful newer products are cards and other collectibles featuring the highly popular Pokémon characters. Although its competition has increased over the years, Topps has remained at the forefront of its field through imaginative leadership.

Early Years: From Chewing Gum to Baseball Cards

The company was founded in 1938 by four brothers experienced in marketing tobacco, fuel, and other products. Abram,

Ira, Philip, and Joseph Shorin named their organization Topps Chewing Gum, Inc. after their ambition to produce the best chewing gum available, adding an extra "p" for distinction. The company's first product, single pieces of chewing gum selling for a penny apiece, promptly became popular throughout the country.

When sugar was rationed during World War II, the fledgling Topps Chewing Gum company bought smaller candy companies, closed them, and used their sugar quotas. With such ingenuity and with the popular slogan "Don't Talk, Chum. Chew Topps Gum" (reflecting the wartime campaign for reminding civilians to keep closemouthed regarding war information), the company was able to thrive while larger gum manufacturers had to cease operations.

To improve business after the war, the Shorin brothers introduced Bazooka Bubble Gum in 1947, the same year that the company was incorporated. (The Bazooka Joe comics found inside the wrapper were introduced later, in 1953, and the main character, Bazooka Joe, was modeled after cofounder Joseph E. Shorin.) Topps also soon introduced "Magic Photos," its first picture products. These cards featured 252 different subjects, including 19 baseball greats. The cards appeared blank when taken from the packages, but when moistened they revealed black-and-white photos "magically."

In the same year Topps Chewing Gum's major competitor, Bowman Gum Company, began to market baseball and football cards as premiums. Baseball cards had first been offered as premiums in cigarette packs during the late 1880s, but the practice had been abandoned amidst World War I's raw material shortages. Topps was intrigued by the premium idea but needed to obtain the legal rights to depict the players and teams. Sy Berger, hired in 1947 to assist with a promotional campaign for Topps salesmen, personally took up the challenge, overseeing the signing of many sport figures of the time to individual contracts. Topps was able, therefore, to enter the baseball card business in 1951.

In that year Topps began marketing two 52-card sets, later known to collectors as "Blue Backs" and "Red Backs," which were designed so that a game of card-baseball could be played by those who had collected all 52 in the set. Each card featured a

Key Dates:

1938: Brothers Abram, Ira, Philip, and Joseph Shorin form Topps Chewing Gum, Inc.

1947: Bazooka Bubble Gum is introduced; company is incorporated.

1951: Company enters the baseball card business.

1953: Bazooka Joe comics are introduced within the Bazooka gum wrapper.

1956: Topps acquires its main trading card rival, Bowman Gum Company, and sells its first set of National Football League cards.

1975: Fleer Corporationfiles federal antitrust suit against Topps and the Major League Baseball Players Association.

1980: Arthur Shorin, son of cofounder Joseph Shorin, becomes chairman and CEO.

1984: Management takes Topps private through a $98 million leveraged buyout.

1987: Company goes public again as The Topps Company, Inc.

1995: Topps acquires U.K.-based Merlin Publishing International Limited for $46.2 million.

1997: Company takes $30 million charge as a result of the closing of its manufacturing plant in Duryea, Pennsylvania.

1999: Topps begins selling Pokémon-related products.

hand-colored picture of a player and instructions on how to play the card-baseball game.

In 1952, Topps introduced the familiar format for its baseball cards, although their size was somewhat larger than the eventual standard. Sy Berger designed these cards to have color pictures of the players with their team emblems on the front and the players' personal history and playing statistics on the back.

During this time, Topps was working on obtaining rights to feature players and logos, while also working to standardize its cards. From 1952 through 1955, Topps competed intensely with Bowman for contracts, and by the end of that period, Topps had managed to secure most of them, purchasing remaining contracts from Bowman. In fact, in January 1956, Topps bought Bowman Gum Company itself, and from that year until 1980 Topps had virtually no competition in the sports trading card market. Standardization efforts were also complete, and in 1957 Topps introduced the standard 2.5- by 3.5-inch cards and began replacing the hand-tinted pictures with color photographs taken by Topps photographers at spring training camps as well as during the official season.

The 1950s also saw Topps enhance its trading card lines with new product lines featuring notable football, hockey, and basketball players. After two years of experimentation, Topps entered the football card market in earnest in 1951 with a 75-card set of college players. Although its football card line would not reappear until the college All-Americans series of 1955, Topps issued football cards every year thereafter. In 1956, Topps sold its first NFL set. Topps also began to compete with the Parkhurst Company for market share in the hockey card

business; Topps introduced a set limited to players from the Boston Bruins, Chicago Blackhawks, Detroit Red Wings, and New York Rangers in 1954. The next Topps hockey set came out in 1957, and thereafter sets were issued each season through 1981. Finally, in 1957 Topps began to market NBA basketball cards. Since these were only mildly successful, another full set of basketball cards was not produced until 1969.

By the early 1960s Topps baseball cards were a well established part of American culture, and production was increasing annually. Football and hockey cards also were selling, particularly after Parkhurst discontinued its hockey line following the 1963–64 season. In 1968, Topps formed a joint venture with the Canadian company O-Pee-Chee to better reach markets for hockey cards in Canada; this relationship continued until 1993.

Topps also began including premiums inside packages of trading cards to entice its young customers. From 1961 until 1971 various lines of Topps cards included collectible items such as stamps or specially embossed cards. Other premium experiments in the 1970s included Topps Story Booklets, Topps Baseball Tattoos, Topps Coins, Topps Posters, Topps Puzzles, and Wacky Packages. Moreover, the company bolstered its lines at the end of the 1974 season to include "Traded" cards for players who had changed teams. This would become standard practice for the sports card industry.

In 1975, the Fleer trading card company filed a $17.8 million federal antitrust suit against Topps and the Major League Baseball Players Association. Specifically, Fleer alleged that Topps's exclusive contracts with the players kept competitors from the baseball card market. Four years of litigation later, Judge Clarence C. Newcomer ruled against Topps and the Players Association in a district court in Philadelphia. Newcomer ordered Topps not to enforce the exclusivity clauses in its contracts and required the Players Association to review applications for licenses to market cards and to enter into at least one agreement by 1981. Although the industry would change considerably as a result of the ruling, the damages awarded to Fleer were miniscule.

1980s: Increased Competition and a Leveraged Buyout

In 1980, with company sales at $60 million, Arthur Shorin, son of founder Joseph Shorin, became chairman and CEO of the company. The younger Shorin had begun working for Topps in 1958 and had gained experience in every department, noting in a 1995 interview in *Topps Magazine,* "I came up principally through the marketing and sales route, but also did my time in manufacturing."

Arthur Shorin's first years as CEO were filled with challenges. As such competitors as Fleer and Donruss (and eventually Upper Deck) were entering the baseball card market, Topps was experiencing some problems. First, the company was focusing on a new product, chocolate bubble gum, to help grow its sales, and that product was failing to provide results; Shorin would later recall, "I don't know a lot about racing, but that was the wrong horse to bet on." Moreover, the company had become unwieldy, with a huge workforce and little focus. Shorin promptly jettisoned the chocolate gum scheme and began scaling down the workforce and implementing cost-cutting measures.

His company also was involved in an appeal of the antitrust suit brought by Fleer. In August 1981, Newcomer's ruling that Topps and the Players Association had violated antitrust violations was overturned. The Third U.S. Circuit Court of Appeals in Philadelphia did not prevent the Players Association from licensing more than one company in the future, however, encouraging increased competition with Topps. Sy Berger noted at the time, ''The Supreme Court confirmed the Court of Appeals decision by not hearing the case. . . . The one thing that the law said is that Topps does not have a monopoly, that others could enter the field and if they worked as hard as Topps, took as long as Topps, maybe they could do as well as Topps.''

Basketball and hockey cards were underperforming during this time. After experimenting with its line of basketball cards, introducing an unusual 176-card set of larger cards displaying pictures of three players, the company returned the cards to their normal size and tried distributing them in a different way, tailoring various sets for different geographic regions. After these experiments failed to bring NBA card sales to an acceptable level, Topps left the basketball card market in 1982 and did not return for ten years. Topps likewise bowed out of the hockey card market during this time, while the company's Canadian partner, O-Pee-Chee, continued these efforts.

Despite such difficulties, Topps was on the rebound by 1984; indeed, baseball card collecting in the 1980s was rapidly becoming an investment market in addition to a hobby. Periodicals emerged featuring price information and describing industry trends. Computer hotlines and investment advising groups helped investors pick out the best cards for their money. In fact, throughout the decade, rookie baseball cards outperformed all other comparable investments—including corporate bonds, common stocks, treasury bills, U.S. coins, and diamonds. During this time, however, Topps underwent a dramatic change. In conjunction with Forstmann Little & Co., Topps management took the company private, paying just $98 million in a leveraged buyout. Three years later, Topps became publicly held again—as The Topps Company, Inc.—selling a limited amount of stock that raised $22 million. In 1988, to reward loyal shareholders who were not seeing increased stock prices during this transition, Topps borrowed $140 million to pay out a special dividend.

By the late 1980s, Topps was reporting a negative net worth, resulting from a heavy debt load and the instability of the trading card market. Indeed, analysts had begun warning investors of a potential decline in the value of their baseball memorabilia. Others, however, remained more optimistic about the future of Topps and its competitors. Topps did, in fact, have a good cash flow, and baby boomer fathers, it seemed, were getting their children interested in card collecting as an investment.

1990s and Beyond

Because Topps's major competitors were concentrating their efforts on higher priced cards and their high-bidding collectors, Topps came to virtually own the market for less expensive cards. Topps even improved the paper stock of the inexpensive cards and boosted prices from 50 cents for 16 cards to 55 cents for 15. At the peak of the baseball memorabilia market, Topps's sales rose 28 percent for the fiscal year ending February 1990.

Moreover, to compete with Upper Deck, which was offering trading cards of a higher quality, Topps introduced premium Stadium Club baseball packs in 1991. The innovative cards featured ''full-bleed'' photographs rather than the traditional ones with cropped borders, glossier laminates, and gold foil stamping. They proved especially popular with collectors, many of whom bid as much as $12 for a pack of 15. Topps introduced Stadium Club lines of its hockey cards the following year.

The company's Bowman subsidiary was experiencing improved sales as well. Topps had brought Bowman back into the baseball card market in 1989, with disappointing results, but in 1992 Topps reduced the Bowman set and added new sets featuring retired ball players. The subsidiary's sales went up, establishing a new card brand for Topps.

By 1992, Topps was free from debt and it resumed its marketing of Topps basketball cards. In addition, the company issued an Archives set that showed NBA stars from the 1980s as they would have appeared had the company kept up the NBA line. Football card lines also were resumed and enhanced. But the company's most profitable line remained its baseball cards, consisting of four brands: Topps, Bowman, Stadium Club, and Stadium Club Dome; these brands were augmented in 1993, when the company premiered its Baseball's Finest line.

Baseball cards remained the biggest seller as the company approached the mid-1990s. After being deluged by all of the new cards marketed by Topps and other companies in these years, however, collectors staged a rebellion of sorts in 1992, and overall sales for the sports card business dropped 20 percent. Topps's profits decreased by 65 percent in the fiscal year ending February 1993, and the following year its stock value fell significantly as well.

The baseball strike that began August 11, 1994, did not help matters. Nevertheless, Topps's response to the strike was unique. The company simulated full season statistics for the backs of its cards by means of a software program that calculated what players might have done if not for the strike. Other new developments at Topps during this time included a move from its old Brooklyn headquarters to new corporate offices in lower Manhattan.

Topps also made efforts at diversifying in the face of the stagnant baseball card market. Indeed, by the mid-1990s, Topps had become quick to introduce trading cards that capitalized on fads unrelated to sports. For example, after learning that children were increasingly interested and apprehensive about the war in the Persian Gulf, Topps took only six weeks to introduce its Desert Storm line of trading cards. Other lines featured pop music stars and characters from such films as *Jurassic Park*.

The company's success was something in which its executives and visionaries took pride. In his introduction to *Topps Baseball Cards: The Complete Picture Collection, A 40 Year History,* Sy Berger, vice-president of sports and licensing at Topps, wrote: ''I must confess that I am proud of what we have achieved. I feel we have given Young America a wholesome interest; we have satisfied the desires of those who are prone to collect; and for the nostalgia buff, we have made something that he can reflect on.'' Moreover, CEO Shorin remained optimistic about the company's future, asserting in a 1995 *Topps Maga-*

zine article: "Anyone who doesn't think the recent unrest has caused real damage to the industry can sell his or her brain for shoe leather. But I think the hobby is resilient, as are the fans, and creativity still works."

Despite Shorin's optimism, the trading card market remained flat during the late 1990s, as did Topps's overall revenue figures. Even more alarming, the company's profits were on the decline. Topps pursued several strategies to attempt to escape from these doldrums. One was to expand its offerings in the nonsports entertainment sector. In addition to continuing a long-running line of *Star Wars* products, Topps found success with comic books and card sets based on the hit television show "The X-Files" and with a card collection based on the bestselling children's book series *Goosebumps*. With many collectors moving away from trading cards to such collectible toys as Beanie Babies, Topps also entered the minicollectible sector with lines of plastic animals packaged with candy called Puppy in My Pocket and Baby Wild Animals.

Another key strategy was overseas expansion. In July 1995 Topps acquired Merlin Publishing International Limited, a leading U.K. publisher and seller of sticker and album collections, for $46.2 million. Among Merlin's products was a line of soccer products connected to Premier League Football in the United Kingdom. Merlin had additional operations throughout Europe, giving Topps a solid platform on which to expand its confectionery lines on that continent. In March 1997 Topps renamed its new subsidiary Topps Europe Limited. Topps established additional subsidiaries in Canada and Mexico during fiscal 1996 and in Brazil and Argentina the following year. The company became more aggressive in pursuing overseas opportunities, gaining soccer licenses in Brazil, Korea, and Denmark and a basketball license in France, and expanding its distribution of confectionery products through agreements with local distributors in Japan, Russia, Australia, New Zealand, and South Africa.

Cost-cutting was also on the agenda in the late 1990s as Topps sought to reverse its profit slide. In late 1996 the company closed its manufacturing plant in Duryea, Pennsylvania, where it had produced gum and cards since 1966. Topps took a $30 million charge related to the closure, leading to a fiscal 1997 net loss of $10.9 million. The company began outsourcing all of its manufacturing, contracting with the Hershey Foods Corporation for the production of Bazooka gum and with several U.S. manufacturers for the making of card products. In April 1998 Topps closed its manufacturing facility in the Republic of Ireland, where it had been producing gum.

Topps returned to profitability in fiscal 1999, posting net income of $15.6 million on sales of $229.4 million. The sales figure, however, was the lowest in more than a decade. Nevertheless, prospects for the early 21st century appeared bright. The confectionery operations were improved through the beefing up of distribution and the introduction of new lollipop brands—Topps Baby Bottle Pop, Flip Pop, and Bazooka Pops—to complement the core Ring Pop and Push Pop brands. In the aftermath of baseball and basketball labor disputes, the sports segment was improving. In entertainment, Topps found success by being very selective in the properties it licensed; the company marketed just three lines during the 1999 fiscal year: "Xena," "The X-Files," and WCW wrestling. More good

news followed in the 2000 fiscal year, including the conclusion of a multiyear license agreement with Marvel Entertainment Group, Inc. whereby Topps would produce sticker/album collections and confectionery items based on Marvel Super Hero Universe characters, such as the X-Men and Spider-Man. Most important, Topps began to profit handsomely from the Pokémon craze among children with the introduction of trading cards, lollipops, and other products during 1999. Topps expected to ring up Pokémon-related sales as high as $100 million for the 2000 fiscal year.

Principal Subsidiaries

Topps Argentina S.A.; Topps Brasil, Ltda. (Brazil); Topps Canada, Inc.; Topps Europe Limited (U.K.); Topps Ireland Limited; Topps Italia SRL; Topps Mexico LLC; Topps UK Limited.

Principal Competitors

Huhtamaki Oy; Marvel Entertainment Group, Inc.; Nabisco Holdings Corp.; Tootsie Roll Industries, Inc.; The Upper Deck Company, LLC; Warner-Lambert Company; Wm. Wrigley Jr. Company.

Further Reading

Ambrosius, Greg, "The History of Topps," *Topps Magazine*, July 1995, pp. 8–13.
——, "Leading Topps Profitably into the 21st Century," *Topps Magazine*, July 1995, pp. 14–15.
——, "One on One with Sy Berger," *Topps Magazine*, July 1995, pp. 16–18.
Baldo, Anthony, "Topps' Stock: The Game Is Over," *Financial World*, April 5, 1988, p. 18.
Bleiberg, Robert M., "Topp of the Market? Baseball Cards Can't Keep Going Up Forever," *Barron's*, June 27, 1988, p. 9.
Jaffe, Thomas, "Topps Pick," *Forbes*, April 30, 1990, p. 456.
Krause, David S., "Baseball Cards Bat .425," *Money*, June 1988, pp. 140–46.
Lazo, Shirley A., "Payment by Topps a Strikeout Victim," *Barron's*, December 19, 1994, p. 32.
Lesly, Elizabeth, "A Burst Bubble at Topps," *Business Week*, August 23, 1993, p. 74.
McLoone, Margo, and Alice Siegel, *Sports Cards, Collecting, Trading, and Playing*, New York: Random House, 1979.
Rubel, Chad, "Players' Strike Hurting Baseball Card Sales," *Marketing News*, January 30, 1995, p. 2.
Sanders, Lisa, "Topps Fights for Bottom Line: Trading-Card Slide Gums Up Works," *Crain's New York Business*, January 19, 1998, p. 4.
Slocum, Frank, *Topps Baseball Cards: The Complete Picture Collection, A 40 Year History, 1951–1990*, New York: Warner Books, 1990.
Teitelbaum, Richard S., "Timeliness Is Everything," *Fortune*, April 20, 1992, pp. 120–21.
"Tempting Takeover Morsels That Could Gain 38% Plus," *Money*, September 1994, p. 62.
Topps Football Cards: The Complete Picture Collection: A History, 1956–1986, New York: Warner Books, 1986.
Welsh, Jonathan, "Trading-Card Firm Hopes Legacy of Mickey Mantle Will End Slump," *Wall Street Journal*, January 17, 1996, p. B9.

—John Myers-Kearns
—updated by David E. Salamie

Travis Perkins plc

Lodge Way House
Harlestone Rd.
Northampton NN5 7UG
United Kingdom
Telephone: (+44) 1604-752-424
Fax: (+44) 1604-587-244
Web site: http://www.travisperkins.co.uk

Public Company
Incorporated: 1988
Employees: 7,000
Sales: £874.3 million (US$1.31 billion) (1999)
Stock Exchanges: London
Ticker Symbol: TPK
NAIC: 444190 Building Materials Supply Dealers

Fast-growing Travis Perkins plc ranks as one of the top three building materials retailers in the United Kingdom, alongside rival Meyer International and behind longtime leader Wolseley. Travis Perkins operates more than 450 branch stores throughout the United Kingdom, under the trade names Travis Perkins Trading Company, Keyline, and D.W. Archer. In all, Travis Perkins' stores stock more than 60,000 items for a customer base drawn almost exclusively from the small builder market. As such, the company has avoided entry into the DIY consumer market. About 50 percent of the company's sales come from building materials and tool rentals; sales of woods contribute another 25 percent of Travis Perkins' annual revenues, while plumbing and heating systems and supplies round out the remainder of the company's sales, which neared £875 million in 1999. Travis Perkins' chain of D.W. Archer stores specializes in the importing, machining, and sales of softwoods, with a focus on wood roofing products. Travis Perkins has joined wholeheartedly into the consolidation of the U.K.'s building materials market. The company has doubled in size since the mid-1990s; in 1999 alone the company made some 18 acquisitions, including that of Keyline, from the CRH Manufacturing Company in Ireland, adding more than 100 Keyline branch stores, and the 38-store chain of Sharpe & Fisher stores, primarily located in

southwest England. The addition of multilingual Frank J. Mc-Kay as company chief executive in 1999 suggests that Travis Perkins is ready to make the leap from its concentration on domestic operations to becoming an international company for the new century.

18th-Century Origins

Travis Perkins itself was the result of a series of significant mergers, which allowed the company to trace its roots back to the late years of the 18th century. One of the company's earliest components was founded in 1797, by Benjamin Ingram, a carpenter, on Beech Street in London. For most of the first half of the next century, the Ingram company operated principally as joiners and carpenters. The changing consumer furniture tastes, from furniture crafted from elm and oak to mahogany, led Ingram to begin supplying hardwoods to third-party joiners and carpenters. This activity in turn led the Ingram company to join with a competitor, operated by the Perkins family. The resulting company was renamed Ingram Perkins, a name it maintained until the 1970s.

Ingram Perkins continued to grow through the 20th century, adding to its number of branch stores in a series of acquisitions. The company's biggest acquisition came in 1970, when Ingram Perkins merged with Sandell Smythe & Drayson—which had been founded in 1785—combining the companies' names under the single banner Sandell Perkins. Sandell Perkins went public in 1986. Two years later, during a consolidation wave then sweeping the United Kingdom's building materials industry, Sandell Perkins merged with Travis & Arnold, of Northhampton.

Travis & Arnold had been founded by Ernest Travis in 1899. Originally operating in London, the company moved to Northampton in 1904. The Midlands became the company's core market, while later expansion took Travis & Arnold into the southwest of England as well. Travis & Arnold's original focus was on the timber and wood products supply side. In the later half of the 20th century, however, Travis & Arnold began to expand its product line, moving into building materials and plumbing supplies. After going public in 1964, Travis & Arnold began making acquisitions, primarily of regional building mate-

Company Perspectives:

To be the most successful company in supplying Timber, Building Materials and Tool Hire from a network of trading branches. Goals: Market Leadership and Financial Strength: To maximise market strength through profitability whilst offering optimum returns on investment. Service and Value for Money: To establish Travis Perkins as the name most renowned for superior service and value for money. Customer Care: To surpass competitors in the anticipation and satisfaction of customer needs. Employment Standards: To maintain exemplary standards within the working environment that attract and retain employees who share a mutual interest in the success of the company. Environment Commitment: To pursue business with respect for environmental concerns locally, nationally and internationally. To achieve these goals we must guarantee: an exceptional, professional level of service and customer care; a continuous programme of service and product training for employees with regular personal appraisals; that customers are made aware that Travis Perkins recognizes their importance and value; to actively investigate and act upon the changing needs of customers; that all communications present a consistent and distinctive corporate identity and character; to cultivate a management style which encourages team work and recognizes change as an opportunity; to sell goods of a proven merchantable quality; to continuously appraise product quality and range, to reflect the requirements of our customers.

Key Dates:

1797:	Benjamin Ingram is founded as a carpentry/joiner shop.
1850s:	Ingram adds hardwood sales to third parties and is renamed Ingram Perkins.
1899:	Travis & Arnold is founded.
1964:	Travis & Arnold goes public.
1970:	Ingram Perkins merges with Sandell Smythe & Dawson and is renamed Sandell Perkins.
1986:	Sandell Perkins goes public.
1988:	Sandell Perkins and Travis & Arnold merge to form Travis Perkins.
1990s:	Company embarks on a period of key acquisitions.
2000:	Travis Perkins announces plans to add 100 new branches before 2002.

rials merchants, such as Page Calnan, Kennedys, and Ellis & Everard's building supplies division. Helping to lead the company was Tony Travis, the grandson of the company's founder.

Sandall Perkins and Travis & Arnold merged in 1988. The resulting company, renamed Travis Perkins plc, boasted a nationwide network of more than 150 stores. Tony Travis took on the dual roles of chairman and chief executive officer. The newly merged company ran headlong into trouble—by the end of the 1980s, the U.K. building market had collapsed. As the country entered into the extended recession of the 1990s, Travis Perkins began to struggle, and by 1991 the company was forced to restructure its operations, taking steps that included the slashing of some 13 percent of its total employees.

Acquisition Drive in the 1990s

Yet the recession and building slump also spelled opportunity for the company. As its smaller rivals faltered, Travis Perkins and its larger competitors, including Meyer International and Wolseley, launched a drive to consolidate the highly fragmented building materials supply industry in the United Kingdom. In 1992, Travis Perkins made its first new acquisition, picking up Ashton Vernon. In 1994 the company added the 46-store chain of AAH building materials stores; the following year it added the 26-store chain of BMSS building materials merchants. With more than 214 branches after the AAH merger, the company had taken a place among the top five in its industry.

With nearly 4,000 employees by 1996, Travis Perkins took a breather from its acquisition drive, while working on integrating its newly acquired operations. The Ashton Vernon, AAH, and BMSS trade names, initially kept in service, were phased out, as stores were converted to the Travis Perkins Trading Company signage. The upturn in the economy beginning in the mid-1990s gave new impetus to Travis Perkins' growth. By the end of 1997, the company was back on its acquisition trail, most notably with the December 1997 purchase of W.H. Newson Holding Limited, and that company's seven-branch timber and builders materials supply stores based in the London area. The company's sales for the year neared £269 million, for net profits of £22 million.

The following year saw Travis Perkins step up its expansion campaign. In January 1998, the company acquired Winser Limited, a drainage merchant specialist operating in North London; two months later, Travis Perkins acquired seven timber and building materials stores as well as two rafter manufacturing facilities when the company purchased Sherry & Haycock. At the same time, the company was preparing an additional acquisition, that of Direct Building Products Limited, completed by the end of March 1998. Together with the company's organic growth—generated through a buoyant market for new housing—Travis Perkins' new acquisitions helped boost the company's revenues to £623 million for the year.

Throughout 1998, Travis Perkins continued making small-scale acquisitions, adding a total of 13 new acquisitions in that year. Yet, the company was already preparing an acquisition on a far larger scale that was to boost it to a solid place among the United Kingdom's top three building materials suppliers. That acquisition came in April 1999, when Travis Perkins announced that it was buying Keyline Builders Merchants, the U.K.'s number five builders' merchant, for £181.5 million. The Keyline acquisition, from CRH of Ireland, added more than 100 new branches, located primarily in the northeast of England and Scotland, complementing Travis Perkins' midlands and southern strengths.

Six months later, Travis Perkins added a new trophy, when it acquired the 38 branch stores of Sharpe & Fisher plc. The company completed the year with the addition of Baseline

Building Supplies Ltd., adding that company's four Devon-area branch stores. While announcing its intention to slow down the pace of new acquisitions, in order to integrate the Keyline and Sharpe & Fisher operations, Travis Perkins also announced that it had taken on CEO Frank J. McKay, formerly of Blueline. McKay's international expertise was expected to aid Travis Perkins as it faced an impasse in the mature U.K. market. With few growth chances left in its home market, Travis Perkins was beginning to see a need to establish itself as an internationally operating company.

The absorption of the Keyline and Sharpe & Fisher operations proved easier than initially forecasted, allowing Travis Perkins to return its attention to the business of growth through acquisition. While large-scale acquisition prospects in the United Kingdom had become scarce, the company looked forward to the addition of a number of small-scale purchases, including two made in January 2000 which boosted its network to more than 465 stores. By March 2000, the company was able to announce its plans to increase its position in the U.K. market by an additional 100 stores before the end of 2002. The market also appeared favorable for organic growth, with suggestions that the company might consider opening a number of ''greenfield'' stores in the early years of the new century. Closing out its 1999 year with sales of nearly £875 million, Travis Perkins had built a solid foundation for its future growth.

Principal Subsidiaries

Travis Perkins Trading Company Limited; D.W. Archer Limited; Travis Perkins (Properties) Limited.

Principal Competitors

Caradon plc; Meyer International PLC; RMC Group p.l.c.; Wolseley plc.

Further Reading

Anderson, Simon, ''Builders' Merchants Trio Tighten Market Grip,'' *Daily Telegraph*, October 26, 1999.

Clark, Andrew, ''Travis Perkins Stacks up the Ballast,'' *Daily Telegraph*, October 26, 1999.

Trefgame, George, ''Travis Perkins Lifts Profile with Keyline Acquisition,'' *Daily Telegraph*, April 29, 1999, p. 67.

——, ''Travis Perkins Profits Build Up,'' *Daily Telegraph*, March 10, 2000.

——, ''Travis Perkins Still Buying,'' *Financial Times*, March 10, 2000.

—M. L. Cohen

Triarc Companies, Inc.

280 Park Avenue
New York, New York 10017
U.S.A.
Telephone: (212) 451-3000
Fax: (212) 230-3023
Web site: http://www.triarc.com

Public Company
Incorporated: 1929 as Deisel-Wemmer-Gilbert Corp.
Employees: 1,800
Sales: $853.97 million (1999)
Stock Exchanges: New York
Ticker Symbol: TRY
NAIC: 551112 Offices of Other Holding Companies;
    312111 Soft Drink Manufacturing; 311942 Spice and
    Extract Manufacturing; 53311 Lessors of Nonfinancial
    Intangible Assets (Except Copyrighted Works); 42272
    Petroleum and Petroleum Products Wholesalers
    (Except Bulk Stations and Terminals)

Triarc Companies, Inc. operates as a beverage producer, a producer of soft drink concentrates, and as a franchiser of restaurants, marketing well-known brand names that include Snapple, Mistic, Stewart's, Royal Crown Cola, and Arby's. Triarc was created in 1993 as the result of a court-ordered reorganization of the DWG Corporation, whose century-long existence established some of the businesses Triarc's management inherited. The company is led by Chairman and CEO Nelson Peltz, who spearheaded the transformation of the company into a branded consumer products concern.

19th-Century Birth of a Cigar Enterprise

Triarc's predecessor, DWG, had two very different lives. The company was first established in 1890 as a small Ohio-based partnership. The founders of the Deisel-Wemmer Company (their full names have disappeared into obscurity) dealt in the importation and manufacturing of cigars. Highly popular during the early years of the 20th century, cigars were a com-

mon male accessory that indicated discretion, affluence, and manliness. The cigar trade was a very profitable business, populated with hundreds of specialty manufacturers.

Deisel-Wemmer was subsequently acquired by an investment group on January 23, 1929, and changed its name to Deisel-Wemmer-Gilbert. The new firm continued to operate as a formidable cigar manufacturer, although not on the same scale as large tobacco companies that maintained stables of several mass-produced brands. Unable to compete with the marketing muscle of these large tobacco combines, the Deisel-Wemmer-Gilbert company was forced to acquire other small competitors simply to maintain market share. It purchased the brand and manufacturing operations of Odin cigars in 1930 and the Bernard Schwartz Cigar Corporation in 1939. On May 15, 1946, the company reduced its cumbersome name to a simple set of initials, and became the DWG Cigar Corporation. The series of acquisitions resumed in 1948, when DWG took over the Nathan Elson Company. In 1955 DWG acquired A. Sensenbrenner & Sons, and a year later bought out Chicago Motor Club Cigar and Reading, Pennsylvania-based Yocum Brothers.

By this time, however, the cigar market had weakened substantially. Years of doctors' advisories about the dangers of smoking, the rise of cancer deaths among smokers, and growing public intolerance with the socially brash habit caused many men to quit. But perhaps most responsible for the demise of cigar smoking was the cigarette industry. Convinced that they should abandon cigars, many men simply switched to cigarettes, which were less obtrusive and carried a less severe health stigma. In addition, cigarette advertising was feverish during the 1950s and led smokers to believe that they gained status by using brands such as Lucky Strike, Chesterfield, and Camel.

The trend toward cigarettes spelled the end for DWG's cigar operations. Quite gradually, the company began to consider other lines of business where its wholesale and distribution skills could be effectively employed. In the meantime, DWG reorganized its stagnant but still profitable tobacco operations. The company purchased the M. Trelles Company in New Orleans in 1961, and in 1963 formed a new subsidiary in Columbia to oversee the company's South American buying and processing operations. By this time, several other cigar operations had

---

Company Perspectives:

The key elements of our business strategy include: focusing our resources on our consumer products businesses— beverage and restaurant franchising; building strong oper- ating management teams for each of the businesses; and providing strategic leadership and financial resources to enable the management teams to develop and implement specific, growth-oriented business plans.

---

been wound up, and the product line was slimmed down. This process helped to derive new efficiencies from DWG's cigar business, but also compacted the widely varied operations into a single unit that could be disposed of quickly and easily.

Victor Posner-Led Diversification Begins in the 1960s

Ready to plunge into new markets, DWG began purchasing small stakes in other businesses, including consumer products. After an attempted takeover of the Allegheny Pepsi bottling company failed in 1965, the New York Stock Exchange delisted DWG from the big board. This removed the final obstacle that prevented DWG from a wholesale divestment of its cigar opera- tions. The dying business was sold in one chunk, while some smaller assets were simply written off. The 1966 sell-off pro- vided DWG with millions of dollars in new acquisition capital. In November 1966—coincident with the company's adoption of a new name, DWG Corporation—the hunt for new busi- nesses turned up an unexpected candidate. DWG purchased a 12 percent share of the National Propane Corporation. Far removed from the cigar business, National Propane marked a clean break from DWG's earlier business ventures.

But it was also at this time that a new force behind DWG came into the picture. Run for decades as a quiet company with a typical consensus-management leadership, DWG became domi- nated by an institutional shareholder called Security Management Company, headed by Victor Posner. Posner began in business at the age of 13, amassing a small pool of capital by delivering groceries for his father. While still a teenager in the 1930s, Posner began buying run-down houses in his native Baltimore. Report- edly, he realized huge gains on his investments by reselling the houses to economically depressed urban blacks. Aware that peo- ple could more easily afford the homes if he retained ownership of the land, Posner's Security Management Company charged buyers a small amount of rent for the land the houses sat upon. Failure to pay land rent could result in foreclosure. This practice earned Posner the unsavory reputation of slumlord. It was this business, however, that formed the basis of Posner's real estate operation and made him a millionaire at an early age.

In 1956, having grown weary of real estate transactions, Posner retired to Sunset Island near Miami. He spent the next ten years without engaging in commercial activity. Posner found a new hobby in 1966, when he began dabbling more actively in the stock market. Familiar with the practice of trading blocks of shares for small profits, Posner now decided to get more deeply involved in the companies he targeted. One of these companies was DWG. Having witnessed DWG's bold but

slow transformation from a sleepy cigar company into a corpo- rate raider, Posner saw huge numbers of investors abandon DWG for its failure to maintain a big board listing. From his experience in real estate, he looked upon DWG differently. Rather than seeing a shrinking company in the middle of a huge transition, he saw an undervalued firm with substantial assets.

But for Victor Posner, DWG was more than a great invest- ment. He decided to use the company as an investment vehicle, engineering additional takeovers of other firms through DWG. In January 1967, Posner used DWG to purchase a controlling share of Wilson Brothers, then a failing shirtmaking concern. Later that year, DWG collected an additional 77 percent of the shares of National Propane. In 1969 DWG acquired 40 percent of the Southeastern Public Service Company, a medium-size utility maintenance and storage company, and the following year increased that holding to more than 50 percent.

DWG became the controlling agent for only half of Posner's empire. He used another company, the vulcanized fiber manu- facturer NVF, to build up a controlling interest in Pennsylvania- based Sharon Steel Corp., one of the country's largest specialty steel manufacturers.

As Posner grew more active, company presidents across the United States feared that their daily mail would bring a dreaded schedule 13D. This Securities and Exchange Commission (SEC) filing announced that someone had acquired more than five percent of their company's shares. Posner had an unusual talent for inspiring wrath in his dealings. He was often attacked, and frequently sued, for installing himself as chairman and chief executive of companies he had taken over. With the titles came paychecks, and Posner drew reasonable compensation from each of his companies. Collectively, however, Posner was one of the highest paid executives in the country, surpassing the heads of IT&T, Exxon, General Motors, and Ford Motor Com- pany. Posner also employed his son and two brothers in impor- tant positions in his growing corporate empire. In addition, Posner's Security Management Company, the ultimate parent of DWG and NVF, still collected land rent from the homes he sold in Baltimore.

In 1971 the SEC sued Posner for improperly compelling the pension fund of Sharon Steel to invest in Posner properties. Some shareholders lambasted Posner at shareholder meetings and threatened to take him to court. These actions were only occasionally successful. Posner's defense was to simply point to the track record of companies he had taken over. Both DWG and Wilson had been ''dead on arrival,'' yet Posner resuscitated them. Other successful companies such as National Propane, NVF, and Sharon Steel were only marginally profitable before Posner became involved with them. Nonetheless, Posner settled his SEC suit by agreeing not to sit on his companies' pension boards. But this did little to improve his image in the business community. Posner's usual recipe for turning companies around mirrored his strategy with Sharon Steel; after gaining control of the steelmaker in 1969, he eliminated a quarter of the salaried jobs and held whomever remained to ambitious productivity goals. Costs were reduced, and output increased.

By 1976, Posner's Security Management Company con- trolled 67 percent of DWG's shares. In addition, the parent

Key Dates:

1890: Earliest predecessor, Deisel-Wemmer Co., begins manufacturing and importing cigars.

1929: Deisel-Wemmer is acquired by investment group and incorporated as Deisel-Wemmer-Gilbert Corp.

1946: Company's name is changed to DWG Cigar Corporation.

1966: Victor Posner begins to exert his influence on the development of DWG Corporation.

1984: Posner-controlled DWG acquires Royal Crown Cola and Arby's.

1992: Posner resigns as chairman of DWG; his shares are acquired by Trian Group, led by Nelson Peltz.

1993: DWG's name is changed to Triarc Companies, Inc.

1995: Mistic Brands, Inc. is acquired.

1997: Two beverage brands, Snapple and Stewart's, are acquired.

1999: Triarc completes its transformation into a consumer products company by selling National Propane.

company held a 44 percent share of NVF and another quasi-investment vehicle, the Pennsylvania Engineering Corporation, a steelmaking equipment manufacturer which Posner acquired in 1966. In turn, DWG held 51 percent of Southeast Public Service Company, 42 percent of Wilson Brothers and 100 percent of National Propane. Posner's corporate conglomerate held few synergies—particularly within DWG. Through his other companies, Posner bought small shares of Burnup & Simms, a small utility service company; UV Industries, a smelting and mining company; and Foremost-McKesson, a large food and drug company. With these similarly undervalued companies in play, and the 13D form on each president's desk, these companies scrambled to keep Posner out of their boardrooms. Their defense strategies varied. Foremost-McKesson sought out a rival bidder and UV Industries broke up. Even in cases where the companies bought up their own shares, Posner usually emerged with a handsome profit. If he met no resistance, he ended up with yet another undervalued company to turn around.

DWG traded over the counter since it was delisted by the New York Stock Exchange. Its share value fluctuated, nearly in the penny stock range, between one and four dollars. But for all its accessibility came volatility. The company could double its value in one year or plunge by half. Over the long run, however, businesses such as steel manufacturing and casting and DWG's storage operations were capable of operating with little additional investment beyond basic maintenance. As long as they continued operating, the combination of taxation, inadequate maintenance, and inflation had the effect of liquidating these marginally performing assets. Posner was allegedly draining them of resources to take advantage of high depreciation on his undervalued properties.

Meanwhile, Posner continued to use DWG to acquire other companies. In 1982 the company took over the Graniteville Company, a textile manufacturer based in South Carolina. In 1984 DWG built up a 25 percent share of Axia Incorporated, and completed a deal in which its Southeastern Public Service

subsidiary acquired Royal Crown Cola, the Arby's fast food restaurant chain, a Texas grapefruit grove, and numerous other small companies. Later that year, DWG added the Evans Products fiber group, and in 1985 took over the Fischbach Corp., an electrical contracting business.

This flurry of activity proved to be the undoing of Victor Posner. The acquisition spree and subsequent earnings failures placed DWG deeply in debt. On more than one occasion Posner was forced to seek a financial bailout from one of his backers, Carl H. Lindner. Their friendly relationship came to an abrupt end in 1986 when Posner received his own 13D schedule, indicating that Lindner's American Financial Corporation had acquired warrants for more than 30 percent of DWG's shares. Posner had become a victim in the takeover game. DWG was rich in assets, had steady cash flow, and was undervalued. It was exactly the kind of company that Posner himself would target. But rather than exercise his warrants on the beleaguered DWG, Lindner presented Posner with a contract that capped the chairman's salary at $3 million—down from $8.4 million the previous year.

Meanwhile, Posner worked to shore up DWG's balance sheet by disposing of the Foxcroft and Enro shirt groups and the citrus operation, while a $200 million deal for Royal Crown fell through. He also had the benefit of talented outside managers, including Leonard Roberts, whom he hired to run Royal Crown after his acquisition of that company caused Arby's management to resign en masse. He had also placed Harold Kingsmore, a veteran of the Cannon and Avondale textile companies, in charge of Graniteville.

While the threat from Lindner subsided, another far more complex battle emerged. A financier that Posner had retained to pull Sharon Steel out of bankruptcy referred a possible sale of Posner's Fischbach electrical contracting unit to his lawyer, Andrew Heine. When it appeared the deal would go through, Heine suddenly backed out and launched a bid for all of DWG. Once again, Posner was on the defensive. He immediately converted his DWG options into voting shares, but was ordered not to vote them by an Ohio judge.

Heine, through his Granada Investments Company, sued Posner for failing to take his $22 per share bid for DWG seriously. Posner countersued, maintaining that the bid was without merit. In 1991 Posner lost to Heine, whose company was awarded $5.5 million for its expenses. In addition, Judge Thomas D. Lambros, noting court investigations of Posner's compensation and charges of illegal stock trading to acquire Fischbach, appointed three directors to DWG's board, with responsibility for the company's audit, compensation, and intercorporate transactions committees.

By the end of 1991, the three directors appointed by Lambros had presented Posner with a critical report on his dealings with DWG. Posner, with eight solid votes on a board of 13, adjourned meetings to discuss the report. In response, Judge Lambros converted half of Posner's share in DWG into nonvoting preferred shares and compelled Posner to sell the remaining common shares. Posner, battered by years of damaging litigation, resigned his chairmanship of DWG in 1992 and walked off with $77 million from his share sales. In return, shareholders agreed to drop their longstanding lawsuits charging the 73-year-old raider with plundering DWG. His shares were purchased by the Trian Group, a New York-based investment partnership led by Nelson Peltz and Peter May.

Trian, the parent company of Triangle Wire and Cable, had amassed a series of canning and packaging companies during the 1980s. They sold Triangle Industries, the parent company of American National Can, to Pechiney S.A. for $1.36 billion. This provided the necessary investment capital to purchase DWG. Trian declared that it had no plans to break up DWG or raid its operations for capital to pay down debt. Instead, with good business prospects the partners proposed only to change the name of DWG to Triarc Companies, Inc.

Peltz was named chairman and chief executive officer of Triarc while May was named president and chief operating officer. The new team appointed a series of new heads for the company's subsidiaries. John Carson was put in charge of Royal Crown, Donald Pierce took over at Arby's, Ronald Paliughi headed National Propane, and Douglas Kingsmore was promoted to the top position at Graniteville. The ouster of Victor Posner, the change in management and, perhaps most importantly, the supervision of the company's activities by Judge Lambros did a great deal to shore up DWG's balance sheet and improve share value. These provided an important base for the company as it began its transformation into Triarc.

Triarc Takes Shape: 1990s

As Triarc set out, it comprised a jumbled mass of unrelated businesses assembled during the Posner era. Triarc's management was intent on giving the company what it had lacked for decades—a defined strategic focus—which meant shedding disparate assets such as lamp manufacturing operations and grapefruit groves and creating a company with a much narrower operating scope. Divestitures ensued, leaving the company focused on four areas of interest: soft drinks, fast food, textiles, and liquefied petroleum gas. The company's strategic focus would be sharpened further, but initially, amid a series of divestitures, attention had to be paid to resolving the operational difficulties bred under the controversial leadership of Posner. By 1995, much of the healing work was completed, enabling executives to devote their energies toward more positive work. With the proceeds gained from asset sales, Triarc assumed an acquisitive posture and began adopting the attributes that described the company at the start of the 21st century.

In August 1995, Triarc acquired the non-alcoholic beverage assets of Joseph Victori Wines, Inc. for $97 million. The purchase added greatly to the beverage business represented by Royal Crown Company, giving the company a new brand called Mistic, a leader in the "new age" beverage segment. Mistic, used as the brand name for a variety of fruit drinks, iced teas, and flavored sparkling waters, was suffering from a somewhat tarnished image, but soon after gaining control of the brand, Triarc restored profitability. In doing so, the company demonstrated its talent for improving relations with distributors, its flair for marketing, and its shrewdness in developing new products for an established brand. These qualities would come to define Triarc during its first decade of business.

By the time Triarc completed its next acquisition—one that would dwarf the purchase of Mistic—management had further refined what its core businesses included and what the company would become. Triarc's ties to the textile business were severed and its involvement in liquefied natural gas was slated to end as soon as an agreement could be reached to divest National Propane, leaving the company focused on two business segments: beverages and restaurants. Management had resolved to turn Triarc into a branded consumer products company, and moved headlong toward such an objective in 1997. In May, Triarc acquired Snapple Beverage Corporation, adding substantially to the branded beverage side of its business. Snapple was acquired from Quaker Oats, which had purchased the popular beverage company from its founders. Quaker Oats paid a staggering $1.7 billion for Snapple, and quickly saw its investment sour as the brand suffered several years of double-digit volume declines. Quaker Oats' mismanagement of the brand turned into Triarc's gain, enabling the company to purchase Snapple at the drastically reduced price of $300 million. Six months later, in November, Triarc bolstered its beverage business further by acquiring Cable Car Beverage Corporation, maker of Stewart's Root Beer and other flavors.

Like Mistic, Snapple was a company in distress when Triarc management took control of the once powerful brand. Quaker Oats had attempted to assimilate the brand into its corporate culture and, consequently, drained Snapple of its strength. The conglomerate began selling Snapple in supermarkets and other large retail channels, ignoring the brand's remarkable success in smaller retail formats, such as delicatessens and convenience stores. Distributors became disgruntled as sales declined, a situation exacerbated by the ouster of the widely popular Wendy Kaufman, who championed the product line in television commercials as "The Snapple Lady." Triarc, which had started to create a reputation for itself as a company with an ameliorative touch following its turnaround of Mistic, cemented its reputation as a savior by quickly reversing the damage done by Quaker Oats. The company worked on improving relations with distributors, rehired Kaufman, and returned Snapple to the retail locations where it had earned its popularity. By 1998, Snapple had regained its luster, buoyed by Triarc's skill as a marketer, which was typified in new product introductions. In April 1998, Triarc launched a new Snapple beverage called WhipperSnapple, a shelf-stable line of fruit smoothies in six flavors. WhipperSnapple was selected as the New Beverage Product of the Year by *Convenience Store News* and awarded the American Marketing Association's Edison Award for Best New Beverage of 1998.

As its beverage business blossomed, Triarc also achieved significant strides in its other business segment. In 1997, all the company-owned Arby's restaurants were sold as part of a strategic decision to operate exclusively as franchiser of the brand. Freed from its role as a restaurant operator, Triarc was able to direct all of its attention toward marketing the Arby's brand and promoting expansion of the concept. Management expanded the restaurant's menu by developing co-brands for Arby's franchisees, such as T.J. Cinnamons, which offered cinnamon rolls and premium coffees. In 1999, another Arby's co-brand, Pasta Connection, was nearing the end of its testing phase, promising the addition of pasta dishes to the Arby's concept.

As Triarc completed its first decade of business, executives completed the transformation of the company into a branded consumer products company. In 1999, Triarc sold its stake in National Propane, leaving it focused on the production and marketing of beverages and the marketing of its franchise restaurant systems. As the company prepared for the 21st century, further brand development in these two core business segments stood as the primary emphasis for the future.

Principal Subsidiaries

Triarc Consumer Products Group LLC; CFC Holdings Corporation; Mistic Brands Inc.; Cable Car Beverage Corporation; Snapple Beverage Corporation; Arby's, Inc.; Royal Crown Company Inc.

Principal Divisions

Triarc Beverage Group; Triarc Restaurant Group.

Principal Competitors

The Coca-Cola Company; McDonald's Corporation; PepsiCo, Inc.; Dr Pepper/7Up Companies, Inc.; KFC Corporation; International Dairy Queen, Inc.; Subway.

Further Reading

"Allegheny Pepsi Board Withdraws Approval of Merger with DWG," *Wall Street Journal,* July 13, 1965, p. 4.

"DWG Corp.," *Moody's Industrial Manual,* 1992, pp. 2913–2914.

"DWG Corp.," *Wall Street Journal,* February 13, 1991, p. C12.

"DWG Investor Group Sees No Sale of Assets," *New York Times,* September 8, 1992, p. C2.

"DWG to Seek the 11% of National Propane It Doesn't Already Hold," *Wall Street Journal,* May 30, 1975, p. 29.

"Is Victor Posner Off His Leash?" *Business Week,* December 30, 1991, p. 39.

"Loosening Posner's Iron Grip," *Business Week,* October 22, 1990, p. 104.

"The Man Who Writes His Own Paycheck," *Forbes,* March 15, 1974, pp. 55–58.

"Ohio Judge Prevents Posner from Voting New Block in DWG," *Wall Street Journal,* May 23, 1989, p. C17.

"Posner Agrees to Quit DWG," *New York Times,* October 5, 1992, p. D2.

"Posner Firms to Up Axia Stake," *American Metal Market,* October 13, 1983, p. 3.

"Posner Set to Reduce DWG Stake," *New York Times,* September 4, 1992, p. D3.

"The Posner Touch," *Barron's,* November 19, 1979, pp. 4–55.

Prince, Greg W., "A Triarc State of Mind," *Beverage World,* October 15, 1997, p. 44.

"Raider Vs. Raider: Is Lindner Stalking Posner?" *Business Week,* June 2, 1986, p. 36.

"There's Action Again in the Posner Suite," *Business Week,* March 29, 1976, pp. 108–14.

"Three Sparkling Turnarounds: Can This Really Be Victor Posner?" *Business Week,* July 27, 1987, pp. 56–57.

"Victor Posner May Soon Taste His Own Medicine," *Business Week,* April 10, 1989, pp. 34–36.

"Wall Street Talks," *Business Week,* November 4, 1967 p. 130.

—John Simley
—updated by Jeffrey L. Covell

TWINLAB®

Twinlab Corporation

150 Motor Parkway
Hauppauge, New York 11788
U.S.A.
Telephone: (516) 467-3140
Fax: (516) 630-3484
Web site: http://www.twinlab.com

Public Company
Incorporated: 1968 as Twin Laboratories, Inc.
Employees: 1,137
Sales: $315.6 million (1999)
Stock Exchanges: NASDAQ
Ticker Symbol: TWLB
NAIC: 325412 Pharmaceutical Preparations
Manufacturing; 51112 Periodical Publishers

Twinlab Corporation manufactures and distributes several hundred different vitamin, mineral, and herbal supplements and nutritional products, thus making it an industry leader. While about 63 percent of its products—such as Twinlab, Nature's Herbs, Changes, and Bronson vitamins and herbal supplements, Alvita Herbal Teas, and Triathlon and PR* Nutrition Bars—are sold in health food stores, the firm is increasing sales through mass retailers and supermarket chains as well, including Wal-Mart and Albertson's. Through its acquisitions Twinlab has also begun using a direct sales approach to customers using catalogs and multilevel marketing. In addition to nutritional products, the company publishes *Muscular Development* magazine and a variety of books on nutrition and fitness. Although 94 percent of Twinlab sales are in the United States, its products are sold in 70 nations. Twinlab operates two production and distribution plants: its historic facility in Ronkonkoma, New York, and one in American Fork, Utah, built in the 1990s.

Origins and a Major Obstacle to Overcome

In 1968 David Blechman, a pharmaceutical detail man, had an idea for a liquid protein product. He and his wife, Jean Blechman, both quit their jobs and with very limited funds between them started Twin Laboratories in their family garage. The firm was named in honor of the founders' two sets of twins.

Sales of Twin Labs' only product, liquid protein, skyrocketed in the 1970s, as liquid protein diet supplements gained widespread fame, in part from the success of a 1976 book entitled *The Last Chance Diet—When Everything Else Has Failed: Dr. Linn's Protein-Sparing Fast Program.* Dr. Robert Linn, a Pennsylvania osteopath, had begun prescribing for his overweight patients a program of fasting and four- to six-ounce daily doses of liquid protein. By 1977 Linn and his staff of 60 were treating over 1,500 patients annually at New York, Philadelphia, Delaware, and Washington, D.C., clinics. At the same time, at least two million people bought Linn's book to read about the latest weight-loss fad diet. This helped spark sales for Twin Labs' over-the-counter liquid protein.

However, the fasting/liquid protein craze came to a halt in the late 1970s. In late 1976 and early 1977 reports of the deaths of people who had followed Linn's diet surfaced, 58 in total. A U.S. Food and Drug Administration (FDA) investigation found that many of the program participants were ingesting fewer than 400 calories a day, and that very low calorie protein diets could cause serious illness or death. The findings and itinerant coverage of what had become a popular diet and its potential side effects, in such magazines as *Newsweek*, *Parents' Magazine*, and *Science Digest,* devastated the liquid protein market, and Twin Labs as well. The company's sales hit rock bottom, as product inventory that formerly sold in one week took two years to sell.

In response to almost nonexistent sales, Twin Labs was forced in the late 1970s to cut almost its entire workforce, which had grown to 150 since the company's founding. Only David and Jean Blechman and their five sons—Ross, Neil, Brian, Steve, and Dean—remained. In spite of the near-collapse, the Blechmans did not quit. "It was a little speed bump along the way," said Ross Blechman, in a videotaped interview, adding "We swore on that day that we'd never let the company be a one-product company."

Diversification and Competition in the 1980s

Twin Labs soon diversified by formulating new vitamin and nutritional supplements. The company also pioneered the use of two-piece hard capsules and time-released herbs. By the 1980s company sales reached $100 million, and the company kept

Company Perspectives:

Twinlab Corporation's mission is to be the best-in-class nutritional and wellness company delivering high quality, innovative products and services globally.

growing. The Blechmans by this time were publishing their own fitness and bodybuilding magazine called *Muscular Development* through an associated family business known as Advanced Research Press.

The nutrition/fitness industry began to boom in the late 1980s, and competition became fairly intense. Among Twin Labs' competitors during this time was Weider Health & Fitness, a supplier of sports nutrition supplements. During this time, Twin Labs had sought to run ads in the two muscle-building and fitness magazines published by Weider, and was denied the opportunity. In response, Twin Labs filed a lawsuit against Weider, in February 1989, for restricting competition.

U.S. District Judge Michael Mukasey dismissed all of Twin's antitrust and tort claims, stating that Weider had made a "legitimate and responsible business decision" by refusing Twin Labs' ads, according to the April 11, 1990 *Wall Street Journal*. Moreover, in 1990 a federal appellate court panel upheld Judge Mukasey's decision, finding that Twin "has remained an effective competitor" without advertising in Weider publications. In a reference to famous muscle-building ads published for many years by Charles Atlas, the appeals court also noted that Twin Labs "is not a 90-pound weakling in whose face Weider has kicked sand. Rather, (Twin Labs) is a muscular competitor who is complaining about the competitive process."

Meanwhile, the Blechmans had begun to grow their holdings through acquisition, purchasing in 1989 NaturPharma, Inc., of Orem, Utah. NaturPharma was a well established producer of herbal products founded as Nature's Herbs, Inc. by Grace Larsen and well-known herbalist John R. Christopher, whom many herbalists regarded as "the pioneer of today's herb renaissance," according to Robert Conrow and Arlene Hecksel in their book *Herbal Pathfinders*. In 1968 Larsen and Christopher started a small herb shop/health food store in Orem and began making their own herbal products. Christopher eventually sold Grace Larsen and her husband, Ernie Larsen, the rights to his herbal products. On January 1, 1988 the firm changed its name to NaturPharma, Inc. The company employed 53 individuals and made over 150 products, marketed under such brands as Nature's Herbs, Herb Masters' Original Formulas, HealthCare Naturals, Certified Potency Power-Herbs, and Pro-Pharma.

NaturPharma was just one of several natural products corporations based or started in Utah; others included Sunrider, Nu Skin, Murdock Madaus Schwabe, Weider Nutrition, Shaperite Concepts, Enrich International, and Nature's Sunshine. By the early 1990s, this concentration of herbal and supplement corporations in Utah, with ties to traditional Mormon use of plant remedies, generated about $1 billion annually and had acquired some political clout as well.

In 1994, Utah Senator Orrin Hatch sponsored the Dietary Supplement Health and Education Act, backed by the Utah

Natural Products Alliance, a Salt Lake City trade group to which NaturPharma belonged. The act sought to prevent the FDA from controlling nutritional supplements as it did prescription drugs, and its passage represented a major victory for the nation's growing supplement and herbal industry. As reported in *The Buying of the President 2000*, Hatch stated that "My bottom-line goal is to allow the one hundred million Americans who regularly consume dietary supplements to continue to reap the ever-growing body of science indicating that dietary supplements can promote health." Of course, some noted that in addition to an interest in health, Hatch maintained a list of long-term financial supporters that included Herbalife and Weider Nutrition, and that Amway Corporation, maker of popular Nutrilite supplements, was another large contributor to Republican politicians.

In 1991 the Blechman family followed its purchase of NaturPharma with the acquisition of Alvita Herbal Teas, a family firm started in 1922 to market alfalfa leaf tea. From modest beginnings in Huntington Beach, California, Alvita gradually added different kinds of herbal teas to its product line, using raw tea ingredients grown all over the world and purchased from distributors within the United States. Following its acquisition, Alvita moved its packaging operations to Twin Labs' facilities on Long Island.

Expansion of production facilities soon became necessary, and in 1993 NaturPharma built a new plant in American Fork, Utah, just a few miles north of its first location in Orem. On a 4.5-acre site in the Utah Valley Business Park, the new 48,000-square-foot building tripled NaturPharma's manufacturing capability and also provided space for other Twin companies. The new facility proved an ideal spot for much of Alvita's operations too, and in 1994 Alvita made the transition from New York to American Fork, Utah.

Reorganizing a Health Empire in the 1990s

By the mid-1990s, the Blechman family holdings had become considerable, and plans were for another acquisition spree, some management changes, and a debut as a public company. In preparation, they formed Twinlab Corporation in 1996, a holding company for the Blechman interests. Thus came together Twin Laboratories Inc.; Twinlab Export Corporation; Twinlab Specialty Corporation; Alvita Products, Inc.; Natur-Pharma, Inc.; B. Bros. Realty Corporation; and Advanced Research Press, Inc. under the parent umbrella of Twinlab Corporation. Also during this time, subsidiary Twin Labs announced that it would sell a 55 percent ownership stake to Leonard Green & Partners, a Los Angeles merchant banking company, for $225 million cash.

With a new corporate structure in place, founders David and Jean Blechman resigned from the board, though they would continue to serve as consultants. Their five sons retained majority control of the firm's eight-member board of directors, while three executives from Leonard Green began serving on the board as well. Ross Blechman was named chairman, president, and chief executive officer of Twinlab, while his four brothers—Brian, Neil, Steve, and Dean—became executive vice-presidents. On November 16, 1996, Twinlab completed the firm's initial public offering of common stock, with the sale of 8.5 million shares at $12 per share on the NASDAQ.

Key Dates:

1968: David and Jean Bleckman found Twin Laboratories.
1977: Sales of Twin Labs' liquid protein product plummet.
1980s: Twin Labs enters the vitamin market.
1989: NaturPharma Inc., with its Nature's Herbs brand name, is acquired.
1996: Company is incorporated as Twinlab Corporation and completes its initial public offering on the NAS-DAQ.
1997: Twinlab embarks on an acquisition program and debuts its web site, called The Health Lab.
1998: *Nutritional Outlook* honors Twinlab as its "Manufacturer of the Year."

The following year, Twinlab entered the multilevel marketing arena when it acquired Changes International, a firm started in 1994 by Scott and Terry Paulson. The new subsidiary offered its own line of nutritional supplements and weight-loss products. According to a company-sponsored article in *Money Maker's Monthly*, the firm's flagship product was Thermo-Lift, a blend of minerals and herbs in capsule or caplet form to help people lose weight and increase their energy. Other Changes International products included protein bars and shakes, as well as a variety of supplements for adults and children.

Under Twinlab, Changes International received a new CEO, Steve Coggin, who came to the company from tenures at competitors Melaleuca and Avon products. Company founders Scott Paulson and Terry Paulson remained at Changes International as president and vice-president, respectively. Coggin oversaw a 1999 strategic alliance with ADoctorInYourHouse .com, a Beverly-Hills-based organization that offered a web site with celebrity endorsements, streaming video, and chat rooms to assist dieters. By early 2000 Changes International's distributors numbered about 100,000, some of whom had successfully expanded outside the United States. Based on good results in Canada and the United Kingdom, the company sought to establish a presence in many other areas including Europe, Australia, Japan, Mexico, South America, Singapore, and elsewhere.

In April 1998 Twinlab completed its purchase of the Bronson Nutritional Division of Jones Medical Industries, Inc. for $55 million in cash. Based in St. Louis, Missouri, Bronson manufactured and distributed over 350 vitamin and herbal supplements and health and beauty products through its catalogs and direct mailings, a sales venue Twinlab would exploit in earnest with the acquisition of the Bronson operations. Bronson contracted with other firms to make private-label supplements, while also producing and selling its own MD Pharmaceutical name brand, sold exclusively through U.S. military commissaries. With over 118,000 active customers, Bronson's annual revenues were about $31 million. Helping finance the Bronson purchase was another offering of common stock, eight million shares, at $36.5 per share.

Twinlab also acquired from Jones Medical Industries a company called Health Factors, International, based in Tempe,

Arizona, and formerly known as JMI-Phoenix Laboratories, Inc. Health Factors would make vitamins and nutritional products for Twinlab and some private-label distributors but did not manufacture its own brand names. The acquired Twinlab subsidiary had annual revenues of about $13.6 million.

In August 1998 Twinlab acquired San-Diego based PR* Nutrition, Inc., a company formed in the early 1990s by Bill Logue and Sheri Sears. Their main product, PR* Nutrition Bars, and other products developed later, used the controversial 40-30-30 formula in which 40 percent of daily calories come from carbohydrates and 30 percent each are derived from protein and dietary fat. Also known as the "Zone" diet, it was developed by Sheri Sears's brother Barry Sears, Ph.D. In the 1990s PR* Nutrition Bars competed against other 40-30-30 bars such as Balance Bars and BioZone Bars. PR* Nutrition also manufactured Ironman Triathlon Bars.

According to Twinlab's 1998 annual report, the company used three main distribution channels, the main one being health and natural food stores, with sales increasing from $164 million in 1996 to $193 million in 1997 and $212 million in 1998. The second largest category was direct sales from multilevel marketing, direct mailings, and catalog sales, which brought in $9.6 million in 1996, $17.1 million in 1997, and $70.5 million in 1998. Mass markets—drugstore chains, supermarkets, and mass market retailers—accounted for $2.8 million of 1996 sales, but this share rapidly increased to $14.1 million in 1997 and $47 million the following year.

By the late 1990s Twinlab faced increased competition as more companies realized the demand for nutritional and herbal supplements, especially from the approximately 76 million middle-aged baby boomers. Large corporations, such as American Home Products Corporation, Bayer Corporation, and Warner-Lambert, had all added herbal products to their lines by December 1998. As the playing field expanded to include major firms, supplement sales continued to rise, and stock values of many supplement firms plummeted. Twinlab's stock price declined 43 percent in 1998, while the stock prices of rivals Nature's Sunshine and Weider Nutrition International fell 39 and 48 percent, respectively.

Some skeptics argued that supplements were unnecessary if one had a good diet, and that in any case the products were often overpriced. However, vitamin and herbal products were generally becoming more accepted by medical doctors and other healthcare professionals. The federal government's creation of an agency to study alternative medicine helped legitimize what many in the medical establishment used to consider quackery.

Thus at the dawn of the new millennium, Twinlab faced the good news of increased consumer demand and growing acceptance by doctors while confronting the bad news of stiff competition from some much larger corporations. Although outside investors owned most of Twinlab, the company's management remained in the hands of the second generation of the Blechman family.

Principal Subsidiaries

Twin Laboratories Inc.; Advanced Research Press, Inc.; Changes International of Fort Walton Beach, Inc.; Bronson

Laboratories, Inc.; PR* Nutrition, Inc.; Health Factors International, Inc.

Principal Divisions

Alvita Herbal Teas; Nature's Herbs.

Principal Competitors

Herbalife International Inc.; Weider Nutrition International, Inc.; Nature's Way Products, Inc.; Nutraceutical International Corporation; Leiner Health Products Inc.; Pharmavite Corporation; Rexall Sundown, Inc.; Balance Bar Company; The Sunrider Corporation; Nature's Sunshine Products, Inc.

Further Reading

Bonventre, Peter, "The Protein Fad," *Newsweek*, December 19, 1977, p. 71.

Carricaburu, Lisa, "The Changing Nature of Supplements," *Salt Lake Tribune*, December 20, 1998, pp. E1, E4.

"Changes International," *Money Maker's Monthly*, February 2000, pp. 1, 4.

Clark, Matt, "Diet Crazes," *Newsweek*, December 19, 1977, pp. 66+.

Conrow, Robert, and Arlene Hecksel, editors, "John Christopher," in *Herbal Pathfinders: Voices of the Herb Renaissance,* Santa Barbara, Calif.: Woodbridge Press, 1983, pp. 230–35.

Cowley, Susan, "The No-Food Diet," *Newsweek*, July 11, 1977, p. 74.

Frank, Arthur, and Stuart Frank, "Fasting for Weight Control," *Mademoiselle*, July 1978, pp. 48, 50.

Lewis, Charles, *The Buying of the President 2000,* New York: Avon Books, 2000, pp. 91, 266–67.

"Liquid Protein: A Deadly Diet," *Science News*, July 29, 1978, p. 70.

Romboy, Dennis, "Orem Health-Food Firm Plans New Plant in Am.F.," *Deseret News*, March 17–18, 1993, p. B3.

"Twin Labs's Claims Against Rival Weider Dismissed by Court," *Wall Street Journal*, April 11, 1990, p. B3.

Unger, Michael, "Twin Labs Selling Stake for $225M/ California Merchant Bank Taking 55% Interest in Firm," *Newsday*, March 13, 1996, p. A45.

Wagner, Jim, "1998 Manufacturer of the Year Twinlab," *Nutritional Outlook*, December 1998

—David M. Walden

UAL Corporation

1200 Algonquin Road
Elk Grove Township, Illinois 60007
P.O. Box 66919
Chicago, Illinois 60666
U.S.A.
Telephone: (847) 700-4000
Toll Free: (800) 241-6522
Fax: (847) 700-4081
Web site: http://www.ual.com

Public Company
Incorporated: 1934 as United Air Lines Transportation
 Company
Employees: 98,000
Sales: $18.03 billion (1999)
Stock Exchanges: New York Chicago Pacific
Ticker Symbol: UAL
NAIC: 481111 Scheduled Passenger Air Transportation;
 481112 Scheduled Freight Air Transportation

UAL Corporation is the holding company for United Airlines, Inc., the world's largest airline, which flies 240,000 passengers a day to 26 countries. It is also the largest employee-owned company in the world. Revenues for 1999 surpassed $18 billion. UAL's plans to acquire US Airways, the sixth largest airline, were the subject of much discussion and uncertainty during mid-2000.

Going Vertical in the 1930s

United Airlines was created in the early 1930s by Bill Boeing's aeronautic conglomerate in order to exploit demand for air transport and to serve as an immediate market for Boeing aircraft. At first United was similar to a consortium, involving the participation of several independent airline companies. One of those companies was Varney Air Lines, credited with being America's first commercial air transport company. Varney's 460-mile network between Pasco, Washington, and Elko, Nevada, was linked with Boeing Air Transport, which operated an airmail service between Chicago and San Francisco. This route crossed Vernon

Gorst's Pacific Air Transport network, which ran mail between Seattle and Los Angeles. The National Air Transport Company, operated by New York financier Clement Keys, connected with Boeing in Chicago, flying mail south to Dallas. Stout Air Services, which had the financial backing of Henry and Edsel Ford, operated an air service between Chicago, Detroit, and Cleveland with Ford tri-motor airplanes. These airline companies cooperated with Boeing, which manufactured aircraft in Seattle, and Pratt & Whitney, an aircraft engine manufacturer in Connecticut operated by Frederick Rentschler. Together they formed a "vertical" aeronautic monopoly, restricting the delivery of new aircraft to its constituent partners and devoting its resources to eliminating competition on its air services. The airline group became known as United Air Lines in 1931.

Among other things, the group was responsible for introducing air-to-ground radio, which improved communication and safety, and stewardesses, all eight of whom were registered nurses hired to allay passengers' fear of flying. A United executive at the time commented, "How is a man going to say he's afraid to fly when a woman is working on the plane?"

In 1934 National, Varney, Pacific, and Boeing officially merged under the name United Air Lines Transportation Company. Pat Patterson, a banker and Boeing official, was placed in charge of the airline at the age of 34. That year, however, congressional legislation outlawed the type of monopoly United had formed with Boeing and Pratt & Whitney, and the airline was forced to divorce itself from the conglomerate. It subsequently became an independent company based at Chicago's Old Orchard (now O'Hare) airport.

In 1936 after several airplane accidents, a series of syndicated newspaper stories sensationalized the horror of airplane crashes and incited a virtual state of panic which drove passengers back to railroads by the thousands. The airline industry was so deeply affected that many smaller companies were faced with bankruptcy. United responded by retaining a popular military test pilot named Major R.W. Schroeder to oversee the company's implementation of new safety codes. With this action United helped to rebuild the public's confidence in air travel.

As one of the nation's larger airline companies United maintained a position of leadership in the industry, constantly demanding newer, more advanced aircraft. United funded many of the developmental costs of the Douglas DC-4, the first four-engine passenger plane. However, when the United States became involved in World War II, all DC-4s were devoted to the war effort before ever having carried a commercial passenger. The company's name was shortened to United Air Lines in 1943 and new plans were made for the airline in anticipation of the end of the war. Two years later United redeployed its aircraft and resumed commercial flying.

Postwar Innovation

In 1954 United became the first airline to employ flight simulators as part of its training and pilot testing programs. The following year United placed an order with Douglas Aircraft for DC-8s, the airline's first passenger jetliners. Although Boeing's 707 jetliner actually became available a few months before the DC-8, United preferred the DC-8 because of its seating arrangement and other cost advantages.

In spite of United's favorable position in the industry, its competitors were growing rapidly and in many cases outperforming United, which had entered a brief period of decline. However, when United acquired Capital Airlines in 1961 its network in the eastern United States was strengthened, helping the company to regain its position as the nation's number one airline.

United President Pat Patterson retired in 1966 and was replaced by George Keck, an engineer who rose to the top position from the company's maintenance department. Keck was generally regarded as arrogant and secretive. According to some reports, his abrupt manner and authoritarian personality offended many people within the company and its unions as well as in the Civil Aeronautics Board, which severely limited his effectiveness and ability to manage the airline in many ways. In 1971 Keck was forcibly removed in what was described as a "corporate coup" instigated by two members of the company's board, Gardner Cowles and Thomas Gleed.

In 1967, during Keck's first year, United became the first airline to surpass $1 billion in annual revenue. On December 30, 1968 United created a subsidiary called UAL to operate its non-airline businesses, and the following year United Air Lines became a subsidiary of UAL.

Going Western in 1970

Western International Hotels was acquired by the UAL holding company in 1970. Western's name was later changed to the Westin Hotel Company and linked to another UAL subsidiary which arranged travel packages. Westin's operations later grew to represent about one-12th of UAL's total business.

Eddie Carlson, who had a record of success while in charge of the Westin Hotel subsidiary, was named to succeed Keck as UAL's new chief executive officer. Carlson's warm and personable demeanor motivated individuals in every division and level at UAL. He flew 186,000 miles one year inspecting the facilities and terminating the employment of what he regarded as redundant company bureaucrats. Despite his lack of experience in the airline industry, Carlson was successful in reversing the company's discouraging trends. Anticipating his own retirement, Carlson chose Richard Ferris, whom he had promoted from the Westin hotel subsidiary, to succeed him. When Carlson was named chairman of UAL and United, Ferris was made president of the airline; and in 1978 Ferris was promoted to chairman of United and president of UAL. Carlson remained as chairman of UAL until his retirement in 1983.

Notwithstanding efforts to improve the relationship the company had with its unions, which had deteriorated during the leadership of George Keck, United remained on cautious terms with its employee representatives. In 1976 the airline agreed to a million-dollar payback settlement with women and minority employees in an anti-discrimination suit. In 1979 United lost $72 million, largely as the result of a month-long labor strike.

Under the leadership of Richard Ferris the airline reached a compromise with its pilots' union. The agreement guaranteed that layoffs would not be authorized in return for more flexible work rules. The lower operating costs that resulted from the agreement were passed on to the consumer with the formation of a discount air service called "Friendship Express." The service was also intended to allow the company to more effectively compete with cut-rate airlines such as People Express and New York Air.

New Frontiers After Deregulation

In 1978 and 1979 UAL continued to diversify its operations when it acquired Mauna Kea Properties and the Olohana Corporation in Hawaii for $78 million. As resort developments, these acquisitions allowed UAL to take more advantage of the tourist business in the airline's most popular destination.

Under the Airline Deregulation Act, airline companies were free to enter new passenger markets without prior government approval. United was the first major airline to support deregulation; however, when Congress passed the legislation in 1978 United was forced to scale down its operations in order to compete profitably. Richard Ferris later commented, "If we did make a mistake, it was in not recognizing the intensity of pricing competition that deregulation would bring, and getting structured to cope with it." Executives with smaller airline companies expressed their fear that the larger airlines would concentrate their resources on contested markets with the goal of forcing the smaller companies out of business. One executive remarked, "What Ferris wants is to have us for lunch, and I don't mean at McDonald's."

In 1985 United acquired Pan Am's Asian traffic rights for $715.5 million. The agreement also included 18 jets, 2,700 Pan Am employees, and all of Pan Am's facilities in Asia. The addition of 65,000 route miles and 30 destinations to United's network made other acquisitions pale in comparison. Ferris

Key Dates:

1934: Three airlines merge with Boeing to form United Air Lines.
1954: United becomes first to train pilots with flight simulators.
1967: Annual revenues exceed $1 billion.
1970: UAL acquires Westin International Hotels.
1987: ''Allegis'' becomes short-lived name for UAL's diverse travel interests.
1994: Employees take 55 percent stake in UAL in exchange for pay cuts.
2000: UAL announces its plan to acquire US Airways Group, Inc., a proposed $4.3 billion merger that faced several obstacles.

said, ''We could spend two or three lifetimes and never get all the traffic [rights] we're buying from Pan Am.''

Ferris joined the board of directors at Procter & Gamble in 1979 with the intention of studying its successful marketing formulas and applying them at UAL. He restructured UAL to reduce costs and improve marketing. After 1982, costs were controlled, productivity rose, and profits were stabilized. Part of the new marketing strategy involved the establishment of additional passenger transfer points, or ''hubs.'' In addition to its main facility at Chicago's O'Hare airport, United operated secondary hubs in Denver, San Francisco, and Dulles airport near Washington, D.C.

In 1986 United's purchase of the bankrupt Frontier Airlines unit from People Express was canceled when the United pilots' union failed to reach an agreement with management over the manner in which Frontier pilots were to be absorbed by United. The $146 million acquisition promised to ease competition at Denver's Stapleton airport, where United, Frontier, and Continental were engaged in a costly battle for passengers. People Express closed Frontier in August 1986, declaring it bankrupt; however, less than a month later Frank Lorenzo's Texas Air Corporation acquired People Express and liquidated Frontier. The following February People Express was absorbed into Continental Airlines. Still competing with United in Denver, Texas Air then controlled airlines with 20 percent of the domestic airline market, compared to United's 16 percent share.

United started to replace its fleet of B-727s with newer wide-body B-767s on more heavily traveled routes. Although United was the last major airline company to still operate the DC-8, federal regulations on noise pollution forced the company to replace the engines on its DC-8s with quieter models. In addition to these aircraft, United flew large numbers of B-737s, B-747s, and DC-10s.

A Change of ''Allegis'' in the Late 1980s

Early in 1987, UAL was renamed ''Allegis,'' a curious computer-generated choice which combined portions of the words ''allegiance'' and ''aegis.'' With an airline, a hotel chain, the Hertz rent-a-car company, and the Apollo computerized reservations system to coordinate them all, Allegis had become

an integrated full-service travel company. Shortly afterward, Allegis encountered a number of problems with Ferris's strategy to create a travel conglomerate. Several investor groups noted that Allegis's subsidiaries would be worth more as separate companies than as divisions of Allegis. On May 26, Coniston Partners announced that it had acquired a 13 percent share of Allegis stock, and that it would be purchasing more in an attempt to gain control of the board and remove Richard Ferris. The Allegis board initialed an anti-takeover defense in which the Boeing Company was given a 16 percent stake ($700 million) in the company in return for a $2.1 billion aircraft order. The defense failed in June, forcing Ferris and several other board members to resign. The new board appointed Frank A. Olson chairman of Allegis.

The unfortunate Allegis name was retired in June 1988. After a brief transition period, the UAL board named Stephen M. Wolf, an airline veteran with executive experience at American, Pan Am, and Continental airlines, as CEO of United. Wolf inherited numerous business troubles, including a contract dispute over company ownership with United's three major employee unions which went unresolved until 1990.

As the U.S. economy weakened going into the 1990s, United began to feel the effects of recession, which reduced the amount of passenger traffic, and fuel prices, which rose in the late 1980s and jumped sharply during the 1990–91 Persian Gulf War. These factors cut into the earnings of all carriers, and in 1991, UAL Corporation suffered a net loss of $331.9 million. United's losses, as well as those of other major U.S. carriers, were exacerbated by recurrent ''fare wars,'' often launched by bankrupt airlines, such as TWA and Continental, whose Chapter 11 protection exempted them—unlike relatively well-off airlines—from paying interest on the debt that they incurred as a result of their sharp promotional price cuts. In 1992, United followed the lead of American Airlines in adopting a four-tiered fare-simplification program in an attempt to eliminate these restricted fares. However, both carriers scrapped this within a few months as budget carriers undercut them in droves.

Nonetheless, United treated the industry's lean period as an opportune time to expand. Such financially troubled airlines as Pan Am and TWA began in the late 1980s to sell routes to raise funds, and governments became increasingly willing to allow foreign carriers air rights within their countries; these two factors prompted United to embark on a strategy of ''globalization.'' United's 1985 purchase, for $750 million, of Pan Am's routes to Asia left the airline well-poised to enter what many industry analysts have described as a transition toward a global free market in transportation. Even American Airlines' Robert Crandall, who rejected the Pan Am Asian routes as too expensive, later conceded that the purchase was an excellent move. In 1990 United placed a record $22 billion order for new airplanes. In 1991 the company purchased six Pan Am routes to London for $400 million, and late that same year finalized a $135 million deal to take over a portion of Pan Am's Latin American operations.

Empowered for the 1990s

Wolf resigned in July 1994 and was replaced by Gerald Greenwald. Later that month, United management and employees reached a historic agreement designed to stave off competition from low-cost, low-wage carriers. In exchange for pay cuts totaling $5 billion and more flexible work rules, employees received a 55 percent stake in UAL Corporation. This made UAL one of the world's largest employee-owned companies. Significantly, the 20,000 flight attendants chose not to participate in the buyout.

In October, the company launched a "shuttle" service to compete in the California Corridor in particular. It mimicked the low-cost, low-fare ways of Southwest Airlines but kept traditional major airline amenities such as assigned seating, a first class section, and a frequent flier club with global travel rewards. However, the pilots' union was skeptical of the lower paying "Shuttle by United" and contractually limited the operation's scope.

After losing more than a billion dollars between 1991 and 1993, UAL posted a profit of $51 million in 1994. It had invested heavily in information technology, and was a pioneer in the use of paperless tickets. The company even sold its proprietary E-Ticket software to other international airlines.

United began flying dedicated cargo aircraft again in 1997 after a 13-year lapse. The DC-10 freighters operated exclusively on Pacific routes. Its charter membership in the Star Alliance with Lufthansa and SAS helped open hundreds of new markets. It upgraded in-flight amenities to recapture high-yield business travelers. It provided electrical outlets for laptop computers, in-flight entertainment systems, and, of course, bigger seats. These factors helped UAL outperform the industry.

The carrier controversially cut travel agency commissions in September 1997. Bookings from online brokers cost airlines an average $10, versus $50 each for traditional travel agents. With the proliferation of online travel sites such as Expedia, Travelocity, Cheap Tickets, and, later, Priceline, UAL began offering the chance to reserve seats on other airlines at its own web site. The strategy sought to appeal directly to the online bargain hunter.

In January 1999, UAL increased its flight frequencies to match moves by US Airways. It had previously boosted operations at its San Francisco, Denver, and Chicago hubs and created a new hub in Los Angeles. United added a daily nonstop flight from LAX to Paris's Charles de Gaulle International Airport in April 2000, connecting the City of Angels directly "to all four corners of the globe." To retain frequent flier and full-fare economy class patrons, United installed roomier Economy Plus seating for them.

James E. Goodwin followed Greenwald as chairman and CEO in July 1999. Both were known for their relatively good relationship with labor. Goodwin had already been with United for 32 years.

Later in the year, United launched an ad campaign in gay newspapers in order to woo gay and lesbian travelers back onto its planes. Proclivity to travel, especially overseas, made gays an attractive demographic target, and American Airlines, Delta, and US Airways also initiated domestic partner benefits. The carrier's protest of a San Francisco ordinance mandating domestic partner health insurance benefits had resulted in a two-year boycott. American Airlines had created a "Rainbow TeAAM" to market to the gay community.

A major announcement came in May 2000, when UAL shared its plans to acquire competitor US Airways Group, Inc. Numerous questions about the proposed $4.3 billion merger remained, including antitrust and union objections, as well as whether US Airways might be the target of a separate offer from another industry heavyweight. If the merger did go through, further consolidation by other carriers, in the interests of staying competitive, could be expected.

Principal Subsidiaries

Air Wis Services, Inc.; Four Star Insurance Company, Ltd. (Bermuda); Four Star Leasing, Inc.; UAL Benefits Management, Inc.; United Airlines, Inc.

Principal Divisions

North America; Pacific; Atlantic; Latin America.

Principal Operating Units

United Shuttle; United Cargo; E-commerce.

Principal Competitors

AMR Corporation; British Airways plc; Delta Air Lines Inc.; US Airways Group Inc.; Northwest Airlines Corporation; Trans World Airlines, Inc.; Southwest Airlines Co.

Further Reading

Biederman, Paul, *The U.S. Airline Industry: End of an Era,* Praeger, 1982.

Carey, Susan, "UAL to Increase Flights from Hub at Dulles Airport," *Wall Street Journal,* p. A10.

——, "UAL Names Goodwin Chairman, CEO; Strong Support from Unions Helped," *Wall Street Journal,* March 26, 1999, p. B9.

Flint, Petty, "United in Battle," *Air Transport World,* October 1994, pp. 28ff.

Harrar, George, "United's Soft Landing," *Forbes,* December 4, 1995, pp. 104f.

Irvine, Martha, "United Airlines Trying to Boost Image with Gay, Lesbian Travelers," *San Francisco Examiner,* March 16, 2000.

Laibich, Kenneth, "Winners in the Air Wars," *Fortune,* May 11, 1987.

Lee, Connie J., "Airline Stocks Advance on Cut in Commissions—Analysts Say Lower Fees for Agents to Aid UAL, But Fallout Is a Concern," *Wall Street Journal,* September 22, 1997, p. B18.

Nelms, Douglas W., "Giant Step in a Small Way," *Air Transport World,* June 1997, pp. 125–27.

Oneal, Michael, "Dogfight! United and American Battle for Global Supremacy," *Business Week,* January 21, 1991.

Ott, James, "United Remakes Itself for Global Competition," *Aviation Week & Space Technology,* July 7, 1997, pp. 54f.

Petzinger, Thomas, Jr., *Hard Landing: The Epic Contest for Power and Profits That Plunged the Airlines into Chaos,* New York: Times Business, 1995.

Smith, Timothy K., "Why Air Travel Doesn't Work," *Fortune,* April 3, 1995, pp. 42ff.

Warner, Bernhard, "Prepare for Takeoff," *Brandweek,* January 19, 1998, pp. 38–40.

—John Simley and James Poniewozik
—updated by Frederick C. Ingram

United Rentals, Inc.

5 Greenwich Office Park
Greenwich, Connecticut 06830
U.S.A.
Telephone: (203) 622-3131
Fax: (203) 622-6080
Web site: http://www.unitedrentals.com

Public Company
Incorporated: 1997
Employees: 13,600
Sales: $2.23 billion (1999)
Stock Exchanges: New York
Ticker Symbol: URI
NAIC: 532299 All Other Consumer Goods Rental; 53231
General Rental Centers; 532412 Construction, Mining,
and Forestry Machinery and Equipment Rental and
Leasing; 53240 Other Commercial and Industrial
Machinery and Equipment Rental and Leasing (pt)

United Rentals, Inc. was founded in 1997 by Bradley S. Jacobs in Greenwich, Connecticut. With more than 722 branches in 45 states, six Canadian provinces, and Mexico, United Rentals is the largest equipment-rental company in North America. The company's rental fleet (original equipment value of approximately $3 billion) consists of more than 500,000 individual units of rental equipment and is the largest in the world. United Rentals rents out more than 600 different types of equipment, such as aerial work platforms, construction equipment, industrial and heavy machinery, traffic control equipment, trench safety equipment, and equipment for special events and for homeowners. Among the company's diversified client base of over one million customers are construction and commercial companies, manufacturers, utilities, municipalities, homeowners, and others. Rental equipment accounts for more than two-thirds of United Rentals' revenues; the company also sells used equipment and supplies and is an authorized dealer for many leading tool and equipment manufacturers. The company took an industry-leading position in e-commerce in February 2000 when it launched a new business-to-business web site: E-Rental Store allows customers to rent or buy equipment on a 24-hour basis, seven days a week. Since going public in 1997, United Rentals has met or exceeded financial analysts' estimates for every quarter of each fiscal year.

Keeping America Beautiful, Global Warming, Legislation, Consolidation: 1979–97

The 1980s' crusade for "The Greening of America," scientific studies of the consequences of global warming, growing awareness of pollution, and continuing publicity about the need to protect the environment precipitated the emergence of many small, privately owned garbage-collection companies throughout the United States. In 1989 Brad Jacobs created United Waste Systems, Inc. with the intention of consolidating these small solid-waste companies into an efficient and profitable organization. By focusing on acquisitions of companies in mid-sized cities and in rural areas, he bypassed competition with industry mammoths, such as Waste Management and Browning-Ferris; small companies in these markets were less expensive to acquire and United Waste could charge higher collection fees without having to worry about competitors.

Jacobs was an experienced administrator. From 1979 to 1983, he had served as chief executive officer of AmerexOil Associates, Inc.—an oil brokerage firm that he cofounded; from 1984 to 1989, he was chairman and chief operating officer of Hamilton Resources Ltd., an international trading company. For eight years Jacobs and his acquisition team built up United Waste by purchasing more than 200 landfills and waste haulers.

By the third quarter of 1997, United Waste serviced over 700,000 commercial, industrial, and residential customers in 16 states. Jacobs sold United Waste to USA Waste Services (at that time the nation's sixth largest waste hauler, later known as Waste Management, Inc.) for $2.2 billion. When United Waste went public in December 1992, its stock was traded at $6 a share. However, the company was sold to USA Waste in September 1997 at $45.42 a share. United Waste had shown that roll-ups (by which a company grows through continuing acquisitions) were a viable way of capitalizing on an investment.

An Industry Ripe for Consolidation: 1997–98

But was United Waste's acquisition and operating strategy applicable to another industry? According to Silvia Sansoni in the June 1, 1998 issue of *Forbes* magazine, Jacobs "enlisted Merrill Lynch to help screen for new opportunities. Equipment rentals popped up and turned out to be a consolidator's dream." The equipment-rental industry was "a $20-billion-a-year market, highly fragmented into more than 20,000 mom-and-pop rental shops; the top 100 companies had less than a 20 percent share of the industry." Equipment rental was "a booming business, growing 15 percent a year, where economies of scale" were a tremendous advantage. For instance, larger companies could obtain "40 percent discounts on equipment that retailed for $50,000 or more." Industry watcher Clifton Linton noted, in the July 6, 1998 issue of *Investor's Business Daily*, that several factors favored "the growth of the rental business. First, contractors lost an equipment deduction when the tax code was changed in 1986. Second, the recession in the early 1990s forced many contractors to sell under-utilized equipment."

Furthermore, the 1991 passage of the Resource Conservation and Recovery Act—which imposed strict regulations on protecting the environment and the design, construction, and operation of landfills—made it even more difficult for small waste-collection companies to meet requirements for garbage disposal and forced them to sell or suspend operations. Only a few weeks after the sale of United Waste, Jacobs founded United Rentals, Inc. According to reporter Steven Lipin of the *Wall Street Journal*, Brad Jacobs concluded that "This industry is ready to be consolidated."

Most of United Waste's senior management team joined Jacobs. They pooled "$46.5 million of their personal wealth, raised another $8 million, and talked to underwriters," wrote *Forbes's* Sansoni. Suitable acquisitions "were tough to find because there's little public record of family-owned rental companies. So Jacobs read five years' worth of trade magazines, downloaded the web sites of hundreds of rental stores and hired a private investigating firm with dozens of databases to identify potential targets."

United Rentals' goal was to create a geographically diversified equipment-rental company in the United States and Can-

ada. The company bought six small leasing companies and in October 1997 began to rent a broad array of equipment to a highly diversified customer base that included construction companies, industrial organizations, and homeowners. The company based its growth strategy on expansion through a highly disciplined acquisition program, the opening of new rental locations, and internal growth that increased equipment categories and customer markets. The company went public in December 1997 and was traded at $13.50 a share.

Initially, much of the company's revenues came from renting equipment to the construction industry and from sales of used equipment. Increasingly, large industrial companies chose to rent, rather than purchase, equipment that they needed for repairing, maintaining, and upgrading their facilities. United Rentals also sold used equipment. By June 1998, United Rentals had acquired 38 rental companies—109 stores—in 20 states. It was now "the fifth largest player in the industry," according to *Forbes's* Sansoni, and its stock had risen to nearly $37 per share. By mid-August United Rentals had completed more acquisitions and was operating in 236 locations in 31 states and Canada.

United Rentals continued to buy small companies and gradually began to seek out the best companies, regardless of their size. In September the company acquired U.S. Rentals, Inc.—at that time the second largest equipment-rental company in the United States—and became the largest and most geographically diverse equipment-rental company in North America. By year-end, United Rentals owned 103 companies located in 439 locations in 39 states, five Canadian provinces, and Mexico. The company offered rentals of more than 600 different types of equipment and served over 900,000 customers. Although renting out equipment accounted for nearly 75 percent of revenues, United Rentals also sold used equipment, acted as an authorized dealer for many types of new equipment, and sold merchandise and parts. Total revenues for fiscal 1998 were $1.22 billion, representing an increase of 149.1 percent over 1997's $489.84 million.

Disciplined Acquisition-Related Growth, Specialty Markets, National Accounts: 1999

United Rentals had quickly positioned itself to benefit from a general trend toward corporate outsourcing. Construction companies and other leading industrial companies, municipalities, government agencies, and utilities recognized the advantages of renting equipment rather than incurring the expense of ownership. They discovered that renting offered many advantages: namely, avoidance of the large capital investment needed for purchasing equipment; access to a broad range of equipment for selecting the specific equipment best suited for each job; reduction of maintenance and storage costs; and the opportunity of renting the latest technology without having to pay for new equipment. "What's driving this business day in and day out is that companies and individuals are discovering the benefits of renting over buying. And this should continue whether we are in a boom or a recession," Chairman Brad Jacobs explained in an interview reported by Robin M. Grugal in the June 9, 1999 issue of *Investor's Business Daily*.

In May 1999 United Rentals acquired seven companies having 21 rental locations in nine states and two Canadian

Key Dates:

1989: Bradley S. Jacobs founds United Waste Systems, Inc.
1991: The Resource Conservation and Recovery Act is passed.
1992: United Waste begins trading on the New York Stock Exchange (NYSE).
1997: United Waste is sold to USA Waste Services, Inc.; Brad Jacobs and six members of his former senior management team found United Rentals; United Rentals is traded on the NYSE.
1998: United Rentals buys U.S. Rentals, Inc. and becomes the largest equipment-rental company in North America.
1999: United Rentals intensifies its acquisitions of companies.
2000: United Rentals enters e-commerce by opening a web site for E-Rental Store.

provinces. The largest acquisition was that of the rental division of Mi-Jack Products, Inc., with ten locations in Illinois, Indiana, Michigan, and Texas. In June United Rentals acquired 12 more companies having combined annual revenues of $125 million in 26 locations. The largest of the 12 was Udelson Equipment Company, which ranked 30th in the business. United Rentals also completed the acquisition of ARAYCO Inc., a unit of Raytheon Co. As part of the ARAYCO deal, United Rentals became the preferred provider of equipment-rental services to Raytheon construction projects in North America for a minimum of three years.

However, United Rentals did not limit its 1999 activities to acquisitions. For example, the company's special events unit, provided portable air conditioners, generators, and trailer kitchens for both the U.S. Open golf tournament in Pinehurst, North Carolina, and for the prestigious Ryder Cup, held that year in Boston.

During the third quarter, United Rentals added 28 new companies, bringing the number of 1999 acquisitions to 91 companies and an additional 295 rental locations in the United States and Canada. According to Salomon Smith Barney analysts Levkovich and Smith, "seven of the 28 newly-acquired companies were in the traffic safety market, which stood to benefit from the Transportation Equity Act for the 21st Century (TIA-21), and stood to impact sales in 2000." In fact, United Rentals had begun to focus on specialty-equipment-rental markets, including companies that required traffic-control equipment to assist in the modernization of the nation's transportation infrastructure. By November 1999, United Rental had bought 13 safety businesses. These businesses provided message boards, traffic control cones, and similar equipment. By the end of 1999 United Rentals owned 14 traffic safety companies with annualized revenues of $250 million, amounting to almost ten percent of total revenues. By means of its ongoing safety program, United Rentals drove down its total cost of risk by more than 20 percent; had 19 percent fewer accidents than did comparable companies; reduced workers' claims for compensation by 45 percent; and lowered the cost of liability claims by 50 percent.

By year-end 1999, United Rentals had the largest and most comprehensive equipment-rental fleet in the industry and could offer "one-stop" shopping to a diverse customer base, thereby reducing its dependence on any particular customer or group of customers. The company served large businesses that needed to be sure that substantial quantities of various types of equipment could be available on a continuing basis. Although United Rentals increased its pace of acquisition, it remained intensely focused on operations and obtained substantial advantages by grouping its branches into clusters of ten to 30 locations in the same geographic area. The company's strong infrastructure was supported by its own information-technology system—dubbed Wynne Systems—which gave each branch access to real-time data about all available equipment within a cluster, facilitated rapid and informed decision making, and enabled management to respond quickly to changing market conditions.

In 1999, approximately 9.4 percent of the company's rental revenues, or $150 million, was attributable to having the branches share equipment rentals. More economies of scale were realized through United Rentals' large purchases of equipment and other items; these high-ticket items enabled the company to negotiate favorable terms with its vendors. The company estimated that these negotiations had reduced the cost of equipment in 1999 by $50 million and hoped to increase these savings to $150 million in 2000. United also reduced the cost of purchasing equipment by making volume purchases from a narrower group of vendors, thereby slashing the cost of equipment by more than $50 million.

Furthermore, United Rentals' geographic spread in many different locations (branches in 45 states, six Canadian provinces, and Mexico) reduced the impact that weather conditions and fluctuations in regional economic conditions could have on its financial performance. Geographic diversity also allowed the company to offer better service to its National Account (a term used in reference to any customer whose operations spanned two or more markets) customers. The company developed these National Accounts in order to achieve a better balance in its business mix. By year-end 1999, United Rentals had more than 500 National Accounts, including such large industrial firms as DuPont. United Rentals gave these clients a single point of contact to handle all their equipment needs, as well as customized information on their equipment usage.

By the end of the fiscal year, United Rentals had completed the acquisition of another 15 equipment-rental companies with 48 locations. In total, the company had acquired 101 companies during the fiscal year. For 1999, United Rentals posted revenues of $2.23 billion, representing an 83 percent increase compared to the previous year. Net income was $153.4 million, a 111 percent increase from the previous year. Not surprisingly, since going public in December 1997, United Rentals had met, or exceeded, financial analysts' estimates for every quarter of each fiscal year.

2000 and Beyond

The U.S. equipment rental industry grew from about $600 million in annual revenues in 1982 to over $25 billion in 2000, an increase representing a compound annual growth rate of approximately 15 percent, according to United Rentals' data.

United Rentals, in February 2000, announced the opening of its E-Rental Store, an Internet business-to-business web site where customers could rent and buy used equipment online. In essence, the store was a 24-hour, seven days a week, branch that customers could access to review equipment specifications, browse through listings of used equipment for sale, locate branches nearest to specific jobs, and gather up-to-the-minute reports on business activity with the company.

At the end of the first quarter of 2000, United Rentals had completed the acquisitions of 17 equipment rental companies with 32 locations and annual revenues of approximately $100 million. Ten of these acquisitions were in the traffic control, trench safety, and special-event segments. These acquisitions established United Rentals as the largest provider of rental equipment for traffic control. Since the beginning of the year, United Rentals had completed 21 acquisitions with total combined annual revenues of approximately $150 million.

Since its founding in 1997, United Rentals, Inc. had grown into the largest equipment-rental company in North America. There was every indication that United Rentals—under the aegis of expert management—would remain focused on its disciplined approach to acquisitions and expansion into new geographic territories—and continue to provide the best level of service in the industry.

Principal Competitors

American United Global, Inc.; Atlas Copco AB; Caterpillar Inc.; The Hertz Corporation; National Equipment Services, Inc.

Further Reading

Grugal, Robin M., ''United Rentals' Jacobs on Renting As Economic Gauge,'' *Investor's Business Daily*, June 9, 1999.

Lee, Edward C., ''URI: Highlighting United Rentals As One of Our Favorite Ideas,'' *Bank of America Securities,* May 17, 1999, p. 1.

Levkovich, Tobias M., and David B. Smith, ''URI: Robust 3Q99 Operating Results Underscore Strong Fundamentals,'' October 28. 1999, p. 3.

Linton, Clifton, ''United Rentals, Inc.: Buying Its Way to Top of Rental Industry,'' *Investor's Business Daily*, July 6, 1998.

Lipin, Steven, ''United Rentals Business Bores All but Holders,'' *Wall Street Journal*, June 17, 1998, pp. C1+.

Perlin, Daniel R., ''URI: No Fundamental Reason for Recent Weakness—Reiterate Buy,'' *Legg Mason Wood Walker, Inc. Report*, September 29, 1999 pp. 1–2.

Redding, Rick, ''Bigger Can Be Better,'' *Business First—Louisville*, August 2, 1999, p. 2.

Sansoni, Silvia, ''The Earth Mover,'' *Forbes*, June 1, 1998, pp. 136+.

Sherer, Paul M., ''Roll-Ups: Ironing Out the Bumps,'' September 3, 1999, pp. C1+.

''The Simple Economics of Rental,'' *RentSmart*, June 1999.

Siwolop, Sana, ''Goods Ready to Rent, Stocks Ready to Grow,'' *New York Times*, August 29, 1999.

—Gloria A. Lemieux

United States Postal Service

475 L'Enfant Plaza S.W.
Washington, D.C. 20260-0010
U.S.A.
Telephone: (202) 268-2500
Fax: (202) 268-4860
Web site: http://www.usps.gov

Government-Owned Company
Founded: 1775
Employees: 792,041
Sales: $62.70 billion (1999)
NAIC: 491110 Postal Services Operated by U.S. Postal
Service

The United States Postal Service (USPS) is an independent government agency that generates income through postage and other fees. With a monopoly on the delivery of noncritical mail, the USPS delivers about 40 percent of the world's mail, or more than 200 billion pieces of mail annually. Beginning in the 1990s, the USPS faced increased competition from rival package delivery and courier services, as well as the Internet. In anticipation of the widespread use of e-mail and other e-commerce services, the USPS focused on developing Internet strategies, such as computerized postage and online delivery tracking of packages.

Early History: The Birth of the United States and the Federal Post Office in the 1700s

The Post Office Department had roots in America dating back to the 17th century, when there was a need for correspondence between colonial settlements and transatlantic exchange of information with England, the native country of most eastern seaboard settlers. The earliest mail services were disorganized at best, with no uniform system in place until 1691, when Thomas Neale established a North American postal service under a British Crown grant and, in absentia, appointed Governor Andrew Hamilton of New Jersey his deputy postmaster general. Thereafter, under the control of the British government, a centralized if erratic postal service operated in the colonies. In 1737, Deputy Postmaster General Alexander Spotswood, who had served as lieutenant governor of Virginia, named Benjamin Franklin, then 31, postmaster of Philadelphia. Franklin became joint postmaster general of the colonies and undertook important reforms that led to a more efficient, regular, and quicker mail service.

Mistrust of the royal postal service led to changes on the eve of the American Revolution. In 1774, the Crown dismissed Franklin because of his activities on behalf of the rebellious colonies. The colonists responded by setting up the separate Constitutional Post under the leadership of William Goddard. At the time of the first Continental Congress in 1775, Goddard's service provided inter-colonial service through 30 post offices operating between New Hampshire and Virginia.

The Continental Congress named Franklin chairman of a committee empowered to make recommendations for the establishment of a postal service. On July 26, 1775, the Congress approved the committee's plans, establishing the organization from which the U.S. Postal Service traces its direct descent and which, after the Bureau of Indian Affairs, is the second oldest federal department. The Congress wisely appointed Franklin the first Postmaster General. Although Franklin served just a brief period, until November 7, 1776, he is generally credited with being the chief architect of the modern postal service.

It was not until after the adoption of the Constitution in 1789 that a law passed on September 22, 1789, created the federal post office under the new government of the United States. It also established the Office of the Postmaster General. President Washington named Samuel Osgood to that post four days later. At the time there were 75 post offices and approximately 2,000 miles of post roads.

Additional legislation in the 1790s strengthened the U.S. Post Office by expanding its responsibilities and codifying its regulations. It remained in Philadelphia, the seat of the federal government, until 1800, when in just two wagons it moved all of its furniture, records, and supplies to Washington, D.C., the nation's new capital.

The chief focus of the efforts of postal officials from the inception of the Post Office to the present day has been on ways to achieve a more efficient and effective mail service. Finding the best methods of transporting and directing mail have always been of primary concern. As a result, the Post Office has played a significant part in the development and subsidization of new modes of transportation. Willing to experiment in the handling and delivery of mail, the Post Office was quick to try out new inventions and policies, even some disastrous ones that led to scornful criticism and ridicule.

Rapid Expansion in the 1800s

During the 19th century, a citizenry hesitant to accept things new and different watched comparatively rapid changes transform the postal service into a remarkable public convenience. By the start of the 1800s, the Post Office Department had bought several stagecoaches for transporting both mail and passengers on the nation's post roads. Its patronage led to better stagecoach design, ensuring improved comfort and safety, and to better roads. In addition, a full ten years before waterways became official post roads in 1823, the Post Office had begun using steamboats to transport mail between river-linked towns that shared no common road. By 1831, it had begun sending mail short distances via trains—the "iron horses" that many people denounced as demonic devices—and five years later awarded its first mail contract to a rail carrier.

Until replaced by automobiles and trucks at the beginning of the 20th century, horses remained major mail carriers, even over long distances, particularly during the period of westward expansion preceding the establishment of transcontinental telegraph and railway services. With the end of the Mexican War and the California gold rush of 1848, the need for effective communication between Atlantic and Pacific coastal cities quickly intensified. In that same year, the Post Office Department contracted a steamship company to carry mail to California. Ships from New York carried mail to Panama, where it was transported across the isthmus, then by ship again to San Francisco. The service was supposed to take between three and four weeks, a goal seldom realized in practice, and the Post Office sought alternative methods for getting the mail across North America in a more expeditious fashion.

In 1858, an overland service was contracted with a stage line, the Overland Mail Company, operating on a 2,800-mile route between Tipton, Missouri, and San Francisco. Semi-weekly stagecoaches began carrying mail in September of that year. The service was prone to problems, however, and the advertised delivery time of 24 days in practice often ran into months. A solution was attempted by the Central Overland California and Pike's Peak Express Company, which, without a contract with the Post Office,

in 1860 began operating a mail carrier service between St Joseph, Missouri, and California. It was popularly known as the Pony Express. Changing mounts at established relay stations, riders could cover more than 100 miles per day. In March 1861, the Pony Express carried President Lincoln's inaugural address over the route in less than eight days, encouraging the Post Office to put the service under federal contract. It began operations under that arrangement in July 1861, but with the transcontinental telegraph hookup on October 24, 1861, the celebrated service, rendered instantly obsolete, was halted.

Some important procedural and organizational changes also marked the pre-Civil War development of the Post Office. In 1829, President Andrew Jackson invited Postmaster General William T. Barry to sit as a cabinet member, although Jackson had no formal authority for the move. Although Barry's predecessor, John McLean, had in fact begun calling the service the Post Office *Department* even earlier, it was not until 1872, after the Civil War, that Congress officially recognized it as such. A year after Barry took his cabinet seat under Jackson, the Office of Instructions and Mail Depredations was created as an investigative arm of the Post Office. It was headed by P.S. Loughborough, generally regarded as the first Chief Postal Inspector. In addition, by 1840 all railroads in the United States had been designated as postal routes, which quickly expanded rail service, the main means of moving large quantities of mail well into the next century.

Initially, mail was not sent in envelopes. Writers would simply fold their letters and address them, then drop them off at post offices where their correspondents would pick them up. In larger cities, there was a local delivery system that charged an extra fee for carrying mail to homes and businesses. An important innovation was the postage stamp, first issued in 1847 and followed by its mandatory prepayment use in 1855. Prepaid postage helped facilitate a new system of free city delivery, which by 1863 was available in 49 cities.

During the Civil War, the Confederacy created its own Post Office Department, with John H. Reagan serving as Postmaster General. Although Reagan was appointed on March 6, 1861, it was a full two months before the Union Postmaster General, Montgomery Blair, stopped the federal mail service to the secessionist states. The war, with Union blockades of Confederate ports and its eventual invasion, seriously impeded postal service in the South. Even at the end of the war, with the restitution of the federal post, mail delivery was irregular. As late as November 1866, less than half of the post offices in the South had been fully restored to service.

After the Civil War, "post offices on wheels," or mail cars, came into rapidly expanding use. They had first appeared during the war, in 1862, but it was not until August 1864 that an official Post Office route was put in operation between Chicago and Clinton, Iowa. Other routes quickly followed, providing mail sorting and handling services while trains were in transit. At first only letters were handled on the postal cars, but by 1869 all other types except parcels were being processed. The use of "post offices on wheels" would continue to grow well into the 20th century. In 1930, when trains were still the most viable means of long-distance hauling, more than 10,000 of them were used to carry mail to every city and rural town in the country. They would still be used into the 1970s, after the reorganization

Key Dates:

1691: An American postal service, under control of the British government, is established.

1737: Benjamin Franklin becomes the postmaster general of the colonies.

1775: A U.S. postal service is established.

1789: The U.S. Constitution is adopted and the federal post office is formed.

1847: The first postage stamp is issued.

1855: Prepayment for postage becomes mandatory.

1872: The postal service is officially recognized by Congress as the Post Office Department.

1914: The Post Office Department forms its own fleet of motorized carriers.

1918: Formal airmail service is introduced.

1963: The Zip Code system is introduced.

1970: The Post Office Department is reorganized as the United States Postal Service (USPS) and becomes an independent agency.

1999: USPS introduces Delivery Confirmation service and PC Postage.

of the Post Office Department as the U.S. Postal Service, but very sparingly. The Transportation Act of 1958 had earlier insured their quick decline, so that by 1965 only 190 trains still carried and processed mail. The last to do so, which ran between New York and Washington, made its final run on June 30, 1977.

Continued Growth in the Early 1900s

The invention of the horseless carriage and the airplane had much to do with declining use of mail cars and railroading in general. Both were extremely important in the changing face of the Post Office as it sought to provide service to the most isolated communities. Near the end of the 19th century, it inaugurated a system of rural free delivery (RFD) in a nation still in the process of shifting from an agrarian to an industrial society. Experiments with RFD were begun in West Virginia in 1896, despite vituperative complaints about its exorbitant cost and general impracticality. It was, however, a great boon to farm residents throughout the United States. It also stimulated the building and improvement of roads and highways, because service was provided only in places that had acceptable roads. So that local residents could qualify for RFD, town and county governments undertook these changes at public cost.

Improved roads were, of course, inevitable, thanks to the automobile. In the same year that it inaugurated RFD, the Post Office began experimenting with the "horseless wagon" and in 1901 awarded its first contract for a horseless carrier covering a short route in Buffalo. For the next decade the Post Office contracted such services through private companies, but in 1914, fed up with excessive charges and fraudulent practices, it requested and obtained the authority to establish its own motorized fleet of carriers. Two years before that, the Post Office had won another fight with private companies when it obtained permission to put in place its parcel post service, a move that stimulated the rapid growth of mail-order merchandising.

After World War I, which provided a proving ground for the flying machine, the Post Office undertook a serious expansion into airmail service. As early as 1911 it had experimented with the airplane, sponsoring several flights at fairs and meets in more than two dozen states. In 1916, during the war, Congress even authorized a transfer of funds for the purpose, but it was not until 1918 that airmail service was begun in earnest. Using planes and pilots on loan from the Army Signal Corps, the Post Office began the first regular airmail service, between New York and Washington, D.C., on May 15 of that year. The date marked an important moment both in the history of the Post Office and commercial aviation.

The Post Office soon took complete control of the service, using its own planes and pilots, and despite reliance on primitive equipment and a lack of all navigational aids and weather data, compiled a remarkable safety record. The public was at first reluctant to pay the 24 cents charged for airmail letters, but interest picked up by 1920, when, on September 8, the last links were made to connect New York and San Francisco. By 1926, when the Post Office began contracting service with commercial airlines, it had won several awards for its pioneer work in night flying, the development of navigational aids, and the general advance of aviation in the United States. The transfer of equipment and stations to the Department of Commerce and municipalities was completed by 1927, when the Post Office put all airmail service under contract to independent carriers.

The Post Office's methods of sorting and distributing of mail were, unfortunately, considerably less innovative. Despite some earlier experimentation with canceling and sorting machines, the old "pigeonhole" method of sorting and distributing mail remained in practice until the mid-1950s, when the Post Office began a serious effort to automate mail handling. It started issuing contracts for the development of a number of mechanical devices—from letter and parcel sorters to facer-cancelers and address readers.

Leading the way toward automation was a parcel sorting machine first used in Baltimore in 1956, but it was quickly followed by the importation and use of the Transmora, a foreign-manufactured, multi-position letter sorter. This was in turn superseded by an American machine, first tested in 1959, which remained in wide use into the 1970s. Other devices placed in service in the 1960s, when the mechanization program greatly accelerated, included Mark II facer-cancelers and a high-speed optical character reader (OCR) capable of sorting mail by the new ZIP (Zoning Improvement Plan) Codes.

The ever-increasing volume and change in the principal type of mail had made the changes mandatory. Most mail sent before World War II had been private correspondence, but by 1963, 80 percent had become business mail. The computer, an indispensable business tool, already had begun to play an important part in the rapid growth of business mail.

Reorganization and Modern Innovation: 1970s Through the 1980s

On August 12, 1970, President Richard M. Nixon signed Public Law 91-375, which reorganized the federal Post Office Department as the United States Postal Service. Under the new law, which went into effect on July 1, 1971, the Service emerged as an independent agency of the executive branch, no longer under the control of Congress. Operational authority passed to a President-appointed and Senate-approved Board of Governors and a managerial infrastructure, headed by the Postmaster General named by the Governors. No longer a cabinet member, the Postmaster General became the Service CEO. The law gave the new agency the authority to issue public bonds to finance operations and to engage in collective bargaining between management and union representatives. It also established a postal rate-setting policy and procedure regulated by the independent Postal Rate Commission.

The reorganization and partial privatization of the Post Office Department was undertaken to solve difficulties that by the 1960s had made its traditional operation an ineffective and financially disastrous albatross for the American taxpayer. Because the rates charged for services no longer bore any relationship to their actual cost, the Post Office had come to depend heavily on federal subsidies, rendering it increasingly susceptible to the vicissitudes of partisan politics. Furthermore, the managerial organization had turned into a bureaucratic maze, with a blurring of the lines of authority and fragmented control. Underfunding also had meant a continued reliance on antiquated facilities and equipment and mail-handling methods that, except for the introduction of the ZIP Code in 1963, had not changed since the turn of the century, despite a vastly expanded volume of mail. The resulting inefficiency led to long delays in service, with jams that from time to time brought it to a virtual standstill, like that at the Chicago Post Office in 1966.

Along with the need to update both equipment and procedures, there was a clear need to reorganize management. In particular, labor-management relations had badly deteriorated in the 1960s. In March 1970, during Congressional deliberations on postal reforms, poor relations led to a six-day work stoppage involving about 152,000 employees at 671 locations. For many postal workers, the proposed changes, including a salary increase, were simply not substantial enough. The workers returned to their jobs, however, when the Postmaster General agreed to give the postal workers' unions a major part in planning reforms.

The most important problem faced by the newly created USPS was the upward spiraling volume of mail and the lack of adequate physical resources and equipment for handling it. Between 1970 and 1980, the volume of mail grew from just less than 85 billion to 106.3 billion pieces, an increase of almost 20 percent. Alarmingly, it grew to 166.3 billion by 1990, and although the rate of growth abated thereafter, the problem of handling that quantity of mail remained formidable.

To deal with the increasing volumes of mail, the U.S. Postal Service updated equipment and sought new methods of improving its mail-handling efficiency. In 1978, it developed an expanded ZIP Code, which helped reduce the number of times mail had to be handled. In 1982, to exploit fully the revised ZIP Codes, the Postal Service installed its first computer-operated OCRs and barcode sorters (BCSs) and the next year introduced the ZIP+4 code to further define address sectors in any geographical area. By 1985, the new equipment and ZIP Code refinements had made it possible for each key postal center to process 24,000 pieces of mail per hour, making it approximately four times as efficient as it had been using older sorting machines. By 1992, the Service also began replacing older facer-cancelers, the Mark II and M-36 models, with a more advanced facer-canceler system (AFCS), which, processing 30,000 pieces of mail per hour, proved twice as fast as the older models. Put in use, too, were multi-line optical character readers (MLOCRs), which, in conjunction with remote bar coding systems (RBCSs), were capable of sorting even hand-addressed envelopes after they had been sprayed with an identifying barcode. These automated mail-handling machines and procedures vastly improved the ability of the Service to handle the growing volume of mail efficiently.

Increased cost was the downside of improved efficiency, however. Between 1975 and 1985, the first-class letter rate rose from ten to 22 cents, and by 1995 it had increased to 32 cents, with proportional increases in other classes and types of mail. The greater expense to customers joined with a general slowdown in the economy quickly led to a slower rate of growth in the volume of mail in the early 1990s. In fact, in 1991, it declined for the first time in 15 years.

The drop was also the result of growing competition, made possible, ironically enough, by the computer, the device that had played such an important role in the growth in the mail volume during the 1970s and 1980s. Fax machines, e-mail on the Internet, electronic money transfers, and increasingly competitive telecommunication rates offered viable and often preferred alternatives to the "snail" mail handled by the Postal Service. Many businesses that traditionally circulated advertisements via third-class mail, unhappy with the increasing rates, sought relief in telemarketing alternatives. Many mail order shippers also turned to USPS competitors including United Parcel Service (UPS), which offered a quicker and more convenient package delivery service.

Restructuring and Meeting the Challenges of the Future: 1990s

That competition caused the USPS, led by Postmaster General Marvin Runyon, who began his tenure in 1992, to undertake some restructuring. Of focal concern were customer needs and how these might best be met. In response, the Service instituted Customer Advisory Councils, made up of groups of interested citizens who worked closely with local postal managers to identify public concerns. There were 500 such councils in place by the summer of 1993. The USPS also issued contracts with private firms to measure customer satisfaction with the mail service. Efforts to reduce bureaucracy and costs, improve customer relations, and stabilize postal rates followed. A downsizing program reduced the upper echelon personnel by one half, and, without layoffs or furloughs, cut other overhead positions by 30,000 through a policy of early retirements and other incentives. At the same time, it made strides toward its automation goals, which by 1994 were less than half realized. Estimates in that year were that 12,000 automation units would be in place and operating by 1997, a considerable increase over the 4,000 put in place between 1991 and 1994.

Downsizing and restructuring helped the Postal Service considerably, but in the mid-1990s it still faced recurring problems that related to its massive size. For example, it was straddled with retirement benefit costs that totaled more than ten percent of its sales, one of many reasons why it operated with an annual deficit. Its size, however, simply reflected the daunting nature of its task. The Postal Service handled 40 percent of the world's mail, processing about 580 million items per day. It employed the largest civilian workforce in the nation, operated a transportation network using more than 200,000 vehicles, and utilized more than 250 million square feet of owned or leased office and storage space. Moreover, despite its ungainly size, it remained doggedly efficient in its primary mission: to get mail where it was supposed to go and, usually, on time.

As the USPS headed toward the 21st century, it continued to focus on implementing its restructuring strategy and to keep pace with its competitors, which included the ever-threatening Internet. By 1998, the Postal Service acknowledged, operations were being affected by the growing popularity of computerized banking and online bill-paying services. Bills, payments, and statements accounted for 25 percent of the USPS's business, and increased usage of online services threatened to significantly hurt the Service's revenues. As the Postal Service strove to function effectively in the competitive atmosphere, it faced criticism from various business groups, particularly UPS, which contended that the USPS was a monopoly that used its revenues to finance products and projects that unfairly competed against private business.

The Postal Service also faced some internal challenges during the mid-1990s when Loren Smith, the senior vice-president of marketing for the USPS from 1994 to 1996, confirmed that he exceeded his 1995 advertising budget of $140 million by 62 percent, or $87 million. Smith was also responsible for launching a variety of new marketing programs, including offering postal paraphernalia, such as T-shirts and mugs, at post offices, redesigning post offices, and selling prepaid phone cards. Although the sale of USPS logo-emblazoned products did well, the Service chose to discontinue the business in 1998 as it strayed a bit too far from the core mission of the USPS. The USPS also faced criticism from the General Accounting Office, which reported in late 1998 that the Postal Service had spent about $234 million since 1995 to develop new business but had only recovered $149 million in new revenues.

Despite these challenges, the USPS enjoyed strong revenues and growth in operations in the late 1990s. A five-year investment program of $17 billion was implemented in 1995, and the USPS committed to investing in modernizing and automating numerous operations and acquiring new vehicles and facilities. In 1998 alone, the Service spent more than $3 billion to improve facilities, purchase vehicles, and acquire mail processing equipment. Also in 1998, the USPS reported positive net income for the fourth consecutive year, lowered debt from $9.9 billion in 1992 to $6.4 billion, and maintained steady postal rates for the fourth straight year. William J. Henderson was named Postmaster General in May when Marvin Runyon returned to the private sector. The Service attempted to update its stodgy image in 1998 as well with a $15 million advertising campaign. The campaign, which included television, print, and radio ads, used the theme, "Fly Like an Eagle," and television commercials employed the Steve Miller Band song of the same name. The

ads were designed to position the USPS as a progressive and modern organization.

The U.S. Postal Service continued to improve operations and prepare for the future in 1999. At the beginning of the year postal rates increased by 2.9 percent, or one cent for standard letters. The rate hike was the first in four years and was also the lowest increase to date. In March the Service launched its Delivery Confirmation service, enabling customers to track packages sent via Priority Mail and Parcel Post. The new service made the USPS more competitive with companies such as UPS and FedEx, which had long offered tracking services. A month later, the USPS introduced Priority Mail Global Guaranteed, which provided two-day guaranteed service to a number of countries in western Europe. The service was available in major metropolitan markets and expansion to additional countries was planned.

Foreseeing the impact of the Internet on its business, the Postal Service explored various Internet opportunities and offered a number of services on its web site, including information about the USPS and the ability to order supplies, calculate rates, and track the location of packages. In August 1999 the USPS introduced online postage services, known as PC Postage. The Service had worked for more than three years with private businesses to develop a standard for digital postage. Companies independently developed PC Postage products, which allowed customers to buy and print postage on their computers, and sought approval by the Postal Service. Two companies, E-Stamp Corporation and Stamps.com Inc., gained approval for commercial distribution in 1999. The USPS also launched a web site—www.usprioritymail.com—designed to generate Priority Mail sales to online retailers. Generally, the majority of e-commerce companies used one delivery company, and the Postal Service hoped to increase its share. The site offered free software for online retailers to download and incorporate into their own web sites. The USPS also worked on developing PostalOne!, an information system geared toward large customers that would support the acceptance of bulk mail, postage payment, transportation, and data exchange.

The USPS enjoyed a fifth consecutive year of positive net income in 1999, reporting net income of $363 million on revenues of $62.7 billion. The Service handled a record 200 billion pieces of mail and achieved increased productivity as well. Despite the positive figures, the USPS noted that unexpected expenses arose, including an additional $100 million for health benefits and an outlay of $300 million for Y2K issues. The postponement of a postal rate increase until January 1999 reduced the Service's projected income by $800 million. The cutting of expenditures by $1 billion, however, helped offset the declines.

Although the USPS was forced to shift gears to remain viable in a rapidly changing environment, its fundamental purpose remained the same—to deliver mail. Postal Service spokesperson Judy de Torok commented on the changing climate in the *Boston Globe*: "Our goal is to have mail remain relevant to the American public.... For us the challenge is, how do we continue to reach customers in the electronic world?" As the USPS entered the new millennium, the question remained unanswered, but the Service was committed to the ongoing search for solutions.

Principal Competitors

United Parcel Service, Inc.; FedEx Corporation; DHL Worldwide Express.

Further Reading

Atkinson, Helen, "Postal Service to Compete for Delivery of Goods Bought Online," *Journal of Commerce,* August 30, 1999, p. 5.

Bruns, James H., *Mail on the Move,* Polo, Ill.: Transportation Trails, 1992.

Cullinan, Gerald, *The Office Department,* New York: Frederick A. Praeger, 1968.

——, *The United States Postal Service,* New York: Frederick A. Praeger, 1973.

Ferrara, Peter J, ed., *Free the Mail: Ending the Postal Monopoly,* Washington, D.C.: Cato Institute, 1990.

Fleishman, Joel L., ed., *The Future of the Postal Service,* New York: Frederick A. Praeger, 1983.

Gay, Lance, "Postal Service Losing Money in Its New Lines," *Houston Chronicle,* November 28, 1998, p. 19.

Jackson, Donald Dale, *Flying the Mail,* Alexandria, Va.: Time-Life Books, 1982.

Lewis, Diane E., "Postal Service Leans Toward Overhaul in E-Mail Era," *Boston Globe,* December 5, 1999, p. E1.

Krause, Kristin S., "USPS Stirs the Pot," *Traffic World,* May 4, 1998, p. 42.

Long, Bryant A., and William J. Dennis, *Mail by Rail: The Story of the Postal Transportation Service,* New York: Simmons-Boardman Publishing Corp., 1951.

Scheele, Carl H., *A Short History of the Mail Service,* Washington, D.C.: Smithsonian Institute Press, 1970.

Sorkin, Alan L., *The Economics of the Postal System: Alternatives and Reform,* Lexington, Mass.: Lexington Books, 1980.

Summerfield, Arthur E., *U.S. Mail: The Story of the United States Postal Service,* New York: Holt, Rinehart and Winston, 1960.

Teinowitz, Ira, "Postal 'Idea Man' Goes $87 Mil Overboard on Ad Plans," *Advertising Age,* October 21, 1996.

The U.S. Postal Service: Status and Prospects of a Public Enterprise, Dover, Mass.: Auburn House Publishing Co., 1992.

U.S. Post Office Department, *A Brief History of the United States Postal Service,* Washington, D.C.: Government Printing Office, 1933.

—John W. Fiero
—updated by Mariko Fujinaka

United States Surgical Corporation

150 Glover Avenue
Norwalk, Connecticut 06856
U.S.A.
Telephone: (203) 845-1000
Fax: (203) 845-4478
Web site: http://www.ussurg.com

Wholly Owned Subsidiary of Tyco International Ltd.
Incorporated: 1964
Employees: 5,400
Sales: $1.17 billion (1997)
NAIC: 339112 Surgical and Medical Instrument
Manufacturing; 339113 Surgical Appliance and
Supplies Manufacturing

United States Surgical Corporation (USSC) is a leading producer of tools for use in surgery, including staplers, sutures, laparoscopic instruments, cardiovascular surgical products, and electrosurgical devices. The company was founded in the 1960s by an entrepreneur who had no background in medicine but had an idea about how to use staples in surgery and pioneered the development of this market in the United States. In the late 1980s USSC introduced another innovation in surgical techniques when it began to market tubes and other devices that allowed operations that were far less invasive than conventional procedures. On the strength of this new technique, the company's fortunes soared in the early 1990s, only to be deflated in the mid-1990s as uncertainty in the healthcare industry as a whole set in. Under increasing pressure from competitors, USSC in 1998 agreed to be bought by Tyco International Ltd., thereby becoming a subsidiary of the Bermuda-based conglomerate.

Surgical Staples Origins

USSC was founded in 1964 by Leon Hirsch, the owner of a small, unsuccessful dry-cleaning equipment business. With only a high school education, Hirsch nevertheless had an avid interest in gadgets and in biology, and he often stopped by the office of a patent broker in New York City, where he lived, to see what was around. One day in the spring of 1963 he happened across a wooden device on the man's desk that looked like a shillelagh. Hirsch was told that the mystery object was used by doctors in Hungary and Russia to make stitches, instead of silk thread, as was used in the United States.

The surgical stapler, as it was known, had first been invented in Hungary in 1908, at a time when many surgery patients died of infection from contamination of their wounds. With the stapler, an area inside the body could be clamped off before any cutting was done, which dramatically reduced the loss of blood and other fluids. However, the stapler was extremely cumbersome and time consuming to use. It took two hours to assemble, and a second person had to feed individual stainless steel staples into it with tweezers in order for a surgeon to use it.

Looking at the stapler, Hirsch had the inspiration that a disposable cartridge of staples would simplify the instrument's use enormously. In the basement of his house, he made a prototype cartridge stapler out of balsa wood, and then spent $75,000 of his savings to have a metal version of his model made. Two surgeons at Johns Hopkins medical school in Baltimore tested the new device, and on the basis of their strong recommendation, Hirsch was able to line up $2 million in financing from two other investors to develop and market the product. In 1964 he incorporated the United States Surgical Corporation, with four employees.

From 1964 to 1967 Hirsch and his partners worked to refine their prototype and to develop a variety of other surgical instruments. They made this effort so that they would be able to spread the costs of their marketing activities among a number of different products. In 1967 USSC finally began to sell its products, distributing them through wholesalers of surgical supplies. The company's main product, the surgical stapler that Hirsch had first developed, looked like a stainless steel wrench. It had a hooked end, and a slot for a staple cartridge. A surgeon placed the hooked end around the area to be closed, tightened the clamp, and then pulled a trigger to insert the staple. With this device, blood loss and injury to tissue was minimized, and time spent in surgery was sharply reduced. The device was used primarily for abdominal and thoracic surgery when it was originally introduced.

In its first two years, USSC successfully sold staplers to a large number of surgeons. In 1967 sales totaled $350,000. By

1969, the company's sales had reached $1 million. The company, however, had also racked up $1 million worth of losses. Surgeons were buying the stapler, but they were not using it; USSC had counted on making its money from sales of the staple cartridges, which were disposable and had to be purchased again and again.

The company found that surgeons were instinctively cautious and conservative in the operating room, reverting in an operation to the techniques they knew best and had been trained to use. Only those surgeons who had been personally trained in the operating room by one of Hirsch's employees had made the switch to regular staple use. USSC tried a number of different solutions to the problem of how to combine sales with training. First, 20 registered nurses were hired to act as technical instructors, training surgeons in the use of staplers in the operating room. This method worked, but it proved too expensive to be practical.

Then, Hirsch hired medics and paramedics leaving the army, and asked them to sell the stapler and to train surgeons. Although they had a sound medical background, Hirsch found that they were poor salespeople. Finally, in 1972 USSC hit upon the solution of hiring experienced salespeople, and then giving them medical training. The company developed a 240-hour course that covered many aspects of basic medicine, which was supplemented by 40 hours of training in an animal laboratory, where actual surgery was done. Overall, the training of each salesperson cost $8,000. To motivate its sales force, the company paid no regular salaries to salespeople, but only commissions, and dismissed employees quickly if they failed to perform well.

By the late 1970s, these efforts, as well as a high pressure corporate culture, had driven USSC's sales to new heights, allowing the company to grow rapidly. From a base line of 20,000 patients who had operations with staples in 1969, the company's market had grown to include 700,000 patients. In addition, the company had expanded its operations to Europe, training sales representatives to begin introducing surgical staples in that market.

At this time, however, clouds began to appear on the horizon. As USSC had contracted out its manufacturing when demand for its product grew, the company's standards of quality control had slipped. To ameliorate this problem, USSC began to build new factories for its products in Puerto Rico and North Haven, Connecticut.

Late 1970s and Early 1980s: Increased Competition and Allegations of Illegal Practices

For many years, USSC had the surgical staple market largely to itself. In 1977, however, one of its main competitors, Johnson & Johnson's Ethicon division, entered the surgical staple market with a disposable stapler, which eliminated the need for the costly cleaning and maintenance of the reusable stapler. The Ethicon stapler immediately became popular, and temporarily captured a large portion of USSC's external wound closure market.

To counter this threat, USSC launched a four-year, $100 million development program to make up lost ground. The company announced that it would market its own disposable stapler, and that it would also move into new areas of medical supplies, such as intravenous feeding sets and electronic vital signs monitors. These new products would have their own sales force.

Also in 1977 USSC decided to replace its network of independent distributors with its own operations. In response, one of its unemployed distributors moved to Australia and set up a competitor to USSC called Hospital Products, Inc., which began to market very similar products in the United States and Australia. USSC responded by suing Hospital Products, Inc., for a variety of infractions, including patent violations and misrepresentation. Hospital Products responded with legal action of its own, charging unfair competition and antitrust violations, and the cluster of suits provoked a frenzy of backbiting and name-calling that went on as the legal actions dragged on into the mid-1980s.

Despite its rapid growth throughout the 1970s, USSC allegedly began in 1979 to engage in a series of illegal practices that were designed to inflate its sales figures. As the Securities and Exchange Commission (SEC) later claimed, the company used fraudulent accounting practices and shipped faked or nonexistent orders to pump up its sales figures. In 1981, for instance, USSC claimed profits of $12.9 million, when in fact the SEC calculated that it had earned only $200,000. In February 1984, under pressure from the SEC, USSC agreed—without admitting or denying the charges—to cut its earnings claims by a total of $26 million for the years 1979 to 1982, and some of its managers agreed to give back bonuses they had earned in earlier years for fraudulently computed sales gains.

In addition, USSC was charged with a variety of illicit sales practices, all of which pointed to an atmosphere of extreme pressure within the company to sell. Salespeople complained that they were forced or encouraged to dump USSC products on hospitals and to engage in a number of dishonest practices, such as hiding products, stealing them, wasting them, writing phony orders, adding zeros to numbers on order forms, and sending products that had not been ordered and then refusing to take them back. In 1980, in response to complaints from hospitals about overshipment, USSC revamped its sales management and fired 20 employees. In 1983 the company also moved to reduce pressure on its sales force by changing the structure of its payment from 100 percent commission on increase in sales, to half salary.

Despite these difficulties, by 1982 USSC's sales had risen to $160 million. Although the company's growth slowed in the

Key Dates:

1964: Leon Hirsch incorporates United States Surgical Corporation (USSC).

1967: First products are sold, most notably the surgical stapler.

1972: Company begins hiring experienced salespeople and giving them medical training.

1980: Following charges of illicit sales practices, USSC revamps its sales management and fires 20 employees.

1984: USSC reduces its earnings claims for 1979 to 1982, following SEC investigation.

1987: USSC introduces absorbable staples and the Surgiport trocar; the latter eventually opens the door to laparoscopic surgery.

1990: USSC introduces the "Endo Clip," which enables laparoscopic gall bladder removal.

1991: Sutures are added to the company's product line.

1992: USSC's stock peaks at $134.50 in January; revenues for the year surpass $1 billion.

1993: Competitive pressure and marketplace changes lead to quarterly losses, a $130 million restructuring, and a year-end stock price of $22.50.

1995: Surgical Dynamics Inc., maker of spinal surgery products, is acquired.

1996: Hostile bid for Circon Corp. is launched.

1998: Electrosurgical device maker Valleylab is acquired; USSC is acquired by Tyco International Ltd.; hostile takeover of Circon is terminated.

following year, as cost-conscious hospitals cut back on inventory, the company's sales nonetheless rose to $180 million. By 1984, USSC controlled 90 percent of the market for internal surgical staples and the majority of the market for external, skin staples.

USSC had diversified its product line to include 13 more products in 1981, and in 1984 it introduced a new technological breakthrough: absorbable staples, which made staple removal unnecessary. While absorbable suture thread had existed for years, the company's new product introduced this quality to the stapling procedure. In the mid-1980s USSC also embarked on a program to enter the suture market. In 1987 the company won a ruling from the Food & Drug Administration streamlining the process for approval of new suture materials, and it announced plans to introduce its suture materials by the early 1990s; USSC entered the suture market in 1991.

Late 1980s and Early 1990s: Skyrocketing Fortunes from Laparoscopic Devices

By far the most important development of 1987 for USSC, however, was the introduction of the Surgiport trocar, a disposable tubelike device through which other surgical instruments were inserted into the body. The company had purchased exclusive rights to this technology from a company called EndoTherapeutics in the previous year. This gadget eventually opened the door to laparoscopic surgery, in which very small incisions were

made in the body so that a camera could be inserted, enabling a surgeon to operate using instruments channeled through narrow tubes. This technique reduced the need for large incisions, which required long periods of recovery for the patient.

In the late 1980s USSC came under fire from animal rights activists for its use of dogs as laboratory animals. For years, the company had used hundreds of dogs to train its sales force in surgical techniques, and also to train doctors in the use of its instruments. Activists complained that these practices were unnecessary and constituted cruelty to animals, and the company was plagued by a number of vociferous protest demonstrations. In 1988 a bomb was placed near Hirsch's parking place by an animal rights protestor, but USSC's company security had infiltrated the movement and was able to prevent the bomb from doing any harm.

Contrary to the wishes of the animal rights protestors, USSC's financial fortunes skyrocketed in the early 1990s. Although the company sold only $10 million worth of laparoscopic tools in 1987, three years later the company introduced the "Endo Clip," which allowed laparoscopic gall bladder removal, and the market for these tools began to grow rapidly. Soon, laparoscopy was also being used for hernia operations, appendectomies, hysterectomies, and other types of abdominal surgery.

With a virtual monopoly on sales of the equipment for these operations, USSC saw its sales grow by 50 percent in 1990 and 75 percent in the first half of 1991. Earnings during that time grew by 78 percent, and by the end of the year, they had nearly doubled since 1990. USSC sold more than $300 million worth of laparoscopic equipment in 1991, to become one of the fastest-growing companies in the United States, with profits of $91 million. The company's stock price kept pace with its spectacular increase in business, and many of USSC's executives who owned stock found themselves millionaires.

Hirsch predicted ample room for growth in the laparoscopic field, as the technique was adapted to an ever greater number of surgical tasks, and USSC set out to market a package of laparoscopic tools, surgical staples, and sutures. In addition, the company began a major push to market its products in Europe, building a new sales and distribution center in France. Overall, one quarter of USSC's revenues came from foreign sales.

By 1992, 85 percent of all gall bladder procedures in the United States were performed using laparoscopic techniques. At the end of that year, USSC's revenues had topped $1 billion, of which half was contributed by laparoscopic products. The company's stupendous success with these instruments had attracted a competitor: industry giant Johnson & Johnson formed Ethicon Endo-Surgery and vowed to introduce 40 competing products. In response to this threat, and the presence of other competitors in the field, USSC brought suit alleging patent infringement.

Mid-1990s: Declining Fortunes

In January 1993, USSC won a suit against a subsidiary of Eli Lilly & Company in which its opponent was ordered to stop making and marketing its products. By the middle of the year, however, the company's luck had changed, as its sales dropped dramatically in the face of fierce price competition from its other competitor, Ethicon. In July 1993, USSC reported a quarterly loss of $22 million. A switch in distribution practices, to a more prompt just-in-time delivery system, caused an unexpectedly sharp fall-off in sales, as hospitals used up the backlog of products that had stockpiled on their shelves, confident that they could acquire more when they needed them.

By September 1993, USSC was still struggling with the effects of a vast oversupply of its products, and its stock price had gone into a steep slide—from its January 1992 high of $134.50 to $22.50. Anxiety over the possible effects of healthcare reform, as well as the maturation of the market for gall bladder instruments and a drop-off in popularity of other laparoscopic procedures, also helped to depress USSC's sales. The company's heavy investments in manufacturing capacity, which had caused it to go into debt, further damaged USSC's financial results, and the company embarked upon a plan to reduce expenditures.

In October 1993, USSC announced another quarter of losses and specified the cost-cutting procedures it would adopt. The company planned to lay off eight percent of its workforce (700 people), cut executive pay, and reduce its stock dividend. In an effort to reduce the oversupply of its products, USSC announced that it would shut down its factories for two weeks in the fall and then reopen them on a four-day work week. In December 1993, the company announced further cuts as its financial woes continued, and it took a $130 million charge against its earnings to pay for its restructuring. An additional 1,600 jobs were lopped off the payroll.

In February 1994, USSC began to seek investors to infuse badly needed cash into the company. This move came after USSC lost a suit it had brought against Ethicon for patent infringement, removing the possibility of a big cash settlement to strengthen its balance sheet. The balance sheet was, however, strengthened through a private stock offering that raised $200 million. USSC, in the face of the managed healthcare revolution, also began altering its sales tactics. Previously, it had sold its products directly to surgeons. But hospitals had developed purchasing groups through which they could demand large discounts. USSC started taking more of a partnership approach as it began dealing with such groups and other cost-conscious buyers. Meanwhile, Hirsch faced a more personal legal battle, a class-action suit alleging insider trading and excessive compensation in connection with his exercise of stock options prior to the spring 1993 stock plunge. It was eventually resolved through an undisclosed settlement.

By 1995 USSC had recovered enough to post respectable profits of $79.2 million on sales of $1.02 billion. The company, however, needed to find new sources of growth as its core stapling, laparoscopic, and suture products were no longer going to be the growth vehicles they once were because of continuing competition, particularly from Johnson & Johnson. USSC, therefore, began seeking acquisitions to expand its product line. In late 1995 the company spent $60 million for Surgical Dynamics Inc., a maker of spinal cages and other devices used in spinal surgery. In August 1996 came a $230 million hostile takeover bid for Circon Corp., a Santa Barbara, California-based maker of endoscopic and sterilization equipment for the

urology and gynecology markets. This product line would fit in well with that of USSC, but Circon fiercely fought to stay independent in what developed into a protracted battle. By August 1997 USSC had gained a 14.9 percent stake in Circon, and in a proxy fight two months later decisively won two seats on Circon's board.

While Circon continued to stave off a complete takeover, USSC pursued other targets. In 1997 and 1998 the company made several acquisitions in the area of women's healthcare, including products used for minimally invasive breast biopsy. In early 1998 USSC acquired Pfizer Inc.'s Valleylab unit for about $425 million. Based in Boulder, Colorado, Valleylab was a maker of surgical ultrasound systems as well as electrosurgical devices used to cut and cauterize.

Late 1990s and Beyond: New Life As a Tyco Subsidiary

In the consolidating late 1990s, USSC itself became an acquisition target and the company agreed to be acquired by Tyco International Ltd., a Bermuda-based acquisitive conglomerate in May 1998. Tyco completed the acquisition in October of that year, through a deal valued at about $3.2 billion in stock. USSC thus became a subsidiary of Tyco and part of the Tyco Healthcare Group, which also included Kendall Healthcare, a maker of a wide range of disposable medical products. In anticipation of its takeover by Tyco, and in light of Tyco's professed antipathy to hostile deals, USSC terminated its tender offer for Circon in September 1998. As was typical, Tyco immediately began a cost-cutting program at USSC, including a workforce reduction of 775. Management changes also ensued. Hirsch, who had reached the age of 71, would no longer head the company he had founded 34 years earlier. Richard A. Gilleland, who was a former chairman and CEO of Kendall, was named to replace him.

Principal Subsidiaries

ARR, Inc.; ASE Continuing Education Center S.A. (France); ASE Partners S.A. (France); Auto Suture Austria GmbH (Austria); Auto Suture Belgium B.V.; Auto Suture Company, Australia; Auto Suture Company, Canada; Auto Suture Company, Netherlands; Auto Suture Company, U.K.; Auto Suture Do Brasil Ltda. (Brazil); Auto Suture Eastern Europe, Inc.; Auto Suture España, S.A. (Spain); Auto Suture Europe Holdings, Inc.; Auto Suture Europe S.A. (France); Auto Suture Europe Service Center, S.A. (France); Auto Suture France, S.A.; Auto Suture International, Inc.; Auto Suture Italia, S.p.A. (Italy); Auto Suture Japan, Inc.; Auto Suture Korea, Inc.; Auto Suture Norden Co.; Auto Suture Poland, sp. z. o. o.; Auto Suture Puerto Rico, Inc.; Auto Suture Russia, Inc.; Auto Suture (Schweiz) AG (Switzerland); Auto Suture Surgical Instruments (Russia); Medolas Gesellschaft fur Medizintechnik gmbH (Germany); Surgical Dynamics Europe, S.A.S. (France); Surgical Dynamics, Inc.; Surgical Dynamics Japan, Inc.; USSC AG (Switzerland); USSC (Deutschland) GmbH (Germany); USSC Financial Services, Inc.; USSC Medical GmbH (Germany); USSC Puerto Rico, Inc.

Principal Competitors

American Home Products Corporation; Baxter International Inc.; Bayer AG; Boston Scientific Corporation; Bristol-Myers Squibb Company; C.R. Bard, Inc.; Cardinal Health, Inc.; CONMED Corporation; Hoffmann-La Roche, Inc.; Johnson & Johnson; McKesson General Medical; Medline Industries, Inc.; Medtronic Sofamor Danek, Inc.; Novartis AG; Stryker Corporation; Teleflex Corporation; Utah Medical Products, Inc.; Vital Signs, Inc.

Further Reading

Collins, Sara, "On the Operating Table: Ailing U.S. Surgical Misjudged the New Health Care Market," *U.S. News and World Report,* September 19, 1994, p. 62.

David, Gregory E., "Cornered," *Financial World,* July 19, 1994, pp. 26–28.

Driscoll, Lisa, "U.S. Surgical Has Hearts Beating Faster," *Business Week,* August 12, 1991.

Feder, Barnaby J., "Feuding by Hospital Suppliers," *New York Times,* August 25, 1981.

Kleinfeld, N.R., "U.S. Surgical's Checkered History," *New York Times,* May 11, 1984.

Kruger, Pamela, "Hanging in There with Leon Hirsch," *New York Times,* December 18, 1994, sec. 3, p. 1.

Lipin, Steven, "U.S. Surgical Launches Takeover Bid for Rival Circon, Valued at $230 Million," *Wall Street Journal,* August 2, 1996, p. B3.

Lublin, Joann S., "Circon CEO Auhll Is Seeking to Regain Board Seat in Battle with U.S. Surgical," *Wall Street Journal,* November 21, 1997, p. B6.

——, "U.S. Surgical's Rx for Circon: Corporate Governance," *Wall Street Journal,* October 6, 1997, p. B4.

Lublin, Joann S., and Mark Maremont, "A CEO with a Motto: 'Let's Make a Deal!,' " *Wall Street Journal,* January 28, 1999, p. B1.

Maremont, Mark, and Ross Kerber, "Tyco to Buy U.S. Surgical for $3.3 Billion in Stock," *Wall Street Journal,* May 26, 1998, p. A3.

Rudnitsky, Howard, "On the Mend," *Forbes,* December 2, 1996, pp. 58+.

Smart, Tim, "Can U.S. Surgical Make a Full Recovery?," *Business Week,* December 5, 1994, p. 68.

——, "Will U.S. Surgical's Cutting Edge Be Enough," *Business Week,* September 21, 1992.

Smith, Geoffrey, "The Guts to Say 'I Was Wrong,' " *Forbes,* May 28, 1979.

Teitelman, Robert, "Case Study," *Forbes,* May 7, 1984.

"U.S. Surgical Battles Back Against Rival Johnson & Johnson," *Health Industry Today,* January 1998, pp. 3–4.

Winslow, Ron, "U.S. Surgical Withdraws Hostile Offer for Circon After Bitter, Two-Year Fight," *Wall Street Journal,* September 16, 1998, p. B12.

—Elizabeth Rourke
—updated by David E. Salamie

United Technologies Corporation

One Financial Plaza
Hartford, Connecticut 06103
U.S.A.
Telephone: (860) 728-7000
Fax: (860) 728-7979
Web site: http://www.utc.com

Public Company
Incorporated: 1934 as United Aircraft Company
Employees: 148,000
Sales: $24.13 billion (1999)
Stock Exchanges: New York London Paris Brussels
Switzerland
Ticker Symbol: UTX
NAIC: 54171 Research and Development in the Physical,
Engineering, and Life Sciences; 333415 Air-
Conditioning and Warm Air Heating Equipment and
Commercial and Industrial Refrigeration Equipment
Manufacturing; 333921 Elevator and Moving Stairway
Manufacturing; 336411 Aircraft Manufacturing;
336412 Aircraft Engine and Engine Parts
Manufacturing

United Technologies Corporation (UTC) is one of the largest conglomerates in the United States and a major military contractor. Although it keeps a low profile, UTC's holdings (Carrier, Hamilton Sundstrand, Otis, Pratt & Whitney, and Sikorsky) are among the leading companies in their respective fields. Stung by global recession in the 1990s, UTC has embarked upon a never-ending quest to cut costs, and jobs, much to the displeasure of its unions.

Origins

United traces its origins to Fred Rentschler, who founded the Pratt & Whitney Aircraft Company in 1925 as one of the first companies to specialize in the manufacture of engines, or "power plants," for airframe builders. Pratt & Whitney's primary customers were Bill Boeing and Chance Vought. Interes-

ted in securing a market for his company's engines, Rentschler convinced Boeing and Vought to join him in forming a new company called the United Aircraft and Transportation Company. The company was formed in 1929, and thereafter Pratt & Whitney, Boeing, and Vought gave exclusive priority to each other's business.

Early in its history, United Aircraft became so successful that it was soon able to purchase other important suppliers and competitors, establishing a strong monopoly. The group grew to include Boeing, Pratt & Whitney, and Vought, as well as Sikorsky, Stearman, and Northrop (airframes); Hamilton Aero Manufacturing and Standard Steel Prop (propellers); and Stout Airlines, in addition to Boeing's airline companies.

The men who led these individual divisions of United Aircraft exchanged stock in their original companies for stock in United. The strong public interest in the larger company drove the value of United Aircraft's stock up in subsequent flotations. The original shareholders quickly became very wealthy; Rentschler himself had turned a meager $253 cash investment into $35.5 million by 1929.

During this time, U.S. Postmaster William Folger Brown cited United Aircraft as the largest airline network and the most stable equipment supplier in the country. Thus, the company was assured of winning the postal service's lucrative airmail contracts before it applied for them. The company's airmail business required the manufacturing division to devote all of its resources to expansion of the airline division. Soon United Aircraft controlled nearly half of the nation's airline and aircraft business, becoming a classic example of an aeronautic monopoly.

Breaking Up in the 1930s

In 1934, Senator Hugo Black initiated an investigation of fraud and improprieties in the aeronautics business. Bill Boeing was called to the witness stand, and subsequent interrogation exposed United Aircraft's monopolistic business practices, eventually leading to the break-up of the huge aeronautic combine. Thereafter, Boeing sold all of his stock in his company and retired. In the reorganization of the corporation, all manufacturing interests west of the Mississippi went to Boeing Airplane in

Seattle, everything east of the river went to Rentschler's United Aircraft in Hartford, and the transport services became a third independent company under the name of United Air Lines which was based in Chicago.

Chance Vought died in 1930, and his company, along with Pratt & Whitney, Sikorsky, Ham Standard and Northrop, became part of the new United Aircraft Company. Sikorsky became a principal manufacturer of helicopters, Pratt & Whitney continued to build engines, and Vought later produced a line of airplanes including the Corsair and the Cutlass.

At the onset of World War II, business increased dramatically at United's Pratt & Whitney division. The company produced several hundred thousand engines for airplanes built by Boeing, Lockheed, McDonnell Douglas, Grumman, and Vought. Over half the engines in American planes were built by Pratt & Whitney. After the war, United Aircraft turned its attention to producing jet engines. The Pratt & Whitney subsidiary's entrance into the jet engine industry was hindered, however, as customers were constantly demanding improvements in the company's piston-driven Wasp engine. In the meantime, Pratt & Whitney's competitors, General Electric and Westinghouse, were free to devote more of their capital to the research and development of jet engines. Thus, when airframe builders started looking for jet engine suppliers, Pratt & Whitney was unprepared. Even United Aircraft's Vought division had to purchase turbo jets for its Cutlass model from Westinghouse.

Postwar Jets

Recognizing the gravity of the situation, United Aircraft began an ambitious program to develop a line of advanced jet engines. When the Korean War began in 1950, Pratt & Whitney was again deluged with orders. The mobilization of forces gave the company the opportunity to reestablish its strong relationship with the Navy and conduct business with its newly created Air Force.

In the early 1950s, United Aircraft experienced a conflict of interest between its airframe and engine manufacturing subsidiaries, as Vought's alternate engine suppliers—Westinghouse and General Motors' Allison division—were reluctant to do business with a company so closely associated with their competitor, Pratt & Whitney. On the other hand, Pratt & Whitney's other customers, Grumman, McDonnell, and Douglas, were concerned that their airframe technology would find its way to Vought. As a result, both of United Aircraft's divisions were suffering, and, in 1954, the board of directors voted to dissolve Vought.

In 1959, Fred Rentschler died, following a long illness, at the age of 68. Commenting on Rentschler's role in developing

engine technology to keep pace with that of the Soviet Union, a reporter in the *New York Times* stated: "This nation's air superiority is due in no small measure to Mr. Rentschler's vision and talents." Rentschler was succeeded as president of United Aircraft by W.P. Gwinn, while Jack Horner became chairman of the company's subsidiary Pratt & Whitney.

United Aircraft continued to manufacture engines and a variety of other aircraft accessories into the 1960s. Much of its business came from Boeing, which had several Pentagon contracts and whose 700-series jets were capturing 60 percent of the commercial airliner market. When Horner retired in 1968, he was succeeded by Gwinn. While this change in leadership was of little consequence to United Aircraft, which was running smoothly, Pratt & Whitney was about to enter a period of crisis.

First, there was considerable trouble with Pratt & Whitney's engines for Boeing's 747 jumbo jet. The problem, traced to a design flaw, cost Pratt & Whitney millions of dollars in research and redevelopment. Moreover, it also cost millions of dollars for Boeing in service calls and lost sales. Commercial airline companies suffered lost revenue from canceled flights and reduced passenger capacity.

A Change of Vision in the 1970s

By 1971, the performance of the Pratt & Whitney division had begun to depress company profits. The directors of United Aircraft acted quickly by hiring a new president, Harry Gray, who was drafted away from Litton Industries. Harry Gray was born Harry Jack Grusin in 1919. He suffered the loss of his mother at age six and was entrusted to the care of his sister in Chicago, when his father's business was ruined in the Depression. In 1936, he entered the University of Illinois at Urbana, earning a degree in journalism before serving in Europe with General Patton's Third Army infantry and artillery during World War II. After the war, he returned to Urbana, where he received a Master's degree in journalism. In Chicago, Grusin went through a succession of jobs, working as a truck salesperson and as a manager of a transport company. In 1951, he changed his name to Harry Gray, according to the court record, for "no reason." He moved to California in 1954 to work for the Litton Industries conglomerate, and he spent the next 17 years at Litton working his way up the corporate ladder.

Hindered in promotion at Litton by superiors who were not due to retire for several years, Gray accepted an offer from United Aircraft. While at Litton, Gray had been invited to tour General Electric's facility in Evandale, Ohio. Litton was a trusted customer of General Electric, and consequently Gray was warmly welcomed. He was made privy to rather detailed information on GE's long-range plans. A few weeks later, officials at GE read that Gray had accepted the presidency at their competitor United Aircraft. The officials protested Gray's actions but were casually reminded that Gray had asked not to be informed of any plans of a "proprietary" nature during his visit to the GE plant.

One of Gray's first acts at United Aircraft was to order an investigation into and reengineering of the Pratt & Whitney engines for Boeing's 747. He then sought to reduce United Aircraft's dependence on the Pentagon and began a purchasing

Key Dates:

1929: Aircraft makers Bill Boeing and Chance Vought join forces with Pratt & Whitney.

1934: United Aircraft officially incorporates from the triumvirate's eastern manufacturing assets.

1945: Pratt & Whitney powers half of all U.S. planes built during World War II.

1954: Aircraft manufacturer Vought dissolves due to conflicts of interest with P&W.

1975: United Aircraft buys majority of Otis Elevator; changes name to United Technologies.

1983: UTC buys Carrier Corporation, an air conditioner manufacturer.

1991: Amid global recession, P&W, Otis, and Carrier post losses.

1992: Major restructuring is launched by new management.

1999: UTC sells its auto parts business and buys aerospace supplier Sundstrand Corp.

program in an effort to diversify the business. In 1974, United Aircraft acquired Essex International, a manufacturer of wire and cables. One year later, the company purchased a majority interest in Otis Elevator for $276 million, and, in 1978, Dynell Electronics, a builder of radar systems, was added to the company's holdings. Next came Ambac Industries, which made diesel power systems and fuel injection devices.

United Aircraft changed its name to United Technologies (UTC) in 1975 in order to emphasize the diversification of the company's business. Acquisitions continued, as UTC purchased Mostek, a maker of semiconductors, for $345 million in 1981. Two years later, the company acquired the Carrier Corporation, a manufacturer of air conditioning systems. In addition, UTC purchased several smaller electronics, software, and computer firms.

Gray was reportedly known to maintain a portfolio of the 50 companies he most wanted to purchase; virtually all of his targets, including the ones he later acquired, viewed Gray's takeovers as hostile. Some of the companies which successfully resisted Gray's takeover attempts were ESB Ray-O-Vac (the battery maker), Signal (which built Mack Trucks), and Babcock and Wilcox (a manufacturer of power generating equipment).

During the 1980s, UTC operated four principal divisions: Power Products, including aircraft engines and spare parts; Flight Systems, which manufactured helicopters, electronics, propellers, instruments and space-related products; Building Systems, encompassing the businesses of Otis and Carrier; and Industrial Products, which produced various automotive parts, electric sensors and motors, and wire and printing products. The company, through its divisions, built aircraft engines for General Dynamic's YF-16 and F-111 bomber, Grumman's F-14 Tomcat, and McDonnell Douglas' F-15 Eagle. In addition, it supplied Boeing with engines for its 700-series jetliners, AWACs, B-52 bombers, and other airplanes. McDonnell Douglas and Airbus also purchased Pratt & Whitney engines.

Gray, who aimed to provide a new direction for UTC away from aerospace and defense, proved to be one of the company's most successful presidents. He learned the business of the company's principal product, jet engines, in a very short time; upon his appointment as president of United Aircraft, sales for the year amounted to $2 billion, and, by 1986, the company was recording $16 billion in sales. A year after he joined the company, Gray was named CEO, and soon thereafter he became chairman as well. In his 15 years at UTC, Gray completely refashioned the company. As Gray's retirement drew near, however, UTC's directors had a difficult time convincing him to relinquish power and name a successor. When a potential new leader appeared to be preparing for the role, Gray would allegedly subvert that person's power. One former UTC executive commented, "Harry equates his corporate position with his own mortality."

One welcome candidate to succeed Gray was Alexander Haig, who had served on UTC's board. However, Haig left the company after being appointed secretary of state in the Reagan administration. The members of the UTC board then created a special committee to persuade Gray to name a successor. Finally, in September 1985, Robert Daniell (formerly head of the Sikorsky division) was appointed to take over Gray's responsibilities as CEO of UTC. Nevertheless, Gray remained chairman.

Getting Rid of Gray in 1986

In light of the poor performances posted by the company's various divisions, some industry analysts were beginning to question Gray's leadership. His refusal to step aside threatened the stability of UTC. With the $424 million write-off of the failed Mostek unit, many analysts began talking of a general dissolution of UTC; the divisions were worth more individually than together. But these critics were silenced when Gray announced in September 1986 that he would retire and that Daniell would take his place.

Even before the official departure of Gray, Daniell had moved quickly to dismantle the company's philosophy of "growth through acquisition." Hundreds of middle-management positions were eliminated, and there was speculation that some of the less promising divisions would be sold. Daniell told the *Wall Street Journal*, "This is a new era for United Technologies. Harry Gray was brought here to grow the company. But now the company is built, the blocks are in place and growth will be a secondary objective." Daniell then had to prove that neither Gray's overstayed welcome nor his departure would affect the company adversely.

Daniell also had more pressing challenges. The U.S.S.R.'s collapse in the late 1980s revealed that it had been a much weaker military foe than previously believed. As a result, the end of the Cold War brought Congressional and public pressure to cut domestic defense budgets. While some other leading defense companies moved to carve out niches in the shrinking market, UTC worked to strengthen its interests in more commercial industries.

UTC's transition was not smooth, and Pratt & Whitney suffered the most. While in 1990 Pratt & Whitney had brought in one-third of UTC's sales and an impressive two-thirds of operating profit, the subsidiary's losses from 1991 to 1993 reached $1.3 billion. Pratt & Whitney was hampered not only by defense cuts, but also by the serious downturn in the commercial airline industry, intense global competition, and a worldwide recession. Moreover, saturation of the commercial real estate market during this time caused declines in demand for elevators and air conditioners, products manufactured by UTC's Otis and Carrier subsidiaries. These companies also recorded losses for 1991. That year, UTC also faced six charges of illegal dumping against its Sikorsky Aircraft division. In the largest penalty levied under the Resource Conservation & Recovery Act up to that time, UTC agreed to pay $3 million in damages.

In 1992, Daniell brought George David, who had been instrumental in the revival of both the Otis and Carrier units, on board as UTC president. David, in turn, tapped Karl Krapek, who was called a ''veteran turnaround artist'' by *Financial World,* to lead the beleaguered Pratt & Whitney subsidiary. Krapek quickly reduced employment at the unit from a high of 50,000 to 40,000 by the beginning of 1993. The divisional reformation also focused on manufacturing, with the goals of shortening lead times, reducing capacity, and expediting processes. Overall employment at UTC was cut by 16,500 from 1991 to 1993.

By the end of 1993, Daniell was able to report positive results; UTC made $487 million on sales of $20.74 billion. In April 1994, after leading the corporation for nearly a decade, Daniell appointed David as the company's CEO, retaining his position as UTC's chairman.

Otis's annual revenues remained in the $4.5 billion range in the early to mid-1990s, while Carrier's rose from $4.3 billion in 1992 to nearly $5 billion in 1994. During the same period, automotive sales rose from $2.4 billion to $2.7 billion. Pratt & Whitney saw commercial engine revenues fall by $800 million, to 2.9 billion. Military and space engine sales fell from $2.5 billion to $1.8 billion while general aviation sales fell by about ten percent to $1.1 billion. During this time, the company paid $180 million for environmental remediation at more than 300 sites. Although cost-cutting improved profits by the mid-1990s, UTC continued cutting jobs.

UTC entered more than a dozen joint ventures overseas while the aerospace industry suffered a recession. The company derived a little over half of its revenues from abroad, and enjoyed strong growth in Asia in the mid-1990s, at least until the Asian financial crisis of 1997. In 1996, UTC had revenues of $1 billion in the People's Republic of China and Hong Kong.

Some technical developments seemed promising. Pratt & Whitney unveiled its most powerful engine ever in 1996. The PW4090 was rated at 90,000 pounds of thrust. (Three years later, the company tested the PW4098, rated at 98,000 pounds.) The new Odyssey system at Otis allowed elevator cars to move both vertically and horizontally.

In January 1997, Sikorsky and Boeing won a $1.7 billion contract to continue developing their RAH-66 Comanche armed reconnaissance helicopter. Sikorsky was able to maintain production levels of its Black Hawk helicopter. Pratt & Whitney engines were chosen for two new military aircraft programs, the

F-22 fighter and the C-17 freighter. On the civilian side, Otis Elevator cut 2,000 jobs as sales fell in the wake of the Asian financial crisis. It also closed its Paris headquarters and most of its engineering centers.

UTC was able to save money on commodities by having its thousands of vendors bid online. These types of products accounted for about a quarter of the $14 billion the company spent on outside goods and services, according to the *Financial Times.* International revenues accounted for about 56 percent of UTC's total in the late 1990s, reaching 60 percent in 1999. Profits were rising in all divisions except UT Automotive.

Reconfiguring for the Future

UTC bought Sundstrand Corp. for about $4 billion in 1999, merging it with Hamilton Standard. Sundstrand derived 60 percent of its $2 billion in annual revenues from aerospace products. On the recommendation of the Goldman, Sachs & Co. investment bank, UTC decided to sell its automotive parts unit in the light of growing price pressure from automakers. Lear Corporation bought the business for $2.3 billion in May 1999. Otis Elevator entered a joint venture with LG Industries in South Korea while Carrier bought out North American competitor International Comfort Products and allied with the Toshiba Corporation.

Layoffs continued at Sikorsky, Carrier, Pratt & Whitney, Hamilton Sundstrand, and Otis—part of a new wave of company-wide restructuring designed to reduce UTC's total workforce by ten percent, or 15,000 jobs. However, in February 2000, a federal judge barred Pratt & Whitney from moving engine repair work out of Connecticut, saying this violated an existing union agreement. Plans to close Hamilton Sundstrand's Connecticut electronics facility also prompted complaints this was aimed at taking away about 400 jobs from the machinists' union.

The company bought Cade Industries, a Michigan aerospace supplier, in February 2000. The next month, UTC announced a new engine overhaul joint venture with KLM, the Dutch airline, which already had a relationship with Hamilton Sundstrand.

Principal Subsidiaries

Carrier Corporation; Hamilton Sundstrand Corporation; Otis Elevator Company; Pratt & Whitney; Sikorsky Aircraft Corporation.

Principal Divisions

Carrier; Otis; Pratt & Whitney; Flight Systems.

Principal Competitors

The Boeing Company; General Electric Company; Textron Inc.

Further Reading

''EPA Levies Record RCRA, CWA Fines,'' *Environment Today,* June 1991, p. 14.
Fernandez, Ronald, *Excess Profits: The Rise of United Technologies,* Reading, Mass.: Addison-Wesley, 1983.

Griffith, Victoria, ''Otis Cuts 2,000 Jobs As Asia Crisis Bites,'' *Financial Times,* April 14, 1998, p. 24.

Jacobs, Karen, ''United Technologies' Job Cuts Spark Labor-Board Inquiry, Action by Judge,'' *Wall Street Journal,* February 23, 2000, p. A6.

Ma, Peter, ''Virtual Auctions Knock Down Costs,'' *Financial Times,* November 3, 1998, pp. 17+.

Norman, James R., ''Welcome to the Real World,'' *Forbes,* February 15, 1993, pp. 46–47.

Smart, Tim, ''UTC Gets a Lift from Its Smaller Engines,'' *Business Week,* December 20, 1993, pp. 109–10.

Stainburn, Samantha, ''Big Names Bow Out,'' *Government Executive,* August 1997, pp. 67–81.

Sullivan, Allanna, ''United Technologies, Looking to Sell Auto-Parts Business, Talks to Buyers,'' *Wall Street Journal,* February 17, 1999, p. A6.

——, ''United Technologies Profit Exceeds Estimates, As Revamping Is Launched,'' *The Wall Street Journal,* July 21, 1999, p. B9.

Velocci, Anthony L., Jr., ''United Technologies Restructures in Bid to Boost Profitability, Competitiveness,'' *Aviation Week & Space Technology,* January 27, 1992, p. 35.

—updated by April Dougal Gasbarre
—updated by Frederick C. Ingram

The Vanguard Group, Inc.

100 Vanguard Boulevard
Malvern, Pennsylvania 19355
U.S.A.
Telephone: (610) 648-6000
Fax: (610) 669-6605
Web site: http://www.vanguard.com

Private Company
Incorporated: 1974 as The Vanguard Group of
  Investment Companies
Employees: 10,500
Sales: $1.2 billion (1998 est.)
NAIC: 52392 Portfolio Management (pt); 52393
  Investment Advice

The Vanguard Group, Inc. is one of the most successful mutual fund companies in the United States. Managing more than $520 billion worth of investors' money, the firm provides an entire family of mutual funds from real estate to bond funds. Its Vanguard 500 Index Fund, a portfolio of stocks that tracks the broad market, is the largest of the 103 domestic funds managed by the firm and is among the largest of U.S. mutual funds. Vanguard's family of mutual funds maintains one of the lowest expense ratios—the relation of management costs for a fund to the amount of assets in the fund—within the financial services industry.

The Birth of the Mutual Fund: 1920s–40s

Although the Vanguard Group of Investment Companies was started in 1974 by John C. Bogle, its predecessor goes back to 1929. The Wellington Fund was started by Walter L. Morgan in July 1929. Morgan, a certified public accountant with a degree from Princeton University, was convinced that the ordinary investor with limited money needed a diversified investment portfolio managed by a professional staff, rather than just venturing out on his own and buying individual company stocks. Massachusetts Mutual Fund, America's first mutual fund, was established in 1924 in Boston, and Morgan immediately recognized the opportunity that such an investment service provided.

When Morgan formed the Wellington Fund, he based the firm's investment strategy on three principles: 1) that the fund was unleveraged rather than leveraged, thus reducing the risk involved in using money that was borrowed; 2) that Wellington would be an open-end fund rather than a closed-end fund, and 3) that Wellington would be a balanced rather than a common stock fund, thereby reducing a customer's risk by including bonds as well as stocks in the individual's investment portfolio. These highly conservative decisions made in the midst of the most rampantly speculative era in stock market history served Morgan well. With the coming of the stock market crash in the autumn of 1929, the Wellington Fund not only remained in business but prospered. Capitalizing on its conservative investment philosophy, the fund's assets passed the $1 million mark by 1935 and grew steadily. By 1943, the Wellington Fund reported over $10 million in assets and by 1949, over $100 million.

Ups and Downs in the 1950s and 1960s

Throughout the 1950s and early 1960s, Wellington Management Company, the formal organization with the responsibility of managing the Wellington Fund's assets, operated on four principles: a conservative investment philosophy, an emphasis on long-term investment performance, a single fund without any related or ''sister'' funds, and a comprehensive, well-organized sales and marketing campaign through brokers and investment advisors across the country.

As the years passed, however, what had worked for the company during the previous years was no longer viable for the era of burgeoning stock market investments. By the late 1960s, the company's strategy of a balanced fund was out of favor with almost all investment advisors. The Wellington Fund, once the leader in balanced fund investing, fell to lower and lower performance levels. At the same time, Walter Morgan decided to retire from active management of the fund, and hired John C. Bogle, a Princeton University graduate. Morgan encouraged Bogle to revive the Wellington Fund by whatever means necessary, and the young man immediately established a strategy which included the acquisition of an aggressive growth fund, the entry into the investment counsel business, and hiring highly capable and experienced portfolio fund managers.

Company Perspectives:

Underpinning our shareholder-focused philosophy is a set of values that guide our day-to-day operations: we manage our funds with prudence, a long-term orientation, and clearly defined objectives. Our overriding goal is to provide investment returns that are competitive with those of similar mutual funds as well as with our unmanaged benchmark indexes; ever mindful of the trust placed in us by our clients, we put our fiduciary duty to them first and foremost, ahead of marketing or other considerations. This ''client-first'' philosophy allows us to focus on getting better, not bigger; we provide accurate and candid information to investors, prominently discussing the risks and costs of investing as well as the rewards; we maintain a spirit of fair dealing, integrity, and honesty in our relationships with clients; we avoid hyperbolic advertising, especially the kind that focuses on past investment performance, which has no predictive value for the future; we foster a commitment to excellence in the crew serving our clients.

Carrying out Bogle's new plan as quickly as possible, The Wellington Company purchased Thorndike, Doran, Paine and Lewis, Inc., a well-established and successful investment firm in Boston, Massachusetts, that managed the Ivest Fund. The new acquisition also included an investment counsel business and four talented portfolio managers. The marriage of The Wellington Company's administrative and marketing operations to Thorndike, Doran, Paine and Lewis's investment expertise was concluded in 1967. It was assumed that Bogle would become the chief executive office of both companies and their respective funds. From the very start of the merger, events seemed to conspire against its success. The stock market declined, both the Wellington and Ivest Funds performed poorly, and business in general was on the downswing. Dissatisfaction began to arise among management and in 1974, because Bogle's associates from the Boston firm had a majority on the Wellington Management Company's board of directors, they summarily fired him.

Shifting Course in the 1970s and 1980s

Although Bogle was heartbroken over his dismissal and the loss of what he considered to be his company, he was determined to revive his fortunes. The Wellington Fund was required by U.S. federal law to have a board of directors independent of the managing company's board of directors. This latter group of directors voted to retain Bogle as chairman of the fund. Bogle then advocated to his board of directors that the Wellington Fund and Ivest Fund should be given complete independence of the Wellington Management Company. Yet the board of directors at the fund decided that Wellington Management Company should continue providing marketing and portfolio management services and also keep its name; at the same time the two *funds,* Wellington and Ivest, should be made independent of the Wellington Management Company and be given a new name. Bogle chose the name Vanguard, in honor of Lord Horatio Nelson's flagship HMS *Vanguard* during the Napoleonic Wars. Incorporated in 1974, The Vanguard Group of Investment Companies opened for business in July 1975.

Bogle had advocated that the Wellington Fund and the Ivest Fund should be their own distributor. At first the board of directors rejected this proposal, but in 1977 it was decided that the two funds should get rid of Wellington Management Company as their distributor and designate Vanguard. The move resulted in an immediate cessation of the traditional broker-dealer distribution network that had always been used by the two funds and the total elimination of any sales charges. The conversion to what is now called a ''no load'' fund was due to the demand from consumers for lower prices in the management of their money. Initially, the company's cash flow reflected a loss of $125 million in 1976, but by 1977 Vanguard proudly reported a complete turnaround—its cash flow had jumped to a positive $50 million.

The 1980s were some of the brightest years for the company. Bogle decided to bring in-house the management of Vanguard's fixed income portfolio, which included six money market and municipal bond funds whose assets were approximately $1.8 billion. During this period, Vanguard's total assets rose from $500 million to almost $4 billion. The company's Windsor Fund, a mixed equities portfolio, was one of the best performing mutual funds in the nation during the entire decade, and its assets increased from $900 million to nearly $8 billion. Assets for the Vanguard Index Trust, the first index mutual fund in the world, skyrocketed from a mere $90 million to an astonishing $7.5 billion. By the end of the decade, Vanguard was acknowledged as the leading no-load mutual fund service which, in turn, led to more profitable returns and greater growth. The assets managed by the company had grown from $3 billion in 1980 to over $50 billion by the fall of 1990.

Vanguard's impressive growth during the 1980s was carried along by one of the most active and positive periods in the worldwide financial markets. During the early 1980s, both stocks and bonds started to produce tremendous returns on investments. On average throughout the decade, the bond market produced an annual rate of return of 13 percent, the highest in the history of the market. At the same time, the stock market came close to its historically highest rate of return, averaging an annual return of just over 18 percent. In addition, tax laws were changed in favor of retirement programs, and individual retirement accounts (IRAs) greatly enhanced the total asset base of the mutual fund industry. In fact, assets for the entire mutual fund industry leaped from $240 billion in 1981 to approximately $1.3 trillion by 1991, a sixfold increase. Although the company's portfolio managers were able and talented, Vanguard doubtless rode the crest of the wave across all the financial markets. Assets managed by Vanguard in December 1991 had increased to $75 billion. Since its inception, Vanguard's asset base had grown at a phenomenal compounded growth rate of 35 percent annually.

Continued Growth in the 1990s

The Vanguard Group was in the vanguard of the mutual fund industry during the early and mid-1990s. The Vanguard Index Trust had grown into one of the largest equity mutual funds in the world, and the company set the standard for market indexing management. Consumerism led the way toward a cost-consciousness within the industry that has had lasting effects. Many of the mutual funds created during the early part of the decade were "no-load" direct marketing funds, following the lead that Vanguard had set years earlier. Ever mindful of the way extra costs decrease a customer's yields, in 1993 Vanguard introduced four new no-load funds with minimal expenses. Called the Admiral funds, these funds had an expense ratio, which includes money management fees and other costs, of a mere 0.15 percent of net assets. Compared with an average of 0.53 percent for United States Treasury money-market funds and 0.93 percent for United States Treasury bond funds, many investors were pleased with the bargain. This difference was telling, since only $100 in expenses would be paid by a customer who invested in the Vanguard Admiral U.S. Treasury Money Market Portfolio as opposed to $440 dollars in expenses in a Fidelity Spartan fund. The only drawback was that the Admiral funds required a minimum investment of $50,000.

In 1994, Vanguard enjoyed one of its best years. Although the market for bonds was highly volatile due to leveraged and risky kinds of derivatives and many mutual funds that specialized in bonds suffered as a result, Vanguard escaped the turmoil because of its supremely efficient bond fund management. In addition, when diversified stock funds lost 1.7 percent across the entire mutual fund industry, Vanguard's low costs and expenses enabled its stock funds to post a 0.6 percent average gain. Not surprisingly, 16 out of Vanguard's 18 diversified stock funds performed better than the industrywide average. By the end of 1994, Vanguard's total asset base had increased to $132 billion.

In July 1995, John J. Brennan was chosen to succeed John C. Bogle as chief executive officer of Vanguard. Brennan, only 40 years old at the time of the appointment, had worked at the company for 13 years and had acted as Bogle's deputy since 1989. Brennan's vision included continuing the emphasis on index funds that his predecessor had started, along with the strategy of low-cost management of all the firm's mutual funds. Brennan also laid plans to invest in new technology that would allow people to transfer money from their bank to buy a Vanguard fund by using a personal home computer. In addition, he hoped to offset the competition from discount brokers by setting up a network so Vanguard would be able to sell non-Vanguard funds for a small transaction fee.

With the stock market climbing to record highs throughout 1995, both institutional investors and private investors began to pour money into mutual funds that were designed to follow the performance of market measures such as Standard & Poor's 500 (S&P 500). These index funds became the leading performers during the year. Index funds that mimicked the S&P 500 re-

ported increases of 19.9 percent during the first six months of 1995, compared to the average equity fund that only gained 16.6 percent during the same period. Vanguard's Index 500 Fund, with more than $13 billion in assets, was the largest such portfolio. In the first half of 1995, the fund had taken in a net $1.5 billion of new money from investors. With the influx of such a large amount of money, the Index 500 became the company's largest stock fund.

At the end of 1995, Vanguard listed a wide range of mutual funds that investors could choose from, including money market funds, tax-exempt income funds, state tax-exempt income funds, fixed-income funds, balanced funds, growth and income funds, growth funds, aggressive growth funds, and international funds. A few of the company's most successful mutual funds included the 500 Portfolio Fund, an index fund that invested in all the 500 stocks of the S&P 500 Composite Stock Price Index and which recorded an average annual return of 16.99 percent over the five-year period ending September 30, 1995; the Growth and Income Portfolio Fund, another index fund that reported an average annual return of 25.63 percent during the recent five-year period ending in September 1995; and the Vanguard Explorer Fund, an aggressive-growth fund that specialized in emerging companies with highly attractive growth potential and which recorded an average annual return of 22.84 percent over the five-year period ending in September 1995.

Vanguard continued to grow its operations and services in the second half of the decade and prospered. At the beginning of 1996 a changing of the guard took place when founder John Bogle stepped down as CEO. Bogle remained the chairman of Vanguard's board. John J. Brennan, who had been with Vanguard since 1982, was appointed CEO. Bogle nominated Brennan to fill his shoes and said in a prepared statement, "I have full confidence that, under his [Brennan's] leadership, Vanguard will maintain the basic principles that have served the company so well over the past two decades. And I know his judgment and decisiveness will enable Vanguard to face the challenges that lie ahead."

Under Brennan's leadership, Vanguard maintained its traditional low costs while expanding operations to remain competitive in the volatile financial services industry. Internationally, the company established Vanguard Investments Australia in 1997 to serve institutional investors. A year later the division began to offer six indexed funds to individual customers. Also in 1998 the company added three indexed mutual funds to its Vanguard Group Ireland offerings. Other notable new events in the mid-1990s included the launch of Vanguard Fiduciary Services in 1998. The unit provided investment management and advisory services to such organizations as foundations, endowments, and tax-exempt organizations. At the end of its first year of operations, the fiduciary group had more than 50 clients and managed about $4.2 billion in assets. The Personal Financial Services (PFS) division, started in 1997, was made up of Vanguard Asset Management and Trust Services and Personal Financial Planning. PFS grew quickly, and by the end of 1998 the unit managed or had produced advisory plans for about $10 billion in assets, an increase of 100 percent since the end of 1997.

Vanguard had an outstanding year in 1998, thanks in large part to the U.S. stock market, which experienced a fourth consecutive year of gains exceeding 20 percent. In 1998 alone,

Vanguard added more than two million new accounts, boosting its total to more than 12 million by the end of the year. The firm's share of U.S. mutual fund assets grew to 7.9 percent, more than twice its market share of 3.8 percent a decade earlier. In addition to adding three new index funds to U.S. investors, Vanguard introduced its 13th state tax-exempt municipal bond fund, launched online trading capabilities as part of the services offered by Vanguard Brokerage Services, and revamped its web site to provide individual clients the capability to open new accounts, view account balances and change options, and access information about Vanguard's funds. Amid all the activity, Vanguard managed to keep its costs low. According to Lipper Inc., which tracks fund performance, Vanguard's operating costs averaged 0.28 percent of assets during 1998, compared to an industry average of 1.25 percent.

As the second largest mutual fund company in the world in 1998, Vanguard received recognition for its innovations and performance. The firm's web site was elected the best mutual fund site of 1998 by *Institutional Investor* magazine's weekly newsletter, *Financial NetNews*. Vanguard also made it onto *InformationWeek*'s list of top technology innovators, and *Working Mother* listed Vanguard as one of the best companies for working mothers. In addition, the firm's 1998 Client Satisfaction Survey determined that more than 99 percent of its individual investor clients were pleased with Vanguard and would recommend the firm to others.

Though Vanguard's financial success continued in the late 1990s, the firm experienced some internal upheaval. Vanguard's board of directors, including Bogle's successor as CEO, sought to force John Bogle into retirement when he reached the age of 70 in May 1999. Though the company had a policy requiring employees who turned 70 to retire, Bogle desired to remain on the board and protested the decision. Employees and investors alike voiced their outrage at the attempted ousting of the legendary founder. The dispute continued through the summer, and in September the board relented, offering Bogle the opportunity to remain on the board. Surprisingly, Bogle turned down the offer. Instead, Bogle continued to work at Vanguard as the head of the newly formed Bogle Financial Markets Research Center.

Heading into the new millennium, Vanguard continued to forge ahead. According to consultancy and fund-tracking firm Financial Research Corporation, Vanguard had net sales of about $45.9 billion in 1999, making it the mutual fund industry's leader, in terms of long-term fund sales, for the fourth consecutive year. In addition, Vanguard's flagship Vanguard 500 Index Fund was on the verge of displacing Fidelity Magellan Fund from the top spot as the world's largest mutual fund in early 2000. Magellan had been the largest mutual fund for nearly a dozen years and in 1992 was three times the size of the Vanguard 500 Index Fund. From 1995 to 2000, however, Vanguard's fund grew quickly, outperforming many actively managed funds and reporting gains of more than 28 percent a year. By early 2000, Vanguard 500 had more than $100 billion in assets.

To maintain its leadership position, Vanguard aimed to increase its international presence and to continue offering a full breadth of stocks, bonds, and mixed funds to the investing public. The company announced plans to add a socially responsible mutual fund to its long list of offerings by early 2000; the Vanguard Calvert Social Index Fund would be the first socially responsible fund offered by a major fund company. Vanguard also intended to invest more energy into its actively managed funds, which did not fare particularly well in the late 1990s, to maintain a better balance of financial offerings. Additionally, industry analysts believed the heyday of the index fund was passing, and Vanguard did not wish to be left behind. By the end of February 2000, for example, more than 75 percent of actively managed funds were outperforming the S&P 500, a feat that had not been matched since 1977. In March 2000 Vanguard said it planned to offer two new actively managed funds and formed a partnership with Turner Investment Partners to reorganize the Turner Growth Equity Fund into the Vanguard Growth Equity Fund. With managed assets exceeding $520 billion and a long history of placing the needs of its investor-shareholders first, Vanguard seemed likely to continue growing and dominating the global mutual fund industry.

Principal Operating Divisions

The Individual Investor Group; The Institutional Investor Group.

Principal Competitors

FMR Corp.; Barclays PLC; Mellon Financial Corporation; Merrill Lynch & Co., Inc.

Further Reading

Bogle, John, *Vanguard: The First Century,* Newcomen Society: New York, 1992.
Calian, Sara, "Vanguard Boosts Its European Presence," *Wall Street Journal,* February 17, 2000, p. C27.
Clements, Jonathan, "Don't Abandon the Vanguard Ship," *Wall Street Journal,* August 17, 1999, p. C1.
Edgerton, Jerry, "Vanguard's New Skipper Will Push High-Tech Service and Index Funds," *Money,* July 1995, p. 53.
Grover, Mary Beth, "Feast or Famine," *Forbes,* July 4, 1994, p. 150.
Hardy, Eric S., and Zweig, Jason, "Vanguard's Achilles Heel," *Forbes,* May 8, 1995, p. 148.
Kaye, Stephen D., "Inside Vanguard," *U.S. News & World Report,* February 6, 1995, p. 70.
Lowenstein, Roger, "It Bogles the Mind: Vanguard's Founder Turned Funds Upside Down—and Not Always for the Better," *SmartMoney,* October 1, 1999, p. 71.
Misra, Prashanta, "The Vanguard Group Comes Begging for Less," *Money,* April 1993, p. 56.
Prial, Dunstan, "Vanguard Founder Shares Views on Tech Fervor, Funds Industry," *Dallas Morning News,* January 30, 2000, p. H11.
Spiro, Leah Nathans, "Vanguard: Cutting Expenses, Boosting Returns," *Business Week,* March 1, 1993, p. 108.
Tam, Pui-Wing, "Vanguard Aims to Perk Up Actively Managed Funds," *Wall Street Journal,* January 24, 2000, p. C1.
Tam, Pui-Wing, and John Hechinger, "Vanguard 500 Set to Pass Magellan," *Wall Street Journal,* January 12, 2000, p. C1.
Ward, Sandra, "A Shifting Vanguard: Why Two Actively Managed Funds Are Being Added to the Lineup," *Barron's,* March 6, 2000, p. F3.
Wiles, Russ, "Vanguard Steps Up to Ethics Challenge," *Chicago Sun-Times,* December 27, 1999, p. 58.
Zweig, Jason, "Vanguard: The Penny-Pincher," *Forbes,* August 28, 1995, p. 164.

—Thomas Derdak
—updated by Mariko Fujinaka

Vitro Corporativo S.A. de C.V.

Avenida del Roble 660
San Pedro, Garcia Garcia, Nueva Leon 66265
Mexico
Telephone: (528) 329-1210
Fax: (528) 335-7210
Web site: http://www.vto.com

Public Company
Incorporated: 1909 as Vidriera Monterrey, S.A.
Employees: 32,535
Sales: 25.88 billion pesos (US$2.63 billion) (1999)
Stock Exchanges: Mexico City New York (ADRs)
Ticker Symbol: VITRO (Mexico City); VTO (New York)
NAIC: 32616 Plastics Bottle Manufacturing; 327211 Flat
Glass Manufacturing; 32712 Other Pressed & Blown
Glass & Glassware Manufacturing; 32713 Glass
Container Manufacturing; 332431 Metal Can
Manufacturing; 333298 All Other Industrial
Machinery Manufacturing; 5551112 Offices of Other
Holding Companies

Vitro Corporativo S.A. de C.V., or Grupo Vitro, is a holding company that, through its subsidiaries, is mainly engaged in the manufacture of such products as glass containers, flat glass for the construction and automotive industries, glassware for table and kitchen use; home appliances and enamelware; silica, sand, soda, and fiberglass; plastic and aluminum can containers; glass-forming machines; and molds for plastic and glass containers. Vitro is the third largest producer of glass containers in the world and one of only two companies in the world—the other being France's Compagnie de Saint-Gobain S.A.—that produces a complete line of glass products, include fiberglass and soda silicate as well as automotive and flat glass, glass containers, and glassware. It serves markets in 70 countries.

Mexican Glass Pioneer: 1899–1974

Vitro was an outgrowth of the Cuauhtemoc brewery founded in Monterrey in 1890 by two generations of three interrelated

Mexican families, but especially by Francisco G. Sada Muguerza and his brother-in-law, Isaac Garza Garza. In order to bottle the product without resorting to imports, Garza established Vidrios y Cristales, S.A. in 1899, with production beginning in 1903. This enterprise was not a success until 1909, when it acquired the Owens patent for automatic mechanical fabrication of the glass bottle and became Vidriera Monterrey, S.A., establishing a separate glass factory in 1911. The company added glassware to its products in 1928, opened a Mexico City plant in 1934, and began exporting to Central America in 1935.

By 1936 the holdings of the Garza and Sada families and their associates had been divided into brewery and glass groups. Although they continued to hold shares within each group, management of the Vidriera group became largely the responsibility of Roberto G. Sada and Andres G. Sada, sons of Francisco Sada Muguerza. In that year Vidriera Monterrey became a holding company named Fomento de Industria y Comercio (FIC). Its units included the Monterrey and Mexico City plants and Vidrio Plano, a newly established unit to manufacture plate glass. Cristaleria was also established in 1936 to manufacture glassware.

In 1943 FIC established a subsidiary to manufacture machinery and equipment because of World War II shortages. The parent company added bottling plants at Los Reyes in 1944 and Guadalajara in 1951. In 1948 it acquired Financiera del Norte, S.A., which later became Banco del Pais, S.A. (Banpais), the nation's fifth-ranking bank. A joint venture, Vitro Fibres S.A., was established with Owens Corning Fiberglass Co. in 1951, a silicates subsidiary in 1964, and a Central American subsidiary for making glass the same year. By 1965 FIC also had added a bottling plant in Ciudad Obregon, and it entered the plastics field soon after. Beginning in 1970, the company started exporting machinery and molds for glass to various American countries, including the United States. In 1973 it acquired a company making safety glass for automobiles.

Boom and Bust Years: 1975–95

In 1974 the tightly held Sada-Garza holdings, known collectively as the Monterrey Group, were divided into four entities:

Company Perspectives:

Grupo Vitro seeks to promote growth and increase value for shareholders by introducing new technology, new products and developing new markets. Through its personnel, products, and suppliers Grupo Vitro seeks to become the most cost-efficient manufacturer in the markets it serves, and to exert a positive influence in the communities in which it has a presence.

Grupo Alfa, Visa, Cydsa, and FIC. FIC, which had sales of 3.4 billion pesos in 1975 (US$272 million, 11th among reporting Mexican companies), became a public company the following year, offering shares on the Bolsa de Valores Mexicanos, Mexico City's stock exchange.

A factory was founded at Queretaro in 1978 and Vitro Flotado, a glass-sheet subsidiary, was launched in 1979. That same year FIC was 16th in size among reporting Mexican firms, with sales of 12.9 billion pesos (US$570 million) and net income of 1.1 billion pesos (US$48.6 million). It employed about 30,000 people. The company had seven marketing divisions: food products, beer, industrials, medicines, perfumes, wines, and soft drinks. Only about ten percent of its output was standard production; the rest was customized to meet the needs of a particular client. The Los Reyes plant housed the world's biggest furnace for glass containers. FIC was exporting 13 percent of its production, at prices about 30 percent below international level, according to company directors.

Also in 1979, Vidrio Plano established a joint venture with Ford Motor Company to fabricate automotive glass in Mexico for sale primarily in Europe and Latin America. Vidrio Plano took 62 percent ownership of the venture. The following year FIC was renamed Vitro. In 1981 it added plastic containers and machinery for making plastics to its products. Vitro and its subsidiaries also owned all of Banpais and 87 percent of Grupo Financiera Banpais, the holding company. Their operating results were excluded from Vitro's consolidated financial statements.

Like many other big Mexican companies that had borrowed heavily during the oil boom of the late 1970s, Vitro was hard hit by the subsequent collapse of petroleum prices and the devaluation of the peso in 1982. Manufacturing capacity in use dropped from 90 percent during 1978–81 to less than 70 percent in 1982–83, and employment peaked at 36,611 in 1980. Moreover, Vitro's stake in Banpais ended with the nationalization of the banks by the Mexican government in 1982. Nevertheless, because other companies did even worse, Vitro was the seventh largest of reporting Mexican companies in 1982, up from 12th the previous year. It had no less than 63 subsidiaries. It made a strong recovery the next year, raising its net profits 64 percent and rising to sixth place. Although the debt to foreign creditors reached about US$840 million in 1984, by 1989 the foreign debt had been almost entirely eliminated. Ernesto Martens became the company's first nonfamily chief executive officer in 1985.

Faced with a curtailed market at home, Vitro began seeking outside markets and formed alliances with foreign companies. These included a joint venture with Samsonite Corp. to make luggage and furniture and with Whirlpool Corporation to produce refrigerators, window air conditioners, and kitchen ranges. The company also added enamelware cooking utensils to its products in 1985 and established a flat-glass joint venture with Pilkington Brothers of Great Britain that year. By 1987 Vitro had ties to some 400 companies in the Americas, together with Cydsa, in which it held a half-interest. The number of joint ventures reached 12 by 1989.

By this time Vitro was strong enough financially to accomplish the first successful hostile takeover of an American company by a Mexican one, purchasing Anchor Glass Container Corp., the second largest U.S. glass-container manufacturer, for more than US$900 million. It also acquired a smaller U.S. company, Latchford Glass Co., that year. State-of-the-art technology for these companies' plants was licensed from Owens-Illinois Inc. Vitro's net sales came to 8.13 trillion pesos (US$2.89 billion) and net income to 611 billion pesos (US$217 million) in 1990. Debt-ridden Anchor ate into Vitro's profits, however, and in 1992 Vitro laid off workers—3,000 of them—for the first time.

Vitro formed its most important alliance in 1992, when it signed an agreement with Corning Inc. to establish two joint ventures. Corning Vitro Corp. was established as a Corning subsidiary 51 percent-owned by Corning and 49 percent by Vitro, while Corning S.A. de C.V. was created as a Vitro subsidiary 51 percent-owned by Vitro and 49 percent by Corning. Corning received a cash payment in excess of US$130 million and 49 percent of Vitro's worldwide consumer business, while Vitro received 49 percent of Corning's worldwide consumer assets and businesses.

Vitro also formed a partnership with AMISILCO Holdings, Inc. that year to create two similar joint ventures—World Tableware International, Inc. and Vitrocrisa Cubiertos, S.A. de C.V., respectively. ACI America, a company with 120 processors and sales offices in the south and west of the United States, was purchased for US$88 million. In 1994 Regioplast, S.A. de C.V. was formed as a joint venture between Vitro and Owens-Illinois to manufacture plastic containers and caps. Vitro sold its share of the luggage business to Samsonite that year but acquired AMSILCO Holdings. As a result of these alliances, in 1995 51 percent of Vitro's sales were outside of Mexico, compared to only 15 percent in 1991, with Anchor alone responsible for 40 percent of total sales.

In Mexico, Vitro opened a new plant in Mexicali for this border area of growing demand for beer and soda. A division for domestic products had ten plants for making washing machines and refrigerators. Nevertheless, all was not rosy for Vitro: sales were only growing slowly, net profits were down, and debt was rising.

Restructuring in the Late 1990s

The peso devaluation of December 1994 affected Vitro less than other Mexican firms because of its dollar holdings, thanks to its alliances with foreign enterprises. Nevertheless, the company, saddled with interest payments on a hefty US$2.2 billion debt, lost money in 1994 and 1996. Anchor Glass continued to be a drain on earnings, as was Vitro's ten percent holding in

---

Key Dates:

1903: Company begins production of beer bottles.
1928: As Vidreira Monterey, begins making glassware products.
1973: Company is now producing safety glass for automobiles.
1981: Named Vitro, company has begun making plastic containers.
1992: Vitro forms two joint ventures with Corning Inc.
1997: Sale of Anchor Glass ends an unprofitable 1989 acquisition.

---

troubled Grupo Financiero Serfin, which it had purchased in 1992 and which also was closely associated with the Monterrey Group. Vitro had to pay US$69 million in 1995 for another ten percent share to keep the bank, Mexico's third largest, from collapsing. In 1996 it put up US$15 million more, but its share of the group fell to 11.4 percent. Adrian Sada Trevino's sons Adrian Sada Gonzalez and Federico Sada Gonzalez became chairman and president/chief executive officer of the firm, respectively, in 1995. (The family's net worth was estimated at US$1 billion in 1993.)

With the continuing transition of U.S. soft-drink manufacturers from glass to plastic containers, Anchor Glass began concentrating on the beer and iced-tea markets. By 1995, however, the latter beverage was falling in sales. Anchor cut its number of plants to 14 (compared to 22 in 1989) and its production by 20 percent (compared to 1991) but continued to founder in red ink. In 1997 Vitro sold the company to Owens Brockway Containers of Canada for US$392.5 million, with Vitro also assuming responsibility for the company's US$70 million pension debt.

To relieve its financial pressures, in 1997 Vitro also agreed to sell its 49.9 percent holding in Cydsa—the Monterrey Group's profitable plastics, chemicals, and fibers group—for the right to receive the proceeds from 47.6 million of its own shares, or 13.2 percent, held by Tomas Gonzalez Sada, Cydsa's president, and his family. These shares were sold in 1998 to Vitro itself, an employee stock-option plan, and a third party, the latter paying 34.46 million pesos (US$3.48 million) for about one-eighth of these shares. Vitro also sold 49 percent of Vitrocrisa, 49 percent of Crisa Corp., and all of Worldcrisa—its glass tableware subsidiaries—to Libbey Inc. for US$100 million. Vitrocrisa represented 14 percent of the parent company's sales. In addition, it sold Materias Primas, S.A., a subsidiary engaged in the mining of silica sand and feldspar, to Unimin Corp. for US$130 million. As a result, Vitro fell from 5th to 12th place among reporting Mexican firms.

Of Vitro's 26.96 billion pesos in sales in 1998 (US$2.49 billion) the flat-glass unit accounted for 34 percent; glass containers for 30 percent; household products for 18 percent; diverse industries for 11 percent; and glassware for seven percent. Export sales accounted for about 27 percent and joint ventures about 67 percent of sales. The company lost some 311 million

pesos (US$28.71 million). Its holdings in Grupo Serfin were down to 5.1 percent by the end of the year.

In September 1999 Vitro announced it would restructure its glass-container division, close a plant, and sell about US$100 million in assets as part of a plan to reduce its debt. Vitro's 1999 sales were down in pesos (25.88 billion) but higher in dollar terms (US$2.63 billion). Flat glass accounted for 33 percent; glass containers, 28 percent; household products, 19 percent; diverse industries, 12 percent; and glassware, eight percent. The company had net income of 1.49 billion pesos (US$151.66 million). The long-term debt at the end of the year was 12.91 billion pesos (US$1.31 billion). In January 2000 Vitro announced the acquisition of Harding Glass, a U.S. distributor of specialty glass products.

Principal Subsidiaries

Ampolletas (49%); Crisa Corporation (U.S.A.); Regioplast, S.A. de C.V. (50%); Vidrio Plano; Vitro-American National Can (France; 50%); Vitro Flex (38%); Vitro Packaging, Inc. (U.S.A.); Vitro Plan (U.K.; 35%); Vitrocrisa Holding (49%); Vitromatic (49%); VVP America (U.S.A.).

Principal Operating Units

Diverse Industries Business Unit; Flat Glass Business Unit; Glass Containers Business Unit; Glassware Business Unit; Household Products Business Unit.

Principal Competitors

Ball-Foster Glass Container Co.; Compagnie de Saint-Gobain S.A.; Owens-Illinois Inc.

Further Reading

Barragan, Maria Antonieta, "Vitro: Caminos de Cristal," *Expansion,* May 12, 1993, pp. 74, 77.

Crawford, Leslie, "Vitro Moves to Reduce $2bn Debt," *Financial Times,* August 11, 1996, p. 25.

"El vidrio sigue en la lucha," *Expansion,* May 2, 1979, pp. 36, 38–39.

"Fixing the Cracks at Vitro," *Business Week,* July 8, 1996, p. 120J.

Gatsiopoulos, Georgina, "Caen utilidades de Vitro en el ultimo trimestre de 1999," *El financiero,* February 15, 2000, p. 27.

"Grupo FIC: genesis desde el vidrio," *Expansion,* November 28, 1979, pp. 67–68, 73–76.

Leal Garcia, Alba, "Cabeza de raton . . . pero vivo," *Expansion,* January 14, 1998, pp. 20–21, 23.

——, "La neuva herejia de Vitro," *Expansion,* August 27, 1997, pp. 18–20, 22–24, 27–28, 31.

"Mexico's Family Groups Struggle with Changes As New Powers Ascend," *Business Latin America,* May 4, 1987, p. 139.

Nichols, Nancy A., "From Complacency to Competitiveness," *Harvard Business Review,* September–October 1993, pp. 162–71.

Rohter, Larry, "Raid Across the Mexican Border," *New York Times,* October 30, 1989, p. D14.

Santiago, Jaime, "Caras de la moneda," *Expansion,* November 8, 1995, p. 23.

—Robert Halasz

Waterford Wedgwood plc

1-2 Upper Hatch Street
Dublin 2
Ireland
Telephone: 1 478 1855
Fax: 1 478 4863
Web site: http://www.wwreview.com

Public Company
Incorporated: 1947 as Waterford Crystal Limited
Employees: 9,271
Sales: EUR 879.6 million (US$969.7 million) (1999)
Stock Exchanges: Dublin London NASDAQ
Ticker Symbol: WATFY
NAIC: 327112 Vitreous China, Fine Earthenware, and
Other Pottery Product Manufacturing; 327212 Other
Pressed and Blown Glass and Glassware
Manufacturing; 332214 Kitchen Utensil, Pot, and Pan
Manufacturing; 339911 Jewelry (except Costume)
Manufacturing; 339912 Silverware and Hollowware
Manufacturing; 551112 Offices of Other Holding
Companies

Waterford Wedgwood plc is a holding company for two of the world's most highly respected names in tableware: Waterford Crystal Limited, which is the world's leading manufacturer of premium cut-glass crystal and one of the most important exporters in Ireland, and Josiah Wedgwood and Sons Limited, a British producer of bone china and fine ceramics that is best known for its distinctive and long-lived patterns. Both of these branches of the company draw upon traditions of craftsmanship that date back to the 18th century. Waterford and Wedgwood merged in 1986. The combined company went on an acquisitions spree in the late 1990s, purchasing Stuart & Sons Ltd., a U.K. premium crystal maker; a majority stake in Rosenthal A.G., a German maker of fine porcelain; and All-Clad Metalcrafters Inc., a U.S.-based maker of premium cookware. Although Waterford Wedgwood sells its luxury items in more than 80 countries worldwide, more than 40 percent of revenues are generated in the United States.

Waterford Crystal Roots and Development

Although the present company was founded in 1947, the firm traces its heritage to the 1780s, when a relaxation of trade restrictions on the Irish glass industry ushered in a 40-year period known as the "Age of Exuberance." Hopeful entrepreneurs established many new glasshouses during this time, among them Quaker brothers George and William Penrose. In 1783 the partners invested a then-hefty IR £10,000 in a crystal factory named for the port county of Waterford in southeast Ireland. They hired more than 50 employees to carry out the extremely labor-intensive crystal-making process.

The operation first involved mixing the "batch" of heavy flint or crystal glass, which contained 35 percent lead to make the highest grade crystal. This batch of glass was then heated for more than 36 hours to 1400 degrees Celsius, where it reached the consistency necessary for forming. Each piece was hand-blown into a water-soaked wooden mold, forming thick glass walls to accommodate the deep, intricate cuts that came to characterize Waterford crystal. After a period of controlled cooling known as "annealing," teams of glass cutters created the complex geometric patterns for which Waterford soon became recognized around the world. Waterford employees have used essentially the same tools and techniques throughout the company's history.

The Waterford Glass Works' first foreman was John Hill, a highly respected craftsman who had brought some of his best craftsmen from England to Ireland to escape excessive glass taxes. Hill was credited with setting up the Waterford factory, but his career there was short-lived. Personal clashes with owner William Penrose's wife led to his premature exit from the company. Before he left, however, Hill passed on valuable technical information to a clerk, Jonathan Gatchell.

The Penrose family sold its enterprise to Gatchell in 1799. In spite of rising taxes and a changing roster of partners, Gatchell was able to pass the Waterford legacy on to his brothers, James and Samuel, and his son-in-law Joseph Walpole, upon his death in 1823. In accordance with Gatchell's will, these three ceded the works to his son, George, upon his 21st birthday in 1835. Unfortunately, a new excise tax had been enacted just two years after Gatchell's death. George found a partner in one of the works' employees, George Saunders, but Saunders sold out by 1850, as heavy taxation eliminated any profits. Gatchell entered a Waterford piece in the Great Exhibition of 1851 (held, ironically, in London's Crystal Palace), then closed the business later that year.

Nearly a century elapsed before the Waterford tradition was revived in 1947 by Joseph McGrath and Joseph Griffin. They established their glass company less than two miles from the site of the original Waterford Glass Works and hired talented employees from Czechoslovakia to staff the operation. Following the lead set by their 18th-century antecedents, their chief designer, Miroslav Havel, adopted historical patterns that had been documented by the National Museum of Ireland. McGrath and Griffin focused their sales efforts on the massive and prosperous postwar American market. By the late 1960s, Waterford had captured the largest share of the fine glassware market.

Maintaining dominance of the industry was effortless throughout the 1970s: Waterford did not introduce any new patterns or revise its advertising from 1972 to 1982. In the early 1980s, however, Waterford began to face challengers; although the market for fine lead crystal tripled from 1979 to 1983, Waterford's sales grew by only about one-fifth, and its market share slid by five points to 25 percent. The company added new patterns, enlisted a new advertising agency, and, in 1986, acquired Josiah Wedgwood and Sons Ltd. in the hopes of finding retail and distribution synergies.

Wedgwood Roots and Development

The roots of Wedgwood ceramics are most often traced to Josiah Wedgwood, himself the descendant of four generations of potters. Josiah embarked on his life's work at the age of nine, when he left school to work under his eldest brother at the family pottery works. An outbreak of smallpox left the youngster physically impaired at the age of 11. (The disease left a lingering infection in his leg, which eventually led to its amputation.) Unable to continue throwing pottery as a result, he turned instead to design and formulation of ceramics and glazes. When Josiah's apprenticeship ended at the age of 19, his brother inexplicably refused to take him on as a partner.

For the next ten years, the young potter cast about for a business associate; during this period his longest partnership, with Thomas Whieldon, lasted for five years. Wedgwood struck out on his own in 1759. Not content to imitate the generally substandard wares on the market, Wedgwood achieved his first important innovation, No. 7 green glaze, shortly thereafter. The potter used his new glaze to produce rococo-style teapots, plates, compotes, and other practical pieces shaped like fruits, vegetables, and leaves. Wedgwood created demand for his pottery by offering innovative products, including asparagus pans, egg spoons and baskets, sandwich sets, and even special plates for ''Dutch fish.''

By 1765, word of Wedgwood's elegant yet durable wares had reached Britain's royal family. That year, Queen Charlotte ordered a tea service made of Wedgwood's second important development, a uniquely cream-colored earthenware. Through this, the first of many ''command performances,'' Wedgwood earned the right to call his ivory-colored pottery ''Queen's Ware.'' Needless to say, the endorsement added to the potter's prestige, popularity, and sales.

Such successes allowed Wedgwood to purchase an estate, which he named Etruria, in 1766. A factory on the site was completed three years later, just in time to accommodate an order from Catherine the Great of Russia for a 952-piece service for 50. The amazing set featured more than 1,200 hand-painted scenes of the English countryside. Wedgwood named a pattern with maroon flowers after Catherine. That style, as well as the Queen's Ware and Shell Edge styles, exemplified the enduring nature of the founder's designs: all were still in production in the 20th century.

Wedgwood capitalized on the popularity of his wares by expanding his line in the 1770s. With the help of an amicable partner, Thomas Bentley, Wedgwood began producing wall tiles and such ornamental wares as plaques, vases, busts, candlesticks, medallions, and even chess sets. Many early decorative pieces were made of a proprietary ceramic called Black Basalt. Although Wedgwood was sure that Black Basalt would enjoy an enduring popularity, it was his Jasper ware, introduced in 1774, that would symbolize Wedgwood for centuries of consumers and collectors. Jasper, an unglazed, translucent stoneware that assimilated colors well, was produced in green, yellow, maroon, black, white, and the shades of blue Jasper that became known as ''Wedgwood blue.'' Historian Alison Kelly, author of *The Story of Wedgwood,* asserted, ''Connoisseurs of pottery since [Wedgwood's] day have valued [Jasper] both as a technical triumph and as an ornament perfect of its kind.''

Wedgwood worked alone for ten years after Bentley died in 1780. He went into semiretirement in 1790, taking his three sons and a nephew into partnership that year. In addition to his artistic achievements, the founder had invented a pyrometer to measure the heat of his kilns and implemented steam-driven potters' wheels and some principles of mass production. Upon his death in 1795, his second son, also named Josiah, shared management of the works with his cousin, Thomas Byerley. Josiah II assumed full control when Byerley died in 1810.

The Napoleonic Wars, which made trade with continental Europe all but impossible, were followed by an economic slowdown that made the early years of the 19th century difficult for Josiah II. In 1828 financial shortfalls compelled him to close the company's London showrooms and sell the bulk of Wedgwood's stock, molds, and models for £16,000. Still, the Etruria works survived both hardship and Josiah II's often-criticized

Key Dates:

1759: Josiah Wedgwood founds a pottery manufacturing concern.

1760s: Wedgwood creates a uniquely cream-colored earthenware, which becomes known as "Queen's Ware."

1769: A factory is completed at Wedgwood's estate, called Etruria.

1774: Wedgwood introduces the innovative and enduring Jasper ware.

1783: George and William Penrose found the Waterford crystal factory in Ireland.

1799: The Penrose family sells Waterford to Jonathan Gatchell.

1810: Josiah Wedgwood II takes full control of the company founded by his father.

1828: Financial difficulties force Wedgwood to close its London showrooms and sell off much of its assets.

1835: George Gatchell, son of Jonathan, takes control of Waterford.

1843: Francis Wedgwood, son of Josiah II, succeeds his father.

1851: Gatchell closes down Waterford, which enters a nearly 100-year-long inactive period.

1875: Wedgwood reopens its London showrooms.

1879: Philipe Rosenthal establishes the Rosenthal company in the Upper Franconian town of Erkersreuth.

1906: The Wedgwood Museum opens, and a U.S. sales office is established.

1940: A new Wedgwood factory, near Barlaston, begins production.

1947: Joseph McGrath and Joseph Griffin revive the Waterford company.

1950: Wedgwood's Etruria factory is closed down.

1963: Sir Arthur Bryan becomes the first non-Wedgwood to serve as managing director.

1966: Josiah Wedgwood and Sons Limited goes public and starts an eight-year acquisition spree.

1986: Waterford acquires Josiah Wedgwood and Sons, forming Waterford Wedgwood plc.

1988: Waterford Wedgwood posts an operating loss for the year, the first of five straight.

1990: Anthony J.F. O'Reilly forms a coalition of investors and purchases about one-third of the company's equity.

1992: The company returns to the black.

1994: O'Reilly is named chairman.

1995: Stuart & Sons, leading U.K. maker of premium crystal, is acquired.

1997: Company gains majority control of Rosenthal AG, a German-based porcelain maker.

1999: Waterford Wedgwood acquires U.S.-based All-Clad Metalcrafters Inc., a maker of premium cookware; designs the Waterford Crystal New Year's Eve Ball used in New York's Times Square to mark the new millennium.

---

management. His third son, Francis, succeeded him upon his death in 1843. Francis had joined the company in 1827 and would control it for 27 years. He revived the founder's legacies of innovation and modernization, adding machines that mixed and dried the clay, as well as new colored ceramics in the tradition of Jasper. His celadon, a pale gray-green ceramic, a lavender clay, and Parian Ware, which featured marbled effects, appealed to Victorian tastes. By 1875, Francis was able to reopen the London showrooms. He also reinstituted production of bone china, which had been offered briefly in the early 1800s. This line would later form the foundation of Wedgwood's export trade.

Successive generations of Wedgwoods took the company into the 20th century, which witnessed a revival of interest in the company's classical designs, both among collectors and consumers. The Wedgwood Museum was opened in 1906, the same year that the company established an American sales office. Overseas trade expanded dramatically during the early decades of the 1900s: by 1920, the U.S. office had grown sufficiently to justify a new subsidiary.

Even the Great Depression did not slow Wedgwood's growth. In 1938 the company laid plans to build a modern facility near Barlaston. The plant, which featured the first electric pottery kilns used in Britain, began production in 1940. Since 80 percent of Wedgwood's production was for export, the company was allowed to continue production throughout World War II. At war's end, Wedgwood was poised for expansion. During the late 1940s and early 1950s, the company incorporated Canadian and Australian subsidiaries, expanded its factory, and inaugurated special "Wedgwood Rooms" in upscale department stores. By the end of the 1950s, the company employed more than 2,000 people at the Barlaston plant. (All production had been transferred from Etruria to Barlaston by 1950.)

In 1963, Sir Arthur Bryan became Wedgwood's managing director, marking the first time in the company's history that an individual who was not related to Josiah Wedgwood held that position. Bryan was named chairman five years later.

Wedgwood's first public offering on the London Stock Exchange in 1966 marked the beginning of an eight-year acquisition spree. The company acquired four competitors in 1966 and 1967, including Coalport, manufacturers of high-quality bone china figurines. Wedgwood doubled in size with the acquisition of Johnson Brothers, which included five tableware factories as well as overseas plants. The company entered the glass market with the 1969 purchase of King's Lynn Glass, then began the 1970s with the acquisition of J & G Meakin and Midwinter companies, manufacturers of fine china and earthenware. These purchases gave Wedgwood access to broader markets without compromising the reputation of their premier brand. Additions in the ensuing years helped Wedgwood integrate vertically. They included Precision Studios, a producer of decorative materials for the ceramics industry, and Gered, a retailer and longtime customer of Wedgwood. By 1975, Wedgwood had nearly 9,000 employees in 20 factories.

The company's growth came to an abrupt halt in the early 1980s, when recession forced Wedgwood to lay off nearly half of its workforce. As the company struggled, threats of hostile takeover necessitated Wedgwood's amicable union with Waterford.

Waterford Wedgwood: Post-Merger Woes in the Late 1980s and Early 1990s

Waterford and Wedgwood merged in 1986, when the crystal manufacturer executed a "white knight" takeover of the china producer for £252.6 million. A recession in the late 1980s and early 1990s brought the premium crystal market's growth to a halt, as price-conscious consumers traded down. From 1989 to 1992, sales in the premium market in the United States (then the world's largest market) dropped by 25 percent, while sales of second-tier crystal increased by half. At the same time, employment costs for both Waterford and Wedgwood had soared: Waterford's labor expenses, which accounted for more than two-thirds of the company's overhead, grew three times faster than inflation in the late 1980s. From 1987 to 1990, Waterford Crystal alone lost more than £60 million, and total corporate debt had swelled to £150 million.

In 1988 Anthony J.F. "Tony" O'Reilly (chairman, president, and CEO of H.J. Heinz Company, as well as "the wealthiest man in Ireland") offered Waterford Wedgwood Chairman Howard Kilroy a buyout. His first attempt was refused, but by early 1990, the struggling company was ready to deal. O'Reilly formed a coalition of investors, including his own Fitzwilton Public Limited Company and New York investment house Morgan Stanley Group Inc. Together, they exchanged an estimated £80 million for about one-third of the tableware firm's equity. Morgan Stanley took 15 percent, 9.4 percent went to Fitzwilton, and O'Reilly personally acquired five percent. The deal valued Waterford Wedgwood at £230 million—less than it had paid for Wedgwood alone just three years earlier.

The company's problems were deeper than O'Reilly had surmised. When Waterford Wedgwood lost IR £1.2 million on IR £71 million sales in 1991, Don Brennan of Morgan Stanley replaced Kilroy as chairman. The new managers traced their financial woes to expensive labor, especially at Waterford. The company trimmed some of its labor costs and simultaneously countered the contraction of the premium crystal market with the 1991 introduction of the Marquis by Waterford line, which retailed at about 30 percent less than traditional Waterford. This new offering—the company's first new brand of crystal in 200 years—was manufactured in Germany and Slovenia, where wages averaged ten percent less than in Ireland. Stylistically, Marquis featured designs less elaborately cut than Waterford patterns. Company executives were careful to assert that they were not reaching "down-market," but that the elegant new designs appealed to more modern, youthful, "continental" tastes. The launch was an unquestionable success: from 1992 to 1993, sales of Marquis increased by 24 percent, and the brand captured the number six spot among premium crystal brands sold in the United States.

At the same time, the company was beset by confrontations with its domestic workforce, including strikes and even a shutdown. In 1992, after management threatened to move more of Waterford's production to Eastern Europe, the unions agreed to a wage freeze and job cuts. In return, the company pledged to keep its Waterford operations in Ireland as long as it could remain competitive.

Although Waterford Wedgwood's share price sank as low as 12p in 1992, the company recorded its first operating profit (IR £500,000) since 1987 that year, with sales 4.5 percent higher than in 1991. In 1993 profits increased again, to IR £10 million, and Waterford Wedgwood's share price grew to 60p. The turnaround was credited to O'Reilly, who advanced from deputy chairman to chairman in 1994. O'Reilly was confident that his stalwart brands would regain their steady and strong profitability, and he targeted future growth for the mature markets of Japan and the United Kingdom.

Mid-1990s and Beyond: Growth Through Acquisitions

Following up on the success of the lower-priced Marquis by Waterford line, the company in 1995 introduced a new Wedgwood line called Embassy, which was positioned in the mid-priced segment, with a five-piece place setting costing about $80. This was also Wedgwood's first porcelain line. Wedgwood also launched an even less expensive—$50–$60 per set—and less formal porcelain line dubbed Home. Also in 1995 Wedgwood debuted a new, bestselling line called Cornucopia, a fine bone china pattern.

Waterford Wedgwood's improved financial condition set the stage for a new round of acquisitions. The first came in 1995 when Stuart & Sons Ltd. was acquired for about IR £4.2 million (US$6.8 million). Stuart & Sons was a leading U.K. maker of premium crystal and claimed to be the last major U.K. manufacturer making all of its glass in its home country. In early 1997 Waterford Wedgwood spent US$1.9 million for a 9.1 percent stake in Rosenthal A.G., a maker of premium porcelain china, tableware, and art; by the end of 1997 the company had gained majority control of Rosenthal after increasing its stake to 61.5 percent. Based in Selb, Germany, Rosenthal had a long history dating back to its establishment in 1879 by Philipe Rosenthal in the Upper Franconian town of Erkersreuth. Rosenthal had sales of US$206 million in 1995, with about 60 percent derived in Germany; the United States and Italy were the company's two largest export markets. In 1998 Waterford Wedgwood further increased its stake in Rosenthal to about 85 percent.

In June 1999 Waterford Wedgwood diversified its line of luxury goods through the acquisition of All-Clad Metalcrafters Inc., a U.S. premium cookware maker, for US$110 million (IR £68 million). Canonsburg, Pennsylvania-based All-Clad was founded in 1973 by John Ulam, a metallurgist who devised a way to bond sheets of aluminum and stainless steel. The combination resulted in cookware that heated evenly but was easy to clean. Sales for the privately held company were about US$52 million in 1998 and were growing rapidly. In fact, high-end cookware was the fastest growing segment of the cookware market, with sales increasing at an annual rate of 18 percent. All-Clad products were sold primarily in upscale department stores, such as Macy's and Bloomingdale's, and in higher-end home furnishings chains, such as Williams Sonoma, Crate & Barrel, and Pottery Barn. Waterford Wedgwood planned to expand the All-Clad brand outside the United States (its overseas sales stood at only three percent of the total in 1998) and also hoped that the addition of All-Clad could help expand the Wedgwood brand into the U.S. home furnishings specialty retail sector, which would represent a new channel.

In addition to pursuing growth through acquisition, Waterford Wedgwood achieved organic growth in the late 1990s through the introduction of new product lines. Particularly successful were cooperative ventures with leading fashion designers—such as Versace, Bulgari, John Rocha, and Jaspar Conran—who helped design ceramics and crystal lines bearing their own names. In 1999 sales in the United States were aided by the employment of Sarah, Duchess of York, as official spokesperson for Waterford Wedgwood in the U.S. market. In November 1999 Waterford Wedgwood purchased a 15 percent stake in British rival Royal Doulton for IR £11.1 million. Calling the transaction a "strategic investment" and not a prelude to an outright bid, Waterford Wedgwood nevertheless declined to rule out a future bid if a rival takeover company emerged. Capping 1999 in typically spectacular fashion, Waterford Wedgwood designed the Waterford Crystal New Year's Eve Ball, which was used to mark the beginning of the new millennium in New York's Times Square.

As the new century approached, Waterford Wedgwood was on a clear upward trajectory. Revenues for 1999 increased 20.4 percent over the previous year, nearing the US$1 billion mark and almost double the figure of five years earlier. In fact, the company had achieved seven straight years of double-digit growth. Operating profits, meanwhile, increased by one-third over the one-year period. In the early 21st century, Waterford Wedgwood was likely to continue to plot its successful course of organic and purchased growth, with the acquisition side likely to lean toward further diversification, along the lines of the All-Clad purchase.

Principal Subsidiaries

Waterford Crystal Limited; Josiah Wedgwood and Sons Limited (U.K.); Rosenthal A.G. (Germany; 84.62%); Stuart & Sons Ltd. (U.K.); All-Clad Metalcrafters Inc. (U.S.A.); Waterford Crystal Gallery Ltd.; Waterford Wedgwood Australia Ltd.; Waterford Wedgwood Canada Inc.; Waterford Wedgwood U.S.A. Inc.; Waterford Wedgwood Japan Ltd.; Waterford Wedgwood Retail Ltd. (U.K.); Josiah Wedgwood & Sons (Exports) Ltd. (U.K.); Josiah Wedgwood (Malaysia) Sdn. Bhd.; Waterford Wedgwood Trading Singapore Pte. Ltd.; Waterford Wedgwood N.V. (Belgium); Wedgwood GmbH (Germany); Stratum Limited (U.K.); Waterford Wedgwood International Financial Services; Waterford Wedgwood International B.V. (Netherlands); Waterford Wedgwood Holdings B.V. (Netherlands); Waterford Wedgwood U.K. plc; Wedgwood Ltd. (U.K.); Waterford Wedgwood Inc. (U.S.A.); Waterford Glass Research and Development Ltd.; Dungarvan Crystal Ltd.; Waterford Wedgwood Employee Share Ownership Plan (Jersey) Ltd.; Waterford Wedgwood GmbH (Germany).

Principal Competitors

Brown-Forman Corporation; Carlsberg A/S; Corning Incorporated; CRISAL; Fitz and Floyd Silvestri Corporation Inc.; Lancaster Colony Corporation; Mikasa, Inc.; Newell Rubbermaid Inc.; Noritake Co., Limited; Oneida Ltd.; Tattinger S.A.; Tiffany & Co.

Further Reading

Brown, John Murray, "Update for Waterford Wedgwood," *Financial Times,* May 1, 1998, p. 25.

Buckley, Christine, "Wedgwood Develops a Pattern for the Future," *London Times,* September 2, 1995, p. 1.

Carnegy, Hugh, "Waterford, in Search of Added Sparkle," *Financial Times,* October 15, 1986, p. 14.

Cheeseright, Paul, "Waterford Proposes to Reshape Crystal," *Financial Times,* June 1, 1995, p. 12.

Cooke, Kieran, "Crystal Gazing into the Future of a Shattered Empire," *Financial Times,* March 5, 1990, p. 22.

——, "Through a Waterford Crystal Glass Darkly," *Financial Times,* May 15, 1990, p. 31.

Craig, Carole, "Home Truths for Ireland: Mixed Fortunes at Waterford Crystal," *International Management,* May 1993, p. 34.

——, "Waterford Seeks Cash Infusion to Trim Debt," *Wall Street Journal,* January 9, 1990, p. A11.

Dunlevy, Mairead, *Waterford Crystal: The History,* Waterford, Ireland: Waterford Crystal Ltd., 1990.

Dyer, Geoff, "Ambitious Goals in the Crystal Ball," *Financial Times,* April 2, 1996, p. 22.

Finn, Edwin A., Jr., and Richard Morais, "Table for Two?," *Forbes,* November 3, 1986, pp. 67+.

Goodhart, David, "Sir Arthur Finds an Irish White Knight," *Financial Times,* October 9, 1986, p. 30.

Hill, Roy, "Why There's a New Gleam at Waterford Glass," *International Management,* May 1985, pp. 70+.

Kehoe, Anne-Margaret, "Waterford Stake in Rosenthal," *HFN—The Weekly Newspaper for the Home Furnishing Network,* March 3, 1997, p. 35.

Kelly, Alison, *The Story of Wedgwood,* New York: Viking Press, 1975.

Lohr, Steve, "At Waterford, Honeymoon Is Over," *New York Times,* April 11, 1989, p. D1.

Murray, Matt, "Dublin's Waterford to Buy All-Clad for $110 Million," *Wall Street Journal,* May 25, 1999, p. B3.

"Reviving Waterford Crystal," *Economist,* April 14, 1990, p. 72.

Rigby, Rhymer, "Wedgwood: Journey to Etruria," *Management Today,* December 1998, p. 86.

Salmans, Sandra, "The Worries of Wedgwood," *Management Today,* June 1980, p. 66.

Toman, Barbara, "Waterford Wedgwood's Chief Resigns As Firm Splits China, Crystal Divisions," *Wall Street Journal,* December 14, 1990, p. A15.

Tomkins, Richard, "A White Knight with Slightly Tarnished Armour," *Financial Times,* March 21, 1989, p. 20.

Valante, Judith, "A New Brand Restores Sparkle to Waterford," *Wall Street Journal,* November 10, 1994, p. B1.

Whiteley, Geoffrey, "Why Wedgwood Wobbled," *Management Today,* August 1983, pp. 26+.

Wilson, Andrew B., and Amy Dunkin, "Waterford Learns Its Lesson: Snob Appeal Isn't Enough," *Business Week,* December 24, 1984, pp. 63+.

Zisko, Allison, "Waterford Acquires Minority Stake in Royal Doulton," *HFN—The Weekly Newspaper for the Home Furnishing Network,* December 13, 1999, p. 48.

Zisko, Allison, and Barbara Thau, "Waterford Buys All-Clad," *HFN—The Weekly Newspaper for the Home Furnishing Network,* June 7, 1999, p. 1.

—April Dougal Gasbarre
—updated by David E. Salamie

Water Pik Technologies, Inc.

23 Corporate Plaza, Suite 246
Newport Beach, California 92660
U.S.A.
Telephone: (949) 719-3700
Toll Free: (800) 525-2774
Fax: (949) 719-6472
Web site: http://www.waterpik.com

Public Company
Incorporated: 1999
Employees: 1,700
Sales: $254.7 million (1999)
Stock Exchanges: New York
Ticker Symbol: PIK
NAIC: 335211 Electric Housewares and Household Fan Manufacturing; 333414 Heating Equipment Manufacturing; 339999 Miscellaneous Manufacturing; 339114 Dental Equipment and Supplies Manufacturing; 333913 Measuring and Dispensing Pumps Manufacturing; 326199 Plastic Products Manufacturing

Water Pik Technologies, Inc. has been developing and manufacturing personal healthcare products—showerheads, filters and oral health products—under the Water Pik brand name for more than 35 years. The company's swimming pool and spa heaters, controls, valves, and water features, many of which have been manufactured for more than 40 years, are sold primarily under the Laars and Jandy brand names. The company's residential and commercial water-heating systems, which have been manufactured for more than 50 years, are sold primarily under the Laars brand name. Water Pik's extensive distribution network allows it to make use of various channels to reach a broad audience of consumers from its manufacturing facilities located in the United States and Canada.

Teledyne Acquires Aqua Tec: 1967

In 1960, Henry E. Singleton and George Kozmetsky each put up $225,000 and launched Los Angeles-based Teledyne, a maker of semiconductors. Singleton, who had received his doctorate in electrical engineering at Massachusetts Institute of Technology, is credited with developing the inertial guidance system used worldwide in commercial and military aircraft. Before founding Teledyne, he had worked for Hughes Aircraft, North American Aviation, and Litton Industries, where he had been in charge of the electronic equipment division from 1954 to 1960. Kozmetsky, also a Litton alumnus, bowed out of management of Teledyne in 1966 to become dean of the College of Business Administration at the University of Texas.

Singleton was an innovator in both the corporate and engineering worlds and soon became a leading corporate merger guru; throughout the 1960s, he specialized in finding companies with undervalued stock, taking them over, and turning a major profit for Teledyne's shareholders. As CEO of Teledyne, he annexed a staggering number of companies—approximately 150 between 1961 and 1970—expanding Teledyne's product base from high technology to include stereo speakers, pilotless aircraft, and consumer durables. Consequently, Teledyne grew from a tiny contractor with sales of $4.5 million to a $1.3 billion giant with earnings of $58 million; it led the *Fortune* 500 in both earnings and earnings-per-share growth for the ten years ending in 1971 and was the biggest gainer on the New York Stock Exchange in 1976.

One of Singleton's acquisitions in 1967 was a company called Aqua Tec, founded in Fort Collins, Colorado, in 1962 by engineer John W. Mattingly and dentist Gerald Moyer. Mattingly and Moyer were makers of the Water Pik Oral Irrigator, which they patented in 1967. As a subsidiary of Teledyne, Water Pik introduced the Original Shower Massage, the first pulsating showerhead, in 1974. This new invention drew on the technology of the Water Pik by combining the pulsating sprays of ten oral irrigators. The Shower Massage immediately became the market leader in showerheads. It was also a success in Canada, where it garnered 65 percent of total sales in its category shortly after its introduction. Water Pik further expanded its product base when it developed its first end-of-faucet water filter in the mid-1970s. It changed its name to Teledyne Water Pik in 1975.

Water Pik proved to be one of Teledyne's star acquisitions. Sales of the Water Pik oral irrigator steadily grew, peaking at about one million units in 1975, and contributing to a $13.1 million profit for the company's consumer products group. The Shower Massage became one of the hottest gift items for the several years after its introduction; its sales grew to nine million units. But the company's meteoric growth faltered when it introduced a string of new products that flopped. The Nurtury food grinder failed to attract the attention of parents, who preferred to use household blenders to pulverize their babies' food, and an electronic counter of a dieter's bites that signaled how fast to chew was dubbed "one of the most absurd consumer products ever devised," according to a 1982 *Business Week* article. The same article described the One Step at a Time cigarette filter, rolled out in the mid-1970s, as "barely profitable." By the early 1980s, the flow of successful new items at Water Pik had dried up, and sales had dropped about 50 percent to about $65 million annually.

From Slump to Surge in Sales: 1980s

Industry observers attributed the reasons for Water Pik's problems largely to Teledyne's—and Singleton's—management style. Manufacturing units had an apparent autonomy in devising their own plans, but the ingrained, tacit imperative at Teledyne was that profit was all that counted, according to one former head of Water Pik quoted in *Business Week* in 1982. Expenditures for research and development tended to get short shrift in order to meet the bottom line. By the early 1980s, Water Pik discontinued product development spending and drastically cut advertising and marketing support. Teledyne, meanwhile, facing shortfalls in others divisions, began to siphon cash from its Water Pik subsidiary.

Beginning in 1979, to address falling sales, Water Pik attempted to revamp its marketing program, changing itself from an engineering-directed to a marketing-oriented firm. New television commercials deemphasized the gift value of the Shower Massage, focusing instead on the appliance's importance as a self-indulgence and its water and energy conservation. Advertising for the Water Pik oral irrigator changed from suggesting its health benefits to emphasizing its importance in "doing something for yourself."

When Frank Marshall moved from Teledyne's Laars subsidiary to take over the helm at Water Pik in May 1984, there had not been a new Water Pik product introduction since 1979. Marshall set out to change this, as well as to develop merchandise that was "counter seasonal" and would sell throughout the year. Under his direction, the company introduced the Ultraviolet Sensor in 1985. The Sensor, a handheld device that measured the amount of ultraviolet rays striking the skin, met with such great demand that its distribution, at least initially, was limited to the West Coast. In addition, Marshall began to explore marketing Water Pik's products through drugstore chains. By 1985, the company's Shower Massage, Water Pik's largest single category, was said to hold about 65 percent of its market, and the Oral Irrigator to have about a 90 percent share of its category. The subsidiary as a whole generated about $100 million in sales annually.

Mel Cruger joined Water Pik as president in 1986, determined to build the business with the company's established products and to expand its revenues via line extensions. Unlike Marshall, he did not have prior experience working at Teledyne, but instead had a 20-year history in marketing packaged goods. Cruger focused on the health-oriented aspects of his company's products and on understanding his customer base better.

Product Expansion, Reorganization, and Merger: 1990s

Responding to the needs of an aging population and the health- and environmentally-conscious spending patterns of middle-aged baby boomers during the first half of the 1990s, Cruger oversaw the introduction of a series of products designed to "meet and exceed consumer needs for protection and enhancement of their well-being," such as the Automatic Toothbrush, introduced by the Oral Health Division in 1990. This product won first prize in the American Society on Aging's second annual design competition for its large handle, which enabled easy use by those with a disability; its "Touchtronic motion" which started the machine when touched to the teeth; and its elliptical brushing movement that simulated the most effective way to clean teeth. The next year, the company's Shower Division updated its market-leading showerhead for the first time since that product's introduction in 1974. Combining "green" marketing and German hydraulics, the new showerhead conformed to new water conservation standards by adding a water-saving feature which used only 2.5 gallons of water per minute. In 1995, the Oral Health Division also updated its toothbrush with the SenSonic Plaque Removal Instrument, which had an internal computer and delivered 30,000 strokes a minute.

Another market area that Cruger and Teledyne Water Pik set out to exploit in 1995 was that of purified water. More than $3 billion was spent annually on bottled waters and an estimated $50 million on filtration products in the mid-1990s. Water Pik introduced a new line called the Pour-Thru Water Filter, which removed 98 percent of lead, 95 percent of chlorine, and 67 percent of pesticides as well as sediment, bad taste, and odors. The filter won two gold medals for quality and performance from the American Tasting Institute in 1996, the same year the company, working in a different vein, customized an Oral Irrigator for use on animals with the help of trainers and veterinarians at Sea World in Florida.

Singleton had resigned from day-to-day management of Teledyne in 1990, leaving oversight of operations to George Roberts, a longtime friend. Before Singleton stepped down, he had begun spinning off entire divisions of his company. By the early 1990s, Teledyne had cut back to about 20 companies in aviation and electronics, specialty metals, and industrial and consumer products. Teledyne Water Pik took over management of two other company units, Teledyne Getz and Teledyne Hanau, both of which manufactured dental products, such as adhesives, oral analgesics, toothpaste, and professional materials. Teledyne Mecca, manufacturer of plastic drinkware and other products, was also assigned to Water Pik. Cruger, interviewed in an article in *HFD* in 1993, praised the reorganization for consolidating ''Teledyne's three highest growth-potential consumer companies into one organization.'' In 1994, Teledyne also moved to consolidate operations by closing three manufacturing plants, including the Hanau facility. It also, temporarily as it turned out, put its Water Pik subsidiary up for sale.

In 1996 Teledyne Inc. merged with Allegheny Ludlum Corporation and formed Pittsburgh-based Allegheny Teledyne Inc., the world's top specialty metals producer, a move that set off another two-year consolidation effort for the conglomerate as a whole. Wayne Brothers, who had joined Teledyne in 1977 as a systems designer in operations, became president of Water Pik, now a subsidiary of Allegheny Teledyne, taking over the reigns from Mel Cruger. Under his leadership, the company set a course to achieve a continuous flow of innovative consumer products within the firm's existing categories and to focus upon growth through acquisition.

The following year, Teledyne Water Pik rolled out its five-year plan to increase its worldwide presence and market share through product development, acquisitions, partnerships, and increased global marketing. With 25 percent of the retail market share in the United States for massaging showerheads and a focus on achieving market leadership in the showerhead, water, and oral care categories, Water Pik began rolling out new products. In 1998 it introduced its Flexible Shower Massage and debuted a new end-of-faucet filtration unit. The Teledyne Water Pik Electronic Faucet Filter took advantage of the move toward greater health consciousness in the United State. In 1999, the company applied its filtering technology to its showerhead, debuting the Shower Filter, designed to remove chlorine from bath water in the interest of softer skin and hair.

A new ad campaign featuring all of the Water Pik products accompanied the new introductions. ''The primary purpose of increasing our advertising commitment is to support the launch of significant new product development initiatives,'' the company's vice-president of marketing and sales was quoted as saying in a 1998 *HFN* article. Teledyne Water Pik spent $15 million in advertising in 1998 and doubled that investment over the next three years.

Teledyne also aimed to expand its product lines and increase its revenues through acquisition. In 1996, it purchased Jandy Industries, Inc., one of the leading producers of electronic pool and spa products. In 1998, it acquired the assets of Trianco Heatmaker, Inc., a manufacturer of high-efficiency gas and oil-fired water-heating products, and in 1999, it acquired substantially all the assets of Les Agences Claude Marchand, Inc., a pool accessories manufacturer and distributor, which did business in Canada as Olympic Pool Accessories.

Partnerships were another means to increased market presence for Teledyne Water Pik. In 1997 with consumers spending $1.7 billion on bottled water and in-home filtration grossing $480 million or more, the company formed an alliance with Pfister, which led to the development of the Price Pfister Pfilter Pfaucet, which incorporated a Water Pik filter. This collaboration was followed by a similar alliance with Rubbermaid Incorporated when in 1998 Teledyne agreed to manufacture filtration cartridges for Rubbermaid's water filtration pitcher systems.

In keeping with its emphasis on conservation, Teledyne Water Pik Canada partnered in 1998 with Tree Canada Foundation to plant new trees to replace thousands destroyed by ice storms. In 1999, the subsidiary joined forces with the Susan G. Komen Breast Cancer Foundation in another activist-oriented effort to fight breast cancer. Packages marked with a pink ribbon offered consumers the choice of receiving a rebate or sending a donation directly to the Komen Foundation.

Spinoff of Water Pik Technologies: 1999

By 1997, Teledyne Water Pik and Teledyne Laars together accounted for seven percent of Allegheny Teledyne's sales and eight percent of its operating profit. The Water Pik, Laars, and Jandy brands generated sales of $235 million in 1998. However, depressed prices for stainless steel forced Allegheny Teledyne to consider cost-cutting measures, including layoffs and early retirement for its workers, in order to continue to turn a profit. Driven by management's desire to focus on its core metals business, the company made the decision to spin off its consumer products businesses as independent entities. In November 1999, Water Pik Technologies, Inc., combining dental equipment, showerheads, water filtration systems, and pool spa products, was spun off to Allegheny Teledyne shareholders at the ratio of one share of the new company for each 20 shares of Allegheny Teledyne's common stock. The new company, so named because management viewed Water Pik as its flagship brand, came under the direction of CEO and President Michael Hoopis, who formerly had held the top position at Allegheny Teledyne's consumer segment. Allegheny also spun off four aerospace and electronics divisions which united to form Teledyne Technologies Inc.

Hoopis continued the direction set by his predecessors. At the start of 2000, the company aimed to represent itself as both more entrepreneurial and more responsive to customers and their needs with the continued introduction of new products. In March 2000, it introduced its new automatic flosser, bringing it into direct competition with Braun. It also piloted the Misting Massage Showerhead, further developing its shower line. By the summer of 2000, the company had eliminated the name Teledyne from its packaging in a move to capitalize on its well known brand name in a highly competitive marketplace. Additionally, it aimed to increase its international business in new and existing markets and to build more strategic alliances.

Principal Divisions

Personal Healthcare Products (Waterpik); Pool Products and Heating Systems (Laars, Jandy, Olympic).

Principal Competitors

Clorox Company (Brita); Proctor & Gamble Co. (PUR); Essef Corporation; Gillette Company (Braun) Optiva (Sonicare); United Dominion Industries.

Further Reading

"Co-founder of Teledyne Dies at 82," *Associated Press,* September 3, 1999.

Ehrbar, A.F., "Henry Singleton's Mystifying $400-Million Flyer," *Fortune,* January 16, 1978, p. 66.

Ellis, Beth R., "Teledyne's Health Plan," *HFD,* June 8, 1987, p. 1.

Fields, Robin, "Allegheny Teledyne Plans Spinoffs," *Los Angeles Times,* September 15, 1999, p. C2.

Murray, Thomas J., "The Trouble at Teledyne," *Dun's,* April 1972, p. 66.

"A Strategy Hooked to Cash Is Faltering," *Business Week,* May 31, 1982, p. 58.

"Teledyne Investing in a Brand Push," *HFN,* August 31, 1998, p. 52.

"The Teledyne Turnaround," *HFD,* November 25, 1985, p. 62.

Zaczklewicz, Arthur, "Water Pik Dives into Transition," *HFN,* December 6, 1999, p. 35.

——, "Water Pik Spinoff Drops Teledyne Name," *HFN,* October 4, 1999, p. 66.

—Carrie Rothburd

West Group

610 Opperman Drive
Eagan, Minnesota 55123
U.S.A.
Telephone: (651) 687-7000
Fax: (651) 687-5827
Web site: http://www.westgroup.com

Division of The Thomson Corporation
Incorporated: 1882 as West Publishing Co.
Employees: 8,000
Sales: $1.4 billion (1998 est.)
NAIC: 511130 Book Publishers; 511140 Database and
Directory Publishers; 514199 All Other Information
Services

West Group, the leading information provider to the U.S. legal market, was formed in early 1997 from the merger of West Publishing Co. and Thomson Legal Publishing. The Thomson Corporation, a Toronto-based information powerhouse, had acquired West Publishing the previous year for $3.4 billion. Thomson became a major player in the legal publishing market in 1989 when it acquired Lawyers Cooperative Publishing Company for $815 million, then added other venerable names in the legal field, including Bancroft-Whitney and Clark Boardman Callaghan. West Publishing held a leading position in the field of indexing and reporting court decisions, from the U.S. Supreme Court on down. Perhaps its most influential and valuable contribution was its late 19th-century invention of the Key Number System, a means of methodically organizing and summarizing the thousands of judicial rulings delivered each year. This indexing grid became so widely used by lawyers that it virtually transformed the adversarial and adjudicatory processes in the United States. West Group continues to use the Key Number System in a number of its products, including such longstanding and widely used series as the *American Digest System* and the *National Reporter System*. Although West has lost ground in the 1990s following court decisions stating that the company does not have copyright protection for some of the key material and citations featured in its products, it has stayed viable through the aggressive development of electronic products and services, including Westlaw, an online service containing more than 10,000 legal, financial, and news databases; westlaw.com, a World Wide Web version of Westlaw; KeyCite, an online citation research service; and lawoffice.com, a comprehensive legal directory listing nearly one million legal professionals.

19th-Century Foundations

In the post-Civil War period, the East was unrivaled for its centers of commerce, intellectual activity, and powerful publishing houses. For a firm to be established on the banks of the Mississippi in the as yet sparsely populated Midwest, create a new print medium, and successfully quell competition from the cultural and business establishment was unthinkable; yet, as historian William W. Marvin recorded, it happened not so much in spite of as *because* of the remote, and therefore inconspicuous, location. A young St. Paul entrepreneur with experience as a traveling book salesman opened his first business in 1872, which he called John B. West, Publisher and Bookseller. West specialized in the sale of law treatises, legal forms, dictionaries, and office supplies. His most promising work, however, was in the trading of new and used court reports, a rare commodity at the time, given the notoriously sluggish official printing of state cases and verdicts. West viewed the lawyers he served as a singularly valuable market for new information; more importantly, he realized that no single publishing company offered both expedient and inclusive case reporting.

In 1876, West convinced his older brother Horatio, an accountant, to join him in a new enterprise that would help to fill at least one identifiable and easily serviced void: that of recording Minnesota Supreme Court rulings. The business now became the John B. West Co. and the chief product, an eight-page weekly pamphlet of legal excerpts entitled *The Syllabi*. By this time, West had already established himself as a valued partner of the local legal community with his "WEST" line of legal blanks, prepared with the assistance of practicing lawyers. He decided to build upon his reputation for quality, authoritativeness, and service by enlisting the expertise of a St. Paul Bar member to edit the content of *The Syllabi*. The publication became an instant hit with the law community and more than

Company Perspectives:

The mission of West Group is to continually enhance its position as the foremost provider of information to the U.S. legal market and to expand its presence by becoming the leading provider of solutions to this market. Furthermore, West Group will work to ensure that The Thomson Corporation achieves its mission of becoming the leading provider of information products and solutions to the global legal market.

fulfilled West's initial advertisement of "prompt and reliable intelligence as to the various questions adjudicated by the Minnesota Courts at a date long prior to the publication of the State Reports." In the words of Marvin, *The Syllabi* "gave the Minnesota Bar what was then unquestionably the most complete current reporting service in the nation."

In a move that proved essential to the long-term survival of the fledgling publisher, West expanded the scope of *The Syllabi* almost immediately, replacing excerpts of Minnesota cases with complete coverage and offering selected case excerpts from neighboring Wisconsin, as a resource tool for lawyers of both states. Soon demand in Wisconsin necessitated the inclusion of all of that state's cases in excerpted form. Ironically, West's first competition came not from Eastern publishers, the concerted response of which might well have proved fatal to the John B. West Company, but from a small Milwaukee printing house. Further expansion was the logical response and so, six months into publication of *The Syllabi,* the company introduced *The North Western Reporter.* This new publication was to include everything currently covered by *The Syllabi* plus all Minnesota U.S. Circuit Court decisions, selected Minnesota and Wisconsin lower court cases, and abstracts of selected cases from other states. Although the *North Western* still functioned as a legal newspaper, the concept of a permanent reference publication was soon to be realized.

Less than three years after *The Syllabi* was introduced, a new series of the *North Western* debuted offering full coverage of current decisions in Minnesota, Wisconsin, Iowa, Michigan, Nebraska, and the Dakota Territory. The flood of orders received by the company was welcome proof that a vast and enthusiastic customer base had been successfully tapped. A *Federal Reporter,* containing decisions by the U.S. Circuit and District Courts around the country, followed in 1880, as did a *U.S. Supreme Court Reporter,* in 1882. What distinguished each of these publications was West's inclusion of a uniform indexing system, complete with headnotes. The medium, particularly its comprehensiveness, was so unlike current practice by printers of state reports that it provoked widespread ridicule. Nevertheless, several publishers realized the profitability of such an approach and soon waged heated competition with West. The company maintained its advantage because of its significant market lead and also because of its low-cost, fast publication, and accurate editing (state-commissioned reports were notoriously error-ridden, often having been produced without benefit of proofing departments or adequate legal knowledge).

The company's rapid growth caused the West brothers to seek outside capital to expand both its staff and manufacturing facilities. In the fall of 1882 Charles W. Ames and Peyton Boyle officially became part of the business, now incorporated as a private concern, West Publishing Co. During the next five years other *Reporter* publications were introduced, including the *Pacific, Atlantic, South Western, South Eastern,* and *Southern.* By 1887 the company was able to boast coast-to-coast coverage. In August of that year, the publisher of the *Eastern Reporter,* Wm. Gould, Jr., & Co., sold its subscription to West Publishing. In November of the following year, another major competitor, Lawyers' Cooperative Publishing Co., ceased publication of its *New England, Central,* and *Western Reporters.* After these milestone victories, West's chief goal for the next several decades became the promotion of the *National Reporter System* as the leading case source for lawyers and judges in all U.S. jurisdictions. A major step toward this goal was the introduction in 1889 of the first permanent *Reporter* editions. Advance sheets for these editions replaced the earlier format of bindable parts but also created a lucrative albeit temporary black market for dealers who would hawk them as West's final, edited version.

While many attorneys began to accept West's publications as fundamental case studies, many of the courts were reluctant to admit the West citations in lieu of actual State Report citations. By the mid-20th century, however, the *National Reporter System* was so successful that West citations had become generally accepted. In 1890, following upon the success of its *National Reporter System,* the company introduced the *American Digest* System, a singularly massive undertaking. The series, when complete, consisted of exhaustive listings and synopses of federal and state cases dating back to 1638. Typically paired to the more detailed *Reporter* volumes, the *Digest* listings were especially notable for their full-scale implementation of the Key Number System, which directed the researcher by category, topic, subtopic, and headnote to pertinent cases on record. Even before publication of its first digest volume, West entered the digest market by negotiating the rights for Little, Brown & Company's *U.S. Digest.* The success of the *National Reporter System,* and its obvious compatibility with the *American Digest System,* made effective competition difficult. The subscription list for John A. Mallory's *Complete Digest,* another potential competitor, was also purchased by West at about the same time. Mallory subsequently accepted a position with West and was crucial in perfecting the *American Digest System* classification scheme. The company closed the century on an especially high note with the unveiling of volume one of the *Century Digest,* intended as the definitive encyclopedia of all existing case law. The volume was unveiled at the American Bar Association (ABA) annual convention in 1897; the following year, the ABA offered its formal endorsement of the *American Digest System* and West's preeminence as a legal publisher was irrevocably ensured.

New Publications and Rapid Growth: 1900s–60s

In 1899 John West left the company to pursue other interests, and the presidency passed to Horatio West. In 1908 Charles W. Ames succeeded Horatio, and since that time every successor to the West presidency has been unrelated, save for a shared, longtime commitment to the private firm. Many company analysts attribute the remarkable development of the com-

Key Dates:

1872: John B. West begins selling law treatises, legal forms, and dictionaries in Minnesota.

1876: John B. West Co. begins publishing *The Syllabi,* a weekly pamphlet of legal excerpts and forerunner to the *National Reporter System.*

1882: Company is incorporated as West Publishing Co.

1890: The *American Digest System* makes its debut, highlighted by its implementation of the Key Number System.

1913: Company completes the compilation of a completely annotated, comprehensive edition of the U.S. statutes.

1926: The 61-volume *United States Code Annotated* is published for the first time.

1956: Teletypesetting is first used by West.

1962: The company's first web offset press is installed.

1975: The Westlaw computer-assisted legal research service is introduced.

1994: Company reaches an agreement with Dow Jones & Co. to provide access to the Dow Jones News/Retrieval service to Westlaw subscribers.

1996: Company is acquired by The Thomson Corporation for $3.4 billion.

1997: West Publishing and Thomson Legal Publishing are merged to form West Group, a division of Thomson Corporation.

1998: Westlaw.com, a Web-based delivery platform for the Westlaw database, is launched.

1999: The U.S. Supreme Court declines to review the decisions of two lower courts that had denied West's claim of copyright protection over the page numbers and page breaks in its reporters.

pany not only to the Wests' dedication and innovations but to the early, conscientious enforcement of two policies at this time—"promotion from within" and prohibition of nepotism in management. In 1913, under Ames, West Publishing fulfilled a plan first announced in 1901: the compilation of a completely annotated, comprehensive edition of the U.S. statutes. By this time, the company was not only revamping the entire field of legal reference but also exerting an impact, through its casebooks, on the manner in which law was taught.

Ames's successor, Homer P. Clark, is generally accorded special status among West presidents. When Clark assumed the presidency in 1921 (after having served the company for nearly 30 years), he inaugurated what was to become known as the "general manager era." Until approximately 1926, when Clark's new approach to managing was adopted, the company had been ruled by a committee, no one member of which was fully cognizant of the day-to-day operations for every department. With Clark, the president gained much closer contact with department heads, thereby solving numerous communication and efficiency problems that had surfaced under the old system. Another means by which Clark ensured the long-term health of the company was through the persistent acquisition of outstanding stock held by disinterested parties and estates; the

stock was then periodically reallocated to key employees, comprising a corporate-reward program that continued under Clark's successors. One of the chief editorial projects during Clark's administration was the *United States Code Annotated,* first published in 1926 after a Congressional joint committee on law revision commissioned both West and the Edward Thompson Company to pool their efforts. The original 61-volume, continually updated series now consists of some 215 permanent hardcovers, which are regularly supplemented by interim pamphlets and statutory supplements.

By the end of World War II, with Clark now serving as chairperson and Henry F. Asmussen in position as president, West began to grow rapidly. Full-time employees numbered 645 in 1945, and five years later the number had swelled to 1,172. Teletypesetting made its debut at West in 1956; further improvements in production efficiency, not to mention printing quality, came with the installation of West's first web offset press in 1962. Under then-president Lee Slater, a former business engineer, West's plant and operational layout underwent a complete modernization and overhaul. In 1968, when Slater handed control of the company to Dwight D. Opperman, West seemed well-positioned to maintain its leadership in the new technological age. When asked why he had joined the firm back in the 1950s, Opperman replied, "In law school it became apparent to me that there was one company above all others whose services were vital to the legal profession. I wanted to be a part of that company."

Late 20th Century: Increased Competition, the Electronic Revolution, and Acquisition by Thomson

As the company entered the 1970s, however, technology and speed competed head-to-head with quality and longstanding service. Chief competitor Mead Data Central introduced its LEXIS service into the field of computer-assisted legal research in 1973, a full two years ahead of West. In 1975, the Westlaw computer-assisted legal research service was introduced. Assessing the situation for *Corporate Report Minnesota,* Brent Stahl wrote, "It is too late in the day for anyone to join West in the comprehensive court reporting field by publishing books. The cost would be prohibitive, and a workable indexing system would be difficult to devise. Computers are another story, and it is by this technology that Mead, or others, might challenge West's territory, which West gained by mastering the technology available in the 1880s." Mead did challenge West, despite the steadily rising popularity of Westlaw, which became competitive with and perhaps even superior to LEXIS by the late 1970s. The battle between Mead and others against West became particularly heated during the middle to late 1980s due to lawsuits and countersuits revolving around the issue of Mead's attempt to use West's compilations of case reports. By 1988, however, West had negotiated a settlement agreement with Mead, after the courts had upheld the copyrightability of West's compilations, which Mead had threatened to integrate with LEXIS. Under the agreement, Mead agreed to pay an undisclosed amount to West for the use of its case report compilations.

The marketing of computerized research—in and outside the legal field—remained ripe territory for West and its Data Retrieval Corporation subsidiary during the 1990s. A 1992 arrangement with Commerce Clearing House to provide Westlaw users with the *Standard Federal Tax Reporter* was one way West worked to expand its subscriber base. In addition, West also pursued state-of-the-art software, such as a simplified natural language search and retrieval process called WIN (Westlaw Is Natural) which was introduced in 1992, in an attempt to open new venues for West as a high-tech information access company. In late 1992 West introduced a document delivery service called Westfax, which allowed a customer to request that individual court decisions be sent to them via fax machine. This service was designed for attorneys and others whose use of computer-assisted legal research was not frequent enough to justify a Westlaw subscription. West also began aggressively pursuing the burgeoning market for CD-ROM-based information products, releasing more than a dozen titles in the first six months of 1993 alone. In August 1993 Vance Opperman, founder and partner of a Minneapolis law firm and son of Dwight, succeeded his father as president of West Publishing. At the time, annual revenues for the company were an estimated $525 million and employment had reached 6,000, up from 3,500 in 1989.

In May 1994 West reached an agreement with Dow Jones & Co. whereby West would be able to provide access to the Dow Jones News/Retrieval service to Westlaw subscribers. The Dow Jones service included electronic access to articles from the *Wall Street Journal* and 1,800 other news and information sources. The deal was significant for Westlaw in its continuing competitive battle with LEXIS-NEXIS, which had long provided its users access to full-text articles from various publications, including exclusive electronic access to the *New York Times*. Later in 1994 Mead Data Central sold LEXIS-NEXIS to Anglo-Dutch publishing giant Reed Elsevier plc. As a result, West had another deep-pocketed competitor to contend with; another was The Thomson Corporation, a Toronto-based publishing behemoth which since 1988 had spent more than $1.3 billion buying U.S. legal publishers.

In March 1995, while West continued to fight legal challenges to its proprietary citation system, the *Minneapolis Star Tribune* newspaper reported that several U.S. Supreme Court justices had taken costly trips at the expense of West Publishing to help select the winner of an award that the company bestowed on a federal judge each year. The paper also reported that since 1983 the high court had declined to review five cases, including two copyright cases, that lower courts had decided in West's favor. No laws were broken in making these gifts, but some legal ethicists raised concerns about the justices accepting the trips from a company with important business before the court. West denied that it had done anything improper, stating that there was no link between the award and the company's court cases and calling the article "just plain wrong."

The growing competitive pressures facing West reached a head in 1995, leading the company to explore all options for the company's future, including its possible sale. West's venerable position was eroding from an explosion of competitors churning out cheap court cases CD-ROMs and from the increasing amounts of legal information available over the Internet. The company's citation system faced new challenges from public-interest advocates and from the Times Mirror Company, owner of legal publisher Matthew Bender, which filed another legal challenge against the proprietary system; West was also battling over

its citations in court with Hyperlaw Inc., a New York-based CD-ROM publisher. West management eventually settled on selling the company, leading to its June 1996 acquisition by Thomson for $3.4 billion. To gain antitrust approval for the combination of the two largest U.S. legal publishers, Thomson had to divest more than 50 legal publications valued at more than $275 million and agreed to license West's copyrighted citation system to any interested party. This settlement at first did not satisfy Reed Elsevier's objections to the acquisition, but the Anglo-Dutch firm dropped its opposition after Thomson agreed to sell Reed about $50 million of the divested publications. By early 1997 Thomson had merged West Publishing with Thomson Legal Publishing—whose units included Lawyers Cooperative Publishing, Bancroft-Whitney, and Clark Boardman Callaghan—to form West Group. Brian H. Hall, who had headed Thomson Legal, was named president and CEO of the new Thomson division, which began its existence as the number one provider of legal information to the U.S. market, with revenues of about $1.1 billion and a 9,500-strong workforce.

In 1998 West Group acquired Washington, D.C.-based Federal Publications, Inc., a leading provider of immigration law and government contracting law information. That year also saw the successful launch of westlaw.com, a Web-based delivery platform for the Westlaw database. This move reflected a Thomson-wide initiative to dramatically increase the company's Internet-based offerings. In early 1999 Thomson created a new operating unit called Thomson Legal & Regulatory Group, which combined the company's operations in the areas of law, tax, accounting, trademark, corporate finance, and human resources. West Group remained a separate division within this new unit, concentrating on the U.S. and Canadian legal markets.

In June 1999 the U.S. Supreme Court declined to review two separate lower court rulings that had found in favor of Matthew Bender and Hyperlaw and against West Group. West had asserted copyright protection over the page numbers and page breaks in its reporters but the decisions denied the company such protection. Matthew Bender, Hyperlaw, and others now had the green light to copy the text of judicial opinions from West publications—as well as such enhancements as the identification of counsel and the page numbers and page break references—although they could not use certain West editorial features, such as synopsis, digest topics, and key numbers. These rulings represented a clear setback for West Group and seemed certain to increase the competitive pressures it already faced. One of West's responses to this development was to look increasingly for opportunities to enhance its products with value-added content.

Principal Competitors

American Lawyer Media Holdings, Inc.; BNA, Inc.; Compass Data Systems; Harcourt General, Inc.; LEXIS-NEXIS; Nolo.com; Reed Elsevier plc; Time Warner Inc.; The Times Mirror Company; Wolters Kluwer nv.

Further Reading

Baenen, Jeff, "West Publishing's Success Brings Antitrust Lawsuit," *Minneapolis Star Tribune*, November 22, 1987.

Berss, Marcia, " 'West Will Always Be There,' " *Forbes,* November 21, 1994, p. 47.

Burrow, Clive, "Legal Research, in English," *New York Times,* October 18, 1992.

Ebbinghouse, Carol, "West Loses Copyright Claim over Page Numbers," *Information Today,* July/August 1999, pp. 20 + .

Ervin, John, Jr., "Publishing for the Law at West," *Publishers Weekly,* November 25, 1988.

Faustmann, John, "Buying Legal History: Thomson's Biggest Takeover Draws Mixed Reaction," *Maclean's,* March 11, 1996, p. 36.

Felsenthal, Edward, "West's Bid to Find a Buyer Comes amid Pressure on Legal Publishers," *Wall Street Journal,* October 23, 1995, p. B6.

Greenhouse, Linda, "Progress Spawns Question: Who Owns the Law?" *New York Times,* February 16, 1990.

Griffith, Cary, "West Aggressively Pursues Electronic Publishing Market," *Information Today,* September 1993, pp. 30–31.

——, "WEST*fax:* An Innovative Service Concludes a Very Bright Year," *Information Today,* February 1993, pp. 18–19.

Hamburger, Tom, and Sharon Schmickle, "West Publishing and the Courts: High Stakes and Hot Competition," *Minneapolis Star Tribune,* March 6, 1995, p. 1A.

"High Court Justices Decline to Comment on Charges in Article," *Wall Street Journal,* March 7, 1995, p. A11.

Karr, Albert R., "Thomson's Pact to Acquire Rival Receives Government Approval," *Wall Street Journal,* June 20, 1996, p. B10.

Lipin, Steven, Raju Narisetti, and Solange De Santis, "Thomson to Purchase West Publishing for $3.43 Billion," *Wall Street Journal,* February 27, 1996, p. A3.

Marcotty, Josephine, "The New West: Publisher Exploring Information Frontiers," *Minneapolis Star Tribune,* August 23, 1993, p. 1D.

Marvin, William W., *West Publishing Co.: Origin-Growth-Leadership,* St. Paul: West Publishing Co., 1969.

McAuliffe, Bill, "West Becomes Past in St. Paul, Present and Future in Eagan," *Minneapolis Star Tribune,* March 25, 1992.

Narisetti, Raju, Bart Ziegler, and Greg Steinmetz, "West Publishing Plans to Provide Dow Jones Service," *Wall Street Journal,* May 18, 1994, p. B7.

Oslund, John J., "For West Publishing, the Gavel Is Coming Down Hard and Loud," *Minneapolis Star Tribune,* November 28, 1994, p. 1D.

——, "West Publishing Co. Sold to Canada's Thomson Corp." *Minneapolis Star Tribune,* February 27, 1996, p. 1D.

Pitzer, Mary J., and Zachary Schiller, "A Searing Courtroom Drama over . . . Page Numbers," *Business Week,* July 4, 1988.

Pritchard, Timothy, "Thomson Jumps Head First into an Electronic Future," *New York Times,* February 21, 2000, p. C11.

Stahl, Brent, "Giant with a Low Profile," *Corporate Report Minnesota,* February 1979, pp. 40–43.

West Publishing Company: Forever Associated with the Practice of Law, Eagan, Minn.: West Publishing Co., 1991.

"West Publishing to Offer Tax Reports," *Minneapolis Star Tribune,* August 19, 1992.

Willis, Judith, "WESTLAW and LEXIS Compete in Market Having Growth Potential," *St. Paul Pioneer Press & Dispatch,* March 18, 1985.

Woo, Junda, "Electronic Publishers of Legal Data Go to Court over Comparative Ads," *Wall Street Journal,* July 13, 1992.

—Jay P. Pederson
—updated by David E. Salamie

Williams Communications Group, Inc.

One Williams Center
Tulsa, Oklahoma 74172
U.S.A.
Telephone: (918) 573-2000
Fax: (918) 573-2296
Web site: http://www.wilcom.com

Public Subsidiary of The Williams Companies, Inc.
Incorporated: 1985 as Williams Telecommunications
    Systems, Inc.
Employees: 9,200
Sales: $2.02 billion (1999)
Stock Exchanges: New York
Ticker Symbol: WCG
NAIC: 513310 Wired Telecommunications Carriers;
    51322 Cable and Other Program Distribution; 513322
    Cellular and Other Wireless Telecommunications;
    51334 Satellite Telecommunications; 51211 Motion
    Picture and Video Production

Headquartered in Tulsa, Oklahoma, Williams Communications Group, Inc., a subsidiary of The Williams Companies, Inc., owns, leases, and operates a nationwide fiber optic network focused on providing voice, data, Internet, and video services to communications services providers. The company also sells, installs, and maintains communications equipment and network services that address the voice and data needs of organizations of all sizes. In the early 1990s, as Williams Telecommunications Systems, Inc. (WilTel), a subsidiary of The Williams Companies and the nation's fourth largest long-distance carrier, the company pioneered advanced data services such as frame relay and asynchronous transfer mode (ATM). WilTel was the first carrier to put traffic on a public network frame relay overlay in early 1991 and offered limited ATM service by the fall of 1993, ahead of both AT&T and MCI. By 1999, Williams Communications Group had facilities serving 50 of the top market segments and was expected by the year 2000 to expand into 125 cities nationwide with its new 32,000-mile network.

The fully integrated architecture of the Williams Multi-Service Broadband Network couples ATM core switching with advanced optical networking technologies to provide carriers with data, voice, and Internet services over any platform. Its customers are companies that require large bandwidth capacity to deliver their own brands of products or services such as voice, data, Internet, or broadcast media services to end-users.

Successful Subsidiary of The Williams Companies Begins Business: 1985

In 1908, the two Williams brothers, S. Miller, Jr., and David, opened a construction business called Williams Brothers that later grew into the world's leading pipeline engineering and construction firm. Their company went public in 1957 with a net worth of about $8 million. In 1985, the company entered the communications business when it began turning decommissioned petroleum pipelines into conduits for fiber optic cable. The idea was that of Roy Wilkens, then president of Williams Pipeline Co., who, after attending a Harvard University program for mid-career executives, was inspired to start the new subsidiary. The Williams Companies committed $50 million to the project and made Wilkens chief executive officer of a team that began stringing fiber in the pipelines to start up its long-distance telecommunications company, Williams Telecommunications Systems, Inc. Four years later, through a combination of construction projects and acquisitions, WilTel had built approximately 11,000 miles of network in the mid-continent and upper Midwest to become the fourth largest digital fiber optic network in the United States.

Wilkens, who had an affinity for high-tech gadgets, such as the company's 30-foot conference table, which, at the press of a button, changed to a podium and four separate tables, or its video-conferencing room with walls of polarized glass that could be controlled to become opaque, nonetheless reported feeling some doubt about the new subsidiary's success. "It was a scary move and we didn't know if it could be done. We really knew nothing about the telecommunications industry going into this thing," he confided in a 1992 article in *Networking Management*. Wilkens served as president and chief executive officer of WilTel from 1985 to 1997.

Company Perspectives:

We recognize and enthusiastically accept our responsibility to the communities we serve, through acting as a good neighbor and through involvement and support for community activities. We are committed to protecting the public, the environment and our natural resources by operating in a safe, reliable manner. We maintain a corporate culture that values originality, invention and creativity, and that nurtures these qualities through openness and reverence for the entrepreneurial spirit. The Company's willingness to take risks in deploying new technology and investing in large capital projects is central to its culture and its success. Efficiency means the difference between success and failure. We will relentlessly pursue a more efficient way to do everything we undertake.

Fortunately for WilTel, it was able to move quickly enough to exploit the two key industry drivers at play in the mid-1980s: fiber technology and regulatory change. Fiber had just entered the scene on a commercial basis; deregulation, in turn, had led to the breakup of AT&T and the creation of opportunities for other long-distance carriers. WilTel early on provided a surprising challenge to industry giants AT&T, MCI, and Sprint. WilTel Network Services, set up in 1990, geared its fiber optic network to medium- and high-end business customers, providing them with reliable, highly secure private lines and data network solutions. WilPak frame relay service, a unit of WilTel, debuted with seven switches in 1991, and by 1992 had cornered approximately 40 percent of the frame relay market; by 1994, its frame relay network expanded to include approximately 30 switches. In 1993, WilPower, another unit of WilTel, offered outsourcing of a firm's internetwork implementation and operations management. WilTel International simultaneously began to develop international private-line services via fiber. Vyvx, WilTel's subsidiary, focused on broadcast and closed-circuit or business television systems, promoting point-to-point or multipoint videoconferencing. It began backhauling broadcasts (transferring the voice and video data) for the Super Bowl in 1990. Among other traffic, Vyvx carried more than three-quarters of the major league sports seen on television.

WilTel's initial growth came at a time when many were predicting a glut in fiber. However, WilTel was able to make use of The Williams Companies' construction experience to lay its fiber optic network quickly and less expensively than most companies. As a result, it offered prices about 20 percent below that of its competitors. Its cables, shielded by pipeline and coordinated by a network control center with an alarm system similar to that used on its energy pipelines, were more reliable than most. WilTel also grew at a time when public networks were undergoing a major transformation to broadband and to technology that could combine voice, data, and video traffic at lower cost and more efficiently. Having already become the fourth largest long-distance carrier, WilTel determined to be out of the gate early with asynchronous transfer mode (ATM) services and deployed switches in eight cities in 1993, eight more in 1994, and another seven in 1995. It also began to package its service with on-premises equipment for customers.

Wholesaling in the Mid-1990s, the Company's New Core Competency

By 1994, WilTel had its heaviest presence in the South, the upper Midwest, and along the East Coast. Its success prompted Long Distance Discount Service (LDDS) to make a move to buy the company for $2 billion as a means of competing with the industry's three long-distance giants: AT&T Corp., MCI, and Sprint. WilTel initially staved off the takeover, then agreed to sell the long-distance portion of its telecommunications business in January 1995, when LDDS renewed its intentions, for $2.5 billion in cash, or about 28 times WilTel's earnings.

Williams signed a three-year non-compete agreement with LDDS (which later became WorldCom, then MCI WorldCom), which restricted WilTel from providing any tariff-based pure voice and data services. However, it retained a single strand of its 24-strand optical fiber through the 11,000-mile network, which it turned over to its newly created WilTech Group, whose mission was to implement new multimedia transmission technologies. It also kept its systems integration and videoconferencing subsidiaries, Solutions and Vyvx. Vyvx, as WilTech's main subsidiary, used the strand to focus on multimedia applications such as video and the Internet. Howard Janzen, from Williams's energy side, was named president of the WilTech Group.

Janzen had joined Williams Pipe Line in 1979, after earning a master's degree in metallurgical engineering from the Colorado School of Mines and completing the Harvard Business School Program for Management Development. In 1987, he moved up to the position of vice-president of the pipeline; in 1991, he became vice-president of operations at Williams Natural Gas Co., and, in 1993, its senior vice-president and general manager. Janzen and Keith Bailey, chief executive officer of The Williams Companies, set about almost immediately to engineer WilTel's 1998 return.

Unlike the old WilTel, whose business had been 80 percent retail and 20 percent wholesale, Williams planned to concentrate on the wholesale end of business as its new core competency and to compete for a larger share of the communications services market. Beginning in 1994, it began to buy up systems integration companies to put together complex networks that combined voice and data communications: ICG Wireless Services in 1995, and Global Access Telecommunications, the nation's second largest reseller of worldwide satellite video transmissions, in 1996.

In 1997, management created The Williams Communications Group, combining its communications and network technology units, Williams Telecommunications Systems, Inc. (WilTel) and The WilTech Group. Janzen became president and chief operating officer and advanced to chief executive officer a few months later. The new subsidiary planned to reemerge as a single-source provider of national business communications systems and international satellite and fiber optic multimedia services. It targeted as new customers service provider-interexchange carriers, incumbent and competitive local exchange carriers, Internet service providers, and cable television companies.

The new Williams Communications chose to organize itself differently than the original WilTel had. It pronounced autonomy its core value and reduced its number of units from four to three: Williams Communications Solutions, Williams Vyvx Services, and Williams Communications Network Applications. Planning for the multi-unit entity was assigned to the business council, made up of the heads of the business units, which dealt with day-to-day operational issues and put recommendations forward to the chief executive officer's cabinet. Both council and cabinet met once a month to discuss larger, long-range issues of management. The rationale behind this decision was to achieve fast decision making, an entrepreneurial spirit, and a sense of accountability at all levels. Williams's Communications also set out to expand services to customers.

The new Williams Communications also shifted its focus away from industrial training with the 1997 decision to divest itself of Williams Learning Network, the leading provider of learning technologies and training services for business and industry. Believing that the communications industry would continue to evolve away from vertical integration, it adopted a strategy it called "eConstruction," targeting for itself the segment of the telecommunications market that provided businesses with connectivity. In 1997, the company became the first interexchange carrier to offer end-to-end frame relay service with its network-to-network interface (NNI) between its own frame relay services and local exchange carriers. Together with Nortel Communications Systems, it created WilTel Communications L.L.C. to sell and maintain telecommunications and networking equipment. Vyvx continued its own innovative work, developing the first mobile, fiber optic switching facility which broadcast the Timothy McVeigh trial from outside the courthouse. In 1996, Vyvx had provided news coverage of the Olympics, the O.J. Simpson trial, and the NATO Summit in Paris.

Debut of New Fiber Optic Network: Late 1990s

As January 1998 approached, Vyvx began to use Transco's right-of-way to install a fiber network between Houston and Washington, D.C. It joined forces with Montana Power Co. and Houston-based Enron Corporation to form FTV Communications, which launched a project to build a long-haul fiber optic network linking Portland and Los Angeles. On the eve of its reentry into the wholesale long-distance market, Williams Communications announced the formation of the Williams Network, a new fiber optic network. It simultaneously began offering capacity to US West Communications, a local exchange carrier called Intermedia Communications, and Internet protocol services provider Concentric Network Corp. Combined, the company had more than $1 billion in contracts to provide long-haul services to these three service providers on the day of its debut. In February 1998, Williams announced plans to build another national fiber network with 32,000 miles of routes, fed by $4.7 billion in investments. It later raised an additional $680 million through its October 1999 initial public offering and an additional $750 million from large blocks of common stock to Intel Corporation, SBC Communications, and Telefonos de Mexico (TELMEX), all of whom planned to use Williams as a preferred provider for one or more of the services it offered.

Originally, the Williams Communications Group considered building its network just like the one it had operated as WilTel, with a traditional infrastructure that included overlay frame relay and ATM networks. However, advances in network and applications technologies combined with a more open regulatory climate had significantly altered the industry landscape since 1995. Most of the traffic on the WilTel network had been voice; now data was becoming predominant. Seizing upon the opportunity to start over with a clean slate, Williams tried to avoid the limitations of using gear that could rapidly become obsolete. It chose to focus instead on a network based on ATM because this was the best technology to provide a multi-service network. Its decision did not go unnoticed. Williams Communications received the InfoVision award of the International Engineering Consortium in 1999 for its innovative public network architecture. It also garnered the SuperQuest award from the SuperCOMM conference for best-built bandwidth and the America's Network readers' choice award for best bandwidth wholesaler.

In mid-1999, Williams Communications sold Williams Conferencing for $39 million at about the same time The Williams Companies began construction on a new facility in downtown Tulsa to house itself and its several subsidiaries. Williams Communications' reentry into the voice market took place in August on a wholesale-only basis with long-distance telephone services to its customers reliant upon the company's own switches. Williams Communications focused its future expansion on the aggressive expansion of its new ATM-switched network, which it expected to complete in 2000 with 32,000 route-miles of fiber. With increased capacity, the $2 billion company aimed to achieve 20 percent of the domestic telecommunications market and to branch out into the global market.

Principal Subsidiaries

Williams Communications Solutions; Williams Communications Network Applications; Williams Vyvx Services; Global Access Telecommunications; Williams Network; Telemetry.

Principal Competitors

AT&T Corp.; Qwest; Sprint Communications Company; MCI WorldCom; Level 3 Communications.

Further Reading

Byrne, Harlan S., "Williams Cos.," *Barron's*, September, 2, 1991, pp. 41–42.

"Free Video: Growing Point-to-Point Power Pitches Network Distribution," *Broadcasting*, July 29, 1991, pp. 43–45.

"Interview: Howard E. Janzen, President and CEO, Williams Communications," *Telecommunications*, February 1999.

Johnson, Johna Till, "Public Frame Relay Gets Rolling," *Data Communications*, December 1991, pp. 67–68.

Masud, Sam, "Williams: Second Time a Charm?," *Telecommunications*, February 1999, pp. 22–23.

Patron, Edward B., "WilTel Rides Again," *Financial World*, June 17, 1996, pp. 37–38.

Stewart, D.R., "Williams Companies Communication Group CEO Leads Revolution," *Tulsa World*, January 10, 1998.

Testa, Bridget Mintz, "Cinderella Complex," *Telephony Upstart Supplement*, May 31, 1999, pp. 84–87.

"Williams System to Install Major Fiber Optic Network," *Oil & Gas Journal*, May 20, 1985, pp. 41–42.

Wilson, Carol, "Quiet WilTel Makes Noise with Fiber Optic Network," *Telephony*, February 2, 1987, p. 22.

—Carrie Rothburd

Wilson Sonsini Goodrich & Rosati
PROFESSIONAL CORPORATION

Wilson Sonsini Goodrich & Rosati

---

650 Page Mill Road
Palo Alto, California 94304
U.S.A.
Telephone: (650) 493-9300
Fax: (650) 493-6811
Web site: http://www.wsgr.com

Partnership
Founded: 1961 as McCloskey, Wilson & Mosher
Employees: 2,100
Sales: $215 million (1998 est.)
NAIC: 54111 Offices of Lawyers

Best known as a full-service law firm that serves mainly high-technology and biotechnology companies, Wilson Sonsini Goodrich & Rosati provides counsel to more than 300 public and 3,000 private companies. Its lawyers represent firms such as Apple Computer, Hewlett-Packard, VA Linux Systems, Novell, Netscape Communications, and Micron Technology. Wilson Sonsini also serves investment banks and venture capital firms that financially support both technology and other clients. Based in the heart of Silicon Valley with a satellite office in San Francisco, the law firm also operates offices in Austin, Texas; McClean, Virginia; and Kirkland, Washington, to serve companies in those regional high-tech centers. Although a young firm compared with many Wall Street law firms, Wilson Sonsini numbers among the leaders in securities, litigation, mergers and acquisitions, intellectual property, and other practice areas of modern corporate law. Probably its most important contribution is serving computer, Internet, and biotechnology firms that are creating the so-called "new economy" in the Information Age or postindustrial society.

Origins and Early Practice

With the advent of the first mainframe computers, American society soon after World War II began to enter the Information Age in which knowledge was the basic commodity, instead of raw materials that fueled the Industrial Revolution. Thus it was in the early stages of what futurist Alvin Toffler called The Third Wave that a new law firm originated. Wilson Sonsini Goodrich & Rosati began in Palo Alto, California, when three attorneys formed a predecessor firm.

After graduating from Princeton and Yale Law School, John Arnot Wilson worked for Cleveland's Thompson, Hine and Flory and the Atomic Energy Commission before deciding to move to California. In 1957 he established a solo practice in 1957 in Redwood City, but then in 1960 he moved to nearby Palo Alto where he shared office space with two other lawyers, Paul McCloskey and Roger Mosher. The three in 1961 created the partnership of McCloskey, Wilson and Mosher to serve such early clients as Tymshare, ESL, ONC Motor Freight, Coherent Laser, and the town of Woodside. They also served Hiller Helicopters, where Wilson earlier had worked as its inhouse counsel.

In 1966 the firm hired Larry W. Sonsini, its first associate and a new graduate of the Boalt Hall School of Law, University of California, Berkeley. "The cultural background of Silicon Valley was embryonic when we started here," recalled Sonsini in the August 25, 1997 *Forbes*. "There weren't a lot of old-line businesses and old-line service support companies like law or accounting firms, banks, or investment banks. We started with a very fresh slate. Consequently, the valley was able to mold itself in such a way as to be responsive to entrepreneurism, growth, and achievement."

At first the law firm had a few high-tech clients who often used prominent San Francisco law firms. Still, the firm's location near Stanford University positioned it to represent companies formed from research conducted there. By 1966 the early partnership had established ties with some key players in the new venture capital field, including Laurance Rockefeller, Davis and Rock, and Draper, Gaither and Anderson, that provided vital private funding for several of the law firm's startup clients.

The small partnership in 1968 completed its first IPO for Wilson's client Behavioral Research Laboratories. Wilson turned that project over to Sonsini, who became the firm's expert on securities.

Company Perspectives:

Our mission is to be a strategic business partner with each of our clients by leveraging our expertise and experience to provide innovative, responsive, and cost-effective legal solutions. We understand that the law is a means to accomplish our clients' business objectives, not an end in itself. Our clients are business people, principally in the technology sector, and the challenges they face must be seen first and foremost as business challenges.

In 1969 the partnership created WM Investment Company to take advantage of stock options that some of its startup clients offered instead of cash for payment of services. Other law firms eventually adopted this pioneering practice as a way to invest in their clients' long-range success.

The 1970s and 1980s

In the 1970s the law firm gained new partners and a new name. John B. Goodrich had earned a J.D. from the University of Southern California in 1966 and an LL.M. in taxation from New York University in 1970 before joining the firm and starting its Tax Department in 1970. In 1971 Mario M. Rosati, a graduate of the Boalt Hall Law School, University of California, Berkeley, was recruited to build the Trust and Estates Practice. After McCloskey left to enter politics, in 1973 the firm changed its name to Wilson, Mosher & Sonsini. Roger Mosher's departure to start his own firm in 1978 led to another name change, Wilson Sonsini Goodrich & Rosati.

The renamed firm in 1980 provided legal counsel to Apple Computer when it went public, which really disappointed Wilson Sonsini's rival Fenwick & West, also based in Palo Alto, which had helped Apple incorporate in 1976. Since that time, both law firms continued to represent Apple, the firm that started the personal computer revolution.

Wilson Sonsini had grown to 32 lawyers by 1981 and by 1984 had gained experience in the first two phases of its business plan, namely serving new firms through the first stage of startup financing and second-stage work such as IPOs, other securities work, intellectual property issues, taxation, employment, environmental issues, and real estate.

In 1984 the firm entered the third stage of providing mature technology firms with counsel concerning mergers and acquisitions when Larry Sonsini represented ROLM Corporation in its $1.8 billion acquisition by IBM. The law firm had helped ROLM get started in 1969 and had handled its IPO in 1975.

The ROLM transaction helped the firm realize that it needed more manpower if it were to provide a full range of legal services. By 1986 it expanded to 97 lawyers, sometimes by lateral hiring of mature attorneys from rival law firms. Historically a rare event, such raiding of other firms for top talent began to be a major trend in the late 1970s and early 1980s after the *National Law Journal* and the *American Lawyer* began publishing articles about law firm internal finances and partner compensation. The general transformation of big law firms to become more business oriented also was influenced by the U.S. Supreme Court ruling that it was unconstitutional to restrict professional advertising.

In the late 1980s Wilson Sonsini gained new opportunities to serve its clients when high-tech firms began being sued by angry stockholders upset over stock declines. These class action lawsuits proliferated in the 1990s when some individuals became known as ''professional plaintiffs'' because they sued literally dozens of companies.

Practice in the 1990s

By the 1990s Wilson Sonsini represented so many technology firms that it sometimes ended up serving one client in a transaction with another client. Several observers questioned the conflicts of interest in such relationships. Clients seldom complained, however. For example, in 1995 Wilson Sonsini represented its client Seagate when it acquired Conner Peripherals, another client. CEO Finis Conner signed a conflict-of-interest waiver and said in the August 3, 1998 *Fortune,* ''Having him [Larry Sonsini] in the deal was okay with me because I felt he would add to it. He is very sensible about things. It all went extremely well.''

Wilson Sonsini continued to help venture capitalists and new business owners get together in the 1990s. It represented venture capital firms like Morgan Stanley Venture Partners, Mayfield Fund, Norwest Venture Capital, and U.S. Venture Partners. Name partner Mario Rosati estimated that he represented about 25 percent of the entrepreneurs who sought his assistance to gain financing from such firms. Wilson Sonsini also helped the National Venture Capital Association work with Congress in 1998 to pass the Internal Revenue Service Reorganization Bill (HR 2676), which clarified some wording in the federal tax code.

Meanwhile, the law firm's stock investments in its clients proved lucrative. For example, in 1998 the firm estimated that it had made $25 million in those investments over the past ten years. The bull market of much of the 1990s proved a real boon to the firm, but the downturn in 2000 hurt some investors.

Wilson Sonsini usually limited its investment in any single firm to $25,000 to $50,000. ''We intentionally keep ownership small to avoid any appearance that our equity participation may affect our legal advice or our legal judgment,'' said Rosati in the October 1, 1999 *Venture Capital Journal.* Some critics, however, argued that any investment, no matter how small, hurt lawyer-client relationships.

With the healthcare and biotechnology industries expanding, Wilson Sonsini represented several life science firms in the 1990s, including Abgenix, ArthroCare, Cardiac Pathways Corporation, Cell Genesys, and Vivus. Nontechnology clients included The Home Depot, U.S. Office Product Company, and Monaco Coach Corporation.

For years Larry Sonsini, as the chairman of the law firm, resisted opening new branch offices. He thought that national and even international practice could be conducted from the firm's home in Palo Alto. Rival firms meanwhile were establishing branch offices in various cities, and some attorneys

Key Dates:

1961: McCloskey, Wilson & Mosher is founded in Palo Alto, California.
1969: Firm creates WM Investment Company to invest in clients' companies.
1970: The firm's Tax Department is started.
1971: A Trust and Estates Department is formed.
1978: The firm is renamed Wilson Sonsini Goodrich & Rosati.
1981: A real estate practice is started.
1985: An environmental practice is created.
1990: The firm starts its Life Sciences Group and organizes its WSGR Foundation.
1998: The firm opens its first branch office, located in Kirkland, Washington.
1999: Offices are started in Austin and San Francisco; Venture/Investment Fund Group is created.

thought that Wilson Sonsini was wrong not to do likewise. In any case, in 1999 Wilson Sonsini opened its Austin, Texas office. In December 1999 the firm announced the opening of a northern Virginia office, effective early 2000. Chairman Larry Sonsini said, "Northern Virginia is our first foothold on the East Coast," in a press release of December 8, 1999, but that the firm also was looking at other East Coast options, including a branch New York City office. The firm's East Coast presence served several Mid-Atlantic clients, including BAAN, GenVec, Rudolph Technologies, and WomenCONNECT.com.

In 2000 Americans heard the big news that the courts had declared Microsoft an illegal monopoly, but many may not have realized that a Wilson Sonsini partner had played a key role in that decision. "Star litigator Gary Reback is Enemy No. 1 at Microsoft," declared *Fortune* on August 3, 1998. For years Reback had argued that Microsoft's linking its Internet Explorer to its Windows operating system and penalizing computer manufacturers who tried to offer other Internet browsers was illegal and stifled technological innovation. Representing such Microsoft rivals as Netscape and assisting the U.S. Justice Department in its lawsuit against Microsoft, Reback and other attorneys won at least the early rounds of this ongoing dispute that some have compared to the breakup of Standard Oil in the early 20th century.

Wilson Sonsini ranked as the 46th largest U.S. law firm based on its 1998 gross revenues of $215 million, up from 1997 when it was number 46 with $174 million in gross revenues. The firm's partners in 1998 received average compensation of $620,000, ranked number 34 by the *American Lawyer* in July 1999. Although more law firms represented high-tech firms in 2000 and several large New York law firms had established California branch offices to serve such clients, it seemed that Wilson Sonsini was well prepared to continue to be a major player helping Information Age clients.

Principal Operating Units

Corporate and Securities; Employee Benefits; Employment Law; Intellectual Property; Litigation; Real Estate/Environmental; Tax; Venture/Investment Funds; Wealth Management.

Principal Competitors

Fenwick & West LLP; Cooley Godward.

Further Reading

Allbritton, Chris, "Silicon Valley's Man with a Mission Faces Off Against Microsoft . . . ," *Los Angeles Times,* May 10, 1998, p. 2.

Baum, Geoff, "Accountant, Lawyer, Banker, Flack," *Forbes,* August 25, 1997, pp. 99–100.

Brandt, Richard L., "Interview: Gary Reback," *Upside,* February 1998, pp. 92–94 +.

Davies, Erin, "Silicon Valley Law," *Fortune,* August 3, 1998, pp. 219–20, 222.

Fineberg, Seth A., "Congress Approves Revised Rollover Law," *Venture Capital Journal,* August 1, 1998, p. 1.

Fryer, Bronwyn, "The Firm," *Gentry,* July 1998, pp. 71–75.

Galanter, Marc, and Thomas Palay, *Tournament of Lawyers: The Transformation of the Big Law Firms,* Chicago: University of Chicago Press, 1991.

Horne, William W., "A Maverick Matures," *American Lawyer,* September 1996.

The Making of Silicon Valley: A One Hundred Year Renaissance, Silicon Valley Historical Association, 1995, p. 43.

Neidorf, Shawn, "Silicon Valley Lawyers Embrace VC-Like Role," *Venture Capital Journal,* October 1, 1999, pp. 35–37.

"Silicon Valley: How It Really Works," *Business Week,* August 18–25, 1997, pp. 66–78.

Stevens, Amy, "Fee-for-All: Savvy Lawyers Find Way to Make Millions: Win Pro Bono Cases – Wilson Sonsini Will Earn $3.5 Million to Represent Abused Prison Inmates – Giving a Chunk to Charity," *Wall Street Journal,* November 29, 1995, p. A1.

Sweeney, Jack, "Busy Plaintiffs Keep Silicon Valley on Edge," *Computer Reseller News,* November 28, 1994, p. 1.

Wild, Joff, "The Battle for Clients in the Golden State," *Managing Intellectual Property* (London), May 1996, p. 14.

—David M. Walden

Zenith Electronics Corporation

1000 Milwaukee Avenue
Glenview, Illinois 60025-2495
U.S.A.
Telephone: (847) 391-7000
Fax: (847) 391-7253
Web site: http://www.zenith.com

Wholly Owned Subsidiary of LG Electronics Inc.
Incorporated: 1923 as Zenith Radio Corporation
Employees: 6,800
Sales: $984.8 million (1998)
NAIC: 421620 Electrical Appliance, Television, and
    Radio Set Wholesalers; 421690 Other Electronic Parts
    and Equipment Wholesalers

Having jettisoned its manufacturing operations in favor of outsourced production, Zenith Electronics Corporation has repositioned itself primarily as a designer and marketer of high-quality consumer electronics products under the Zenith brand. Among the products it sells are high-definition, flat-screen, and other television sets, set-top boxes for cable and satellite systems, DVD players, and digital audio products, such as MP3 players and CD recording systems. From its start Zenith advertised that its reputation would be built and sustained by the superior workmanship, reliability, and innovation of all products bearing the Zenith name. The company became a huge American success as a top producer first in the radio industry and later in television. Low-priced imports from Asia, however, began to rock Zenith in the mid-to-late 1970s. Although continuing to produce innovative products—including the high-definition television (HDTV) technology chosen as the standard by the industry alliance in the United States—Zenith posted losses through much of the 1980s and the entire decade of the 1990s. With no end in sight to the mounting losses, Zenith sold a controlling interest to South Korea-based LG Electronics Inc. (part of the LG Group conglomerate) in 1995, then emerged in late 1999 from a prepackaged bankruptcy as a wholly owned subsidiary of LG.

Radio-centric Beginnings

Zenith's beginnings were very modest. Two ham radio operators, Karl E. Hassel and R.H.G. Mathews, began manufacturing radio equipment at a kitchen table in 1918 under the name Chicago Radio Laboratory. Hassel ran an amateur radio station with the call letters 9ZN, from which they named their first product Z-Nith—the origin of the later name Zenith. These two men were joined by Commander Eugene F. McDonald, Jr., in 1921. McDonald, already a self-made millionaire when he joined the company, was pivotal to Zenith's growth. He was much more than a financial backer. McDonald's flamboyant style was echoed in the company's dramatic advertising methods and this style, coupled with innovative genius and an ability to sense changes in public tastes, meant that for more than three decades, in the public perception, McDonald was Zenith.

McDonald was counterbalanced by Hugh Robertson, who joined the company as treasurer in 1923. Robertson's financial expertise and careful planning led Zenith through many difficulties, including the Great Depression. The year 1923 was significant in many other ways. The company was incorporated as Zenith Radio Corporation that year, and 30,000 shares of stock were issued at $10 per share, with the largest single block going to McDonald. At that time, Zenith Radio Corporation took over sales and marketing for the Chicago Radio Laboratory, a maker of radio equipment. Zenith later acquired all of Chicago Radio Laboratory's assets and officially began to manufacture under its own name.

Soon McDonald, who preferred to be addressed as The Commander (as a lieutenant commander in the Navy during World War I he was entitled to the name), began to show his flair for drama. He persuaded Admiral Donald B. MacMillan to take a shortwave radio with him on his Arctic expedition. MacMillan's transmissions proved to be exciting demonstrations of the efficiency of shortwave communication. In addition to his advertising schemes, McDonald organized and became president of the National Association of Broadcasters in 1923.

Meanwhile, Zenith's inventors and technicians were developing landmark products. In 1924 Zenith introduced the world's first portable radio. Then in 1925, McDonald helped MacMillan

Company Perspectives:

Zenith Electronics Corporation has a proud heritage of leadership in home entertainment products. For more than eight decades, beginning with the advent of radio, the Zenith name has been synonymous with quality and innovation. A pioneer in electronics technology, Zenith has invented countless industry-leading developments, including the first portable and push-button radios, the first wireless TV remote controls and the first HDTV system using digital technology.

organize another expedition, this time to the North Pole. McDonald was part of the expedition as a ship commander, but went only as far as Greenland. His shortwave radio broadcasts of Eskimos singing into the microphone were a great success, and Zenith's advertising always reminded the public that Zenith shortwave radios were the choice of the Arctic explorers.

More innovations followed. In 1926 Zenith introduced the first home radio receiver that operated directly from regular AC electric current, and automatic push-button tuning came in 1927. Also in 1927, the company's famous slogan, "The Quality Goes In Before The Name Goes On," was used for the first time. By the late 1920s Zenith was in 12th place in a $400 million industry.

But when the Great Depression hit after the stock market crash of 1929, the radio industry was thrown into chaos. Zenith's sales went from $10 million in 1929 to less than $2 million in 1932. Although the company suffered five successive years of losses, Treasurer Hugh Robertson managed to get the company through without borrowing until profitability returned.

McDonald, even during those times, did not give up his attempts to get Zenith technology into new areas. In 1934, he sent a wire to all U.S. oil and tire companies: "Watch absence of people on streets between eleven and eleven thirty during presidential talk." After the talk, he sent letters urging them to become Zenith auto-radio dealers and get rich.

One of McDonald's most popular ideas during the 1930s was the big black dial for radios. Its large clock-style numbers were designed to be read from a distance or without glasses. McDonald also promoted portable shortwave radios for $75—predecessors of Zenith's famous Trans-Oceanic radios—an idea that was ridiculed at the time but was extremely successful in the end.

Zenith management valued and encouraged worker loyalty. Therefore, when the company began to be profitable again in 1936 for the first time in five years, Zenith paid its workers, rather than its stockholders, a dividend, in appreciation for sticking out the tough times with little money. Net sales of $8.5 million in 1936 resulted in net income of $1.2 million. By 1937 sales were up to almost $17 million, and net income was nearly $2 million.

Mid-Century Move into Television

By the late 1930s, Zenith was exporting to 96 countries and was a pioneer in television and FM broadcasting. In 1939

Zenith's station W9XZV, the first all-electric television station, went on the air. This was followed the next year by W9XEN, one of the first FM stations in the United States. By 1941 Zenith had risen to second place in a $600 million industry, behind only RCA.

Although World War II meant a decline in normal consumer business, this decline was more than offset by war production. Zenith manufactured radar, communications equipment, and high-sensitivity frequency meters. Net sales were $23.8 million in 1941, and $34.2 million in 1942, with $1.4 million in net income that year.

Zenith's major product outside of war-related materials during World War II was a highly successful line of hearing aids that retailed for $40. A miniature adaptation of a radio receiving set, it made hearing assistance affordable for thousands of people. Zenith became the largest marketer of hearing aids in the world, outselling all other companies combined.

Once it was able to resume civilian research and production, Zenith concentrated on improving television, even though McDonald had resisted television for almost a decade. The company introduced its first line of black-and-white television receivers in 1948. Also in 1948, to meet an immediate increased demand, Zenith purchased the Rauland Corporation, a noted Chicago manufacturer of television picture tubes. One year after this purchase, the combined talents of the Zenith and Rauland researchers produced the nonreflective black tube.

While Zenith continued research and development on color television throughout the early 1950s, and even participated in the development of industry standards for a compatible color television system, it still did not get into the color TV market. McDonald was even more adamant about color television than he had been about black-and-white, saying, "Someday, the technical and service problems of color TV will be solved. When that day comes, we will offer you a line of outstanding color sets. In the meantime, we will not try to make an experimental laboratory of dealers and the public. We will keep color in our laboratories until it is ready." Zenith continued to work on its black-and-white televisions, inventing the first wireless remote control in 1956, and held the leading position in black-and-white television from 1959 on.

The color television breakthrough came in 1961, when Zenith introduced a ten-receiver line of color sets. Demand for these sets grew so quickly that it had to expand its facilities. Also that year Zenith's experimental stereophonic FM broadcasting system was approved by the FCC as the national standard.

1970s: Fierce Competition and Restructuring

Color television improvements continued steadily. In 1969 Zenith introduced the patented Chromacolor picture tube, which set the standard for brightness in the color TV industry for many years. In 1970, the company received awards from the American Association for the Advancement of Science in recognition of its years of technological achievements. By 1972, the year it introduced a line of 25-inch televisions, Zenith was number one in production of color television sets.

Key Dates:

1918: Two ham radio operators form Chicago Radio Laboratory.

1921: Commander Eugene F. McDonald, Jr., joins the company.

1923: Company is reincorporated as Zenith Radio Corporation.

1924: Zenith introduces the world's first portable radio.

1926: Company introduces the first AC-powered radio.

1927: Company debuts the first push-button radio.

1939: The first all-electric TV station, Zenith's W9XZV, goes on the air.

1948: Company's first line of black-and-white TV receivers makes its debut.

1956: Zenith invents the first wireless remote control.

1961: Company's first line of color TVs is introduced; Zenith's FM stereo broadcasting system is approved by the FCC as the national standard.

1969: Company introduces the revolutionary Chromacolor picture tube.

1979: Heath Company, maker of do-it-yourself electronic kits, including a personal computer, is acquired.

1980: Zenith Data Systems is created as a computer subsidiary.

1981: The first Zenith computer, the Z-100, is introduced.

1982: Company suffers a net loss of $24 million and fails to pay a dividend for the first time in nearly 50 years.

1984: The electronics industry adopts a Zenith-developed system as the standard for MTS stereo TV broadcast and reception; company changes its name to Zenith Electronics Corporation.

1989: Company sells its computer business to Paris-based Groupe Bull for $511.4 million.

1991: South Korea-based Lucky-Goldstar, later LG Group (LG), purchases a five percent stake in the company for $15 million.

1994: The industry chooses Zenith's transmission system as the U.S. standard for HDTV.

1995: LG gains a 58 percent controlling stake in Zenith by buying $351 million in company stock.

1996: Company announces the layoff of 25 percent of its U.S. workforce; FCC adopts Zenith's digital transmission technology as part of the HDTV standard.

1998: Zenith closes its last U.S. manufacturing plant.

1999: Zenith begins shipping its first HDTV sets; the company emerges from a prepackaged bankruptcy filing as a wholly owned subsidiary of LG and as purely a designer and marketer—not a manufacturer—of electronics products.

Enormous profitability led to expansion. In 1971 Zenith acquired a 93 percent interest in Movado-Zenith-Mondia Holding, a watch manufacturer. It also acquired a one-third interest in a Venezuelan television company in 1974 and significantly increased its U.S. product distributors. Zenith was able to maintain the leading position in the fiercely competitive U.S. color television market between 1972 and 1978, but was overtaken by RCA in 1979.

Domestic competition, however, did not prove to be Zenith's greatest problem. Manufacturers in Japan, Taiwan, and Korea began selling great numbers of electronic consumer goods in the United States at prices below what American companies could afford to offer. Zenith's then-chairman, John Nevin, filed suits against the Japanese and testified in Congress, accusing the Japanese of dumping goods on the American market at below-cost prices. Nevin's demand that the federal government enforce its antidumping laws was finally met, but not before significant damage had been done.

In 1977, Zenith sold most of its domestic hearing aid instrumentation operation. Also that year, Zenith contracted with Japan's Sony Corporation to market Sony's Betamax home video television recorder in the United States under the Zenith label. By 1978, Zenith had sold most of its Movado watch assets and laid off 25 percent of its American workforce, having established plants in Mexico and Taiwan. The latter move was intended to take advantage of the cheaper labor available in those countries and to address the increasing price competition.

Zenith President and CEO Revone Kluckman realized that action outside Washington was needed to combat the pricing

crisis. Kluckman was credited with refocusing Zenith's competitive energies from legal battles back to the factory floor by implementing cost-cutting measures and improved manufacturing procedures.

A sweeping reorganization also began in 1978. The corporate structure was rebuilt along product lines, with each group receiving a charter to move aggressively into new businesses. Jerry Pearlman, then a senior Zenith finance executive, later chairman and president, was instrumental in pushing for one business in particular: computers. In 1979, Zenith acquired the Heath Company, a longtime maker of do-it-yourself electronic kits. The shrewd and inexpensive ($64.5 million) purchase occurred right after Heath announced its first personal computer kit and only months after Apple introduced its first personal computer.

1980s: Entry into and Exit from Computer Industry

Zenith Data Systems, a wholly owned subsidiary, was born in 1980 after the Heath acquisition. The parent company required that any new business tap at least two of three Zenith capabilities: technology, manufacturing, and distribution. Zenith Data Systems was a perfect match on all three counts. The first Zenith computer, the Z-100, was introduced in 1981; 35,000 Z-100s were shipped that first year.

In addition to complete computer systems, Zenith began to sell video terminals compatible with virtually all personal computers on the market. These became very successful, as were the components Zenith sold to other computer companies. Zenith also entered the market for decoders for the growing cable TV and wireless markets.

Nevertheless, the early success of Zenith Data Systems was not enough to offset the impact of price competition in the consumer electronics business. The company suffered a net loss of $24 million on revenues of $1.2 billion in 1982 and did not pay a dividend that year for the first time in almost half a century.

Zenith continued to push for cost reductions. These were achieved through the use of robotics and other improvements in design and manufacturing, which led to a higher sales volume to offset lower prices. By 1983, although it lacked the advertising dollars to mount the campaigns of other industry manufacturers, Zenith Data Systems boasted an installed base of 95,000 micro-computers. Computer sales mounted to $135 million that year, and Zenith was profitable. It also celebrated a short-lived victory in an antitrust suit against Japanese television manufacturers that year, a suit later overturned on appeal.

Zenith worked to win large contracts with educational institutions and the federal government, greatly broadening its impact on the personal computer market. It also held a virtual monopoly on the do-it-yourself computer market through more than 70 Heathkit Electronic Centers. Whereas overall computer sales accounted for 1.4 percent of Zenith sales in 1979 (exclusively Heath), they were up to 15 percent in 1984. Also in 1984, the electronics industry adopted a Zenith-developed system as the standard for MTS stereo TV broadcast and reception. It was another profitable year, marked by a name change from the long outdated Zenith Radio Corporation to Zenith Electronics Corporation.

The roller coaster went down again for Zenith in 1985. Although computer products sales rose from $249 in 1984 to $352 million in 1985, computer sales did not offset the $125 million loss in consumer electronics. The company was nearly $8 million in the red at year's end.

In 1986 Zenith introduced more new products than at any time in its history, especially in the home entertainment and computer improvement areas. Record numbers of videocassette recorders were shipped, up 34 percent, and cable operations were up 16 percent. Computer systems and components were up 56 percent to $548 million, accounting for 29 percent of total sales. Nevertheless, 1986 was another year of losses—of $10 million—due to pricing pressures and lower profit margins. Japanese, Taiwanese, and Korean prices in the United States were ten percent lower in 1986 than in 1985.

Zenith Chairman Jerry Pearlman eventually asked the federal government to once again monitor foreign manufacturers' illegal dumping of inexpensive TV sets on the American market. His request did little good, however, because the government took years to investigate and act on the charges. As Zenith continued to lose money, pressure from investors to sell its consumer electronics unit mounted. Pearlman, however, could not attract an acceptable bid.

In 1988 Zenith reported a modest $12 million profit, ending a four-year streak of losses. But the company was saddled with heavy debt (incurred primarily in financing the growth of its computer business), and competition in both the consumer electronics and computer industries was heating up.

It was becoming increasingly evident to Pearlman that Zenith's continued participation in two tough business areas was hurting the company's competitiveness; although both were more than $1 billion in sales by 1988, neither was profitable. In 1989 Pearlman and the Zenith board suddenly decided to sell Zenith's computer business to Paris-based Groupe Bull. Zenith used the $511.4 million it received from Bull to pay off its short-term debt and some of its long-term obligations as well. Zenith management hoped this trimming would improve its ability to compete in consumer electronics in the 1990s.

1990s and Beyond: Continuing Red Ink, HDTV, and the Loss of Independence

But starting with 1989, Zenith posted five straight years of heavy losses—the smallest, the 1991 loss of $52 million; the largest, the 1992 loss of $106 million. In the midst of these losses—primarily caused by continued depressed prices for televisions—the company moved forward with the development of new, innovative products.

The company's most publicized foray involved high-definition television (HDTV), the super-sharp digital television technology that was supposed to replace the standard analog television. With the prodding of the U.S. government, which feared that Japanese manufacturers would completely dominate the television industry unless American companies moved quickly to develop HDTV, three company partnerships were formed in the late 1980s, each working on their own HDTV standard. Zenith and its partner AT&T Microelectronics developed a digital transmission technology that was among the finalists for adoption. In 1993, however, the government wanted to speed up the adoption process by having all seven company finalists cooperate on developing a digital HDTV system, forming the Grand Alliance. The following year, Zenith's transmission system was chosen by the alliance to be the U.S. standard to be submitted to the Federal Communications Commission (FCC) for final approval. With the alliance arrangement, Zenith would receive a royalty for its role—a slice of perhaps $10 to $20 per television set—but could not expect a sizable return on its $15 million HDTV investment until the early 21st century when the market for HDTV sets was expected to approach that of regular TVs.

With its HDTV payoff years away, Zenith faced a proxy fight in 1991 from a dissident stockholder dissatisfied with the management of the company. Pearlman was able to ward off this attempt for his ouster by wooing a foreign investor. South Korea-based Lucky-Goldstar Group, a huge conglomerate and maker of low-end consumer electronics products, purchased a five percent stake in the company for $15 million. Zenith and Lucky-Goldstar (LG) had a relationship dating back to the 1970s when the Korean firm began making radios for Zenith. Later, LG started buying picture tubes and other components from Zenith, while Zenith bought LG-made VCRs and combination TV-VCR sets. Following the equity purchase, LG also gained access to Zenith's work on HDTV and on flat, high-resolution screens for computers and televisions.

Starting in 1992, Zenith attempted to improve operating results through a series of reengineering efforts initiated by the firm's president and chief operating officer, Albin F. Moschner. In addition to reducing its workforce by 25 percent over the next two years, the program aimed to improve new product development and get products to market faster, increase quality, and establish greater integration between factories. These efforts, however, did not produce immediate results, and continuing pressure from shareholders over the lack of improvement led the Zenith board of directors to begin closely monitoring Pearlman's performance through frequent and lengthy meetings and the tracking of numerous performance measures. A further blow came in early 1993 when one of Zenith's creditors, the Bank of New York, found the company in violation of the net worth covenant in its credit agreement.

Zenith's performance did improve in 1994, but not enough to put it back in the black. The company continued to suffer from price erosion—$48 million worth—brought on by its foreign competitors, leading to another loss, this time of $14.2 million. This represented an $83 million improvement over 1993 results, in part attributed to savings of $40 million in costs from the reengineering efforts.

Early in 1995, Pearlman retired as CEO, naming Moschner to the position. Pearlman also announced that he would retire as chairman at the end of the year. Shortly thereafter, Moschner and Pearlman revealed that the firm planned to concentrate on the production of large-screen TV sets, those with screens larger than 30 inches. This segment of the market was predicted to enjoy much greater revenue growth than the industry overall. To begin production of the large-screen TVs, Zenith needed $150 million to upgrade its production facilities, money it did not have and needed to secure from the outside. Once again, Zenith turned to the Lucky-Goldstar Group, later known as LG Group, for an infusion of cash. LG Electronics Inc., a subsidiary of LG Group, acquired a nearly 58 percent controlling interest in Zenith through the purchase of $351 million in Zenith stock. The last of the American-controlled television manufacturers was thus in the hands of foreign ownership.

Through the sale, Zenith acquired the immediate capital it needed for its plans to produce large-screen picture tubes and large-screen TV sets. The deal was synergistic in that Zenith would also be able to make large-screen picture tubes for Goldstar TVs sold via LG's distribution system to such emerging markets as Latin America and Asia. The cash infusion and the potential for further LG investment in Zenith if the need arose placed Zenith in a stronger position to survive until it could benefit from its commitment to large-screen TVs and from its investment in HDTV.

But with the payoff from its high-end consumer electronics products still off on the horizon, and with sales and prices of television sets falling, Zenith continued to bleed red ink—at an accelerating pace. The company posted losses of $92.4 million, $178 million, and $299.4 million in 1995, 1996, and 1997, respectively. Moschner resigned abruptly in July 1996 and was replaced by Peter S. Willmott, first as interim CEO and president and then on a permanent basis. In late 1996 Willmott announced the layoff of 25 percent of the company's U.S. workforce, or about 1,175 workers; the indefinite postponement of the construction of a $100 million large-screen picture tube plant in Woodridge, Illinois; as well as layoffs at the company's four plants in Mexico. Early the next year, Zenith attempted to revitalize its brand image through a redesign of the corporate Z-bolt logo and a $10 million national ad campaign, the company's first in five years, which promoted its sleeker and more technologically advanced line of standard and large-screen television sets. It also began using a subbrand, Inteq, on its high-end products to differentiate them from lower-end models. At the same time, Zenith continued to pursue cutting-edge products. In 1996 it joined with U.S. Robotics Corporation to build a cable modem for accessing the Internet through a cable television wire, and it won a $1 billion contract to build three million digital television set-top boxes for Americast, an alternative cable consortium owned by several Baby Bell phone companies and the Walt Disney Company. In addition, in late 1996 the FCC adopted Zenith's digital transmission technology as part of the HDTV standard in the United States.

During 1997, Zenith shipped its first DVD player, which actually had been manufactured by Toshiba. In August it canceled outright plans for the Woodridge large-screen picture tube plant. Instead, it focused its capital expenditures on its existing picture tube plant in Melrose Park, Illinois. The following month, Willmott, after only ten months on the job, announced that he would retire earlier than expected, sometime during the following winter. Following a successor search, Jeffrey P. Gannon, a 24-year veteran of General Electric Company, was hired as the new president and CEO in January 1998.

Under Gannon's leadership, Zenith moved ahead on the HDTV front, shipping its first HDTV set in August 1999, a 64-inch widescreen rear-projection model. The market for HDTV remained small, however—there were only 70 digital TV stations on the air by September 1999—and the company posted another substantial loss in 1998 of $275.5 million (on sales of just $984.8 million). Zenith began planning a more radical remake centering on its exit from manufacturing. In late 1998 Zenith closed its only remaining U.S. factory, the Melrose Park picture tube plant. Then in August 1999 the company filed a prepackaged bankruptcy plan with the support of its creditors as well as LG. It emerged from bankruptcy in November of that year as a wholly owned subsidiary of LG, and as a company focused solely on designing, marketing, and distributing consumer electronics products. Of the company's remaining Mexican manufacturing plants, three were sold off and one was transferred to LG ownership. Zenith began outsourcing all of its manufacturing, with most of the products built by LG itself. These moves left the company with a workforce of fewer than 7,000, after having started the decade with 32,000 employees.

After leading the company through its reorganization, Gannon resigned from his leadership position. The new president and CEO was Australia native Ian G. Woods, a senior LG executive who had served previously as CFO of Australia-based Matrix Telecommunications Limited. With its finances on more stable ground and its new leadership in place, Zenith in early 2000 unveiled a revamped product lineup, which featured HDTV sets, flat-screen plasma displays, liquid crystal display (LCD) TVs, a KidsView line of TVs for children, home theater projection TV systems, HDTV satellite receivers, a five-disc DVD player, digital audio products, and a variety of accessories. This impressive range of projects and the company's improved financial performance during 1999 appeared to signal the beginning of a long-awaited Zenith turnaround.

Principal Subsidiaries

Interocean Advertising Corporation of Illinois; Zenith Distributing Corporation of Illinois; Zenith Electronics Corporation of Arizona; Zenith Electronics Corporation of Pennsylvania; Zenith Electronics Corporation of Texas; Zenith/Inteq, Inc.; Zenith Video Tech Corporation; Zenith Video Tech Corporation—Florida; Zenith Radio Canada, Ltd.; Zenith Taiwan Corporation; Zenith Electronics (Ireland), Ltd.; Zenith Electronics (Europe), Ltd.; Cableproducts de Chihuahua, S.A. de C.V. (Mexico); Zenith Partes De Matamoros, S.A. de C.V. (Mexico); Productos Magneticos de Chihuahua, S.A. de C.V. (Mexico); Telson, S.A. de C.V. (Mexico); Zenco de Chihuahua, S.A. de C.V. (Mexico); Radio Componentes de Mexico, S.A. de C.V.

Principal Competitors

Emerson Radio Corp.; Hitachi America, Ltd.; Matsushita Electric Industrial Co., Ltd.; Motorola, Inc.; Philips Electronics North America Corp.; Pioneer Electronics (USA) Inc.; Samsung Electronics America, Inc.; SANYO North America Corporation; Scientific-Atlanta, Inc.; Sharp Electronics Corporation; Sony Corporation; Thomson S.A.; Universal Electronics Inc.

Further Reading

"Brightening Picture," *Barron's*, March 20, 1989, pp. 13+.

Cahill, Joseph B., "Closing Plants Zenith's Only Survival Hope," *Crain's Chicago Business*, April 6, 1998, p. 3.

——, "Korean Crisis Blurs Zenith's Credit Picture," *Crain's Chicago Business*, December 22, 1997, p. 4.

——, "Zenith's Quest for Recovery," *Crain's Chicago Business*, January 13, 1997, p. 13.

Carey, Susan, "South Korean Company Seeks Control of Zenith, Last of the U.S. TV Makers," *Wall Street Journal*, July 18, 1995, pp. A3, A4.

Cones, Harold N., and John H. Bryant, *Zenith Radio: The Early Years, 1919–1935*, Atglen, Penn.: Schiffer Publishing, 1997.

Curtis, Philip J., *The Fall of the U.S. Consumer Electronics Industry: An American Trade Tragedy*, Westport, Conn.: Quorum Books, 1994.

Darlin, Damon, "Eager to Learn," *Forbes*, August 12, 1996, p. 92.

Dobrzynski, Judith H., "How to Handle a CEO," *Business Week*, February 24, 1994, pp. 64–65.

Dreyfack, Kenneth, "Zenith's Side Road to Success in Personal Computers," *Business Week*, December 8, 1986, pp. 100+.

Dreyfack, Kenneth, and Judith H. Dobrzynski, "Zenith Wants to Give the Boob Tube a Brain," *Business Week*, May 6, 1985, pp. 69+.

Elstrom, Peter, "The Angry Angels at Zenith," *Business Week*, August 12, 1996, p. 32.

Frank, Allan Dodds, "Why Is This Man Smiling?," *Forbes*, March 10, 1986, pp. 40+.

Gatland, Laura, "Zenith Tunes In to Younger Set in Attempt to Boost TV Sales," *Crain's Chicago Business*, September 15, 1997, p. 37.

Gerson, Bob, "A Revamped Zenith Bound for CES Splash," *Twice*, December 20, 1999, pp. 3, 10.

Glain, Steve, "New-Look LG Tunes in to Faster Times," *Wall Street Journal*, August 8, 1995, p. A8.

Kartus, Lisa, "The Strange Folks Picking on Zenith," *Fortune*, December 19, 1988, pp. 79+.

——, "Zenith: Tail Wags Dog," *Financial World*, November 3, 1987, pp. 22+.

Miller, James P., "HDTV Panel Picks Zenith Signal System," *Wall Street Journal*, February 17, 1994, p. B6.

——, "Zenith Shares Surge As It Wins a $1 Billion Digital-TV Contract," *Wall Street Journal*, August 23, 1996, p. B3.

——, "Zenith's Pearlman Plans to Step Down As CEO, Chairman," *Wall Street Journal*, February 24, 1995, pp. B2, B8.

Murphy, H. Lee, "Zenith CEO Vows More Changes," *Twice*, June 2, 1997, pp. 3, 42.

Nakarmi, Laxmi, Richard A. Melcher, and Edith Updike, "Will Lucky Goldstar Reach Its Peak with Zenith?," *Business Week*, August 7, 1995, p. 40.

Oloroso, Arsenio, Jr., "Zenith's Revamp on High Wire," *Crain's Chicago Business*, September 14, 1998, p. 1.

Quintanilla, Carl, "Zenith Plans to Lay Off 25% of U.S. Staff," *Wall Street Journal*, December 19, 1996, p. A4.

Slutsker, Gary, "Zenith's Bright Side and Its Dark Side," *Forbes*, May 2, 1988, pp. 112+.

Stevens, Shannon, "Zenith's Sharper Image," *Brandweek*, September 8, 1997, pp. 20–21.

Taub, Stephen, "Defining What Zenith Does Best," *Financial World*, April 4–17, 1984, pp. 104+.

Therrien, Lois, "HDTV Isn't Clearing Up Zenith's Picture," *Business Week*, February 25, 1991, pp. 56–57.

——, "Zenith Is Sticking Its Neck Out in a Cutthroat Market," *Business Week*, August 17, 1987, pp. 72+.

——, "Zenith's Jerry Pearlman Sure Is Persistent," *Business Week*, October 2, 1989, pp. 67+.

——, "Zenith Wishes on a Lucky-Goldstar," *Business Week*, March 11, 1991, p. 50.

Zenith: Highlights of the First 60 Years, Glenview, Ill.: Zenith Radio Corporation, 1978.

"Zenith: The Surprise in Personal Computers," *Business Week*, December 12, 1983, pp. 102+.

—updated by David E. Salamie

INDEX TO COMPANIES

Index to Companies

Listings in this index are arranged in alphabetical order under the company name. Company names beginning with a letter or proper name such as Eli Lilly & Co. will be found under the first letter of the company name. Definite articles (The, Le, La) are ignored for alphabetical purposes as are forms of incorporation that precede the company name (AB, NV). Company names printed in bold type have full, historical essays on the page numbers appearing in bold. Updates to entries that appeared in earlier volumes are signified by the notation (upd.). Company names in light type are references within an essay to that company, not full historical essays. This index is cumulative with volume numbers printed in bold type.

China National Cereals, Oils & Foodstuffs Import and Export Corporation, **24** 359
China National Chemicals Import and Export Corp., **IV** 395; **31** 120
China National Heavy Duty Truck Corporation, **21** 274
China National Machinery Import and Export Corporation, **8** 279
China National Petroleum Corp. (SINOPEC), **18** 483
China Navigation Co., **I** 521; **16** 479–80
China Orient Leasing Co., **II** 442
China Resources (Shenyang) Snowflake Brewery Co., **21** 320
China Southern Airlines Company Ltd., 31 102; **33 98–100**
China Zhouyang Fishery Co. Ltd., **II** 578
Chinese Electronics Import and Export Corp., **I** 535
Chinese Metallurgical Import and Export Corp., **IV** 61
Chinese Petroleum Corporation, IV 388–90, 493, 519; **31 105–108 (upd.)**
Chinese Steel Corp., **IV** 184
The Chinet Company, **30** 397
Chino Mines Co., **IV** 179
Chinon Industries, **III** 477; **7** 163
Chipcom, **16** 392
Chippewa Shoe, **19** 232
CHIPS and Technologies, Inc., 6 217; **9 114–17**
Chiquita Brands International, Inc., II 595–96; **III** 28; **7 84–86**; **21 110–13 (upd.)**
Chiro Tool Manufacturing Corp., **III** 629
Chiron Corporation, 7 427; **10 213–14**; **25** 56
Chisso Chemical, **II** 301
Chiswick Products, **II** 566
Chita Oil Co., **IV** 476
Chitaka Foods International, **24** 365
Chivers, **II** 477
Chiyoda Bank, **I** 503; **II** 321
Chiyoda Chemical, **I** 433
Chiyoda Fire and Marine, **III** 404
Chiyoda Kogaku Seiko Kabushiki Kaisha, **III** 574–75
Chiyoda Konpo Kogyo Co. Ltd., **V** 536
Chiyoda Mutual, **II** 374
Chloé Chimie, **I** 303
Chloride S.A., **I** 423
Choay, **I** 676–77
Chock Full o'Nuts Corp., 17 97–100; **20** 83
Chocoladefabriken Lindt & Sprüngli AG, 27 102–05; **30** 220
Chocolat Ibled S.A., **II** 569
Chocolat Poulait, **II** 478
Chocolat-Menier S.A., **II** 569
Chogoku Kogyo, **II** 325
Choice Hotels International Inc., 6 187, 189; **14 105–07**; **25** 309–10; **26** 460
ChoiceCare Corporation, **24** 231
ChoicePoint Services, Inc., **31** 358
Chorlton Metal Co., **I** 531
Chorus Line Corporation, 25 247; **30 121–23**
Chosen Sekiyu, **IV** 554
Chotin Transportation Co., **6** 487
Chouinard Equipment. *See* Lost Arrow Inc.
Chow Tai Fook Jewellery Co., **IV** 717
Chris-Craft Industries, Inc., II 176, 403; **III** 599–600; **9** 118–19; **26** 32; **31 109–112 (upd.)**

Christal Radio, **6** 33
Christensen Boyles Corporation, 19 247; **26 68–71**
Christensen Company, **8** 397
Christiaensen, **26** 160
Christian Bourgois, **IV** 614–15
Christian Broadcasting Network, **13** 279
Christian Dior S.A., I 272; **19 86–88**; **23** 237, 242
Christie, Mitchell & Mitchell, **7** 344
Christie's International plc, 15 98–101
Christopher Charters, Inc. *See* Kitty Hawk, Inc.
Chromalloy American Corp., **13** 461
Chromalloy Gas Turbine Corp., **13** 462
Chromatic Color, **13** 227–28
Chromcraft Revington, Inc., 15 102–05; **26** 100
The Chronicle Publishing Company, Inc., 23 119–22
Chronimed Inc., 26 72–75
Chronoservice, **27** 475
Chrysalis Records, **22** 194
Chrysler Corporation, I 10, 17, 28, 38, 59, 79, 136, **144–45**, 152, 162–63, 172, 178, 182, 188, 190, 207, 420, 504, 516, 525, 540; **II** 5, 313, 403, 448; **III** 439, 517, 544, 568, 591, 607, 637–38; **IV** 22, 449, 676, 703; **7** 205, 233, 461; **8** 74–75, 315, 505–07; **9** 118, 349–51, 472; **10** 174, 198, 264–65, 290, 317, 353, 430; **11 53–55 (upd.)**, 103–04, 429; **13** 28–29, 61, 448, 501, 555; **14** 321, 367, 457; **16** 184, 322, 484; **17** 184; **18** 173–74, 308, 493; **20** 359–60; **22** 52, 55, 175, 330; **23** 352–54; **25** 89–91, 93, 142–44, 329; **26** 403, 501; **31** 130. *See also* DaimlerChrysler AG
CH2M Hill Ltd., 22 136–38
Chu Ito & Co., **IV** 476
Chubb Corporation, II 84; **III** 190, **220–22**, 368; **11** 481; **14 108–10 (upd.)**; **29** 256
Chubu Electric Power Co., **IV** 492
Chuck E. Cheese, **13** 472–74; **31** 94
Chugai Pharmaceutical Company, **8** 215–16; **10** 79
Chugai Shogyo Shimposha, **IV** 654–55
Chugoku Electric Power Company Inc., V 574–76
Chunghwa Picture Tubes, **23** 469
Chuo Trust & Banking Co. *See* Yasuda Trust and Banking Company, Limited.
Church & Dwight Co., Inc., 29 112–15
Church and Tower Group, **19** 254
Church, Goodman, and Donnelley, **IV** 660
Church's Fried Chicken, Inc., **I** 260; **7** 26–28; **15** 345; **23** 468; **32** 13–14
Churchill Downs Incorporated, 29 116–19
Churchill Insurance Co. Ltd., **III** 404
Churny Co. Inc., **II** 534
Cianbro Corporation, 14 111–13
Cianchette Brothers, Inc. *See* Cianbro Corporation.
Ciba-Geigy Ltd., I 625, **632–34**, 671, 690, 701; **III** 55; **IV** 288; **8** 63, **108–11 (upd.)**, 376–77; **9** 153, 441; **10** 53–54, 213; **15** 229; **18** 51; **21** 386; **23** 195–96; **25** 55; **27** 69; **28** 193, 195; **30** 327
CIBC. *See* Canadian Imperial Bank of Commerce.
CIBC Wood Gundy Securities Corp., **24** 482

Ciber, Inc., **18 110–12**
Ciby 2000, **24** 79
CICI, **11** 184
CIDLA, **IV** 504–06
Cie Continental d'Importation, **10** 249
Cie des Lampes, **9** 9
Cie Générale d'Electro-Ceramique, **9** 9
Cie. Generale des Eaux S.A., **24** 327
Cifra, S.A. de C.V., 8 556; **12 63–65**; **26** 524; **34 197–98**
Cigarrera La Moderna, **21** 260; **22** 73
Cigarros la Tabacelera Mexicana (Cigatam), **21** 259
CIGNA Corporation, III 197, **223–27**, 389; **10** 30; **11** 243; **22 139–44 (upd.)**, 269
CIGWELD, **19** 442
Cii-HB, **III** 123, 678; **16** 122
Cilag-Chemie, **III** 35–36; **8** 282
Cilbarco, **II** 25
Cilva Holdings PLC, **6** 358
Cima, **14** 224–25
Cimarron Utilities Company, **6** 580
CIMCO Ltd., **21** 499–501
Cimenteries CBR S.A., **23** 325, 327
Ciments d'Obourg, **III** 701
Ciments de Chalkis Portland Artificiels, **III** 701
Ciments de Champagnole, **III** 702
Ciments de l'Adour, **III** 702
Ciments Lafarge France, **III** 704
Ciments Lafarge Quebec, **III** 704
Cimos, **7** 37
Cincinnati Bell, Inc., 6 316–18; **29** 250, 252
Cincinnati Chemical Works, **I** 633
Cincinnati Electronics Corp., **II** 25
Cincinnati Financial Corporation, 16 102–04
Cincinnati Gas & Electric Company, 6 465–68, 481–82
Cincinnati Milacron Inc., 12 66–69
Cincom Systems Inc., 15 106–08
Cineamerica, **IV** 676
Cinecentrum, **IV** 591
Cinema International Corp., **II** 149
Cinemark, **21** 362; **23** 125
Cinemax, **IV** 675; **7** 222–24, 528–29; **23** 276
Cineplex Odeon Corporation, II 145, **6 161–63**; **14** 87; **23 123–26 (upd.)**; **33** 432
Cinnabon Inc., 13 435–37; **23 127–29**; **32** 12, 15
Cintas Corporation, 16 228; **21 114–16**, 507; **30** 455
Cintel, **II** 158
Cintra. *See* Corporacion Internacional de Aviacion, S.A. de C.V.
Cipal-Parc Astérix, **27** 10
Ciprial S.A., **27** 260
CIPSCO Inc., 6 469–72, 505–06
Circa Pharmaceuticals, **16** 529
Circle A Ginger Ale Company, **9** 177
Circle International, Inc., **17** 216
The Circle K Company, II 619–20; **V** 210; **7** 113–14, 372, 374; **20 138–40 (upd.)**; **25** 125; **26** 447
Circle Plastics, **9** 323
Circon Corporation, 21 117–20
Circuit City Stores, Inc., 9 65–66, **120–22**; **10** 235, 305–06, 334–35, 468–69; **12** 335; **14** 61; **15** 215; **16** 73, 75; **17** 489; **18** 533; **19** 362; **23** *51–53*,

E. & J. Gallo Winery, I 27, **242–44**, 260; **7** 154–56 (upd.); **15** 391; **28 109–11** (upd.), 223
E&M Laboratories, **18** 514
E & S Retail Ltd. *See* Powerhouse.
E! Entertainment Television Inc., 17 148–50; 24 120, 123
E*Trade Group, Inc., 20 206–08
E.A. Miller, Inc., **II** 494
E.A. Pierce & Co., **II** 424; **13** 340
E.A. Stearns & Co., **III** 627
E.B. Badger Co., **11** 413
E.B. Eddy Forest Products, **II** 631
E.C. Snodgrass Company, **14** 112
E.C. Steed, **13** 103
E. de Trey & Sons, **10** 270–71
E.F. Hutton Group, **I** 402; **II** 399, 450–51; **8** 139; **9** 469; **10** 63
E.F. Hutton LBO, **24** 148
E. Gluck Trading Co., **III** 645
E.H. Bindley & Company, **9** 67
E.I. du Pont de Nemours & Company, I 21, 28, 305, 317–19, 323, **328–30**, 334, 337–38, 343–44, 346–48, 351–53, 365, 377, 379, 383, 402–03, 545, 548, 675; **III** 21; **IV** 69, 78, 263, 371, 399, 401–02, 409, 481, 599; **V** 360; **7** 546; **8 151–54** (upd.), 485; **9** 154, 216, 352, 466; **10** 289; **11** 432; **12** 68, 365, 416–17; **13** 21, 124; **16** 127, 130, 201, 439, 461–62; **19** 11, 223; **21** 544; **22** 147, 260, 405; **24** 111, 388; **25** 152, 540; **26 123–27** (upd.); **34** 80, 283–84
E.J. Brach & Sons, **II** 521. *See also* Brach and Brock Confections, Inc.
E.J. Longyear Company. *See* Boart Longyear Company.
E. Katz Special Advertising Agency. *See* Katz Communications, Inc.
E.L. Phillips and Company, **V** 652–53
E.M. Warburg Pincus & Co., **7** 305; **13** 176; **16** 319; **25** 313; **29** 262
E. Missel GmbH, **20** 363
E.N.V. Engineering, **I** 154
E.R. Squibb, **I** 695; **21** 54–55
E. Rabinowe & Co., Inc., **13** 367
E.S. Friedman & Co., **II** 241
E.S. International Holding S.A. *See* Banco Espírito Santo e Comercial de Lisboa S.A.
E-Stamp Corporation, **34** 474
E-Systems, Inc., I 490; **9 182–85**
E-II Holdings Inc., **II** 468; **9** 449; **12** 87. *See also* Astrum International Corp.
E.W. Bliss, **I** 452
E.W. Oakes & Co. Ltd., **IV** 118
The E.W. Scripps Company, IV 606–09; 7 157–59 (upd.); **24** 122; **25** 507; **28 122–26** (upd.)
E.W.T. Mayer Ltd., **III** 681
E-Z Haul, **24** 409
E-Z Serve Corporation, 15 270; **17 169–71**
EADS. *See* European Aeronautic Defence and Space Company.
Eagle Airways Ltd., **23** 161
Eagle Credit Corp., **10** 248
Eagle Family Foods, Inc., **22** 95
Eagle Floor Care, Inc., **13** 501; **33** 392
Eagle Gaming, L.P., **16** 263
Eagle Hardware & Garden, Inc., 9 399; **16 186–89; 17** 539–40
Eagle Industries Inc., **8** 230; **22** 282; **25** 536

Eagle Managed Care Corp., **19** 354, 357
Eagle Oil Transport Co. Ltd., **IV** 657
Eagle Plastics, **19** 414
Eagle Printing Co. Ltd., **IV** 295; **19** 225
Eagle Sentry Inc., **32** 373
Eagle Snacks Inc., **I** 219; **34** 36–37
Eagle Square Manufacturing Co., **III** 627
Eagle Star Insurance Co., **I** 426–27; **III** 185, 200
Eagle Supermarket, **II** 571
Eagle Thrifty Drug, **14** 397
Eagle Travel Ltd., **IV** 241
Eagle-Lion Films, **II** 147; **25** 328
Eagle-Picher Industries, Inc., 8 155–58; 23 179–83 (upd.)
Earl Scheib, Inc., 32 158–61
Early American Insurance Co., **22** 230
Earth Resources Company, **IV** 459; **17** 320
Earth Wise, Inc., **16** 90
Earth's Best, **21** 56
EarthLink, **33** 92
EAS. *See* Executive Aircraft Services.
Easco Hand Tools, Inc., **7** 117
Eason Oil Company, **6** 578; **11** 198
East African External Communications Limited, **25** 100
East Chicago Iron and Forge Co., **IV** 113
East Hartford Trust Co., **13** 467
East India Co., **I** 468; **III** 521, 696; **IV** 48; **20** 309
East Japan Heavy Industries, **III** 578–79; **7** 348
East Japan Railway Company, V 448–50
East Midlands Electricity, **V** 605
The East New York Savings Bank, **11** 108–09
East of Scotland, **III** 359
East Texas Pulp and Paper Co., **IV** 342, 674; **7** 528
East-West Airlines, **27** 475
East-West Federal Bank, **16** 484
Easter Enterprises, **8** 380; **23** 358
Easterday Supply Company, **25** 15
Eastern Air Group Co., **31** 102
Eastern Airlines, I 41, 66, 78, 90, 98–99, **101–03**, 116, 118, 123–25; **III** 102; **6** 73, 81–82, 104–05; **8** 416; **9** 17–18, 80; **11** 268, 427; **12** 191, 487; **21** 142, 143; **23** 483; **26** 339, 439
Eastern Associated Coal Corp., **6** 487
Eastern Australia Airlines, **24** 396
Eastern Aviation Group, **23** 408
Eastern Bank, **II** 357
Eastern Carolina Bottling Company, **10** 223
Eastern Coal Corp., **IV** 181
Eastern Coalfields Ltd., **IV** 48–49
Eastern Corp., **IV** 703
Eastern Electricity, **13** 485
Eastern Enterprises, IV 171; **6 486–88**
Eastern Gas and Fuel Associates, **I** 354; **IV** 171
Eastern Indiana Gas Corporation, **6** 466
Eastern Kansas Utilities, **6** 511
Eastern Machine Screw Products Co., **13** 7
Eastern Market Beef Processing Corp., **20** 120
Eastern Operating Co., **III** 23
Eastern Pine Sales Corporation, **13** 249
Eastern Software Distributors, Inc., **16** 125
Eastern States Farmers Exchange, **7** 17
Eastern Telegraph Company, **V** 283–84; **25** 99–100

Eastern Texas Electric. *See* Gulf States Utilities Company.
Eastern Tool Co., **IV** 249
Eastern Torpedo Company, **25** 74
Eastern Wisconsin Power, **6** 604
Eastern Wisconsin Railway and Light Company, **6** 601
Eastex Pulp and Paper Co., **IV** 341–42
Eastman Chemical Company, 14 174–75; 25 22
Eastman Christensen Company, **22** 68
Eastman Kodak Company, I 19, 30, 90, 323, 337–38, 690; **II** 103; **III** 171–72, **474–77**, 486–88, 547–48, 550, 584, 607–09; **IV** 260–61; **6** 288–89; **7 160–64** (upd.), 436–38; **8** 376–77; **9** 62, 231; **10** 24; **12** 342; **14** 174–75, 534; **16** 168, 449; **18** 184–86, 342, 510; **25** 153; **29** 370
Eastman Radio, **6** 33
Eastmaque Gold Mines, Ltd., **7** 356
Eastover Mining, **27** 130
Eastpak, Inc., **30** 138
Eatco, Inc., **15** 246
Eateries, Inc., 33 138–40
Eaton Axle Co., **I** 154
Eaton, Cole & Burnham Company, **8** 134
Eaton Corporation, I 154–55, 186; **III** 645; **10 279–80** (upd.); **12** 547; **27** 100
Eaton Vance Corporation, 18 150–53
Eavey Co., **II** 668
Ebamsa, **II** 474
EBASCO. *See* Electric Bond and Share Company.
Ebasco Services, **III** 499; **V** 612; **IV** 255–56
eBay Inc., 32 162–65
EBC Amro Ltd., **II** 186
Eberhard Faber, **12** 115
Eberhard Foods, **8** 482
EBIC. *See* European Banks' International Co.
Ebiex S.A., **25** 312
EBS. *See* Electric Bond & Share Company *or* Electronic Bookshelf.
EBSCO Industries, Inc., 17 151–53
EC Comics, **25** 139
EC Erdolchemie GmbH, **7** 141
ECC Group plc, III 689–91. *See also* English China Clays plc.
Echigoya Saburobei Shoten, **IV** 292
Echlin Inc., I 156–57; 11 83–85 (upd.); **15** 310
Echo Bay Mines Ltd., IV 75–77; 23 40
Les Echos, **IV** 659
EchoStar Communications Corporation, **18** 355; **27** 307
ECI Telecom Ltd., 18 154–56
Eckerd Corporation, 9 186–87; 18 272; **24** 263;
Eckert-Mauchly Corp., **III** 166
Ecko Products, **I** 527
Ecko-Ensign Design, **I** 531
ECL, **16** 238
Eclipse Candles, Ltd., **18** 67, 69
Eclipse Machine Co., **I** 141
Eclipse Telecommunications, Inc., **29** 252
Eco Hotels, **14** 107
Ecolab Inc., I 331–33; 13 197–200 (upd.); **26** 306; **34 151–56** (upd.), 205, 208
Econo Lodges of America, **25** 309
Econo-Travel Corporation, **13** 362
Economist Group, **15** 265

M. Samuel & Co., **II** 208

M. Sobol, Inc., **28** 12

M Stores Inc., **II** 664

M.T.G.I. Textile Manufacturers Group, **25** 121

M.W. Carr, **14** 245

M.W. Kellogg Co., **III** 470; **IV** 408, 534; **34** 81

M-Web Holdings Ltd., **31** 329–30

Ma. Ma-Macaroni Co., **II** 554

Maakauppiaitten Oy, **8** 293–94

Maakuntain Keskus-Pankki, **II** 303

MaasGlas, **III** 667

Maatschappij tot Exploitatie van de Onderneming Krasnapolsky. *See* Grand Hotel Krasnapolsky N.V.

Maatschappij tot Exploitatie van Steenfabrieken Udenhout, voorheen Weyers, **14** 249

MABAG Maschinen- und Apparatebau GmbH, **IV** 198

Mabley & Carew, **10** 282

Mac Frugal's Bargains - Closeouts Inc., **17 297–99**

Mac Publications LLC, **25** 240

Mac Tools, **III** 628

MacAndrews & Forbes Holdings Inc., II 679; **III** 56; **9** 129; **11** 334; **28** 246–49; **30** 138

MacArthur Foundation. *See* The John D. and Catherine T. MacArthur Foundation.

Macau Telephone, **18** 114

Maccabees Life Insurance Co., **III** 350

MacCall Management, **19** 158

MacDermid Incorporated, 32 318–21

MacDonald Companies, **15** 87

MacDonald Dettwiler and Associates, **32** 436

MacDonald, Halsted, and Laybourne, **10** 127

Macdonald Hamilton & Co., **III** 522–23

Macey Furniture Co., **7** 493

Macfarlane Lang & Co., **II** 592–93

Macfield Inc., **12** 502

MacFrugal's Bargains Close-Outs Inc., **29** 312

MacGregor Sporting Goods Inc., **III** 443; **22** 115, 458; **23** 449

Mach Performance, Inc., **28** 147

Machine Vision International Inc., **10** 232

Macintosh. *See* Apple Computer, Inc.

Mack Trucks, Inc., I 147, 177–79; **9** 416; **12** 90; **22 329–32 (upd.)**

MacKay-Shields Financial Corp., **III** 316

MacKenzie & Co., **II** 361

Mackenzie Hill, **IV** 724

Mackenzie Mann & Co. Limited, **6** 360

Mackey Airways, **I** 102

Mackie Designs Inc., 30 406; **33 278–81**

Mackinnon Mackenzie & Co., **III** 521–22

Maclaren Power and Paper Co., **IV** 165

Maclean Hunter Limited, III 65; **IV** **638–40, 22** 442; **23** 98

Maclean Hunter Publishing Limited, 26 **270–74 (upd.); 30** 388

Maclin Co., **12** 127

The MacManus Group, **32** 140

MacMark Corp., **22** 459

MacMarr Stores, **II** 654

MacMillan Bloedel Limited, IV 165, 272, **306–09,** 721; **9** 391; **19** 444, 446; **25** 12; **26** 445

Macmillan, Inc., IV 637, 641–43; **7** **284–86,** 311–12, 343; **9** 63; **12** 226; **13**

91, 93; **17** 399; **18** 329; **22** 441–42; **23** 350, 503; **25** 484; **27** 222–23

Macnaughton Blair, **III** 671

The MacNeal-Schwendler Corporation, **25 303–05**

Macneill & Co., **III** 522

Macon Gas Company, **6** 447; **23** 28

Macon Kraft Co., **IV** 311; **11** 421; **19** 267

Maconochie Bros., **II** 569

Macrodata, **18** 87

Macwhyte Company, **27** 415

Macy's. *See* R.H. Macy & Co., Inc.

Macy's California, **21** 129

Mad Dog Athletics, **19** 385

Maddingley Brown Coal Pty Ltd., **IV** 249

Maddux Air Lines, **I** 125; **12** 487

Madge Networks N.V., 18 346; **26** **275–77**

Madison & Sullivan, Inc., **10** 215

Madison Financial Corp., **16** 145

Madison Foods, **14** 557

Madison Furniture Industries, **14** 436

Madison Gas & Electric Company, **6** 605–06

Madison Resources, Inc., **13** 502

Madison Square Garden, **I** 452

MAEFORT Hungarian Air Transport Joint Stock Company, **24** 310

Maersk Lines, **22** 167

Maes Group Breweries, **II** 475

Maeva Group, **6** 206

Mafco Holdings, Inc., **28** 248

Magasins Armand Thiéry et Sigrand, **V** 11; **19** 308

Magazine and Book Services, **13** 48

Magazins Réal Stores, **II** 651

Magcobar, **III** 472

MagCorp, **28** 198

Magdeburg Insurance Group, **III** 377

Magdeburger Versicherungsgruppe, **III** 377

Magee Company, **31** 435–36

Magellan Corporation, **22** 403

Magic Chef Co., **III** 573; **8** 298; **22** 349

Magic City Food Products Company. *See* Golden Enterprises, Inc.

Magic Marker, **29** 372

Magic Pan, **II** 559–60; **12** 410

Magic Pantry Foods, **10** 382

Magicsilk, Inc., **22** 133

MagicSoft, Inc., **10** 557

Magirus, **IV** 126

Maglificio di Ponzano Veneto dei Fratelli Benetton. *See* Benetton.

Magma Copper Company, 7 287–90, 385–87; **22** 107

Magma Power Company, 11 270–72

Magna Computer Corporation, **12** 149; **13** 97

Magnaflux, **III** 519; **22** 282

Magnavox Co., **13** 398; **19** 393

Magne Corp., **IV** 160

Magnesium Metal Co., **IV** 118

Magnet Cove Barium Corp., **III** 472

MagneTek, Inc., 15 287–89

Magnetic Controls Company, **10** 18

Magnetic Peripherals Inc., **19** 513–14

Magnivision, **22** 35

Magnolia Petroleum Co., **III** 497; **IV** 82, 464

Magnus Co., **I** 331; **13** 197

La Magona d'Italia, **IV** 228

Magor Railcar Co., **I** 170

MAGroup Inc., **11** 123

Mahalo Air, **22** 252; **24** 22

Maharam Fabric, **8** 455

Mahir, **I** 37

Mahou, **II** 474

Mai Nap Rt, **IV** 652; **7** 392

MAI PLC, **28** 504

MAI Systems Corporation, 10 242; **11** 273–76; **26** 497, 499

Maidenform Worldwide Inc., 20 352–55

Mail Boxes Etc., 18 315–17; 25 500. *See* *also* U.S. Office Products Company.

Mail-Well, Inc., 25 184; **28 250–52**

Mailson Ferreira da Nobrega, **II** 200

Mailtek, Inc., **18** 518

MAIN. *See* Mid-American Interpool Network.

Main Event Management Corp., **III** 194

Main Plaza Corporation, **25** 115

Main Street Advertising USA, **IV** 597

Maine Central Railroad Company, 16 **348–50**

Mainline Industrial Distributors, Inc., **13** 79

Mainline Travel, **I** 114

Maison Bouygues, **I** 563

Maison de Schreiber and Aronson, **25** 283

Maison de Valérie, **19** 309

Maison Louis Jadot, 24 307–09

Maizuru Heavy Industries, **III** 514

Majestic Contractors Ltd., **8** 419–20

Majestic Wine Warehouses Ltd., **II** 656

Major League Baseball, **12** 457

Major Video Concepts, **6** 410

Major Video, Inc., **9** 74

MaK Maschinenbau GmbH, **IV** 88

Mak van Waay, **11** 453

Makepeace Preserving Co., **25** 365

Makhteshim Chemical Works Ltd., **II** 47; **25** 266–67

Makita Corporation, III 436; **20** 66; **22** **333–35**

Makiyama, **I** 363

Makovsky & Company, **12** 394

Makro Inc., **18** 286

Malama Pacific Corporation, **9** 276

Malapai Resources, **6** 546

Malayan Breweries, **I** 256

Malayan Motor and General Underwriters, **III** 201

Malaysia LNG, **IV** 518–19

Malaysian Airlines System Berhad, 6 71, **100–02,** 117, 415; **29 300–03 (upd.)**

Malaysian International Shipping Co., **IV** 518

Malaysian Sheet Glass, **III** 715

Malbak Ltd., **IV** 92–93

Malcolm's Diary & Time-Table, **III** 256

Malcus Industri, **III** 624

Malden Mills Industries, Inc., 16 351–53

Malév Plc, 24 310–12; 27 474; **29** 17

Malheur Cooperative Electric Association, **12** 265

Malibu, **25** 141

Mallard Bay Drilling, Inc., **28** 347–48

Malleable Iron Works, **II** 34

Mallinckrodt Group Inc., III 16; **IV** 146; **8** 85; **19** 28, **251–53**

Malmö Flygindustri, **I** 198

Malmö Woodworking Factory. *See* Tarkett Sommer AG.

Malmsten & Bergvalls, **I** 664

Malone & Hyde, Inc., **II** 625, 670–71; **9** 52–53; **14** 147; **18** 506

Malrite Communications Group, **IV** 596

Malt-A-Milk Co., **II** 487

Malt-O-Meal Company, 15 189; **22 336–38**

Mameco International, **8** 455

Mammoet Transport B.V., 26 241, **278–80**

Man Aktiengesellschaft, III 301, **561–63**

MAN Gutehoffnungshütte AG, **15** 226

Management and Training Corporation, 28 253–56

Management Decision Systems, Inc., **10** 358

Management Engineering and Development Co., **IV** 310; **19** 266

Management Recruiters International, **6** 140

Management Science America, Inc., **11** 77; **25** 20

Manbré and Garton, **II** 582

Manchester and Liverpool District Banking Co., **II** 307, 333

Manchester Board and Paper Co., **19** 77

Manchester Commercial Buildings Co., **IV** 711

Manchester United Football Club plc, 30 296–98

Manco, Inc., **13** 166. *See also* Henkel Manco Inc.

Mancuso & Co., **22** 116

Mandabach & Simms, **6** 40

Mandalay Resort Group, 32 322–26 (upd.)

Mandarin, Inc., **33** 128

Mandarin Oriental Hotel Group International Ltd., **I** 471; **IV** 700; **20** 312

Mandel Bros., **IV** 660

Manetta Mills, Inc., **19** 304

Manhattan Card Co., **18** 114

Manhattan Co., **II** 217, 247

Manhattan Construction Company. *See* Rooney Brothers Co.

Manhattan Electrical Supply Co., **9** 517

Manhattan Fund, **I** 614

Manhattan International Limousine Network Ltd., **26** 62

Manhattan Trust Co., **II** 229

Manheim Auctions, Inc. *See* Cox Enterprises, Inc.

Manifatture Cotoniere Meridionali, **I** 466

Manischewitz Company. *See* B. Manischewitz Company.

Manistique Papers Inc., **17** 282

Manistique Pulp and Paper Co., **IV** 311; **19** 266

Manitoba Bridge and Engineering Works Ltd., **8** 544

Manitoba Paper Co., **IV** 245–46; **25** 10

Manitoba Rolling Mill Ltd., **8** 544

Manitou BF S.A., 27 294–96

Manitowoc Company, Inc., 18 318–21

Mann Egerton & Co., **III** 523

Mann Theatres Chain, **I** 245; **25** 177

Mann's Wine Company, Ltd., **14** 288

Mannatech Inc., 33 282–85

Manne Tossbergs Eftr., **II** 639

Mannesmann AG, I 411; **III 564–67; IV** 222, 469; **14 326–29 (upd.); 34** 319

Mannheimer Bank, **IV** 558

Manning, Selvage & Lee, **6** 22

Mannstaedt, **IV** 128

Manor Care, Inc., 6 187–90; 14 105–07; **15** 522; **25 306–10 (upd.)**

Manor Healthcare Corporation, **26** 459

Manorfield Investments, **II** 158

Manos Enterprises, **14** 87

Manpower, Inc., 6 10, 140; **9 326–27; 16** 48; **25** 432; **30 299–302 (upd.)**

Mantrec S.A., **27** 296

Mantua Metal Products. *See* Tyco Toys, Inc.

Manufactured Home Communities, Inc., 22 339–41

Manufacturers & Merchants Indemnity Co., **III** 191

Manufacturers and Traders Trust Company, **11** 108–09

Manufacturers Casualty Insurance Co., **26** 486

Manufacturers Fire Insurance Co., **26** 486

Manufacturers Hanover Corporation, II 230, 254, **312–14**, 403; **III** 194; **9** 124; **11** 16, 54, 415; **13** 536; **14** 103; **16** 207; **17** 559; **22** 406; **26** 453

Manufacturers National Bank of Brooklyn, **II** 312

Manufacturers National Bank of Detroit, **I** 165; **11** 137

Manufacturers Railway, **I** 219; **34** 36

Manufacturing Management Inc., **19** 381

Manus Nu-Pulse, **III** 420

Manville Corporation, III 706–09, 721; **7 291–95 (upd.); 10** 43, 45; **11** 420–22

Manweb plc, **19** 389–90

MAPCO Inc., IV 458–59; 26 234; **31** 469, 471

Mapelli Brothers Food Distribution Co., **13** 350

Maple Leaf Mills, **II** 513–14

MAPP. *See* Mid-Continent Area Power Planner.

Mapra Industria e Comercio Ltda., **32** 40

Mar-O-Bar Company, **7** 299

A.B. Marabou, **II** 511

Marantha! Music, **14** 499

Marantz Co., **14** 118

Marathon Insurance Co., **26** 486

Marathon Oil Co., **IV** 365, 454, 487, 572, 574; **7** 549, 551; **13** 458

Marathon Paper Products, **I** 612, 614

Marauder Company, **26** 433

Maraven, **IV** 508

Marblehead Communications, Inc., **23** 101

Marbodal, **12** 464

Marboro Books, Inc., **10** 136

Marbro Lamp Co., **III** 571; **20** 362

Marc's Big Boy. *See* The Marcus Corporation.

Marcade Group. *See* Aris Industries, Inc.

Marceau Investments, **II** 356

March of Dimes, 31 322–25

March-Davis Bicycle Company, **19** 383

Marchand, **13** 27

marchFIRST, Inc., 34 261–64

Marchland Holdings Ltd., **II** 649

Marchon Eyewear, **22** 123

Marciano Investments, Inc., **24** 157

Marcillat, **19** 49

Marcon Coating, Inc., **22** 347

Marconi plc, 33 286–90 (upd.)

Marconi Wireless Telegraph Co. of America, **II** 25, 88

Marconiphone, **I** 531

The Marcus Corporation, 21 359–63

Marcus Samuel & Co., **IV** 530

Marcy Fitness Products, Inc., **19** 142, 144

Mardon Packaging International, **I** 426–27

Mardorf, Peach and Co., **II** 466

Maremont Corporation, **8** 39–40

Margarete Steiff GmbH, 23 334–37

Margarine Unie N.V. *See* Unilever PLC (Unilever N.V.).

Marge Carson, Inc., **III** 571; **20** 362

Margo's La Mode, **10** 281–82

Marico Acquisition Corporation, **8** 448, 450

Marie Brizard & Roger International S.A., 22 342–44

Marie Callender's Restaurant & Bakery, Inc., 13 66; **28 257–59**

Marie-Claire Album, **III** 47

Marigold Foods Inc., **II** 528

Marinduque Mining & Industrial Corp., **IV** 146

Marine Bank and Trust Co., **11** 105

Marine Bank of Erie, **II** 342

Marine Computer Systems, **6** 242

Marine Diamond Corp., **IV** 66; **7** 123

Marine Group, **III** 444; **22** 116

Marine Harvest International, **13** 103

Marine Midland Corp., **I** 548; **II** 298; **9** 475–76; **11** 108; **17** 325

Marine Office of America, **III** 220, 241–42

Marine-Firminy, **IV** 227

Marinela, **19** 192–93

Marineland Amusements Corp., **IV** 623

MarineMax, Inc., 30 303–05

Marion Brick, **14** 249

Marion Foods, Inc., **17** 434

Marion Freight Lines, **6** 370

Marion Laboratories Inc., I 648–49; 8 149; **9 328–29; 16** 438

Marion Manufacturing, **9** 72

Marion Merrell Dow, Inc., 9 328–29 (upd.)

Marionet Corp., **IV** 680–81

Marisa Christina, Inc., 15 290–92; 25 245

Maritime Electric Company, Limited, **15** 182

Mark Controls Corporation, **30** 157

Mark Cross, Inc., **17** 4–5

Mark Goldston, **8** 305

Mark Hopkins, **12** 316

Mark IV Industries, Inc., 7 296–98; 21 418; **28 260–64 (upd.)**

Mark Travel Corporation, **30** 448

Mark Trouser, Inc., **17** 338

Markborough Properties, **II** 222; **V** 81; **8** . 525; **25** 221

Market Growth Resources, **23** 480

Market Horizons, **6** 27

Market National Bank, **13** 465

Marketime, **V** 55

Marketing Data Systems, Inc., **18** 24

Marketing Equities International, **26** 136

Marketing Information Services, **6** 24

MarketSpan Corp. *See* KeySpan Energy Co.

Markham & Co., **I** 573–74

Marks and Spencer p.l.c., I 588; **II** 513, 678; **V 124–26; 10** 442; **17** 42, 124; **22** 109, 111; **24** 268, 270; **313–17 (upd.)**, 474; **28** 96

Marks Brothers Jewelers, Inc., 24 318–20

Marks-Baer Inc., **11** 64

Marland Refining Co., **IV** 399–400

Marlene Industries Corp., **16** 36–37

MarLennan Corp., **III** 283

Marley Co., **19** 360

Marley Holdings, L.P., **19** 246

Marley Tile, **III** 735

Marlin-Rockwell Corp., **I** 539; **14** 510

INDEX TO INDUSTRIES

Index to Industries

CONGLOMERATES

Accor SA, 10; 27 (upd.)
AEG A.G., I
Alcatel Alsthom Compagnie Générale
    d'Electricité, 9
Alco Standard Corporation, I
Alfa, S.A. de C.V., 19
Allied Domecq PLC, 29
Allied-Signal Inc., I
AMFAC Inc., I
Aramark Corporation, 13
Archer-Daniels-Midland Company, I; 11
    (upd.)
Arkansas Best Corporation, 16
BAA plc, 33 (upd.)
Barlow Rand Ltd., I
Bat Industries PLC, I
Bond Corporation Holdings Limited, 10
BTR PLC, I
Bunzl plc, 31 (upd.)
Burlington Northern Santa Fe Corporation,
    27 (upd.)
C. Itoh & Company Ltd., I
Cargill Inc., 13 (upd.)
CBI Industries, Inc., 7
Chemed Corporation, 13
Chesebrough-Pond's USA, Inc., 8
CITIC Pacific Ltd., 18
Colt Industries Inc., I
The Connell Company, 29
CSR Limited, 28 (upd.)
Daewoo Group, 18 (upd.)
De Dietrich & Cie., 31
Deere & Company, 21 (upd.)
Delaware North Companies Incorporated, 7
Desc, S.A. de C.V., 23
The Dial Corp., 8
El Corte Inglés Group, 26 (upd.)
Elders IXL Ltd., I
Engelhard Corporation, 21 (upd.)
Farley Northwest Industries, Inc., I
First Pacific Company Limited, 18
Fisher Companies, Inc., 15
Fletcher Challenge Ltd., 19 (upd.)
FMC Corporation, I; 11 (upd.)
Fortune Brands, Inc., 29 (upd.)
Fuqua Industries, Inc., I
General Electric Company, 34 (upd.)
GIB Group, 26 (upd.)
Gillett Holdings, Inc., 7
Grand Metropolitan PLC, 14 (upd.)
Great American Management and
    Investment, Inc., 8
Greyhound Corporation, I
Grupo Carso, S.A. de C.V., 21
Grupo Industrial Bimbo, 19
Gulf & Western Inc., I
Hankyu Corporation, 23 (upd.)
Hanson PLC, III; 7 (upd.)
Hitachi Ltd., I; 12 (upd.)
Hutchison Whampoa Ltd., 18
IC Industries, Inc., I
Inchcape plc, 16 (upd.)
Ingram Industries, Inc., 11
Instituto Nacional de Industria, I
International Controls Corporation, 10
International Telephone & Telegraph
    Corporation, I; 11 (upd.)
Istituto per la Ricostruzione Industriale, I
ITOCHU Corporation, 32 (upd.)
Jardine Matheson Holdings Limited, I; 20
    (upd.)
Jason Incorporated, 23
Jefferson Smurfit Group plc, 19 (upd.)
Justin Industries, Inc., 19
Kanematsu Corporation, 24 (upd.)
Kao Corporation, 20 (upd.)

Katy Industries, Inc., I
Kesko Ltd. (Kesko Oy), 8; 27 (upd.)
Kidde, Inc., I
KOC Holding A.S., I
Koninklijke Nedlloyd N.V., 26 (upd.)
Koor Industries Ltd., 25 (upd.)
K2 Inc., 16
The L.L. Knickerbocker Co., Inc., 25
Lancaster Colony Corporation, 8
Larry H. Miller Group, 29
Lear Siegler, Inc., I
Lefrak Organization Inc., 26
Leucadia National Corporation, 11
Litton Industries, Inc., I; 11 (upd.)
Loews Corporation, I; 12 (upd.)
Loral Corporation, 8
LTV Corporation, I
LVMH Moët Hennessy Louis Vuitton SA,
    33 (upd.)
Marubeni Corporation, 24 (upd.)
Marubeni K.K., I
MAXXAM Inc., 8
McKesson Corporation, I
Menasha Corporation, 8
Metallgesellschaft AG, 16 (upd.)
Metromedia Co., 7
Minnesota Mining & Manufacturing
    Company (3M), I; 8 (upd.); 26 (upd.)
Mitsubishi Corporation, I; 12 (upd.)
Mitsui & Co., Ltd., 28 (upd.)
Mitsui Bussan K.K., I
The Molson Companies Limited, I; 26
    (upd.)
Montedison S.p.A., 24 (upd.)
NACCO Industries, Inc., 7
National Service Industries, Inc., 11
Nichimen Corporation, 24 (upd.)
Nissho Iwai K.K., I
Norsk Hydro A.S., 10
Ogden Corporation, I
Onex Corporation, 16
Orkla A/S, 18
Park-Ohio Industries Inc., 17
Pentair, Inc., 7
Poliet S.A., 33
Powell Duffryn plc, 31
Preussag AG, 17
Pubco Corporation, 17
Pulsar Internacional S.A., 21
The Rank Organisation Plc, 14 (upd.)
Red Apple Group, Inc., 23
Rubbermaid Incorporated, 20 (upd.)
Samsung Group, I
San Miguel Corporation, 15
Sara Lee Corporation, 15 (upd.)
Schindler Holding AG, 29
Sea Containers Ltd., 29
ServiceMaster Inc., 23 (upd.)
Sime Darby Berhad, 14
Société du Louvre, 27
Standex International Corporation, 17
Stinnes AG, 23 (upd.)
Sudbury Inc., 16
Sumitomo Corporation, I; 11 (upd.)
Swire Pacific Ltd., I; 16 (upd.)
Talley Industries, Inc., 16
Tandycrafts, Inc., 31
Teledyne, Inc., I; 10 (upd.)
Tenneco Inc., I; 10 (upd.)
Textron Inc., I; 34 (upd.)
Thomas H. Lee Co., 24
Thorn Emi PLC, I
Thorn plc, 24
TI Group plc, 17
Time Warner Inc., IV; 7 (upd.)
Tomen Corporation, 24 (upd.)
Tomkins plc, 11
Toshiba Corporation, I; 12 (upd.)

Tractebel S.A., 20
Transamerica Corporation, I; 13 (upd.)
The Tranzonic Cos., 15
Triarc Companies, Inc., 8
TRW Inc., I; 11 (upd.)
Unilever, 32 (upd.)
Unilever PLC, II; 7 (upd.)
United Technologies Corporation, 34 (upd.)
Universal Studios, Inc., 33
Valhi, Inc., 19
Valores Industriales S.A., 19
Veba A.G., I; 15 (upd.)
Vendôme Luxury Group plc, 27
Viacom Inc., 23 (upd.)
Virgin Group, 32 (upd.)
Virgin Group PLC, 12
W.R. Grace & Company, I
The Washington Companies, 33
Wheaton Industries, 8
Whitbread PLC, 20 (upd.)
Whitman Corporation, 10 (upd.)
Whittaker Corporation, I
WorldCorp, Inc., 10
Worms et Cie, 27

CONSTRUCTION

A. Johnson & Company H.B., I
ABC Supply Co., Inc., 22
Abrams Industries Inc., 23
AMREP Corporation, 21
ASV, Inc., 34
The Austin Company, 8
Baratt Developments PLC, I
Beazer Homes USA, Inc., 17
Bechtel Group, Inc., I; 24 (upd.)
BFC Construction Corporation, 25
Bilfinger & Berger Bau A.G., I
Bird Corporation, 19
Black & Veatch LLP, 22
Bouygues S.A., I; 24 (upd.)
Brown & Root, Inc., 13
Bufete Industrial, S.A. de C.V., 34
CalMat Co., 19
Centex Corporation, 8; 29 (upd.)
Cianbro Corporation, 14
The Clark Construction Group, Inc., 8
Colas S.A., 31
Day & Zimmermann, Inc., 31 (upd.)
Dillingham Corporation, I
Dominion Homes, Inc., 19
Eiffage, 27
Encompass Services Corporation, 33
Environmental Industries, Inc., 31
Eurotunnel PLC, 13
Fairclough Construction Group PLC, I
Fleetwood Enterprises, Inc., 22 (upd.)
Fluor Corporation, I; 8 (upd.); 34 (upd.)
George Wimpey PLC, 12
Gilbane, Inc., 34
Granite Rock Company, 26
Hillsdown Holdings plc, 24 (upd.)
Hochtief AG, 33
Horton Homes, Inc., 25
Hospitality Worldwide Services, Inc., 26
Hovnanian Enterprises, Inc., 29
J.A. Jones, Inc., 16
John Brown PLC, I
John Laing PLC, I
Kajima Corporation, I
Kaufman and Broad Home Corporation, 8
Kitchell Corporation, 14
The Koll Company, 8
Komatsu Ltd., 16 (upd.)
Kumagai Gumi Company, Ltd., I
L'Entreprise Jean Lefebvre, 23
Lennar Corporation, 11
Lincoln Property Company, 8

Lindal Cedar Homes, Inc., 29
Linde A.G., I
Mellon-Stuart Company, I
Michael Baker Corp., 14
Morrison Knudsen Corporation, 7; 28
  (upd.)
New Holland N.V., 22
NVR L.P., 8
Ohbayashi Corporation, I
Opus Group, 34
The Peninsular & Oriental Steam
  Navigation Company (Bovis Division), I
Perini Corporation, 8
Peter Kiewit Sons' Inc., 8
Philipp Holzmann AG, 17
Post Properties, Inc., 26
Pulte Corporation, 8
Redrow Group plc, 31
RMC Group p.l.c., 34 (upd.)
Rooney Brothers Co., 25
The Rottlund Company, Inc., 28
The Ryland Group, Inc., 8
Sandvik AB, 32 (upd.)
Schuff Steel Company, 26
Shorewood Packaging Corporation, 28
Simon Property Group, Inc., 27
Sundt Corp., 24
Taylor Woodrow PLC, I
Thyssen Krupp AG, 28 (upd.)
Toll Brothers Inc., 15
Trammell Crow Company, 8
Tridel Enterprises Inc., 9
The Turner Corporation, 8; 23 (upd.)
U.S. Home Corporation, 8
Walter Industries, Inc., 22 (upd.)
Wood Hall Trust PLC, I

CONTAINERS

Ball Corporation, I; 10 (upd.)
BWAY Corporation, 24
Clarcor Inc., 17
Continental Can Co., Inc., 15
Continental Group Company, I
Crown Cork & Seal Company, Inc., I; 13
  (upd.); 32 (upd.)
Gaylord Container Corporation, 8
Golden Belt Manufacturing Co., 16
Greif Bros. Corporation, 15
Inland Container Corporation, 8
Kerr Group Inc., 24
Keyes Fibre Company, 9
Liqui-Box Corporation, 16
The Longaberger Company, 12
Longview Fibre Company, 8
The Mead Corporation, 19 (upd.)
Metal Box PLC, I
National Can Corporation, I
Owens-Illinois, Inc., I; 26 (upd.)
Primerica Corporation, I
Reynolds Metals Company, 19 (upd.)
Royal Packaging Industries Van Leer N.V.,
  30
Sealright Co., Inc., 17
Smurfit-Stone Container Corporation, 26
  (upd.)
Sonoco Products Company, 8
Thermos Company, 16
Toyo Seikan Kaisha, Ltd., I
U.S. Can Corporation, 30
Ultra Pac, Inc., 24
Viatech Continental Can Company, Inc., 25
  (upd.)
Vitro Corporativo S.A. de C.V., 34

DRUGS/PHARMACEUTICALS

A.L. Pharma Inc., 12
Abbott Laboratories, I; 11 (upd.)

Akorn, Inc., 32
ALZA Corporation, 10
American Home Products, I; 10 (upd.)
Amgen, Inc., 10
Astra AB, I; 20 (upd.)
Barr Laboratories, Inc., 26
Bayer A.G., I; 13 (upd.)
Block Drug Company, Inc., 8
Bristol-Myers Squibb Company, III; 9
  (upd.)
Carter-Wallace, Inc., 8
Chiron Corporation, 10
Ciba-Geigy Ltd., I; 8 (upd.)
D&K Wholesale Drug, Inc., 14
Eli Lilly & Company, I; 11 (upd.)
F. Hoffmann-Laroche & Company A.G., I
Fisons plc, 9; 23 (upd.)
FoxMeyer Health Corporation, 16
Fujisawa Pharmaceutical Company Ltd., I
G.D. Searle & Co., 34 I; 12 (upd.); (upd.)
GEHE AG, 27
Genentech, Inc., I; 8 (upd.)
Genetics Institute, Inc., 8
Genzyme Corporation, 13
Glaxo Holdings PLC, I; 9 (upd.)
Johnson & Johnson, III; 8 (upd.)
Jones Medical Industries, Inc., 24
Leiner Health Products Inc., 34
Marion Merrell Dow, Inc., I; 9 (upd.)
McKesson Corporation, 12
Merck & Co., Inc., I; 11 (upd.)
Miles Laboratories, I
Monsanto Company, 29 (upd.)
Moore Medical Corp., 17
Murdock Madaus Schwabe, 26
Mylan Laboratories Inc., I; 20 (upd.)
National Patent Development Corporation,
  13
Novo Industri A/S, I
Pfizer Inc., I; 9 (upd.)
Pharmacia & Upjohn Inc., 25 (upd.)
Pharmacia A.B., I
Quintiles Transnational Corporation, 21
R.P. Scherer, I
Roberts Pharmaceutical Corporation, 16
Roche Bioscience, 14 (upd.)
Rorer Group, I
Roussel Uclaf, I; 8 (upd.)
Sandoz Ltd., I
Sankyo Company, Ltd., I
Sanofi Group, I
Schering A.G., I
Schering-Plough Corporation, I; 14 (upd.)
Shionogi & Co., Ltd., 17 (upd.)
Sigma-Aldrich, I
SmithKline Beckman Corporation, I
SmithKline Beecham plc, 32 (upd.)
Squibb Corporation, I
Sterling Drug, Inc., I
The Sunrider Corporation, 26
Syntex Corporation, I
Takeda Chemical Industries, Ltd., I
Teva Pharmaceutical Industries Ltd., 22
The Upjohn Company, I; 8 (upd.)
Vitalink Pharmacy Services, Inc., 15
Warner-Lambert Co., I; 10 (upd.)
Watson Pharmaceuticals Inc., 16
The Wellcome Foundation Ltd., I

ELECTRICAL & ELECTRONICS

ABB ASEA Brown Boveri Ltd., II; 22
  (upd.)
Acer Inc., 16
Acuson Corporation, 10
ADC Telecommunications, Inc., 30 (upd.)
Adtran Inc., 22
Advanced Micro Devices, Inc., 30 (upd.)

Advanced Technology Laboratories, Inc., 9
Aiwa Co., Ltd., 30
Alliant Techsystems Inc., 30 (upd.)
AlliedSignal Inc., 22 (upd.)
Alpine Electronics, Inc., 13
Alps Electric Co., Ltd., II
Altera Corporation, 18
Altron Incorporated, 20
American Power Conversion Corporation,
  24
AMP Incorporated, II; 14 (upd.)
Analog Devices, Inc., 10
Analogic Corporation, 23
Anam Group, 23
Anaren Microwave, Inc., 33
Andrew Corporation, 10; 32 (upd.)
Applied Power Inc., 32 (upd.)
Arrow Electronics, Inc., 10
Ascend Communications, Inc., 24
Atari Corporation, 9; 23 (upd.)
Atmel Corporation, 17
Audiovox Corporation, 34
Ault Incorporated, 34
Autodesk, Inc., 10
Avnet Inc., 9
Bicoastal Corporation, II
Bose Corporation, 13
Boston Acoustics, Inc., 22
Bowthorpe plc, 33
Broadcom Corporation, 34
Burr-Brown Corporation, 19
Cabletron Systems, Inc., 10
Canon Inc., 18 (upd.)
Carbone Lorraine S.A., 33
Carl-Zeiss-Stiftung, 34 (upd.)
Casio Computer Co., Ltd., 16 (upd.)
Cisco Systems, Inc., 34 (upd.)
Citizen Watch Co., Ltd., 21 (upd.)
Cobham plc, 30
Cobra Electronics Corporation, 14
Coherent, Inc., 31
Cohu, Inc., 32
Compagnie Générale d'Électricité, II
Cooper Industries, Inc., II
Cray Research, Inc., 16 (upd.)
Cubic Corporation, 19
Cypress Semiconductor Corporation, 20
Daktronics, Inc., 32
Dallas Semiconductor Corporation, 13; 31
  (upd.)
De La Rue plc, 34 (upd.)
Dell Computer Corporation, 31 (upd.)
DH Technology, Inc., 18
Digi International Inc., 9
Discreet Logic Inc., 20
Dixons Group plc, 19 (upd.)
Dolby Laboratories Inc., 20
Dynatech Corporation, 13
E-Systems, Inc., 9
Electronics for Imaging, Inc., 15
Emerson Electric Co., II
Emerson Radio Corp., 30
ENCAD, Incorporated, 25
ESS Technology, Inc., 22
Everex Systems, Inc., 16
Exar Corp., 14
Exide Electronics Group, Inc., 20
Fluke Corporation, 15
Foxboro Company, 13
Fuji Electric Co., Ltd., II
Fujitsu Limited, 16 (upd.)
General Electric Company, II; 12 (upd.)
General Electric Company, PLC, II
General Instrument Corporation, 10
General Signal Corporation, 9
GenRad, Inc., 24
GM Hughes Electronics Corporation, II
Goldstar Co., Ltd., 12

ENGINEERING & MANAGEMENT SERVICES

ENTERTAINMENT & LEISURE

FINANCIAL SERVICES: BANKS

FINANCIAL SERVICES: NON-BANKS

FOOD PRODUCTS

FOOD SERVICES & RETAILERS

HEALTH & PERSONAL CARE PRODUCTS

HEALTH CARE SERVICES

INSURANCE

Principal Mutual Life Insurance Company, III
Progressive Corporation, 11
The Progressive Corporation, 29 (upd.)
Provident Life and Accident Insurance Company of America, III
Prudential Corporation PLC, III
The Prudential Insurance Company of America, III; 30 (upd.)
Reliance Group Holdings, Inc., III
Riunione Adriatica di Sicurtà SpA, III
Royal Insurance Holdings PLC, III
SAFECO Corporaton, III
The St. Paul Companies, Inc., III; 22 (upd.)
SCOR S.A., 20
The Standard Life Assurance Company, III
State Farm Mutual Automobile Insurance Company, III
Sumitomo Life Insurance Company, III
The Sumitomo Marine and Fire Insurance Company, Limited, III
Sun Alliance Group PLC, III
SunAmerica Inc., 11
Swiss Reinsurance Company (Schweizerische Rückversicherungs-Gesellschaft), III
Teachers Insurance and Annuity Association, III
Texas Industries, Inc., 8
TIG Holdings, Inc., 26
The Tokio Marine and Fire Insurance Co., Ltd., III
Torchmark Corporation, 9; 33 (upd.)
Transatlantic Holdings, Inc., 11
The Travelers Corporation, III
UICI, 33
Union des Assurances de Pans, III
Unitrin Inc., 16
UNUM Corp., 13
USAA, 10
USF&G Corporation, III
VICTORIA Holding AG, III
W.R. Berkley Corp., 15
Washington National Corporation, 12
Willis Corroon Group plc, 25
"Winterthur" Schweizerische Versicherungs-Gesellschaft, III
The Yasuda Fire and Marine Insurance Company, Limited, III
The Yasuda Mutual Life Insurance Company, Limited, III
"Zürich" Versicherungs-Gesellschaft, III

LEGAL SERVICES

Akin, Gump, Strauss, Hauer & Feld, L.L.P., 33
American Lawyer Media Holdings, Inc., 32
Baker & McKenzie, 10
Baker and Botts, L.L.P., 28
Brobeck, Phleger & Harrison, LLP, 31
Cadwalader, Wickersham & Taft, 32
Coudert Brothers, 30
Fenwick & West LLP, 34
Foley & Lardner, 28
Hildebrandt International, 29
Holme Roberts & Owen LLP, 28
Jones, Day, Reavis & Pogue, 33
King & Spalding, 23
Latham & Watkins, 33
LeBoeuf, Lamb, Greene & MacRae, L.L.P., 29
Milbank, Tweed, Hadley & McCloy, 27
Morgan, Lewis & Bockius LLP, 29
Paul, Hastings, Janofsky & Walker LLP, 27
Pillsbury Madison & Sutro LLP, 29
Pre-Paid Legal Services, Inc., 20

Shearman & Sterling, 32
Skadden, Arps, Slate, Meagher & Flom, 18
Snell & Wilmer L.L.P., 28
Sullivan & Cromwell, 26
Vinson & Elkins L.L.P., 30
Wilson Sonsini Goodrich & Rosati, 34

MANUFACTURING

A.B.Dick Company, 28
A.O. Smith Corporation, 11
A.T. Cross Company, 17
AAF-McQuay Incorporated, 26
AAON, Inc., 22
AAR Corp., 28
ABC Rail Products Corporation, 18
ACCO World Corporation, 7
Acme-Cleveland Corp., 13
Ag-Chem Equipment Company, Inc., 17
AGCO Corp., 13
Aisin Seiki Co., Ltd., III
Aktiebolaget Electrolux, 22 (upd.)
Aktiebolaget SKF, III
Alamo Group Inc., 32
Alfa-Laval AB, III
Allen Organ Company, 33
Alliant Techsystems Inc., 8; 30 (upd.)
Allied Healthcare Products, Inc., 24
Allied Products Corporation, 21
Allied Signal Engines, 9
AlliedSignal Inc., 22 (upd.)
Allison Gas Turbine Division, 9
Alltrista Corporation, 30
American Business Products, Inc., 20
American Homestar Corporation, 18
American Locker Group Incorporated, 34
American Standard Companies Inc., 30 (upd.)
American Tourister, Inc., 16
American Woodmark Corporation, 31
Ameriwood Industries International Corp., 17
AMETEK, Inc., 9
Ampex Corporation, 17
Amway Corporation, 30 (upd.)
Analogic Corporation, 23
Anchor Hocking Glassware, 13
Andersen Corporation, 10
The Andersons, Inc., 31
Andreas Stihl, 16
Anthem Electronics, Inc., 13
Applied Materials, Inc., 10
Applied Power Inc., 9; 32 (upd.)
ARBED S.A., 22 (upd.)
Arctco, Inc., 16
Armor All Products Corp., 16
Armstrong World Industries, Inc., III; 22 (upd.)
ASV, Inc., 34
Atlas Copco AB, III; 28 (upd.)
Avery Dennison Corporation, 17 (upd.)
Avondale Industries, Inc., 7
Badger Meter, Inc., 22
Baker Hughes Incorporated, III
Baldor Electric Company, 21
Baldwin Piano & Organ Company, 18
Baldwin Technology Company, Inc., 25
Ballantyne of Omaha, Inc., 27
Ballard Medical Products, 21
Bally Manufacturing Corporation, III
Baltek Corporation, 34
Barnes Group Inc., 13
Barry Callebaut AG, 29
Bassett Furniture Industries, Inc., 18
Bath Iron Works Corporation, 12
Beckman Coulter, Inc., 22
Beckman Instruments, Inc., 14
Beiersdorf AG, 29

Belden Inc., 19
Bell Sports Corporation, 16
Beloit Corporation, 14
Benjamin Moore and Co., 13
Berry Plastics Corporation, 21
BIC Corporation, 8; 23 (upd.)
BICC PLC, III
Binks Sames Corporation, 21
Binney & Smith Inc., 25
Biomet, Inc., 10
BISSELL Inc., 9; 30 (upd.)
The Black & Decker Corporation, III; 20 (upd.)
Blount, Inc., 12
Blyth Industries, Inc., 18
BMC Industries, Inc., 17
Borden, Inc., 22 (upd.)
Borg-Warner Automotive, Inc., 14
Borg-Warner Corporation, III
The Boyds Collection, Ltd., 29
Brass Eagle Inc., 34
Bridgeport Machines, Inc., 17
Briggs & Stratton Corporation, 8; 27 (upd.)
BRIO AB, 24
British Vita plc, 33 (upd.)
Brother Industries, Ltd., 14
Brown & Sharpe Manufacturing Co., 23
Broyhill Furniture Industries, Inc., 10
Brunswick Corporation, III; 22 (upd.)
BTR Siebe plc, 27
Bucyrus International, Inc., 17
Bugle Boy Industries, Inc., 18
Bulgari S.p.A., 20
Bulova Corporation, 13
Bundy Corporation, 17
Burelle S.A., 23
Burton Snowboards Inc., 22
Bush Boake Allen Inc., 30
Bush Industries, Inc., 20
Butler Manufacturing Co., 12
Callaway Golf Company, 15
Cannondale Corporation, 21
Caradon plc, 20 (upd.)
Carbone Lorraine S.A., 33
Carl-Zeiss-Stiftung, III; 34 (upd.)
Carrier Corporation, 7
Casio Computer Co., Ltd., III
Caterpillar Inc., III; 15 (upd.)
Central Sprinkler Corporation, 29
Cessna Aircraft Company, 27 (upd.)
Champion Enterprises, Inc., 17
Chanel, 12
Chart Industries, Inc., 21
Chris-Craft Industries, Inc., 31 (upd.)
Chromcraft Revington, Inc., 15
Cincinnati Milacron Inc., 12
Circon Corporation, 21
Citizen Watch Co., Ltd., III
Clarcor Inc., 17
Clark Equipment Company, 8
Clayton Homes Incorporated, 13
The Clorox Company, 22 (upd.)
Cobra Golf Inc., 16
Cockerill Sambre Group, 26 (upd.)
Cohu, Inc., 32
Colas S.A., 31
The Coleman Company, Inc., 30 (upd.)
Collins Industries, Inc., 33
Colt's Manufacturing Company, Inc., 12
Columbia Sportswear Company, 19
Congoleum Corp., 18
Conso International Corporation, 29
Converse Inc., 9
Corrpro Companies, Inc., 20
Crane Co., 8; 30 (upd.)
Crown Equipment Corporation, 15
Cuisinart Corporation, 24
Culligan International Company, 12

REAL ESTATE

RETAIL & WHOLESALE

RUBBER & TIRE

TELECOMMUNICATIONS

TEXTILES & APPAREL

UTILITIES

WASTE SERVICES

NOTES ON CONTRIBUTORS

Notes on Contributors

BIANCO, David P. Freelance writer.

BRYNILDSSEN, Shawna. Freelance writer and editor based in Bloomington, Indiana.

COHEN, M. L. Novelist and freelance writer living in Paris.

COVELL, Jeffrey L. Freelance writer and corporate history contractor.

FUJINAKA, Mariko. Freelance writer and editor living in Paso Robles, California.

HALASZ, Robert. Former editor in chief of *World Progress* and *Funk & Wagnalls New Encyclopedia Yearbook*; author, *The U.S. Marines* (Millbrook Press, 1993).

INGRAM, Frederick C. South Carolina-based business writer who has contributed to *GSA Business, Appalachian Trailway News,* the *Encyclopedia of Business,* the *Encyclopedia of Global Industries,* the *Encyclopedia of Consumer Brands,* and other regional and trade publications.

LEMIEUX, Gloria. Freelance writer and editor living in Nashua, New Hampshire.

MALLETT, Daryl F. Freelance writer and editor; actor; contributing editor and series editor at The Borgo Press; series editor of SFRA Press's *Studies in Science Fiction, Fantasy and Horror*; associate editor of Gryphon Publica-

tions and for *Other Worlds Magazine*; founder and owner of Angel Enterprises, Jacob's Ladder Books, and Dustbunny Productions.

PEIPPO, Kathleen. Minneapolis-based freelance writer.

RHODES, Nelson. Freelance editor, writer, and consultant in the Chicago area.

ROTHBURD, Carrie. Freelance writer and editor specializing in corporate profiles, academic texts, and academic journal articles.

SALAMIE, David E. Part-owner of InfoWorks Development Group, a reference publication development and editorial services company.

TRADII, Mary. Freelance writer based in Denver, Colorado.

UHLE, Frank. Ann Arbor-based freelance writer; movie projectionist, disc jockey, and staff member of *Psychotronic Video* magazine.

WALDEN, David M. Freelance writer and historian in Salt Lake City; adjunct history instructor at Salt Lake City Community College.

WERNICK, Ellen D. Freelance writer and editor.

WOODWARD, A. Freelance writer.

EXPLORERS

*From Ancient Times
to the Space Age*

EXPLORERS

From Ancient Times to the Space Age

Volume 1

Consulting Editors

John Logan Allen
Professor of Geography
University of Connecticut

E. Julius Dasch
Manager/Scientist
NASA National Space Grant Program

Barry M. Gough
Professor of History
Wilfrid Laurier University

Macmillan Library Reference USA

Simon & Schuster Macmillan
New York

Simon & Schuster and Prentice Hall International
London Mexico City New Delhi Singapore Sydney Toronto

EDITORIAL CREDITS

Developed for Simon & Schuster Macmillan by Visual Education Corporation, Princeton, N.J.

For Macmillan

Editor: Hélène G. Potter
Cover Designer: Judy Kahn

For Visual Education

DIRECTOR OF REFERENCE: Darryl Kestler
PROJECT EDITOR: Guy Austrian
ASSOCIATE EDITOR: Doriann Markey
WRITERS: Michael Burgan, John Haley, Rebecca Stefoff, Elizabeth Trundle
RESEARCH ASSISTANT: Christopher Binkley
COPYEDITING SUPERVISOR: Maureen Pancza
COPY EDITOR: Joanna Foster
INTERIOR DESIGN: Maxson Crandall
PHOTO RESEARCH: Sara Matthews
CARTOGRAPHER: Gyula Pauer
PRODUCTION SUPERVISORS: Ellen Foos, Christine Osborne
PRODUCTION ASSISTANT: Rob Ehlers
ELECTRONIC PREPARATION: Cynthia C. Feldner, Fiona Torphy
ELECTRONIC PRODUCTION: Elise Dodeles, Lisa Evans-Skopas, Deirdre Sheean, Isabelle Verret

Simon & Schuster Macmillan
1633 Broadway
New York, NY 10019

Library of Congress Catalog Card Number: 98-8809

PRINTED IN THE UNITED STATES OF AMERICA

Printing Number

1 2 3 4 5 6 7 8 9 10

Library of Congress Cataloging-in-Publication Data

Explorers and discoverers: from ancient times to the space age/consulting editors,
    John Logan Allen, E. Julius Dasch, Barry Gough.
        p. cm.
    Includes bibliographical references and index.
    ISBN 0-02-864893-5 (set).—ISBN 0-02-864890-0 (v. 1).—ISBN 0-02-864891-9 (v. 2).—
ISBN 0-02-864892-7 (v. 3)
    1. Explorers—Biography—Dictionaries.   I. Allen, John Logan. 1941–   .
II. Dasch, E. Julius.   III. Gough, Barry M.
G200.E877   1998
910´.92´2—dc21   98-8809
[B]   CIP

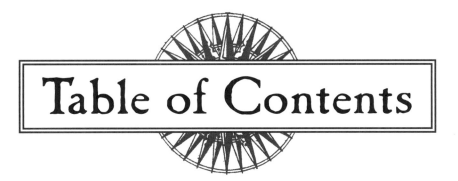

Table of Contents

Volume 1

A section of color plates, *Ancient Times and Middle Ages,* appears between pages 116 and 117.

Introductory Essays

Biographical Profiles

A

B

Volume 2

A section of color plates, *The Renaissance,* appears between pages 124 and 125.

Volume 3

A section of color plates, *Modern Times,* appears between pages 124 and 125.

List of Maps

Volume 1

Volume 2

Volume 3

Preface

This encyclopedia of *Explorers and Discoverers* contains profiles of 333 men and women who expanded our knowledge of the world and beyond. These individuals made difficult—even fatal—journeys, discovered unknown lands, mapped unfamiliar regions, and described the peoples, flora, and fauna that they encountered in their travels.

A board of distinguished consultants—experts in history, geography, and space science—selected the subjects of these profiles. The choices reflect the range of interests, skills, and professions that lead people to abandon their established lives for the uncertainty of an expedition into uncharted territory. Among the explorers profiled, readers will find geographers, merchants, navigators, botanists, archaeologists, and treasure hunters. Also profiled are people who made essential contributions to the process of discovery by working in their own countries as cartographers, inventors, and historians.

The pioneers of space exploration have carried the spirit of discovery into our own time, and some of those men and women are included in these volumes. However, the full story of the exploits of the individuals who have blazed the way in mountaineering, aviation, and undersea exploration will have to be the subject of another work.

Introductory Essays

Volume 1 of *Explorers and Discoverers* begins with three essays: "The Technology of Exploration," "Causes and Effects of Exploration," and "The History of Exploration." These three summaries provide some technical and historical background and help students to understand how each explorer's efforts were a part of the long and complex process of discovery.

Within the text, SMALL CAPS call attention to the names by which profiled individuals are alphabetized in these volumes. Words in **boldface** are defined in the margin. Some of these terms are given fuller explanations in the Glossary at the end of Volume 3.

Biographical Profiles

The biographical profiles, which follow the essays, are arranged in alphabetical order and run through all three volumes. Each profile begins with a headnote that lists the explorer's nationality, dates of birth and death, and main activities. The text of a profile usually begins with a brief summary of the individual's accomplishments, followed by an account of the person's life before, during, and after the events that earned him or her a place in the history of discovery. Each article ends with a short list of books about the profiled individual. Students may also refer to the Bibliography at the end of Volume 3 for works that deal more generally with the topic of exploration.

The text is accompanied by over 250 photographs, paintings, drawings, and etchings. These illustrate the men and women profiled, as well as vessels, equipment, and historical events. In addition, 50 maps show the routes taken by explorers across oceans and continents.

Appendices

At the end of Volume 3, students will find four additional resources—a Glossary, a List of Explorers by Nationality, a List of Explorers by Area of Exploration, and a Bibliography.

The Glossary presents detailed information about some of the key terms used in the profiles. The two lists of explorers will help readers to study the efforts of individuals and their countries to explore the world's geographical regions. The Bibliography contains further references that are organized in two sections: General Works and Works by Region.

Acknowledgments

This reference work represents the collaboration of many people, including researchers, writers, editors, designers, layout artists, consultants, and publishers. We invite you to share the great adventures of exploration and discovery that are recounted in the following pages.

The Technology of Exploration

Christopher COLUMBUS spent eight years trying to win support for his first voyage of discovery. He studied ancient maps and made calculations to prove that he could reach Asia from Europe by sailing across the Atlantic Ocean. His wait ended in 1492, when the king and queen of Spain gave him money for three ships. For 33 days, Columbus sailed over open waters. He then landed on an island in the Caribbean Sea that he named San Salvador. However, because he had only the imprecise instruments of his time to track his course, the measurements he made were not reliable. To this day, historians who have tried to retrace his route are not sure on just which island he first landed. Eventually, Columbus returned to Spain with the information he had gathered during his voyage. Other explorers followed Columbus, and they soon realized that the ancient maps were wrong. Two unknown continents—the Americas—lay between Europe and Asia. European mapmakers began to redraw the world.

Columbus faced basic concerns that are shared by all explorers. He needed the skills of navigation that made it possible both to determine where he was going and to tell people where he had been. He needed transportation to get there and—with luck and skill—back again. Navigation and transportation are the technologies of exploration. The needs of explorers can encourage inventors to make advances in technology. New technologies, in turn, can create new opportunities for exploration.

Tools and Techniques of Navigation

The simplest way to keep track of location is by following landmarks, such as mountains or rivers. Sailors can go from one port to the next along a familiar coastline. When traveling in unknown areas or sailing on the open sea, people learned to look to the sky. From the sun by day and from the moon and stars by night, navigators could get a rough idea of time and direction. This method, known as celestial navigation, is not very precise—and is made impossible by fog and clouds.

Navigators acquired a powerful tool around the year 1000. It was discovered that lodestone, a type of magnetic iron ore, could make a needle point northward. Soon mariners were using magnetized needles that floated in bowls of water—the first compasses. These allowed people to measure direction quite accurately.

The ancient Greeks knew of another tool, the **astrolabe,** a metal disk on which navigators could measure the height of the sun or a star above the horizon. Medieval Arabs perfected this

astrolabe navigational instrument used since ancient times to determine distance north or south of the equator

This astrolabe had a rotating bar that a navigator could line up with the sun or stars. The angle on the rim showed the height of the sun or stars in the sky.

latitude distance north or south of the equator

quadrant navigational instrument used since the Middle Ages to determine distance north or south of the equator

sextant optical instrument used by navigators since the 1750s to determine distance north or south of the equator

longitude distance east or west of an imaginary line on the earth's surface; in 1884, most nations agreed to draw the line through Greenwich, England

chronometer clock designed to keep precise time in the rough conditions of sea travel

Inuit people of the Canadian Arctic, sometimes known as the Eskimo

For detailed descriptions of navigational tools, such as the astrolabe, quadrant, and chronometer, see the Glossary in Volume 3. Additional photographs can be found in the color sections of Volumes 1 and 2.

device, adding tables and formulas that revealed the navigator's **latitude.** By the 1500s, mariners had replaced the astrolabe with the cross-staff, a simpler tool that provided the same information. The cross-staff was an early version of the **quadrant,** which was later developed into the **sextants** and octants that are still in use today. These tools allowed mariners to determine latitude in most regions near and north of the equator. They were not as useful far south of the equator until the 1600s, when astronomers began including southern constellations in their star charts.

Mariners also needed to know their **longitude,** but for centuries they had no easy, reliable way to find this information. Using a method called dead reckoning, a navigator could estimate longitude with rough calculations of speed and direction. Dead reckoning was useful over short distances, but a small error on a long ocean voyage could lead a ship hundreds of miles off course, possibly into unknown and dangerous waters.

Mariners were making ocean crossings routinely by the 1600s, and they were desperate for an accurate way to find their longitude. The English Parliament offered a great sum of money for a solution. The prize went unclaimed for decades, until John HARRISON invented the **chronometer** in 1762. This clock kept precise time at sea despite the rough weather. The accurate measurement of time made possible an accurate calculation of longitude. As a result, explorers and mapmakers were able to determine their position at any point on the earth's surface.

Maps and Mapmaking

Maps are central to exploration. They show the boundaries of the known world, challenging adventurers to go beyond. When explorers return from unknown regions, they bring information that fills in our maps—and enlarges our understanding of the earth. Many explorers and discoverers have also been mapmakers.

The Development of Maps

The oldest known maps come from the Middle East and date from about 2500 B.C. Many cultures invented their own styles of mapmaking. The people of the Marshall Islands in the Pacific Ocean made sailing charts on stick frameworks, attaching curved sticks and seashells that represented currents and islands. The seafaring **Inuit** showed the positions of islands by stitching bits of wood or fur onto sealskin. North American Indians drew or carved maps on tree bark, skins, wood, and stone.

By A.D. 200, the Chinese were drawing maps based on square grids. Each square represented an equal area of the earth's surface, so measuring distance on the map was easy. At about the same time, the Greek scholar PTOLEMY summed up European knowledge of geography in his *Guide to Geography.* In this book, he listed the positions of 8,000 places in Europe, Africa, and Asia. He also gave instructions for using projections to create maps. Projections are ways to represent the round earth on flat paper—though only a globe can accurately represent the shape of the earth.

cartographer mapmaker

cartography the science of mapmaking

By the Middle Ages, Ptolemy's work had been lost to most Europeans. Some **cartographers** drew on Christian beliefs to create maps that were symbolic as well as geographic. These maps are often called "T-and-O" maps because they are circular in shape and show Europe, Africa, and Asia divided by a *T* that is formed by the Mediterranean Sea and various rivers. With Jerusalem at their center and imaginary monsters at the edges, these maps reflected a medieval Christian view of the world.

Medieval Arab geographers preserved knowledge of Ptolemy's work, and their maps more closely resembled Ptolemy's. Although Arab maps, like those of Europeans, contained many geographical errors, they made important advances in **cartography.** Their maps also included new information provided by Arab travelers and traders who had visited much of Africa and Asia.

The Modern Age of Mapmaking

Europeans rediscovered Ptolemy's writings in the 1400s. New world maps based on his ideas, methods, and information began the era of modern cartography. Although the Ptolemaic maps contained inaccuracies, they contributed to a new and growing interest in geography and exploration.

Meanwhile, sailors had developed another kind of map, the sea chart, to help them locate ports and avoid dangerous waters. The early charts were little more than sketches of coastlines. After magnetic compasses came into use in the Mediterranean region around 1200, mariners began to make more detailed and accurate charts called portolans. Networks of lines showed the directions of winds that would carry ships between ports. In time, cartography became a science based on precise measurements and careful calculations. Mapmakers developed hundreds of new projections that let them produce larger and more accurate maps.

European nations began to focus their efforts on exploration and mapmaking. In 1419 Prince Henry of Portugal created a center at Sagres, Portugal, for the study of maps, geography, and navigation. He sent ships on voyages of discovery that marked the beginning of the Age of Exploration. In the following centuries, opportunities for conquest, trade, and knowledge expanded. Hundreds of expeditions were organized by governments, merchants, and scientific societies. Explorers visited every part of the world, and by the early 1900s, cartographers had filled in most of the blank spots on their maps.

Smaller and easier to use than the quadrant, this sextant of the 1800s had mirrors that reflected the sun or stars along the navigator's line of sight.

For detailed descriptions of vehicles such as the caravel, sledge, and space capsule, see the Glossary in Volume 3. Additional photographs can be found in the color sections of all three volumes.

Vessels and Vehicles

Explorers needed ways to reach the places they located on maps. Naturally, the earliest travel was on foot, but people found that they could move beyond local areas more easily on rivers and seas. With the invention of aircraft, people have extended their reach into the air and even into outer space. Explorers have led the way into unknown areas, traveling by land, sea, and air. Their success—and their lives—have often depended on their transportation.

Travel over Land

Various forms of land transportation developed in different areas to fit local conditions. Wise explorers often learned the best methods from local peoples. For example, on the long, hot trade routes of North Africa, Arabia, and Asia, travelers joined camel **caravans** that might include 10,000 camels or more. In tropical central Africa, on the other hand, pack animals could not survive the humidity and the insects. Explorers of Africa's rain forests and rivers often hired (or forced) large numbers of local tribesmen to carry their supplies.

After the arrival of Europeans, horses and wagons became the most widely used form of transport on the plains and deserts of the Americas and Australia. But in some areas, small, lightly equipped groups could move more easily than huge expeditions could. Through forests, over mountains, and along rivers, trappers and scouts traveled by foot and canoe. Often they had to **portage** from one river to another. For teams of explorers in the icy polar regions, disciplined travel was even more important. Explorers had to follow precise plans, setting up supply **depots** and using dogs to pull **sledges** and **boat-sledges** over the ice and snow. Eventually, exploration of the continents was completed from the air, but for many centuries, people had to travel over land.

Ancient and Medieval Ships

Water transportation was well developed in ancient times. The people who lived around the Mediterranean Sea were skilled sailors. By 3000 B.C., the Egyptians had seagoing vessels made of short wooden planks, held together by pegs and ropes. These ships were propelled by oarsmen and a single large sail. By 2000 B.C., the Phoenicians (of what is now Lebanon) were well known in the Mediterranean region for their abilities as sailors. They eventually traveled as far west as modern-day Morocco and Spain in sturdy ships built of cedar and fir timbers.

Around 700 B.C., Greek traders began to compete with the Phoenicians. Greek cargo vessels sailed for distant ports carrying large crews to fight pirates, the seagoing bandits who attacked ships at sea. The Greeks also built oar-driven warships called **galleys.** The Romans built galleys, too, but they also developed wide, round cargo ships that could move by wind power alone.

The Norsemen of Scandinavia, Iceland, and Greenland had two main types of wooden ships powered by both oars and sails. The longships, used for fighting and raiding, may have been as long as 150 feet, with 34 pairs of oars. The *knorr,* designed for trading, was shorter and had higher sides. Norse ships could bend slightly to withstand the battering of the rough northern seas.

The Chinese sailed the western Pacific Ocean and the Indian Ocean in flat-bottomed boats called **junks.** These ships had several masts with sails made of fiber mats. In the late 1200s, Marco POLO reported seeing junks 200 to 300 feet long, with cabins for up to 60 merchants. At that time, the Arabs were the most skilled sailors in the Mediterranean Sea and the Arabian Sea. Their **dhows** may have been the first **lateen-rigged** ships.

caravan large group of people traveling together, often with pack animals, across a desert or other dangerous region

portage transport of boats and supplies overland between waterways

depot place where supplies are stored

sledge heavy sled, often mounted on runners, that is pulled over snow or ice

boat-sledge boat mounted on sled runners to allow travel on both ice and water

galley ship with oars and sails, used in ancient and medieval times

junk Chinese ship with sails made of fiber mats

dhow Arab vessel with triangular sails, widely used in the Mediterranean Sea and Indian Ocean

lateen-rigged having triangular sails that can catch wind from either side of a mast, making a ship easy to maneuver

This woodcut shows a caravel of the 1400s. The Portuguese began the Age of Exploration by sailing ships like this one along the west coast of Africa.

caravel small ship with three masts and both square and triangular sails

galleon large sailing ship used for war and trade

brig small, fast sailing ship with two masts and square sails

brigantine two-masted sailing ship with both square and triangular sails

schooner fast, easy-to-maneuver sailing ship with two or more masts and triangular sails

dirigible large aircraft filled with a lighter-than-air gas that keeps it aloft; similar to a blimp but with a rigid frame

satellite object launched into space to circle a planet or moon

orbit stable, circular route; one trip around; to revolve around

Modern European Ships

European shipbuilding took a great leap forward with the age of European exploration. Before that time, most voyages were short trips close to shore. But sailors were able to make longer ocean voyages as European shipyards began to produce new types of vessels. First, shipbuilders replaced the single mast, carrying a single large sail, with two or even three masts. These masts could hold a number of smaller sails, allowing a captain to position the sails at appropriate angles to catch the wind.

The Portuguese used **caravels** in their voyages along the coast of Africa in the 1400s. These ships were the workhorses of early European exploration of the seas. They had both triangular sails, which could catch shifting coastal winds, and square sails, which caught more wind on the open sea. Two of Columbus's ships, the *Niña* and the *Pinta,* were caravels. The **galleon** was the main warship of the 1500s, but like the later **brig, brigantine,** and **schooner,** it sometimes served for exploration. Explorers' vessels were adapted from many other uses. Between 1768 and 1771, for example, James COOK sailed around the world in a converted coal-hauling ship. In the 1800s and 1900s, ships were built from iron and steel, with engines powered by steam, gasoline, and nuclear reactors.

Some ships sail beneath the waves. The first submarines were built in the 1600s, but they were not truly useful for many years. In the 1900s, the vast ocean floors were opened to explorers such as Jacques-Yves COUSTEAU. A great success in undersea exploration came in 1958, when the American nuclear-powered submarine *Nautilus* reached the North Pole—under the ice cap.

Aerial Exploration

Exploration took to the air in the late 1700s. The early hot-air balloons and **dirigibles** crashed often, however, and most explorers of the 1900s preferred to use the airplane. The first attempt to fly into the Arctic failed in 1909, but in the 1920s, Richard BYRD flew over both the North and South Poles. Aerial explorers photographed and mapped huge stretches of remote territory in the continental interiors. They also provided cartographers with images of the tops of the highest mountain ranges.

The Space Age

Waves of new technology continued to open new frontiers of exploration in the second half of the 1900s. Navigators at sea and in the air benefited from loran, a system that calculates position by means of radio signals broadcast from various places around the planet. The next step was to broadcast the signals from space. Today's Global Positioning System (GPS) has 24 **satellites** in **orbit** around the earth. A handheld GPS receiver can calculate latitude and longitude for anyone from a cartographer to a polar explorer to a backwoods hiker.

rocket vehicle propelled by exploding fuel

Soviet Union nation that existed from 1922 to 1991, made up of Russia and 14 other republics in eastern Europe and northern Asia

capsule small early spacecraft designed to carry a person around the earth

cosmonaut Russian term for a person who travels into space; literally, "traveler to the universe"

astronaut American term for a person who travels into space; literally, "traveler to the stars"

space suit protective gear that allows a person who wears it to survive in space

space station spacecraft that circles the earth for months or years with a human crew

space shuttle reusable spacecraft designed to transport people and cargo between the earth and space

interstellar between the stars

Hundreds of other satellites gather up-to-the-minute information and broadcast it to earth. The familiar television weather map is a triumph of satellite mapping. In the 1990s, the United States began its Mission to Planet Earth, a program that uses satellites to study the atmosphere and ocean currents. These satellites also helped cartographers to make extremely accurate maps of the earth's surface. Other satellites aim their instruments at planets, stars, and galaxies throughout the universe.

Satellites are carried into space on **rockets.** When a rocket reaches space, it separates from the satellite and falls toward the earth. It burns up from heat caused by friction with the earth's atmosphere. The world's first satellite, named *Sputnik 1,* was launched by the **Soviet Union** in 1957. The Soviets went on to launch *Swallow,* the first spacecraft that held a person, in 1961. Like most early spacecraft, the *Swallow* was a tiny metal **capsule** with flight controls and a supply of air for its pilot, the **cosmonaut** Yuri GAGARIN. A heat shield protected the *Swallow* from burning up when it parachuted back to earth. Later that year, American **astronauts** Alan SHEPARD and John GLENN also rode capsules into space. In 1965 cosmonaut Aleksei LEONOV, wearing a **space suit,** made the first "space walk," floating while tethered outside his capsule for about 10 minutes.

The United States operated the Apollo space program from 1967 to 1972. Apollo spacecraft entered into orbit around the moon and then released a landing craft to the surface. When the astronauts had finished their work on the moon's surface, they blasted off, rejoined the spacecraft in orbit, and then flew back to the earth. Some Apollo missions carried four-wheeled vehicles called rovers, which were driven by astronauts on the moon's surface.

Astronauts and cosmonauts have done valuable scientific research while living on **space stations.** These spacecraft often have separate quarters for sleeping, exercising, and working. In the 1970s, the Soviet Salyut and American Skylab stations had varying amounts of success. The Soviet station *Mir* was launched in 1986 and remained in use into the 1990s. Meanwhile, the United States developed a spacecraft called the **space shuttle.** Two rockets—one on each side of a giant fuel tank—lift the shuttle into orbit around the earth. The shuttle can carry up to eight crew members and fly for up to three weeks. It returns to earth by landing on a runway, just like an airplane.

The space shuttle does not go farther than its orbit around the earth, but the United States and the Soviet Union have both sent spacecraft to other planets. These craft, called probes, have no human pilots. They are controlled by computers that communicate with the earth by radio. Some have gone into orbit around other planets and moons, and a few have made surface landings. A small number have flown beyond the solar system into **interstellar** space. For now, however, most scientists continue to explore space from the surface of the earth.

Atop this 363-foot-tall Saturn V rocket, the Apollo 11 astronauts escaped the earth's gravity on July 16, 1969. They reached the moon four days later.

Causes and Effects of Exploration

Exploration began when the earliest humans searched for food and better living conditions. It continued throughout the ages as people attempted to gain knowledge of their world and to initiate trade with people in other regions. In the 1400s, Europeans began to accelerate and organize the process of exploration, sending many expeditions into areas about which they knew little. Lasting 500 years, the European Age of Exploration resulted in the first complete and accurate geographic picture of the world. Like all periods of discovery, it was driven by a combination of forces.

Motives for Exploration

Although exploration was often a national effort, the people who traveled to the far corners of the globe for their countries were a diverse group. Why did they risk hunger, disease, and shipwreck—and worse—as explorers? Nations had a variety of political, economic, religious, and scientific motives for launching expeditions. Individual explorers often shared these goals and also sought adventure, fortune, and personal glory in journeys of discovery.

Politics

The desire to control territory drove many nations to explore new lands. In the late 1800s and early 1900s, Britain and Russia competed for control of Tibet. The two countries sent explorers, spies, and diplomats to learn about the country and its capital, Lhasa. These complex political maneuvers came to an end in 1904, when a British army fought its way into Lhasa under the command of Francis YOUNGHUSBAND. National glory was a motive for Chinese exploration in the 1400s. The Chinese emperor sent ZHENG He with large fleets to visit ports in Asia, Arabia, and eastern Africa. Zheng's goal was not to conquer but to demonstrate China's wealth and power to other nations. Glory was also an inspiration for many individual explorers. For example, in the 1800s, dozens of men and women competed to discover the source of the Nile River in Africa. The winner of this race, Britain's John Hanning SPEKE, stood to gain worldwide fame—as well as political control over the river valley for his country. However, the fierce criticism and doubt he faced in Britain was not overcome for many years, and Britain eventually had to give up the African empire Speke had helped to build.

Spanish conquistadors—covered in metal armor and seated on horses—were a strange sight to the Indian tribes living in the Americas.

Commerce

The desire for trade, precious metals, slaves, and natural resources lay behind many voyages and expeditions. The European Age of Exploration began with Portugal's search for a sea route to the spices and silks of southern Asia. The Portuguese hoped to avoid the overland routes controlled by merchants in the Middle East and Italian city-states such as Venice and Genoa.

In the 1500s, Portugal, Spain, and other nations began to establish colonies in Asia and the Americas that would become important sources of income. Spanish mines in the Americas produced vast quantities of gold and silver at a time when Europe's own mines could not keep up with the needs of commerce and industry. Spain used much of its new wealth to pay its debts and finance its armies, while the **conquistadors** reaped huge personal fortunes. Meanwhile, the known territory of North America expanded constantly as French, Dutch, and British explorers hunted for valuable furs. The European colonial powers tried to control the flow of trade in their empires in ways that would bring them the greatest possible profit.

Religion

For some explorers, religious faith was the strongest motive of all. The quest of Xuan Zang, a Chinese Buddhist pilgrim, was a personal one. He made a difficult journey to India in the 600s in order to study ancient holy writings. In later centuries, Christians of the Society of Jesus, known as **Jesuits,** went to distant parts of the world to convert other peoples to Christianity. Their successes helped the Society of Jesus gain considerable influence in both European and colonial politics. Among these priests were the Italian Matteo Ricci in China, the Frenchman Jacques Marquette on the Mississippi River, and the Spaniard Eusebio Francisco Kino in the American Southwest.

Science

Much exploration was based on the desire to know what lay beyond a mountain range or across an ocean. In the 1700s, scientists began to organize their studies into separate fields, such as **botany** and **geology.** It became common for naturalists such as England's Joseph Banks to travel with naval vessels. Other scientists, including the German Alexander von Humboldt, organized their own expeditions to observe the wonders of the natural world and collect samples of rocks, plants, and animals. Nations also mounted large, well-funded voyages to answer scientific questions. The U.S. South Seas Exploring Expedition gathered many volumes of scientific data between 1838 and 1842. But the voyage was also intended to demonstrate the strength of the young American nation and allow it to claim territory in Antarctica. The mission grew out of a complicated set of motives and goals, as had the European Age of Exploration.

Europe and the Age of Exploration

By the end of the Middle Ages, highly developed civilizations had emerged in many parts of the world. The Islamic world of North Africa and the Middle East had made great achievements in science,

conquistador Spanish or Portuguese explorer and military leader in the Americas

Jesuit member of the Society of Jesus, a Roman Catholic order founded by Ignatius of Loyola in 1534

botany the scientific study of plants

geology the scientific study of the earth's natural history

medicine, and the arts. The Aztec and Inca Empires of the Americas had large populations ruled by stable governments, as did China and India. Asia's rich trade network stretched from the Mediterranean Sea to the Pacific Ocean. Yet only Europe set out to explore and colonize the rest of the world. Why this happened is an important question.

A Time of Transition

In the 1400s, Europe was changing. Using new methods of agriculture, farmers produced larger crops, making it possible to support cities and towns with larger populations. Craftspeople in the cities produced many more items, such as woolen cloth and iron tools, that could be traded. European merchants and trading companies wanted to sell these goods in foreign markets. They also looked for foreign goods to bring to Europe, especially Asia's rare and costly spices, fabrics, and gemstones.

At the same time, Europe was entering a new period in its centuries-old conflict with the Islamic world. Empires in central Asia were converting to the Muslim faith and preventing Christians from using the trade roads across Asia. When goods did reach Europe, trade was controlled by Italian merchants. Wanting to bypass the Muslims and the Italians, people in the western and northern parts of Europe searched for new sea routes to Asia.

Europeans were also facing Muslims on the battlefield. Christian armies began campaigns to force the Muslims out of Spain and eastern Europe, but the struggle was long and difficult. Europeans hoped to find or convert Christians in Africa and Asia and join with them against the Muslims. Many explorers were encouraged by the legend of Prester John, a Christian emperor who was thought to rule somewhere in India, central Asia, or Africa.

Europeans were looking outward. But the great civilizations of east Asia had little interest in the rest of the world. The Chinese in particular felt that their culture was superior to all others and that China could supply goods to meet all the needs of its people. Also, Asians did not place as high a value on converting others to their religions as Christians and Muslims did. For these reasons, Asians rarely traveled to foreign lands.

The Impact of Technology

Europeans' leap into world exploration got a boost from new technology—and their willingness to use it. Arab **dhows** performed well in the relatively calm waters of the Mediterranean Sea, the Persian Gulf, and the Indian Ocean. But sailors in western and northern Europe were faced with the rough and stormy Atlantic Ocean, North Sea, and Baltic Sea. European shipbuilders developed vessels with strong hulls, high sides, and multiple masts and sails that were well suited to long ocean crossings.

These European ships were also sturdy enough to carry hundreds of cannons, which overwhelmed Arab and Asian navies. Gunpowder had originated in China, where it was used mainly for fireworks. But Europeans made gunpowder into a weapon, using it first in cannons and then in handheld guns. Early firearms were too

dhow Arab vessel with triangular sails, widely used in the Mediterranean Sea and Indian Ocean

inaccurate and awkward to be truly useful. Sometimes the shock they created among people who had never seen them was more effective than the weapons themselves. In the 1800s, however, firearms were improved and became a major force in battle.

Printing was another technology that changed the world. Before the printing press was invented in the 1400s, books in Europe were usually handwritten in Latin. The printing press could produce books much more quickly. By writing and printing in the languages they spoke, such as English and French, Europeans were able to spread new information about the world more easily than before. By contrast, Muslims rejected printing and permitted only classical Arabic to be used in writing. These decisions limited the spread of information and ideas in the Islamic world.

Exploration's Effects on Europe

The Age of Exploration changed everything from the way Europeans ate to the way they thought of the world around them. It changed the fortunes of western Europe's nations and brought them new responsibilities as the rulers of distant colonial empires. It also led to new conflicts.

Wealth and Warfare

Beginning with the efforts of well-armed Portuguese and Spanish explorers in the 1400s and 1500s, Europeans won greater access to

This painting shows Christopher Columbus at the court of King Ferdinand and Queen Isabella, presenting treasure and Indians brought from the Americas.

many trade routes and opened new routes as well. New foods from around the world changed the diets of Europeans. Corn, tobacco, potatoes, squash, and chocolate came from the Americas, tea and spices from eastern Asia, coffee from the Middle East, and bananas from Africa. Other products flowed across the seas to European ports, including silk and gemstones from Asia, rare woods and dyes from Brazil, gold and ivory from Africa, and above all, gold and silver from Central and South America. Portugal and Spain—and later the Netherlands, France, and England—prospered and became the major powers of Europe and the world.

With explorers continuing to lead the way, European nations made ambitious efforts to map, claim, and conquer lands that possessed desirable resources, goods, or locations. They established settlements, trading posts, military bases, and colonial governments. Europeans gradually brought much of the world under their influence, if not always under their direct control.

But the Age of Empire, as it came to be called, was as costly as it was profitable. European governments faced conflict not only with the people they had conquered but often with their own colonists as well. The competition for empires also fueled the rivalries that existed among European nations and contributed to several wars, including the Seven Years' War (1756 to 1763) and World War I (1914 to 1918).

A New Way of Seeing

The changes in diet, wealth, and borders were accompanied by changes in the way Europeans viewed the world. Before the Age of Exploration, Europeans thought that the Bible and some ancient Greek and Roman writings contained all human knowledge. But explorers found many things that those texts did not mention—such as whole continents with strange plants and animals. They also found religions other than the Jewish, Christian, and Muslim faiths they already knew. The world turned out to be bigger and more varied than they had dreamed.

Even so, Europeans' faith in Christianity was powerful and constant. Confronted with exotic beliefs and cultures, most Europeans insisted that their own way of life was superior. However, some people began to see value in other cultures. For example, in the 1500s and 1600s, Jesuits arrived at royal courts in China and India and found lively debates among scholars of Asian religions such as Hinduism and Buddhism. The missionaries could not easily convert such men to Christianity. They first had to gain respect at court by learning the dress, language, and customs of the land. Only then would they be invited to join in the discussions. Later, in the 1700s and 1800s, some English and French sailors who visited Pacific islands such as Tahiti thought that the Tahitians enjoyed a simple, pleasant life, even without Christianity. Despite the less peaceful aspects of the islanders' culture, such as human sacrifice, some sailors chose to stay in the islands rather than return to Europe.

As they learned about new lands and peoples, some explorers made an effort to describe what they found as fully and accurately as they could. They began to rely more on evidence and science

Made in the early 1700s, this engraving depicts Christian missionaries performing a baptism ceremony in the Congo region of central Africa.

than on myth and faith when studying their surroundings. This shift occurred slowly, but it helped to shape the modern world.

Exploration's Effects on Other Continents

The arrival of Europeans brought enormous changes to Asia, Africa, Australia, and the Americas. Many societies on these continents came under the rule of Europeans. The native peoples struggled to retain their cultures while living in the colonial empires.

Conquest

Many explorers were officers in their nations' armies and navies, and they arrived in new lands with soldiers at their sides. Their willingness to use force was strengthened by the belief that it was their right—and even their duty—to control the world. Some individuals spoke out powerfully against the mistreatment of conquered peoples. One such defender was Bartolomé de LAS CASAS, a Spanish priest who worked through the Roman Catholic Church to protect the Indians of Mexico during the 1500s. Nevertheless, European armies fought and defeated many peoples in the Americas, Africa, and Asia.

Deadlier than their guns were the diseases the Europeans carried. People living in the Americas, long isolated from the rest of the world, had no resistance to certain European diseases, including measles, influenza, and smallpox. The effect was devastating. Soon after the Europeans landed, Indians began dying by the thousands. Smallpox helped Hernán CORTÉS conquer the stricken Aztecs in the 1500s. A century later, the Puritan settlers found New England almost empty. Diseases introduced earlier by European fishermen and traders had nearly wiped out the local Indian population.

Colonization

Along with conquest came colonization. In North America and elsewhere, Europeans claimed land for settlement and displaced the people who were already there. In other places, such as India and Indonesia, European officials took control of local governments. European customs, languages, and laws became standard. European commercial systems based on cash and private property replaced systems based on **barter** and tribal ownership of land. Missionaries worked to convert colonial subjects to Christianity. In some colonies, especially in Central and South America, Europeans and non-Europeans intermarried, leading to a mixing of their cultures.

European culture also spread new ideas that eventually led to the end of colonial practices such as slavery. The slave trade had long existed in parts of Africa, Asia, and the Americas, but Europeans expanded and organized the trade. To provide labor for their plantations in the Americas, they forcibly shipped millions of Africans across the Atlantic Ocean.

In the 1600s and 1700s, many Europeans—as well as some of their descendants in North and South America—came to believe in the right of all people to equality, liberty, and religious freedom. Europeans began to look hard at both slavery and colonial rule, and some began to feel that such practices were no longer acceptable.

In the early and mid-1800s, the fight against the slave trade was led by the British. During and after that same period, colonies in the Americas and elsewhere demanded independence from their parent

barter exchange of goods without the use of money

When India was ruled by the British, Indians and Britons both cooperated and clashed as fellow soldiers in the British army.

countries, as the United States had done in 1776. Europeans found it more and more difficult to refuse—especially when faced with fierce fighting in colonies such as Algeria and Vietnam. By the mid-1900s, most European countries were willing to let go of their empires.

Legacy

The long-term effects of exploration and the colonial rule that followed are still felt strongly today. Many colonies became new nations just a few decades ago, and they continue to suffer from problems that existed under their colonial rulers. Corrupt officials, as well as tensions among different groups of people, have made life in modern times difficult for these countries. Meanwhile, a few colonies still exist, such as the islands of French Polynesia. Traces of the old European empires remain in organizations such as the Commonwealth of Nations, a group of former British colonies that maintain cultural and commercial ties with Britain.

The Age of Exploration brought a diverse world closer together. Traders carried goods to and from every corner of the globe. Scientists made the entire world their laboratory. People of all cultures came into contact, and whether they learned from each other, fought with each other, or both, they knew that they shared a single planet. This interaction has created a global civilization that is still taking shape today.

The History of Exploration

Turn to the profiles of explorers to learn more about their lives and travels. Some profiles also contain maps of the explorers' routes.

No map or globe could exist without the efforts of the men and women who have explored the world. Since ancient times, people of all cultures have gathered information about their surroundings. This process entered a new phase in the late 1400s, when western Europeans launched what came to be known as the Age of Exploration. Over many years, mapmakers received reports from explorers and sketched the outlines of the world's continents and oceans. As explorers began to investigate inland areas, mapmakers drew in rivers, mountains, and cities. The story of how a region came to be known is the story of many hundreds of explorers, guides, soldiers, priests, traders, historians, and mapmakers.

North America

When mapmakers in Europe, Africa, and Asia began to describe the world they knew, they had no evidence that the Americas existed. Separated from the rest of the inhabited world by the vast waters of the Atlantic and Pacific Oceans, North and South America were inhabited by many different tribes. In all likelihood, these people had come from Asia across a land bridge that connected Siberia and Alaska thousands of years earlier, when sea levels were low.

Sturdy wooden ships carried Norse explorers, settlers, and raiders across the stormy northern seas.

The Coasts

Around A.D. 800, the Norse—seagoing warriors and traders from Scandinavia—began building ships that could sail the rough northern Atlantic. They pushed westward, settling the islands of Iceland and Greenland. In about the year 1001, Leif ERIKSON sailed west from a Norse colony in Greenland and landed on an island off the eastern coast of what is now Canada. He and his crew are the first Europeans known to have reached North America. The Norse eventually gave up their attempts to establish a permanent settlement on the island of Newfoundland (in present-day eastern Canada). Their adventures there remained largely unknown to other Europeans.

The next step in the exploration of North America did not occur until almost 500 years later, when the nations of western Europe were eagerly searching for a sea route to Asia. Christopher COLUMBUS sailed west from southern Europe in 1492 and arrived at islands in the Caribbean Sea. Five years later, John CABOT also sailed west, but in waters north of those explored by Columbus. Cabot probably landed on Newfoundland. Soon the English, French, and Dutch sent many more explorers to the Americas. French crews under Giovanni da VERRAZANO explored the coast from what is now Florida to Canada and proved that this area was a single landmass, not a string of islands. Spain's Alonso ALVAREZ DE PINEDA charted the coast of the Gulf of Mexico and was the first European to see the Mississippi River. Jacques CARTIER sailed up the St. Lawrence River, establishing France's claims in the northeast. Henry HUDSON also followed water routes inland, investigating the Hudson River for the Dutch and Hudson Bay for the English. By the early 1600s, Samuel de CHAMPLAIN and other explorers had mapped most of the continent's east coast.

The exploration of the west coast began in the 1500s. European ships usually reached the coast by following Ferdinand MAGELLAN's sea route around the southern tip of South America and into the Pacific Ocean. After the Spanish established settlements on the west coast of the area now known as Mexico and Central America, ships sailed north from those ports. Juan Rodriguez CABRILLO and Sebastián VIZCAÍNO extended Spanish claims along the coast of what is now California. Parts of California were also claimed by Sir Francis DRAKE for England, but Spain built settlements there to ensure that the area remained in Spanish hands. Farther north, British navigators including James COOK and George VANCOUVER charted the west coast of Canada.

The northernmost stretches of the Pacific coast were under Russian control, thanks to Vitus BERING and Otto von KOTZEBUE, who had crossed the Bering Sea to what is now Alaska. Spaniards such as Alejandro MALASPINA and Juan Francisco de la BODEGA Y QUADRA sailed to Alaska from the south but did not interfere with Russian settlements.

United States

As explorers moved into the interior of North America, the land that is now the United States became a focus for rivalries among Spain, France, and Britain. After setting up colonies on the Caribbean islands and in Mexico, Spanish **conquistadors** pushed north in search of wealthy cities and empires to conquer. Juan PONCE DE LEÓN led the way, claiming Florida for Spain in 1513. Some 20 years later, Spain sent a large expedition to conquer lands along the Gulf of Mexico. The expedition ended in disaster. One survivor, Álvar Núñez CABEZA DE VACA, walked back to Spanish territory through the lands that are now Texas and New Mexico. As a result of his reports, new expeditions were sent north from Mexico.

Hernando de SOTO explored the Mississippi River and the American southeast from 1539 to 1542. During that same time, Francisco Vásquez de CORONADO entered regions farther west, and some of his men saw the Grand Canyon—but neither he nor Soto found the riches they sought. Spain focused its attention on its gold-producing colonies in Mexico, the Caribbean, and South America. Spain did

conquistador Spanish or Portuguese explorer and military leader in the Americas

THE EXPLORATION OF NORTH AMERICA

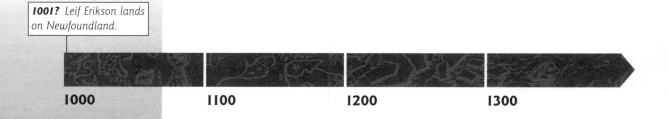

1001? Leif Erikson lands on Newfoundland.

1000   1100   1200   1300

Trade in furs and other goods brought French and British colonists into contact with Indian tribes and spurred the exploration of North America.

establish settlements to protect Mexico's northern frontier, in what became California, Arizona, New Mexico, and Texas. This area was explored by missionaries such as Eusebio Francisco KINO and governors such as Juan Bautista de ANZA.

Unlike the Spanish, who had to fight their way northward through mountains and deserts, the French controlled waterways to the heart of the continent: the St. Lawrence River and its links to the Great Lakes and the Mississippi River. The fur trade they established was extremely profitable for many years. The French were also more skilled than other Europeans at getting along with Indians, who helped them explore much of northern and central North America.

After Champlain opened a fur-trading route to the Great Lakes, Jean NICOLLET DE BELLEBORNE, Pierre Esprit RADISSON, and Médard Chouart des GROSEILLIERS further explored the lake regions. Expeditions under Louis JOLLIET and René-Robert Cavelier de LA SALLE traveled south along the Mississippi River, claiming the lands around it for France. Adventurers such as Pierre Gaultier de Varennes de LA VÉRENDRYE and his sons pushed west into the Great Plains and the fringes of the Rocky Mountains. France's efforts ended in 1763, when it lost the Seven Years' War and gave up its North American territory to Britain and Spain. But French culture has remained in North America, particularly in the present-day Canadian province of Québec.

The British concentrated on colonizing the Atlantic coast, beginning with Sir Walter RALEIGH's failed attempt to found a colony on the shores of what is now North Carolina. When Britain's American colonies became the United States in 1783, they received Britain's formerly French territory between the original colonies and the Mississippi River. The formerly French land west of the Mississippi, known as the Louisiana Territory, was given back to France by Spain in 1801. Concerned about its access to the river and the port of New Orleans, the United States purchased the western lands in 1803 in a deal known as the Louisiana Purchase. The land was bounded by the Mississippi River to the east, Canada to the north, and the Rocky Mountains to the southwest. The following American exploration

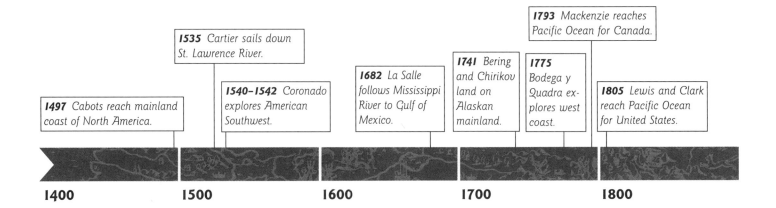

1497 *Cabots reach mainland coast of North America.*

1535 *Cartier sails down St. Lawrence River.*

1540–1542 *Coronado explores American Southwest.*

1682 *La Salle follows Mississippi River to Gulf of Mexico.*

1741 *Bering and Chirikov land on Alaskan mainland.*

1775 *Bodega y Quadra explores west coast.*

1793 *Mackenzie reaches Pacific Ocean for Canada.*

1805 *Lewis and Clark reach Pacific Ocean for United States.*

1400   **1500**   **1600**   **1700**   **1800**

The U.S. Army had a major role in the exploration and conquest of the American West, fighting bitter wars against Indians and Mexicans. This regiment of African-American cavalry won fame in the late 1800s.

of the West was a huge undertaking carried out in large part by military officers such as Meriwether LEWIS and Zebulon PIKE and fur traders such as Wilson Price HUNT and Robert STUART.

Some of the most colorful explorers were known as the Mountain Men. These trappers and traders traveled in the Rocky Mountains and the far west during the first half of the 1800s. Jedediah SMITH, James BRIDGER, Christopher "Kit" CARSON, Peter Skene OGDEN, and Joseph WALKER found routes that soon led settlers to the West. The Mountain Men were also a great help to army officers assigned to map the West, such as John Charles FRÉMONT and Benjamin Louis Eulalie de BONNEVILLE.

Canada

The exploration of inland Canada began with Champlain. He not only traveled widely but also sent men such as Etienne BRULÉ to live with the Indians, learn their languages, and explore their territory, especially around the Great Lakes. But the French were not the only Europeans active in Canada. The British wanted a share of the fur trade, too. In the late 1660s, the Frenchmen Groseilliers and Radisson helped the British launch the Hudson's Bay Company, which established many posts in the far north. After the British defeated France in the Seven Years' War and gained possession of Canada, they carried on the exploration and mapping of its northern and western reaches. Between 1770 and 1811, Samuel HEARNE, Alexander MACKENZIE, David THOMPSON, and Simon FRASER traveled through much of this rugged region of Canada. The rivers followed by Mackenzie, Thompson, and Fraser bear their names today.

Central and South America

trade winds winds that blow from east to west in the tropics

European seafarers knew that the **trade winds** blow toward the west in the tropical zones of the Atlantic Ocean for much of the year. When Christopher COLUMBUS decided to sail across the Atlantic,

This painting is one of many depicting Christopher Columbus's historic landing, which marked the beginning of the modern exploration of the Americas.

conquistador Spanish or Portuguese explorer and military leader in the Americas

Spanish Main area of the Spanish Empire including the Caribbean coasts of Central America and South America

he used these winds to propel his ships westward, arriving among the islands in the Caribbean Sea. Columbus thought that he had reached the shores of Asia. But other Europeans soon realized that the Americas were a "new world"—and a new source of wealth. Spain, having paid for Columbus's voyage, took the lead in exploring and colonizing the Caribbean islands. Using them as bases, the Spanish moved west and south into Mexico, Central America, and South America.

Mexico and Central America form a long, slender bridge between the mainlands of North America and South America. Communities of Indians existed from the coral and volcanic islands of the Caribbean to the windswept southern tip of Cape Horn. However, they were often separated by wide grasslands and deserts or by dense rain forest. Some of these Indians—especially the Aztecs of Mexico and the Inca of Peru—had built large cities and wealthy empires. The gold and silver they possessed were irresistible targets for the Spanish **conquistadors.** Despite the efforts of priests such as Bartolomé de Las Casas and Cristóbal de Acuña to protect the Indians, the history of exploration in this region is largely one of conquest.

The Caribbean

Columbus's four voyages, from 1492 to 1504, took him to the Bahamas, Cuba, Hispaniola, Guadeloupe, and other islands in the Caribbean. After founding a colony on Hispaniola, he sailed along the coasts of South America and Central America. Still determined to reach the markets of Asia, Columbus searched without success for a passage westward through the lands he had discovered.

But by the end of the 1400s, Spain was focusing less on reaching Asia and more on exploring the American islands and continents. Many of the men who completed the mapping of the Caribbean had sailed with Columbus. Among them were Vicente Yáñez Pinzón, who visited the coast of Mexico, and Juan Ponce de León, whose pilot discovered the powerful ocean current now known as the Gulf Stream. In 1500 Juan de La Cosa drew a world map that is believed to be the first to show the Americas. He and Rodrigo de Bastidas made the earliest landing on the Central American mainland, part of the area later known as the **Spanish Main.**

Central America and Mexico

Another of Columbus's former officers, the greedy and cruel Alonso de Ojeda, began the Spanish conquest of the mainland in 1499, in what later became Venezuela and Colombia. A few years later, Vasco Nuñez de Balboa crossed Central America at its narrowest point and was the first European to see the Pacific Ocean from the Americas. Spain next turned its attention to central Mexico. Having learned from the Indians that a powerful empire existed there, Hernán Cortés marched boldly inland from the coast with the help of Indian guides. In 1521 he conquered the Aztec Empire and laid the foundations of the colony of New Spain. Cortés then sent some of his ambitious officers on missions of their own—partly to keep them from threatening his own control of Mexico. Pedro de AL-VARADO, Cristóbal de Olid, and Francisco de Montejo made conquests to the south, in lands that are now Guatemala, Honduras, and the Yucatán Peninsula. Once the Spanish were firmly in control of central Mexico, they expanded northward. Juan Rodriguez CABRILLO's explorations on the Pacific coast gave Spain its first claim to California.

South America

While probing the edges of the Caribbean Sea, Columbus, Ojeda, Vicente Yáñez Pinzón, and others found the northeastern shores of South America. Amerigo VESPUCCI, in the service of Spain and Portugal, sailed south along the eastern coast on two voyages between 1499 and 1502. He described the continent in letters that were published throughout Europe. The German mapmaker Martin Waldseemüller was inspired to call the continent "America" in Vespucci's honor, and the name stuck.

Portugal became more active in South America after Pedro Álvares CABRAL made an unplanned landing on the coast of Brazil in 1500. Under the **Treaty of Tordesillas,** Cabral's landfall was in Portuguese territory. The Portuguese crown soon began founding colonies in Brazil. The next milestone came in 1520, when Ferdinand MAGELLAN led Spanish ships through a strait at the continent's southern tip. He had found the passage to the Pacific Ocean that so many explorers had sought.

A few years later, Europeans entered the South American interior. Sebastian CABOT journeyed up the Río de la Plata and its **tributaries** on the continent's southeast coast. In 1533 Francisco PIZARRO, following the example of Cortés, invaded and conquered the great Inca civilization on South America's west coast. The new Spanish territory of Peru was the base for expeditions to the north, south, and east by Diego de ALMAGRO and Francisco de ORELLANA, among others. Rumors of a rich king or city called **El Dorado** drew Sebastián de BENALCÁZAR, Gonzalo JIMÉNEZ DE QUESADA, and Nikolaus FEDERMANN into the mountains of what is now Colombia.

By the middle of the 1500s, Europeans knew the general outline and geography of South America, but much of the interior remained unexplored. Several Spanish explorers, including Álvar Núñez CABEZA DE VACA, had tried and failed to travel from east to

Treaty of Tordesillas agreement between Spain and Portugal dividing the rights to discovered lands along a north-south line

tributary stream or river that flows into a larger stream or river

El Dorado mythical ruler, city, or area of South America believed to possess much gold

THE EXPLORATION OF CENTRAL AMERICA AND SOUTH AMERICA

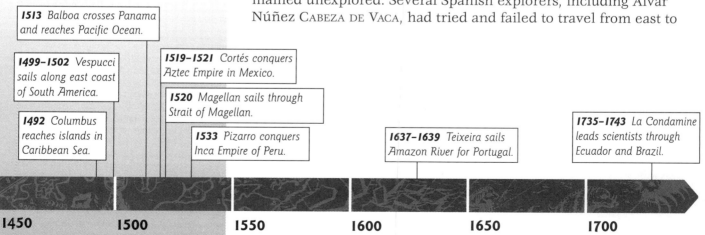

1513 Balboa crosses Panama and reaches Pacific Ocean.

1499–1502 Vespucci sails along east coast of South America.

1492 Columbus reaches islands in Caribbean Sea.

1519–1521 Cortés conquers Aztec Empire in Mexico.

1520 Magellan sails through Strait of Magellan.

1533 Pizarro conquers Inca Empire of Peru.

1637–1639 Teixeira sails Amazon River for Portugal.

1735–1743 La Condamine leads scientists through Ecuador and Brazil.

1450   1500   1550   1600   1650   1700

In 1911 an American professor named Hiram Bingham found the ruins of the Inca city of Machu Picchu, high in the mountains of Peru.

west across the southern part of the continent. But in the 1600s, Portuguese missionaries and adventurers began moving inward from the Brazilian coast. Pedro de TEIXEIRA's explorations gave Portugal control over most of the great Amazon River basin. In their quests for gold, gems, and slaves, **bandeirantes** such as Antonio RAPÔSO DE TAVARES crossed much ground.

South America presented scientists with many opportunities for research, especially in the Amazon rain forest. In 1735 Charles-Marie de LA CONDAMINE arrived to measure the length of one degree of **latitude** at the equator. Later, naturalists such as Alexander von HUMBOLDT, Charles DARWIN, and Alfred Russell WALLACE came to collect **specimens** and left with new scientific theories. Other scholarly explorers cast light on Indian civilizations such as the Inca, who had been conquered nearly 400 years before Hiram BINGHAM came to find the ruins they had left behind.

bandeirante member of a Portuguese raid into Brazil during the 1600s

latitude distance north or south of the equator

specimen sample of a plant, animal, or mineral, usually collected for scientific study or display

The Middle East and North Africa

To the ancient Greeks and Romans, the Middle East and North Africa were quite familiar. These lands are located where trade routes to Europe, Asia, and Africa meet. In its long history, this crossroads has drawn merchants and armies from all directions.

Ancient and Medieval Visitors

HERODOTUS of Halicarnassus traveled in Greece, Persia, and Egypt in the 400s B.C., and his writings summarize what the ancient Greeks knew about those lands. In the centuries that followed, military campaigns—especially those of ALEXANDER the Great—extended Greek knowledge of western Asia. But after the fall of the Roman Empire in the late A.D. 400s, much ancient knowledge was lost to the people of Europe.

Fortunately, Greek and Roman learning was preserved—and expanded—by the people of North Africa and the Middle East. The

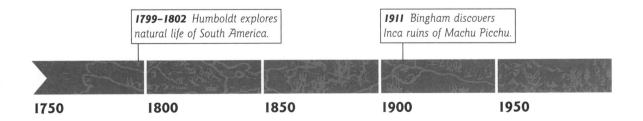

1799–1802 Humboldt explores natural life of South America.

1911 Bingham discovers Inca ruins of Machu Picchu.

1750   1800   1850   1900   1950

Crusades series of Christian holy wars fought against Muslims in the Middle East, mainly between 1095 and 1270

caravan large group of people traveling together, often with pack animals, across a desert or other dangerous region

pilgrimage journey to a sacred place

religion of Islam appeared in the Arabian peninsula in the 600s. In less than 200 years, it spread west to Spain and east to Persia. Unified by Islam and the Arabic language, the Islamic world became more powerful, and it once again received the attention of Europeans. The Jewish traveler BENJAMIN of Tudela and the Christian missionary ODORIC of Pordenone were among many who visited the Middle East and published accounts of their journeys. For many years, Muslims battled huge Christian armies that swept eastward in religious wars known as the **Crusades.** Meanwhile, Asians continued to travel to the region. For example, the Chinese diplomat ZHENG He commanded large fleets that visited the coast of Arabia in the 1400s.

Muslim Travelers
Islamic culture had its own tradition of travel and exploration. Trade, which took ships and **caravans** from one end of the vast Islamic empire to the other and beyond, encouraged people to make great journeys. So did the **pilgrimage** that each Muslim hoped to make to the holy city of Mecca (in what is now Saudi Arabia). Many pilgrims extended their journeys in order to visit other parts of the world. Among the Muslims who contributed to Islamic geographical knowledge were the traveler IBN FADLAN, the geographers al-MAS'UDI and IBN HAWQAL, and the mapmaker al-IDRISI. The greatest of the Muslim travelers was IBN BATTUTA, a keen observer of life in many lands from Morocco to China. Also notable was LEO AFRICANUS, a Muslim scholar who, after traveling through much of North Africa, became a Christian and wrote an important history of Africa.

Europeans in the Islamic World
After the Crusades failed to defeat the Muslims, Europeans began looking for new trade routes to Asia. This search was part of Europeans' growing interest in foreign lands. Some people also became more curious about the ancient world. Many ruins of ancient civilizations lay in areas that were controlled by Muslims. But since the Crusades, Christians were not welcome in Islamic countries. Those forbidden lands became all the more fascinating to Europeans. Driven by curiosity and love of adventure, travelers and scholars such as Ludovico di VARTHEMA, Johann BURCKHARDT, and Sir Richard Francis BURTON began exploring the Middle East and North Africa. They risked their lives to do so and often had to travel disguised as Arabs.

THE EXPLORATION OF THE MIDDLE EAST AND NORTH AFRICA

400s B.C. *Herodotus travels to Egypt and writes* Histories.

334–324 B.C. *Alexander conquers Middle East and central Asia.*

| 400 B.C. | 200 | A.D. 1 | 200 | 400 | 600 |

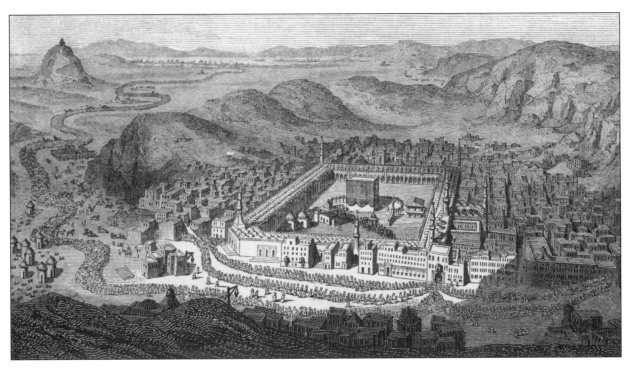

European explorers had to disguise themselves as Muslims to visit the Al-Haram mosque in Mecca, Saudi Arabia, the holiest site of Islam.

In the 1860s, George Sadlier and William Palgrave began the systematic exploration of Arabia. This task was carried on by Charles DOUGHTY, Anne Blunt, Gertrude BELL, and Freya STARK. The last blank spot on maps of Arabia was the southern desert known as the Empty Quarter. It was explored by the modern travelers Bertram Thomas, Harry St. John Philby, and Wilfred THESIGER.

Another desert, the harsh and vast Sahara, covers hundreds of thousands of square miles in North Africa. Like Arabia, it posed a challenge to Europeans. Its climate and terrain make travel difficult, and those who lived there were often hostile to non-Muslims. Muslim travelers, however, passed freely along the caravan routes that crisscrossed the Sahara. Ibn Battuta visited the Saharan kingdom of Mali at the height of its splendor.

French, Italian, and Portuguese explorers began probing the northern part of the Sahara in the Middle Ages. But modern scientific exploration did not get under way until the 1800s, when travelers such as Heinrich BARTH, Alexine TINNÉ, and Gustav NACHTIGAL embarked

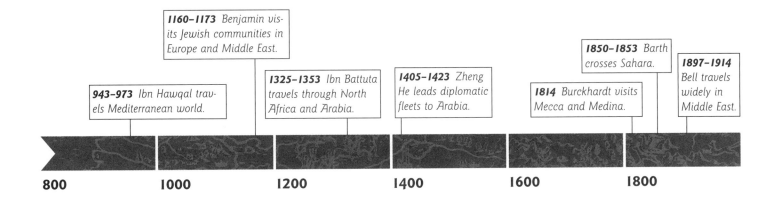

1160–1173 Benjamin visits Jewish communities in Europe and Middle East.

943–973 Ibn Hawqal travels Mediterranean world.

1325–1353 Ibn Battuta travels through North Africa and Arabia.

1405–1423 Zheng He leads diplomatic fleets to Arabia.

1850–1853 Barth crosses Sahara.

1814 Burckhardt visits Mecca and Medina.

1897–1914 Bell travels widely in Middle East.

800   1000   1200   1400   1600   1800

on ambitious journeys across the desert. France took the lead, and by the early 1900s, it had established its control over the region.

Africa South of the Sahara

South of the Sahara are the grasslands, forests, rivers, and lakes of the African continent. These lands remained a mystery to Europeans until the 1800s because the Sahara presented such a formidable barrier to travel from the north. Africa has no extremely high mountain ranges to block the way of explorers. However, the huge rain forests near the equator, as well as the Kalahari desert in the south, made travel difficult. Although the major rivers—the Nile, Niger, Congo, and Zambezi—seemed to offer passage to the interior, their many waterfalls and marshes prevented long-distance travel by boat. The greatest hazards were the tropical diseases that claimed the lives of many explorers.

Ancient Knowledge

The ancient Greek historian HERODOTUS relates the story of ancient Phoenicians who sailed all the way around Africa. Although there is no proof that this voyage took place, many modern historians consider it possible. Better documented is the story of HANNO, a citizen of Carthage, a city-state on the Mediterranean coast of North Africa. In the 500s B.C., he led a large expedition to establish colonies on Africa's west coast. Another Greek historian, PTOLEMY, produced the most complete geography of the ancient world. But he had little accurate knowledge of Africa south of the Sahara. He believed that it was connected to Asia and that ships could not sail around it. Europeans also remained unfamiliar with Africa's east coast, which borders the Indian Ocean. However, Arabs and Asians, including the Chinese diplomat ZHENG He, had long traded and traveled in eastern Africa.

The Portuguese Voyages

Portugal launched a new era of African exploration in the 1400s. Its explorers searched for a sea route around the Muslim lands of North Africa in order to reach the wealthy trade markets of India and eastern Asia. Over several decades, Portuguese ships cautiously sailed south, each voyage going farther than the last. Gil EANNES, Diogo CÃO, and Bartolomeu DIAS were among those who led the way for Vasco da GAMA, who reached the Indian Ocean by rounding Africa. A mapmaker at the Portuguese court, Martin Behaim, used the Portuguese discoveries to make a globe in 1492 that is the oldest still in existence.

THE EXPLORATION OF AFRICA SOUTH OF THE SAHARA

1488 Dias rounds Africa's Cape of Good Hope.

1486–1493 Covilhã searches for Prester John in Abyssinia.

1400   1500   1600

Traveling along Africa's Zambezi River, David Livingstone became the first European to see the falls of Mosi-oa-tunya, which he renamed Victoria Falls.

tributary stream or river that flows into a larger stream or river

The Portuguese ventured into the African interior as well, but they kept many of their findings so secret that even today we know little about their activities. Francisco ALVARES, Pedro Páez, and Pêro da COVILHÃ visited the kingdom of Abyssinia (now Ethiopia) in northeastern Africa. Abyssinia was one of several regions where Europeans hoped to find a mythical Christian ruler named Prester John. The Portuguese established gold mines and trading posts on both the west and east coasts of Africa. They also began Europe's involvement in the slave trade, capturing and enslaving Africans or buying them from Arab and African slave dealers.

The Nile and Niger Rivers

The interior remained unmapped long after Europeans had become familiar with the coasts. But in the late 1700s, Europeans began to focus on the exploration of eastern and central Africa. They were trying to solve one of the great geographical mysteries of the time: Where was the source of the Nile River? Over more than a century, Richard BURTON, Alexine TINNÉ, James BRUCE, John Hanning SPEKE, Samuel BAKER, David LIVINGSTONE, Henry Morton STANLEY, Charles CHAILLÉ-LONG, and Eduard SCHNITZER mapped the river, its **tributaries,** and the lakes of central Africa. They endured great hardships, much confusion, and bitter personal disputes.

Explorers from the late 1700s to the mid-1800s also worked to map the Niger River in western Africa and explore the lands around it. Daniel HOUGHTON, Mungo PARK, Hugh CLAPPERTON, and Alexander Gordon LAING were key figures in this effort. In 1828 René-Auguste CAILLIÉ, traveling alone, was the first European to visit the Muslim city of Timbuktu on the Niger and live to tell about it. The mapping of the river was completed by Richard Lemon LANDER.

The Continental Interior

The exploration of Africa's interior was often carried out during searches for the sources of the Nile and Niger Rivers. It was also closely linked to European nations' colonial ambitions. Baker, Livingstone, Stanley, and Verney Lovett CAMERON explored for Britain and Belgium and made the first crossings of the continent by Europeans. A new burst of exploration in the late 1800s and early 1900s helped to complete maps, advance scientific knowledge, and expand European

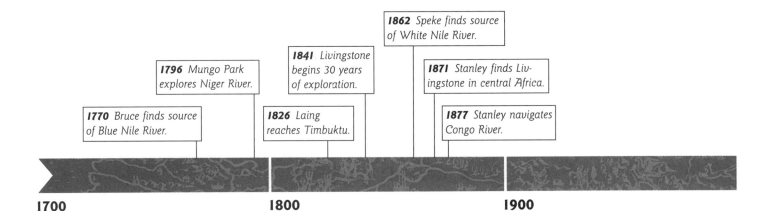

1862 Speke finds source of White Nile River.

1841 Livingstone begins 30 years of exploration.

1796 Mungo Park explores Niger River.

1871 Stanley finds Livingstone in central Africa.

1770 Bruce finds source of Blue Nile River.

1826 Laing reaches Timbuktu.

1877 Stanley navigates Congo River.

1700   **1800**   **1900**

empires. During those years, Joseph THOMSON, Paul Belloni DU CHAILLU, Pierre-Paul-François-Camille Savorgnan de BRAZZA, and many others traveled widely. Africa also drew a new generation of women explorers, such as May French SHELDON, Mary KINGSLEY, and Delia Denning AKELEY. These men and women relied heavily on the help of Africans, who worked as porters, guides, and interpreters.

Asia

Western Asia is near enough to the Mediterranean Sea to have been familiar to the ancient Greeks and Romans. But eastern lands such as India, China, and Japan were hardly known to them at all. To ancient Europeans, eastern Asia was the edge of the world. Even medieval Europeans knew these lands only as the remote sources of silk, spices, and other exotic goods.

Asia, the world's largest continent, stretches from the Mediterranean Sea to the Pacific Ocean. Its western edge merges with eastern Europe—geographers use the Ural Mountains in Russia as the border between Asia and Europe. Asia is home to a wide variety of peoples. Some of them made journeys of exploration throughout the continent well before Europeans began traveling there.

India

Separated from the rest of Asia by the Himalaya mountain range, India is a peninsula so large that it is called a subcontinent. To HERODOTUS, India was a land of marvels at the edge of the known world. ALEXANDER the Great reached the Indus River (in present-day Pakistan, northwest of modern India), and his general NEARCHUS explored part of the Indian Ocean, but the Greeks knew nothing of the rest of India. The Romans traded with India and gained somewhat broader knowledge of the region. Medieval Chinese travelers and explorers also reached India by sea and land. Among them was the admiral ZHENG He. The Chinese Buddhist monks FAXIAN, XUAN Zang, and YI Jing made pilgrimages to India, the birthplace of Buddhism.

From the 1200s on, some Europeans sought more contact between Europe and Asia. Marco POLO, Nicolò de CONTI, Pêro da COVILHÃ, Vasco da GAMA, and Ludovico di VARTHEMA were among those who visited India. Their descriptions of its spices and gems made European nations more eager than ever to trade in "the Indies"—a term that often included Southeast Asia as well as India. The British East India Company became a major force in India's politics, and by the mid-1800s, Britain had conquered and colonized the Indian subcontinent. During this time, British **surveyors** such as George EVEREST carried out the mapping of this enormous area.

surveyor one who makes precise measurements of a location's geography

Central Asia

Central Asia consists mostly of deserts and mountains. It is the region north of India and south of Russia, east of the Middle East and west of China. Though surrounded by great centers of civilization, central Asia was somewhat isolated. Travelers were often discouraged at the thought of braving the Hindu Kush Mountains, tribes of fierce horsemen, and the hostile defenders of Tibet. But as early as

Many explorers risked their lives to see the Potala, the palace of Tibet's spiritual leader, the Dalai Lama.

Jesuit member of the Society of Jesus, a Roman Catholic order founded by Ignatius of Loyola in 1534

plateau high, flat area of land

Roman times, traders passed through central Asia along the Silk Road, a caravan route linking the Middle East and China. The Silk Road was partly the result of the efforts of a Chinese diplomat and explorer named ZHANG Qian, who traveled to central Asia in the A.D. 100s. The Chinese Buddhist pilgrim Xuan Zang visited in the 600s, and Europeans, including WILLIAM of Rubruck and Marco Polo, followed in the 1200s. **Jesuits** such as Bento de GOES began making extended visits in the late 1500s.

In the 1700s, Europeans developed a great fascination with central Asia, fueled by the mystery of the city of Lhasa, located on the high Tibetan **plateau.** At that time, only a few foreigners had visited the city, which was difficult to reach and closely guarded. When European interest began to increase, Tibetan officials closed Lhasa to all foreigners.

The Europeans were not easily kept out. During the 1800s, Russia and Britain both had ambitions to control central Asia. Spies, soldiers, diplomats, and surveyors from both nations entered the region. The British writer Rudyard Kipling called these activities "the Great Game." Russians such as Nikolai PRZHEVALSKI pushed south toward Tibet, while Francis YOUNGHUSBAND and others came north from British India. Many British achievements, both in surveying and in spying, were made by Indians called "pundits." Nain SINGH, Kishen

SINGH, and KINTUP were among the Indians hired by the British to risk their lives on secret missions to the north. In 1904 Younghusband, at the head of a British army, forced his way into Lhasa, winning the "game" for Britain. Other travelers and scholars, including Sven HEDIN, Mark Aurel STEIN, Isabella Bird BISHOP, and Alexandra DAVID-NEEL, continued to explore the region well into the 1900s.

Siberia

Siberia is the immense part of northern Asia that stretches from the Ural Mountains to the Pacific Ocean. It is a land of plains, mountains, forests, rivers, and snow. The people native to Siberia were tribes of hunters and farmers scattered across the continent. Tribes in southern Siberia were related to the Mongols, an Asian people, while those in the north were related to the **Inuit** people of the North American polar region.

Inuit people of the Canadian Arctic, sometimes known as the Eskimo

The exploration and conquest of Siberia was a long process carried out almost entirely by Russians. In the 1500s, the Russian state based in Moscow began looking east toward the unknown land beyond the Ural Mountains. Timofeyevich YERMAK led an early Russian attempt to conquer part of Siberia. In the following decades, Russian fur trappers and military commanders advanced eastward, exploring rivers and building forts. They insisted that the local tribes hand over furs as a sign of respect for the distant rulers in Moscow.

Almost all the great rivers of Siberia, including the Ob, the Yenisei, and the Lena, flow from south to north. As the Russians reached each of these rivers, they were frustrated to realize that they could not simply sail across the continent. But in 1639, only 60 years after Yermak's expedition, a small party of explorers led by Ivan Moskvitin became the first Russians to reach the Pacific Ocean. Later in the 1600s, Yerofei Pavlovich KHABAROV explored the Amur River along the border with China. Semyon Ivanov DEZHNEV made early progress in mapping Siberia's far northern reaches. The full outline of Siberia would not be known until the 1800s, after the explorations of Vitus BERING, Aleksei CHIRIKOV, and Gennady Ivanovich Nevelskoy.

China

China, the home of an ancient civilization, is one of Asia's largest, most varied, and most heavily populated lands. Romans knew China mainly as the source of silk fabric. A few scattered Chinese and Roman records suggest that the two empires exchanged visitors in the A.D. 100s and 200s. However, very few Europeans traveled to

THE EXPLORATION OF ASIA

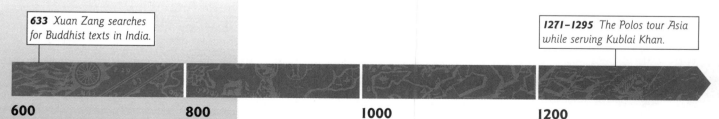

633 *Xuan Zang searches for Buddhist texts in India.*

1271–1295 *The Polos tour Asia while serving Kublai Khan.*

600   800   1000   1200

This Arabic illustration from the 1500s depicts the court of Genghis Khan, the Mongol emperor whose grandson Kublai was served by Marco Polo in the 1200s.

China before the 1200s. At that time, the Mongols gained control of China and central Asia. They maintained order along the trade routes and permitted foreigners to travel in the empire. Dozens of merchants, missionaries, and diplomats did so, and many left accounts of their journeys. Among the best known of these explorers were the Polo family, ODORIC of Pordenone, and IBN BATTUTA. XU Hongzu, one of several important Chinese explorers, roamed across China and into Tibet, seeking the sources of the Mekong and Salween rivers in the 1600s.

Soon a new wave of Europeans reached the Far East, using the sea route pioneered by the Portuguese. Matteo RICCI and Bento de Goes were among a handful of Europeans whom the Chinese permitted to enter during this period. But by the 1800s, the European powers had pressured China into allowing greater freedom to outsiders. Explorers such as Alexandra David-Neel and Ferdinand Paul Wilhelm von RICHTHOFEN traveled widely.

Japan
To medieval Europeans, Japan seemed even more remote, mysterious, and exotic than China. Marco Polo called this island kingdom Cipangu, and that name appeared on many European maps from the 1300s on. Polo did not claim to have visited the island, but he wrote that he had heard in China that Cipangu possessed "gold in the greatest abundance." Of course, this remark made Europeans very eager to go there.

At the time, Japan had little contact with the rest of the world, although it traded with Korea and China and knew of the existence of India. The arrival of Portuguese traders and missionaries such as Francis XAVIER in the mid-1500s was unsettling to some Japanese. Japan's rulers tried several times to drive out the Europeans and to limit contact between Japanese and foreigners. Explorers of the Pacific Ocean, such as Jean-François de Galaup de LA PÉROUSE and Adam Ivan von KRUSENSTERN, slowly added to Europe's knowledge of Japan. As had been the case with China, by the 1800s, travelers

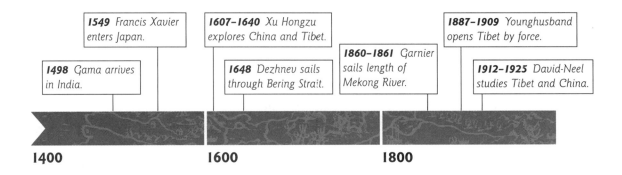

1549 Francis Xavier enters Japan.

1498 Gama arrives in India.

1607–1640 Xu Hongzu explores China and Tibet.

1648 Dezhnev sails through Bering Strait.

1860–1861 Garnier sails length of Mekong River.

1887–1909 Younghusband opens Tibet by force.

1912–1925 David-Neel studies Tibet and China.

1400　　　　**1600**　　　　**1800**

such as Isabella Bishop were visiting and traveling the country with relative freedom.

Southeast Asia

Today, Southeast Asia includes the nations of Bangladesh, Myanmar, Thailand, Cambodia, Laos, Vietnam, Malaysia, and Indonesia. It is a region of mountains, rain forests, and islands and is home to many different peoples who practice a wide variety of religions. Traders and diplomats from India and China began carrying their merchandise, culture, and politics to Southeast Asia in the A.D. 100s and 200s. The European exploration of the region began 1,000 years later, when Marco Polo and Odoric passed through it, followed by Ibn Battuta and Nicolò de Conti. The accounts of these travelers made Europeans aware that the spices of India actually came from the Spice Islands (now the Moluccas) of Indonesia.

Vasco da Gama's voyage to India opened the way for Portuguese settlement and exploration in Southeast Asia. Those activities were begun by Afonso de ALBUQUERQUE in the early 1500s. During that century, Portuguese and Spanish explorers entered dense jungles to reach the interior of the region's mainland. But their accounts of these journeys went unnoticed in their home countries. Soon the Dutch, British, and French were also active in the region, setting up trading posts and claiming territory. By the mid-1700s, Europeans had mapped the coasts of most of Southeast Asia, but many areas were still largely unknown. During the 1800s, remarkable efforts were made by explorers such as Francis GARNIER and Auguste PAVIE. They learned much about the region's geography and history, and their findings helped France gain control over much of the area that is now Vietnam, Cambodia, and Laos. Expeditions with different goals were made by scientists such as Alfred Russel WALLACE, who explored Borneo and other islands.

The Pacific Ocean and Australia

The Pacific Ocean covers one-third of the earth's surface and contains thousands of islands of all shapes and sizes. Australia is large enough to be a continent in itself, while Melanesia, Micronesia, and Polynesia are groups of thousands of tiny, widely scattered islands.

THE EXPLORATION OF THE PACIFIC OCEAN AND AUSTRALIA

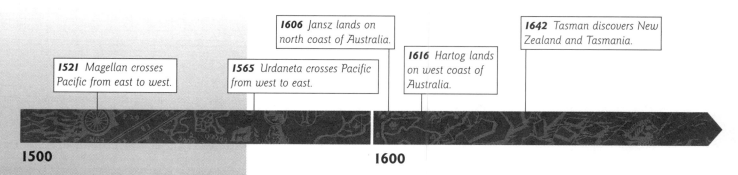

1606 *Jansz lands on north coast of Australia.*

1642 *Tasman discovers New Zealand and Tasmania.*

1521 *Magellan crosses Pacific from east to west.*

1565 *Urdaneta crosses Pacific from west to east.*

1616 *Hartog lands on west coast of Australia.*

1500

1600

The Dutch explorer Jacob Roggeveen was astounded to find these enormous stone statues on Easter Island, which lies in the southern Pacific Ocean.

circumnavigation journey around the world

This vast and varied world is sometimes called Oceania. Before the European Age of Exploration, the inhabitants of these islands were rarely in contact with the peoples of Asia or the Americas. But the seafaring ancestors of the Polynesians had sailed great distances to colonize tiny islands in the middle of the ocean.

The Pacific Islands

By the 1300s, Europeans knew that there was an ocean to the east of Asia, but they believed that body of water to be the same Atlantic Ocean that bordered Europe. Once Europeans realized that across the Atlantic lay the Americas, they continued to search for the ocean east of Asia. Vasco Nuñez de BALBOA sighted that body of water from a hilltop in what is now Panama, and Ferdinand MAGELLAN named it the Pacific when he sailed into it seven years later. Balboa and Magellan were right to believe that Asia would be found on the far edge of those waters—but neither of them imagined how far away that was.

Magellan made the first known crossing of the Pacific Ocean and reached what were later called the Philippine Islands. The Portuguese proceeded to explore the western Pacific from Southeast Asia. After Magellan's death in the Philippines, a member of his crew named Juan Sebastián de ELCANO led survivors back to Europe, completing the first **circumnavigation.** Soon navigators such as Miguel López de LEGAZPI, Andrés de URDANETA, Alvaro de MENDAÑA DE NEHRA, and Pedro Fernandez de QUIRÓS were crossing and re-crossing the Pacific for Spain. They brought the Philippines under Spanish control and established regular sailing routes between those islands and Mexico.

The Dutch and the English were also interested in Oceania. In the early and middle 1600s, Dutch mariners Jacob Le Maire, Willem SCHOUTEN, and Abel TASMAN visited many tropical island groups, including the Tuamotu, Tonga, and Fiji Islands. Jacob ROGGEVEEN led the last major Dutch voyage in the Pacific, discovering Easter Island in 1722. English explorers of the Pacific included Francis DRAKE in the 1500s, William DAMPIER in the 1600s, and George ANSON in the early 1700s.

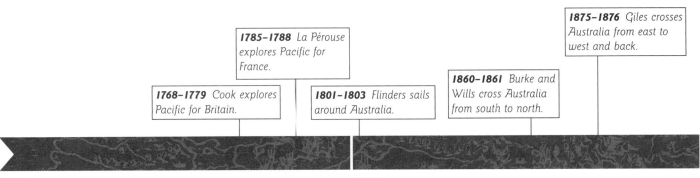

1875–1876 Giles crosses Australia from east to west and back.

1785–1788 La Pérouse explores Pacific for France.

1768–1779 Cook explores Pacific for Britain.

1801–1803 Flinders sails around Australia.

1860–1861 Burke and Wills cross Australia from south to north.

1700

1800

The next stage of Pacific exploration was largely scientific. John Byron, Samuel Wallis, and Philip Carteret led English expeditions to chart parts of Oceania. They also searched for an enormous continent that geographers such as Alexander Dalrymple expected to find in the southern hemisphere. In the late 1700s, James Cook mapped much of the Pacific, proving that the huge southern continent was a myth. Around the same time, Louis-Antoine de Bougainville, Jean François de Galaup de La Pérouse, and Antoine Raymond Joseph de Bruni d'Entrecasteaux sailed the Pacific for France. In the mid-1800s, Charles Wilkes led a major expedition for the United States.

Australia, New Guinea, and New Zealand

Some early explorers of Southeast Asia and the Pacific Ocean caught glimpses of Australia's coast. Willem Jansz made the first known sighting in 1605. Because he was Dutch, the land he saw was long known as New Holland. Dirck Hartog, Abel Tasman, and William Dampier also explored parts of New Holland's coast. It was difficult to explore the dozens of islands, both large and small, that lie off the mainland's northern and eastern coasts. For years mariners did not know whether places they found were separate islands or were connected to the mainland. The work of James Cook, Entrecasteaux, Matthew Flinders, and Nicolas Baudin finally produced a complete map of the coast.

Cook's explorations gave Britain its claim to Australia, which was populated by the Aborigine people. At first the British developed Australia as a prison colony, sending only prisoners and guards to live there. But by the early 1800s, several settlements of free men and women existed on the east coast. Gregory Blaxland and William Charles Wentworth crossed the Blue Mountains in 1813, opening new areas to settlers. Hamilton Hume, Charles Sturt, Edward John Eyre, John McDouall Stuart, and Friedrich Wilhelm Ludwig Leichhardt probed the continent's harsh desert plains. Robert O'Hara Burke and William John Wills were the first to cross the continent from south to north. Ernest Giles made the first journey from east to west and back again. The map of Australia was largely completed by 1880, but not without many disasters.

The early explorers of Australia also investigated the large, nearby islands of New Guinea and New Zealand. New Guinea, a large, mountainous, forested island north of Australia, was first sighted in 1526 by a Portuguese sailor named Jorge de Meneses. In the early 1600s, Spain's Luis Vaez de Torres made a survey of the island's south coast. He was followed by Willem Schouten, Abel Tasman, William Dampier, Philip Carteret, and James Cook. In the mid-1800s, Germany, the Netherlands, and Great Britain competed for the island, which is now divided between the nations of Indonesia and Papua New Guinea.

New Zealand's two main islands lie to the southeast of Australia. Europeans found them populated by a Polynesian people called the Maori. Tasman made the first recorded European sighting of the islands in 1642, and more than a century later, Cook circled and mapped them. After Cook's voyage, the British claimed New Zealand. For a time part of the Australian colony, it is now an independent nation.

The Polar Regions

The frozen Arctic Ocean around the North Pole and the continent of Antarctica around the South Pole were among the last of the earth's regions to be explored. The Arctic is bordered by populated lands: northern Europe, Russia, North America, and Greenland. Peoples such as the Inuit and the Chukchi have lived in Arctic territory for thousands of years. But Antarctica is far from other continents and has never had a human population until explorers found it in the early 1800s. At each end of the globe, travelers in these regions must overcome extreme cold, long winters, and sea ice that can trap or wreck ships.

The Northwest Passage

Northwest Passage water route connecting the Atlantic Ocean and Pacific Ocean through the Arctic islands of northern Canada

Around 1500 the English began the epic, four-century search for the **Northwest Passage.** What they sought was a waterway, far from the southern ocean routes controlled by Spain and Portugal, that would allow ships to cut across North America and sail to Asia. In the late 1500s, the English mariners Martin FROBISHER and John DAVIS searched for the passage in the far north, among ice-choked waterways and snow-covered islands. For the next 350 years, the dream of a Northwest Passage lured hundreds of explorers into the Arctic.

Henry HUDSON thought that he had found the passage, but Hudson Bay proved to be a dead end. William BAFFIN and Robert BYLOT sailed farther north than anyone else had up to that point, but they found no westward route. The English lost interest in the passage for a time and instead built the colonies that became the United States. But by the late 1700s, explorers were again searching the Arctic for the Northwest Passage. James COOK, George VANCOUVER, and other British navigators looked for the western end of the passage as they explored the Pacific coast of North America. Spanish explorers also probed this coast, without success.

By about 1800, geographers realized that there is no easy way to sail through or around North America. They knew that if the passage existed, it would certainly be dangerous, narrow, and clogged with ice. Merchants carrying cargo would not be able to use it. But in the early 1800s, Britain launched a new effort to find the passage, mainly to satisfy scientific curiosity and national pride. William Edward PARRY made much progress, but John FRANKLIN's expedition was never heard from again. During the long search for Franklin and his crew, explorers such as Francis Leopold McCLINTOCK and Robert John Le Mesurier McCLURE filled in the map of the Canadian Arctic. McClure also found the long-sought Northwest Passage, but he had to abandon his ship without sailing through it. This feat was at last completed by Roald AMUNDSEN of Norway in a small boat, on a voyage that lasted from 1903 to 1906.

The Northeast Passage

To sail from Europe to Asia was a cherished goal for many nations. In the 1500s, Portugal controlled the southern route around Africa. The western route across the Atlantic turned out to be blocked by

Northeast Passage water route connecting the Atlantic Ocean and Pacific Ocean along the Arctic coastline of Europe and Asia

the Americas, so some people looked to the northeast. They hoped to find a **Northeast Passage**—a sea route to Asia through the Arctic Ocean north of Europe and Russia. By the end of the 1500s, England's Sebastian Cabot and Richard Chancellor and the Netherlands' Willem Barents had sailed north of Norway and reached ports in northern Russia. In the mid-1700s, Vitus Bering led a massive nine-year expedition to map Russia's Arctic coastline. Most people still believed that the Northeast Passage was too cold and dangerous for safe shipping. Nils Adolf Erik Nordenskiöld proved them wrong in 1879 by becoming the first explorer to sail through the entire Northeast Passage. He had to spend the winter in a harbor along the way, but 53 years later, an icebreaking ship called the *Sibiryakov* crossed the passage in a single season. Since that time, the Northeast Passage has been used regularly to ship cargo between western Russia and Siberia.

The Arctic

boat-sledge boat mounted on sled runners to allow travel on both ice and water

The explorers who searched for the Northwest and Northeast Passages sometimes tried to sail as far north as possible. They were always forced to turn back where the Arctic Ocean had frozen to ice. William Parry tried to travel north over the ice, using **boat-sledges,** but he had little success. Some geographers and explorers believed that the ice was only a ring, beyond which the polar sea was open and free of ice. Elisha Kent Kane, Charles Francis Hall, and George Washington De Long were among the Americans who tried to cross the ice. Austro-Hungarians Julius von Payer and Karl Weyprecht discovered land north of Russia that they named Franz Josef Land. Fridtjof Nansen of Norway followed the drift of the polar ice, and Sweden's Salomon August Andrée tried to reach the North Pole in a balloon.

By the time people realized that ice covered the entire polar region, Arctic exploration had become a race to reach the North Pole. Americans Frederick Albert Cook and Robert Edwin Peary both claimed to have been first. The public accepted Peary as the victor, but today some researchers believe that both men's claims were false. There is no doubt that Walter William Herbert crossed the pole by dogsled in 1969, and both the Russian icebreaker *Arktika* and the American submarine *Nautilus* reached it by sea. But by that time, people had long been exploring the Arctic by air. As early as the 1920s, Roald Amundsen, Richard Evelyn Byrd, Lincoln

THE EXPLORATION OF THE POLAR REGIONS

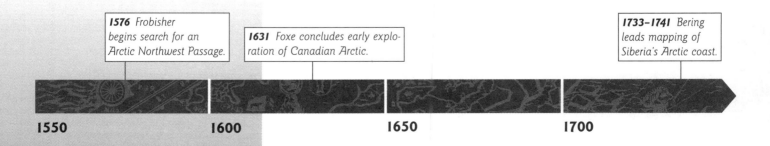

1576 *Frobisher begins search for an Arctic Northwest Passage.*

1631 *Foxe concludes early exploration of Canadian Arctic.*

1733–1741 *Bering leads mapping of Siberia's Arctic coast.*

1550   1600   1650   1700

In the polar regions, many explorers relied on sleds that were pulled by dogs and steered by a driver.

dirigible large aircraft filled with a lighter-than-air gas that keeps it aloft; similar to a blimp but with a rigid frame

ELLSWORTH, and Umberto NOBILE crossed over the pole in airplanes or **dirigibles.** An American Air Force plane landed at the pole in 1952, making Joseph Fletcher the first person known to have set foot there.

Antarctica

During the 1700s, mariners such as James COOK sailed far enough south to encounter the ice around Antarctica, but they could not see the continent itself. By 1800, ships hunting whales and seals were visiting seas and islands in the far south, and some of these crews may have seen the mainland. In 1820 Fabian von BELLING-SHAUSEN of Russia made the first confirmed sightings of the Antarctic coast. Jules-Sébastien-César DUMONT D'URVILLE, Charles WILKES, and James ROSS also sailed to Antarctica in the next few decades.

Like the North Pole, the South Pole became a magnet for explorers and nations seeking glory. Frederick Cook and Ernest SHACKLETON tried and failed to reach the pole. Roald Amundsen succeeded in 1911, beating Robert Falcon SCOTT by a matter of days. In the

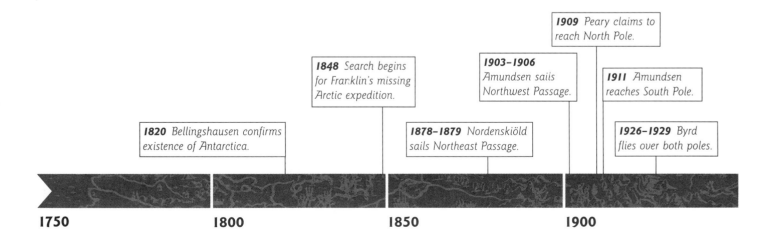

1820 *Bellingshausen confirms existence of Antarctica.*

1848 *Search begins for Franklin's missing Arctic expedition.*

1878–1879 *Nordenskiöld sails Northeast Passage.*

1903–1906 *Amundsen sails Northwest Passage.*

1909 *Peary claims to reach North Pole.*

1911 *Amundsen reaches South Pole.*

1926–1929 *Byrd flies over both poles.*

1750   1800   1850   1900

years that followed, George Hubert WILKINS, Lincoln Ellsworth, and Richard Byrd competed to reach the pole and to explore the continent by air. Fifteen nations have established bases in Antarctica, partly to support scientific research and partly to stake a claim to land and natural resources. The international Antarctic Treaty, signed in 1959, prohibits both commercial and military activities on the continent.

Space

Scientists have studied the solar system and outer space for many centuries by looking at the night sky. But the physical exploration of space began in the mid-1900s, when people first began using **rockets** to leave the earth. Rockets were developed mainly by military scientists, and the specially trained pilots who go into space are often officers in their nations' armed forces. The early exploration of space was in some ways a military competition between the United States and the **Soviet Union.** It was also a great scientific effort.

In 1957 the Soviets launched *Sputnik 1,* the first **satellite** to **orbit** the earth. Space scientists in both nations then raced feverishly toward the next goal: to send a human being into space. They trained elite groups of **astronauts** and **cosmonauts** to fly the next generation of spacecraft.

Orbiting the Earth

In 1961 cosmonaut Yuri GAGARIN began the Soviet Union's Vostok program in a **capsule** named *Swallow.* He was the first person to travel into space. Gagarin orbited the earth once and then piloted the *Swallow* back to the Soviet Union. A month later, American astronaut Alan SHEPARD rode a Mercury capsule called *Freedom 7* into space, and John GLENN made three orbits of the earth the following year in *Friendship 7.*

It was a period of intense rivalry between the United States and the Soviet Union. Both nations made rapid advances in space technology. For a time, the Soviets led the way, and they made history

rocket vehicle propelled by exploding fuel

Soviet Union nation that existed from 1922 to 1991, made up of Russia and 14 other republics in eastern Europe and northern Asia

satellite object launched into space to circle a planet or moon

orbit stable, circular route; one trip around; to revolve around

astronaut American term for a person who travels into space; literally, "traveler to the stars"

cosmonaut Russian term for a person who travels into space; literally, "traveler to the universe"

capsule small early spacecraft designed to carry a person around the earth

THE EXPLORATION OF SPACE

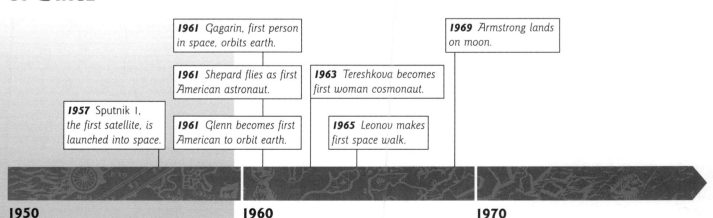

1961 Gagarin, first person in space, orbits earth.

1969 Armstrong lands on moon.

1961 Shepard flies as first American astronaut.

1963 Tereshkova becomes first woman cosmonaut.

1957 Sputnik 1, the first satellite, is launched into space.

1961 Glenn becomes first American to orbit earth.

1965 Leonov makes first space walk.

1950   1960   1970

In a new era of discovery, people have left the earth and begun the exploration of space.

space station spacecraft that circles the earth for months or years with a human crew

NASA National Aeronautics and Space Administration, the U.S. space agency

space shuttle reusable spacecraft designed to transport both people and cargo between the earth and space

again when Valentina TERESHKOVA became the first woman in space, aboard Vostok 6, the *Sea Gull.* The Soviets launched the first two spacecraft to link together in space, as well as the first spacecraft to carry more than one person. Cosmonaut Aleksei LEONOV was the first person to "walk" in space, floating at the end of a cable outside the Voskhod 2 capsule *Diamond.*

Soon, however, American astronauts were setting new records for time spent in space. They were also the first to link two spacecraft flying in orbit around the earth. Such maneuvers were part of the American effort to reach a new goal, set by President John F. Kennedy: to land on the moon.

Missions to the Moon

For many years, Soviet and American space scientists launched small spacecraft without crews to photograph and study the moon. These probes prepared the way for the Soviet Soyuz and American Apollo programs. The United States won this stage of the "space race." In 1968 the crew of Apollo 8 made ten orbits of the moon. A year later, Apollo 11 landed Neil ARMSTRONG and Edwin "Buzz" Aldrin, Jr., on the moon's surface.

The United States sent six more missions to the moon, partly to demonstrate the nation's superiority in space and partly to conduct scientific research. The high cost of the missions and a decline in public interest ended the Apollo program in 1972. But some scientists predict that people will return to the moon at a later stage of space exploration—perhaps to establish bases, mines, or colonies.

Stations and Shuttles

While Americans explored the moon, Soviets experimented with **space stations,** on which cosmonauts could live and work for long periods. In 1971 the Soviet Union launched its first space station, *Salyut 1,* and cosmonauts began setting new records for time spent in space. Five more Salyut stations reached orbit, as did an American station, *Skylab.*

Meanwhile, **NASA** developed a series of **space shuttles** that took crews into orbit around the earth. Dozens of astronauts—including Sally RIDE, the first American woman to travel in space—conducted

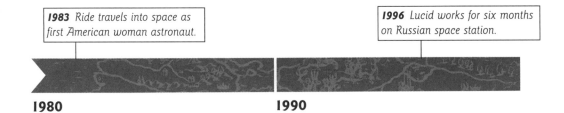

1983 Ride travels into space as first American woman astronaut.

1996 Lucid works for six months on Russian space station.

1980   **1990**

scientific experiments in the shuttles. The shuttles were also useful for retrieving old satellites and placing new ones in orbit. The program suffered a major setback when the shuttle *Challenger* exploded during a launch in 1986, but flights resumed at the end of the decade.

In 1986 the Soviet Union launched a large space station named *Mir,* which means "peace." As competition between the United States and the Soviet Union eased, *Mir* was visited by astronauts from several nations. Shannon LUCID, an American astronaut, spent six months aboard the station. In the 1990s, after the Soviet Union disbanded, the governments of Russia, the United States, and other countries began considering more international projects. Their ideas included a new space station and a landing on Mars. At the end of the decade, these nations practiced using space shuttles to assemble a space station in orbit around the earth.

European nations—as well as China, Japan, India, and others—continued to become more active in space in the 1980s. They launched satellites that joined the hundreds now orbiting the earth. These devices perform a wide range of services, from broadcasting television to predicting the weather.

The first human-made objects to leave our solar system were probes such as *Pioneer 10* and *Voyager 1.* But most space exploration is still carried out by scientists on the earth. They receive information from probes and satellites. For example, in 1997 the U.S. Mars Pathfinder project sent a remote-controlled robotic vehicle to the surface of Mars. Instruments such as telescopes—both on the earth and in orbit—are also used to study the planets and stars of the universe.

Biographical Profiles

Acuña, Cristóbal de

Spanish
b 1597?; Burgos, Spain
d 1676; Lima, Peru
***Produced earliest published account
of Amazon River***

Jesuit member of the Society of Jesus, a Roman Catholic order founded by Ignatius of Loyola in 1534

Treaty of Tordesillas agreement between Spain and Portugal dividing the rights to discovered lands along a north-south line

league unit of distance, usually used at sea, roughly equal to 3.5 miles

In the first published description of South America's Amazon region, Father Cristóbal de Acuña described more than 150 Indian nations.

In 1639 Father Cristóbal de Acuña left his post as head of a **Jesuit** college in Spain to make an extraordinary journey. Acuña was part of an expedition that sailed from Peru to Pará (now Belém), Brazil, along the mighty Amazon River. During the trip, the Jesuit priest wrote about everything he saw. His journal became the first published description of South America's Amazon region.

From Priest to Explorer

Acuña was born in Burgos, a city in northern Spain. The exact date of his birth is unknown, as are the details of his life before and after his Amazon adventure. Acuña arrived in Peru in the 1620s, and he was named the head of the college at Cuenca, then part of Peru.

At the time, Spain and Portugal were competing to control South America, particularly the regions near the Amazon River. In 1638 a Portuguese captain, Pedro de Teixeira, sailed up the Amazon River from Pará, Brazil, to the Spanish town of Quito (in modern-day Ecuador). His journey alarmed Spanish officials, who worried that the Portuguese would try to take control of Peru. The Spanish realized that a better knowledge of the Amazon would help them to protect their territory and to support their claim to the Amazon as stated in the **Treaty of Tordesillas.**

The Spanish decided that Teixeira could not be allowed to return to Portuguese territory unless he took a Spaniard with him. The governor of Quito, Don Juan Vásquez de Acuña, volunteered to make the trip. His brother, Father Cristóbal de Acuña, was chosen instead. Acuña's instructions were to "describe, with clearness, the distance in **leagues,** the provinces, tribes of Indians, rivers, and districts. . . ."

The Teixeira expedition left Quito on February 16, 1639, heading down the Napo River toward the Amazon. Acuña noted the many small rivers that fed into the Amazon from the upper Amazon Valley. These rivers would allow colonists to ship goods from the Spanish territories of Peru and New Granada (now Colombia) directly to the Atlantic Ocean. The Teixeira expedition traveled down the Marañón River (the upper Amazon). Acuña was particularly impressed by the Agua Indians, whom he described as the "most intelligent and best governed of any tribe on the river."

The Wonders of the Amazon

When Acuña finally saw the Amazon itself, he wrote that it was "the largest and most celebrated river in the world." Acuña's writings reflected the excitement he felt in seeing what seemed like a paradise. He wrote that "the river is full of fish, the forests with game, the air of birds, the trees are covered with fruit. . . ."

Acuña recommended that the Spanish develop the resources along the river. He imagined a day when Spanish plantations would grow tobacco and sugar cane, and shipyards would build with Amazon lumber. Medicines could be produced by learning from the Indians' knowledge of herbs. Acuña also found the climate pleasing, neither too hot nor too cold.

Nearly everything the Jesuit priest saw impressed him, from the land to the people who lived on it. He carefully documented more than 150 Indian nations, describing their customs, languages, trading practices, and wars with one another.

Acuña took an interest in the Indians' turtle roundups. Captured turtles were kept in wooden holding tanks until the Indians needed them for food. Acuña reported that "turtle eggs were almost as good as hen's eggs," though harder to digest. He was also fascinated by an unusual method of fishing. The Indians beat the water with poisonous vines, causing the stunned fish to float to the surface.

Acuña was upset only by the Portuguese, who made raids along the river to kidnap Indians as slaves. This practice made the Indians fearful of all Europeans. The tribes either fled inland as Acuña's expedition passed or treated the Europeans with false kindness. Once, when the Portuguese soldiers wanted to capture Indians, Acuña protested strongly to Teixeira. The captain agreed to call off the raid and continue down the river.

Science and Legends

In his journal, Acuña wrote scientific reports about the creatures he saw. These included the manatee and what is now called the electric eel. In Acuña's words, the manatee "has hair all over its body, not very long, like soft bristles, and the animal moves in the water with short fins. . . ." The eel, Acuña wrote, "has the peculiarity that, when [it is] alive, whoever touches it trembles all over his body. . . ." These notes were the first recorded descriptions of the animals to reach Europe.

As they proceeded down the river, the explorers met the Tupinambá Indians, who had migrated 3,500 miles to escape the Portuguese invasion of Brazil. Acuña described these Indians as "noble-hearted" and welcoming. The Tupinambá told him the legends of the Amazons, a civilization of women warriors. They also repeated legends he had heard from other tribes, about lands filled with giants, pygmies, and men whose feet were turned backward. Acuña never judged the stories he heard; he simply wrote them down, believing that "time will discover the truth."

After the Journey

The expedition reached Pará on December 16, 1639. Acuña immediately wrote to the king of Spain, recommending that the king act quickly to take control of "Amazonia." The priest also urged the king to stop the Indian wars and to support a plan to convert the Indians to Christianity. Acuña eventually traveled to Spain to present his report in person.

Acuña's account of his journey, *New Discovery of the Great River of the Amazons,* was published in 1641. By that time, however, Spain had lost its claim to the Amazon. Captain Teixeira had succeeded in extending Portuguese control over the region. A disappointed Acuña returned to his religious duties in Peru. Though his efforts had not helped Spain, he was the first to provide a detailed account of the Amazon region and the vast potential of its natural resources.

Suggested Reading Cristóbal de Acuña, *Expeditions into the Valley of the Amazons,* edited by Clements R. Markham (Hakluyt Society, 1859).

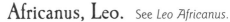

Africanus, Leo. *See Leo Africanus.*

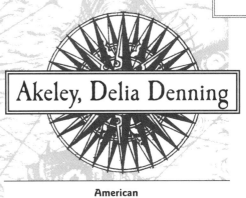

Akeley, Delia Denning

American
b December 5, 1875; Beaver Dam, Wisconsin
d May 22, 1970; Daytona Beach, Florida
*Explored Africa, collecting plants and
animals for museums*

specimen sample of a plant, animal, or
mineral, usually collected for scientific study
or display

Delia Denning Akeley pursued a successful
career as a scientific explorer of Africa.

Delia Denning Akeley studied the wildlife and peoples of Africa. Working mostly in the tropical lands along the equator, she collected **specimens** of the plants and animals she found. Akeley's work helped educate Americans, who were eager to learn about a distant, exotic continent.

African Adventures

We know very little about Delia Denning's life before she met the man who became her husband, Carl F. Akeley. He was a sculptor at the Milwaukee Art Museum. Working as his assistant, Delia helped him create realistic animal exhibits for museums. Akeley took a job at the Field Museum in Chicago, and shortly after, he and Delia were married.

At the Field Museum, Carl Akeley became famous for the lifelike animals in his exhibits. In 1905 he traveled to Kenya, in East Africa, to collect specimens for a new exhibit. Delia joined him on the journey.

The Akeleys spent 18 months in East Africa, searching for birds and animals to bring to America. Delia fell in love with Africa, and her strong passion for the continent deepened throughout her life.

In 1909 the Akeleys returned to Africa to collect elephants for the American Museum of Natural History in New York City. During the trip, Carl was often sick or injured, but Delia carried on with their work. In addition to searching for specimens, Delia also studied families of baboons, noting their similarities to humans.

On Her Own

Carl and Delia divorced in 1923, and in 1924 Carl married Mary Lee Jobe AKELEY. He died two years later. Delia did not generally receive credit for the contributions she had made to his early work. In the meantime, however, she had become a respected explorer herself. The Brooklyn Museum of Arts and Sciences sent her to East Africa to collect specimens for an exhibit.

Delia Akeley spent 10 weeks traveling on the Tana River and then crossed the desert of Somalia. From Kenya, she sent her completed collection to the United States. After finishing this work, she made a difficult journey into the Ituri Forest of the Belgian Congo (now the Democratic Republic of Congo). There she lived with and studied a local tribe, the Pygmies, who were known for their short stature. When she returned to the United States, Akeley wrote and lectured about her many African adventures.

Suggested Reading Delia Akeley, *J. T., Jr.: The Biography of an African Monkey* (Macmillan, 1928) and *Jungle Portraits* (Macmillan, 1930); Elizabeth Flagg Olds, *Women of the Four Winds* (Houghton Mifflin, 1985); Mignon Rittenhouse, *Seven Women Explorers* (Lippincott, 1964).

Akeley, Mary Lee Jobe

American
b January 28, 1878; Tappan, Ohio
d July 19, 1966; Stonington, Connecticut
Explored Africa and Canada

specimen sample of a plant, animal, or mineral, usually collected for scientific study or display

On her trips through the Canadian Rocky Mountains, Mary Lee Jobe Akeley won fame as a mountain climber, and a peak is named for her.

Mary Lee Jobe Akeley is best known for bringing public attention to the natural wonders of Africa. First with her husband and then on her own, she explored central and eastern Africa, photographing the beauty of the region's scenery and wildlife.

After studying in both Ohio and Pennsylvania, Mary Lee Jobe taught at Hunter College in New York City. In 1909 she took a break from teaching to make an expedition to British Columbia, Canada. That monthlong trip stirred her interest in exploration. She returned many times to the Canadian northwest to study the region's tribes and vegetation. In 1924 she married the naturalist Carl F. Akeley and turned her attention to his primary interest, Africa.

Bringing Africa to America

Carl Akeley wanted to create an exhibit called the Great African Hall at the American Museum of Natural History in New York City. In 1926 he led a trip to the Belgian Congo (now the Democratic Republic of Congo) to collect plant and animal **specimens** for the exhibit. He also intended to study the region's gorillas.

On the trip, Carl died of a fever, but Mary Lee completed the study of the gorillas and collected additional specimens for the museum. She also mapped areas of East Africa that had not yet been explored, and she studied the languages and cultures of local tribes.

The next year, Mary Lee Akeley came to New York with her specimens and helped assemble the African Hall exhibit. She returned to Africa in 1935 to gather more materials for the exhibit. Akeley's groundbreaking work led people to call her the woman who "brought the jungle to Central Park West." (The American Museum of Natural History is located on Central Park West in New York City.)

Preserving the Beauty of Africa

In the years between her first two trips to Africa, Akeley reported her work to King Albert of Belgium, who awarded her the Cross of the Knight. She also helped the Belgians expand a national park in the Congo.

Akeley became one of the leading voices in the growing effort to preserve Africa's natural beauty. Her numerous books and photos persuaded others to protect the continent's unique cultures and wildlife.

Suggested Reading Mary Lee Jobe Akeley, *Carl Akeley's Africa* (Dodd, Mead and Company, 1929) and *The Wilderness Lives Again* (Dodd, Mead and Company, 1940); Crowther Dawn-Starr, *Mary L. Jobe Akeley* (School of Art, Arizona State University, 1989).

Albuquerque, Afonso de

Portuguese
b 1453; Alhandra, near Lisbon, Portugal
d December 15, 1515; at sea off Goa, India
Strengthened Portuguese power in East Asia

courtier attendant at a royal court

corsair fast pirate ship

Afonso de Albuquerque was a brilliant but cruel admiral who made the most of his limited resources.

Afonso de Albuquerque was a charming **courtier,** a ruthless warrior, and a successful naval commander. While serving Portugal in India in the early 1500s, Albuquerque worked to strengthen his country's weak hold on these distant lands. He tried to create naval bases in the region to preserve the empire and to control the valuable spice trade.

Early Military Career

Albuquerque was born in 1453 in Alhandra, near Lisbon. He came from a wealthy military family with close ties to the royal family of Portugal. As a young soldier, Albuquerque fought in North Africa against Portugal's Muslim enemies. After 10 years in Africa, he returned to the court of Manuel I, king of Portugal.

At the time, Portugal was influential in the spice trade, thanks to its early expeditions to Asia. Vasco da GAMA had reached India in 1499, an achievement that led to a series of Portuguese trading posts along India's southwestern coast. The Asian spice trade was extremely profitable. Many Indian rulers, however, were hostile to the Europeans. To protect Portugal's interests in India, King Manuel sent a naval squadron there in 1503, led by Albuquerque.

Albuquerque's mission was to secure trade routes around the southern tip of Africa and into the Indian Ocean. A clever diplomat, he used words, not guns, to achieve his first victory. Albuquerque persuaded the ruler of Cochin, in southwest India, to let the Portuguese build a fortress there. It was Portugal's first military base in Asia.

Years of Battle

In 1506 Albuquerque led a naval expedition against the Muslims who lived near the Persian Gulf. He wanted to close off their way to India. The next year, the Portuguese captured the city of Hormuz, which overlooks the entrance to the Persian Gulf. After the battle, Albuquerque showed his savage side, ordering his men to cut off the noses and ears of the female prisoners. The male prisoners lost their noses and right hands.

In 1509 Albuquerque was named governor-general of Portugal's Indian lands. Seeking a better harbor for his ships, he invaded the port city of Goa. Backed by 23 ships as well as by Indian **corsairs,** the Portuguese waged a bitter struggle with Goa's Muslim forces. When Albuquerque's troops finally took the city, they slaughtered the defenders.

Using Goa as a base, Albuquerque continued to expand Portuguese power in Asia. He captured the city of Malacca, on the Malay Peninsula. Control of the nearby waterways gave Portugal a secure sea route to China.

Despite Albuquerque's successes, however, Portugal was unable to maintain its empire. The nation's forces were spread too thin to defend their territory against the Muslims and other European powers. During yet another military expedition in 1515, Albuquerque fell ill and died on board a ship near Goa.

Greek
b 356 B.C.; Pella, Macedonia
d June 13, 323 B.C.; Babylon
*Explored and conquered Middle East
and central Asia*

As a young man, Alexander claimed to be a relative of Achilles, one of ancient Greece's greatest heroes.

Suggested Reading Afonso de Albuquerque, *The Commentaries of the Great Alfonso Dalboquerque, Second Viceroy of India*, translated by Walter de Gray Birch (B. Franklin, 1970); Elaine Sanceau, *Indies Adventure: The Amazing Career of Afonso de Albuquerque, Captain-General and Governor of India (1509–1515)* (Blackie, 1936).

Alexander the Great, king of Macedonia, was one of the most successful generals in history. By the time he was 30 years old, he had created a huge empire in Asia, Europe, and Africa. He led his army to regions that no European had ever fully explored.

More than just a skilled military leader, Alexander was also a learned man who appreciated science and the arts. As a young man, he had been tutored by Aristotle, the great thinker and scientist of ancient Greece. Exploration became one of Alexander's main goals as he led his armies through foreign lands. Although he could be cruel in war, he had the wisdom to treat his enemies well when they came under his rule. He built cities in the lands he conquered and spread Greek culture in Asia. His empire could not survive without him, however, and it collapsed after he died suddenly at the age of 33.

A Prince Becomes King

Alexander was born in 356 B.C. at Pella, north of Greece. He was the son of King Philip II of Macedonia and Queen Olympias. While Alexander was still a child, his parents divorced, and he and his mother fled the court. Alexander was later reunited with his father and fought by his side. Philip and Alexander defeated the Greeks and then led them against their common enemy, the Persians.

When Philip was assassinated in 336 B.C., Alexander acted quickly to take power. He executed the people he thought were responsible for his father's death—and anyone else who challenged his authority. At the age of 21, Alexander was secure as king, and he decided to carry out his father's plan to destroy the Persian Empire.

In the spring of 334 B.C., Alexander set out with an army of 35,000 soldiers. Along the Aegean coast (in what is now Turkey), he captured Greek cities that had been occupied by the Persians. Proceeding east, he defeated an army led by the Persian king Darius III at the Battle of Issus. Darius, however, managed to escape.

Conquering the Persians

Alexander next turned to Tyre (in modern-day Lebanon), Persia's main port on the Mediterranean Sea. After fierce fighting, the Greeks took Tyre in 332 B.C., and Alexander ordered that the city's women and children be sold as slaves. With this victory, Alexander was the master of the eastern Mediterranean. Later that year, Alexander reached Egypt. He was crowned pharaoh and founded the city of Alexandria.

Alexander returned north in pursuit of Darius. Greek and Persian forces clashed near the city of Nineveh (in present-day Iraq), and the Persians suffered their worst defeat of the war. Once again, Darius escaped, but he was later assassinated by one of his own generals. Alexander had reached the heart of the Persian Empire. He marched triumphantly to the great city of Persepolis and then occupied the Persian capital of Ecbatana (present-day Hamadan, Iran). After these victories, Alexander ruled all of Persia and commanded an army of more than 200,000.

East to India

For two years, Alexander remained in central Asia. Based in Tehran, his armies roamed eastward through the lands now known as Afghanistan, Turkmenistan, and Uzbekistan. Next, Alexander set his sights on India. He led his troops across the Hindu Kush mountain range, and in the summer of 327 B.C., they reached the northern part of the Indus River.

Alexander and his army marched across the plains of Punjab, the edge of the world known to Europeans at that time. Even the Persians had not crossed this region. After defeating a local army, Alexander heard about another great river to the east (most likely the Ganges River). He was determined to push deeper into India. He hoped to find the great sea that ancient Europeans believed surrounded the lands of the earth. Having already crossed the known world, Alexander's weary troops refused to go any further.

Alexander ordered a general named NEARCHUS to build a fleet to sail down the Indus River. He believed that the Indus was the source of the Nile River and would lead his army back to Egypt.

Like others in his time, Alexander did not know that east of India was the vast kingdom of China.

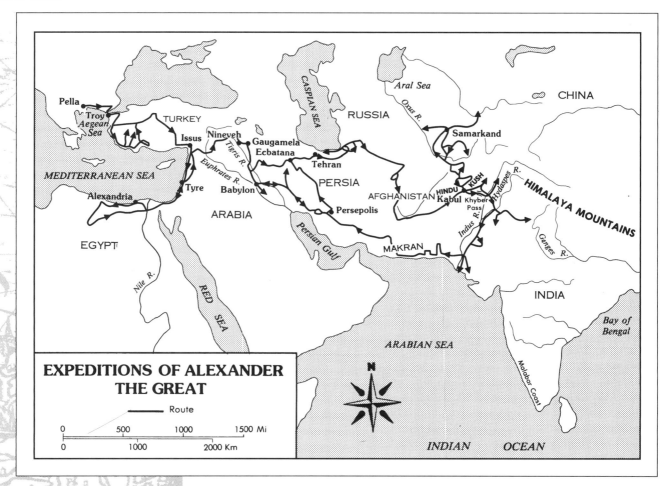

EXPEDITIONS OF ALEXANDER THE GREAT

—— Route

0   500   1000   1500 Mi
0   1000   2000 Km

The local people, however, told Alexander that the Indus led south to a great sea—the Indian Ocean. He decided to explore this sea, still convinced that it would take him back to Egypt.

A Disastrous Return Trip

Alexander loaded part of his army onto his new fleet of ships. He and the rest of his troops marched along the riverbank, battling local warriors as they went. For nine months, the army trudged on, covering 1,000 miles to the mouth of the Indus River on the Arabian Sea.

Alexander then divided his soldiers into three groups. The sick and wounded were ordered to march back to Persia. Nearchus and the fleet were to sail west along the coast, exploring the Arabian Sea and the Persian Gulf. Alexander's army was to march along the shore, providing the fleet with supplies.

In the fall of 325 B.C., the fleet set sail, but Alexander's plan soon went horribly wrong. During its 130-day voyage, Nearchus's fleet met Alexander's army only once. Food and water were scarce along the barren coast. Many of the men on the ships died before the fleet reached the mouth of the Euphrates River in Persia.

Meanwhile, the rough terrain along the shore forced Alexander to march inland. This trek was also a disaster. Crossing the Makran desert in the region now called Pakistan, the troops found little food or water. Many died from hunger or thirst. Eventually the soldiers found a **caravan** route that led back to Persepolis and on to what is now Iran.

The End of an Empire

Since the start of its expedition, Alexander's army had marched more than 25,000 miles. But Alexander's days of exploration and conquest were over. He spent his last two years trying to strengthen his control over his new lands. He hoped to combine the best of the Greek and Persian cultures by having his Greek officers marry Persian wives. Alexander himself married a daughter of King Darius.

Alexander, however, was showing signs of mental strain. He claimed he was a son of the gods and had divine powers. In fact, he was all too human. He fell ill after a long bout of drinking and died of a fever on June 13, 323 B.C.

Without his leadership, the empire quickly collapsed into several smaller parts ruled by his quarreling relatives and generals. Still, Alexander's achievements truly earned him the nickname "the Great." His travels and military conquests united the known world, planting the seeds for increased trade and the sharing of culture and knowledge among distant lands.

Suggested Reading Robin L. Fox, *The Search for Alexander* (Little, Brown, 1980); Harold Lamb, *Alexander of Macedon: The Journey to World's End* (Doubleday, 1946); Aubrey de Selincourt, *The Campaigns of Alexander* (Penguin, 1976).

caravan large group of people traveling together, often with pack animals, across a desert or other dangerous region

---

al-Idrisi. See *Idrisi, al-*.

Almagro, Diego de

Spanish
b 1474?; Almagro, Spain
d July, 1538; near Cuzco, Peru
Explored Chile by land

conquistador Spanish or Portuguese explorer and military leader in the Americas

adelantado Spanish leader of a military expedition to America during the 1500s who also served as governor and judge

league unit of distance, usually used at sea, roughly equal to 3.5 miles

Diego de Almagro was described in his time as "a man of short stature, with ugly features, but of great courage and endurance."

Diego de Almagro, an explorer and **conquistador,** took part in one of the greatest adventures in the history of exploration. It was also one of the most brutal attacks on a native population. With Francisco PIZARRO, Almagro discovered and conquered the great Inca civilization of what is now Peru. Hoping to discover a vast fortune in gold, Almagro then led the first European expedition to explore the area that is now Chile by land.

Diego de Almagro was probably born about 1474 in the town of Almagro, in the Estremadura region of Spain. Until he was 40, he wandered across Spain, looking for adventure, and he once murdered a man in a brawl. In 1514 Almagro traveled to the Americas and arrived in what is now Colombia.

In Search of the Inca

After a decade in South America, Almagro teamed up with Francisco Pizarro. The two men pooled resources with a wealthy priest to invest in farming, mining, and the slave trade. The men then planned an expedition to find the Inca Empire, which was called Birú. The Inca were rumored to possess incredible wealth.

Almagro and Pizarro set out in 1525. During the first of two unsuccessful trips, Almagro lost an eye and several fingers in a battle with Indians. At the end of 1530, Pizarro tricked Almagro and made another trip, this time alone. He had won permission from the Spanish government to lead the Peruvian conquest and keep most of the Inca fortunes he found for himself. Almagro was angry, but he was apparently satisfied after Pizarro promised to share his future riches.

Almagro gathered recruits and supplies and met Pizarro at Cajamarca, Peru, in 1533. The combined forces of Almagro, Pizarro, and Hernando de SOTO marched 750 miles from Cajamarca to Cuzco, the Inca capital. The Spanish captured the city, and Pizarro named Almagro governor of Cuzco.

Exploration of Chile

In 1534 the king of Spain named Almagro **adelantado** of New Toledo, a province that extended some 200 **leagues** south from Pizarro's territory of New Castile. The two leaders quarreled over whose lands included the Inca capital. Pizarro avoided a war by encouraging Almagro to explore New Toledo along the Pacific Ocean.

Almagro left Cuzco on July 3, 1535. His forces included 750 Spaniards and 12,000 Indians, and he hoped to find a rich civilization like that of the Inca. Following the route used by the Incas, the expedition passed Lake Titicaca (on the border of modern Peru and Bolivia). Almagro then tried to march during the winter—a costly mistake. He lost many soldiers, Indians, and horses before he finally stopped in the Salta Valley.

When the journey was resumed, the expedition made a difficult trek across the Andes and then turned south into the plain of northern Chile. Almagro and his forces eventually reached the site of Santiago, today the capital of Chile.

During the long march, Almagro's forces committed many gruesome acts of violence against the Indians they met and captured.

Father Cristóbal de Molina, a priest who kept notes on the journey, described some of these brutal scenes. He wrote that the Indian prisoners walked in long lines, chained together at the neck. When a prisoner died, his head was cut off so that his body could be removed without undoing the chains.

Failure and Death

After months of exploration, Almagro and his forces had not found great treasures. Weary and disappointed, the expedition headed back to Cuzco. The explorers took a coastal route north, and they became the first Europeans to cross the 600-mile-long Atacama Desert in northern Chile.

When Almagro returned to Cuzco, he found the city under attack by Manco, an Inca leader. Almagro defeated Manco and claimed the city for himself. This action led to war between Almagro and his old partner, Pizarro, who was supported by his three half brothers. Almagro won an early battle but was eventually defeated and captured. After an unjust trial, held only for show, he was beheaded in July 1538. His son later took revenge by murdering Francisco Pizarro.

Diego de Almagro won wealth, power, and fame for his part in the conquest of Peru. His place among explorers, however, was guaranteed by his remarkable expedition through Chile.

Suggested Reading Gerald Green, *The Sword and the Sun: A Story of the Spanish Civil Wars in Peru* (Scribner, 1953).

---

al-Mas'udi. See *Mas'udi, al-*.

---

al-Nasibi, ibn Hawqal. See *Ibn Hawqal*.

Alvarado, Pedro de

Spanish
b 1485?; Badajoz, Spain
d June 29, 1541; Jalisco, Mexico
Explored Guatemala, El Salvador, Mexico, and Ecuador

conquistador Spanish or Portuguese explorer and military leader in the Americas

Beginning with his first expedition to Mexico in 1518, Pedro de Alvarado always sought unknown regions to explore. He first served under the command of others, then became a **conquistador** himself. He led a successful mission to Guatemala and El Salvador. Later Alvarado entered the province of Quito (present-day Ecuador) to look for Inca riches, only to find that Francisco PIZARRO had already arrived there.

Alvarado was born in about 1485 in Badajoz, in the Spanish province of Estremadura. We know little about his life before 1510, when he landed in the West Indies with his four brothers. For the next eight years, Alvarado helped run a plantation in Santo Domingo (now the capital of the Dominican Republic). He was then named commander of a ship sent to the Yucatán peninsula of Mexico. During the journey, Alvarado earned a reputation as a brave though sometimes cruel man.

Pedro de Alvarado survived bitter cold while exploring the Andes, but many of his soldiers froze to death in the heavy mountain snow.

plateau high, flat area of land

Trouble with the Aztecs

Alvarado next joined Hernán CORTÉS to push farther into Mexico. Cortés and his forces discovered and conquered the Aztecs, who had ruled the most powerful empire in Mexico. During this time, Alvarado became Cortés's second-in-command. When Cortés had to leave the Aztec capital of Tenochtitlán, he left Alvarado in charge.

Alvarado tried to intervene in the Aztec religious ceremonies, hoping to stop the practice of human sacrifice. The Aztecs' resistance resulted in the death of 200 of their nobles. When Cortés returned to the city, he and his forces had to retreat to avoid war with the Aztecs. By 1523, however, Cortés had regained Tenochtitlán as well as the rest of Mexico. Alvarado received permission to explore and conquer Central America.

Fighting Through Unknown Territory

During his expedition to Central America, Alvarado proved to be a strong leader. He won the loyalty of his men and the respect of the Indians he conquered. Details of this trip come primarily from two letters that Alvarado sent to Cortés.

Alvarado and his forces traveled south along the western coast of Mexico, reaching the city of Tehuantepac with little trouble. From there on, Alvarado constantly battled Indians as he headed east into Guatemala. The Indians' resistance, however, was greatly weakened by an epidemic of smallpox, a disease that had come with the Europeans to the Americas.

The expedition crossed "two rivers with very steep, rocky banks" and climbed a mountain pass. The pass led Alvarado to the great interior **plateau** of Guatemala. He called the scenery "magnificent," and he counted 16 volcanoes along the Pacific Ocean. Alvarado moved into an abandoned Indian city, where his forces later fought off an Indian attack. When he resumed his march, Alvarado took advantage of a war between two major Indian tribes. He won the friendship of one tribe, the Cakchiquel, by aiding them in their battle against the Quiché.

By autumn, Alvarado had reached the city of Tecpán and defeated the Atitlán Indians. He had also begun to build the first capital of Guatemala at the site of modern-day Guatemala City. Alvarado then continued into what is now El Salvador, going as far south as Cuzcaclan (near the present capital, San Salvador). Alvarado was eventually given full authority in Guatemala and El Salvador.

Jungles and Mountains

In 1533 Alvarado turned his attention to South America and the province of Quito. He hoped to find great wealth there, as Pizarro had done. Alvarado sailed to the coast and led his expedition into the rain forest. The heavy humidity of these interior lands rusted the men's weapons and armor. When the party reached the mountains of the Andes, they suffered greatly in the icy conditions. They also had trouble breathing because of ash from an erupting volcano.

When he finally reached Quito, Alvarado found that the land had already been claimed by Pizarro and his partner, Diego de ALMAGRO.

To avoid a war between the competing conquistadors, Almagro bought Alvarado's remaining army and supplies.

After returning to Guatemala, Alvarado planned a trip to the Spice Islands, in the East Indies, in 1540. Instead, the Spanish governor of Mexico persuaded him to lead an expedition to search for the legendary Mexican cities of Cíbola. Alvarado never accomplished either goal. He was killed on June 29, 1541, when a rearing horse fell on him.

Suggested Reading John E. Kelly, *Pedro de Alvarado, Conquistador* (Kennikat Press, 1971).

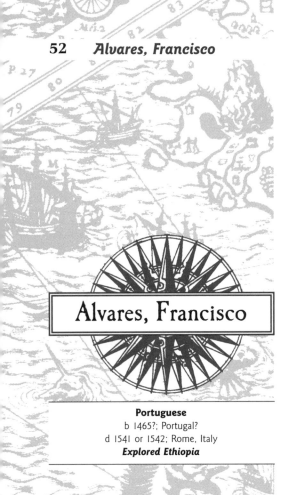

Alvares, Francisco

Portuguese
b 1465?; Portugal?
d 1541 or 1542; Rome, Italy
Explored Ethiopia

Francisco Alvares was a Roman Catholic priest. In 1515 he served as chaplain on an expedition to Abyssinia (now known as Ethiopia). Alvares wrote about his journey to this East African nation near the Red Sea. European readers were fascinated by their first look at Abyssinia's customs, society, and people.

The Search for a Mysterious King

Alvares was a member of a Portuguese expedition in search of Prester John, a great Christian king. Prester John later turned out to be a myth, but many Europeans believed that his kingdom existed somewhere in Africa or Asia. Alvares and his companions also hoped to establish official ties between Portugal and Abyssinia.

The expedition's commander died during the voyage from Portugal to East Africa, which took five years. In 1520, however, the party arrived at the court of Lebna Dengel, the emperor of Abyssinia.

Alvares, of course, did not discover Prester John or his fabled kingdom, but he did find a fellow Portuguese, Pêro da COVILHÃ. Once an explorer himself, Covilhã had been missing for almost 30 years. He had been captured by the Abyssinians, who forbade him to leave. During his captivity, he had learned a great deal about Abyssinia, and he helped Alvares to understand this foreign land.

Record of a Lost Empire

Alvares also made his own careful observations of the country and its people. When he returned to Portugal in 1527, he wrote a detailed description of Abyssinia. He called his work *True Information on the Countries of Prester John of the Indies.* The book was translated into several languages and read all across Europe. Alvares became famous. The book was also historically valuable. Not long after Alvares left Abyssinia, the country was destroyed by Muslim invaders. His book was the only detailed record of the Abyssinian Empire. Five years after he returned to Portugal, Alvares traveled to Italy. He delivered letters from the Abyssinian emperor to Pope Clement VII, the leader of the Roman Catholic Church. Alvares remained in Italy until his death.

Suggested Reading Francisco Alvares, *The Prester John of the Indies; A True Relation of the Lands of the Prester John, Being the Narrative of the Portuguese Embassy to Ethiopia in 1520,* translated by Lord Stanley of Alderley (Hakluyt Society, 1961).

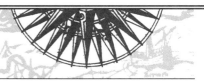

Alvarez de Pineda, Alonso

Spanish?
b 1400s?; ?
d 1520; Pánuco River, Mexico
Explored Gulf of Mexico and was first
European to see Mississippi River

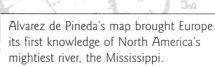
Alvarez de Pineda's map brought Europe its first knowledge of North America's mightiest river, the Mississippi.

In 1519 Alonso Alvarez de Pineda commanded a Spanish ship along the coast of the Gulf of Mexico, exploring from the southern tip of Florida to Veracruz, Mexico. During his expedition, Alvarez de Pineda proved that Florida was not an island, as most people believed at the time. He also became the first European explorer to see the mouth of the Mississippi River.

Nothing is known of Alvarez de Pineda's life before his historic journey. Historians have tried to trace his background through Spanish records, but they cannot find any mention of him. He was probably not actually Spanish. In any case, by 1519 Alvarez de Pineda had reached the Americas, where he met Francisco de Garay, the Spanish governor of Jamaica. Garay was in financial trouble and desperately needed money. He hoped that if he discovered new lands, he would find great riches. Garay received permission to send four ships to explore the mainland of North America. He hired Alvarez de Pineda to lead the expedition.

The Gulf of Mexico

Garay's four ships sailed from Jamaica with a combined crew of approximately 270. Their mission was to explore the area between Florida, which had been discovered by Juan PONCE DE LEÓN, and eastern Mexico, where Hernán CORTÉS was already active. Alvarez de Pineda and his crew were looking for a strait connecting the Gulf of Mexico with the South Sea. The South Sea, later known as the Pacific Ocean, had been discovered by Vasco Nuñez de BALBOA.

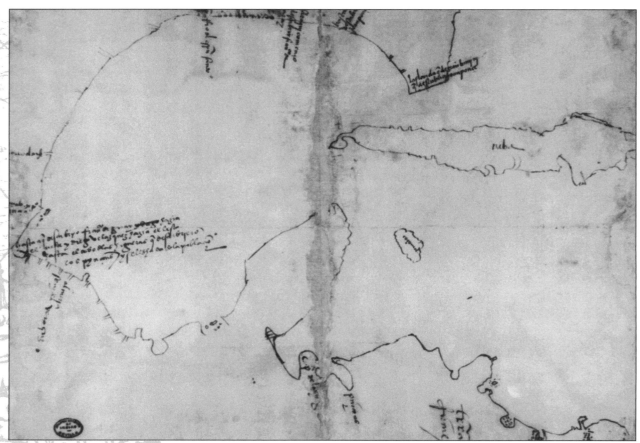

The explorers sailed through the Yucatán Channel between Mexico and Cuba and headed north until they sighted Florida. Ponce de León believed that Florida was an island, so the explorers looked for a waterway between Florida and the mainland. When they failed to find a channel, they knew that Florida was not an island after all.

Alvarez de Pineda then wanted to sail up Florida's east coast, but the wind and ocean currents forced him to change his plans. From Florida's west coast, he began to follow the Gulf of Mexico coastline toward Mexico. On the way, the expedition saw the waters of the Mississippi River pouring into the gulf. That day, June 2, 1519, was the feast day of the Holy Spirit, a Catholic holiday. Alvarez de Pineda named the river Rio del Espiritu Santo—the river of the Holy Spirit.

Conflict with Cortés

As Alvarez de Pineda sailed along the coast of the Gulf of Mexico, he observed "a very good land"—peaceful and fertile. The trees produced a variety of fruits, and he was sure that the rivers contained gold. He noted that the Indians wore gold jewelry "in their nostrils, on their ear lobes, and on other parts of their body."

Eventually the expedition came to Villa Rica de Vera Cruz (modern-day Veracruz). There, Hernán Cortés was preparing to launch an attack against the great Aztec Empire. Alvarez de Pineda sent four men ashore to inform Cortés that he planned to found a settlement nearby. Cortés was not happy about the arrival of another Spanish explorer in this region, which he wanted to claim for himself. However, he was too busy with his military planning to pay much attention to this nuisance. He seized the four messengers, but he let Alvarez de Pineda's ships sail north, to the mouth of the Pánuco River.

The ships traveled about 20 miles up the river, observing 40 villages of the friendly Huastec Indians. After about 40 days on the river, the expedition returned to Jamaica.

Mexico Becomes Deadly

Alvarez de Pineda gave Governor Garay the map he had made during the voyage. The map showed a fairly accurate outline of the Gulf of Mexico, and it was sent to Spain with the rest of the expedition's records. Even before Spanish officials granted their permission, Garay planned to settle the Mexican land that Alvarez de Pineda had explored. In fact, some historians believe that Alvarez de Pineda did not return to Jamaica with the original expedition. Instead, he may have stayed near the Pánuco River to start a settlement.

If Alvarez de Pineda did not stay in Mexico, then he certainly went back to the Pánuco region from Jamaica. Either way, this adventure was less successful than his first. The Huastec Indians, who had been friendly during the first visit, turned against the Spanish. Early in 1520, they killed all of the Spaniards' horses and all but 60 of the several hundred settlers. Alvarez de Pineda died in the fighting.

Suggested Reading Clotilde Garcia, *Captain Alonso Alvarez de Pineda and the Exploration of the Texas Coast and the Gulf of Mexico* (San Felipe, 1982).

Amundsen, Roald Engelbregt Gravning

Norwegian
b July 16, 1872; Borge, near Oslo, Norway
d June 1928; near Spitsbergen, Norway
*Sailed Northwest Passage; reached South Pole;
explored polar regions by sea, land, and air*

Northwest Passage water route connecting the Atlantic Ocean and Pacific Ocean through the Arctic islands of northern Canada

Northeast Passage water route connecting the Atlantic Ocean and Pacific Ocean along the Arctic coastline of Europe and Asia

plateau high, flat area of land

Sometimes called the last Viking, Roald Amundsen was 54 years old when his airplane crashed in the Arctic.

In 1903 Roald Engelbregt Gravning Amundsen launched his exploring career with a stunning success. He sailed through the **Northwest Passage,** a feat other explorers had failed to accomplish for hundreds of years. During the trip, Amundsen spent three sleepless weeks navigating through shallow, icy waters that threatened to wreck his tiny ship at any moment. The historic journey was only the first of his many spectacular explorations in the world's polar regions.

Amundsen later became the first to reach the South Pole. He also sailed through the **Northeast Passage** and pioneered the use of aircraft to explore the Arctic Ocean. Sometimes called the last Viking, Amundsen had trouble getting along in respectable society. But throughout his life he showed skill, cunning, and bravery that few explorers ever matched.

An Early Inspiration

Amundsen came from a middle-class Norwegian family. Although his father and uncles made their living in the shipping business, Roald Amundsen grew up in the city of Oslo. The only chance the boy had to explore nature came when his family spent holidays on a farm.

When he was 15, Amundsen read the works of John FRANKLIN, a British explorer. These writings, Amundsen later said, "shaped the whole course of my life." Franklin wrote vividly of his first Arctic expedition and the great suffering he had endured. Amundsen was particularly impressed by this account, and he later wrote: "A strange ambition burned within me to endure those same sufferings."

Amundsen's mother, however, had other plans. After her husband died, Mrs. Amundsen wanted her son to become a doctor. He tried to obey her wishes but never did well in medical school. His passion was to become an explorer. Amundsen stayed in school until he was 21, when his mother died. He then decided to explore the Arctic.

A Brush with Death

Before tackling the Arctic, Amundsen took on an exploration closer to home. Along with his brother, he set out to cross the Norwegian **plateau** in the dead of winter. If Amundsen wanted to suffer as his hero Franklin had, he was off to a good start. Amundsen did not prepare as carefully for this trip as he would for his future expeditions. The two young men set out with only a small amount of food and two sleeping bags. Without a tent, they were soon freezing and starving.

One night Amundsen burrowed into the snow to sleep. When the weather changed, the surrounding snow turned into "a ghastly coffin of ice." It took his brother three hours to chip Roald free. By the end of their ordeal, the brothers were horribly thin and sickly, their skin a shade of greenish yellow.

mate assistant to the commander of a ship

scurvy disease caused by a lack of vitamin C and once a major cause of death among sailors; symptoms include internal bleeding, loosened teeth, and extreme fatigue

In case he did not return from the South Pole, Amundsen left a letter there for Robert Scott to take to Norway. The letter was found on Scott's frozen body.

Explorer in Training

Amundsen called his first experience a training exercise. It also marked his break from the civilized Norwegian society to which his family had belonged. Amundsen continued his training by working as a common sailor on a ship that often sailed the Arctic waters. He sailed for three summers and then qualified as a **mate.** In 1897 he was named first mate of the Belgian Antarctic Expedition. The trip was nearly a disaster, but Amundsen made it a triumph of survival.

The Belgian ship was not prepared for winter and became caught in an ice field near Graham Land, south of the tip of Chile. The situation worsened when the commanding officers were unable to provide fresh meat for the crew. As a result, the officers and many crew members developed **scurvy,** and Amundsen took command of the ship. He and the ship's physician, Dr. Frederick Cook, saved the expedition. They nursed everyone back to health, then maneuvered the ship out of the ice the following spring.

Adventure or Science?

When he returned to Norway, Amundsen received his captain's license and began preparing for his journey through the Northwest Passage. He thoroughly studied the British attempts of the past. His reading of

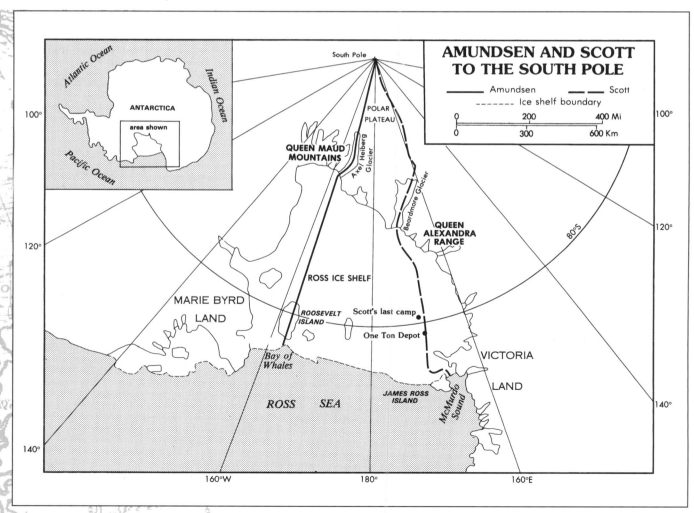

Francis Leopold MCCLINTOCK's book convinced him that John Franklin's route offered the best chance of success. At the same time, Amundsen had in mind several improvements over Franklin's methods.

Rather than follow the main ice pack west of Canada's King William Island, Amundsen would sail east of the island. The waters there were more frequently free of ice. Amundsen also decided to use a new invention, the diesel engine, to power his small yacht, the *Gjoa.* Luckily the Arctic was enjoying some unusually warm weather at the time. He took his plan to Fridtjof NANSEN, a famous polar explorer. Nansen approved the plan and gave his encouragement.

To some, Amundsen's planned journey did not seem like a serious expedition. The lands through which he would be traveling had already been explored, and no one thought that the passage would ever be useful for shipping. Amundsen's critics charged that his voyage was a only a stunt to win public attention. Like the American polar explorer Robert PEARY, Amundsen was an adventurer who made his living by speaking and writing about his exploits. To raise money for this trip, he had to convince scientific organizations that his expedition would produce useful research.

Amundsen had no interest in science, but for the sake of his plan, he studied relentlessly and became an expert on magnetism. He promised to provide new information about the North Magnetic Pole, the place pointed to by magnetic compasses in the Northern Hemisphere. It had been 70 years since an earlier explorer, Sir

Amundsen wrote that on his yacht, the *Gjoa,* he and his crew felt like "seven as light-hearted pirates as ever flew the black flag. . . ."

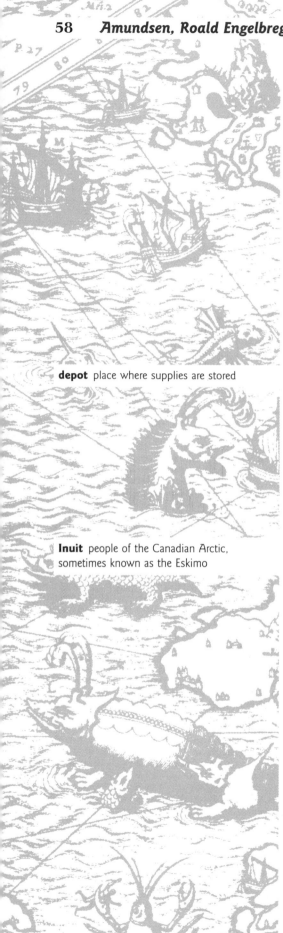

depot place where supplies are stored

Inuit people of the Canadian Arctic, sometimes known as the Eskimo

James Clark Ross, had studied the magnetic pole. During the winter and spring of 1903, Amundsen found educational societies and wealthy individuals who would fund his journey.

Still, many of Norway's scientists sensed that Amundsen was not sincere about his scientific interest. Funding for the trip soon dried up, and his debts mounted. Rather than go bankrupt and lose his yacht, Amundsen set sail in secret, one step ahead of his creditors.

Three Years' Voyage

It was midnight, June 16, 1903, when the *Gjoa* and its seven crew members sneaked out of Oslo. Amundsen was an untraditional captain. He did not believe in strict discipline and acted more like a president than a dictator. "Good work," Amundsen said, "can be done without the fear of the law."

Though the *Gjoa* was heavily loaded, the ship made good progress. By mid-August, the explorers were off the coast of northern Greenland, where they met fellow explorer Knud RASMUSSEN and the Danish Literary Greenland Expedition. Amundsen's party picked up supplies from a **depot** set up earlier and went on their way.

By August 22, they had arrived in the Canadian Arctic, at a camp once used by Amundsen's hero, John Franklin. From there, the party sailed to the point in Franklin Strait beyond which no one had sailed since Franklin's own journey. They pressed on, hoping that the waterway would remain clear of ice.

In early September, the *Gjoa* ran aground and was nearly wrecked. Finally the ship returned to the water, and the party reached its winter harbor on the south coast of King William Island. Amundsen spent two winters there, making observations and trading with the local **Inuit** people. In August 1905, he set sail again. In the shallow waters of Simpson Strait, Amundsen endured his three-week sleepless ordeal. But on August 27, a ship that had come east from the Bering Strait sailed into sight. Amundsen knew that he had made it through the Northwest Passage.

Unfortunately, the ice closed in too fast for the *Gjoa* to reach the Pacific Ocean that year. After another winter in the Arctic, the expedition arrived in San Francisco in October 1906. While still traveling along the Arctic coast, Amundsen had managed to come ashore and hike to a telegraph station on the Yukon River. He had sent word of his success, and a celebration was already organized when the *Gjoa* sailed into San Francisco Bay. When Amundsen finally returned to Norway, no one minded that he had left without paying his debts. Instead, he received a hero's welcome.

Plans and New Plans

With his new fame, Amundsen had no trouble raising money for his next adventure. He wanted to be the first person to reach the North Pole, and he planned to drift with the polar ice pack, as Fridtjof Nansen had done. But while Amundsen made his preparations, Robert Peary made his own attempt at the pole. On April 6, 1909, Peary announced that he had reached his goal.

Amundsen immediately decided to focus instead on the South Pole, which had also never been reached. But Amundsen had a competitor for that destination, too. Robert Falcon SCOTT, a British explorer, was already planning a trip to the southern continent. Amundsen feared that Scott would speed up his plans if he knew that the Norwegian was heading south. So instead of announcing his new plan, Amundsen lied. He claimed he was still going to the Arctic.

In the meantime, Amundsen built a house to serve as his base on the coast of Antarctica. He also bought 100 Greenland sled dogs. On August 9, 1910, Amundsen and his crew left Oslo on the *Fram,* the ship once used by Nansen. Their destination was Alaska—or so everyone thought. At Madeira, an island off the coast of Spain, Amundsen announced his real plan, both to the world and to his enthusiastic crew. Scott, upset that he had been deceived, hurried his own preparations. The race to the South Pole was on.

Amundsen had developed a brilliant but risky plan for his expedition. He had studied recent charts of the ice shelf that extended over the Ross Sea. By comparing these to earlier charts, Amundsen had guessed that part of the ice shelf was on top of land. Most other explorers assumed that the ice floated on water. By setting up his base on the ice over land in the Bay of Whales, he was 69 miles closer to the pole than Scott, who camped on James Ross Island. Luckily, Amundsen's conclusion about the ice shelf was correct. If he had been wrong, his camp could have dropped off the floating ice into the sea at any moment.

Amundsen's plan had another possible flaw. No one had ever explored the area he wanted to cross. He could not map out an exact route, and he might have run into a wall of mountains that he could not cross. Again, by good luck, Amundsen's risks paid off.

Harsh Realities

On October 19, 1911, Amundsen set off from his base with four **sledges,** four human companions, and 13 dogs. He had only limited experience in sledging, but Helmer Hanssen, who led the team, was an expert. They followed Amundsen's time schedule closely, though they faced dangers along the way. On the ice shelf, they were threatened by steep inclines and huge, bottomless cracks in the ice. But the team reached the Polar Plateau in early December, and the rest of the journey went smoothly.

To make his plan work, Amundsen had to follow an unpleasant but necessary strategy. Fewer sled dogs were needed to pull the sledges as the food was eaten. All the dogs, however, still would have to be fed with the remaining food. Amundsen had calculated that he could travel farther without the unneeded dogs. He was bothered by the idea of using the dogs for weeks and then killing them, but he stuck to this plan. It was practical but cruel, and it made him even less popular with some people.

The dogs were shot at the party's camp at the base of the plateau, a spot they named the Butcher Shop. The explorers, near starvation, were forced to join the remaining dogs in eating the dead animals. "But on this first evening," Amundsen later wrote, "we put a restraint on ourselves; we thought we could not fall upon our four-footed friends and devour them before they had time to grow cold. . . ."

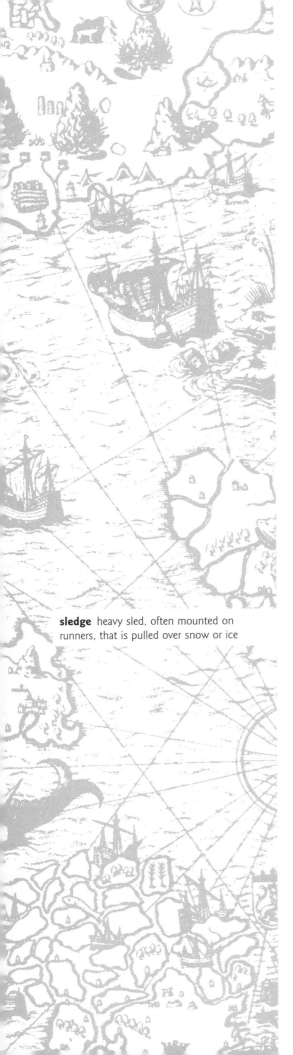

sledge heavy sled, often mounted on runners, that is pulled over snow or ice

Amundsen, a loyal subject of Norway's King Haakon VII, planted the Norwegian flag at the South Pole.

On December 6, the party reached its highest point on the plateau (11,024 feet), going on to arrive at the pole itself on December 14. All five men assisted in planting the Norwegian flag. Amundsen reported: "Five weather-beaten, frostbitten fists . . . grasped the waving flag in the air and planted it as the first at the geographic South Pole." The team then headed back to their base camp, reaching it on January 11, 1912. The expedition had covered 1,860 miles in 99 days.

Wartime Activities

Amundsen returned to Norway secretly. He wanted to write his book about the successful expedition quickly and then move on to his next adventure. He was once again bankrupt, but he found a wealthy Norwegian who was willing to support him. Amundsen returned to an old plan, to drift along with the polar ice pack in the Arctic. World War I, however, delayed this expedition.

Amundsen decided that the war could be an opportunity to earn money. He bought Norwegian ships and sold them at a profit to countries allied against Germany. With this money, he had the ship *Maud* built especially for his drift on the ice. Amundsen left in July 1918, planning to sail the Northeast Passage before heading into the pack ice. The crossing was successful, but before he could begin the polar drift, his ship was locked in ice for two years near the Bering Strait. During that time, Amundsen was injured in a fall and mauled by a bear. He decided to call off the expedition.

More Trouble than Money

During those two years, Amundsen's financial problems returned. He spent more than he had, always hopeful that he would find more money. The Norwegian government gave him some aid, but it was not enough to keep him out of debt. Still, even as he struggled with money, Amundsen discovered an exciting new way to undertake polar exploration—by airplane.

While waiting in Seattle to begin his intended polar drift, he bought a Junker—a German plane—and stored it on the *Maud*. Amundsen hoped to fly it from Point Barrow, Alaska, to Spitsbergen, Norway, across the Arctic Ocean. The *Maud* finally set sail in the summer of 1922, but Amundsen was not on it. He had decided to take his airplane to Point Barrow on a merchant ship. It was a lucky move, since the *Maud* was soon taken away by Amundsen's creditors. Meanwhile, Amundsen was finally ready to fly the Junker, but he damaged it in a trial flight.

At this point, Amundsen was deeply in debt. Even his brother gave up helping him. The great explorer tried to earn money by speaking across America, but this lecture tour did not bring in enough money. In his own words, he was "nearer to black despair than ever before in the 54 years of my life." Then an unexpected telephone call restored his hope.

While Amundsen was sitting in a hotel room, wondering how he was going to pay his bill, he received a call from an American, Lincoln ELLSWORTH. A college dropout and the son of a millionaire, Ellsworth was desperately searching for something to do with his life. He said that he would give Amundsen the necessary funds. In exchange,

Ellsworth wanted to share the command of a flight to the North Pole. Delighted and relieved, Amundsen agreed. "The gloom of the past year rolled away," Amundsen wrote, "and even the horrors of my business experience faded into forgetfulness in the activities of preparation."

Amundsen the Aviator

Amundsen and Ellsworth left for the North Pole in 1925, using two planes. In one sense, the journey was a failure because they never reached their destination. But the drama of the trip captivated the world. The two planes went down into the ice near the pole, and the explorers worked heroically to get the one working plane back into the air. The craft was overloaded, but the men managed to return safely. Amundsen was once again hailed as the brave and resourceful explorer of old.

A year later, Amundsen took part in another astounding flight. On the Italian **dirigible** *Norge,* he flew across the Arctic from Norway to Alaska. The dirigible floated over the polar ocean, dangerously weighed down by glittering blankets of ice. The trip was a marvel of technology, and Amundsen was once again at the center of the world's attention.

Unfortunately, Amundsen's later actions spoiled the glory of these achievements. In his autobiography, he attacked Umberto No-BILE, the Italian who had designed and piloted the *Norge.* He also criticized other explorers, including many of his partners and even his brother. When he could have appeared as a grand hero of exploration, he came across as a bitter old man.

Amundsen's image was restored on one last voyage. In 1928 Nobile tried to repeat his flight across the Arctic. He wanted to clear his name after the charges Amundsen had made against him. During the flight, however, Nobile's dirigible crashed. When he heard of the accident, Amundsen immediately put aside his conflicts with Nobile and boarded a plane to join in the search. Nobile was eventually rescued, but Amundsen did not return. His plane had gone down, and the Norwegian explorer sank unseen into the Arctic Ocean.

Suggested Reading Roald Amundsen, *My Life as an Explorer* (Doubleday, Doran and Company, 1928); Gerald Bowman, *Men of Antarctica* (Fleet, 1958); Roland Huntford, *Scott and Amundsen* (Atheneum, 1984); Theodore K. Mason, *Two Against the Ice: Amundsen and Ellsworth* (Dodd, Mead and Company, 1982); J. Gordon Naeth, *To the Ends of the Earth: The Explorations of Roald Amundsen* (Harper and Row, 1962); L.H. Neatby, *Conquest of the Last Frontier* (Ohio University Press, 1966); Bellamy Partridge, *Amundsen* (Robert Hale, 1933); Charles Turley, *Roald Amundsen Explorer* (Methuen, 1935).

dirigible large aircraft filled with a lighter-than-air gas that keeps it aloft; similar to a blimp but with a rigid frame

Andrée, Salomon August

Swedish
b October 18, 1854; Grenna, Sweden
d 1897?; White Island, Norway
Attempted balloon flight to North Pole

In July of 1897, Salomon August Andrée set out from Spitsbergen Island in his balloon, the *Ornen,* seeking to reach the North Pole. It was the last time he would be seen alive. His fate and the story of his trip would remain unknown for more than 30 years.

A Love of Science and Ballooning

Andrée was born in 1854, one of seven children of a pharmacist. He showed an early interest in science, and in 1869 he entered the Royal Institute of Technology in Stockholm. He graduated four

Salomon August Andrée named his balloon *Ornen*, which means Eagle.

sledge heavy sled, often mounted on runners, that is pulled over snow or ice

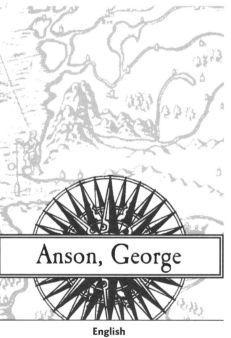

Anson, George

English
b April 23, 1697; Shrughborough Park, England
d June 6, 1762; Moor Park, England
Sailed around world, reformed British navy

years later and remained in Stockholm for two more years, working as a draftsman and designer. He went on to become chief engineer in the Swedish patent office.

Andrée became interested in balloons when he read a book called *Laws of the Wind.* In 1876 he traveled to Philadelphia to visit the exhibition celebrating the hundredth anniversary of the United States. There he met with an experienced balloon pilot who taught him the basics of ballooning. In 1894 Andrée received a grant to buy a balloon, the *Svea,* from which he conducted many scientific experiments.

The next year, Andrée announced his plan to travel by balloon to the North Pole. At that time, no one had ever reached the pole. Andrée began by making careful studies of the geography and winds of the Arctic. He designed special equipment that would allow him to steer his new balloon. He also gathered money to support the expedition. One of his sponsors was Alfred Nobel, the man who established the Nobel Prizes.

Forced Down

On July 11, 1897, Andrée and two companions took off from Spitsbergen aboard his new balloon. Problems at the launch caused some important equipment to be left behind. What happened next remained a mystery until August 6, 1930, when the remains and the records of the expedition were found on White Island, near Spitsbergen.

The records showed that the flight had lasted for 325 miles and three days. Then an unexpected lack of wind forced the balloon, weighted down by frost, to land on the ice. The men tried to return home by **sledge,** but heavy equipment, polar bears, and cold weather made the trip difficult. By early October, they had traveled 200 miles, but no one knows how much longer they might have survived. The bodies of Andrée and one companion were found in their tent. They had probably been poisoned by carbon monoxide gas that leaked from their kerosene stove. The journals, photos, and equipment they left behind told a moving story of a courageous and difficult journey.

Suggested Reading Edward Adams-Ray, translator, *Andrée's Story: The Complete Record of His Polar Flight, 1897,* revised edition (Viking, 1960); George Palmer Putnam, *Andrée: The Record of a Tragic Adventure* (Brewer and Warren, 1939); Per Olof Sundman *The Flight of the Eagle,* translated by Mary Sandbach (Pantheon, 1970).

George Anson was born into a distinguished family in Staffordshire in 1697 and went to sea with the navy when he was 15. He rose through the ranks and became a captain. From 1724 to 1739, Anson commanded three different ships, protecting Britain's territories in the Americas from Spanish attacks. Most of this military action took place along the southeast coast of North America. From 1740 to 1744, Anson led a British fleet on a voyage around the globe. When he returned home, he worked to turn the British navy into an efficient, professional force.

In 1748 Baron George Anson published a book describing his four-year global voyage. The work became a best-seller and was later translated into French.

scurvy disease caused by a lack of vitamin C and once a major cause of death among sailors; symptoms include internal bleeding, loosened teeth, and extreme fatigue

galleon large sailing ship used for war and trade

Anza, Juan Bautista de

Spanish
b 1735? Fronteras, Mexico
d December 19, 1788; Arizpe, Mexico
Established Sonora-California Trail

Setting Out to Circle the Globe

On September 18, 1740, Anson left Britain with six ships for the first part of a four-year trip around the world. His first task was to sail to the west coast of South America and attack Spanish settlements. Before reaching his goal, Anson lost half his fleet to shipwrecks, and many of his sailors died of **scurvy,** but Anson sailed on. He eventually captured the Spanish town of Paita on the coast of Peru and destroyed many Spanish ships in the region.

By that time, Anson's remaining ships had suffered damage. He put all his men on the most seaworthy of his vessels and sailed west to Tinian, an island in the western Pacific. They rested briefly there, then sailed farther west, reaching Macao, on the southern coast of China, in November 1742. The following summer, Anson captured a Spanish **galleon** sailing between the Philippines and the Americas. The ship carried a fortune in gold bars and coins. Back at Macao, Anson sold 32 wagonloads of this Spanish treasure to the Chinese and then headed home. When he reached Britain in 1744, Anson was a rich man for life.

Building a Better Navy

The determination Anson showed on his difficult global voyage appeared again during his next mission. At the time, the British navy was badly run and poorly organized. In 1745 Anson was named a rear admiral and began to reform the service.

Under his command, the navy dockyards were improved, and fleets were inspected regularly. To reduce theft and bribery, Anson checked the navy's finances carefully. He established new rules for awarding promotions and enforcing discipline. These reforms were partly why, for example, the wealthy civilian Alexander DALRYMPLE was denied the command of an expedition to the Pacific Ocean in 1768. Captain James COOK was the skilled naval officer who was chosen instead.

After making his reforms, Anson went back to active duty. In 1747 he commanded a British fleet against the French. He won a key victory, was promoted to vice admiral, and was given the title of baron. He continued working for the navy, and in 1755 he established the British marine corps.

When Anson died at Moor Park in 1762, he was Britain's highest-ranking admiral. His four-year trip around the world had stirred his country's interest in the Pacific, and he had turned the British navy into perhaps the best fleet in the world.

Suggested Reading Patrick O'Brian, *The Golden Ocean* (Norton, 1984); Richard Walter, *Anson's Voyage Round the World* (Charles E. Lauriat, 1928).

Colonel Juan Bautista de Anza has been called the last **conquistador.** He was born in **New Spain** and dedicated himself to defending its northern frontiers. He also blazed new trails to connect the widespread Spanish territories in North America. These trails included important land routes from Sonora (in what is now the state of Arizona) to upper California and from Sonora to Santa Fe (in what is now the state of New Mexico). In 1775 Anza led an expedition

conquistador Spanish or Portuguese explorer and military leader in the Americas

New Spain region of Spanish colonial empire that included the areas now occupied by Mexico, Florida, Texas, New Mexico, Arizona, California, and various Caribbean islands

presidio Spanish settlement in the Americas that was defended by soldiers

viceroy governor of a Spanish colony in the Americas

mission settlement founded by priests in a land where they hoped to convert people to Christianity

that established the first European settlement in the area of San Francisco Bay.

Young Soldier

Juan Bautista de Anza was born at the **presidio** of Fronteras, in the Sonora province in New Spain. Historians are unsure whether he was born in 1735 or 1736, and little is known of his early life. In 1752 he enlisted as a volunteer in Fronteras's armed forces, and by 1760 he had reached the rank of captain. That same year, he was named commander of the presidio of Tubac (near the present-day city of Douglas, Arizona). During the next 10 years, he led many successful campaigns against the Apache Indians.

The Sonora-California Trail

By 1770 the Spanish settlements in upper California were in trouble. The settlers had difficulty getting the supplies they needed by sea, and Russians in Alaska were pushing south toward California. Anza responded to these threats by suggesting a plan that his father had proposed 30 years earlier. Anza volunteered to open a land route from Sonora to upper California, using his own money to fund the expedition. Both the king of Spain and the **viceroy** of New Spain approved the plan.

Anza set out in January 1774 with 34 men, including Father Francisco GARCES. They headed north along the Gila River and followed it to the point where it flowed into the Colorado River. There Anza befriended the Yuma Indians, who controlled the lower Colorado River area. In his report on the journey, Anza emphasized the importance of friendly relations with the Yuma.

The expedition crossed the Colorado River, but Anza's party got lost in the desert west of the river and had to return to Yuma territory. They set out again, this time circling around the desert to the southwest and traveling through the Cocopah Mountains. Heading northwest, they reached the **mission** of San Gabriel. Anza left some soldiers at San Gabriel as reinforcements and then traveled north to the Monterey mission, which he also reinforced. Satisfied that the missions were safe, Anza then returned to Sonora, where he was promoted to lieutenant colonel. He was also chosen to lead a group of colonists to upper California and to find a site for a new presidio at San Francisco Bay.

Expedition to San Francisco

The new expedition left Tubac on October 23, 1775, with 240 colonists, 165 pack animals, 340 horses, and 300 cattle. Anza followed much the same route that he had taken on his previous expedition. This time, however, he marched across the desert instead of traveling around it. He divided the colonists into three groups that traveled a day apart. This way, the watering holes in the desert would have time to fill up again before the next group arrived. Rain, snow, and freezing temperatures made the winter journey difficult, and many of the animals died. At one point, Anza wrote, a storm was followed "with an earthquake which lasted four minutes." Despite the hardships, only one colonist died

Colonel Juan Bautista de Anza devoted himself to defending the northern frontier of Spain's empire in the Americas.

on the trip, and three healthy infants were born along the way.

Anza led the colonists to Monterey and then pushed on to explore the San Francisco Bay area. He discovered the Guadalupe River and found a good location for a presidio on a cliff at the mouth of San Francisco Bay. This expedition proved that Anza was an excellent leader. His outstanding performance earned him a promotion to colonel and an appointment as governor of New Mexico in 1777.

Anza's Governorship and His Legacy

Anza proved to be as capable a governor as he was an explorer. He brought peace to the northern frontier of New Mexico by defeating and befriending the Comanche, who then joined him against the Apache. He also continued to lead journeys of exploration, establishing the Sonora–Santa Fe Trail in 1780. The following year, he was unfairly blamed for an uprising by the Yuma and briefly lost his post as governor. In 1786 he requested a transfer to a more healthful climate, and two years later, he was named commander of the presidio at Tubac. However, he died in Arizpe, Mexico, on December 19, 1788, less than two months after being appointed to his new position.

Anza was one of the best commanders and governors in New Spain. He established important routes connecting the heart of New Spain with remote outposts in California. He also kept detailed notes on the landscape, water supply, natural resources, and Indian tribes of the areas he explored. This information was valuable to later efforts at exploration and colonization. In the early 1900s, a legend grew that Anza was the founder of the city of San Francisco. In fact, the site of the city was chosen after Anza's expedition, although it was within the area that Anza had explored. Descendants of some of the settlers he led in 1775 still live in San Francisco today.

Suggested Reading Herbert E. Bolton, *Anza's California Expeditions,* 5 volumes (Russell and Russell, 1966), and *Outpost of Empire: The Story of the Founding of San Francisco* (Alfred A. Knopf, 1931); Frederick J. Teggart, editor, *The Anza Expedition of 1775-1776: Diary of Pedro Font* (University of California Press, 1913).

Armstrong, Neil Alden

American
b August 5, 1930; Wapakoneta, Ohio
living
First person on moon

Neil Alden Armstrong did something that no other explorer had ever done and none can ever repeat—he was the first person from the earth to set foot on another world. Millions of people watched on television in 1969 as Armstrong walked across the dusty, dark gray surface of the moon. The mission, named Apollo 11, was more than a personal achievement. Like all space flights, it was a triumph of technology and teamwork. For Americans, it was also a welcome victory in the "space race" with the **Soviet Union.** The whole world looked to Neil Armstrong as a symbol of what humanity could accomplish.

Dreams of Flying

As a boy living in small towns in Ohio, Armstrong built model airplanes and read about **aeronautics.** Sometimes he used a neighbor's telescope to look at the moon and stars in the night sky. His passion for airplanes led him to take flying lessons as a teenager, and he earned a pilot's license before he graduated from high school. He entered Purdue University in Indiana to study aeronautical engineering, but two years later, the United States became involved in the Korean War. Armstrong received flight training in Florida and then went to Korea as a fighter pilot. He flew 78 combat missions, winning three medals for what he called "bridge breaking, train stopping, tank shooting and that sort of thing." When his military service was completed, Armstrong returned to Purdue and finished his studies.

Into Space

Now an experienced flyer and an aeronautics engineer, Armstrong found a job as a research pilot for the National Advisory Committee for Aeronautics (NACA). The job took him to Edwards Air Force base in California, where he continued to work after NACA was replaced by **NASA** in 1958. As a test pilot, Armstrong flew more than 1,100 hours in new and experimental jets, trying to find out how high and how fast people and machines could travel. He flew **supersonic** fighter planes, and between 1960 and 1962, he flew six missions in a **rocket**-powered plane called the X-15. This plane was built to go to the highest parts of the earth's atmosphere—the very edge of space. Flying the X-15, Armstrong reached heights of 40 miles and speeds of 4,000 miles per hour.

By now, NASA had begun training **astronauts** to fly in small **capsules** that were launched into space by rockets. In early 1962, John GLENN became the first American to **orbit** the earth, kindling Armstrong's enthusiasm. Later that year, Armstrong was chosen by NASA to be one of the second group of astronauts. He was the first astronaut who was not a military officer.

Armstrong's first space flight was the Gemini 8 mission in 1966. He and copilot David Scott performed the first successful docking in space when their capsule met another spacecraft and joined with it. Despite problems that forced Armstrong to end the mission ahead of schedule, the docking was important to the progress of the American space program.

To the Moon

Armstrong's second space flight was his greatest contribution to exploration and one of mankind's greatest achievements. The United States had begun the Apollo program to reach the moon, and previous Apollo flights had taken astronauts near the moon and around it. Apollo 11 was intended to land astronauts on the moon's surface. NASA chose Armstrong to command the mission. Edwin "Buzz" Aldrin, Jr., and Michael Collins would accompany him.

On July 16, 1969, a Saturn 5 rocket blasted off from Cape Kennedy, Florida. It carried the command spacecraft, called the *Columbia,* and the landing craft, the *Eagle.* Three days later, the

space suit protective gear that allows a person who wears it to survive in space

From left to right: Neil Armstrong, Edwin Aldrin, Jr., and Michael Collins, the crew of the United States's Apollo 11 mission to the moon.

craft entered into orbit around the moon. While Collins stayed in the *Columbia,* Armstrong and Aldrin piloted the *Eagle* to a flat plain on the moon called the Sea of Tranquility. Six hours later, after adjusting his **space suit,** Armstrong opened the outer door and slowly climbed down a ladder to the powdery ground. Looking at his footprints on the moon's surface, he declared: "That's one small step for a man, one giant leap for mankind."

Armstrong and Aldrin spent two and a half hours walking on the moon. They set scientific instruments in place to record information about the moon's environment. They also gathered samples of soil and rocks and planted the American flag. A plaque they left behind reads: "Here men from the planet Earth first set foot upon the Moon, July 1969 A.D. We came in peace for all mankind." The next day they lifted off to dock with the *Columbia.* The three astronauts in the capsule splashed down in the Pacific Ocean on July 24. A navy ship picked them up and took them home.

Although Apollo 11 brought Armstrong worldwide fame, he did not enjoy the publicity. He preferred to work quietly at NASA's headquarters in Washington, D.C. He left the agency in 1971 for a career in education and business. In 1986 he served on the committee that investigated the explosion of the space shuttle *Challenger.*

Suggested Reading Carmen Bredeson, *Neil Armstrong: A Space Biography* (Enslow, 1998); Andrew Chaikin, *A Man on the Moon: The Voyages of the Apollo Astronauts* (Viking, 1994); Michael D. Cole, *Apollo 11: First Moon Landing* (Enslow, 1995); Alan Shepard and Deke Slayton, *Moon Shot: The Inside Story of America's Race to the Moon* (Turner, 1994).

Ashley, William Henry

American
b 1778?; Powhatan, Virginia
d March 26, 1838; Cooper County, Missouri
Explored Green River

Although William Henry Ashley made only one journey of exploration in his life, he played a major role in opening the American West. His fur-trapping company employed many men who explored the Rocky Mountains in their search for beaver skins. During their travels, these men discovered new river routes and mountain passes that enabled settlers to cross the Rocky Mountains and push westward to the Pacific Ocean.

The Rocky Mountain Fur Company

Ashley was born in Virginia around 1778, but he migrated west to Missouri in 1805. He soon became a businessman in St. Louis, dealing in firearms and real estate. In fact, his involvement with exploration came more from his desire to make money than from the love of adventure. Ashley realized that there were great profits to be made from fur trapping in the Rocky Mountains, which were largely unexplored. In 1822 he and his partner Andrew Henry founded the Rocky Mountain Fur Company. They advertised for "enterprising young men" to go into the wilderness and make their fortunes by trapping beaver. Some of the men who joined Ashley's company would later be among the most important American explorers, such as Jedediah SMITH.

In 1823 Ashley led a party of men west along the Missouri River route established 20 years earlier by Meriwether LEWIS and William CLARK. They hoped to follow this route all the way to the Rockies.

William Ashley founded the first annual rendezvous, a meeting of traders and trappers in the Rocky Mountains.

Unfortunately, the group was attacked by Arikara Indians while traveling up the Missouri River, near the present-day border between North Dakota and South Dakota. Twelve of Ashley's men were killed, and the others were forced to turn back. One thousand armed men set out to subdue the Arikara, but the Indians defeated these men, too. With his first route blocked by the Arikara, Ashley had to rethink his plans. Since he was heavily in debt, he did not want to miss the entire trapping season and the profits that might be made. He decided to send his men to the Rockies by land instead of by river.

Two parties set out, one led by Jed Smith and the other by Andrew Henry. A year later, four men from Smith's group limped into St. Louis with both good news and bad news. The good news was that Smith had discovered rich fur-trapping territory around a river they called Seedskeedee, a name that means Prairie Hen (later named the Green River). The bad news was that Smith and his men were desperately in need of supplies.

A Businessman Becomes an Explorer

Ashley himself led the expedition to resupply his men, leaving Fort Atkinson, Missouri, in early November 1824 with 25 men, 50 pack horses, and several wagons. He followed the Platte River west before heading out across the open prairies and into the mountains. Despite the harsh winter weather, the party found excellent trapping in the Medicine Bow Mountains, in what is now southern Wyoming. After crossing the mountains, Ashley led his party south and west until they reached the Green River on April 15, 1825. Having resupplied Smith, he split his men into four groups and sent them out in different directions to trap beaver. The groups were instructed to meet 50 miles down the Green River on or before July 10.

Ashley led one group south on the Green River, hoping to find a river that would lead farther west. Traveling in buffalo-skin boats, the party explored the rough and often dangerous river. As the boats passed through deep, dark canyons, Ashley noticed the fear and gloom on his men's faces. They had heard tales of a giant whirlpool that would suck them all down to the center of the earth. Although they did come across several large whirlpools, none was as terrible as they had feared. Ashley, who could not swim, once nearly fell out of his boat. Still, the party pressed on until May 16, when they met two fur trappers who were traveling north from Taos, in the area now called New Mexico. These trappers told Ashley that there were no beaver farther south, so Ashley and his men turned back. Their journey on the Green River lasted 31 days and took them as far as what is now the state of Utah.

The Trappers' Rendezvous

Ashley's four groups met as planned. Their skillful trapping was a great success for Ashley, who had collected enough furs to pay off his debts and become a wealthy man. This gathering of trappers, called a rendezvous (the French word for meeting), started an annual tradition. The mountain men normally worked alone in the woods, but every year they came together at the rendezvous for a few weeks of trading, drinking, gambling, and storytelling.

Ashley went back to St. Louis, but he returned the next year for the rendezvous, which took place in Cache Valley, near the Great Salt Lake. There he sold his trapping business to Jed Smith and Smith's two partners. Ashley returned East to pursue a career in politics and was elected to the U.S. House of Representatives in 1831.

Ashley contributed in many ways to the exploration and settlement of the West. He personally explored the Green River, and the men he sent into the wilderness to trap furs found the South Pass through the Rockies. This pass, in present-day Wyoming, became a major route for settlers traveling to the west coast. Ashley's men also discovered and explored the Great Salt Lake. As a politician, Ashley used his enthusiasm for the riches of the West to encourage large groups of people to settle in that region.

Suggested Reading Harrison C. Dale, *The Ashley-Smith Explorations and the Discovery of a Central Route to the Pacific, 1822–1829* (Arthur H. Clark, 1941); Dale L. Morgan, *The West of William Ashley* (Old West, 1964).

---

ash-Sharif al Idrisi. See *Idrisi, al.*

Audubon, John James

French
b April 26, 1785; Cayes, Haiti
d January 27, 1851; New York, New York
Studied and drew birds of North America

Creole person of European ancestry born in Spanish colonies in the Americas; or, person descended from French settlers of what is now the southern United States

John James Audubon was not the usual kind of explorer. He did not blaze trails into the wilderness or discover new continents. But he added as much to the world's knowledge of North American wildlife as did any of the explorers whose trails he followed. Audubon's observations and drawings of birds in the wild provided a stunning record of the birds of North America in their natural environments.

Audubon's Early Life

Audubon was born on a plantation in what is now Haiti. He was the son of a French merchant and his **Creole** mistress. Before Audubon was a year old, his mother died, and his father took him and his half sister to live in France. His father's wife adopted both children as her own. By the age of 15, Audubon had become interested in drawing and in natural history, and he began a series of drawings of French birds. This passion would become his life's work.

In 1803 Audubon left France to avoid that country's political troubles. He moved to an estate that his father had bought in Pennsylvania and began his study of American birds. Audubon loved to draw his subjects, but he was also curious about their habits, which he studied closely. In one experiment, he tied silver threads around the legs of some young birds and noted that two returned to the same place the following year.

The Birth of an Idea

Audubon married in 1808 and spent most of the next 12 years in Kentucky, trying to support his family. He tried his hand at several businesses while continuing to draw birds. In 1820, while working

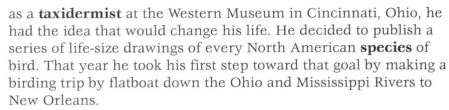

taxidermist scientist who preserves the bodies of animals by stuffing them for display

species type of plant or animal

specimen sample of a plant, animal, or mineral, usually collected for scientific study or display

John James Audubon's drawings of North American birds are among the most accurate and beautiful ever produced.

as a **taxidermist** at the Western Museum in Cincinnati, Ohio, he had the idea that would change his life. He decided to publish a series of life-size drawings of every North American **species** of bird. That year he took his first step toward that goal by making a birding trip by flatboat down the Ohio and Mississippi Rivers to New Orleans.

Audubon could not find an American publisher who was interested in his project. In 1826 he traveled to England and Scotland, where his work was more highly regarded. A printer in Scotland agreed to publish full-size reproductions of the drawings. Audubon and the printer found buyers who paid in advance to receive each new drawing as it was published. For the next 12 years, Audubon divided his time between business trips in England and Scotland and birding trips in North America.

Birds of America

In 1832 Audubon made two birding trips to Florida. The first was a difficult journey on the St. Johns River. He collected very few birds, but there were so many insects in the air that they put out his candle as he tried to write in his journal. His second try, a trip south along Florida's east coast, was more successful. Although he discovered only two new species, he collected over 1,000 **specimens** and made many drawings.

The following summer, Audubon organized an expedition to the coast of Labrador, in Canada. He hoped to discover new species and to study the feathers and breeding habits of the birds that spent the summer there. But Audubon saw few new species and found Labrador unbearable. He complained in his journal of the cold and the mosquitoes, and he later wrote about "the wonderful dreariness of the country."

In the spring of 1837, he traveled to the Republic of Texas, which had recently been created, and met its president, Sam Houston. Audubon failed to identify any new species of birds, but he learned much about the habits of birds west of the Mississippi River. Despite the difficulties of his travels, his project was completed the next year. In all, 435 color drawings were published as part of his series, *Birds of America.*

Audubon immediately began work on a series about four-legged animals, which was to be called *Quadrupeds of North America.* In March 1843, he set out to collect specimens for his new project. He also hoped to identify new species of birds for a new edition of *Birds of America.* He planned an eight-month journey and traveled to the regions of the upper Missouri and Yellowstone Rivers, but he never reached his goal, the Rocky Mountains. Audubon spent the rest of his life on his estate on the Hudson River. He died there in 1851.

Suggested Reading John J. Audubon, *Delineations of American Scenery and Character* (reprint, Ayer, 1970); Alice Ford, editor, *Audubon, By Himself* (Doubleday, 1969).

English
b November 2, 1796; Stockport, England
d June 23, 1878; London, England
Explored central Canadian Arctic

Admiral Sir George Back was famous not only for his work as an explorer but also for his illustrations of the Arctic region.

Admiralty governing body of Britain's Royal Navy until 1964

Admiral Sir George Back was called "in bravery, intelligence, and love of adventure . . . the very model of an English sailor." During his explorations of the Canadian Arctic, Back covered more than 10,000 miles on foot and by canoe. He not only led his own expeditions but also made significant contributions to the efforts and survival of others.

Before becoming an explorer, Back fought in naval battles against the French. While jailed in France as a prisoner of war, he studied mathematics and drawing. He continued to study art in Naples, Italy, after he was released. His first experience in exploration came in 1819, when he sailed with Sir John FRANKLIN's first Arctic expedition. Several of Franklin's starving men died, but more would have been lost without George Back's help.

Old Man of the Arctic

An attempt to save yet another expedition from disaster resulted in Back's most important discovery. When the British explorer John Ross disappeared in the Arctic, Back planned a voyage to find him. Ross turned up unexpectedly, but Back decided to go to the Arctic anyway, in 1833, to locate the mouth of Canada's Great Fish River, which was later renamed the Back River in his honor. He traveled the length of the river from the Great Slave Lake to the Arctic Ocean. When he returned to England, he published his account of the journey, together with his own illustrations.

In 1836 he accepted a new mission: to chart parts of the northern coast of Canada. The expedition ended in failure when his ship, the H.M.S. *Terror,* was trapped by ice in Hudson Bay. But Back won great admiration for his cool command during the crisis. When he returned to England in 1837, he was awarded the Royal Geographical Society's highest honors, and in 1839 he was knighted. He also served on the British **Admiralty's** Arctic Council. In late old age, he unveiled a monument in honor of John Franklin in Westminster Abbey, the church where many of Britain's great men and women are buried.

Suggested Reading George Back, *Arctic Artist: The Journal and Paintings of George Back, Midshipman with Franklin, 1819–1822,* edited by C. Stuart Houston, commentary by I. S. MacLaren (McGill-Queen's University Press, 1994) and *Narrative of the Arctic Land Expedition to the North of the Great Fish River, and Along the Shores of the Arctic Ocean, in the Years 1833, 1834, and 1835,* (reprint, M. G. Hurtig, 1970).

English
b 1584?; England?
d January 23, 1622; Qeshm, Iran
***Explored Greenland and attempted
Northwest Passage***

William Baffin was a brilliant navigator of the Arctic Ocean. In 1615 and 1616, he served as pilot for two expeditions that explored and charted the bay between northern Greenland and the largest Canadian island. Both the bay and the island now bear his name. Baffin also had an amazing natural talent for observation and measurement. His skills were so keen that he was able to make measurements nearly as accurate as those made by precision instruments hundreds of years later.

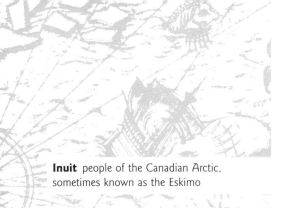

Inuit people of the Canadian Arctic, sometimes known as the Eskimo

longitude distance east or west of an imaginary line on the earth's surface; in 1884 most nations agreed to draw the line through Greenwich, England

Northwest Passage water route connecting the Atlantic Ocean and Pacific Ocean through the Arctic islands of northern Canada

mate assistant to the commander of a ship

Baffin's Early Voyages

Nothing is known about Baffin's early life. He does not appear in any records before 1612, when he sailed to Greenland with Captain James Hall. Baffin served as pilot of Hall's ship. The mission ended tragically when Hall was killed by the local **Inuit** people. Hall had taken part in an earlier expedition with a Danish party that had treated the Inuit badly, and the Inuit had not forgotten.

While in Greenland, Baffin was the first navigator to try to determine **longitude** at sea by observing the position of the moon. Unfortunately, his results were not precise enough to be useful. After writing an account of that voyage, Baffin joined the English Muscovy Company as a pilot on several successful whaling expeditions to Spitsbergen, an island north of Norway. His experiences there sharpened his skills as an Arctic navigator.

Ice in the Arctic

In 1615 Baffin piloted Henry HUDSON's old ship, the *Discovery,* now under the command of Robert BYLOT. The expedition was sponsored by the **Northwest Passage** Company, which hoped to find a direct route to Asia by sailing north of Canada. Baffin sailed to the waters northwest of Hudson Strait, where his readings of the tides indicated that there was no passage to the north. Baffin's measurements were so accurate that 200 years later, they impressed the Arctic explorer William PARRY, who was using much better instruments. It was Parry who named Baffin Bay and Baffin Island.

The next year, again with Bylot, Baffin piloted the *Discovery* up Baffin Bay to Smith Sound. Although the voyage was a highly successful exploration, it was a failure for the Northwest Passage Company. The waters of Smith Sound were blocked by ice, and Baffin was forced to turn back. When he returned to England, Baffin wrote a detailed account of his voyage. He reported that there was no passage through the bay. This was not strictly correct, and Matthew Perry found a way out of the bay in 1821. However, this route was so badly blocked with ice that it was not only unprofitable but also extremely dangerous. In the end, Baffin saved the merchants much time and money by convincing them that it was best to focus their efforts elsewhere.

Despite his careful observations, many geographers doubted Baffin's story because of errors made by his publisher, Samuel PURCHAS. Purchas was rather careless with the text of Baffin's report, and he left out the detailed map that Baffin had drawn. In 1635 Luke FOXE published a map that included the bay described in Baffin's report, but later maps left the area blank. It was not until Captain John Ross rediscovered the bay in 1818 that Baffin received full credit.

Travels in the Middle East

Baffin wanted to try to find the Northwest Passage's western end in the Pacific Ocean. In 1617 he sailed from England to India as **mate** aboard the ship *Anne Royal,* which was owned by the British East India Company. The ship was sent to establish trade in the Red Sea. Baffin charted the waters there and in the Persian Gulf. He returned to England in 1619, having apparently given up on the Arctic.

The next year, Baffin signed on with the *London,* one of four ships sailing to the Middle East. At the entrance to the Persian Gulf, the fleet fought a combined force of two Portuguese ships and two Dutch ships. The captain of the *London* was killed in the battle, but the fleet sailed on, helping the ruler of Persia (now Iran) to drive out the Portuguese.

Baffin lost his life on this mission, but it seems fitting that he was taking measurements when he died. He had gone ashore near the castle of Qeshm to measure the height and distance of the castle walls so that the British could aim their guns more accurately. During a skirmish outside the walls, Baffin was killed. The British took the castle without the help of his measurements.

Baffin's Contributions to Navigation

Baffin's observations and notes proved invaluable to many later explorers and discoverers. His readings of **latitude** were always nearly perfect. He made brilliant attempts to determine longitude before the invention of the **chronometer.** Baffin also measured the earth's magnetic field in various places around the world. The first magnetic chart, published in 1701, would not have been possible without his efforts. Although Baffin's fame was delayed, his place in history is now secure.

Suggested Reading Clements R. Markham, *Voyages of William Baffin* (Hakluyt Society, 1881).

latitude distance north or south of the equator

chronometer clock designed to keep precise time in the rough conditions of sea travel

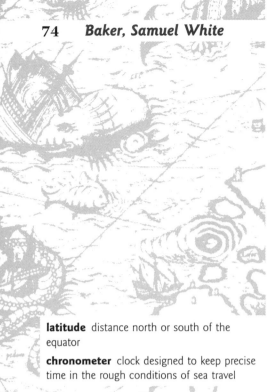

Baker, Samuel White

English
b June 8, 1821; London, England
d September 30, 1893; Devonshire, England
Explored Nile River and Lake Albert

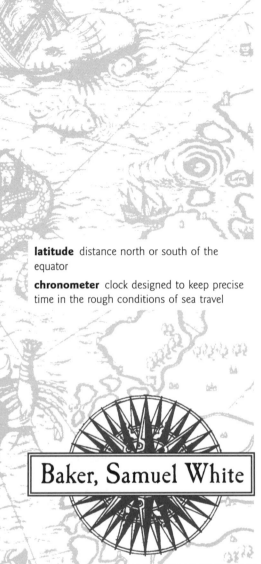

typhus disease that causes high fever, dizziness, and rashes; often transmitted by body lice

Samuel White Baker went to Africa to search for the source of the Nile River. He is best known, however, for his attempts to create British colonies in Africa and to stop the slave trade in the Sudan. He and his second wife, Florence Baker, also explored the White Nile River and discovered Lake Albert.

Early Life and Travels

Baker was born into a wealthy English family. He was educated in Germany and developed a love of travel, hunting, and adventure. In his early 20s, he married a minister's daughter and managed his father's plantations on the island of Mauritius in the Indian Ocean. He later started his own successful agricultural business on the island of Ceylon (present-day Sri Lanka). After about 10 years overseas, Baker returned to England with his wife, Henrietta, who died of **typhus** shortly after.

Baker spent the next few years traveling in Asia Minor, the Crimea, and the Balkans. In 1860 Baker married a young Hungarian woman, Florence Ninian von Sass. Florence shared Baker's love of adventure, and the newlyweds decided to organize an expedition to search for the source of the Nile River.

Explorations and Emergencies

The Bakers arrived in Cairo, Egypt, in 1861. They had plenty of time and money for their journey because they were wealthy, independent travelers rather than military officers or hired adventurers.

tributary stream or river that flows into a larger stream or river

Samuel Baker was motivated by his love of adventure and his hatred of the African slave trade.

They spent their first year in Africa exploring the Nile and its **tributaries** at an easy pace. They traveled south on the Nile to Berber, in the Sudan, learning Arabic along the way. Then, when they reached Khartoum, the situation changed. The office of the Royal Geographical Society in Khartoum asked the Bakers to lead an expedition to locate two missing explorers, John Hanning Speke and James Augustus Grant. The two explorers, who had been sponsored by the society, had disappeared during the previous year while searching for the source of the Nile. The Bakers agreed to help find Speke and Grant, and they spent the next six months organizing the rescue expedition.

In December 1862, the Bakers began the 1,000-mile trip to Gondokoro. They arrived in six weeks, and the missing explorers showed up unharmed just two weeks later. Though they were relieved that the two men were safe, the Bakers were disappointed to learn that Speke and Grant had located the Nile's source. The two men suggested that the Bakers study a portion of the Nile that remained unexplored, as well as a lake that was rumored to be linked to the river. Speke and Grant gave the Bakers a map of their route, and the couple headed south.

The Bakers had to join a slave trader's caravan to travel safely through the kingdom of Bunyoro (in what is now Uganda). The ruler of Bunyoro and his people were not happy to have Europeans on their land. Even so, one year after leaving Gondokoro, the couple reached the eastern shore of the lake they had sought. The local tribes called the lake Luta N'zige, but Baker renamed it Lake Albert in honor of the husband of England's Queen Victoria. The Bakers also found Murchison Falls (now called Kabalega Falls), which they named for the president of the Royal Geographical Society. The society awarded Samuel Baker its gold medal for his accomplishments, and he was knighted by the queen in 1866. That year, Baker published a book entitled *The Albert N'yanza, Great Basin of the Nile, and Explorations of the Nile Sources.* Two years later, he released a second book, *Exploration of the Nile Tributaries.*

Fighting the Slave Trade

In 1869 Baker and his wife were in Egypt for the opening of the Suez Canal. Ismail, the ruler of Egypt, asked Baker to make a four-year expedition to claim for Egypt the lands that lay south along the White Nile toward Lake Victoria. It was a dangerous job, but Baker was eager for adventure, and he wanted to help Ismail wipe out the slave trade in the region. He was given command of a force of 1,200 men.

It took Baker a year to struggle through the Nile's swamps to Gondokoro. During the years since his previous journeys, the area had become poorer, the slave traders more powerful, and the local tribes more hostile. Baker was able to gain the confidence of some tribes by offering Egypt's protection. He established several military stations in 1871, but he also aroused the anger of many local chiefs and slave traders. More and more, Baker depended on military force to put down local uprisings, and he angered many tribes by taking their supplies for his soldiers.

One of Baker's toughest opponents was the ruler of the Bunyoro kingdom. During the Bakers' expedition of 1863, this ruler had forced Baker to surrender most of his possessions to buy passage through the Bunyoro kingdom. Now Baker and his troops were forced to fight the Bunyoro people. Baker captured the region for Ismail's empire, but Egypt's control over it was never secure.

Baker was unsuccessful in shutting down the slave traders, who had become the rulers of many areas. After Baker returned to Britain in 1873, Egyptian officials often simply took over the local slave trade from those who had run it before.

Although this expedition was a failure, Baker is credited with the first serious attempt to combat slavery in the Sudan. In addition, his extensive travels made him one of Britain's leading experts on the Nile River and central Africa.

Suggested Reading Richard Hall, *Lovers on the Nile: The Incredible African Journeys of Sam and Florence Baker* (Random House, 1980); Dorothy Middleton, *Baker of the Nile* (Falcon Press, 1949).

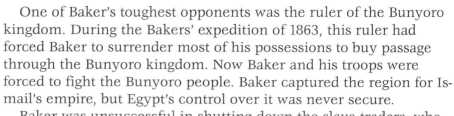

Balboa, Vasco Nuñez de

Spanish
b 1475; Jerez de los Caballeros, Spain
d January 21, 1519; Acla, Panama
Discovered Pacific Ocean

Vasco Nuñez de Balboa founded the Spanish town of Darién (now in Colombia) and explored the areas nearby. In 1513 he left Darién without permission from Spanish authorities. Using information given him by local Indians, Balboa led an expedition to find the "Great Waters." He became the first European to see the Pacific Ocean from North America.

Caribbean Troubles

Balboa was born in 1475 into a family of poor nobles in the province of Badajoz, Spain. We know very little about his youth. In 1501 he sailed for Hispaniola, the island where Haiti and the Dominican Republic are located today.

On Hispaniola, Balboa settled down as a planter, but he was not suited for that life and soon ran up very large debts. To escape the men to whom he owed money, he hid himself and his dog Leoncico in a huge jug. They were smuggled onto a ship carrying supplies for the Spanish colony at San Sebastián on the Gulf of Urabá. On the way, the ship met a **brigantine** commanded by Francisco PIZARRO. Pizarro had come from San Sebastián and said that all the members of the colony, except his crew, had died from disease and Indian attacks. Pizarro and the commander of the supply ship, Martín Fernández de Enciso, sailed together to the shore and found San Sebastián in ashes.

brigantine two-masted sailing ship with both square and triangular sails

Rise to Power

By then, Balboa had been accepted as a member of Enciso's crew. He told Enciso about an Indian village on the mainland (in what is now Panama) that he had seen on his way to Hispaniola. The Spaniards went to the village, where they seized control of the Indians and their rich supplies of food, cotton, and treasures. The Spaniards set up a headquarters, and Balboa officially founded the

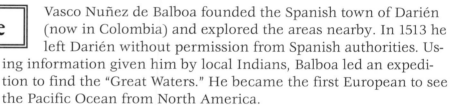

Vasco Nuñez de Balboa crossed land that cost many later explorers their health and strength—and even their lives.

pirogue canoe usually made from a hollow tree trunk

plateau high, flat area of land

town of Santa María la Antigua del Darién. He quickly set about building his power.

Balboa convinced the Spanish colonists that Enciso, a weak leader, had no authority in Darién. Enciso was forced to return to Spain to ask for help from King Ferdinand. Diego de Nicuesa arrived as the king's new governor, but Balboa pressured the colonists to reject him. The colonists picked Balboa and a man named Zamudio to rule as mayors. Balboa then got rid of Zamudio, too, by sending him to Spain to defend Balboa against the accusations made by Enciso.

Balboa ruled wisely for two years and had a talent for making friends with the local Indians. On the other hand, he conquered and looted the villages of any Indians who were hostile. He collected a fortune in gold and jewels. Many Indians told Balboa stories about "Great Waters" beyond the mountains. He was convinced that a large sea existed, so he wrote to King Ferdinand, asking for 1,000 men for an expedition of discovery. Before Balboa got his answer, he learned that the king was going to order him back to Spain. Realizing that he had to act quickly, Balboa started the expedition on his own.

The Far Side of America

Bolboa's party left Darién on September 1, 1513, in one brigantine and ten **pirogues,** with 190 Spaniards, 800 Indians, and several dogs, including Leoncico. They dropped anchor near the colony of Acla. The spot was at the narrowest part of Panama—a lucky choice. Balboa made an alliance with the local Indian chief, Careta, who presented the Spaniard with his daughter as a bride. Leaving with about half of his men, Balboa started south. Carrying heavy weapons and armor in the hot and humid climate, the Spanish found the going extremely tough. Few parts of the world were as hard to pass through, but after three days, they reached a deserted Indian village. Balboa needed new guides for the rest of the trip, so he found the Indians who had left that village and befriended them. Their chief was so impressed that he gave Balboa guides to take him to a mountain ridge. From there, the chief said, the "Great Waters" could be seen.

Travel was no easier when they continued, and it took the group four days to cover about 30 miles. They met a tribe of hostile Indians and defeated them in a bloody battle. The Spanish tortured many of the captured Indians and looted their village, collecting much treasure. Finally the Spanish party reached a small **plateau** near the top of a high mountain. On September 27, 1513, Balboa climbed alone to the summit and gazed past the rocks and greenery. He became the first European to see the vast Pacific Ocean from North America. When the rest of his party joined him, they sang the Te Deum, a Christian hymn, and built a cross.

Balboa sent out three separate groups to find the best way to the shore. They decided on a path and went together to the ocean's edge. Balboa waded into the water carrying his sword in one hand and the banner of Spain's royal family in the other. He claimed the

The Spanish flag, as it appeared in Balboa's time, combined the symbols of the provinces of Castile and León.

ocean, its islands, and all the lands around it as the property of Spain. He named the ocean the Mar del Sur, which means South Sea in Spanish.

Glory and Conflict

For the return trip, Balboa chose a different route, but it was as difficult as the first. The explorers nearly died of hunger because they were carrying so much treasure instead of food. They won even more treasure when they surprised and captured a powerful chief called Tubanama and held him for ransom. (His name may be the source of the name of the country of Panama.) Balboa then caught a feverish illness and had to be carried into town when his party reached Darién, about four and a half months after they had left.

While Balboa had been away, King Ferdinand had made Pedro Arias de Ávila, known as Pedrarias, the new mayor of Darién. Pedrarias asked Balboa if it was true that Leoncico was getting the same share of the booty as a soldier. Balboa said that it was true, because the soldiers had agreed that the dog was worth several fighting men.

Pedrarias was not a strong leader, and he was always jealous of Balboa's popularity. At a rare time when there was less tension between them, Balboa began a bold new adventure. He built ships on the shore of the Pacific Ocean, intending to explore the unknown coastline. Hundreds of Indian slaves died while carrying the parts of the ships over the mountains and through the jungles. Balboa managed to have two ships built. He set sail and soon encountered the Pearl Islands off the coast. However, poor winds forced him to return to the mainland.

Trouble Catches Up with Balboa

Meanwhile, Pedrarias had become certain that Balboa was plotting to set up a separate government on the west coast of Panama. Pedrarias sent a message to Balboa, asking him to come to Darién. He said he wanted to hold discussions, but he actually planned to arrest Balboa. Soon Pedrarias worried that Balboa might not show up, so he ordered Pizarro to take an armed force to the west coast. Balboa met Pizarro, who had once been his lieutenant, halfway across Panama. He went with Pizarro without fighting. When they reached Darién, Pedrarias had Balboa put on trial and convicted of treason. Although the colonists supported their popular hero, he was sentenced to die. Balboa was beheaded in Acla on January 21, 1519, not far from the town he had founded and made famous in the world of his time.

Vasco Nuñez de Balboa was always loyal to Spain, but he was also a brash and independent explorer. He often ignored his leaders, set his own goals, and organized his own plans. The area he explored was fairly small, but it included some of the most forbidding terrain in the world. His discovery of the Pacific Ocean stands out in history as a tremendous feat.

Suggested Reading Charles L. G. Anderson, *Life and Letters of Vasco Nuñez de Balboa* (Fleming H. Revell Company, 1941); Kathleen Romoli, *Balboa of Darién: Discoverer of the Pacific* (Doubleday, 1953).

Banks, Joseph

English
b February 15, 1743; London, England
d June 19, 1820; London, England
Sailed as naturalist with James Cook

circumnavigation journey around the world

specimen sample of a plant, animal, or mineral, usually collected for scientific study or display

botany the scientific study of plants

Joseph Banks's descriptions of the culture of Tahiti sparked Europe's scientific interest in the Pacific.

Sir Joseph Banks was a naturalist who accompanied Captain James Cook on Cook's first **circumnavigation** of the globe and exploration of the South Pacific. Banks and his assistants collected thousands of **specimens,** drawings, and descriptions of exotic plant and animal life from South America, Tahiti, New Holland (now called Australia), and the Great Barrier Reef. He was so successful that it became common practice for naturalists to sail with such expeditions.

Young Man with a Bright Future

Banks was born in 1743, the son of a wealthy doctor. He was educated at Harrow, Eton, and Oxford—the finest schools in Britain. As a student, he showed a keen interest in **botany** and the natural sciences. When he was 15, he took part in a voyage to Newfoundland to collect specimens and nearly died of a fever. The collection of plants he gathered is now on display in the British Museum.

Banks was 18 when his father died. The young man inherited an annual income and was able to live comfortably while pursuing his interest in the natural sciences. Seven years later, he persuaded the British government to allow him to join James Cook's expedition to the Pacific Ocean. Cook's mission was to observe the planet Venus as it passed between the earth and the sun.

Banks contributed a substantial amount of money to hire a team of assistants and artists. Such a well-equipped group of scientists had never before sailed with an expedition. They brought with them an entire library of books about natural history. One man who knew Banks reported that the team had "all sorts of machines for catching and preserving insects, all types of nets, trawls, drags, and hooks for coral fishing, they even have a curious contrivance of a telescope by which, put into the water, you can see the bottom at great depth."

Island Adventures

Cook's ship, the *Endeavour,* left Britain in August 1768, headed for the Pacific Ocean by way of South America. Banks and his team spent the days at sea dragging nets through the water and cataloging their finds. In December the ship reached the large island known as Tierra del Fuego, at the southern tip of South America. The scientists went ashore to study plants in the mountains, where two of Banks's servants froze to death.

The next stop was Tahiti, a tropical island with a more pleasant climate than Tierra del Fuego. Banks learned to speak the islanders' language and served as an interpreter for the Tahitians and the British. Presenting gifts, he went to great lengths to win the trust of the islanders. He even removed his clothes and darkened his skin with charcoal and water in order to fit in better. With or without this disguise, the Tahitians seemed to accept him. He was allowed to visit burial grounds that no European had ever seen before.

Banks was a sharp observer of Tahitian culture, and his journal provided a fascinating picture of their way of life. He recorded every detail of daily living, describing how the islanders made

dysentery disease that causes severe diarrhea

fishhooks from bones and wove nets from jungle vines. He also provided the first descriptions of surfing ever to reach Europe. Not content just to observe, he allowed himself to be tattooed. The tradition of sailors being tattooed may have begun in this way. Like so many Europeans who visited Tahiti, Banks also noted the charms of Tahitian women, including one named Queen Obarea.

The voyage continued to New Zealand, Australia, and the Great Barrier Reef, where Banks added to his growing collection of specimens. The Australian Aborigines were not as friendly as the Tahitians. Skirmishes with the people of New Guinea, along with an outbreak of **dysentery,** cut short his activities there. Even so, Banks made several discoveries. He was the first European to describe a kangaroo, and he found a spot near what is now Sydney, Australia, that was so rich in plant life that he called it Botany Bay. He later recommended Botany Bay as the site for a new British prison colony.

Life as a Famous Scientist

The trip was a huge success for Banks, who collected more than 1,000 plants, 500 fish, 500 birds, and countless insects, shells, corals, and rocks. He also acquired many small objects, cloths, and carvings made by the peoples of the Pacific. In fact, upon his return to Britain in 1771, the public considered Banks, rather than Cook, to be the hero of the voyage. Banks found himself very popular in the circles of London's high society, and he was honored when even King George III asked to meet with him.

One year later, Banks planned to accompany Cook on a second voyage, this time with an even larger team, including several musicians. But Cook's ship could not sail with the extra cabins and cargo, so the captain asked Banks to make do with fewer assistants. Banks angrily refused and instead made a private journey to conduct research in Iceland and the Hebrides, islands in the Atlantic Ocean northwest of Scotland.

Despite this disagreement, the captain and the naturalist remained friends. When Cook returned to Britain from his next voyage, he brought with him a young Tahitian man named Omai. Banks took the visitor in, dressed him in the finest clothes, and introduced him to London society. He even took him on hunting trips to Yorkshire. Omai soon returned to the Pacific with Cook, who continued to bring Banks new specimens.

In 1777 Banks was named president of the Royal Society, an organization of British scientists, and he held this post for the next 42 years. When Cook died, Banks persuaded the society to produce a medal to commemorate the captain's achievements. He also promoted many new expeditions and explorers, such as William BLIGH, Mungo PARK, and Matthew FLINDERS. He served as royal adviser for London's Kew Gardens and played a key role in establishing botanical gardens in Jamaica, St. Vincent, and Ceylon (now known as Sri Lanka). After his death, a statue in his honor was placed in London's Natural History Museum.

Suggested Reading J. C. Beaglehole, *The Endeavour Journal of Joseph Banks,* 2 volumes (Angus and Robertson, 1962); Harold B. Carter, *Sir Joseph Banks, 1743–1820* (Omnigraphics, 1987).

Barbosa, Duarte

Portuguese
b 1480?; Portugal
d June 6, 1521; Cebu, Philippines
*Explored Indian Ocean;
sailed with Magellan in service of Spain*

Duarte Barbosa was related to the wife of Ferdinand MAGELLAN and became one of Magellan's most loyal supporters on the first journey around the world. Barbosa was already an experienced seaman when he played a major role in Magellan's historic expedition.

In Love with the Sea

Barbosa was born in Portugal in the late 1400s, but he may have grown up in Spain. Historians believe that he was the son or nephew of Diogo Barbosa, an official in the Spanish government. Duarte was lured to the sea, as were many young Portuguese men at that exciting time. He traveled widely, sailing to the Cape of Good Hope, the east coast of Africa, and Arabia. He helped make important trade deals at Aden and Hormuz, on the Persian Gulf. He proceeded from there to western India and as far east as Sumatra, in present-day Indonesia. India was probably where Barbosa first met Magellan, who was traveling there with a Portuguese official.

Duarte returned to Lisbon, Portugal, around 1516 and published a book about his adventures, *The Book of Duarte Barbosa.* He was eager to continue his explorations but received little support from Portugal's King Manuel I. Disappointed, Barbosa headed to the city of Pôrto, where many discontented sailors gathered. There he met Magellan and interested him in sailing around South America to the Spice Islands (now called the Moluccas). The two men left Pôrto in October 1517 and traveled to Spain. They stayed in the household of Diogo Barbosa, and Magellan married Diogo's daughter, Beatriz. Spain's King Charles I gave Magellan his support for the ocean voyage.

Leadership on a Difficult Journey

Tensions were high from the start between the Spanish and Portuguese crew members of Magellan's expedition. On April 2, 1520, the fleet was off the southern coast of South America when 30 sailors seized one of the ships. Barbosa handpicked a group of reliable crewmen, and they easily recaptured the ship of rebels. For his loyalty, Barbosa was rewarded by Magellan with command of the *Victoria,* which would be the only ship to complete the voyage.

Barbosa proved to be a natural leader. He set an example by showing the physical and mental strength to endure the hardships of the journey. The explorers sailed in uncharted waters for months without seeing land. When the food ran out, the men were forced to eat rats and leather. They reached Asia in the spring of 1521, but Magellan was killed in the Philippines soon afterward. Barbosa and his countryman Juan Serrano were chosen as the new leaders of the expedition.

Barbosa did not survive much longer than Magellan. The ruler of the island of Cebu in the Philippines invited Barbosa and 26 crewmen to a banquet on shore. Serrano was opposed to the idea, but Barbosa persuaded him to go along. At the banquet, all the sailors except Serrano and one other were ambushed and killed. Serrano was stripped naked and bound in chains—his shipmates had to abandon him to die on the island. Although Barbosa never made it back to Europe, the *Victoria* did complete the journey, thanks in part to his leadership and courage.

Barents, Willem

Dutch
b 1550?; Terschelling Island, Netherlands
d June 20, 1597; Barents Sea
*Explored Northeast Passage and
discovered Spitsbergen Island*

Northeast Passage water route connecting
the Atlantic Ocean and Pacific Ocean along
the Arctic coastline of Europe and Asia

Suggested Reading Duarte Barbosa, *The Book of Duarte Barbosa*, 2 volumes, translated by M. L. Dames (Hakluyt Society, 1921).

At a time when many explorers sailed to East Asia around the southern tip of Africa, Willem Barents searched for a route through the Arctic. Between 1594 and 1597, Barents made three voyages to locate a **Northeast Passage** that would make trade with China easier. Although he never found a passage free of ice, he did discover Spitsbergen Island, the largest of a group of islands that are now part of Norway.

Two Early Failures

On Barents's first expedition in 1594, two of his ships, piloted by other captains, made significant progress in the Northeast Passage. The *Swan* and the *Mercury* sailed through the Pet Strait, which lies between the northern coast of Russia and the island of Novaya Zemlya. The strait was named after the English explorer Arthur Pet, whose sailing directions Barents had translated. The ships reached the Kara Sea and then turned back, for their captains were sure that they had discovered the passage to China. In fact, they were many hundreds of miles away. Barents himself tried to sail north of Novaya Zemlya but was stopped by ice.

A second expedition was organized the next year by Dutch leaders who were confident that Barents could reach China. Seven ships in four Dutch ports were loaded with goods to be traded in the East. This expedition was a failure. The ships found the Pet Strait clogged by ice, and they returned home. Both of Barents's voyages had been funded with public money, and the Dutch government now voted to waste no more money exploring this route.

Over 200 years later, the Swedish explorer Nils Adolf Erik Nor-denskiöld studied Barents's voyages. Nordenskiöld believed that if Barents had persevered, he could have passed the ice and reached the Russian settlements on the Obi and Yenisei Rivers. In this way, Barents could have established trade between Europe and central Asia. But the lure of trade with China must have been much stronger for both Barents and his sponsors.

The Discovery of Spitsbergen

Barents refused to give up on the route to China. Both he and his scientific adviser, the Reverend Peter Plancius, believed that ice was a problem only near the shore. They hoped that ships sailing far north of Novaya Zemlya would find open waters. Barents persuaded the merchants of Amsterdam to finance another voyage, and he set out again in 1596.

Barents piloted a vessel commanded by Jacob van Heemskerck. A second ship was commanded by Jan Cornelius Rijp. On June 9 both ships discovered Bear Island, and 10 days later, they found Spitsbergen Island, which they thought was Greenland. The two captains then disagreed about the best course to take, and the ships separated. Rijp sailed a short distance farther north and then returned home. Barents headed for Novaya Zemlya, but on August 26

The islands discovered by Willem Barents were later a rich source of profits for Dutch and English hunters of whales, seals, and walrus.

scurvy disease caused by lack of vitamin C and once a major cause of death among sailors; symptoms include internal bleeding, loosened teeth, and extreme fatigue

the ship was trapped in ice near the island. The crew was forced to abandon the ship and spend the winter on the ice.

Survival in the Arctic

Barents and his men knew of only one crew that had wintered in the Arctic before then. Those English sailors, led by Hugh Willoughby 40 years earlier, had all frozen to death. The Dutch knew that their chances of survival were not good. With driftwood and some of the ship's timbers, they built a cabin with a fireplace. The area's many foxes were a good supply of food. Polar bears were the biggest problem, but the men overcame even this danger. They also made careful astronomical and geographical observations.

Of the 17 men on the ice, 15 survived the winter. (The other two probably died of **scurvy.**) But when summer came, the ship remained stuck in the ice. The men had no choice but to use the ship's two small boats. Before leaving the cabin, Captain Heemskerck wrote out two copies of an account of the voyage—one copy for each boat. Barents wrote his own account, which he placed in the cabin's chimney. It was found 274 years later, just where Barents had left it.

The two small boats set out in June 1597. Barents never reached home—on the seventh day of the journey, he died of scurvy. After 80 days of rowing and sailing over 1,600 miles, the boats reached a Dutch trading settlement on the coast of Russia. There they met Captain Rijp, who took them home. All of Europe marveled at their story.

Suggested Reading Rayner Unwin, *A Winter Away from Home: William Barents and the North-east Passage* (Seafarer Books, 1995); Gerrit de Veer, *The Three Voyages of William Barents to the Arctic Regions (1594, 1595, and 1596)*, edited by Charles T. Beke (B. Franklin, 1964).

Barrow, John

English
b June 19, 1764; Ulverston, England
d November 23, 1848; London, England
Founded Royal Geographical Society

Admiralty governing body of Britain's Royal Navy until 1964

Northwest Passage water route connecting the Atlantic Ocean and Pacific Ocean through the Arctic islands of northern Canada

As a young man, John Barrow showed himself to be a hard worker with a sense of adventure. When he grew up, these qualities led him to support Arctic exploration and to found England's Royal Geographical Society.

England, China, and Africa

Barrow had an active and difficult youth. In his early teens, he worked in an iron factory in Liverpool, England. At the age of 15, he became a crewman on a whaling ship in the Arctic Ocean. This sailing experience marked the beginning of his interest in Arctic exploration. He was also the first person to make a balloon flight in England. Barrow later worked as a tutor to the son of Sir George Leonard Staunton. Sir George was the chief assistant of a British nobleman named Lord Macartney. This connection would launch Barrow's brilliant career in the service of his country.

Lord Macartney was named Britain's ambassador to China, and Barrow was invited to join him as a scientific adviser. Barrow's observations and writings helped shape Europe's understanding of China's culture and history. Macartney was then appointed governor of Cape Colony in South Africa. He again invited Barrow to join him as an adviser, and Barrow accepted. In 1803 Barrow returned to Britain and became permanent secretary of the **Admiralty.** He held this post for almost 40 years.

The Arctic and the World

When the Napoleonic Wars ended in 1815, large numbers of skilled British naval officers were released from duty. Barrow used his influence with the Admiralty to employ many of these sailors in the search for a **Northwest Passage.** In the early 1800s, European ships sailing to Asia had to make a long and dangerous journey around either South America or Africa. Barrow hoped to find a shorter sea route to Asia across the Arctic Ocean. The passage was not found until years after Barrow's death. However, the expeditions he sent out made many important geographic discoveries. Explorers of the Canadian Arctic named Barrow Strait and Cape Barrow after the secretary who supported their work.

In 1830 Barrow made perhaps his most important contribution to exploration. Together with six others, he founded the Royal Geographical Society. The society soon became the world's leading independent sponsor of exploration. It backed many of history's most important explorers, including David LIVINGSTONE and John Hanning SPEKE.

John Barrow founded the Royal Geographical Society, which sponsored the work of hundreds of explorers.

Suggested Reading John Barrow, *The Mutiny of the Bounty* (Oxford University Press, 1975); Christopher Lloyd, *Mr. Barrow of the Admiralty: A Life of Sir John Barrow, 1764-1848* (Collins, 1970).

Barth, Heinrich

German
b February 16, 1821; Hamburg, Germany
d November 25, 1865; Berlin, Germany
Explored North Africa and central Africa

Heinrich Barth covered 10,000 miles during his six-year exploration of the African interior.

Heinrich Barth is now considered one of the leading explorers and scholars of Africa, although his work was not fully appreciated during his lifetime. He traveled in the Sahara and the Sudan regions for nearly six years through territory that was largely unknown to Europeans. His knowledge of history, geography, and archaeology enabled him to make important observations about these lands and the people who lived there.

Young Loner

Barth was the son of a wealthy merchant. As a child, he became obsessed with the desire to impress his mother by becoming more successful than his father. The young Barth applied himself to his schoolwork, ignoring all social activities. He spent his time reading books on science, geography, and languages. As a student at the University of Berlin, he excelled in archaeology, history, and geography, but he did not develop any social skills.

Concerned about his son's lack of personal contact, Barth's father sent him on a lengthy tour of London, Paris, and the Mediterranean region. He hoped that new people and places would bring his son out of his shell. The trip did nothing to cure Barth's inability to relate to others, but it did spark his interest in Africa. After visiting the North African coast, he became fascinated with the idea of exploring the vast lands to the south. Instead, he returned to Germany after three years to take a teaching position at the University of Berlin.

Barth's social difficulties continued to be a problem. He was so unpopular with his students and fellow instructors that the archaeology course he taught was canceled. Barth suffered another blow when the woman he had been seeing suddenly ended their relationship. Those disappointments were soon forgotten. The batch of mail that brought his sweetheart's letter also included an invitation to join an expedition to the African interior. The 28-year-old Barth accepted immediately, and two months later, he was back in North Africa as a member of the English Mixed Scientific and Commercial Expedition.

Explorations in Libya

The leader of the expedition was a British former missionary, James Richardson, who was an accomplished explorer. He planned to gather information about the Sahara while making trade arrangements for British merchants. In March 1850, the party left the Libyan city of Tripoli and traveled south toward the city of Kano in what is now Nigeria.

Barth made his first major discovery about 500 miles south of Tripoli, near the desert town of Murzuch. He found the ruins of an ancient Roman settlement along a dry river valley. Farther south, he found rock paintings made by peoples who had lived there from the Stone Age to about A.D. 100. The paintings showed how the once fertile land had gradually become a desert. The earliest paintings showed tropical animals, such as elephants and ostriches. Later images featured cattle and horses, which thrive on grassy plains. The most recent paintings were of the desert's best-known animal, the camel.

sultan ruler of a Muslim nation

malaria disease that is spread by mosquitoes in tropical areas

sheikh Arab chief

Barth's social skills were still not as good as his scientific skills. He and Richardson quickly grew to dislike each other. But Barth had the support of a German geologist on the expedition, Adolf Overweg. The two Germans began riding and camping apart from their leader. Several times they left the party to explore on their own, but one such trip nearly cost Barth his life. While climbing the supposedly haunted Mount Idinen, Barth and Overweg became separated. Barth was trapped on the hot, barren mountain. At one point, he became so thirsty that he sucked blood from his own veins. He almost died before he was rescued.

The journey was also made difficult by the Tuareg people of the Sahara. The explorers faced the constant threat of attack as they made their way to the city of Ghat. After a few months, though, they made a truce with the Tuareg and were allowed safe passage. Barth then struck out on his own to visit Agadès, where he was an honored guest at the crowning of the new **sultan.** He spent several weeks investigating the ancient town and befriending its citizens, who called him *Abd-el-Kerim,* which means "servant of God." In October, Barth rejoined his companions at the oasis of Tintellust in the Aïr Mountains. Three months later, they parted company to pursue three separate paths to Lake Chad. They agreed to meet in the city of Kuka (now Kukawa, Nigeria), near the lake's western shore.

The Loner Becomes a Diplomat

Within three weeks, Barth traveled 375 miles south, reaching the city of Kano in February 1851. Although his supplies were running low, he wisely offered expensive gifts to the chief officials of the province. They rewarded him with their full hospitality during his monthlong stay. In addition to studying the society and geography of the area, Barth paved the way for profitable trade agreements between Kano and Europe. While on his way to meet Richardson and Overweg at Kuka, he learned that Richardson had died of **malaria.**

Barth was becoming much more skilled at dealing with people, and he received a warm welcome from Sultan Omar of Bornu. The sultan gave him access to the entire territory and provided guides to help him explore Lake Chad. But Barth left that task to Overweg and traveled south to Yola, where he discovered parts of the Benue River. He then went east to explore the Shari River.

Barth was now almost out of money, so he wrote to his sponsors in London to ask for more. The funds arrived with instructions to head west to Timbuktu (in present-day Mali). While the explorers prepared for this journey, Overweg died of malaria.

The Dangerous Journey to Timbuktu

Barth left Bornu and headed west across the plains to Sokoto (in present-day Nigeria). Without the sultan's protection, Barth and his six-man party had to beware of the area's tribesmen and bandits. He kept his men constantly on guard and posed as a holy man delivering religious books to the **sheikh** of Timbuktu. His disguise was so convincing that some local people believed that he was the Messiah.

Timbuktu proved to be a disappointment. Europeans had thought that it was a rich and beautiful city, but Barth discovered that it was a dull, poor place. The city's residents disliked foreigners and accused him of being a spy. Barth later said that he was safe in Timbuktu only because people feared his Colt six-shooter pistol, a recent invention. When he was permitted to leave Timbuktu in May 1854, Barth returned to Kuka, where he was welcomed by the tribes he had befriended earlier.

In Kuka he learned that his sponsors in Europe feared that he was dead and had sent an explorer named Eduard Vogel to discover his fate. Barth met Vogel in the Bundi jungle and brought him to Kuka. In August 1855, Barth returned to Tripoli and then to Europe, exhausted after nearly six years in Africa.

Return to Europe

When Barth arrived in London, he was honored with the Patron's Medal of the Royal Geographical Society. He again withdrew from the company of others and spent the next three years writing a full account of his experiences. The five-volume work met with a mixed reception from its readers, who considered it believable but dull. Years later the book was more fully appreciated for its wealth of useful facts, keen insights, and detailed maps and drawings.

Barth returned to Germany and was welcomed back to the University of Berlin as a professor of geography. He remained disappointed that the public did not acclaim his work, but he did not live long enough to see that opinion change. Two years after coming home, he died at the age of 44 from a stomach ailment that had begun in Africa.

Suggested Reading Brian Gardner, *The Quest for Timbuctoo* (Harcourt, Brace and World 1968); Robert I. Rotberg, *Africa and its Explorers* (Harvard University Press, 1970).

For a map of Barth's travels, see the article about Gustav NACHTIGAL in Volume 2.

Bartram, John

American
b March 23, 1699; near Darby, Pennsylvania
d September 22, 1777; Kingsessing, Pennsylvania
Studied plants of eastern North America

botanist scientist who studies plants
botany the scientific study of plants

John Bartram has been called the first American **botanist.** His passion for collecting and studying plants led him throughout eastern North America. His studies took him as far north as Lake Ontario and as far south as Florida.

Bartram became interested in plants while growing up on a farm in colonial Pennsylvania. He later traveled to Philadelphia to buy books about plants, and he taught himself **botany.** At the age of 29, he bought property on the Schuylkill River near Philadelphia. He planted gardens and conducted experiments in creating new types of plants. George Washington and Benjamin Franklin often came to Bartram's gardens to relax and talk.

Travels in the American Wilderness

Bartram made the first of many trips to study America's plant life in 1738. He began in Williamsburg, Virginia, and then traveled up the James River and across the Blue Ridge Mountains, covering more than 1,000 miles in five weeks. In 1751 he published his journals from a trip to Lake Ontario. Over the next decade, he visited the Catskill Mountains, North Carolina, South Carolina, and the frontier fort that became the city of Pittsburgh.

Soon afterward, a British friend managed to have Bartram named botanist to King George III, a position with a comfortable salary.

Bartram was grateful and relieved, since he had always traveled at his own expense. In 1765 he traveled as royal botanist to Charleston, South Carolina, where he joined his son William. Together father and son explored the Carolina wilderness for two months and then found a trail to Georgia. They continued south to Florida, where they charted the St. Johns River. Enduring swamps and mosquitoes, they studied Florida's natural world—trees, flowers, fruits, birds, fish, and minerals.

Although this effort was Bartram's last major expedition, he had a great influence on the exploration of America. He suggested the importance of studying the American West to Benjamin Franklin. Franklin took the idea to Thomas Jefferson, who sent Meriwether Lewis and William Clark on their famous journey from 1803 to 1806. Jefferson's instructions to Lewis and Clark were very similar to John Bartram's original proposal.

Suggested Reading Edmund Berkeley, *The Life and Travels of John Bartram* (University Presses of Florida, 1990); Helen Gere Cruickshank, editor, *John and William Bartram's America* (Devin-Adair, 1957); Thomas Slaughter, *The Natures of John and William Bartram* (Alfred A. Knopf, 1996).

Bastidas, Rodrigo de

Spanish
b 1460?; Triana, Spain
d 1526; Caribbean Sea
Explored coasts of Colombia and Panama

Rodrigo de Bastidas made his fortune as a merchant and sailor before he became an explorer. He was motivated to begin his new career by the profits other Spaniards had made in the Americas. He explored most of the coastline of present-day Colombia, and he became the first European to reach Central America.

Shipwrecked by Worms

Bastidas was about 40 years old when the Spanish crown gave him permission to discover new lands in South America. He was not, however, allowed to enter areas that had been discovered by Christopher Columbus or were controlled by Portugal. Teaming up with the great mapmaker Juan de La Cosa, Bastidas sailed in February 1501, following Columbus's route across the Atlantic Ocean.

Bastidas found an island rich in vegetation and called it Isla Verde, which means "Green Island" in Spanish. This island is either present-day Barbados or Grenada. He reached the coast of South America in what is now Colombia and traded with the Sinu (or Zenu) Indians. He then sailed north along the coast to Panama. It was the first expedition to reach Central America, but he could not take time to explore. He was forced to turn back because worms were slowly eating the wood of his ships. The collapsing vessels were wrecked on the southwest coast of Hispaniola (the island now occupied by Haiti and the Dominican Republic). Bastidas and La Cosa walked to the island's capital carrying a treasure of gold and pearls. For their trouble, they were arrested for trading in an area that was off-limits to them. After their release, they returned to Spain in 1504.

A Troubled Colony

Twenty years later, Bastidas was granted a license to found a colony on the **Spanish Main.** He recruited 500 settlers on Hispaniola and took them to the coast of Colombia, where he founded the city of Santa Marta. Unlike most Spanish explorers, Bastidas protected the

Spanish Main area of the Spanish Empire including the Caribbean coasts of Central America and South America

local Indians from slavery. He encouraged the colonists to do their own manual labor, but they rebelled against him. The settlement also suffered an epidemic of **dysentery.** Under such difficult conditions, Bastidas had to seek help in Hispaniola. He too had come down with dysentery, and he died aboard ship 12 days after leaving Santa Marta.

Suggested Reading Washington Irving, *Voyages and Discoveries of the Companions of Columbus* (reprint, Twayne, 1986).

Bates, Henry Walter

English
b February 8, 1825; Leicester, England
d February 16, 1892; London, England
Explored upper Amazon River valley

dysentery disease that causes severe diarrhea

species type of plant or animal

zoology the scientific study of animals

specimen sample of a plant, animal, or mineral, usually collected for scientific study or display

A famous naturalist, Henry Walter Bates was also a skilled student of human cultures and languages.

Henry Walter Bates was an expert on insects. He journeyed to the Amazon River valley in Brazil in 1848 and explored the region for 11 years. He studied the lives of its people and discovered thousands of insect **species** that had been unknown to European scientists. In Britain he was greatly honored for his work.

Bates had little formal education. His father, a manufacturer, pushed him into business by getting him a job at a company that made stockings. Bates worked long hours during the day, but he found time to attend school at night. He read as much as he could and became interested in **zoology.** He began to roam the countryside, collecting **specimens** of animal life. At 18, he published a paper about beetles in a new scientific magazine.

The next year, his life was changed when he met Alfred Russel WALLACE, a schoolteacher. The two friends shared a love for zoology and collected specimens together outside of town. Then Wallace suggested that they study a more exciting region: the Amazon River valley in South America. Bates jumped at the chance to make zoology more than just a hobby.

Into the Jungle

In May 1848, the two young scientists arrived in the Brazilian town of Pará (now called Belém), where the Amazon River meets the Atlantic Ocean. Journeying inland, they explored the Tocantins River and the Black River (Río Negro). Then they separated to cover a wider area. Bates worked near Pará for more than a year. He collected specimens of many animals, including anteaters and bats. He then headed upriver for Óbidos, a town on the Amazon River. He studied insects and spider monkeys for several months and then reunited with Wallace.

The two friends soon split up again. For the next seven years, Bates explored the upper Amazon region. Most of this time was spent near two smaller rivers, the Solimões and the Tapajós. He gathered 14,500 specimens, of which 8,000 types had been unknown. He discovered more than 500 species of butterflies alone. While studying insects, he noticed that some species try to escape their enemies by imitating the shape or color of a different species. Bates's research proved to be very valuable to later scientists who studied insects.

An Honored Return Home

Bates had hoped to follow the Amazon as far west as the Andes, but his years in the jungle had damaged his health. He had no choice but to return to Britain. His work met with great praise from his fellow scientists, and he took an important position with the Royal Geographical Society. He wrote a very popular book about his travels and also won a high honor from Brazil, a country that rarely praised foreign scientists. His home in England is now a museum where thousands of his specimens are still on display. However, a desire for fame was not what drove him. Though he had suffered through illness, loneliness, hunger, and hard work, he wrote that the "pleasure of finding another new species . . . supports one against everything."

Suggested Reading Henry Walter Bates, *The Naturalist on the River Amazon*, abridged edition (University of California Press, 1962); Monica Lee, *300 Year Journey: Leicester Naturalist Henry Walter Bates, F.R.S., and His Family, 1665-1985* (Penguin, 1989).

Battuta, Ibn. *See Ibn Battuta.*

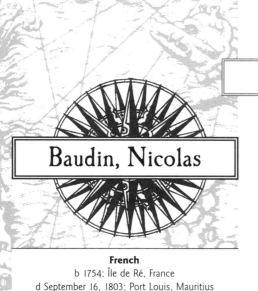

Baudin, Nicolas

French
b 1754; Île de Ré, France
d September 16, 1803; Port Louis, Mauritius
Explored coastline of Australia

specimen sample of a plant, animal, or mineral, usually collected for scientific study or display

species type of plant or animal

scurvy disease caused by a lack of vitamin C and once a major cause of death among sailors; symptoms include internal bleeding, loosened teeth, and extreme fatigue

The French scientist Nicolas Baudin led an expedition along the coast of New Holland (now Australia). He was a tough commander who pushed his crew members beyond their limits. Many of the scientists and sailors under Baudin's command deserted the mission. Others died along the way—including Baudin himself. Still, the Frenchmen managed to collect more than 10,000 plant and animal **specimens** and to discover 2,500 **species** that had been unknown to science.

Science and Sickness

After an early career in the French navy, Baudin sailed on an Austrian ship for 12 years, exploring parts of Asia and South America. He gathered many samples of the plant and animal life that he found. His career took a new turn in 1800, when Napoleon, the emperor of France, ordered him to explore New Holland. The east coast of that continent had already been claimed by the British. If Baudin found that the western part of New Holland was separated from the eastern part by water, he could claim the west for France.

Baudin set sail with two ships. It was five months before they stopped at an island port in the Indian Ocean. Forty crewmen, officers, and scientists went ashore and refused to return to the ships. Some were physically ill. Others were simply tired of Baudin's harsh command. The rest of the team reached New Holland three months later. The two ships were soon separated in a storm, and each charted sections of the coastline before they met again at Timor, an island to the north. Again many crew members went ashore, most of them suffering from **scurvy.**

A Suffering Crew

The ships set sail again, this time for the island of Van Diemen's Land (now called Tasmania). With little fresh food or water, crew members were dying every day. But Baudin would not give up. He pushed his men onward, reaching the Tasmanian rain forest in early 1802. Half the crew became too ill to sail the ships. When the

sloop small ship with one mast and triangular sails

expedition struggled into the port of Sydney, a **sloop** had to be sent to bring the sick men to shore.

After a short rest, the expedition headed south again to explore more of the coast of New Holland. The British settlers watched suspiciously. In June 1803, Baudin sent one ship back to France and took the other to Timor. He wanted to continue exploring, but now his own ill health held him back. The next month, he began the return trip to France, but he never got there. The surviving crew members arrived home more than three years after their disastrous expedition had left.

Suggested Reading Frank Horner, *The French Reconnaissance: Baudin in Australia, 1801-1803* (Melbourne University Press, 1987); N. J. B. Plomley, *The Baudin Expedition and the Tasmanian Aborigines* (Blubber Head, 1983).

Bautista de Anza, Juan. See *Anza, Juan Bautista de.*

Belalcázar, Sebastinán, de. See *Benalcázar, Sebastián de.*

Bell, Gertrude Margaret Lowthian

English
b July 14, 1868; Washington, England
d July 12, 1926; Baghdad, Iraq
Traveled in Middle East

Gertrude Bell was a scholar of the culture and history of the Middle East, and she took great risks to travel and study in that region. She was highly respected for her knowledge of the Arab world. Her understanding enabled her not only to translate medieval Persian poetry but also to serve Great Britain as a diplomat and adviser.

Exploring the Mysteries of Persia

Bell showed her talent early, earning a university degree in natural history in less time than it took most students. In 1892, at the age of 23, she made her first trip to Persia (modern-day Iran). She wrote in a letter to a friend that it was "the place I have always longed to see."

Bell was introduced to Persia by her uncle, a British diplomat in the city of Tehran. She was thrilled by the beauty of the land and its language. She quickly learned to read Persian and began to translate Persian poetry into English. She won high praise for her translations of poems by Divan of Hafiz, a Persian poet of the 1300s.

In 1897 Bell went on a six-month trip around the world. She then returned to her studies of the Middle East. She visited Jerusalem and the desert region east of the Dead Sea. Seeing the ruins of a grand Persian palace was, she wrote, "a thing one will never forget as long as one lives." She then traveled through the flat Syrian Desert, enduring a slow and exhausting caravan journey to see ruins from the time of the ancient Roman Empire.

Bell returned to Europe and spent several summers climbing mountains in France. But she found herself traveling to the Middle East again and again between 1900 and 1914. She was often the first European woman to see the places she visited. Although Arab women

Gertrude Bell risked her life to study ancient ruins and modern kingdoms in the deserts of the Middle East.

often lived separately from the men, the desert leaders treated Bell with the courtesy and respect they showed to male visitors. They helped her to find sites that would teach her more about the history of the Middle East. Her quest took her all the way to Constantinople (now Istanbul), a Turkish city with a long and rich history.

Dangers of the Desert

Bell again proved her daring and courage during her last desert expedition. In 1913 she traveled to Damascus in the Turkish Ottoman Empire, where she bought 20 camels and hired three camel drivers and two servants. In great secrecy, she set out for Hail, a city in the Arabian desert. She feared that the government would try to stop her from traveling through the harsh desert areas that were controlled by bandits. In fact, a Turkish official did try to bar her way soon after she began her journey. He let her continue only after she signed a letter saying that he was not to blame for anything that might happen to her.

As expected, Bell's caravan ran into trouble with a desert ruler. Bell offered him gifts, but the bandit suggested to her servants and drivers that they murder her and take her belongings. Luckily, they stayed loyal and refused to hurt her. At last the caravan was allowed to travel on, but matters only got worse when they reached their destination. The prince of Hail was away fighting a war. His grandmother suspected that Bell was an enemy spy, so she had her arrested. When one of the prince's advisers set them free, Bell spent a day taking photographs of the city before traveling north to Baghdad. She arrived in May 1914, a few months before World War I broke out.

Service to Britain

When Britain entered the war, Bell was sent to Egypt to gather information for Britain's Arab allies. After the war ended, she settled in Baghdad to work for the British government and was later put in charge of the British collections of historical objects in Iraq. She worked to have a museum built to preserve and display these collections. Even after her death in 1926, her devotion to historical study was felt. In her will, she left money to create the British School of Archaeology in Iraq.

Suggested Reading Janet Wallach, *Desert Queen: The Extraordinary Life of Gertrude Bell, Adventurer, Adviser to Kings, Ally of Lawrence of Arabia* (Doubleday, 1996); H. V. F. Winstone, *Gertrude Bell* (Quartet Books, 1978).

Belleborne, Jean Nicolett de. See *Nicolett de Belleborne, Jean.*

Bellingshausen, Fabian Gottlieb von

Russian
b September 9, 1778; Saaremaa, Estonia
d January 13, 1852; Kronstadt, Russia
Discovered mainland of Antarctica

Fabian Gottlieb von Bellingshausen, an officer in the Russian navy, led the first major expedition to Antarctica. Bellingshausen observed and wrote descriptions of parts of the continent during this journey, but he did not formally claim it for Russia. In the years that followed, explorers from several other countries continued Bellingshausen's explorations of Antarctica.

When Fabian Gottlieb von Bellingshausen sailed around Antarctica, he found it hard to tell whether icebergs were actually snow-covered mountains.

frigate small, agile warship with three masts and square sails

czar title of Russian monarchs from the 1200s to 1917

Their territorial claims have left the status of the continent in question to this day.

Bellingshausen was born into a family of German nobles who lived on the coast of the Baltic Sea. He joined the Russian navy when he was only 10 years old and became an officer at 19. His first assignment as an officer was to serve under Adam Ivan von KRUSEN-STERN on a voyage around the world. Bellingshausen was next given command of a **frigate** in the Black Sea.

The New Continent

In 1819 **Czar** Alexander I chose Bellingshausen to lead an expedition to the southern polar seas. At that time, no one was sure whether a continent existed there. In the 1700s, James COOK and several whaling captains had reported seeing only islands and ice. The czar wanted to investigate this mysterious region and find harbors that could hold supplies for Russian ships. In the winter of 1819 to 1820, Bellingshausen investigated these islands and found that they were not connected to a mainland. As he sailed, he corrected errors in existing maps and added details.

He then headed farther south into uncharted territory, pushing into the icy seas that had stopped Cook. Sailing east around the pole, he sighted the mainland, exploring the coasts of what would later be called Queen Maud Land and Enderby Land. When the southern winter came, he sailed north to avoid being caught in the ice. The following spring, he hurried south again and continued to follow the coast, reaching what is now known as the Bellingshausen Sea. He loyally named two islands, Peter I Island and Alexander Island, after Russian czars.

The fleet returned to Russia on August 5, 1821, three years after setting sail. Many people were now convinced that an entire continent existed at the South Pole. The story of its exploration had only just begun. Bellingshausen himself never visited such remote seas again, but he served the Russian navy for many years and retired with the rank of admiral.

Suggested Reading Glynn Barratt, *Bellingshausen: A Visit to New Zealand* (Dunmore Press, 1979); Charles Neider, *Antarctica: Authentic Accounts of Life and Exploration in the World's Highest, Driest, Windiest, Coldest and Most Remote Continent* (Random House, 1972).

Benalcázar, Sebastián de

Spanish
b 1495?; Belalcázar, Spain
d April 1551; Cartagena, Colombia
Explored parts of Ecuador, Peru, and Colombia

conquistador Spanish or Portuguese explorer and military leader in the Americas

encomendero Spanish colonist who received a grant of land in the Americas and had control over the Indians who lived there

Sebastián de Benalcázar was a Spanish **conquistador** whose life was ruled by greed and ambition. He fought the Indians of South America—and sometimes even his own countrymen—to gain wealth and power. As a soldier, he helped conquer Peru and Ecuador. As an explorer and colonial official, he founded several cities that still stand in Ecuador and Colombia.

Sebastián de Benalcázar's real name was Sebastián Moyano, but he was known by the name of Belalcázar, his hometown in southern Spain. He was born into a poor family and never learned to read. As a young man, he began his quest for fame and fortune in the West Indies. Within a few years, he had become an **encomendero** in what is now Panama and was involved in heavy fighting. The Spanish waged war against Indian tribes for control of regions that are

El Dorado mythical ruler, city, or area of South America believed to possess much gold

adelantado Spanish leader of a military expedition to America during the 1500s who also served as governor and judge

now Nicaragua and Honduras. When the Spanish were victorious after three years of battle, they founded the city of Léon. Benalcázar helped to found the city and served as its first mayor.

Fortunes Rising

Five years later, Benalcázar went to Peru to help Francisco PIZARRO and Diego de ALMAGRO conquer the Inca Empire. Benalcázar was the captain of the Spanish horsemen and received a share of the enormous riches won by the conquistadors. He was also named the commander of San Miguel de Piura, a city in northern Peru. As a result, he was no longer a part of the Spanish military force that continued to move through Peru.

But he was not out of the fighting for long. When the Inca general Rumiñavi attacked the city of Quito, Pizarro asked Benalcázar to crush the uprising. Benalcázar left Piura and headed north over a wide, empty plain. He convinced local enemies of the Inca, the Cañari Indians, to join him. The Inca surprised the war party on a slippery mountain road, but Benalcázar's troops won this first battle. As the Spanish and Cañari marched through the Andes toward Quito, the Inca attacked again and again.

Benalcázar arrived at Quito to find that the Inca had deserted the city and burned it to the ground. Taking control of the ruined city, he fought off one last Inca attack and then rebuilt the city for the Spanish. He cruelly tortured his Inca prisoners to find out where they had hidden their treasures of gold and silver.

The Land of the Golden Man

Benalcázar pushed on into southern Ecuador and founded two cities, Riobamba and Guayaquil. He then turned his attention to rumors of a golden man whose country was full of great riches. This legendary land became known to the Spanish as **El Dorado.** It may have been Benalcázar who first used this name. Excited by the stories of wealth, he led several expeditions in search of El Dorado. In his travels, he explored much of what is now Colombia. He crossed rugged lands and followed the Cauca River valley north to the lands of the Popayán Indians, whom he conquered. He founded two cities in the region, Popayán and Cali. He then crossed a mountain range and discovered the source of a major river, the Magdalena. As he made his way along this river, the Pijáo Indians attacked with poison darts, killing 20 men. One Spanish soldier said that this march was filled with "bad mountains, bad roads, and bad Indians."

When Benalcázar finally came to a land of wealth, he was upset to find out that Gonzalo JIMÉNEZ DE QUESADA had already claimed the area. This area, which had belonged to the Chibcha Indians and was rich in emeralds, was also claimed by Nikolaus FEDERMANN. The three rivals returned to Spain and asked the king to resolve the conflict. The king named Benalcázar captain general and **adelantado** of a large part of eastern Colombia. Benalcázar returned to South America and fought for the king in the Peruvian Civil Wars, which lasted for five years. During the fighting he killed another Spaniard, Jorge Robeldo, who had tried to take control of some of Benalcázar's lands. Robeldo's widow took revenge by having Benalcázar arrested for murder. He was ordered to travel to the coast of Colombia, where he was to board a ship for Spain. But he died on the way to the coast, still on the continent he had explored and looted for over 30 years.

Suggested Reading James Lockhart, *The Men of Cajamarca, a Social and Biographical Study of the Conquerers of Peru* (University of Texas Press, 1972).

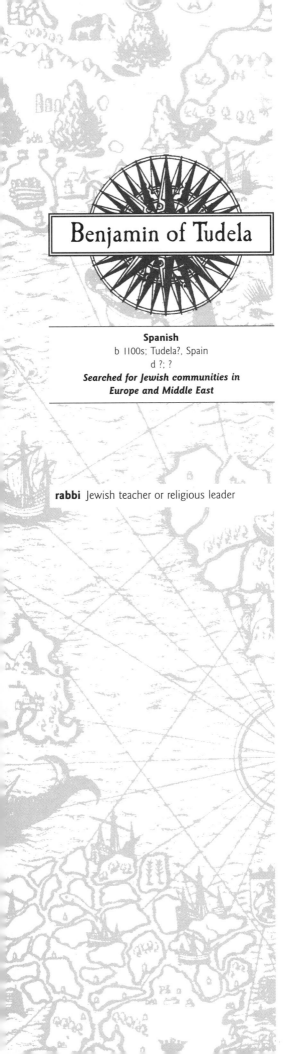

Benjamin of Tudela

Spanish
b 1100s; Tudela?, Spain
d ?; ?
Searched for Jewish communities in Europe and Middle East

rabbi Jewish teacher or religious leader

Benjamin of Tudela spent years traveling to Jewish communities in Europe, North Africa, and the Middle East. Upon his return to his home in Spain, he wrote a book about what he had seen and heard. It was first published in printed form as *The Itinerary of Benjamin of Tudela* in 1543. Like other medieval writers, Benjamin did not always distinguish between legends and facts. He may have stretched the truth for the sake of a colorful tale, or he may have been mistaken. Even so, historians consider his account to be one of the most complete and accurate travel narratives of the Middle Ages. Modern scholars value its record of the life and customs of medieval Jews in many parts of the world.

Traveling with a Mission

Other than a few hints contained in his writings, the details of Benjamin's life are a mystery. He was born sometime in the 1100s and lived in the town of Tudela near the city of Saragossa in northern Spain. People knew him as Benjamin ben Jonah or **Rabbi** Benjamin. But scholars who have studied his book think that he was most likely a merchant, not a rabbi. He may have been called Rabbi Benjamin simply out of respect for his learning.

Benjamin's travels were inspired by the situation of the Jews who lived in Europe during the Middle Ages. In many nations, Jews suffered verbal and physical attacks by Christians. Spain's large Jewish population lived in relative comfort, but some Spanish Jews feared that one day the Christians would force them to leave. Benjamin wanted to give Spanish Jews useful information about places where they could live if they had to leave their country.

The Beginning of a Long Journey

Benjamin left Saragossa around 1160. He traveled to the port of Barcelona and then to southern France, where he boarded a ship for the Italian city of Genoa. His account of the trip lists every town and city in which he stopped. It is a practical guide, in which he noted how many days' travel separated each place from the next. Benjamin also recorded how many Jews lived in each community, and sometimes named their leading citizens. He described the circumstances in which the Jews lived, what kinds of work they did, and whether they were on good terms with Christian rulers and citizens. He also discussed many political and economic matters, such as the democratic government of Genoa and the bustling docks at Montpellier, France.

Constantinople and the Holy Land

From Italy, Benjamin traveled to Greece, which was then part of the great empire of the Byzantine Christians. The empire's capital was Constantinople, where Jews had to live in a separate section of the city. "They are exposed to be beaten in the streets," he wrote, "and must submit to all sorts of bad treatment." Despite the Jews' oppression, he was impressed with the city's magnificence and wealth. He wrote that people came to Constantinople "from all parts of the world for purposes of trade."

Benjamin then traveled south through the region of greatest interest to the Jews—Palestine, the ancient Holy Land of the Bible. At the time of his visit, Jerusalem was in the hands of European Christian knights who had captured it from Muslims. Benjamin described the Christians' activities, the city's temples and shrines, and other points of interest. For example, he claimed to have seen the pillar of salt into which Lot's wife was transformed, as told in the Bible. Benjamin wrote that "although the sheep continually lick it, the pillar grows again, and retains its original state." He also mentioned an early tourist attraction in the city of Hebron, where visitors paid to see fake tombs of biblical heroes. For an extra fee, Benjamin explained, Jews could see the real tombs.

The Distant Lands of Islam

From Jerusalem, Benjamin traveled to Damascus, in Syria, where he admired the lush gardens and the splendid **mosque.** Moving on, he went east into the region called Mesopotamia (present-day Iraq), where he found large and prosperous communities of Jews. They lived peacefully under the rule of the **caliph** of Baghdad. The leader of Mesopotamia's Jews was treated with respect by the Muslims. Benjamin painted a favorable picture of Jewish life in Mesopotamia. Some scholars think that he exaggerated, especially in his high estimate of the number of Jews living there. Still, it is known that a large Jewish community had long existed in Mesopotamia and was on good terms with the Muslim people at the time of Benjamin's visit.

Benjamin also described the ruins of Babylon, one of the great cities of ancient Mesopotamia. It is impossible to tell whether Benjamin really saw the ruins or merely heard about them from other travelers. Similarly, he discussed the eastern lands of Persia, now known as Iran, as well as Samarkand and other cities in central Asia. He even mentioned such distant lands as China, India, and Tibet. He did not claim to have visited these places, and it is very unlikely that he did so. Like other medieval writers, Benjamin probably expanded on his own firsthand observations by including common knowledge and travelers' tales in his writings.

He was on more familiar ground when he visited North Africa and described the cities and **caravan** routes of Egypt and the Sahara. He wrote that Alexandria in Egypt was home to about 3,000 Jews and was "an excellent market to all nations," filled with Christian, Muslim, and Asian traders. From Egypt he sailed to the island of Sicily and then returned home by way

mosque Muslim house of prayer and worship

caliph Muslim political and religious ruler

caravan large group of people traveling together, often with pack animals, across a desert or other dangerous region

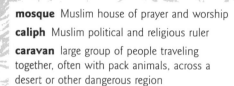
Fearing that Spanish Jews might be forced to leave Spain, Benjamin of Tudela traveled widely to learn about life in other Jewish communities.

of Italy, Germany, and France. He reached Tudela around 1173, after completing an impressive tour of the parts of the world known to medieval Europeans. Jewish scholars learned of Benjamin's journey and admired his book. After his writings were translated from Hebrew into Latin in 1575, other Europeans also became aware of his achievement.

Suggested Reading Sandra Benjamin, *The World of Benjamin of Tudela* (Fairleigh Dickinson University Press, 1995); Manuel Komroff, editor, *Contemporaries of Marco Polo* (Dorset Press, 1989); Yosef Levanon, *The Jewish Travellers in the Twelfth Century* (University Press of America, 1980).

Bennett, Floyd

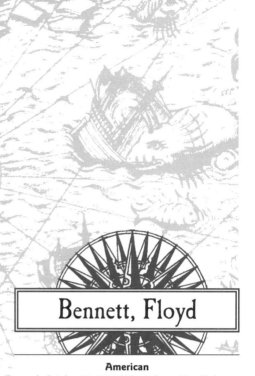

American
b October 25, 1890; Warrensburg, New York
d April 25, 1928; Québec, Canada
Piloted Richard Byrd's plane over North Pole

Floyd Bennett's heroism as a pilot and explorer won him the Congressional Medal of Honor for his role in the first flight over the North Pole.

Floyd Bennett was an expert pilot and mechanic. He flew for Richard BYRD from 1925 until his early death at the age of 37. The two men were the first to fly over the North Pole.

Bennett worked as a car mechanic before joining the navy in 1917. There he learned how to fly and fix airplanes. Byrd, a navy pilot, spotted Bennett's talent and recruited him to be his copilot. They both flew in the Arctic region with Donald B. MacMILLAN in 1925. The next year, Bennett and Byrd set out to make the first flight over the North Pole. They took off from Spitsbergen, an island north of Norway. They had a scare when an engine began to leak oil, but when the oil level dropped below the hole, the leak stopped. The successful journey lasted 15½ hours and covered 1,360 miles. The U.S. Congress awarded Bennett the Medal of Honor.

Byrd and Bennett then aimed to be the first pilots to carry passengers across the Atlantic Ocean. In a test flight, the front of the plane was too heavy, and they made a crash landing. Everyone survived, but Bennett was seriously injured. He did not recover in time to make the ocean crossing in 1927. One year later, Byrd made Bennett his second-in-command for a flight to the South Pole. Before they were ready to leave the United States, Bennett flew off to rescue two German pilots who had crashed into a river in Canada. He made the rescue in the wet cold of early spring. Still weak from his own crash, he caught pneumonia and died. Byrd later flew over the South Pole in a plane named *Floyd Bennett*. He tied an American flag to a stone from Bennett's grave and dropped it from the plane into the snow below.

Suggested Reading Cora L. Bennett, *Floyd Bennett* (W. F. Payson, 1932); Basil Clarke, *Polar Flight* (Ian Allen, 1964).

Bering, Vitus Jonassen

Danish
b August 12, 1681; Horsens, Denmark
d December 6, 1741; Bering Island, Russia
***Commanded first European crossing
from Siberia to Alaska***

Vitus Jonassen Bering was a Danish naval officer who led two difficult Russian expeditions to the coast of Alaska. He was sent to find out whether North America and Russia were connected by land or divided by water. Bering showed himself to be a strong leader, a capable organizer, and a skilled navigator. He led hundreds of men across Siberia, which is more than three times as wide as North America. His explorations helped the Russian fur trade expand along the Alaskan coastline. The strait between Siberia and Alaska had already been found in 1648 by a Russian pioneer named Semyon Ivanov DEZHNEV. But Dezhnev's report had gone unnoticed at the time. Bering repeated Dezhnev's discovery on a much larger and more challenging scale.

The Captain and the Czar

Little is known about Bering's life before he led these missions. After he returned from an ocean voyage to the East Indies in 1703, he was asked to join the Russian navy. He served with Russian fleets in battles on the Baltic, Black, and White Seas for 20 years. By 1723 he had achieved the rank of captain second class. When he applied to become a captain first class, he was turned down, so he retired from the navy. But within a year, Bering was asked to return as captain first class to lead a voyage of exploration.

Czar Peter the Great had written the mission's instructions before he died. The explorers were to start from the western city of St. Petersburg, march across Siberia, sail to the Kamchatka Peninsula, then cross Kamchatka to its east coast on the Pacific Ocean. There they would build ships to explore the area between Russia and North America. It would have been easier to sail ships from western Russia around Africa to the East Indies and then sail north past Japan. But Czar Peter had purposely chosen the exhausting overland route. Because it passed only through Russian territory, other

czar title of Russian monarchs from the 1200s to 1917

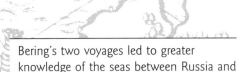

Bering's two voyages led to greater knowledge of the seas between Russia and Alaska.

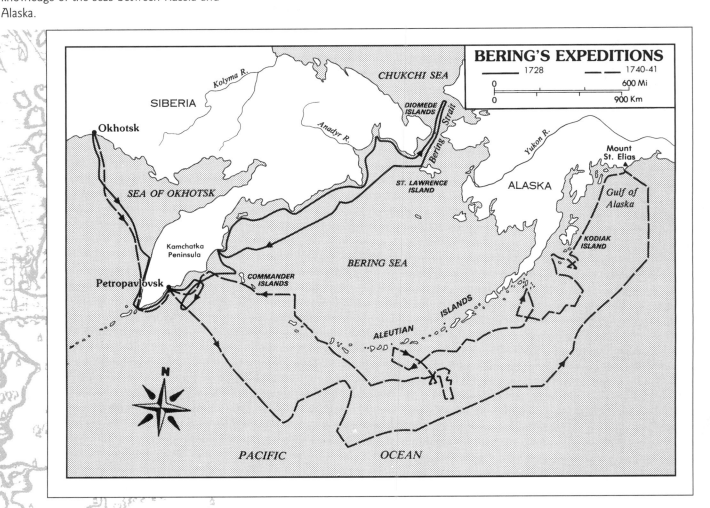

Vitus Jonassen Bering was among the hundreds of western Europeans whom Czar Peter enlisted to help modernize Russia.

caravan large group of people traveling together, often with pack animals, across a desert or other dangerous region

countries would have no idea that Russia intended to explore North America. Peter also wanted to impress his new subjects in Siberia, which had recently come under his empire's control. By sending a large and well-equipped expedition through Siberia, he could show the people that their distant ruler was quite powerful.

Hard Roads and Foggy Seas

Bering accepted the challenge and left St. Petersburg in 1725 with 100 men. He had two lieutenants, Martin Spanberg and Aleksei CHIRIKOV. As they crossed Siberia, they gathered hundreds of laborers. The growing party crossed mountain ranges and floated down rivers, sometimes fighting Siberian tribes along the way. They carried supplies and boats through a frozen land where the snow was deeper than the horses were high.

The **caravan** finally reached Okhotsk, on the Siberian coast, more than two years after setting out. There the men built a ship and moved their supplies across the Sea of Okhotsk to Kamchatka. They crossed Kamchatka and built another ship, the *St. Gabriel*. After 3½ years, the actual voyage of discovery could finally begin.

Through the Bering Strait

The *St. Gabriel* followed the shore northeast toward the distant corner of Asia. In the sea north of the Pacific Ocean, Bering landed on an island, which he named after Saint Lawrence. The island is now part of Alaska, and the sea is now known as the Bering Sea. The ship continued north, and after two days, it had passed out of sight of land. The czar's orders had been to travel along the coast. If the ship looped around Asia and back to the west, it would mean that water separated Asia from America. If the shore turned east, away from Russia, it would prove that the continents were connected by land.

Lieutenant Chirikov wanted to continue the search, even if it meant spending the entire winter in that barren region after the waters froze. But Bering felt that wintering so far north would be dangerous. He sailed on for a few more days and entered the narrow strait he had been looking for. Bering should have been able to see North America, but there was too much fog, and he returned to Kamchatka. Although he did not have solid proof, he was convinced that the strait existed. The Russian public was not so certain.

Another Chance at Discovery

When Bering returned to St. Petersburg two years later, his superiors scolded him for failing to complete his mission. Still, they admired his ability to organize and lead such a large and lengthy expedition. After all, Bering had had to cope with many details, such as providing food and clothing for all the men. He had ensured that the weary and homesick officers and workers got along well and performed their duties. He had also had to deal with the people in the hundreds of villages he passed.

Bering proposed a new mission to the eastern seas. He also wanted to explore the northern coast of Siberia. The Russian government set aside its doubts about Bering's first journey and named

This Russian flag would have flown over Bering's expeditions as they advanced eastward across northern Asia.

surveyor one who makes precise measurements of a location's geography

scurvy disease caused by a lack of vitamin C and once a major cause of death among sailors; symptoms include internal bleeding, loosened teeth, and extreme fatigue

Bethencourt, Jean de

French
b 1360?; Normandy, France
d 1422; Grainville, France
Explored Canary Islands for Spain

him captain commander of the Great Northern Expedition. This huge project would take nine years to chart the hundreds of miles of Siberia's Arctic coastline. Bering commanded 13 ships and 3,000 men. He hired two landscape painters, five **surveyors,** and 30 scientists with hundreds of books and nine wagons full of instruments. Bering himself would study the easternmost section of the coast. Each time the expedition met with problems, the government sent him angry letters, and it took his men eight years just to reach Okhotsk. By the time he sailed for Alaska with two ships, he was exhausted and dispirited.

The two ships were separated in a summer storm. Bering's ship, the *St. Peter,* sailed southeast to the Gulf of Alaska, where Bering finally sighted the Alaskan mainland. Even this discovery, toward which Bering had worked for 15 years, did not lift his spirits. He was too busy worrying about the challenges ahead. The crew made several landings to explore the Alaskan coast, and the chief scientist wanted to stay there and do research all winter. Bering, however, insisted on returning to Kamchatka before the winter weather struck. Storms blew the ship to a group of islands now known as the Commander Islands.

The party was forced to winter in an unsafe harbor with no hope of receiving supplies. Bering was one of 30 men who died that winter from **scurvy** and cold weather. The following summer, the survivors built another boat from what was left of the *St. Peter* and made their way back to Kamchatka. The other ship, captained by Chirikov, was waiting for them there.

A Place in History

Historians still argue about Bering's importance as an explorer. After all, Dezhnev had already discovered the strait almost a hundred years earlier. But it was Bering's mission that brought back the news that Alaska was rich in furs of many kinds. Russian trappers headed for North America, and the Russian Empire slowly expanded down the North American coast. Today's maps also show that Bering's hard work has been remembered. The Bering Strait, the Bering Sea, and even Bering Island, where he died and was buried, still carry the name of this dedicated explorer.

Suggested Reading Raymond H. Fisher, *Bering's Voyages: Whither and Why* (University of Washington Press, 1977); F. A. Golder, *Russian Expansion on the Pacific, 1641–1850* (Peter Smith, 1960); Gerhard Friedrich Müller, *Bering's Voyages: The Reports from Russia,* translated by Carol Urness (University of Alaska Press, 1986); Georg Wilhelm Steller, *Journal of a Voyage with Bering, 1741–1742,* translated by Margritt A. Engel and O. W. Frost, edited by O. W. Frost (Stanford University Press, 1988).

Jean de Bethencourt was a French nobleman who conquered the Canary Islands, which lie off the coast of Africa. He brought the islands under the rule of King Henry III of Spain. They later became a major port where ships stopped to pick up supplies for journeys to the Americas and beyond.

Bethencourt was raised to live in the luxurious style of French nobles. Then, at the court of King Charles VI of France, he heard exciting stories of exploration and adventure. These tales of glory gave him an idea: he would conquer the Canary Islands and teach the people there about his religion, Christianity.

Mysterious Islands

There are 14 small islands that make up the Canaries, located 700 miles south of Spain and 70 miles west of Morocco. In Bethencourt's time, Europeans knew little about them. Decades earlier, Portuguese and Italian sailors had been to the Canaries. Since then, however, only a handful of merchants and pirates paid any attention to these islands.

Bethencourt used his own money to pay for the expedition. On May 1, 1402, he sailed from France with two ships. During the voyage, he was threatened by crew members who were planning a mutiny. He squashed the rebellion and safely reached the Canary Island known as Lanzarote in a few weeks. The people who lived on the island wore clothes made from animal skins and woven grass. Bethencourt conquered these people and settled on Lanzarote. However, he felt that he needed more men to fight for control of the other islands. He traveled to Spain and sought help from the Spanish king, Henry III, who was a family friend.

A New Spanish Colony

Bethencourt soon returned as the royally appointed ruler of the Canary Islands, which he claimed for Spain. While he was gone, his second-in-command had conquered another island, Fuerteventura. With two islands under his control, Bethencourt hurried home to Normandy to gather colonists and take them to a third island, Hierro.

At the end of 1406, Bethencourt left the Canary Islands for good. He kept his royal title and his rights to the colony's profits, but he hired his nephew to live there and govern. Bethencourt returned to Normandy and wrote an account of his expeditions, but many historians doubt his truthfulness. He died in Normandy in 1422.

Suggested Reading Jean de Bethencourt, *The Canarian; or, Book of the Conquest and Conversion of the Canarians in the Year 1402: by Messire Jean de Béthencourt,* translated and edited by Richard Henry Major (B. Franklin, 1969).

In the early 1400s, Jean de Bethencourt explored the Canary Islands, which later became an important point of departure for voyages to the Americas.

Bilot, Robert. See *Bylot, Robert.*

Bingham, Hiram

American
b November 19, 1875; Honolulu, Hawaii
d June 6, 1956; Washington, D.C.
Discovered Machu Picchu and Vitcos in Peru

Hiram Bingham held many impressive positions in his lifetime. He was a professor of Latin American history and geography at Yale University. He was the governor of Connecticut and a United States senator. He was even the pastor of a small church in Hawaii. But he always listed "explorer" as his main occupation. He made several trips to South America, and in 1911 he discovered the ruins of two lost Inca cities, Machu Picchu and Vitcos.

Hiram Bingham discovered Machu Picchu. The ancient Inca city is built on terraces, which look like steps carved out of the mountainside.

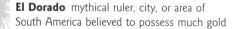

El Dorado mythical ruler, city, or area of South America believed to possess much gold

Although he led a life of great adventure, Bingham had been raised to be a humble, religious man. His parents were missionaries who had moved to Honolulu just before he was born. One of his grandfathers had also been a missionary in the Pacific, and Hiram grew up in the shadow of his family's history. In 1894 he entered Yale University, where he was drawn toward a more worldly life. But when he graduated, he returned to Hawaii and served as pastor of the Palama Chapel in a poor neighborhood in Honolulu.

The Road to Adventure

Bingham's outlook on life changed when he fell in love with the young and wealthy Alfreda Mitchell, who was vacationing in Hawaii with her family. He wanted to marry her, but he knew that he would have to earn a better living. He left his job as a pastor and earned a master's degree in South American history from the University of California at Berkeley. After that, he and Alfreda were married. Bingham then studied at Harvard University and was later hired to teach at Princeton University, but he soon became bored with the life he led at these schools. Within a year, he was off on his first field trip. He traveled across Venezuela and Colombia, tracing the route of Simon Bolívar, who had freed much of South America from Spanish rule in the 1800s.

When Bingham returned, he was hired as a lecturer at Yale. The president of the United States, Theodore ROOSEVELT, then asked him to attend a scientific conference in Santiago, Chile. This trip gave Bingham a chance to explore the old Spanish trade route from Buenos Aires, Argentina, to Lima, Peru. He also visited the ruins of Choqquequirau. This ancient city had once been thought to be the last capital of the Inca Empire and maybe even **El Dorado,** the legendary city of gold. Bingham became interested in searching for Vitcos, the true last capital of the Inca.

To Find a Lost City

In 1911 Bingham set out on the most important trip of his career, the Yale Peruvian Expedition. One of his goals was to search for Inca ruins in the Urubamba Valley of the Andes in Peru. On July 24, Bingham discovered the ruins of Machu Picchu perched atop a high cliff between steep mountain peaks. The Inca city was almost impossible to reach. Bingham crawled on his hands and knees across a decaying bridge over a roaring river. He then climbed the mountainside leading to the ancient city. "I felt utterly alone," he wrote later. But when at last he saw the grand ruins up close, "breathless with excitement, I forgot my fatigue. . . ." Still, Bingham did not believe that this was Vitcos, the last capital of the Inca Empire. A local guide helped him continue his search. They arrived at a place called Nūsta Isppana. Seeing a landmark, a large white rock near the ruins of a temple, he felt certain that he had found Vitcos.

Return to a Life of Service

Back in the United States, some historians questioned whether Bingham had been the first to discover Machu Picchu in 1911. He had found the name "Lizarraga" and the date "1902" written in charcoal on a temple wall. It turned out that a man named Augustine Lizarraga had in fact been there and left this inscription but had never reported his find. Bingham is usually credited as the "scientific discoverer" of Machu Picchu. His careful records and notes added much to earlier knowledge about the Inca. His work also created new interest in scientific exploration of both South America and North America.

Bingham made two other expeditions to Peru with the support of Yale University and the National Geographic Society. He served in World War I and was elected governor of Connecticut in 1924. He resigned as governor soon after taking office, when he was appointed to fill an open seat in the United States Senate. He was a senator for eight years. Bingham had lived up to his early sense of duty. He added to human knowledge and led a life of service. At the same time, he was a man who loved to have adventures, dance at parties, and socialize with the rich and powerful.

Suggested Reading Alfred M. Bingham, *Portrait of an Explorer: Hiram Bingham, Discoverer of Machu Picchu* (Iowa State University Press, 1989); Hiram Bingham, *Lost City of the Incas* (reprint, Greenwood, 1981).

Bird, Isabella. See *Bishop, Isabella Bird.*

Bishop, Isabella Bird

English
b October 15, 1831; Yorkshire, England
d October 7, 1904; Edinburgh, Scotland
Traveled widely; was famous for travel

During the 1800s, a number of strong-willed, adventurous women traveled to remote parts of the world. Many of them later wrote popular books about their journeys. They proved that exploration was not only for men, and they expanded people's ideas about what women could do. One of the best-known and most widely traveled of these women was Isabella Bird, who became Isabella Bird Bishop when she married in 1881. Her journeys through North America and Asia and across the Pacific Ocean sometimes seemed like ordinary sightseeing—but at other times, they held all the mystery of true exploration.

Traveling for Her Health

Bird, a daughter of an English minister, grew up in a household that emphasized service to others. Her family shared the belief, commonly held in England and elsewhere in the 1800s, that a woman's place was in the home. Bird was often sick as a child. During her early 20s, she felt so weak, ill, and tired that she sometimes spent months in bed. A doctor recommended a sea voyage. Bird's father gave her some money and told her that she could go anywhere she wanted for as long as the money lasted. She boarded a ship and crossed the Atlantic Ocean to visit a cousin in Canada.

The experience of traveling on her own filled Bird with humor and energy. She toured part of North America by train and

stagecoach, writing lively letters home to her beloved sister, Henrietta. When she returned home, her family encouraged her to make a book out of the letters. *The Englishwoman in America,* Bird's first book, appeared in 1856. In the years that followed, however, she again became weary and sick. Short trips to North America and the Mediterranean Sea failed to improve her health or her spirits. In 1872 a doctor suggested another long sea voyage, and Bird decided to visit Australia and New Zealand. At the age of 40, she stood on the edge of a new life.

Delights and Dangers of Travel

Bird was not impressed with Australia or New Zealand, so she set sail for San Francisco. When her ship stopped in Hawaii (then called the Sandwich Islands), she decided to stay. For six months, she rode over the islands on horseback, exploring volcanoes and delighting in her freedom. She experienced what she called "the height of enjoyment in traveling" when she camped under a tree with her saddle for a pillow. Bird had discovered the great love of her life, travel in wild places.

From Hawaii she went to San Francisco and toured the American West, determined to visit a remote valley in Colorado that she had heard about. Her adventures in Colorado included mountain climbs, blizzards, and a romance with "Mountain Jim" Nugent, a tattered but generous character whom Bird called a "Desperado." Bird eventually returned home after a two-year absence.

The books she wrote about her visits to Hawaii and the Rocky Mountains, *The Hawaiian Archipelago* and *A Lady's Life in the Rocky Mountains,* became immensely popular. By the time the second book appeared, she had already left on her next long trip, this time to Japan. There she immersed herself in the daily lives of people in remote rural districts seldom visited by tourists. She also passed through several Chinese cities before reaching the island of Singapore. She was offered a chance to board a ship bound for Malaysia, then a little-known land of rain forests in southeast Asia. "I was only allowed five minutes for decision," she wrote, "but I have no difficulty in making up my mind when an escape from civilization is possible." After returning from her Asian trip, Bird seemed to settle down, writing books and marrying Dr. John Bishop, who had proposed marriage on many occasions. During this time, her sister Henrietta died. Five years later, Isabella's husband also died.

Last Adventures

In 1888, with her loved ones gone, Isabella Bird Bishop left England for Tibet, a region that had long fascinated her. Starting in India, she made a horseback journey to Ladakh, a mountain kingdom in the Himalayas, and reached the fringes of Tibet. She then joined a British army officer who was riding through Persia (now Iran). They traveled together for several months before Bishop joined a **caravan** to the Black Sea.

Back in Europe, politicians sought her opinion on conditions in Persia and the Middle East, and she once again published her

The daring and determined Isabella Bird Bishop gained worldwide fame through the books she wrote about her travels.

adventures. By now many people had realized that Bishop was more than a tireless traveler and a good writer. She was also a careful observer, whose reports on the places she visited contained valuable geographic information. In 1892 Britain's Royal Geographical Society made Bishop its first woman member.

Bishop's last long trip began in 1894. After passing through Korea, she spent almost three years in China. Several times she came close to dying at the hands of mobs who were hostile to foreigners, and she began carrying a pistol. Despite these dangers, Bishop did not turn back. She continued the trip she had planned, advanced to the foothills of Tibet, and spent the rest of her time camping with Buddhist nomads whom she met there. Although she was by then close to 70, Bishop refused to give up the travel that had given meaning and purpose to her life. After a trip to Morocco in 1900, her health failed, and she remained at home until her death three years later.

Suggested Reading Pat Barr, *A Curious Life for a Lady: The Story of Isabella Bird, a Remarkable Victorian Traveller* (Doubleday, 1970); Cicely P. Havely, editor, *This Grand Beyond: Travels of Isabella Bird Bishop* (Century, 1984); Dorothy Middleton, *Victorian Lady Travellers* (Dutton, 1965); Rebecca Stefoff, *Women of the World: Women Travelers and Explorers* (Oxford University Press, 1992).

Blaxland, Gregory

English
b June 27, 1778; Newington, England
d January 1853; North Parramatta, Australia
Explored Australia's Blue Mountains

Gregory Blaxland was the first European to cross Australia's Blue Mountains, part of the Great Dividing Range that separates Australia's east coast from the rest of the continent. His journey opened the way for other important explorations of Australia.

He was born into a wealthy English family and had many important and influential friends. One of these friends was the naturalist Sir Joseph BANKS, who had explored Australia's Botany Bay in 1770

with Captain James COOK. At Banks's suggestion, Britain created a prison colony in Australia. In 1805 Blaxland became one of the first free men to move to Australia, hoping to start a farm there. The British government gave him 4,000 acres of land and 40 convicts to do the farmwork. The government also agreed to pay for the prisoners' food and clothing for the first 18 months.

The Search for Greener Grass

Blaxland settled at the foot of the Blue Mountains. In 1813 a lack of rain ruined his harvest. He and two other landowners, William Lawson and William Charles WENTWORTH, decided to look for more fertile land on the other side of the mountains. Previous explorers had tried and failed to cross the mountains by traveling in the valleys between peaks—but Blaxland and his group stayed atop the ridges, and they succeeded.

After about three weeks of hiking, the group reached a **tributary** of the Nepean River. On both sides of the river, later named the Lett River, rich grasslands stretched for miles. The men compared the area to the biblical land of Canaan. Blaxland said that it had enough grass to support all the colony's cattle for 30 years.

It turned out that they had not actually crossed the whole mountain range. The land they saw was only a valley known as the Bathurst Plains. Even so, their technique of staying on the ridges proved that the mountains could be crossed. Other colonists were convinced that the continent west of the mountains was worth exploring. Blaxland wrote an account of the trip in 1823 and spent the rest of his life as a farmer. He killed himself 30 years later in a fit of severe depression.

Suggested Reading Victor Hyde, *Gregory Blaxland* (Oxford University Press, 1958); Arthur W. Jose, *Builders and Pioneers of Australia* (Books for Libraries, 1970).

tributary stream or river that flows into a larger stream or river

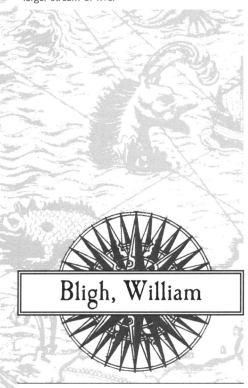

Bligh, William

English
b September 9, 1754; Tyntan, England
d December 7, 1817; London, England
Charted northeast coast of Australia; explored southern Pacific Ocean

mutiny rebellion by a ship's crew against the officers

William Bligh was a skilled seaman who had an adventurous and troublesome career. He showed early promise as a navigator, and at 22 he served on the *Resolution* under Captain James COOK. He must have learned a great deal from Cook as they visited the southern Pacific Ocean, North America, and the Arctic Ocean. Bligh himself commanded British warships in several major battles. Late in his career, he served as a colonial governor in Australia. He is best known, however, as the captain of the *Bounty.* His crew staged a **mutiny,** setting him and 19 loyal crew members adrift in a small boat.

The Floating Greenhouse

At the age of 33, Bligh was a lieutenant in the British navy. He was given command of the *Bounty* on a mission to Tahiti, an island in the South Pacific Ocean. Sir Joseph BANKS, a well-known scientist, had proposed that breadfruit trees be taken from Tahiti and replanted in the West Indies. The new breadfruit crops would feed the slaves on West Indian plantations. The *Bounty* was remodeled as a floating greenhouse to carry the young trees.

Bligh set sail from Britain in the winter of 1787 with a crew of 44 men. He was the only naval officer on board and had hired an old

The crew of the *Bounty* rebelled against William Bligh, setting him and 19 loyal men adrift in a small boat.

---

mate assistant to the commander of a ship

circumnavigation journey around the world

friend, Fletcher Christian, as a **mate.** The trip got off to a bad start. Crew members were frustrated by rough weather, cramped living quarters, and short supplies of bad food. They got no sympathy from Bligh, a strict and moody commander. He planned to sail west around the southern tip of South America. This was not the safest route to the South Pacific, especially in winter, but he wanted to make this trip a complete **circumnavigation.** The overworked crew was very unhappy with this plan, and Bligh finally agreed to sail east around the southern tip of Africa instead.

The Mutiny on the Bounty

The expedition reached Tahiti 10 months after leaving Britain and spent 5 months there. This period was longer than the usual visit, but they had to wait for the breadfruit seedlings to sprout. During these months, many of the crewmen formed relationships with Tahitian women and came to enjoy the island's simple life. They also grew even more tired of Bligh's strict discipline and bad temper.

When the *Bounty* left Tahiti for the Friendly Islands (present-day Tonga), Bligh was frustrated by the crew's sulky attitude. He punished the men who did not work hard enough to suit him by putting them in chains. He even accused Christian of stealing coconuts from him. Christian grew angry and started planning to escape to Tahiti. About three weeks after the *Bounty* had left the

chronometer clock designed to keep precise time in the rough conditions of sea travel

island, Christian led a mutiny. Bligh and the crewmen who stayed loyal to him were put aboard a 23-foot-long boat and set adrift with some food and a **chronometer.**

Luckily, Bligh was a skillful navigator. He brought the small boat safely across nearly 4,000 miles of ocean to Timor, an island that is now part of Indonesia. Bligh and his men were taken back to Britain, where he was not blamed for losing the *Bounty.* In fact, he was praised as a hero for having survived.

Meanwhile, Christian had taken the *Bounty* back to Tahiti, where another British ship soon arrived to capture the rebels. Christian escaped with 11 other mutineers and 12 Tahitian women to Pitcairn Island. They burned the *Bounty* when they arrived, so that passing ships would not see it and know where they were hiding. When an American whaling ship visited Pitcairn about 20 years later, only one mutineer was still alive. Five had been killed in quarrels over land and women, and the rest had died of natural causes. But their children survived, and by 1825 the Pitcairn settlement had become a colony of 65 people.

Back in Command

Bligh repeated his expedition to Tahiti in 1791. This time he did carry breadfruit trees to Jamaica. He also charted Australia's northern coast on the way. In later years, Bligh commanded ships in battle, winning honors for his service in the Napoleonic Wars. But he had not seen his last mutiny.

In 1805 he was named governor of New South Wales (now a province of Australia). When he arrived at the colony, he found that the soldiers there were more interested in moneymaking schemes than in their military duties. Bligh tried to whip these corrupt men into shape. After three years under Bligh's strict dicipline, the officers rebelled and put him in prison. He was held for two years, until he was recalled to Britain. The soldiers were put on trial and dismissed from the army. Despite his misfortune, Bligh continued his career in the navy and died with the rank of vice admiral.

Suggested Reading Gavin Kennedy, *Captain Bligh: The Man and his Mutinies* (Duckworth, 1989); Richard A. Mansir, *The Journal of Bounty's Launch* (Kittiwake, 1989); Sam McKinney, *Bligh: A True Account of the Mutiny Aboard His Majesty's Ship Bounty* (International Marine Publishing, 1989); Charles Nordhoff and James Norman Hall, *Mutiny on the Bounty* (Little, Brown, 1932).

Bodega y Quadra, Juan Francisco de la

Spanish
b 1743; Lima, Peru
d March 26, 1794; Mexico City, Mexico
Explored northwest coast of North America

Juan Francisco de la Bodega y Quadra was a Spanish naval officer who explored the Pacific coast of North America. Known as a gentleman who loved to entertain guests, he was also a friend to the Indians he met. In 1775 and 1779, he sailed north as far as Alaska, making Spain's northernmost claims of territory.

Overcoming Prejudice

In the late 1700s, Spain was working to strengthen its control of areas north of Mexico. San Blas, a city on the west coast of Mexico, was the base for Spanish exploration of North America's Pacific coast. In 1774 Bodega and five other young officers were sent to San

Blas to lead sea voyages to the north. To his dismay, Bodega was passed over for command in favor of the younger Bruno de HEZETA. Bodega was probably discriminated against because he was a **Creole** born in Peru. Spanish authorities often looked down on Creoles and preferred people who were born in Spain, such as Hezeta. Despite this prejudice, Bodega volunteered to serve as second-in-command of another ship, the *Sonora,* a light, narrow **schooner.** The ship was intended only for short trips, and 10 of the 17 crew members had never before been to sea.

Hezeta's instructions were to sail far to the north, going ashore to claim land for Spain wherever he could do so safely. He was to avoid the settlements of other nations. He was also ordered to be friendly to the Indians and find out what goods they had to trade. Shortly after the Spaniards left San Blas, the captain of one ship began to show signs of insanity. He was replaced by the captain of the *Sonora,* who left his own ship to Bodega's command.

Parting Ways

The mission began to have more problems. When the ships anchored off the coast of what is now the state of Washington, a party went ashore to find fresh water. Several men were killed in a sudden attack by Indians. Also, some of Hezeta's crewmen were beginning to suffer from **scurvy.** Hezeta decided to turn back and return to San Blas. When the sun rose the next morning, the *Sonora* and Hezeta's ship had become separated. Most historians agree that Bodega lost Hezeta on purpose, thinking his commander too timid. Bodega and his pilot, Mourelle, felt that it was their duty to sail as far north as they could in their small, fragile craft.

Fresh water was in short supply, and food had to be divided carefully, but the crew agreed to continue. They sailed north along the coast for two more weeks and then landed on an island now known as Prince of Wales Island, near the southern tip of Alaska. Bodega explored every inlet and bay he could find, searching for the **Northwest Passage.**

The *Sonora* entered a calm bay of warmer water. Bodega thought that the water was warmed by the glowing volcanoes that could be seen from the ship at night. He claimed the bay for Spain and named it for Antonio Bucareli, the **viceroy** of **New Spain.** He headed north again, but he soon turned back because five men had scurvy. By the time the *Sonora* reached Monterey Bay in California a month later, every man on board had become ill. Bodega and his crew were nursed back to health by Spanish priests.

Sailing North Again

Four years later, Bodega served as second-in-command of a new expedition to the north. The Spanish had learned that the British captain James COOK would be arriving in the northwest Pacific Ocean. The Spanish ships were sent to warn Cook away from Spanish territory and also to find out how far the Russians had expanded into Alaska.

The Spaniards left San Blas in February 1779 and arrived in May at Bucareli Sound. They explored the area for a month and then

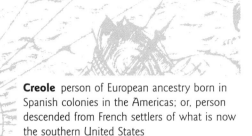

Creole person of European ancestry born in Spanish colonies in the Americas; or, person descended from French settlers of what is now the southern United States

schooner fast, easy-to-maneuver sailing ship with two or more masts and triangular sails

scurvy disease caused by a lack of vitamin C and once a major cause of death among sailors; symptoms include internal bleeding, loosened teeth, and extreme fatigue

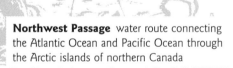

Northwest Passage water route connecting the Atlantic Ocean and Pacific Ocean through the Arctic islands of northern Canada

viceroy governor of a Spanish colony in the Americas

New Spain region of Spanish colonial empire that included the areas now occupied by Mexico, Florida, Texas, New Mexico, Arizona, California, and various Caribbean islands

sailed north. In Alaska the party went ashore near what is now Prince William Sound and claimed the land for Spain. It was the northernmost territory that Spain would ever claim in the Americas. Heavy rains, several cases of scurvy, and seven deaths forced the explorers to return to San Blas.

Bodega continued to serve Spain in North America. He commanded the Nootka settlement off the coast of what is now called Vancouver Island. He oversaw exploration of the nearby coast, continuing the search for the Northwest Passage. He was still in command in 1792 when Captain George VANCOUVER came to reclaim British land from Spain. Although Spain eventually lost its hold on the Alaskan and Canadian coastlines, Bodega's work long delayed that day. Throughout his career, he was a courageous explorer who faced many dangers to carry out orders.

Suggested Reading Warren L. Cook, *Flood Tide of Empire: Spain and the Pacific Northwest, 1543-1819* (Yale University Press, 1973).

Bonneville, Benjamin Louis Eulalie de

American
b April 14,1796; Paris, France
d June 12, 1878; Fort Smith, Arkansas
Explored American West

Benjamin Bonneville claimed that he explored the West to seek his fortune in the fur trade, but he may have been a spy for the U.S. government.

Captain Benjamin Louis Eulalie de Bonneville traveled widely over the Rocky Mountains and beyond. He did not discover any new territory, but his research added greatly to the United States government's knowledge of the West. Although he claimed to be a fur trapper, many historians suggest that he was actually a spy. In any case, Bonneville was an important figure who helped open the Rockies and California to American settlers.

Businessman or Spy?

When he was a boy, his family moved from France to the United States. He graduated from the U.S. Military Academy at West Point at age 19. For the next several years, he served on the frontier at two army posts in what are now the states of Arkansas and Oklahoma. He also became interested in the fur trade. In 1830 he requested a leave of absence from the army, saying that he wanted to travel west and try his luck at trapping furs. He easily found wealthy people who loaned him money to help him start his new business.

Bonneville's true reasons for going west are one of the unsolved mysteries of American history. Perhaps he really did want to get rich in the fur trade. Some historians, however, claim that Bonneville was a spy for the U.S. government. Much of the territory he explored was also claimed by Great Britain. The army had granted him a leave of absence but had also given him detailed instructions as to what he was to do in that time.

Bonneville was ordered to explore the country as far as the Rocky Mountains and the territory beyond. He was to study the soil, mineral deposits, natural history, and climate of the lands he explored. He was also to observe the Indian tribes, noting opportunities for trade, the number of warriors in each tribe, and their methods of warfare. In sum, his mission was to gather any information that might help the United States expand westward.

Western Trails

On May 1, 1832, Bonneville led a caravan of wagons with 110 men out of Fort Osage, Missouri. They headed through the South Pass in the Rockies and arrived at the Green River. It was the first time that wagons had come so far west. Bonneville immediately built a fort as his headquarters. Other fur trappers called the fort "Bonneville's Folly." They knew that it was too far north to be useful for trapping in winter—or even late fall and early spring. However, the fort was in a good place for watching who came and went through the Rockies. The location of Bonneville's fort supports the theory that he was a spy.

During his first winter, Bonneville and his men set traps near the Snake and Salmon Rivers with little success. The next summer, he sent his field commander, Joseph Reddeford WALKER, with about 50 men to explore land west of the Great Salt Lake. It is not known whether Walker had orders to reach the west coast of California, but he did end up at the Pacific Ocean. The trail Walker blazed would later be the main route for settlers going to California.

Bonneville himself made two expeditions to the Columbia River, which runs through present-day Washington and Oregon. He may have been trying to find out more about the British settlements in that area. Both times the British at Fort Walla Walla forced him to turn back. He also sent a party into the northern Rockies to contact the Crow Indians. Just before leaving the West, he himself made a lengthy tour of Crow territory.

Surprise and Success

After three years in the Rockies, Bonneville returned to the East. He was surprised to find that he had been discharged from the army for staying in the West longer than his leave of absence allowed. He had sent a letter asking for more time, but the letter never made it to Washington. President Andrew Jackson personally made sure that Bonneville was readmitted to the army. Bonneville later served in the Mexican War and retired with the rank of brigadier general.

Although he failed to make any money from his fur trapping, Benjamin Bonneville's time in the West was well spent. His report to the government gave detailed information on each of the subjects he had been asked to investigate. It was thought to be one of the best intelligence reports ever written about the West.

Suggested Reading Washington Irving, *The Adventures of Captain Bonneville* (Twayne, 1977); Edith Haroldsen Lovell, *Benjamin Bonneville: Soldier of the American Frontier* (Horizon, 1992).

Boone, Daniel

American
b November 2, 1734; Pennsylvania
d September 26, 1820; Missouri
Explored Kentucky

Daniel Boone may be the most famous pioneer in the history of the American frontier. He was a skilled woodsman who was never happier than when he was alone in the wilderness. Yet he devoted himself to helping others settle lands west of the British colonies that would soon become the United States. His greatest achievement was to blaze the Wilderness Road to Kentucky through the Cumberland Gap, a pass in the Appalachian Mountains.

Daniel Boone defended early settlements in Kentucky from Indian attacks. He was captured by the Shawnee in 1778, but he managed to escape.

The Call of Bluegrass Country

Boone fought for the British during the French and Indian War, which lasted from 1754 to 1763. A fellow soldier named John Finley told him about a fertile bluegrass region west of the Appalachian Mountains. In the winter of 1767 to 1768, Boone tried and failed to reach bluegrass country from his home in Yadkin County, North Carolina. The next winter, Finley arrived in Yadkin County, and the two friends planned a spring expedition through the Cumberland Gap with four other men. This trip was a success. The travelers camped by a small creek near the edge of the bluegrass plain. By day they hunted and explored, and by night they read *Gulliver's Travels* by the British writer Jonathan Swift.

Unfortunately, one member of the party was killed by Indians. Boone refused to leave the plain, but the others returned to North Carolina before the end of the year. Boone's brother Squire came for several visits. During his time alone, Daniel explored the Kentucky and Licking River valleys. After two years, he packed up his furs and headed home. He was passing through the Cumberland Gap when a band of Cherokee Indians stole his supplies and every fur that he had collected during the last two years. It was neither the first nor the last time he would encounter conflict with Indians.

The Wilderness Road

In 1773 Boone attempted to lead seven families, including his own, through the Cumberland Gap into Kentucky. They were ambushed by Indians. Boone's son and five other members of the party were killed in the attack. Boone wanted to press on toward Kentucky, but the other survivors persuaded him to end the expedition and turn back.

Two years later, a man named Judge Henderson bought land from the Cherokee through an illegal treaty. He planned to sell the land to settlers. He hired Boone and 28 other men to mark a trail across Cherokee territory to the Cumberland Gap and into Kentucky. This trail was the famous Wilderness Road. On the south bank of the Kentucky River, Boone and his men built a few crude cabins. This settlement grew to become Boonesborough, the first white settlement in Kentucky.

Boone later found that Kentucky was getting too crowded for him, so he moved on. He settled first in what is now West Virginia and then in Spanish territory in what is now Missouri. He died there in 1820. Since then many myths and legends have grown up around his life. What is certain is that his love of the wilderness was unmatched. Without him, the first settlements in Kentucky would probably not have survived.

Suggested Reading John Bakeless, *Daniel Boone* (William Morrow, 1939); Lawrence Elliot, *The Long Hunter: A New Life of Daniel Boone* (Reader's Digest Press, 1976); Timothy Flint, *The Life and Adventures of Daniel Boone* (U. P. James, 1958).

Borchgrevink, Carstens Egeberg

Norwegian
b December 1, 1864; Oslo, Norway
d April 21, 1934; Oslo, Norway
Explored Antarctica

surveyor one who makes precise
measurements of a location's geography

sledge heavy sled, often mounted on
runners, that is pulled over snow or ice

Carstens Egeberg Borchgrevink was one of the first people to set foot on the mainland of Antarctica. He later led the first expedition to spend a winter on that frozen continent. His stay set the stage for a new period of Antarctic exploration. Teams of scientists and explorers learned to work there all year round.

In just four years, Borchgrevink went from being an unknown language teacher and **surveyor** in Australia to leading a major expedition. In 1894 he quit his job to follow his dream of going to Antarctica. He volunteered to serve on the *Antarctic,* a Norwegian whaling ship. A party landed on the shore of Antarctica, near Cape Adare in Victoria Land. They were the first people known to have set foot on the mainland. They were astonished to find plants in this frozen world. Borchgrevink was determined to return to the harbor with a team of scientists.

Penniless, he managed to raise money for a trip to London, where a conference on geography was to be held. Although he was neither famous nor experienced, he gave a passionate speech that caused a stir of excitement. He was soon sharing his plans with the leaders of the conference. But he did not realize that he had offended the president of the conference, who was also planning an Antarctic expedition. Unwilling to be upstaged, the president opposed Borchgrevink's plans. Luckily, a British newspaper saw a good story and offered to pay for Borchgrevink's voyage.

The Long Winter

In December 1898, the 34-year-old Norwegian set sail from an island south of Australia on the *Southern Cross.* The ship arrived off Cape Adare two months later. The team members built a house on the shore, and the ship left them to spend the winter in the most severe climate in the world. Borchgrevink's nine-person staff included experts on magnetism, weather, and natural science. Two men from Finland were in charge of a team of **sledge** dogs. Borchgrevink climbed to the highest point on the cape and studied the area in detail. After nearly a year, the *Southern Cross* returned. With new supplies, a sledge party was sent across the Ross Ice Shelf. The scientists gathered much useful information. Even more important, Borchgrevink had proved that it was physically possible to spend the winter in Antarctica. Within the next 10 years, explorers such as Robert Falcon Scott and Ernest Shackleton were doing just that.

Suggested Reading C. E. Borchgrevink, *First on the Antarctic Continent: Being an Account of the British Antarctic Expedition, 1898–1900* (C. Hurst and Company, 1992).

Bougainville, Louis-Antoine de

French
b November 12, 1729; Paris, France
d August 31, 1811; Paris, France
Sailed around world; explored Pacific Ocean

Louis-Antoine de Bougainville led the first French expedition to **circumnavigate** the globe. His voyage took place soon after the Seven Years' War with Britain. France was discouraged after losing its colonies in Canada and India to the British. Bougainville boosted French spirits by exploring, charting, and claiming islands in the South Pacific Ocean.

He was the son of a lawyer in Paris and studied law as a young man. His real interests, though, were mathematics and science. A

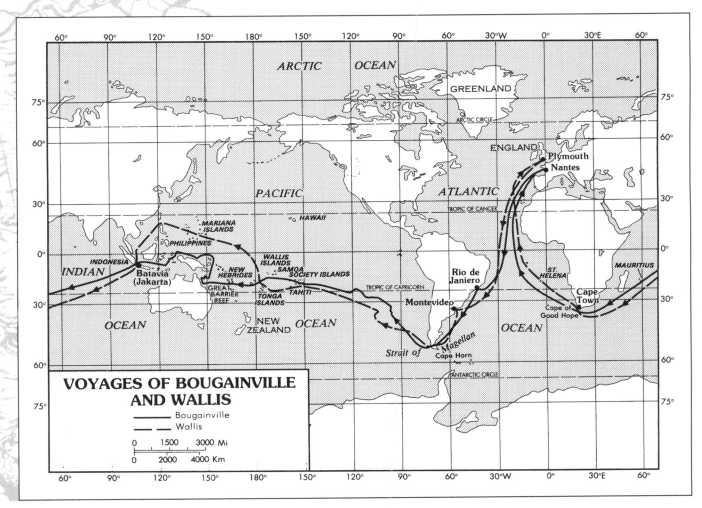

VOYAGES OF BOUGAINVILLE AND WALLIS

—— Bougainville
---- Wallis

0   1500   3000 Mi
0   2000   4000 Km

France's Louis-Antoine de Bougainville and Britain's Samuel WALLIS both commanded voyages around the world in the 1760s.

circumnavigate to travel around

aide-de-camp assistant to a high-ranking military officer

botanist scientist who studies plants

scurvy disease caused by a lack of vitamin C and once a major cause of death among sailors; symptoms include internal bleeding, loosened teeth, and extreme fatigue

mathematical paper he wrote was well received, and he was elected to the British Royal Society. In 1756, during the Seven Years' War, Bougainville served in Canada as **aide-de-camp** to a general. When he returned to France, he searched for a new way to serve his country. He decided to explore the Pacific Ocean for new islands. As a first step, he started a French settlement in the Falkland Islands (also called the Malvinas), off the southeast coast of South America. The British and Spanish governments saw the colony as a threat and asked King Louis XV of France to abandon it. Louis backed down, and the Spanish refunded Bougainville the money he had spent to establish the colony.

Around the World

In 1766 King Louis sent Bougainville on a voyage through the Pacific Ocean and around the world. Bougainville had no formal training as a sea captain, but he had learned a great deal while crossing the Atlantic Ocean during the war. He hired skilled men to serve as second-in-command, pilot, and **botanist.** Two ships set sail from Nantes, France. They stopped in South America and formally gave up the colony in the Falklands. Then they sailed west around Cape Horn into the Pacific Ocean.

The crews endured foul weather and **scurvy** until they found a safe harbor on the island of Tahiti. Although Bougainville knew

After long service to France, Louis-Antoine de Bougainville made scientific studies at his estate and was honored by Emperor Napoleon I.

that he was not the first European to reach Tahiti, he claimed the island for France. He also took a guest on board, Ahu-toru, the son of a Tahitian chief. After 12 days on Tahiti, the French sailed on. Supplies ran so low that the sailors had to eat the rats that lived on board. With a sick and starving crew, Bougainville decided to avoid the dangerous Australian coast, passing up the chance to claim Australia for France. Meanwhile, it was discovered that the botanist's chief assistant was a woman named Jeanne Baret disguised as a man. Baret may have been the first woman to sail around the world.

Public Success

After charting the Solomon Islands and picking up supplies in the Dutch East Indies, the two ships arrived in France. In over two years, only nine men out of 200 had died, an impressively low number for that time. Ahu-toru, who had been eager to visit France, created a public sensation on his arrival. Bougainville himself became a popular hero, and his book, *Voyage Around the World,* was widely read.

In 1772 Bougainville became secretary to Louis XV and commanded the French fleet that helped the Americans during their revolution against the British. An island and a strait in the South Pacific bear his name, as does Bougainvillea, a South American plant that he introduced to Europe.

Suggested Reading David Hammond, *News from New Cythera: A Report of Bougainville's Voyage 1766–69* (Minnesota University Press, 1970); Maurice Thiery, *Bougainville: Soldier and Sailor* (Grayson and Grayson, 1932).

Boyd, Louise Arner

American
b September 16, 1887; San Rafael, California
d September 14, 1972; San Francisco, California
Explored Greenland

For her Arctic rescue work, Louise Boyd was awarded Norway's Chevalier Cross of the Order of Saint Olav and France's Cross of the Legion of Honor.

Louise Arner Boyd was a highly respected leader of expeditions to the Arctic. A wealthy heiress, she used her money to break into a scientific world that was dominated by men. Boyd began as a tourist but became an expert on the geography and natural history of Greenland. She was also a skilled photographer and the first woman to fly over the North Pole.

The Lure of the Arctic

Boyd inherited her family's fortune in 1920. Four years later, without any special purpose in life, she took a summer cruise to the Arctic on a Norwegian tour boat. It was on this cruise that she first felt what she called the "Arctic lure." Her second trip was just as lighthearted as the first. She passed her time hunting polar bears and taking photographs.

Boyd soon had a chance to work with "real" explorers, as she called them. Back in the Arctic in 1928, she had intended to do more hunting, but an emergency changed her plans. The **dirigible** flown by the Italian Umberto NOBILE went down in the Arctic Ocean. During a rescue attempt, the famous Norwegian explorer Roald AMUNDSEN disappeared. Boyd joined the international search for Amundsen and his plane, working closely with members of his earlier expeditions for four months. Though Nobile was rescued, Amundsen was never found. By the time the searchers gave up, Boyd was determined to become an Arctic explorer herself.

dirigible large aircraft filled with a lighter-than-air gas that keeps it aloft; similar to a blimp but with a rigid frame

fjord narrow inlet where the sea meets the shore between steep cliffs

For Science and Country

In 1931 she made the first of four important scientific studies in the Greenland **fjord** named after Franz Josef, a former emperor of Austria. Her writings and photographs greatly impressed the American Geographical Society, which funded her work. During World War II, Greenland became an important area, and the U.S. War Department recruited Boyd as an adviser.

In 1955 Boyd became the first woman to fly over the North Pole. She was also the first woman elected to the council of the American Geographical Society in 1960. She succeeded brilliantly as a woman working in a world of men.

Suggested Reading Louise Boyd, *The Coast of Northeast Greenland, with Hydrographic Studies in the Greenland Sea* (American Geographical Society, 1948) and *The Fjord Region of East Greenland* (American Geographical Society, 1935).

Brandon. See *Brendan.*

Brazza, Pierre-Paul-François-Camille Savorgnan de

Italian-French
b January 25, 1852; Rome, Italy
d September 14, 1905; Dakar, Senegal
Explored central Africa

Pierre Savorgnan de Brazza spent most of his adult life in central Africa, working to protect the rights of Africans in the French colonies he had helped to create.

Thanks to the explorations of Count Pierre Savorgnan de Brazza, France came to control a large part of Africa near the equator. Brazza represented France in the race among European nations to establish colonies in Africa. He argued that Europeans should sign treaties with African peoples rather than conquer them by force. He strongly opposed the mistreatment that many Africans suffered at the hands of Europeans.

Competition in the Congo

An Italian noble by birth, Brazza studied at France's naval academy and served in the French navy. He later became a citizen of France. In 1874, while stationed in Gabon on the west coast of Africa, Brazza received permission to explore the Ogowe River. He discovered the Ogowe's source, and with the help of the friendly Bateke tribe, he almost reached the Congo River. Attacks by cannibals in the region forced him to turn back in 1878. Later that year, Brazza was outraged to learn that Henry Morton STANLEY had succeeded in traveling down the Congo. Brazza returned to France and asked the government to fund another trip. The French agreed when they realized that Belgium had hired Stanley to colonize the area.

Brazza returned to Gabon, traveled up the Ogowe, and stopped at the village of Mbe. During his monthlong stay, he convinced the Bateke ruler to sign a treaty that placed the Bateke kingdom under French control. The Bateke allowed Brazza to build a fort in Mbe, which later became known as Brazzaville, the capital of the Republic of the Congo.

The Dark Side of Colonial Rule

Thanks in part to Brazza's explorations, France created a large colonial empire in central Africa. Brazza remained there as a French governor. He stirred up controversy by exposing the way

Ancient Times and Middle Ages

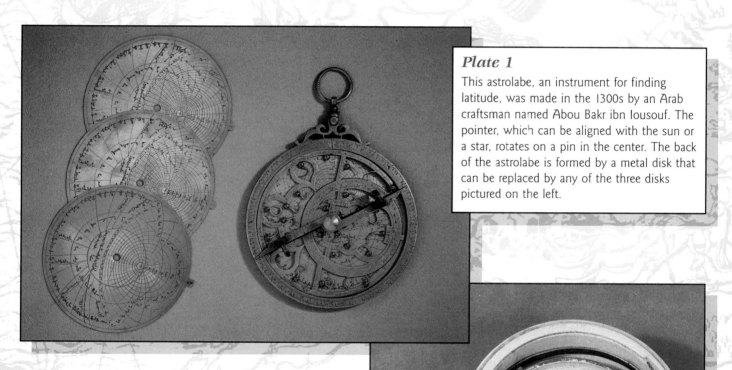

Plate 1

This astrolabe, an instrument for finding latitude, was made in the 1300s by an Arab craftsman named Abou Bakr ibn Iousouf. The pointer, which can be aligned with the sun or a star, rotates on a pin in the center. The back of the astrolabe is formed by a metal disk that can be replaced by any of the three disks pictured on the left.

Plate 2

Navigators have used compasses as the principal instruments for determining direction since the 1200s. The first compasses were probably just pieces of lodestone, a mineral that aligns itself with the earth's magnetic field. The mariner's compass consisted of a magnetized needle stuck through a piece of wood, cork, or straw. An ivory case houses this Italian mariner's compass dating from the 1500s.

Plate 3

Phoenicians were among the greatest mariners, explorers, and traders of the ancient world. This relief sculpture, dating from between 721 B.C. and 705 B.C., depicts ancient Phoenician sailors hauling cargoes of timber on galleys.

Plate 4

This mosaic from the early 500s, found in a cathedral in Ravenna, Italy, shows ancient Roman sailing vessels. The ships, with single masts and square sails, carried Roman merchants and soldiers throughout the Mediterranean Sea.

Plate 5

Arab merchants and sailors of the 700s and 800s used a type of ship called a dhow. These ships carried exotic items such as cloves, pepper, silks, and tea—goods that later attracted Europeans to the region.

Plate 6

A port city welcomes the fleet of the emperor Yang Di, who ruled China in the early 600s. In this Chinese painting, the ships, known as junks, display common features including tall sterns, ornate figureheads, and rectangular sails made of fiber mats.

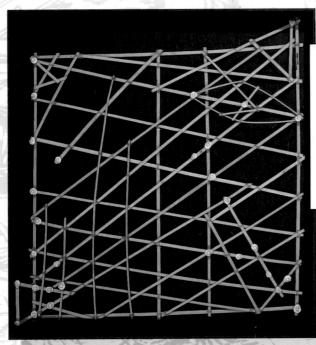

Plate 7

Long before the arrival of European explorers, people sailed across the vast expanses of the Pacific Ocean. Some charted its widely scattered island chains. Maps made by the people of the Marshall Islands had grids formed of straight sticks. Curved sticks represented wave swells, and small shells showed the locations of islands.

Plate 8

This map appears in an English book of Psalms from the early 1200s. Its "T-and-O" organization places Asia at the top, Europe at bottom left, and Africa at bottom right. Such maps often had a religious, symbolic purpose.

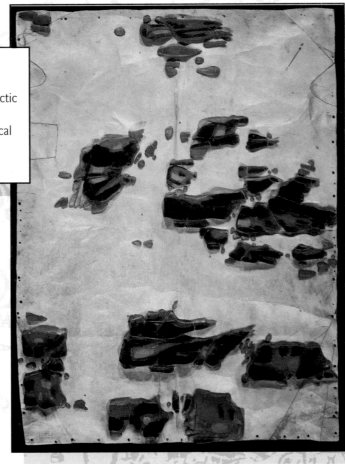

Plate 9

The Inuit people of northern Canada made three-dimensional maps of islands in the Arctic Ocean. They affixed pieces of fur or carved driftwood to sealskin. The Inuit's geographical knowledge was crucial to the survival and success of European explorers in the Arctic.

Plate 10

After magnetic compasses came into use around 1200, sailors began making portolans, or sea charts. Networks of lines indicated the directions of winds. This portolan shows the eastern Mediterranean coast.

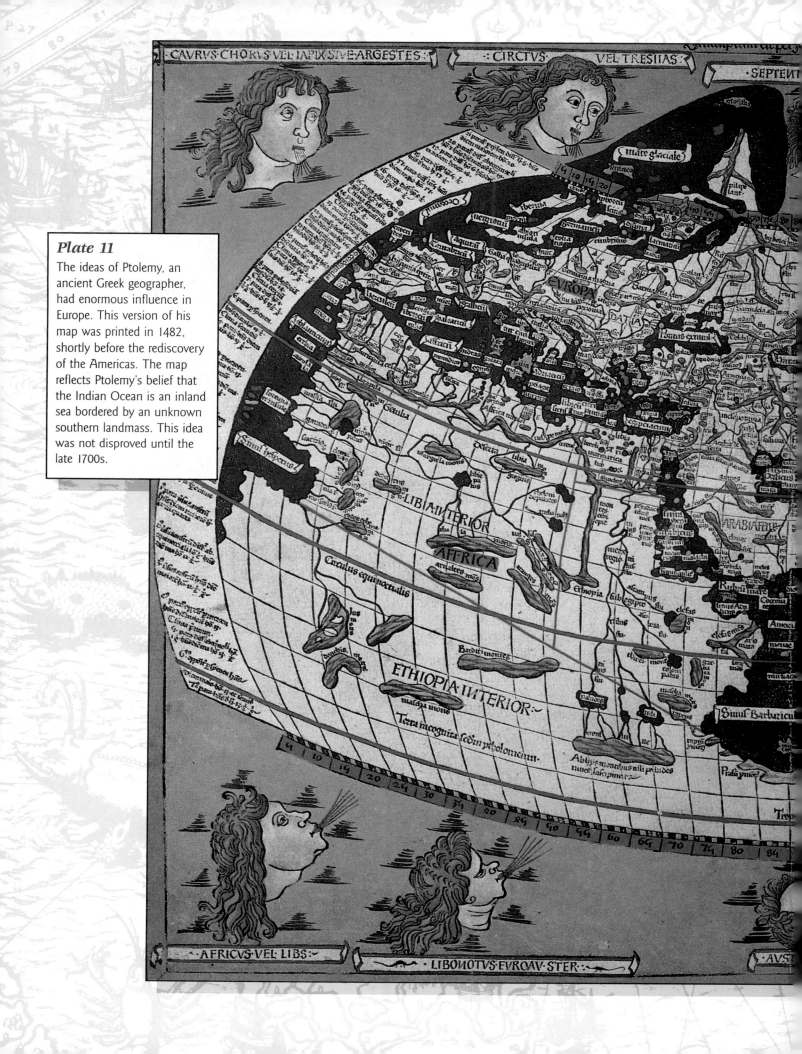

Plate 11

The ideas of Ptolemy, an ancient Greek geographer, had enormous influence in Europe. This version of his map was printed in 1482, shortly before the rediscovery of the Americas. The map reflects Ptolemy's belief that the Indian Ocean is an inland sea bordered by an unknown southern landmass. This idea was not disproved until the late 1700s.

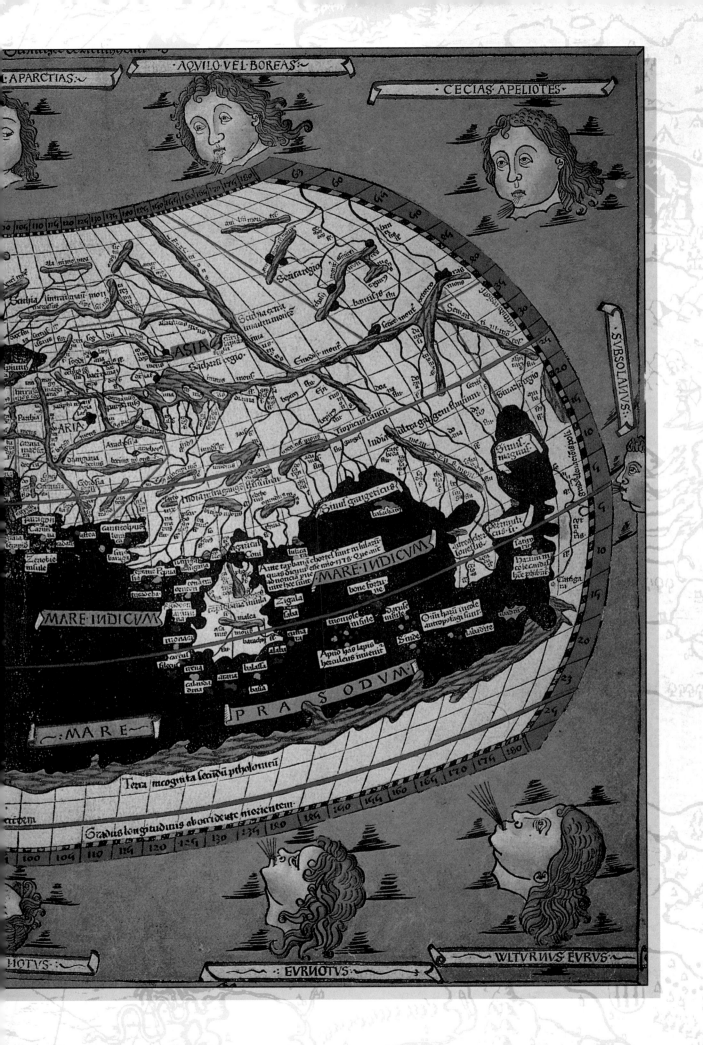

Plate 12

In the imaginations of medieval Europeans, the far reaches of the globe were populated by strange creatures, including humans with monstrous deformities. This image is a detail of a French illustration from about 1460.

Plate 13

The story of the Polo family's journey through Asia in the late 1200s was very popular in medieval Europe and inspired much exploration in the following centuries. This illustration of the Polo family decorated a manuscript produced in 1375.

Plate 14

According to legend, an Irish abbot named Brendan, who lived in the A.D. 500s, may have been the first European to reach North America. This colored woodcut shows Brendan and several other monks on a missionary voyage, with a sea monster lurking near their boat.

French soldiers and officials abused the rights of Africans. The French government began to work on reforms, but Brazza died before he could see these take effect.

Suggested Reading Jean Carbonnier, *Congo Explorer, Pierre Savorgnan de Brazza* (Scribner, 1960); Richard West, *Brazza of the Congo: European Exploration and Exploitation in French Equatorial Africa* (Victorian Book Club, 1973).

Brendan

Irish
b between 484 and 489?; Tralee, Ireland
d between 577 and 583?; ?
May have reached the Americas

This map illustrates part of the tale of Saint Brendan's voyage, in which the monks built an altar to God on the back of a whale.

Brendan, later called Saint Brendan, became a Christian monk in 512 and founded several monasteries. He himself headed the Clonfert monastery in Galway, Ireland. Centuries later, Brendan became associated in legend with at least one fantastic ocean voyage. Some historians believe that Brendan and several other monks, or other Irish explorers of his time, may have been the first Europeans to reach the Americas.

A book was written in the 800s called *Navigatio Sancti Brendani*, which means, in Latin, "The Voyage of Saint Brendan." According to this book, Brendan and 17 other monks made a sea journey in a 30-foot-long boat made of animal skins. They were searching for a mythical place called the Saints' Promised Land, which they believed was in the Atlantic Ocean.

On their journey, Brendan and his monks came to several islands, which may have been the Outer Hebrides and the Faeroes, north of Ireland. They crossed a spot where the sea resembled a "thick, curdled mass." This may be history's first description of seaweed in the Sargasso Sea. Eventually they reached large, flat islands in clear water, possibly the Bahamas. One monk was left behind

there as a missionary. They also found a "fragrant island of mountains" which may have been Jamaica. Brendan and his crew sailed north to a large continent and then returned to Ireland.

"St. Brendan's Isle" remained on many maps until as late as 1759, although mapmakers could not agree on its location. Known also as Brendan the Voyager, Brendan is considered the patron saint of sailors.

Suggested Reading Geoffrey Ashe, *Land to the West: St. Brendan's Voyage to America* (Collins, 1962); Timothy Severin, *The Brendan Voyage* (McGraw-Hill, 1978); George Simms, *Brendan the Voyager* (O'Brien, 1989).

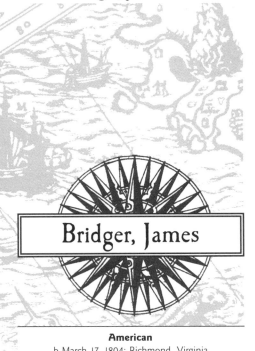

Bridger, James

American
b March 17, 1804; Richmond, Virginia
d July 17, 1881; Washington, Missouri
Explored American West

surveyor one who makes precise measurements of a location's geography

Many tales and legends surround the adventures of Jim Bridger, Mountain Man of the American West.

The exploration of the American West was carried out in part by a loosely knit group known as the Mountain Men. These rough and ready trailblazers pushed west of the Mississippi River in the early 1800s in search of beaver furs, which were in great demand. Jim Bridger was one of the first and best-known of the Mountain Men. He spent much time among Indians, and over the course of his life, he married three Indian women. He learned a great deal from the western tribes about local geography and wildlife, and he put this knowledge to use as a guide for many travelers. In so doing, he helped open the West to other Americans, who settled the lands he had explored.

An Orphan on the Frontier

Jim Bridger spent the first years of his life in Virginia, where his father was an innkeeper and **surveyor.** The frontier appealed to many Americans in the early 1800s, and in 1812 Bridger's father moved the family to a farm near St. Louis, Missouri. The move did not turn out well. Within a year, every member of the family except Jim was dead. Now an orphan, the nine-year-old boy went to work for a blacksmith in St. Louis.

When Jim was 18, he heard about an advertisement that called for "enterprising young men" to follow the Missouri River to its source and work there as fur trappers. The ad had been placed by the lieutenant governor of Missouri, General William Henry ASHLEY. Like other Americans, Ashley was eager to take part in the profitable trade that Canadian fur trappers had already established west of the Mississippi River. The United States had bought the region from France in 1803, and Meriwether LEWIS and William CLARK had explored it. Their glowing reports encouraged other adventurers to go west.

Adventures in the Rockies

Bridger signed on with Ashley's venture and was soon on his way up the Missouri River. The trip was an eventful one. Another trapper, Hugh Glass, was savagely attacked by a grizzly bear. According to some sources, Bridger was one of two men assigned to bury their companion. Bridger and the other man did not bury Glass but simply took his rifle. Luckily, it turned out that Glass was not dead after all. Despite his horrible injuries, he managed to crawl many miles to a fort, where he regained his health.

Another story involving Bridger is set in the winter of 1824 to 1825, when he and another of Ashley's men reached the shore of the Great Salt Lake, in what is now Utah. Upon tasting the water and finding it salty, Bridger mistakenly thought that he had arrived at the Pacific Ocean. For years Bridger was credited with being the first person, other than Indians, to see the Great Salt Lake. Although historians now believe that others probably came across the lake before him, his name is still linked to its discovery.

"Old Gabe" the Mountain Man

Bridger's first trip into the West introduced him to a land and a way of life that he made his own. From then on, he spent much of his time exploring and guiding others through the territory now occupied by the states of Montana, Idaho, Utah, Wyoming, North Dakota, and South Dakota.

In the 20 years following the Ashley expedition, Bridger supported himself by trapping and trading furs. For a time, he and some partners owned a trading company. He attended many rendezvous, the rowdy annual gatherings of fur trappers that were part business meeting and part festival. His fellow Mountain Men called him "Old Gabe" and knew him as a skilled frontiersman and an inspired teller of tall tales. They scoffed at his wild stories about a strange land of multicolored fountains and odd-smelling springs. But Bridger's account proved to be accurate when other explorers followed his trail to what is now Yellowstone National Park.

Opening the Way to the West

By the early 1840s, few beaver were left to be trapped, and the demand for beaver hats in Europe had ended. But the number of people heading west for other reasons was increasing, and Bridger saw a new opportunity to make a living. He and a partner sold supplies and services to these travelers at a fort and trading post on the Green River in southwestern Wyoming. Fort Bridger became a landmark of the Oregon Trail and a gateway to the West. Travelers who passed through included the explorers John Charles FRÉMONT and Benjamin BONNEVILLE, as well as Brigham Young, leader of a new religious group known as the Mormons. After the Mormons settled near the Great Salt Lake, Bridger came into conflict with them and was forced to surrender his fort to them.

Bridger retired to a farm he had bought in Missouri. He seems to have missed the mountain life, and he soon returned to the West as a guide. One of his missions was to lead U.S. Army troops to the Salt Lake region, where they fought with the Mormons. The army took control of Fort Bridger and used it as a post until 1890. Bridger was also employed by mapmakers and surveyors and by army units that protected shipments of mail. He finally retired in 1868 and spent his final years on his farm, ill and blind.

During his time in the West, Bridger's knowledge and skills won him great fame. An official of the Montana Historical Society wrote in 1900,

"James Bridger was the Daniel BOONE of the Rocky Mountains . . . yet most of his life history is lost to us. We obtain glimpses of him here and there, but the many eventful scenes of his life are now forever lost."

Suggested Reading J. Cecil Alter, *Jim Bridger* (University of Oklahoma Press, 1962); Gene Caesar, *King of the Mountain Men: The Life of Jim Bridger* (Dutton, 1961); Clide Hollman, *Jim Bridger, King of Scouts* (Vantage, 1953); William Luce, *Jim Bridger, Man of the Mountains* (Chelsea Juniors, 1992); Dan Zadra, *Jim Bridger: The Mountain Man* (Creative Education, 1988).

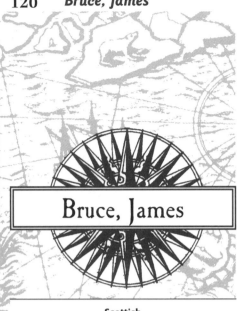

Bruce, James

Scottish
b December 14, 1730; Stirling, Scotland
d April 27, 1794; Stirling, Scotland
Explored Blue Nile River

tributary stream or river that flows into a larger stream or river

headwaters source of a river

From the first time he visited Africa, James Bruce had one goal as an explorer: to find the source of the Nile River. This river, the longest in the world, has two main **tributaries,** the White Nile and the Blue Nile. When Bruce reached the **headwaters** of the Blue Nile, he rejoiced in his success, but in fact the Nile River's source is at the head of the White Nile. Still, Bruce's exploration of the Blue Nile stands out as an impressive feat.

Tragedy Strikes Early

Bruce came from a wealthy Scottish family. As a young man, he studied both law and medicine, but a severe illness forced him to give up his studies. After he recovered, he married the daughter of a Scottish wine merchant and joined her family's business. His wife died just one year later, and the grieving Bruce left Scotland to cope with his loss.

He visited Spain and Portugal and studied a number of languages, including Arabic. In 1758, his father died. Bruce inherited a large sum of money and decided to continue traveling. First, however, he served in the British military. The British government then made him a diplomat in Algiers, a North African city on the Mediterranean Sea. Bruce's fascination with Africa deepened. Two years later, he traveled to Egypt to make plans for the journey he dreamed of, an expedition up the Blue Nile.

River, Desert, and War

Bruce left Cairo in 1768 with about 20 men. They sailed up the river to Aswan, then crossed the Eastern Desert to Abyssinia (modern-day Ethiopia), where Bruce believed that he would find the source of the Blue Nile. The expedition arrived at the Abyssinian capital of Gondar to find a country torn by civil war. The party's survival depended on the good will of the emperor of Abyssinia. By the end of 1770, Bruce reached Lake Tana, the source of the Blue Nile. He believed that he had succeeded where others had failed for centuries. He wrote: "I triumphed here, in my own mind, over kings and their armies." But he still faced a difficult return trip. He arrived in Cairo only after another year in Abyssinia and a 20-day trip across the desert of Sudan.

Doubts and Attacks at Home

When he returned to Britain, Bruce found that many people did not believe his written account of the journey. He was a colorful writer and displayed a high opinion of himself. Some critics charged that everything he had written was a lie.

James Bruce's tales of war in Abyssinia were so shocking that many people in Britain doubted his claim to have found the source of the Nile River.

Frustrated and disgusted, Bruce returned to his family's home in Scotland. He married again, but this marriage also ended in the death of his wife. Bruce spent his time compiling the writings and drawings from his trip. A five-volume work was published in 1790. The book became very popular, especially after later explorers confirmed much of what he wrote. Soon after, Bruce died of a fall down the front steps of his manor.

Suggested Reading James Macarthur Reid, *Traveller Extraordinary, the Life of James Bruce of Kinnaird* (Norton, 1968).

Brulé, Etienne

French
b 1592?; Champigny-sur-Marne?, France
d June 1632?; Huron lands near the Great Lakes
***Explored Great Lakes, Susquehanna River,
and Chesapeake Bay***

Etienne Brulé may have been the first European to explore four of the five Great Lakes.

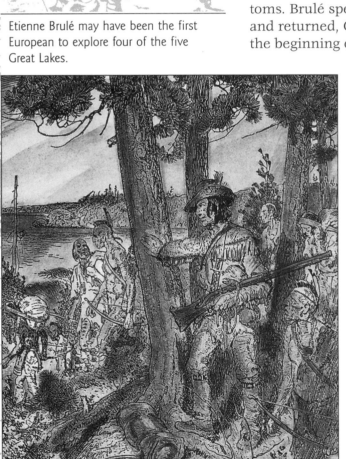

Since Etienne Brulé produced no written record of his explorations, much of his life remains a mystery. It is known, however, that he lived among the Huron Indians for many years. He also traveled the length of the Susquehanna River, so that he was probably the first European to set foot in what is now Pennsylvania. According to the reports of other explorers, he may have also been the first European to see four of the five Great Lakes.

Brulé arrived in Québec, in French Canada, in 1608. Two years later, the French explorer and colonizer Samuel de CHAMPLAIN sent him to live among the Indians and learn their languages and customs. Brulé spent a year with the Algonquin in the Ottawa Valley and returned, Champlain wrote, "dressed like an Indian." It was only the beginning of Brulé's fascination with the Indian way of life.

Huron Country

Little is known about Brulé's travels between 1611 and 1615. He probably stayed with the Huron near Georgian Bay on the east side of Lake Huron. He is credited with being the first European to see that lake. In 1615 he served as Champlain's interpreter on a trip to Huron country. The French hoped to arrange fur trading with the Indians and to add new territory to the French Empire.

Champlain and his Huron allies prepared to attack the Iroquois near Oneida Lake. Meanwhile, Brulé went with a small party of Hurons to seek the support of the Andaste, a tribe in what is now the state of New York. The journey led around the west end of Lake Ontario, so it is likely that Brulé was the first European to see that lake as well.

Conflicts near the Great Lakes

When Brulé and the Andaste arrived at the Iroquois village that had been targeted for attack, Champlain was gone. He and the Huron had been defeated by the Iroquois and had left two days earlier. Brulé then returned to the Andaste village, near the source of the Susquehanna River. Always ready for adventure, he set out on his own to explore. He followed the Susquehanna south and eventually reached Chesapeake Bay. He explored the bay and some of its many islands. As he traveled back to Québec, he was captured by the Iroquois. The Indians tortured Brulé until a violent thunderstorm struck. Seeing the storm as an omen, the Iroquois allowed Brulé to leave.

In 1618 he met Champlain again and told him of his travels. Champlain urged him to continue exploring, so Brulé and another Frenchman named Grenolle explored the north shore of Lake Huron as far as Lake Superior. Some accounts say that several years later, Brulé was in the country of the Neutrals, a tribe of Indians who lived near Lake Erie. If Brulé really did visit the Neutrals, he was the first European to see Lake Erie.

In 1629 the British attacked the city of Québec. Brulé abandoned Champlain and joined the British, who may have lured him with money. After the French surrendered Québec, Brulé returned to Huron country. Sometime around 1632, for reasons that no one else ever learned, the Hurons killed and ate him. It was a strange end for a man who had admired the Huron culture and had adopted it so well.

Suggested Reading C. W. Butterfield, *History of Brulé's Discoveries and Explorations* (Helman-Taylor, 1898) James Herbert Cranston, *Etienne Brulé, Immortal Scoundrel* (Ryerson, 1949).

Bruni, Antoine Raymond Joseph de. See *Entrecasteaux, Antoine Raymond Joseph de Bruni d'*.

Burckhardt, Johann Ludwig

Swiss
b November 24, 1784; Lausanne, Switzerland
d October 15, 1817; Cairo, Egypt
Explored Arabian Peninsula and East Africa

Johann Ludwig Burckhardt was one of the first Europeans to combine the two careers of scholar and explorer. In the early 1800s, he made detailed studies of Muslim communities and cities in Arabia and traveled south along the Nile River. He learned about ancient cultures that were largely unknown—and even forbidden—to Europeans. Burckhardt was highly regarded by other explorers for the many facts he provided on obscure areas and customs of the Muslim world.

Burckhardt came from a wealthy Swiss family, but he spent much of his youth in Germany. He was an excellent student at German universities, where he studied science and languages. In 1806 he traveled to Britain, looking for work. Intrigued with the idea of visiting foreign lands, Burckhardt applied to the Association for Promoting the Discovery of the Interior Parts of Africa, known as the African Association. Its founder, Sir Joseph BANKS, hired Burckhardt to explore the Niger River and the city of Timbuktu in western Africa. Banks suggested that Burckhardt study the Arabic language before beginning his travels.

Studies Become an Obsession

Burckhardt's studies went far beyond what the African Association had expected. Determined to be an effective explorer, the dedicated young scholar spent more than four years in training. In Britain he

sheikh Arab chief

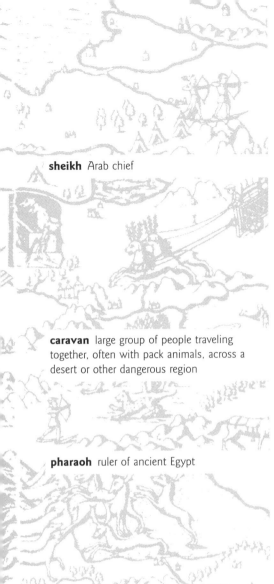

caravan large group of people traveling together, often with pack animals, across a desert or other dangerous region

pharaoh ruler of ancient Egypt

To travel in Muslim lands, the Swiss scholar Johann Ludwig Burckhardt disguised himself as Sheikh Ibrahim ibn Abdullah.

studied Arabic and researched Muslim culture. He walked barefoot, slept outdoors, and lived on a diet of vegetables and water. In early 1809, he traveled to Syria, where he continued to study the region's language and customs. He also created a disguise, pretending to be a **sheikh** named Ibrahim ibn Abdullah. Dressed in Arab clothing, he made three trial journeys in Syria before heading for Egypt in June 1812.

Burckhardt had planned to start from Cairo on his trip southwest to the Niger River and Timbuktu. Even before he reached Cairo, however, he changed his route. By now he was completely immersed in Muslim culture, and he wanted to learn more. He decided to visit Muslim cities that were closed to outsiders and became the first European since the Middle Ages to see Petra, a city in what is now Jordan. Arriving in Cairo later that year, he could not locate a **caravan** heading west and decided instead to follow the Nile River south.

Ancient Lands

Traveling by donkey, Burckhardt covered more than 1,000 miles and made one of his few actual discoveries. At the village of Abu Simbel in southern Egypt, he came upon the temples of Ramses II, a great **pharaoh.** The temples had been carved into the side of a cliff approximately 3,000 years before Burckhardt's visit. He was the first European traveler to see these impressive monuments since ancient times. Farther south, in the region of Nubia, Burckhardt found more temples and ruins. Taking detailed notes, he provided keen insights into the history and geography of this ancient region and its people. Although he admired the Nubians he met, he was also at risk among them. Their customs allowed robbers to take what they wanted from travelers—and kill those who refused to give up their valuables. Burckhardt had several narrow escapes.

The Swiss scholar developed an eye infection and had to stay in the area for several months to recover. In March 1814 he set out again, taking a caravan route south across the Nubian Desert and then continuing to follow the Nile River. He eventually turned east, reached the Red Sea, and sailed across it to Arabia.

Forbidden Cities

Arriving in the town of Jidda, Burckhardt wrote to the African Association to tell them of his detour. He planned to stay in Arabia until he could join the annual caravan from Cairo to the Niger River. He was anxious to explore the Muslim region known as the Hejaz. Its capital, Mecca, is the holiest city of Islam, and non-Muslims were forbidden to enter.

In his Egyptian disguise, Burckhardt visited Mecca and another holy city, Medina. His descriptions of those cities and their citizens were the most accurate yet written by a European. He returned to Cairo the following year to find that an epidemic of disease had broken out. He left quickly and headed east once again. This time he traveled to the Sinai Peninsula, where he studied manuscripts kept in a monastery at Mount Sinai.

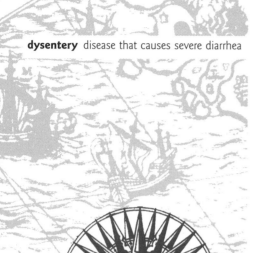

dysentery disease that causes severe diarrhea

The Mission Uncompleted

In 1816 Burckhardt returned to Cairo to wait for the caravan to take him to Timbuktu. While he prepared for his journey, he came down with **dysentery** and died the following year. He was buried as Sheikh Ibrahim ibn Abdullah in a Muslim funeral. Although Burckhardt never made the expedition for which he had been hired, the African Association was impressed with the length and quality of his journals. He had written in great detail about the terrain, climate, people, and wildlife of the regions he had visited. Over the next few years, the association published his accounts. They were too scholarly to be popular with the general public, but they proved invaluable to later students of the Muslim world.

Suggested Reading Katherine Sim, *Desert Traveller: The Life of Jean Louis Burckhardt* (Victor Gollancz, 1969).

Burke, Robert O'Hara

Irish
b 1821; St. Clerans, Ireland
d June 28, 1861; Cooper's Creek, Australia
Led Great Northern Exploration Expedition across Australia

Robert O'Hara Burke commanded perhaps the most tragic expedition in Australia's history. Burke had courage, but he was inexperienced and impatient. His first trip into Australia's barren interior was his last. However, he and William John WILLS did succeed in crossing the continent from south to north.

A Police Officer Enters History

Burke was born in Ireland and educated in Belgium. At the age of 20 he joined the army of Austria-Hungary, then one of Europe's most powerful nations. He achieved the rank of captain but then returned to Ireland and became a police officer. In 1853 he went to live in Tasmania, an island south of Australia, and soon moved to Melbourne, a city on the mainland. Burke served in Melbourne as a police sergeant and inspector.

In 1860 he was selected to lead an expedition across Australia from south to north. His sponsors wanted to build a telegraph line across the continent. Burke unfortunately lacked many of the qualities that explorers need. He was not a careful planner, and he had no real experience in the harsh Australian interior. But he did have the finest expedition money could buy. He left Melbourne with 18 men, 24 camels, 28 horses, and 21 tons of supplies. The camels were imported from India and were cared for by three handlers from Pakistan.

Early Troubles

At Menindee, some 400 miles north of Melbourne, Burke faced his first major problem. Tired of Burke's fiery temper, the group's second-in-command, camel master, and doctor all quit. Burke made William John Wills his new second-in-command. He then decided to leave most of his staff and supplies at Menindee and move quickly with just six men to Cooper's Creek, a river to the north. He instructed a guide, William Wright, to follow with the rest of the men and supplies.

A stubborn and sometimes misguided man, Robert Burke (left) ignored the advice of the younger William Wills (right), a decision that led both to their deaths.

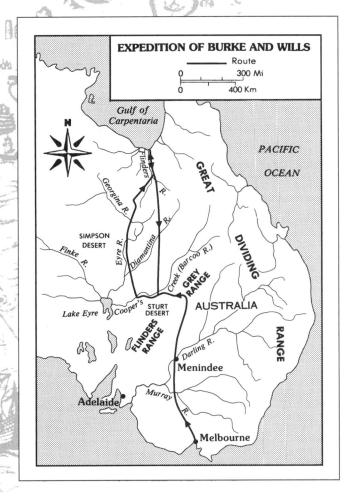

EXPEDITION OF BURKE AND WILLS

After crossing Australia, Burke and Wills became lost in the desert interior and never made it back to Melbourne.

depot place where supplies are stored

dysentery disease that causes severe diarrhea

When Burke reached Cooper's Creek, he set up a **depot.** He had planned to stay there until Wright arrived, but he became too impatient. Leaving William Brahe at the depot, Burke set out with Wills, John King, and Charles Gray. They took six camels, a horse, and supplies for 12 weeks. Brahe was told to wait three months for their return.

The Struggle North and South

The four explorers faced a brutal journey. They marched 12 hours a day for two months in searing heat. The temperature rose as high as 140 degrees Fahrenheit. They ate little along the way. Exhausted, the men finally reached the mouth of the Flinders River at the Gulf of Carpentaria. They never actually saw the Indian Ocean because wide marshes lay between them and the shore. But they were close enough to know that they had completed their mission. They began the return journey almost immediately.

The trek south was as wet as the trip north had been hot and dry. Burke, Wills, King, and Gray traveled slowly through heavy rains and lightning storms. Once they ran over a snake almost as thick as a log. They killed it and ate it. As they grew more desperate for food, the men had to eat their horse and two of their camels. When Gray came down with **dysentery,** the others thought that he was faking, but he died two weeks later.

The three remaining explorers spent a day burying their dead companion. That delay in their trip probably cost them their lives. When they arrived back at Cooper's Creek on April 21, the depot was deserted. William Brahe had left the camp earlier that day. He had headed back toward Menindee and had left some food and a note saying what route he was taking. Brahe was only about 14 miles away. Wills and King wanted to try to follow him, but Burke was sure that they could not catch up. Instead, Burke insisted on heading for Mount Hopeless, some 150 miles to the southwest, which was the nearest inhabited area.

The Last Journey

The three men headed southwest, but they soon lost their way and ended up wandering in circles. They were forced to eat nardoo, a type of grass seed, along with fish and rats. Each day the search for food became more difficult, and the men grew weaker. Burke and Wills died of starvation within two days of each other at the end of June 1861. King was found by a group of Aborigines, the people native to Australia. They cared for him until he was rescued by a search party. Back in Melbourne, the public was critical of Burke's foolish decisions. In later years, however, he and Wills were recognized for their bravery in reaching their goal. They had covered 1,500 miles and had established a land route across the continent.

Suggested Reading Tim Bonyhady, *Burke and Wills: From Melbourne to Myth* (David Ell, 1991); Max Colwell, *The Journey of Burke and Wills* (Hamlyn, 1971); Randal Flynn, *Burke and Wills, Crossing the Continent* (Macmillan Australia, 1991).

Burton, Richard Francis

English
b March 19, 1821; Torquay, England
d October 20, 1890; Trieste, Italy
Explored Africa and Asia;
discovered Lake Tanganyika

The explorer Richard Burton gained fame and notoriety for his translations of Eastern classics such as the *Arabian Nights* and the *Kama Sutra.*

Sir Richard Francis Burton was among the most notable and controversial explorers of the 1800s. He discovered Lake Tanganyika in central Africa and went on two expeditions to search for the source of the Nile River. He later traveled through much of western Africa and the Arabian Peninsula. A sharp observer and talented student of languages, Burton gathered an enormous amount of information about the lands and people he saw. He shared his knowledge in more than 50 books. These included volumes of poetry and translations of works from Arabia and India, as well as original accounts of his travels. Burton's works have often been criticized—both then and now—for their racist attitudes and shocking content. However, they are widely respected for their contributions to the study of Africa and Asia.

Interest in Foreign Lands

The son of a British army colonel, Burton traveled through Europe with his family as a boy. Even then he showed signs of being a rebel. He fought often in school and did poorly in his classes. At Oxford University, he developed what became a lifelong interest in foreign languages, but he was expelled for disobedience. He learned 6 languages before he was 18 years old, and he eventually mastered some 25 more.

Thrilled with travel and adventure, Burton joined the army of the British East India Company, which controlled much of India's trade and politics. During a seven-year stay, he researched the history and culture of Indian cities, also learning Arabic and 10 other languages. In 1849 he took an extended leave from the army to perfect his command of Arabic and prepare for his next adventure.

Holy Cities

Burton was fascinated by the famed Islamic cities of Mecca and Medina on the Arabian Peninsula. Christians were forbidden to enter these heavily guarded cities. Burton wore Arab clothing and darkened his skin with henna, a natural dye. In 1853 he spent several months in Mecca and Medina, posing as a doctor from Afghanistan. He wrote about his experiences in a book called *Personal Narrative of a Pilgrimage to Mecca and El Medina,* which is considered one of his best travel books. Burton's disguise also enabled him to be the first European to visit the holy city of Harar in Ethiopia.

Burton was in Ethiopia as part of an expedition with a fellow army officer named John Hanning SPEKE. The two men explored eastern Ethiopia and Somaliland (now known as Somalia) and searched for the source of the Nile River. They were both wounded in an

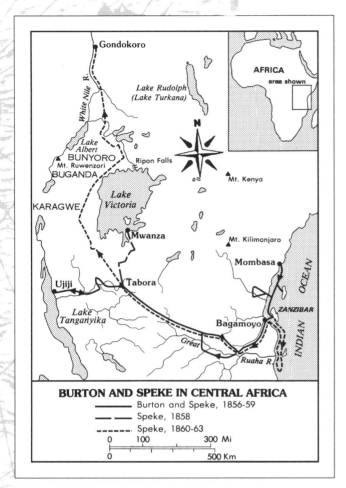

BURTON AND SPEKE IN CENTRAL AFRICA
——— Burton and Speke, 1856-59
— — — Speke, 1858
- - - - Speke, 1860-63

| 0 | 100 | 300 Mi |
| 0 | | 500 Km |

Richard Burton and John Speke had angry public disagreements over whether Speke had found the source of the Nile River.

tributary stream or river that flows into a larger stream or river

malaria disease that is spread by mosquitoes in tropical areas

attack by Somalis at Berbera in 1855, and they were forced to flee the country. After recovering from their injuries, they returned to Africa for a second journey. It would prove more successful than the first, but it would also lead to a bitter feud.

Searching for the Source of Nile

Burton won the support of Britain's Royal Geographical Society and was named the mission's leader. His assignment was to find the origin of the White Nile, the Nile River's largest **tributary.** He was also to locate an unexplored body of water called the Sea of Ujiji, which is now known as Lake Tanganyika. The party traveled west from the coastal region of Zanzibar to Kazeh (now Tabora, Tanzania). By the time the party reached the Sea of Ujiji in February 1858, Burton was suffering from **malaria,** and Speke was temporarily blinded by a tropical eye disease. They explored the lake only briefly before returning to Kazeh to regain their health.

Speke recovered more quickly than Burton and set out on his own to locate a larger body of water rumored to be northeast of the Sea of Ujiji. He found Lake Ukerewe in late July and renamed it in honor of Britain's Queen Victoria. Speke learned from local tribes and missionaries that a large river flowed from the lake's north side. He correctly assumed that he had discovered the source of the Nile, and he rushed back to Kazeh to share the good news with Burton. The fiercely competitive Burton doubted Speke's claim and ridiculed him for lacking proof. Speke returned to Britain first and claimed that he had indeed found the source of the Nile. He received funds from the Royal Geographical Society to continue exploring Lake Victoria on his own. As Speke's reputation grew, so did Burton's anger.

New Travels and Studies

Burton recovered from his malaria in 1860 while traveling across the United States. He studied the Mormon communities of Utah and wrote a book about them the following year. He then took an unimportant position as a British official in West Africa. He also became involved in another bitter controversy. In this case, however, Burton supported the explorer in question, Paul Belloni Du CHAILLU. This French-American traveler claimed to have observed gorillas in the highlands of West Africa. Burton believed that Du Chaillu was telling the truth and defended him at a public debate. Burton was also inspired to travel to the Gabon River region eight months later, and he too caught a brief glimpse of a gorilla. He also studied the area's Fang people, also know as Oahouins, who were known to practice cannibalism.

Burton's travels west and south led him through Nigeria, Cameroon, and Angola. He was assigned to visit Benin to try to reduce the slave trade there. He failed to persuade Benin's King

Gelele to stop the practice, but he did study the region and produce a two-volume account of what he learned. He wrote several other books about the lands and peoples of West Africa.

Burton's work for the British government next took him to continents other than Africa. He traveled extensively in Brazil, Syria, Palestine, Iceland, Italy, and the Balkans. He also made a return visit to India and tried unsuccessfully to find gold in Arabia and West Africa. This tireless traveler spent his last years as a diplomat in Italy, where he died at the age of 69.

In his writings, Burton often offended the readers of his day. He described the peoples he met in very unflattering ways, making fun of their appearance, habits, and religious beliefs. He also insulted other groups, such as Jews and the French. Few would deny, however, that Burton was an extraordinary man who achieved greatness as both an explorer and a writer.

Suggested Reading Thomas J. Assad, *Three Victorian Travelers* (Routledge and Kegan Paul, 1964); Fawn M. Brodie, *The Devil Drives; A Life of Sir Richard Burton* (W. W. Norton, 1967); Byron Farwell, *Burton* (Holt, Rinehart, and Winston, 1963); Edward Rice, *Captain Sir Richard Francis Burton* (Charles Scribner's Sons, 1990).

Button, Thomas

Welsh
b 1500s; St. Lythans, Wales
d April 1634; Worlton, Wales
Searched for Northwest Passage

Northwest Passage water route connecting the Atlantic Ocean and Pacific Ocean through the Arctic islands of northern Canada

mutiny rebellion by a ship's crew against the officers

In 1613, while sailing in northern Canada in search of the **Northwest Passage,** Admiral Sir Thomas Button discovered the west side of what is now Hudson Bay. The discovery was not an occasion for joy, since it meant that the bay was not part of the passage. Button had followed the route of Henry HUDSON, who had sailed those waters one year before. After a **mutiny** by his crew, Hudson had been set adrift on the bay in a small, open boat. The rebellious crew had returned to England, and now Button was back on the bay on Hudson's ship, the *Discovery,* sailed by Hudson's treacherous pilot, Robert BYLOT. Though Hudson, his son, and the loyal members of his crew may still have been alive, the Button expedition did not try to find them.

After reaching the west end of the bay, Button and his crew wintered at Port Nelson, where several sailors froze to death. Button kept the surviving men in order with strict discipline. When summer came, they explored 600 miles of the bay's coastline and then sailed home. The area would prove to be a rich source of furs for Britain. Button continued to succeed in the navy, reaching the rank of admiral. His later years were troubled by charges that he was involved in illegal financial dealings.

Suggested Reading George Thomas Clark, *Some Account of Sir Robert Mansel Kt, Vice Admiral of England, and Member of Parliament for the County of Glamorgan, and of Admiral Sir Thomas Button Kt, of Worlton and of Cardiff in the County of Glamorgan* (Dowlais, 1883).

Bylot, Robert

English
b 1500s; England?
d 1600s; ?
Searched for Northwest Passage

Robert Bylot was a natural leader who won the respect of everyone who sailed with him. In 1611, however, he damaged his reputation forever by joining a **mutiny** against Henry HUDSON, captain of the *Discovery.* Bylot had certainly earned Hudson's respect. After Hudson fired the first **mate** during the voyage, he gave the position to Bylot. But when the mutiny occurred, Bylot chose not to support his captain, who was left to die in the freezing Canadian wilderness.

mutiny rebellion by a ship's crew against the officers

mate assistant to the commander of a ship

Northwest Passage water route connecting the Atlantic Ocean and Pacific Ocean through the Arctic islands of northern Canada

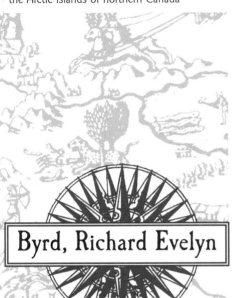

Byrd, Richard Evelyn

American
b October 25, 1888; Winchester, Virginia
d March 11, 1957; Boston, Massachusetts
***Explored Arctic Ocean and Antarctica by plane;
flew over North and South Poles***

Inuit people of the Canadian Arctic, sometimes known as the Eskimo

sledge heavy sled, often mounted on runners, that is pulled over snow or ice

The rebel crew put Bylot in charge of the return trip to England. He proved his abilities by sailing the ship with only seven crewmen, who were ill. They were all arrested when they arrived in England. The usual penalty for mutiny was death by hanging, but Bylot persuaded the navy to let them live. In fact, he was soon back on the *Discovery,* sailing in search of the **Northwest Passage.**

Within a year after his trial, he piloted that ship for Sir Thomas BUTTON on an expedition to Hudson Bay. Bylot then sailed as the *Discovery*'s captain on two important voyages to the Canadian Arctic in 1615 and 1616. Although Bylot led those missions, his pilot, William BAFFIN, has received all the credit for discovering Baffin Bay and the south shore of Baffin Island. History does not record how Bylot spent the rest of his life. The circumstances of his death, like those of his birth, are a mystery.

Suggested Reading Christy Miller, *The Voyages of Captain Luke Foxe of Hull, and Captain Thomas James of Bristol, in Search of a Northwest Passage in 1631-32 with Narratives of the Earlier Northwest Voyages of Frobisher, David, Weymouth, Hall, Knight, Hudson, Button, Gibbons, Bylot, Hawkridge, and Others* (B. Franklin, 1963).

Admiral Richard Evelyn Byrd brought modern machines to the world's polar regions. Until Byrd's time, explorers in the Arctic and Antarctica used **Inuit** methods of travel, such as **sledges** pulled by dogs. Byrd relied on airplanes and snow tractors, which he equipped with cameras and radios. Although these machines could be very dangerous, they put the poles in easy reach. When the American explorer Robert PEARY conquered the North Pole in 1909, he risked his life for five hard weeks on a dog sledge. Seventeen years later, Byrd's round-trip to the pole from the Norwegian island of Spitsbergen took only 15½ hours. "To think," Byrd wrote in his log, "that men toiled for years over this ice, a few hard-won miles a day; and we travel luxuriously a hundred miles an hour. How motors have changed the burdens of man."

Career in the Navy

Byrd's adventures began at an early age. He came from an upper-class Virginia family, and his parents sent him on a trip around the world when he was just 12 years old. Two years later, he decided that someday he would reach the North Pole. After high school, he entered the U.S. Naval Academy, where he was a gifted athlete in football and gymnastics. However, he broke his foot twice in school. When he injured it again while serving on the battleship *Wyoming,* he had no choice but to retire from active duty in 1916.

Byrd had already decided that he wanted to fly planes on missions of exploration. The United States was close to entering World War I, however, and the navy needed instructors. Byrd trained sailors in Rhode Island and briefly held a command position. When the United States declared war on Germany in 1917, he took a desk job, but he was eager to see action. He persuaded the navy to train him as a pilot. Byrd quickly showed his skills and was made a flight instructor in Florida. There he helped invent a device for navigating a new flying boat called the NC-1. In the summer of 1917, he went

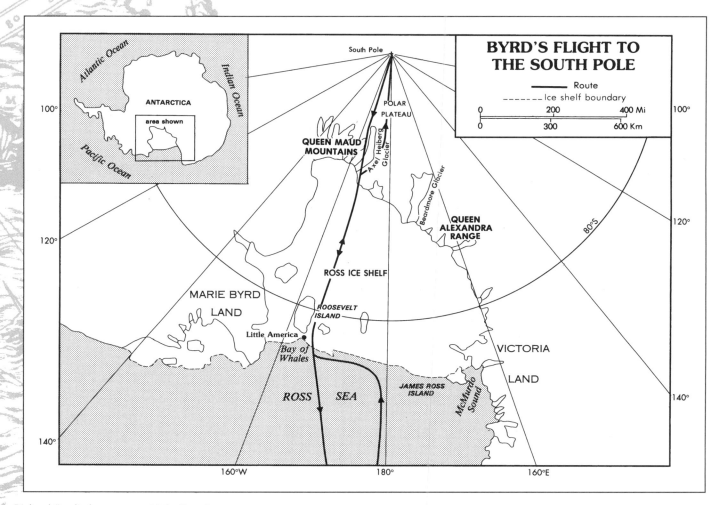

Richard Byrd's base camp, Little America, was built on the same site that Roald Amundsen used for his 1911 overland journey to the South Pole.

dirigible large aircraft filled with a lighter-than-air gas that keeps it aloft; similar to a blimp but with a rigid frame

to a base in Nova Scotia, Canada, to train pilots to fly the NC-1 across the Atlantic Ocean. The war ended before his work in Canada was finished. For the next five years, he worked for the navy in Washington, D.C. He helped persuade Congress to let the navy pursue the use of airplanes in combat.

Dreams Come True

Byrd began to realize his ambitions as an explorer in 1925, when he was put in charge of the airplanes on an expedition to Greenland led by Donald MacMillan. In those early days of flight, mechanical failures were not the only dangers. A plane could easily run out of fuel if the pilot made an error in navigation. That would mean a crash landing in the ice and water of the Arctic Ocean. But Byrd and MacMillan proved that planes could be useful tools for exploring the Arctic.

The next year, Byrd had a chance to achieve his boyhood goal of traveling to the North Pole. He and his copilot, Floyd BENNETT, set up camp on Spitsbergen Island, north of Norway. They had company—the famous Norwegian explorer Roald AMUNDSEN was there planning his own flight in an Italian **dirigible.** Byrd and Bennett reached the pole first, however, in their three-motor plane, the

Richard Byrd devoted his life to exploring the earth's polar regions. He was the first to fly over both the North Pole and the South Pole.

Josephine Ford. During the flight, oil began to leak from one of the engines. Bennett wanted to land to make repairs, but the risks of landing on the rough and unstable ice were too great. Luckily, the leak stopped when the oil level dropped below the hole in the tank. The relieved pilots circled the pole and returned safely to their base. Even Amundsen greeted them with embraces and praise. He said that "few more hazardous ventures have ever been undertaken in history."

Byrd's next feat was to cross the Atlantic Ocean in a plane large enough to carry passengers. On June 29, 1927, he flew from New York to Paris, France, with a cargo of 15,000 pounds. Just as he approached Europe, a faulty compass and bad weather forced him to bring the plane down in the ocean. Still, he had shown that airplanes could be used for trade and travel across the Atlantic. He and his crew received a hero's welcome in both Paris and New York.

The South Pole Is Next

Byrd turned his attention south. He prepared the largest and most expensive expedition ever to visit Antarctica. He raised close to one million dollars and bought four ships, four planes, and a variety of advanced cameras for photographs and motion pictures. Little America, his camp at the Bay of Whales on the Ross Ice Shelf, was more like a village, housing 42 workers and 94 dogs. Byrd began by making short trips with planes and sledges. He then turned to his main goal, a flight to the South Pole.

His plane was named *Floyd Bennett* after his former partner, who had died the year before. On November 28, 1929, Byrd took to the air with the Norwegian-American pilot Bernt Balchen at the controls. Their greatest fear was that the plane would not make it over a mountain range that lay between their base and the pole. But the two men dumped some of their cargo, and the plane cleared the icy mountains at a height of 10,500 feet. The flight was a success.

No Escape from Danger

The 1930s were tough times economically for Americans, and Byrd had trouble raising money for another trip to Antarctica. After deciding on less ambitious plans, he raised enough money for a two-year expedition. On this visit, he and his teams covered more ground than before and recorded a great deal of scientific information. The mission was a success, but Byrd almost died.

He was alone at a scientific station 125 miles from his base camp. A leaking stovepipe released carbon monoxide, a poisonous gas, into the station. His radio messages to the base camp were strange and confused, so his staff knew that something was seriously wrong. Because of bad weather, he could not be rescued for more than a month. Byrd later wrote about this experience in *Alone,* published in 1938. In this book, he doubted the value and wisdom of exploration. He realized that he had nearly killed himself to collect a "tiny heap of data" that might have no practical use. He was, he wrote, "a fool, lost on a fool's errand. . . ."

However, Byrd did not abandon his work in Antarctica. In 1939 he led the first Antarctic expedition to be sponsored by the U.S. government. Over the next few years, he led several more trips, one with 13 ships and 4,000 crew members. He made his last flight over the South Pole in 1956. A year later, he died in his sleep, and the world mourned the loss of the explorer it had admired for 30 years.

Suggested Reading Richard Evelyn Byrd, *Alone* (reprint, Island, 1984) and *Discovery: The Story of the Second Byrd Antarctic Expedition* (reprint, Gale, 1971); Edwin P. Hoyt, *The Last Explorer: The Adventures of Admiral Byrd* (John Day, 1968); Lisle A. Rose, *Assault on Eternity: Richard E. Byrd and the Exploration of Antarctica* (Naval Institute Press, 1980).

Byron, John

English
b November 8, 1723; Newstead Abbey, England
d April 10, 1786; London, England
***Explored southern Pacific Ocean
and Falkland Islands***

circumnavigation journey around the world

Northwest Passage water route connecting the Atlantic Ocean and Pacific Ocean through the Arctic islands of northern Canada

frigate small, agile warship with three masts and square sails

sloop small ship with one mast and triangular sails

John Byron led one of the first British voyages of discovery in the Pacific Ocean. He also set a long-standing record for the fastest **circumnavigation.** Byron joined the navy as a youth and at 17 served under George ANSON aboard the *Wager.* The ship was one of six on a mission to raid Spanish settlements on the west coast of South America. In 1741 the *Wager* was shipwrecked on the coast of Patagonia, the southernmost region of the South American mainland. Byron and his shipmates were captured by a local tribe of Patagonians and held for a year. The Patagonians then turned the sailors over to Spanish officials, who also imprisoned the Englishmen. Byron did not return home until four years after the shipwreck. Back in England, he published an account of his difficult time in Patagonia. But those experiences did not keep him from going back to sea. In 1758 he served bravely in naval battles against France and was promoted to the rank of commodore.

Competition at Sea

In the mid-1700s, both Britain and France took pride in the successes of their navies. They competed for control of distant lands and new sources of wealth. These territories were also important as ports for ships on long voyages. Byron was named commander of an expedition to find and claim new lands for England in the southern Atlantic Ocean, between the Cape of Good Hope in Africa and the Strait of Magellan in South America. The commodore was asked to look for a large and fertile land, known as Pepys Island, that was rumored to be somewhere in the southern Atlantic. He was also instructed to explore the area of the California coast that Sir Francis DRAKE had named New Albion in 1579. Farther north in the Pacific Ocean, he was to search for the western end of the **Northwest Passage.**

On June 21, 1764, Byron sailed with the *Dolphin,* one of the first **frigates** covered with copper, and the *Tamar,* a **sloop.** To keep the plans secret, the crews were told that the expedition was headed for

After sailing through some of the worst storms ever recorded at sea, Byron earned the nickname "Foul Weather Jack."

the Caribbean Sea. Only after the ships reached Brazil did Byron tell them their real orders. He promised to double their pay if they would carry out the mission. They agreed, and the ships continued down the South American coast, staying at Port Desire in Patagonia for two weeks before heading south.

On to the Pacific

Byron never found Pepys Island, but in early 1765 he reached the Falkland Islands and claimed them for England. He did not know that the explorer Louis-Antoine de BOUGAINVILLE had just established a French colony in those islands. Entering the Pacific Ocean shortly after, Byron tried to anchor at the Tuamotu Islands. When he could not find a suitable harbor, he named two of the islands the Disappointment Islands. He also named two islands for England's King George and one for himself, but the names would not be permanent.

From this point on, Byron ignored his instructions. He did not sail north to explore California or seek the Northwest Passage. Instead, he continued sailing west and reached Batavia (now Jakarta, Indonesia) in November 1765. He may have been worried about the condition of the copper on his experimental ship. He raced toward Cape Town, South Africa, and reached it in three months. Byron and his crew returned to England having set a record for the fastest circumnavigation—less than two years. But since Byron had not completed his assignment, the voyage was considered a failure.

Naval Duty

In 1769 Byron was named governor of Newfoundland, a British colony in what is now Canada. During the American Revolution, the navy called him back to active service. His fleet brought English troops to the war and tracked the movements of French ships off the American coast. In 1779 Byron took part in his last naval campaign, fighting the French at the Battle of Grenada in the Caribbean Sea. He then returned to England and retired with the rank of vice admiral. The family name was carried on by his grandson, the famous Romantic poet George Gordon Lord Byron.

Suggested Reading John Byron, *The Wreck of the* Wager (Book Club of California, 1940); Peter Shankland, *Byron of the* Wager (Coward, McCann and Geoghegan, 1975).

Cabeza de Vaca, Álvar Núñez

Spanish
b 1490?; Jerez, Spain
d 1556; Seville?, Spain
*Explored American Southwest
and northern Mexico*

Bad luck and poor planning helped make Álvar Núñez Cabeza de Vaca an explorer, and his unexpected travels had lasting effects on the history of Spanish America. After a failed expedition left him stranded in Florida, he and three other men wandered for eight years in the lands between Florida and Mexico. They were the first Europeans to cross North America from the Gulf of Mexico to the Gulf of California. Cabeza de Vaca's travels proved that there was a massive continent north of **New Spain.** His reports inspired Francisco Vásquez de CORONADO, Hernando de SOTO, and others to explore a land about which Europeans knew almost nothing.

This engraving shows Cabeza de Vaca and his companions trading with Indians.

New Spain region of Spanish colonial empire that included the areas now occupied by Mexico, Florida, Texas, New Mexico, Arizona, California, and various Caribbean islands

barge flat-bottomed boat without sails

Early Struggles and Later Disasters

There are few details known of Cabeza de Vaca's early life. Both his mother and father came from distinguished military families, and he too joined the military as a young man. He took part in several battles in Italy and Spain before joining an expedition to Florida led by Pánfilo de NARVÁEZ.

Cabeza de Vaca served as treasurer of the mission, which sailed from Spain on June 27, 1527, with five ships and about 600 men. Problems began as soon as the ships landed at Santo Domingo on the island of Hispaniola in the Caribbean Sea. There, about 140 men deserted, thinking they would enjoy an easier life on the island.

Narváez recruited more soldiers in Cuba and then sailed to Vera Cruz, Mexico. He left Cabeza de Vaca in command of two ships and sent him to another island, Trinidad, for more supplies. Cabeza de Vaca was ashore with about 30 men when a hurricane struck the island. The storm wrecked both ships and drowned the 60 crew members left on board. A few days later, Narváez arrived and picked up the survivors. The reunited force then spent the winter at Spanish settlements along the Gulf of Mexico. Narváez purchased two more ships, and in the spring of 1528, he set sail with about 400 men. They sighted Florida on April 12. Two days later, they landed at Tampa Bay and took official possession of the land that Juan PONCE DE LEÓN had claimed for Spain 15 years before.

Deadly Decisions

The Spaniards' supply of food was already low, but Indians near Tampa Bay told the Spaniards that they would find food and gold farther north, in a city called Apalachen. Narváez then made a fatal error. He took about 300 men and set out for Apalachen on foot. He ordered his fleet to follow the coastline and meet him and his soldiers to the north.

Harassed by hostile Indians, Narváez, Cabeza de Vaca, and the other hungry Spaniards trudged north to Apalachen. They found corn but little else. They moved on, looking for food and waiting for the ships, which never appeared. The ships had spent nearly a year searching for Narváez's party and had sailed back to New Spain.

As they marched along the west coast of Florida, the Spanish soldiers died one by one from hunger, disease, and Indian arrows. Narváez decided to build **barges** and float across the Gulf of Mexico to the Spanish settlement at Pánuco. It was about 600 miles away, much farther than he realized. On September 22, the Spaniards slaughtered and ate the last of their horses. They then sailed west in five barges.

For a map of the route taken by Cabeza de Vaca, see the profile of Hernando de SOTO in Volume 3.

The Sole Survivors

The men sailed the barges close to the coast, but the poorly built boats were difficult to control and barely stayed afloat. Narváez ordered the crews to fend for themselves, and the barges slowly drifted apart. Later, Cabeza de Vaca learned from local Indians what had happened to three of the barges. The crewmen of one, weak from hunger and thirst, went ashore and were killed by Indians. Another barge was stranded on the water, and all aboard starved to death. The barge led by Narváez disappeared at sea and was never seen again.

In November 1528, the two remaining barges, one of which carried Cabeza de Vaca, were wrecked on what is now Galveston Island in Texas. There were now only 90 men left of the 300 who had begun the long march through Florida. The Indians who now greeted the Spaniards were friendly, but an unusually cold winter struck hard. Many Spaniards and Indians died from hunger, disease, and cold, and Cabeza de Vaca fell ill. When spring came, most of the Spanish survivors left the region, but he remained behind, too weak to travel.

Life Among the Indians

For the next five years, Cabeza de Vaca lived among the Indians. At first he was held captive. Later he wandered alone, trading with various tribes along Galveston Bay and elsewhere in the Texas region. In the winter of 1534 to 1535, he met two Spanish soldiers and their Arab slave—the only other survivors of his expedition. The four men decided to make another attempt to reach Spanish territory by heading inland to the west. They began their trek in 1535 at a point near modern-day San Antonio. Accompanied by Indian guides, they crossed into the region that is now New Mexico and possibly Arizona. They then headed south through the Mexican province of Sonora, toward the Gulf of California.

A Happy Return and a Bitter End

In July 1536, Cabeza de Vaca and his companions reached Mexico City, where they were hailed as heroes. They submitted a report of their adventures before Cabeza de Vaca left for Spain the following year. Five years later, he published *The Shipwrecks*, a more personal story of his years in the wilderness.

Back in Spain, Cabeza de Vaca turned down an invitation from Hernando de Soto to join a new expedition to Florida. But he had not completely lost his taste for adventure. In 1540 he went to Asunción (in present-day Paraguay) to govern Spanish settlements in the area. To get there, he had to make a difficult four-month journey by land from Brazil. On the way, he probably became the first European to see Iguaçu Falls, on the border between Argentina and Brazil.

Unfortunately, Cabeza de Vaca's time in Paraguay did not turn out well. In 1542 he led an unsuccessful search for gold. When he returned to Asunción, he was arrested—for reasons that are unclear—and was taken back to Spain to stand trial. The case dragged on for six years. He was found guilty and was banished to Africa, but the king of Spain overturned the sentence and allowed Cabeza de Vaca to remain in Spain with a small income.

Suggested Reading Morris Bishop, *The Odyssey of Cabeza de Vaca* (Century, 1933); Álvar Núñez Cabeza de Vaca, *Adventures in the Unknown Interiors of America*, edited and translated by Cyclone Covey (University of New Mexico Press, 1966); Lissa Jones Johnston, *Crossing a Continent: The Incredible Journey of Cabeza de Vaca* (Eakin Press, 1997).

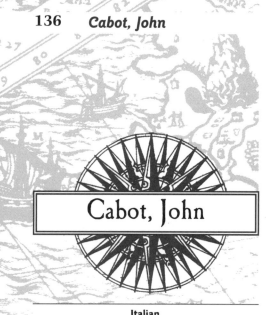

Cabot, John

Italian
b 1450?; Genoa?, Italy
d 1499?
*Made first landfall in North America
after Leif Erikson*

caravan large group of people traveling together, often with pack animals, across a desert or other dangerous region

latitude distance north or south of the equator

John Cabot was an Italian who believed that he could find a quick route to the spices of eastern Asia by sailing west across the northern Atlantic Ocean. He was unable to interest the rulers of Spain and Portugal in his idea, so he approached King Henry VII of England, who encouraged and supported his plan. In 1497 Cabot led the first European expedition to land in North America since the Norseman Leif ERIKSON's expedition 500 years before. Cabot's voyage would prove to be as important for England as Christopher Columbus's had been for Spain.

Italy and the Spice Trade

Like most details about his life, the date and place of John Cabot's birth are unknown. Letters about Cabot mention that he came from Genoa, a city-state in what is now Italy. However, official records in Genoa do not include a "Caboto" family living there at that time. Other records indicate that he became a citizen of Venice, another Italian city-state, in 1476.

These Italian port cities thrived on the spice trade, and Cabot became interested in the money that could be made. In the days before refrigerators, spices were not simply a luxury—they were a necessity to hide the unpleasant taste of spoiling meat. Demand for spices was high in Europe. Italian merchants grew rich by buying spices from Arab traders and then selling them at a higher price in western and northern Europe. To avoid paying the high prices of the Italian and Arab middlemen, the buyers wished for a way to get the spices directly from Asia.

Cabot thought that he knew of such a way. He claimed that as a young man, he had traveled east to Mecca (in modern-day Saudi Arabia) to buy spices from Arab traders. According to Cabot, when he asked the Arabs where the spices came from, they told him they did not know. They said that the spices were brought from the east by traders in **caravans,** and that these traders had bought the spices from other traders who came from even more distant lands. It was apparent to Cabot that the spices came from lands very far to the east of Europe. Believing that the earth was round, he reasoned that he could reach the spices' source by sailing west across the Atlantic Ocean.

It is not known whether Cabot developed this idea on his own, or whether he was inspired by the similar voyage made by Christopher Columbus in 1492. There is evidence that Cabot was in Valencia, Spain, when Columbus returned from that journey. If so, Cabot may have witnessed Columbus's triumphant arrival. In any case, Cabot improved upon Columbus's idea. He suggested that since the circumference of the globe is smaller at a northern **latitude** than at

John Cabot (with flag), pictured here with his son Sebastian, may have been the first European to land in North America since the time of the Vikings.

the equator, ships sailing in the north would have a shorter trip around the world. Thus, Cabot could make the trip more quickly than Columbus. At the time, of course, neither man realized that Columbus had not reached Asia at all—he had found an unknown continent.

Cabot for the English

Cabot took his idea to the royal courts of both Spain and Portugal, but neither wanted to fund his voyage. He then moved his family to England to see if he could interest King Henry VII in the plan. Since England was at the very end of the route of the spice trade, the English paid the highest price for spices. Cabot believed that they would be very interested in a shorter, cheaper route to Asia.

Cabot chose to settle in the port of Bristol on the west coast of England. It was a good choice, because the merchants of Bristol were already looking for new ways to obtain spices. About 40 years earlier, a Bristol merchant named Robert Stormy had tried to bypass the Italians by sending two ships to Arab lands on the Mediterranean Sea. One of the ships was wrecked. The other was destroyed by Italian cargo shippers, who did not appreciate Stormy's attempts to deny them their usual profits.

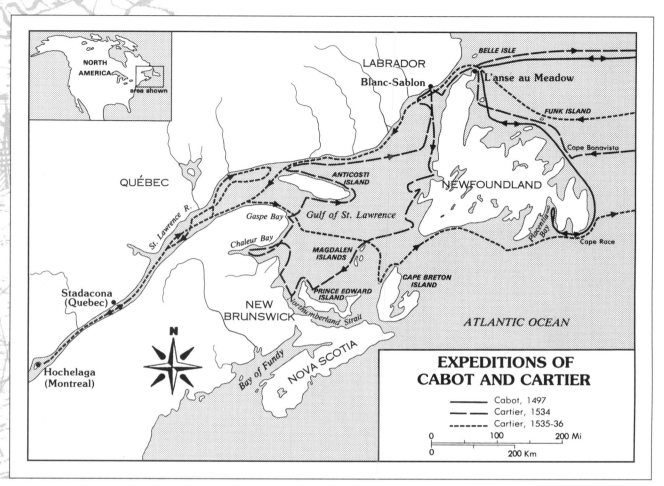

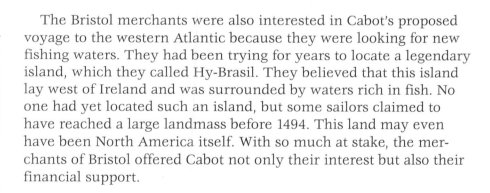

EXPEDITIONS OF
CABOT AND CARTIER

——— Cabot, 1497
— · — · Cartier, 1534
- - - - Cartier, 1535-36

John Cabot and Jacques Cartier were among the earliest explorers of the St. Lawrence River region.

The Bristol merchants were also interested in Cabot's proposed voyage to the western Atlantic because they were looking for new fishing waters. They had been trying for years to locate a legendary island, which they called Hy-Brasil. They believed that this island lay west of Ireland and was surrounded by waters rich in fish. No one had yet located such an island, but some sailors claimed to have reached a large landmass before 1494. This land may even have been North America itself. With so much at stake, the merchants of Bristol offered Cabot not only their interest but also their financial support.

Preparing for Discovery

Cabot still needed the approval of the king. He presented his plan to Henry, who reacted with great enthusiasm. England's rival, Spain, was already profiting from newly discovered lands to the west, and Henry was eager for England to do so as well. On March 5, 1496, he granted permission to Cabot and Cabot's three sons to sail under the flag of England. He wrote a letter that granted the family of explorers permission to find new lands "in whatsoever part of the world they may be, which before this time were unknown to Christians." Cabot was also allowed to bring any spices or other products back to England and sell them. In return, the king was to receive one-fifth of the profits.

quadrant navigational instrument used since the Middle Ages to determine distance north or south of the equator

Cabot's instructions allowed him five ships, but he was able to find only one. It was called the *Matthew* and was about the same size as the *Niña,* the smallest of Columbus's three ships. He hired about 20 sailors, and it is likely that his son Sebastian CABOT was also on board. On May 20, 1497, the ship sailed west from Bristol to Dursey Head, on the west coast of Ireland. John Cabot then used a method of navigation called latitude sailing. He sailed the Atlantic at a single chosen latitude and maintained his course by finding the North Star at night. He also used a compass and **quadrant** to help him find the correct latitude if he was blown off course. Thirty-three days after leaving Dursey Head, the *Matthew* reached the coast of North America. Although Cabot had traveled a much shorter distance than Columbus had, it took about the same amount of time because the winds in the north were less favorable.

Landfall in North America

No one is sure exactly where Cabot landed, since neither he nor any member of his crew kept a journal during the voyage. Because of Cabot's practice of latitude sailing, many historians locate his landfall at present-day Griquet Harbor. This bay, on the northern tip of what is now called Newfoundland, lies on the same latitude as Dursey Head, Ireland. This theory is supported by Cabot's report of a large island, which could be Belle Isle, about 15 miles to the north of his landfall. If so, it would mean that Cabot landed within five miles of where Leif ERIKSON had landed nearly 500 years before. Other historians have placed Cabot's landfall father south, perhaps at Cape Breton Island.

The exact spot remains a mystery, but the time when land was sighted was 5 A.M. on June 24, according to an inscription on a map made by Sebastian. For some reason, this was the only landing made by John Cabot and his crew. The captain apparently feared that any people who lived there might be hostile. Though the Europeans did not see anyone else, they did see signs of life: snares, fishing nets, and a red stick with holes at both ends that was probably used for weaving the nets. Cabot forbade his men to go farther from the ship than the distance a crossbow could be shot. At least one historian has suggested that the explorers might also have been discouraged by the swarms of mosquitoes that plague Newfoundland during the summer. Whatever the reason, Cabot chose to spend the rest of the voyage observing the coast from the relative safety of his ship.

The extent of Cabot's exploration is also unknown. Historians who think that he landed in Griquet Harbor believe that he sailed south along Newfoundland's east coast before heading back to England. Those who believe that he landed farther south assume that he sailed north before turning homeward. Wherever he was, Cabot noted that fish were so plentiful that the crew could let down weighted buckets and draw them up full of cod. On the shore they saw tall trees that would make excellent masts, as well as tended fields of plants that may have been blueberry bushes. At one point, they also saw two figures chasing each other in the woods, but they could not tell whether the figures were animals or humans.

khan title of an Asian ruler

Northwest Passage water route connecting the Atlantic Ocean and Pacific Ocean through the Arctic islands of northern Canada

Return to Bristol, Return to America

Heading home, Cabot sailed east for 15 days and found himself off the coast of Brittany, France. He then turned north and arrived back in Bristol on August 6. After he had made his own map and globe to show his route and discoveries, he went to London to inform the king. Cabot was convinced that he had reached the northern shores of Asia—"the land of the Great **Khan.**" Though he had not returned with spices or jewels, he told Henry about the rich fishing he had found and falsely claimed that the new land produced exotic wood and silk.

King Henry named the discovery New Isle, but by 1502 he was calling it "the newe founde lande", the name that it bears today. Henry was excited by the reports, but his rewards to Cabot were modest. Cabot received a prize from the royal treasury and a small yearly income to be paid by the city of Bristol. But what Cabot lacked in riches was made up for in fame. A letter written at the time says that Cabot "is called the Great Admiral and vast honour is paid to him and he goes dressed in silk, and these English run after him like mad."

With this new status, Cabot was able to plan a second trip. He intended to sail farther to the southwest to look for Cipangu, which is now known as Japan. According to Marco POLO, the great Italian traveler of the 1200s, all the spices and jewels of the world came from Cipangu. King Henry granted Cabot permission to sail with six English ships and to enlist any English sailor willing to make the trip. The king paid for one ship, and the merchants of Bristol provided four more. The fleet set sail from Bristol early in May 1498.

The fate of Cabot's second voyage is still a mystery. One book written in the 1500s claims that the expedition sailed up the west coast of Greenland before it was stopped by huge icebergs. That account goes on to say that Cabot sailed south along the coasts of what are now called Baffin Island, Newfoundland, Nova Scotia, and New England, and as far south as Chesapeake Bay, before returning to England empty-handed. Other historians believe that this source confuses Cabot's second voyage with one made much later by his son Sebastian, who was searching for a **Northwest Passage.** These historians believe that one of John Cabot's ships was forced to return to England for reasons that are not clear, and that the other four were never heard from again.

Cabot's Place in History

Only one fact is known for certain about Cabot after he departed on his second voyage. Records show that his reward money was last collected from the Bristol city government on the holiday of Michaelmas, September 29, 1498. It is not clear whether the money was collected by Cabot himself or by his wife. After that, John Cabot does not appear in history. His son Sebastian may be one reason why. Although Sebastian became an accomplished explorer himself, he also took credit for much of his father's work. Not until the 1800s did historians realize that John Cabot, not Sebastian, was the man who led England's first voyage of exploration across the Atlantic.

Cabot, Sebastian

Italian
b 1476?; Venice, Italy
d 1557; London, England
***Explored waterways in South America
and Canada***

Northwest Passage water route connecting the Atlantic Ocean and Pacific Ocean through the Arctic islands of northern Canada

Northeast Passage water route connecting the Atlantic Ocean and Pacific Ocean along the Arctic coastline of Europe and Asia

cartography the science of mapmaking

cosmography the scientific study of the structure of the universe

Opinions of John Cabot written by those who lived in his time say that he was an excellent navigator and a skilled maker of maps and globes. He also seems to have been a careful explorer who would not needlessly risk the lives of his crew. Although he believed to the end that he had found a sea route to Asia, he had in fact discovered something equally valuable. His idea of crossing the Atlantic at a more northernly latitude than Columbus brought many benefits to England. In the short run, it gave the English food and profits from fertile new fishing waters. In the long run, it opened the English exploration of North America, the continent they would eventually claim and colonize.

Suggested Reading C. Raymond Beazley, *John and Sebastian Cabot; the Discovery of North America* (B. Franklin, 1964); Brian Cuthbertson, *John Cabot and the Voyage of the* Matthew (Formac, 1997); Henry Kurtz, *John and Sebastian Cabot* (Franklin Watts, 1973); James A. Williamson, *The Cabot Voyages and Bristol Discovery Under Henry VII* (Hakluyt Society, 1962).

Sebastian Cabot, one of the most accomplished mapmakers of his time, was the first explorer to search for a **Northwest Passage** to Asia. On an expedition sponsored by England, he explored the coast of Labrador and reached Hudson Bay. He later organized three missions to seek a **Northeast Passage** to Asia. One of these missions led to trade between England and Russia. Cabot's most famous journey, however, was one he made to South America. Sponsored by Spain, he explored the Río de la Plata, the Paraná River, and part of the Paraguay River.

A Family of Explorers

Sebastian Cabot was a son of the famed navigator and explorer, John CABOT. Although he probably learned navigation, **cartography,** and **cosmography** from his father, the two men had little else in common. John was friendly and good-natured. Sebastian, on the other hand, was vain and self-centered and had a habit of exaggerating his own importance. He even claimed credit for some of his father's accomplishments.

In the 1490s, the Cabot family moved to Bristol, England. Sebastian probably accompanied his father in 1497 on a voyage to North America sponsored by King Henry VII of England. On this expedition, the Cabots sailed along the east coast of what is now Canada. It was the first journey across the North Atlantic since Leif ERIKSON had landed on those same shores 500 years before.

Historians disagree about how many voyages Sebastian himself led, as well as about the extent of his explorations. Several authors list as his first voyage an expedition across the North Atlantic from 1508 to 1509, which was sponsored by Henry VII. The goal was to find a direct route to Asia by sailing north of Canada. Cabot sailed northward along the coasts of Newfoundland and Labrador and reached Hudson Bay. At the entrance to the bay, he mistakenly believed that he had found the Northwest Passage, and he did not press forward. He may have sailed as far north as Foxe Channel, between present-day Baffin Island and the Northwest Territories.

Sebastian Cabot was famous both as an explorer and as a mapmaker, but he spent much of his time chasing legends.

cartographer mapmaker

Council of the Indies governing body of Spain's colonial empire from 1524 to 1834

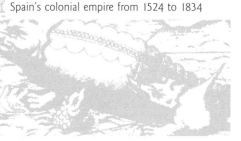

tributary stream or river that flows into a larger stream or river

There, dangerous chunks of floating ice would have caused Cabot to abandon the journey and head back to England.

Sailing for Spain

For three years after his return, Cabot served as royal **cartographer** for the new English king, Henry VIII. In 1512 Cabot accompanied English troops who were sent to help the Spanish king, Ferdinand of Aragon, in his war against the French. Since Henry VIII was not really interested in exploration, Cabot offered his services to King Ferdinand. Ferdinand hired Cabot as Spain's royal cartographer. Within a few years, Cabot was awarded the rank of pilot major and became a member of the **Council of the Indies.**

In 1526 Charles I, the new king of Spain, asked Cabot to sail to eastern Asia in search of trade and riches. Cabot had a theory that there was a shorter route to Asia than the one taken by Ferdinand MAGELLAN just five years earlier. To that end, he was instructed to map the coast of South America in detail. On April 3, 1526, he sailed west from the Spanish port of Sanlúcar de Barrameda with four ships and about 200 men. On September 29, he reached a harbor that today is the site of the Brazilian city Recife.

From Indians living on the Brazilian coast, Cabot heard the first of several reports of the "White King." This king supposedly dressed like Europeans and ruled a wealthy realm that included a mountain of silver. Continuing south along the coast, Cabot found an island he named Ilha de Santa Catarina, in honor of his wife. Farther south, he picked up two castaways from an earlier, ill-fated expedition. These men repeated the tale of the White King, claiming that his kingdom was located north of the region now called Paraguay. Cabot, attracted by the tales of great wealth, changed his plans in order to search for the legendary king. When several of his officers objected, he simply abandoned them on the coast.

The Search for the White King

On February 21, 1527, Cabot entered the mouth of a large river that led into the interior of Argentina. He named it the Río de la Plata (Silver River) after the pieces of silver he obtained from local Indians. The silver had come from the Inca civilization in Peru, but Cabot thought its source was much closer. He built a fort on the Río Carcarañá, a **tributary** of the Río de la Plata. Then he left in search of the silver. He sailed up another tributary, the Paraná River, going about 50 miles past the point where it meets the Paraguay River. At the end of March, he began exploring the Paraguay River, but he was forced to turn back because food was running low and Indians had begun to attack.

Cabot returned to the fort he had built. Soon he heard another local legend, this one about the "Enchanted City of the Caesars."

According to the legend, the city was part of a wealthy, advanced, and peaceful civilization, perhaps in the Andes of Peru. After failing to find the city, Cabot met another explorer, Diego Garcia, and the two men decided to combine forces to look for the White King. Attacks by Indians once again forced Cabot to retreat to the fort, but he found that it had been destroyed, and the troops there had been killed. With nothing but seal meat left to eat, Cabot decided to return to Spain in November 1529. He reached Spain the following year without any of the Asian treasure that the Spanish had expected. He was stripped of his rank and banished to Africa for two years for disobeying his orders.

New Honors in Later Years

Eventually Cabot's rank as pilot major was restored, and in 1547 he returned to England at the invitation of King Edward VI. He became a founder of the Company of Merchant Adventurers (also known as the Muscovy Company), which had the right to claim lands north of the British Isles. In the 1550s, Cabot organized three expeditions that searched for a Northeast Passage to Asia by sailing north of Russia. Although none of the explorers found such a passage, one ship, piloted by Richard CHANCELLOR, entered the White Sea north of Russia in 1553. Chancellor and his crew traveled south by land to Moscow, where he negotiated a trade agreement between England and Russia.

Cabot never found a northern sea route to Asia, but his maps and voyages greatly influenced the next generation of European explorers. His map of the world was a landmark in the history of cartography, and his voyages to Canada and South America paved the way for future expeditions. Many explorers, inspired by Cabot's stories about the White King and the Enchanted City of the Caesars, risked everything to find the sources of these legends.

Suggested Reading Raymond Beazley, *John and Sebastian Cabot* (Burt Franklin, 1964); Henry Kurtz, *John and Sebastian Cabot* (Franklin Watts, 1973); John Williamson, *The Cabot Voyages and Bristol Discovery Under Henry VII* (Hakluyt Society, 1962).

Caboto, Giovanni. See *Cabot, John.*

Caboto, Sebastiano. See *Cabot, Sebastian.*

Cabral, Pedro Álvares

Portuguese
b 1467?; Belmonte, Portugal
d 1520; Santarém, Portugal
Discovered Brazil

As the leader of the first successful trade mission to India, Pedro Álvares Cabral was the first person to sign treaties for direct trade between Europe and the East Indies. He is best known, however, as the man who discovered Brazil. Historians are still unsure whether the discovery was intentional or accidental. They are not even certain whether Cabral should receive credit for finding Brazil. But Brazilians today celebrate him as the discoverer of their country.

Pedro Álvares Cabral discovered Brazil while on an expedition to establish trading posts in India.

trade winds winds that blow from east to west in the tropics

Noble Service to the Crown

Cabral was born in about 1467 on an estate in Belmonte, Portugal, to a wealthy noble family that had influence at the Portuguese royal court. As a boy, Cabral served as a page to King John II. Other details of his life as a young man are unknown, except that he grew up to serve on the council of Portugal's King Manuel I and was made a knight of the Order of Christ.

In 1499 Cabral was named chief captain of a fleet sent to establish trading posts on the west coast of southern India, known as the Malabar Coast. The expedition sailed from the Tagus River in Lisbon, Portugal, on March 9, 1500, with 13 ships and 1,000 men. The commander of one of Cabral's ships was Bartolomeu DIAS, who had reached the Cape of Good Hope at the southern tip of Africa 12 years before.

The Discovery of Brazil

On his earlier voyage, Dias had had no choice but to follow the unknown west coast of Africa. This time Cabral decided to take the route first charted by Vasco da GAMA a year earlier. Cabral first sailed to the Canary Islands and then continued southwest past the Cape Verde Islands off the coast of Africa. He turned south on March 22 but soon switched to a southwesterly course to take advantage of the strong **trade winds.** When he reached the southern latitude of the Cape of Good Hope, he tried to turn east, but winds and currents continued to push him farther west. On April 22, near Easter, the crew sighted Mount Pascal in Brazil. Cabral claimed the land for Portugal and named it Terra da Vera Cruz, which means "land of the true cross" in Portuguese. In later years, the land came to be known as Terra do Brazil, named for the brazilwood that traders valued for its red dye. The name Brazil was the one that stuck.

Cabral spent little time in this new land, exploring about 50 miles of the coast in 12 days. He landed on an island just north of the site of the present-day city of Rio de Janeiro. Cabral planted a cross on the island, and the crew celebrated mass. They also met Indians, whom Cabral described in a letter to King Manuel as friendly and peaceful. In the same letter, he described the Indians' houses and their custom of wearing feathers as decorations.

No official log of the journey exists, but some details are provided by Cabral's letters to the king and by the eyewitness account of one of the crew, Pêro Vaz. At one point, Cabral asked the crew to vote on whether to send a ship back to Portugal with news of the discovery and whether the ship should take some Indians along. Such a democratic approach was quite unusual at the time. Most captains exercised complete authority over their missions and their men. Cabral's crew voted to send the ship to Portugal but without the Indians.

Trade Mission to the Indies

On May 2, Cabral resumed his journey to the Cape of Good Hope, but three weeks later, a storm at sea sank four of the ships and scattered the rest. The remaining ships regrouped off the east coast of Africa and reached Calicut on the Malabar Coast in September.

Cabral set up a trading post, but the Muslims of Calicut did not want the Portuguese there. A party of Muslims attacked the post, killing about 50 Europeans. Cabral retaliated by burning Arab ships and firing his own ships' cannons at the city. He finally left Calicut, sailing south along the coast to Cochin and Cannanore, where he received a warmer welcome. He established trading posts in these towns and signed trade treaties on behalf of Portugal.

Cabral returned to Lisbon in 1501, carrying pearls, diamonds, porcelain, and valuable spices such as pepper, ginger, cinnamon, and cloves. The trip had cost many lives, including that of Dias, who had gone down with his ship during the storm off the Cape of Good Hope. Cabral was welcomed home by King Manuel, but the two men seem to have had a disagreement later. Vasco da Gama was chosen over Cabral to lead the next Portuguese voyage to the Indies. Cabral left the royal court at this time and never returned. He settled on his estate near Santarém, married, and had six children.

Questions About the Discovery

Some historians believe that Cabral's discovery of Brazil was not an accident. Under the **Treaty of Tordesillas,** Portugal was given the right to claim lands lying east of a line drawn through the Atlantic Ocean on maps. King Manuel may have given Cabral secret orders to sail as far west as possible without crossing that line, to see if Portugal could claim any new lands.

Another difficult question is whether Cabral was actually the first European to discover Brazil. At least three other explorers—Amerigo VESPUCCI, Vicente Yáñez PINZÓN, and Diego de Lepe—landed on the Brazilian coast before Cabral. These explorers, however, were mainly interested in the Caribbean islands. When they reached the north coast of Brazil, they were not surprised to have found land south of those islands. Cabral was the first to discover Brazilian land where it was not expected to be. Today monuments in both Lisbon and Rio de Janeiro honor him as the discoverer of Brazil.

Suggested Reading William Brooks Greenlee, *The Voyage of Pedro Álvares Cabral to Brazil and India, from Contemporary Documents and Narratives* (Hakluyt Society, 1938).

Treaty of Tordesillas agreement between Spain and Portugal dividing the rights to discovered lands along a north-south line

Cabrillo, Juan Rodriguez

Portuguese
b 1498?; ?
d January 3, 1543; San Miguel Island, California
Explored California and Central America

During a lifetime filled with adventure, Juan Rodriguez Cabrillo was a soldier, sailor, shipbuilder, miner, explorer, and author. His travels took him to many parts of the Americas. In 1518 he served under Pánfilo de Narváez during the exploration and conquest of Cuba. In the years that followed, he helped Hernán Cortés to conquer the Aztec capital of Tenochtitlán (present-day Mexico City). With Tenochtitlán secure, he joined Pedro de Alvarado in the region that is now Honduras, Guatemala, and El Salvador. Today Cabrillo is known in the United States as the first European explorer of the coast of California.

Seeking Adventure and Wealth

Nothing is known about Cabrillo's parents or the date and place of his birth. The first recorded information about him shows that he

encomendero Spanish colonist who received a grant of land in the Americas and had control over the Indians who lived there

brigantine two-masted sailing ship with both square and triangular sails

received military training in Cuba from 1510 to 1511. He was reported to be in his early 20s when he left for Mexico in 1520, so he was probably born around 1498. It is unlikely that he came from a noble family, but as an adult, he earned the privileges of an **encomendero** in both Cuba and Guatemala. Most historians have believed that Cabrillo was a Portuguese who had entered the service of Spain, but recently some scholars have claimed that he was actually Spanish.

Cabrillo proved to be an outstanding soldier and seaman during Narváez's conquest of Cuba in 1518. Two years later, he went to Mexico with Narváez on a mission to control the ambitious activities of Cortés. A battle ensued, and Cortés defeated Narváez. Like many of the remaining men in Narváez's army, Cabrillo then changed sides, and Cortés put him in charge of building 13 **brigantines** for the final assault on Tenochtitlán. During the battle, Cabrillo was wounded, but the Spanish were victorious. He recovered in time to join Francisco de Orozco on an expedition in late 1521. Orozco founded the Mexican city of Oaxaca.

Beginning in 1523, Cabrillo spent several years under the command of Pedro de Alvarado, exploring and conquering large parts of Central America. Cabrillo became a citizen of the colonial province of Guatemala. He lived with his Indian wife and their children, and he became wealthy from gold mines that he had discovered. In 1532 he sailed to Spain to marry the sister of a friend and then returned to Guatemala the following year. Upon his arrival, he received a commission to build a fleet for an expedition to the Spice Islands (also called the Moluccas) that Alvarado was planning.

The Exploration of California

In 1542 Cabrillo was chosen to lead a journey along the Pacific coast to the northern limits of Spanish territory. He was instructed to find and claim new lands. One of the vessels built for Alvarado, the *San Salvador,* served as Cabrillo's flagship. He sailed on June 27, and by July 2, he had reached the Baja California peninsula. He is the first European known to have made contact with the Indians of that area.

Cabrillo explored every inlet and bay along the coast. One of these he named San Diego Bay after the smallest of his ships. Today it is the site of the city of San Diego. He sailed as far north as the Russian River but then turned back to find a safe port in which to spend the winter. While spending the winter on San Miguel Island, one of several large islands off the coast, his party was attacked by Indians. His leg was broken in the fighting, and the injury led to his death soon after. In the spring, Cabrillo's chosen successor, Bartolomé Ferrera, led the Spanish force as far north as Oregon before returning to Mexico.

Cabrillo's account of this expedition was not published until the 1800s. However, it is the oldest written record of human activity on the west coast of the United States. Today Cabrillo is remembered as the discoverer and explorer of the California coast, and his name can be found on schools, monuments, and roads throughout the state.

Suggested Reading Harry Kelsey, *Juan Rodriguez Cabrillo* (Huntington Library, 1986); Nancy Lemke, *Cabrillo: First European Explorer of the California Coast* (EZ Nature, 1991); Francis J. Weber, *Explorer of California: Juan Rodriguez Cabrillo* (Opuscula, 1992).

Cadamosto, Alvise da

Italian
b 1432; Venice, Italy
d 1480?; Venice, Italy
Explored west coast of Africa

galley ship with oars and sails, used in ancient and medieval times

caravel small ship with three masts and both square and triangular sails

Alvise da Cadamosto was one of the first Europeans to explore the seas south of Spain and Portugal. He made two journeys of discovery along the west coast of Africa, sailing as far south as what is now Gambia. He may also have discovered the Cape Verde Islands.

In the Service of Henry the Navigator

As a young man, Cadamosto decided to become a sailor. In 1454 he left Venice, Italy, on a **galley** bound for Flanders, a region that is now part of France and Belgium. When winds delayed the ship off Portugal's Cape St. Vincent, he met the famous prince of Portugal, Henry the Navigator. Prince Henry, who sponsored many voyages of discovery, persuaded Cadamosto to lead a Portuguese trading fleet to the west coast of Africa.

The prince provided Cadamosto with a **caravel** in return for half of the profits of the voyage. Cadamosto set sail on March 22, 1455. Within a week, his ship reached the island of Madeira, off the northwest coast of Africa. From Madeira, Cadamosto continued south past the Canary Islands. He then headed to an island known as Arguin Island. For a third of the trip to Arguin Island, the ship sailed out of sight of land—a daring feat at the time. Eventually Cadamosto reached the mouth of the Senegal River (in modern-day Senegal). He and his crew spent about a month in the area. At a local marketplace, Cadamosto saw many unfamiliar plants and foods, as well as such animals as lions, panthers, and elephants. The Africans were fascinated by Cadamosto. They rubbed his hands to see if the light color of his skin would come off.

After leaving the Senegal River region, Cadamosto searched for riches farther south. He was joined by two other ships, one belonging to Prince Henry and another commanded by an Italian named Uso di Mare. They discovered a river about 60 miles south of Cape Verde, Senegal, but hostile Africans prevented them from exploring it. When they reached the Gambia River (in what is now Gambia), they traveled upstream. They were soon followed by canoes filled with Africans who carried shields and wore white clothes and feathered headdresses. The Europeans attempted to show that they were on a peaceful mission, but fighting broke out. Although the Europeans had superior weapons, they tried to frighten the Africans away rather than harm them.

A Second Voyage to Africa

Cadamosto returned to Portugal around 1456. Four years later, he and Uso di Mare went to Africa again. As they were sailing along the African coast, their ships were blown out to sea by a storm. Three days later, they spotted two large islands that may have been the Cape Verde Islands. Returning to the Gambia River, they followed it inland for 10 miles and met a group of Mandingo people. The Mandingo king, Batti, welcomed the Europeans kindly. Cadamosto and di Mare traded with the Mandingo for slaves, gold, exotic animals, nuts, cotton, and ivory. After two weeks, the Europeans continued south, traveling about 150 miles to explore the mouths of five smaller rivers before returning to Portugal.

Cadamosto's colorful account of his travels was published in Venice in 1507.

Suggested Reading G. R. Crone, *The Voyages of Cadamosto and Other Documents on Western Africa in the Second Half of the Fifteenth Century* (Hakluyt Society, 1937).

Caillié, René-Auguste

French
b November 19, 1799; Mauzé, France
d May 17, 1838; Mauzé, France
Explored Africa

René-Auguste Caillié was the first European to return alive from Timbuktu.

caravan large group of people traveling together, often with pack animals, across a desert or other dangerous region

scurvy disease caused by a lack of vitamin C and once a major cause of death among sailors; symptoms include internal bleeding, loosened teeth, and extreme fatigue

René-Auguste Caillié was the first explorer to travel to the African city of Timbuktu (in present-day Mali) and live to tell about it. He traveled through many miles of desert, often while severely ill. After he left the city, hostile Africans made his return trip every bit as difficult. Caillié's account of his trip was widely doubted and criticized in Europe, but other explorers confirmed his reports after his death.

Chasing a Childhood Dream

As a child, Caillié was left on his own after his mother died and his father was sent to prison. He dropped out of school to learn to be a shoemaker, but his greatest interest was Africa. He read a great deal about the continent and was especially fascinated by tales of a fabulous city called Timbuktu.

At age 16, Caillé left his village and found a job as a cabin boy aboard a ship bound for Africa. He arrived at Cape Verde, the westernmost point in Africa, in July 1816. He deserted his ship to join an expedition traveling up the Senegal River. He soon became seriously ill, however, and he returned to France, where he remained for three years. His second trip was also cut short by illness, but the attempt would not be his last.

In 1824 Caillié returned to Senegal, but this time he decided to prepare more thoroughly for his journey inland. For eight months, he lived among the area's Arab tribes, studying their languages and customs. He sought money from the French government to fund his travels, but his request was denied. Luckily, a British colonial official gave him a job to help him raise the needed money. In 1827 Caillié set out with a small Arab **caravan.** He posed as an Egyptian Arab who wanted to pass through Timbuktu on the way back to Egypt.

Difficulties and Disappointments

Caillié's skin was fairly dark, and he was fluent in the local language, so he had little trouble with his disguise. Still, the journey was very difficult, and he suffered tremendous physical hardships. He fell ill with **scurvy** and fever and was forced to interrupt his trip for several days. He finally reached Timbuktu in April 1828.

What he saw in Timbuktu was a great disappointment. Some Arab histories, as well as the famous book *Arabian Nights,* had portrayed Timbuktu as a lively, wealthy, and exotic city. Caillié found a city of "badly built houses of clay" and streets that were "monotonous and melancholy like the desert."

To add to his disappointment, he was not, after all, the first European to see Timbuktu. He found out that the Scottish explorer Alexander Gordon LAING had visited the city two years earlier. Laing had been killed before he was able to return to Europe to tell of his travels. Despite the fact that the journey had lost much of its glamor and glory, Caillié took detailed notes on the city and its residents during his two-week visit.

Triumph and Heartbreak

From Timbuktu, Caillié began the 1,200-mile trek across the western Sahara to Morocco. He traveled through the desert with a caravan that included 600 camels. At first he was able to ride a camel, but his fellow travelers gradually became hostile toward him. They began to treat him like a slave, forcing him to walk and even beating him. Caillié left the caravan to travel on his own. He made a dangerous journey through Moroccan territory that was forbidden to Christians. After three months, he arrived in the Moroccan city of Fès. The French colonial official there did not believe that this dark, ragged stranger was French, and he refused to help Caillié. Continuing north, Caillié reached Tangier, where a sympathetic official arranged for his passage home.

Caillié received a hero's welcome in France. He was made a knight of the Legion of Honor. The Paris Geographical Society gave him a large reward for being the first traveler to return from Timbuktu. He published an account of his journey, but many readers refused to believe that Timbuktu was not a magnificent city. Some pointed to Caillié's humble background and lack of scientific training. They claimed that he had invented his entire story. Heartbroken, Caillié returned to his childhood village, where he died of **tuberculosis** in 1838. Ten years later, the German explorer Heinrich BARTH confirmed Caillié's reports and praised him as "one of the most reliable explorers of Africa."

Suggested Reading Gailbraith Welch, *The Unveiling of Timbuktoo: The Astounding Adventures of Caillié* (Carroll and Graf, 1991).

tuberculosis infection of the lungs

Cam, Diego. See *Cão, Diogo.*

Cameron, Verney Lovett

English
b July 1, 1844; Radipole, England
d March 27, 1894; near Leighton Buzzard, England
Explored central Africa

---

tributary stream or river that flows into a larger stream or river

Verney Lovett Cameron was the first European to travel across central Africa from coast to coast. He explored Lake Tanganyika and located the outlet where the lake water flows into a **tributary** of the Congo River. He also led an expedition to locate the missing explorer David LIVINGSTONE. Cameron became known for his strong opposition to the African slave trade and for his efforts to develop trade and transportation in Africa.

The Search for David Livingstone

Cameron, the son of a clergyman, left his village at age 13 to join the British navy. He took part in Britain's military campaign in Abyssinia (present-day Ethiopia) in 1868. He also joined patrols on Zanzibar, an island off the coast of Tanzania, that were organized to find and arrest slave traders. After spending so much time in eastern Africa, he became interested in exploring the continent's

malaria disease that is spread by mosquitoes in tropical areas

interior. When he was 28, Britain's Royal Geographical Society offered him a chance to lead a search for Livingstone.

Members of the expedition met at Bagamoyo on the east coast of Tanzania in February 1873 and departed for the interior the next month. By the time they reached Tabora (in central Tanzania), one man had died of **malaria,** and the rest were seriously ill. On October 20, while still in Tabora, Cameron received a letter announcing Livingstone's death. A few days later, Livingstone's servants arrived with the explorer's body, which was returned to England. Some members of Cameron's expedition, believing their mission complete, left with Livingstone's servants. Cameron, though, was determined to continue exploring with the help of Livingstone's papers and equipment.

Across Africa

Cameron traveled to the southern end of Lake Tanganyika, where he identified the Lukuga River as the lake's outlet. He tried to reach the Congo River by sailing north on the Lualaba River, but he failed and was uncertain what to do next. He then met one of Livingstone's former guides, an Arab slave trader named Tippoo Tib. Learning of Cameron's difficulties, Tippoo Tib suggested that Cameron travel west to what is now Angola, on Africa's west coast. Cameron agreed and left the town of Nyangwe (in modern-day Democratic Republic of Congo) in August 1874. He crossed the Congo River basin and arrived at the coastal village of Catumbela, in Angola, on November 7, 1875. He was the first European to travel all the way across tropical Africa.

Upon his return to England a few months later, Cameron was awarded the Founder's Medal of the Royal Geographical Society. In 1877 he published an account of his journey, entitled *Across Africa.* For the rest of his life, he was an active spokesman for British involvement in Africa. He took part in several efforts to develop trade on the continent, and he proposed building a railway across Africa from north to south. He also spoke publicly against the slave trade. In 1883 he returned to Africa with Richard Francis Burton. The two men wrote a book about their adventures, *To the Gold Coast for Gold.*

Suggested Reading Verney Lovett Cameron, *Across Africa* (Negro Universities Press, 1969); Robert W. Foran, *African Odyssey: The Life of Verney Lovett Cameron* (Hutchinson, 1937).

Verney Lovett Cameron was the first European to cross tropical Africa from coast to coast.

Campbell, Robert

Scottish
b February 21, 1808; Glenlyon, Scotland
d May 9, 1894; Manitoba, Canada
Explored sources of Yukon River

Fur trader Robert Campbell was one of the first explorers of the Yukon region of Canada. From 1834 to 1852, he investigated the far northwest of North America. He is particularly known for his accomplishments on the Yukon River, which flows from Canada through Alaska to the Bering Sea.

Early Explorations of the Northwest

In 1830 Campbell joined the Hudson's Bay Company, a British company involved in trade in Canada. Four years later, he was assigned to the Mackenzie River region in northwestern Canada. He

was instructed to explore the area and to build a network of trading posts there. In 1837 he traveled up the Stikine River (in what is now British Columbia), and a year later, he built a post on Dease Lake. In his journal, he described how he and his companions were forced to endure "a winter of constant danger...and of much suffering from starvation." They were so short of food, he wrote, that "our last meal before abandoning Dease Lake on 8th May, 1839, consisted of the lacing of our snow-shoes."

The following year, Campbell and seven others explored the northern branch of the Liard River. They also discovered a body of water Campbell called a "beautiful lake." He named it Frances Lake after the wife of Sir George Simpson, an official of the Hudson's Bay Company. Leaving their canoe and continuing on foot, the explorers eventually came to a stream that flowed to the west. Campbell named the stream Pelly after the company's governor. Campbell would later discover that the Pelly River was one of the main branches of the Yukon River. He would also learn that the Yukon River system can be navigated for over 1,500 miles to its mouth in the Bering Sea.

Expanding Trade in the Northwest

Campbell and his men built a trading post at Frances Lake and then set off on a journey down the Pelly River by canoe in June 1843. Eventually they came to a place where the upper Yukon River joins the Pelly to form the main flow of the Yukon River. A group of Wood Indians there warned the explorers that many fierce Indians lived farther down the Yukon. Campbell's companions were alarmed by this information, and rather than risk their lives, they forced him to call off the trip and turn back.

In 1850 Campbell followed the Yukon to the place where it meets one of its large northern **tributaries,** the Porcupine River. He traveled up the Porcupine River and crossed the Richardson Mountains to the Mackenzie River, which empties into the Arctic Ocean. Following the Mackenzie River inland, he reached Fort Simpson, a major trading post west of Great Slave Lake. Campbell's discovery of the routes between the Mackenzie, the Porcupine, and the Yukon Rivers was valuable information that provided a great boost to trade in the region. He left the Yukon territory in 1852 and traveled south and east to Montréal. He made that entire journey of over 3,000 miles on snowshoes.

Robert Campbell braved the cold and isolation of the far northwest of North America mainly to expand the business activities of the Hudson's Bay Company. As an explorer, he also greatly expanded knowledge of one of the most remote regions of the earth. He demonstrated his remarkable courage, skill, and endurance in that harsh terrain for 18 years.

Suggested Reading Clifford Wilson, *Campbell of the Yukon* (Macmillan of Canada, 1970).

tributary stream or river that flows into a larger stream or river

---

Candish, Thomas. See *Cavendish, Thomas.*

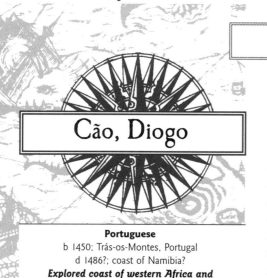

Cão, Diogo

Portuguese
b 1450; Trás-os-Montes, Portugal
d 1486?; coast of Namibia?
*Explored coast of western Africa and
discovered mouth of Congo River*

cartographer mapmaker

Cano, Juan Sebastián del. See *Elcano, Juan Sebastián de.*

Diogo Cão was one of the most capable navigators of his day. He discovered the lower course of Africa's Congo River and gave it and the surrounding region the name Zaire. He was chosen by King John II of Portugal to sail down the Atlantic coast of Africa. King John hoped that Cão would find the southern tip of Africa, sail around it, and reach the trade markets of Asia. Cão's first expedition covered some 800 miles of mostly unexplored coastline and took him to the mouth of the Congo River and beyond. A second journey, from which he apparently never returned, covered nearly twice this distance. Even so, he never found the southern tip of Africa and could not complete his mission.

The Discovery of the Congo River

Cão was born into a Portuguese military family. He joined the Portuguese navy as a youth, eventually becoming a captain and proving his skill in combat off the west coast of Africa. In his early 30s, his reputation as a brave and talented navigator brought him to the attention of the king of Portugal, John II.

King John gave Cão the opportunity to explore Africa's western coastline. The king supplied him with limestone pillars to use as markers for claiming new territory. The pillars, known as *padrãos,* were five feet tall and featured a cross at the top. Each *padrão* was inscribed with the names of the king and the expedition's commander.

Cão left Portugal in June, 1482, sailing down the coast of Africa by way of the Canary Islands and the Gulf of Guinea. He made his way along the rugged coastline against dangerous currents, traveling 280 miles past the southernmost point previously explored. Late in the year, he reached the mouth of the Congo River and left a *padrão* on the river's southern bank.

Cão spent a month near the river, known to the native Bakongo people as the Nzadi, meaning "great water." Because Cão misunderstood the Bakongo name for the river, the Portuguese royal **cartographers** would later list the river and the surrounding area, as Zaire or Kongo.

The friendly Bakongo told Cão that far upriver was the royal city of the Mani Kongo, Lord of the Kongo. Cão hoped that the Mani Kongo might prove to be Prester John, a legendary Christian king whom the Portuguese had long hoped to find. Before leaving the area, Cão sent four of his African slaves on a mission to the city of the Mani Kongo, bearing gifts for the ruler.

The rest of the expedition continued 500 miles farther south along the coast, reaching Cape St. Mary (in present-day Angola), where Cão erected another *padrão*. When he returned to the Congo River for his slaves, he found no trace of them nor any explanation for their disappearance. Certain that his men were being held captive, Cão kidnapped four of the Bakongo and sent word to the Mani Kongo that the captives would be held until Cão's men were freed. He then sailed for Portugal, promising to return to the Congo region.

The Disappearance of Diogo Cão

Cão arrived in Portugal in April 1484 and was knighted for his accomplishments. King John treated the Bakongo captives as honored guests, since he believed that they would help him find Prester John. Confident that Cão had almost found the route around Africa, the king agreed to finance a second journey.

Cão left Portugal on his second voyage in late 1485. First he went to the Congo River to exchange his Bakongo hostages for the slaves he had left behind. He sailed about 100 miles up the river but was forced to turn back when he reached dangerous rapids. He returned to the coast and continued south, still searching for a route to Asia. He reached Cape Negro (now in Angola) and Cape Cross (now in Namibia), placing *padrãos* at both sites. Here his story abruptly ends. There is no further record of Cão's journey, and his disappearance remains a mystery to this day.

Historians have speculated that Cão may have been shipwrecked on Cape Cross or lost at sea on his way back to Portugal. His slaves, however, arrived safely in Lisbon. Some scholars suggest that Cão returned to Portugal but was executed by King John for twice failing to find the route around Africa.

Suggested Reading Eric Axelson, *Congo to Cape: Early Portuguese Explorers* (Barnes and Noble, 1973); Ernest Ravenstein, *The Voyages of Diogo Cão and Bartholomeu Dias, 1482–1488* (State Library, 1986).

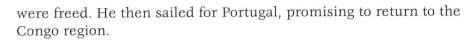

Carpini, Giovanni de Plano

Italian
b 1180?; Umbria, near Perugia, Italy
d August 1, 1252; Italy?
***Traveled across Europe and Asia
to Mongol Empire***

Giovanni de Plano Carpini, a member of the Franciscan order of monks, made a historic journey across Asia when he was 65 years old. He was sent by Pope Innocent IV as an ambassador to the powerful Mongols (also called Tartars), whose warriors had invaded eastern Europe. During his mission to the Mongol court, Carpini traveled over 15,000 miles, finding routes to the previously unknown lands of eastern Asia. His description of Asia and the Mongols is considered one of the best provided by a Christian writer of the Middle Ages.

In the Service of the Church

Carpini was a follower of Saint Francis of Assisi, the founder of the Franciscan order. As a monk, Carpini became a leading teacher in northern Europe and one of the pope's most trusted representatives. He made lengthy trips to both Spain and Scandinavia on behalf of the Franciscan order. When Pope Innocent IV decided to send an ambassador to the Mongols in 1245, he chose Carpini.

The pope had two reasons to communicate with the Mongols. The first was the Mongol invasion of eastern Europe in 1241. The pope hoped to discover why the Mongols had attacked. The second reason was the fall of Jerusalem to the Saracens, a Muslim tribe from the Arabian desert. The pope hoped to enlist the Mongols' aid in driving the Saracens from Jerusalem and the surrounding area.

khan title of an Asian ruler

European leaders knew little about the Mongols. Stories about a Christian kingdom in Asia, ruled by the legendary Prester John, had fascinated Europeans for many years. Some people suggested that the Mongols were descendants of Prester John's followers. But, Europeans asked, if the Mongols were somehow connected with Prester John, why were they invading Christian Europe? To find out, Pope Innocent wrote a letter to the Mongol ruler, known as the Great **Khan.** Carpini was instructed to deliver this letter and bring back a reply.

Journey into the Unknown

Since the Great Khan's location was unknown, Innocent decided to increase his chances of success by sending two separate groups. Carpini led one party. The other was led by Laurentius of Portugal, who did not succeed in reaching the khan.

Carpini set out from Lyon, France, on Easter Day, 1245. He and the other members of the mission traveled to Prague (in the present-day Czech Republic), where they were told to continue east into Poland. There they would meet a Russian prince who would escort them to meet Batu, the Mongol conqueror of eastern Europe. This general was camped near the Volga River in Russia. After weeks of winter travel, they arrived at the city of Kiev (now in Ukraine), which had been almost totally destroyed by the Mongols. Some Mongols in Kiev offered to take Carpini's group on horseback to Batu's camp. According to Carpini, they rode as fast as the horses could run, changing horses three or four times a day. Even so, they did not reach Batu's camp until the day before the next Easter, nearly a year after they had left France.

The Heart of the Mongol Empire

Batu ordered Carpini's group to continue east to Mongolia, where they could meet with the khan, whose name was Guyug. Accompanied by two Mongol escorts, they traveled into the heart of Mongol territory. Heading north of the Caspian and Aral Seas, they rode through a bitterly cold June snowstorm. They arrived at Guyug's palace on July 22, just in time to see Mongol leaders elect him as their ruler.

Over 4,000 foreign ambassadors were present for the election. Carpini was one of only a handful of Europeans. After Guyug had been officially named khan, Carpini was given an opportunity to present the pope's message. Guyug gave Carpini a letter in response and instructed him to begin his trip back to Europe.

Carpini's Return

Carpini's group left immediately and traveled right through the winter. Carpini later wrote: "We often had to lie in snow in the wilderness. . . . When we awoke in the morning, we often found ourselves completely covered with snow that the wind had blown over us." They arrived at Batu's camp on May 9, 1247. When Carpini asked if Batu had any message of his own for the pope, Batu said that he had nothing to add to Guyug's reply. Carpini sensed some tension between Batu and the new emperor. This observation would be welcome news to the Europeans, who hoped that the Mongols would be too busy fighting among themselves to continue their attacks against Europe.

Carpini reached France in November and made a full report to the pope. Guyug's letter was not encouraging. The khan claimed that eastern Europe had been conquered by the Mongols because the people there "did not comply with the commandments of God and [the] Khan, but rather, in their infamy, deliberately murdered Our ambassadors." His message to the Europeans was: "Today you shall say from the depths of your heart: we wish to be Your subjects and give You some of our power." Of course, the leaders of Europe would not choose to submit to the khan, but they continued to fear the powerful Mongol armies.

Although Carpini's expedition did not achieve friendly relations between the Europeans and the Mongols, he brought back much valuable information. In his book, *History of the Mongols,* Carpini described the climate and geography of the Mongol lands as well as the Mongols' religion, history, customs, leaders, and armies. Carpini's journey also opened a route to the east that was soon followed by others. One such traveler was another Franciscan monk, WILLIAM OF RUBRUCK, who unraveled the story of Prester John and the Asian Christians.

Suggested Reading Christopher Dawson, *Mission to Asia* (reprint, Toronto University Press, 1980); Manuel Komroff, *Contemporaries of Marco Polo* (reprint, Dorset, 1989); Sherwood Merriam, *The Road to Cathay* (Macmillan, 1928).

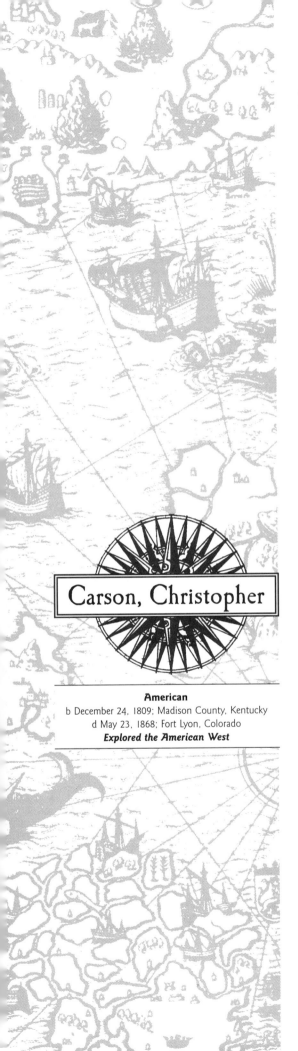

Carson, Christopher

American
b December 24, 1809; Madison County, Kentucky
d May 23, 1868; Fort Lyon, Colorado
Explored the American West

Christopher Carson, better known as Kit, was one of those Americans known as the Mountain Men. From the 1820s to the 1840s, they roamed the West, trapping beaver and selling furs. Along the way, the Mountain Men came to know more about the mountains, rivers, and plains of the West than any geographer. They were also popular heroes, famous for their astonishing adventures and colorful personalities. Perhaps none was better known or more admired than Kit Carson.

To the Mountains

Carson's father had fought in the American Revolution, and after the war, he headed west to Kentucky. Christopher was born in 1809, and the family moved to Missouri a year later. Carson's childhood on the frontier was not an easy one. The community he lived in was always in danger of attack by Indians. He received no schooling and did not know how to read or write. When he was nine years old, his father died, and his mother found him work with a saddlemaker in a nearby town. Carson did not stay with this man for long. Years later he recalled: "The business did not suit me and, having heard so many tales of life in the Mountains of the West, I concluded to leave him."

For a young man like Carson, the mysterious western lands held the promise of freedom and adventure. Only 20 years had passed since Meriwether LEWIS and William CLARK had returned from their

Many tales and legends were told about Christopher "Kit" Carson, but his real life as a Mountain Man was more than enough to secure his fame.

famous expedition to the Pacific Northwest. Large portions of the West were still unexplored and unmapped, but already some people were seeking their fortunes there. In 1826 Carson joined a group of traders bound for Santa Fe, which was then in Mexican territory.

After spending some time in Taos, north of Santa Fe, Carson joined a party of trappers led by Ewing Young, one of the first Mountain Men. They made a hard journey through mountains and deserts to California, trapping beaver in every river along the way. Carson then headed northwest and spent about 10 years in the Rocky Mountains, hunting beaver and buffalo. Sometimes the group in which he traveled included another Mountain Man, James BRIDGER. By the early 1840s, however, beaver were becoming scarce, and trappers found it hard to make a living. When Carson's Indian wife died in 1842, he took their daughter to Missouri to be raised. During this trip, a chance meeting changed his life and led to his fame throughout the nation.

Carson and Frémont

On a steamboat, Carson met John Charles FRÉMONT, a U.S. Army officer who was leading the exploration and mapping of the Oregon Trail through the Rocky Mountains. Frémont discovered that Carson knew the territory well, and he eventually hired him as a guide for two expeditions through the Rockies, Oregon, Utah, and California. In 1845 the government published Frémont's report, which became a huge public success. Americans had developed a great interest in the West. Thousands of people were moving to the frontier on the Oregon Trail. Also, a growing number of Americans felt that U.S. territory should include western regions that belonged to Mexico. People eagerly bought and read Frémont's report, which included glowing descriptions of the man Frémont called "My good and reliable friend, Kit Carson." The tough but soft-spoken Mountain Man became a hero.

In 1845 Carson made a third journey with Frémont. They crossed the Great Basin of Nevada and the Sierra Nevada mountain range on their way to California. There they became involved in a war between the United States and Mexico. Among other activities, Carson guided American soldiers over the Sierra Nevada. The war ended with the United States in control of California and the Southwest.

Military Career

In 1847 Frémont sent Carson to Washington, D.C., with reports of the events in California. President James K. Polk was impressed with Carson and made him a lieutenant in the Mounted Riflemen, an army unit. About a year later, members of Congress who opposed Frémont's activities in the West had Carson's appointment canceled. But there was nothing they could do about his fame.

Carson returned to Taos—by then part of the United States as a result of the war—and spent the next few years farming, fighting

Indians, and driving sheep to market. In the mid-1850s, increasing numbers of Indians were coming under U.S. control. The federal government put Carson in charge of relations between whites and Indians in his area. His job was to maintain order, supervise trade, and see that the Indians received the benefits that the government had promised them. Carson tried to represent the Indians fairly and often came into conflict with the territory's governor. The governor did not agree with some of Carson's suggestions for improving conditions for the Indians. On one occasion, he went so far as have Carson arrested.

In 1861, when the Civil War broke out, Carson resigned his post to serve with the Union army. He fought in the West against the Apache, Navajo, and Comanche Indians, who were allied with the Confederacy. After the war, the army sent Carson to Colorado, but he left the service in 1867 because of ill health. He was appointed superintendent of Indian affairs for Colorado, but he died before taking up the job.

The Real Kit Carson

Kit Carson became a legend in his own lifetime. Once Frémont's reports had made him known to the public, other people began telling and publishing colorful stories about him. Some of these were exaggerations of events that had really happened, and some were completely false. Carson even became the hero of several works of fiction, such as the novel *Kit Carson, Prince of the Gold Hunters,* published in 1849. More recently, scholars have worked to replace the myths with a more accurate picture of the honest, loyal, and courageous Mountain Man who helped open the American West.

Suggested Reading Harvey L. Carter, *"Dear Old Kit": The Historical Christopher Carson* (Oklahoma University Press, 1968); Thelma S. Carter and Harvey L. Carter, *Kit Carson: A Pattern for Heroes* (Nebraska University Press, 1984); R. C. Gordon-McCutchan, editor, *Kit Carson: Indian Fighter or Indian Killer?* (Colorado University Press, 1996); Edward L. Sabin, *Kit Carson Days,* 2 volumes (reprint, Nebraska University Press, 1995).

Carteret, Philip

English
b January 22, 1733; Jersey Island, England
d July 21, 1796; Southampton, England
Discovered Pitcairn Island; sailed around world

frigate small, agile warship with three masts and square sails

sloop small ship with one mast and triangular sails

Philip Carteret was an English naval officer and explorer who survived a difficult 31-month sea voyage around the world. During his long journey, he made several discoveries in the Pacific Ocean, pointing the way for later explorers. At the time, however, he did not gain the recognition he deserved. His achievements were overshadowed by those of other famed English explorers, such as Samuel WALLIS and James COOK.

The Dolphin Voyages

Carteret was born into a distinguished family on the island of Jersey in the English Channel. He joined the navy as a teenager and served bravely during the Seven Years' War against France. One of the officers under whom he served was a commander named John BYRON. When Byron was planning an expedition on the **frigate** *Dolphin* in 1764, he asked Carteret to join him. Carteret agreed to serve as first lieutenant on the **sloop** *Tamar,* which was to sail alongside the *Dolphin.* The expedition lasted two years and traveled to the

Though his ship was barely seaworthy and his crew was desperately ill, Philip Carteret led a voyage around the world in the 1760s.

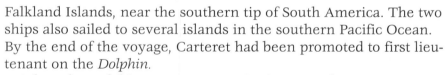

Falkland Islands, near the southern tip of South America. The two ships also sailed to several islands in the southern Pacific Ocean. By the end of the voyage, Carteret had been promoted to first lieutenant on the *Dolphin.*

When the *Dolphin* went to sea again, it was under a new commander, Samuel Wallis. The purpose of this voyage was to search for *Terra Australis Incognita,* an undiscovered southern continent believed to lie somewhere in the Pacific Ocean. Carteret was to command the *Swallow,* an old ship in poor condition. He was disappointed with the *Swallow,* but he was told that it would be replaced in the Falkland Islands. Carteret set sail with Wallis from Plymouth, England, late in the summer of 1766.

When they arrived in the Falklands, Carteret found that no new ship was waiting for him. He wanted to turn back, but Wallis would not allow it. To make sure that Carteret did not try to return to England, Wallis forced him to lead the way through the dangerous Strait of Magellan. This strait would take them across the southern tip of South America and into the Pacific Ocean.

In bad weather and high seas, the passage through the strait took four months. Just before the ships reached the Pacific Ocean, a strong wind pushed Wallis's *Dolphin* far ahead of the *Swallow,* and the two ships were separated. Carteret was now free of Wallis and could choose his own route. Although his ship was in terrible condition and many of his crew members were suffering from **scurvy,** Carteret continued to sail west.

scurvy disease caused by a lack of vitamin C and once a major cause of death among sailors; symptoms include internal bleeding, loosened teeth, and extreme fatigue

Surviving on the High Seas

The *Swallow*'s voyage lasted for the next two years. In the southern Pacific Ocean, Carteret discovered Pitcairn Island, which later served as a hiding place for rebel sailors on the *Bounty,* a ship commanded by William BLIGH. Carteret also sailed to Santa Cruz and the Solomon Islands, which no European had seen since the 1500s. He did not realize that these islands had already been discovered by Alvaro de MENDAÑA DE NEHRA and Pedro Fernandez de QUIRÓS.

Sailing west from the Solomon Islands, Carteret reached New Britain, off the east coast of New Guinea. He discovered that New Britain was part of a group of three islands, not two as previously thought. He claimed New Britain and named the other two islands New Ireland and New Hanover. He also discovered and named the St. George Channel, which lay between New Britain and New Ireland. He named the strait between New Ireland and New Hanover after Byron and a harbor on New Ireland after himself. Further north and west, he reached another island group, which had been explored earlier by the Dutch navigator Abel TASMAN. Carteret named this group the Admiralty Islands.

More than a year after leaving England, Carteret reached an island in Indonesia. He hoped that he could finally repair his damaged ship, but Dutch officials there refused to help him. Carteret continued west, reaching what is now Jakarta, Indonesia, a year later. He spent four months there while the *Swallow* was repaired at last.

On his return journey to Britain, Carteret met a mysterious French navigator, who gave him news of the *Dolphin* but would say nothing about himself. He was Louis-Antoine de BOUGAINVILLE, another explorer sailing around the world. After this strange meeting, Carteret sailed on. He reached Britain in March 1769, after 31 months at sea. Half his crew had died during the voyage.

Ten years later, Carteret was again given command of a ship, the *Endymion.* He held this post for three years. Afterwards he remained a navy officer, but he never again went to sea.

Suggested Reading Helen Wallis, editor, *Carteret's Voyage Around the World,* (Hakluyt Society, 1965).

Cartier, Jacques

French
b 1491; St.-Malo, France
d September 1, 1557; St.-Malo, France
Explored Gulf of St. Lawrence and St. Lawrence River

Jacques Cartier was an expert navigator who led three French expeditions to North America. In 1534 he sailed into the Gulf of St. Lawrence but did not find the St. Lawrence River. On the second voyage, a year later, he discovered the river and explored it as far as the site of present-day Montréal. In 1541 Cartier returned to the region to search for a mythical kingdom of great wealth and to start a French colony. Although he accomplished neither of these goals, Cartier was honored in his home country. His careful explorations were the first steps toward the empire France would build in North America.

On his three ocean crossings from France to North America, Jacques Cartier never lost a single ship or crew member to an accident at sea.

Treaty of Tordesillas agreement between Spain and Portugal dividing rights to discovered lands along a north-south line

Northwest Passage water route connecting the Atlantic Ocean and Pacific Ocean through the Arctic islands of northern Canada

A Search for Historical Evidence

Little is known of Jacques Cartier's life before he made his voyage to North America in 1534. Some historians believe that he took part in Giovanni da VERRAZANO's voyages to the Americas in the 1520s. In his writings, Cartier mentioned the food and native people of Brazil, one of the places explored by Verrazano. Records show that Cartier was away from France during Verrazano's expeditions. But other scholars point out that Cartier never wrote about those voyages or about the sections of the North American coast that Verrazano also explored.

Whether or not Cartier visited North America with Verrazano, he did become known as a skillful sailor. The abbot of the monastery at Mont-Saint-Michel, France, brought Cartier to the attention of the French king Francis I. At the time, Francis was looking for someone to lead a French expedition to North America. The abbot told the king that Cartier had traveled to both Brazil and Newfoundland (in present-day Canada).

Eyes on North America

King Francis hoped to find riches in the Americas like the gold and silver which Spain and Portugal had been mining for the last 30 years. However, a church decree of 1494, called the **Treaty of Tordesillas,** had given Spain and Portugal the right to claim newly discovered lands. The treaty excluded other nations. In 1533 King Francis persuaded Pope Clement VII to change the decree so that it would apply only to lands that were already known. Under the revised decree, any other lands could be claimed by the country that found them. Francis had won the opportunity for his country to join Spain and Portugal as a colonial power.

The king asked Cartier to lead the first French voyage to North America. In April 1534, Cartier sailed from St.-Malo in Brittany, France, with two ships and 61 men. His goals were to find new sources of precious metals and to discover a **Northwest Passage** to eastern Asia. Thanks to fair weather, the trip across the Atlantic Ocean was easy, taking only 20 days. The two ships reached land at what is now Cape Bonavista, Newfoundland. The island of Newfoundland was already being visited by French fishermen who needed to resupply or repair their vessels.

The Bleak and Rocky Coast

Even though it was early May, there was still much ice floating in the water. Cartier's ships sailed southeast to a warmer harbor before heading north again to what is now Funk Island. The French paused there to hunt sea birds called great auks for food. Soon the ships entered the Strait of Belle Isle between Newfoundland and the mainland coast of Labrador. This strait was the way into the bay later known as the Gulf of St. Lawrence.

As Cartier sailed along the rocky coast of Labrador, he was disappointed by what he saw. Although he landed in many places, he wrote that he found "nothing but moss and stunted shrubs." He described the few Indians he met as "untamed." Cartier soon grew weary of the bleak coast and headed south along the west coast of Newfoundland. When he reached the island's southern end, he guessed that there was a channel between Newfoundland and Nova Scotia, which was known to lie to the south. For some reason, he did not try to find this channel. Instead, he turned west and crossed over to what are now called the Magdalen Islands. Cartier did not name these islands—he thought that they were part of the mainland.

On June 29, Cartier's ships left the islands and sailed west all night. The crew sighted what is now called Prince Edward Island in the morning. Cartier mistakenly thought that this island, too, was part of the mainland. He took the ships across the entrance to the Northumberland Strait and sailed into Miramichi Bay, on the coast of modern-day New Brunswick. He then headed farther north and discovered another waterway, which he named Chaleur Bay. At last Cartier had found something to delight him, for he thought this bay lovelier than any other place he had seen during the voyage. He praised the warm air and water, the plentiful fish, and the rich soil. Chaleur Bay was long and narrow and seemed to stretch on without end. Cartier hoped that he had discovered a passage to China.

New Friends in North America

On the north shore of Chaleur Bay, Cartier had his first meeting with the Micmac Indians. They surrounded his ships in their canoes. Cartier wrote that the Indians made "signs of joy" to indicate friendship. Still, Cartier did not trust them, so his men shot small guns over the Indians' heads. The Micmac paid no attention to Cartier's threats. They returned the next day and offered fur pelts for sale. The French and Indians traded peacefully. Cartier sailed on, but he soon reached the end of the bay and knew that he would not find a Northwest Passage there.

The expedition sailed back out of the bay and then north to the tip of the Gaspé Peninsula. There the French met about 200 Huron Indians, who had come from what is now called Québec to fish along the coast. Cartier did not realize that the Indians were a fishing party, and he wrote that they were the "poorest people that can be in the world," because they carried so little with them.

The French raised a 30-foot-high cross at Gaspé Harbor. On the cross they wrote, "Long live the King of France." The Indians' chief, Donnaconna, could not understand the French language, but he could tell that these strangers were claiming the land. Donnaconna quickly made it clear to the French that the territory belonged to his people. The French were apparently able to reassure Donnaconna as to their peaceful intentions. The chief agreed to send his two sons, Domagaya and Taignoagny, to France to learn to speak French. Cartier promised to return the next year with Donnaconna's sons, who would then be able to serve as interpreters.

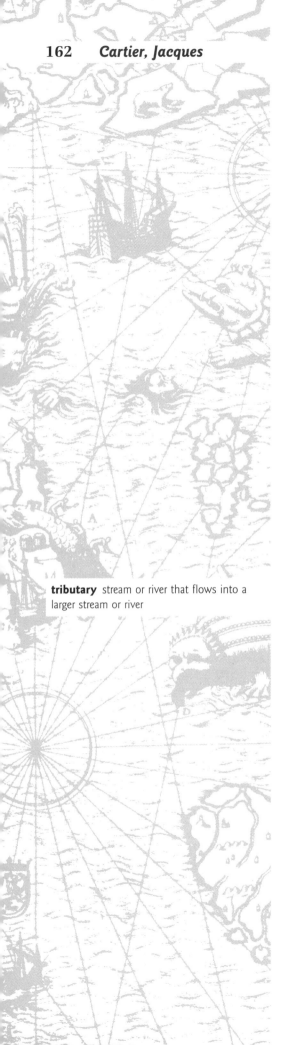

tributary stream or river that flows into a larger stream or river

Cartier set sail from Gaspé Harbor and explored nearby Anticosti Island. With summer nearly over, Cartier and his crew decided to return to France. They reached St.-Malo with both ships in good condition. Not one member of the crew had been lost. Although Cartier had failed to find gold, jewels, or a route to Asia, he was given a hero's welcome in France. He had added to European knowledge of North America, and he had made valuable allies among the Huron Indians.

The St. Lawrence River

Cartier had been back in France for less than two months when the king hired him to lead another expedition. This time Cartier was given three ships and 110 men. They set sail in the late spring of 1535. Bad weather and strong winds caused the ocean crossing to take more than twice as long as it had the first time. The ships finally landed at Funk Island in early July. Cartier then headed directly to the Strait of Belle Isle to search for a water route into the interior of the continent. He named a harbor after St. Lawrence on August 10, the feast day of that saint. In later years, that name would also be applied to the Gulf of St. Lawrence and the St. Lawrence River.

With Donnaconna's two sons as guides, Cartier easily found the mouth of the St. Lawrence River. Domagaya and Taignoagny told Cartier that this river was the route to "Canada," meaning the area that is now the province of Québec. They told him that the waters came from so far away that no one had ever seen their source. Cartier decided that this river must be the passage to Asia that he was seeking. Soon after entering the St. Lawrence River, the explorers saw a deep and rapid river joining the flow from the west. The Huron guides told them that this **tributary** was the way to Saguenay, a kingdom of great riches. The search for Saguenay later became the main purpose of Cartier's final voyage.

Demons and Deceptions

In September the ships reached the village of Stadacona, where the city of Québec is located today. Donnaconna was there to greet them. Donnaconna's sons had promised to lead Cartier all the way to the village of Hochelaga, the site of modern-day Montréal. Then, however, the guides began to stall. Cartier later learned that Hochelaga's chief claimed to rule Donnaconna's people. Donnaconna wanted to keep his French allies to himself.

Cartier decided to go to Hochelaga, even without the two guides, so Donnaconna tried to scare the French into staying at Stadacona. He had three Indians dress up as devils. They blackened their faces and wore long horns and dog skins. They warned the French that snow and ice upriver would cause the death of the entire crew if they tried to go to Hochelaga. The French only laughed at this trick. Donnaconna laughed along, pretending that he had meant the incident as a joke. Unsure of the chief's intentions, Cartier proceeded with his plans.

Cartier left part of his crew behind with Donnaconna's tribe and sailed up the river aboard one of his ships. He arrived at Hochelaga

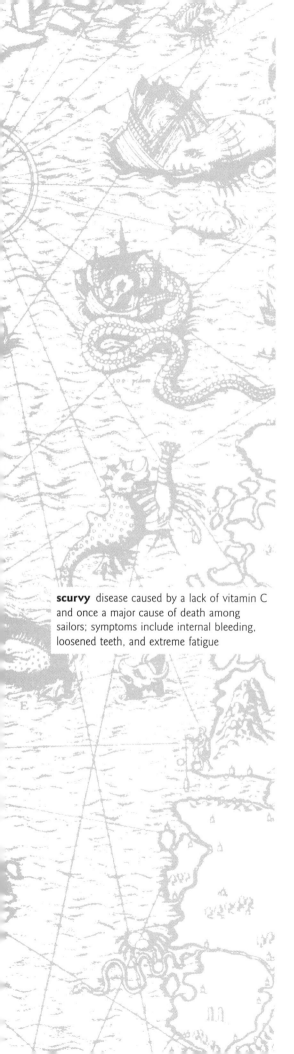

scurvy disease caused by a lack of vitamin C and once a major cause of death among sailors; symptoms include internal bleeding, loosened teeth, and extreme fatigue

about two weeks later. One thousand Huron Indians came to the riverbank to greet the explorers. They offered gifts and threw corn bread to the sailors. The Huron brought sick members of the tribe to Cartier, believing that he could heal with the touch of his hands. A grand ceremony was staged in the village's main plaza to welcome the visitors.

Some of the Frenchmen climbed a peak that Cartier named Mont Réal, which means "Royal Mountain" in French. From the top, they could see rapids on the river, just beyond Hochelaga. These rapids made it impossible to travel farther up the St. Lawrence River without canoes, which the French did not have. Cartier was very disappointed that he could not continue up the river, for he believed that it would have led him to Asia. He was forced to return to Stadacona. Before leaving Hochelaga, he asked the Indians about the legendary land of Saguenay. They told him that the stories he had heard earlier were true. They described the land's precious metals and said that its people had a reputation as skilled warriors.

Long Winter Nights

Unable to search for Saguenay, Cartier headed back east to the mouth of what is now called the St. Charles River. Near Stadacona, at a port that he named Ste.-Croix, he rejoined the sailors he had left behind. Those men had built a fort, and Cartier's entire party spent the winter there. Cartier used the time to write about the customs of local Indians. His notes contain the first written mention of tobacco in northern North America.

The winter was extremely cold. From mid-November to mid-April, the French ships were frozen in ice at the mouth of the St. Charles River. Many of the sailors suffered from **scurvy.** The disease caused their legs to swell up, their gums to turn black, and their teeth to fall out. Cartier wrote, "Out of the 110 men that we were, not 10 were well enough to help the others, a thing pitiful to see." Some of the crew were saved by a cure that they had learned from Domagaya. He had taught them to prepare a kind of tea from the bark and needles of the white cedar tree. Everyone who took this medicine recovered. At the end of the winter, 85 men were still alive.

Dreams of Saguenay

The relationship between the French and the Indians had become tense. Even so, many of the long winter nights were spent around fires, listening to Donnaconna tell stories. His elaborate and detailed accounts of the land of Saguenay were more amazing than any the French had yet heard. He gave glowing descriptions of Saguenay's gold and jewels. He claimed that the land's people included white men and one-legged monsters. Cartier did not realize that this kind of storytelling was a tradition among the Huron. Eager to please and entertain their guests, they said whatever they thought the French wanted to hear. The Huron saw the Frenchmen's eyes light up at the mention of gold, so they made sure to talk about gold as often as possible.

Donnaconna soon regretted having told these tales. Cartier decided that King Francis should hear the stories of Saguenay directly from the chief. Just before leaving for France, he kidnapped Donnaconna, Domagaya, Taignoagny, and several other important members of the tribe. The Huron people raised a great cry for the return of their captured chief. Cartier promised to bring Donnaconna back within a year with gifts from the French king.

The ships set sail in May 1536. During the voyage, Cartier made progress in his exploration of the Gulf of St. Lawrence. He had seen the Magdalen Islands two years earlier but had thought that they were part of the mainland. Now, sailing past them again, he realized that they were islands. He also became the first French explorer to sail between Newfoundland and Nova Scotia.

When the ships reached France, Cartier presented Donnaconna to the royal court. The Huron chief became very popular, once again spinning his tales about the kingdom of Saguenay. Donnaconna noticed that King Francis was interested in spices and exotic fruits as well as gold. Soon the stories were full of cloves, nutmeg, pepper, oranges, and pomegranates. King Francis decided to send Cartier back to North America to find Saguenay.

Journey of Disappointments

Cartier's departure was held up for five years. France was at war with Spain, and all of its money was spent on the French army and navy. The king could not afford to sponsor Cartier at that time. Once the war was over, Cartier spent three years preparing five ships. Intending to establish the first French colony in North America, he took hundreds of people on board to settle there.

By January 1541, Cartier was ready to set sail. Suddenly, the king placed Jean-François de la Rocque de Roberval in command in place of Cartier. All the settlers and crewmen, including Cartier, had to swear an oath of loyalty to Roberval. Cartier would still be the chief navigator, but he was no longer in charge. There is no record of his feeling about being replaced.

Cartier and the five ships left St.-Malo in May. Roberval would follow as soon as his own ships were ready. Three months later, Cartier's party arrived in Stadacona. A Huron named Agona had taken Donnaconna's place as chief of the tribe. Agona was relieved to hear that his rival Donnaconna had died in France. Cartier had a feeling that the Huron were not as friendly as they seemed. To prevent a conflict, he lied and said that the others were happy in France and did not want to return. In fact, except for one girl, all of the kidnapped Indians had died.

It was probably this same feeling of distrust that caused Cartier to abandon his old fort at Ste.-Croix. The French built a new fort several miles farther from Stadacona. They called it Charlesbourg-Royal, and the colonists planted a garden there. In the surrounding area, they began to collect what they thought were diamonds and gold. Actually, they had only found quartz and iron pyrite, which is also known as "fool's gold."

Meanwhile, Cartier and some of his men began the search for Saguenay. They traveled west toward Hochelaga, passing through

For a map of Cartier's routes, see the profile of John CABOT *in this volume.*

the territory of Achelacy, a chief whom Cartier had met on the previous expedition. Cartier left two French youths with Achelacy to learn the tribe's language. This example was later followed by other French explorers, such as Samuel de CHAMPLAIN, who sent Etienne BRULÉ and other young men to live among the Indians.

Just before reaching Hochelaga, Cartier's party reached a waterfall. The explorers left their boats and followed an Indian trail along the shore. The path led them to a village called Tutonaguy, where the French were treated kindly. Four Indians joined Cartier to help him reach Saguenay. These guides took the French to another village and drew a map with sticks to show the way to Saguenay. However, they also told Cartier that another series of waterfalls blocked the way. At this news, Cartier had to turn back again.

The Colony in Ruins

When Cartier got back to Charlesbourg-Royal, he found that he had been right to mistrust the Huron. The Indians had become violent, probably because they realized that the French visitors intended to stay. There are no records to show what actually happened during the long winter of 1541 to 1542. According to hearsay later gathered from French sailors, the Indians attacked the settlement more than once. They killed about 35 people during the winter. Scurvy broke out, but it was quickly cured with the medicine made from the white cedar tree. The settlers were depressed and miserable, and to make matters worse, no one knew why Roberval had not yet arrived.

In early summer, the French ships headed back to France with all of the colonists aboard. The settlers brought back barrels of what they thought were gold, silver, and jewels. On the way, the ships anchored in the harbor of St. John's in Newfoundland. There they found Roberval with three ships. Roberval ordered Cartier to turn around and go back to Stadacona. Cartier may have thought that his crew and the colonists would rebel against this plan. He may also have been eager to show his cargo to the king. Whatever his reasons, Cartier and his ships slipped away in the night and returned to St.-Malo.

Cartier was not punished for disobeying Roberval's order. Instead, the king rewarded him by giving him two of the ships. Cartier lived out the rest of his life in St.-Malo and at his nearby manor, Limoïlou. He died at the age of 66.

The riches that Cartier brought back turned out to be worthless rocks. No one ever found the land of Saguenay—it had existed only in the Indians' stories and in the Frenchmen's greedy imaginations. But Cartier is rightly remembered for his skill and leadership. His three missions were among the most important voyages of discovery ever made. The St. Lawrence River region became the heart of the French empire in North America.

Suggested Reading Henry S. Burrage, editor, *Early English and French Voyages Chiefly from Hakluyt, 1534-1608* (Barnes and Noble, 1934); Josef Berger, *Discoverers of the New World* (American Heritage Publishing Company, 1960); Harold Lamb, *New Found World* (Doubleday, 1955); Samuel Eliot Morison, *The European Discovery of America* (Oxford University Press, 1971); David B. Quinn, *North America from Earliest Discovery to First Settlements* (Harper and Row, 1977).

Cavelier, René Robert de La Salle. *See La Salle, René Robert Cavelier de.*

Cavendish, Thomas

English
b 1560; England
d October 1592; southern Atlantic Ocean
*Sailed around world;
discovered Port Desire, Argentina*

Thomas Cavendish commanded the third sea voyage around the world—and captured dozens of Spanish treasure ships along the way.

circumnavigate to travel around

courtier attendant at a royal court

buccaneer pirate, especially one who attacked Spanish colonies and ships in the 1600s

topsail second-lowest sail on the mast of a ship

Sir Thomas Cavendish was an English navigator who led the third expedition to **circumnavigate** the globe. His journey around the world followed those of Ferdinand MAGELLAN and Sir Francis DRAKE. Cavendish also spent time in South America, where he explored Patagonia and discovered Port Desire (in what is now Argentina).

High Hopes for Success

Cavendish attended Cambridge University in England but left without earning a degree. He was a **courtier** and a member of the English Parliament. During this time, he enjoyed an expensive lifestyle and almost ran out of money. He decided to seek his fortune at sea.

In 1585 he joined the British admiral Sir Richard Grenville on a voyage to the colony of Virginia in North America. When he returned to England, Cavendish began to plan his own ocean adventure. He wanted to make a full journey around the world, similar to that completed by Sir Francis Drake in 1580. In July 1586, Cavendish set sail from Plymouth, England, with 123 men in three ships. The ships were named the *Desire,* the *Content,* and the *Gallant.* They sailed south along the west coast of Africa to Sierra Leone, then crossed the Atlantic Ocean to Cape Frio, Brazil. Cavendish continued south and explored Patagonia (now part of southern Argentina). On the coast of Argentina, he made his major discovery—Port Desire, which he named for his ship. In later years, ships preparing to sail through the Strait of Magellan would often stop at Port Desire for supplies and repairs.

Pirates of the Pacific Ocean

Cavendish and his crew continued south and then sailed west through the Strait of Magellan into the Pacific Ocean. They made their way up the west coasts of South America, Central America, and Mexico. Like Sir Francis Drake, Cavendish and his men were **buccaneers**—they raided settlements and other ships.

Cavendish and his men captured some 19 vessels as they crossed the Pacific Ocean. Their route took them to many islands, including the Philippines and Java (in modern-day Indonesia). They then crossed the Indian Ocean and rounded the Cape of Good Hope at the southern tip of Africa. They reached England in September 1588 after two years and 50 days at sea.

Although Cavendish returned with only one ship, the *Desire,* he brought home the riches he had set out to find. When his ship reached England, the crew was wearing silk, and the **topsail** was said to be of gold cloth. Three years later, however, Cavendish again found himself in financial trouble. He decided to repeat his earlier journey. He gathered five ships and set sail, but he never made it back to England. He died at sea in 1592, somewhere in the southern Atlantic Ocean.

Suggested Reading Thomas Cavendish, *The Last Voyage of Thomas Cavendish, 1591–1592: The Autograph Manuscript of his Own Account of the Voyage, Written Shortly Before his Death,* edited by David Beers Quinn (Chicago University Press, 1975); Philip Edwards, editor, *Last Voyages—Cavendish, Hudson, Raleigh: The Original Narratives* (Oxford University Press, 1988).

Chaillé-Long, Charles

American
b July 2, 1842; Somerset County, Maryland
d March 24, 1917; Virginia Beach, Virginia
Explored Nile River region of Africa

In the late 1800s, Egypt and central Africa attracted explorers from all over the world. Charles Chaillé-Long, an American soldier, was one of these adventurers. He worked in Africa for the Egyptian government as a diplomat, officer, and geographer. During his journeys, he discovered a lake that is now in Uganda. He also gathered information about the White Nile River and other rivers of the region.

Into Central Africa

Chaillé-Long was born in Maryland. In 1861 he left school to fight in the Civil War, serving as a captain in the Union army. After the war, Chaillé-Long traveled to Egypt in hopes of finding more excitement. In 1869 he was appointed a lieutenant colonel in the Egyptian army. Within five years, he became chief of staff to General Charles "China" Gordon.

Gordon sent Chaillé-Long to explore the lands south of the Sudan in central Africa. Chaillé-Long was instructed to study the region's geography and to gather any information about the land and its people that might help Egypt gain control of the area. In Buganda (now Uganda), Chaillé-Long discussed a treaty with the local ruler, King Mutesa. They met in Rubaga, the capital city of Buganda. Chaillé-Long later reported that Rubaga was a large settlement that covered the hills for several miles around. He described the luxurious housing that was offered to visitors. He also noted that King Mutesa had an army of 150,000 warriors and a fleet of war canoes on Lake Victoria.

The Geographer Adds to the Maps

Chaillé-Long examined the geography of the lake regions of East Africa. He charted the course of the upper part of the Nile River, known as the White Nile River. He followed the White Nile from its source to Karuma Falls in central Uganda. This work added to the earlier discoveries of John Hanning SPEKE. While in Uganda, Chaillé-Long discovered Lake Ibrahim (now known as Lake Kyoga). In 1875 he traveled to the region between the Nile and Congo Rivers. Here, too, he added to knowledge that had been obtained by earlier explorers. After his journey into the continental interior, he worked at a new career as an official of the United States government in Egypt and Korea.

In later life, Chaillé-Long gained a reputation for boasting about his accomplishments. In his writings, he described his discoveries in grander terms than they really deserved. He wrote about his work as an explorer and diplomat in his autobiography, *My Life in Four Continents.*

Charles Chaillé-Long explored the Nile River region and was known for his boastful nature.

Suggested Reading Charles Chaillé-Long, *My Life in Four Continents* (Hutchinson and Company, 1912); Pierre Crabitès, *Americans in the Egyptian Army* (Routledge, 1938).

Chaillu, Paul Belloni Du. See *Du Chaillu, Paul Belloni.*

Champlain, Samuel de

French
b 1567?; Brouage, France
d December 25, 1635; Québec, Canada
Explored and colonized eastern Canada

Samuel de Champlain was an adventurer, a mapmaker, and a leader of colonists. He devoted the last 30 years of his life to building France's North American empire. He founded the first permanent French colony on the continent and explored the Atlantic coast as far south as Cape Cod, Massachusetts. He journeyed inland as far west as Lake Huron and was the first European to reach the lake that bears his name, Lake Champlain (in present-day New York).

The son of a French sea captain, Champlain was born around 1567 on the coast of the Bay of Biscay. He fought for France's King Henry IV in religious wars between Protestants and Roman Catholics during the late 1500s. In 1599 Champlain spent two years in the West Indies as part of a Spanish expedition. During this time, he suggested that a canal connecting the Atlantic and the Pacific Oceans be built across Panama. His idea was ahead of his time—the canal was built about 300 years later.

The Geographer's Adventure

When Champlain returned to France, he wrote and illustrated a book about his experiences. King Henry was so impressed by the book that he made Champlain the royal geographer. Champlain, however, was bored by the easy life at the French court. He persuaded Henry to let him go to North America. At that time, France could not afford to send colonists to settle in the Americas. King Henry knew, though, that France needed to compete with Portugal, Spain, and England, which were already creating empires around the world. He offered a deal to French businessmen, giving them the right to trap and trade furs in North America if they used some of their profits to build and support French colonies.

In 1603 Champlain traveled to North America as the geographer for a party of fur traders. He and a few others sailed up the St. Lawrence River to the Indian village of Tadoussac. From there they continued 60 miles up the Saguenay River and also surveyed the St.-Maurice River. They traveled as far as the site of the modern-day city of Montréal. There the Indians spoke of a lake to the west that was so large that they were afraid to sail on it. Champlain thought that this might be the Pacific Ocean. He headed west, hoping to discover a sea route to China, but his travel on the St. Lawrence was blocked just west of Montréal by the dangerous Lachine Rapids. Frustrated, Champlain realized that the way to navigate North America's rivers was to use lightweight canoes like those of the Indians. Explorers who encountered rapids or falls could simply carry their canoes along the riverbanks until they passed the dangerous waters. This solution became the key to future French exploration in North America.

While traveling these rivers, Champlain formed an **alliance** with the Algonquin Indians against their enemies, the Iroquois Indians.

alliance formal agreement of friendship or common defense

Samuel de Champlain never gave up on his dream of building a strong French colony in North America.

New France French colony that included the St. Lawrence River valley, the Great Lakes region, and until 1713, Acadia (now called Nova Scotia)

The friendship of the Algonquin was helpful to Champlain at the time, but the Iroquois became bitter enemies of France. They later allied themselves with the British and helped cause the downfall of the French empire in Canada.

"The Narrowing of the Waters"

Champlain returned to France to report his findings and was back in North America less than a year later, now with a different fur company. He scouted the east coast as far south as Cape Cod in search of a good location for a settlement. He finally chose the east coast of the Bay of Fundy in the area the French called Acadie (Acadia, now Nova Scotia). After two years, however, the king took away the fur company's trading rights. Champlain's new colony had depended on the fur traders' profits, so Champlain and the other colonists were forced to return to France.

In 1608 the fur company regained its trading rights for a year, and Champlain again crossed the Atlantic. This time he started a colony on the St. Lawrence River at a place the Indians called Kebec, which means "the narrowing of the waters." Champlain named the settlement Québec. He hoped to use it as a base for more exploration. Just as he was about to leave for the west, a group of Algonquin and Huron Indians came to Québec to ask for his help in an attack on the Iroquois. He traveled south with them toward the homeland of the Mohawk Iroquois. On the way, they came upon the lake that now bears Champlain's name.

When the war party finally faced the Iroquois, Champlain's allies gathered around him. As they marched towards the Iroquois, the Algonquin suddenly stepped aside to reveal Champlain, a light-skinned stranger in gleaming steel armor and helmet. The sight surely amazed the Iroquois, who were even more shocked when Champlain raised his small musket and fired four shots. He killed two chiefs and wounded another. The Iroquois scattered in dismay while the Algonquin and Huron celebrated their powerful new ally.

Champlain returned to **New France** from Iroquois country in 1610. He built a trading post at what is now Montréal. By this time, many different fur companies were competing to trade with the Indians. Champlain spent most of his time building friendly relations between the French and the Indians. Yet he made sure that the work of exploration was continued by others even when he could not do it himself. He also sent selected young men, including Etienne BRULÉ, to live with the Indians in order to learn their customs and languages and explore their lands.

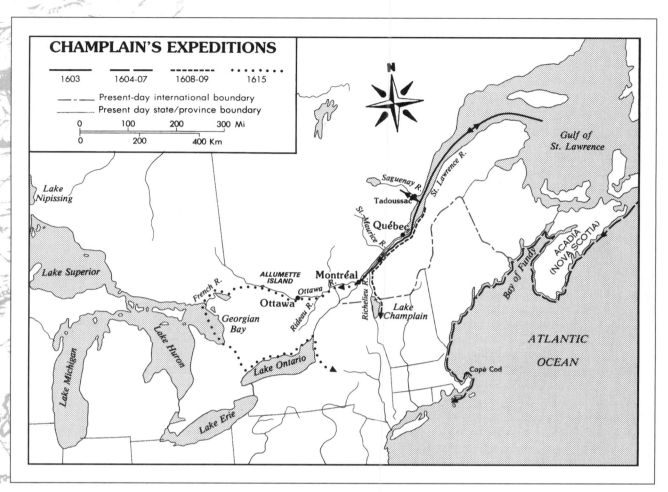

CHAMPLAIN'S EXPEDITIONS

For his work exploring, mapping, and settling French America, Champlain was called the "Father of New France."

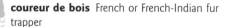

coureur de bois French or French-Indian fur trapper

The Wrong River

In 1613 a **coureur de bois** named Vignau told Champlain that the source of the Ottawa River was a lake that emptied into a northern sea. Vignau, who had lived with the Algonquin, claimed that he had visited this sea and that it could be reached by a journey of 17 days from Montréal. Champlain was again hopeful that he might find a water route to Asia, so he decided to travel up the Ottawa River himself. The trip was difficult—the men sometimes had to tie their canoes to their wrists and pull them over the rapids. Champlain nearly drowned doing this, and all the explorers suffered from swarms of mosquitoes. They also had to struggle around an enormous waterfall at the mouth of the Rideau River, near what is now Ottawa. Champlain wrote that the waterfall "forms an archway nearly four hundred yards in width. The Indians, for the fun of it, pass underneath this without getting wet, except for the spray made by the falling water."

The party arrived at Allumette Island in the Ottawa River, where the Algonquin told Champlain that Vignau's story was false. Vignau was probably talking about Hudson Bay, far to the north. But the Algonquin held back this information because they did not want the French to know too much about the territory. Champlain was furious with Vignau, and the explorers returned to Montréal just three weeks after setting out.

Champlain carried the flag of the French monarchy. The emblem on the flag is called a *fleur-de-lis.*

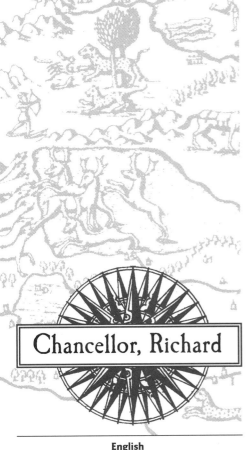

Years of Conflict

Champlain made his last great journey into the North American wilderness in 1615. He got as far west as Georgian Bay on the eastern shore of Lake Huron, where he saw the villages and beautiful lands of his Huron allies. The route that Champlain took to get there became the fur traders' road west for many decades.

At Georgian Bay, Champlain and the Huron prepared for another attack against the Iroquois. Etienne Brulé went as interpreter with a small group of Huron to gather more Indian allies. Champlain and the main Huron war party made their way south around the eastern end of Lake Ontario to the home of the Onondaga Iroquois. The Huron launched a wild and disordered attack and were badly defeated. Even French firearms could not save the day, and Champlain was wounded in the battle. He and his allies were forced to retreat before Brulé and the additional warriors even arrived. Champlain had to spend the winter with the Huron near Lake Ontario. He used the time to visit tribes and explore areas he had not seen before, returning to Montréal in the spring.

In 1616 Champlain sailed back to France, where the king gave him official authority in Québec. Champlain spent the rest of his life trying to make his colony stable and prosperous. In 1629 Québec was captured by the English, and Champlain was taken to England as a prisoner. When the city was given back to France by a treaty in 1633, Champlain returned to Québec, where he lived a short while longer and then died in his late 60s.

Suggested Reading Morris Bishop, *Champlain* (Macdonald, 1949); Samuel Eliot Morison, *Samuel de Champlain: Father of New France* (Little, Brown, 1972); Francis Parkman, *Pioneers of France in the New World* (Little, Brown, 1897).

Chancellor, Richard

English
b 1500s?; England?
d November 10, 1556; Aberdour Bay, Scotland
Opened trade with Russia on White Sea

Northeast Passage water route connecting the Atlantic Ocean and Pacific Ocean along the Arctic coastline of Europe and Asia

The facts of Richard Chancellor's birth and background are unknown, but it is clear that he was a skilled navigator. In 1553 he was assigned to pilot a small English fleet eastward to China by sailing through the seas north of Europe. It was one of the first attempts to find what became known as the **Northeast Passage.** Although he did not find such a route, he made a great success out of a voyage that was in other ways a terrible disaster. Piloting the expedition's only ship that survived the Arctic seas, Chancellor discovered the northern sea route to Russia. His mission opened the first political and commercial relations between Russia and England.

The Muscovy Company

The idea of searching for a Northeast Passage to eastern Asia came from John Dudley, the English duke of Northumberland. Dudley had been lord admiral under England's King Henry VIII. During the reign of Henry's successor, the young and sickly Edward VI, Dudley was a major force on the ruling council that held power. He gathered some 200 traders to form the new Company of Merchant Adventurers. The company had a royal charter that made it the only company allowed to sail along northern trade routes. The merchants hoped to find the same kind of wealth that the Spanish and

Portuguese had gained through their voyages of discovery to the south. The explorer Sebastian CABOT was appointed governor of the company. His first duty was to organize an expedition to China, which Europeans then called Cathay.

Cabot named Sir Hugh Willoughby commander of the voyage and fitted out three ships: the *Bona Esperanza,* captained by Willoughby; the *Edward Bonaventure,* captained by Chancellor; and the *Bona Confidentia.* Willoughby was a curious choice, since he had no experience as a navigator. He was a soldier who had been knighted for his role in a campaign against the Scots in 1544, but more recently he had fallen out of favor with the royal court. After he was removed from his command of a castle on the Scottish border, Willoughby's friends persuaded him to try his luck as a navigator. Cabot must have believed that as long as Willoughby kept the crews in order, Chancellor would take care of the sailing.

Separated at Sea

The expedition left England on May 10, 1553. In July the ships were separated by a storm off the coast of Finnmark (now the northern part of Norway). Chancellor took his ship to the meeting place that had been agreed on in case of such a separation. When Willoughby and the other two ships failed to arrive after seven days, Chancellor sailed on into the White Sea, north of Russia. At the mouth of Russia's Northern Dvina River, he met Russian fishermen. According to an account written in the late 1500s, the Russians were "amazed with the strange greatnesse of his shippe" and began to flee in terror. Chancellor caught up with them and "looked pleasantly upon them, comforting them by signs and gestures." The reassured fishermen soon supplied Chancellor and his crew with food and information.

Trade with Ivan's Russia

When the Russian **czar** Ivan IV (also known as Ivan the Terrible) received word of the visitors, he invited them to his capital, Moscow. Ivan welcomed the chance to open a new trade route with England. At the time, the only way for Russia to trade with western Europe was through the German merchants of central Europe. A sea route to the north would allow Russia and western European countries to trade with each other directly. Ivan gave Chancellor letters for King Edward VI, offering free and open trade between their two nations.

When Chancellor returned to England, he found that Edward had died two months after the expedition had set sail. John Dudley had been executed for opposing the new queen, Mary. The Company of Merchant Adventurers was reorganized as the Muscovy Company, and Queen Mary granted it a new charter.

The company's first agents in northern Russia learned the fate of the Willoughby expedition. Willoughby had sailed his two remaining ships in a wild series of zigzags and landed on Novaya Zemlya, a large island off the north coast of Russia. A leak in one ship forced him to sail back toward England, but the ships were trapped in the Arctic ice on the northern coast of Scandinavia. The men had

czar title of Russian monarchs from the 1200s to 1917

plenty of food, but they were unprepared for the cold. Russian fishermen had found their frozen bodies and turned them over to the agents of the Muscovy Company, who had shipped them back to England.

Chancellor's Second Voyage

In October 1555, Chancellor returned to Russia with the ships *Edward Bonaventure* and *Philip and Mary* to establish English markets there. After completing that task, he sailed for home with the first Russian ambassador to England on board. Off the coast of Scotland, his good luck ran out. A storm dashed the *Edward Bonaventure* against the shore, breaking the ship apart. Chancellor was killed, but the ambassador was one of a few survivors. He was rescued by some Scots, who held him captive for months. After his release, agents of the Muscovy Company escorted him to London.

Thanks to the ambassador's safe arrival, trade relations between Russia and England continued to thrive after Chancellor's death. However, the Muscovy Company still viewed Russia only as a step on the way to the riches of China. Two of Chancellor's crewmen, William Burrough and Arthur Pet, continued the search for a Northeast Passage.

Suggested Reading Foster Rhea Dulles, *Eastward Ho! The First English Adventurers to the Orient: Richard Chancellor, Anthony Jenkinson, James Lancaster, William Adams, Sir Thomas Roe* (Books for Libraries, 1969); Joseph Gamel, *England and Russia: Comprising the Voyages of John Tradescant the Elder, Sir Hugh Willoughby, Richard Chancellor, Nelson, and Others to the White Sea*, translated by John Leigh (reprint, Da Capo, 1968).

Chang Ch'ien. *See Zhang Qian.*

Chang K'ien. *See Zhang Qian.*

Charlevoix, Pierre François Xavier de

French
b October 24, 1682; St.-Quentin, France
d February 1, 1761; La Flèche, France
Traveled St. Lawrence River, Great Lakes, and Mississippi River

Jesuit member of the Society of Jesus, a Roman Catholic order founded by Ignatius of Loyola in 1534

New France French colony that included the St. Lawrence River valley, the Great Lakes region, and until 1713, Acadia (now called Nova Scotia)

Pierre François Xavier de Charlevoix was a French **Jesuit** priest who was sent to North America to search for an inland sea. This fabled "Western Sea" supposedly gave rise to rivers that emptied into the Pacific Ocean. His search led him through the Great Lakes region and down the Mississippi River. Upon his return to France, Charlevoix wrote the first detailed and reasonably accurate account of the interior of eastern North America.

The Explorer-Priest

Charlevoix was born to noble parents in France. He joined the Jesuit order as a young man and became a deacon. In 1705 he was sent to **New France** to teach at the Jesuit college in Québec, on the St. Lawrence River. He returned to France four years later, was made a priest, and took a teaching position in France. In 1719 aides to King Louis XV drew on his knowledge of the St. Lawrence River area. He was asked to recommend boundaries for Acadia (now

When Pierre François Xavier de Charlevoix's expedition arrived in New Orleans in 1722, he found a village of only "a hundred or so shacks."

mission settlement founded by priests in a land where they hoped to convert people to Christianity

latitude distance north or south of the equator

cartographer mapmaker

voyageur expert French woodsman, boatman, and guide

jaundice a condition in which excess bile, a chemical produced by the liver, causes yellowish discoloring of the body

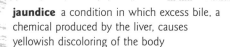

headwaters source of a river

Nova Scotia), a region claimed by both France and England. While involved in this task, he was asked to travel again to New France to research rumors about the Western Sea. This exploration was a secret, so his official reason for going was to examine the Jesuit **missions** in New France.

Charlevoix arrived in Québec on September 23, 1720, and spent the winter there. When spring arrived, he headed west. He traveled up the St. Lawrence River and then canoed through the Great Lakes. In his journal, he described the lakes' coastlines, estimated distances, and made readings of **latitudes.** His extensive notes later helped **cartographers** make more accurate maps of the Great Lakes.

Charlevoix asked everyone he met about the Western Sea. The missionaries and French officials knew nothing helpful, and the **voyageurs** and Indians made up stories. In July 1721 he decided to travel down the Mississippi River and continue his research in Louisiana. He planned to return north a year later to visit the outposts on Lake Superior, since he had not yet been there.

Travels on the Mississippi

On July 29, Charlevoix's party headed from Lake Michigan to the St. Joseph River, but bad weather and illness kept him at Fort St. Joseph for about a month. When he recovered, he continued southwest down the Kankakee and Illinois Rivers before reaching the Mississippi River. Traveling in canoes made of hollowed tree trunks, the men had a rough trip. The river was full of sandbanks and fallen trees, and the weather was unexpectedly cold. They spent Christmas Day in the settlement of Natchez, arriving in New Orleans on January 10, 1722. Charlevoix predicted that although New Orleans then consisted of only "a hundred or so shacks," it would someday be a great city.

The priest made his way to the mouth of the Mississippi River and from there traveled east to the settlement of Biloxi, on the Gulf of Mexico. There he came down with **jaundice.** He decided that in his weakened condition, he could not return up the Mississippi River to Lake Superior as planned. He attempted to return to Québec by sea but was shipwrecked on the Gulf of Mexico. All aboard survived—and spent 50 days walking back to Biloxi.

Return to France

Charlevoix tried again to sail north, but his ship took two months to get from Biloxi to the island of Hispaniola (now Haiti and the Dominican Republic). When he finally reached the island at the end of September, he decided that it was too late in the year to go north to Québec, so he sailed instead for France to make his report.

From the information he had gathered, Charlevoix concluded that the Western Sea lay between 40° and 50° north latitude, and that Indian tribes who lived west of the Sioux Indians probably knew of it. He also believed that rivers flowing west to the Pacific Ocean would be found near the **headwaters** of the Missouri River. He, therefore, offered the king's ministers two proposals for reaching the Western Sea. One was to send an expedition up the Missouri River. The other was to send missionaries to the Sioux Indians in the hope that the missionaries would also make contact with tribes to the west. Charlevoix favored the first plan, but the royal aides chose the second.

As it turned out, the Western Sea did not exist, but this fact would not be known for some time. Even so, Charlevoix's explorations were invaluable. His journal became a classic, for it combined lively stories, sharp descriptions, and scholarly records.

Suggested Reading Charles E. O'Neill, editor, *Charlevoix's Louisiana: Selections from the History and the Journal* (Louisiana State University Press, 1977).

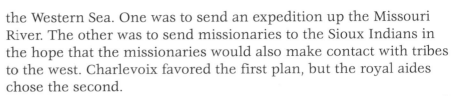

Cheng Ho. See *Zheng He.*

Ch'ien, Chang. See *Zhang Qian.*

Ching, I. See *Yi Jing.*

Chini, Eusebio Francisco. See *Kino, Eusebio Francisco.*

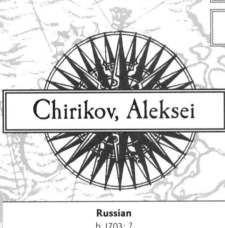

Chirikov, Aleksei

Russian
b 1703; ?
d November 1748; Moscow, Russia
Explored Siberia and Alaska

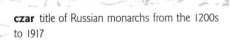

czar title of Russian monarchs from the 1200s to 1917

Captain Commander Aleksei Chirikov was second-in-command to Vitus BERING on two voyages to the Kamchatka Peninsula of eastern Russia, from 1725 to 1730 and from 1733 to 1741. On the second expedition, Chirikov was the captain of the first ship to reach Alaska from Siberia. He landed a day and a half earlier than Bering himself.

The First Kamchatka Expedition
Chirikov earned his job as Bering's chief aide by rising quickly through the ranks of the Russian navy. He graduated from the naval academy in 1721 and was immediately made a sublieutenant, skipping the rank of midshipman. After a brief tour of duty at sea, he returned to the academy to teach navigation. There he attracted the attention of the organizers of Bering's first expedition. They made Chirikov second-in-command, along with Martin Spanberg. In early 1725, Bering led the party east from the Russian capital of St. Petersburg.

The mission had been ordered by **Czar** Peter the Great to determine whether Siberia and the Americas were connected by land or separated by a strait. The plan was to travel by land across the entire width of Asia, about 12,000 miles. Along the way, the original party of 100 men picked up hundreds of laborers. When they arrived at the Siberian port of Okhotsk, they built a ship to carry men and supplies across the Sea of Okhotsk to Kamchatka. They then spent four months crossing Kamchatka, after which they built another ship, the *St. Gabriel,* for the voyage across the northern Pacific Ocean.

On July 13, 1728, the *St. Gabriel* left port and headed northeast along the coastline. Four weeks later, the explorers landed on an

island that Bering named for St. Lawrence. After sailing north for two more days, the ship was out of sight of land—with winter approaching. Chirikov argued that they should press on along the coastline, according to Czar Peter's instructions. Chirikov was willing to spend the winter in the harsh Siberian climate. Spanberg, however, suggested that they continue for only a few more days before turning back.

Bering agreed with Spanberg that it was too dangerous to spend the winter so far north. On August 16, the *St. Gabriel* turned around. Had the next day's weather been clear instead of foggy, the explorers would have seen the western edge of North America, and they would have known that they were in a narrow strait. They spent the winter in Kamchatka and then returned to St. Petersburg to make their report. Although Bering was criticized for not completing his mission, he was placed in command of a second expedition.

The Great Northern Expedition

The new plan was even more ambitious than the first. One of its purposes was to resume the search for the border of Asia and America. In addition, Bering was to investigate the route from Siberia to Japan and organize the charting of the entire Arctic coastline of Siberia. Once again the party was required to travel across Russia, a journey that took them eight years. On June 4, 1741, Bering and Chirikov were at last ready to sail from Kamchatka in search of Alaska.

Shortly after leaving the peninsula, Chirikov's and Bering's ships were separated in a storm. In mid-July, Chirikov reached Prince of Wales Island, off the Alaskan coast in what is now known as the Alexander Archipelago. A landing party went ashore, but these men failed to return. Chirikov then sent a second party, which also disappeared. He never learned their fate. Both parties were apparently taken prisoner by the island's inhabitants. The loss of 20 men with whom he had traveled for eight years seems to have broken Chirikov's spirit. Until then he had held up well under the intense pressure of the difficult journey. The disappearance of the landing parties also meant the end of any land exploration, since the lost men had taken the ship's only two boats.

The End of a Costly Mission

Chirikov was forced to return to Kamchatka, but he had little fresh water aboard his vessel. Without the boats, he could not go ashore to find food or water. Sailing through the Aleutian Islands, he received some water—but not nearly enough—from a group of cautious Aleuts, the people native to the area. By the time he reached Avatcha Bay on the Kamchatka Peninsula, 20 of his men had died from **scurvy,** and he too was suffering from that disease.

The surviving explorers spent the winter recovering. In the spring, Chirikov sailed again to search for his missing commander. He sailed close to what is now Bering Island, just east of Kamchatka. Chirikov could not have known that Bering's men had been on that island since their ship had been blown into its harbor. Bering was one of 30 men who had died on the island over the

scurvy disease caused by a lack of vitamin C and once a major cause of death among sailors; symptoms include internal bleeding, loosened teeth, and extreme fatigue

winter from scurvy and cold weather. The remaining crew members were preparing their escape at about the time Chirikov sailed past. Bad weather forced Chirikov to turn back before reaching Alaska. He settled in Moscow, but he never fully recovered from the scurvy and died at the age of 45.

Many historians, especially Russians, believe that Chirikov was a more able commander than Bering. They point to the fact that he successfully guided his crippled crew back to Siberia, while Bering failed to do so. Chirikov also made more or less the same discoveries as Bering did. Some historians argue that the Bering Strait would have been found on the first expedition if Bering had followed Chirikov's advice.

Suggested Reading Raymond H. Fisher, *Bering's Voyages: Whither and Why* (University of Washington Press, 1978); Gerhard Friedrich Müller, *Bering's Voyages: The Reports from Russia,* translated by Carol Urness (University of Alaska Press, 1986).

Chouart, Médard. See *Groseilliers, Médard Chouart des.*

Cintra, Pêro da. See *Sintra, Pedro de.*

Clapperton, Hugh

Scottish
b May 18, 1788; Annan, Scotland
d April 13, 1827; Sokoto, Nigeria
Explored western Africa

Hugh Clapperton was an outspoken opponent of the African slave trade.

sultan ruler of a Muslim nation

Hugh Clapperton, who explored much of the interior of West Africa, was a member of the first European expedition known to have reached Lake Chad. His attempts to trace the path of the Niger River were not wholly successful, but he still uncovered important information about the river's course.

Clapperton was one of 21 children of a Scottish surgeon. He left home at the age of 13 and took a job as a cabin boy on a trading ship. He joined the navy and had become a lieutenant when he was chosen for his first African expedition, led by Dr. Walter Oudney in 1820. The goal was to discover whether the Niger River ran through Bornu (in modern-day Nigeria). In Tripoli (in what is now Libya) in 1821, they were met by Dixon Denham, an army major who insisted that he had been assigned to lead the expedition.

Clapperton sided with Oudney, and the two went south to Murzuch in the Sahara without Dixon, who conducted his own explorations of villages in the area. Clapperton and Oudney reached Bornu in 1822, and within two months, they had found Lake Chad. There they learned that the Niger ran south rather than east, so they continued southwest to trace the river's path. Oudney died in early 1824, and Clapperton went west to Sokoto (in what is now northern Nigeria). Although Clapperton objected to the local slave trade, he became friendly with Sokoto's **sultan,** Bello.

Clapperton returned to London in 1825 and arranged to have his journal published. He left again for Africa later that year, but shortly after reaching Sokoto, he fell ill and died. His account of this trip was later published by his servant, Richard Lemon LANDER.

Suggested Reading Richard Lander, *Records of Captain Clapperton's Last Expedition to Africa, by Richard Lander, his Faithful Attendant and the Only Surviving Member of the Expedition; with the Subsequent Adventures of the Author* (Cass, 1967); Harry Williams, *Quest Beyond the Sahara* (R. Hale, 1965).

Clark, William

American
b August 1, 1770; Caroline County, Virginia
d September 1, 1838; St. Louis, Missouri
***Explored Missouri River and
northwestern United States***

The even-tempered William Clark was a perfect match for the moody Meriwether Lewis as co-commander of the Corps of Discovery.

William Clark and Meriwether LEWIS were the two commanders of the Corps of Discovery, better known as the Lewis and Clark Expedition. From St. Louis, they followed the Missouri River upstream, crossed the Rocky Mountains, and followed the Columbia River to the Pacific Ocean. In crossing the North American continent, they completed what may be the most important journey of exploration ever launched by the U.S. government. Their successful expedition played a major role in the territorial expansion of the young American nation.

A Family History

William Clark was the younger brother of George Rogers Clark, a hero of the American Revolutionary War. William grew up hearing tales of his older brother's daring deeds. After the war, the Clarks, like many American families, moved west—to what is now the state of Kentucky. From 1789 to 1791, Clark took part in several skirmishes with the region's Indian tribes, who were trying to protect their lands from the settlers' claims. Clark became a lieutenant in the U.S. Army in 1792. He served for four years under General Anthony Wayne during Wayne's military and diplomatic efforts against the Indian tribes of the lower Great Lakes region. During this time, Clark met Meriwether Lewis, a fellow officer in Wayne's army. Clark began to tire of military life, however, and he resigned in 1796, one year after Wayne's final victory over the Indians. After leaving the army, Clark traveled between Indiana and Virginia for several years. In 1803 he received a letter from his former comrade Lewis, who invited Clark to join him in commanding the Corps of Discovery, which had recently been created by President Thomas Jefferson.

The Corps of Discovery

President Jefferson gave the Corps the task of exploring the enormous Louisiana Territory, which the United States had recently bought from France. This transaction, known as the Louisiana Purchase, extended the United States westward from the Mississippi River to the Rocky Mountains. Although the territory had become a part of the United States, the government in Washington, D.C., had little knowledge of the region—and even less control over it. The Corps of Discovery was asked to enter and explore these new lands on behalf of the United States and to describe their geography, natural life, and Indian tribes. Jefferson also wanted Lewis to establish a useful water route between the Mississippi River and the Pacific Ocean. The president hoped to strengthen the American claim on the Pacific Northwest that had begun with the discovery of the Columbia River by Captain Robert GRAY in 1792. That region was also being claimed by Britain and Spain.

In Lewis and Clark's time, the American flag had a stripe and a star added to it for each new state. The flag they carried had 15 stars and 15 stripes.

Lewis requested that Clark be named co-commander of the expedition, and Jefferson agreed. Clark accepted the invitation, and Lewis met him at Clark's home in Kentucky. They traveled to St. Louis, and the Corps camped outside the city during the winter of 1803 to 1804. The expedition started up the Missouri River on May 14, 1804, with about 40 men, including Clark's black slave, York. By autumn they had traveled some 1,600 miles upriver to the villages of the Mandan Indians, in what is now North Dakota. There they built winter quarters and settled in to wait for spring.

Sacajawea and Pomp

During the winter, Lewis and Clark met a French-Canadian fur trader from Montréal named Toussaint Charbonneau, who asked to join the expedition. The trader's wife was a Shoshone Indian named Sacajawea, who had been captured by the Minetaree Indians and sold to Charbonneau. Sacajawea gave birth to a son while in the Corps of Discovery's winter quarters. Lewis and Clark realized that Sacajawea and her child would be valuable as a symbol of the Corps's peaceful mission, since no war party would travel with a woman and child. Sacajawea would be a great help in establishing friendly relations with western Indian tribes.

Clark took an interest in Sacajawea's child, Jean-Baptiste Charbonneau, whom he nicknamed "Pomp." In later years, Clark saw to the education of Pomp and other Charbonneau children. On April 9, 1805, the eight-week-old infant was strapped to his mother's back, and the Corps left the Mandan villages, heading west.

Lewis and Clark

During the long journey up the Missouri River, Lewis and Clark showed why they were an ideal pair of commanders. They had nearly opposite personalities, so that it was easy to divide their duties. Lewis, moody and restless, often went on long side trips off the river to explore and hunt. Meanwhile, the sociable Clark stayed with the boats. He took measurements of the land, drew maps, wrote in his journal, and enjoyed the companionship of the rest of the party.

Despite their differences as people, Lewis and Clark respected each other and worked well together. Clark was the older of the two men, and he had more experience as a frontiersman. He was also a skilled artist who drew birds, fish, and mammals with great care and accuracy. Being so even-tempered, he made the difficult journey a harmonious one.

To the Source of the Missouri River

On the way to the Mandan villages, the Corps had faced several hazards. There were minor nuisances, such as rains, strong winds, and dust storms. The party also had dangerous run-ins with grizzly bears and buffalo. One night a buffalo ran through the center of the camp, nearly crushing some of the sleeping explorers. Clark himself narrowly escaped being bitten by a rattlesnake. Yet once the group had parted from their Mandan hosts, the journey became even more uncomfortable.

portage transport of boats and supplies overland between waterways

Just below the Great Falls (in modern-day Montana), the Missouri River passed through foothills of the Rocky Mountains. The water became shallower, and the weather turned cold and wet. According to Clark, the men were often "up to their armpits in the cold water, and sometimes walk[ed] for several yards over the sharp fragments of rocks." Working with "great patience and humour," the party slowly **portaged** around 10 miles of falls. During the portage, they endured severe heat, thunderstorms, hailstorms, and even a tornado. They were attacked by mosquitoes, and the moccasins on their feet were torn by rocks and thorns, but still they marched on. By July 15, they were back on the river, but 10 days later, they reached a place now called Three Forks. There, 2,300 miles upstream from St. Louis, the river split into three streams. Lewis and Clark named the streams Jefferson, Madison, and Gallatin (after President Jefferson, Secretary of State James Madison, and Secretary of the Treasury Albert Gallatin).

Crossing the Rocky Mountains

From Three Forks, Lewis and a small group set off on foot. Clark, Sacajawea, and the rest of the expedition followed on the Jefferson River. Sacajawea was beginning to recognize landmarks from her youth, but there were still no signs of her tribe, the Shoshone. On August 17, Clark caught up with Lewis, who had made contact with the Shoshone. According to the expedition's journals, Sacajawea began to "dance and show every mark of the most extravagant joy . . . to indicate that [the Indians] were of her native tribe." Sacajawea was taken to a meeting of the tribal council and recognized the chief, Cameahwait, as her brother.

The Shoshone provided the Corps of Discovery with horses and a guide, and Lewis and Clark lost no time in moving on. The two commanders knew that they had a long way to go to reach the Pacific coast before winter. Their guide led them through the valley of the Salmon River and into the Bitterroot Range of the Rocky Mountains. The next month was the most difficult yet, as the explorers hacked their way through the wilderness. A snowfall on September 16 wiped out all signs of the trail they were following. Their troubles worsened when the party's hunters could not find enough food. Some of the explorers began to grow thin and to suffer from **dysentery** and **scurvy.**

dysentery disease that causes severe diarrhea

scurvy disease caused by a lack of vitamin C and once a major cause of death among sailors; symptoms include internal bleeding, loosened teeth, and extreme fatigue

The expedition finally reached the villages of the Nez Percé tribe. There the Shoshone guide left the explorers with two Nez Percé chiefs, who volunteered to take them to the Pacific Ocean. They started down the Clearwater River on October 7, entered the Snake River three days later, and reached the Columbia River on October 16. Thanks to Sacajawea and the Nez Percé, Lewis and Clark received a friendly welcome at all the Indian villages along the way. Around evening campfires, Lewis and Clark entertained their hosts with tobacco and with violin music.

The Pacific and Back

On October 22, the Corps came face to face with the Cascade Mountains, which stood between the explorers and the Pacific Ocean.

tributary stream or river that flows into a larger stream or river

For a map of Clark's route, see the profile of Meriwether LEWIS in Volume 2.

Although the river pass through those mountains is a difficult one, the explorers had had much experience by then and managed it easily. By November 2, they had reached tidewater, the point where salt water from the ocean meets the fresh water of a river. The party followed the river until November 15, when they caught their first sight of the Pacific. They built winter quarters, which they named Fort Clatsop, and heavy rains and snows kept them indoors for months. They spent the time eating, sleeping, and looking at the stormy ocean.

The weather cleared in March, and the Corps retraced its route to the Bitterroot River. Near the site of present-day Missoula, Montana, the group split up again. Lewis led one party through an Indian shortcut to the Missouri River and explored a northern **tributary,** the Marias River. Clark led the other group through Shoshone territory and then down the Jefferson River, to where it meets the Missouri River at Three Forks. From there Clark sent a small party down the Missouri River to Great Falls to join Lewis's men. Clark took his main group south by land to the Yellowstone River and canoed down it to where it joined the Missouri.

Lewis and Clark reunited on August 12 near the mouth of the Yellowstone River. Two days later, at the Mandan villages, they bid farewell to Sacajawea and her family. On September 23, 1806, the Corps of Discovery returned to St. Louis to the cheers of a welcoming crowd.

In the following months, Clark intended to edit the several diaries—including his own and Lewis's—that had been written by members of the party. However, he was not confident of his editing skills and decided to find a professional to complete the task. He eventually hired Nicholas Biddle of Philadelphia, but the accounts of the trip were not published until 1815. In the meantime, Clark was appointed brigadier general of militia and superintendent of Indian affairs for the Louisiana Territory. He proved to be a strong supporter of Indian causes. From 1813 on, he served as governor of the territory and lived in St. Louis until his death at the age of 68.

Although Lewis and Clark did not discover a direct water route to the Pacific, they collected a great deal of information. They gave the government a measurement of the continent's width, a new understanding of the richness of the West, and a claim to the Columbia River region. They also helped the nation to realize that the West was not merely a passageway to Asia but was also quite valuable in itself.

Suggested Reading John L. Allen, *Lewis and Clark and the Image of the American Northwest* (Dover Publications, 1991); Stephen E. Ambrose, *Undaunted Courage: Meriwether Lewis, Thomas Jefferson, and the Opening of the American West* (Simon and Schuster, 1996); Bernard DeVoto, editor, *The Journals of Lewis and Clark* (Houghton Mifflin, 1997); James P. Ronda, *Lewis and Clark Among the Indians* (University of Nebraska Press, 1984).

Claudius, Ptolemaeus. See *Ptolemy.*

Colom, Cristovão. See *Columbus, Christopher.*

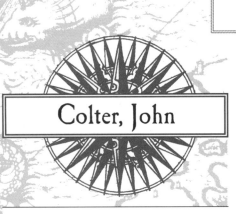

> ## Colombo, Cristoforo. See *Columbus, Christopher.*
>
> ## Colón, Cristóbal. See *Columbus, Christopher.*

Colter, John

American
b 1775?; Staunton, Virginia
d November 1813; near Missouri River
Explored Wyoming, Montana, and Idaho

John Colter was a member of the Corps of Discovery led by Meriwether LEWIS and William CLARK. He joined them on their famous expedition to the American West from 1804 to 1806. Later, Colter made one of the most remarkable journeys ever attempted in North America. He traveled alone through land that is now part of the states of Wyoming, Montana, and Idaho. He spent several months in territory that had previously been seen only by Indians. Among the many wonders he saw were the hot springs, boiling mudholes, and geysers of what is now Yellowstone National Park. Colter was the model for the type of American Mountain Man that would soon flourish in the West.

Travels with Lewis and Clark

Little is known of Colter's life before he joined the Corps of Discovery. Lewis and Clark's historic expedition traveled up the Missouri River to its source in the Rocky Mountains and then made its way to the shores of the Pacific Ocean. Both Lewis and Clark mentioned Colter frequently in their journals. They showed their confidence in him by choosing him for some especially difficult missions.

On the way back to St. Louis in the summer of 1806, the Corps of Discovery met two fur trappers named Joseph Dickson and Forrest Hancock. These two men realized that they would have an easier time finding and trapping beaver if they were guided by someone who knew the territory. They approached Colter, who was given permission by Lewis and Clark to leave the Corps early. Colter guided Dickson and Hancock around the valley of the Yellowstone River for a successful trapping season. He then started back toward St. Louis.

His journey home was interrupted yet again when he reached the mouth of the Platte River (near present-day Omaha, Nebraska). He met a businessman named Manuel Lisa, who was generally disliked but who employed many trappers. Lisa had recognized early that there was money to be made from Lewis and Clark's exploration of the West. In 1807 he hired several former members of the Corps to establish a fur-trading post on the Missouri River. He persuaded Colter to join him, and at Colter's suggestion, he built a fort and trading center where the Yellowstone River flows into the Missouri River. Lisa named it Fort Raymond after his son.

Travels Alone

Lisa's party spent the winter of 1807 to 1808 trapping beaver. Colter, meanwhile, set out on the most extraordinary solo exploration of North America ever attempted by a non-Indian. Lisa had given him two missions: to scout for new beaver territory and to encourage the Crow and other Indian tribes to the south and west to bring

their furs to Fort Raymond. From the route that Colter took, some historians have guessed that he was also looking for Spanish settlers in the southwest who could also become active in the fur trade.

Colter traveled over 500 miles in the middle of winter through the region that is now Wyoming, Montana, and Idaho. Since he left no journals, historians can only guess at the route he took, but they believe that he made a large figure eight to the south and west of Fort Raymond. After leaving the fort, he probably traveled west across the Pryor Mountains, which are part of the Bighorn Mountains. He then turned southwest and crossed the basin of the Bighorn River to the foot of the Absaroka Mountains, just east of modern-day Yellowstone National Park. After that he went southeast, following the mountains to the Shoshone River. Here he saw Yellowstone's hot springs and geysers. Still traveling south, he went around the Absaroka Mountains into the Wind River valley, turned north up the valley, and crossed into Jackson Hole. The magnificent sight of the Grand Teton Mountains stood before him.

By then it was near January, and Colter was probably running low on supplies. He was also quite far from Fort Raymond, and it was unlikely that any tribes living farther away would bring their furs to the fort. However, he decided not to turn back. He crossed the Tetons, probably on a pair of homemade snowshoes. More than a century later, in 1931, a farmer plowing near the Tetons uncovered a rock that had the name "John Colter" scratched on one side and the date "1808" on the other.

Colter turned south after crossing the Tetons, possibly still looking for Spanish settlements. He then quickly turned back north and crossed the Tetons a second time, following them into the area of Yellowstone National Park. Finally, he headed back east to Fort Raymond.

Running for His Life

Colter did not stay at the fort for long. He set out for the area in southwestern Montana where the Missouri River splits into the three lesser rivers that Lewis and Clark named the Jefferson, the Madison, and the Gallatin. He trapped beaver there in October 1808 with a man named John Potts. The two men kept a careful watch for the Blackfoot Indians. They knew that the Blackfoot were looking to avenge the death of two of their tribe who had been killed in a skirmish with Lewis in 1806. Despite their caution, Colter and Potts were surprised by Blackfoot warriors, and Potts was killed instantly when he tried to defend himself.

The Indians tormented Colter by debating what would be the most interesting way of putting him to death. At last they asked him how fast he could run. Colter understood what they were up to, and although he was a swift runner, he told them that he was slow as a turtle. Colter was then stripped naked and given a 30-second head start before the Blackfoot warriors would begin to chase him. To their surprise, Colter quickly dashed ahead and had soon outrun all but one of the Indians. With precise timing, Colter turned around, tripped the warrior, wrestled a spear away from him, and killed him.

Colter then raced for the Jefferson River. He jumped into the water and hid beneath drifting logs while the angry Blackfoot warriors searched for him. That night he swam five miles downstream in freezing waters. When he got out of river, he started running again. A week or two later, he arrived at Fort Raymond, having traveled 150 miles barefoot. His feet were badly cut, and he was naked, sunburned, and covered with insect bites. Colter took a few weeks to regain his strength. Then he set out for another season of fur trapping.

Return to Civilization

Colter had two more narrow escapes from the Blackfoot tribe. In the last encounter, his five companions fell dead around him, cut down by Blackfoot arrows. After this incident, Colter returned to Fort Raymond early in 1810 and announced his retirement with these words: "If God will only forgive me this time and let me off I will leave the country . . . and be damned if I ever come into it again." He was true to his word. A few days later, he got into his canoe and paddled the 2,000 miles to St. Louis, never again to return to the western wilderness.

Colter was well received in St. Louis by his former captain, William Clark. Clark kept a map to which he added information brought him by his former followers when they visited and discussed their travels. He added Colter's information to his map, and this was the closest Colter ever came to providing a record of his extraordinary achievements. Colter was given little credit in his time because he left neither charts nor journals of his travels. In fact, when he described to people in St. Louis some of the wonders he had seen, they found his stories of hot springs and geysers unbelievable. They gave his amazing discovery the mocking name "Colter's Hell."

Despite this early lack of recognition, John Colter has come to be known as possibly the finest example of the American mountaineer and trapper. During his journeys in the American northwest, he showed the incredible physical and mental toughness needed to survive alone for long periods. His act was a hard one to follow for later Mountain Men such as Jedediah SMITH, James BRIDGER, and Christopher CARSON.

Suggested Reading Lillian Frick, *Courageous Colter and His Companions* (L. R. Colter-Frick, 1997); Burton Harris, *John Colter: His Years in the Rockies* (Big Horn Book Company, 1977); Harriet Upton, *Trailblazers* (Rourke, 1990).

Columbus, Christopher

Italian
b August 25 to October 31, 1451?; Genoa, Italy?
d May 20, 1506; Valladolid, Spain
Discovered the Americas

On October 12, 1492, Christopher Columbus carried the flag of Spain onto a small island in the Caribbean Sea. Though he believed he had reached the shores of eastern Asia, he had in fact landed in the Americas and was probably the first European to do so since Leif ERIKSON had arrived 500 years earlier. Columbus's discovery led directly to Europe's intense long-term interest in the American continents. But historians have found it difficult to agree on the details of the voyage and of Columbus's life before it.

Some historians believe that the first European to have reached the North American coast may have been BRENDAN (later known as

Christopher Columbus earned the title "Admiral of the Ocean Sea" for his four crossings of the Atlantic.

Saint Brendan), an Irish monk of the 500s. However, it is better documented that the Norse merchant Bjarni HERJOLFSSON saw the continent in about 986, and his countryman Leif Erikson landed there around 1001. But they had little or no contact with the peoples who had inhabited the Americas for thousands of years. Other Europeans barely noticed or quickly forgot the Norse voyages. In contrast, when Columbus made his landfall in 1492 and met the Arawak and Carib Indians, Europe was ready to listen—and to act. Whether Columbus himself believed that he had found a new continent is just one of the many questions surrounding his history.

Who Was Christopher Columbus?

The questions about Columbus start with his birth. Most historians agree that he was born sometime between August 25 and October 31, 1451. But other dates have been proposed, from as early as 1435 to as late as 1460. Many suggestions have also been made about his birthplace, including the Italian city-state of Genoa, the Greek island of Khíos, the Spanish island of Majorca, and the Spanish province of Galicia. The theory that Columbus was Spanish is based on the 40 known documents and letters that bear his authentic signature. All of these are written in Spanish, as are most of the notes written in the margins of the books he owned. Columbus himself stated that he was born in Genoa, and writers of his time referred to him as Genoese.

Columbus's family background and education are also something of a mystery. Many historians describe Columbus as the eldest of five children born to a poor family of wool weavers. Others have argued that he came from a more distinguished family, perhaps even a royal one. These historians point out that his marriage to a Portuguese noblewoman would have been very unlikely had he not also been a noble.

It is widely agreed that Columbus had little formal education. His son Fernando, who wrote a biography of his famous father, claimed that Columbus had attended a university in Italy. Most scholars doubt that, but it is quite clear that Columbus understood the science and philosophy of his day, especially navigational science. He was also a student of history, a keen observer of his time, and a great reader. In particular, he was influenced by the works of the Greek philosopher Aristotle, as well as several Arab philosophers and astronomers. PTOLEMY's *Guide to Geography* and Marco POLO's *Travels* also helped form his ideas.

Columbus himself may actually have intended to cause all this confusion. Fernando wrote that his father often chose to conceal information about his birth and family. Some scholars have suggested that Columbus may have fought in a battle against Spain as a young man and may have wisely hidden that fact later in life. After all, the Spanish might not have wanted to sponsor the voyages of a former enemy.

Other scholars have recently collected evidence that Columbus was trying to hide Jewish heritage on one side of his family. In the 1490s, life in Spain was very difficult for both Jews and Muslims. In 1492, both groups were forced to convert to Christianity or leave the country. If Columbus had Jewish ancestry, he would probably have preferred to keep it secret. Whatever the truth may be, little is

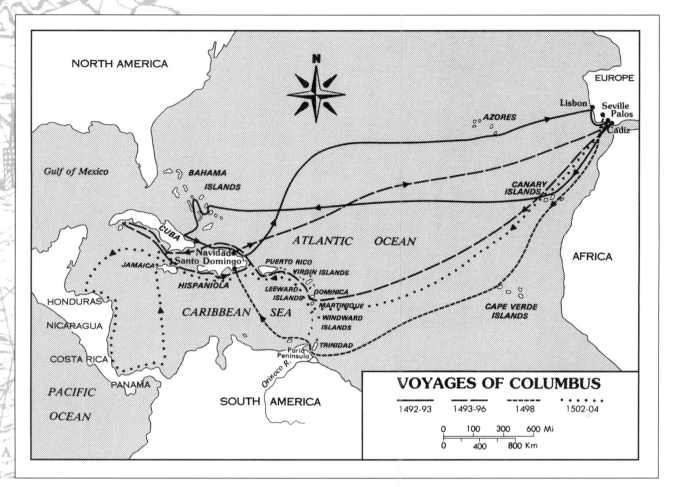

VOYAGES OF COLUMBUS

—— 1492-93	—— 1493-96	------ 1498	······ 1502-04

| 0 | 100 | 300 | 600 Mi |
| 0 | 400 | 800 Km | |

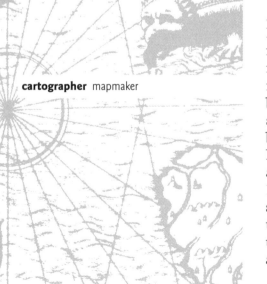

Though he believed that he had reached Asia, Columbus made important discoveries on all four of his voyages to the Caribbean.

cartographer mapmaker

known about Columbus's boyhood or early adulthood. Most historians do agree that he first went to sea at an early age with his brother Bartolomé, who was his closest friend and adviser.

An Early Career at Sea

In 1476 Columbus traveled to Lisbon, Portugal, where there was already a community of Genoese sailors who were known for their navigational skills. Bartolomé was also in Lisbon and had become a noted **cartographer.** The popular story of Columbus's arrival in Lisbon, as related by Fernando, is that he swam ashore after his ship sank during a battle off the coast. Between 1476 and 1485, Columbus sailed with the Portuguese in the Mediterranean Sea and the Atlantic Ocean, as far south as west Africa and as far north as England and Ireland. He may also have made a trip to Iceland in 1477. In 1479 he married the Portuguese noblewoman Doná Felipa Perestrello e Moriz. The couple settled in Madeira, a group of Portuguese islands off the northwest coast of Africa. The next year, they had a son, Diego. Doná Felipa died sometime between 1481 and 1485, and Columbus returned to Lisbon.

"The Enterprise of the Indies"

As early as 1483, Columbus had developed a plan to reach "the Indies," the European name for the Asian lands that were the source

crusade Christian holy war

caravel small ship with three masts and both square and triangular sails

trade winds winds that blow from east to west in the tropics

mutiny rebellion by a ship's crew against the officers

of valuable goods such as spices and silks. European merchants and monarchs were excited about the profits they could make by trading in the Indies. But at the time, the only known sea route was a long and dangerous voyage south and east, around Africa's Cape of Good Hope. Columbus believed that by sailing west across the Atlantic Ocean, he could make the trip more quickly and thus more inexpensively. His proposal for an "Enterprise of the Indies" was rejected in late 1483 by Portugal's King John II. Columbus then decided to take the plan to the king and queen of Spain, Ferdinand and Isabella. Meanwhile, his brother Bartolomé promoted the idea at the royal courts of England and France.

Columbus traveled to the Spanish city of Córdoba in 1485. While there, he had a mistress named Beatriz Enríque de Arana. She gave birth to Columbus's son Fernando in 1488. Columbus presented his plan to the Spanish court on two occasions, but both times a council of experts rejected the project. His ideas were ridiculed by some at the court, but he did receive the support of several powerful people. The voices in his favor included Luis de Santangel, treasurer of the royal household, and Prior Juan Perez, the queen's priest. In 1491 these men convinced Queen Isabella to approve Columbus's voyage.

The primary goal of the expedition was to find a shorter route to the Indies. Columbus was also instructed to look for gold and to convert any foreign peoples he met to Christianity. Columbus obtained a promise that he would be named governor of any lands he might discover during the voyage. He would also be given the title "Admiral of the Ocean Sea." All of these titles would pass to his sons upon his death. Columbus hoped that the wealth he would gain from these lands and titles could pay for a new **crusade** to capture Jerusalem from the Muslims who ruled it.

Unknown Waters

A crew and supplies were gathered in the town of Palos, where three ships were readied for the voyage. The flagship *Santa Maria* and two smaller **caravels,** the *Niña* and the *Pinta,* carried 90 men out of the harbor on August 3, 1492. Columbus commanded the *Santa Maria,* while the *Pinta* and the *Niña* were captained by two brothers, Martín Alonso PINZÓN and Vicente Yáñez PINZÓN. The small fleet stopped at the Canary Islands for repairs to the *Pinta* and improvements to the *Niña.* The ships finally left the Canaries on September 6 for a voyage that would test all of Columbus's skill and determination and the ability of the crews.

Columbus navigated by dead reckoning. With this method, a navigator tracks a ship's position by combining compass readings of direction with careful estimates of speed. Columbus headed west from the Canaries and let the **trade winds** carry him south and west. He believed that it would take 21 days to sail to Cipangu (the island now known as Japan), off the east coast of Asia. But it took longer to cross the Atlantic than Columbus had expected. As the days continued to pass without sight of land, he constantly had to calm the fears of his crew to prevent a **mutiny.** Columbus himself trusted his compass and had faith that the voyage was a holy

This drawing shows Christopher Columbus's first small fleet (from left to right): the *Santa Maria,* the *Pinta,* and the *Niña.*

mission, blessed by God. At last the sailors began to see birds and floating tree branches—signs that land was near.

The original log of the voyage has been lost, but a crew member named Bartolomé de LAS CASAS kept a summary of it. In the log, the sharp-eyed Columbus described weather conditions, water color, cloud formations, plants, and animals. Although the 2,300-mile voyage was made during the hurricane season, Columbus found the sea "like a river and the air sweet. . . ."

Discovery of America

At two hours after midnight on October 12, Rodrigo de Triana, a sailor on the *Pinta,* peered out into the moonlight and sighted land. The voyage had taken a little over 33 days. That morning the ships anchored off an island. Columbus went ashore, named the island San Salvador, and claimed it for Spain. He met and traded with the people living on the island, who called themselves the Arawak. Columbus admired the Arawak and expressed in his journal his belief that they would make good converts to Christianity. He referred to them as Indians, mistakenly believing that he had reached the Indies of eastern Asia.

Columbus had certainly not landed in Asia, but the exact location of San Salvador remains unknown. At least nine islands have been proposed as the site of Columbus's first landfall, including what are now called Watling Island, Samana Cay, and Grand Turk Island. Many scholars today believe that it was Watling Island.

Columbus's personal banner combined the Christian cross with the initials of Ferdinand and Isabella (also spelled Ysabel), the king and queen of Spain.

Columbus left the island on October 14 after trading glass beads for parrots and "a kind of dry leaf." This plant was tobacco, which Europeans were soon to make a habit of smoking. After bringing six or seven Indians on board, Columbus sailed south to look for a king who the Indians said had much gold. He reached three more islands and named them Santa Maria de la Concepción, Fernandina, and Isabella. He then gave up the search for the king and headed west-southwest. He reached what is now Cuba on October 28 and traveled about 360 miles along the coast, observing several good harbors and making more landings. In Cuba he first encountered the fierce Carib, an Indian tribe who were known to eat human flesh. He promised to help the Arawak against this enemy and later enslaved some of the Carib.

On November 21, the captain of the *Pinta,* Martín Alonso Pinzón, took his ship to search for gold without Columbus's permission. The other ships went on, reaching a large island now called Hispaniola. On Christmas Eve, the *Santa Maria* ran aground while exploring the coast and had to be abandoned. A young Indian chief named Guacanaqari sent people to help Columbus and his crew transfer supplies to the *Niña.* The two leaders established a warm friendship. Before leaving the island, Columbus founded the first European settlement in the Americas since the time of the Vikings. He called it La Villa de La Navidad, which means Christmas Town in Spanish, and left 40 Spaniards there.

Soon Pinzón returned with the *Pinta,* and after Columbus had pardoned him for his desertion, the two remaining ships headed back to Spain. A terrible storm struck, but Columbus sailed the violent ocean with great skill. Las Casas was moved to write that "Christopher Columbus surpassed all his contemporaries in the art of navigation."

Columbus's Second Voyage

Columbus and his men received a triumphant welcome in Barcelona, Spain. He immediately began planning a second voyage. Ferdinand and Isabella showed how pleased they were by supplying a much larger fleet than before—17 ships, carrying 1,500 men. The expedition left Cadiz, Spain, on September 25, 1493, with the objectives of creating a permanent trading colony in Asia and converting the Indians to Christianity. Columbus was also ordered to explore Cuba to see whether it was an island or part of the Asian mainland.

On November 3, the island now known as Dominica was sighted. From there Columbus sailed north and west, discovering and naming the Leeward Islands. After spending six days on the large island now known as Guadeloupe, he continued northwest. After charting several other islands Columbus dropped anchor at the island now called St. Croix on November 14. Heading north, he found that St. Croix was the largest in a group of islands he named the Virgin Islands. He then sailed west to Hispaniola. There he found La Navidad in ruins. All the Spaniards left there the previous year had been killed. According to the Indians, the settlers had become violent and abusive toward the Indians, who eventually attacked the

malaria disease that is spread by mosquitoes in tropical areas

Spanish village. Columbus abandoned the site and set up a new colony called Isabella farther east, near an area where the settlers had found gold. He loaded 12 ships with gold and sent them back to Spain with a request for additional supplies.

Columbus spent the next few months exploring Hispaniola and building fortresses throughout the island. He then sailed to Cuba. After six weeks of picking his way among the small islands and dangerous shoals along the Cuban coast, he reached Cape Cruz, the island's southernmost point. Columbus was confident—but mistaken—in his belief that Cuba was not an island but a peninsula of the Asian mainland. He left off his exploration of Cuba and sailed east and south, finding the island now known as Jamaica. Already suffering from arthritis, Columbus then contracted **malaria.** He fell into a feverish daze and was forced to return to Isabella. The colony was in disorder, and the settlers had enslaved local Taino Indians in the effort to mine gold. Fortunately, his brother Bartolomé arrived from Spain with supplies and helped to restore calm. Columbus lay ill at Isabella for five months. He moved the colonists from Isabella to a new colony, Santo Domingo, and put Bartolomé in charge. Then he returned to Spain to defend himself against his enemies at court.

Columbus's Third Voyage

When he arrived in Spain, Columbus found that the king and queen still had confidence in him. They approved a third expedition to find the mainland that Columbus believed lay south of the islands he had discovered. After two years of preparation, Columbus left in 1498 with six ships. He sent three of the ships to supply Hispaniola and took the other three south to the Cape Verde Islands, off the coast of western Africa. From there he sailed west, reaching the island he named Trinidad on July 31. He followed its southern shore and then entered the Gulf of Paria. Columbus observed fresh water flowing into the gulf from northern branches of the Orinoco River and realized that he was sailing along the coast of a continent, now known as South America. He wanted to explore more of this coast, but he decided to go to Hispaniola instead. On the way, he landed on the Paria Peninsula (in present-day Venezuela), becoming the first European to set foot in South America.

When he reached Santo Domingo, Columbus had to put down a rebellion among the colonists. As a result, complaints were made against him to the royal court. The Spanish monarchs sent Francisco de Bobadilla to Hispaniola to investigate these complaints. Bobadilla had both Columbus brothers arrested and sent back to Spain for trial. Although they were found innocent of any wrongdoing, neither was allowed to return to Hispaniola for some time.

Columbus's Last Voyage

Since the time of Columbus's first discoveries in 1492, other explorers had crossed the Atlantic as well. Many people were coming to believe that Columbus had not reached Asia at all but had discovered a "new world." Columbus was eager to prove that he had indeed reached the Indies, so he asked Ferdinand and Isabella for

permission to lead another voyage. He intended to search for a water route leading to the Indian Ocean. He was allowed to sail on May 11, 1502, with four ships and 140 men. The crew included his son Fernando, and Bartolomé commanded one of the ships.

Columbus followed the route he had taken on his second voyage, sighting the island now called Martinique on June 15. He wound his way through the Leeward Islands, past what is now Puerto Rico to Hispaniola. The settlement's new governor, Nicolás de Ovando, refused him permission to land at Santo Domingo. Columbus sailed on, passing between Jamaica and Cuba and reaching the coast of (modern-day) Honduras in August. He tried to explore the coast to the east. Bad weather forced him to turn south along the coast of the area that is now Nicaragua and Costa Rica. When he reached what is now Panama, the Indians there told him that he had reached a narrow piece of land between two seas. Columbus believed that it was the Malay Peninsula in Asia. He was sure that China lay to the north, with India across the sea on the other side of the land. He was about to try to prove his theory, but he postponed his plans after finding gold in Panama.

In February 1503, Columbus attempted to found a settlement at Santa Maria de Belén in Panama, but fighting with the Indians cost him a ship and the lives of 10 men. He set sail and encountered a storm that wrecked one ship and damaged the other two badly. Unable to continue to Hispaniola, Columbus landed at St. Ann's Bay, Jamaica. Stranded, he sent two canoes carrying 12 crewmen and 20 natives to Santo Domingo for help. It took almost a year for a rescue mission to arrive. By then Columbus was completely exhausted and discouraged. He was suffering from arthritis and probably **gout** as well. He returned to Spain in November 1504 and spent the rest of his life trying to obtain the titles and awards that had been promised to him.

Passing into History

Columbus died on May 20, 1506 in Valladolid, Spain. His son Fernando wrote that the explorer's death was caused by "the gout, and by grief at seeing himself fallen from his high estate, as well as by other ills." Columbus's death went largely unnoticed at the time. His fame had been overshadowed by that of Amerigo VESPUCCI, the explorer who had declared that Columbus had discovered a "new world." Scholars still debate whether Columbus himself ever came to the same conclusion.

One final mystery hangs over the story of Columbus. To this day, no one knows where his remains are buried. They were moved from his home to Seville in 1509, to Santo Domingo in 1541, to Havana in 1796, and back to Seville in 1899. There are at least eight containers that supposedly hold his remains, in places as far apart as Rome and New York City. Though much about his life and death is uncertain, Columbus's place among the first rank of explorers is secure.

Suggested Reading Silvio A. Bedini, editor, *The Christopher Columbus Encyclopedia* (Simon and Schuster, 1992); Fernando Colón, *The Life of the Admiral Christopher Columbus* translated by Benjamin Keen (Rutgers University Press, 1959); Robert H. Fuson, translator, *The Log of Christopher Columbus* (International Marine

gout disease characterized by painful swelling of the joints

Publishing Company, 1987); Samuel Eliot Morison, *Admiral of the Ocean Sea* (Little, Brown and Company, 1942); Paolo Emilio Taviani, *Christopher Columbus: The Grand Design* (Orbis, 1985); John Boyd Thatcher, *Christopher Columbus: His Life, His Work, His Remains,* 3 volumes (AMS Press, 1967).

Conti, Nicolò de

Italian
b 1395?; Chioggia?, near Venice, Italy
d 1469; Venice?, Italy
Traveled throughout southern Asia

caravan large group of people traveling together, often with pack animals, across a desert or other dangerous region

Religion has often played a major role in exploration and in the records left by explorers. This was true of Nicolò de Conti, although he was a merchant and not a priest. He had traveled to southern Asia and was passing through Egypt on his way home to Italy when he was forced to abandon his Christian beliefs and convert to Islam. Once back in Italy, he begged the pope to forgive him. The pope agreed—as long as Conti would give a detailed account of his travels to the pope's secretary. That account, later published in English as *India in the Fifteenth Century,* is a valuable record of life in southern Asia during the Middle Ages.

Travel to India

Conti was born in Italy but lived as a young man in the city of Damascus in Syria. There he worked as a merchant and learned to speak Arabic. In 1414 Conti and 600 other merchants set off in a **caravan** to the east. They traveled along the Euphrates River, through Baghdad (now in Iraq) to the port city of Basra. From Basra they crossed the Persian Gulf to Hormuz. Conti eventually reached Calacatia, a port on the Indian Ocean, where he stayed long enough to learn the Persian language. He next sailed with a group of merchants to the Indian state of Cambay. He married an Indian woman who traveled south with him along the coast to Goa. From there he turned inland to visit the kingdom of Deccan. Some historians believe that he was the first European to enter the Indian interior. It is not clear whether Conti crossed to India's east coast by land or water. In any case, he visited Ceylon (now Sri Lanka), remained there for a year, and became the first European to describe how cinnamon was grown there.

Sailing east across the Bay of Bengal, Conti found cannibals on the Andaman Islands. Then he landed on the coast of Burma (now Myanmar). Turning northwest, he sailed up the Ganges River, coming to what he called "cities unvisited." He arrived at a place "where aloes, gold, silver, precious stones and pearls were to be found in abundance." On this inland part of his journey, he visited many of the same places that Marco Polo had explored about 150 years earlier. Conti reported seeing tattooed men, elephant hunts, pythons, and rhinoceroses.

Lands of Spice

Conti once again returned to the sea, this time sailing to Sumatra and Java (now part of Indonesia). He and his wife now had children, and the family stayed on these islands for nine months. But Conti thought the people there were "more inhumane and cruel than any other people." During this time, he visited the Banda Islands, the only place in the world where cloves were then grown. The islands were also an important source of nutmeg and other spices.

From Java, Conti may have sailed up the eastern coast of China as far as Nanking. Some scholars, on the other hand, say that he then began his homeward journey, passing through Ciampa (now Thailand) on his way back to Ceylon. His return trip next took him across the Arabian Sea to Aden, and then up the Red Sea to Jidda (in present-day Saudi Arabia). At Jidda, Conti, his family, and his many servants began an overland trek to Cairo, Egypt.

Hardships in Cairo

Cairo is probably where Conti was forced to give up his Christian faith and adopt the Islamic religion. Conti felt that this act was a terrible sin, but he did it to protect his family. In the end, however, his wife, two of his children, and all of his servants died in Cairo from the **plague.**

In 1444 Conti finally reached Italy. The written record of his great adventure describes his return in simple words: "At last, as fortune would have it, after all his journeys by land and by sea, he arrived with his two surviving children in his native city of Venice." In 25 years, he had traveled almost as widely as Marco Polo. But unlike Polo, Conti did not have the protection of a powerful prince during his journey. It is remarkable that Conti survived his trip at all.

The record he provided helped fill in some of the blank spaces in Europe's maps of the East. Thirteen years after he returned to Venice, the great Italian mapmaker Fra Mauro began to draw his map of the world. There is no doubt that Conti's report supplied many of the details on Mauro's map.

Suggested Reading Norman Penzer, editor, *The Most Noble and Famous Travels of Marco Polo, Together with the Travels of Nicolò de' Conti* (A. and C. Black, 1937).

Cooes, Bento de. See *Goes, Bento de.*

Cook, Frederick Albert

American
b June 10 1865; Hortonville, New York
d August 5, 1940; New Rochelle, New York
*Explored Arctic and Antarctica;
claimed to reach North Pole*

Dr. Frederick Albert Cook was one of the world's most colorful explorers—and one of the most controversial. In the autumn of 1909, he was honored around the world as the first person to have reached the North Pole. This American physician was briefly the most famous explorer in the world. Fourteen years later, he was sitting in prison, and his claims of reaching the pole had been viciously attacked by his rival, Robert PEARY. Cook's ruined reputation was the result of a long and bizarre story.

Boyhood in Brooklyn, Adulthood in the Arctic

Growing up in New York's Catskill Mountains, Cook learned to appreciate nature's beauty and danger. He also learned to survive difficult times after his father died and his family moved to Brooklyn, New York. He worked at a vegetable stand while attending night school, then delivered milk every morning while attending medical school. The young doctor joined his first Arctic expedition in 1891,

plague contagious disease that quickly kills large numbers of people

After returning from his harrowing Arctic adventures, Frederick Cook said that he felt "exotic" in civilized society and was "native to Nowhere."

anthropologist scientist who studies human societies

Inuit people of the Canadian Arctic, sometimes known as the Eskimo

sledge heavy sled, often mounted on runners, that is pulled over snow or ice

depot place where supplies are stored

when he answered an advertisement placed by the Arctic explorer Robert Peary. Cook was hired as a medic for Peary's crossing of northern Greenland.

Two years later, Cook led his own expedition to Greenland aboard the ship *Zeta*. He returned the next year on the *Miranda*. That ship was crippled by an iceberg, ruining Cook's chance to lead an important scientific mission. For the next three years, Cook practiced medicine, but he then sailed with the Belgian Antarctic Expedition in 1898. Cook served as the surgeon, photographer, and **anthropologist,** and he was part of the first crew ever to spend a winter in Antarctica. On this voyage, Cook worked with the Norwegian explorer Roald AMUNDSEN, who thought highly of his American shipmate. After Cook and Amundsen saved the expedition from near disaster, Amundsen credited Cook with the success.

In 1901 Cook sailed north at his own expense to treat Peary, who had fallen ill during his first attempt to reach the North Pole. Cook arrived at Ellesmere Island, Canada, and found Peary in a sour and difficult mood after his failure to reach the pole. Cook swore that he would never work with his former employer again.

The First Controversy

While Peary continued his efforts in the Arctic, Cook set out on a new adventure. In 1903 he led an unsuccessful attempt to climb Alaska's Mount McKinley, the highest mountain in North America. Three years later, he tried again with Edward M. Barrill. The two men claimed to have succeeded, but recent research suggests that Cook faked a photograph showing himself at the mountain's peak.

Racing to the Pole

In 1907, while Peary was planning his final trek to the North Pole, Cook and a wealthy friend quickly made a plan of their own. They wanted the fame that would surely come to the first explorer to reach the pole. For Cook, there would also be the pleasure of robbing Peary of that great honor.

The ship *John R. Bradley* dropped off Cook and his supplies at Annoatok, 32 miles north of Etah, Greenland, on August 27, 1907. The following February, Cook began a crossing of Ellesmere Island with nine **Inuit** companions and 103 sled dogs. By March 18, he was ready to venture onto the frozen polar sea with only two of the Inuit guides. In addition to **sledges** and dogs, Cook used a folding boat made of canvas to cross the open channels of water that cut through the ice pack.

Cook claimed that on April 21, 1908, he reached the North Pole, preceding Peary's own claimed success by a year. The return trip proved even more dangerous. Cook and the two Inuit were low on supplies by the time they reached land. They were also far off course, nowhere near their supply **depot.** The three men wintered in an underground shelter near Ellesmere Island. They lived off the land, using the traditional methods of the Inuit, and returned to Annoatok in April 1909.

Claims and Questions

News of Cook's adventure did not reach Europe or the United States until September 1, 1909, just five days before Peary sent word of his own success. During that time, Cook arrived in Copenhagen, Denmark, where he was given a hero's welcome. Within days, however, Peary challenged Cook's claim, sparking a bitter and vicious controversy that continues even today.

Each explorer was backed by rival newspapers that kept the feud alive in an effort to sell papers. In fact, there were holes and contradictions in the evidence both men offered to support their claims. By the start of World War I in 1914, most scholars—and the public—thought that Cook's account was less believable than Peary's. Cook's biggest problem may have been conflicting statements made by his two Inuit companions. Peary's claim, on the other hand, was backed by the U.S. government agencies that had supported his expedition.

Continued Troubles

Cook did not give up after the controversy with Peary, even though most people now considered him a tremendous liar. In 1915 he traveled around the world, and later he made money in the Texas oil business. His dealings led to legal problems, and he was accused of selling worthless real estate. In 1923 he was found guilty of mail fraud and sentenced to a federal prison at Leavenworth, Kansas. Cook held up fairly well behind bars, considering all he had been through. He worked as a doctor in the prison hospital and edited the prison's newspaper. He also wrote about his experiences in the Arctic. Respected by his fellow inmates and the prison authorities alike, he was paroled in 1929.

Shortly before his death in 1940, Cook received a pardon from President Franklin D. Roosevelt, erasing his criminal record. No one has denied that Cook's survival in the hostile Arctic environment was an impressive feat. But nothing has erased the blemishes on his reputation as an explorer.

Suggested Reading Robert M. Bryce, *Cook and Peary: The Polar Controversy, Resolved* (Stackpole Books, 1997); Frederick Albert Cook, *My Attainment of the Pole* (Polar, 1911) and *Return from the Pole*, edited by Frederick J. Pohl (Pellegrini and Cudahy, 1951); Andrew A. Freeman, *The Case for Doctor Cook* (Coward-McCann, 1961); William R. Hunt, *To Stand at the Pole: The Dr. Cook-Admiral Peary North Pole Controversy* (Stein and Day, 1982).

Cook, James

English
b October 27, 1728; Marton-in-Cleveland, England
d February 14, 1779; Hawaii
Explored Pacific Ocean, searched for Antarctica

scurvy disease caused by a lack of vitamin C and once a major cause of death among sailors; symptoms include internal bleeding, loosened teeth, and extreme fatigue

Captain James Cook is one of the outstanding figures in the history of exploration. He made great contributions to our knowledge of the Pacific Ocean, including its islands, waters, and peoples. He also conquered **scurvy,** a disease that had long troubled sailors, and helped turn exploration into a science.

Cook may have been the greatest explorer of the 1700s, but he came from quite a humble background. He was the second of nine children born to a poor Scottish couple in a small farming village. At the age of 13, he dropped out of school to help his father in the fields and at 14 went to work for a grocer. Soon after that, the future Captain Cook went to sea.

Born in a poor English village, James Cook went on to sail around the world three times and become honored as the greatest explorer of the 1700s.

longitude distance east or west of an imaginary line on the earth's surface; in 1884 most nations agreed to draw the line through Greenwich, England

specimen sample of a plant, animal, or mineral, usually collected for scientific study or display

From Cabin Boy to Commander

Cook began his career as a cabin boy aboard the *Freelove,* a coal-hauling ship. He learned to navigate in the rough Baltic Sea and North Sea. He came to appreciate these sturdy ships as well as the seafaring life. The owner of the *Freelove* was about to promote Cook when talk spread of war against France and Germany. The young sailor then enlisted in the British Royal Navy.

Smarter and more determined than most sailors, Cook quickly worked his way up through the ranks. During the Seven Years' War against France, he was given command of the *Mercury* and sent to map the St. Lawrence River in Canada. His work helped the British capture Québec, the French city on the river.

Back in England, Cook married Elizabeth Batts in 1762. He then returned to sea. This time he went to Newfoundland, Nova Scotia, and Labrador. He drew charts of the Grand Banks that were very helpful to fishermen. While he was there, he observed a solar eclipse and used it to calculate Newfoundland's **longitude.** This achievement brought Cook to the attention of the Royal Society, an organization of British scientists.

Science on the Seas

Astronomers knew that in the summer of 1769, the planet Venus would pass across the face of the sun. This rare event could be seen from the island of Tahiti in the southern Pacific Ocean. The Royal Society wanted to send a ship to Tahiti to make observations. The government realized that such a mission would also be an ideal opportunity to search for *Terra Australis Incognita.* This Latin term means "the unknown southern continent." Many scientists of the 1700s believed that a large landmass must exist in the southern half of the earth to balance the known lands of the north.

Cook was chosen to command the *Endeavour* on a voyage to Tahiti. He was also given secret orders to search for the southern continent. The ship was a coal hauler like those which Cook had sailed as a boy, and its crew of 94 included the naturalists Joseph BANKS and Daniel Carl Solander. The expedition left Britain on August 26, 1768, crossed the Atlantic, and sailed around South America's Cape Horn. Cook stopped at Tierra del Fuego and other sites along the way so that Banks and Solander could gather plant and animal **specimens.**

Knowing how deadly disease could be on such a long journey, Cook insisted that the ship be kept clean. He also made sure that the crew ate plenty of fresh vegetables, citrus fruits, and sauerkraut. At first the sailors resisted eating the sauerkraut. But after seeing it served and eaten at the officers' dining table, the other men began to request it for themselves. For the first time in the history of naval exploration, not a single man died from scurvy.

Paradise of the South Seas

On April 13, 1769, the ship anchored at Matavai Bay, on the northwest side of Tahiti. There Cook directed the construction of Fort Venus, the crew's base for their three-month stay. During that time, Cook explored the entire island, closely observing the carefree

circumnavigation journey around the world

lifestyle of the Tahitians. He recorded details of burial ceremonies, tattooing rituals, and other aspects of the island's society.

Cook was strict but fair with his crew during their time on Tahiti, just as he was at sea. The men worked hard, but Cook also allowed them to enjoy the relaxed Tahitian social life. When it came time to leave the beautiful island, only two men thought of deserting the ship and staying behind. It is clear that Cook demanded and received the loyalty and trust of his crew. His leadership may also explain why the crew was so willing to continue the expedition, even though Cook had not yet revealed their mission.

With a Tahitian guide named Tupia, Cook sailed west to other islands near Tahiti. He claimed the entire group for England and named them the Society Islands. From there he sailed south, and in October 1769, he rediscovered the islands that Abel TASMAN had called Staaten Land in 1642. Cook spent several months circling the two main islands, proving that they were not the tip of *Terra Australis Incognita.* Today the islands are known as New Zealand, and the waterway between them is called Cook Strait. The naturalists explored the islands in great detail. Their task was difficult, since the islands' fierce Maori warriors were not as welcoming as the Tahitians.

Avoiding Disaster in Australia

Leaving New Zealand, Cook sailed west again, reaching the unexplored east coast of New Holland (now Australia). He landed at a place that Banks and Solander called Botany Bay because they collected an astonishing number of plants there. After a week, the *Endeavour* headed north as Cook guided the sturdy vessel through the maze of sea coral now known as the Great Barrier Reef. Despite his skill, the ship struck the reef and began to take on water through a gash in the hull.

The accident could have been a disaster, but Cook and his crew stayed calm and kept the ship afloat. The men patched the hole and managed to reach the Australian shore, where they made permanent repairs. The spot where they landed is today the site of Cooktown. The ship sailed again after a month of repairs. Cook headed north and charted some 2,000 miles of the Australian coastline before setting course for England. He sailed by way of New Guinea, Batavia (present-day Jakarta, Indonesia), the Indian Ocean, and Africa's Cape of Good Hope. This route completed Cook's first **circumnavigation.**

The Southern Continent

Cook came home on July 12, 1771. A year and a day later, he set sail once again. Some people, especially the scientist Alexander DALRYMPLE, still believed that *Terra Australis Incognita* existed somewhere in the south seas. Dalrymple, a wealthy Scottish nobleman, wanted to lead the search expedition. But thanks to reforms of the navy initiated by Admiral George ANSON, the more qualified Cook was given command.

This time his ship was the *Resolution,* and he was joined by a second ship, the *Adventure.* The two vessels sailed down the African

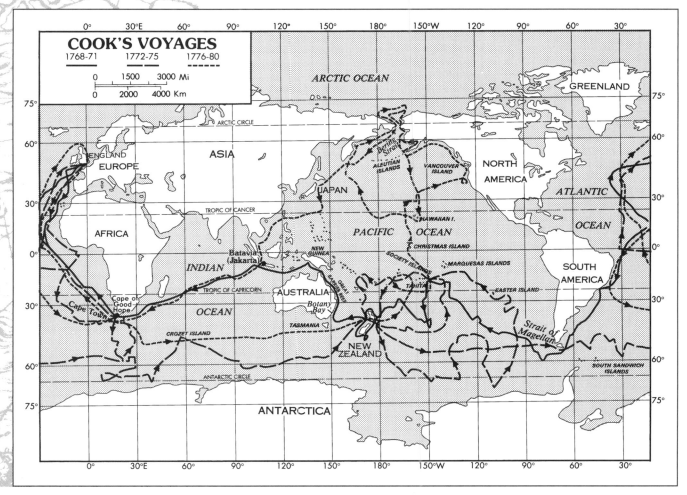

COOK'S VOYAGES

1768-71	1772-75	1776-80

On his three voyages, Cook added dozens of new islands to European maps of the world.

coast. Instead of rounding the Cape of Good Hope into the Indian Ocean, they continued south, becoming the first crews to sail into Antarctic waters. Cook led the ships south through bitter cold and icebergs, but the broken ice soon turned solid, and Cook was forced to return north—much to the crews' relief. In a dense fog, the two ships became separated, but they met as planned in New Zealand three months later. In New Zealand, a landing party from the *Adventure* disappeared, probably killed by Maori warriors.

Cook spent the following months sailing the unknown waters between Australia and South America. He hoped to find *Terra Australis Incognita,* but all he saw was endless ocean and a few small islands. In August 1773, he returned to Tahiti for a month. He then visited other Society Islands, the Friendly (or Tonga) Islands, and New Zealand. In the meantime, the ships became separated and failed to meet again. The *Adventure* returned to England.

In November 1774, Cook turned the *Resolution* to the south once again. By December the ship was surrounded by icebergs, and Cook was suffering from a problem with his gallbladder, a gland near the liver. One of the naturalists on board, Johann Reinhold FORSTER, sacrificed his pet dog so that Cook would have the meat he needed to regain his strength.

When he recovered, Cook sailed for warmer waters. The crew hoped that they were finally heading home, but Cook made another

latitude distance north or south of the equator

turn southward. By the end of the voyage, he had sailed around the world at a **latitude** very far to the south. Although he could not get past the floating polar ice, he was able to rule out the existence of a major southern continent. Even so, he correctly suspected that a polar landmass could exist. In his journal, he wrote: "That there may be a continent or large tract of land near the Pole I will not deny; on the contrary I am of the opinion that there is, and it is probable that we have seen a part of it."

From Ice to Fire

At that point, Cook could have turned the *Resolution* back toward England, but he thought that he could still learn more about the Pacific. In early March 1775, the *Resolution* reached Easter Island and made its first landfall in four months. Cook was the first European to visit the island since the Dutchman Jacob ROGGEVEEN had discovered it 53 years before. Cook found about 700 people living on this island of fiery volcanoes. The people were friendly, but they had a practice of stealing from the Europeans nearly anything they could carry. Cook noted with interest that the islanders could easily communicate with Oddidy, a Tahitian whom he was taking to England. This led Cook to believe that the many island peoples of the southern Pacific were related.

After three days on Easter Island, Cook sailed north to the Marquesas, another group of islands that Europeans had already discovered but had not yet charted. He then sailed to Tahiti, where he and his crew received a warm welcome. Continuing west, he charted and named the New Hebrides, New Caledonia, and Norfolk Island. Next, he sailed east to return home by way of Cape Horn, the tip of South America, just in case he had missed something in his search for *Terra Australis Incognita*. He did not find the continent, but he did find and name South Georgia Island and the South Sandwich Islands.

The Third Voyage Begins

Three years and 18 days after leaving England, the *Resolution* returned to its harbor, having sailed more than 70,000 miles. Cook had lost only four men, none from scurvy. He received many honors and was promoted to captain, but he did not take much time to enjoy his increasing fame. He began recruiting for yet another voyage. Since Cook had just answered one of his day's greatest geographical questions, the British navy asked him to answer another. His new mission was to search for a **Northwest Passage.**

The navy sent two expeditions to search for the passage's Atlantic entrance. Meanwhile, Cook was to explore the Pacific north of the Bering Strait, which separated Asia and North America. He once again commanded the *Resolution,* leaving Plymouth, England, along with the *Discovery* on July 12, 1776.

The two ships sailed south to Cape Town (in present-day South Africa) and then headed into the southern Indian Ocean, where they found a group of rocky islands. Cook named them the Crozet Islands after the French explorer who had first sighted them four years earlier. He continued eastward, sailing for nearly a month through thick fog, until he reached Tasmania, an island south of

Northwest Passage water route connecting the Atlantic Ocean and Pacific Ocean through the Arctic islands of northern Canada

This 1902 oil painting by the Australian artist E. Phillips Fox (1865–1915) is titled *The Landing of Captain Cook at Botany Bay 1770.*

Australia, in January 1777. He anchored for four days at Adventure Bay and observed what he called the "wretched" lives of the islanders.

Lands Familiar and Unknown

Cook made several stops in the South Seas: at New Zealand, Tahiti, the Friendly Islands, and a group now known as the Cook Islands. Tensions ran high during the few weeks he spent on New Zealand. The Maori believed that Cook had come to take revenge for the deaths of the *Adventure*'s landing party. Fortunately, there were no major incidents on this visit.

Cook spent most of the summer and fall as an honored guest throughout Polynesia, the vast island region of the southern Pacific. He offered the islanders gifts of livestock from England, and again he took the opportunity to study the peoples' customs. He was the first European to note the islanders' idea of taboo, meaning something forbidden by culture or religion. He also recorded his disgust with the human sacrifices and cannibalism he saw even in Tahiti. He left the Society Islands in early December and sailed north.

On December 25, the British landed on a deserted island just above the equator and named it Christmas Island (now called Kiritimati). On January 20, 1778, they reached a group of islands that Cook named after the earl of Sandwich. These islands are now the American state of Hawaii. Cook was probably the first European to see them.

Captain Cook carried this version of the British Union Jack around the world.

On this visit to the Sandwich Islands, Cook stayed less than two weeks. He noted the similarities between the people who lived there and those on other Polynesian islands, and he wondered how they had come to inhabit such a vast expanse of ocean. During their short stay, the British sailors also made a strong impression on the islanders, who included the pale-skinned strangers in their spoken histories.

The Arctic Ocean

The expedition spent the spring and summer of 1778 charting the North American coast from what is now Oregon to the Bering Strait, searching for the Northwest Passage. Cook anchored his ships in what is now called Nootka Sound, where he and his men were greeted by Nootka Indians in elaborate costumes—headdresses, masks, and painted faces.

Continuing north and west, the *Resolution* and the *Discovery* sailed past the Pacific coasts of Canada and southern Alaska. The farther west they sailed, the less convinced Cook was that he would find a clear passage to the Atlantic Ocean. He sailed along the Aleutian Islands and on into the Bering Sea, heading north until ice blocked his path. With the ships taking a beating from the surrounding ice, Cook decided to head for the safety and warmth of the south to make repairs. He set course for the Sandwich Islands, planning to renew his search for the Northwest Passage the following summer.

Trouble in Hawaii

When he anchored in Kealakekua Bay, he was greeted by crowds of islanders bearing gifts. On that day, January 17, 1779, Cook made the last entry in his journal. The events of the next few weeks, up to the captain's death, were recorded only by his crew.

At first the visit went well. To the Hawaiians, Cook was a god who had come to earth by sailing into their sacred bay. The island chiefs feasted with him and called him "Orono" or "Lorono," the name of their god of peace and prosperity. After two weeks or so, Cook tried to leave Hawaii, but bad weather forced him to return the ships to the bay.

Although the Hawaiians thought that Cook was a god, they did not hesitate to steal from the crew. At his many stops in the Pacific islands, Cook had grown accustomed to the islanders' habit of thievery. They simply did not think of objects as property that someone owned. Cook usually punished offenders to prevent further thefts, but he was never harsh, and he avoided the use of real force. But on Hawaii, the islanders overran the *Resolution* and *Discovery,* practically trying to take the ships apart. Frustrated, Cook allowed his men to display their weapons. The Hawaiians seemed more surprised than frightened by this threat, and the number of thefts increased. On the morning of February 14, 1779, one of the ship's small boats was missing, and Cook decided that things had gone too far.

The Death of Captain Cook

Cook decided to bring a Hawaiian chief on board and hold him until the boat was returned. When Cook went ashore, a great crowd of islanders gathered. Offshore, crewmen waited in boats, holding their guns. Tensions rose on both sides. When some of the islanders advanced toward the British landing party, a crewman fired, killing an important chief. Cook turned around to tell his men to hold their fire, but at that moment, the Hawaiians fell on him in a fury. They stabbed him in the back and then hacked his body to pieces. Four of Cook's crewmen died with him.

The captain's death left the British in a state of shock. After the islanders dispersed, some of the crew went ashore and gathered as much of Cook's body as they could, then gave him a burial at sea. The captain was 50 when he died, leaving behind his widow and three children.

tuberculosis infection of the lungs

Charles Clerke, commander of the *Discovery,* then took charge of the expedition, but he died soon after of **tuberculosis.** Command then fell to Lieutenant John Gore. The two ships sailed to eastern Russia, where they sent word of Cook's death back to England. They then attempted to complete their mission, heading north once again to search for the Northwest Passage. They failed, just as Cook had the year before. After a stop in Russia to repair damage caused by the ice, the two ships sailed west to England and arrived on August 22, 1780.

The Work of an Explorer

Cook once wrote that his ambition was "to go as far as it was possible for a man to go, and to make an exact recording of all that I saw." He succeeded, and in the process, he helped turn exploration into a modern science.

Cook opened possibilities for trade on the northwest coast of North America and throughout the Pacific. But his main accomplishments were scientific. His journals from his voyages contained detailed observations of the peoples and customs of the Pacific island cultures. He mapped thousands of miles of coastlines, and his experiments with shipboard diet virtually ended death at sea from scurvy. In his searches for *Terra Australis Incognita* and the Northwest Passage, he devoted his life to answering questions about the world.

Suggested Reading J. C. Beaglehole, *The Life of Captain James Cook* (Stanford University Press, 1974); James Cook, *Seventy North to Fifty South,* edited by Paul W. Dale (Prentice Hall, 1969); Robin Fisher and Hugh Johnson, editors, *Captain James Cook and His Times,* (University of Washington Press, 1979); A. Grenfell Price, editor, *The Explorations of Captain James Cook in the Pacific as Told by Selections of His Own Journals, 1768-1779* (Heritage, 1976); Alan Villiers, *Captain James Cook: A Definitive Biography* (Scribners, 1970).

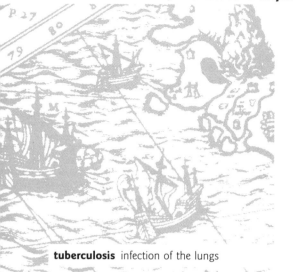

Coronado, Francisco Vásquez de

Spanish
b 1510?; Salamanca, Spain
d 1554; Mexico City, Mexico
Explored southwestern North America

In 1540 Francisco Vásquez de Coronado was the wealthy, respected governor of New Galicia, a province of **New Spain.** But he left his comfortable position to make an extraordinary search for lands of great riches. He never found those legendary places, but he did explore the land that became the states of Arizona, New Mexico, Texas, and Oklahoma. This **conquistador** traveled as far as central Kansas—farther north than anyone had gone from New Spain. Coronado's travels, along with those of Hernando de Soto, helped reveal the size and diversity of the North American continent.

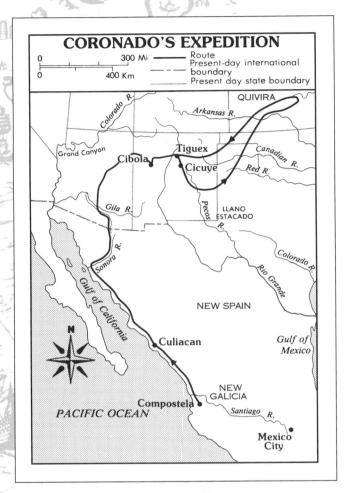

CORONADO'S EXPEDITION

Francisco Vásquez de Coronado led his exhausted Spanish troops on a futile search for gold in the dusty plains of the American Southwest.

New Spain region of Spanish colonial empire that included the areas now occupied by Mexico, Florida, Texas, New Mexico, Arizona, California, and various Caribbean islands

conquistador Spanish or Portuguese explorer and military leader in the Americas

viceroy governor of a Spanish colony in the Americas

pueblo Indian village or dwelling in the American Southwest, often built of sun-dried bricks

Privilege and Power

Coronado came from a noble Spanish family. Little is known of his life before he came to New Spain in 1535 with the new **viceroy,** Antonio de Mendoza. Two years later, Coronado gained fame for ending a revolt by miners in Amatepeque (near modern-day Taxco, Mexico). He also advanced his position when he married Beatriz de Estrada, a wealthy cousin of the Spanish king Charles I.

Thanks to his skills and status, Coronado was named the governor of New Galicia in 1538. In that role, he helped prepare the expedition of Father Mar-cos de Niza, who had been assigned by Viceroy Mendoza to explore the lands north of New Spain. Marcos returned from his journey with tales of a realm called Cíbola that consisted of seven fabulously wealthy cities. Marcos claimed to have seen the cities from a distance, and Mendoza immediately made plans to find and conquer them. He chose Coronado for the task, with Marcos to serve as a guide.

Slow Progress

During the first few weeks of 1540, Coronado assembled his expedition in Compostela, a city on the Pacific coast of central Mexico. He gathered about 340 Spaniards, 300 Mexican Indian allies, and 1,000 Indian and black slaves. For food he took herds of cattle, sheep, pigs, and goats. On February 23, this enormous group left Compostela and marched along the coast of the Gulf of California to Culiacán. At that time, Culiacán was farther northwest than any other European settlement in North America.

Coronado was frustrated by the slow pace of his large expedition. There were too many causes for delay, such as the need to carry the cattle one at a time across rivers. Coronado decided to move ahead with 100 lightly equipped Spaniards and some of the Indians. He sent a soldier named Melchior Diaz to scout a route. The main body of the expedition would follow Coronado at a slower pace.

The conquistador proceeded into northern Arizona. Crossing the Gila River, he and his men headed northeast across the area that is now the Fort Apache Indian Reservation. Many of the men became ill from eating berries they found there. Then Diaz reappeared with disappointing news. He had seen what was thought to be the first city of Cíbola—merely an overcrowded village of huts.

The Great Plains and the Grand Canyon

Despite the bad news, Coronado traveled on. He crossed into what is now New Mexico and reached the Zuñi Indian **pueblo** of Hawikuh about July 4, 1540. What Father Marcos had described as a fabulous city was in fact a collection of huts made of stone and sun-dried clay. Marcos was sent back to Mexico City in disgrace. With food and morale both running low, Coronado attacked and conquered the pueblo. He made it his headquarters, allowing

Coronado's travels took him to the Texas prairie. There, he and his men were amazed to see bison, which they called "humpback oxen."

his men to rest and sending Diaz to retrieve the rest of the expeditionary force. He then sent small parties to explore other Zuñi pueblos in the area.

Next, Coronado sent a scouting party to the northwest, where his men found seven Hopi Indian villages and learned of a great river farther west. Intrigued, Coronado sent a soldier named Garcia López de Cárdenas to search for this river. That journey ended abruptly when Cárdenas reached the Grand Canyon. It was impossible to descend the steep canyon walls to the Colorado River below. Cárdenas and his men were the first Europeans to find the Grand Canyon and the first to record a sighting of the Colorado River.

Coronado also sent scouting parties to the east. One party found villages along the Rio Grande that were larger and could provide more food than the Zuñi pueblos. Coronado moved his headquarters to Tiguex, the largest of these villages. During the winter of 1540 to 1541, the Spanish endured severe weather and constant Indian attacks. Coronado brought an end to the attacks by burning several Indian prisoners to death.

The Search for Quivira

On one of his many trips away from Tiguex, Coronado met a Plains Indian whom he called "the Turk." This Indian told Coronado of a rich land to the northeast, known as Quivira. The Indian described fish as large as horses, gold jugs and bowls used for eating, and gold bells hanging from a tree. Coronado was impressed by these stories, and not wanting to return to New Spain empty-handed, he decided to seek the riches of Quivira.

On April 23, 1541, Coronado's expedition left Tiguex with "the Turk" as its guide. Heading east to Cicuye (present-day Pecos, New Mexico) and crossing the Pecos River, the men marched across what they called the Llano Estacado (the modern-day Staked Plain in Texas). Though the Indians they met gave them food, pottery, cloth, and some turquoise, the Spanish were disappointed not to find any gold or silver. Often the Indians simply fled in fear of the Spaniards' horses, a type of animal that they had never seen before.

After five weeks of wandering eastward across Texas, Coronado began to mistrust his guide. Coronado became convinced that "the Turk" was lying in an effort to get the Spaniards lost in the wilderness. When the guide confessed that this was true, Coronado executed him. Food was by then running low, so Coronado sent most of his soldiers back to Tiguex. He and 30 horsemen headed north, where the local Tejas Indians had suggested that he might find Quivira.

Disappointment in the North

The Spaniards traveled north for 42 days. They crossed the Canadian River and rode through the western part of Oklahoma before turning northeast. Reaching the Arkansas River, they crossed it and followed it downstream. At last they met some Quivira Indians (later referred to as the Wichita), who guided the Spanish to their village.

The Quivira settlement was a small group of thatched huts, not the wealthy civilization described by "the Turk." But Coronado could not bring himself to give up his search for treasure. He made several journeys into the surrounding area. He never found gold, and he did not consider the region suitable for Spanish settlements. At last he decided to rejoin his men in Tiguex.

A few Quivira Indians guided the Spanish back to Tiguex, following a shorter route than the party had originally taken. This route later became part of the Santa Fe Trail, famous for the wagons that traveled it between New Mexico and Missouri in the 1800s. Coronado spent the winter of 1541 to 1542 in Tiguex. During that time, he was seriously injured when he fell off a horse.

A Beaten Conquistador

In April 1542, the Spanish began the long march back to New Spain. It was a terrible journey. The exhausted soldiers complained constantly, and they began deserting the group as soon as they saw Spanish settlements. By the time Coronado reached Mexico City to report to Viceroy Mendoza, he had fewer than 100 men left. One soldier wrote that Coronado was "very sad and very weary, completely worn out and shame-faced."

Although he had failed to meet his goals, Coronado was allowed to continue to serve as governor of New Galicia until 1544. He then retired to Mexico City. Spanish officials questioned him for executing "the Turk" and for leaving the northern lands without setting up permanent Spanish control. A royal court found him innocent of misconduct, and he returned to his quiet retirement. But he never fully recovered from his fall, and his health remained poor until he died 10 years later.

Coronado may have considered his mission a failure, but historians see it as a remarkable feat of exploration. He opened up a vast region to the Spanish and greatly expanded the boundaries of New Spain. The names of Coronado Mountain in Arizona, the Coronado State Monument in New Mexico, and Coronado City in Kansas are reminders of his lasting importance.

Suggested Reading Herbert E. Bolton, *Coronado on the Turquoise Trail: Knight of Pueblos and Plains* (University of New Mexico, 1949); Pedro de Castañeda, *The Journey of Coronado, 1540–1542*, translated by George Parker Winship (Readex Microprint, 1966); Arthur Grove Day, *Coronado's Quest: The Discovery of the Southwestern States* (Greenwood, 1982); George Parker Winship, *The Coronado Expedition, 1540–1542* (Rio Grande Press, 1964).

Cortés, Hernán

Spanish
b 1485; Medellín, Spain
d December 2, 1547; near Seville, Spain
Explored Mexico; conquered Aztec Empire

New Spain region of Spanish colonial empire that included the areas now occupied by Mexico, Florida, Texas, New Mexico, Arizona, California, and various Caribbean islands

arquebusier soldier who carried a type of long, heavy gun invented about 1400

Hernán Cortés invaded Central America in 1519 with a small force of Spanish soldiers. He conquered the empire of the Aztec Indians through a combination of trickery, military skill, diplomacy, and cruelty. He then quickly brought a huge area which he named **New Spain** under Spanish control. His efforts on behalf of Spain made him a controversial figure both in his own time and today.

Choosing a Life of Danger

At the age of 14, Cortés left the Spanish town in which he grew up. He went to college to study law but left after two years for unknown reasons. The academic life may not have suited him. After a couple of aimless years, he decided to pursue a life of adventure.

In 1504 Cortés sailed on a merchant ship headed for Spanish colonies in the Caribbean Sea. He settled on Hispaniola (the island now occupied by Haiti and the Dominican Republic) and became a minor public official in the town of Azua. During the Spanish conquest of Cuba from 1511 to 1518, he served under Diego Velásquez, who became Cuba's governor.

At first Cortés had a good relationship with Velásquez. The governor appreciated Cortés's military skills, lively personality, and talent as a writer. Velásquez named Cortés mayor of the Spanish settlement at Santiago de Cuba. But trouble soon arose between the two men. Cortés was a free spirit who resisted anyone else's authority. He was accused of trying to overthrow Velásquez. Although he was pardoned, he and the governor had a strained relationship from then on.

Despite the tension, Velásquez named Cortés commander of an expedition to Mexico in 1518. Velásquez was eager to investigate the reports of two Spanish explorers that gold and fabulous temples could be found on the Yucatán Peninsula. While preparing for his new mission, Cortés learned that the governor had decided to remove him from command. On November 18, 1518, before the order could be delivered, Cortés quietly sailed out of the harbor. He got the rest of the supplies he needed at the ports of Trinidad and Havana. His final count of men and supplies included 780 soldiers, 100 sailors, 32 crossbowmen, 13 **arquebusiers,** 16 horses, and 10 canoes.

The First Encounters

Cortés first landed on the island of Cozumel, off the coast of the Yucatán Peninsula. He conquered the local Indians, pulled down their

Hernán Cortés's independent spirit helped him conquer Mexico, but as governor of a new colony, he had trouble controlling his political enemies.

conquistador Spanish or Portuguese explorer and military leader in the Americas

cacique Indian chief in Central America and South America

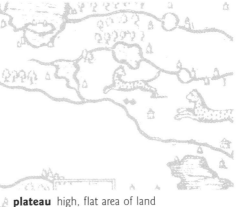

plateau high, flat area of land

religious statues, and began converting them to Christianity. Like all **conquistadors,** Cortés explored in the name of "God and King." If the Indians refused to convert, they were killed for being in league with the devil. On Cozumel, Cortés also found Jerónimo de Aguilar, a Spaniard who had been captured during an expedition eight years earlier. Aguilar joined Cortés as an interpreter, having learned the Mayan language from his captors.

Cortés then sailed to the coast of the mainland. He won his battle with the Indians there when they fled at the sight of horses, which had never before been seen in the Americas. Later, a group of **caciques** brought food, gold, and women to win Cortés's favor. One of the women, named Malinche (also known as Malintzin), was a noble of the Aztecs, the most powerful tribe in Central America. Malinche became Cortés's interpreter and mistress. Her skill with languages and diplomacy made her a very important member of the Spanish expedition. The Spaniards baptized her, naming her Doña Marina.

Contact with the Aztec Empire

Cortés sailed again, heading north along the eastern coast of Mexico. He landed at the harbor called San Juan de Ulúa. There he met with an ambassador sent by Montezuma, the emperor of the Aztecs. The ambassador had been instructed to find out whether the Spaniards were human invaders or messengers of the Aztec god Quetzalcoatl. The ambassador reported that the newcomers were humans, not gods, but Montezuma was still uncertain. He wondered if Cortés was Quetzalcoatl himself. The emperor sent more representatives bearing gifts of gold, hoping that the Spanish would leave.

Realizing just how wealthy the Aztec Empire was, Cortés began planning a military attack. However, he knew that he did not have permission to conquer Mexico. He solved this problem by creating his own colony, Villa Rica de Vera Cruz (now Veracruz), and named himself its leader. Having built this settlement, Cortés had all his ships destroyed so that his men would not be tempted to return to Cuba. Then he made detailed plans for the attack. He would march inland, defeat the local Indian tribes, and persuade them to fight with him against the Aztecs. During his battles with the Aztecs, he would put his Indian allies in the front lines.

On August 16, 1519, Cortés left Vera Cruz, marching his men from the hot, swampy coastal lands to the bleak **plateau** where the Tlaxcala Indians lived. The Spanish defeated the Tlaxcala, who then became Cortés's most loyal allies. Next the invasion force moved south to the city of Cholula and then headed west to a high point overlooking the Valley of Mexico. Cortés could see the center of the fabulous Aztec Empire, with its great cities and acres of farmland surrounded by lakes and volcanoes.

A Royal Prisoner

Cortés and his men marched through the valley, passing lakes and irrigated fields before crossing a drawbridge into the Aztec capital

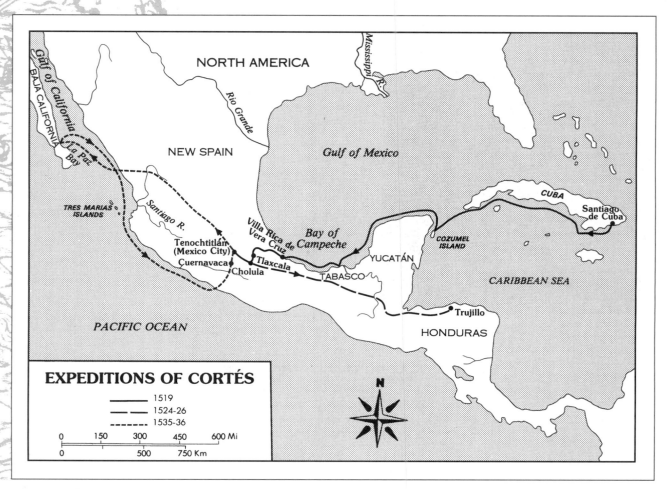

NORTH AMERICA

NEW SPAIN

Gulf of Mexico

Gulf of California

BAJA CALIFORNIA

La Paz Bay

Rio Grande

Mississippi R.

TRES MARIAS ISLANDS

Santiago R.

Tenochtitlán (Mexico City)

Cuernavaca

Cholula

Tlaxcala

Villa Rica de Vera Cruz

Bay of Campeche

TABASCO

YUCATÁN

COZUMEL ISLAND

CUBA

Santiago de Cuba

CARIBBEAN SEA

PACIFIC OCEAN

Trujillo

HONDURAS

EXPEDITIONS OF CORTÉS

——— 1519
— — 1524-26
- - - - 1535-36

0   150   300   450   600 Mi
0   500   750 Km

N

Cortés's conquests and explorations helped extend Spanish influence throughout Central America.

city, Tenochtitlán. The Spanish were greeted with much ceremony by many Aztec chiefs—and finally by Montezuma himself. The Aztecs gave their visitors a palace of their own to stay in.

Cortés realized that he could not attack as he had planned. Since the drawbridge was the only way out of the city, the Spaniards could easily be trapped there. He decided instead to take Montezuma prisoner. At a meeting with the emperor, Cortés first threatened Montezuma but then promised to treat him well if he cooperated. The Aztec leader reluctantly agreed to live with the Spaniards at their palace. By controlling Montezuma, Cortés now controlled the empire—but much fighting was yet to come.

Trouble on All Sides

Cortés received word that a new enemy was on the way. Governor Velásquez had sent Pánfilo de NARVÁEZ with a Spanish army to relieve Cortés of his command. But Cortés launched a surprise attack. He captured Narváez and won the support of Narváez's troops.

When Cortés returned to Tenochtitlán with his new army, he found the city on the verge of warfare. Pedro de ALVARADO, in command during Cortés's absence, had tried to stop the Aztec religious practice of human sacrifice. Alvarado had executed some 200 nobles, and the Aztecs were furious. Trying to restore calm, Cortés released some Aztec prisoners and asked Montezuma to talk to his angry people. They responded by pelting their emperor with rocks, and he later died from his wounds.

Cortés was forced to abandon Tenochtitlán. He fought his way out of the city on the night of June 30, 1520, which the Spanish later called the "Sorrowful Night." In the battle, Cortés lost half his men, all of his horses, and most of his captured treasure. He retreated to the plateau of the Tlaxcala, the only Indian tribe that did not desert him.

A Hard Conquest

Cortés was not ready to give up. With his usual quick thinking, he planned a naval attack on Tenochtitlán. Juan Rodriguez CABRILLO, an expert shipbuilder who had arrived with Narváez, oversaw the construction of 13 **brigantines.**

This Aztec drawing shows messengers bringing gifts to Cortés at the Spanish camp.

brigantine two-masted sailing ship with both square and triangular sails

The ships were then taken apart and carried to lakes and rivers around Tenochtitlán, where they were put back together. Meanwhile, smallpox, a highly contagious and fatal disease, was sweeping through Mexico, killing many thousands of Indians. The Spanish attacked the weakened Aztecs and took the city on August 13, 1521, after three months of heavy fighting.

Back in Spain, Cortés's actions in Mexico were being investigated. Velásquez and other enemies worked hard to stir up trouble, but a royal committee decided that Cortés had not done anything wrong. He received honors for his conquests, and in 1522 he was named the political and military leader of the colony of New Spain.

Cortés began to build a new capital city, which he called Mexico City, on the site of Tenochtitlán. He also sent out many expeditions to explore the surrounding area. One of these missions was led by Cristóbal de Olid to what is now Honduras. When Olid reached Honduras, he decided to set up his own colony. In 1524 Cortés was forced to travel to Honduras to arrest him, but Olid had died by the time Cortés arrived.

Less Success in Later Life

While Cortés was dealing with the problem of Olid, his enemies in Mexico City spread rumors that he was dead. When he returned, he had been replaced as governor. Cortés sailed to Spain in 1528 to try to correct this situation. The Spanish people gave him a thunderous welcome, and he was honored by the king, but he was not restored to his position as governor.

Cortés returned to Mexico and financed several explorations in search of treasure. In 1535 he led an expedition himself and tried to start a colony on the peninsula called Baja California. The mission was a failure. Cortés eventually returned to Spain, where he fell ill and died in 1547.

Throughout his career as a conquistador, Cortés was determined and brilliant—but also brutal. His conquest of the Aztec Empire was an impressive military feat. It was also a political act that helped the Spanish take control of all the lands and peoples of Central America.

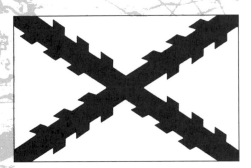

Setting out for Tenochtitlán, one of Cortés's men wrote, "We left the camp with our banner unfurled and four of our company guarding its bearer. . . ."

Suggested Reading Francisco Lopez de Gomara, *Cortés: The Life of the Conqueror by His Secretary*, translated and edited by Byrd Simpson (University of California Press, 1964); Salvador de Madariaga, *Hernan*

Cortés, Conqueror of Mexico (University of Miami Press, 1967); Albert Marrin, *Aztecs and Spaniards: Cortés and the Conquest of Mexico* (Atheneum, 1986).

Cosa, Juan de La. See *La Cosa, Juan de.*

Cousteau, Jacques-Yves

French
b June 11, 1910; St. André-de-Cubzac, France
d June 25, 1997; Paris, France
Explored oceans underwater

oceanographer scientist who studies the ocean and underwater life

scuba equipment that allows a diver to carry oxygen underwater; letters stand for "self-contained underwater breathing apparatus"

Audiences around the world were fascinated by the underwater explorations of Jacques-Yves Cousteau.

Many explorers have sailed on the oceans, but few have taken the time to look beneath the waves. Captain Jacques-Yves Cousteau explored the earth's underwater world and shared the wonders he saw through films, books, and television programs. His global audience probably made him the most famous **oceanographer** in history.

Above and Below the Oceans

Cousteau had an early interest in the water. He grew up in France, but it was at a summer camp in Vermont that he learned to swim at the age of 10. During the early 1930s, as a young officer in the French navy, he obtained a pair of underwater goggles. He wore them in the Mediterranean Sea, where he saw "a jungle of fish. That was like an electric shock. . . ." His lifelong interest in the oceans had begun.

In 1943 Cousteau and an engineer named Émile Gagnan introduced the Aqua-Lung, the first **scuba** gear. With the Aqua-Lung, divers could stay underwater for long periods without using air hoses or bulky diving suits. Scuba gear is now widely used for both scientific and recreational purposes.

After World War II, Cousteau organized a research company, and in 1950 he acquired the ship *Calypso*. With his entire family, he sailed the world's oceans, taking cameras underwater and capturing marine life on film. In 1956 his motion picture *The Silent World* won an Academy Award.

Later Research Projects

In the early 1960s, Cousteau was intrigued by the idea that humans could live under the water. His *Conshelf* project proved that this was possible. He and four others lived in an underwater structure for a month in 1963. The experiment was filmed and shown on television.

At the age of 75, Cousteau began his most ambitious project ever. "Rediscovery of the World" was a years-long study of the health of the earth's waters. In 1996 the famous *Calypso* was hit by another ship, and it sank in the harbor of Singapore. Not one to give up, Cousteau was planning to build a new research vessel at the time of his death in 1997.

Suggested Reading Jacques-Yves Cousteau, Frédéric Dumas, and James Dugan, *Silent World* (Harper and Row, 1953); James Dugan, *Man Under the Sea* (Harper and Row, 1956); Richard Munson, *Cousteau: The Captain and His World* (Paragon House, 1991).

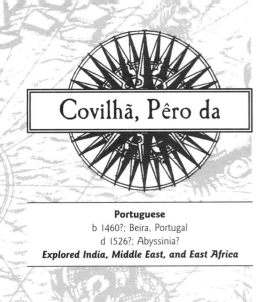

Portuguese
b 1460?; Beira, Portugal
d 1526?; Abyssinia?
Explored India, Middle East, and East Africa

Crusades series of Christian holy wars fought against Muslims in the Middle East, mainly between 1095 and 1270

caravan large group of people traveling together, often with pack animals, across a desert or other dangerous region

Pêro da Covilhã was a Portuguese explorer who traveled to India, Arabia, and Africa. His goals were to identify trade routes to Asia and to find a Christian king named Prester John. Covilhã explored the trade centers of India and visited the Islamic holy cities of Mecca and Medina. When he traveled to Abyssinia (now Ethiopia), he was welcomed and given an official position. He was also forbidden to leave the country, and he never again returned to Portugal.

As a young man, Covilhã served King Alfonso V of Portugal. When Alfonso died, Covilhã served the next Portuguese king, John II, carrying messages to Spain and perhaps also spying in North Africa. On one mission, he disguised himself as a merchant in order to befriend the ruler of Tlemcen (in present-day Algeria). In 1487 King John chose Covilhã to travel to the kingdom of Abyssinia in eastern Africa. The Portuguese believed that this region was the land of Prester John.

The Legend of Prester John

The idea that a fabulously wealthy Christian kingdom existed somewhere in the east had been popular in Europe for centuries. This land's ruler, Prester John, was believed to be immortal, thanks to a nearby "fountain of youth." Rumors of Christians in Africa or Asia may well have been based in fact. Christian missionaries may have reached those continents during the time of the **Crusades** or before. In 1165 a letter from Prester John to European rulers stirred much interest. The letter described a kingdom where beds were made of sapphires and tables were made of emeralds. The letter also called Prester John and his powerful armies the protectors of Christians everywhere.

Although the letter turned out to be a fake, it fueled Europeans' desire to find such a strong ally against the Islamic empire. By Covilhã's time, no one imagined that Prester John was quite so wealthy and powerful. But most people still believed in the existence of a kingdom ruled by Prester John's descendants. This belief encouraged many voyages of exploration and discovery.

Traveling in Disguise

Covilhã left Portugal in 1487. At that time, Prester John's kingdom was thought to be in Abyssinia. Covilhã passed through Spain and Italy on his way to Alexandria, Egypt. To protect himself where Christians were unwelcome, Covilhã disguised himself as a Muslim merchant and joined a **caravan** headed for Cairo. He traveled south from Cairo, crossing the Red Sea to Aden (in present-day Yemen). He accompanied Arab traders to the Malabar Coast of India and then turned back west through the Persian Gulf and Arabia. Still disguised, Covilhã entered the Islamic holy cities of Mecca and Medina, which were strictly closed to Christians. Covilhã then returned to Cairo in about 1493, having visited many of the leading trade centers of the east. The reports he sent to King John became very useful to later explorers such as Vasco da GAMA.

Prisoner in Abyssinia

Covilhã then went to Abyssinia to search for Prester John. When he got there, Emperor Eskender offered him a friendly welcome. The emperor gave him a house, servants, and a prestigious post as governor of one of the empire's districts. Eskender then forbade Covilhã ever to leave Abyssinia.

While Covilhã was gone, King John sent other explorers in search of Prester John. They often started on Africa's west coast and traveled inland. African slaves who had been converted to Christianity were also sent to various locations with gifts for Prester John. Thirty years passed before Europe learned of Covilhã's fate. The Portuguese king sent Francisco ALVARES as an ambassador to Abyssinia. Alvares arrived to find Covilhã, who was now an elderly man, a healthy and happy captive. Covilhã did not want to leave his African home, but he permitted his 23-year-old son to return to Portugal to be educated. As late as 1526, Covilhã was reported to be alive and well in Abyssinia.

Suggested Reading Francisco Alvares, *The Prester John of the Indies: A True Relation of the Lands of the Prester John, Being the Narrative of the Portuguese Embassy to Ethiopia in 1520,* translated by Lord Stanley of Alderley (Hakluyt Society, 1961); Eric Axelson, *Congo to Cape: Early Portuguese Explorers* (Faber, 1973).

---

da Gama, Vasco. *See Gama, Vasco de.*

Dalrymple, Alexander

Scottish
b July 24, 1737; New Hailes, Scotland
d June 19, 1808; London, England
Promoted search for southern continent

hydrographer scientist who studies bodies of water to make navigation easier

Alexander Dalrymple was certain of the existence of a legendary southern continent, but he was passed over for command of a mission to find it.

Alexander Dalrymple was a Scottish scholar, seaman, and geographer. He considered himself an expert on a mythical southern land called *Terra Australis Incognita.* His book on the subject sparked Britain's interest in a complete exploration of the Pacific Ocean. Dalrymple was also the first to hold the post of **hydrographer** to the British Royal Navy.

Dalrymple was born in 1737 into an ancient and noble Scottish family. When he was a young man, his heroes were the great explorers Christopher COLUMBUS and Ferdinand MAGELLAN. He later went to work for the British East India Company in the Pacific and eventually became its staff hydrographer. However, when Dalrymple boldly told his employers that they should change their way of working, move the company's headquarters, and put him in charge, they sent him back to England.

The Invisible Continent

Dalrymple had studied the writings of the ancient Greek geographer and astronomer PTOLEMY, who had been the first to suggest that a great southern continent existed. Ptolemy believed that landmasses, not oceans, covered most of the earth's surface. He pictured an enormous continent stretching from Africa to Asia, with the Indian Ocean an inland sea. His book *Geography* greatly influenced the European geographers who followed him.

Explorers such as Bartolomeu DIAS, Ferdinand Magellan, and Abel TASMAN had proved that Africa, South America, and Australia were not parts of one great southern continent. But geographers, including Dalrymple, refused to rule out the unknown land's existence, believing that earlier explorers had simply missed it. Dalrymple wrote a book in which he used various scientific theories to support his claims. In 1768 the British navy planned an expedition to find and claim the continent. Dalrymple offered his services as the perfect commander for the mission.

Stubborn to the End

Because Dalrymple was a member of the Royal Society, an organization of British scientists, he was asked to take part as an observer. James COOK, a highly skilled navy officer, was chosen to command the voyage. Dalrymple was so angry that he refused to go at all. Cook's expedition proved that *Terra Australis Incognita* did not exist. Dalrymple alone did not accept Cook's findings. Despite this conflict, Dalrymple remained a respected scientist. He was an expert in charting winds and currents, and in 1795 he was the first to be named hydrographer to the Royal Navy. He died 13 years later at the age of 70.

Suggested Reading Howard Tyrell Fry, *Alexander Dalrymple (1737-1808) and the Expansion of British Trade* (University of Toronto Press, 1970).

English
b 1652?; Yoevil, England
d March 1715; England
Discovered New Britain; explored Australia

buccaneer pirate, especially one who attacked Spanish colonies and ships in the 1600s

William Cecil Dampier may have been the most famous **buccaneer** of the 1600s. His sharp eye and talent for observation helped him to write popular books that turned Europe's attention to the Pacific. He circled the world three times and explored the west coasts of Central and South America as well as Australia and New Zealand. Dampier kept a careful journal in which he documented winds, currents, and plant and animal life.

Dampier was born around 1652 in a small village in southwestern England. He went to sea as a youth and worked in Newfoundland and the Caribbean. In 1674 Dampier signed on at a log-cutting camp on the Gulf of Mexico. He worked there for four years, until a hurricane destroyed most of the area's timber. This disaster left him penniless.

A Pirate's Journal

Despite his problems, Dampier did not lose his adventurous spirit. He joined a band of over 300 buccaneers led by John Coxon and Bartholomew Sharp. They crossed Panama to the Pacific Ocean and sailed down the west coast of South America, raiding villages along the way. In the spring of 1681, Dampier and nearly 50 of the others set out to seek their own fortunes. Dampier started keeping a journal and wrote in it faithfully until he returned to England. He protected the journal in a hollow bamboo case sealed with wax. For 10 years, Dampier moved from ship to ship and from adventure to adventure. He wrote that he was a pirate "more to indulge my curiosity than to get wealth." His travels from South America's Cape Horn took him north to Mexico and west to the Galápagos Islands. Dampier was not a typical pirate. He drank little and stayed away from the rough men who worked alongside him.

In 1686 Dampier guided Captain Charles Swan's buccaneer ship *Cygnet* and another vessel from Mexico to Guam, an island in the Pacific Ocean. They traveled 7,300 miles in 51 days, fortunately reaching land before their supplies ran out. The *Cygnet* sailed on to the Philippines and New Holland (present-day Australia). Dampier left the *Cygnet* at the Nicobar Islands in the Indian Ocean. He spent the next three years working aboard merchant ships in Southeast Asian waters.

NIEUWE REYSTOGT
R O N D O M D E
WERRELD,
waarin omſtandiglyk beſchꝛeeven woꝛden
De Land-engte van Amerika, verſcheydene Kuſten
en Eylanden in Weſtindie, de eylanden van Kabo Verde, de door-
togt van de Straat Le Maire na de Zuydzee, de kuſten van Chili,
Peru, Mexiko; 't eyland Guam een van de Ladrones, 't eyland Min-
danao een van de Filippines; en de Ooſtindiſche eylanden ontrent Kam-
bodia, Cina, Formoſa, Lukonia, Celebes, enz. voorts Nieuw
Holland, Sumatra, de eylanden van Nikobar, de Kaap van Goede
Hoop, en 't eyland Sante Helena.

M I T S G A D E R S
Derzelver Landsdouw / Rivieren / Havens / Gewaſſen / Vꝛugten /
Gedierten / en Inwooners / beneffens hunne Gewoonten /
Godsdienſt / Regering / Handel / enz.

In 't Engelſch beſchreeven dooꝛ
W I L L I A M D A M P I E R ,
en daarupt vertaald dooꝛ
W. S E W E L .
Met naauwkeurige Landkaarten, en kopere Plaaten vercierd.

In 'S G R A V E N H A G E ,
By ABRAHAM DE HONDT, Boekverkooper op de
Zaal van 't Hof / in de Foꝛtupn 1698.

Above is the title page in Dutch of William Dampier's *A New Voyage Around the World*, which may have inspired parts of Jonathan Swift's *Gulliver's Travels*.

privateer privately owned ship hired by a government to attack enemy ships

Darwin, Charles Robert

English
b February 12, 1809; Shrewsbury, England
d April 19, 1882; Down, England
Explored South America and Pacific; developed theory of evolution

Dampier returned to England in 1691 with his journal, which is now kept in the British Library. Six years later, he published his first book, *A New Voyage Round the World.* It quickly became a best-seller. Dampier's later books included geographical information and charts, which JAMES COOK and other explorers used on their own voyages.

Troubles at the Top

Dampier's reputation as a navigator spread. In 1698 he was chosen to command the H.M.S. *Roebuck* on an expedition to search for *Terra Australis Incognita,* the unknown southern continent. The *Roebuck* was barely seaworthy, and Dampier was not well liked by his crew, who resented taking orders from a former pirate.

Dampier explored New Holland's west and northwest coast and the island chain that now bears his name. He also discovered New Britain Island off the coast of New Guinea. On the way back to England, the *Roebuck* went down off Ascension Island in the southern Atlantic Ocean. Some weeks later, passing English merchant ships rescued both captain and crew.

Dampier was brought to trial in 1699 for his actions as commander of the sunken ship. A military court decided that he was "not a fit person to command any of Her Majesty's ships." But three years later, he was back on the high seas. He obtained a license to sail as a **privateer** off the coast of South America. But by that time, he had lost his buccaneering touch. His license was stolen, and he was thrown into jail in the Dutch East Indies for being a pirate.

A Quiet Conclusion

Dampier was eventually released, and he returned to England in 1707. A year later, another privateer hired him as ship's pilot. He roamed the Pacific for three very profitable years, but he had to sue his employer in order to get his share of the riches. After several years of legal battles, he received a large sum of money. But by then his fame had faded, and when he died a few years later, he was an unknown man.

Suggested Reading Christopher Lloyd, *William Dampier* (Faber, 1966); Leslie R. Marchant, *An Island unto Itself: William Dampier and New Holland* (Hesperian, 1988); Joseph C. Shipman, *William Dampier, Seaman-Scientist* (University of Kansas Press, 1962).

Charles Darwin was a naturalist who spent five years on a scientific expedition to South America and the Pacific Ocean. Sailing aboard the British research ship *Beagle,* Darwin studied the natural history and plant and animal life of the regions he visited. What he saw led him to develop the theory of evolution, in which he suggested that plant and animal **species** change over long spans of time to fit their environments. This theory caused a great public debate when he first described it in his book *The Origin of Species,* published in 1859.

Charles Darwin's theory of evolution is now the basis of modern biology, but it continues to cause religious and scientific debates.

species type of plant or animal

specimen sample of a plant, animal, or mineral, usually collected for scientific study or display

fossil trace left in rocks by a plant or animal that lived long ago

A Hobby Becomes a Career

Darwin's family taught him a love of science. His grandfather was a poet and a naturalist, and his father was a doctor. As a boy of eight, Darwin also showed an interest in science. He began collecting flowers, insects, birds, rocks, and butterflies. But he was only an average student in school, and it seemed that he could never have a career as a scientist. He tried attending medical school in Scotland but left because he disliked the sight of blood.

When he was 19, he entered Cambridge University to study to become a minister. Three years later, just weeks away from completing his studies, Darwin received an exciting offer. His friend and professor John Stevens Henslow had recommended him for an unpaid post as naturalist aboard the *Beagle*. The ship's mission was to chart the coasts of South America. Darwin accepted, and this decision was a turning point for him. He later wrote: "The voyage of the *Beagle* has been by far the most important event in my life."

Science Across the Ocean

The *Beagle*'s commander was Captain Robert FITZROY. Fitzroy's view of science was typical of the time. He believed that the goal of science was to prove that the Bible was literally true. Like most Christians of that period, he thought that the earth and all of the species on it were created together about 6,000 years ago and had stayed the same ever since. Although Fitzroy and Darwin came to disagree on such questions, they became good friends during the voyage.

The *Beagle* set sail in the winter of 1831. Darwin collected **specimens** at sea by towing a net through the water behind the boat. He continued working even when he was terribly seasick. He also went ashore whenever he could and often made long journeys on foot. He would arrange for the *Beagle* to drop him off and pick him up days or even weeks later. He explored the high mountains and the wide grasslands of South America. He also traveled up rivers to places that no European had ever seen before.

Darwin was struck by the way in which even the smallest animals struggled for survival in the natural world. He carefully studied the way different animals lived together in the same area. He also observed how they were affected by their natural environment. Darwin and an assistant collected and preserved many plants, animals, and rocks. The cabin he shared with Captain Fitzroy started to look like a museum.

The Secrets of Fossils

In 1832, on the Atlantic coast of Argentina, Darwin made an important discovery. He found **fossils** of giant prehistoric mammals. These extinct creatures resembled animals that existed in his own time. Darwin began to doubt the biblical idea that certain species had become extinct because they had not boarded Noah's ark in time to be saved from the flood. Darwin thought that too many species had disappeared for that story to be true. The fossils that he found set his new ideas in motion. He began to believe that the earth and the creatures on it do not stay the same but are constantly changing.

In 1834 Darwin spent six weeks high in the Andes Mountains. He was 12,000 feet above sea level and about 700 miles from the Atlantic Ocean. In that place so far from water, he found fossils of seashells. Beneath a layer of seashell fossils, he found fossils of pine forests. These discoveries led him to a revolutionary idea. He came to think that the area had been a forest that was later submerged, remained underwater until it was covered in seashells, and then was thrust back out of the water in the form of mountains. He believed that these incredible changes must have taken millions of years, not just 6,000.

In 1835, three Andean volcanoes that were thousands of miles apart erupted at the same time. A month later, there was a major earthquake farther south, in Chile. Darwin noticed that the earthquake lifted the land in some areas by two or three feet. He was now more convinced than ever that the earth is highly unstable.

Evidence for Evolution

Darwin was not the first scientist to suggest that animal species evolve and change over time. In fact, his own grandfather had hinted at this possibility. But no one had figured out how evolution actually took place. Darwin found evidence to explain such a process on the Galápagos Islands. These islands are in the Pacific Ocean, about 600 miles west of South America.

While in the Galápagos, Darwin studied more than 12 different species of finches in different areas of the islands. All of these birds looked alike, but each species had a different beak. Each finch's beak matched the kind of food it ate. Those with strong beaks ate large, hard seeds that were difficult to crush. Those with more delicate beaks ate smaller seeds. Darwin realized that the finches' beaks were suited to eat the food that they could find nearby. He suggested that in an area where most of the seeds were hard, birds with strong beaks would have an easier time surviving than birds with smaller beaks. The surviving birds would reproduce, and after some time, most of the birds in the area would have large beaks. Darwin referred to this process of survival and evolution as "natural selection."

Troubling Questions and Answers

A year later, the expedition returned to Britain. After 5 years aboard the *Beagle,* Darwin was homesick, and he never again went out to sea. He spent 10 years making a catalog of all the specimens he had collected. He spent another 8 years studying one species of **barnacle** that he had found during the voyage. In 1839 he married a cousin, Emma Wedgewood. Three years later, the couple moved to the village of Down, outside London, where the family grew to include 10 children. Darwin continued his research, studying sheep, pigs, goldfish, bees, and pigeons.

He came to some shocking conclusions. He probably realized that many people would refuse to accept his theory of evolution because it went against the accepted Christian beliefs about nature. In fact, his own religious beliefs were deeply shaken. He waited until 1858 to present his ideas, in a paper written with another naturalist,

barnacle small, hard-shelled sea animal that often attaches itself to the bottoms of boats

Alfred Russel WALLACE. A year later, he published *The Origin of Species.* At first the book was attacked angrily, but later it was praised and translated into almost every European language. Darwin went on to publish eight more major works.

Though he had been a healthy man during the *Beagle* expedition, Darwin never enjoyed good health after returning to Britain. His long illness may have been the result of mosquito bites that he suffered in South America. He died in Downs at the age of 73 and is buried alongside other British heroes in London's Westminster Abbey.

Suggested Reading Nora Barlow, editor, *Charles Darwin and the Voyage of the* Beagle (Philosophical Library, 1946); Charles Darwin, *The Origin of Species* (New American Library, 1986); Robert S. Hopkins, *Darwin's South America* (John Day, 1969); Alan Moorehead, *Darwin and the* Beagle, revised edition (Penguin, 1979).

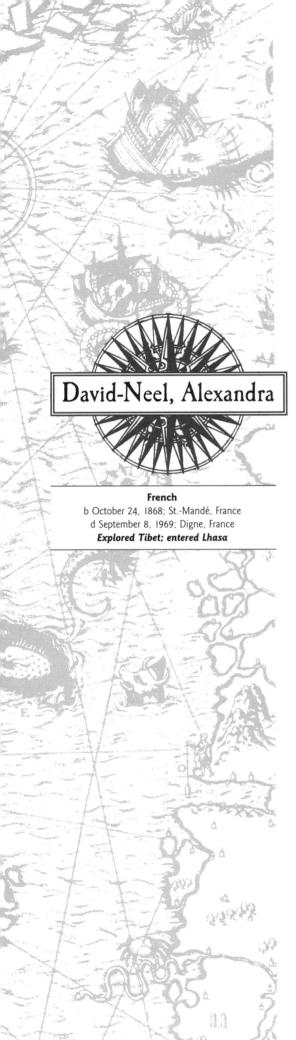

David-Neel, Alexandra

French
b October 24, 1868; St.-Mandé, France
d September 8, 1969; Digne, France
Explored Tibet; entered Lhasa

Alexandra David-Neel became famous as the first European woman to enter the forbidden city of Lhasa, Tibet. Lhasa was the home of Tibet's spiritual leader, the Dalai Lama. At the time, Tibetans considered Lhasa sacred and off-limits to foreigners. Many famous travelers, such as the great Swedish explorer Sven Anders HEDIN, had tried and failed to enter the holy city. In 1924, at the age of 55, David-Neel made the dangerous trek from China to Tibet. Disguised as a Mongolian peasant, she was able to enter Lhasa. This journey captured the imagination of the world. Her sudden fame rewarded long years of dedicated study and travel in Asia.

An Outrageous Young Woman

David-Neel was born into a wealthy French family. Her father, Louis David, was the nephew of the French painter Jacques-Louis David. He was also a friend of the novelist Victor Hugo. Political trouble in France forced Louis David to move to Belgium, where he met and married Alexandrine Borghmans. The couple returned to France in 1867, and their daughter Alexandra was born a year later.

Alexandra was a good student with an interest in religion. She also had an independent spirit. As a teenager, she often traveled alone to far-off places without telling anyone where she was going. She went to Italy by train and to Spain by bicycle. In those days, such behavior was thought to be outrageous for a young woman from a respected family. During a trip to London, Alexandra David became interested in Eastern religions. At the age of 21, she spent all the money she had inherited from her family so that she could visit India and Ceylon (now Sri Lanka).

From the Opera House to a Cave

When she returned to Europe, David studied music in Belgium and France. In 1893 she began working as an opera singer and pianist in eastern Asia, the Mediterranean, and North Africa. She also wrote essays on a wide range of topics, including women's rights and Buddhism.

In 1900 she met Philippe Neel, a passionate man who was the chief engineer of a French railroad company. These two free spirits married

A recognized authority on Tibetan Buddhism, Alexandra David-Neel gave Europeans a wider insight into the spiritual world of Asia.

maharaja king or prince in India

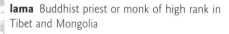

lama Buddhist priest or monk of high rank in Tibet and Mongolia

prilgrimage journey to a sacred place

in Tunisia in 1904. Philippe preferred to live in Europe, but he did not mind his wife traveling as much as she wished. In fact, he funded many of her trips to the East. Alexandra wrote to her husband whenever she could. When he died in 1941, she said that she had lost her greatest friend.

David-Neel became a successful writer, and she gave lectures across Europe. In 1910 she finished a book on Buddhism. A year later, she sailed to India, where she studied Eastern religions and continued to write. She also learned to speak many Asian languages.

In 1912 she traveled to the kingdom of Sikkim in the Himalaya Mountains, on India's northeastern border. She befriended the **maharaja,** who introduced her to the Dalai Lama. The Dalai Lama had fled to Sikkim to escape a Chinese invasion of Tibet. David-Neel lived for several months in a mountain cave. She then entered a Buddhist monastery, where she met a 15-year-old boy named Aphur Yongden, who later became her adopted son. Some people in the region believed that she was a goddess who had died and returned to earth.

Daring Journeys

The British were furious when they learned that David-Neel, who was French, had been crossing the border into Tibet. They wanted to keep other Europeans out of Tibet because it bordered on British territory in India. David-Neel was ordered to leave the area. She decided to return to Tibet by way of China, but first she and Yongden traveled to Burma (now Myanmar), Vietnam, Korea, and Japan. In October 1917, they arrived in Beijing, China. That winter they began a 2,000-mile trek westward across China. It was a difficult and dangerous journey. China was in the midst of a civil war, and bandits often attacked travelers on the roads.

After six months, David-Neel and Yongden reached Kumbum, on the border between China and Tibet. They stayed there for more than three years. They studied Buddhism, translated sacred texts, and made occasional trips into Mongolia and Tibet. Meanwhile, the situation in Asia grew worse. A civil war in Russia spread to Mongolia. Fighting increased in China and along the border between China and Tibet. In February 1921, David-Neel and Yongden left Kumbum.

They wandered for nearly three years. In the fall of 1923, they entered Tibet, determined to reach Lhasa. David-Neel spoke Tibetan almost perfectly. She dyed her skin and her hair with ink and dressed in ragged peasant clothes. Yongden posed as a **lama,** and David-Neel pretended to be his mother. They told anyone who asked that they were making a **pilgrimage** to Lhasa. They traveled by night and slept by day. The mountain passes were lonely, cold, and dangerous. Thieves tried to rob them, but David-Neel scared them off by firing her pistol. She and Yongden used an Eastern method to fight the cold weather—they raised their body temperatures through intense concentration. On Christmas Day, they rested in a cave.

They had nothing to eat but soup made from boiling water and pieces of leather which they had cut from their shoes.

Disguised in a Holy City

After four months of travel, they caught sight of the highest point in Lhasa—the golden roof of the Dalai Lama's palace, the Potala. David-Neel's disguise was successful, and she and Yongden entered the city safely. They wandered in Lhasa for the next two months. They even visited the Potala, which was open to pilgrims for a New Year festival. Then they happened to witness a domestic quarrel. The Tibetan police asked them to attend a court hearing. David-Neel was afraid that if she went to court, the Tibetans would discover that she was a European, so she and Yongden left the city and returned to India. In 1925 David-Neel came home to France, after 14 years in the East.

Fame and Honors

David-Neel was not the first European to enter Lhasa. But this fact did not stop the French from making her a national hero. France named her a **chevalier** of the Legion of Honor. The geographic societies of France and Belgium awarded her gold medals. Audiences packed the halls where she gave lectures, and her books became best-sellers.

In 1937 she received money from the French government to return to China and continue her studies. As World War II spread in the East, she moved to southeastern Tibet and then again to China. After the war, she returned to her home in Digne, a mountain town in the French Alps. Yongden lived with her until he died in 1955. David-Neel continued to write, and when she died at the age of 100, she was working on four major books.

Suggested Reading Tiziana Baldizzone, *Tibet: Journey to the Forbidden City: Retracing the Steps of Alexandra David-Neel* (Stewart, Tabori and Chang, 1996); Alexandra David-Neel, *My Journey to Lhasa* (Beacon, 1993); Barbara Foster, *Forbidden Journey: The Life of Alexandra David-Neel* (Overlook, 1997).

chevalier member of the French knighthood

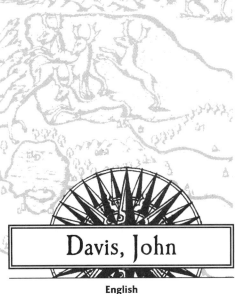

Davis, John

English
b 1550?; Sandridge, England
d December 29 or 30, 1605;
Bintan Island, near Singapore
Explored Canadian Arctic

quadrant navigational instrument used since the Middle Ages to determine distance north or south of the equator

longitude distance east or west of an imaginary line on the earth's surface; in 1884 most nations agreed to draw the line through Greenwich, England

Northwest Passage water route connecting the Atlantic Ocean and Pacific Ocean through the Arctic islands of northern Canada

John Davis was an expert navigator who invented a version of the **quadrant.** He was also a first-rate explorer. In 1587 he sailed into the waters west of Greenland and traveled farther north than Sir Martin FROBISHER had traveled 10 years earlier. But neither Frobisher nor Davis had an accurate instrument to measure **longitude,** and both were confused by faulty maps made by Nicolo Zeno. They did not realize that they had both "discovered" the same region. They both thought that Frobisher had been on the east coast of Greenland, when in fact he was on the east coast of what is now called Baffin Island. Davis was the first to chart that coast, and he left the area believing that a **Northwest Passage** might begin there. It would be up to William BAFFIN to test that theory about 30 years later.

Ready for the Land of Desolation

Davis grew up in southwestern England. As a youth, he was friends with Walter RALEIGH and Humphrey GILBERT. Gilbert was excited about the possibility of a Northwest Passage, and his enthusiasm eventually inspired Davis to undertake his own explorations. Davis

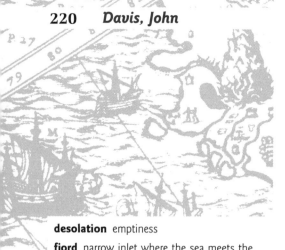

desolation emptiness

fjord narrow inlet where the sea meets the shore between steep cliffs

Inuit people of the Canadian Arctic, sometimes known as the Eskimo

kayak small canoe, usually made of sealskin stretched over a light frame of bone or wood

pinnace small boat that can sail in shallow waters

latitude distance north or south of the equator

spent 14 years at sea, becoming a trusted and skilled captain. He decided that he was ready for the Arctic Ocean.

In the 1580s, Davis, Raleigh, and Adrian Gilbert (Humphrey's brother) formed a company to carry out the adventure. They planned it with the help of John Dee, a mathematician and geographer. They also consulted Sir Francis Walsingham, an advisor to Queen Elizabeth I. A wealthy merchant named William Sanderson directed the preparations and handled the money.

In June 1585, Davis headed out to sea with two small vessels, the *Sunshine* and the *Moonshine.* On July 20 he sighted the east coast of Greenland, which he called "the Land of **Desolation.**" He rounded its southern tip and anchored in a **fjord** that he named Gilbert Sound (now known as Godthaab Fjord). When he came across a group of **Inuit,** he enchanted them with music played by four crewmen. Soon the fjord was full of Inuit in **kayaks.** The English and the Inuit traded, and Davis acquired five of the kayaks.

He then took his ships into the sea west of Greenland, in what is now called Davis Strait. He made careful notes about the local plant and animal life. Eventually the winds changed, and signs of bad weather appeared. Davis had to return to England, but he was optimistic about finding a sea route to Asia in those waters.

A Second Chance at Success

The next year, Davis led a second expedition back to Davis Strait. His two ships were joined by a larger ship, the *Mermaid,* and a **pinnace,** the *North Star.* At that time, most scientists and navigators believed that there was an open Arctic sea beyond the wall of ice near Greenland. Two of the ships were sent to try to break through this ice, but it was impossible. Those two ships returned to England. Meanwhile, Davis took the *Mermaid* and the *Moonshine* back to Godthaab Fjord, where his crew again befriended the Inuit. The English and the Inuit traded briskly and even held soccer and wrestling matches. Curious about the area's natural history, Davis took time to explore some coastal and inland areas of Greenland before heading back to sea.

When the ships encountered dangerous pack ice, most of the crewmen were frightened and wanted to turn back. Davis talked some of the men into continuing the mission aboard the *Moonshine.* He allowed the rest of the crew to return to England aboard the *Mermaid.* Although the *Moonshine* made little progress, its crew caught a large number of fish in Davis Strait. Profits from the catch helped to pay some of the voyage's costs. Davis's investors were encouraged enough to fund yet another journey to the Arctic Ocean.

Fighting Ice, Wind, and the Spanish Fleet

The third expedition began in 1587 with three ships. Soon it was just Davis and a few sailors aboard the small pinnace *Ellen.* As before, most of the men had turned back, and Davis had inspired a few volunteers to push on. He made sure that he would make a profit by setting up a fishery off Godthaab Fjord before he took the *Ellen* up the coast of Greenland to a high northern **latitude.** Ice and winds kept Davis from sailing farther north and forced him back to the south. The *Ellen* barely escaped being frozen in the ice. Davis then explored the coast of Baffin Island, where both he and Frobisher had been before. Encouraged by strong winds at the opening of Frobisher's "Mistaken Strait" (present-day Hudson Strait), Davis hoped that he had found the beginning of the Northwest Passage.

After the *Ellen* returned home, war broke out between England and Spain. Davis commanded the *Black Dog* against the Spanish Armada in 1588. The English won the battle, and as the ruined Spanish fleet drifted helplessly north to Scotland, Davis took the *Drake* to attack what was left.

Bad Luck on the High Seas

With the money he had made from his efforts against the Spanish, Davis hoped to search for the Northwest Passage from the Pacific coast of North America. He sailed to the south of Africa with Thomas CAVENDISH's expedition of 1592. But that venture failed badly, and Davis lost most of his fortune. On his way back to England, he discovered what are now the Falkland Islands (also known as the Malvinas).

Though no longer wealthy, Davis still had an estate in England. He retired there and wrote two books that summed up his experiences as a navigator and explorer. He also provided information for a globe that was designed in 1592. This globe was of great interest to those who saw it, because the outlines of the earth's continents were beginning to be known.

Davis's retirement did not last long. In 1596 and 1597, he served in the English navy. The next year, he was hired by the Dutch to pilot their first voyage to the East Indies. Davis wrote the only known account of this difficult voyage, in which the mission's commander was killed in a battle on the Malay Peninsula. Because of his experience, Davis was hired by the English East India Company for its own first voyage to the Indies, from 1601 to 1603.

A rival company hired him to sail the same route two years later. His ship was attacked by Japanese pirates off the coast of the Malay Peninsula. The pirates had boarded the ship peacefully and were having dinner with their English hosts when they suddenly drew their swords. John Davis was one of the first to be killed.

Suggested Reading Albert Hastings Markam, editor, *The Voyages and Works of John Davis, the Navigator* (reprint, Burt Franklin, 1970).

For more information about Nicolo Zeno, see the profile of Antonio ZENO in Volume 3.

---

del Cano, Juan Sebastián. See *Elcano, Juan Sebastián de.*

De Long, George Washington

American
b August 22, 1844; New York City, New York
d October 30, 1881; Lena River, Russia
Explored Russian and Alaskan Arctic

Lieutenant Commander George Washington De Long of the U.S. Navy led a daring and dangerous expedition into the Arctic Ocean. He was testing a theory that the warm summer waters of the Pacific Ocean might melt a passage through the polar ice pack. He hoped to follow such a waterway as far as possible, perhaps even to the pole itself. The voyage was financed by Gordon Bennett, a New York newspaper publisher.

George Washington De Long searched for the missing Arctic explorer Charles Francis HALL. In later years, rescuers would search the Arctic for De Long.

Bennett knew that if the theory was correct, the results would be spectacular. In exchange for Bennett's support, De Long promised to let Bennett's newspaper publish the mission's daily log. De Long made entries in the log right up to the day he died from starvation and severe cold weather.

Frozen in the Ice

In the summer of 1879, De Long entered the Arctic Ocean through the Bering Strait, which separates Siberia and Alaska. His ship, the *Jeannette,* was caught by rapidly freezing ice near Herald Island on September 5. The ship drifted northwest, trapped in the ice pack, for almost two years. In the summer of 1881, a sudden shift of the ice crushed the *Jeannette* to pieces. De Long and 32 crew members managed to escape the wreck in three small boats. They turned the boats into sleds and dragged their supplies over the frozen sea, hoping to reach Russian settlements.

After a long and difficult haul, the explorers reached the New Siberian Islands at the end of July. They sailed the boats on the open waters of the Laptev Sea but were separated in a storm. One boat was never heard from again, but the other two landed successfully at the mouth of the Lena River, on the coast of Siberia. Tragically, the survivors were separated again. A party led by George Melville, the expedition's chief engineer, made it to Yakutsk in December 1881. Melville immediately set out to save De Long's group. He found only two survivors. De Long had died over two months earlier, at the age of 37.

The Jeannette's Surprising Journey

Though many expeditions had met with disaster in the course of Arctic exploration, De Long's voyage was set apart from the rest by a strange event. Three years after the sinking of the *Jeannette,* the ship's wrecked remains washed up on the shores of Greenland, having floated halfway around the world. Scientists realized that the polar ice pack drifts clockwise around the North Pole. A few years later, this knowledge inspired the Norwegian explorer Fridtjof NANSEN to repeat the *Jeannette*'s drift in a specially designed research vessel called the *Fram.*

Suggested Reading Emma Wotton De Long, *Explorer's Wife* (Dodd, Mead and Company, 1938); Leonard F. Guttridge, *Icebound: The* Jeannette *Expedition's Quest for the North Pole* (Paragon House, 1988); A. A. Hoehling, *The* Jeannette *Expedition: An Ill-Fated Journey to the Arctic* (Abelard-Schuman, 1969).

---

de Novaes, Bartolomeu. See *Dias, Bartolomeu.*

D'Entrecasteaux, Antoine Raymond Joseph de Bruni.
See *Entrecasteaux, Antoine Raymond Joseph de Bruni d'.*

---

de Soto, Hernando. See *Soto, Hernando de.*

Dezhnev, Semyon Ivanov

Russian
b 1605; Veliki Ustyug, Russia
d 1672; Moscow, Russia
Sailed through Bering Strait; explored Siberia

czar title of Russian monarchs from the 1200s to 1917

sable mammal of northern Europe and Asia, related to the mink and the weasel

Semyon Dezhnev made a major discovery in 1648, but he failed to report it properly, and his feats were almost forgotten. He was the first European known to have sailed through what is now called the Bering Strait. This narrow northern waterway separates Siberia and Alaska. By sailing through it, Dezhnev discovered that Asia and North America are not connected by land. But because he could neither read nor write, Dezhnev kept no written records of his voyage. The news of his discovery did not make it back to Europe from the distant outposts of Siberia. Vitus BERING sailed into the same strait 80 years later and announced his own success right away. Bering is now well known to history, and the strait is named after him. Dezhnev's achievement was finally recognized many years later.

Not much is known about Dezhnev's early years. He probably grew up in the European part of Russia. Somehow he gained experience as a sailor and then signed on to work for the Russian **czar.** He was sent to Siberia to collect tribute from the people. Siberian villages were forced to pay tribute as a sign that the czar was their ruler. In this way, Russia extended its influence all the way from the Ural Mountains to the Pacific Ocean.

The Sea of Ice

Records show that Dezhnev was sent to work in northeastern Siberia, where he helped build the first Russian outpost on the Kolyma River. Many Russian traders were drawn to this area, attracted by reports of rivers farther to the east. They had heard that the region was a rich source of **sable** furs, walrus tusks, and silver. There was soon great interest in exploring that area east of the Kolyma River. The terrain was rough, and great risk and hardship would be involved. But adventurers dreamed of great fortunes and were willing to face the challenge.

In 1648 Dezhnev was selected to lead an expedition to the east. He was told to find villages along the way that had not yet paid tribute to the czar. Dezhnev and about 90 explorers and traders sailed north on the Kolyma River and into the Arctic Ocean. They traveled east along the Arctic coast in seven ships called *koches.* These ships had strong hulls designed to survive the pounding they would take in the ice-filled waters of the Arctic Ocean. Even so, four ships were lost by the time the small fleet sailed out of the Arctic. Explorers who braved the Arctic seas later on were amazed that any of the ships had made it through at all. Dezhnev then led the three remaining koches south through what is now called the Bering Strait and into the sea beyond, which was later named the Bering Sea. With Siberia on the west side of the strait and Alaska to the east, Dezhnev could see that Asia and North America were separate continents.

Little else is known about the actual voyage. The next time Dezhnev's party was sighted was in September 1648. The Russians fought with the Chukchi people who lived on the nearby Chukotski Peninsula (also called the Chukchi Peninsula). By then they had lost another ship, and before long the last two ships were also wrecked.

In the Service of the Czar

It took Dezhnev and his men about 10 weeks to walk from the site of their last shipwreck to the mouth of the Anadyr River. They built new boats and continued up the river to the region of the Anual people. There Dezhnev began to carry out his task of collecting tribute. His usual method was simply to take control of a village—by force if necessary. Then he would take hostages and hold them until the proper amount of tribute was presented. Dezhnev also used his position to build his personal fortune. He often collected furs and ivory tusks for himself in addition to what he collected for the czar.

Dezhnev spent the next 12 years exploring the uncharted areas of Siberia and gathering tribute from the people he encountered. His work took him to regions along the Lena and the Yana Rivers. In 1654 he asked to be taken off the job, but another five years passed before his replacement arrived.

In 1661 Dezhnev traveled to the Russian city of Irkutsk with furs, silver, and more than two tons of walrus tusks. He gave a full report of his mission, describing in detail his hardships, wounds, debts, and costs. He then requested that he be paid the salary owed to him for his 19 years of service.

In the end, Dezhnev had to go all the way to Moscow, the Russian capital. He presented his case to the czar's agency in charge of Siberia and finally received his pay. He then returned to eastern Siberia with his nephew. There he served as an officer on the Olenek River for several years. After a short time on the Vilyui River, he took a job protecting a shipment of furs to Moscow. The trip took two years. He arrived in Moscow safely and died there two years later.

Suggested Reading Raymond H. Fisher, *The Voyage of Semen Dezhnev in 1648: Bering's Precursor* (Hakluyt Society, 1981).

Dias, Bartolomeu

Portuguese
b 1450?; Portugal
d May 24, 1500; at sea, off South Africa
**Explored African Congo;
discovered Cape of Good Hope**

Bartolomeu Dias commanded the first European expedition to sail past the Cape of Good Hope, the southernmost tip of Africa. He found that point almost by accident. But his discovery opened the sea route to Asia that Europeans had been hoping to find for decades. On his historic voyage, Dias added some 1,260 miles to maps of the African coast. In later years, he took part in the Portuguese discovery of Brazil.

The Unknown South

Dias was born in Portugal sometime around 1450. Some historians believe that several of his older relatives were also sailors. In 1481 he joined an expedition to the part of Africa's west coast that was known as the Gold Coast. Six years later, Portugal's King John II gave Dias command of three ships and sent him to find the southern tip of Africa. Since the early 1400s, the Portuguese had sent sea captains such as Gil EANNES and Diogo CÃO south along Africa's west coast. The missions had made steady progress, but no one had found the end of the coastline. It seemed to stretch on forever. Dias was instructed to continue his countrymen's work, find the southern

Bartolomeu Dias was honored by his country with this stamp, issued by Portugal in 1945.

cape, and sail around it. On the other side of Africa, he was to search for the legendary land of Prester John, a Christian king who was said to rule a land of great riches in the east. King John of Portugal was also eager to find a sea route to the Indies because trouble in eastern Europe and central Asia had closed overland trade routes between western Europe and eastern Asia.

Dias left Lisbon in the summer of 1487. Of his three ships, he used one—commanded by his brother Pedro—only to carry supplies. That way he and his men would have enough food and water to stay at sea for many months. He also brought several Africans who had lived in Europe and so could help communicate with any African peoples the explorers might meet. Dias sailed south for four months, stopping along the way to trade, and soon passed the stone pillar left by Cão in what is now Namibia. The stone marked the southernmost point yet reached by the Portuguese. As he continued south, Dias left pillars of his own along the coast.

A Stormy Discovery

By the end of December, Dias's ships had passed the Orange River, just to the north of present-day South Africa. The ships then sailed into a terrible storm. Fierce winds blew them southward for the next 13 days. When the storm finally ended, Dias sailed east, expecting to spot Africa's west coast once again. When he did not find any land, he headed north, reaching Bahia dos Vaquieros (present-day Mossel Bay) on February 3, 1488. The coast certainly looked like part of Africa, but Dias did not yet realize that he had rounded the cape. He was on the southern shores of Africa, about 200 miles east of the Cape of Good Hope.

Dias did not stay long at Bahia dos Vaquieros. Warriors of the Hottentot tribe that lived there greeted the Portuguese by throwing stones, and Dias killed one of these attackers. He then sailed east and landed on an island in Algoa Bay, which he named Santa Cruz. This was probably the first ground past the cape ever walked on by a European. Dias continued sailing east for a few more days until he reached a river, which he named Rio de Infante in honor of the commander of his second ship.

Dias would have sailed on in search of the Indies, but his frightened crew begged him to turn around. He did so only after they signed letters that said that he was a brave and skilled navigator. Dias hoped that these documents would support him if the king demanded to know why he had turned back before reaching Asia.

Return to Portugal

As he sailed west on his way home, Dias finally spotted the cape he had been sent to find. He did not know that the Cape of Good Hope was actually not the southernmost point in Africa. That honor belongs to Cape Agulhas, about 160 miles to the east. The rest of the return voyage was uneventful—with one exception. Dias had left the supply ship behind at Guinea, and when he found it, six of its nine crewmen were dead, and all of the supplies on board had been stolen.

Dias brought his expedition back to the port of Lisbon in December 1488, 16 months and 17 days after leaving. His success frustrated

the hopes of a little-known Italian navigator named Christopher COLUMBUS. At that time, Columbus was trying to convince King John II to finance a voyage to the Indies that would sail west, not east as Dias had done. The king might have been interested had Dias not found the cape. But now it looked as if Portugal's route to Asia was open, so Columbus had to look to Spain for support.

A Little Fame and an Early Death

World maps based on the ideas of the Greek scientist PTOLEMY showed land connecting southern Africa with Asia, making the Indian Ocean an inland sea. Dias's voyage, and that of Vasco da GAMA nine years later, showed that the tip of Africa was not connected to land to the east. Dias began the long process by which Europeans abandoned their faith in Ptolemy's writings and began to form their own opinions about the world.

But Portugal could not follow up on Dias's discoveries right away. The country had a tense relationship with Spain as well as other problems within Portugal. In those difficult times, Dias did not receive the honors he deserved as a hero of exploration. Even so, in 1494 he was named to prepare a fleet of ships to be led by Gama. Three years later, the ships sailed for India by way of the Cape of Good Hope. Dias made the trip as far as the Cape Verde Islands, off Africa's west coast. The new Portuguese king, Manuel I, had ordered him to leave Gama and set up a trading post on the islands. The post was a success, and Dias then started another one on the continent's east coast.

In March 1500, Dias sailed on his last voyage. He commanded a **caravel** headed for India with the fleet of Pedro Álvares CABRAL. The ships sailed south from the Cape Verde Islands and crossed the equator. When they encountered the **trade winds,** Cabral was forced to the west. As a result, the explorers landed on the coast of Brazil at what is now Pôrto Seguro. After about a month, the fleet left Brazil to return to its original route south of Africa. Somewhere near the Cape of Good Hope, a tremendous storm sank four of the ships, including the one commanded by Dias.

Suggested Reading Eric Victor Axelson, *Congo to Cape: Early Portuguese Explorers* (Barnes and Noble, 1973).

For a map of Dias's route, see the profile of Vasco da GAMA in Volume 2.

caravel small ship with three masts and both square and triangular sails

trade winds winds that blow from east to west in the tropics

---

d' Iberville, Pierre Le Moyne. See *Iberville, Pierre Le Moyne d'*.

Doughty, Charles Montagu

English
b August 19, 1843; Leiston, England
d January 20, 1926; Sissinghurst, England
Wrote about his travels in Arabia

geology the scientific study of the earth's natural history

Charles Doughty lived for two years among the bedouin, the wandering tribes of the Arabian desert. He wrote a detailed account of the region and its people. This volume, *Travels in Arabia Deserta,* attracted little attention when it was published in 1888. But since then it has been recognized as a masterpiece of travel writing.

A Passion for the Desert

Doughty studied **geology** and literature at Cambridge University. A trip he had made as a young man to the Middle East inspired his

caravan large group of people traveling together, often with pack animals, across a desert or other dangerous region

plateau high, flat area of land

Charles Doughty was a serious, quiet scholar whose greatest passion was the history and daily life of Arabia.

life-long interest in Arabia. When his studies were completed, he spent a year in Damascus (in present-day Syria) learning Arabic. He then disguised himself as a Syrian Christian and joined a **caravan** bound for Mecca (in what is now Saudi Arabia). Doughty traveled with the caravan as far as Madayin Salah (now in eastern Syria). He stayed there for several months, studying tombs and monuments in the region. He made copies of their engravings by placing paper against hard surfaces and rubbing the paper with a special crayon. Doughty sent his rubbings to British officials in Damascus. He then spent the next few months living with a bedouin family in the Arabian wilderness.

Doughty shared many adventures and hardships with his Muslim hosts. He moved with them as they sought fresh pasture for their camels. Each day he recorded details of bedouin household activities and daily life. Doughty and the bedouins wandered south through the hills and deserts of Arabia. Then he decided to join a party headed for the Harra **Plateau,** which is made of black lava. Doughty described this region as an "iron wilderness" where he found a "bare and black shining beach of heated volcanic stones."

Seeing and Learning

Doughty also spent some time with the Moahib tribe and the Bishr tribe as they traveled to Hail (now in Saudi Arabia). Along the way, he saw many strange animals, including antelope with straight horns. The weary scholar pushed on, making his way to several other cities that are now in Saudi Arabia and studying the area's Jewish history. Finally, Doughty returned to Damascus to collect his rubbings. He then traveled to Naples, Italy, where he wrote his account of his travels. His work is a classic description of the land and people of the Arabian desert.

Suggested Reading Charles Doughty, *Travels in Arabia Deserta,* edited by H. L. MacRitchie (Bloomsbury, 1989); Stephen E. Tabachnik, editor, *Explorations in Doughty's Arabia Deserta* (University of Georgia Press, 1987).

WITHDRAWN